INTERNATIONAL ENCYCLOPEDIA OF ADULT EDUCATION

INTERNATIONAL ENCYCLOPEDIA OF ADULT EDUCATION

Edited by
Leona M. English

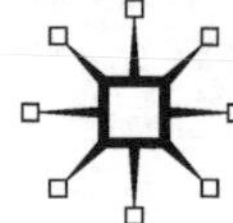

First published 2005 by
PALGRAVE MACMILLAN
Houndmills, Basingstoke, Hampshire RG21 6XS and
175 Fifth Avenue, New York, N.Y. 10010
Companies and representatives throughout the world

PALGRAVE MACMILLAN is the global academic imprint of the Palgrave Macmillan division of St. Martin's Press, LLC and of Palgrave Macmillan Ltd. Macmillan® is a registered trademark in the United States, United Kingdom and other countries. Palgrave is a registered trademark in the European Union and other countries.

ISBN-13 978–1–4039–1735–5
ISBN-10 1–4039–1735–3

This book is printed on paper suitable for recycling and made from fully managed and sustained forest sources.

A catalogue record for this book is available from the British Library.

Library of Congress Cataloging-in-Publication Data
International encyclopedia of adult education / edited by Leone M. English.
p. cm.
Includes bibliographical references and index.
ISBN 1–4039–1735–3
1. Adult education—Encyclopedias. I. English, Leona M., 1963–
LC5211.I56 2005
374′003—dc22 2004059171

10 9 8 7 6 5 4 3 2 1
14 13 12 11 10 09 08 07 06 05

Printed in China

Contents

Editorial Board

List of Contributors

Sue Adams
Coady International Institute, St. Francis Xavier University, Canada

Katerina Ananiadou
Institute of Education, University of London, UK

Barbara Shaw Anderson
North Carolina State University, USA

Clinton L. Anderson
United States Department of Defense, Voluntary Education Program, USA

James Athanasou
University of Technology Sydney, Australia

Elsa Auerbach
University of Massachusetts, USA

Paul Bélanger
Université du Québec a Montréal, Canada

John Benseman
University of Auckland, New Zealand

Laura Bierema
University of Georgia, USA

Adrian Blunt
University of Saskatchewan, Canada

Roger Boshier
University of British Columbia, Canada

Marcie Boucouvalas
Virginia Polytechnic Institute and State University, USA

David Boud
University of Technology Sydney, Australia

Stephen Brookfield
University of St. Thomas, USA

Judith O. Brown
Barry University, USA

Shauna Butterwick
University of British Columbia, Canada

Valerie-Lee Chapman
North Carolina State University, USA

M. Carolyn Clark
Texas A&M University, USA

Darlene E. Clover
University of Victoria, Canada

Dianne Conrad
University of New Brunswick, Canada

Ian R. Cornford
University of Technology Sydney, Australia

Patricia Cranton
St. Francis Xavier University, Canada

L. A. Parks Daloz
Whidbey Institute, USA

Jane Dawson
St. Francis Xavier University, Canada

Pierre Dominicé
University of Geneva, Switzerland

Richard Edwards
University of Stirling, Scotland

John Egan
University of Sydney, Australia

Leona M. English
St. Francis Xavier University, Canada

Roger Etkind
University of the Western Cape, South Africa

Tara Fenwick
University of Alberta, Canada

Brian Findsen
University of Glasgow

Matthias Finger
Swiss Federal Institute of Technology, Switzerland

Maria Clara Bueno Fischer
Universidade do Vale do Rio dos Sinos–UNISINOS, Brazil

Patricia Gouthro
Mt. Saint Vincent University, Canada

André P. Grace
University of Alberta, Canada

Fyre Jean Graveline
Brandon University, Canada

Shibao Guo
University of Alberta, Canada

Talmadge C. Guy
University of Georgia, USA

Budd L. Hall
University of Victoria, Canada

Mike Healy
University of Georgia, USA

Lilian H. Hill
Virginia Commonwealth University, USA

Robert J. Hill
University of Georgia, USA

Mohamed Hrimech
Université de Montréal, Canada

Cheryl Hunt
University of Exeter, UK

Susan Imel
Ohio State University

Peter Jarvis
University of Surrey, UK

Juanita Johnson-Bailey
University of Georgia, USA

David James Jones
University of Nottingham, UK

Georg Karlsson
University of Linköping, Sweden

Irene Karpiak
University of Oklahoma, USA

Jennifer Kelly
University of Alberta, Canada

Sandra Kerka
Ohio State University

Kathleen P. King
Fordham University, USA

Carolin Kreber
University of Alberta, Canada.

Jeffrey S. Kuhn
Columbia University, USA

Dorothy A. Lander
St. Francis Xavier University, Canada

Staffan Larsson
Linköping University

Al Lauzon
University of Guelph, Canada

Michael Law
University of Waikato, New Zealand

Linda Leach
Massey University, New Zealand

Moira Lee
Temasek Polytechnic Institute, Singapore

Victoria J. Marsick
Columbia University, USA

Peter Mayo
University of Malta

Katherine McManus
Simon Fraser University, Canada

Olutoyin Mejiuni
Obafemi Awolowo University, Nigeria

Carlos Zarco Mera
Latin American Council for Adult Education (CEAAL), Mexico

Sharan B. Merriam
University of Georgia, USA

Shahrzad Mojab
Ontario Institute for Studies in Education/ University of Toronto, Canada

Jenny Moon
University of Exeter, UK

Roger K. Morris
University of Technology Sydney, Australia

Mazanah Muhamad
Universiti Putia, Malaysia

Tom Nesbit
Simon Fraser University, Canada

Michael Newman
University of Technology Sydney, Australia

Oluyemisi O. Obilade
Obafemi Awolowo University, Nigeria

Edmée Ollagnier
University of Geneva, Switzerland

Donovan Plumb
Mt. Saint Vincent University, Canada

Daniel D. Pratt
University of British Columbia, Canada

Julia Preece
University of Botswana

B. Allan Quigley
St. Francis Xavier University, Canada

Jost Reischmann
Bamberg University, Germany

Anne Reuss
University of Abertay, Scotland

Amy Rose
Northern Illinois University, USA

Marsha Rossiter
University of Wisconsin, USA

Birgitte Simonsen
Danish University of Education, Denmark

Mark K. Smith
YMCA George Williams College, UK

Nicky Solomon
University of Technology Sydney, Australia

Thomas J. Sork
University of British Columbia, Canada

Bruce Spencer
Athabasca University, Canada

Joyce Stalker
University of Waikato, New Zealand

Jennifer Sumner
Ontario Institute for Studies in Education/University of Toronto, Canada

Edward W. Taylor
Pennsylvania State University, USA

Mark Tennant
University of Technology Sydney, Australia

Lyn Tett
University of Edinburgh, Scotland

Alan Thomas
Ontario Institute for Studies in Education/University of Toronto, Canada

Elizabeth J. Tisdell
Pennsylvania State University, USA

Joanne Tompkins
St. Francis Xavier University, Canada

Thomas Mark Turay
Coady International Institute, St. Francis Xavier University, Canada

Shirley Walters
University of the Western Cape, South Africa

Karen E. Watkins
University of Georgia, USA

Michael Welton
Mount St. Vincent University, Canada

Faye Wiesenberg
University of Calgary, Canada

Arthur L. Wilson
Cornell University, USA

Raymond J. Wlodkowski
Regis University, USA

Nick Zepke
Massey University, New Zealand.

Miriam Zukas
University of Leeds, UK

Dedication

This encyclopedia is dedicated to two brave and courageous women.

Dedicated to the memory of **Florence Mary O'Neill** (1905–90) of Witless Bay, Newfoundland, an adult educator who dedicated her life to everyone's improvement "whether they wanted to or not." An itinerant teacher of adult education beginning in 1936, she was the first Canadian to earn a doctorate in adult education (Columbia University, 1944). She became the director of adult education for Newfoundland (1946–58) and then director of adult education programs for the federal Department of Indian Affairs in Ottawa, until her retirement in 1969. Her achievements in the field remain exemplars of practice and an inspiration for all who value knowledge and learning.

KATHERINE MCMANUS

Dedicated to **Valerie-Lee Chapman**, Ph.D. (d. 2004) courageous woman and adult education professor at North Carolina State University. This is to your life and the beautiful and amazing way that you evidenced power and knowledge in your work. You said YES when you were awarded the prestigious SSHRC and Killam fellowships; when you found a great doctoral advisor in Tom Sork; and when you were challenged to fight your illness. You said yes to life and dared to "rage against the dying of the light." You, Valerie-Lee, were an adult education exemplar of a gifted writer and thinker. You were passionately dedicated to adult education and to doing it in new ways . . . feminist, collaborative, qualitative and above all reflectively and with reflexivity. In your own words, you were "all about letting in fresh air from women's work, poststructuralism, narrative and all the exciting stuff happening in the social sciences and cultural geography." Adult educators are truly blessed to count you among them. Valerie-Lee, you were a phenomenal woman if ever there was one.

LEONA M. ENGLISH

Foreword

In such a diverse and fast expanding domain, the publication of the *International Encyclopedia of Adult Education* is a timely step in the development of the field. Indeed, the national educational scene in every country has been profoundly transformed over the last three decades. Nowadays, in most post-industrial societies, adults participating in organized learning activities well outnumber the young people undertaking their initial education in schools and colleges. However, this reality is not yet recognized and still only partially documented. Actors in adult education need support to help them understand and reconstruct their diffuse field. The components of our learning societies are extremely dispersed among a vast array of agencies, into a variety of learning contexts, through many modes of provision and educational approaches, while a growing and very diversified group of adults participate actively. And this visible part of adult learning is only the tip of an iceberg, hiding the pervasive reality of non-formal and experiential learning taking place everyday at home, in the community and at the workplace.

The *International Encyclopedia of Adult Education* is a necessary contribution in reconstructing this reality, while identifying and taking into account a diversity of discourses and disciplines. It is a great challenge to present an overview of a field where the knowledge base is so diffuse and still in development. This encyclopedia, with over 170 entries, has succeeded not only in presenting the key concepts and typical thematics of the field, but also in providing us with insights into emerging subjects and concerns, regarding the new forms of learning, the recent theoretical approaches, the current geo-political dimensions and the emerging philosophical issues.

We will not be able to ensure to all citizens the full exercise of their right to learn without grasping the tremendous changes that adult education has undergone over the last 30 years. We will not be able to contribute to the emergence of sustainable and fair learning societies without having an encompassing view of the field much too often confined to one of its dimensions and constructed with a single discourse. We will not be able to build adult education locally without understanding the trends and debates taking place at the global level. And all this is precisely what this new encyclopedia on adult education accomplishes.

As president of the International Council of Adult Education and the General Secretary of the International Conference of Adult Education sponsored by UNESCO in 1997 (CONFINTEA, Hamburg), I can appreciate how much such a "tool" will be useful for so many actors involved in the ongoing multifaceted development of adult education. The encyclopaedia will be of valuable help for thousands of isolated practitioners in community organizations, in institutions, at the work place and in the new media, for political, economic, educational and cultural decision-makers, for researchers striving to understand the contributions of other disciplines studying the complex reality of adult learning, as well as for a larger public searching to grasp the multidimensional reality behind the now prevailing discourse on lifelong learning.

On behalf, I am sure, of all these future readers and users, I wish to thank the editor and the publisher for having taken the risk of such a great initiative.

Paul Bélanger
President, International Council of Adult Education & Professor
Université du Québec a Montréal
Canada

Acknowledgements

As I began to think of who to acknowledge in the making of this encyclopedia, I was overwhelmed by the enormity of the intellectual support and academic assistance I have received. This has been invaluable to me and integral to the final product. I share with Yeats (1938) the sentiment that "My glory was I had such friends" ("The Municipal Gallery Revisited").

To begin, I would like to thank my colleagues here at St. Francis Xavier University – Patricia Cranton, Jane Dawson, and Allan Quigley – for unwavering support of this project. I would also like to thank the editorial board members – David Boud, Tara Fenwick, Matthias Finger, Cheryl Hunt, Dorothy Lander, Sharan Merriam, Tom Nesbit, Elizabeth Tisdell, Shirley Walters, and Arthur Wilson – who gave generously of their time to think about this project and its possibilities, and to offer considerable academic advice. They not only performed editorial work but also wrote many of the entries. Thank you, as well, to the many contributors to this project – with your fine conceptual and authorial ability this project has seen the light of day. And to Stephen Brookfield who came to the rescue on so many last-minute entries without a moment's pause, I am very grateful. Dorothy Lander, friend and colleague at St. Francis Xavier University, gave intellectual energy and personal support to every stage of this project – this would never have come to fruition without her.

A special thank you to the library staff of the Angus L. MacDonald and Coady International Institute at St. Francis Xavier University, especially to Catherine Irving, for tireless help in the location of those hard-to-find books and article page numbers. My appreciation for you is immense. Bernadine Raiskums, author of her own dictionary of adult education, generously volunteered to spend untold hours cross-referencing the entries and in editing. Your considerable knowledge of the field and its resources were an invaluable scholarly resource. Brandon Rama Vaidyanathan helped with the indexing and worked tirelessly to make every word count. Thank you also to Matthew Puddicombe and Dylan Quinn, student research assistants, for compiling endless lists and doing library research. Angela Stewart, Jim Stewart, and Denise Morrow gave extensive editorial assistance in the production process and for this I am most thankful. To the editors at Palgrave Macmillan – Ruth Lefèvre and Alison Jones – thank you so much for taking this on; your unending patience every time I changed a deadline or a contributor is so very much appreciated. Most of all I thank my Master of Adult Education students at St. Francis Xavier University who kept asking, "Can you explain that to me? What does that mean?" Without their questions I never would have realized the need for a volume such as this one. Thank you all so very much.

LEONA M. ENGLISH

The Production of Knowledge and the Un/Making of an Encyclopedia of Adult Education: An Introduction

The process of un/making an encyclopedia is inherently and deliberately complex and ambiguous. Yet, the gaze of academic readers and the ever-vigilant eye of the marketer/publisher suggest that such ambiguity is theoretically sanctioned but practically outlawed. The predilection of many readers for false clarity and of many publishers for "accessible" work is in itself a contestable political position (Lather, 1996). Yet, the un/makers of this encyclopedia have resisted simplicity in favor of a more complex re-reading of our field of adult education. Indeed, our entire process has been an unfolding one that has invited many voices and challenging points of view, all of which confer value on the nuanced readings that ambiguity affords.

This ambiguity of process, and the concomitant discomfort with it, mirrors a scene from the play "The Archbishop's Ceiling" (Miller, 1984) when one character asks, "You don't like ambiguity?" to which he receives a reply, "Oh sure, providing it's clear" (p. 67). Indeed, ambiguity has been embedded in this encyclopedia project from the onset. To begin with, this was intended as an act of unmaking previous encyclopedias (Jarvis, 1999; Tuijnman, 1996). This new encyclopedia is an act of resistance to these existing compendia, and at the same time an epistemological attempt to gather cacophonous global voices, to challenge contributors to stretch intellectual boundaries by unmasking the unspoken struggles and debates about what constitutes knowledge in our field. Indeed, this encyclopedia follows in function, though not in form, the *Handbook of Adult and Continuing Education* (Wilson & Hayes, 2000) in its attempts to surface contradictions and ambiguities.

That this encyclopedia was being labored on in the early years of the 21st century ties this knowledge-focused project acutely to the global human condition that assails us daily in the media. As scholars and practitioners we are living in a time in which uncertainty and flux are the norm; static knowledge positions are no longer tenable; the very ground beneath the encyclopedia is shifting. Yet, those who have been brokers of knowledge in the past have encountered equally troubling times. In *God's Secretaries: The Making of the King James Bible*, Adam Nicholson (2003) describes a no-less turbulent Jacobean England as "the England of Shakespeare, Jonson, and Bacon; of the Gunpowder Plot; the worst outbreak of the plague England had ever seen; Arcadian landscapes; murderous, toxic slums" (p. 3). We can see here similarities to our own Western context, though ours is given to increasingly conservative politics and the cooptation of lifelong learning by a market-driven discourse. Yet, this age has the socio-critical tools to analyse these conditions, so that we can challenge and resist the power that limits our agency.

Conceptual Framework

Our principal intellectual tasks were to complete a compendium of useful and complicated knowledge for those who are already immersed in adult education, as well as for students and those coming into the field. We wanted to create a useful taxonomy of adult education knowledge that did not replicate existing compendia but rather allowed for interrogation of issues in our field and its intersectoral activity. Even a cursory reading of the entries will indicate that adult education has become thoroughly cross-disciplinary, saturated as it is in areas of politics, religion, health, development, and work. Adult education has become the exemplar of 21st century knowledge work – crossing boundaries to create useful knowledge that assists in the establishment of global civil society.

As such, our encyclopedia project is situated at the intersection of knowledge, power, and relational learning. Among the multiple shapers of this project are the myriad reviewers, publishers, board members, and contributors, not to mention the anticipated gaze of the reader and the critic. The socio-political context of all participants has also been an influential force in its development, as have the written texts in our field (journals, encyclopedia, books, articles, websites) that have been analysed as a way to extend the project beyond our perspectives.

The making of this encyclopedia has been positioned on the border of information and interrogation. We want to bring contested knowledges to the fore and yet retain the balance of providing useful information. Our intellectual goal is to retain the tension between providing standard accessible information for the reader, especially the graduate student, and yet let questions permeate the text. As such, this encyclopedia borders on the intellectual terrain of unknowing and uncertainty. It is a book of partial knowledge(s) and partial truth(s). It valorizes questioning, and takes the advice of Rilke (1984), "to love the questions themselves . . . Live the questions now . . . someday far into the future, you will . . . live your way into the answer" (p. 34).

Critique

Yet, we did not allow ourselves to be guided solely by the gaze of the reader, nor by endless critique or skepticism of knowledge. In many ways, as Latour (2004) says, our age has spent all too much time critiquing, and not knowing always what we were critiquing. Latour, no slouch himself when it comes to critique, insightfully observes that "a certain form of critical spirit has sent us down the worn path" (p. 231). Latour is more concerned with spending time on "*matters of concern,* not *matters of fact*" (p. 231, italics in the original). Our field's preoccupation with critical discourse, critical theory, and postfoundational challenges to knowledge has in many ways been very beneficial. Yet, it has also resulted in exclusionary practices such as deciding that the only worthy knowledge is found under the rubric of criticality. We wonder with Latour if we have gone too far and in so doing lost sight of some things that are still precious to us, our matters of concern. Are there no facts anymore? Is everything in dispute? When Latour raised this issue in *Critical Inquiry* many wondered with him if we have questioned everything to the point where there is nothing left to believe in, or to work with. This encyclopedia plays with Latour's challenge, offering entries that balance information (he calls this fact) with questioning of the information.

In valorizing the commitment to critique, we run the risk of alienating already confused students and colleagues, and we become further invested in breaking down and not building up. This was seen most clearly in the editorial process when several contributors resisted the instruction to define or describe their term at the beginning of the entry – an instruction that in itself highlights clarity as a political position (Lather, 1996). Our commitment to heterogeneity at times conflicts with our commitment to students and to other scholars. Perhaps this resistance is a way of embodying our allegiance to multivocality, yet we realize it can also immobilize us. However, as makers of this encyclopedia we knew at the outset that such tensions were part of the process. We became wary of classification, codification, and labels that did not at the same time challenge these activities. This tension and our commitment to matters of concern was our guide. Can we be the type of critic that Latour (2004) challenges us to be: "the one who assembles, not the one who lifts the rugs from under the feet of the naïve believers but the one who offers arenas in which to gather" (p. 246)? This encyclopedia is one such attempt to move with Latour beyond "critical barbarity" (p. 240), to become "associated with more not less" (p. 248), and to generate "more ideas than we have received" (p. 248). Our "fair position" is to allow at least some structure for the reader, and to posit that some ideas in adult education are important in terms of adult learning and social change.

Making of Books and Writing

We are people who like to classify, as Foucault has observed, absolutely everything. One only has to think of the Bible, the Koran, the Code of Hammurabi, and the *Odyssey*, to realize just how much we have been interested in the compilation of knowledge. The *Odyssey*, for instance, was more than an epic. It was a running record of the geography, history, science, politics and knowledge of the ancient Greek world (Heer, 2003). And along with classifying, we like to search these compendia using a variety of devices, the latest search engine being the omnipresent Google. Libraries, even the earliest known ones from 2500 BCE, were established by kings as ways to collate and search for information. This task of being a keeper of books and knowledge was seen to be so important that Ashurbanipal, King of Assyria, claimed that he personally had collated all the tablets and information in his palace (see Heer, p. 24).

An encyclopedia is but an extension of these efforts to classify and codify knowledge. Not surprisingly the *Oxford English Dictionary* (*OED*) defines the encyclopedia as "a literary work containing extensive information on all branches of knowledge" (Simpson & Weiner, 1989, p. 219). Many encyclopedia intend to encompass everything and in so doing become wrapped in controversy. One of the first encyclopedias, the French Enlightenment *Encyclopédie* by Denis Diderot, was 26 years in the making and is said to have prepared the intellectual groundwork for the Revolution. For its generation of controversy and its incitement of unrest, it was banned. Yet, efforts to compile information and to make compendia have continued, as has the public's fascination with the people and the processes involved (see Pashley, 2003). A case in point is the *Meaning of Everything: The Story of the Oxford English Dictionary* (Winchester, 2003), which is a historical fictional account that focuses on the personal relationships and dynamics behind the book itself. Yet another book about the *OED* and written by same author, is *The Professor and the Madman* (1998); it too has caught the popular imagination and interest.The madman is W.C. Minor one of the main *OED* contributors, and the professor is Sir James Murray, the self-taught editor of the *OED*. Other popular accounts of book and knowledge-making include the stories of the Roman alphabet and how it has been used and manipulated (Sacks, 2003). *Language Visible* (Sacks) includes in its pages the story of the American lexicographer Noah Webster who set out to make American and British spellings different so as to establish a distinct national identity for the United States. Webster's was a very political act, and ours is no less so. The politics of knowledge has always been an integral part of book-making, and certainly of encyclopedia- making.

Consequently, editing an encyclopedia of adult education is quite a challenge, given the scope and diversity of the field and the ever unfolding and contested nature of knowledge. Even the best of encyclopedias can go only so far, making a definitive and permanent delineation of the field impossible and undesirable. Our purpose is to provide a starting point for further research and exploration, both for those new to the field and to those more senior, knowing as we do that finite knowledge of a topic is impossible and is necessarily influenced by the writer, reader, context, and the positionality of the writers and the readers. In providing a starting point for further exploration, our intellectual labor came to include synthesizing, defining, classifying, and challenging. The reality is that instead of order in the universe, dare we say adult education, we have chaos and complexity that caused considerable resistance to our manifold attempts to make this volume global, representative, and a challenge to existing encyclopedia. Perhaps the most telling aspect of the work is the resistance to all things "training"-related. Despite the allegiance to practice in our field, there was great resistance to writing or being associated with the term training, in particular. After some searching, however, we found a superb writer and thinker in the person of Edmée Ollagnier from the University of Geneva. Not lost on any of us is the reality that human resource development (HRD) and training are areas very important to many of our students, yet seemingly anathema to many writers in the field.

The resistance included resistance to the unknown genre of encyclopedia. Our field of adult education has consistently concerned itself with several genres, including research articles, chapters, books, sourcebooks, and handbook chapters. Fewer in number are those adult educators who write scholarly book reviews, book review essays, or dictionary entries. Basically unknown to most is the genre of encyclopedia entry, which was reflected in the diversity of writing styles submitted, and the uncertainty around the genre and its concomitant expectations. Indeed, a specific academic genre is increasingly difficult to isolate as authors experiment with various forms; one only has to think of the self-reflexive turn in our field to realize that mémoire and autobiography have become part and parcel of our academic texts. Indeed, many authors do not even always know what form they are using or how they will be classified, and many are not concerned. Canadian writer Sharon Butala (2004) tells of how she found out what her particular genre was. Having published her most successful book ever, *The Perfection of Morning* (1997) she searched *Quill and Quire* to find out how they classified her. When they described her as a memoirist, a memoirist she became. Perhaps the genre of encyclopedia entry will enter our vernacular and become a mainstay.

Engaging the Issues

The making of this encyclopedia also gave rise to many political issues and discussions. Even our roundtable discussion at the CASAE/AERC conference (English et al., 2004) was political, with conversation riding "naturally" to what was missing, and who was not included. The roundtable was intended to provide an occasion for an open exchange on the un/making of an encyclopedia of adult education in 2003–04, and the very discussion centered on the politics and power dynamics of the project.

One of the most substantive issues that arose was: What does the academy value about this work? The academic world (that is, us) does not count this work as important (really useful knowledge, maybe, which is an established adult education term for learning that is enduring and valuable). In terms of tenure and promotion at a university, writing and editing an encyclopedia count for very little, since an encyclopedia is not peer-reviewed in a traditional sense. The sense of value was reflected in the somewhat lackadaisical way some of the contributors approached the writing task. Dealing with tardiness and no-shows is to be expected in editing a volume this size, but it was exacerbated by the fact that there were no academic brownie points to be accrued. This is unfortunate but clearly a question of knowledge that many of us are in key positions to address and challenge.

A second issue was: Who has access to this knowledge? What are the class issues inherent in publishing an expensive, hard-bound, library edition of an encyclopedia? This is no small matter when one of the goals of the work is to assist students and researchers who are typically underresourced. The conundrums of the publishing process are legion. What publisher would take this on if not to make money? Would the Internet be a more helpful medium? We reply, there are Internet encyclopedia such as Mark Smith's *Encyclopaedia of Informal Education* www.infed.org and the *Encyclopedia of Canadian Adult Education* developed by Don Chapman and Ian Hunt <http://www.ucfv.bc.ca/aded/encyclopedia/>.

The inclusions/exclusions of terms, people, countries and worldviews generate yet another issue, and one that speaks to the hierarchies of truth and knowledge in the field of adult education. The categorization of terms and the guidelines for writers, which we used, are also signifiers of the exercise of power, although our extensive consultative processes have tried to honor Mary Parker Follett's (1924) "power with" instead of power over. This has indeed been an unsettling experience.

The issue that affected the editor most directly has been the relationship between the writers and the editor. The editor became the one whom writers hid from and told stories to. In some cases, the editor was cast in the role of confessor, an anonymous listener who knew only the writer's name but who had a listening ear and a "thinking heart" (Hillesum, 1985, p. 236). In such cases, one imagines, the partial anonymity of editor and unknown writer allows for truth-telling and for the sharing of life stories. Often, the editor and the scribe became friends in the telling, in the typing on keyboards as mind connected to fingers. Yet in physical meetings at conferences we experienced pregnant pauses, awkwardness and shyness, never too sure of what we should say or do in the bodily meeting, fearful of the nakedness of not having a computer between us. A number of writers became sick or had to deal with major life events during this process, including accidents, divorce, death, family emergencies, overwork, exhaustion, and overcommitment. This speaks to the general health of knowledge workers in our field and to the reality that many of us are aging. How have we managed to exclude youth from our ranks and from this project?

The editor unwittingly became the supervisor, the big sister (sovereign power), who sent the reminder emails, who begged and cajoled for entries, and who became the recipient of many an excuse ("my computer collapsed" is the 21st century version of the "dog ate my homework"). The editor took on the unexpected role of parent or stereotypic pedagogue, wary of the errant student or child, anticipating misbehavior, and resisting the role of villain and disciplinarian. And in some cases the editor became the beneficiary of writer angst and resentment, as if she were the one who signed the writer up, and agreed to a deadline to write an entry. In the absence of a sovereign power, the writers exercised self-discipline, and conducted themselves as if the editor were keeping watch in the Panopticon.

Other issues include: What is the nature of adult education knowledge and can it be codified in an encyclopedia? Should academics decide who and what is included or not? Where is the voice of the practitioner? How international is our field in the face of language constraints, cultural difference, technological access, and varying purposes? We claim not to answer these but to raise them and to allow them to saturate our work and our thinking about this encyclopedia.

Our Matters of Concern

In choosing our final list of terms we concentrated on what matters to our field, to the degree that we could establish what matters. There was no attempt to intentionally speak to the language of general education, though there is overlap. For instance, it is hard to conceive of an adult education encyclopedia that does not discuss learning, literacy, or critical thinking, concepts that also have resonance with scholars of teacher education. Similarly, the boundaries between adult education and its sometime home, the social sciences, are blurred. Entries on feminism(s), gender, and research methods as they relate to adult education are inevitable in an encyclopedia for the field.

Coming to a common understanding of the field of adult education is an elusive and not necessarily productive task. That is one of the reasons why we did not include an entry on adult aducation itself, preferring instead to leave that term open to the interpretation of each author. We acknowledge that the boundaries of the field are stretching, porous and infinite and that others have tried, with varying degrees of success, to come to a consensus on what the term means (see Selman, Cooke, Selman, & Dampier, 1998). More helpful than mapping the boundaries is working with the "matters of concern" to members of the field, to borrow a phrase from Bruno Latour (2004). We know intuitively and empirically what we are concerned with, and our multiple texts tell the tale of where we have spent our research and practice energies as a field in the past 20 years or so. These matters of concern are as various as world events, globalization, classroom teaching, and complexity science; we are a field deeply imbricated in the various ways that learning affects our lives in its many manifestations.

So, we began by scouring our texts: conference presentations, dialogue with students, conversations with colleagues, and most of all in our writing: articles, books, chapters, proceedings. We studied the journals and the compendia of existing books, asking: what counts for knowledge in adult education at this time?

We went to the existing reference books to see what had been done. Although we do not have a great number of these books in our field, one of the few that exists is the American *Handbook of Adult and Continuing Education*, which is published every 10 years, and which is the most promoted and recognized reference book in the field. The current volume (Wilson & Hayes, 2000) contains a collection of *essays*, including our own, on key topics in North American adult education such as literacy, critical reflection, and labor education. Similar volumes include *Learning for Life: Canadian Readings in Adult Education* (Scott, Spencer, & Thomas, 1998), *Learning in Adulthood* (Merriam & Caffarella, 1999), and *Foundations of Adult Education in Canada* (Selman et al., 1998). Again, we examined each of these volumes to see how our time has been spent.

We also turned to previous encyclopedias such as Tuijnman's (1996) *International Encyclopedia of Adult Education* which contains 161 international entries, but which is in fact similar in genre (without the emphasis on contested positions) to the *Handbook*, discussed above. Tuijnnman's book is a second edition of a similar handbook edited by Colin Titmus in 1989 (*Lifelong Education for Adults: An International Handbook*). Yet another reference book, the *International Dictionary of Adult and Continuing Education* (1999) by Peter Jarvis, provided us with useful information, especially categories of adult education knowledge.

In developing the tentative word list we consulted Merriam and Brockett's (1997) *The Profession and Practice of Adult Education* (1997), Sheared and Sissel's (2001) *Making Space*, Finger and Asún's (2001) *Adult Education at the Crossroads*, and Bernadine Raiskums' (2001) *Principles and Principals: A Dictionary of Contemporary Adult Education Terms*. We also closely examined works in cognate areas, such as Lorraine Code's (2000) *Encyclopedia of Feminist Theories*, and dialogued with Dr. Code about her process and experience.

Anonymous reviewers of the publishing proposal responded to the initial list of terms, as did the editorial board. Board members suggested writers, possible length of items, and made other adjustments. Some of our guiding principles were: inclusiveness, representativeness, helpfulness, intellectual challenge and student-centeredness. We did not include biographical entries, in part because establishing the criteria for these would be an endless task. Rather we chose to allow people's names to arise naturally in the discussion of relevant terms. For instance, when conscientization is discussed Freire is part of the conversation. The terms that are presented here are as close a rendering of our matters of concern as we had time, writers, publisher permission, and word length to accommodate.

The final list of writers is indeed a bricolage. The contributors locate themselves in critical theory, humanism, feminist theory, queer theory, multiculturalism, and postfoundational studies. They write in a variety of genres (practical workshop books, complex academic texts, journal articles, etc.) and we have included them all. We allowed their voices to be heard in the piece without over-editing them. Even with the omissions, this encyclopedia provides a good selection of terms and a strong rendering of our field and our matters of concern. We are proud to put our names behind it. Thank you to the contributors, the writers we had access to who could write in English, and whose ability to communicate complex concepts in an understandable way is most appreciated.

Features

In structure and organization, this encyclopedia contains 171 entries varying from 1,000–3,000 words, and 105 contributors. Each entry provides a description of the term, identifies the key figures associated with it, and provides a bibliography of significant references. The organization is A–Z, for ease of use. The encyclopedia includes terms from each of four main categories:

- Concepts (learning models, criticism, schools of thought, etc.) such as feminisms, constructivism, and postmodernism.
- Strategies such as journal writing, evaluation and action learning.
- Institutions and organizations.
- Areas of practice such as military education, HRD, religious education, and community development.

Within these main categories there were many subcategories distributed across the 171 entries.

To make this volume more useful we have used the following features.

1. A thorough index that includes subjects, books cited, and cross-references to terms.
2. A comprehensive cross-referencing feature at the end of each

entry. This allows for easy access and cross referencing to other entries which might not be immediately obvious.

References and Further Reading

Butala, S. (1997). *The perfection of morning: A woman's awakening in nature*. Saint Paul, MN: Hungry Mind Press.

Butala, S. (2004). Keynote speech. Narrative Matters Conference, Fredericton, New Brunswick, Canada, May 20, 2004.

Code, L. (Ed.). (2000). *Encyclopedia of feminist theories*. London: Routledge.

English, L. M., Lander, D. L, Hunt, C., Nesbit, T., Tisdell, E. J., Boud, D., Finger, M., Fenwick, T.J., Wilson, A. L., & Walters, S. (2004). Scribes and sorcerers – the production of knowledge and the un/making of an encyclopedia of adult education. In D. E. Clover (Ed.), *Proceedings of the Joint International Conference of the Adult Education Research Conference and the Canadian Association for the Study of Adult Education* (pp. 572–573). University of Victoria, British Columbia, Canada, May, 2004.

Finger, M., & Asún, J. (2001). *Adult education at the crossroads: Learning our way out*. London & New York: ZED Books.

Follett, M. P. (1924). *Dynamic administration*. New York: Longmans, Green.

Heer, J. (2003). A brief history of search engines. *The Walrus*, 1 (2), 24–25.

Hillesum, E. (1985). *An interrupted life: The diaries of Etty Hillesum 1941–43*. New York: Washington Square Press.

Jarvis, P. (1999). *International dictionary of adult and continuing education* (2nd ed.). London: Kogan Page.

Lather, P. (1996). The politics of accessible language. *Harvard Educational Review, 66* (3), 525–545.

Latour, B. (2004). Why has critique run out of steam? From matters of fact to matters of concern. *Critical Inquiry, 30*(2), 225–248.

Merriam, S. B., & Brockett, R. G. (1997). *The profession and practice of adult education*. San Francisco: Jossey-Bass.

Merriam, S. B., & Caffarella, R. S. (1999). *Learning in adulthood* (2nd ed.). San Francisco: Jossey-Bass.

Miller, A. (1984). *The archbishop's ceiling*. London: Methuen.

Nicholson, A. (2003). *God's secretaries: The making of the King James Bible*. New York: HarperCollins.

Pashley, N. (2003). Paragraphs about words and letters. *University of Toronto Bookstore Review, 17*(1), 27–28.

Raiskums, B. W. (2001). *Principles and principals: A dictionary of contemporary adult education terms and their users*. Anchorage, AK: PWR & Associates.

Rilke, R. M. (1984). Letter 4, *Letters to a young poet*. (S. Mitchell, Trans.). New York: Random House.

Sacks, D. (2003). *Language visible: Unraveling the mystery of the alphabet from A to Z*. Toronto: Knopf Canada.

Scott, S. M., Spencer, B., & Thomas A. M. (1998). *Learning for life: Canadian readings in adult education*. Toronto: Thompson Educational.

Selman, G., Cooke, M., Selman, M., & Dampier, P. (1998). *The foundations of adult education in Canada*. Toronto: Thompson Educational.

Sheared, V., & Sissel, P. A. (2001). *Making space: Merging theory and practice in adult education*. Westport, CN: Bergin & Garvey.

Simpson, J. A. & Weiner, E. S. C. (Eds.) (1989) *Oxford English Dictionary* (2nd ed.). 20 vols. Oxford: Clarendon Press and New York: Oxford University Press).

Titmus C. J. (Ed.). (1989). *Lifelong education for adults: An international handbook*. New York: Pergamon.

Tuijnman, A. C. (Ed.). (1996) *International encyclopedia of adult education and training* (2nd ed.). Oxford, UK: Pergamon.

Wilson, A. L., & Hayes, E. R. (Eds.). (2000). *Handbook of adult and continuing education*. San Francisco: Jossey-Bass.

Winchester, S. (1998). *The professor and the madman: A tale of murder, insanity, and the making of the Oxford English Dictionary*. New York: HarperCollins.

Winchester, S. (2003). *The meaning of everything: The story of the OED*. Oxford, New York: Oxford University Press.

Entries A–Z

A

Accelerated Learning

Accelerated learning refers to those courses and programs that are structured to take less time to complete than what has been traditionally required. Compared to courses in most conventional colleges, accelerated courses are offered in less than 15 weeks and for fewer than 45 clock hours of instruction. Typically, accelerated courses are between 5 and 8 weeks duration with 20 to 32 contact hours of instruction. Accelerated degree programs have increased significantly within the last decade with more than 250 colleges and universities offering them in the United States (Wlodkowski, 2003). Adults often prefer accelerated programs because they can earn their degrees more quickly and courses are more convenient to their work schedules. Some academics have criticized accelerated programs as being too compressed to offer consistent educational quality (Traub, 1997).

In a national survey, Carol Aslanian (2001) found that among adults in the United States studying for undergraduate degrees, 13% were enrolled in accelerated degree programs. Estimates are that 25% or more of all adult students will be enrolled in accelerated programs by 2013 (Wlodkowski, 2003). This expansion is projected because adults with work and family responsibilities need efficient educational formats to advance their careers and reduce the stress of competing obligations. In addition, colleges and universities, with for-profit institutions like the University of Phoenix, compete for adult students by making courses and programs more flexible and responsive to their needs. Growth is also occurring internationally with universities offering accelerated programs in Puerto Rico, the Philippines, Ireland, Germany, and Australia.

Quality of Accelerated Learning

Critics mainly question accelerated learning because, in their opinion, these courses and programs do not offer enough time to cover the appropriate content and allow rigorous analysis and reflection of course material (Wolfe, 1998). However, Herbert Walberg's synthesis (1988) of time and learning research concluded that time is a necessary but not sufficient condition for learning and that time in and of itself is only a modest predictor of achievement. Other factors that influence learning as much or more so than time spent on learning are student capability, quality of instruction, and personal motivation (Wlodkowski, 1999). In addition, the neural networks that make up long term memory, the part of learning that lasts, fade unless the memory unit is used or reinforced in relationships relevant to one's life (Ratey, 2001).

Modest studies of accelerated courses, using summative assessments, have generally found adult student learning to meet a standard of satisfactory to excellent as judged by faculty experts (Wlodkowski & Westover, 1999). These studies required adult students to demonstrate writing skills, critical thinking, and application of a learned knowledge base. Similar research, conducted in Spanish in Puerto Rico (Wlodkowski, Iturralde-Albert, & Mauldin, 2000), found that the average performance of older students in accelerated courses was significantly higher than the average performance of younger students in traditional courses with the same teachers and content. However, the average family income and formal education experience were higher for the older students than for the younger students.

The initial evidence is that adults in accelerated courses do learn satisfactorily and in a manner that meets the challenge of conventional college coursework (Wlodkowski, 2003). Recent research supports the conclusion of Patricia Scott and Clifton Conrad (1992) in their comprehensive critique of accelerated courses: "the large number of studies across all fields with no preference between compressed and traditional formats suggest that all courses – regardless of field – can utilize intensive course designs without diminishing educational outcomes" (p. 443).

Characteristics of adults such as motivation for career advancement, work experience, and practice with self-directed responsibilities fit readily with characteristics of accelerated formats such as pragmatic courses, efficient academic progress, and faculty who are working professionals. This symmetry and interaction may catalyze overall learning. Just as online learning has fostered society's appetite for asynchronous learning, accelerated learning is enhancing society's desire for learning unrestricted by conventional expectations of time or tradition.

Needed Research and Assessment

Most studies in the field of accelerated learning are modest. The expansion of accelerated learning programs in adult education has far exceeded rigorous assessment and longitudinal research in areas such as student learning and persistence. Most studies are directed toward undergraduate business management programs. The majority of other accelerated programs are in disciplines such as teaching, nursing, and computer science. Studies of the effectiveness of accelerated learning need to be expanded to areas such as the physical and natural sciences and medicine and engineering to understand how widely applicable this approach to learning is. Research about how well younger adults, under the age of 25, learn in accelerated courses and programs is lacking. Responsible expansion of accelerated learning to a wider population and greater scope of academic disciplines requires substantially more research and assessment.

See also: continuing education, facilitation, motivation, prior learning and assessment recognition, teaching.

References and Further Reading

Aslanian, C. B. (2001). *Adult students today*. New York: The College Board.

Ratey, J. J. (2001). *A user's guide to the brain: Perception, attention, and the four theatres of the brain*. New York: Pantheon.

Scott, P.A., & Conrad, C. F. (1992). A critique of intensive courses and an agenda for research. In J. C. Smart (Ed.), *Higher education: Handbook of theory and research* (pp. 411–459). New York: Agathon Press.

Traub, J. (1997). Drive-thru U.: Higher education for people who mean business. *New Yorker*, October 20–27, 114–123.

Walberg, H. J. (1988). Synthesis of research

on time and learning, *Educational Leadership, 45*(6), 76–85.
Wlodkowski, R. J. (1999). *Enhancing adult motivation to learn: A comprehensive guide for teaching all adults*. San Francisco: Jossey-Bass.
Wlodkowski, R. J. (2003). Accelerated learning in colleges and universities. In R. J. Wlodkowski & C.E. Kasworm (Eds.), *Accelerated learning for adults: The promise and practice of intensive educational formats* (pp. 5–15). *New Directions for Adult and Continuing Education*, No. 97. San Francisco: Jossey-Bass.
Wlodkowski, R. J., Iturralde-Albert, L., & Mauldin, J. (2000). *Report on accelerated learning project: Phase 4*. Denver, CO: Center for the Study of Accelerated Learning at Regis University.
Wlodkowski, R. J., & Westover, T. (1999). Accelerated courses as a learning format for adults. *Canadian Journal for the Study of Adult Education,13*(1), 1–20.
Wolfe, A. (1998). How a for-profit university can be invaluable to the traditional liberal arts. *Chronicle of Higher Education* (December 4) B4–B5.

Raymond J. Wlodkowski

Action Learning

Action learning is an approach to developing people that emphasizes learning from and through experience by working on an actual problem or project. Action learning builds the capacity of individuals and systems to learn how to learn (Marsick & O'Neil, 1999). Participants work in small groups to examine and take action on a problem, and to learn how to learn from that action. A learning coach often works with the group to help the members learn how to balance task accomplishment and learning (Yorks, O'Neil, & Marsick, 1999). Action learning is practiced worldwide across a broad spectrum of contexts ranging from community-based initiatives to senior-level executive development. A program can last from several days to up to a year. This diverse application has spawned a number of "schools" and varieties of practice under the umbrella name of action learning. All varieties, however, share a common focus on helping people learn through using real work as the vehicle for learning (Yorks et al., 1999). The use of a real problem or project distinguishes action learning from other types of experienced-based learning such as outdoor experiential activities, role-playing, and simulations, which seek to draw out poignant lessons in the course of the learning activity for subsequent application in another context.

Origins of an Idea

The term action learning was coined in the 1940s by the late Reg Revans (1907–2003), often called its founder. The seeds of action learning were sown in the 1920s while Revans, a physicist, worked alongside five Nobel Prize winners at the Cavendish Laboratory at the University of Cambridge. Revans observed how the scientists met periodically in a collaborative, non-hierarchical forum to generate fresh insights and solutions into complex problems vexing them individually via a process of questioning and dialogue.

In 1945, Revans became the Director of Education with the National Coal Board. It was here that he conceptualized the notion of action learning, an approach to learning reminiscent of his early years at Cavendish. Facing an acute shortage of qualified managers following the war, Revans organized managers into small groups or "sets," as he called them, facilitating a questioning and dialogue process to share best practices and identify solutions to operational problems. Revans called this process action learning, a philosophy and method that stood in stark contrast to dominant notions of education that emphasized dissemination of static content to passive learners.

Action learning can be called a form of action research (Reason & Bradbury, 2001), that is, an iterative cycle of problem formulation, data collection and analysis, intervention, monitoring, assessment and problem re-formulation. But its emphasis is on learning with less attention paid to rigorous research methods.

L = P + Q

Revans defined learning as the product of two elements – programmed knowledge and questioning insight – captured in an equation: L = P + Q. Programmed knowledge (P) is found in books and experts. Questioning insight (Q) occurs when people question themselves and experts to shed new light on perplexing problems. Revans held that the key to learning is asking the right questions (Revans, 1998). Questioning insight opens the manager to new interpretations of experience and is essential to navigating an increasingly complex, uncertain world.

Essential Features

Revans' original conceptualization of action learning had three main elements: an action learning "set" of up to six members who met at regular intervals, a problem brought to the group by each individual set member, and a facilitator or "set advisor" who guided the process initially and then ideally worked himself or herself out of a job as participants gained greater confidence and skill in learning from one another, essentially "self-facilitating" the process (Weinstein, 2002).

Action learning has evolved considerably from Revans' original construction. In some program designs, participants work on individual projects and in others, the team works as a whole on one project (Marsick & O'Neil, 1999). The focus on individual versus team projects influences the degree of emphasis on individual versus organizational change. Team projects often focus on organizational goals, while individual projects focus on personal development.

The choice of a problem is a critical success factor in action learning (Lawrence, 1991). The design of the program is affected differently when the problem is a familiar or unfamiliar one, and when the team addresses the challenge in a familiar or unfamiliar setting (Revans, 1998). Depending on the learning context, an action learning project can focus on shop floor production issues, middle-level operational problems, or senior-level strategic issues. A learning coach may or may not be used depending on the approach, goal, organizational context, and the stage of the action learning program (O'Neil, 1999).

Action learning programs held in large, complex organizations often involve many stakeholders with vested interests in the project. It is not uncommon to have an overall executive sponsor as well as individual "clients" or business owners for each project, who themselves must interface with various constituencies on behalf of the project team.

Alternative Approaches

Action learning is best viewed as a tree with many branches. Two branches in particular, Action Reflection Learning™ and Business-

Driven Action Learning, offer alternative approaches and represent an evolution of Revans' original model.

Action Reflection Learning™ was developed independently by the Management Institute of Lund (MiL) and its United States counterpart, Leadership in International Management (LIM) and trademarked by both groups. As the name suggests, Action Reflection Learning™ emphasizes critical reflection, transformation, and change (Yorks et al., 1999). Proponents believe that learning coaches should draw out a deeper set of lessons learned through intentional reflection and challenges to assumptions underlying the thinking of participants (Marsick, 2002). The goal is to achieve personal and organizational transformation by changing one's whole assumptive frame of reference through learning (Yorks et al., 1999).

Business-Driven Action Learning (Boshyk, 2002) is practiced primarily in senior-level executive development programs. As the name implies, learning is grounded in business realities and drives business performance. This approach serves a dual mission of delivering tangible business results while developing strategic leadership capability among participants. Programs are typically sponsored by senior executives and focus on enterprise-level strategic issues and opportunities, as opposed to middle management operational issues.

Four Schools

O'Neil (1999) identified four distinct approaches or schools of action learning: (a) the tacit school, (b) the scientific school, (c) the experiential school, and (d) the critical reflection school. Moving hierarchically from the tacit school to the critical reflection school, each level involves a deeper focus around questioning insight that is increasingly more critical and complex (Yorks et al., 1999).

The tacit school is grounded in an assumption that significant learning will take place, with limited intervention, so long as carefully chosen participants are put together, some team building is done, and information is provided by experts (Yorks et al., 1999). Action learning programs that fall under the tacit school place strong emphasis on the project itself, reflecting a belief that leadership competencies will be developed "in action" in the natural course of the project.

The scientific school is grounded in the early work of Reg Revans who, as a physicist, based his thinking on the scientific method. This approach is highly rational and endeavors to apply the scientific method to social and workplace problems. The scientific school places a heavy emphasis on reformulating and solving problems and understanding how the problem fits into the broader system. Revans (1987) emphasized the importance of learning from peers or "comrades in adversity," as he called them, each wrestling with a complex problem with no clear solution. Followers of this school emphasize the ability of set members to learn on their own with only limited intervention by a learning coach early in the program.

The experiential school is grounded in Kolb's (1984) experiential learning model, which presents a continuous cycle of "doing, reflecting, consolidating, and planning" (Weinstein, 2002). Followers of this school place a strong emphasis on reflection via ongoing learning reviews guided by the learning coach. Group members engage in repeated cycles of action and reflection as a way to learn from experience and improve individual and organizational performance. The experiential school intentionally seeks personal development outcomes by helping people set and monitor progress toward personal learning goals (Yorks et al., 1999).

In the critical reflection school, there is an added dimension of challenging personal and organizational assumptions (Marsick, 2002). These practitioners begin with theories of learning from experience, as do practitioners in the experiential school, but they differ in how they use reflection (O'Neil, 1999). Reflection is taken to a deeper level by focusing on underlying premises in the thinking of participants. A learning coach plays a key role in this process by challenging the premises underlying the thinking of participants, along with taken-for-granted norms of their organization (Yorks et al., 1999). The strength of critically reflective action learning programs is their focus on transformative learning. They are most successful when a need for change is recognized and various levels of the organization are open to learning.

The "fit" among program design, goals, and organizational culture must be carefully considered when deciding upon a particular approach. Action learning programs become more complex, critical, contextual, and "noisy" as one moves up the ladder from tacit to critical reflection. Tacit programs are best suited to organizations that seek to reinforce their existing culture and way of doing business, while critical reflection programs are best suited to organizations facing massive sea change or discontinuity in the external environment.

Critique

Action learning has been critiqued. Programs are said to lack research rigor or quality control. Scholars find them too instrumental, not deeply critical, or too manager-centered. Practitioners disagree with one another's designs: e.g., not enough focus on action, reflection, learning, or results; too much "P" content or facilitator guidance; not enough questioning; too focused on consulting rather than one's own problem. Organizations resist changes growing from programs. Finally, a focus on past problems can preclude future-oriented vision.

See also: collaborative learning, learning organizations, problem-based learning, study circles, work-based learning, workplace learning.

References and Further Reading

Boshyk, Y. (Ed.). (2002). *Action learning worldwide: Experiences of leadership and organizational development.* Hampshire, UK, & New York: Palgrave Macmillan.

Kolb, D. A. (1984). *Experiential learning.* Englewood Cliffs, NJ: Prentice Hall.

Lawrence, J. (1991). Action learning – A questioning approach. In A. Mumford (Ed.), *Handbook of management development* (3rd ed., pp. 214–247). Brookfield, VT: Gower.

Marquardt, M. J. (1999). *Action learning in action: Transforming problems and people for world-class organizational learning.* Palo Alto, CA: Davies-Black Publishing.

Marsick, V. J. (2002). Exploring the many meanings of action learning and ARL. In L. Rohlin, K. Billing, A. Lindberg, & M. Wickelgren (Eds.), *Earning while learning in global leadership: The Volvo MiL partnership* (pp. 297–314). Lund, Sweden: Management Institute of Lund (MiL) Publishers.

Marsick, V. J., & O'Neil, J. (1999). The many faces of action learning. *Management Learning, 30*(2), 159–176.

O'Neil, J. (1999). *The role of the learning advisor in action learning.* Unpublished doctoral dissertation. Teachers College, Columbia University, New York.

Pedler, M. (1996). *Action learning for managers*. London: Lemos & Crane.

Reason, P., & Bradbury, H. (Eds.). (2001). *Handbook of action research: Participative inquiry and practice*. Thousand Oaks, CA: Sage.

Revans, R. W. (1987). *International Institute of Development Policy and Management on Action Learning: Manchester training handbook* No. 9. Manchester, UK: IDPM Publications.

Revans, R. W. (1998). *The ABC of action learning*. London: Lemos & Crane.

Weinstein, K. (2002). Action learning: The classic approach. In Y. Boshyk (Ed.), *Action learning worldwide: Experiences of leadership and organizational development* (pp. 3–18). Basingstoke, UK & New York: Palgrave Macmillan.

Yorks, L, O'Neil, J., & Marsick, V. J. (Eds.). (1999). Action learning: Successful strategies for individual, team, and organizational development. *Advances in Developing Human Resources*, no. 2 (pp. 1–18). San Francisco: Berrett Koehler.

Victoria J. Marsick and Jeffrey S. Kuhn

Action Research

Action research is a participative inquiry method in the qualitative research tradition (Reason & Bradbury, 2001). It has seen increased in recognition and usage throughout the social sciences over the past two decades and gained sweeping popularity in various sectors of adult education practice – in part because it helps make the connection between practice and research. Nevertheless, despite its growth in the field, it remains the subject of some controversy in the research literature.

Looking first at its growing usage, it was named by Bryant and Usher (1986) as the *preferred* style of adult education research in England as early as 1986. Meanwhile, in North America, adult education community-based contexts (Folkman & Rai, 2001) and corporate settings (Watkins, 2001) are widely utilizing this method. Action research is now so well-established across adult literacy practice in Australia, England, and North America (Quigley & Norton, 2003) that it is accepted as a key method in the research-in-practice movement among literacy practitioners (Brooks & Watkins, 1994; Quigley, 1997a, 1997b). In Australia, the UK, and the USA, the development of the literacy Research-In-Practice Move-ment has received considerable federal and provincial/territorial governmental and corporate support as well; nevertheless, it is one of the research methods that challenge traditional research paradigms and the role of the researcher, as seen next.

Action research has grown in terms of acceptability. Where once it was considered less rigorous and not generalizable, now these very weaknesses are seen as strengths. Merriam and Simpson (1995) note: "Because it [action research] lacks external and internal controls, generalizability of *results are limited to the specific circumstances and condition in which the research was done*" (italics added, p. 125). While researchers have argued that threats to internal and external validity, such as these, can be at least partially addressed in qualitative research, the real issue emerging in adult education is not techniques or methods or terminology. It is about the inherent values of researchers, the politics of research, and the credibility of research-based knowledge itself (Garrison & Shale, 1994). This was seen as early as 1995 when Merriam and Simpson categorized action research with participatory, critical, and feminist research designs, stating: "These less conventional paradigms differ in their definition of what is considered valid knowledge" (p. 121).

While action research is now a widely accepted *method* in the growing, ever-changing list of adult education research methods, controversy around valid, reliable, credible knowledge mounts. This larger issue has generated considerable discourse in other disciplines, such as in education and sociology (e.g., Denzin & Lincoln, 2000; Reason & Bradbury, 2001), to the point where authors such as Greenwood and Levin (1998) have asserted with some exasperation that action research is "not some kind of a social science dead end. It is a disciplined way of developing valid knowledge and theory while promoting social change" (p. 98). Clearly frustrated with the difficulties in establishing this and similar methods in the pantheon of methods, they advocate "restarting Western intellectual history just before the wrong turn begun in the 17th century with the emergence of the Cartesian model" (p. 97).

While the debates on knowledge and the role of the researcher evolve, it may also be noted that action research is an example of how research language, assumptions, and ideologies can become confusing – and confused – when they cross discipline boundaries. While many will agree that action research, as a method, has inherent principles in virtually all applications – such as the cogeneration of knowledge among researchers and participants (Greenwood & Levin, 1998, p. 97), the collective intent that the results are "for immediate application by those engaged in the research and by those for whom the research was initiated" (Merriam & Simpson, 1995, p. 122), and the tenet that the research process is both inductive and not so predetermined that the design cannot be modified during the study itself (Kemmis & McTagggart, 1986) – the question of where social change ends with action research, and begins with other methods such as participatory research, is very hard to determine. While action research is typically more concerned with professional development issues and participatory research more with social change, and while they have very different histories (Hall, 1979), their purposes and the intent of the researchers is a matter of debate. Meanwhile, the surge of similar methods like participatory action research (Borda, 2001), emancipatory action research (Kemmis, 2001), action inquiry (Torbert, 2001), and others such as action reflection learning (O'Neil & Marsick, 1994), all make the distinction between methods and purposes and ideologies very challenging. Some in adult education, such as Cervero (1991), Blunt (1994) and Quigley (1997a), have attempted to provide a framework for the many methodologies that continue to arise, but the research landscape keeps expanding.

See also: action learning, aesthetic education, appreciative inquiry, health education, HRD, participatory action research, research methods.

References and Further Reading

Blunt, A. (1994). The future of adult education research. In D. R. Garrison (Ed.), *Research perspectives in adult education* (pp. 167–210). Malabar, FL: Krieger.

Borda, O. (2001). Participatory (action) research in social theory: Origins and challenges. In P. Reason & H. Bradbury (Eds.), *Handbook of action research: Participative inquiry and practice* (pp. 27–37). Thousand Oaks, CA: Sage.

Brooks, A., & Watkins, K. E. (Eds.). (1994). *The emerging power of action inquiry technologies. New Directions for Adult and*

Continuing Education, No. 63. San Francisco: Jossey-Bass.

Bryant, I., & Usher, R. (1986, June). *Tension points in the adult education research*. Paper presented at the annual meeting of the Standing Committee of University Teaching and Research in the Education of Adults, (SCUTREA) University of Hull, England.

Cervero, R. M. (1991). Changing relationships between theory and practice. In J. Peters, P. Jarvis & Associates (Eds.), *Adult education: Evolution and achievements in a developing field of study* (pp. 19–41). San Francisco: Jossey-Bass.

Denzin, N. K., & Lincoln, Y. S. (Eds.). (2000). *Handbook of qualitative research* (2nd ed.). Thousand Oaks, CA: Sage.

Folkman, D., & Rai, K. (2001). Practicing action learning in a community context. *Adult Learning, 11*(3), 15–17.

Garrison, D. R., & Shale, D. (1994). Methodological issues: Philosophical differences and complementary methodologies. In D. R. Garrison (Ed.), *Research perspectives in adult education* (pp. 17–38). Malabar, FL: Krieger.

Greenwood, D., & Levin, M. (1998). *Introduction to action research: Social research for social change*. Thousand Oaks, CA: Sage.

Hall, B. L. (1979). Participatory research: Breaking the academic monopoly. In J. Niemi (Ed.), *Viewpoints on adult education research*. Columbus: Ohio State University. Retrieved December 2, 2003 from the database. (ERIC Document Reproduction No. ED179762)

Kemmis, S. (2001). Exploring the relevance of critical theory for action research: Emancipatory action research in the footsteps of Jürgen Habermas. In P. Reason & H. Bradbury (Eds.). *Handbook of action research: Participative inquiry and practice* (pp. 91–102). Thousand Oaks, CA: Sage.

Kemmis, S., & McTaggart, R. (1986). *The action research reader* (3rd ed.). Geelong, Victoria: Deakin University Press.

Merriam, S. B., & Simpson, E. L. (1995). *A guide to research for educators and trainers of adults* (2nd ed.). Malabar, FL: Krieger.

O'Neil, J., & Marsick, V. J. (1994). Becoming critically reflective through action research. In A. Brooks & K. E. Watkins (Eds.), *The emerging power of action inquiry technologies* (pp. 17–30). *New Directions for Adult and Continuing Education*, No. 63. San Francisco: Jossey-Bass.

Quigley, B. A. (1997a). The role of research in the practice of adult education. In B. A. Quigley & G. Kuhne (Eds.), *Creating practical knowledge through action research: Posing problems, solving problems, and improving daily practice* (pp. 3–22). *New Directions for Adult and Continuing Education*, No. 73. San Francisco: Jossey-Bass.

Quigley, B. A. (1997b). *Rethinking literacy education: The critical need for practice-based change*. San Francisco: Jossey-Bass.

Quigley, B. A., & Norton, M. (2003). It simply makes us better: Literacy research-in-practice in the USA, UK, and Canada. *Perspectives: The New York Journal of Adult Learning, 1*(2), 5–17.

Reason, P., & Bradbury, H. (Eds.). (2001). *Handbook of action research: Participative inquiry and practice*. Thousand Oaks, CA: Sage.

Torbert, W. (2001). The practice of action inquiry. In P. Reason & H. Bradbury (Eds.), *Handbook of action research: Participative inquiry and practice* (pp. 250–260). Thousand Oaks, CA: Sage.

Watkins, K. E. (2001). Learning by change: Action science and virtual organization development. *Adult Learning, 11*(3), 15–17.

B. Allan Quigley

Activism

Activism involves people in advancing a project or strengthening the hold of political ideas within their communities. As a process, activism can both strengthen excluded communities and, through collective action, promote the citizenship of individuals within those communities. As Ruth Lister (1997) points out, this type of action can boost individual and collective self-confidence because individuals and groups come to see themselves as political actors and effective citizens. "This is especially true for women for whom involvement in community organizations can be more personally fruitful than engagement in formal politics that are often experienced as more alienating than empowering" (p. 33).

When adult educators' work together with others to involve activists it encourages the active participation of ordinary people in creating the learning that shapes their selves, as well as the communities in which they live. Adult educators thus have an important role in generating activism within communities where apathy has prevailed. Activism helps to promote people's fundamental right as citizens to be listened to as part of the process of decision-making. Activism means that people can become involved in taking and influencing the decisions that affect their lives. Sometimes this can be difficult as activists may have very different views of what is important and what needs to be changed in their communities. Activist members of communities need to recognize each other as citizens who share a common status and equal rights. This can be difficult given that we live increasingly within communities of difference. We live in heterogeneous societies with many different voices so the challenge for progressive activism is to reconcile the valuing of difference with the need for shared understanding and agreement about purpose. An inclusive activism requires the recognition of different voices as well as the fair distribution of resources that provide the conditions for equal participation.

Difference and Solidarity

Communities need to be open to mutual recognition of the different perspectives and alternative views of the world in ways that allow pre-judgments to be challenged so that assumptions can be amended and an enriched understanding of others can be developed. The role of adult educators is to develop discussion and dialogue because this lies at the heart of learning. Through dialogue people learn to take a wider, more differentiated view and thus acquire sensitivity, subtlety and capacity for judgment. Identities are respected and compromises, if not consensus, are reached between rival traditions. By providing forums for participation and voice, adult educators can create conditions for mutual accountability so that activists can take each other's needs and claims into account in order to create the conditions for each other's development. Education for activism means the nurturing of a capacity and willingness to debate, to ask awkward questions and to see through obfuscation and lies. It requires the cultivation of awareness that individual fulfillment needs to be combined with the larger demands of solidarity and concern for the public good.

Social Movements

One way in which adult educators can become involved in working with activists and promoting activism is through social movements. Social movements, such as the women's movement, or the disability rights campaign or the coalition against globalization, all act to critique the existing social order, highlighting inadequacies and offering new ways of thinking. For example, the women's movement emphasized that apparently personal issues, such as the time spent on caring for the family, were actually political issues that required public action. Members of social movements subscribe to a common cause that is expressed collectively and embody a set of beliefs that reflect their shared values and purposes.

Social movements contribute to social change through the politicizing of areas of experience that were previously excluded from the political agenda. For example, the disability movement has challenged the discourse of personal handicap and shown instead how society erects disabling attitudinal, organizational and environmental barriers that exclude many of its citizens. Engaging in principled action has also been an effective way in which social movements have challenged the climate of opinion. For example, media images of activists protesting against environmental exploitation and pollution, potentially putting their lives at risk for a wider cause, have forced these issues on to the political agenda and made the link between the global and local.

People who participate in social movements engage in significant collective learning experiences but their educative potential often goes unnoticed by adult educators. These contribute to the creation of a critically informed public through the dissemination of ideas, values and beliefs that are in opposition to the *status quo*. The important task, therefore, is to find ways of systematizing a curriculum that extends what is learned whilst, at the same time, achieving successful social action. This type of relationship suggests a very different educational process from the traditional one where the educator defines what it is relevant to learn. Instead educators become resources for social movements and the curriculum consists of topics that their members see as relevant to their interests.

The ability of activists to define their own problems and develop their own organizational structures leads to a more genuinely democratic structure. The educational opportunities presented by working with such groups that are committed to progressive social change can be enormous. Working to develop a curriculum from the social context of individual experience requires identifying the contradictions that experience raises. For example, the experience of being disabled includes dependency and the analysis of what this means should be regarded as an educational resource rather than a problem to be solved. The idea of activists as learners also connects with the historical tradition of radical social action that emerged out of industrialization and the consequential changes in social structures in which political analysis was regarded as a prerequisite for transformative social change. As Paulo Freire (1972) has argued: "there is no such thing as a neutral education process. Education either functions as an instrument that is used to facilitate the integration of the young into the logic of the present system and bring about conformity to it or it becomes the practice of freedom" (p. 56). Education from this perspective "becomes the means by which men and women deal critically and creatively with reality and discover how to participate in the transformation of the world" (p. 56).

The articulation of a vision that expresses the social nature of our experience, which aims to turn personal troubles into public issues and to support social movements that act to transform the world, are therefore legitimate educational aims.

Educating Desire

Social movements have also played an important part in stretching our imagination about alternative ways of being because they open up questions about what we value and how we want to live. They ask questions about what type of society we want for the future and thus "inject critique, vision and imagination into what we have learnt to take for granted" (Crowther, 1999, p. 36). By seeing the world as it is and how it might be, social movements are intrinsically utopian. In this sense utopia's proper role is to stir the imagination and challenge comfortable habits – a place to be desired rather than a place that does not exist. Adult educators, too, should be concerned with the world as it could be, as much as with the world as it is. It is important to begin questioning our desires and to test them against other desires in order to explore what is possible for the future. As E. P. Thompson (1976) commented, utopia's proper space is the education of desire in order "to desire better, to desire more, and above all to desire in a different way" (p. 790).

One example of the education of desire is the disability movement, which aims to bring about structural and cultural changes to ensure that disabled people can have the same possibilities, and be supported by the same rights, as their contemporaries who do not have disabilities. The movement changed the focus of activity in relation to disability away from organizations *for* disabled people to organizations controlled and run *by* disabled people. They stress autonomy and the importance of self-organization as a challenge to the myth of passivity and the objectification of disabled people that results from underlying oppressive ideologies and social relations. As Tom Shakespeare (1993) points out, "in making 'personal troubles' into 'public issues' disabled people are affirming the validity and importance of their own identity, rejecting the victimizing tendencies of society at large, and their own socialization" (p. 263).

An aspect of this change of consciousness has been for disabled people to adopt a disabled identity with the same vigor and sense of purpose as has been achieved in other social movements such as the lesbian and gay movement. The process of positive identification for people with disabilities is made difficult by the existence of internalized oppression, coupled with segregation and isolation from sources of collective support and strength. Nevertheless, the movement has been an educational force for change both within disability organizations and through its campaigning role in educating the wider world. It has enabled disabled people to desire a better life and thus to campaign actively for their human, civil and political rights through consciousness-raising and education. This shows the strong link between activism and learning and the important role that adult educators can play in this process.

Activism and Democracy

It is at the level of communities that people often get their first experience of democracy. Therefore, expanding opportunities for democratic life should start here where, for many people, they can engage directly in issues that affect their everyday lives. In the current context, however, a good deal of interest in participation may work against democratic life, rather than for it. For example, when community activists become incorporated into an externally created partnership that seeks to achieve goals that are not in the community's interest, criticism can be silenced. There are also problems with tokenism, in which, for example, the one Black person on a committee is burdened with the expectation of being able to "speak for" the entire community from which he or she comes. The development of local coalitions against exclusion such as those pursued through social movements, however, can lead to the development of a political culture that emphasizes the fundamentally unequal nature of society rather than people's individual deficits. Emphasizing the importance of redistributing resources also shows that there are alternatives to increasing inequalities that do not entirely rely on individual action.

In order to do this, the knowledge and experiences of those who have been excluded need to be valued and the mystification caused by expert knowledge needs to be interrogated. The democratic approach is about more than having a voice in services, however important that is. It is also about how we are treated and regarded more generally, and with having a greater say and control over the whole of our lives. Members of communities can become active citizens making demands for change when their different ways of knowing and understanding the world being valued as a resource for learning. Rather than seeking to minimise risk, adult educators should be educating desire through promoting activism and challenging activists to define and solve their problems for themselves.

See also: conscientization, environmental adult education, ethnography, human capital theory, popular education, praxis, problematizing learning, social justice, social movement learning.

References and Further Reading

Crowther J. (1999). Popular education and the struggle for democracy. In J. Crowther, I. Martin, & M. Shaw (Eds.), *Popular education and social movements in Scotland today* (pp. 29–40). Leicester: NIACE.

Freire, P. (1972). *Pedagogy of the oppressed.* (M. B. Ramos, Trans.). Harmondsworth: Penguin.

Lister, R. (1997). Citizenship: Towards a feminist synthesis. *Feminist Review*, 57, Autumn, 28–48.

Shakespeare, T. (1993). Disabled people's self-organization: A new social movement? *Disability, Handicap and Society*, 8 (3), 249–264.

Thompson, E. P. (1976). *William Morris*. New York: Pantheon Books.

Lyn Tett

Activity Theory

Activity theory (often referred to in the USA as situated cognition) defines human learning and cognition as communicative social processes rather than psychological mental activities. From this viewpoint understanding learning and cognition requires understanding how their social, tool-dependent, and experiential nature shapes their construction in and through the everyday activities of real people acting in the real world: "cognition observed in everyday practice is distributed – stretched over, not divided among – mind, body, activity and culturally organized settings (which include other actors)" (Lave, 1988, p. 1). Learning and cognition are social because they are produced by and through communicative processes as people interact with each other in specific communities (which have histories, rules and social patterns, norms and assumptions shaping communication); they are not individual mental activities "inside the head." Learning and cognition are tool-dependent in that people acting in communities typically act/interact with culturally-defined social and material mechanisms that both aid and structure cognition (things such as tools, technology, language). Learning and cognition are experiential in that adults act in, interact with, and act on context itself (in terms of producing, reproducing, or altering purposes, norms, and specific activities). As depicted by Tara Fenwick (2000), "knowledge emerges as a result of these elements interacting. Thus, knowing is interminably inventive and entwined with doing" (p. 253). Understanding cognition as "entwined with doing" is key to understanding how activity theory "situates" acting humans in the real world (Chaiklin & Lave, 1993; Engestrom & Miettinen, 1999; Kirshner & Whitson, 1997; Lave & Wenger, 1991). Only by knowing the setting, activities, and cultural accoutrements can we understand cognition.

Related Concepts

Activity theory and situated cognition take the position that there is more to human cognition than individual mental activity. Human cognitive practices are understood as inherently *in* the world of actors interacting with each other in socially organized settings with culturally-provided tools. This point of view challenges the dominant psychological construction of cognition as individually acquired stocks of stable knowledge that knowers can transport for use in any setting. In situating cognition and learning in the real world, proponents of situated analyses have introduced a number of related concepts which sometimes are erroneously used as synonyms for the broader theories but actually are subconstructs representing specific aspects of situated views. For example, "legitimate peripheral participation" (Lave & Wenger, 1991) is sometimes used as a substitute for activity theory in the United States. The term really refers to the "central defining characteristic" of situated activity in which "learners inevitably participate in communities of practitioners and that the mastery of knowledge and skill requires newcomers to move [from peripheral] toward full participation in the sociocultural practices of a community" (Lave & Wenger, p. 29). Here, Lave and Wenger also introduce the related construct of communities of practice which refers to the highly specialized activities, discourses, skills, tools, and norms of interaction that constitute any one community of activity such as midwifery or tailoring or navigating a ship or designing a park, and so on.

Situating cognition thus depends upon the idea of authentic activity. Learning and cognition are therefore processes of enculturation in authentic situated social practices, not matters of knowledge acquisition and internalized mental processes. Enculturation through legitimate participation in communities of practice introduces the central role of apprenticeship in situated analyses: "cognitive apprenticeship methods try to enculturate students into authentic practices through activity and social interaction in a way similar to that evident – and evidently successful – in craft apprenticeship" (Brown, Collins, & Duguid, 1989, p.37). For millennia humans have adopted apprenticeship as a crucial instructional mechanism for gaining the cultural proficiency necessary to operate in the world. In the situated perspective, learning and cognition are not simply learning *from* experience because they are themselves located *in* tool-mediated social interaction.

History

One strand of situated activity theories begins with "the problem of context" (Chaiklin & Lave, 1993; Kirshner & Whitson, 1997; Lave, 1988). Psychological models of learning and knowing have depicted cognition as a complex but decontextualized individual neurological process. In this view learning occurs "inside" the physiological "mind" in a process that acquires and stores "knowledge" to be used at will in any circumstance. This conception of cognition as the ability to acquire, transfer, and apply knowledge has not only dominated our understanding and practice of education (Brown et al., 1989), it has also helped to sustain a false separation between knowing and doing (Lave). Jean Lave, along with and among others (e.g., Chaiklin & Lave; Kirshner & Whitson; Lave & Wenger,1991; Rogoff & Lave, 1984), has challenged this acquisition and transfer model by showing how knowing and learning are inherently, integratively, and irremovably situated in the everyday real world of social actors: "knowledge-in-practice, constituted in settings of practice, is the locus of the most powerful knowledgeability of people in the lived-in world" (Lave, p. 14). This view, prevalent in the United States under the term "situated cognition," typically tends to questions of learning particularly in schooling contexts (such as child and adolescent education) and contexts of professional development (such as learning in various professions) (see Kirshner & Whitson, 1997; McLellan,1996). The situated cognition strand is preceded by and derived from the strand known as activity theory which is used to describe the theory and research of the cultural-historical school of Russian psychology in the 1920s and 1930s (Engestrom & Miettinen,1999).

Although intimations of activity theory can be discerned in Marx's social analysis and American pragmatism (Engestrom & Miettinen,1999), L. S. Vygotsky, A.N. Leont'ev, and A.R. Luria are routinely identified in both strands as key originators to what has come to be termed "the social formation of mind" (Wertsch, 1985). Translations and interpretations of their work began appearing in the West in the 1970s and 1980s inspiring both the development of American interpretations of situated cognition and the continued development of activity theory in Eastern European and Scandinavian countries. Whereas the American interpretations have come to focus on questions of learning and education, the European tradition has continued to focus on the analysis of cognition to understand how thought, meaning, communication, and activity are socially constructed and interpreted (Engestrom & Miettinen). Such analysis specifically investigates how humans construct and communicate meaning through language but also more broadly how meaning is semiotically constructed and conveyed as well as interpreted and contested. Since the early 1990s the journal *Mind, Culture, and Activity* has presented a steady stream of theoretical and empirical analyses using activity theory to investigate a wide range of human activities representing the social formation of mind.

Contributions

Activity theory and situated cognition are prominent contributors to the larger movement in recent decades of what some have called the "cultural turn" in social and educational analysis. What was once thought to be generic and nomological is now understood to be local and idiographic; what was once thought to be structural and stable is now understood to be constructed and mediated. Such depictions, however, still envision the world as bifurcated between structure and agency, between voluntarism and determinism, between synchronic and diachronic, between macro and micro. By investigating the social formation of mind, Engestrom and Miettinen (1999) suggest that activity theory has transcended its origins in Russian psychology to contribute to the "ongoing multidisciplinary wave of interest in cultural practices and practice-bound cognition" (p. 8). They argue that there is a demand for a new unit of analysis which activity theory furnishes. For example, much social analysis leans to one side or the other of traditional dichotomies such as structure–agency questions and macro–micro analyses. Activity theory, with its unit of analysis as the activity network, integrates such dichotomies as the local and the general, the specific and the historical as "culturally mediated human activity" (Engestrom & Miettinen; see also Kirshner & Whitson, 1997). By transcending false dichotomies, activity theory can get beyond the unsatisfactory "linear and monocausal concepts of causation taken from classical physics" (Engestrom & Miettinen, p. 9) by examining the socially recursive construction of human learning and knowing. Activity theory has also added new dimensions to social constructivism by broadening it to include more than the single actor's perception of meaning; meaning is co-authored as well as contested by many interacting social agents through continual community creation and recreation. Kirshner and Whitson further posit that situated cognition can contribute to the question of locating thought: "thoughts are generally considered to be in the head, leading to the usual dualism of a world of mental representations separated from the real, outside-the-head world" (p. 10). Lave (1988) and others have challenged this alleged split by showing how the thinking of "just plain folks" is a product of their interaction with the world, that is, entwined with doing. The promise of situated cognition and activity theory lies in leading us away from dichotomous entrapments and towards situated interpretations of human activity, although operationalising such analyses remains a challenge in educational investigations (Kirshner & Whitson).

Issues in Adult Education

Like many other forms of educational inquiry, adult education has uncritically adopted functionalist interpretations of mind–body dichotomies. In addition, by emulating more established social science disciplines, adult education often has sought knowledge of itself in nomological and decontextualized forms. But adult education has not been immune to the increasing call to consider context in analysis, although it has largely escaped so far the more significant cultural turn in social and educational analysis. As the call developed in the 1980s to "analyse the context" of educational practice, situated cognition in some small way contributed to that impetus in adult education. Beginning in the 1990s situated interpretations of educational phenomenon began appearing in the adult education literature in the United States and the United Kingdom. For the most part, researchers in the USA attempting to use situated cognition perspectives have tended to utilize sub-constructs such as legitimate peripheral participation, communities of practice, and authentic activity while not incorporating the more significant dimensions of activity theory itself. Context thus tends to get included as an "add on" to preexisting frames of analysis such as functionalism and psychological humanism rather than constituting cognition. Consequently, the theoretical origins of activity theory in its "social formation of mind" Russian psychology or, more recently, situated cognition's derivations from Pierre Bourdieu's cultural capital and Anthony Giddens' structuration theories have never really become evident in adult education. Similarly, as intimated by Fenwick (2000), activity theory/situated cognition's potential to reconstitute a theory of experiential learning in adult education has yet to be realized. Adult education tends to conceive of experiential learning as Dewey- and Kolb-like reflections *on* experience whereas activity theory locates cognition *in* experience. Further, as Fenwick has noted, the political potential of situated cognition is never realized. In Lave's (1988) earlier work, she drew upon Bourdieu and Giddens to question cultural reproduction in schooling. In US education more generally such political analysis has never really appeared in situated analyses. Indeed, as situated theories have become more visible in American education, their employment has become instrumental rather than analytical (see, for example, their use in "teaching technology" in the USA; for an exception to this dominant trend, see Lea & Nicoll, 2002). That political potential has not surfaced in adult education either.

See also: actor network theory, communities of practice, experiential learning, social constructivism.

References and Further Reading

Brown, J., Collins, A., & Duguid, P. (1989). Situated cognition and the culture of learning. *Educational Researcher, 18*(1), 32–42.

Chaiklin, S., & Lave, J. (Eds.). (1993). *Understanding practice: Perspectives on activity and context.* Cambridge: Cambridge University Press.

Engestrom, Y., & Miettinen, R. (1999). Introduction. In Y. Engestrom, R. Miettinen, & R. Punamaki (Eds.), *Perspectives on activity theory* (pp. 1–16). Cambridge, UK: Cambridge University Press.

Fenwick, T. J. (2000). Expanding conceptions of experiential learning: A review of the five contemporary perspectives on cognition. *Adult Education Quarterly, 50*(4), 243–272.

Kirshner, D., & Whitson, J. (Eds.). (1997). *Situated cognition: Social, semiotic, and psychological perspectives.* Mahwah, NJ: Lawrence Erlbaum.

Lave, J. (1988). *Cognition in practice: Mind, mathematics, and culture in everyday life.* Cambridge, UK: Cambridge University Press.

Lave, J., & Wenger, E. (1991). *Situated learning: Legitimate peripheral participation.* Cambridge, UK: Cambridge University Press.

Lea, M., & Nicoll, K. (Eds.). (2002). *Distributed learning: Social and cultural approaches to practice.* London: Routledge/Falmer.

McLellan, H. (Ed.). (1996). *Situated learning perspectives*. Englewood Cliffs, NJ: Educational Technology Publications.

Rogoff, B., & Lave, J. (Eds.). (1984). *Everyday cognition: Its development in social context*. Cambridge, MA: Harvard University Press.

Wertsch, J. (1985). *Vygotsky and the social formation of mind*. Cambridge, MA: Harvard University Press.

Arthur L. Wilson

Actor-Network Theory

Actor-network theory (ANT) was developed in the sociology of science and technology, but has become increasingly influential in the social sciences more generally, and latterly in adult education. Sometimes referred to as the sociology of translation, it was influenced by post-structuralism, in particular the work of Michel Foucault. Perhaps its most defining principle is that human and non-human objects are treated as equivalent, what is referred to as the principle of symmetry. Unlike most social theories, therefore, which privilege human intentions and actions, actor-network theory holds that humans can only act because of objects and that objects can themselves act. This means that human and non-human actors must all be written or talked about within the same genre. Human actors are not privileged over non-human actors. Actors have the power to act only insofar as they are elements in a network, which suggests that action is relational. Thus, one can think of teachers and students as nodes in the network, what is referred to as a "knowing location." This challenges fundamental binaries such as the human/non-human, subject/object, structure/agency and nature/technology. For Bruno Latour (1993), one of the main exponents of ANT, all objects are hybrid. These hybrids are ordered in space and time and it is this ordering that constitute the networks through which certain things become possible and sayable and other things not. This poses major challenges to how we theoretically conceive the various practices of adult education, as it asks us to look at the complex relations that make up practice rather than focus on a selection of factors. Given its roots in the sociology of science and technology, it may not be surprising that it is amongst those interested in networked learning that ANT has emerged most strongly (Fox, 2000), where notions of the cyborg have been used as a metaphor to indicate the hybrid forms of human/technology actors through which learning takes place. However, debates in the areas of literacy (Clarke, 2002) and lifelong learning (Edwards, 2002) have also seen contributions drawing upon ANT.

From Individual to Social Understandings of Practices

In general ANT is part of the shift from individualized, psychological approaches to the understanding of social practices, knowledge-building and subjectivity to more social and cultural interpretations. Learning is taken to involve spatio-temporal orderings of actors, the actors and ordering involved resulting in certain forms of learning over others. The what, who and how they are brought together for human resource development will therefore be very different from that for community activism. Both might be identified as adult education, but they signify very different relational practices.

Knowledge-building then is taken to be a joint exercise within a network that is spread across space and time and includes inanimate – for example, books, journals, pens, computers – as well as animate objects. The symmetry between inanimate and animate objects in actor-network theory arises because "human powers increasingly derive from the complex *interconnections* of humans with material objects . . . This means that the human and physical worlds are elaborately intertwined and cannot be analyzed separate from each other" (Urry, 2000, p. 14). In adult education, this means that learning and subjectivity are themselves distributed through the range of networks within which one is interconnected. These networks can expand and contract and some will be more stable than others over time. Adult educational practices therefore can be seen as actor-networks in which participants and participation are ordered in time and space, whether this is in the classroom, the workplace, the community, online, or in the complex interplay of all of these. ANT therefore provides a framework for analysing the exercises of power by which cultural, social and economic power is circulated and exercised at the micro level of social practices.

Methodologically, therefore, research influenced by ANT tends to provide detailed ethnographies. While these have mostly been carried out to date in the science and technology domains, work has started to emerge that is relevant to adult education. For example, Nespor (1994) provides ethnographies of business studies and physics students' different networking practices to examine the knowledge and identity productions in which they are engaged. He uses this to critique the notion of communities of practice as representing too static an understanding of learning. Given this methodological approach, ANT does not provide the grounds for large-scale generalizations about adult education practices *per se*, but opens up possibilities for the detailed understanding of how difference is engendered among those practices. The actor-networks of HIV education, agricultural development and flower arranging may all constitute forms of adult education, but the mobilization of those practices as adult education obviously takes very different forms. ANT provides important resources through which to understand those differences in terms of performative practices and not in terms of somewhat static notions of context or structure.

The Constitution of Actor-Networks

In one of its earliest formulations, four moments to networking practices are identified. These are problematization, interessement, enrolment and mobilization (Callon, 1986). Problematisation is about what subjectivities and interests are allowable within specific networks. In other words, what objects are included and excluded. This is done through defining the problem, which acts as a powerful form of gate-keeping. Interessement identifies the practices through which barriers are built between those who are part of the network and those who are not, which can take many different forms, for example, material, discursive, taste. They are the actions through which other interests are excluded. While interessement sets the barriers to participation, enrolment fashions the alliances within the network. It signifies the internal rather than foreign policy. Mobilizations are the practices through which enrolled networks are stabilized, however temporarily, and made manageable and mobile. Thus, ANT emphasizes the performative nature of social practice, as "left to their own devices *human actions and words do not spread very far at all*" (Law, 1994, p. 24). These performances are the translations through which networks form, reform and dissolve. Without translation, the capacity of one actor to represent the interests of others, the network is not stabilized. It is through translation or mediation that networks are formed. Without such practices, there is no network. ANT therefore emphasizes the changing nature of human knowledge and practices and the actions through which power is exercised. Thus, for instance, in thinking about a learning episode, we need to examine the network of actors through which it is constituted. Learning can be examined not as a state, disposition or process, but as actor-networks in which participants and participation are choreographed, thereby constituting particular orderings of space and time through particular mediations. As a result, specific possibilities for learning and subjectivity emerge.

Nouns and Verbs

To call ANT a theory is to suggest a settled body of understanding. However, this does not do justice to the ways in which it is constantly changing and developing as a way of understanding social practices. Most of its well-known proponents reject the idea that it is a theory as such. In a sense ANT may be better understood as a way of theorizing than a theory *per se*, as a verb rather than noun. This way of understanding ANT is consistent with its own understanding of social practices as forms of action. For adult educators, this means that all actions have to be conceptualized as practices with performative effects, and the actors involved are more numerous and more complexly related than can be encompassed by discourses of teachers and learners. However, this also points to a possible relationship between ANT and activity theory, although the latter privileges human over non-human actors, as the former are felt to be imbued with agency independent of the latter.

See also: activity theory, communities of practice.

References and Further Reading

Callon, M. (1986). Some elements of a sociology of translation: Domestication of the scallops and the fishermen of St. Briue Bay. In J. Law (Ed.), *Power, action, belief: A new sociology of knowledge* (pp. 196–233). London: Routledge & Kegan Paul.

Clarke, J. (2002). A new kind of symmetry: Actor-network. Theories and the new literacy studies. *Studies in the Education of Adults*, *34*(2), 107–121.

Edwards, R. (2002). Mobilising lifelong learning: Governmentality in educational practices. *Journal of Education Policy*, *17*(3), 353–365.

Fox, S. (2000). Communities of practice, Foucault and actor-network theory. *Journal of Management Studies*, *37*(6), 853–867.

Latour, B. (1993). *We have never been modern*. London: Sage.

Law, J. (1994). *Organising modernity*. London: Sage.

Nespor, J. (1994). *Knowledge in motion: Space, time and curriculum in undergraduate physics and management*. London: Falmer.

Urry, J. (2000). *Sociology beyond societies*. London: Routledge.

Richard Edwards

Adult

Adult is a concept that is readily understood but difficult to define. Dictionaries indicate that adult means grown-up, mature, or a person who has reached the age of majority. The roots of the term can be traced back to the Old English word *ald* and the Latin *alere,* both of which encompass ideas about growth, nourishment/preparation, old age and becoming "head of a family" (meaning a senior community member or a forebear, as in "alderman" and "elder"). *Alere* also gives rise to *adolescere,* from which is derived +"adolescence," denoting a period of "growing up." The past-participle of *adolescere* gives *adultus,* from which we obtain "adult." Thus, deeply-embedded in the term is an understanding that the person to whom it is applied has completed a period of growth and preparation and so passed from a state of immaturity and dependency to one of maturity and independence, thereby achieving a position of responsibility within, and towards, their society. Studies of adult life and the aging process became popular in the 1960s and 1970s. Translated into models of development based on "ages and stages," they continue to underpin much of the theory and practice of adult education. However, the basis of developmental theory is now in question.

Adulthood Defined by Age

D. B. Bromley (1974) noted the "fundamental importance of the juvenile phase of the life-cycle" (p. 9), but pointed out that it seemed to claim an inordinate amount of intellectual attention and material resources, since: "We spend about one quarter of our lives growing up and three quarters growing old." Bromley suggested that the transition between growing up and growing old occurred somewhere between the ages of 16 and 20, when "a person completes his [*sic*] genetically regulated programme of growth" (p. 17).

In these terms, becoming an adult is simply a matter of biology. It happens when the physical transformations which take place between birth and puberty are complete and the human body enters a relatively stable state in which, barring injury or the onset of disease, change becomes a slow, albeit cumulative, process. Bluntly, adulthood is a period of aging, a slow deterioration culminating in death. However, in human societies, adulthood is additionally defined by psychological, social and cultural factors and there is a dynamic interplay between these factors and the physical process of aging (see Tennant & Pogson, 1995).

Aristotle's view of aging was that all living organisms, including humans, began life containing a latent heat which gradually dissipated over time until it disappeared completely at death – but he thought that, while the human body reached its prime between the ages of 30–35, the mind did not reach this state until a person was about 49 years old. In Roman times, Cicero suggested that the process of aging might be temporarily resisted by physical exercise, diet and intellectual activity. His advocacy of the benefits of learning in later life anticipated much current thinking about the role of adult education in the lives of older people, as well as the notion of "functional age" as a more useful measure of psychological and physical capabilities than chronological age. By itself, chronological age is a relatively poor determinant of capabilities, attitudes or behaviors. Nevertheless, many social and legal conventions are age-linked, often inconsistently. A common definition of an adult is a person who has reached the age of majority. The phrase is associated in Western democratic societies with the right to vote in the election of political representatives – but the age when this right can be exercised varies between countries and at different times, and does not always coincide with the age at which it is deemed legal to participate in other adult activities over which the state may hold jurisdiction, such as having sex, driving a vehicle or drinking alcohol.

While the socio-political drivers for such conventions and legislation vary across cultures and history, there seems to be a universal assumption that a boundary exists between the mid/late teens and early 20s, and that crossing it denotes a significant rite of passage into adulthood. The ritual of coming of age is often associated with the 21st birthday even when, as in the UK, voting rights are obtained at the age of 18.

In East Africa, the Masai culture has been deliberately shaped by an "age-set" system which places those of the same age band in groups in order to inculcate, and take collective advantage of, the particular skills, knowledge and expertise associated with the age-set. By the age of 16, young people are expected to be sufficiently prepared for a move into the next age-set and this transition has traditionally been marked by the ritual of circumcision. After this, adulthood is assumed: girls deemed ready to marry and have children; boys to be admitted to the warrior group, remaining there for 10–12 years before undergoing a further ritual and obtaining admission to the tribal elder group overseeing community affairs (Burger, 1990, pp. 54–55).

Ages, Phases and Stages

The idea that chronological age is not simply a marker of the passage of time but of distinct stages in a human life has long been prevalent: William Shakespeare wrote of the Seven Ages of Man; in the Talmud, the Sayings of the Fathers refer to 14 stages; Confucius thought there were 6. Twentieth-century theories of human development have endorsed the notion of "life-stages": they remain divided on the number of stages and how to define them but similarly assume a linear progression from one stage to the next.

A slightly different image is invoked by the term life-cycle. Although he initially used this, Bromley (1974) subsequently noted a preference for the term life-path arguing that it allowed a distinction and a contrast to be made between "*juvenile* and *adult* phases" of life, as well the identification of *stages* within each *phase* (pp. 18–32, original emphases). Belief in two distinct phases of human development, subdivided into successive stages, underpins the view that the processes of thinking, reasoning and learning are qualitatively different in adulthood than during childhood and adolescence; and that education, especially for those in the first phase, should be arranged on a hierarchical basis with each level providing preparation for the next. Although they continue to give shape to complex educational systems, such understandings, and the developmental theories that support them, are increasingly being contested.

Within the so-called adult phase of life, Bromley (1974) postulated seven stages: early, middle and late adulthood, occurring, respectively, between the ages of 20–25, 25–40, and 40–60; pre-retirement (60–65);

retirement (65–70); old age (from 70 onwards); and a "terminal stage" to acknowledge the process of dying as an aspect of life rather than death. Voicing a belief commonly held in Western societies, especially in the 20th century, Rhona and Robert Rapoport (1980) claim that experiences up to the age of 25 are effectively rehearsals, preparing people for the main act of their lives. They assert that this occurs, approximately, from the ages of 25 to 55 and constitutes "the prime of life, full adulthood, the productive years" (p. 72). The assertion is clearly based on their view that: "We live in a society which measures much of the value of its adult members by their *production* (in which we include . . . *reproduction*). . . peoples' self-esteem depends a good deal on feeling that they are fulfilling an occupational role, or a parental role (or both). . . [it] is one reason why most people dread old age" (p. 100, original emphasis).

This linear, developmental model of preparation and production/reproduction, followed by a period spent, once again, outside the mainstream of society, is a feature of a peculiarly Western mindset. It derives from a mechanistic and reductionist worldview in which people are like cogs in a machine: they are moulded during their formative years to fulfill various useful functions within the economic machinery of society but, after a specified period of time, they are regarded as redundant or obsolete. The Rapoports' (1980) vignette clearly assumes that, at the end of a period of "full adulthood," older people no longer have a valuable function in the machinery of society, rather than, as in other times and cultures, that they are able to take on a different, but still-valued, role as an elder with knowledge and wisdom to contribute to their communities.

Developmental Theories and Critiques

Developmental theories help to underpin, and are a product of, a mechanistic approach to education. Among the most frequently cited in adult education are those of Robert Havighurst, Daniel Levinson and Erik Erikson. Havighurst (1972) made a clear distinction between the "developmental tasks" of different age-groups: those of early adulthood, between the ages of 18–30, encompass marriage, parenthood, home- and career-making, and social responsibility. Levinson et al. (1978) located early adulthood between the ages of 20–39 and similarly noted that it is characterized by moving out of the family home, creating personal stability and developing life-structuring goals.

Erikson (1978) located eight levels of development, also based on chronological age, but suggested that at each level a particular kind of conflict needs to be met and resolved, thereby enabling the individual to develop greater autonomy and self-awareness. If conflicts remain unresolved this is likely to result in psychological difficulties associated with states of loneliness, uselessness and despair. In these terms, becoming an adult is not simply about accomplishing certain tasks but, through these tasks, achieving an integrated psychological state.

Shauna Pomerantz and Amanda Benjamin (2000) note that answers to the question "What is an adult?" generally involve lists of "typical" adult behaviors which draw heavily on such theories. However, they argue that the traditional view of adulthood as a linear trajectory along which societal hoops are jumped in some sort of ascending order no longer matches either the reality of many people's lives or popular cultural images of adulthood. Using situation comedies presented on American television as a lens through which to view popular conceptions of adults, they suggest that, in the 1950s and 1960s, "The line between adult and child was solid and rarely, if ever, transgressed. . . . Ages and stages were respected as the "natural" order of things" (pp. 342–343). By the 1990s, the distinction between adult behavior and that of children had virtually disappeared, with television characters slipping between adult and juvenile "personas" and often struggling actively against the traditional expectations of adulthood.

Even before such images became common, one of the main critiques of developmental theories was that they sought to be universal and therefore ignored the dynamics of change over time and the variability of individuals. Moreover, they were often based on research undertaken with boys and men within a particular society and value system in which the state had already institutionalized the life course.

New postmodern understandings of the self as a changing narrative, together with an emerging worldview shaped by holistic rather than mechanistic principles, suggest that the time is ripe for a re-examination of what it means to be an adult in the 21st century.

See also: adult development, adult learning, andragogy, life history, motivation, older adults' learning, young adult education.

References and Further Reading

Bromley, D. B. (1974). *The psychology of human ageing* (2nd ed.). Harmondsworth: Penguin.

Burger, J. (1990). *Gaia atlas of First Peoples.* London: Gaia Books/Robertson McCarta.

Erikson, E. H. (1978). *Adulthood.* New York: Norton.

Havighurst, R. (1972). *Developmental tasks and education* (3rd ed.). New York: MacKay.

Levinson, D. J., Darrow, D., Klein, E. B., Levinson, M., & McKee, B. (1978). *The seasons of a man's life.* New York: Knopf.

Pomerantz, S., & Benjamin, A. (2000). "When you act like an adult, I'll treat you like one . . .": Investigating representations of adulthood in popular culture. In T. J. Sork, V.-L. Chapman, & R. St. Clair (Eds.), *AERC 2000*: Proceedings of the 41st Adult Education Research Conference (pp. 341–345). Vancouver, University of British Columbia.

Rapoport, R., & Rapoport, R. (1980). *Growing through life.* London: Harper & Row.

Tennant, M. C., & Pogson, P. (1995). *Learning and change in the adult years.* San Francisco: Jossey-Bass.

Cheryl Hunt

Adult Development

Adult development, defined as change over time or change with age, is central to the practice of adult education. But defining development as change over time belies the complexity of the concept. What triggers change and what is the process? Some view development as an orderly unfolding or progression (e.g., Erikson, 1963), while others find little about the process that is preprogrammed; instead, development is an adaptation response to new priorities and expectations associated with the life course. The goal of development is also unclear. Is it to achieve an end point such as self-actualization (Maslow, 1970), or a more permeable and inclusive perspective (Mezirow, 2000)? Or, is development dialectic in nature, that is, a constant interactive process between the person and the environment with no end point.

Defining development as change over time or change with age means that change can involve increases or decreases, gains or losses, moving forwards according to some normative model, or slipping "backwards." This movement is most easily seen when considering development from a biological perspective. Changes in sight and hearing, changes in the central nervous system, and changes as a result of major disease processes, can be evaluated in terms of gains and losses, all of which directly and indirectly influence adults' ability to learn. It bears pointing out, however, that the vast majority of literature on adult development especially as it is relates to adult learning, portrays development as change towards increasingly higher, more mature, more integrated levels of functioning.

This positive growth perspective associated with development is firmly embedded in the humanistic orientation of adult education. Knowles (1980) for example, writes, "the urge for growth is an especially strong motivation for learning, since education is by definition, growth – in knowledge, understanding, skills, attitudes, interests, and appreciation. The mere act of learning something new gives one a sense of growth" (p. 85). Daloz (1986) writes that "development is more than simply change. The word implies *direction*" (p. 22). He goes on to say that as adults develop, they move, "from relatively narrow and self-centered filters through increasingly inclusive, differentiated, and compassionate perspectives" (p. 149).

However, while most adult educators see development as growth-oriented, leading to more complex, more mature, more integrated systems, some acknowledge that change can be in the opposite direction. Dewey (1938/1963) recognized that some experiences can be "mis-educative" which in turn "has the effect of arresting or distorting the growth of further experience (p. 25). Jarvis (1987) also notes that for some people, learning experiences "may be ones which induce other emotions [than growth] from which they learn to restrict their activities . . . change need not be developmental, in the normal sense of the term; indeed it can be detrimental to the development of the person" (p. 129). Indeed, a qualitative study of 18 adults who self-identified a negative outcome from learning found that if a life experience challenges some central defining aspect of the self, and this challenge is interpreted as too threatening to the self, growth-inhibiting responses are learned to protect the self (Merriam, Mott, & Lee, 1996).

The Context of Development

How a person develops is also a function of time – historical, chronological, and social. Historical time, or history-graded influences (Baltes, 1987), are the "long-term processes, such as industrialization and Urbanization," and "economic, political, and social events that directly influence the life course of the individuals who experience those events" (Neugarten & Datan, 1973, p. 58). As an example, the worldwide war on terrorism is affecting different age cohorts and different ethnic groups in distinct ways. Young adults may be on the battlefields in this war, middle-aged adults may be warily comparing it to the Vietnam War, citizens of Arab heritage may be restricted in their travel, and so on.

Chronological or life time is simply the number of years one has lived since birth and is most useful when thinking about biological change; it is also a proxy for any number of factors in the study of adult development. Finally, social time is probably the most powerful construct in understanding adult development. Social time, "the socially prescribed timetable for the ordering of major life events" exists in all cultures (Neugarten, 1976, p. 16). It is the timetable for which certain behaviors are expected. And although there is variation in the actual experiencing of these events, and the norms may change over time, the overall "normative pattern is adhered to, more or less consistently, by most persons within a given social group" (p. 16). This "overall normative pattern" implicitly signals the appropriate time to marry, have children, retire, and so on.

Perhaps equally powerful in defining one's learning and development are nonnormative (Baltes, 1987) or unanticipated life events (Schlossberg, Waters, & Goodman, 1995). These are events that occur in some people's lives and are not time-dependent, such as a health condition, an accident, achieving fame, and so on. There is also the nonevent which is what we expected to occur, such as getting promoted, or having children, but did not.

Finally, there is a growing awareness that the sociocultual context of adult lives is an important factor in shaping both development and learning. "Learning is located at the interface of people's biography and the sociocultural milieu in which they live, for it is at this intersection that experiences occur" (Jarvis, 1992, p. 17). These experiences are the product of cultures and subcultures, normative expectations of behavior at certain stages in the life cycle, and an individual's genetic make up. How an individual "develops" is a function of historical and cultural norms in conjunction with chronological age.

Thus the social and historical context sets up expectations that vary by culture and historical period as to what adults learn and how they will develop. Other contextual factors include the social constructions of race, class, gender, ethnicity, sexual orientation, ability/disability, and so on. These constructions and how they intersect with development can also initiate a political analysis as "different versions of development serve the interests of different groups" (Tennant & Pogson, 1995, p. 199).

Models of Adult Development

Development from an adult education perspective has been predominately viewed as an internal psychological process. Emanating from this perspective are the age and stage theories wherein development is conceptualized as a patterned or orderly progression tied to chronological time expressed as specific ages or life stages. The most prominent of the stage models linked to age are the Levinsons' studies of male and female adult development (Levinson, Darrow, Klein, Levinson, & Mckee, 1978; Levinson & Levinson, 1996), Kohlberg's model of moral development (1973), Gould's psychoanalytical theory of development (1978), and Loevinger's (1976) stages of ego development.

Erikson's (1963) 8-stage life-span model is the best-known of these. Each stage represents a crisis or issue to be resolved in either a negative or positive fashion. In order to move from stage to stage, that is, develop, one must achieve a favorable ratio of positive over negative. In young adulthood, the issue needing resolution is between establishing intimacy with another or remaining isolated; middle adulthood is the struggle between generativity, or caring for the next generation, and self-absorption; in older adulthood, one must achieve a sense of integrity versus despair. These age/stage models of development are often referred to as a basis for identifying age/stage-appropriate adult educational programs (Knowles, 1980; Knowles & Associates, 1984).

Moving away from sequential, age/stage frameworks, adult development can also be understood from the perspective of life events and transitions. Life events are occurrences in people's lives that require adaptations or adjustments to behavior, beliefs or attitudes, in other words, change or development. Life events, if viewed as a process, can be considered transitions. For example, becoming a parent, undertaking a career change, or becoming ill can be seen as both discrete life events and as transitions. Much of adult learning is tied to life events and transitions. In fact, a landmark study by Aslanian and Brickell (1980) found that 83% of adults engaged in learning were doing so due to some transition in their lives. These transitions for the most part were work-related, followed by family life events.

Although the psychological framework for development has been prevalent in framing the connection to adult learning, other perspectives are equally informative. From programs for immigrants to learn to be "citizens" in the early decades of the 20th century, to parent education programs, to worker training in business and industry, the learning of social roles has been one basis for adult education programming. First published in 1952, Havighurst's (1972) book on developmental tasks and education further reinforced the link between the learning of social roles and adult education. Havighurst defined developmental tasks as those tasks that arise at a certain period in a person's life, such as getting started in an occupation in young adulthood, dealing with teenagers in mid-life, or adjusting to loss of health in late adulthood. In providing what he termed the teachable moment, these tasks and their accompanying social roles are still referenced today in adult education program planning.

Adult Cognitive Development

Of the many dimensions of development including psychological, biological, and social, adult *cognitive* development is most strongly connected to adult learning and education. How does adult thinking change over time, and how can education facilitate this change? Piaget's (1972) 4-stage model of cognitive development is considered foundational to a number of other models. According to Piaget, the fourth stage of formal operations is reached in the teen years, and is the ability to reason hypothetically and think abstractly; it is the apex of mature adult thought. The best-known model to draw from Piaget is Perry's (1970) developmental scheme. In this scheme, there are nine positions moving from relatively simple dualistic thinking patterns to highly complex ways of perceiving and evaluating knowledge.

More recent models of adult cognitive development have recognized the centrality of contextual knowledge and the importance of constructing one's own knowledge (Goldberger, Tarule, Clinchy, & Belenky, 1996). This emphasis on knowledge construction allows for more contextualization of adult cognitive development. Goldberger et al.'s research on women, for example, incorporates themes "related to the experience of silencing and disempowerment, lack of voice, the importance of personal experience in knowing, connected strategies in knowing, and resistance to disempassioned knowing" (p. 7).

A dialectical perspective on cognitive development also incorporates the adult life context (Riegel, 1975). In dealing with life's inherent complexities and its contradictions, "dialectic thinking allows for the acceptance of alternative truths or ways of thinking about similar phenomena that abound in everyday adult life" (Merriam & Caffarella, 1999, p. 153). As an example, one might be opposed to capital punishment, "yet silently applaud the gentle person who switches off the life-support system of her spouse who is suffering beyond relief from a terminal illness" (p. 153). By integrating abstract thinking with very pragmatic life concerns, one tolerates ambiguity if not outright contradiction.

Perhaps more than other researchers, Kegan (1994) incorporates psychological and contextual variables into his model of cognitive development. In order to deal with "the mental demands of modern life," adults' thinking needs to continue to evolve through higher levels of consciousness. In today's world, adults have extraordinary demands on both their personal world of home and family, and their public worlds of work and community. Kegan's model of cognitive development sets two powerful desires at odds with each other – the desire to be connected to others, and the desire to be independent of others. At the same time, we move through different consciousness thresholds from very concrete views of the world to more abstract inferences, to abstract systems (building relations between abstractions), to dialectical thinking, the signature of mature adult thinking. The pressing demands of our "culture's curriculum" necessitates continued development so that we can function within contradictions and ideological differences. Cognitive development is in fact Kegan's agenda for adult learning.

Finally, Mezirow's (2000) model of transformational learning can be seen as a model of cognitive development. When our present meaning system fails to "make sense of" or accommodate something we encounter as part of our everyday lives, we either reject it, or we must examine our assumptions with an eye to changing the way we think. Through trying to make sense of such experiences, the meaning structures are themselves changed: "Transformative learning refers to the process by which we transform our taken-for-granted frames of reference (meaning perspectives, habits of mind, mindsets) to make them more inclusive, discriminating, open, emotionally capable of change, and reflective so that they may generate beliefs and opinions that will prove more true or justified to guide action" (pp. 7–8).

Adult Development and Adult Education

At the center of the adult education enterprise is the adult learner. Adult development, defined as change with age, allows us to better understand how changes in adulthood intersect with adult learner needs and interests. Indeed, learning is often the way in which adults deal with change. And in turn, the learning that adults engage in may precipitate further development.

When linking adult development with adult learning several issues emerge. First is the usefulness of particular models of adult development. Since some of these models were derived from small, mainly white North American samples, one cannot assume they apply to all or even many adults. Whether any of the models of development apply to non-Western cultures is also not known. For example, becoming more independent and autonomous is a distinctly Western value. Developmental models with this as the most developed state are inappropriate for cultures that value interdependence and community. It is also not clear how some of the concepts such as "generativity" (Erikson, 1963) or dialectic thinking (Riegel, 1975) can be used in programming for adults.

A particularly contentious issue is whether it is the adult educator's place to "push" development; that is, should adult educators set about to change the perspective of a learner, for example, or seek to move learners to "higher" stages of development? If so, how exactly does one go about doing this? Further, intervening in an adult's developmental journey may have unintended consequences for both the learner and the educator (Robertson, 1996).

In summary, learning is about change and so is development. Adult development and adult learning are so intertwined that it would be difficult to even try to separate them. The better route is to appreciate what we do know about how adults grow and change, and be aware of the complexity of development. As Merriam and Caffarella (1999) observe, a full understanding of adult development would require an integrated model drawing from biological, psychological, and sociological perspectives.

See also: adult learning, journals, life history, lifespan development, meaning-making, motivation, narrative, older adults' learning, young adult education.

References and Further Reading

Aslanian, C. B., & Brickell, H. M. (1980). *Americans in transition: Life changes as reasons for adult learning*. New York: College Entrance Examination Board.

Baltes, P. B. (1987). Theoretical proposition of life-span developmental psychology: On the dynamics between growth and decline. *Developmental Psychology, 23*, 611–626.

Daloz, L. A. (1986). *Effective teaching and mentoring: Realizing the transformational power of adult learning experiences*. San Francisco: Jossey-Bass.

Dewey, J. (1938/1963). *Experience and education*. New York: Collier Books.

Erikson, E. H. (1963). *Childhood and society* (2nd ed.). New York: Norton.

Goldberger, N. R., Tarule, J. M., Clinchy, B. M., & Belenky, M. F. (Eds.). (1996). *Knowledge, difference, and power: Essays inspired by Women's Ways of Knowing*. New York: Basic Books.

Gould, R. (1978). *Transformations: Growth and change in adult life*. New York: Simon & Schuster.

Havighurst, R.J. (1972). *Developmental tasks and education* (3rd ed.). New York: Mckay.

Jarvis, P. (1987). *Adult learning in the social context*. London: Croom Helm.

Jarvis, P. (1992). *Paradoxes of learning: On becoming an individual in society*. San Francisco: Jossey-Bass.

Kegan, R. (1994). *In over our heads: The mental demands of modern life*. Cambridge, MA: Harvard University Press.

Knowles, M. S. (1980). *The modern practice of adult education: From pedagogy to andragogy* (2nd ed.). New York: Cambridge Books.

Knowles, M. S. & Associates (1984). *Andragogy in action: Applying modern principles of adult learning*. San Francisco: Jossey-Bass.

Kohlberg, L. (1973). Continuities in childhood and adult moral development. In P. Baltes & K. Schaie (Eds.), *Life-span developmental psychology: Personality and socialization* (pp. 179–204). Orlando, FL: Academic Press.

Levinson, D. J., Darrow, D., Klein, E. B., Levinson, M., & Mckee, B. (1978). *Seasons of a man's life.* New York: Academic Press.

Levinson, D. J., & Levinson, D. M. (1996). *The seasons of a woman's life.* New York: Ballantine.

Loevinger, J. (1976). *Ego development: Conceptions and theories.* San Francisco: Jossey-Bass.

Maslow, A. H. (1970). *Motivation and personality* (2nd ed.). New York: HarperCollins.

Merriam, S.B., & Caffarella, R. S. (1999). *Learning in adulthood: A comprehensive guide* (2nd ed.). San Francisco: Jossey-Bass.

Merriam, S. B., Mott, V. W., & Lee, M. (1996). Learning that comes from the negative interpretation of life experience. *Studies in Continuing Education, 18*(1), 1–23.

Mezirow, J. (2000). Learning to think like an adult: Core concepts of transformation theory. In J. Mezirow & Associates, *Learning as transformation* (pp. 3–33). San Francisco: Jossey-Bass.

Neugarten, B. (1976). Adaptation and the life cycle. *Counseling Psychologist, 6,* 16–20.

Neugarten, B., & Datan, N. (1973). Sociological perspectives on the life cycle. In P. Baltes & K. W. Schaie (Eds.), *Life-span developmental psychology: Personality and socialization.* Orlando, FL: Academic Press.

Perry, W. G. (1970). *Forms of intellectual and ethical development in the college years.* Austin, TX: Holt, Rinehart & Winston.

Piaget, J. (1972). Intellectual evolution from adolescence to adulthood. *Human Development, 16,* 346–370.

Riegel, K. F. (1975). Dialectic operations: The final period of cognitive development. In N. Datan & L. H. Ginsberg (Eds.), *Life-span developmental psychology: Normative life crises.* Orlando, FL: Academic Press.

Robertson, D. L. (1996). Facilitating transformative learning: Attending to the dynamics of the educational helping relationship. *Adult Education Quarterly, 47*(1), 41–53.

Schlossberg, N. K., Waters, E. B., & Goodman, J. (1995). *Counseling adults in transition* (2nd ed.). New York: Springer.

Tennant, M. C., & Pogson, P. (1995). *Learning and change in the adult years: A developmental perspective.* San Francisco: Jossey-Bass.

Sharan B. Merriam

Adult Learning

A definition of adult learning can be at once deceptively simple, yet enormously complex. It is simple because we know that learning "is of the essence of everyday living and of conscious experience; it is the process of transforming that experience into knowledge, skills, attitudes, values, and beliefs" (Jarvis, 1992, p. 11). But it is also complex because there is no one definition, model, or theory that explains how adults learn, why adults learn, or how best to facilitate the process. Yet the learning of adults is the one key theme that unites the otherwise widely disparate field of adult education. Whether in adult basic education, human resource development, or continuing professional education, practitioners share the common goal of facilitating adult learning. Rather than a single definition or description of adult learning, what we have is a colorful mosaic of theories, models, sets of principles, and explanations that combined, form the knowledge base of adult learning.

Until the mid-20th century, what we knew about adult learning was embedded in studies by behavioral and cognitive psychologists, studies that focused on problem solving, information processing, memory, intelligence, and motivation. Much of this research was conducted in laboratory settings, and if adults were included, what was of interest was how advancing age affected the learning activity. Thorndike, Bregman, Tilton, and Woodyard's *Adult Learning* published in 1928 is an example of this early research. This book reports the results of adults being tested in a laboratory under timed conditions on various learning and memory tasks. The authors concluded that adults between 25 and 45 could learn "at nearly the same rate" as 20-year-olds (p. 178). Research in the 1940s found that when time pressure was removed, adults up to age 70 did as well as younger people.

Adult learning from a psychological, and in particular a behaviorist perspective, shaped adult learning research and theory building in North America until the 1970s when other traditions and European influences broadened inquiry. Research on information processing, memory, cognitive development and intelligence is ongoing and continues to inform the field of adult education. More recently, however, these same topics have been investigated from a perspective that takes into account the adult's life situation, life experiences, and social and cultural influences. Even wisdom, which from a cognitive development perspective is considered to be the pinnacle of intellectual maturity, is being studied from a sociocultural perspective (Sternberg, 1990).

Adults as Learners

By the mid-20th century, adult education was a recognized field of practice with its own professional associations, journals, and conferences. Rather than extrapolating from research with children or research that placed adults under the same conditions as children, adult educators began to consider how learning in adulthood could be distinguished from learning in childhood. This shift in focus resulted in three major contributions to the mosaic that is adult learning – andragogy, self-directed learning, and transformative learning.

The European concept of andragogy was introduced to North America by Malcolm Knowles in 1968 as "a new label and a new technology" distinguishing adult learning from children's learning or pedagogy (p. 351). Andragogy consists of five assumptions about the adult learner. Working from these assumptions, Knowles proposed a program-planning model for designing, implementing, and evaluating educational activities with adults. For example, with regard to the first assumption that as adults mature, they become more independent and self-directing, Knowles suggested that the classroom climate be one of "adultness," both physically and psychologically.

At first heralded as *the* explanation of adult learning, andragogy underwent intense examination by educators of both adults and children. It was recognized, for example, that some children and adolescents are independent, self-directed learners while some adults are highly dependent on a teacher for structure and guidance. Further, adults may be externally motivated to learn as when an employer requires attendance at a training program, and some children may be motivated by curiosity or the internal pleasure of learning. By 1980 Knowles had acknowledged that the dichotomy between andragogy and pedagogy was not as stark as originally drawn. He wrote that both approaches are appropriate with children and adults, depending on the situation.

Andragogy has been most severely critiqued for its assumption that the individual adult learner is autonomous and in control of his or her learning. Lacking is any recognition that both the learner and the learning that takes place are shaped by a person's history and culture in conjunction with the institutional context where it occurs. Despite these critiques, for those new to or on the periphery of adult education, andragogy enjoys widespread recognition as one understanding of adult learning and a tested guide to working with adults in practice.

Self-directed learning (SDL) is a second dimension of adult learning theory to be considered adult-specific. The major impetus for this model of adult learning came from Tough's (1971) research with Canadian adult learners. He found that 90% of the participants in his study had engaged in an average of 100 hours of self-planned learning projects in the previous year. The uncovering and documenting of self-directed learning – learning that is widespread, that occurs as part of adults' everyday life, and that is systematic yet does not depend on an instructor or a classroom – has been a major contribution towards understanding and defining adult learning.

More than 30 years of research in North America and Europe on self-directed learning has verified its widespread presence among adults, documented the process by which it occurs, and developed assessment tools to measure the extent of individual self-directedness. Of these foci, the process of SDL speaks most directly to adult learning. How one actually moves through a self-directed learning experience has generated a number of models of the process. Earlier models, including those of Tough (1971) and Knowles (1975) tend to be more linear, whereas more recent models take into account the learner, the context in which the learning takes place, and the type of learning. Spear and Mocker (1984), for example, presented a model that takes into account opportunities for learning found in one's environment, past or new knowledge, and chance occurrences. These opportunities cluster into the "organizing circumstance" which in turn, structures the self-directed learning activity, and the "circumstances created during one episode become the circumstances for the next" (p. 5).

The third contribution to adult learning that helped define what is different about learning in adulthood, is transformational learning. While it has long been recognized that adults can be profoundly changed through learning, it wasn't until Freire's (1970) and more recently Mezirow's (2000) work that this type of learning was documented. Rather than focusing on the learner as andragogy and to a large extent self-directed learning do, transformational learning is about the cognitive process of meaning making. It is particularly an adult learning theory because transformational learning is dependent on adult life experiences and a more mature level of cognitive functioning than found in childhood. The essence of transformational learning is that through sudden or dramatic experiences, people are changed in ways that they themselves and others can recognize.

Mezirow (2000) is considered the primary architect of transformational learning, although he readily acknowledges being influenced by the Brazilian educator, Paulo Freire. Freire (1970) emphasized the need for this type of learning to deal with oppression and to bring about social change. Mezirow focuses more on the process of individual transformation, a process that is personally empowering. This 10-step learning process is initiated by a disorienting dilemma – a life experience that cannot be accommodated by one's present worldview. This leads the adult to examine and critically reflect on the assumptions and beliefs that have guided meaning making in the past, but now are no longer adequate. From an examination of current beliefs, the learner moves to exploring new ways of dealing with the dilemma, often in conjunction with others confronting a similar crisis. It is in dialogue with others that the learner tests out new assumptions, understandings, and perspectives. A plan of action is then formulated and put into motion. The new or transformed perspective is more inclusive and accommodating than the previous perspective.

Since the 1990s, transformational learning has moved center-stage in terms of the volume of research and writing. Transformational learning conferences occurring every 2 years with the most recent in 2003, have also contributed to the burgeoning knowledge base about this type of learning. Further, connections between transformational learning and adult development (Merriam & Clark, in press), and transformational learning and spirituality (Dirkx, 1998), have expanded our understanding of adult learning and the meaning-making process.

In summary, andragogy, self-directed learning, and transformational learning have come to define much of adult learning today. Both andragogy and self-directed learning were instrumental in distinguishing adult learning from childhood learning at a time when the field of adult education was defining itself. They remain dominant in the real world of practice, perhaps because of their humanistic foundations and the fact that they capture what is popularly and intuitively understood about adult learning. Transformational learning, though powerful and emancipatory when it occurs, is more difficult to plan for, implement, and assess.

Expanding our Understanding of Adult Learning

Several new ways of thinking about adult learning are drawing attention to the complexity of learning in adulthood. As was the case in the early decades of the 20th century, adult educators are once again drawing from other disciplines and perspectives to illuminate our understanding of adult learning. Discussed here are critical perspectives on learning, situated cognition or context-based learning, and learning through emotions, body, and spirit.

Rather than focusing on the individual adult learner, a critical lens on adult learning considers sociocultural and historical conditions that shape the context in which learning takes place. Based in Marxism, critical theory, multiculturalism, and feminist theory, questions are raised about the institutions that provide learning, the cultural context, what is valued as knowledge, who has power to define what is learned, and so on. Key themes that characterize the critical perspective are (a) power and oppression, (b) race, class, and gender, and (c) knowledge and truth. These themes are interrelated and it is impossible "to talk about racism, classism, sexism, and other 'isms' without reference to power and oppression; nor can power be considered apart from issues surrounding knowledge construction" (Merriam & Caffarella, 1999, p. 342).

From a critical perspective, there is no "generic" adult learner irrespective of race, class, gender or other characteristics that can marginalize learners. Analyses of these forces and how they play out in the teaching-learning situation are becoming more prevalent in the adult education literature. In particular, backed by a voluminous literature in feminist theory and feminist pedagogy, women's learning has been a topic of much interest especially since the publication of *Women's Ways of Knowing* (Belenky, Clinchy, Goldberger, & Tarule, 1986). In this study, five categories of knowledge construction were uncovered ranging from silence, where women are passive and what they know is defined by others, to constructed knowledge in which women are active creators of their own knowledge. In the critical approach to women's learning, intellectual and emotional aspects of learning are seen as embedded in the larger patriarchal, sociopolitical framework of adult education practice.

The context in which learning takes place is also key to understanding another approach to adult learning – situated cognition; however, rather than the sociopolitical dimensions of the context, in a situated cognition approach, learning is what is constructed by the interaction of people in a particular situation with particular tools or artifacts including language, signs, and symbols. Situated cognition posits that learning is context bound, tool dependent, and socially interactive. The place in which situated cognition occurs is the community of practice, which might be a family, a classroom, a workplace, and online community, a town, or a corporation. This approach "contextualizes" learning, moving beyond a preoccupation with the individual learner.

What this approach has contributed to adult learning is to underscore the location of adult learning in the real-life, or "authentic" experiences of adults; that is, learning is most effective and meaningful in situations where actual cognitive processes are required, rather than in simulated activities typically found in school. Research has shown for example, that adults are considerably more accurate in comparison pricing when actually shopping (98% correct answers) than when doing identical calculations on a paper-and-pencil test (59% correct) (Lave, 1988). What this means for adult education practice is that learning is most effective through apprenticeships, internships, and practicums where one can learn through modeling, coaching, trial and error, shadowing, site visits, and job-embedded activities.

A third way in which our understanding of adult learning has been expanded is through the work on emotions, body, and spirit. The mind/body split so ingrained in Western notions of learning has dominated adult learning until recently. Scholars are now trying to explain and legitimize the role played by emotions, the body, and the spirit in learning.

Dirkx (2001), in a discussion of emotions and learning, argues that learning itself is inherently an imaginative, emotional act and that significant learning is inconceivable without emotion. It is through emotions that "deeply personal, meaningful connections" are made so that really significant learning can take place (p. 66). There are two kinds of connections. First, is the connection to one's own inner experiences; emotions are "gateways to the unconscious and our emotional, feeling selves" (p. 66). Second, emotions and feelings connect to the "shared ideas within the world" and are "reflected in big words or concepts, such as Truth, Power, Justice, and Love" (p. 64).

Closely aligned with the emotional components of learning is somatic knowing, or knowing through our bodies. This is easy to grasp when we consider how stress is manifested in our bodies. In fact it is now understood that because receptors are found throughout the body, emotions can be stored and mediated by parts of the body other than just the brain. Thus, active physical engagement in addition to cognitive activity can promote learning. Weiss (2001, p. 63) cites the president of Brainergy, Gessner Geyer, as saying, "In essence, we are kinesthetic learners. Learning isn't all in our heads, and our brains don't sit disembodied in a bucket. Our minds and bodies work together to help us pay attention, solve problems, and remember solutions . . . Movement and exercise can enhance optimal learning states" (p. 63).

Finally, spirituality and its connection to adult learning have attracted substantial attention in recent years. Spirituality, like learning, is about connection and meaning-making. Tisdell (1999) writes that educators should recognize that "a search for or an acknowledgement of the spiritual in the lives of adult learners is connected to the search for meaning that gives our lives coherence. For all adults, this is connected to how we create meaning in our relationships with others. It is in our living and loving" (p. 93).

Adult learning then, is not easily defined in a few words. There is a substantial body of research and literature dating back to the early decades of the 20th century where adult learning was conceived of as problem solving, memory, and information processing. From that foundation, adult educators began to differentiate adult learning from preadult learning, a move that led to a focus on the adult learner him or herself. Andragogy, self-directed learning, and more recently, transformational learning are major distinguishing aspects of adult learning today. In addition, our understanding of adult learning has been expanded to include consideration of the larger sociocultural and political context in which it takes place, and how the context itself both shapes and is an integral part of the learning transaction. Finally, an even more holistic conception of adult learning acknowledges the role of emotions, the body, and the spirit in learning.

See also: andragogy, autobiography, critical thinking, cultural learning, dialogue, embodied learning, motivation, peer learning, reflective learning, self-directed learning.

References and Further Reading

Belenky, M. F., Clinchy, B. M., Goldberger, N. R., & Tarule, J. M. (1986). *Women's ways of knowing: The development of self, voice, and mind.* New York: Basic Books.

Dirkx, J. M. (1998). Transformative learning theory in the practice of adult education: An overview. *PAACE Journal of Lifelong Learning, 7,* 1–14. (Pennsylvania Association for Adult Continuing Education)

Dirkx, J. M. (2001). The power of feelings: Emotion, imagination, and the construction of meaning in adult learning. In S. B. Merriam (Ed.), *The new update on adult learning theory* (pp.

63–72). *New Directions for Adult and Continuing Education,* No. 89. San Francisco: Jossey-Bass.

Freire, P. (1970). Cultural action for freedom. *Harvard educational review monograph series No. 1.* Cambridge, MA: Center for the Study of Development and Social Change.

Jarvis, P. (1992). *Paradoxes of learning: On becoming an individual in society.* San Francisco: Jossey-Bass.

Knowles, M. S. (1968). Andragogy, not pedagogy. *Adult Leadership, 16*(10), 350–352, 386.

Knowles, M. S. (1975). *Self-directed learning.* New York: Association Press.

Knowles, M. S. (1980). *The modern practice of adult education: From pedagogy to andragogy* (2nd ed.). New York: Cambridge Books.

Lave, J. (1988). *Cognition in practice: Mind, mathematics and culture in everyday life.* Cambridge: Cambridge University Press.

Merriam, S. B., & Caffarella, R. S. (1999). *Learning in adulthood: A comprehensive guide* (2nd ed.). San Francisco: Jossey-Bass.

Merriam, S. B., & Clark, M. C. (in press). Learning and development: The connection in adulthood. In C. H. Hoare (Ed.), *Oxford handbook of adult development and learning.* London: Oxford University Press.

Mezirow, J. (2000). Learning to think like an adult: Core concepts of transformation theory. In J. Mezirow & Associates, *Learning as transformation* (pp. 3–33). San Francisco: Jossey-Bass.

Spear, G. E., & Mocker, D. W. (1984). The organizing circumstance: Environmental determinants in self-directed learning. *Adult Education Quarterly, 35*(1), 1–10.

Sternberg, R. J. (Ed.). (1990). *Wisdom: Its nature, origins, and development.* Cambridge, UK: Cambridge University Press.

Thorndike, E. L., Bregman, E. O., Tilton, J. W., & Woodyard, E. (1928). *Adult learning.* New York: Macmillan.

Tisdell, E. J. (1999). The spiritual dimension of adult development. In M. C. Clark & R. S. Caffarella (Eds.), *An update on adult development theory* (pp. 87–96). San Francisco: Jossey-Bass.

Tough, A. (1971). *The adult's learning projects: A fresh approach to theory and practice in adult learning.* Toronto: Ontario Institute for Studies in Education.

Weiss, R. P. (2001). The mind-body connection in learning. *T+D, 55*(9), 60–67.

Sharan B. Merriam

Aesthetic Education

For a large part of the 20th century the term aesthetic education was usually used to refer to those classes and other activities concerned to help adults become familiar with and appreciate the acknowledged canon of great and good works of art. At the beginning of the 21st century the idea of the canon has largely been rejected and the term aesthetic education has come to refer to classes concerned with identifying, appreciating and enjoying art from any and all sources.

Whilst this entry is concerned with aesthetic education, it is important to acknowledge that, in adult education around the world, the arts are often used as a teaching method in areas like health education, human resource development, management training, political education and in many action research projects. Examples of this sort of work can be found in the proceedings of the conferences on adult education and the arts edited by Elias, Jones, and Normie (1989); Jones, McConnel, and Normie (1996); Jones and Normie (2001); and Jones and Normie (2002); and papers by Butterwick (2002) and Conrad (2002). The ERIC Digest no. 236, *Adult Learning in and through the Arts,* by Sandra Kerka (2002) is also useful.

Such courses are not concerned primarily with aesthetic education, though some of the skills and abilities required for developing aesthetic awareness may well be acquired. The success of such courses is measured in terms of awareness of health issues, political awareness and action, improved management skills, and better performance in the workplace, rather that in terms of increased aesthetic sensitivity.

Aesthetic Values

In the context of postmodernism it is accepted that aesthetic values are not universal and are culturally determined. The defining characteristics of cultures are discussed in the entry on creativity, but it is worth mentioning that it is better to understand the nature of cultures if we think of them as being quite small and existing in a given period of time (Jones, 2001).

Nowadays, it is accepted that aesthetic education can deal with anything from the music of the French Court in the 18th century to the tattoos and body piercing of sections of English youth in the 21st century. The focus has changed from the canon to the experiencing of artworks. The education service and adult education in particular, played an important catalytic role in bringing about these changes.

In many countries, the changes began with a challenge to the dominant cultural value system. In the UK, the grand narrative of European art, which epitomized a largely aristocratic cultural value system, was challenged by a range of cultural minority groups. In some countries, ethnic minority groups demanded a platform for their art, and the community arts movement brought about the making and enjoyment of art by and for ordinary people. People with disabilities demanded that their art be given more exposure, and feminist groups demanded that the history of art pay more attention to women practitioners. The young, as always, challenged the prevailing value system of the academy. The ideology which had been based on a belief that an artist was a special sort of person to be revered and studied changed to one which held that every person had the potential to work as a creative artist within their own cultural context. All people were now seen as having the potential to work creatively.

It became clear that the idea that there was a canon of great and good works of art which every educated citizen ought to appreciate was no longer tenable. There was not just one cultural value system, there were many, and it was the business of education to acknowledge this and reflect it in practice.

Educational Developments

The educational task has changed from one of inducting the next generation into the canon of great and good art to one of developing the knowledge, skills and abilities to enjoy and appreciate work from any cultural context. The curriculum for aesthetic education has changed from one which focused on content, historical and, to some extent, contemporary art, to one which focuses on process, on the ways in which we look at, listen to, watch and read works of art.

It is the experiencing of works of art which has come to be seen as important. It was always acknowledged that works of art had the ability to evoke strong emotional reactions in the viewer or audience, but in order for this to happen one had to approach the work in a certain way.

This involved allowing oneself to suspend judgment and approach the work with an innocent eye. Viewers had to disregard any preconceptions about the nature of art and give themselves over to the work.

Perception

Because of this, attention came to focus on the nature of perception, in particular, visual perception. It was known that in everyday life we perceive minimally; we perceive as little as we need to perceive in order to survive. Appreciation of the arts demanded higher levels of perceptual acuity, particularly if one was engaging with works of art from a different cultural context.

Coinciding with this change in our understanding of the nature of aesthetic value systems, psychologists were discovering that perception was, itself, culturally determined. The ways in which we make sense of the images which hit our retina, the sound waves which bounce on our ear drums or the smells and tastes which invade our senses is determined by where we learned to perceive (Jones, 1988, pp. 58–73). The growing body of evidence suggested that perception is largely a learned skill and that the way we perceive is conditioned by the cultural context in which we learned to perceive.

Since we cannot assume that all members of a group are experiencing and perceiving, a work of art in the same way, it becomes impossible to build a value system on the premise that there is only one way to perceive a work of art. It was this realization that led to the belief that the development of perceptual acuity was a central aim of aesthetic education. Aesthetic education was no longer seen as a means of inculcating good taste but rather as a way of making people see what was there and relate it to its cultural context. In this sense, aesthetic education can be seen as a means of crossing cultural boundaries and as a means of promoting multicultural attitudes.

The Aesthetic Experience

Of course, not all people have the same reaction to a given work of art. One person may experience an intense emotional reaction to a particular painting which leaves another person cold. There is little empirical research into the question of why we get strong reactions to some works and not others. It is accepted that throughout a lifetime reactions can change, some works no longer interesting us whilst others begin to excite us. Theoretical explanations are usually derived from the Jungian idea of archetypal symbols (Jung, 1964), which itself is an area in need of further research.

This change in attitudes meant that arts providers began to question what they were doing. Theatres, museums and galleries began to appoint education officers in an attempt to make their provision more accessible.

Art galleries which housed large collections of historical work found themselves faced by a dilemma; they housed the canon but this was no longer seen as the sole focus of aesthetic education. The canon was not, of course, excluded from the educational gaze, and these galleries sought to find ways of making their collections more accessible. They tried to contextualize the works in their collections and began to become interested in their role as interpreters of the arts.

Interpreting Art

This is a problematic area. The idea of interpretation suggests that it is possible to translate a work of art, say a painting, into another medium, language, and still evoke the same reaction. It is possible to argue, for example, that the experience of a painting, like the experience of music, cannot be replicated in an alternative medium like language. Words, quite simply, do not have the capacity to evoke the same responses in us. We are moving into the affective area here. We are concerned with the ability of a work of art, in any medium, to engage with our emotions, and whether it is possible to translate that artwork into another medium, say the medium of language, so that it evokes the same emotional response.

In his 2003 Reith Lecture, "Phantoms in the Brain," Ramachandran (2003) describes the processes involved in the act of seeing. He points out that it is not a simple process. It is easy to assume that it is effortless and instantaneous, but Ramachandran points out that we have a distorted upside-down image on our retina which excites the photoreceptors and the signals then go through the optic nerve to the brain. Here they are analysed in 30 different visual areas in the rear part of our brain, before, finally, we identify what we are looking at.

Language operates differently, is processed in different areas of the brain and relates to our emotions differently. Ramachandran (2003) goes on to point out that once the image is recognized the message goes to a structure called the amygdala which is the emotional core of the brain, sometimes known as the gateway to the limbic system. This, he says, allows us to gauge the emotional significance of the image, whether or not it appeals to us, whether or not it has significance for us and excites an emotional reaction.

It appears that it is not physiologically possible to evoke the same responses, to convey meaning, in the same way using a different medium. Ramachandran (2003) explains that humans have not just one visual area, the visual cortex, but 30 areas in the back of the brain which enable us to see, to perceive the world. He speculates that each of these 30 areas has a different function, specialized for a different aspect of vision. He quotes as an example one area called V4 which seems to be concerned with processing color information, seeing colors, whereas another area in the parietal lobe called MT, or the middle temporal area, is concerned mainly with seeing motion.

Thus the idea of interpretation also becomes a contested area. It appears that the human brain is simply not wired up in a way that will allow us to have the same experience when a visual work of art is translated into the different medium of words. The educational purposes of gallery talks and written information about paintings were thus challenged.

The activities that galleries could undertake in this field of aesthetic education were to do with developing levels of perception, pointing out different qualities of the form and color of the painting, and contextualization, providing information about the artist and the socio-economic context in which the painting was created. They could not make someone have an emotional reaction to the work if that person was not predisposed to connect with the work, and they could not argue that a particular work was aesthetically better than another.

Providers

Aesthetic education for adults is provided by a variety of agencies. In many countries, national and local government educational providers are involved in this work, as are voluntary organizations. Arts providers, over the last 50 years, have become increasingly involved and these agencies stress the educational nature of their work.

The community arts movement is an international phenomenon. Community arts practitioners are concerned to empower ordinary members of a community to create and enjoy their own art, as opposed to the art that is on offer in professional art galleries, concert halls, theatres and libraries, to which they often do not relate. Typically a community arts project involves what have been called sociocultural animateurs working within usually deprived communities to raise levels of awareness and to empower those communities through artistic activity. Given that perception is culturally determined and that the arts are culturally defined, and that aesthetic value systems are culturally developed, and given that cultures are quite small units, this seems to be an ideal way in which to promote aesthetic education. Aesthetic education needs to begin with the student's own culture before moving on to the experience of works from other cultures.

See also: creativity, cultural learning, cultural studies, multiple intelligences.

References and Further Reading

Butterwick, S. (2002). Your story/my story/ our story: Performing interpretation in participatory theatre. *Alberta Journal of Educational Research, 48*(3), 240–254.

Conrad, D. (2002). Drama as arts-based pedagogy and research: Media advertising and inner-city youth. *Alberta Journal of Educational Research, 48*(3), 254–269.

Elias. W., Jones, D.J., & Normie, G. (Eds.). (1989). *Truth without facts, selected papers from the first three international conferences on adult education and the arts.* Brussels: Vrije Universiteit Press.

Jones, D. J. (1988). *Adult education and cultural development.* London and New York: Routledge.

Jones, D. J. (2001). Learning culture. In *Proceedings of the 42nd Annual Adult Education Research Conference.* East Lansing, MI: Michigan State University.

Jones, D. J., McConnel, B., & Normie, G., (Eds.). (1996). *One world many cultures, papers from the fourth International Conference on Adult Education and the Arts.* Cardenden, Scotland: Fife Regional Council.

Jones, D. J., & Normie, G. (Eds.). (2001). *A spatial odyssey, Papers from the 6th International Conference on Adult Education and the Arts.* University of Nottingham in conjunction with SCUTREA, Standing Conference on University Teaching and Research in the Education of Adults. Nottingham, England: Continuing Education Press.

Jones, D. J., & Normie, G. (Eds.). (2002). *Life's rich pattern: Cultural diversity and the education of adults.* Boston, UK: SCUTREA in conjunction with Pilgrim College.

Jung, C. G. (1964). *Man and his symbols.* London: Aldus.

Kerka, S. (2002). *Adult learning in and through the arts. ERIC Clearinghouse on Adult, Career, and Vocational Education.* Washington DC. Retrieved January 1, 2003, from ERIC Document Reproduction Service, no. ED467239.

Ramachandran, V. S. (2003). Phantoms in the brain. In *The emerging mind, The Reith Lectures.* London: British Broadcasting Corporation. Retrieved June 22, 2004 from Reith Lectures website: http://www.bbc.co.uk/radio4/reith2003/lecture1.shtml

David James Jones

Africa and Adult Education

Adult education in Africa today must be understood in relation to its colonial history, its historical traditions of adult education, and African value systems. Contemporary adult education in Africa also has to compete with the negative effects of globalization, war, drought and famine, health, democracy, and scarce resources. These challenges are contextualized by an African renaissance that emphasizes sustainable development through the privileging of indigenous knowledge systems, which are specific to a local area and belong to a particular group of people; indigenous knowledge is knowledge that people have developed over time, which has to do with their context and immediate environment and which continues to develop (Letsoko, 2003, p. 3).

Colonial Influences

Countries have experienced different colonial influences that directly affect the official languages of communication, and also contribute to divisions within the continent. The division of Africa in 1884 by European colonial powers introduced regulations and languages, so there are Francophone, Anglophone and Portuguese speaking countries, with Afrikaans and German speaking parts as well. The colonial goal of adult education and literacy was primarily to support the colonial administration, so that only a few male indigenous people were offered basic schooling. In British colonies, women were treated in the same way that women in Victorian England were treated, so their education was confined to domestic matters that reinforced their subordinate status to men (Mulenga, 2000).

The post-independence initiatives in many countries included the establishment of government adult education agencies – usually for literacy and distance education. Departments of Extra Mural Education emerged, following the patterns of the country of origin of their colonial masters. Adult education is usually offered through colonial languages rather than the myriad of local, indigenous languages.

African Traditions of Adult Education and Lifelong Learning

There is not a single unique African position since Africa is a vast continent, but nevertheless some generic African perspectives can be articulated that are in contradistinction to most Western perspectives. There are three features of African traditional adult education and lifelong learning: practices, educational goals and value systems. In terms of practice, Afrik (2000) points to a tradition of learning by doing, which has usually been exercised through an oral tradition under the leadership of chiefs, headmen and elders over the community as a whole. A particular feature of this learning has been the initiation training into adulthood, and instruction into local crafts through apprenticeships. Through the generations moral and historical values have been transmitted through proverbs, folklore, and songs that represent the wisdom of time. The unique feature of this oral tradition is that the proverbs and folklore are adapted and change with each new generation, although their basic concepts remain constant and hence their potential as an indigenous knowledge resource, remains strong.

The lifelong learning goal in most of Africa is essentially a collective, rather than individual, concept. Its emphasis is on building social (for community), rather than human (for economic prosperity), capital. The aim is for communities and families to rear honest, respectable, skilled, cooperative people.

Avoseh (2001, p. 480) makes a number of observations about traditional African value systems and lifelong learning. They consist of three generic dimensions. A spiritual dimension is influenced by the metaphysical world, and is encapsulated in a spiritual obligation to one's ancestors and God, resulting in a sense of obligation to the community. The communal aspect emphasizes a commitment to the interests of the "corporate existence of the community." The political dimension is understood in the form of duty, to serve the interest of the nation before oneself through community, family and spiritual responsibilities.

These African values are encapsulated by one word in different African languages. For instance in South Africa it is *Ubuntu*, in Botswana it is *Botho*. They all emphasize ideas of reverence for human life, mutual help, generosity, cooperation, respect for older people, and harmony and preservation of the sacred. Commitment to the family includes an obligation to the living and the dead and those yet to be born.

While these values do not analyse or explain current issues of gender or poverty imbalances, they indicate that there is a potential conflict of interest with Western notions of lifelong learning where acquisition of qualifications is promoted more than acquisition of social values. The African voice is relatively weak in the global lifelong learning debate, and there are still only a few centers in Africa devoted to lifelong learning (for example, the University of the Western Cape in Cape Town, South Africa). The external image of developing countries is that they are still developing, their initial schooling infrastructure is incomplete and that literacy is the main focus for adult education.

These two histories have influenced both the style and nature of today's adult education provision; they set the pattern for development around a number of key concerns, of which literacy education is only one.

Adult Education in the Context of Development

Education policies designed by international donor agencies often focus on basic education. However, in many African countries initial schooling is not compulsory and literacy rates are some of the lowest in the world. In 1998, for instance, adult female literacy rates in Sub-Saharan Africa were 51% compared with 82% for the world; and for men the figure was 68% compared with 82% for the world (DFID, 2000). These figures hide vast disparities across Africa. In Mozambique the adult literacy rate was 43%, in Botswana it was 75.6% and in Zimbabwe it was 87.2% (SARPN, 2003).

Adult education initiatives in reality have a much broader remit than literacy. They are organized by a variety of organizations, ranging from churches, businesses and voluntary organizations to government departments. They cover a wide range of activities such as literacy classes in communities, distance learning, continuing professional development in the workplace, education for women, income-generation projects, community development, prison education, poverty-alleviation projects, rural-transformation strategies, and extension work initiatives. Extension workers are government-employed professionals who live and work in village communities; their goals include increasing agricultural productivity, reducing malnutrition and other health risks, enhancing skills training, and promoting literacy and income-generation projects in order to reduce poverty and increase women's involvement in public affairs and general democratic participation.

The formal sector consists of specialized institutions including providers of open and distance learning with an increasing emphasis on the use of information technologies. The non-formal and informal sector consists of civil societies, public and private-sector organizations where education and training is not the core business but may be part of a project or public-service relationship. More recently the emphasis has been on local capacity-building, sustainable development (including environmental and ecological sustainability) and empowerment for self-reliance through decentralized and participatory programmes. Initiatives in this respect include programmes for gender sensitivity, citizenship, and voter education.

The above initiatives, however, are plagued by numerous challenges in different parts of Africa. Some of these are political, others are social or environmental. Representations at the 2003 CONFINTEA V Mid-Term Review, a conference sponsored by UNESCO, listed a number of issues including inadequate resources; a culture of dependency brought about by previous donor and government policies for infrastructure development that ignored traditional practices and values; high levels of poverty, war, drought, famine and political instability; unemployment; the burden of debt; human-rights abuse; environmental degradation; few well-articulated policies for youth and adults; and the need for more post-literacy programmes. Other issues that affect progress in adult education can be attributed to the use of European rather than local languages, a weak civil society in contributing to policy-making, and the need for accurate documentation and data, such as national surveys and qualitative studies of practice. Research, it is argued, must be relevant, participatory and based on indigenous cultures and languages that would serve the needs of local communities (Chilisa & Preece, 2005).

There are a number of key organizations for African adult education. The Pan-African Association for Literacy and Adult Education (PAALAE) is an interactive network of adult educators across 30 African countries. Its e-mail address is nafa@metissacana.sn. Pamoja is a non-profit organization based in Vermont, USA, and Tanzania, East Africa (the word Pamoja means "altogether" in the East African Kiswahili language). Their website is http://www.pamoja.net/. The Africa Network Campaign on Education For All (ANCEFA) aims to promote and build capacity of African civil society to advocate for access to free quality education for all. Its website is http://www.ancefa.org/. The Association for the Development of Education in Africa (ADEA) is a network of partners promoting the development of effective education policies based on African leadership and ownership. Its website is http://www.adeanet.org/.

See also: culturally relevant adult education, English as a second language, extension, health education, identity, international adult education, libraries, peace education, popular education, womanism.

References and Further Reading

Afrik, T. (2000). Significant post independence developments in adult and continuing education in sub-Saharan Africa. In S.A. Indabawa, A. Oduaran, T. Afrik, & S. Walters (Eds.), *The state of adult and continuing education in Africa* (pp. 19–30). Bonn: Department of Nonformal Education (DNFE), Namibia & Institute for International Cooperation of the German Adult Education Association (IIZ/DVV).

Avoseh, M. B. M. (2001). Learning to be an active citizen: lessons of traditional Africa for lifelong learning. *International Journal of Lifelong Education, 20*, 479–486.

Chilisa, B., & Preece, J. (2005). *Research methods for adult educators in Africa.* Cape Town, South Africa: Pearson Education Publishers.

CONFINTEA V Mid-Term Review *Synthesis Report* (2003). Hamburg, Germany: UNESCO Institute for Education.

Department for International Development (DFID). (2000). *Poverty elimination and the empowerment of women.* London: DFID.

Letsoko, S. P. (2003). *Is the idea of local "traditional" or "indigenous" knowledge plausible*? Presentation to University of Witwatersrand School of Education, Witwatersrand.

Mulenga, D. (2000). The development and provision of adult education and literacy in Zambia. In S.A. Indabawa, A. Oduaran, T. Afrik, & S. Walters (Eds.), *The state of adult and continuing education in Africa* (pp. 173–182). Bonn, Germany: Department of Non-Formal Education (DNFE) Namibia & Institute for International Cooperation of the German Adult Education Association (IIZ/DVV).

Southern African Regional Poverty Network. *SARPN Poverty Indicators*. Retrieved July 1, 2003 from http://www.sarpn.org.za/RegionalViews/botswana.php

Julia Preece

Africentrism

Africentrism is a philosophical paradigm that places the experiences of peoples of African descent at the center rather than the periphery of human experiences enabling Africans to be the makers of their own history. The term Africentrism is etymologically correct and can be used to highlight the continent and its historical experiences more accurately than the United States-focused term, Afrocentrism. However, the terms Afrocentrism and Africentrism are both used widely and interchangeably.

According to Asante (1992), who coined the term, Afrocentrism is "a simple idea . . . at its base it is concerned with African people being subjects of historical social experiences rather than objects in the margins in European experiences" (p. 20). Viewing itself as a critique of Eurocentrism and White supremacy, Afrocentrism challenges the positivistic epistemological basis of mainstream Western intellectual ideas and knowledge, believing in spirituality and validation of knowledge through a combination of historical understanding and intuition (Keto, 1995; Mazama, 2001).

Institutionalization has helped to develop and disseminate Afrocentricity in philosophical, political and cultural realms. In particular, the graduate programme in the Department of African American Studies at Temple University and the annual Diop Conference have been rich sites for production and reproduction of the tenets of Afrocentrism (Karenga, 1988). Further dissemination of discourses associated with Afrocentrism can be found in the *Journal of Black Studies* and *Imhotep*, which provide not only visibility but also a venue for scholarship. The relationship between African American Studies and Afrocentricity are close as the latter acts as a meta-paradigm providing the former with perspectives, theories and methods that define it as the discipline of Africology.

The discourse of Afrocentrism can be viewed as producing/enabling at least three types of subjects, according to Reed, Lawson, and Gibbs (1997): "race-distancing elitists" who have a monopoly on the sophisticated and cultural gaze of Afrocentrism; the "race-embracing" rebels who often view themselves in the tradition of Malcolm X; and the "for-profit" Afrocentric who is usually self-taught in Egyptian history and African continent histories (p. 176).

Debates and Contestation

Is Afrocentrism a 20th century paradigm? While Asante (1987, 1988) coined and developed the term Afrocentricity, the underlying philosophy and historiography of the concept can be applied to the work of earlier theorists of African descent. Some would argue that the roots of Afrocentricity lie in the 19th century with Africentric intellectuals such as Martin Delaney, Du Bois, and Woodson rather than in the 20th century. For example, while Tunde Adeleke (2001) recognizes differences between earlier forms of Africentricism (aimed at integration and acceptance) and present-day variants (Black distinctiveness and separatism), he also perceives underlying similarities. As he argues, "Delaney affirmed the dominance and preeminence of Africa. His writings affirm the wealth and antiquity of civilization in Africa and contributions of Africans in various intellectual fields" (p. 24). Conceptually, both pan-Africanism (early 19th century), the Negritude movement (1930s, 1940s, and 1950s), and the Black Power movement (1960s) can be seen as similar in their philosophical orientations of developing a Black Consciousness.

While Afrocentrism can be viewed as having an African epistemology and worldview at its heart, not everything that is centered on Africa can be regarded as Afrocentric. Afrocentricity has a specific philosophy, as Asante argues; Afrocentricity cannot be reduced to the practicing of African culture. Central to the Afrocentric idea is self-consciousness that is the deliberate and systematic effort to fully assume one's place in the world.

Afrocentrism has been charged with essentialism by poststructuralist and critical cultural studies theorists (Gilroy, 1993, 2000; McCarthy, 1997) who question its philosophical assumptions that there exists an overarching and collective African consciousness. In line with this critique, the North American cultural critic bell hooks identifies the necessity and advantages of challenging essentialism within the African American community. For hooks (1990), such a challenge provides the opportunity to undermine racism in the guise of the "authentic Black." Further, she sees it as a way of "acknowledging how class mobility has altered collective black experiences as well as enabling us to affirm multiple black identities" (p.10). Asante's (2001) response to critics such as hooks and Gilroy is that "such false separation, particularly in the context of White racial hierarchy and domination, is nothing more than a White definition of Blackness. I reject such a notion as an attempt to isolate Africans in the Americas from their brothers and sisters on the continent" (p. 847). Acknowledgment of gender issues is through the concept of womanism, whereby race-based unity is maintained in opposition to a mainstream feminism that is regarded as conflictual and Eurocentric in its theorization of relations between the sexes.

Communitarian impulses within Afrocentrism highlight it as not just an intellectual exercise, but also a political project. How might Afrocentrism be applied to adult education that uses African origins as a unifying source for social action? Any unified action would have to be provisional. If we accept the claim of critical cultural studies theorists that Black identity is a political construct, then Afrocentrism's epistemological claims to unity through authenticity become very difficult to maintain; especially in poststructuralist/postmodern times of plurality, hybridity and translation. For adult educators working within an Africentric paradigm, empowerment would be based primarily on exposure to "African" culture (*Kwanza* celebrations, for example) rather than understanding aspects related to social class, gender and so on. Adoption of Afrocentrism makes problematic the notion of community as something that is fluid; that has to be worked at. That empowerment is based on raising consciousness, via exposing a different reality through knowledge, indicates similarities with feminist epistemologies as well as Freirian understandings of conscientization.

See also: Africa, postcolonialism.

References and Further Readings

Adeleke, T. (2001). Will the real father of Afrocentricity please stand. *Western Journal of Black Studies, 25*(1), 21–29.

Asante, M. K. (1987). *The Afrocentric idea.* Lawrenceville, NJ: Africa World Press.

Asante, M. G. (1988). *Afrocentricity.* Lawrenceville, NJ: Africa World Press.

Asante, M. K. (1992). African American studies: The future of the discipline. *The Black Scholar, 22*(3), 20–29.

Asante, M. K. (2001). Against race: Imagining political culture beyond the color line. [Review of the book *Between Camps*]. *Journal of Black Studies, 31*(6), 847–851.

Gilroy, P. (1993). *Black Atlantic.* Cambridge, MA: Harvard University Press.

Gilroy, P. (2000). *Between camps*. London: Allen Lane/Penguin Press.

hooks, b. (1990). Postmodern blackness. *Postmodern Culture, 1*(1), 1–14.

Karenga, M. (1988). *Introduction to Black studies*. Los Angeles: The University of Sankore Press.

Keto, C. (1995). *Vision, identity and time: The Afrocentric paradigm*. Dubuque, IA: Kendall/Hunt.

Mazama, A. (2001). The Afrocentric paradigm. *Journal of Black Studies, 31*(4), 387–405.

McCarthy, C. (1997). Nonsynchrony and social difference: An alternative to the current radical accounts of race and schooling. In A. H. Halsey, H. Lauder, P. Brown & A. Stuart Wells (Eds.), *Education, culture economy society* (pp. 541–556). London: Oxford University Press.

Reed, W. E., Lawson, E. J., & T. Gibbs. (1997). Afrocentrism in the 21st Century. *Western Journal of Black Studies, 21*(3), 173–179.

Jennifer Kelly

Andragogy

The term andragogy has been used in different times and countries with various connotations. There are three main understandings: (a) andragogy as the scholarly approach to the learning of adults, viewed as the science of understanding and supporting their lifelong and lifewide education; (b) andragogy in the tradition of Malcolm Knowles, which refers to a specific theoretical and practical approach based on a humanistic conception of learners who are self-directed and autonomous, where teachers who work with learners to facilitate their learning are also in a learning mode; this understanding is most common in the United States; and (c) andragogy used in an unclear way, with its meaning changing from "adult education practice" or "desirable values" or "specific teaching methods," to refer to "reflections" or a specific "academic discipline," as well as the "opposite of childish pedagogy." Terms make sense in relation to the object they name. Relating the development of the term to the historical context may explain the differences.

The History of Andragogy

The first person to use the term andragogy, as far as we know, was the German high-school teacher Alexander Kapp in 1833. In a book entitled *Plato's Educational Ideas* he describes the lifelong necessity to learn. Midway through that book, which begins with a section on early childhood, there is a section on adulthood entitled "Die Andragogik oder Bildung im maennlichen Alter" (Andragogy or Education in the Man's Age); a replica of this book can be found on www.andragogy.net. In 60 pages, Kapp argues that education, self-reflection, and character education are the first values of human life. He then refers to vocational education for those in the healing professions, soldiers, educators, orators, rulers, and men as fathers. In a common pedagogical pattern, Kapp includes and combines the education of inner, subjective personality (character) and outer, objective competencies; for Kapp, learning happens not only through teachers, but also through self-reflection and life experience, and is about more than teaching adults.

Kapp does not explain the term andragogik, and it is not clear whether he invented it or whether he borrowed it from somebody else. He does not develop a theory, but justifies andragogy as the practical necessity of the education of adults. Yet it was not considered unique, which may be the reason why the term lay fallow: other terms and ideas were available. The idea of adult learning was not unusual in the time around 1833, neither in Europe (Enlightenment movement, reading-societies, workers' education, educational work of churches), nor in America (Franklin Institute in Philadelphia, Lowell Institute in Boston, Lyceum Movement, town libraries, museums, agricultural societies); all had important dates between 1820–40. The existing initiatives had their own terminology, so a new term was not needed.

The Second and Third Invention

In the 1920s, Germany adult education became a field of theorizing, especially among a group of scholars from various disciplines, the so-called "Hohenrodter Bund," who developed in theory and practice the Neue Richtung (new direction) in adult education. Here some authors gave a second birth to the term andragogik, now used to describe sets of explicit reflections related to the why, what-for, and how of teaching adults. Andragogy became a sophisticated, theory-oriented concept, used as an antonym to "demagogy" – too difficult to handle, not really shared. So again the term fell into disuse and was forgotten. But a new phenomenon was arising: a scholarly, academic reflection level "above" practical adult education. The scholars came from various disciplines, working in adult education as individuals, not representing university institutes or disciplines. The idea of adult education as a discipline was not yet born.

It is not clear where the third wave of using andragogy originated. In the 1950s, andragogy can suddenly be found in publications in Switzerland (Hanselmann), Yugoslavia (Ogrizovic), the Netherlands (ten Have), and Germany (Pöggeler). Still the term was known only to insiders, and was sometimes more oriented to practice, sometimes more to theory. Perhaps this mirrors the reality of adult education at that time. There was little formal training for adult educators, some very limited theoretical knowledge, no institutionalized continuity of developing such knowledge, and no academic course of study. Adult education was still an unclear mixture of practice, commitment, ideologies, reflections, theories, mostly local institutions, and some academic involvement of individuals. As the situation was unclear, the term could not be any clearer. But the increasing use of the term signalled that a sharp distinction between "doing" and "reflecting" was developing, one that was perhaps in need of a separate term.

Andragogy: A Banner for Identity

The heyday for the term andragogy for the English-speaking adult education world came with Malcolm Knowles, a scholar of adult education in the USA. In his 1989 book, Knowles describes his 1967 encounter with the term. A Yugoslavian adult educator, Dusan Savicevic, participated in a class Knowles was giving at summer session in Boston University. Savicevic explained the German roots of the term to Knowles. Following Kapp's use of the term, andragogy lay fallow until it was once more introduced by a German social scientist, Eugen Rosenstock, in 1921, but it did not receive general recognition. The term was resurrected when in "1957 a German teacher, Franz Pöggeler, published a book, *Introduction into Andragogy: Basic Issues in Adult Education*, and this term was then picked up by adult educators in Germany, Austria, the Netherlands, and Yugoslavia . . ." (Knowles, p. 79).

Knowles published his first article (1968) about his understanding of andragogy with the provocative title "Andragogy, Not Pedagogy." In a short time the term andragogy, now intimately connected to Knowles, received general recognition throughout North America and other English-speaking countries; "within North America, no view of teaching adults is more widely known, or more enthusiastically embraced, than Knowles' description of andragogy" (Pratt & Associates, 1998, p. 13).

Knowles' concept of andragogy – "the art and science of helping adults learn . . . is built upon two central, defining attributes: First, a conception of learners as self-directed and autonomous; and second, a conception of the role of the teacher as facilitator of learning rather than presenter of content" (Pratt & Associates, 1998, p. 12), emphasizing learner choice more than expert control. Both attributes fit into the specific socio-historic thoughts in and after the 1970s, for example the deschooling theory (Illich, 1971), Rogers's person-centered approach, and Freire's conscientization. Perhaps a third attribute added to the attraction of Knowles' concept: constructing andragogy as opposed to pedagogy provided an opportunity for educators to be seen as "good teachers" instead of pedantic ones. This flattered adult educators in a time when most were andragogical amateurs, doing adult education based on their content expertise, experience, and a mission they felt, rather than on specific training or educational competence. To be offered understandable, humanistic values and beliefs, some specific methods and a good-sounding label strengthened a group that felt inferior to comparable professionals. And this was accompanied by a significant growth of the field of practice plus an increased scholarly approach, including the emerging possibility of studying adult education at universities. All these elements document a new period ("art and science") in adult education; it made sense to concentrate them in a new term.

Providing a unifying idea and identity, connected with the term andragogy, to the amorphous group of adult educators was certainly the main contribution that Knowles gave to the field of adult education at that time. Another was that he strengthened the already existing scholarly access to adult education by publishing, theorizing, researching and educating students who themselves through academic research became scholars, and by explicitly defining andragogy as science (Cooper & Henschke, 2003).

Issues with Andragogy

Nevertheless, over the years a critique has developed against Knowles' understanding of andragogy. A first critique argues that Knowles claimed to offer a general concept of adult education, but like all educational theories in history andragogy is but one concept, born into a specific historical context. For example, one of Knowles' basic assumptions is that becoming adult means becoming self-directed, a view that is often rejected because many adults are not self-directed. Critics do not agree that the American prototype of the self-directed lonesome fighter is the ultimate educational goal: in family, church, or civic education, for instance, the "we" is more important than the "self." The andragogy concept of Knowles is, as the Dutch scholar van Gent (1996) observes, not a general-descriptive, but a "specific, prescriptive approach" (p. 116). Another critique is Knowles' conception of pedagogy as a pedantic schoolmasters' practice, not as an academic discipline.

This hostility towards pedagogy has had two negative outcomes. On a strategic level, scholars of adult education could make no alliances with their colleagues from pedagogy; on a content level, knowledge developed in pedagogy over 400 years could not be utilized by those in andragogy (for more critical remarks see Merriam & Caffarella, 1999, p. 273ff, Savicevic, 1999, p. 113ff). Thus, attaching andragogy exclusively to Knowles' specific approach meant that the term was lost to those in pedagogy.

The European Development

In most countries of Europe Knowles' view of andragogy has played at best a marginal role. Its use and development in the different countries and languages has been more hidden, dispersed and uncoordinated, yet steady. Andragogy has nowhere been used to describe one specific concept, but from 1970 on it was connected with the development of coming academic and professional institutions, publications and programs, triggered by a similar growth of adult education in practice and theory in the USA. Andragogy functioned in Europe as a header for (in place of) systematic reflection, parallel to other academic headers like biology, medicine, and physics. Examples of this use of andragogy are the Yugoslavian (scholarly) journal for adult education, named "*Andragogija*" in 1969; the Yugoslavian Society for Andragogy formed in 1993; Slovenia's "Andragoski Center Republike Slovenije" founded with the journal "*Andragoska Spoznanja*"; Prague University's (Czechia) "Katedra Andragogiky"; Bamberg University's (Germany) "Lehrstuhl Andragogik", named in 1995; while the Internet address of the Estonian adult education society is "andra.ee." On this formal level "above" practice and specific approaches, the term andragogy could be used in communist countries as well as in capitalistic ones, relating to all types of theories, for reflection, analysis and training, in person-oriented programs as well as human resource development.

A similar professional and academic expansion developed worldwide, using variations of the concept of andragogy: Venezuela has the "Instituto Internacional de Andragogía"; since 1998 the Adult & Continuing Education Society of Korea has published the journal *Andragogy Today*. This documents the growth of new types of professional institutions, functions and roles, with fulltime employed and academically trained professionals. Some of the new professional institutions have used the name andragogy in the same sense as adult education, but sounding more like a science-based discipline, but throughout Europe in general, "adult education," "further education," or "adult pedagogy" are used more than andragogy.

Andragogy: Academic Discipline

An academic discipline of andragogy with university programs, professors and students, focusing on the education of adults, exists today in many countries. But in the membership-list of the Commission of Professors of Adult Education of the USA (2003) not one university program/institute in the USA uses the name andragogy; in Germany one out of 35, in Eastern Europe 6 out of 26 use the term. Many actors in the field seem not to need the label andragogy. However, other scholars, for example Dusan Savicevic who provided Knowles with the term andragogy, explicitly claim "andragogy as a discipline, the subject of which is the study of education and learning of adults in all its forms of expression" (Savicevic, 1999, p. 97; Henschke 2003; Reischmann 2003). This claim is not a mere definition, but includes the prospective function to influence the future: to challenge "outside" (demanding a respected discipline in the university context), to confront "inside" (challenging colleagues to clarify their understanding and consensus of their function, and science), and overall to stand up with a self-confident academic identity.

The future will show whether the ongoing differentiation in institutions, functions, and roles will result in a need for further clarification of the term andragogy.

See also: adult learning, facilitation, informal learning, learning, pedagogic identity, self-directed learning, teaching, women's learning.

References and Further Reading

Cooper, M. K., & Henschke, J. A. (2003). *An update on andragogy: The international foundation for its research, theory and practice*. Paper presented at the Commission of Professors of Adult

Education (CPAE) Conference, Detroit, MI, November 2003.

Henschke, J. A. (2003). *Andragogical concepts*. Retrieved December 1, 2003, from Studies in Andragogy and Adult Education website: http://www.umsl.edu/~henschke

Illich, I. (1971) *De-schooling society*. New York: Harper & Row.

Kapp, A. (1833). *Plato's educational ideas* (originally in German). Minden & Leipzig: Ferdinand Essmann.

Knowles, M. S. (1968). Andragogy, not pedagogy! *Adult Leadership, 16*, 350–352, 386.

Knowles, M. S. (1989). *The making of an adult educator*. San Francisco: Jossey-Bass.

Merriam, S. B., & Caffarella, R. S. (1999). *Learning in adulthood* (2nd ed.). San Francisco: Jossey-Bass.

Pöggelner, F. (1957). *Introduction to Andragogy: Basic Issues in Adult Education* (originally in German). Ratingen: Henn Verlag.

Pratt, D. D., & Associates. (1998). *Five perspectives on teaching in adult and higher education*. Malabar, FL: Krieger.

Reischmann, J. (2003). *Why andragogy?* Bamberg University, Germany. Retrieved January 10, 2004 from andragogy.net website: http://www.Andragogy.net

Savicevic, D. (1999). Understanding andragogy in Europe and America: Comparing and contrasting. In J. Reischmann, M. Bron, & Z. Jelenc (Eds.), *Comparative adult education 1998: The contribution of ISCAE to an emerging field of study* (pp. 97–119). Ljubljana, Slovenia: Slovenian Institute for Adult Education.

van Gent, B. (1996). Andragogy. In A. C. Tuijnman (Ed.), *International encyclopedia of adult education and training* (2nd ed., pp. 114–117). Oxford, UK: Pergamon.

Jost Reischmann

Appreciative Inquiry

Appreciative inquiry (AI) is an action research methodology, rooted in discourses of organizational development, chaos theory, and spirituality. AI focuses attention on what is working well for individuals and organizations. Adult educators embed methods and principles of experiential learning (e.g., Ricketts & Willis, 2001) and spiritual literacy (English, Fenwick, & Parsons, 2003) into AI as a way of facilitating whole-person learning and creating preferred future conditions for learning and social action. The socio-rationalist or social constructionist underpinning of AI contends that what we focus on becomes our reality. Accordingly, AI seeks to redirect attention away from problems and adversarial, blame-oriented conversations towards understanding or researching the best of "what is." Similarly, one of the central tasks of adult education, writes Eduard Lindeman (1926), is to evoke aesthetic appreciations, not merely as a way of finding values but also of discovering, creating values (p. 69). Accordingly, AI offers an aesthetic approach to program evaluation and evaluation research.

The power of language in creating our reality is another assumption of social constructionism and AI. Words and questions are fateful, write appreciative inquiry advocates, Ludema, Cooperrider and Barrett (2001). They go on to promote the "unconditional positive question, . . . [which] guides inquiry agendas and focuses attention towards the most life-giving, life-sustaining aspects of organizational [and human] existence" (p. 189).

The comprehensive framework most often used for appreciative inquiry is known as the 5-D step model. DEFINE, the first process of AI, asks unconditional positive questions and leads the other 5-D core processes of appreciative inquiry for studying a topic (Ludema et al., pp. 192–196; Watkins & Mohr, 2001, pp. 25, 40–41).

The second process is to DISCOVER – to appreciate the best of "what is." The third process is to DREAM – to envision what "might be." The fourth process is to DESIGN – to construct what "should be." The last process, DESTINY, refers to innovating what "will be" and to sustain that change (also called DELIVERY).

Whitney, Cooperrider, Trosten-Bloom, and Kaplin's (2002) encyclopedia on AI provides samples of unconditional positive questions and interview guides, which are applicable to many fields of adult education practice. For example, they pose an unconditional positive question that seeks out the best of continuous learning and the possibilities for a learning organization: "How did you and others grow and change, as a result of being in this environment?" (p. 31).

In the transitional process between Discover and Dream, the researcher extrapolates and prioritizes from the "best of what is" to envision "what might be" as the basis for constructing "provocative propositions," or "possibility statements" that propose an ideal action written in the present tense as if it already exists. Provocative propositions, according to Blair (1998), are "gems of clarity and filled with purpose (p. 198) as this statement in the human resource development (HRD) context exemplifies: "We train all rookie editors and desktoppers in our style. . . . Whenever we get feedback from a client, we send e-mail to everyone" (p. 211).

Problem-Posing versus Problem-Solving

Appreciative inquiry theorists often present the basic assumptions of problem-solving and AI in opposing columns, contrasting the basic assumptions of each approach (e.g., Hammond & Royal, 1998, pp. 12–13). The basic assumption of problem-solving is that an organization/ learner is broken and needs to be fixed, while the basic assumption of appreciative inquiry is that an organization/learner is a mystery to be embraced (p. 24). An example of problem-solving is Freire's (1970) concept of "banking" education, in which educators identify adult learners' life problems for them and proceed to design learning activities that deposit in students' minds the knowledge and skills they need to solve those problems. In contrast, problem-posing acts as AI's "unconditional positive question" in which the educator has unconditional "faith in the people"; in the context of Freire's literacy education, problem-posing evokes generative words and themes – rather than vocabularies of deficit – that learners use to "name their world." The generative and spiritual capacity of appreciative inquiry developed by Cooperrider and Srivastva (1987), described as "more than a method or technique," also animates Freirian popular education: "The appreciative mode of inquiry . . . engenders a reverence for life. . . . [T]he action researcher is drawn to affirm, and thereby illuminate, the factors and forces involved in organizing [educating, and learning] that serve to nourish the human spirit" (p. 131).

English, Fenwick, and Parsons (2003) present appreciative inquiry as a way of effecting a spiritually based vision of change in the adult education and training world and as an alternative to starting the change process with a focus on problems (pp. 142–143). They offer a systematic approach to AI (pp. 146–149) beginning with the unconditional positive question: "Can you recall a special moment when you felt spiritually connected to others in your practice?" Rose (undated) frames the spiritual dimension of appreciative inquiry in terms of its potential for increasing our practice of authenticity, by which she means "being fully present, fully oneself, truthful in one's interactions with others, and communicating one's true self (not depending on roles or other social constructs to do the communicating for us)" (p. 2). Like English et al., Rose draws on Václav Havel's writings to support her claim that AI is not so much about being *positive* as being real. AI allows learners and participants to share their "shadow side" in a compassionate way, acknowledging that lies, brokenness, dysfunctions, and incompleteness can only exist "because of the greater reality of the human desire and gravitation towards authenticity" (p. 3). AI is consistent with Havel's vision of a "transcendental anchor," which English et al. elaborate as an authentic vision of education within the workplace that includes human and spiritual values "without subjugating these to the material gain of the organization and its elite" (p. 106). Barge and Oliver's (2003) poststructuralist challenge to AI protocols also honors the dark side of appreciation, respecting the complexity of the context and the whole person/whole organization complete with fragilities, vulnerabilities, distresses, and criticisms as well as moments of excellence (p. 131). AI becomes authentic education "when 'negative' emotions such as anger, disgust, and sadness . . . are viewed as life-giving" and learners approach inquiry reflexively, highlighting "potentially harmful effects of positive emotions and the potentially constructive consequences of negative emotions" (Barge & Oliver, pp. 137–138).

Both appreciative inquiry and asset-based community development (ABCD) pioneered by Kretzmann and McKnight (1993), challenge the vocabularies of deficit and problems, and mark a shift from the "needs-based" approach (see Hall, 1998; Mathie & Cunningham, 2002). To illustrate the shaping power of language, Patton (2003) examines the five premises of AI and its corollaries (and disjunctions) in comparison to traditional needs assessment and utilization-focused evaluation. Rose (n. d.) suggests that what the "compare and contrast" approach gains in simplicity and symmetry, it loses in nuance. She makes the distinction between the *philosophy* of AI, which is foundational, and its *methodology*, which is infinitely malleable (p. 4). "An appreciative stance – which flows from philosophy – can always be present, even if the method of choice is problem-solving" (p. 4). Critics charge AI with glossing over the negative and the imperfect problems and looking at the world through rose-colored glasses (see Barge & Oliver, 2003; Kerka, 2003). Rose illustrates how "problem" does not have a monolithic meaning, with the distinction between *problems* – "things that happen to people" or "situations that people experience" – and *problem-solving*, which is a practical, purposive activity. The unconditional positive question that sets the tone for AI's Define process could be problems or needs such as those identified in Freire's problem-posing approach. The generative themes and issues provide the bases for a praxis of reflection-analysis and action (AI's Dream and Destiny processes). Appreciative inquiry becomes critical pedagogy by actively involving educators and learners in identifying generative themes around the organizing categories of oppression (e.g., gender, class, race, sexual orientation, ethnicity, age). Conversely, problem-posing popular educators could benefit from the explicitly appreciative stance of asset-based community development and AI by identifying learners' talents, and building on their skills, knowledge, attitudes and values in addressing and potentially transforming oppressive relations.

AI Practitioners

Watkins and Mohr (2001) differentiate between AI facilitators and AI practitioners on the basis of practitioners' more advanced professional development in experiential educational methods and group process (pp. 48–50). Professional development for adult education is often in these knowledge and content areas. Ricketts and Willis (2001) believe that integrating the Continuous Learning Cycle (refined from David Kolb's Experiential Learning Cycle) into the AI process enhances the potential in the Destiny phase for living the provocative propositions. They recommend a self-facilitated learning approach in which the learning journal guides the process and contains everything that the participants need to create their own stories of quality moments, and facilitate their own learning processes (p. 63). Odell's (1998) practice of grassroots village planning and mobilization in Nepal, Sikkim, Tibet and the USA, expands AI and offers guiding principles for AI practitioners by building on complementary methodologies of Participatory Rural Appraisal (PRA) and Harrison Owen's Open Space Technology.

Barge and Oliver (2003) add a reflexive dimension to Barrett's (1995) description of the competencies (affirmative competence, expansive competence, generative competence, and collaborative competence) for transforming organization's problem-solving culture into an appreciative and generative learning culture: affirmative competence, expansive competence, generative competence, and collaborative competence. Barge and Oliver object to these competencies that bracket out agonistic emotions, such as anger, disgust, and sadness; they call on facilitators and managers to add a reflexive competence, which involves conversational structures that emphasize "role taking and perspective taking . . . [and] making explicit the multiple [including agonistic negative] meanings that constitute a situation" (p. 136). They also recommend that participants ponder on their constructions of the situation, and the partial truth of selective story-telling.

The potential of the new sciences of chaos and complexity for facilitating adult learning is gaining attention in adult education (see Fenwick, 2003) and, as a central metaphor of AI, is congruent with Barge and Oliver's call for contingent, multiple, and emergent meanings of appreciation. Fenwick poses the example of conversation or dialogue to explicate learning as the co-emergence of learner and setting, in which "interaction enfolds the participants and moves beyond them in a 'commingling of consciousness' " (p. 35). The metaphor of chaos theory so central to the five principles of AI shifts notions of human intentionality that underpin humanism and andragogy, to a post-foundational and poststructuralist philosophy (Barge & Oliver, 2003) in which meaning and learning emerge *between* learners and systems, situated in language use and its effects. Quantum language underpins the guiding principles for facilitating the appreciative inquiry process and emphasizes the *synergies* of collaborative inquiry, including the *constructionist* aspect (what we observe, or attend to, activates the moment of choice and creates our reality); *simul-*

taneity (the butterfly effect in which inquiry effects change simultaneously); the *poetic* (human systems emerge between multiple and contested interpretations of stories); the *anticipatory* (what we imagine is a rehearsal for the moment of choice); and the *positive* (attending to the positive enacts the positive).

Adult Education Applications of AI

Kerka's (2003) brief annotations of research reports on adult education applications of appreciative inquiry highlight the transformative potential of AI as well as some of the challenges in the process: complexity, group size, difficulty measuring results, and moving from vision to action (p. 1). Kerka offers researchers new to AI a starting point for applying this change process, with examples from graduate studies in adult education, workplace learning, gender equity and diversity development, prison education, faith communities, community development, extension education, and career development. Hammond and Royal (1998) provide stories or case studies of AI from diverse cultures and bring alive the complexities of AI processes that defy a "Pure AI." Many of these case studies experiment with adult learning practices. The Family Rehabilitation Center (FRC) in Sri Lanka, an NGO that provides island-wide care for those affected by armed conflict, used AI to evaluate its programs and concluded that staff "came to own the resulting recommendations that came out of the provocative propositions" (Jacobsgaard, 2003, p. 62). Hall (1998) calls for reflective evaluation practice as a way to weave together youth engagement, asset-based community development and appreciative inquiry; he also highlights learner-centered evaluation techniques, including shared story-telling, asking the "so what" questions, and self-assessment.

Mathie and Cunningham (2002), program staff for the Coady International Institute in Nova Scotia, present a strategy that combines AI and asset-based community development (ABCD) for mobilizing social capital and sustainable community-driven development in collaborative partnerships with NGOs in rural communities in Southern Ethiopia, the Philippines and Kenya, as well as in the urban setting of Curitiba, Brazil. They present possibilities for community associations to mobilize "bonding" social capital which enables people to "get by," and to increase "bridging" social capital which enables people to "get ahead," by relying on "linkages between community level actors and macro-level actors in public and private sectors" (pp. 4, 7). Fostering these linkages also leads to active citizenship engagement and thus a potential effect of AI and ABCD interventions is a strengthened civil society.

Appreciative inquiry is an attractive evaluation methodology for adult educators whose practice or applied research involves marginalized individuals, organizations/groups that face turmoil and low morale difficulties, and environments in which vocabularies of deficit persist, including literacy, addictions, welfare-to-work programs, prisons, and human rights violations.

See also: action research, dialogue, indigenous learning, problematizing learning, relational learning, research methods, women's learning.

References and Further Reading

Barge, J. K., & Oliver, C. (2003). Working with appreciation in managerial practice. *The Academy of Management Review, 28*(1), 124–142.

Barrett, F. J. (1995). Creating appreciative learning cultures. *Organizational Dynamics, 24*(1), 36–49.

Blair, M. (1998). Lessons using AI in a planning exercise. In S. A. Hammond & C. Royal (Eds.), *Lessons from the field: Applying appreciative inquiry* (pp. 187–214). Plano, TX: Practical Press.

Cooperrider, D. L., & Srivastva, S. (1987). Appreciative inquiry in organizational life. In W. Pasmore & R. Woodman (Eds.), *Research in organization change and development* (Vol. 1., pp. 129–169). Greenwich, CT: JAI Press.

English, L. M., Fenwick, T. J., & Parsons, J. (2003). *Spirituality of adult education and training*. Malabar, FL: Krieger.

Fenwick, T. J. (2003). *Learning through experience: Troubling orthodoxies and intersecting questions*. Malabar, FL: Krieger.

Freire, P. (1970). *Pedagogy of the oppressed*. New York: Continuum.

Hall, J. (1998). The banana kelly experience: Strength-based youth development. In S. A. Hammond & C. Royal (Eds.), *Lessons from the field: Applying appreciative inquiry* (pp. 112–123). Plano, TX: Practical Press.

Hammond, S. A., & Royal, C. (Eds.). (1998). *Lessons from the field: Applying appreciative inquiry*. Plano, TX: Practical Press.

Jacobsgaard, M. (2003). Using appreciative inquiry to evaluate project activities of a nongovernmental organization supporting victims of trauma in Sri Lanka. In H. Preskill & A. T. Coghlan (Eds.), *Using appreciative inquiry in evaluation* (pp. 53–62). *New Directions for Evaluation*, No. 100. San Francisco: Jossey-Bass.

Kerka, S. (2003). Appreciative inquiry. *Trends and issues alert, No. 41* from ERIC Clearinghouse on Adult, Career, and Vocational Education. Retrieved November 29, 2003, from the ERIC database (ERIC Document Reproduction Service No. ED473671).

Kretzmann, J., & McKnight, J. (1993). *Building communities from the inside out: A path toward finding and mobilizing a community's assets*. Chicago: ACTA Publications.

Lindeman, E. C. L. (1961). *The meaning of adult education*. Montreal: Harvester (Originally published in 1926).

Ludema, J. D., Cooperrider, D. L., & Barrett, F. J. (2001). Appreciative inquiry: The power of the unconditional positive question. In P. Reason & H. Bradbury (Eds.), *Action research: Participatory inquiry and practice* (pp. 189–199). London: Sage.

Mathie, A., & Cunningham, G. (2002). *From clients to citizens: Asset-based community development as a strategy for community-driven development* (Occasional Paper). Antigonish, NS: Coady International Institute, 2002. Retrieved November 26, 2003 from http://www.stfx.ca/institutes/coady/about_publications_occasional_citizens.html

Odell, M. (1998). Appreciative planning and action: Experience from the field. In S. A. Hammond & C. Royal (Eds.), *Lessons from the field: Applying appreciative inquiry* (pp. 127–143). Plano, TX: Practical Press.

Patton, M. Q. (2003). Inquiry into appreciative evaluation. In H. Preskill & A. T. Coghlan (Eds.), *Using appreciative inquiry in evaluation* (pp. 85–98). *New Directions for Evaluation*, No. 100. San Francisco: Jossey-Bass.

Ricketts, M. W., & Willis, J. E. (2001). *Experience AI: A practitioner's guide to integrating appreciative inquiry with experiential learning*. Chagrin Falls, OH: Taos Institute Publication.

Rose, L. (undated). Appreciative inquiry and problem solving: Contradiction or complementary? Retrieved November 30, 2003 from Appreciative Inquiry Canada website http://members.shaw.ca/lornedaniel/problem_solving2.htm.

Rose, L. (2003). Appreciative inquiry: Embracing the shadow side and reaching toward authenticity. Retrieved November 30, 2003 from Appreciative Inquiry Canada website: http://members.shaw.ca/lornedaniel/embracing2.htm.

Watkins, J. M, & Mohr, B. M. (2001). *Appreciative inquiry: Change at the speed of imagination*. San Francisco: Jossey-Bass/Pfeiffer.

Whitney, D. L., Cooperrider, D., Trosten-Bloom, A., & Kaplin, B. S. (2002). *Encyclopedia of positive questions* (Vol. 1). Euclid, OH: Lakeshore Com-munications.

Dorothy A. Lander

Asia and Adult Education

Asia is the largest continent with 60% of the world's population and the highest number of illiterates. It is highly diverse, economically, politically, socially and culturally. Japan is the world's second largest economy, with an almost 100% literacy rate and well-developed adult education system. At the other end of the spectrum, Afghanistan is one of the poorest nations with a low literacy rate and hardly any systematic adult education opportunities. The widely diverse adult education practice in Asia is little understood, simply because there is a dearth of information on the subject. This is especially true for the developing and less developed countries.

Asia can be divided into five regions: Central, East, South, Southeast, and Australasia. This entry covers adult education as practiced in select countries in Central, East, South, and Southeast Asia. To capture the diverse learning activities engaged in by adults in Asia, this entry conceptualizes adult education broadly, similar to how it has been defined in the *Hamburg Declaration on Adult Learning* (1997, p. 253). A number of terms are commonly used in referring to adult education in Asia, including social education (Japan), non-formal education (India, Bangladesh), continuing education (Korea), education for workers and peasants or free-time education (China), lifelong education (Thailand), and lifelong learning (Singapore).

Purposes and Programs

Adult education in Asia serves a wide array of purposes and goals, which can be described by Titmus's (1989) framework – second-chance education, role education, vocational education, and personal enrichment.

Second-chance education offers some adults an entrance to the education system, and may range from basic literacy skill to fulfilling credential requirements for university entrance. Illiteracy is the major challenge in Asia, since 70% of the 860 million adult illiterates in the world are in the Asia and Pacific region (UNESCO, 2002). Despite years of effort to provide education for all, literacy remains low, and a major program is therefore basic literacy. Some countries have reported significant progress in this area while others question the outcome of such programs. In India, for example, the massive total literacy campaign over 4 decades has apparently failed to produce a substantial impact (Ahmed, 2002). Reservations with basic literacy programs have therefore prompted Asia to focus on functional literacy. The educational objective of functional literacy is not just the ability to read and write, but also to use literacy skills for particular purposes in the home, community or workplace.

The number of adults who have never had the chance to attend any formal school or who drop out of school is alarming. Through equivalency programs they can acquire a formal education, and a great demand for second-chance education is reported in the Maldives, Mongolia, Nepal, Myanmar, and the Philippines.

Vocational education is concerned with the acquisition of skills and knowledge required in employment, and includes apprenticeship, vocational training and learning in the workplace. Vocational education is a big industry in more developed economies like Japan, Korea, Taiwan, Hong Kong and Singapore.

Demand for continuing education grows with the availability of higher education, new learning modes and advancements in communications technology. Diverse learning programs and methods are enabling millions of Chinese, Indians, Koreans, Thais and other Asians of all ages and professions to pursue further education and beyond.

Role education serves to meet social functions outside the workplace. This includes social role education (for example as a citizen) and personal role education (for example as a parent). Adult education in Asia provides an avenue for citizen voice, a place where democratic values are nurtured and promoted. One of Thailand's adult education policies is dedicated to helping adults live in a democratic society and to provide them with tools to build national ideology and social cohesion (Jariyavidyanont, 2002). Education for peace for the former Khmer Rouge population in Cambodia aims at building a culture of peace (ACCU, 2004). Concern with sustainable development prompts countries such as China and Nepal to pursue educational programs on the environment, and family and health issues are also common agendas in the region.

The goal of personal enrichment helps to develop individual potential, as opposed to promoting social and economic productivity. Expanded agendas include leisure, recreation, and culture. For example, the Japanese participate in programs related to hobbies and personal interests such as music, calligraphy, and flower arrangement (Gordon, 1998).

Adult education in Asia is provided by the state and civil society, the latter made up of the private sector and NGOs. In Malaysia, profit-oriented private-sector involvement is encouraged by market demand (Muhamad & Associates, 2001), and NGOs play an important role in non-formal education activities in most Asian countries.

Influencing Factors and Issues

Adult education in Asia is shaped by various factors, external and internal to the nations. External elements include the adult learning movement and forces outside the region. Internal variables may be historical factors, or political, economic, and social cultural contacts. These factors pose challenges to Asia.

Political influence manifests in terms of policies, structures, resources and programs. In Japan the enactment of a 1990 law promotes lifelong learning (Gordon, 1998). In Thailand a comprehensive policy helps to integrate formal, non-formal and informal adult education into a broad and holistic vision (Somtrakool, 2002). The absence of a precise policy on adult education affects its practice in Malaysia (Muhamad & Associates, 2001), where, unlike many other Asian nations, there is no specific public institution responsible for planning and coordinating the diverse providers. On the other hand, centralization and hierarchical structure may stifle local initiatives and contributions by other sectors as observed in Bangladesh (Bobillier, 2002).

As a vehicle for socio-economic development, Asian economies invest heavily in adult education, although programs vary with developmental levels and challenges. For example, Malaysia's shift to industrialization has led to a growth in technical training (Muhamad & Associates, 2001), while elsewhere, current trends towards globalization create a demand for multicultural and multilingual skills.

Social-cultural situations and

value systems also affect adult education. Two-thirds of the illiterates in the Asia Pacific region are women, for example (UNESCO, 2002), and literacy efforts seek to address this issue and promote women's social and economic standing. A rural women's program in India serves to empower them to participate as equal citizens in the economic, political and sustainable development of society (ACCU, 2004). A program in Laos seeks to meet the minority indigenous group's needs (ACCU), while the multicultural and multi-religious Malaysia and Singapore societies necessitate programs to promote ethnic harmony. Educational programs for the Japanese elderly exist to cater to the nation's aging population.

Social and cultural values may hamper the growth of adult education. For example, the Japanese emphasis on academic achievement for career purposes puts lifelong learning on the margin (Maehira, 1994). To meet local situations and needs, Asia will be challenged to harness traditional knowledge, wisdom, and cultural values.

Technological advancements in communications systems have also altered the Asian adult education scenario, making education available to anybody at any place, any time. Nevertheless, traditional learning modes remain useful and are preferred by some. Economic and technological change calls for retraining and retooling, with an increasing emphasis on individual learning for economic gains (human resource development through training for job-related skill) that puts adult education for social purposes onto the back burner.

In summary, the diverse adult education scenarios in Asia have evolved from basic literacy to lifelong learning in response to the changing regional and world scenarios and needs. Although significant progress has been made, challenges still abound.

See also: civil society, continuing education, cultural studies, educational foundations, Europe and adult education, higher education, international adult education, journals, literacy, Mediterranean adult education, non-governmental organizations, rural learning.

References and Further Reading

ACCU (Asia/Pacific Cultural Center for UNESCO). (2004). Retrieved January 13, 2004 from Literacy Breakthroughs website: http://www.accu.or.jp/litdbase/break/index.htm

Ahmed, M. (2002). Lifelong learning and the learning society. In M. Singh (Ed.), *Institutionalising lifelong learning: Creating conducive environments for adult learning in the Asian context* (pp. 22–42). Hamburg, Germany: UNESCO Institute for Education.

Bobillier, C. (2002). Effective delivery of learning in Bangladesh. In M. Singh (Ed.), *Institutionalising lifelong learning: Creating conducive environments for adult learning in the Asian context* (pp. 163–176). Hamburg, Germany: UNESCO Institute for Education.

Gordon, B. (1998). Lifelong learning in Japan. Retrieved January 5, 2004 from http://wgordon.web.wesleyan.edu/papers/lifelrn.htm

Hamburg Declaration on Adult Learning (1997). *Adult Education and Development, 49*, 251–260.

Jariyavidyanont, P. (2002). Legislation, policies, and accreditation of lifelong learning in Thailand. In M. Singh (Ed.), *Institutionalising lifelong learning: Creating conducive environments for adult learning in the Asian context* (pp. 239–248). Hamburg, Germany: UNESCO Institute for Education.

Maehira, Y. (1994). Patterns of lifelong education in Japan. *International Review of Education, 40*(3–5), 333–338.

Muhamad, M., & Associates (2001). *Adult*

and continuing education in Malaysia. Kuala Lumpur: UNESCO Institute for Education and University Putra Malaysia Press.

Somtrakool, K. (2002). Building bridges between formal, non-formal and informal: Policies and strategies for lifelong learning in Thailand. In M. Singh (Ed.), *Institutionalising lifelong learning: Creating conducive environments for adult learning in the Asian context* (pp. 111–116). Hamburg, Germany: UNESCO Institute for Education.

Titmus, C. J. (Ed.). (1989). *Lifelong education for adults: An international handbook*. New York: Pergamon Press.

UNESCO. (2002). Literacy facts and figures in Asia and the Pacific. Retrieved January 12, 2004, from Asian/Pacific Cultural Centre for UNESCO website: http://www.accu.or.jp/litdbase/stats/index.htm

Mazanah Muhamad

Attitudes

Broadly conceived, attitudes towards adult education are persons' dispositions, preferences, prejudices and beliefs, usually expressed as opinions, that influence adult education participation decisions. Attitudes shape how individuals value and assess the importance of adult education for themselves, others and the larger society. Directly and indirectly, attitudes influence individuals' decisions to participate, persist and withdraw from adult education programs and activities. Attitudes towards adult education are therefore important psychological objects of study in participation, program planning and policy research, and an integral component of adult education participation theory. However, attitudes are subject to change, are not perfect predictors of behavior, and are not easily quantified.

Usually when researchers use the term attitude they are referring to its evaluative property, that is to how positively or negatively a person feels towards an attitude object. Attitudes often have a number of associated beliefs that represent dimensions of attitude such as affect, belief and cognition, each of which can be defined and measured as a discrete factor or component. Psychometric instruments to measure attitudes usually consist of a series of statements of opinion, to which respondents are asked to agree or disagree. Two such instruments have been developed by adult education researchers following two distinct research traditions: the Education Participation Scale (EPS) (Boshier & Collins, 1985) within the motivational orientations research tradition, and the Adult Attitudes Towards Continuing Education Scale (AACES) (Darkenwald & Hayes, 1988) within the attitudes research tradition. The major projects in these two research traditions have their conceptual origins in Houle's classic study, *The Inquiring Mind* (1961). According to Houle, "Every adult has a basic orientation to education, an underlying conviction of its nature and value which influences his or her opinion about, and participation in, learning" (p. 67).

Motivational Orientations

A substantial body of research findings has been accumulated over the last 4 decades to establish motivational orientation as the most highly developed theoretical contribution to participation research (Courtney, 1992). The Education Participation Scale (EPS), adult education research's most widely recognized instrument, has been confirmed with diverse international participant populations to yield valid and reliable scores on sub-scales indicating adults' particular reasons for participating in adult education (Boshier & Collins, 1985). The current version of the EPS (A-form) (Boshier, 1991) extends beyond Houle's original three orientations (goal, learning, and activity) derived from a qualitative study of 22 participants, to identify 7 discrete categories of motivation to participate from a pool of over 14,000 respondents. The 7 motivational orientations identified by the A-form are: Communication Improvement; Social Contact; Educational Preparation; Professional Advancement; Family Togetherness; Social Stimulation and Cognitive Interest. EPS research confirms that adult education participants enroll for more than one set of reasons and that differences in orientation are also attributable to personal characteristics including gender, age and ethnicity.

Attitude Scale Development

North American researchers have produced all of the small body of published research on the development of instruments to measure attitudes towards adult education, and it is difficult to even find the term "attitude" in European adult education texts and journals. Since participation is the most studied phenomenon in adult education research it is surprising that so little effort has been directed by researchers, on both sides of the Atlantic, to the measurement of attitude as a factor influencing adults' decisions to participate in adult education programs. Since Brunner, Wilder, Kirchner and Newberry's (1959) assessment of the importance of psychological research in adult education, made almost 5 decades ago, there have been only five well-documented projects to develop valid and reliable instruments. In chronological order these projects are: Adolph and Whaley (1967), Seaman and Schroeder (1970), Blunt (1983), Darkenwald and Hayes (1988), and Blunt and Yang (2002).

Three of these projects are flawed, two methodologically, and one both methodologically and theoretically (Blunt, 1983; Blunt & Yang, 2002). The sample used by Adolph and Whaley (1967) to develop a Thurstone-type scale was both too small and not representative of a typical adult education participant population; non-expert judges selected the scale items; and evidence of the scale's validity was weak. Seaman and Schroeder's (1970) instrument failed to satisfactorily predict educative behavior and its semantic differential structure made it inappropriate for widespread use. A second Thurstone scale (Blunt), while methodologically sound, failed to meet researchers' needs for an easily applied instrument that yielded simple-to-interpret results, such as those yielded by more popular Likert scaling techniques. In addition, further study was needed to confirm the scale's factor structure and the journal that published it omitted the table of item values necessary for its use.

Darkenwald and Hayes (1988) established a new approach to scale development with the Adult Attitudes Toward Continuing Education Scale (AACES). AACES was linked conceptually to Houle's (1961) notion of motivational orientations and used a Likert rather than a Thurstone scaling technique. Houle's work was cited in this project to support the importance of attitude research and his term "orientation" was equated with the project's operational definition of attitude. However, Darkenwald and Hayes' work did not build on prior research findings indicating that attitude towards adult education was a multi-factorial construct and their results failed to empirically confirm the theoretical structure they relied upon to conceptualize their instrument. Also they misinterpreted their original factor analyses, and while these analyses were later corrected (Hayes & Darkenwald, 1990) the 22-item AACES remains suspect on both methodological and theoretical grounds.

The Revised Adult Attitudes Towards Continuing Education Scale (RAACES) (Blunt & Yang, 2002) is the most recently published instrument. This 9-item scale, developed by confirmatory factor analysis from the original 22-item AACES with data from a Canadian population, is based on three attitude components: Enjoyment of Learning, Intrinsic Value and Perceived Importance. A causal model of the three factors and an index of participation behavior explained almost 90% of the variance and covariance of the attitude and that participation measures. The model confirmed participation behavior was directly influenced by Enjoyment of Learning (.37), interpreted to be a mediating affect factor, which was in turn impacted by Perceived Importance (.39) and Intrinsic Value of Adult Education (.36), with the latter two factors being strongly associated (.74). While further research, internationally and with a variety of populations, is desirable to fully confirm the properties, validity and reliability of RAACES, its use is warranted as a replacement for AACES.

Relationship between Motivational Orientations and Attitudes

Both the EPS and AACES have been developed using Likert scaling of opinion items and factor-analytic procedures and it is likely they are not measuring discrete psychological constructs. When a 9 × 9 matrix of six EPS and three AACES factors was factor analysed a four-factor solution was derived demonstrating that the scales were measuring related phenomena (Blunt & Yang, 1995). Similarly, when individual responses to the 40-item EPS and 22-item AACES were analysed together, 29 EPS and 11 AACES items combined to form eight factors. It is possible, and an idea worthy of future investigation, that these two projects are measuring attitude constructs that can be differentiated as group and general factors, two kinds of factors that together with specific and error factors that are the products of factor-analysis procedures. General factors are found in all measures and group factors are involved in more than one but not all measures. The motivational orientations project may have identified group factors. The attitude assessment project may be a search for a general factor within which a hierarchical or nested structure of specific factors will eventually be located.

Attitude Theory and Participation

Social science research confirms that relationships between attitudes and behavior are highly complex. Positive attitudes towards adult education tend to be held by those in society who are: more highly educated; of moderate to high socio-economic status; female; socially active; frequent participants in adult education; and those who believe they exert personal control over their life situations. Yet attitude is only a moderately significant direct predictor of behavior as the decision to participate is mediated by many personal and situational variables. Affect, often established through prior life experience, plays an important role in decision-making and can serve as a force for, or a deterrent to, participation. Attitude formation through direct experience with an attitude object results in more strongly held attitudes than does attitude formation through indirect, nonbehavioral experience. Information also has an effect on attitude formation; the more information a person has about the attitude object, the greater the effect of attitude on behavior. Consequently the same attitude scale scores do not necessarily have the same effects on respondents' behaviors.

Recent participation research has focused on theoretical models of reasoned action (TRA) that combine behavioral intentions with the effects of attitudes and subjective social norms to predict participation (Ajzen & Fishbein, 1980). TRA recognizes that a person's intention to participate is the single best predictor of the eventual behavior, and that intentions are formed by individuals within social contexts where the views of others (social norms) exert a powerful influence on decision-making. In some groups social norms may be so strong that an individual's behavior is constrained to the point where a person with a positive attitude may decide not to participate or the decision to participate renders their participation involuntary rather than voluntary: "I am here because my family thinks this course will be good for me," rather than, "I am here because I want to learn about relaxation techniques." TRA posits that a person's attitude towards participation (affect) and their beliefs about what important-others think (subjective social norm) shape their behavioral intentions in powerful ways. A growing body of research findings currently serves to confirm the use of TRA to predict intentions to participate in continuing professional education and to explain the participation decision process (See Yang, Blunt, & Butler, 1994). These research findings also confirm that the empirical mapping of psychological influences on participation is far from complete.

See also: motivation, participation.

References and Further Reading

Adolph, T., & Whaley, R. F. (1967). Attitudes toward adult education. *Adult Education, 17*(3), 152–157.

Ajzen, I., & Fishbein, M. (1980). *Understanding attitude and predicting social behavior*. Englewood Cliffs, NJ: Prentice Hall.

Blunt, A. (1983). Development of a Thurstone scale to measure attitudes toward adult education. *Adult Education Quarterly, 34*(1), 16–28.

Blunt, A., & Yang, B. (1995). An examination of the validity of the Education Participation Scale (EPS) and the Adult Attitudes Toward Continuing Education Scale (AACES). Proceedings of the Adult Education Research Conference (AERC) (pp. 13–18). University of Alberta, May 19–21.

Blunt, A., & Yang, B. (2002). Factor structure of the Adult Attitudes Toward Continuing Education Scale and its capacity to predict participation behavior: Evidence for adoption of a revised scale. *Adult Education Quarterly, 52*(4), 299–314.

Boshier, R. W. (1991). Psychometric properties of the alternative form of the Education Participation Scale. *Adult Education Quarterly, 41*(3), 150–167.

Boshier, R. W., & Collins, J. (1985). The Houle typology after twenty-two years: A large scale empirical test. *Adult Education Quarterly, 35*(3), 113–130.

Brunner, E. de S., Wilder, D. S., Kirchner, C., & Newberry, J. S. (1959). *An overview of adult education research*. Chicago, IL: Adult Education Association of the USA.

Courtney, S. (1992). *Why adults learn: Towards a theory of participation in adult education*. London: Routledge.

Darkenwald, G. G., & Hayes, E. R. (1988). Assessment of adult attitudes towards continuing education. *International Journal of Lifelong Education, 7*(3), 197–204.

Hayes, E. R., & Darkenwald, G. G. (1990). Attitudes toward adult education: An empirically based conceptualization. *Adult Education Quarterly, 40*(3), 158–168.

Houle, C. O. (1961). *The inquiring mind: A study of the adult who continues to learn*. Madison, WI: University of Wisconsin Press.

Seaman, D. F., & Schroeder, W. L. (1970). The relationship between extent of educative behavior by adults and their attitudes toward continuing education. *Adult Education, 20*(2), 99–105.

Yang, B., Blunt, A., & Butler, R. (1994). Prediction of participation in continuing professional education: A test of two behavioral intention models. *Adult Education Quarterly, 44*(2), 83–96.

Adrian Blunt

Australia and Adult Education

In spite of Australia's relatively small population (fewer than 20 million), it is difficult to describe briefly the development and present provision of Australian adult education. Australia is a federation, made up of six states and two territories occupying a continent of some 8 million square kilometers, in which the principal responsibility for education remains with the states and territories.

Origins and History of Australian Adult Education

The earliest attempts at European adult education in the Australian colonies were missionary activities directed at "saving" the convicts (Australia was first settled as a penal colony) and the original Aboriginal inhabitants. These attempts, although high-minded, were almost completely unsuccessful. Within a decade of the foundation of the original institutes in Scotland, the first colonial Mechanics' Institutes were operating in Australia. Though they may not have met their proponents' high expectations, they were a powerful force for adult education and popular culture in the 19th century. From the beginning of public education, colonial schools offered night classes for undereducated adults. As local industry grew and public infrastructure was laid down, technical education was established, first, as part of the Mechanics' Institute movement. By the 1890s, the colonial universities had established extension boards, on the British model, and were offering extramural classes. Other more uniquely Australian forms of university adult education were also evolving at this time, including late afternoon part-time classes and correspondence courses of study.

As the labor movement grew, education in political and industrial matters became an important component of informal adult education. The first formal involvement of the labor movement in adult education came with its partnership with local universities in the formation of the Workers' Educational Association (WEA), and the WEA model soon became the standard for the provision of "official" adult education in Australia. During the Second World War, the

AAES (Australian Army Education Service) provided a useful example of what a well-resourced comprehensive adult education service could accomplish. After the war, and in the spirit of postwar reconstruction, there was a renewed interest in adult education and what it could contribute. The growth of postwar immigration led to the establishment of the Adult Migrant Educational Service (AMES), and the adult night schools were revamped as Evening Colleges, providing general education and leisure-time activities for adult learners. As the baby boom developed and suburbia spread, the parent education movement grew. In 1964, Australia hosted a UNESCO regional seminar on adult education, out of which grew ASPBAE (Asian South Pacific Bureau of Adult Education), which today is the world's largest regional adult education grouping. As the 1960s proceeded, formal higher education opportunities for adults continued to expand as Australia pioneered many initiatives in mature-age entry and distance education. As a result, the role of traditional university non-credit adult education or, as it had become known, continuing education was increasingly under question.

The 1970s was a lively decade in which Australian society changed direction. The new federal government was strongly reformist and nowhere was the possibilities for change more apparent than in education. For adult education, the more significant of these were: a strong emphasis on access and equity; the development of a new community focus; and a repositioning of technical education as technical and further education (TAFE). Control of the evening colleges passed from the state bureaucracy to local community management. The Neighborhood Houses and Learning Centers movement emerged as an offshoot of the women's movement. In 1975, the Trade Union Training Authority (TUTA) was established as a federally funded body to conduct trade-union education. And, for the first time, serious and sustained attempts were made to address the educational needs of the Aboriginal community, both child and adult, and a number of important initiatives within existing educational institutions and, more significantly, under direct Aboriginal community control were begun. There was an increasing interest in the initial preparation and continuing professional development of adult educators. A number of formal courses of study were established. Thus from about the mid-1980s a critical mass of issues – lifelong learning, retraining, up-skilling, second-chance learning, access and equity – came together to create a very positive climate for adult education. Governments came to see adult education as a sector of education that they could use to achieve important priorities.

Policies and Legislation

Over much of its history, adult education in Australia has operated without the benefit of a formal legislative foundation or overt policy. Governments have seemed to believe that adult education was a good idea as long as it did not cost too much. However, economic and social issues came together in such a way as to prompt a closer governmental involvement in adult education. There were a number of reports on post-compulsory education and the economy, all of which addressed the need for a fundamental rethinking of the education and training system. The overarching idea to emerge was that education, training and work should fit together better so that the acquisition of knowledge and skills, no matter where it occurred, would be encouraged, recognized, and rewarded. In the early 1990s the states, the territories and the federal government established the Australian National Training Authority (ANTA) to oversee and fund the National Training Reform Agenda. Significantly, the ANTA Board decided to include adult and community education within its sphere of operations.

Administration and Financing

Adult education is a responsibility of the states and territories. A full range of providers from private teachers, through voluntary associations and community groups, to statutory authorities and government departments, carries out the actual delivery of that education. Generally in terms of funding the nature of the provision determines the degree of public money provided. Labor-market programs, some other forms of vocational education and training (VET), many second-chance and other access programs are funded by government. General adult education, leisure learning, and hobby programs are usually offered on a full direct-cost recovery/user-pays basis, The state or territory agency with responsibility for adult education maintains control through its management of the quality assurance processes that determine the distribution of the limited funding that the government provides to meet basic infrastructure costs and the needs of its target groups. Thus through the expenditure of quite small amounts of money, the agency can generate a considerable amount of adult education, the direct costs of which are largely borne by the learner.

Provision and Participation

Studies have shown that almost 80% of Australian adults have participated in adult education activities at some time in their lives. It is also reported that each year about 25% of all adults (about 3 million) participate in some form of further education or training. Australian writers generally recognize four major categories of provision: adult basic education; general-interest adult education; public or informational education; and VET. About half of all adult education classes taken each year are employer-provided or work-related. Women make greater use of the community providers than men – 75% compared to 25%. However, men are more likely than women to participate in courses run by employers or related to work. Men and women make about equal use of courses provided by formal educational institutions.

Practitioners, Professional Education and Research

Traditionally, in Australia, people have entered the vocation of adult education from some other occupation, often in a part-time or voluntary capacity. Many hold occupational qualifications, which are usually regarded as adequate for their new role. Often the volunteers and/or part-timers do not possess any relevant formal qualifications. However, about 20 universities provide courses of professional education leading to formal awards for the educators of adults – ranging in level from the undergraduate diploma to the doctorate – involving almost 4,000 students and about 150 full-time academics. In the past, the study of adult education in Australia has been over-dependent on the work of British and North American scholars. Today, this situation is beginning to change as graduate study grows and local research and scholarly writing increases.

Lifelong Learning

Perhaps the most significant recent change in Australian adult education has been the repositioning of adult education as adult learning. Adult education, reconceptualized as adult learning, is ubiquitous and to large extent is no longer recognizable as a separate form of provision, or as a distinct sector of education, or as a movement. While there are many positive consequences of this repositioning, such as the wider official acceptance of ideas like lifelong learning and the learning society, there are also some dangers, such as the narrowness of the official definitions being adopted. Lifelong learning will become an increasing reality for many Australians but such learning must be more than lifelong VET.

See also: extension, indigenous learning, Internet resources, journals, vocation, workplace literacy.

References and Further Reading

Duke, C. (1984). Australian adult education: Origins, influences and tendencies. Canberra Papers in Continuing Education. Canberra, Australia: Australian National University/CCE.

Foley, G. (2000). *Understanding adult education and training* (2nd ed.). St Leonards: Allen & Unwin.

Morris, R., Gonczi, A., & Tennant, M. C. (1995). *Formal courses of professional development for Australian adult educators*. International Conference on Educating the Adult Educator. Canmore, Alberta, May, 14–17.

Tennant, M. C. (1991). *Adult and continuing education in Australia*. London: Routledge.

Tennant, M. C., & Morris, R. K. (2001). Adult education in Australia: Shifting identities 1980–2000. *International Journal of Lifelong Education, 20*(1/2), 44–54.

Whitelock, D. (1974). *The great tradition: A history of adult education in Australia*. St Lucia: University of Queensland Press.

Roger K. Morris

Authenticity

Authenticity is a multi-faceted concept which includes: (a) being genuine, (b) showing consistency between values and actions, (c) relating to others in such a way as to encourage their authenticity, and (d) living a critical life. Although authenticity is not often directly referred to in the adult education literature, it underlies both humanism and critical pedagogy, which together comprise a substantial proportion of adult education theory and practice. Authenticity is often mentioned in passing – Brookfield (1995), for example, advises us of the importance of being authentic in our role as an educator, and Scott (1998) lists freedom, democracy, and authenticity as the goals of transformative learning. Freire (1972) refers to authentic witness based on a critical knowledge of the context of practice. Cranton (2001) suggests that authenticity is at the core of meaningful teaching and contributes to the spiral-like journey of individuation and transformative learning.

Being Genuine

Cranton (2001) defines authenticity as the expression of the genuine self in the community and presents a process by which educators come to know themselves and their preferences within the social context of their work. She describes teaching as a specialized form of communication which has learning as its goal and points out that meaningful communication rests on the premise that those involved are speaking genuinely and honestly rather than with intent to manipulate or deceive. Brookfield (1990) suggests that educators reveal personal aspects of themselves and their experiences, insofar as they are comfortable doing that, as a part of being genuine.

Taylor (1991) is highly critical of the modern ethic of authenticity which contains the notion of self-determining freedom where individuals make judgments for themselves alone without external impositions. As opposed to earlier moral views where people relied on some source, such as God or the idea of good, in the modern ideal of authenticity, individuals find a license to "do their own thing" and find self-fulfillment at the expense of others and society. Taylor emphasizes that human beings are fundamentally dialogical in character. We become full human agents and identify ourselves through relationship and expression. Narcissistic authenticity is inadequate – alone, we cannot determine what is significant. At a broader social level, the purely personal understanding of self-fulfillment denies commitment to a community and marginalizes political citizenship.

To take this back to adult education, it is important to go beyond a definition of authenticity that focuses only on the self. Authenticity develops in relationship, through dialogue and in a social and political context. Educators communicate with learners as a way of fostering their development, and this is done within a framework of the social responsibilities of the educator.

Showing Consistency Between Values and Actions

Brookfield (1990) proposes that being an authentic teacher includes making sure our behaviors are congruent with our words and admitting we do not have all the answers and can make mistakes. Brookfield (1997) balances credibility and authenticity; educators should practice what they preach and be sure not to espouse one way of working then behave in a different way in their own teaching. Similarly, in discussing personal authenticity, Ray and Anderson (2000) emphasize that actions need to be consistent with beliefs. They see reliance on personal experience rather than "meaningless hype" (p. 8) and falsely objective journalism as the way to develop authenticity.

In a variation on this theme, the terms "authentic evaluation" (Fenwick & Parsons, 2000) and "authentic performance tasks" (Wlodkowski, 1999) appear in the adult education literature. Essentially, these authors advocate that we use evaluation strategies which accurately represent or are consistent with the expected student learning. For example, if educators expect learners to be able to engage in a critical debate, they should evaluate their actual performance as they participate in a debate.

Relating to Others

Jarvis (1992) sees people as being authentic when they choose to act so as to "foster the growth and development of each other's being" (p. 113). Jarvis sees this as an experimental and creative act where adult educators consciously have the goal of helping another person develop. In other words, teachers and students learn together through dialogue as Freire (1972) advocates, and the result of authentic teaching is that "teachers learn and grow together with their students" (Jarvis, p. 114). As we know from Buber's (1961) work, it is only through relationships with others that authenticity can be fostered. Brookfield (1990) also emphasizes building trust with students, and respecting students as people. He provides educators with a practical focus – what we can *do* in the classroom to be authentic.

Freire (1972) outlines six attitudes that need to be present for meaningful and authentic dialogue (dialogue which is not oppressive) to occur: (a) love for the world and human beings, (b) humility, (c) faith in people and their power to create and recreate, (d) trust, (e) hope that the dialogue will lead to meaning, and (f) critical thinking and the continuing transformation of reality. Authenticity develops in relationships among people and is expressed in dialogue.

Hollis (1998), a Jungian, helps integrates an understanding of persona (the masks we wear) with the importance of relationships in authenticity. To enter into an authentic relationship requires self-understanding. "The quality of all our relationships is a direct function of our relationship to ourselves . . . The best thing we can do for our relationships with others, and with the transcendent, then, is to render our relationship to ourselves more conscious" (Hollis, p. 13). The quality of relationships depends on how well we know ourselves and how authentically we bring ourselves to the relationship. Hollis proposes four principles of relationship: what we do not know or want to accept about ourselves, we project onto others; we project our wounds and longings onto others; when the other person refuses responsibility for our wounds and longings, projection gives away to resentment and issues of power; and the only way to heal a faltering relationship is to take personal responsibility for our own individuation.

Although Jung does not write directly about authenticity, the notion of persona plays a vital role in his understanding of human psychology. The persona is that aspect of an individual's psyche that lives up to what is expected and proper. We cover up our inferiorities with a persona; we are vulnerable without it. As Sharp (1998) says, "Civilized society depends on interactions between people through the persona" (p. 27). It becomes unhealthy when a person believes he or she is nothing but a persona or mask – no more than what is shown to others. This is inauthentic. Personality and a sense of the self need to be consciously developed, and this clearly falls into the realm of adult education and adult development.

Leading a Critical Life

Jarvis (1992) suggests that authenticity is linked with reflective learning. People need to develop as autonomous and rational individuals within their social context. When people's actions are "controlled by others and their performance is repetitive and ritualistic" (pp. 115–116), they are inauthentic. Heidegger (1962) sees authenticity as involving critical participation in life. By critical participation, he means we question how we are different from the community and live accordingly; we do not do something just because it is done that way by others or believe what others believe without considering whether it is true for us. This is a good way of understanding authenticity – we need to know who we are and what we believe and then act on that. However, keeping Taylor's (1991) cautions in mind, this does not mean that we make such decisions in isolation. Authenticity involves knowing and understanding the collective, and carefully, critically determining how we are different from and the same as that collective. Sharp (1995) suggests the first fruit of consciously developing as an authentic person is the "segregation of the individual from the undifferentiated and unconscious herd" (p. 48). In Jungian terms, this is individuation, and it includes not only separation from the herd, but also a simultaneous rejoining in a more meaningful way with the collective of humanity.

Thinking along parallel lines, Freire (1972) argues that authenticity comes through having a critical knowledge of the context within which we work and seeing the principal contradictions of that society. To be authentic, the educator is bold, dares to take risks, and recognizes that he or she will not always win over the people.

Authenticity is the expression of the genuine self in the community. In order to create that genuine self, we need to critically participate in life rather than run with the unconscious herd. Part of this journey is understanding how others are different from us without attempting to make them into our own image; that is, we help others discover their authenticity as a way of fostering our own authenticity.

See also: appreciative inquiry, identity, lifespan development, narrative, pedagogic identity, teaching.

References and Further Reading

Brookfield, S. D. (1990). *The skillful teacher*. San Francisco: Jossey-Bass.

Brookfield, S. D. (1995). *Becoming a critically reflective teacher*. San Francisco: Jossey-Bass.

Brookfield, S. D. (1997). Through the lens of learning: How the visceral experience of learning reframes teaching. In D. Boud, R. Cohen, & D. Walker (Eds.), *Using experience for learning* (pp. 21–32). Buckingham, UK: Society for Research into Higher Education,

Buber, M. (1961). *Between man and man*. Glasgow: Fontana Library.

Cranton, P. (2001). *Becoming an authentic teacher in higher education*. Malabar, FL: Krieger.

Fenwick, T. J., & Parsons, J. (2000). *The art of evaluation: A handbook for educators and trainers*. Toronto: Thompson Educational.

Freire, P. (1972). *Pedagogy of the oppressed*. Harmondsworth, England: Penguin.

Heidegger, M. (1962). *Being and time*. (J. MacQuarrie & E. Robinson, Trans.). San Francisco: Harper.

Hollis, J. (1998). *The Eden project: In search of the magical other*. Toronto: Inner City Books.

Jarvis, P. (1992). *Paradoxes of learning: On becoming an individual in society*. San Francisco: Jossey-Bass.

Ray, P., & Anderson, S. (2000). *The cultural creatives*. New York: Three Rivers Press.

Scott, S. M. (1998). An overview of transformation theory in adult education. In S. M. Scott, B. Spencer & A. M. Thomas (Eds.), *Learning for life: Canadian readings in adult education* (pp. 188–199). Toronto: Thompson Educational.

Sharp, D. (1995). *Who am I really? Personality, soul and individuation*. Toronto: Inner City Books.

Sharp, D. (1998). *Jungian psychology unplugged: My life as an elephant*. Toronto: Inner City Books.

Taylor, C. (1991). *The malaise of modernity*. Concord, ON: House of Anansi Press.

Wlodkowski, R. J. (1999). *Enhancing adult motivation to learn: A comprehensive guide for teaching all adults*. (Rev. ed.). San Francisco: Jossey-Bass.

Patricia Cranton

Autobiography

Autobiography was first incorporated into adult education as a writing tool in literacy and language learning, but more recently it has emerged as an instructional method for students' personal learning concerning their life as learners, as teachers, or as growing individuals. Writing one's autobiography involves reassembling the events of a life into a comprehensive sketch. Educators who take seriously both the quest for life's meaning and the meaning of each individual's life are recognizing that autobiography can enhance personal knowing, critical consciousness, and personal transformation. Increasingly this method is being incorporated into educational programs in continuing and higher education, the workplace, and the community. It has been said that life is lived forwards, but understood backwards. And it is perhaps this aspect of life that has brought autobiography – transforming one's life into text – to increasing importance in literature, literary criticism, counseling, and more recently in adult education.

Historical Progression

Autobiography emerged as a literary genre at the end of the 18th century from a tradition that has variously been called a "memoir" or "confession" (the most notable being the religious *Confessions* of St. Augustine). For a time it was employed by men who had achieved some notoriety in the community, either artistically or politically. For women it was used initially as a means of detailing their faith in God, and later developed into a method of self-analysis, self-understanding, personal reflection, and healing. The past quarter century has seen a renewed interest in autobiography as a distinct literary genre that, in turn, has spawned a specific area of literary criticism through the psychoanalytic and philosophical analysis in James Olney's (1980) edited writings, and through the feminist literary analysis of Smith and Watson's (1998) edited collections.

The ever-growing interest in autobiography is evidenced in the number of such writings by political leaders and other more or less famous people and by the large readership of these books. In psychotherapy, autobiography has become established as a tool for self-understanding and self-reflection, and in the field of aging as a way for older adults to engage in life review. Educators have advanced autobiography as a source for narrative research and have examined story and narrative as the primary tools in the work that teachers and counselors do. Feminist scholars have given increased attention to autobiography as a research method, as have the social sciences concerned with the study of lives in a historical or social context.

Within Adult Education

Turning to the field of adult education, more than 20 years ago Catherine Warren (1982) foretold the role of life history for adult education, highlighting its potential for an enlarged understanding of adult learners' lives. Since then a growing number of educators have examined the use of life stories as primary tools in the work of teachers and counselors. Among adult educators, William Randall (1995) approached autobiography from a psychological and developmental perspective, focusing on the benefits of "re-storying" personal experience to learning and development. He and others are continuing to research the use of autobiography in a variety of adult education and higher education settings as a means of fostering self-reflection, personal knowing, perspective transformation, and growth of consciousness (Dominicé, 2000; Karpiak, 2000; Rossiter, 1999).

Definitions and Perspectives

Autobiography, or "self-life-writing" has been variously defined as a "self-portrait," an "archeological dig," or a "voyage of discovery." French autobiographer and literary critic, Philippe Lejeune (1989), provides a formal and enduring definition of autobiography as "retrospective prose narrative written by a real person concerning his own existence, where the focus is his individual life, in particular the story of his personality" (p. 4). This definition establishes an "autobiographical pact" between the author and the reader that the author is, indeed, writing in earnest and is reporting from his or her lived experience (Lejeune). In this definition Lejeune highlights the process of writing as integrating the outer and inner life of the individual toward an appreciation of the growth of his or her personality.

Although the term, autobiography, is sometimes used interchangeably with memoir and journal or diary, Lejeune (1989) distinguishes it from other forms of personal writing. Autobiography is unlike a private journal or diary that records the writer's experiences, impressions, and mental states; and it is different from the memoir, in which the subject may be a particular moment or period of an individual's life, rather than of its entirety. In autobiography, the view taken is retrospective of an entire life. It has the distinction of being a narrative prose, in which the author, the narrator (of the life story), and the protagonist are one and the same (Lejeune).

While Lejeune's definitions and Olney's (1980) psychological approach have dominated the autobiography scene, recent feminist theorists have pointed out the limitations of these conceptions, with respect to both issues of race and gender and the sociocultural influences of life. For example, in Smith and Watson's (1998) edited collection, writers analyse the way in which autobiographers comment upon the sociocultural aspects of life, especially if these writers were born as women. They also highlight the apparent differences between the writings of men and women. Men, for instance, write to present themselves as successfully overcoming various obstacles, or to justify their actions. Women, on the other hand, are more likely to reflect on their interdependent existence with others and their community, focusing on both the personal and contextual relationships that have shaped their life; and rather than presenting a success story, women tend to reveal their fears, anxieties, and struggles as developing selves.

Autobiography as Adult Learning and Instruction

When employed as an instructional method, autobiography reflects a more complex and closer association of adult education with adult development than do other methods. It aligns most closely with those approaches in adult education where the focus is on personal and transformative learning, that is, where the goal of education is to help learners make meaning out of their world through their experience of it. Cranton and Roy (2003) define transformative learning as the process by which we critically reflect on our assumptions, beliefs, values and perspectives concerning the world around us. Essential to this process is our capacity to bring to consciousness those beliefs, assumptions, and experiences that were previously unconscious. Through transformative learning we develop perspectives that are more integrated, more complex, and more open or permeable. Autobiography and re-storying our life is central to transformative learning. In Rossiter's (1999) words, "the re-storying process tells the story of perspective transformation" (p. 84), leading adults not only to reflect on and interpret their life, but also to change it.

The use of autobiography as an instructional method for personal and transformative learning extends into many areas of the world, including Europe, Australia, the United States and Canada, where educators in various settings are exploring ways to incorporate autobiography into their programs. In some cases the student autobiographies, written in the context of a course, are shared with others in the class. Dominicé (2000) describes a process whereby students in both educational and work settings in Switzerland prepare both oral and written versions of their "educational biographies," which they then share in small groups as a reflective and interpretive process. Alternatively, Karpiak (2000) outlines her method of having graduate and continuing education students in the United States and Canada prepare only written versions of five chapters of their life story as a final elective course assignment.

Autobiography in the context of adult education offers adult learners perhaps their first opportunity to review their life and to write about it as though it were another's. This exercise appears to serve various functions for writers. Karpiak (2000) reports that some use this opportunity to reflect on the class experience and on the authors they have studied, and to integrate these into their life as learners. Many outline the turning points and challenges that have marked and directed their life as growing professionals. Others use the opportunity to write about the personal events that have shaped their life, to reflect upon them, and in some cases to analyse them, even *to relive* them (as is evidenced by their occasional shift to writing in the present tense).

In the course of writing, students achieve a deeper awareness of themselves and of others and of their relationship with others and the world. Dominicé (2000) noted the growing sense of empowerment and identity formation as writers gained insight into their past and the ways in which personal and societal influences had intersected. As learners, they came to appreciate their own history with learning and of themselves as learners. Karpiak (2000), who conducted research on those students who had written their life story, found that the exercise helped them to perceive their patterns of behavior and the various roles they had unwittingly played; sometimes it served to bring a new sense of order to their life, or affirmation of their accomplishments, and in some instances it helped to bring closure to painful events. There was evidence to suggest that when adult learners write their life story they embark on a process of gaining self- and other-awareness that can lead to a transformation of their view of themselves and the world around them.

Autobiography for Inquiry

Adult learners who write the story of

their life offer a perspective, an "inside view" to readers that most other means and methods do not. Many of the theories about learning and development that have shaped scientific thought were in part derived from analysing personal narratives and autobiographical materials; similarly, these autobiographies provide mediums for gaining insight into the lives of students (Dominicé, 2000). They reveal the ways in which social and cultural factors have shaped their lives as learners, how early school experiences can condition subsequent successes or failures, and how present educational environments can influence learning (Dominicé). Their stories remind us that these students have lives lived, which yield a storehouse of experiences that in turn can be tapped, brought forth, explored, and shared in the classroom or other educational setting. Further, in the course of reading these stories, educators may become inspired to reflect on their own story, and thereby to know more about their life and how it has shaped their educational philosophies and practices (Dominicé). Finally, prospective students who read the stories of fellow students may garner hope for their prospect of overcoming the many obstacles to learning, both those that came earlier in life and those that come later. These stories act as roadmaps for working through and prevailing over life events.

See also: life history, narrative, writing, research methods.

References and Further Reading

Cranton, P., & Roy, M. (2003). When the bottom falls out of the bucket: Toward a holistic perspective on transformative learning. *Journal of Transformative Education, 2*(2), 86–98.

Dominicé, P. (2000). *Learning from our lives: Using educational biographies with adults*. San Francisco: Jossey-Bass.

Karpiak, I. E. (2000). Writing our life: Adult learning and teaching through autobiography. *Canadian Journal of University Continuing Education, 26*(1), 31–50.

Lejeune, P. (1989). *On autobiography*. (K. Leary, Trans.). Minneapolis, MN: University of Minnesota Press.

Olney, J. (1980). Autobiography and the cultural moment: A thematic, historical and bibliographical introduction. In *Autobiography: Essays theoretical and critical* (pp. 3–27). Princeton, NJ: Princeton University Press.

Randall, W. L. (1995). *The stories we are: An essay on self-creation*. Toronto: University of Toronto Press.

Rossiter, M. (1999). Understanding adult development as narrative. In M.C. Clark & R. S. Caffarella (Eds.), *An update on adult development theory: New ways of thinking about the life course* (pp. 77–85). *New Directions for Adult and Continuing Education*, No. 84. San Francisco: Jossey-Bass.

Smith, S., & Watson, J. (1998). Introduction: Situating subjectivity in women's autobiographical practices. In *Women, autobiography, theory: A reader*. Madison, WI: University of Wisconsin Press.

Warren, C. E. (1982). The written life history as a prime research tool in adult education, *Adult Education, 32*(4), 214–228.

Irene Karpiak

C

Canada and Adult Education

Canada, the second biggest country in the world, has 99,846,70 square kilometers, over five time zones. The climate is temperate to arctic. Arable land is 4.94%, and the population at 32,207,113 is spread like a string of beads across the northern part of the continent, with 85% living within 300 km. from the southern border. It was settled by Aboriginals, British, French, and in the 20th century, principally by other nationals. The French, comprising 23% of the population, remain centered in the province of Quebec. In the 20th century Canada has turned from a rural to an industrial and urban society. In 2003, Toronto, its largest city, had nearly half its population born in another country. It is a democratic federation, with education being a provincial responsibility, resulting in the development of a patchwork of educational systems.

Pre-World War I

It is impossible to understand the education of adults in Canada, without referring to the dialectic between *learning* and *education*, an invisible contest in all societies, at varying epochs. In the settlement of the country in the 17th to 19th centuries – a new land, a new agriculture, a new forestry, new unfamiliar threats to physical health, and new people – learning was paramount. There were few "teachers" for the dominating practical exigencies of everyday survival (see Moodie, 1987). As a result they grouped together, in families, and then in meager but growing voluntary associations, the engines of learning that persist today as the humus of civil society. In the early years they borrowed from the "home countries," – the Mechanics' Institutes (1830), the Workers' Educational Associations (1918), the YMCA (1868) – and they formed their own, among them the Granges (1872) agricultural organizations, the Canadian Reading Camp Association (1899) and the Women's Institutes (1897). At the same time, education began to appear, primarily devoted to the young, but slowly and steadily including provision for adults. Universities began to provide extension services and local school boards opened "night classes" for adults. The dominant agencies were the military and the Church. And the dominant themes that have dominated adult education in Canada have been languages (since the beginnings of the European invasion and settlement, someone, somewhere, in Canada, was teaching or learning a language), literacy, and citizenship (see Selman, 1995).

1914–45

The training of a citizen-army, in both wars, involved the greatest programs of adult education in Canada's history. Nevertheless, despite the evidence of millions of adults learning new, martial, survival skills, the lesson was lost on Canada until the 1960s. Yet the intervening 21 years was a fertile time for the invention of forms of adult education in Canada that became models for the world. The Antigonish Movement (1920s) initiated by St. Francis Xavier University in the province of Nova Scotia demonstrated that poverty-stricken adults, by reading, discussion and action, could transform their lives. During the same decade, under the impetus of the novel radio-broadcasting, and the creation of a public-financed Canadian Broadcasting Corporation (1936), the Canadian Association for Adult Education (1935) introduced first "Farm Radio Forum," and second, "Citizens Forum," educational programs that involved, every week, at the same time, all of Canada.

During those years, the Canadian Federal Government, prevented by constitutional arrangements from intervening in formal education, and clearly responsible for the economy, began its 90-year program of "training," as distinct from "education" (1913), by subsidizing provinces, except Quebec, to engage in the training of adults in various industrial skills. By the end of the period it had trained millions of adult workers, although those workers, because of their lack of formal credentials, could not transfer to the formal education system and were barred from the main passage to economic and personal success. Similar influences caused a number of large industries, particularly the oil industry, to invest in their own employee training in the 1930s.

The need for *learning* outside of the educational system began to reassert itself, and 40 years later one high-technology large corporation in the province of Ontario, "maintained 19 teaching centers through which passed some 8,000 to 10,000 students per year" (Thomas, 2001, p. 334). Supported by the military who had discovered the same conditions, these developments became a mainstay of the education of adults following 1945.

1945–80

In the postwar years the education of adults boomed and became a part of every major institution in Canada. A succession of national conferences, extending from 1958, beginning with two on education, and concluding with a Conference on Youth in 1971, established a political agenda for Canada for the next 20 years, and created a model for adult learning. In the 1960s differing systems of community colleges were established in every province. These attempted to create an alternative to the universities, and made it possible for a whole new social sector of young adults to become students. The colleges engaged in forms of community development in their early days, but in the financial crunch of the 1980s they retreated to more conventional programs of evening classes. The universities, providing the same services during 1950 to 1980, under the same financial rigors, virtually abandoned extension, and created schools of continuing education mostly for university graduates. The public school boards found an unexpected clientele in Canadians who had not finished high school, or who were attracted to the pubic schools as their "familiar" agencies. During the late 1950s and early 1960s, the province of Ontario was operating three "all-night" secondary schools, and also running a substantial Guidance and Counseling Center for adults. Canadian adults were making novel uses of educational agencies beyond their intended uses. They were attending both concurrently with employment and, consecutively, as part-time and full-time students. The age of the part-time student had arrived. In the same era, formal professions were developing mandatory continuing education for their members, often by legislation.

Canada, in concert with other Western countries, has developed "academic" adult education in the sense of providing instruction for prospective adult educators. The first university program at graduate level appeared in the province of British Columbia in 1958. Subsequently there are programs in every province, two at undergraduate level, and in many community colleges. Canada does not have the ability to control entrance to the profession, though the power of the degree has influenced employment of adult educators considerably. In terms of the universities, research and publishing about adult education has increased considerably partly through the creation of a new organization, the Canadian Association for the Study of Adult Education (1981), and its associated refereed journal, the *Canadian Journal for the Study of Adult Education*.

The divided educational jurisdictions in Canada have always made it difficult to ascertain the precise number of adults participating in education, and the only way to find reliable figures is by national polling. There have been several such polls in Canada: for example, "If those who are still involved in full-time education are excluded, the study indicates that approximately 33% took part in adult education in 1991 (Selman, Cooke, Selman, & Dampier, 1998, p. 121). The lifelong learning movement, current in the 1990s, blurred the distinction between adult and formal education, although Canada, the United States, and many other countries, particularly immigrant and settlement countries, had always been lifelong learning societies.

1980–the Present

The 1990s produced a financial crisis in Canada that devastated the education of adults. Public programs were severely curtailed, and the attitude grew amongst public and private providers that achieving competence and knowledge was primarily the individual's responsibility. Most programs were maintained but at increased cost to the individual. The cost to the country was the diminution of other than purely vocational programs. The traditional dominant themes in Canada – languages (less than the others), literacy, and citizenship – have suffered. Canada has discovered that the same disadvantages that plagued "public education" of children and youth, have applied equally to the education of adults. Similarly, the same conditions have plagued adult education as formal education – the educated and well-off have received more than the poor and uneducated. The one promising introduction to the education of adults has been prior learning assessment and recognition (PLAR).

Officially introduced in the 1990s, primarily in the colleges, and later in universities, PLAR frees *learning* from *education*, and allows any individual, subject to various assessments and regardless of how and where he or she has learned, to enter and re-enter the formal education system. It has been slow to develop, mostly because of the deep-seated conservatism of Canadians about any change in education, but it is being used by increasing numbers of people (Thomas, 2000).

The education of adults in Canada has assumed various forms, and has experienced ups and, recently, downs; but it has always been based on Enlightenment optimism about human nature and its ability to change and grow. There are indications that the contestation between *learning* and *education* is entering a new and more amicable and functional relationship, and that a genuine new form of continuing education, that has always been available for some, is about to be born – again in public, and accessible to many more Canadians.

See also: civil society, continuing education, extension, indigenous learning, journals, labor education, literacy, women's voluntary organizations.

References and Further Reading

Moodie, S. (1987). *Roughing it in the bush.* Boston: Beacon Press.

Selman, G. (1995). *Adult education in Canada: Historical essays*. Toronto: Thompson Educational.

Selman, G., Cooke, M., Selman, M., & Dampier, P. (1998). *The foundations of adult education in Canada.* (2nd ed.). Toronto: Thompson Educational.

Thomas, A. M. (2000). Prior learning assessment: The quiet revolution. In A. L. Wilson & E. R. Hayes (Eds.), *The handbook of adult and continuing education* (pp. 508–522). San Francisco: Jossey-Bass.

Thomas, A. M. (2001). The past, present, and future of adult education. In T. Barer-Stein & M. Kompf (Eds.), *The craft of teaching adults* (3rd ed., pp. 325–347). Toronto: Irwin Publishing & Culture Concepts.

Alan Thomas

Career Education

Career education is the totality of programs and services that seek to enhance a person's educational, vocational and social development. Specifically, career education refers to the imparting of knowledge about occupations and work and to developing the skills that are necessary to fashion one's career. It is a key component of the field of adult education since the term career encompasses the general path or progress of a person throughout their life, not only in some vocation but also their avocational, cognitive, emotional and social development.

Background

There are substantive historical links between adult, career and vocational education. For instance, in 1895 the School of Mechanical Arts in San Francisco offered one of the earliest programs of career guidance. Moreover, Frank Parsons who is considered the founder of vocational guidance established a continuing education program in Boston in 1905 through the Breadwinners Institute. He set out the original framework as a model triarchy for helping an individual select a career:

- First, a clear understanding of yourself, aptitudes, abilities, interests, resources, limitations and other qualities.
- Second, a knowledge of the requirements and conditions of success, advantages and disadvantages, compensations, opportunities, and prospects in different lines of work.
- Third, true reasoning on the relations of these two groups of facts (Parsons, 1909, p. 5).

Vocational guidance, however, was limited to individual services and could not meet the demands of large populations. Career education in

Western societies evolved as a distinct field in the 1970s as a response to the needs of groups and also for the provision of career services in institutional settings. It began as a component of formal education programs in secondary schooling and as a means of giving expression to ideas of vocational development throughout the lifespan. At that time, Hoyt, Evans, Mackin and Mangum (1972) saw career education as a curriculum approach that assisted with career decision-making and provided information.

Purpose of Career Education

The purpose of career education was to prepare individuals for the world of work, but the concept of career education has broadened even further as a general preparation for life. While many might consider that career education is focused only in secondary education, it occurs to a large extent in adult education settings both formally and informally in universities, colleges, institutes, community colleges, professions, employment services, welfare organizations and government agencies.

Career education finds expression in adult education settings through various means; it is not a single, unified or homogeneous process. Also, there is no substantive theory of career education although, at times, career education is infused into curriculum aims and objectives. As a form of experience-based learning it is evident in community contacts and collaboration with occupations, employer and employee organizations. Career education may transpire with the exploration of specific occupations or preparation for job-seeking or coaching and mentoring. More importantly, it occurs through educational processes whenever they act as a catalyst for the enhancement of personal development.

Assumptions of Career Development

Theoretical notions of career development have provided a varied basis for career education activities and approaches, and at least 18 different career development theories have been listed (see Brown, 2004). Whereas earlier ideas about career development included traits and factors such as life-span and social cognitive aspects, the newer perspectives on career education are being built on emerging research focused on gender, race, ethnicity and social class, as well as constructivist ideas (see Brown). There have been criticisms (Sharf, 1997) that career development theories (and hence career education) have been based mainly on White, male, middle-class perceptions; or have made assumptions about social and economic equality; or have not been relevant for minority groups. Indeed, Zunkner (1998, pp. 431–444) summarized how Native Americans, African Americans, Asian Americans, Hispanic Americans and multicultural groups had vastly varying cultural opinions about work and careers.

This recognizes that life-course patterns (i.e., careers) occur in cultural and historical contexts. It emphasizes the point that career education has a different nature, function and scope across different global contexts, wherever cultural, social and economic conditions vary. For example, Athanasou and Torrance (2002) studied the Pacific Islands and noted that cultural heterogeneity compounded with economic, historical and geographic backgrounds limited the scope for educational and vocational achievement. Even though education was a regional priority, there were few formal systems of assistance for career development and for the most part career education was embedded within personal self-direction or family traditions.

Even within a society, the nature and scope of career education is being challenged in other ways. The traditional concept of a stable, linear and single career throughout one's life has also undergone substantial changes. This is now accompanied by varied rates of labor-force participation throughout the life-span. The increased participation of women has also changed the labor market, and the economic value of education or qualifications has assumed greater importance in employment. Visible labor-force changes are increased part-time or casual employment, a propensity for job mobility, and substantial downsizing or retrenchments across many occupations with reduced employment stability or security for those with few transferable skills.

Adult and Career Education

Career education as a component of adult education is an area that will develop to fit contemporary society. Multiple career education responses will be gathered to respond to diverse career development needs in adult education. These will include a primary emphasis on maintaining employment potential through adult education, as well as directly or indirectly providing information that will permit adults to discover opportunities and prepare them for changes. Adult career education will also feature in promoting those avocational activities that still occupy people's lives. Accordingly, career education has the potential to reinforce the liberating and transformative aspects of adult education in its many guises throughout the lifespan since it seeks to enhance a person's educational, vocational and social development. Reader with an interest in the field are referred *inter alia* to the following journals that provide a coverage of career education issues for adults: *International Journal of Educational and Vocational Guidance, Journal of Employment Counseling, Career Development Quarterly, Journal of Vocational Behavior, Australian Journal of Career Development, British Journal of Guidance and Counselling, Journal of Career Development, Career Development International*, and *Journal of Career Assessment*.

See also: continuing professional education, human resource development, mentor, military education, training, vocational education, workplace learning.

References and Further Reading

Athanasou, J. A., & Torrance, J. (2002). Career development in the Pacific Islands: Key issues influencing educational and vocational achievement. *International Journal of Educational and Vocational Guidance*, 2, 7–20.

Brown, D. (2004). *Career information, career counselling, and career development* (8th ed.). Boston: Allyn & Bacon.

Hoyt, K. B., Evans, R. N., Mackin, E. F., & Mangum, G. L. (1972). *Career education: What it is and how to do it.* Salt Lake City, UT: Olympus.

Parsons, F. (1909). *Choosing a vocation.* Boston: Houghton Mifflin.

Sharf, R. S. (1997). *Applying career development theory to counseling* (2nd ed.). Pacific Grove, CA: Brooks/Cole.

Zunkner, V. G. (1998). *Career counselling. Applied concepts of life planning* (5th ed.). Pacific Grove, CA: Brooks-Cole.

James Athanasou

Case Study Research

A case study is an intensive description and analysis of a single unit or bounded system such as an individual, program, event, group, intervention, or community. A case study research design is used when one wants to gain a holistic understanding of the "case" and when the phenomenon of interest is intertwined with the context in which it exists. In fact, case study research attends to the context rather than a single variable, the process rather than cause and effect. The case study offers a means of investigating complex social units consisting of multiple variables of potential importance in understanding a phenomenon. Anchored in real-life situations, the case study results in a rich and holistic account of a phenomenon. Insights derived from case study research can directly influence policy, practice, and future research in adult education.

Most of us have encountered case studies in our training as professionals and in our practice as adult educators. The fact that a lawyer, a social worker, a medical doctor and even a detective can be involved in research on a "case" has led to some confusion as to just what constitutes case study research. While some define case study research in terms of the process of doing a case study, or in terms of the end product, most scholars define the case in terms of the unit of analysis. As Stake (2000) suggests, case study is less of a methodological choice than "a choice of what is to be studied" (p. 435).The "what" is a single entity, a unit around which there are boundaries. The case then has a finite quality about it either in terms of time (the evolution or history of a particular program), space (the case is located in a particular place), and/or components comprising the case (number of participants, for example). Stake (1995) clarifies the bounded system as follows:

> The case could be a child. It could be a classroom of children or a particular mobilization of professionals to study a childhood condition. The case is one among others . . . An innovative program may be a case. All the schools in Sweden can be a case. But a relationship among schools, the reasons for innovative teaching, or the policies of school reform are less commonly considered a case. These topics are generalities rather than specifics. The case is a specific, complex, functioning thing. (p. 2)

It is clear what is within the boundaries of the case, and what is not.

Types of Case Studies

Case studies are common to a number of disciplines such as anthropology, psychology, sociology, political science, and applied fields such as social work, administration and all areas of education. Within any of these fields, the case study can be primarily descriptive, interpretive, or evaluative (Merriam, 1998). Case studies can also be collective. Each of these types will be discussed in turn.

A descriptive case study presents a detailed account of the unit under study. Stake (2000) identifies this type of study as an intrinsic case study; its purpose is not to represent other cases or to illustrate an abstract concept or to build theory. Rather, "in all its particularity *and* ordinariness, this case itself is of interest (p. 437, emphasis in original). Lijphart (1971) calls a purely descriptive case study "atheoretical." They are "entirely descriptive and move in a theoretical vacuum; they are neither guided by established or hypothesized generalizations nor motivated by a desire to formulate general hypotheses" (p. 691). Nevertheless, this type of case study is useful in presenting basic information about a phenomenon where little research has been conducted. For example, Houle's (1984) vivid account of one of Billy Graham's crusade meetings is a descriptive case study of oratory as a basic teaching method in adult education.

Interpretive case studies include rich description, but this description is the basis for developing conceptual categories or to illustrate, support, or challenge theoretical assumptions held prior to the study. The researcher gathers as much data about the case as possible with the intent of analyzing, interpreting, or theorizing about the phenomenon. Stake (2000) calls this type of case study "instrumental." In an instrumental case study, the intent is "to provide insight into an issue or to redraw a generalization. The case is of secondary interest, it plays a supporting role, and it facilitates our understanding of something else" (p. 437). Most case studies in adult education are interpretive as for example Tisdell's (1993) investigation of power, privilege, and oppression in two adult higher education classes.

Yin (2003) extends the notion of interpretive case studies with his concept of "explanatory" case studies. An explanatory case study "presents data on cause–effect relationships – explaining how events happened" (p. 5). He illustrates this type of case study with a study of nine cases of funded research projects and the extent the results were utilized in practice. Three different theories of research utilization were tested with these cases.

A third type of case study is evaluative in nature. Evaluative case studies include both description and interpretation but also judgment. Using a case study design when doing an evaluation allows the results of a study to be more easily communicated to various stakeholders most of whom are likely to be non-researchers. Adult educators and human resource development personnel are likely to find this methodology particularly amenable to program evaluations.

When studying more than one case, whether the cases be descriptive, interpretive or evaluative, a number of terms are used including multiple or collective case studies, multicase or multisite studies, or comparative case studies. Cross-case analysis is also used. A researcher collects and analyzes data from several cases, comparing findings across the individual cases. Collective case studies should not be confused with a single case where subunits are embedded (learners within a particular educational program for example). Often a case description is given for each individual case, and then generalizations are made across cases. Instead of studying the role of human resource development in a single small business, for example, Rowden (1995) studied three successful small businesses. A case description of each business is followed by a cross-case analysis presenting generalizations common to all three businesses. The more cases included in a study and the greater the variation across the cases, the more compelling an interpretation is likely to be.

Conducting a Case Study

The process of conducting a case study begins with the selection of the "case." The selection is done purposefully, not randomly; that is, a particular person, site, program, process, community, or other bounded system is selected because it exhibits characteristics of interest to the researcher. The case might be unique or typical, representative of a common practice, or never before encountered. The selection depends upon what you want to learn and the significance that knowledge might have for extending theory or improving practice.

Often, one must select samples within the case, as for example when studying a large hospital patient education program, a corporate training program, or a statewide adult literacy program. While each of these – the patient education program, the training program, the literacy program – constitutes a single bounded system or case, decisions have to be made regarding subunits *within* the case. Who should be interviewed? When and which activities should be observed? Sometimes several levels of selection are necessary. In studying a statewide literacy program for example, you would first determine, based on variables of interest such as location, funding, size, and student diversity, which sites to include, then which classes to observe at those sites and which staff and students to interview.

Data collection is a comprehensive process in case study research. Depending on the question of interest in the case, both quantitative and qualitative methods might be employed. At a minimum, one would want to become intimately familiar with the case through some combination of observations, interviews, and reading documents relevant to the case. Surveys or other forms of measurement might also be employed. How one analyses the data collected depends on the questions being asked about the case and the type of case study employed. For example, an interpretive case study would require that data be analysed in relation to some conceptual or theoretical frame as Tisdell (1993) did when she employed critical theory to analyse the power dynamics in two adult higher education classes. Yin (2003) illustrates how, depending on the variables of interest, even the highly statistical technique of factor analyses can be used in causal case studies. He presents an example of a collective case study of nine high-tech or industrial parks to find out which factors attract high-tech firms to new locations. Yin comments that "the study could have been designed as a survey or secondary analysis of economic data. . . . However, such investigations do not permit in-depth examination of the factors themselves. . . . The illustrative case study was intended to examine the factors more closely" (p. 18).

The findings of the investigation are written up as a comprehensive description of the case. And as Stake (2000) notes, there are a number of stylistic options for this case write-up including "how much to make the report a story," and "how much to compare with other cases" (p. 448). Perhaps because a case study focuses on a single unit, a single instance, the issue of generalizability looms larger here than with other types of qualitative research. However, as several writers point out, much can be learned from a particular case (Merriam, 1998). Readers can learn vicariously from an encounter with the case through the researcher's narrative description (Stake). The vivid description in a case study can create an image – "a vivid portrait of excellent teaching, for example – can become a prototype that can be used in the education of teachers or for the appraisal of teaching" (Eisner, 1991,

p. 1999). Further, Erickson (1986) argues that since the general lies in the particular, what we learn in a particular case can be transferred to similar situations. It is the reader, not the researcher, who determines what can apply to his or her situation. Stake explains how this knowledge transfer works:

> Case researchers, like others, pass along to readers some of their personal meanings of events and relationship – and fail to pass along others. They know that the reader, too, will add and subtract, invent and shape – reconstructing the knowledge in ways that leave it . . . more likely to be personally useful. (p. 442)

In summary, case study research is a particularly powerful tool for understanding and illuminating particular aspects of adult education practice. The unit of analysis, the bounded system, defines the case itself. It is from an in-depth analysis of the case that we can learn about some aspect of practice. Case studies can be primarily descriptive, interpretive, or evaluative. However, comprehensive description forms the foundation for each of these three types. A number of separate case studies can be combined in what are known as collective, multi-site, or comparative case studies. Collective case studies can enhance both the power and the applicability of findings. Finally, once the "case" has been identified, the researcher can employ any and all appropriate data collection and analysis techniques in the service of presenting case findings. And because case studies are about the phenomenon in context, they are typically highly readable and accessible to educators and policy advocates who can make a difference in practice.

See also: research methods.

References and Further Reading

Eisner, E. W. (1991). *The enlightened eye: Qualitative inquiry and the enhancement of educational practice*. Old Tappan, NJ: Macmillan.

Erickson, F. (1986). Qualitative methods in research on teaching. In M. C. Wittrock (Ed.), *Handbook of research on teaching* (3rd ed., pp. 119–161). Old Tappan, NJ: Palgrave Macmillan.

Houle, C. O. (1984). *Pattern of learning: New perspectives on life-span education*. San Francisco: Jossey-Bass.

Lijphart, A. (1971). Comparative politics and the comparative method. *American Political Science Review*, 65, 682–694.

Merriam, S. B. (1998). *Qualitative research and case study applications in education* (2nd ed.). San Francisco: Jossey-Bass.

Rowden, R. W. (1995). The role of human resource development in successful small to mid-sized manufacturing businesses: A comprehensive case study. *Human Resource Development Quarterly*, *6*(4), 355–373.

Stake, R. E. (1995). *The art of case study research*. Thousand Oaks, CA: Sage.

Stake, R. E. (2000). Case study. In N. K. Denzin & Y. S. Lincoln (Eds.), *Handbook of qualitative research* (2nd ed., pp. 435–454). Thousand Oaks, CA: Sage.

Tisdell, E. J. (1993). Interlocking systems of power, privilege, and oppression in adult higher education classes. *Adult Education Quarterly*, *43*(4), 203–226.

Yin, R. K. (2003). *Applications of case study research* (2nd ed.). Thousand Oaks, CA: Sage.

Sharan B. Merriam

Chaos Theory

The new sciences are reconceptualizing chaos as complexity in the range of behaviors and richness of information in and among non-linear systems, a view which itself has led to the science of chaos now being more commonly called the science of complexity. This study of chaos as complexity, as systems of patterns, is prompting a revisioning in the sciences and humanities that is touching every discipline, including economics, management, literature, and education. Many have commented on the chaos that seems to characterize modern society, referring to the disorder, turbulence, and randomness of our present-day families, institutions, and political affairs. In this regard chaos is perceived as opposition to order, harmony, and goodness. And it is this common belief about chaos that has been challenged by contemporary sciences where a contrasting and more complex view of chaos is presented – chaos as "orderly disorder." They argue that complex order may be hidden within chaos (Hayles, 1991), or, correspondingly, that chaos may give rise to a new order (Prigogine & Stengers, 1984).

Signs of chaos theory are beginning to appear in the literature of adult education, and with these the corresponding challenges to the basic assumptions concerning learners, the nature of knowledge, and the processes of acquiring knowledge. Like other fields, adult education is possibly "at the edge" where "complexity thinking" is putting forward new principles, practices, and perspectives (Domaingue, 1988; Karpiak, 2000; Osberg & Biesta, 2003).

Antecedents

Physicist, Fritjof Capra, with his publication of *The Tao of Physics* in 1975, not only contested the principles of "classical science," but also foreshadowed the more recently acknowledged congruence between chaos and complexity science and the Eastern philosophies, such as Buddhism and Taoism, as noted by Waldrop (1992). Capra traced the erosion of classical science to Einstein's theory of relativity, and Heisenberg's "uncertainly principle," both of whose views represented at that time a departure from Newton's 17th century characterization of the world as "a giant clockwork." According to that prevailing perspective, nature could be viewed objectively, laws were time-reversible and deterministic, and problems could be predicted, explained, and in some way controlled. Contemporary science, wrote Capra, has shaken the very foundations of the well-established belief system about the certainty of science.

Nobel laureate, Ilya Prigogine, and philosopher of science, Isabella Stengers, pronounced the end of certainty in their 1984 publication, *Order Out of Chaos,* and went on to describe a world that is responsive, non-linear, relational, and self-modifying, in stark contrast to the earlier mechanistic, Newtonian world that was isolated, solitary, linear, orderly, and stable. They also advocated a shift in our understanding of nature, noting that nature is less machine-like than previously believed, and more human-like, that is, unpredictable, highly sensitive to the surrounding world, and affected by seemingly slight variations. And they challenged the classical view of time as reversible, arguing instead that for human beings time is not reversible, that time matters immensely, that *time is creation*.

According to chaos theory, living systems – from one-celled organisms to human beings, groups, and social systems – are self-organizing; that is, operating according to their own internal principles of organization. At the same time, these are open systems, in constant interaction, response, and dialogue with their environment (Prigogine & Stengers, 1984). Further, living, complex systems have the capacity, when faced with sudden changes, to maintain themselves in a stable state but also, most strikingly, either to collapse into chaos, or, alternatively, to rise to a new, more complex order. This potential for self-renewal and self-transcendence – for "order out of chaos" – represented a turning point in science, and called for "a new dialogue" with nature about order, predictability, and control.

Contemporary Definitions and Features of Chaos

Since then, contemporary science has continued to refine the notions of chaos and complexity. Chaos is now viewed as "dynamic instability" and defined not as the absence of order, but rather as a more complex relation to order. Correspondingly, the study of chaos is the study of patterns and processes of non-linear systems, and how these evolve and change. Hayles (1991) observes, "At the center of chaos theory is the discovery that hidden within the unpredictability of chaotic systems are deep structures of order" (p. 1). Nature, when left to develop and change randomly, creates complexity and harmony through patterns and relationships. This view of chaos as "disorderly order" has challenged earlier notions of objectivity, validity, prediction, and control, leading to the study of different kinds of phenomena that have previously overwhelmed the usual methods of inquiry (Hayles). She concludes, "Although it is too soon to say where the discoveries associated with complex systems will end, it is already apparent that chaos theory is part of a paradigm shift of remarkable scope and significance" (p. 2).

Contemporary scientists have identified several major properties associated with chaotic systems: sensitivity to initial conditions, strange attractors, and emergence. The first property refers to the "extreme sensitivity" to and dependence of systems upon their initial conditions. Based upon earlier studies of atmospheric currents, it gradually became known that even the smallest difference in initial starting values could result in very different behaviors and outcomes. Moreover, small changes at crucial points anywhere in the system could result in major effects; this is sometimes referred to as the "butterfly effect" (Domaingue, 1988).

"Strange attractors" refers to the tendency of life processes to self-organize, that is, to gravitate to some relatively stable dynamic that brings order or pattern to chaotic behavior. In nature birds form flocks, a dripping faucet develops a regular rhythm, and tornados form funnels. In human life strange attractors can be understood as those values or human desires (longevity, power, knowledge, freedom) that can act as driving forces and motivations for actions.

Finally, "emergence" refers to the tendency of complex systems to develop new structures and dynamic patterns that are more complex, more integrated, and more coherent. Building blocks at one level combine into new building blocks at a higher level. Through interaction and accommodation systems manage to transcend themselves and to become something more (Waldrop, 1992). In summary, these various properties associated with chaos and complexity theory describe a world not only of systems, but also of emergent and evolving systems, and of connections both maintained and transcended in the face of change.

Chaos in Learning and Education

American educator, William Doll (1993), is one among a growing number of educators who have for the past 2 decades interpreted and applied the ideas of chaos and complexity theory into a new vision of education. Focusing on the changes occurring in the chaos-complexity sciences, he envisions "a major turning point in our relations with the world, nature, and ourselves" (p. 97). And turning to education, he predicts a revisioning in many aspects of our orientation:

> I believe a new sense of educational order will emerge, as well as new relations between teachers and students, culminating in a new concept of curriculum. The linear, sequential, easily quantifiable ordering system dominating education today – one focusing on clear beginnings and definite endings – could give way to a more complex, pluralistic, unpredictable system or network. (p. 3)

While Doll (1993) writes from the perspective of general education, his ideas pertain equally to the field of adult and continuing education. Chaos theory challenges some of the most powerful and pervasive educational theories underlying current educational practices. Challenge and disturbance, qualities that are assumed to be disruptive and inefficient in the traditional curriculum, are seen to be essential in the emerging paradigm. Learning occurs not only in the zone of comfort, but especially during times of confusion. Teaching rests not on student compliance, but on student challenge. The goal of teaching is not to transmit knowledge, but to transform it. And finally, the role of the teacher is not to instill the known, but to inspire a desire to explore the unknown. Doll advocates a "dancing curriculum" that emerges out of the interactions of teacher, student, and text.

Chaos Theory in Adult Education

Although a number of educators have explored the significance of chaos theory in grade school (K-12) education, adult educators have been slower to touch on its epistemological implications. Among the early exceptions was adult educator Robert Domaingue (1988), who generated new metaphors for adult education arising from chaos theory, among these being the rain forest, flocking of birds, and growth of a plant. Consistent with Doll's (1993) pronouncements opposing the Tylerian step-by-step approach to educational objectives, he proposed the analogy of a computer program, in which learners journey through various "hypercards" that correspond to their learning interests. Concerning the principle of sensitive dependence on initial conditions, he interpreted it to mean that learners come with unique histories and learning experiences; therefore, learning objectives and evaluation of outcomes would need to take into account that this uniqueness of the individual's initial conditions would lead each to a different place with respect to knowledge.

In a more recent paper that explores the relationship of chaos theory with transformative dimensions of teaching and learning, Karpiak (2000) speculates on a curriculum for adult and continuing education in which learners are conceived of as "a work in progress," still "becoming." She suggest that the task of the teacher is to become finely attuned not only to the bolder but also to the more subtle signals of curiosity, confusion, wonder, and distress, and to act as a guide to learners as they traverse the unknown.

More recently, Osberg and Biesta (2003) have proposed a different way of understanding educational practice were we to follow the tenets of chaos theory. According to chaos theory, knowing is transactional and never complete, and there will always be something that is not yet apparent. In this regard, knowledge would not be sought for the purpose of understanding the world *as it is*, but rather for the purpose of finding novel and creative ways of interacting with our world, and through this process of our interacting, to discover ways to create greater novelty and complexity.

Chaos theory is still in its infancy and will surely continue to develop and change. And to the extent that adult education adopts this theory, the field will embark on a process of continued exploration and modification of the theory and its implications for research and practice. Embracing chaos and complexity is akin to leaving the clearing and venturing into the forbidden forest. What we have traditionally assumed to be thorough needs assessment may at best be only one part of a much larger and ever-changing entity. What we thought to be careful planning following well-defined models might be suddenly confounded. What we considered to be legitimate evaluation of our work and that of learners may be denying others the feedback that could actually promote further growth. Could it be that chaos and complexity theory are heralding a crossroads, an impending bifurcation in adult education? Do we continue on the paths of our predecessors, who were well socialized into the modernist, mechanistic view, or do we take the alternate path? Only time will tell, and time, according to chaos theory, is change.

See also: actor-network theory, appreciative inquiry, spirituality, teaching, transformative learning.

References and Further Reading

Capra, F. (1975). *The tao of physics*. New York: Bantam Books.

Doll, W. E., Jr. (1993). *A post-modern perspective on curriculum*. New York: Teachers College Press.

Domaingue, R. (1988). Introducing metaphors of chaos to adult education. *New Horizons in Adult Education, 2*(11/21), 55–59.

Hayles, N. K. (1991). Introduction: Complex dynamics in literature and science. In N. K. Hayles (Ed.), *Chaos and order: Complex dynamics in literature and science* (pp. 1–33). Chicago: University of Chicago Press.

Karpiak, I. E., (2000). Evolutionary theory and the "new sciences": Rekindling our imagination for transformation. *Studies in Continuing Education, 22*(1), 29–44.

Osberg, D., & Biesta, G. (2003). *Complexity, representation and the epistemology of schooling*. Paper presented at Complexity Science and Educational Research Conference, University of Alberta, Edmonton, Alberta, October, 2003.

Prigogine, I., & Stengers, I. (1984). *Order out of chaos: Man's new dialogue with nature*. New York: Bantam Books.

Waldrop, M. (1992). *Complexity: The emerging science at the edge of order and chaos*. New York: Simon & Schuster.

Irene Karpiak

Civil Society

Civil society is a social space, with emancipatory potential, influenced by but not completely absorbed into the state and economy. The discourse of civil society burst dramatically into the global, political and academic scene in the 1970s with the advent of the Polish Solidarity movement. This "new" language permitted theorists and activists alike to make sense of attempts to reform Soviet-style state socialism without armed resistance. It also helped them to grasp the struggle against bureaucratic authoritarianism in the south and the emergence of the new social movements in the West.

This new, hopeful political discourse didn't take long emigrating into academia. During the 1980s the vocabulary of civil society pervaded the social science literature. By the 1990s, the discipline of adult education had begun to host this conceptual stranger, working its emergent understanding of social learning in terms of the new orientation to understanding the dynamics of social life. But the scholarly world soon discovered that the discourse of civil society had an ancient pedigree. Scholars trace its genealogy to Aristotle, who imagined man as a political animal who expressed his essence in a political community (a kind of public) of "free and equal citizens." But he didn't distinguish the "political sphere" (the *polis*) from "civil society." In Latin, the Aristotelian concept is *societas civilis* (Cohen & Arato, 1992).

Civil Society and the State

It was not until the early modern period of European history, however, that the concept of civil society took on a contemporary feel. In fact, the distinction between civil society and the state has been very important in the Western intellectual tradition, central to different variants of anti-absolutist thinking in the West since the 17th century. During the 17th and 18th centuries, the emergent market economy freed some individuals (entrepreneurs) to pursue their own economic interests, and with the appearance of individualism, intellectuals began to grapple with the unsettled relationships between individual passions and interests and those of the public, or commonweal. The English philosopher John Locke (1632–1704) believed that human beings now had to enter into a contract based on mutual consent in order for a commonwealth (under God) to be firmly established. He also thought that, for society to be properly ordered, individuals required "rights and privileges" protected under law. One can see that the idea of a social space, not under tutelage of state power, is emerging in Western consciousness. In the 18th century, Scottish enlightenment philosophers like Adam Smith (1723–90) and Adam Ferguson (1723–1815) pushed onward from Locke to conceptualize civil society as a social space held together by the force of moral sentiments and natural affections.

During the late 18th century, the Age of Revolutions, the German philosopher Immanuel Kant (1724–1804) contributed significantly to the Western understanding of civil society. Like Locke and the Scottish Enlightenment thinkers, Kant argued that the state was not coterminous with civil society. But Kant pursued the epochal idea that civil society was fundamentally the arena for rational debate and critique, where a critical citizenry could be created through dialogue. In the 19th century, two German philosophers of different temperaments, Georg Hegel (1770–1831) and Karl Marx (1818–83), thought that the earlier thinkers had overly idealized civil society; on the ground, 18th century ideals of a society bound together by natural sentiment seemed ill-considered. Both Hegel and Marx thought that civil society (economic associations were viewed as part of civil society) was bristling with self-interest and conflict, hardly a lovely, reasonable place! But they imagined that the resolution lay in differing directions. Hegel thought that an authentic community could only be created by the state, while for his part Marx turned Hegel on his head by insisting that only a revolutionary transformation of the mode of production could create the preconditions for an authentic political life. This rather startling idea contained ambiguities, however (Seligman, 2002).

During the 20th century, critical theorists began to break with Marx's economic reductionism. Gradually, thinkers associated with the Frankfurt School such as Theodor Adorno (1903–1969) and Max Horkheimer (1895–1973), and the Italian revolutionary Antonio Gramsci (1891–1937), developed ideas that enabled civil society to be uncoupled from both state and economy. Puzzling over the question of why the European masses weren't revolutionary, both Gramsci and the Frankfurt intellectuals turned to the cultural sphere for answers. They discovered that the network of institutions comprising the modern civil society (churches, schools, clubs, associations, social movements) were used instrumentally by the dominant classes to establish their hegemony over the lower orders. The family was also included in civil society's domain because it was an institution central to shaping the character and political disposition of its members. This cultural turn within critical theory made ideas (about self, others, the world) less the economy's prisoner, more an actor on their own terms. Today civil society is understood as the sphere of identity formation, social integration and cultural reproduction. The family is "in," the economy is "out."

Habermas and Civil Society

The stage was set for Jürgen Habermas, the inheritor of the Frankfurt mantle, to wed his communication theory to the discourse of civil society. Habermas' now famous argument that Marx had reduced the evolution of the human species to its remaking of the natural world through labor and had not taken account of how inner and sociocultural worlds are made through the generations through symbolic interaction, burst into the social sciences. Unlike liberal thinkers, Habermas postulated communicative autonomy as the defining feature of civil society. The system realm – dominated by power and money – operated differently from that of the lifeworld realm. Administrative systems coordinated action through coercion, and the economy pursued profit, efficiency and instrumental success. In contrast, civil society (the lifeworld expressed in institutions) required communicative interaction oriented to understanding for its reproduction. Habermas' decisive argument was that relationships within civil society were not governed by an instrumental logic. One could now consider how the System realm could colonize the lifeworld realm, introducing distorting dynamics into the communication process (Chambers, 2002).

Habermas' accentuation of civil society as the preeminent communicative learning domain staked out a controversial theoretical and political position. Those thinkers (like Griff Foley, 1999) who gave precedence to overturning the capitalist economy accused Habermas and his followers of acceding to capitalism and a reformist approach to social change. Foley believes that the economy rules, and, until it is socialized, all talk of a vital civil society replete with emancipatory potential is futile. Thus, orthodox Marxist critics of civil societarians argue that its proponents avoid the struggle to gain the real, essential levers of power. Feminists have also queried idealized versions of civil society that assume that it is a nice place, far away from the nastiness of the economy and polity, and violence, racism or sexism in daily life. Indeed, voluntary organizations can engage in disturbingly oppressive practices free from any monitoring attuned to universalist principles. Organizations like the Ku Klux Klan or Al-Qaeda are, after all, voluntary. Sharp criticism of "bad civil society" alerts adult educators to the way sexism or racism can be manifest in civil society organizations. But, generally speaking, Habermas' "critical liberalism" found many followers within the field of adult education thought and practice. Specifically, Habermas' identification of civil society as the primary site of resistance and emancipation, targeting of social movements as exemplary actors, naming of the public sphere as the salient arena of action and democratic deliberation as the fundamental social learning process caught the imagination of activists and theorists alike.

Civil Society and Socially Responsible Adult Education

Over the last decade or so, propelled by a desire to develop a social learning theory, adult education scholars have increasingly found a home in the evolving discourse of civil society. The core value structure of adult education – our affirmation that the lifeworld is the foundation of meaning, social solidarity and stable personality, our commitment to the enlightened, autonomous and reflective learner and to the centrality of social learning processes to the formation of the active citizen, and to the fostering of discussion, debate and dialogue among divergent views – leads us straight to the civil society camp. This is our natural home, implicit in our voluntarist, community development and personal growth traditions (Welton, 1997, 1998, 2001).

When Habermas executed his famous transformation of critical social theory into a critical communications theory, this move was fortuitous for the discipline of adult education, enabling adult educators to link communication and learning theory. The very act of communication creates the possibility of interactions that open the dialogue partners to new ways of thinking and acting in the world. Where communication is blocked, silenced or distorted, the deeply intersubjective learning process is thwarted. One can imagine, then, that the putting in place of a civil society over time can be reconceptualized as the building of society's learning infrastructure. The struggle to build a democratic civil learning infrastructure is closely allied, in western societies, to modernization processes. In Canada, for instance, the struggle for responsible government in the first decades of the 19th century was, essentially, a struggle by excluded citizens to extend the possibilities for conversations and engagement over salient matters facing the people.

To be sure, important learning dynamics occur within the spheres of economy and polity; one need only think of the impact of technological innovations throughout history. But civil society is the privileged domain for non-instrumental learning processes. It is here, within the network of family, school, associational, movement and public life, that citizens are able to raise issues or topics requiring public attention and system-action. Here, for example, associations like trade unions (which bridge the lifeworld and the system) can raise pertinent issues pertaining to exploitation and oppression within the workplace, on the shopfloor. Left to their own logic and devices, neither economic nor administrative systems are hospitable to learning new ways of seeing and being. The risks of genetic engineering, ecological threats, global warming, feminism's plethora of themes, skyrocketing impoverishment of the Third World, the HIV/AIDS epidemic in Africa – these issues swirl out of learning conversations of radical intellectuals, ordinary suffering citizens, and citizen advocates and organizations. The general tendency, therefore, is for learning conversations to crystallize into publicly persuasive formulations, and for these demands to migrate into the system realms for attention and action. Thus, there must be fluid learning gateways constructed between civil society, the economy and the state.

Several axioms pertinent to adult education theory and practice emerge through our engagement with the discourse (and practices) within civil society. We have already suggested that, filtered through the learning lens, civil society can be revisioned as society's essential learning infrastructure. From here, we can then make the following observations. First, it is within the realm of civil society that social capital is produced. Concepts like physical and human capital are well known, social capital less so. Social capital refers to the way the dynamics of associational life produce norms of reciprocity and trustworthiness. We form connections to benefit our own interests (networking or jobs). But social capital also affects the wider community – a well-connected community permits individuals to accrue benefits. Social capital is clearly both a "private good" and a "public good." Service clubs, for instance, produce friendships and business connections while mobilizing resources to fight disease. Social capital is vital to the learning climate of the civil infrastructure. If relations of trust and reciprocity are damaged or only thinly present, persons will not be open to each other. Indeed, they may look out for number-one and exclude any willingness to walk down a conversational road.

Second, the scope and vitality of a society's associational life is a prerequisite for building a deliberative democracy. We learn to be citizens not by participating in politics first, but in the "free spaces" of school, church, 4-H club, and YWCA. Associations carry considerable potential to create opportunities for people to learn to respect and trust others, fulfil social obligations and how to press one's claims communicatively. Tyrannical and oppressive states understand the potential of civil society associations. They will inevitably move to create elaborate surveillance mechanisms to spy on citizens and prevent learning from crystallizing into outright opposition. Canadian adult educators from the 1930s until the present have been acutely aware that citizens needed to have institutional opportunities to deliberate with one another across time and space. The study group is an enduring illustration of commitment to the vitality of civil society as means to creating democracy.

Third, the new social movements are an integral, if disruptive, part of the civil society infrastructure in late modern societies. New social movements are not perfect places; they are flawed, human, and contentious. However, the movement's task is to produce a broad shift in public opinion; to alter the parameters of organized will-formation, and to exert pressure on parliaments, courts and administrations in favor of specific policies. Movements may also act defensively to maintain the existing structure of associations and public influence. Certainly there are social movements – like religious fundamentalism – that occupy the terrain of civil society and compete to undermine other's conceptions of the good life or vital democracy. Here, the state's role is to ensure that rules of tolerance and respect for the other's viewpoint are adhered to. The new social movements (such as the women's, peace, and ecology movements) are salient learning spaces within modern societies. They raise issues relevant to the entire society, define new ways of approaching problems, propose solutions, supply new information, offer different interpretations of prevalent values, and mobilize good reasons while criticizing bad ones.

Fourth, the creation and maintenance of exuberant public spheres is central to civil societarian adult education. Certainly, the new social movements often serve as public spaces creating learning opportunities (through forums, etc.). But in late modern societies, the public sphere is substantively differentiated. Following Habermas (1996), we can talk of popular science and literary publics, religious and artistic publics, feminist and "alternative" publics and publics concerned with healthcare issues, social welfare or environmental policy. We can also differentiate publics in terms of the density of communication, organizational complexity and the spatial range.

The media – the complex of information-processors and image creators – play an enormously powerful role in influencing how we see the world. To be sure, most adult educators insist that the mass media be committed normatively to creating an enlightened public who are perceived to have a capacity to learn and to be criticized. However, with globalization has come both an avalanche of information and the transformation of corporate-dominated media into instruments for powerful, special interests. The central question for civil societarian adult educators and citizens is this: who can place issues on the agenda and determine what direction the lines of communication take? Evidence abounds in contemporary, international political life that many demonstrations against organizations like the World Trade Organization come about because such organizations are perceived to block communicative learning processes.

The discourse on civil society and the public sphere in the contemporary social sciences and humanities is richly suggestive for adult learning theorists and practising adult educators who are designing intervention strategies for a just and honest learning society.

See also: extension, non-governmental organizations, social movements, social policy, women's voluntary organizations.

References and Further Reading

Chambers, S. (2002). A critical theory of civil society. In S. Chambers & W. Kymlicka (Eds.), *Alternative conceptions of civil society* (pp. 90–110). Princeton, MA: Princeton University Press.

Cohen, J., & Arato, A. (1992). *Civil society and political theory.* Cambridge, MA: MIT Massachusetts Institute of Technology Press.

Foley, G. (1999). *Learning in social action: A contribution to understanding informal education.* London: Zed Books.

Habermas, J. (1996). *Beyond facts and norms: Contribution to a discourse theory of law and democracy.* Cambridge, MA: MIT Press.

Seligman, A. (2002). Civil society as idea and ideal. In S. Chambers & W. Kymlicka (Eds.), *Alternative conceptions of civil society* (pp. 13–33). Princeton, NJ: Princeton University Press.

Welton, M. R. (1997). Civil society as theory and project: Adult education and the renewal of global citizenship. In D. Wildemeersch, M. Finger, & T. Jansen (Eds.), *Adult education and social responsibility* (pp. 187–220). Sonderdruck: Peter Lang.

Welton, M. R. (1998). Educating for a deliberative democracy. In S. Scott, B. Spencer, & A. Thomas (Eds.), *Learning for life: Canadian readings in adult education* (pp. 365–372). Toronto: Thompson Educational.

Welton, M. R. (2001). Civil society and the public sphere: Habermas's recent learning theory. *Studies in the Education of Adults, 33*(1), 20–34.

Michael Welton

Class

Class refers to the economic, social and cultural divisions within society and the struggles between different social groups for control over status, prosperity and opportunity. It is an ambiguous concept, subject to different interpretations, and variously referred to as a descriptive category, a process, a social position, or a relationship. Regardless of specific definition, most analyses of class and adult education (a) draw clear links between educational institutions, the world of work, and the economic system that underpins them, and (b) highlight how educational institutions function for the maintenance and inculcation of societal ideology and values. A focus on class can also alert us to the unexamined patterns of behavior through which social classes are produced and reproduced in the dynamics between adult education and the wider cultural politics of societies. As class is one of the major determining elements in shaping the lives we lead, examining its operation provides a means of figuring out the values and purposes inherent not only in who we are, but also in where we stand, and in how we treat (and are treated by) other people.

Class is a fairly recent concept. Originally based on "*classis*" – the six orders into which the Romans were divided for taxation purposes – its present use dates from mid-18th century France. At that time, the *Encylopédistes*, a group of intellectuals who sought to assemble all available knowledge, developed a systematic classification first of plants, animals, minerals, and natural phenomena and then of the social and economic positions of people in society. The concept of class later gained wider currency with the changes brought about by the Industrial Revolution. By the mid-19th century Karl Marx (Marx & Engels, 1845/1970) was using class as the foundational concept for explaining social organization in terms of understanding the ownership, means, and control of work processes. He claimed that societies consisted of two classes: the bourgeoisie (who owned and controlled the mills, mines, and factories) and the proletariat (workers with only their labor power to sell). For Marx, the relationship between these two classes is essentially unequal and exploitative. The working class generates surplus wealth but does not profit from it as much as they might because the bourgeoisie disproportionally appropriates and accumulates it. All social life is marked by the struggles and conflicts over the generation and distribution of wealth and the status attached to it. Societal transformation was only possible when workers developed class consciousness about the sources of exploitation: the sense of a shared predicament, an awareness of the capitalist class as their common enemy, and a realization of their common strength and destiny.

Not everyone regards class in such materialistic terms. Max Weber (1930), for instance, argued that class is better defined by also including notions of culture, politics, and lifestyle. People who fall within the same *economic* class may nevertheless occupy different *social* class positions and have differing opportunities for work, income, developing skills, obtaining education, and owning property. For Weber, one's class is based more on these "life chances," cultural background, status, and life outside of work than it is on one's relationship to the ownership and control of the means of production. Rather than see society as a two-class system, Weber posited a system of social stratification of many different classes that sometimes overlap. This less-deterministic approach can also be seen in the work of Pierre Bourdieu (Bourdieu & Passeron, 1977) for whom a class is any grouping of individuals sharing similar conditions of existence and tendencies or "dispositions." Equally important as one's location in an economic order is the possession of various forms of capital – economic, cultural, social or symbolic – which can constellate differently in different societies. Bourdieu's concept of class thus takes into account other stratifying factors, such as gender, race, ethnicity, place of residence, and age. Finally, these class structures are not predetermined or imposed from without but subtly reproduced by people acting within preexisting contexts. Although both Weber and Bourdieu allow more scope for human agency than did Marx, they still regard external class structures as fundamental and quite constant. In other words, class relationships transcend the individuals who occupy the positions: people may move around (or stay put) but they still divide into exploiters and exploited.

These two broad views have shaped current understandings of class. Throughout the social upheavals of industrialization, definitions of class in Europe continued to be affected by older ideas of rank. The "lower orders," the laboring classes, and the middling ranks of society (such as merchants or teachers) existed alongside the aristocracy and the gentry. However, as the stratification of industrial society became more rigid, these definitions settled into the familiar classification of working, middle, and upper class. This depiction treats class as essentially static. Although it underlines the essentially economic nature of class, such a definition ignores the dynamic and shifting nature of the relationships between those who possess wealth and power and those who do not. More recently, class has come to be regarded as a relation that is constantly changing. As British historian E. P. Thompson (1971) puts it, "class is not a category . . . but rather an historical relationship between one group of people and another . . . It is defined by men [*sic*] as they live their own history" (pp. 9–10).

North American countries, which evolved in reaction to European feudalism, tend to see themselves as free from the archaic categories of class where people's rank is determined by birth. Here, immigration, mobility, the ideologies of egalitarianism and meritocracy and the advent of the consumer society have been powerful forces that have flattened class differences. As a result, existential rather than social factors are more likely to influence who North Americans think they are. For example, people in those countries today define themselves as Black, Jewish, Latino, lesbian, gay, or mobility-challenged before they describe themselves as working-class. Also, identity and other subjective politics (usually less opposed to capitalism) continue to appeal. So, even though vast institutionalized social inequalities persist throughout North America, the discussion of class remains relatively ignored. Social injustice tends to be discussed more in terms of identity, inequality, or status rather than opposing social classes.

With these different and competing notions of class, discussing it can be difficult. However, several clear elements can be identified. First, a concern with class focuses on materialist concepts regarding the production and reproduction of social life, and the importance of human activity in shaping both subsistence and consciousness. Second, attentiveness to class helps explore the fundamental and dynamic relationships between economic and social structures, the ideologies that frame our perspective, and the ways we experience, understand, and shape the world. Third, class suggests that social phenomena are not explained by their surface manifestations or how they are individually experienced but are, instead, representations of external divisions of power. Fourth, class provides a basis for explaining why people organize themselves into collective forces to resist injustice and exploitation. Finally, for those with a commitment to social justice, a focus on class also raises several important questions: How are dominant ideologies and relations of ruling negotiated or internalized? How might alternative ones develop? How can marginalized people, silenced by social, economic, and cultural relations of power, recover their voices and the right to be heard?

Class and Adult Education

Although educational researchers and commentators often refer to the triad of "class, race, and gender" as linked analytic vectors, they clearly have a bit of a problem with class. A keyword search of the ERIC (Educational Resources Information Centre) database produces over 18,000 hits for the descriptor gender, almost 13,000 hits for race, and fewer than 3,500 hits for social class. When the descriptor adult education is added, the number of hits diminishes dramatically: 459 for gender and adult education, 293 for race and adult education, and only 74 for social class and adult education. Assuming that the number of ERIC references correlates roughly with researchers' interests, then why is class so significantly less acknowledged than its counterparts? Why is class ignored as "the elephant in the room" (hooks, 2000)?

Answers to these questions can be

found by examining the hegemonic function of educational systems in capitalist societies. Educational policies and practices are not neutral phenomena but, instead, profoundly political. Of course, most educators will acknowledge that education is a political process, but they're much less certain about how it reflects underlying political structures, let alone economic systems. It's much easier to observe the effects of power and privilege than to determine their causes. Yet, there are several guides to how education reproduces existing patterns of power. Economists Samuel Bowles and Herb Gintis (1976) demonstrated how educational systems can best be understood as part of a system of broader capitalist class relations. Their "correspondence principle" explains how schools reproduce the social relations required for capitalist production. Capital requires, first, workers of specific types and, also, relative social stability and ideological acceptance of class relations. The capitalist class thus has a broadly shared set of interests pertaining to public education systems and the capacity to promote such interests.

For some, the correspondence principle is too mechanistic or reductive; it allows little agency for those involved. One less deterministic approach came from Pierre Bourdieu (Bourdieu & Passeron, 1977) who suggested that education serves the interests of the privileged by structuring learners' access to, and uses of, "social and cultural capital." Others have introduced the notions of struggle and resistance into this process. Most notably, Paul Willis (1977) showed how several working-class teenage "lads" resisted and rebelled against school and classroom authority. Tellingly, however, this resistance worked better within the school environment than outside it: when the lads left school they still remained unable to find anything but unskilled and unrewarding jobs. The work of Peter McLaren (1995) and Michael Apple (1996) also shows how social and cultural oppression can be resisted and contested in educational settings. They document the complex relationships between cultural reproduction and economic reproduction and explore how class interrelates with the dynamics of race and gender in education. Finally, adult educators Paula Allman (2001) and Shirley Walters (1997) have examined the dramatic effects of the increasingly globalized nature of capitalism on educational practices, policies, and discourses.

All these studies indicate the essential role of education in promoting and maintaining the social relations required for capitalist production and, further, that education can only be fully understood as part of a broader capitalist class system. Although we now recognize that the relationships between educational practices and political structures are much more complex than correspondence theory suggests, teachers who work in such areas as adult basic education literacy, vocational education, and the pernicious Welfare-to-Work programs will recognize how often their work, the policies about it, and the rhetoric surrounding it is still closely tied to the needs of employers (Kincheloe, 1999; Livingstone, 1999).

Despite these concerns, too few adult educators raise questions about, or encourage examination of, the relations between education and class. Perhaps this is not so surprising: education is meant to inculcate dominant values, not confront them. So, in capitalist societies where class is the primary structuring of social inequality, class perspectives get ignored or buried. Yet, there are several reasons why adult educators should raise, rather than hide, these ideas. First, education is a function of the state and is therefore regulated according to certain economic, political, and cultural interests and pressures. Second, educational institutions are situated in historical and social contexts which suggest that education is intimately linked with maintaining particular cultural and social arrangements. In capitalist societies, these arrangements are structured around inequalities, as capitalism foundationally depends upon a labor force of differing levels of skill. Educational institutions, by creating and maintaining a steady supply of workers with these differing levels, ensure that existing and future workforces can adapt to changes in investment, production, and trade circumstances. Educational credentials, selection mechanisms, and cognitive classifications are all used in this endeavor. Thus by transmitting, sustaining, and legitimizing particular systems of structured inequality, educational systems uphold the characteristics of a particular order of social relations. This is best seen in Freire's oft-repeated comment that education either domesticates or it liberates; classroom activities either support the status quo or challenge it, there is no middle ground. So, a third reason for adult educators to consider class lies in the exploration of these issues in their own practice. What is taught and how to teach are choices made from a wider universe of knowledge and values. Such choices always benefit and privilege some while ignoring, downplaying, or deprivileging others. In other words, curricular and pedagogical choices reflect different ways of understanding and responding to social relations. Fourth, the adult education profession is imbricated with political choices. For example, consider the practice and contexts of teaching. Some people are considered worthy or accredited to teach; others are not. There are concomitant struggles over autonomy, respect, wages and control. The practice of teaching attests to the ways some people think that their cultures should be passed on. Is it appropriate to always assume the teacher is a neutral, objective and benevolent agent of the state who is there to impart solely the basic information required for learners to survive within a capitalist system? Should adult educators infuse their teaching with a critique of capitalism? How far can they go to resist and challenge what Paula Allman calls the postmodern condition – "skepticism, uncertainty, fragmentation, nihilism, and incoherence? " (2001, p. 209).

See also: cultural studies, emancipatory education, human capital theory, ideology, marginality, philosophy, social movements.

References and Further Reading

Allman, P. (2001). *Critical education against global capitalism*. Westport, CT: Bergin & Garvey.

Apple, M. W. (1996). *Cultural politics and education*. New York: Teachers College Press.

Bourdieu, P., & Passeron, J. C. (1977). *Reproduction in education, society, and culture*. Newbury Park, CA: Sage.

Bowles, S., & Gintis, H. (1976). *Schooling in capitalist America*. New York: Basic Books.

hooks, b. (2000). *Where we stand: Class matters*. New York: Routledge.

Kincheloe, J. L. (1999). *How do we tell the workers?* Boulder, CO: Westview Press.

Livingstone, D. W. (1999). *The education–jobs gap*. Boulder, CO: Westview Press.

Marx, K., & Engels, F. (1845/1970). *The German ideology*. (C. J. Arthur, Ed. &

Trans.). London: Lawrence & Wishart.
McLaren, P. L. (1995). *Critical pedagogy and predatory culture*. New York: Routledge.
Thompson, E. P. (1971). *The making of the English working class*. Oxford: Oxford University Press.
Walters, S. (Ed.). (1997). *Globalization, adult education, and training: Impacts and issues*. London: Zed Books.
Weber, M. (1930). *The Protestant ethic and the spirit of capitalism* (T. Parsons, Trans.). London: Allen & Unwin.
Willis, P. (1977). *Learning to labour*. Farnborough, UK: Saxon House.

Tom Nesbit

Cognition

As defined in the *Oxford English Dictionary*, and derived from the Latin (*cognosco, cognoscere, cognovi, cognitum*), cognition is "the action or faculty of knowing; knowledge; consciousness." In academic dialogue, however, the term is often unfortunately restricted to thinking, which is actually derived from a different Latin root (*cogito, cogitare, cogitavi, cogitatum*), reflected in the English word "cogitate." Thinking, while important, is only one way of knowing.

This broader view of cognition enables us to cast a wider net in considering research being done from various perspectives including the cognitive unconsciousness, as well as the cognitive neurosciences, social cognition, and all the various personal and transpersonal ways of knowing, along with the resurging interest in intuitive and contemplative knowing. A multi-modal epistemological orientation and a multidisciplinary perspective allow an expanded space for understanding cognition. Given that attention in the field of adult education is already being paid to areas such as situated cognition, consciousness studies, and others, the field has the potential to provide leadership to the world of learning and education in embracing this broader conceptualization of cognition.

Foundational Research in Cognition

Jean Piaget, a Swiss psychologist, is often considered the pioneer in cognitive development research. Cognitive maturation for Piaget refers to the incremental manifestation of a genetic plan that affects development, hence his interest in biological factors of influence. Knowledge, however, is an active construction from interaction with one's world via assimilation and accommodation, twin cognitive processes that Piaget found central. Assimilation refers to taking in, forming, and incorporating new knowledge into one's framework. When new knowledge does not fit, however, an accommodation process of restructuring (or possibly holding matters in abeyance) will ensue, unless of course one ignores, discards, or rejects the new when it does not fit. Repeated testing of Piaget's scheme has resulted in claims of hierarchical levels of cognitive development, beginning with sensori-motor, moving to preoperational, then to concrete, and concluding with formal operations.

Formal operational thinking enables systematic problem-solving, with abstract reasoning finely honed. Working in the Piagetian frame, a host of researchers have moved towards understanding postformal thinking, in order to indicate the complexity of adult cognition. Seminal figures include Alexander (& Langner), Arlin, Arman, Cook-Greuter, Commons, Basseches, King,

Kitchener, Miller, Richards, Sinnott, and others. Among the key markers of post-formal thinking are the ability to think relativistically, sustain contradiction and paradox, integrate, and reconcile alternatives in moving towards dialectical thinking. Metacognition (thinking about how one thinks) is integral to postformal thought.

Social Cognition

Paralleling Piaget in influence, but more focused on how the social context affects thinking, the Russian psychologist Vygotsky (1987) placed added emphasis on the importance of social interaction and modeling in learning during childhood. Vygotsky's theory is reminiscent of Bandura's social learning theory. Vygotsky's voluminous work has attracted interest from researchers in adult cognition, particularly as translations of his work have become more available. In a similar vein, the term situated-cognition is increasingly used among those interested in the adult years, to refer to the notion that cognition is contextually bound. Terms such as "everyday cognition" also appear in articulating the sometimes "tacit" modes of learning characteristic of adult cognition. Perspective-taking and reading social cues are equally important parts of social cognition and are increasingly being recognized by adult educators, beyond the learning disabilities literature.

Interdisciplinary Influences

In addition to psychology, the disciplines of sociology, anthropology, and neuroscience help deepen our understanding of cognition. Interdisciplinary publications such as Sternberg and Grigorenko's (2001), explore the influences of nutrition, environmental pollutants, as well as caste and class on cognition. Moreover, even as early as the 1970s, and continuing to the present, Schaie (2004) developed a "stage-theory" model of adult cognitive development that addressed the environment and contextual factors in adult cognition; and Labouvie-Vief has for decades emphasized the integration of both intellect and affect in postformal development, as well as "adaptive logic" that balances objective and subjective knowing.

Moreover, the "cognitive unconscious," rooted in the earlier literature on subliminal perception, or perception without conscious awareness, has now become well-established empirically. The influence of the context is apparent in that literature as well (see for example Greenwald, 1992). An understanding of information processing from that literature base complements the "limits on loss" position of Cerella (1993).

While age-related declines are still of vital importance to our understanding, the advent of the cognitive neurosciences (Lane & Nadel, 2000; Rugg, 1997) over the last several decades has afforded sharper tools such as brain imaging to better understand the workings of the adult brain, and the balances between decrement, stability, and regeneration – barring of course disease or disuse. Increased understanding of the role of the frontal lobes in adulthood in their capacity to govern reflective thought has also arisen, as have new insights into the interplay between reason and emotion in both processing information and in "knowing." Moreover, the continuing research of Gage at the Salk Institute and others on the phenomenon of adult neurogenesis holds promise for better understanding the renewed potential of cognition in the adult years. The brain's plasticity is also shaped by interaction with the culture and environments, a finding that has afforded insights into the seminal works of anthropologists, such as Spradley (1972), as to the role of culture in cognition.

Wisdom and Cognition

Finally, renewed attention is being directed to the philosophical and theological literature of the ages, in better understanding how wisdom emerges as an aspect of cognition. Moreover, recognition of transpersonal cognition and ways of knowing has matured over the last 30 years to help us better appreciate a variety of non-rational, non-ego-based ways of knowing, and their commonalities across cultures, that hold promise for an expanded understanding of cognition.

Advances continue to unfold, but the very existence of unconscious cognition, transpersonal knowing, and so on, suggests that all may not be within our conscious control. Such a realization will serve a healthy function in reducing any potential arrogance, increasing our humbleness and reverence for our "knowing" faculties, and maybe even catalyzing the development of wisdom so sorely needed in today's world.

Embracing an expanded view of cognition consistent with its etymological root that includes, but is broader than, one's "thinking" faculties, that addresses the whole adult in both internal and external environments, has import for the study and practice of adult education. Multidisciplinary sources are providing a growing dynamic framework which expands our view of who the adult learner is or could be, and creates a 21st century vision for research and practice (see Wilber, 1999, 2000).

See also: activity theory, adult development, adult learning, critical thinking, learning, lifespan development, philosophy, transfer of learning.

References and Further Reading

Cerella, J. (1993). *Adult information processing: Limits on loss*. San Diego, CA: Academic Press.

Greenwald, A. G. (1992). New look 3: Unconscious cognition reclaimed. *American Psychologist, 47*(6), 766–769.

Lane, R. D., & Nadel, L. (Ed.). (2000). *Cognitive neuroscience of emotion*. London: Oxford University Press.

Rugg, M. D. (1997). *Cognitive neuroscience*. Cambridge, MA: MIT (Massachusetts Institute of Technology) Press.

Schaie, K. W. (2004). *Developmental influences on adult intelligence: The Seattle longitudinal study*. New York: Oxford University Press.

Spradley, H. J. P. (Ed.). (1972). *Culture and cognition*. San Francisco: Chandler.

Sternberg, R. J., & Grigorenko, E. (Eds.). (2001). *Environmental effects on cognitive abilities*. Mahwah, NJ: Laurence Erlbaum Associates.

Vygotsky, L. S. (1987). *The collected works of L.S. Vygotsky (Volumes 1–6)*. (R. W. Rieber & A. S. Carton, Eds.). (N. Minick, Trans.). New York and London: Plenum Press.

Wilber, K. (1999, 2000). *Collected works (Volumes 1–4, 1999; Volumes 5–8, 2000)*. Boston, MA: Shambala.

Marcie Boucouvalas

Cohort Learning

Saltiel and Russo (2001) define cohorts as groups of individuals entering a program at the same time and proceeding through all program requirements (i.e., classes) together to complete it as an intact group. More than just an administrative structure, cohorts in academia, often known as learning cohorts, are designed to maximize learning outcomes by building on a number of well established learning principles from adult and group-learning theory (see Imel, 2002).

Advantages of Cohort Learning as Conceived in the Literature

Three key advantages that appear most frequently in the literature on cohort learning are described as (1) its ability to enhance academic achievement; (2) to improve student retention rates; and (3) to assist in the development of team skills that are highly valued in today's modern workplace.

1. *Cohorts enhance academic achievement* – while there is not yet a large body of empirical evidence, a number of authors describe the positive effect that cohort learning has on cognitive and affective learning outcomes. Reynolds (1997) found that cohort, compared to non-cohort, learning groups in higher education achieved slightly higher affective and cognitive learning, as well as transfer of learning. Lawrence (1997, 2002) and Drago-Severson, Kegan, Popp, Broderick, and Portnow (2001) describe small-scale qualitative studies of cohort learning in graduate students at US universities who experienced a deeper transformational level of learning triggered by collaborative, or co-created, learning that they hypothesize more readily facilitates critical analysis and self-reflection. These researchers believe that the strong community of learning that cohorts create encourages a personal support system and deeper comfort level that, in turn, results in more risk-taking and self-disclosure. In another small-scale study of an online graduate program, Tisdell and cohort members (2002) came to similar conclusions about the ability of cohort learning to produce transformative learning facilitated by a strong emotional support system.

   This power of intact groups of learners to develop a stronger sense of commitment to the learning outcomes, as well as motivation and persistence in working towards them, has long been documented in group learning studies (Johnson & Johnson, 1997). Huber and Lowry (2003) support this hypothesis in their analysis of the best practices for online programs documented by eight regional accrediting commissions of higher education programs in the United States.
2. *Cohort learning enhances students' retention rate* – related to the above, is the claim that cohort learning reduces the drop-out rate in academic programs. This appears to be due primarily to the strength of the community of learning and subsequent personal support system that develops when a small intact group of students move through a program together (Johnson & Johnson, 1997; Lawrence, 1997, 2002; Tisdell et al. 2002). This could be related to the well-documented evidence that peer support in both face-to-face (Schlossberg, Lynch, & Chickering, 1989) and online programs (Cain, Marrara, Pitre, & Amour, 2003) positively influences graduation rates.
3. *The development of highly transferable team workplace skills* – team

skills, or the ability to work collaboratively with others – is an important asset in today's modern work (Watkins, 1995). As individuals in learning cohorts require these skills in order to succeed in this kind of program, an important secondary benefit of this kind of learning environment is the acquisition of these highly transferable skills. While evidence for this is most clearly presented in Johnson and Johnson's (1997) classic literature review of group theory and skill development, Saltiel and Russo (2001) and Lawrence (1997) also describe the learning transfer of team skills from academia to the workplace. Reynolds (1997) bases her similar claim in a larger scale comparative study of US institutions of higher education. Barnett and Norris (1994) draw related conclusions from a small-scale qualitative study of cohort programs across the western US, arguing that the resulting interdependence of students in these programs creates great potential for high-quality organizational teamwork. Dent (2000) describes this development of mutual interdependence as fostering leadership and problem-solving skills that are highly valued by organizations who use learning cohorts in their professional development programs.

Key Issues

Yet, cohort learning is not without its issues. Four key issues found in the literature deal with the challenges that cohort learning presents to traditional institutions of higher education in terms of (1) administration; (2) program design; (3) teaching approach; and (4) the nature of the teacher–student relationship.

1. *Educational administrative structure* – Saltiel and Russo (2001) and Dent (2000) most clearly address the issue of how the administrative structure of cohort learning groups differs from that of traditional open-entry programs. Dent describes the key challenges that this kind of student grouping present to traditional institutions of higher education as the need for institution-organization contracts to be more flexible regarding student qualifications and institutional accountability, and to move towards greater equity in student–teacher interactions as teachers deal with students as collectives who have more consumer-oriented expectations of faculty and the program. Not downplaying the degree of shift that cohort learning requires in order to succeed, Saltiel and Russo focus on the administrative advantages as: stable registration numbers for both programming and staffing of courses purposes; enhanced student motivation to persist and succeed; and an enhanced opportunity for developmental programming that promotes higher academic achievement.
2. *Program design approach* – those who have taught cohorts of learners emphasize the need for a systematic approach to designing these programs (Tisdell et al., 2002). Saltiel and Russo (2001) clearly describe the need for courses in these programs to be offered in a logical sequence that builds student learning and skills in a progressive and developmental manner in order to build the

advantages of cohort learning to be realized. They also recommend that program developers take group dynamics theory into consideration in order for strong learning communities or networks that provide students with strong emotional and intellectual support.

3. *Teaching/program delivery approaches* – in a similar manner, those with experience of teaching and learning cohorts recommend a different approach to teaching than the traditional teacher-as-expert model still commonly found in institutions of higher education. Generally, this means developing more democratic classrooms where students and teacher interact as peers and colleagues to challenge and learn from one another. Saltiel and Russo (2001) describe this approach as requiring the unlearning of individualism and learning of collaboration. Johnson and Johnson (1997) describe it as cooperative interdependence. Salmon (2000) describes it as co-constructing knowledge in an inter- or mutually-dependent learning environment.
4. *Teacher–student roles and relationships in the classroom* – related to all three points above, the teaching/learning environment most recommended by experienced teachers of learning cohorts requires a shift from the traditional institutional transmission to a more egalitarian developmental approach (see Pratt & Associates, 1998). The accompanying shift from teacher as expert in control of the classroom dynamics, towards teacher as resource who shares control of the learning process with students is consistent with the central principles of both adult learning and group learning theory.

   Merriam and Caffarella (1999) describe the compatibility of this shift in their comprehensive compendium of adult learning theory, while Johnson and Johnson (1997) do likewise in their definitive study of group theory and skills. More recently, Tisdell et al. (2002) discuss the interdependence of the roles of teacher and student within a democratically negotiated power-sharing classroom as of critical importance to the success of online graduate cohort programs. Salmon's (2000) five-step model of teaching learning cohorts online stresses the importance of shifting from a teacher-directed to a student-directed approach if students are to become successful mutually-dependent learners.

The common practical and theoretical threads found within cohort learning are derived from adult education and learning (see Merriam & Caffarella, 1999) and group learning theory (see Johnson & Johnson, 1997). As these and other related fields of practice and theory evolve, so will our understanding and application of this complex and multifaceted concept of cohort learning.

See also: action learning, collaborative learning, cooperative education, learning, study circles.

References and Further Reading

Barnett, B., & Norris, C. J. (1994). *Cultivating a new leadership paradigm: From cohorts to communities*. Paper presented at the Annual Meeting of the University Council for Educational

Administration. Philadelphia, PA. (ERIC Document Reproduction Service No. ED387877).

Cain, D. L., Marrara, C., Pitre, P.E., & Armour, S. (2003). Support services that matter: An exploration of the experiences and needs of graduate students in a distance learning environment. *Journal of Distance Education, 18*(1), 42–56.

Dent, E. E. B. (2000). The unique governance challenges of graduate contract-cohort programs. *Journal of Management Education, 24*(1), 55–73.

Drago-Severson, E., Kegan, R., Popp, N., Broderick, M., & Portnow, K. (2001). The power of a cohort and of collaborative groups. *Focus on basics: Connecting research and practice 5* (Iss. B), 15–22. Retrieved January 1, 2002 from http://ncsall.gse.harvard.edu/fob/2001/fob_5ib.pdf

Huber, H. E., & Lowry, J. C. (2003). Meeting the needs of consumers: Lessons from postsecondary environment. In S. R. Aragon (Ed.), *Facilitating learning in online environments* (pp. 79–88). *New Directions for Adult and Continuing Education,* No. 100. San Francisco: Jossey-Bass.

Imel, S. (2002). Adult learning in cohort groups. ERIC Document Reproduction Service No. ED472604.

Johnson, D. W., & Johnson, F. P. (1997). *Joining together: Group theory and group skills* (6th ed.). Boston, MA: Allyn & Bacon.

Lawrence, R. L. (1997). The interconnecting web: Adult learning cohorts as sites for collaborative learning, feminist pedagogy and experiential ways of knowing. In 38th Annual Adult Education Research Conference Proceedings (pp. 179–184). Stillwater, OK, May 16–18, 1997. (ERIC Document Reproduction Service No. ED409 460).

Lawrence, R. L. (2002). A small circle of friends: Cohort groups as learning communities. In D. S. Stern & S. Imel (Eds.), *Adult learning in community* (pp. 83–92). *New Directions for Adult and Continuing Education,* No. 95. San Francisco: Jossey-Bass.

Merriam, S. B., & Caffarella, R. S. (1999). *Learning in adulthood: A comprehensive guide* (2nd ed.). San Francisco: Jossey-Bass.

Pratt, D. D., & Associates (1998). *Five perspectives on teaching in adult higher education.* Malabar, FL: Krieger.

Reynolds, K. C. (1997). Postsecondary education in cohort groups: Does familiarity breed learning? Paper presented at the Annual Meeting of the American Educational Research Association, Chicago, IL, March 24–28. (ERIC Document Reproduction Service No. ED461 308).

Salmon, G. (2000). *E-moderating: The key to teaching and learning online.* London, UK: Kogan Page.

Saltiel, I. M., & Russo, C. S. (2001). *Cohort programming and learning: Improving educational experiences for adult learners.* Malabar, FL: Krieger.

Schlossberg, N. K., Lynch, A. Q., & Chickering, A. W. (1989). *Improving higher education environments for adults.* San Francisco: Jossey-Bass.

Tisdell, E. J., & Cohort Members, (2002). High tech meets high touch: Cohort learning online in graduate higher education (pp. 114–119). Proceedings of the 21st Midwest Research-to-Practice Conference in Adult, Continuing and Community Education, DeKalb, IL, October 9–11. Retrieved September 1, 2003 from College of Education, Northern Illinois University website: http://www.cedu.niu.edu/reps/Document/Midwest_Conference_Papers_part2.pdf

Watkins, K. E. (1995). Workplace learning: Changing times, changing practices. In W. F. Spikes (Ed.), *Workplace learning* (pp. 3–16). *New Directions for Adult and Continuing Education,* No. 68. San Francisco: Jossey-Bass.

Faye Wiesenberg

Collaborative Learning

Collaborative learning is often used as an umbrella term for a variety of educational approaches involving joint intellectual effort by participants, or participants and facilitators together. In most collaborative learning contexts, participants are working in groups of two or more, mutually searching for understanding, solutions or meanings, or creating something new. There is wide variability in collaborative learning activities, but most centre on the participants' exploration or application of the topic at hand, not simply on the facilitator's presentation or explication of it. Collaborative learning mobilizes the social synergy that resides within a group of co-learners engaged in a dynamic process of shared inquiry. Through dialogue, learning as shared inquiry evolves by critically exploring the perspectives of others. New dimensions of interpretations are fuelled, issues clarified and interdependence valued. There is an ongoing negotiation of roles among the community of learners (Lee, 1998, 2003). The implicit assumption in collaborative learning is that adult learners are experienced social beings that can function in collaborative paradigms possess intrinsic motivation and are self-directed in their desire to unravel problems that have direct relevance to them (Knowles, 1980). Related terms and concepts include peer learning, learning community, experiential learning, dialogical education and negotiated learning, peer collaboration, co-ordinated learning, collective learning, and collaborative inquiry.

The Conceptual Framework of Collaborative Learning

The etymological roots of the term *collaborate* come from the Latin *colabore* which means to work together, implying a concept of shared goals. The term *collaborate* has an explicit intention to "add value." For example, people create something new or different through the collaborative process as opposed to simply exchanging information or disseminating data. Collaboration requires "a mutual task in which the partners work together to produce something that neither could have produced alone" (Forman & Cazden, 1985, p. 329).

The terms "cooperative learning" and "collaborative learning" are often used interchangeably. They are similar in that they were both originally developed for educating people with different ages, degrees of experience and interdependence. Collaborative learning in higher and adult education arenas complements the cooperative learning that children may experience in primary school. Most cooperative learning researchers and theoreticians are social psychologists or sociologists whose original work was intended for application at the 4 to 12-year age levels. Second, cooperative learning approaches tend to be more structured and focused upon specific behaviors and rewards (Johnson & Johnson, 1994). In contrast, collaborative learning tends not to "micro manage," not to break tasks into small component parts and not to provide rewards. Third, these two learning approaches have different epistemological bases. Cooperative learning typically deals with traditional (canonical) knowledge. In contrast, collaborative learning holds to knowledge-creation as a social act. Fourth, there is a major difference in the locus of authority. Cooperative learning authorizes the teacher to oversee student participation and to ensure that the process works as predetermined by the teacher. In contrast, collaborative learning emphasizes co-responsibility and the negotiating of agendas. There is perambulating authority and crossing of power lines. Learning tasks are deliberately "open-ended." The "teacher" is facilitator and a partner-in-learning. Recognizing dissent and then collectively accounting for it emerges as a powerful tool for increasing understanding in collaborative learning communities (Bruffee, 1993, 1995; Matthews, Cooper, Davidson, & Hawkes, 1995).

Explicit Use of the Term Collaborative Learning and Related Concepts

Although collaborative learning as an educational term was introduced and elaborated in higher education, most notably by Kenneth Bruffee (1993, 1995), it is a concept that permeates the theories and practices of adult education. For example, Lindeman (1926) conceptualizes adult education as a *collaborative*, informal, yet critical exercise in which participation is non-coercive and the learner is of prime importance. Freire (2000) maintains that *collaborative* engagement is an integral part of the dialogical process. Paterson (1979) emphasizes that teaching is a *collaborative* process involving exchanges, outgoings and interaction. Knowles (1980) asserts that *collaboration* is integral to the establishment of effective cooperation among adult learners. Brookfield (1986) includes commitment to *collaborative* facilitation as one of the characteristics of effective facilitation of adult learning.

Antecedents

Collaborative learning has a long history of practice in action. Thousands of years ago the Talmud stated that in order to understand the Talmud one must have a learning partner. As early as the first century the rhetorician Quintillian argued that students could benefit from teaching one another, while the Roman philosopher Seneca advocated cooperative learning through statements such as "*Qui Docet Discet*" ("when you teach, you learn twice"). The 17th century church theologian and educator Comenius, an early exponent of student-led curricula, believed that students could benefit both by teaching and being taught by other students.

The Danish Folk High School Movement is notably a remarkable and successful example of collaborative learning as radical resistance to cultural imperialism. It subsumes ideas of experiential learning, holistic learning, dialogue, open-ended inquiry, and symmetry of power relations between teachers and learners and among learners. The Movement started in 1844 in Rodding as a community adult education venture. Nikolaj Frederick Severin Grundtvig (1783–1872) was the intellectual source behind the methods, aims and assumptions of the Schools. According to Grundtvig, the spirit in which the teaching is conducted is more important than the subject matter. He did not want the schools to focus on books and homework but on the "living word," that is, the spoken word in narrative and dialogue. The Danish Folk High Schools are committed to individual growth in and through the social communal medium of shared learning. The educational operative of encouragement and the living word foster three important interplays: teacher– student; student–student; and national poet–educational community. In the Grundtvigian classroom, teachers would exhibit nourishing attitudes, an energetic spirit and dialogical behavior. Reciprocal teaching was Grundtvig's idea of the ideal learning process.

The Antigonish Movement based at St. Francis Xavier University, Nova Scotia, is another example of collaborative learning. It consisted of a blending of adult education, Christian ethics and a program of social justice, directed through a university extension department in which poor people working in the primary industries of Nova Scotia were encouraged to discuss their own problems, engage in self-help and create their own cooperative movement. The Antigonish Movement considered study clubs or discussion circles as the key educational techniques illustrating its learner-centeredness. Moses Coady, a leader in the movement, proposed the discussion circle as a better technique whereby the people of eastern Canada could be mobilized to think, to study and to get enlightenment. In curriculum terms, Coady advocated principles and implemented practices that were learner-centred. Coady was concerned with creativity, originality, discovery, awareness and the value of experience. For him, the purpose of education was the collaborative development of attitudes and values that encourage individuals to develop to the utmost limit of their capacities rather than the traditional acquisition of knowledge.

A Critique of Collaborative Learning

The consensus–dissensus debate appears to be the most controversial and frequently misunderstood aspect of collaborative learning; it assumes community as inherently universalizing and that the multiplicity of diverse perspectives need to be unified into an ideological whole. Critics of collaborative learning (Burnett, 1992; Johnson, 1986; Myers, 1986; Stewart, 1988) take issue with Bruffee's (1993, 1995) works. They allege that Bruffee's lack of analysis concerning the notion of consensus is the weak point in his works. Contrary to the critics, Karis (1989) asserts that Bruffee's statement regarding the value of substantive conflict has often been overlooked. In responding to Johnson's allegation that consensus is enforced in collaborative learning Bruffee (1986) clarifies that "collaborative negotiation of knowledge allows the option of dissent" (p.78). According to Bruffee, the importance of dissent in collaborative learning is that it serves to enable learners to recognize the value of other perspectives.

These challenges to Bruffee's (1993, 1995) emphasis on consensus seem to arise out of a lack of clarity concerning the nature of consensus, a holistic understanding of which necessarily encompasses dissensus. The two concepts need not be polarized; they can function as a composite. Consensus may be seen in terms of difference and not just of agreements; as the result of conflicts, not as a monolith (Myers, 1986). Participants should be reassured that disagreements over substantive matters may be a positive development and an integral dimension in the collaborative process (Karis, 1989). Consensus represents "generativity of group life" (Trimbur, 1989). The social synergy inherent in group life unleashes the capacity for collaboration, shared decision-making and collective action.

A further objection raised in the consensus–dissensus debate involves the allegation of "peer indoctrination" (Johnson, 1986). Critics of collaborative learning contend that peer indoctrination classes or "inherent groupiness" (Stewart, 1988) slide into "potentially totalitarian practices" (Beade, 1987), stifling individual voice and creativity, suppressing differences and enforcing conformity. The literature notes that the "power of influence" (Stewart) is closely aligned with "peer indoctrination." Stewart inquires: How does one account for the originality of genius? How does genius transcend the influences that have molded the individual? For Stewart the "most damning criticism of all" is that collaborative learning is "psychologically unsound" in that it does not take into account the range of human personality traits. In being aware of the criticism that collaboration may result in "groupthink" and prevent people from exercising their individual strengths, Qualley and Chiseri-Strater (1994) respond that they have more often seen collaborative learning serving as a catalyst for individual transformation. They also observe that collaborative learning maximizes the creative and ongoing dialogical tension that is always present between individuals and their worlds.

See also: action learning, cooperative education, learning, peer learning, study circles.

References and Further Reading

Beade, P. (1987). Comment. *College English, 49*(6), 707–708.

Brookfield, S. D. (1986). *Understanding and facilitating adult learning.* San Francisco: Jossey-Bass.

Bruffee, K. (1986). Comment and response to Thomas S. Johnson. *College English, 48*(1), 77–78.

Bruffee, K. (1993). *Collaborative learning: Higher education, interdependence, and the authority of knowledge.* Baltimore, MD: John Hopkins University Press.

Bruffee, K. (1995). Sharing our toys. *Change, 27*(1), 12–19.

Burnett, R. E. (1992). Interpretation: Conflict in collaborative decision-making. In N. R. Blyer & C. Thralls (Eds.), *Professional communication: The social perspective* (pp. 144–162). London: Sage.

Forman, E. A., & Cazden, C. B. (1985). Exploring Vygotskian perspectives in education: The cognitive value of peer interaction. In J.V. Wertsch (Ed.), *Culture, communication and cognition. Vygotskian perspectives* (pp. 323–347). Cambridge, UK: Cambridge University Press.

Freire, P. (2000). *Pedagogy of the oppressed.* (M. Ramos, Trans.) New York: Herder & Herder. Original work published in 1970.

Johnson, D. A., & Johnson, R. T. (1994). *Learning together and alone* (4th ed.). London: Allyn & Bacon.

Johnson, T. S. (1986). Comment. *College English, 48*(1), 76.

Karis, B. (1989). Conflict in collaboration: A Burkean perspective. *Rhetoric Review, 8*(1), 113–126.

Knowles, M. S. (1980). *The modern practice of adult education: From pedagogy to andragogy* (2nd ed.). New York: Cambridge Books.

Lee, G. C. M. (1998). *Collaborative learning in three British adult education schemes.* Unpublished doctoral thesis. University of Nottingham.

Lee, G. C. M. (2003). Engaging the whole person through the practice of collaborative learning. *International Journal of Lifelong Education, 22*(1), 78–93.

Lindeman, E. C. L. (1926). *The meaning of adult education.* New York: New Republic.

Matthews, R. S., Cooper, J. L., Davidson, N., & Hawkes, P. (1995). Building bridges between cooperative and collaborative learning. *Change, 27*, 35–40.

Myers, M. (1986). Reality, consensus and reform in the rhetoric of composition teaching. *College English, 48*(2), 154–174.

Paterson, R. W. K. (1979). *Education and the adult.* Boston: Routledge.

Qualley, D. A., & Chiseri-Strater, E. (1994). Collaboration as reflexive dialogue: A knowing "deeper than reason." *Journal of Advanced Composition, 14*(1), 111–130.

Stewart, D. C. (1988). Collaborative learning and composition: Boon or bane? *Rhetoric Review*, *7*(1), 58–83.
Trimbur, J. (1989). Consensus and difference in collaborative learning. *College English*, *51*(6), 602–616.

Moira Lee

Community (of Practice)

Communities of practice are informal groups of people who interact regularly to use collective learning and shared expertise to solve mutually engaging problems. Jean Lave and Etienne Wenger (1991) are credited with naming this concept that describes the sociocultural process by which newcomers learn to become full participants of communities engaged in expressing knowledge in practice and in which established members share knowledge while also gaining from new perspectives to deepen their expertise. The term practice in this sense refers to the activities involved in accomplishing work. The community's identity and structure are defined by its members and by the shared ways in which they perform work and understand events. Wenger (1998), the writer of many books and articles on the topic, maintains that communities of practice are ubiquitous in society and that each person is a member of multiple networks. Nevertheless, the term has become strongly associated with organizational learning and knowledge management.

The concept is rooted in a social theory of learning, or social constructionism, in which learning and knowledge are understood to be cultural and social phenomena created in relationship with others within a social context (Nicolini, Gherardi, & Yanow, 2003; Wenger, 1998). Knowledge construction is a social process that occurs when people congregate for a joint purpose whether that occurs in a kitchen, community meeting, work setting, or other places where people purposefully gather. This contrasts with the conventional notion emanating from a Western, European tradition in which knowledge is composed of information stored in individual's minds, that can be organized sequentially and recorded as symbolic, material artifacts, "mastered" by individuals, and then transmitted and measured in classrooms. Although a place remains for the transmission of codified knowledge, knowing primarily requires the active participation of people in practice in a social-historical context. Learning doesn't merely produce people who *know about* or *know how*; people learning to become community members also *learn to be* in the sense of creating a mutual social identity (Brown & Duguid, 2000; Gherardi & Nicolini, 2000; Mutch, 2003; Wenger).

The concept of communities of practice is related to adult learning theories of experiential learning and situated cognition. The role of experience is central to adult learning theory, and a basic principle of classroom practice is the recognition of the life experience that participants bring to new learning situations. In situated cognition, the social context is inextricable from learning, meaning that learning is a social activity tied to the life experiences, interactions, and activities of people. Learning and knowledge are socially constructed and structured by the setting, the tools used by learners, the interactions among learners, and their social context (Hansman, 2001). Gustavsson (1997) cautions that while situated learning theory offers the potential for gaining new understandings of the theory/practice relationship, learning tied to the personal and the process of doing is insufficient by itself. In a multicultural, global society we need a learning process in which we can distance ourselves from our everyday patterns and self-evident interpretations and reach beyond our immediate social group.

In a community of practice, learning necessarily involves engagement and participation in authentic activities. Novices are socialized into the distinctive practices that emerge in the community and gain a stock of practical knowledge and expertise. As individuals gain competence and assimilate the character and viewpoint of the community, they gain a new identity and the esteem of other members. This is not an asymmetrical relationship. Novices are not merely passive observers; rather they have their own unique contributions to make, and the notion of competence is defined in community. "Since knowledge is integrated and distributed in the life of the community, learning is an act of belonging" (Nicolini et al., 2003, p. 15). Since the knowledge of a community of practice is not a static entity, learning also involves collaboration and reciprocation as members solve problems of mutual interest.

We are urged by Wenger (1998; Wenger, McDermott, & Snyder, 2002) to consider the words "communities of practice" as a unit containing three dimensions: the (a) mutual engagement of people, who are (b) informally bound together within a purpose or enterprise, and (c) who use a shared repertoire of expertise. Community is considered essential for the creation and maintenance of knowledge and knowledge is sustained by its transmission to newcomers, or novices, that enter the community (Gherardi & Nicolini, 2000). Community used in this sense is not something restricted to geographical place, but rather refers to a dynamic whole that emerges when a group of people participate in common practices, depend on and make decisions together, and commit themselves to the long-term well-being of the group. Practice involves the application of both explicit and tacit knowledge, in other words, both articulated/codified knowledge and the unarticulated knowledge that resides in the knowledge, skills, practices, intuition, and values acquired by community members. Tacit knowledge consists of embodied expertise and deep understanding that allows for the interpretation of new, complex experiences and forms patterns of behavior for action.

Characteristics

People engage in communities of practice to share information, insight, and advice to help each other solve common problems and explore ideas. They value learning together not just because it helps them to complete their work effectively, but also because they derive personal satisfaction from working with colleagues who share their perspectives. Over time, they develop common tools and a shared body of knowledge, practices and approaches to problem solving. People develop and maintain personal relationships and a common sense of identity. Their social relationships both reify the community of practice and are used to solve problems and transmit learning (Wenger et al., 2002). What binds people together is the shared interpretation, or the common structural framework with which community members interpret information (Brown & Duguid, 2000).

Saint-Onge and Wallace (2003) suggest that communities of practice: (a) exist to answer questions that arise in practice and hence need to make use of productive inquiry, (b) generate knowledge that supports practice by using both internal and external information and through the contributions of its members create new knowledge methods, practices, or products within the community's domain of their practice, (c) self-organize to meet a shared purpose and develop norms for self-governance, (d) assume accountability for supporting each other, (e) develop channels of regular communication, and (f) collaborate along multiple channels of communication, both through face-to-face interaction and technological mediation. Physical or geographical proximity is not required; however, these do facilitate the constant engagement involved in discussion and solution of practice problems.

It is tempting to consider a profession, or even a professional specialization, as a community of practice. However, members may only solve similar problems in parallel but not in regular communication with each other. Activities required to maintain licensure such as attending conferences, reading professional journals, or having irregular consultations with other members of the profession to solve practice problems, do not constitute the dense network of interpersonal communications required to maintain community and engage in the complex, collective process of negotiation involved in creating meaning and pursuing work to be completed. Although professions such as medicine, social work, or community development are practiced in different countries, the values of the profession and its social and legal requirements are influenced by the sociocultural context and may differ from country to country.

Organizational Learning and Knowledge Management

A post-industrial economy has focused the interests of business managers on the organization's intangible assets, including the knowledge of employees in the organization. The interest in practice-based theories of knowing reflects the growing importance of knowledge-related issues in business and society and the inadequacy of early theories based in economic and cognitive assumptions (Nicolini et al., 2003; Wenger et al., 2002). Early attempts to manage knowledge tried to capture expert's knowledge in *expert systems* databases that were made accessible to other employees. Unfortunately, expert systems were found to be unable to replicate the social, dynamic nature of knowledge or the complexities of human judgment. As society increasingly relies on expert knowledge, it is urgent to understand the organizational, interpersonal processes that foster its creation, sustenance, and reproduction. In a knowledge economy, the attraction of nourishing existing communities of practice or cultivating new ones is that they are thought to be able to solve practice problems quickly, because members know how to access relevant information from their peers, transfer best practices to other parts of a company, foster professional development, and assist with the recruitment and retention of talented people. Indeed, several recently published texts suggest steps for nourishing communities of practice in order to leverage them for business success (Saint-Onge & Wallace, 2003; Wenger et al.). However, the informal nature of communities of practice makes them resistant to management, supervision, or interference.

Because of their closed nature, communities of practice may be resistant to changes imposed from without, which can be counterproductive if they perpetuate practices that compromise safety or circumvent the law. For example, Gherardi and Nicolini (2000) describe construction workers who learned to organize the exterior of their worksites to manipulate the inspectors' attention so that the worksite was not selected for inspection and fines; however, once inside the site the scaffolding or electrical wiring may not be up to standard. They comment that repeated warnings and insistence on compliance will be ineffective; rather people may simply find more creative ways to avoid compliance. Instead, collective and participatory action both perpetuate the knowledge of the community of practice and allow for change. Another consequence of the closed nature of communities of practice is that they may stifle the introduction of new knowledge, claim to have the right to ownership of knowledge, and practice exclusion of certain people and therefore reproduce discrimination of minorities.

Practice knowledge is thought to be the product of communities of practice, and therefore business interests in the topic can also be related to social capital theory; Saint-Onge and Wallace (2003) go so far as to refer to knowledge capital as if knowledge can exist outside or without knowers. Linking education with economic growth and the global economy risks equating human knowledge and productivity as a commodity to be managed for the benefit of business, rather than for human benefit. Critically reflective adult education practice challenges economic and international modernization because of the resulting cultural homogenization, environmental destruction and displacement of people, most often minorities, for the benefit of business. It must also be questioned whether communities of practice is a term that will stand the test of time. It has undeniable intuitive appeal as can be attested by the variety of authors who have applied the concept in their work, albeit somewhat loosely.

See also: activity theory, cognition, continuing professional education, cultural learning, organizational learning.

References and Further Reading

Brown, J. S., & Duguid, P. (2000). *The social life of information*. Boston, MA: Harvard Business School Press.

Gherardi, S., & Nicolini, D. (2000). The organizational learning of safety in communities of practice. *Journal of Management Inquiry, 9*(1), 7–18.

Gustavsson, B. (1997). Life-long learning reconsidered. In S. Walters (Ed.) *Globalization, adult education and training* (pp. 237–249). London and Cape Town, South Africa: Zed Books and CACE Publications.

Hansman, C. A. (2001). Context-based adult learning. In S. B. Merriam (Ed.), *The new update on adult learning* (pp. 43–51). *New Directions for Adult and Continuing Education*, No. 89. San Francisco: Jossey-Bass.

Lave, J., & Wenger, E. (1991). *Situated learning: Legitimate peripheral participation*. Cambridge, UK: Cambridge University Press.

Mutch, A. (2003). Communities of practice and habitus: A critique. *Organization Studies, 24*(3), 383–401.

Nicolini, D. S., Gherardi, S., & Yanow, D. (2003). *Knowing in organizations: A practice-based approach*. Armonk, NY: M. E. Sharpe.

Saint-Onge, H., & Wallace, D. (2003). *Leveraging communities of practice for strategic advantage*. New York: Butterworth Heinemann.

Wenger, E. (1998). *Communities of practice: Learning, meaning and identity*. Cambridge, UK: Cambridge University Press.

Wenger, E., McDermott, R., & Snyder, W. M. (2002). *Cultivating communities of practice: A guide to managing knowledge*. Boston, MA: Harvard Business School Press.

Lilian H. Hill

Community Development

Community development refers to the process of ensuring that people living in a variety of communities are involved in defining and taking action on the issues that affect them. It tries to involve those who are usually excluded from the decision-making processes that affect their lives because they do not have the power or authority to have their voices heard. This process of empowerment has as its ultimate aim the challenging of discrimination and inequality.

The process of community development involves: identification of ideas, problems or issues for further development; analysis of the causes or effects of these; consideration of possible action to achieve change; and organization of learning, development and change at individual, group and community levels. This can lead to a greater understanding of social issues in their political context, and of how participative and democratic decision-making processes can be enacted.

Effective community development has a strong adult education component. To build communities there must be a process of learning occurring whereby members are involved in recognizing, discovering and acquiring skills, finding out how to do things, acknowledging and sharing knowledge and developing awareness of the issues and problems that face them. Community development also requires strong organizational skills in order to mobilize energies and knowledge, engage people, build networks and organizations and to take action to bring about change. Learning and organizing depend on each other: people learn by doing, and they gain knowledge through mobilizing to take action. Learning is what gives community action its transformative potential and organizing helps to institutionalize and sustain collective learning.

One of the areas that community development workers in adult education have a particular focus on is supporting young people and adults to return to learning throughout life, using community-based guidance and provision, particularly for those who are disadvantaged. They are also involved in supporting young people and adults in improving their communities through increasing self-help and voluntary community action in tackling problems. They have a role in enhancing the ability of agencies to listen to the needs and concerns of local people and in raising awareness of issues through public education campaigns such as crime prevention and environmental action. Overall they are involved in stimulating the effective involvement of local people in personal, social, cultural, economic and political development, and through this, helping people to participate actively in determining change.

Community

Community development takes place

outside of formal institutions and responds to the notion of community, a concept that has many meanings. Communities may be defined in terms of the common characteristics that their members share. These may be personal characteristics; common beliefs; activities; use or provision of services and goods (commuters, dog-owners, and parents); where members live or work. Not everyone will be fully engaged in these different types of community and its strength within any group is determined by the degree to which its members experience both a sense of solidarity and a sense of significance within it.

Just because people have characteristics in common does not mean that they identify themselves as a community – this requires that they have common interests. One type of interest is a common cultural heritage that arises from a common tradition or identity, or from a sense of belonging and loyalty, perhaps in faith communities or ethnic communities. Social relationships such as the social ties of family, neighborhood, mutual support and social interaction that are derived from kinship, or a common residence base or common experience can also give rise to common interests. Another kind of community is formed among those who share common economic interests such as belonging to the same social class, or being home-owners; or share a common profession such as adult educators. Lastly, common experiences of power or oppression for example, being wealthy; refugees; working-class people; ethnic minorities can also provide the basis for an awareness of common interests (Taylor, 2003, p. 35).

Although the meanings of community have been separated out here they also overlap. An ethnic minority community may have meaning for its members because of its common traditions and history, because of the social relations between its members, because of a common heritage or because of a common experience of discrimination and powerlessness.

Building Communities

If people can develop the confidence, skills and networks, both within and beyond their own neighborhood or community, they can then challenge the ways in which outsiders treat them and the ways they are portrayed. A confident community that is respected by the outside world can then become a place where people want to live and work, which reinforces the self-esteem of those who live there, and so on. To set such a positive cycle in motion requires, firstly, building confidence and social capital in these communities and realizing existing strengths, so that members no longer see themselves and their neighbors as failures. It also involves building new relationships with outsiders (service providers; business; the media) that empower people as service users, consumers and workers, as well as changing the image of the locality. It requires the development of jobs and assets that bring people into these communities, the creating of stronger links between them and the mainstream economy and empowering community members as co-producers. Finally it involves building new forms of governance that empower people as citizens (Stewart & Taylor, 1995).

The work that is done with communities is often described as capacity-building, which involves drawing out potential that is already there but may be lying dormant or unrecognized (Banks & Shenton,

2001). This potential needs to be released at both the individual and collective levels. Individuals need to build their skills, knowledge, confidence and experience, but to engage collectively also requires an awareness of common knowledge and interests, active networks and organizations, and networking and organizational skills. Individual skills can be seen as human capital, while the networks and norms that are built up through collective action can be seen as "social capital"; habits of organizing and a willingness to take action might be seen as "organizational capital." Together these forms of capital enhance the ability of communities to become active agents and to release the power of the community.

Releasing community potential and capacity-building are the essential foundations for effective community development initiatives. Without effective approaches to community learning, engagement and organization, initiatives that are designed to improve and develop communities are unlikely to be sustainable. The first step in empowerment is to build the confidence and self-esteem of the people who live in excluded communities. The next step is to release the assets that already exist in the area but which are undervalued through shared activity and learning. The strengths of engaging in shared activity are the acknowledgement of local assets, the ability to start from small beginnings, the potential for involvement and ownership, and the fact that relatively limited resources can release considerable energies.

It is important that investment in community development, from the state or other organizations, is provided at an early stage, that it is given the time to bear fruit and that a moderate pace, rather than accelerated action, is adopted. If communities are to be involved effectively, a development phase needs to be built into new initiatives, which gives communities the time and the resources to develop the organizational capacity that will be essential to effective representation.

A strong community infrastructure can serve as a focus for channeling the views of local communities to power-holders and providing legitimacy. It can act as a channel for accounting back to those communities, and it can provide the information backup that government and state agencies take for granted. Such an infrastructure will also develop the capacity of others in communities so that tasks of leadership can be spread so that succession is assured. However, there are considerable challenges. The challenge of reconciling the diversity of interests within any community requires identifying common ground that can unite people while providing channels for them to represent their different interests. Without this infrastructure, conflict and competition can erode scarce resources, community representation can become divorced from its constituency, and activities can become very dependent on one or two individuals. Just as participation cannot be imposed from above, neither can community infrastructure if it is to be owned and trusted by communities. It needs to be built up from below and be accountable and accessible to all (Taylor, 2003, p. 190).

Knowledge and Learning

Community development focuses on particular life circumstances and structures in society, and attempts to effect change in these through learning and education. Education, which grows out of the experiences of ordinary people and the social interests that are generated within communities, has a different focus from mainstream education both in its curriculum and in its methods. Community development is about encouraging and engaging people throughout life into learning that is based on their interests. Education is developed that is enjoyable and relevant to the participating learners and is responsive to community priorities and needs that are identified *with* people rather than *for* them. The motivation and purpose for learning of the participants will change over time but if education is rooted in the community "it will allow genuinely alternative and democratic agendas to emerge at the local level" (Martin, 1996, p. 140).

Community development involves supporting people to improve their personal, community, social and economic well-being through creating learning opportunities within and for communities. The engagement of people in creating their own knowledge involves developing a capacity for self-determination and evolution and emphasizes the social embeddedness of learning rather than its individual focus. Community-based knowledge learnt from experience is a valuable asset because it is derived from the issues that are important to people. The choices people make, once they have had the opportunity to engage in dialogue about the focus of their learning, are more open and are no longer limited by what providers wish to offer. These choices could be about the acquisition of vocational skills or qualifications, but are equally likely to be about fulfilling social or cultural objectives. Such an approach to knowledge recognizes that learning is located in social participation and dialogue as well as in the heads of individuals and treats teaching and learning not as two distinct activities, but as elements of a single, reciprocal process.

It is important to develop learning that builds on experience and emphasizes the wealth of people's knowledge rather than what they do not know. This approach requires the joint development of a curriculum based on the valuing of the knowledge that people bring from their own family and community contexts. The curriculum also needs to enable the development of a critical understanding of the social, political and economic factors that shape experience. Building knowledge and a curriculum that reflects the issues and concerns of ordinary people is an empowering process that does lead to "learning how to change your life. Really useful knowledge is knowledge calculated to make you free" (Johnson, 1988, pp. 21–22). The challenge for the educator is to capture the positive and enthusiastic belief in the power of learning and in the potential of all people that comes from engaging in more democratic decision-making. This leads to genuine engagement in deciding what is important knowledge in the construction of the curriculum. A "whole life – all life" approach would place the learner's needs and experience at the center and help people to engage in the wide range of political roles and social relationships that occur outside both the workplace and the marketplace.

It is important to respond to the voices of those who are excluded from making decisions. When people do not have their voices heard their only other option is to exit from participation in decision-making to the detriment of the wider society which then creates policies *for* people rather than *with* them. Community development is about evolving more open, participatory and democratic relationships between educators and their constituencies. The reciprocal quality of these relationships is crucial, otherwise development work focuses on what people lack rather than what they have. This fundamental element of role redefinition and reversal has wide-ranging implications for the nature of educative relationships, the context of learning and the potential for redistribution of educational opportunities.

An emphasis on whose experiences count, and how they are interpreted and understood, helps to challenge the commonsense of everyday assumptions about experience and its relationship to knowledge production. This allows new claims to be made for the legitimacy of reflexive experience leading to really useful knowledge for those who are involved in generating it. In questioning the discourses that frame the ways of thinking, problems, and practices which are regarded as legitimate, it begins to be possible for people to open up new ways of reflexively thinking about the social construction of their experiences. When people create their own knowledge and have their voices heard, narrow definitions of what is thought to be "educated knowledge" and who it is that makes it, are thrown into question. In this way the experiences and stories that have been excluded, and the mystification caused by "expert" knowledge, can be interrogated as a way of articulating views that come from below rather than above. This is important "because, in identifying and making spaces where alternative ways of thinking and being can be worked up, such practices increase the possibilities of knowledge – that is knowledge that is useful to those who generate it" (Barr, 1999, p. 82).

Having a greater say in services is important, but being treated as capable citizens, with a right to dissent from provided solutions, is much more empowering and can lead to democratic renewal for all people. A popular curriculum that addresses the concerns of ordinary people and actively draws upon their experience as a resource for educational work in communities increases the possibilities of developing knowledge that is useful to those who generate it.

See also: civil society, community education, educational foundations, learning region, popular education.

References and Further Reading

Banks, S., & Shenton, F. (2001). Regenerating neighbourhoods: A critical look at the role of community capacity building. *Local Economy, 16*(4) 286–98.

Barr, J. (1999). Women, adult education and really useful knowledge. In J. Crowther, I. Martin, & M. Shaw (Eds.), *Popular education and social movements in Scotland today* (pp. 70–82). Leicester: NIACE National Institute for Adult, Continuing Education.

Johnson, R. (1988). Really useful knowledge, 1790 – 1850. In T. Lovett (Ed.), *Radical approaches to adult education: A reader* (pp. 3–34). London: Routledge.

Martin, I. (1996). Community education: The dialectics of development. In R. Fieldhouse et al. (Eds.), *A history of modern British adult education* (pp. 109–141). Leicester, UK: NIACE National Institute for Adult, Constinuing Education.

Stewart, M., & Taylor, M. (1995). *Empowerment and estate regeneration: A critical review*. Bristol: The Policy Press.

Taylor, M. (2003). *Public policy in the community*. London: Palgrave Macmillan.

Lyn Tett

Community Education

The primary focus of community education is on education *within* and *for* community: thus, the "community" prefix refers not simply to a context in which education takes place, but to a vital component of an educational process designed to foster, articulate and work with a sense of community, often with the intention of bringing about social change. Community education generally involves a blurring of traditional boundaries, such as those between formal educational institutions and their surrounding communities. Community education may be regarded as a way of thinking rather than as a particular form or sector of education. It is difficult to define because the concept of community is itself notoriously slippery and contested; also, community education activities encompass a wide range of educational practices and intentions which derive from different traditions, including adult education, youth work, democratic schooling, and community participation.

Community

The concept of community became popular in the 19th century as a reaction to social fragmentation brought about by the industrialization and urbanization of many Western societies. This was a particular interest of social theorists in Germany where, in 1887, Ferdinand Tönnies, identified two different forms of human relationships: *Gemeinschaft* and *Gesellschaft*. The former term is usually associated with "community"; the latter with "society." *Gemeinschaft* relationships are characteristically intimate and whole; values are shared so there are no fundamental moral conflicts; roles and relationships cohere and do not conflict; and the group in question is stable both geographically and in terms of its internal structures. *Gesellschaft* relationships are often distant and impersonal; determined by increasingly specialized social roles and contracts; and affected by geographical and social mobility.

These ideal types have formed the basis of much subsequent thinking about the nature of community and are partially responsible for the association of community with "warm" and desirable values and a view of "us against them." As Raymond Williams (1976) noted, "community" never seems to be used unfavorably (p. 66). Consequently, it has often been utilized politically to encourage acceptance of policy initiatives by, in Ian Martin's (1987) terms, creating "a smokescreen to fudge some of the key issues . . . about power, accountability and resource allocation" (p. 13).

In 1955, George Hillery famously identified 94 definitions of community. Less than a quarter produced anything approaching a common formula; and about one-fifth contained mutually exclusive elements. Although such conceptual confusion and potential for abuse has led some sociologists to reject it, Crow and Allan (1994, p. 193) maintain that, if it did not exist, the term "community" would have to be invented. In Habermasian terms, its significance lies in representing a form of social organization that is situated, and mediates, between the personal "life-world" of the individual and the "systems world" of the state and its institutions.

There are three distinctive aspects of community, all associated with individuals having something in common. The commonality may be through links with a particular place;

shared interests; or a sense of "communion" or "solidarity" with one another, often expressed in collective social action. They may all be present simultaneously, though this is unusual. Different approaches to community education place varying degrees of importance upon each aspect.

Precursors of Community Education

In the 19th century, philanthropic organizations, many influenced by Christian socialism, were responsible for an expansion of educational opportunities. As the following examples illustrate, their emphasis on local developments, mutual support and social welfare as key components of the educational process foreshadowed later developments in adult and community education (see www.infed.org, and Fieldhouse & Associates, 1996, for further elaboration).

- *Youth organizations.* The Young Men's Christian Association (YMCA) was founded in London in 1844, and within a decade had become established in other parts of Britain as well as France, North America, India and Australia. Its intention was to improve social conditions and promote learning as a way of bearing witness in everyday life to faith in Jesus Christ. It was distinctive in its design as a movement of, by and for young men, and in its emphasis on collective effort in the formation of local associations. The Young Women's Christian Association (YWCA), created in 1877, focused on the welfare and spiritual and mental development of working girls. In the 1970s it initiated several key community-based youth work projects. Both organizations continue to flourish around the world and to support activities for young people near their homes.
- *Adult schools.* The first adult schools in Britain were designed to give direct access to the Bible by teaching adults to read. Quaker influence was strong, especially in establishing "Friends' Meeting Houses." These provided accommodation for reading classes and other social activities designed to promote the moral and social welfare of working people. Contemporary developments in the mid- to late 1800s included the founding of the Co-operative Movement which emphasized improvement through education, including that of the social and political position of women within the movement itself; and the establishment of Mechanics' Institutes whose origins lay in the earlier working men's libraries and mutual improvement societies of the 18th century. These Institutes, in turn, gave shape to working men's colleges which were designed as communities of teachers and students sharing in a common life.
- *Folk high schools.* These originated in Denmark in 1844 as residential forms of schooling for a largely rural population. They placed less emphasis on reading than most contemporary British developments, and more on the notion of a "useful and enjoyable human life" shaped by living and working cooperatively, a factor which, following the Danish example subsequently became significant within the British working men's colleges and later university settlements. Intellectual and spiritual growth was regarded as being

linked to, and enhanced by, a strong sense of identity within a clearly-defined social and cultural group. The model of the folk schools was particularly attractive to early 20th century progressive educators seeking to integrate political, economic and educational issues. It is reflected in many ideas about community schooling.

Several intentions are evident in these examples: to assist the intellectual development of the individual; to improve the situation of the "working class" through moral and social welfare; and to develop shared interests through local associations and cooperative activities. Although the terms "adult education" and "community education" are often used interchangeably, adult education is particularly associated with the first of these intentions, especially in Britain where its early development was strongly linked to the belief of the Enlightenment; that intellectual development is a precursor of good citizenship.

Community education has closer links with intentions to develop shared interests for mutual benefit, generally within a specific locality and often as a form of "compensation" for social/educational disadvantage. In these respects, as Tony Jeffs and Mark Smith (1999) illustrate, it is sometimes indistinguishable from other community-based activities with an educational focus. More radical approaches to community education were developed in the latter part of the 20th century. They moved away from philanthropic notions of "provision" and "welfare" and sought to harness common interests in order to challenge and effect change in prevailing social and political circumstances.

Forms of Community Education

Categorizing community-based activities as separate "forms" of education can become an exercise in semantics. However, it highlights some of the issues and values associated with education beyond the regulatory frameworks of formal educational institutions as well as confusions about terminology. The following terms are significant in the debate about what constitutes community education:

- *Non-formal/informal education.* "Non-formal education" is sometimes used to define organized educational activities arranged outside the "formal" regimes of schools and other institutions. "Informal education" then encompasses non-organized activities with an educational component, including individual pursuits and interactions with friends, family and workmates. In practice, this distinction is easily blurred and the terms used interchangeably. Thinking about education as "formal" *versus* "non-formal/informal" can reinforce a crude distinction between what happens inside and outside educational institutions and an assumption that institutions are not part of, or influential within, the communities in which they are located.
- *Community schooling/learning.* The first documented use of the term "community school" is attributed to Henry Morris who, in the 1930s, sought to create a cultural focus for villagers in Cambridgeshire, England, to counteract the pull of the cities at a time of agricultural depression. Like some of his contemporaries in the USA, Morris's concerns

were to respond to the local effects of a wider socio-economic crisis and to create more cost-effective use of school buildings and resources by opening them up to adults for education and recreation. The model became popular, economically and socially, in many parts of Britain. It deliberately blurs boundaries between educational provision for different age-groups; schools and local communities; and education and leisure. "Community learning centers" are a more recent development in the USA, designed primarily to extend opportunities for children. By enabling schools to stay open longer and widen the nature of their provision they, too, have a socio-economic underpinning and work across boundaries between educational and other agencies. Models now being adopted through overseas aid in countries like Ghana make specific provision for adults and encourage links with local businesses, societies and municipal administration. Community schooling/learning tends to focus on educational provision for individuals in the community, with some provision made by local community members. With the exception of schools associated with particular faith communities, education *for* community is less evident, although the idea of sharing in a "common life" for the betterment of all is present in educational philosophies and practices linked to notions of democratic schooling.

- *Community organization/development.* Interest in community self-help and development grew following the Second World War. In 1948, *A Report on Community Organization and Adult Education* in the USA examined a range of community development projects and identified key characteristics of "community organization." It noted that there was much common ground between community organization and adult education but that, while adult education placed emphasis on "the growth in learning by the individual," community organization "must concentrate upon the strategy and tactics of achieving results directly related to community-wide projects" (www.infed.org/archives/e-texts/aea.htm). Britain sought to develop such activities in its colonies to promote literacy training and self-help groups focusing on health, welfare and agriculture. The United Nations subsequently embraced the idea of community development and encouraged sponsorship of local projects by national governments. By the 1970s, conflicts between national and local interests, exacerbated by inadequate financial support, had led to widespread disillusionment in many Southern countries and a view that community development continued to be associated with colonial attitudes. Nevertheless, acknowledgment of the importance of group participation aimed at achieving locally-significant results remains a crucial aspect of some community education practices and was influential in shaping a more radical agenda in community education in Britain from the late 1960s.
- *Popular education.* Associated particularly with South America and the work of Paulo Freire, "popular education" is, to some degree, an antidote to the disillu-

sionment with government-sponsored community development initiatives. It is an overtly political movement designed to empower groups that have traditionally lacked full participation in political processes. Popular education sees communities themselves as sources of knowledge; the role of the community educator in popular education is to help people to reclaim and assert their own collective history in order to bring about change in political and social structures. In Scotland, concerns that new policy initiatives have reconstructed community education within an economic and managerialist frame have led many erstwhile community education practitioners/researchers to embrace the concept of popular education as more representative of community education's traditional values (see Crowther, Martin, & Shaw, 1999).

Models of Community Education

Community education has been notoriously undertheorized but several typologies were developed in the 1980s to try to fit the complexity of practice into a theoretical framework (Allen, Bastiani, Martin, & Richards, 1987). Essentially, these comprise three discrete models, each highlighting particular ideas about education, community and practice.

Model 1 focuses on *economics, individuals and specific places*: education is an economic tool and the cost-effective use of buildings and resources is important. "Provision" is made for individuals, often shaped by the Enlightenment tradition of developing intellectual capacity to create a better-informed citizenry. Activities center on a geographical locality, emphasizing the "commonality of place" aspect of community.

Model 2 builds on a "commonality of shared interests." It is concerned with *social justice, individuals-in-communities and place linked to lifestyle*: education is a means of redressing imbalances in society by "compensating" groups of individuals who have been forced to adopt particular lifestyles because of a lack of other opportunities. The purpose of community education is to address the perceived needs of "deprived" or alienated groups by helping them to adjust better to life in the wider society. The possibility that the wider society itself might need "adjustment" is not addressed.

Model 3 is predicated on an understanding of community as a "sense of solidarity." It allows for, and often encourages, *political challenge*. The locus of control of activities moves from "providers" of education to *local communities*. Acting collectively and drawing on the expertise of community education facilitators whose job it is to help them to articulate their own forms of knowledge, these communities are expected to be able to effect change in their conditions. They are not necessarily (though may be) located in a specific place, but may be representative of shared interests, orientations or cultures within a single country or across the world. The term *"un-place"* is useful to indicate the non-specific location of some of the communities – such as "working class," gay, or ethnic – most often associated with this approach.

Cheryl Hunt (2000) suggests that these models are underpinned by three expanding discourses, the key dimensions of which are italicized in the descriptions above. An "Economic-Political" discourse expands from discussion of cost-effectiveness in what is regarded as an essentially homogenous society to encompass the notion of social justice in, and the "enrichment" of, a plural society; it culminates in an overtly political interpretation of community education as a means of challenging and changing existing structures. A "Psychological-Sociological" discourse shifts its emphasis from the individual as consumer of educational provision for personal growth to the education of individuals for the "betterment" of particular groups, and finally to the whole group rather than the individual as the locus of educational development. The third discourse, "Geographical-Ecological," moves from the specifics of place into the more abstract notion of lifestyle and ultimately encompasses the "unplace" of the symbolic dimensions of community.

Absent from these discourses is any reference to the spiritual dimensions of community which inspired many early developments in the field. Given the expanding nature of the discourses, however, and renewed interests in spirituality as an aspect of adult learning, the ground is ripe for new understandings of community education.

See also: community development, comparative adult education, environmental adult education, extension, folk high schools, informal learning, libraries, popular education, voluntary organizations, women's voluntary organizations.

References and Further Reading

http://www.infed.org.htm *Encyclopedia of Informal Education.*

Allen, G., Bastiani, J., Martin, I., & Richards, K. (Eds.). (1987). *Community education: An agenda for educational reform.* Milton Keynes, UK: Open University Press.

Crow, G., & Allan, G. (1994). *Community life.* London: Harvester Wheatsheaf.

Crowther, J., Martin, I., & Shaw, M. (Eds.). (1999). *Popular education and social movements in Scotland today.* Leicester: National Institute of Adult Continuing Education (NIACE).

Fieldhouse, R., & Associates (1996). *A history of modern British adult education.* Leicester: NIACE.

Hunt, C. (2000). Wyrd questions: Reframing adult/community education. In T. Sork, V.-L. Chapman, & R. St. Clair (Eds), *AERC 2000*: Proceedings of the 41st Adult Education Research Conference (pp. 185–189). University of British Columbia, Vancouver, AERC.

Jeffs, T., & Smith, M. (1999). *Informal education: Conversation, democracy and learning.* Ticknall, UK: Education Now Publishing Cooperative.

Martin I. (1987). Community education: Towards a theoretical analysis. In G. Allen, J. Bastiani, I. Martin, & K. Richards (Eds.), *Community education: An agenda for educational reform* (pp. 9–32). Milton Keynes, UK: Open University Press.

Williams, R. (1976). *Key-words: Vocabulary of culture and society.* London: Fontana.

Cheryl Hunt

Comparative Adult Education

Comparative adult education (CAE) describes a scholarly approach to understanding adult education, in which two or more aspects are compared. "Comparison" methodically identifies similarities and differences between the aspects under study; their significance for theory and practice should be explained.

This general definition needs two additional specifications:

1. Although comparison within a single country (intra-national)

can occur, the term mostly – in North America as well as in Europe – stands for "international comparative adult education," meaning the comparison between two or more countries.

2. Also, many types of international comparative research do not include explicit comparison: "It is generally accepted that most of what is included under the rubric of comparative studies in adult education . . . does not include comparison in the strict sense" (Titmus, 1999, p. 36). Perhaps in these cases "comparison" refers to the implicit comparison with one's own country that inevitably happens when analysing a foreign country.

Why International Comparison?

A first reason is *knowledge and understanding* – to become better informed about adult education in other countries, its historical, societal, and cultural roots, "and thus to develop criteria for assessing contemporary developments and testing possible outcomes" (Kidd, 1975, p. 7). This understanding reflects back to one's own country: Observations made in a foreign context help to better perceive and understand adult education not only in the other, but also in one's own country.

A practical reason for international comparison is *"borrowing"*: it is hoped that learning from experiences abroad helps to adapt foreign experiences to one's own practice, avoids repeating mistakes and "reinventing the wheel." On a theoretical level it is argued that the international-comparative perspective assists to *overcome one's own ethnocentric blindness*: international comparison helps "to better understand oneself, and to reveal how one's own cultural biases and personal attributes affect one's judgment" (Kidd, 1975, p. 7).

And it is expected that learning from each other supports *peace and tolerance*: "One of the foremost challenges of our age is . . . to construct a culture of peace based on justice and tolerance within which dialogue, mutual recognition and negotiation will replace violence, in homes and countries, within nations and between countries" (UNESCO, *Hamburg Declaration on Adult Education*, 1997, chapter 14).

In smaller countries it is certainly easier to experience international knowledge, understanding, and respect through everyday experiences. For the United States of America, spanning an entire continent and having armed forces, business presence, and cultural influence all over the world, this is more difficult.

The International Interest in Andragogy

In the history of adult education and andragogy we find a continuous interest in adult education in other countries. In the century between the lives of Grundtvig (Denmark) and Freire (Brazil) a number of names and ideas attained international currency. The Danish "Folkehojskole," the English university extension movement, the Swedish study circle, and the American encounter-group movement became models for adult education in other countries; often the differences between the "borrowed" and the original have not been perceived.

International travel and exchange has, from the early years, offered key-persons in the adult education movement an important way to shape their understanding: Lindeman (USA) traveled to Germany, Mansbridge (Great

Britain) to Australia and Canada, and Borinski (Germany) to Scandinavia. And conferences have also contributed to the international exchange: At the first conference of the World Council for Comparative Education 1960 in Ottawa, Alexander N. Charters, Professor of Adult Education at Syracuse University, New York, and Roby Kidd, Canadian expert and scholar, conferred in a working group on international and comparative adult education. In 1966 the legendary Exeter conference took place in New Hampshire; the "Exeter papers" were published by the Syracuse University Publications in Continuing Education. In 1970 Alexander Charters and Beverly Cassara, Professor at the University of District of Columbia, published the papers from the World Council of Comparative and International Education in Montreal. In Prague, Czechoslovakia, 1992, Colin Titmus, Great Britain, leading researcher in this field, chaired a working group at the VIIIth World Council of Comparative Education Societies. The 1993 conference "Rethinking Adult Education for Development" assembled the comparativists in Ljubljana, Slovenia. Hamburg, Germany, hosted the UNESCO CONFINTEA V Conference in 1997, and the International Society for Adult Comparative Education (ISCAE) held its 2002 conference in St. Louis, Missouri, USA, in conjunction with the American Association for Adult and Continuing Education (AAACE) and the International Association of Adult Education.

These examples indicate that in many countries an international interest occurs in adult education. Certainly, cultural differences limit the transfer from one country to another. Comparative research, by helping to understand the differences and similarities among countries and their significance for adult education, clarifies the possibilities and limits of understanding and borrowing.

Types of International Comparative Adult Education

Knowledge about the education of adults in other countries can be gained from various sources, and several types of comparative research can be categorized. A first, "pre-scientific" source is the reports given by international travelers, mostly characterized as "subjective-impressionistic." More systematic descriptions are categorized as "travelers' reports" and less systematic "travelers' tales." Their value is debatable. Because of random observation and subjective description, it is not clear how reliable and how representative the descriptions are. On the other hand, the plea is made that just this subjective focus of eye witnesses can mean a specific strength.

At the scientific level, six different types of international-comparative research are identified:

- The first is country reports, which try to describe the system of adult education in one country, as proposed, for example, at the 1966 Exeter conference: "to identify and describe the existing adult education programs within each country in order to make the relevant data available to scholars in their own and in other countries for comparative analysis" (Charters & Siddiqui, 1989, p. 3). Country reports were presented mainly during the 1970s and 1980s; some are rather impressionistic, others follow a well-developed outline and structure.
- The second is program reports, or topic-oriented studies. During

and after the 1980s an increasing number of program reports can be found. Because attempts to describe a whole national system were seldom successful, this type focuses on descriptions of adult education programs, institutions, and organizations in a distinct country. Included in this category (sometimes categorized separately) are the *topic-oriented studies* or the *problem approach*, where not a program, but a certain topic or problem is discussed in the context of a nation. These reports/studies are more "international" and less "comparative." Because only one country or program is presented, no comparable object is available; the readers have to draw the comparative conclusions themselves.

- The third, juxtaposition, collects and presents data from two or more countries, but no explicit comparison is given. Statistical reports represent this type, as well as collections of country reports (for example Jarvis, 1992). Juxtaposition can also be topic- or problem-oriented when a topic is discussed in relation to various countries. For example, Pöggeler's (1990) *The State and Adult Education*, brings together articles discussing the role of the state in different countries.
- The fourth is comparison, in the strict understanding of "international comparative adult education" reports from two or more countries, and offers an explicit comparison making the similarities and differences understandable:

> A study in comparative international adult education . . . must include one or more aspects of adult education in two or more countries or regions. Comparative study is not the mere placing side by side of data . . . such juxtaposition is only the prerequisite for comparison. At the next stage one attempts to identify the similarities and differences between the aspects under study . . . The real value of comparative study emerges only from . . . the attempt to understand why the differences and similarities occur and what their significance is for adult education in the countries under examination (Charters & Hilton, 1989, p. 3)

- The fifth, field- and method-reflecting text, reflects the methods, strategies, and concepts of international comparison, and includes summarizing reports about developments in the international comparative field on a material or meta level. The article at hand is an example for this category.
- Finally, there are the reports from international organizations. A bit outside of this system, but still counted as part of the international tradition, are reports from transnational institutions such as UNESCO, OECD, or the World Bank. Joachim Knoll, Professor (emeritus) at Bochum University, Germany, is one of the key persons supplying such information.

Difficulties and Problems of International Comparative Work

One problem is that the continuity of scholarly work is not guaranteed. Only a small number of scholars work in international comparative adult education as their main field; others enter for only a short period of time. The knowledge developed in comparative adult education is spread over many places, languages, and countries, which makes it difficult for new researchers to start working in this field. To build up continuity it is necessary to bring together the knowledge, experiences, discussions, and standards of the "why" and "how" of international comparison so that researchers can refer to and build upon an internationally shared set of research methods. To serve the continuity in this field through networking, conferences, and publications, the International Society for Comparative Adult Education ISCAE (www.ISCAE.org) was founded.

Often discussed is how comparison can be done between *different cultures*: are researchers knowledgeable enough to understand the aspects under study in a foreign cultural context? This can be a problem especially for American researchers who typically lack international experience. But the reality of international comparative studies shows that this problem can be reduced when the aim is not "perfect" but "better" understanding, and when the work is carried out in dialogue with foreign partners for communicative validation (Knox, 1993).

A clear handicap is *language*. International communication takes place in English, yet for the majority of the world this is a foreign language. Communicating – and even more, publishing – in this foreign language takes many times more effort than in one's native context. English literature is often not available, and it makes no sense to refer to non-English research literature, because the latter does not exist for the international readership. Researchers from non-English countries, when working in the international context, lose most of their scholarly background – theory, methodology, and content – that is based on their native language. On the other hand, native English speakers with no command of a foreign language always depend on more or less reliable translations.

Another problem is the regular *attendance at central international meetings*. To enter this field and to stay in its networks entails traveling and being visible. This is difficult, especially for junior scholars. International comparative projects have *higher costs* and *more problems* than research carried out in one country. When weighing the potential outcome of these investments for one's career, it may be more beneficial to work at the national level.

In spite of these problems, those working in international comparative adult education report personal enrichment and reward from experiencing the wider international world.

See also: dialogue, international adult education.

References and Further Reading

Charters, A. N., & Hilton, R. J. (Eds.).(1989). *Landmarks in international adult education: A comparative analysis*. London: Routledge.

Charters, A. N., & Siddiqui, D. A. (1989). *Comparative adult education: State of the art. With annotated resource guide*. Vancouver: Center for Continuing Education, University of British Columbia.

Jarvis, P. (Ed.).(1992). *Perspectives on adult education and training in Europe*. Malabar, FL: Krieger.

Kidd, J. R. (1975). Comparative adult education: The first decade. In C. Bennett, J. R. Kidd, & J. Kulich (Eds.), *Comparative studies in adult education: An anthology* (pp. 5–24). Syracuse, NY: Syracuse University.

Knox, A. B. (1993). *Strengthening adult and continuing education: A global perspective*

on synergistic leadership. San Francisco: Jossey-Bass.
Pöggeler, F. (Ed.).(1990). *The state and adult education*. Frankfurt, Germany: Verlag P. Lang.
Titmus, C. (1999). Comparative adult education: Some reflections on the process. In J. Reischmann, M. Bron, & Z. Jelenc (Eds.), *Comparative adult education 1998: The contribution of ISCAE to an emerging field of study* (pp. 33–50). Ljubljana, Slovenia: Slovenian Institute for Adult Education.
UNESCO Institute for Education (1997). *The Hamburg Declaration on Adult Learning*. Hamburg, Germany: UNESCO, 1997, retrieved Jan. 21, 2004, from www.unesco.org/education/uie/confintea/documents.htm)
www.ISCAE.org International Society for Comparative Adult Education.
www.hku.hk/cerc/wcces/ World Council of Comparative Education Societies.

Jost Reischmann

Competency-Based Education

Competency-based education/learning (CBE) in essence involves the education/training and evaluation of individuals to predetermined standards to establish or predict effective performance (competency). In practice, however, competence or competency is difficult to define (see Wolf, 1995). While there is disagreement among writers about the defining characteristics of CBE, these include: training to agreed performance standards with expected outcomes explicitly stated to learners; carefully delineated programs which include only skills and knowledge relevant to the immediate training objectives; employment of criterion-referenced rather than normative assessment; and movement from time-based training, characteristic of traditional apprenticeship systems, to outcomes-based concerns. The competency standards involved are perceived by proponents of the approach to be essentially "real world" standards derived from business requirements.

CBE reemerged as an important force in English-speaking countries in adult vocational education through the last decade of the 20th century because of technological, economic and social revolutions and increased international competition from Japan, Germany and the emerging Asian economies that threatened the economic supremacy of English-speaking countries. High youth unemployment then also created the need for quick, political solutions (Wolf, 2002).

The origins of CBE lie in Taylorist principles of scientific management, and more specifically the application of those principles in the war effort to reduce skills shortages in welding, etc. and to produce battle-ready military personnel quickly during the Second World War in the USA (see Kanigel, 1997). The more recent resurgence of CBE is also closely linked to the economic rationalist policies of politicians like Margaret Thatcher in the UK, and hence this approach has ideological dimensions that focus upon cost-cutting and efficiency in achieving outcomes.

In CBE, summative assessment, in the form of outcome standards, dictates procedures adopted including final assessment and the construction of precise learning programs to achieve the stated outcomes. Regardless of the possibilities in theory, in practice little attention is paid to learning processes in CBE curricula, with this resulting more in training than education. Consequently, CBE is frequently referred to as competency-based training (CBT). Michael Collins (1995), among many others, has argued strongly that CBE involves deskilling, and that its behaviorist thrust is a challenge to the lifeworld in that it promotes surveillance and social control while returning educators and learners to authoritarian pedagogic practices.

Collins (1995) has also perceptively noted that CBE can "withstand epistemological analysis of its shortcomings" (p. 86). An essential problem is that it is difficult to argue against effectiveness in learning using only value judgments (e.g., Hager, 1994). The failure of such criticisms to alter governments' CBE policy initiatives necessitates analyses of the practical problems associated with CBE implementation, and failure to achieve desired policy outcomes (Cornford, 2000).

CBE and Some Related Approaches

CBE is related to other approaches such as performance-based assessment and mastery learning, with all these concerned with achieving higher levels of performance. Mastery learning is concerned with the education of individuals until they achieve predetermined standards. It differs from CBE in that there is very considerable attention to the teaching/ learning elements to achieve the desired outcome with less concern about the time and resources needed to achieve this. Essentially there is considerable attention to formative assessment in mastery learning via good teaching, practice and constructive feedback, with this approach largely used in schools. In CBE the emphasis is upon summative assessment, that is assessment to determine the final level of achievement, rather than formative assessment that is concerned with assisting learning through stages towards the final goals.

Performance-based assessment, long used in vocational education and a "parent" of competency-based assessment, requires carefully worded, specific learning outcomes since such precision increases the reliability of assessment. Generally, performance-based assessment has been associated with occupational rather than just job or skill-specific preparation. Drawing upon a broader educational outlook, performance-based assessment has included more sympathetic consideration of future problem-solving skill needs in an occupation, and also specific attention to learning through traditional curricula and formative assessment, than has CBE. All three forms of assessment – mastery learning, performance-based assessment and CBE – have focused upon observable, demonstrable performance as opposed to assessment of theory.

Establishment of Competency Standards

A major problem for CBE is that only very rarely is there one set of standards that is universally recognized across any one industry in any country. Business organizations, motivated by profit and survival in a competitive environment, draw upon a range of different standards internally that can encompass their own enterprise standards, state standards and federal standards depending upon the extent and degree to which there are varying levels of legal compliance and professional regulation. In many trades- or craft-based skill areas there are at least three distinct sets of standards for products or services, with these ranging from high quality through middle standards to low-level, cheap and satisfactory but only for a limited duration (Cornford, 2000). Thus gaining agreement on national standards is very difficult.

There are basically two distinct approaches to a statement of assessment standards in CBE: atomistic and holistic. Atomistic approaches attempt to identify every single element and step or stage in skilled performance. Holistic approaches attempt to overcome the problems of many statements of outcomes, with the attendant need for extensive assessment using detailed checklists, and all statements of outcomes assuming the same relative importance. Holistic assessment focuses more upon the effectiveness of performance overall. It also places more responsibility upon the assessor since all elements relating to standards are not stated explicitly and thus are more subject to individual interpretation. Consequently, holistic assessment encounters more problems with validity and reliability which are reliant on a precise statement of objectives.

Precision of Statements of Competencies and Cognitive and Affective Elements

Other than identification of standards, the exact statement of standards or formulation of criteria for criterion-referenced assessment in CBE is often problematic (see Wolf, 1995), except for relatively simple, performance skills. Historically, earlier statements of standards in CBE were expressed in strictly behavioral terms with these closely allied to the types of skills used in training. However, during the 1950s and 1960s, Bloom and others' work on the Taxonomy of Educational Objectives, incorporating cognitive, psychomotor and affective domains, probably did much to curtail the enthusiasm for CBE.

Cognitive and affective processes, i.e. thinking and emotion, have again been recognized as important elements in effective occupational performance since the 1990s. Partly this is due to changes to the nature of knowledge, skill and work in an increasingly cognitive direction with more widespread use of computers and information technology. Governments now widely recognize the need for thinking, problem-solving and effective communication skills, as any of the sets of core competencies or skills produced in the USA, UK, Canada, Australia, and New Zealand demonstrate.

The inadequacy of the older performance-based statements as competency standards was recognized in the early 1990s, and attempts were made to expand their behavioral nature to include both affective and cognitive elements. However, there are problems in creating competency statements beyond performance levels with these problems not satisfactorily resolved. It is difficult to formulate exact competency standard statements where these involve diverse tastes and opinions, as with aesthetic standards, or involve complex problem-solving with multiple, competing and varying factors, as for example in complex management decision-making. Ethical issues, as important as they are in business, are also difficult to capture in competency standards. Perhaps more importantly, when essentially behavioral competency standards are expended to include cognitive and affective elements, this results in loss of validity and reliability in assessment because the standards become markedly more abstract and less precise (see Cornford, 2000).

Class Bias of CBE

The majority of CBE programs have been developed for lower to middle-level skills and the working class. For example in the health area, programs tend to remain restricted to the para-professional health level, rather than extending to doctors and surgeons. Although there have been attempts to develop competency-based programs for management, these programs have not extended to senior levels. This is not withstanding the fact that the greatest need for competent performance in modern societies arguably lies with political leaders and bureaucrats.

There was a movement to develop higher-order competencies in the mid-1990s but this was relatively short-lived. Apart from the problems of capturing complex judgments and cognitive elements in standards, there were the logical problems of distinguishing between lower and higher-order skills and making value judgments about their relative importance. What may be judged to be a higher or lower-order skill is extremely context and situation-specific. For example everyday language skills, which may generally be assumed as lower-order, can assume great important when a doctor speaking a different language is dealing with a patient presenting as a medical emergency.

Contributions of CBE

The most recent manifestation of CBE has resulted in a decidedly mixed legacy. Employment of CBE has resulted in benefits for lower-level skills where the objectives are specifically concentrated upon performance rather than cognitive outcomes, or where inadequate standards existed previously. A more substantial legacy is the tendency for assessment objectives to be stated explicitly to learners early in education/training programs. However, the degree of incorporation of CBE by business into workplace training, with business intended to be the chief beneficiary, is relatively low as can be judged by the limited research available. There also appears to have been limited use made by business of competency assessment in promoting individuals and awarding wage increments.

A serious concern is that there has been a remarkable reluctance of governments that have adopted CBE, as a major plank in vocational education policies, to commission and publish results of evaluations of CBE policy effectiveness. This is despite the facts that economic rationalist ideology was supposedly about economic benefits and accountability, and the huge amounts of public money that have been spent on trying to revolutionize vocational education systems. Generally, evidence to date suggests that the CBE policies have not been effective on a number of levels (Cornford, 2000; Wolf, 2002). Although research comparing current and past standards is problematic, in addition to qualitative and anecdotal evidence, in Australia there is empirical evidence that skill standards in some trade areas have declined under CBT policy (Mills & Cornford, 2002).

There is an intrinsic weakness in the use of competency standards for program design and assessment regardless of the variations in policies and approaches adopted. Competency standards do not contribute in any substantial way to formative assessment and learning through different skill and knowledge levels before the ultimate, summative assessment. The CBE movement has generally ignored important curriculum issues, and also theory and research from the areas of skill learning and the development of expertise since these bodies of literature point to the importance of time and the quality of teaching and learning in the attainment of substantial skills.

See also: evaluation, portfolio, program planning, training.

References and Further Reading

Collins, M. (1995). Critical commentaries on the role of the adult educator: From self-directed learning to postmodernist sensibilities. In M. R. Welton (Ed.), *In defense of the lifeworld* (pp. 71–97). Albany, NY: State University of New York Press.

Cornford, I. R. (2000). Competency-based training: Evidence of a failed policy in training reform. *Australian Journal of Education, 44*, 135–154.

Hager, P. (1994). Is there a cogent philosophical argument against competency standards? *Australian Journal of Education, 38*, 3–18.

Kanigel, R. (1997). *The one best way: Frederick Winslow Taylor and the enigma of efficiency*. New York: Penguin.

Mills, H., & Cornford, I. (2002). A preliminary exploration of the knowledge/skills of third year metal trades apprentices after the introduction of CBT. *Australian Vocational Education Review, 9*(2), 24–30.

Wolf, A. (1995). *Competency-based assessment*. Buckingham, UK: Open University Press.

Wolf, A. (2002). *Does education matter? Myths about education and economic growth*. London: Penguin.

Ian R. Cornford

Conscientization

Conscientization is before all a pedagogical practice in adult education, and as such inseparably linked to the name of Paulo Freire (1921–97; see Freire, 1971, 1994, 1998a, 1998b). Philosophically, conscientization is rooted in a combination between Marxism and Enlightenment, which, translated into pedagogy, means that individuals become aware, or must be made aware, of the social and political conditions in which they exist. Adult education is thus identical to social and political awareness-raising.

The Philosophical Roots of Conscientization

Freire's conceptualization of conscientization can be traced back to three different intellectual roots, namely Roman Catholic humanism, Marxism, and German philosophy. The very origin of Freire's thinking must be located in Christian Personalism (e.g., Maritain, Bernanos, Marcel, Mounier, and the Brazilian Ataide), into which he later incorporated critical theory (e.g., Marcuse, Fromm). With this combination, he thus perfectly fits into the emerging intellectual movement in Latin America called liberation theology, which constitutes a form of "political theology." The writings of the young Marx form another basis of Freire's analysis, and consequently he conceives pedagogy as a way of educating for liberation. For Freire, critical consciousness, or *concientizaçao* (conscientization) is basically the critique of the false consciousness, or critique of ideology in Marxist terms. It is via Marxism that Freire accessed the German tradition of existentialism, and especially phenomenology, sharpening his thinking about language. Indeed, language, according to this tradition, is not neutral but rather conveys a certain culturally transmitted worldview, and as such is much more than a simple means of communication. Rather, language is directly linked to culture. Through language, one can both question and strengthen culture. Freire incorporated this view into his liberation pedagogy, which might also be seen as a way of becoming aware and transforming the dominant and oppressive culture through questioning the language it imposes upon us. Freire's conscientization thus takes place in a situation of oppression. Yet, influenced by critical theory and phenomenology, Freire is less interested in physical or institutional oppression, than in cultural and internalized oppression.

Following Marcuse and Fromm, Freire pays particular attention to language and worldviews, which are manipulated and manipulating, leading to the internalization of the oppression, i.e., ultimately leading to the oppressed identifying themselves with their oppressors. Freire's liberation pedagogy is thus a cultural action or process towards liberation. As such, it has two phases, namely critical consciousness (conscientization) and critical praxis. Conscientization is the process by which a group (class) becomes aware of their cultural oppression, of their "colonized mentality," and by doing so discover that they have a popular culture, a political identity and a societal role. Conscientization is in itself a liberatory process, as one is freed from self-depreciation. It is important to mention that, for Freire, the oppressors must be considered, as they also must become aware of their dehumanizing situation, which maintains injustice. But, as a second phase, conscientization requires "critical praxis." Such praxis is not a revolutionary seizure of power from the oppressors; rather, it is a peaceful intervention in order to develop alternatives. Developing such alternatives must include the oppressors by transforming unjust power relationships through dialogue.

Freire's Pedagogical Practice

Freire implemented his ideas through adult literacy programs with the rural populations who had immigrated to the north-east of Brazil from the newly industrialized cities. But for him, literacy work was embedded in a much broader political program, aimed at addressing issues of rural development and immigration. Freire's literacy programs taught people to read and to write, and at the same time to become aware of their internalized cultural oppression. This was done through the selection of literacy subjects, pertinent to the people and related to their existential issues. There was therefore a political intention, conscientization being the hidden agenda of literacy (see Freire & Macedo, 1987).

Freire's pedagogical model takes people from a situation of "magical consciousness" – where people are not able to analyse their situation (they are "voiceless") – to a stage of "naïve consciousness" – they recognize their oppressors, but are afraid of them – to "critical consciousness." This is the stage when people envision the possibility of acting upon the situation, and ultimately take concrete steps towards such action. Critical consciousness therefore encompasses two elements, namely (a) a critical understanding of society and culture within which people live; where the relevant question is: What is our oppression situation? Critical consciousness also implies (b) a comprehension of peoples' capacity to change the situation; where the relevant question is: What is our capacity to influence this situation?

According to Freire there are four distinct steps in leading a group of people from naïve consciousness to critical consciousness:

- The *investigation of the thematic universe* of the people. In this first step, external researchers investigate the language and culture of the people, in order to understand their cultural universe.
- The *identification of the generative themes*. In this second step, this thematic universe is being structured collectively by the people, distinguishing between the roots causes and the symptoms, which are simply the expressions of the root causes.
- The *codification of generative themes*. In this third step, particularly relevant root causes are selected and translated into meaningful themes. For each of these so-called generative themes a collection of relevant expressions or sentences is developed, through role play, drawings, posters, theatre, and other activities.
- The *dialogue within the cultural circle*. This is the final, yet most important step of Freire's liberation pedagogy. Here the previously developed expressions or sentences are being codified. In other words, they are being decomposed into their basic elements. Their pronunciations and ways of writing are being identified, the goal being to get at the most meaningful words for that particular group of people. The cultural circle is where *literacy* and critical consciousness actually take place.

Critical Appreciation of Liberation Pedagogy

Without doubt Freire is one of the greatest authors of adult education. In addition to his life committed to the cause of the disenfranchised, he has left an important body of work which has become the object of numerous dissertations, books, and critical discussions. Freire stresses the collective dimension of learning, especially in his cultural circle: it is collectively that people not only solve problems, but moreover transform their socio-political conditions. Freire's approach is anti-authoritarian yet politically and ideologically oriented. Even if he does change the wording over time – for example from "conscientization" to "dialogical critical consciousness," or from "revolution" to "radical democracy" – ultimately the "true" path is known by the animator. It is the animator who knows the "overall vision which has to be always retained" (Freire & Faundez, 1989, p. 123). To be fair, this is the problem of the entire Enlightenment education project. Nevertheless, it is possible to challenge, today, the assumption of class coherence and a common oppressor, which are however the pedagogical instruments Freire works with. More generally, one can argue that in fact Freire confuses epistemology (i.e. learning) and politics (i.e. freedom from oppression). In Freire's theory and praxis epistemology and politics mix (learning to be free from oppression), which is at the same time adult education's greatest strength and identity and its greatest conceptual weakness. This is even more so because Freire remains unspecific about the concrete action or result of the pedagogical praxis: on the one hand he clearly rejects revolution and violence, i.e. a violent revolt in order to seize power from the oppressors and to establish a proletariat dictatorship, convinced as he is that the oppressors must also undergo a learning process. But on the other hand, his suggestions for alternatives remain unspecific beyond acknowledging that it has to be political. This might be viewed as an strength, i.e. there is no "one" solution, and the solution has to be invented by the people given their particular situations, but it might also be seen as a weakness, where liberation pedagogy might simply not be able to live up to peoples' expectations.

See also: andragogy, critical theory, emancipatory education, popular education, problematizing learning, transformative learning.

References and Further Reading

Freire, P. (1971). *Pedagogy of the oppressed.* (M. R. Ramos, Trans.) New York: Herder & Herder.

Freire, P. (1994). *Pedagogy of hope.* (R. R. Barr, Trans.) New York: Continuum.

Freire, P. (1998a). *Pedagogy of freedom: Ethics, democracy and civic courage* (P. Clarke, Trans.). New York: Rowan and Littlefield.

Freire, P. (1998b). *Pedagogy of the heart* (D. Macedo, Trans.). New York: Continuum.

Freire, P., & Faundez, A. (1989). *Learning to question: A pedagogy of liberation.* (T. Coates, Trans.) New York: Continuum.

Freire, P., & Macedo, D. (1987). *Literacy: Reading the word and the world.* South Hadley, MA: Bergin & Garvey.

Matthias Finger

Continuing Education

Within the broad rubric of adult education, the term continuing education refers, somewhat awkwardly, both to education that is pursued beyond the period of one's formal education and to the non-degree credit education that is offered by degree-granting institutions. Continuing education counts as its students those working adults who are in some way continuing their educational efforts on a part-time basis. At times, and in certain jurisdictions, continuing education is also referred to as further education, extension education, community education, or recurrent education. It is now well-understood, in this era of lifelong learning, that adults continue their learning not only after completing their initial education, training, or baccalaureate degrees, but also during their work lives and into retirement.

In North America and some parts of Europe, the term continuing education, or continuing higher education, is used most frequently to describe institutionalized provision of ongoing opportunities for adults' personal and professional growth. These programs are generally offered by faculties, schools, or centers for continuing education that are attached to, or housed within, formal post-secondary institutions. Large school boards may also offer continuing education programs. The strength of continuing education programs lies in their emphasis on academic and theoretical foundations and use of highly-skilled instructors. Continuing education "units" offer a wide range of programs that usually include liberal arts courses, language study, fine arts, personal development, and perhaps travel courses. In addition, large providers of continuing education may offer programs of professional development in the areas of business management, managerial and supervisory practice, human resources, accounting, health or wellness, safety, adult education, social services, project management, construction, or engineering sciences. Where unique economic opportunities exist – for example, Alberta's oilfields – continuing education units may work collaboratively with private or public sectors to offer programs that accommodate workplace demands through certification in training or safety standards.

Continuing education may take place using distance education formats if learners are separated geographically from their instructors. Before the advent of communication technologies, correspondence education might have served as a vehicle for continuing education opportunities for some adult learners.

Many continuing education units offer non-degree credentials such as certificates, diplomas, or citations. In some cases, credits from continuing education courses are transferable to degree-level study. Courses, designed for maximum accessibility by working adults, are scheduled in innovative and flexible ways – on weekends, evenings, and in short, intense bursts of 2 or 3 days. Continuing education courses usually have no formal entry requirements beyond being an adult. Since the recent introduction of communication technologies into delivery formats, programs are also offered online and in mixed mode, using blended models that combine face-to-face attendance with web-based platforms.

The History of Continuing Education

Adults have been engaged in organized adult and continuing education activities for centuries. The term "Socratic method," in fact, derives from the system of discourse practiced by Socrates and his followers as they furthered their own education through discussion. More recently, continuing education in North America has taken its shape from practices in Europe, specifically Great Britain and the Scandinavian countries.

In Britain, the industrial era gave rise to institutions such as the YMCA, Mechanics' Institutes, and the Workers' Educational Association (WEA). These agencies provided the burgeoning working class with opportunities for education that was social, personal, and professional. Young men who left their farm homes seeking employment in urban areas were able to learn social skills and engage in constructive personal activities at the YMCA. They received scientific and technical information related to their trades from the network of Mechanics' Institutes that sprang up across the country.

University extension education, originating from both Oxford and Cambridge universities in England, served as a major influence on the development of modern continuing education in North America. Following the British model, early universities in urbanized central Canada reached out to rural populations by offering lectures on "university-type" subjects (Selman, 1994). This lecture-based form of extension education was not well-suited to the evolving North American society and was eventually supplanted by a second, more successful model of continuing education called the Wisconsin Model, after initiatives begun by the University of Wisconsin in 1907. Instead of relying on exporting traditional academic lectures to populations beyond the university, extension educators "devised other ways of serving the educational needs of adult citizens – correspondence instruction, audio-visual devices of various kinds, short courses and workshops, information pamphlets, [and] traveling 'field' men" who were experts in their content areas were some of the ways in which knowledge was taken *to* the people (Selman, Cooke, Selman, & Dampier, 1998, p. 39).

Another pioneering model of continuing education was the early to mid-20th century Chautauqua movement, where cavalcades of entertainers and educators traveled across the country setting up their tents in rural areas. "Chautauquas" took their name from the late-19th century Chautauqua Institute, centered in upstate New York, which was best-known for its work with correspondence education – the print-based, "first generation" of distance education.

Continuing Education as a Reflection of Society

Institutions of continuing education developed as mechanisms through which citizens could access educational programs for personal or professional enhancement. In the past, especially in times of conflict or war, nations exhibited increased dependence on adult and continuing education to educate individuals in issues of citizenship and democracy. The 1919 Report of the British Ministry of Reconstruction (Adult Education Committee, 1919) exhorted men and women to take up their responsibilities as citizens through renewed education. Denmark's folk high schools emerged mid-19th century amid that country's political-economic disasters and its fall from power that resulted from losses in its war with Prussia.

In North America, continuing education experienced a golden age through the mid-20th century, and many notable continuing education organizations were founded by men and women of vision: Moses Coady's cooperatives of Antigonish, Adelaide Hoodless's Women's Institutes, Alfred Fitzpatrick's Frontier College, the Banff Centre, Myles Horton's Highlander Institute, and John Grierson's National Film Board. In times of growth and civil unrest, these agencies of continuing education gave voice to social and emancipatory pedagogies.

In the 1960s, rapidly-growing populations made it necessary to dramatically expand post-secondary systems, and, with the creation of new community colleges, continuing education efforts become increasingly institutionalized. Changing social and economic contexts led to the demise of grassroots institutions such as the National Farm Forum, and a rising sense of professionalism, first noticeable in the 1950s, supported a growing awareness of credentialing which was in turn supported by increased population and new job markets. The effect, overall, made it more possible for adults to avail themselves of opportunities for continuing education in academic, vocational, and general education areas (Selman et al., 1998).

In the 1990s, however, shifting fiscal policies, combined with an enhanced need for training in increasingly competitive economies, resulted in a noticeable shift in continuing education's priorities. "An increased emphasis on accountability and assessment in business, government, and educational institutions focuses learning and teaching on things measurable and transferable" (Fenwick, 2000, p. 54). Continuing education units in Canada and the United States struggled to maintain their existence as they were forced to adopt cost-recovery status. Philosophically, continuing educators debated the tension between responding to community needs and becoming profit centers.

Foreshadowing similar reflections on continuing education issues by Haughey (1998) and Lauzon (2000), McLean (1996) noted that "although a strong sense of social responsibility still pervades much university continuing education in Canada, social and institutional changes are making politically and community-oriented educational practices more difficult to undertake" (p. 9).

The Practice of Continuing Education

As a result of economic changes and fiscal restraint in the last decade, many Canadian universities have dramatically reorganized, or even disbanded, their continuing education units. In traditional postsecondary systems that value research and scholarship, those still engaged in continuing education often describe themselves as marginalized or disempowered. Arising from mandates that define them as providers of non-degree credit education to working adults, their administrative and financial structures are often unique within their institution. While continuing education units may include academic or professorial faculty, the majority of their staffs are managerial in nature, organized to design, develop, market, deliver, and assess programs and courses that are required to be revenue-producing.

Continuing education's historic commitment to enhancing the quality of working adults' personal and professional lives demands academic expertise, business acumen, and environmental sensitivity. Successful continuing education units must respond quickly to societal and workplace demands by providing high-quality and relevant programming. To do so, continuing education management maintains close ties with community, using environmental scanning techniques and advisory committees to guide programming decisions. Continuing education courses are often staffed by instructors who are hired from the workplace because of their specific expertise in content areas. The autonomy afforded some continuing education units because of contract hiring and unique governance assists them in serving community needs while at the same time reinforcing their separation from other more traditional parts of post-secondary institutions.

Many continuing education units also provide contract training to clients within the public and private sectors. Incorporating a consulting function into their operations assists them in creating revenue that in turn sustains their ability to offer a variety of courses to the general public.

See also: career education, continuing professional education, extension, higher education, professional development, training, workshops.

References and Further Reading

Adult Education Committee, Ministry of Reconstruction. (1919). *The 1919 Report: The Final and Interim Reports of the Ministry of Reconstruction*. London: His Majesty's Stationery Office.

Fenwick, T. J. (2000). Adventure guides, outfitters, firestarters, and caregivers: Continuing educators' images of identity. *Canadian Journal of University Continuing Education, 26*(2), 53–77.

Haughey, D. (1998). From passion to passivity: The decline of university extension. In S. M. Scott, B. Spencer, & A. M. Thomas (Eds.), *Learning for life: Canadian readings in adult education* (pp. 200–212). Toronto: Thompson Educational.

Lauzon, A. (2000). University extension and public service in the age of economic globalization: A response to

Thompson and Lamble. *Canadian Journal of University Continuing Education, 26*(1), 79–96.

McLean, S. (1996). Continuing education and the postmodern arts of power. *Canadian Journal of University Continuing Education, 22*(2), 7–26.

Selman, G. (1994). Continuing education and the Canadian mosaic. In M. Brooke & M. Waldron (Eds.), *University continuing education in Canada: Current challenges and future opportunities* (pp. 4–18). Toronto: Thompson Educational.

Selman, G., Cooke, M., Selman, M., & Dampier, P. (1998). *The foundations of adult education in Canada* (2nd ed.). Toronto: Thompson Educational Publishers.

Dianne Conrad

Continuing Professional Education

Continuing professional education (CPE) refers to the education of professionals subsequent to their preparatory or pre-professional education that continues throughout their careers (Queeney, 2000). The underlying assumption of CPE is that practicing professionals (i.e., those whose practice is based upon a specific body of knowledge and skills) must engage in ongoing learning activities in order to maintain their competence. This assumption has remained fairly consistent since its introduction in North America during the 1960s. However, the concept of CPE defined in the literature, as well as who is responsible for its provision, has evolved considerably over the past few decades. Houle's (1980) idea was that CPE is essentially "learning that advances from a previously established level of accomplishment to extend and amplify knowledge, sensitivities and skill" (p.77), to be generally provided in formal workshop settings by institutes of higher education, or professional associations. Since then, the concept has expanded to currently encompass non-formal and self-directed "lifelong" professional learning activities that are generally situated within the professional's own workplace (Roscoe, 2002; Spikes, 1995).

This evolving view of CPE raises critical questions in terms of its content (i.e., what must a competent professional know, and know how to do?) and context (i.e., who is responsible for keeping professionals up-to-date and competent?) (Mott, 2000). Closely related to these are questions dealing with motivation (i.e., how can professions keep members up-to-date?), delivery (i.e., where/how does advanced educational technology play a role?), and relationship to aligned fields of practice, such as human resource development, career development, and workplace learning.

Key Questions

1. *"What must a competent professional know, and know how to do?"* Nowlen (in Mott, 2000) describes three models of CPE that have emerged in North America as the "update," "competency," and "performance" models. The "update" model springs from an information-deficit view of CPE that assumes that professional knowledge is a commodity consisting of externally provided information used in practice. The "competency" model, also primarily a deficit view, assumes that this externally created knowledge/information must be supplemented with profession-

specific skills, professionally appropriate personal traits, and a self-image that is consistent with the values and norms of the profession in question. The third "performance" model both encompasses and moves beyond this individualistic focus to acknowledge the relevance of the professionals' complex network of interdependent multiprofessional teams, as well as forms of interventions (Mott). This most recent conceptualization of CPE has transformed the question from "what should the professional know?" to the broader question of "what is the profession all about?" (Mott). At the same time, this transforms CPE from a primarily knowledge and skill-development focus to a more dynamic "constructivist" and "transformative" learning focus (Daley, 2000). This latter view emphasizes authentic, practice-based, collaborative, and future-oriented expertise (Mott).

2. *"Who is responsible for keeping professionals up-to-date?"* When CPE was initially acknowledged as critical to the credibility, as well as growth, of practicing professionals, the same institutions of higher education that were developing and providing pre-professional (or pre-service) education became the key developers and providers of CPE (Queeney, 2000). CPE within this context consisted of formally structured and centrally located classes taught by academics or accredited professionals within a time-limited period. To a large extent, this is still the case in North America today, but a number of economic, institutional and social changes/trends have contributed to a much more diverse picture of CPE in terms of who is responsible for keeping professionals up-to-date, as well as a major shift in the location and form of CPE.

   Today, the responsibility for CPE is shared amongst three key stakeholders: the individual professional; the professional body that accredits/regulates him/her; and her/his employer. Also, CPE activities now take place in a number of diverse settings.

   - *The individual professional.* The "new employment contract" between employer and professional employee means that today's professional practices more as an independent contractor whose value to an employer depends upon her/his ability to stay current in the field (Patton & McMachon, 1999). This requires that professionals take responsibility for deciding what they need to learn, when they need to learn it, and where to best learn it. This is true for both salaried and contract professionals, as post-industrial North America increasingly depends on up-dated "knowledge workers" to keep the economy growing and individual industries/organizations globally competitive (Collins & Young, 2000). Professionals, who are also increasingly becoming free agents/contractors in the global economy, now view CPE as a critical component of their career development and success and professional knowledge as something that they can take with them wherever they go (Arthur & Peiperl, 2000; Watkins, 1995).

- *The professional body*. Today, professional bodies share the responsibility for keeping professional members up-to-date by offering annual conferences and occasional CPE workshops to their members, or by contracting with institutions of higher education to develop and deliver formal CPE programs to their members.
- *The employer*. While the "new employment contract" between employers and professional employees essentially transfers responsibility for CPE onto the shoulders of individual employees, an increasing number of employers recognize the importance of "investing in" these employees to the tune of several billions of dollars in the US economy (somewhat less in the Canadian economy) (Doyle, 2000). As a result, today the proportion of CPE that occurs in the workplace far exceeds that offered by institutions of higher education, or professional associations. Also, the form that CPE takes in the workplace is typically "just-in-time" information-giving or skill-training sessions conducted by workplace learning specialists, self-directed learning modules available through advanced technology, or non-formal learning projects devised and undertaken by employees during and after work hours (Spikes, 1995).

Secondary Questions

1. *"How does the profession keep its members up-to-date?"* One key issue emerging in the literature related to motivating professionals to keep up-to-date has to do with the motivating influence of "professional communities of practice" (Wenger, 1998). While not a new phenomenon, the importance of such "communities" regarding CPE arises from the new employee–employer contract shifting the professional's career development from within the more narrow employing organization, to the broader external field of professional practice (Parker & Arthur, 2000). As professional careers become increasingly boundaryless (i.e., no longer bound to one organizational setting but spanning several) keeping up-to-date becomes a critical career-development issue. In addition, CPE is becoming a basis for professional re-licensure within many fields of practice in the USA (Cervero, 2000).
2. *"Does advanced communication technology have a role to play in CPE?"* The increasing use of distributed forms of communication is greatly influencing "where" CPE takes place. No longer are professionals limited to time and place-specific forms of CPE offered face-to-face (Carchidi, 2002). Now, they are able to access CPE via audio, video and computer conferencing during any time of the day or week. With one's workplace increasingly becoming one's laptop (Watkins, 1995), professionals are finding it easier to access CPE via the internet in a form that best matches their

individual learning needs and goals (King, 2003). Also, the Internet provides them with a valuable tool for keeping in touch with their "community of practice," a critical (and often unrecognized) vehicle for keeping up-to-date in the field (Parker & Arthur, 2000).

Fields of Practice Related to CPE

Adult education theory and practice forms the original foundation underlying CPE (Brookfield, 1990; Knowles, 1980; Merriam & Caffarella, 1999). Today, CPE is being enriched by aligned fields of theory and practice, primarily human resource development, career education and development and workplace learning.

Human resource development (HRD) practice, situated within organizational settings, is a field of practice primarily based on organizational development theory (Doyle, 2000). HRD departments typically custom design and deliver "just-in-time" learning to meet the organization's development goals, as well as those individual professional employee's career development needs that complement these goals.

Career development is a field of practice that focuses on enabling an individual to meet her/his career goals from pre-professional education to the end of one's engagement in the world of work (Patton & MacMachon, 1999). As such, it encompasses CPE at many points along this lifelong journey, influencing in a fundamental manner its nature, direction, and timing. Today, this field of theory and practice is changing from a solely individual focus to a much more complex interactive and systemic view that recognizes the multiple factors involved in managing one's career in a complex global economy.

Workplace learning, a newly emerging field of theory and practice, is at the intersection of adult education and human resource development practice and theory (Peterson & Provo, 2000). It is the dynamic interplay between organizational and individual needs that provides the foundation for this new field (Bratton, Calder, & Gold, 2001) which occurs within the workplace. Dymock's (2003) model of lifelong learning in the 21st century views adult education methods applied to an understanding of the modern workplace (i.e., HRD) as key to professionals' abilities to meet their company's strategic development goals and stay competitive in today's global marketplace.

The newly evolving view of CPE as informed by these three related fields of theory and practice transforms the question "what should the professional know?" to the broader "what is the profession all about?," enlarging its scope and nature to become lifelong and transformative. This view of CPE as lifelong throughout a professional's entire career is supported by its move from traditional institutions of higher education to the workplace (Lawler & King, 2003), as well as the demands of the new employment contract (Collins & Young, 2000).

The transformative aspect of CPE is supported by this shift from a static to dynamic activity fuelled by critical self-reflection, and the continuous revising of one's perspective on practice (Daley, 2000). This view of professional practice as continually "socially constructed and re-constructed" is one in which the self-reflective professional transforms his/her perspective through the ongoing application of professional knowledge to practice. Such dynamism underlies Daley's concept of CPE as "learning how to learn" about what one's profession is all about.

See also: career education, professional development, training, workshops.

References and Further Reading

Arthur, M. B., & Peiperl, M. A. (2000). Continuing the conversation about career theory and practice. In M. A. Peiperl, M. B. Arthur, R. Goffee, & T. Morris (Ed.), *Career frontiers: New conceptions of working lives* (pp. 273–281). Oxford, UK: Oxford University Press.

Bratton, J., Calder, K., & Gold, J. (2001). An integrative framework for work-related learning. Paper presented at the Researching Work and Learning Conference, Calgary, Alberta.

Brookfield, S. D. (1990). *Understanding and facilitating adult learning*. San Francisco: Jossey-Bass.

Carchidi, D. M. (2002). The virtual delivery and virtual organization of postsecondary education. In Altbach (Ed.), *Studies in Higher Education*, Dissertation Series. New York: Routledge.

Cervero, R. M. (2000). Trends and issues in continuing professional education. In V. M. Mott & B. J. Daley (Eds.), *Charting a course for continuing professional education* (pp. 3–12). *New Directions for Adult and Continuing Education*, No. 86. San Francisco: Jossey-Bass.

Collins, A. C., & Young, R. A. (2000). *The future of career*. Cambridge, UK: Cambridge University Press.

Daley, B. J. (2000). Learning in professional practice. In V. M. Mott & B. J. Daley (Eds.), *Charting a course for continuing professional education* (pp. 33–42). *New Directions for Adult and Continuing Education*, No. 86. San Francisco: Jossey-Bass.

Doyle, M. (2000). Managing careers in organizations. In A. Collins & R.A. Young (Eds.), *The future of career* (pp. 228–242). Cambridge, UK: Cambridge University Press.

Dymock, D. (2003). Towards a model of lifelong learning in the workplace. Paper presented at the 3rd International Conference on Work and Learning, University of Tampere, Finland.

Houle, C. O. (1980). *Continuing learning in the professions*. San Francisco: Jossey-Bass.

King, K. P. (2003). Learning the new technologies: Strategies for success. In K. P. King & P. A. Lawler (Eds.), *New perspectives on designing and implementing professional development of teachers of adults* (pp. 49–57). *New Directions for Adult and Continuing Education*, No. 98. San Francisco: Jossey-Bass.

Knowles, M. S. (1980). *The modern practice of adult education: From pedagogy to andragogy* (2nd ed.). New York: Cambridge Books.

Lawler, P. A., & King, P. K. (2003). Challenges and the future. In K. P. King & P. A. Lawler (Eds.), *New perspectives on designing and implementing professional development of teachers of adults* (pp. 83–91). *New Directions for Adult and Continuing Education*, No. 98. San Francisco: Jossey-Bass.

Merriam, S. B., & Caffarella, R. S. (1999). *Learning in adulthood: A comprehensive guide* (2nd ed.). San Francisco: Jossey-Bass.

Mott,V. W. (2000). The development of professional expertise in the workplace. In V. M. Mott & B. J. Daley (Eds.), *Charting a course for continuing professional education* (pp. 23–31). *New Directions for Adult and Continuing Education*, No. 86. San Francisco: Jossey-Bass.

Parker, P., & Arthur, M. B. (2000). Careers, organizing and community. In M. A. Peiperl, M. B. Arthur, R. Goffee, & T. Morris (Eds.), *Career frontiers: New conceptions of working lives* (pp. 99–121). Oxford, UK: Oxford University Press.

Patton, W., & McMachon, M. (1999). *Career development and systems theory: A new relationship*. Pacific Grove, CA: Brooks Cole.

Peterson, S. L., & Provo, J. (2000). A case study of academic programme integration in the USA: Andragogical, philosophical, theoretical and practical perspectives. *International Journal of Lifelong Education, 19*(2), 103–114.

Queeney, D. S. (2000). Continuing professional education. In A.Wilson & E. Hayes (Eds.), *Handbook of adult and continuing education* (pp. 375–391). San Francisco: Jossey-Bass.

Roscoe, J. (2002). Continuing professional development in higher education. *Human Resource Development International*, *5*(1), 309.

Spikes, W. F. (1995). Preparing workplace learning professionals. In W. F. Spikes (Ed.), *Workplace learning* (pp. 55–61). *New Directions for Adult and Continuing Education*, No. 68. San Francisco: Jossey-Bass.

Watkins, K. E. (1995). Workplace learning: Changing times, changing practices. In W. F. Spikes (Ed.), *Workplace learning* (pp. 3–16). *New Directions for Adult and Continuing Education*, No. 68. San Francisco: Jossey-Bass.

Wenger, E. (1998). *Communities of practice: Learning, meaning, and identity*. Cambridge, UK: Cambridge University Press.

Faye Wiesenberg

Co-operative Education

The idea, or ideal, of *co-operative education* is related to formal or non-formal education processes that aim to develop co-operative human beings from an ethical, political, economic, social or even intellectual point of view. This generic concept of co-operative education can be, and is in fact, related to historically contextualized policies and practices of education that are quite different from each other. One could identify, for instance: (a) co-operative education associated with self management and a solidarity-based economy, that emerged from the emancipatory working-class struggles in international history, and whose main reference is the Co-operative Movement; (b) *Toyotist* co-operative education, related to the development of people able to act co-operatively in order to attend to the demands of the current Japanese restructured workplace in capitalist firms; (c) co-operative education related to preparing human beings to accept different cultures and people and, also, to develop a co-operative relationship with nature in times of (self) destruction of humanity and the planet; (d) cognitive co-operative education in distance education, which takes place in virtual learning environments, as another possible variation and, also, (e) the co-operation between employers and universities to place students in firms to develop practical skills. This is also labelled, formally, co-operative education.

Co-operative Movement and Education

Co-operative education associated with self-management and a solidarity-based economy played a key role in the emergence of the Co-operative Movement. This movement – struggling to create co-operatives as associations of people working together, as owners of the means of production aiming to produce and distribute consumer goods – emerged in the 19th century in Great Britain and, since the beginning, has taken co-operative education as one of its principals and considered it as a *sine qua non* for the success of co-operatives:

> Co-operatives provide education and training for their members, elected representatives, managers and employees so they can effectively contribute to the development of their co-operatives. They inform the general public – particularly young people and opinion leaders – about the nature and benefits of co-operation. (ICA News, 1995, n. p.)

In countries of the South, the reemergence of economic activities based on self-management and solidarity brings together, consequently, the demand for co-operative education. In Latin America the theory and practice of the popular education tradition enriches it. From this perspective, knowledge is conceived as a historic and social praxis and dialogue is assumed as a critical (and radical) epistemological and pedagogical perspective, more than a didactic method, aiming to contribute to people's emancipatory goals.

Contemporary co-operative education, in this conceptual context, also integrates theoretical references related to environmental education to help people to run co-operatives from an economically and socially sustainable development perspective. Another important aspect here is that educational programmes include a demand for critical understanding of the *work*, as a social and cultural fact and as a concept within capitalism, as a key analysis that workers must make to help in their struggle to create another kind of work relations and culture in and for co-operatives.

> Co-operation: an attitude and a practice of "operating with" in order to reinforce work and not capital; to develop solidarity; to be able to share the collective results of the work; to construct knowledge collectively and democratically and develop people's attitudes to co-operation.

Co-operative Education in the Toyotist Workplace

Under current Toyotist workplace rules, workers work co-operatively in a very different way than they used to under a Taylorist working routine. Working in times or cells and as partners in the pursuit of a firm's strategic goals is a current practice in several work environments; workers are openly referred to as "partners" rather than "workers." Employers demand that formal and non-formal education programmes for children and adults integrate co-operative education in the curricula to prepare workers to perform in this new environment.

> Co-operation: an attitude and a practice to "operate with" to augment capital; co-operation is in permanent tension with competition and individualism.

Co-operative Education for a New World Order

We have seen the emergence of education proposals that we have also labelled as co-operative education or education for co-operation. Here we categorize educational proposals and practices oriented to the contemporaneous worldwide agenda in which there is a claim, at least at the discourse level of progressive forces in society, for people around the planet to relearn to live together as human beings and with nature; to recognize and respect each other's cultural perspectives, the "other"; to co-operate and develop solidarity with those socially, politically, culturally and economically excluded people. The political and educational aims and programs, identified by the traditional co-operative movement and by the new forms of economy based on the value of solidarity, tend to be incorporated or, on the reverse side, incorporate, the theoretical and political framework of the new social movements including in the educational process gender, ecological and race issues, and the attitude and practical forms of networking (O'Sullivan, 1999).

Co-operation: attitudes and practices of "operating with" the development of a sustainable society based on the utopia of solidarity. Networking is a key element.

Co-operative Education in Virtual Learning Environments

Co-operative education based on co-operative learning in virtual learning environments assumes co-operation as a central attitude and competency for a collective construction of knowledge. Piaget, the well-known cognitive psychologist and Vygotsky the theoretician from the social-historic school of psychology are icons who have contributed indirectly to this theoretical perspective of co-operative education, which seeks to overcome the limited idea of interaction in the educational goals of Internet use. Some tools used in this perspective are electronic mail, newsgroups, webchat, conferences via TV and the www.

Co-operation: attitude and practice of "operating with," networking, for the development of collective knowledge.

Co-operative Education: Partnership Between University and Firms

Co-operative education is also used to refer to forms of collaboration between firms and universities in order to create opportunities for students to learn professional practical skills, as part of their academic curricula. This is sometimes called work-based learning.

Co-operation: attitude and practice of firms and university "operating with" each other to educate new professionals.

In conclusion, to be educated in and for the experience of co-operation means to have developed and to be open to develop in practice values, attitudes and competencies for co-operation. One could identify the main competencies for co-operation as: to be able to associate with, to manage something or someone and to self-manage, to communicate, to transfer ideas, learning or other things, to run one's own business, among others. Therefore, co-operation means to be, or to become, able to work with, to dialogue with, to write with, to think with, to decide with, to participate and network. It is a condition to create another model of society based on solidarity or, from a very different perspective, to be functional and to meet the demands of the contemporary restructured capitalist firms. Therefore, it is an integral part of formal and non-formal adult education programmes and strategies.

See also: action learning, collaborative learning, community education, peer learning, problem-based learning, work-based learning.

References and Further Reading

Holland, C., Frank, F., & Code, T. (1998). *Literacy and the new work order: An international literature review*. Leicester: National Institute of Adult Continuing Education.

ICA News (1995). Statement on the Co-operative Identity. Retrieved on June 22, 2004 from the International Co-operative Information Center websit http://www.wisc.edu/uwcc/icic/orgs/ica/pubs/ica-news/1995/5-6/index.html, No. 5/6.

O'Sullivan, E. (1999). *Transformative learning: Educational vision for the 21st century*. Toronto: OISE/UT in association with University of Toronto Press, and London/New York: Zed Books.

World Association for Cooperative Education: http://www.waceinc.org/

Maria Clara Bueno Fischer

Creativity

In adult education, the term creativity is used to identify all those activities that aim to help adults to become involved in the creative process, and this involves the communication of meaning. This distinguishes them from those activities which are sometimes concerned solely with making (cookery, gardening, dressmaking, woodwork). Adult education classes which adopt a "how to do it" approach are considered not to be concerned with the development of creative ability. This is because the creative act is about someone making a statement which involves their own particular view of or reaction to the world they inhabit.

Classes concerned with the development of creativity are also distinguished from those classes which use the arts as a method to achieve non-arts learning outcomes in, say, health education and political education.

The term creativity is associated with the Arts and it is recognized that definitions of the Arts are culturally determined. In this respect, as with aesthetic education, the cultural context can be defined in terms of ethnicity, socio-economic class, age, location and historic period. Thus we can identify the cultural values of Asian working-class youth in Bradford in the 1960s. Other defining characteristics of a culture such as gender and disability are problematic but not excluded. Cultures, then, are quite small and located in a particular geographical area at a particular period in time. The idea of European culture becomes impossible when one tries to identify what values, beliefs and behaviors the peoples of Europe are supposed to share.

In most 20th-century cultures, definitions of the Arts usually include the visual arts (including photography and performance art), music, dance, theatre (including film and television drama) and literature. Here, no distinction is made between so-called popular and classical forms of these arts. In some cultures, circus and acrobatics are also included. Adults engage with these arts as either creative artists, performers or as audiences for the arts. For many years the creative act was shrouded in mystique and it was believed that an individual had to be born talented in order to work as a creative artist. Nowadays it is understood that the skills and behaviors required to operate creatively can be learned, given the motivation to do so.

How is Creativity Recognized?

Much research into the nature of creativity was engendered by the Cold War and the Space Race when, after the Russians had launched the first Sputnik, the Americans decided they needed more creative scientists. There was a spate of research in the 1960s into creativity, but not much empirical work has been done since then. The research and writing on creativity falls into one of three categories. There are those who see creativity as a quality of a work of art, those who see it as an aspect of personality, and those who see it as a process (Jones, 1988, pp. 73–89).

The research which identifies creativity as a quality of a work of art was carried out mainly by Child (1970, pp. 390–404). According to this argument, the attribution that a work of art is or is not creative depends on our being able to identify objectively its aesthetic value. Child attempted to demonstrate that objective aesthetic value exists by measuring agreement amongst individuals in aesthetic preference. His findings were inconclusive and one is forced to assume that, to date, we are not able to demonstrate that either aesthetic value or creativity can be established as an objectively identifiable quality of a work of art. This conclusion challenges the notion of the canon of great and good work, an argument rehearsed more fully in the entry on aesthetic education.

Those researchers who see creativity as an aspect of personality usually conceptualize it as a problem-solving operation. What is tested is the ability to find novel solutions to problems set by the researcher. Such tests of creativity were devised so that scores on these tests might be correlated with scores on tests of other aspects of personality. There was generally a consensus amongst researchers in this area that the creative personality was independent, able to tolerate disorder or chaos, tolerant, occasionally rebellious and energetically committed. It was not possible to establish any correlation between creative ability and intelligence as measured on IQ tests.

Researchers who see creativity as a process have attempted to identify and analyse the nature of that process. Maslow (1968, pp. 135–145), using a Freudian model, saw it as an aspect of self-actualization and identified three types of creativity, Primary, Secondary and Integrated.

- *Primary creativity* was located in the Freudian "primary processes" and concerned dreams, myths, legends, fantasies. It was the stuff of daydreams, and concerned images and symbolic forms.
- *Secondary creativity* was located in the secondary processes and concerned the more cognitive and intellectual activity of design. It was about designing bridges, houses, cars and other manufactured items.
- *Integrated creativity* occurred when primary and secondary creativity worked together; when the images arising from the primary processes were organized within a designed structure. It was this type of creativity which educators saw as relating most closely to their educational goals.

With the development of this conceptual framework, adult educators began to see their task as developing creative ability rather than technical proficiency. They were also concerned to develop levels of perceptual acuity as well as an individual and novel approach to the use of a chosen medium. They were not concerned to teach adults a particular way of using the medium, but rather to give them the confidence to find their own way of exploiting the potential of that medium. The acquisition of knowledge about the nature of the creative process and about the arts in general was also seen to be important.

Creative Ability

As more research into the nature of the creative process was carried out, the task of the adult educator was further clarified. In Freudian terms, the process involved both conscious and unconscious processes. In some cultures these unconscious processes are seen as spiritual in nature, relating to dreamtime or states of transcendant meditation.

It was also noted that the process engenders anxiety states (May, 1975) and part of the creative capacity is the ability to tolerate these anxiety states. Anxiety grows mainly from unconscious activity where the creator feels that the work is out of control, not subject to a conscious effort to organize. As many artists have stated, it feels as though the work has a life of its own, not subject to the will of the creator. Ehrenzweig (1968) identified a paranoid-schizoid phase to the creative process, where individuals feel out of control and unwilling to trust their unconscious processes to organize the apparent chaos before them. They have to resist the temptation to throw their work away and start again. This ability to cope with these feelings and continue with the work is seen as being of the utmost importance.

This obviously creates problems for adult educators, particularly in non-vocational adult education where many of these creativity classes take place. Adult students become concerned about their anxiety states and, rather than seeing them as a positive indicator that they are really working creatively, see them as a symptom of possible failure. This is an area of adult education where enabling students to work at an unconscious level, to trust their instincts and to give up conscious control of their work is of paramount importance. It is not an intellectual activity where participants can consciously work out what to do next. Often, against all their instincts, adult students have to be persuaded to stop thinking about what they are doing. Only in this way can the unconscious primary processes take over and generate the metaphorical images which are central to the creation of a work of art.

Students surprise themselves. They create works which are outside their previous experience. They do not always like what they produce and have to be persuaded of its value. Often they would like to paint, compose or write like an artist they admire. They have to be persuaded to value their own creative work.

In adult education courses, arts centers, community arts projects, arts laboratories and other venues where creative arts classes take place, it becomes important to prepare students for the trials which lie ahead. There is a case for discussing the nature of creative activity at the beginning of each course so that students understand, at a cognitive level, what is happening to them. This does not mean that they will avoid these anxiety states, but at least they will realize that they are an indicator of real creative involvement.

See also: aesthetic education, learning festivals, journal writing, writing.

References and Further Reading

Child, I. L. (1970). The problem of objectivity in esthetic value. In G. Pappas (Ed.), *Concepts in art and education* (pp. 390–404). New York: Macmillan.

Ehrenzweig, A. (1968). *The hidden order of art*. London: Weidenfield & Nicolson.

Jones, D. (1988). *Adult education and cultural development*. London and New York: Routledge.

Maslow, A. H. (1968). *Towards a psychology of being*. New York: Van Nostrand Reinhold Co.

May, R. (1975). *The courage to create*. London: Collins.

David James Jones

Critical Multiculturalism

Critical multiculturalism is a term used to distinguish forms of multicultural education that specifically focus on challenging power relations based on *social structures* of race or culture, gender, class, etc. and on challenging the "isms" that result from those power relations, as in rac*ism* or sex*ism*. The term *critical* multiculturalism, or more accurately, *critical multicultural education*, is meant to distinguish it from those "multicultural education" approaches that simply focus on individual differences, but never deal directly with challenging systemic racism, sexism, heterosexism, classism, and so on. Within the field of adult education, the discourses of critical multicultural education draw on the discourses within the grade school or more general education theory literature that deals with challenging power relations based on social structures of race, gender, class, sexual orientation, religion, language, national origin, and disability. These discourses include many of the emancipatory education discourses including critical pedagogy, feminist pedagogy, queer pedagogy, resistance postmodernism, and postcolonial pedagogies. Like most emancipatory education discourses, all of these have the work of Paulo Freire (1970), that gave rise to critical pedagogy, as one theoretical strand as well many of the race or culture-based or anti-racist educational theories (Darder, Torres, & Baltodano, 2002; Gay, 2000) at their root. These multiple theoretical influences are evident in the work of the contributing authors in recent edited texts dealing with these critical multicultural pedagogies (Banks & Banks, 2001; Darder et al., 2002; May, 1998; Sleeter & McLaren, 1995). Some authors refer to these discourses specifically as critical multiculturalism when discussing the confluence of these pedagogies, whereas others use the term "revolutionary multiculturalism" (McLaren, 1997), and the black feminist writer bell hooks (1994) uses the term radical or engaged pedagogy.

To gain a better understanding of the *critical* multicultural education discourses, it is helpful to have some understanding of the development and use of this term. As suggested above, some versions of the term "multicultural education" simply focus on cultural differences from an individual's perspective without attention to power differentials based on race, ethnicity or culture; other approaches focus very specifically on challenging power relations. Building on their earlier work, Christine Sleeter and Carl Grant (see Grant & Sleeter, 1999; Sleeter, 1996) identify five different approaches to multicultural education that are in use by educators who have somewhat different epistemological assumptions and different implicit definitions of what "multicultural" means. They note that these approaches include: (a) teaching the culturally different; (b) using a human relations approach; (c) employing single group studies; (d) utilizing "the multicultural education" approach; and (e) engaging in education that is multicultural and social reconstructionist.

As discussed elsewhere (Tisdell, 1995), some of the differences in underlying assumptions are that the first two approaches tend to be more individual and psychological, and more or less accept the epistemological grounding that has traditionally been operative in K-12 education based on the belief that knowledge is neutral. There is no real attention to who is represented in the curriculum, or who determines what counts as knowledge, or the power relations that may have shaped the knowledge-production process. More particularly, the educational emphasis of the "teaching the culturally different" approach is on how to educate culturally different "others" to assimilate and be more successful in the dominant culture, rather than on challenging or changing the system. The "human relations approach" has similar underlying assumptions but focuses more on helping people of different cultural groups learn to live together harmoniously, particularly as individuals, from a psychological perspective. The emphasis is the development of interpersonal communication skills to reduce prejudice and to create understanding among human beings, by promoting positive feelings and attitudes that students have about themselves and others as members of various racial, ethnic, gender or cultural groups; but again, there is no real direct attention to how unequal structural power relations have shaped society or direct discussion of racism. An assumption underlying this approach is that students learn better in an environment that promotes individual and psychological safety among its members.

Grant and Sleeter's (1999) last three approaches – single-group studies approaches, what they refer to as "the multicultural education" approach, and the social reconstructionist approach – focus more on social structures and emphasize the significance of power relations in shaping the knowledge production and dissemination process. These last three approaches collectively are termed critical multicultural approaches because of their focus on power relations, and are based on the assumption, as hooks (1994) observes, "no education is politically neutral" (p. 37). Single-group studies approaches, rather than focusing on several groups at a time, focus more on the detailed historical, social, and cultural experience of one particular group to promote an in-depth understanding of the educational needs of that group, such as African Americans, American Indians, gays and lesbians, or people with disabilities. The curriculum is based on the work of members of the particular group and the way knowledge is defined in their own communities. Single-group studies approaches are equivalent to some of the pedagogies discussed in adult education that focus on a particular group, such as queer pedagogy which focuses on the experience of gays and lesbians; Africentric teaching approaches and "culturally relevant" approaches tend to focus on the educational needs of a particular cultural group, while trying to challenge power relations based on race or culture that have shaped the lived realities of members of that race or cultural group.

By contrast, the multicultural education approach examines power relations of multiple groups from a comparative perspective, while the social reconstructionist approach blends a comparative perspective with direct strategies for social change. In the reconstructionist approach, not only is knowledge seen as political, it also emphasizes that participants themselves can and should take control in challenging the way knowledge has been defined, constructed, and disseminated. While most critical multicultural education discourses would consider the *intersections* of multiple social structures of race or culture, gender, class, sexual orientation, national origin, language and disability, all the critical multicultural discourses would use race or culture as a social structure as the *primary* unit of analysis. Whereas in critical pedagogy class has been primary, and in feminist pedagogy, gender has been primary, in critical multicultural education race or culture are primary, but not to the exclusion of other social structures such as language or disability.

See also: activism, conscientization, critical theory, cultural studies, difference, problematizing learning, social movement learning.

References and Further Reading

Banks, J., & Banks, C. (2001). *Multicultural education* (4th ed.). San Francisco: Wiley.

Dardar, A., Torres, R. D., & Baltodano, M. (Eds.) (2002). *The critical pedagogy reader*. New York: Routledge Falmer.

Freire, P. (1970). *Pedagogy of the oppressed*. (M. B. Ramos, Trans.) New York: Continuum.

Gay, G. (2000). *Culturally responsive teaching: Theory, research, and practice*. New York: Teachers College Press.

Grant, C., & Sleeter, C. (1999). *Turning on learning: Five approaches to multicultural teaching plans*, (2nd ed.). San Francisco: John Wiley.

hooks, b. (1994). *Teaching to transgress: Education as the practice of freedom*. New York: Routledge.

May, S. (Ed.). (1998). *Critical multicultralism: Rethinking multicultural and antiracist education*. London: Taylor & Francis.

McLaren, P. (1997). *Revolutionary multiculturalism: Pedagogies of dissent for the new millennium*. Boulder, CO: Westview.

Sleeter, C. (1996). *Multicultural education as social action*. Albany, NY: State University of New York Press.

Sleeter, C., & McLaren, P. (Eds.). (1995). *Multicultural education, critical pedagogy, and the politics of difference*. Albany, NY: State University of New York Press.

Tisdell, E.J. (1995). *Creating inclusive learning environments for adults: Insights from multicultural education and feminist pedagogy*, Information Series No. 361. Columbus, OH: ERIC Clearinghouse on Adult, Career, and Vocational Education. Retrieved January 1, 2004, from ERIC database (ERIC Document Reproduction Service No. ED384827).

Elizabeth J. Tisdell

Critical Theory

Critical theory defines a critical look at the existing reality from an abstract social position of truth and justice. It refers to a particular tradition of Marxist German philosophy which was prominent during the 1930s up to the 1980s, and as such is associated with names such as Theodor Adorno, Walter Benjamin, Max Horkheimer, Erich Fromm, Ernst Bloch, Herbert Marcuse, and Jürgen Habermas. Though educational considerations can be derived from critical theory, this tradition has no direct pedagogical implications; critical theory has mainly become important in the field of adult education because a series of authors have referred to it. In the 1980s, adult educators such as Brookfield (1991, 1995) and Mezirow (1991) used the concepts of "critical thinking," to refer explicitly or implicitly to critical theory. Sometimes Paulo Freire and his approach to conscientization is also placed in the context of critical theory, even though this is not entirely accurate.

What is Critical Theory?

Critical theory is grounded in German idealist thought (e.g., claims on reason and truth), including Marxism. Critical theorists believe in the emanicpatory powers of reason (*Vernunft*), and oppose it to its diminished version of rationality (*Rationalität*). They are/were preoccupied with the study as well as the actual influence of the evolution of society towards "reasonable" institutions, creating ultimately the conditions for a true, free, and just life.

The main idea of critical theory is that there exists an objective or independent vantage point from which a social critique can be formulated.

Reason, so-to-speak, can serve as an objective vantage point against which society can be compared and critically judged. The early critical theorists considered this vantage point to be located in the very humanness, i.e., the humans' capacity to reason, know, and understand. Second-generation critical theorist Jürgen Habermas somewhat narrowed this vantage point to science and language (i.e., the fact that human languages allow for rational reasoning). It is from this vantage point that critical theorists felt entitled to criticize the evolution of society as they saw it unfolding, i.e., mainly the Second World War and the process leading up to it. They interpreted this evolution as symptomatic of the contradictions of capitalist society preventing both society and individuals from the potential of emancipation.

As a matter of fact, critical theorists mainly identified and criticized the obstacles to emancipation, yet offered few solutions, even though they claimed to be simultaneously concerned with interpretation (philosophy) and transformation (action) (e.g., Held, 1980). More precisely, critical theorists offered two pedagogically relevant approaches towards emancipation, namely (a) critical theory or the critique of society and its evolution, including the critique of the role of education in perpetuating non-emancipatory institutions, and (b) critical thinking, by which they meant the process of reasoning critically, so as to become aware of the non-emancipatory institutions. It is this second approach which translated during the 1980s and the 1990s into critical pedagogy. The first approach, instead, was mainly used by sociologists of education in order to critique educational practices and institutions.

History of Critical Theory

Critical theory can be divided into at least two generations, both of which are directly relevant for education (Jay, 1973). The first generation is constituted by Marxist German intellectuals who gathered in the 1920s around the Institute for Social Research at the University of Frankfurt. They were basically concerned with a political-cultural understanding of fascism. How was it possible that fascism arrived? And they interpreted fascism not as an accident of history but rather as a perversion of the entire Enlightenment project (e.g., Adorno & Horkheimer, 1944). They further asked how it was possible that the proletariat (the subject of revolution) supported Hitler? Again, they did not answer by simply saying that the masses were alienated and manipulated. Instead, they embarked on a complete revision of Marxism trying to update it through a new analysis of contemporary society, analyzing the emergence of mass culture, as well as the commodification of art and culture (Fromm, 1941; Marcuse, 1964). The basic idea was that there were new, much more subtle, and culturally deeply embedded ways of domination from which humanity had to emancipate itself. These ways of domination further cemented economic domination. Consequently, a much more radical negation of the dominant system and a much deeper form of critical reflection was needed in order to free humanity, a reflection which would even question what the system presented as a fact, namely instrumental rationality. The only direct pedagogical contribution here stems from Adorno.

The second generation of the Frankfurt school is constituted by the late Fromm and Marcuse in the

United States, but especially by German philosopher Jürgen Habermas (born 1929). All three wrote under the very optimistic impression of the New Left (Europe) and counter-cultural movements (USA). Habermas now tries to locate the emancipatory potential within language and discourse, especially in his seminal book *A Theory of Communicative Action* (1984). In a nutshell, Habermas tries to reaffirm the possibility of a critical reason against what he calls the "colonization of the lifeworld" by instrumental reason (McCarthy, 1978). His is an attempt to outline a rational theory of emancipation, conceived as a cognitive consciousness-raising process among socially interacting individuals. This approach has been picked up by educational philosophers and turned into what has since become "critical pedagogy."

Critical Pedagogy

Indeed, educators have quickly identified Habermas' critical theory, especially his theory of communicative action, and tried to translate it into critical pedagogical practice. This is especially the case in Germany, where many authors have taken up Habermas' ideas and translated them into educational consciousness-raising tools or theories. In the English-speaking language area the translation of Habermas into critical pedagogy was more indirect and passed through his disciples Bernstein (1985), Fay (1987), and others, mainly during the 1970s. Particularly well-known promoters of such critical pedagogy are Michael Apple (1996), Stanley Aronowitz and Henry Giroux (1993), Wilfred Carr and Stephen Kemmis (1986), Henry Giroux (1997), and Ira Shor (1992).

More concretely, the theory and practice of critical pedagogy means to lead individuals, and not groups, along a process of critical reasoning, to become aware of the non-emancipatory structures in which they are caught. Such structures can be both institutions and worldviews, of which individuals can be made critically aware. Thus critical pedagogy has two meanings, namely (a) the fact of being or becoming aware of non-emancipatory institutions and worldviews, which is a form of ideology critique, and (b) the process of reasoning critically, which is a form of awareness-raising. It is exclusively this second meaning which has been retained in the field of adult education.

Critical Adult Education

Indeed, during the late 1980s and 1990s, critical pedagogy also translated into what has come to be called "critical adult education." Again, critical adult educators, or rather adult education theorists, were mainly influenced by Habermas, yet many of them ground their thinking in plain Marxism. Well-known adult education authors inspired by Marxism and critical theory are Susan Collard, Phyllis Cunningham, Ramon Flecha, Mechthild Hart (1992), Michael Collins (1991), and Michael Welton (1995). Given the American context within which these authors write, they focus mainly on the process of critical thinking, as opposed to ideology critique. This is particularly the case of adult education professors Jack Mezirow and Stephen Brookfield who both mixed critical thinking together with pragmatism.

In general, the main problem with both critical adult education and critical pedagogy is that there is little practice and much theory. Critical pedagogy and critical adult education is therefore mainly a discourse about the importance and the necessity of "becoming critical" (Carr & Kemmis, 1986). It is a discourse that often leaves practitioners frustrated, as it focuses on the very process of so-called critical thinking, as opposed to the substance to which such critical thinking should be applied.

See also: conscientization, critical multiculturalism, critical thinking, problematizing learning, theory, transformative learning.

References and Further Reading

Adorno, T., & Horkheimer, M. (1944). *Dialectic of enlightenment*. New York: Social Studies Association.

Apple, M. W. (1996). *Cultural politics and education*. New York: Teachers College Press.

Aronowitz, S., & Giroux, H. (1993). *Education still under siege*. Westport: Bergin & Garvey.

Bernstein, R. J. (Ed.). (1985). *Habermas and modernity*. Cambridge, MA: MIT Press.

Bottomore, T. (1984). *The Frankfurt School*. London: Tavistock Publications.

Brookfield, S. D. (1991). *Developing critical thinkers: challenging adults to explore alternative ways of thinking and acting*. San Francisco: Jossey-Bass.

Brookfield, S. (1995). *Becoming a critically reflective teacher*. San Francisco: Jossey-Bass.

Carr, W., & Kemmis, S. (1986). *Becoming critical: Education, knowledge and action research*. London: Francis & Taylor.

Collins, M. (1991). *Adult education as vocation: A critical role for the adult educator*. New York: Routledge.

Fay, B. (1987). *Critical social science*. Ithaca, NY: Cornell University Press.

Fromm, E. (1941). *Escape from freedom*. New York: Farrar & Rinehart.

Giroux, H. (1997). *Pedagogy and the politics of hope: theory, culture and schooling*. Boulder, CO: Westview Press.

Habermas, J. (1984). *The theory of communicative action* (2 Vols.). Boston: Beacon Press.

Hart, M. (1992). *Working and educating for life: Feminist and international perspective on adult education*. New York: Routledge.

Held, D. (1980). *Introduction to critical theory: Horkheimer to Habermas*. London: Hutchinson.

Jay, M. (1973). *The dialectical imagination: The history of the Institute of Social Research and the Frankfurt School 1923–1950*. Boston: Little, Brown & Co.

Marcuse, H. (1964). *One-dimensional man: Studies in the ideology of advanced industrial society*. Boston: Beacon Press.

McCarthy, T. (1978). *The critical theory of Jürgen Habermas*. Cambridge, MA: MIT Press.

Mezirow, J. (1991). *Transformative dimensions of adult learning*. San Francisco: Jossey-Bass.

Shor, I. (1992). *Empowering education. Critical teaching for social change*. Chicago: University of Chicago Press.

Welton, M. R. (Ed.).(1995). *In defense of the lifeworld: Critical perspectives on adult learning*. Albany, NY: State University of New York Press.

Matthias Finger

Critical Thinking

Critical thinking is a continuous learning process comprising four interrelated processes: (a) the experience of questioning and then replacing or reframing an assumption, or assumptive cluster, which is unquestioningly accepted as representing dominant commonsense by a majority; (b) the experience of taking a perspective on social and political structures, or on personal and collective actions, which is strongly alternative to that held by a majority; (c) the experience of analysing commonly held ideas for the extent to which they perpetuate economic inequity, deny compassion, foster a culture of silence and prevent adults from realizing a sense of common connectedness; and (d) the taking of informed democratic action grounded in well-researched assumptions. Understood in this way critical thinking is a reflexive habit, a stance towards the world in which the deconstruction of ideas and practices for the interests they serve becomes second nature. In adult education the concept is a contested idea, one with a confusing variety of meanings and indicators informed by different intellectual traditions – ideology critique, psychoanalysis and psychotherapy, analytic philosophy and logic, and pragmatism (Allman, 2001; Brookfield, 1991; Mayo & Thompson, 1995; Mezirow and Associates, 1990).

Ideology critique, the first tradition, is a term associated with thinkers from the Frankfurt School of critical social theory. It describes the process by which adults learn to recognize how uncritically accepted and unjust dominant ideologies are embedded in everyday situations and practices. Critical thinking conceived as ideology critique focuses on helping people come to an awareness of how capitalism shapes social relations and imposes – often without our knowledge – belief systems and assumptions (i.e., ideologies) that justify and maintain economic and political inequity. Since capitalism will do its utmost to convince us that we should live in ways that support its workings, we cannot be fully human unless we use critical thought to unearth and challenge the ideology that justifies this system. Critical thinking in this perspective involves people learning how ideology lives within them as well as understanding how it buttresses the structures of the outside world that stand against them.

A second more psychoanalytically and psychotherapeutically inclined tradition within adult education emphasizes critical thinking as the identification and reappraisal of inhibitions acquired in childhood as a result of various traumas. Using the framework of transformative learning, theorists emphasize critical thinking as the process whereby adults come to realize how childhood inhibitions serve to frustrate them from realizing their full development as persons. This realization is the first step to slaying these demons, laying them to rest, and living in a more integrated, authentic manner.

A third tradition shaping how critical thinking is understood is that of analytic philosophy and logic. Here critical thinking describes the process by which we become more skillful in argument analysis. In this tradition we act critically when we recognize logical fallacies, when we distinguish between bias and fact, opinion and evidence, valid and invalid inference, and when we become skilled at using different forms of reasoning (inductive, deductive, analogical, etc.). This kind of relentless critique of unexamined and possible faulty assumptions is represented by the principle of falsifiability. From this perspective, to be critical is to be skilled at conceptual analysis, at deconstructing others' assertions and at recognizing false inferences and logical fallacies. The analytic philosophy tradition comprises a set of valuable, even essential, intellectual functions, but it focuses on cognitive processes to the neglect of social and political critique.

A fourth tradition informing critical thinking is that of pragmatism, which emphasizes the role people play in constructing their own experiences and meanings in a world that can be shaped and reshaped by human intervention. The goal of pragmatism is to use whatever means possible to bring about beautiful consequences. In adult educational terms it is associated with creating democratic classrooms, with democracy privileged as a beautiful social form. In its search for democratic beauty, pragmatism rejects universal truths and focuses instead on the variability of how people make idiosyncratic interpretations of their experience and the different approaches they take to build democracy. Elements of this tradition have filtered, via the work of Eduard Lindeman (1961), into adult education's concern with helping people understand their experience, and with the field's preference for experiential methods. In Myles Horton's (1990) renowned work at Highlander a largely pragmatist approach was allied with a tradition of ideology critique to help activists realize that their own experience – properly analysed in a collaborative but critical way – could be an invaluable resource in their fight for social justice. Critical thinkers informed by the pragmatic tradition are those who strive to extend participatory democracy in all spheres of their lives while not being tied to any methodological template to accomplish this.

Understanding the Process

The process of critical thinking usually begins with an event that points out a discrepancy between assumptions and perspectives that explain the world satisfactorily, and what happens in real life. When people get fired with no notice after spending decades working loyally for a company, when marriages fail after people have faithfully followed the rules for successful relationships, or when open and democratic processes are encouraged in organizations and then sabotaged by those same people encouraging them, adults start to question the assumptions by which they have lived their lives and to scrutinize these assumptions for their accuracy and validity. During this process of scrutiny, alternative perspectives on thought or action that are embedded in alternative assumptions start to suggest themselves. The final phase of the cycle (which keeps on repeating itself as we go through more experiences characterized by depth, breadth, and intensity) is the taking of informed action. Informed action is action that is grounded in an accurate assessment of the context in which the action is placed, so that the anticipated consequences of the action are as close as possible to those that actually occur. Action, as understood here, includes cognitive action as well as behavioral.

In developmental psychology a body of literature argues that a propensity for critical thought is a distinctively adult capacity not extensively found in children and adolescents (Sinnott, 1998). Critical thinking occurs as adults pass through experiences in their interpersonal, work and political lives that are characterized by breadth, depth, diversity and different degrees of intensity that only comes with time. We cannot critically scrutinize the validity of our unquestioned assumptions about interpersonal relationships, work and politics until we have lived through the building and decay of several intimate relationships, until we have felt the conflicts and pressures of workplaces, and until we have acted politically and lived with the consequences of our political actions. How can we assess the truth of rules we learned in childhood regarding relationships, work and politics, until we have experienced directly these complex, contradictory and ambiguous realities? According to this interpretation of adulthood, what is distinctive about adult learning is the search for meaning in these realities, and the process by which critically reflective capacities are developed in this search.

A number of different concepts inform this understanding of critical thinking. The concept of dialectical thinking is at the center of one cluster of theorizing on adult reasoning (Basseches, 1984), and is described as a form of general reasoning in adulthood in which universalistic and relativistic modes of thought coexist. Its essence is the continuous exploration of the interrelationships between general rules and contextual judgments. Contradictions and discrepancies between these two modes of thought are regarded as opportunities for creative development, for the development of increasing inclusiveness, differentiation and integration.

In terms of a theory of critical thinking in adulthood, the relevance of the cluster of concepts with dialectical thinking at its center is clear. The contextual contradictions and ambiguities of adult life – in particular the discrepancies between uncritically assimilated norms governing relationships, work and politics and our experience of these complex realities – impel us to find meaning and create order in the midst of this confusion. We become attentive to the importance of context and the validity of situational or relativistic reasoning, while at the same time committing ourselves to those values and general beliefs we find most valid for our experience. Adult life is marked by learning how to fuse universal logic with the pragmatic constraints of relationships, work and community involvement. Adults become aware of how context alters the neat application of rational logic, of how the rules of reasoning learned at earlier stages of life are reinterpreted and contextualized because of their experience of the complexities of adult life.

A second cluster of concepts informing understandings of the critical thinking process focuses on the ways adults develop a critical awareness of the oppressive features embedded in existing political arrangements (Newman, 1994). The overarching concept for this process is that of emancipatory learning interpreted as the process by which adults learn to free themselves from oppressive social structures and constraining ways of thinking. The process leads to a more accurate and authentic view of reality, in which adults see through the distortions of media images and common-sense rules, to understand that education systems, like all other social structures, serve the interests of a dominant class. In emancipatory learning people realize that "natural" givens, "obvious" truths and commonly accepted values are part of a set of dominant cultural values, the purpose of which is to maintain oppressive social structures.

Advocates of emancipatory learning tend to envision a dualism of oppressor and oppressed, of all-powerful, omniscient demagogues who, through a subtle manipulation of education, church and media (or a brutal torturing of dissidents), keep the mass of people in a state of cognitive and emotional stupefaction, a culture of silence. This dualistic paradigm inevitably erects a model of the liberatory educator as one who has a more authentic and accurate view of the prevailing, oppressive reality, and who has a duty to awaken learners from their intellectual slumbers. The role of the educator as animateur of critical consciousness is central to this concept. The confident claims to accurate perceptions of reality made by some proponents of this approach, and the arrogance regarding the apparent gullibility or ignorance of working people embedded within these claims, has done some damage to the prospects for making this view of learning accessible to a wide number of practicing educators. Nonetheless, it has served to focus attention on the centrality of values to all educational activities, and made it harder to assert that adult education is solely concerned with technique and with the provision of whatever learners say they need in the most effective way possible.

A third cluster of concepts relating to critical thinking in adulthood has evolved within the field of adult education research, and, as such, represents one of the few attempts to develop theoretical propositions about adult learning which does not rely on perspectives drawn from an allied discipline. The central component here is learning to learn, defined as the capacity adults possess of becoming self-consciously aware of their learning styles and being able to adjust these according to the situations in which they find themselves (Tuijnman & Van Der Kamp, 1992). Fundamental to the concept is some form of epistemological awareness; that is, a self-conscious awareness of how we come to know what we know and an ability to appraise the accuracy of the grounds for truth that undergird the assertions and practices to which we subscribe. This is often described as epistemic cognition.

Considerable differences exist regarding the facilitation of critical thinking. Those subscribing to a critical thinking as ideology critique position emphasize the role of the teacher as a necessary trigger to critical analysis. If learners are hoodwinked by dominant ideology and unable to escape the tentacles of hegemony, then their ability to challenge and contest these forces depends partly on skilled educators confronting them with these uncomfortable realities. The psychotherapeutic and psychoanalytic traditions also privilege the role of the therapist or analyst. Again, the responsibility of these professionals is to help adults understand the forces inhibiting their development and take steps to respond to these. Both the ideology critique and psychotherapeutic schools emphasize the importance of action in critical thinking. The circle of critical praxis is not closed until adults take action to challenge ideology, contest hegemony or confront inhibitions.

Although the analytic philosophy position also emphasizes the teacher's role, the importance of action receives less emphasis in this tradition. Or, perhaps more accurately, cognitive action is viewed as an end in itself. A critical thinker here is one who thinks more clearly, not necessarily one whose life or actions have any connection to such thought. The greatest emphasis on method is found in the pragmatic tradition since this values experimentation so highly. Pragmatist critical thinkers are consistently seeking new perspectives, new practices and new approaches to developing this capacity. In particular they link the facilitation of critical thinking to the development of democratic, participatory learning communities. Such communities are held to be inclusive and diverse and therefore to encourage the widest range of perspectives possible.

Several criticisms are leveled at the literature on critical thinking in adult education. One concerns the Eurocentric bias of the research and theoretical base. The most cited authorities are all White, European and male and the samples informing their theorizing are overwhelmingly White Anglo-Americans. Additionally, critical thinking elevates a Western form of cognitive, rational knowing above other forms of comprehension. There is little attention to affect, to emotion, to spirituality, to holistic modes of being and knowing and little consideration of how critical reflection can be triggered through aesthetic experiences, meditation, and contemplation. Books such as *Women's Ways of Knowing* (Belenky, Clinchy, Goldberger, & Tarule, 1986) have also argued that critical thinking is mostly conceived in a masculinist way as an exclusionary, inherently skeptical form of separate knowing. The recent upsurge of postmodernist thought has also questioned the linear, developmental manner in which narratives of adult critical thinking are often presented. Finally, the literature of critical thinking has been criticized for its overly exclusionary language which intimidates many of those same learners it seeks to help. Despite these criticisms, the idea of critical thinking continues to hold a powerful sway on adult educators' imaginations.

See also: critical multiculturalism, critical theory, emancipatory education, transformative learning.

References and Further Reading

Allman, P. (2001). *Critical education against global capitalism: Karl Marx and revolutionary critical education*. Westport, CT: Bergin and Gravey.

Basseches, M. (1984). *Dialectical thinking and adult development*. Norwood, NJ: Ablex Publishing.

Belenky, M. F., Clinchy, B. M., Goldberger, N. R., & Tarule, J. M. (1986). *Women's ways of knowing: The development of self, voice, and mind*. New York: Basic Books.

Brookfield, S. D. (1991). *Developing critical thinkers: Challenging adults to explore alternative ways of thinking and acting*. San Francisco: Jossey-Bass.

Horton, M. (1990). *The long haul: An autobiography*. New York: Doubleday.

Lindeman, E. C. L. (1961). *The meaning of adult education*. Montreal: Harvest House (first published by New Republic, 1926).

Mayo, M., & Thompson, J. (Eds.). (1995). *Adult learing, critical intelligence and social change*. Leicester, UK: National Institute for Adult Continuing Education.

Mezirow, J., and Associates. (1990). *Fostering critical reflection in adulthood: A guide to transformative and emancipatory learning*. San Francisco: Jossey-Bass.

Newman, M. (1994). *Defining the enemy: Adult education in social action*. Sydney, Australia: Stewart Victor Publishing.

Sinnott, J. D. (1998). *The development of logic in adulthood: Postformal thought and its operations*. New York: Plenum Press.

Tuijnman, A., & Van Der Kamp, M. (Eds.). (1992). *Learning across the lifespan: Theories, research, policies*. New York: Pergamon.

Stephen Brookfield

Cultural Learning

Cultural learning refers to the unique capacity of human beings to link their individual minds together through communication to form intersubjective learning entities (communities of practice) that are capable of forms of cognition that are beyond the ability of any single person. While adult educators have yet to fully incorporate the implications of cultural learning ideas for the theory and practices of their field, learning theorists throughout the social sciences are recognizing the profound impact of cultural learning for our species.

While a capacity for cultural learning has had long phylogenetic preparation in human evolution, the full emergence of this capacity is widely believed to be of relatively recent origin. According to Michael Tomasello, a leading cognitive development researcher who has investigated the learning capacities of both primates and of human children, while our closest primate relatives share many cognitive capacities possessed by humans, they do not display a crucial facility for cultural learning. It is this capacity that has enabled humans to produce and reproduce sophisticated and meaningful cultures; develop intricate social systems; forge distinct, dynamic and autonomous personal identities; and coordinate complex social actions.

The capacity for cultural learning hinges on our unique human tendency and ability to identify with and understand other humans as intentional beings. This capacity, which extended existing primate capacities to form representations of ourselves as intentional beings, first emerged in humans between 40,000 and 100,000 years ago and, according to Tomasello (1999), normally develops in each new member of our species between 9 and 12 months of age. A key requirement of cultural learning is being able to represent another person as someone like oneself who sees the world from an alternative perspective and with their own goals or intentions. With this capacity, human beings can enter into learning relationships with each other within which they can forge common interpretations of the world. As these interpretations are taken up in subsequent moments of cultural learning they are renegotiated, reproduced and elaborated to form increasingly complex patterns of cultural order that can extend over vast regions of time and space.

One of the great advantages of the capacity of cultural learning is that humans are able to share and learn from the experiences of each other. Being able to understand another person as intentional like oneself makes it easier to learn new skills from them. It is possible, for instance, to discern that there is a *reason* why a person should hold the rock in such a manner while crushing seeds. Being able to share joint attention with another person makes it possible for someone to see the world through their eyes and with their goals. In this fashion, skills learned by one human over a lifetime need not be reinvented by members of a succeeding generation. Cultural learning enables people, not only to see the actions of the experienced member but to understand the meaning and purpose of these actions in meeting the member's goals.

Another key element of cultural learning theory is the *cultural artifact*. Artifacts form when humans negotiate shared meanings for an object or event that are incidental to the material affordances of that object or event. For instance, two humans can reach an understanding that a particular object is the possession of one of them. There is nothing inherent in the object that would make this so. The object is an artifact because it signifies something to both people, it has meaning because both people agree it does.

The important feature of cultural artifacts is that they can be used symbolically. Meanings attached to elements of the material world under direct control of intentional humans (a person's own gestures or vocalizations, for example) can be drawn upon in intersubjective contexts to negotiate subsequent meanings. The capacity of humans for cultural learning has made it possible for us to develop verbal and non-verbal systems of communication. Over time, humans have built up extensive systems of symbols that can be chained in endlessly varied ways to enable increasingly sophisticated, complex and abstract cultural representations.

In order to sustain cultural learning processes, humans must engage one another in contexts that permit shared joint attention. According to learning theorist, Etienne Wenger, cultural learning transpires when people share a focus of attention (or joint enterprise), when they have opportunities to participate in a process of negotiating new understandings, and when they possess a shared history that provides a common stock of shared interpretations that they can use to reach these new understandings. For the most part, the conditions required for cultural learning are easily met in the face-to face-contexts of everyday life. The existence of complex cultural tools in these contexts – conversational protocols, story-telling conventions, rites and rituals, symbolic objects and edifices, and so forth – further magnify the power of cultural learning processes.

Wenger (1999) identifies three simultaneous effects of cultural learning in "communities of practice" (his term for the intersubjective contexts of cultural learning): (a) cultural learning produces understandings that are shared by a community of practice; (b) as members of a community of practice experience engagement in processes of shared joint attention, they also derive a deepened sense of their own subject position within the community of practice, and as they learn with others, they constitute a sense of their own *cultural* identity; and (c) the great potential of cultural learning is that it produces understandings that coordinate social action. People in communities of practice possess effective, collaborative means for changing their material world in ways individuals alone could not manage.

Drawing on the ideas of Jürgen Habermas (1989), it is possible to add a fourth effect of cultural learning in communities of practice unnamed by Wenger. Habermas contends that a key effect of the learning processes that transpire in what he terms the "lifeworld," is the reproduction of social solidarity. As people participate in communities of practice, they not only gain a sense of themselves, they also gain a sense of others as beings like themselves. The human capacity for care and empathy is both condition of and effect of cultural learning processes.

Perhaps one of the more remarkable features of the theoretical foundations of adult education is the *absence* of explicit or critical discourse on the nature of human learning processes. As transformational learning theorist, Jack Mezirow, observes, while adult education is rich with "practice injunctions" intended to enable adult educators to achieve various desired ends, it has not been the context for rigorous investigation of adult learning processes (personal communication, August, 1994). As many have observed, for the most part, throughout the 20th century, adult education unquestioningly adopted the highly individualistic views of learning espoused by the discipline of psychology. Behaviorist notions of learning, based for the most part on experimental studies of animal behavior, and, later, cognitive theories of human learning, inspired by burgeoning interest in computer information processing, offered tidy but highly oversimplified models of human learning processes. Adult educators, intent on controlling interpersonal contexts to produce specific learning outcomes (defined, for the most part in behavioral terms), easily adopted these models of learning as the foundation for an array of adult education technologies. Over the past two decades, deepening skepticism about the social purposes of adult education has raised questions about its reliance on individualist learning theory.

While adult education largely retains its uncritical stance towards adult learning, in recent years a few adult education theorists have begun to explore alternative conceptions of human learning processes. The notion of "cultural learning" has much to contribute to this emerging foundational discourse in adult education.

See also: collaborative learning, community of practice, dialogue.

References and Further Reading

Habermas, J. (1989). *The theory of communicative action, Volume 2*. Cambridge, UK: Polity Press.

Tomasello, M. (1999). *The cultural origins of human cognition*. Cambridge, MA: Harvard University Press.

Wenger, E. (1999). *Communities of practice: Learning, meaning, and identity*. Cambridge, UK: Cambridge University Press.

Donovan Plumb

Cultural Studies

Cultural studies, part social movement and part interdisciplinary academic study, aims to reveal the relationships between culture and power in order to understand and change inequitable social practices and structures. Most authorities agree, however, that cultural studies represents multiple definitions depending on its historical and institutional locations, that those engaging in cultural studies use multiple methods loosely amalgamated as semiotic and discursive analyses, and that cultural studies draws upon many intellectual traditions such as Marxism, anthropology, linguistics, semiotics, critical theory, feminism and poststructuralism, for example. From an initial focus in the United Kingdom in the 1940s and 1950s on revealing and altering how culture functioned to produce differential relations of power in the British class system, students of cultural studies have examined gender, sexuality, popular culture, colonial and postcolonial identity, music, film, television, science, race, ethnicity, subjectivity, postmodernism, globalization, and various other interests in order to ask how cultural practices produce relations of dominance and how those relations of dominance can be resisted. Within an increasingly diverse set of interests and initiatives, if there is a "centering" thematic to cultural studies it would be "showing the pervasiveness of the inequalities of power relations through which the world is ordered; and thinking about how that order can be upset" (Dirks, Eley, & Ortner, 1994, p. x). As such, students of cultural studies bring both activist and theoretical efforts to questions of social justice. Because adult education represents a specific cultural practice that produces and reproduces relationships of power (Cervero & Wilson, 2001), cultural studies can be used to examine adult education's role in serving and/or challenging dominant interests.

History and People

Given that a premise of cultural studies is to challenge the construction of "selective traditions," major reviews (Davies, 1995; During, 1999; Grossberg, Nelson, & Treichler, 1992; Sardar & Van Loon, 1998) nonetheless tell a similar tale, particularly in terms of the origins of cultural studies in the United Kingdom in the 1940s, 1950s, and 1960s. A key component of that tale is cultural studies' consistent location on the Left as a response to various historical manifestations of the Right, from its Marxist analyses of mass culture in the 1940s and 1950s, to its association with the New Left in the 1960s and 1970s, and to its echoing of the continuing fragmentation of the Left during the Conservative Restoration of the Reagan–Thatcher years and beyond to the continued ascent of neo-liberal world marketization. Most sources identify Raymond Williams and Richard Hoggart as major intellectual and practical architects of cultural studies who have initiated questions about the relationships between culture and power within the broad social change agenda of the Left. Williams' *Culture and Society 1780–1950* (1958) and Hoggart's *The Uses of Literacy* (1957) are cited as canonical texts (in a discipline which seeks to question canons whenever possible) representing starting points for the construction of the academic discipline of cultural studies. Williams is noted for his project to articulate the relationships between culture and society (Grossberg et al.), while Hoggart is known for examining the tension between canonical cultural texts ("great literature") and "mass culture" (During). Hoggart is also noted for founding the Centre for Contemporary Cultural Studies at Birmingham University, a key location for cultural studies since the 1960s. A third major contributor to constructing the discipline of cultural studies is E.P. Thompson whose *The Making of the English Working Class* (1963) furthered the initial themes of cultural studies that culture and politics were not separable (During). These initial efforts of Williams, Hoggart, Thompson, and others were trying to understand and respond to what they perceived to be the erosion of traditional British working class values and communities by a colonizing and disruptive mass culture.

It will be noted that the recognized originators of the theory and practice of cultural studies are White, male, albeit working-class individuals, who can be charged with a certain "Anglocentrism" (Sardar & Van Loon, 1998). They nonetheless pursued important questions of class construction. Whereas it is always dangerous to essentialize any historical movement, those initially practicing cultural studies in Britain did introduce key theoretical and practical questions about the relationship of culture and politics. Those questions began spreading beyond the United Kingdom in the 1970s to Australia, Canada, France, India, South Asia, and the United States (where cultural studies contributed significantly to the "canon wars" in the 1980s and 1990s in American higher education's literary and history departments). As cultural studies developed, its focus shifted from questions of class to other cultural systems and practices that produced relations of dominance as many different marginalized cultural groups sought to understand and respond to the cultural politics they participated in and helped construct. As different cultural questions were asked, students of cultural studies incorporated an ever-diverse set of theoretical analyses (such as Gramsci's hegemony, Bourdieu's cultural capital, Foucault's discursive analyses of knowledge–power regimes, feminists and poststructuralists' notion of "the other," and so on) which further fueled the migration of cultural studies in terms of its geographical and intellectual diversification. One of the reasons that the major reviews of the evolution of cultural studies (Davies, 1995; During, 1999; Grossberg et al., 1992; Sardar & Van Loon, 1998) claim that there is no essential definition of cultural studies, that there is no definitive method of analysis, and that there are no stable intellectual traditions is because of the proliferation of schools of cultural studies, methods, and objects of study and resistance. The contemporary landscape of cultural studies is one of multiple but sometimes conflicting possibilities with a staggering range of inquiry into relationships between culture and power. A selective listing of topics of inquiry represented in recent cultural studies would include but not be limited to: gender and sexuality, nationhood, colonialism and postcolonialism, race and ethnicity, popular culture, identity politics, education, science, globalization, space and time, multiculturalism, media, consumption and market, leisure, literature, esthetics, music, and history. Readers interested in examining cultural studies in terms of its multiple theoretical manifestations, its array of analyses, its topics of cultural inquiry, and its critical thematics are urged to consult especially the edited collections by During, Grossberg et al., as well as Davies.

The Analysis of Culture

One of the earliest tasks of cultural studies was to ask whose culture was being used to selectively define what constituted a whole society's "way of life" (Williams, 1958). By analysing the selective cultural representation of dominant interests, Williams exemplified cultural studies' initial focus on "texts" from his insider (British subject) and outsider (Welsh culture) locations to ask how British society was possible (Davies, 1995). Identifying and defining relationships between culture and society requires "efforts to theorize and grasp mutual determinations and interrelations of cultural forms and historical forces" (Grossberg et al., 1992, p. 3). Given the array and richness of these efforts to theorize and grasp relationships among culture, society, power, and individual lives, it is only possible in this setting to briefly illustrate "how cultural studies works." During (1999) provides an analysis of a rather ubiquitous North American, if not worldwide, cultural "text," the advertising image known as the "Marlboro Man," from several different theoretical perspectives to produce different "readings" of the icon's various cultural messages. The Marlboro Man as corporate symbol of a cigarette brand, depicted as a tall, lean, ruggedly sturdy man (masculine used deliberately) dressed in complete iconic Western cowboy attire, standing beside or astride his (again deliberately) horse, backdropped by rugged snow-capped wilderness, can semiotically "connote masculinity, freedom and transcendence of workaday life" (During, p. 5). Because such semiotic "decoding," an early analytical method, only begins to show the meaning of cultural messages but not their effect, During presents a "structuralist" reading, based on Althusser, to show how a cultural message can represent an ideological order that socializes specific values. In this way male adolescents and adults use the culturally produced iconography of the Marlboro Man to "make sense of the world" by self-identifying with the image of independence and strength. During further argues, however, that structuralist cultural studies tend to underestimate the ability of individuals and communities to produce their own meanings from cultural messages and that any discrete cultural message, such as the Marlboro Man, is "polysemic," that is, representing multiple meanings:

> the tobacco industry, the medical profession, and a certain stream with the women's movement might *struggle* [original emphasis] over the meaning of Marlboro Man for political and commercial reasons: one in order to sell more product; the other to promote health . . . the last to reject an insensitive mode of masculinity. (p. 6)

This limited example represents semiotic and discursive analyses used to reveal and question relationships between culture and individuals and/or groups. It also represents the historical movement from decoding to multiple, sometimes conflicting meaning appropriations to resistance (see Sardar & Van Loon, 1998, for a similar analysis of how changing names of Indian cuisine restaurants in the UK demonstrate Indians' resistance to dominant relations of power; see During, and Grossberg et al., for extensive examples of cultural studies).

Issues and Relevance to Adult Education

Cultural studies has succeeded in challenging interpretations of culture as a convivially shared set of behavioral practices and norms, what Williams once referred to as "the whole way of life," in order to demonstrate culture's multiple and contested meanings. A major agenda from its early days in the postwar UK has been an interest in cultural groups with lesser power and how they can develop their own readings and uses of cultural products and practices (During, 1999). So the question is not what is culture, but whose culture and to what repressive ends it is directed (Dirks et al., 1994). Beginning as an attempt by the British Left to understand and resist the erosion of working-class culture (Davies, 1995), cultural studies still holds promise, because of its great proliferation of perspective and method, to provide a socially just response to the current effects of the ascendancy of the Right worldwide. As Grossberg et al. (1992) argue, cultural studies represent an intellectual and practical space where the "new" politics of difference can be articulated and strategized. Even so, numerous issues face cultural studies. Taking a lead from Stuart Hall, a major leader of the Birmingham Centre, who proclaimed that cultural studies needs a "moment of clarification," Grossberg et al. ask that as cultural studies becomes more institutionalized in academic settings, as its "rough" edges get smoothed to fit in discipline boundaries, as its political intentions get challenged by institutional norms, will cultural studies still matter in terms of what kind of work will be identified with it and what its social and political effects will be.

That UK cultural study was initiated by working-class adult educators doing working-class adult education, a well-accorded effort in the UK, is virtually unknown in the United States. Further, elsewhere in the English-speaking world, the notion of adult education as a "cultural practice" is not an alien thought, whereas in the USA adult educators have tended to understand their practice in technical and humanist terms. Clearly, though, adult education is deeply implicated in the struggle for knowledge and power throughout the world (Cervero & Wilson, 2001), and cultural studies offers an analysis capable of asking how adult education contributes to the cultural production and reproduction of power in the furtherance of dominant interests. Specific questions might include the use of culture in literacy work, the ways in which culture is implicated in neo-liberal marketization, and how culture is used to produce dominant political relationships.

See also: class, critical multiculturalism, critical theory, difference, power, race.

References and Further Reading

Cervero, R. M., & Wilson, A. L. (2001). *Power in practice*. San Francisco: Jossey-Bass.

Davies, I. (1995). *Cultural studies and beyond: Fragments of empire*. London: Routledge.

Dirks, N., Eley, G., & Ortner, S. (Eds.). (1994). *Culture/power/history*. Princeton, NJ: Princeton University Press.

During, S. (Ed.).(1999). *The cultural studies reader* (2nd ed.). London: Routledge.

Grossberg, L., Nelson, C., & Treichler, P. (Eds.). (1992). *Cultural studies*. London: Routledge.

Hoggart, R. (1957). *The uses of literacy*. London: Chatto & Windus.

Sardar, Z., & Van Loon, B. (1998). *Introducing cultural studies*. New York: Totem.

Thompson, E. P. (1963). *The making of the English working class*. New York: Vintage.

Williams, R. (1958). *Culture and society 1780–1950*. New York: Columbia University Press.

Arthur L. Wilson

Culturally Relevant Adult Education

Culturally relevant adult education refers to educational models, programs, processes and strategies that incorporate learners' cultural practices and values in the teaching–learning process with the goal of engaging learners to become critically aware of their own agency.

Similar terms include: culturally responsive, culturally appropriate, culturally congruent, and culturally grounded, which are sometimes used interchangeably. Related ideas include: cultural sensitivity, tolerance of and openness to cultural differences or to persons of different cultural, ethnic, racial or linguistic backgrounds. Terms such as "culturally responsive" and "culturally appropriate" are sometimes used synonymously with culturally relevant. Conceptually, these terms are linked to a broader multicultural framework where group-based differences are seen as linked to social hierarchies and structured oppression. The term culturally grounded emanates from a more focused Africentric theoretical stance where the ownership of as well as educational methods and strategies reflect the culture and history of African Americans or other people of color.

Theoretical Assumptions

Culturally relevant adult education

draws on the theoretical traditions concerned with socio-cultural and resistance theory in education. Key theoretical assumptions that undergird culturally relevant education are: (a) that teaching and learning are accomplished through interaction, communication, and language use; (b) that conventions for meaningful interaction are culturally learned initially and primarily through processes of family and community socialization; (c) that classrooms are essentially communicative environments that are influenced by the culturally situated practices by which educators and learners interact; and (d) that socio-cultural differences become the basis for a range of learners' negative reactions. Within the framework, cultural practices are seen as constituted in webs of signification, meaning systems, which are learned and shared by members of particular social groups. For any given action or practice, multiple interpretations are possible based on learners' particular cultural backgrounds. Some sets of shared actions and practices are privileged because they are tied to social groups whose status within a particular society is itself privileged. Thus, for researchers and educators, understanding cultural differences in the learning environment is an important factor in gaining a deeper and more valid understanding of the nature of adult learning.

The classroom is conceptualized as a place where educators and learners interact via culturally constituted symbolic systems. Adult learners bring to the learning environment a set of communicative and interaction strategies that may or may not serve them well depending on the way in which the educational activity itself is culturally framed. Where differences exist between the cultural frame that educators use to organize and deliver the educational activity and the cultural frame that learner(s) bring to the classroom, there will result a conflict, a kind of cultural incongruity that negatively influences the teaching–learning (communicative) interaction.

In culturally relevant adult education, the relationship of learners' cultures to that of the educators is different for different cultural groups. Community and family patterns among persons from a dominant culture background are assumed to be more congruent with that of the culture of the institution or agency that provides or sponsors the educational activity. One reason for this might include the fact that the institution or agency is controlled by individuals from the dominant class. Another reason might be because middle-class adults have already spent much successful time in school. On the other hand, dominated social groups exercise less control over institutional educational processes and practices. Their experience with formal education and different cultural systems may place them in a position of being in conflict and opposition to the dominant culture of the classroom or program.

Classroom Connections to Societal Structures of Power

Because cultural differences between learners and educational agencies are linked to broader structural inequities between different social groups in society, cultural differences are also understood as tied to broader structural relations. Consequently, identifying cultural differences in a classroom is essential in helping educators to mediate the tension between learners' cultural backgrounds and institutionalized educational practices. Thus, for different societies, different group relations will exist, but the underlying relations of power, oppression, and marginalization are similar.

For example, in America, when non-White middle-class adults engage in an adult education activity they might experience interactions and situations that range from mildly strange and uncomfortable to genuinely problematic because the content or format is not appropriate in the community from which they come. When these cultural mismatches occur, they represent, on a micro social level, conflictual relations between dominant and subordinate social groups that exist on a macro level. Studies that investigate difficulties experienced by learners in institutional settings focus on the challenges and difficulties faced by learners whose reactions can range from indifference and apathy (Wlodkowski & Ginsberg, 1995) to open resistance (Quigley, 1992). In North America, culturally relevant research has focused on the educational experiences of a variety of ethnic, language, and cultural groups. While the cultural frames for each group are quite different, research on various ethnic, racial, or language groups all share an analysis of the historical experience of oppression and marginalization within the affected group. When adult educators modify program design and teaching practices to be more reflective of the cultural experiences of the learners they serve, the result is increased engagement in the educational process by participants.

Using an Africentric feminist framework, Sheared (1999) found that by changing the patterns of interaction to be more reflective of those patterns indigenous to the African American community, learners interacted with each other in accomplishing instructional tasks in what she refers to as the polyrhythmic nature of African American culture. She notes that this results in the learners becoming more interactive and engaged.

A few studies have focused on Native American culture. Lockard (1999) described a successful American Indian (Navajo) educational project aimed at teaching traditional Navajo language and culture by using that culture as both curriculum and pedagogy. In her study, she described the significance to learners of participating in a culturally relevant program that connects to traditional Navajo language and culture because so much of it was being lost among the current generation of Navajo adults and youth. Advances in literacy were achieved as a result. Working within a diverse community that includes Native Americans, Cajete (1994) documents the significance of traditional Native American culture in helping Native Americans work within the dominant Anglo society. Similarly, Osterling (2001) explores a family literacy program for Salvadoran refugees in the United States designed and implemented by grassroots organizations that serve an increasingly diverse, multicultural/multilingual community. The program addresses the educational needs of poor illiterate families while drawing on parents' culture and extensive life experiences.

Identifying and Addressing Cultural Differences

Some studies have focused less on the relationship between societal structures of inequality and cultural differences by emphasizing the importance of adjusting professional practice to become more relevant to the culture of specific communities. In their study of the African American religious experience and adult education, Isaac and Rowland (2002) discuss how preachers shape the form and content of sermons to appeal to African American audiences. Some professional organizations, such as the Association for Multicultural Counseling and Development (Fuertes & Ponterotto, 2003), have identified professional competencies related to serving culturally diverse populations.

New Directions for Culturally Relevant Research

Technology and spirituality represent two recent areas of culturally relevant research. With the advent of web-based technologies for distance education, studies have recently been made to investigate the role of culture in online teaching and learning. Research has identified the limitations imposed by technology on educators to develop culturally relevant instruction. More recently, studies have begun to identify ways that technology can incorporate or adjust to learners' cultures. Berkshire and Smith (2000) describe the Rural Alaska Native Adult Program of Alaska Pacific University. This program is specifically designed for adult Native learners. The asynchronous instructional design provides an opportunity for learners to discuss course content and topics with local mentors and elders, a format that is very culturally appropriate and relevant for the Alaska Native learner. McLoughlin (1999) argues that computer technologies are themselves the product of a particular cultural frame and that these technologies do not adequately contextualize computer interface or learning environments. She describes an Australian program that targets Indigenous learners and accommodates their learning and communication styles.

Tisdell (2003) has proposed a link between spirituality and culture. She discusses how spiritual development is informed by culture and how this knowledge is relevant to teaching and learning. For educators, knowledge of how culture helps to shape one's spirituality, and how spirituality promotes meaning-making, can support adult educators in their efforts to help their learners' educational experiences become more transformative and culturally relevant.

Culturally relevant adult education is a relatively new area of inquiry and practice. While its meaning varies across studies, its common focus is on the relationship between the micro social level such as components of professional practice and learning and broader socio-cultural and societal issues of power and difference.

See also: Africentrism, class, difference, gender, indigenous learning, power, race.

References and Further Reading

Berkshire, S., & Smith, G. (2000). *Bridging the great divide: Connecting Alaska Native learners and leaders via "High Touch-High Tech" distance learning.* Houston, TX: National Association of African American Studies and National Association of Hispanic and Latino Studies. National Association of Native American Studies Section.

Cajete, G. (1994). *Look to the mountain: An ecology of indigenous education.* Durango, CO: Kivaki Press.

Fuertes, J. N., & Ponterotto, J. G. (2003). Culturally appropriate intervention strategies. In G. Roysircar, P. Arredondo, J. N. Fuertes, J. G. Ponterotto, & R. L. Toporek (Eds.), *Multicultural counseling competencies,*

2003: Association for Multicultural Counseling and Development. Alexandria, VA: Association for Multicultural Counseling and Development, A division of the American Counseling Association, p. 148 ff.

Isaac, E. P., & Rowland, M. L. (2002). *The African American sermon as an exemplar of culturally relevant adult education.* Paper presented at the Adult Education Research Conference. Raleigh, NC, May 24–26, 2002. Retrieved March 13, 2004 from ERIC database (ERIC Document Reproduction No. ED 472065).

Lockard, L. (1999).Navajo language and culture in adult education. In T.C. Guy (Ed.), *Providing culturally relevant adult education: A challenge for the twenty-first century* (pp. 81–91). *New Directions for Adult and Continuing Education,* No. 82. San Francisco: Jossey-Bass.

McLoughlin, C. (1999). Culturally responsive technology use: Developing an online community of learners. *British Journal of Educational Technology, 30*(3), 231–243.

Osterling, J. (2001). Waking the sleeping giant: Engaging and capitalizing on the sociocultural strengths of the Latino community. *Bilingual Research Journal, 25*(1–2), 59–88.

Quigley, B. A. (1992). Opposing views: An analysis of resistance to adult literacy and basic education. *International Journal of Lifelong Education, 11*(1), 41–49.

Sheared, V. (1999). Giving voice: Inclusion of Afro-American students' polyrhythmic realities in adult basic education. In T.C. Guy (Ed.), *Providing culturally relevant adult education: A challenge for the twenty first century* (pp. 49–61). *New Directions for Adult and Continuing Education,* No. 82. San Francisco: Jossey-Bass.

Tisdell, E. J. (2003). *Exploring spirituality and culture in adult and higher education.* San Francisco: Jossey-Bass.

Wlodkowski, R. J., & Ginsberg, M. B. (1995). *Diversity and motivation: Culturally responsive teaching.* San Francisco: Jossey-Bass.

Talmadge C. Guy

D

Dialogue

The term "dialogue" is Greek, from the two roots, *dia* meaning "through" or "with each other," and *logos* meaning "the word." The origins of dialogue go back to ancient Athens. It was the main teaching method used by Socrates and immortalized in Plato's famous dialogues. This derivation suggests that dialogue is a stream of meaning flowing among, through and between persons.

Many adult educators observe that adult learning is best achieved in dialogue (e.g., Freire, 2000; Knowles, 1980; Vella, 1994). Vella's dialogical approach to adult learning is based on 12 principles: needs assessment; safety in the environment and the process; sound relationship between teacher and learner; sequence of content and reinforcement; praxis; respect for learners as subjects of their own learning; cognitive, affective and psychomotor aspects; immediacy of the learning; clear roles and role development; teamwork; engagement of the learners in what they are learning; and, accountability. Andragogy in Malcolm Knowles' terms holds that adults have a repertoire of life experience that positions them to be in dialogue with one another. The concept of dialogue spans a spectrum of discourses such as emancipatory education, literary theory, educational philosophy, feminist pedagogy, and organizational learning.

Difference Between Dialogue and Discussion

The etymological distinction between the terms "dialogue" and "discussion," often used interchangeably, is instructive. The term "discussion" shares its root meaning with "percussion" and "concussion," both of which involve breaking things up, and stems from the Latin *discutere*, "to smash to pieces." In dialogue, there is the free and creative exploration of complex issues, a deep listening to one another and suspending of one's own views, while, by contrast, in discussion different views are presented and defended and there is a search for the best view to support decisions that must be made. Dialogue and discussion are potentially complementary but it seems necessary to distinguish between the two and to move consciously between them (Ellinor & Gerard, 1998; Isaacs, 1993). The term "dialogue" is more consonant with the discursive relational dynamics of collaborative learning; there is a constant movement towards "shared minds" rather than a single overpowering position.

Emancipatory Education and Dialogue

In adult education, Paulo Freire is best known as the emancipatory educator who popularized the notion of dialogue as an educational form. Freire's pedagogy articulates that the central feature of dialogue is the recovery of the voice of the oppressed as the fundamental condition for human emancipation. For Freire, the essence of dialogue is "the true word." True words are unities of reflection and action "in such radical interaction that if one is sacrificed, even in part, the other immediately suffers" (Freire, 2000, p. 87). To speak a true word is to engage in praxis: to transform the world in accordance with reflection: to name the world.

Critical and libratory Freirian dialogue is problem-posing that begins with an investigation of the cultural situation of the participants. This cultural situation provides the curriculum of problems that are to be engaged with in the educational process. As a result of dialogue over these problems, facilitators and participants become actively involved in attending to their problems. Freire emphasizes that dialogic encounters take place between teacher–learner, learner–teacher and learner–learner.

Literary Theory and Dialogue

Dialogue is pivotal to Mikhail Bakhtin's (1981) literary theory. A "dialogic penetration into the word . . . opens up fresh aspects in the word" (p. 352). This occurs through interaction, which brings more and more features of the other's word into understanding and into a position where it can be related to the listener's own words and so create new discourses. Bakhtin uses the concept of dialogue to focus on the continuous flow of interaction and response among individuals; language, as dialogue, is always in the process of becoming. His concept *heteroglossia* implies that culture and society, as well as individuals, are constituted by multiple voices. This legitimates differences of opinion and restores the individual's voice in the creation of cultural patterns.

Bakhtin (1981) points out that we do not use language; language uses us. The nature of discourse is that the language we encounter already has a history: the words that we speak have been spoken by others before us ("the internal dialogism of the word"). What we speak always means more than we mean to say; the language that we use carries with it implications, connotations and consequences that we can only partly intend. The words that others hear from us, how they understand them, and what they say in response, is beyond our unilateral control. This relation of speaker, hearer, and language is reflected not only in spoken communication but with authors, readers, and a variety of texts.

Educational Philosophy

For the educational philosopher, Nicholas Burbules, dialogue entails a particular kind of relationship and interaction; it is at the heart a social relation that engages its participants (Burbules, 1993). He defines dialogue as representing "a continuous developmental communicative interchange through which we stand to gain a fuller appreciation of the world, ourselves, and one another" (p. 8). In *Dialogue in Teaching,* Burbules recommends the interaction of at least two distinct spectrums to characterize different forms of dialogue: the degree to which an interchange is critical or inclusive, and the degree to which the investigation is intended to be convergent (upon a single answer) or divergent (allowing for multiple perspectives).

Burbules discusses the forms of inquiry, conversation, instruction, and debate as varied types of dialogical engagement. Inquiry involves a co-investigation of a question, the resolution of a disagreement, the formulation of a compromise, all as ways of addressing a specific problem to be addressed. Conversation involves a more open-ended discussion in which the aim of intersubjective understanding, rather than the answering of any specific question or problem, is paramount. Instruction involves an intentional process in which a teacher leads a student, through questioning and guidance, to formulating certain answers or understandings. Debate involves an exchange less about reaching agreement or finding common answers than about teasing out positions through an engagement for and against other positions. The key point is that the actual form and tone of utterances may vary widely: some are more critical, others more inclusive; some tend towards convergent answers, others towards a divergent multiplicity of possibilities. Yet all can be dialogical in spirit, and many examples for each type can be found in the philosophical and pedagogical literature on dialogue (Burbules, 1993).

Several virtues and emotions are integral within dialogical engagements: *concern* – in being with our partners in conversation, to engage them in the flow of the dialogue, with a social bond that ignites a commitment to the other; *trust* – taking what others say in faith alongside the risk that comes with it; *respect* – a recognition that each person is equal in some basic way and entails a commitment to being fair-minded, opposing degradation and rejecting exploitation; *appreciation* – valuing the unique quality that others bring; *affection* – involves a feeling with, and for, our partners-in-learning; *hope* – engaging in dialogue with the belief that it holds much possibilities.

Feminist Pedagogy

The metaphor of developing a voice, and of joining with other voices in dialogue, has become central in the literature surrounding feminist pedagogy (Maher, 1987; Weiler, 1991) and other approaches in learning such as collaborative learning and peer learning. The inquiry based on women's experience articulated in *Women's Ways of Knowing* (Belenky, Clinchy, Goldberger, & Tarule, 1986) showed that women emphasize relationships in their development – an emphasis that stresses voice, listening, and talking as the medium for connecting with others; and the power of a speaking voice is embodied in the lives of women in terms of "speaking out," "being silenced," "really talking," "saying what you mean," and "listening to be heard." The development of a sense of voice, mind, and self are inextricably entwined.

Feminist pedagogy is linked to the theoretical and practical concerns of feminist theory and seeks to uncover, understand, and transform gender, race and class oppression and domination. It is committed to the development of a critical consciousness empowered to apply learning to social action and social transformation. Feminist pedagogy embraces the critical, oppositional and activist stance of the Freirean model of education, yet expands his vision by considering not only the class and race aspects of knowledge production and dissemination, but also the gender aspects as well as the intersections of these categories in people's lives. To achieve emancipatory goals, feminist educators develop and use classroom process skills that are explicitly designed to empower learners to apply their learning to social action and transformation, recognize their ability to act to create a more humane social order, and become effective voices of change within the wider social world.

Organizational Learning

In elaborating on the integral role of dialogue in collaborative learning, Lee (1998) draws upon developments in contemporary management circles and organizational learning where dialogue process is a linchpin. The interface of dialogue and its application to organizational change can be traced to organizational theorists such as Senge (1993) and Isaacs (1993). Dialogue experiences aim to explore communication patterns and expose assumptions and tacit cultural "theories-in-use" which hinder the generation of collaborative learning efforts and result in counterproductive decision-making and dysfunctional organizational practices.

Dialogue process as articulated by Bohm (1996) and Isaacs (1993) entails four movements: suspension of assumptions, shared inquiry, generative listening, and holding the tension of opposites. Dialogue process facilitates and creates new possibilities for communication. The whole group is the object of learning and members share the potential excitement of collectively discovering ideas that individually none of them might have thought of. Through dialogue, people help one another to become aware of the incoherence of each other's thoughts, and in this way the collective thought becomes more and more coherent (from the Latin *cohaerere*, "hanging together").

Dialogic mentoring (Bokeno & Gantt, 2000) involves a collaborative, mutually constructive, critically reflective, participatory and emergent engagement of relationships among self, other and world. It is a form of mentoring that cultivates generative or double-loop learning via the relational processes that contextualize learning. The characteristics of generative learning that emerge through dialogic mentoring include celebrating contradiction and difference rather than resolving, reconciling, preventing, or otherwise managing it; focusing on the pursuit of openness in terms of ongoing communication that is left tentative; and celebrating equity of voice in that no one person's voice carries special privileges except possibly the experienced ability to frame more intriguing questions.

See also: collaborative learning, feminist pedagogy, organizational learning, praxis, problematizing learning, relational learning.

References and Further Reading

Bakhtin, M. M. (1981). *The dialogic imagination: Four essays by M. M. Bakhtin* (M. Holquist Ed., C. Emerson, & M. Holquist, Trans.). Austin: University of Texas Press.

Belenky, M. F., Clinchy, B. M., Goldberger, N. & Tarule, J. M. (1986). *Women's ways of knowing: The development of self, voice, and mind*. New York: Basic Books.

Bohm, D. (1996). *On dialogue*. London: Routledge.

Bokeno, R. M., & Gantt, V. W. (2000). Dialogic mentoring. *Management Communication Quarterly, 14*(2), 237–270.

Burbules, N. C. (1993). *Dialogue in teaching: Theory and practice*. New York: Teachers College Press.

Ellinor, L., & Gerard, G. (1998). *Dialogue: Rediscover the transforming power of conversation*. New York: John Wiley.

Forman, E. A., & Cazden, C. B. (1985). Exploring Vygotskian perspectives in education: The cognitive value of peer interaction. In J.V. Wertsch (Ed.), *Culture, communication and cognition. Vygotskian perspectives* (pp. 323–347). Cambridge: Cambridge University Press.

Freire, P. (2000). *Pedagogy of the oppressed.* (M. B. Ramos, Trans.) New York: Continuum, 30th anniversary edition.

Isaacs, W. (1993). Taking flight: Dialogue, collective thinking, and organizational learning. *Organisational Dynamics, 22*(2), 24–39.

Knowles, M. S. (1980). *The modern practice of adult education: From pedagogy to andragogy* (2nd ed.). New York: Cambridge Books.

Lee, G. C. M. (1998). *Collaborative learning in three British adult education schemes.* Unpublished doctorial dissertation. University of Nottingham, UK.

Maher, F. (1987). Toward a richer theory of feminist pedagogy. *Journal of Education, 169*(3), 91–99.

Senge, P. (1993). *The fifth discipline.* London: Doubleday Dell.

Vella, J. (1994). *Learning to listen, learning to teach: The power of dialogue in educating adults.* San Francisco: Jossey-Bass.

Weiler, K. (1991). Freire and a feminist pedagogy of difference. *Harvard Educational Review, 61*, 449–474.

Moira Lee

Difference

The notion of diversity implies dissimilarities, multiples, discontinuities, and difference. Multiculturalism and diversity include the celebration of difference. Adult education related to civil rights, social justice, feminism, and gay and lesbian discourses, among many others, was built at the end of the 20th century on the idea that difference matters. Notions of difference offer adult educators an opportunity to reclaim our past tradition of learning for social change. Hill (2001) positions difference in adult education as a fundamental human right related to democratic learning and comparable to values proposed in the Report of the UNESCO Commission for Education in the 21st Century: the right to know, to do, to be, to live together (Delors, 1996, p. 108). Difference in these contexts is a critical project with the potential to liberate. On the other hand, those who desire to distribute power unevenly construct, use, or make difference necessary through "othering." Thus, processes of marginalization are also enacted through discourses of difference.

Difference intersects with adult education at many locations. Several significant junctures include those with multiculturalism and diversity, democracy, identity, critical theory, and postmodernism. In the early 1990s, adult educators lamented the field's lack of regard for difference. Adult education was labeled "Eurocentric, racist, gender insensitive, elitist, and exclusionary" (Cunningham, 2001, p. xi) for its lack of diversification. Difference allows for sharing of particular standpoints or points of view, and permits challenges to a unitary, referential universe or a central perspective espoused by dominant members in society. Intersubjectivity – the sharing of subject-position knowledge – may produce a fuller understanding of an object, event or process. However, Ellsworth (1989) and others warn that sharing different viewpoints is "a vehicle for regulating conflict and the power to speak, for transforming conflict into rational argument by means of universalized capacities for language and reason" (p. 301).

Post-Colonial Perspective

Homi Bhabha (2001) distinguishes between the multiculturalism/diversity cited above and cultural difference/hybridity, suggesting that the former is a Western concept that permits examination of relations with non-Western culture based on a binary structure of opposition. To Bhabha, contested relationships built on difference are ambivalent; those othered/oppressed are always difficult to situate, thus the dominant group undermines its own power. This ambivalence makes a space for resistance available to those who are marginalized. Once universalized, different cultures – labeled "incommensurables" – become transparent, mysterious, vague, and elude a taxonomy or classification within a regime of power. Bhabha (1994) pursues a "third space" which is a "hybrid" location that simultaneously disrupts the processes that create it, and, more importantly, allows for the construction of new possibilities of legitimization for the Other. It is these "in-between spaces [that] provide the terrain for elaborating strategies of selfhood – singular or communal – that initiate new signs of identity, and innovative sites of collaboration, and contestation, in the act of defining the idea of society . . ." (pp. 1–2). These are contradictory and ambivalent spaces.

As a critique of totalizing narratives and monolithic claims, arguments built on difference suggest that there are dissimilar – sometimes radically dissimilar – "realities," dissimilar "truths," dissimilar meanings and ways to make those meanings, and dissimilar ways of knowing something. Difference is about differentiation from "the identical" in which oppositions are announced. An undertaking of postmodernism is to celebrate difference in multiple ways. Binary oppositions that categorize and essentialize are rooted in foundational (enlightenment/modernist) thinking. Postmodern notions of difference move beyond the oppositional identity binaries that are constructed as clear-cut and "natural" – and therefore seemingly unimpeachable. These include the oppositional couplets: normal/abnormal, natural/unnatural, man/woman, black/white, and gay/straight each of which can be troubled by difference. This postmodern notion understands difference as "specificity, variation, heterogeneity" (Young, 1990, p. 171) and looks with suspicion on dualisms.

Identities that are border-crossing make binaries problematic and they unsettle stereotypes. For instance, the complexity of interracial combinations, transgender expressions, and fluid (Queer) sexualities subvert the reciprocity of the binaries constructed around race, gender, and sexual orientation. Difference can disturb such monolithic narratives as institutional racism, feminist notions of gender subordination, and other social constructions. Some, like Stuart Hall (1992), promote intentional transgression by representing the complexities of identities. A consequence of differences in representation may be to weaken the solidarity of a definable "us." As a corollary, it is no longer possible to say "we" in regard to the shared aims of identity politics. To claim to be "multiracial" rather than black, or Queer rather than lesbian or gay, challenges the fundamental binary divisions of white/black and gay/straight, which are themselves constructed on sharp contrasts of difference designed to trouble the dominant white and straight discourses. Such difference, when constructed on *"altérité radicale*" or "radical otherness," disrupts sense-making, refuses to assimilate, and rejects grand theories and metanarratives about the world.

Post-Structuralist Perspectives

Jacques Derrida suggests that language produces rather than reflects meaning. Meaning is constructed through a process of *difference*. This process is a continuous deferral of meaning that leaves traces of other different signs that have to be excluded for the sign to be itself (Derrida, 1981, p. 702; 1982). To name the instability of meaning, he uses the neologism *différance* (signifying both "to differ" and "to defer"). Meaning is always different from itself, a condition that makes politics possible since a specific meaning is only fixed in time and space by force. These notions are central to Derrida's formulation of deconstruction or dismantling "truths." Everything is a text, subject to *différance*, the questioning of the originality, fixity, immediacy of meaning, and subject to the deferral of meaning. Jean-François Lyotard (1984) posits a postmodern construction that contests totalizing narratives and regimentation because such narratives minimize, devalue, deny, and erase difference.

Difference and Adult Education

So what does difference have to say to adult education? Hemphill (2001) reminds us that "the canon of received knowledge regarding theory and practice in the field of adult education implies a sweeping claim of universality" (p. 15). He posits that "our intellectual perspectives to accommodate diverse contributions . . . [makes] many more ideas available to us regarding motivation, self, community, or complex adult cognition than those traditionally promoted in the adult education mainstream" (p. 15).

Lifelong learning enterprises make vital contributions to the social, economic, technological, political, and cultural lives of individuals and communities. Invoking difference, which makes politics possible, can be generatively troublesome to the field, and opens new ways to realize these contributions. There is a maxim that offers, "What we know is determined by the way in which we know it." Difference allows us to understand what and how others know, and challenges our own ways of knowing. Yet, questions linger: If in fact there is always a "remainder," and it is not possible to order an irreconcilable world, as postmodern notions of difference suggest, how do we proceed in the practice of adult education? If difference means we can no longer trust in the faithful representation of reality and truth through objectivity and detachment, how do we conduct adult education research? If modernist, empiricist claims to rationality are now less tenable, how do we teach and learn? Will recognizing the contingency, fragmentation, and historicity of knowledge be enough? In response, we can say at least that difference allows us to: (a) redraw our ideas; (b) adopt unruly perspectives; (c) critique what and who structures meaning, thus opening up possibilities of resistance; (d) abandon our desire for a seamless narrative and in the process engage in complexity; (e) challenge power relations by utilizing spaces that are shifting and dynamic; and (f) celebrate the condition that all forms of culture and identity are continually in process. The result may be a new and different vision for adult education.

See also: gender, identity, marginality, postcolonialism, poststructuralism.

References and Further Reading

Bhabha, H. K. (1994). *The location of culture*. New York: Routledge.

Bhabha, H. K. (2001). The commitment to theory. In V. B. Leitch, W. E. Cain, L. Finke, & B. Johnson (Eds.), *The Norton anthology of theory and criticism* (pp. 2,379–2,397). New York: Norton.

Cunningham, P. M. (2001). Forward. In V. Sheared & P. A. Sissel (Eds.), *Making space: Merging theory and practice in adult education* (pp. xi–xiv). Westport, CT: Bergin & Garvey.

Delors, J. (Chairperson). (1996). *Learning: The treasure within*. Paris: UNESCO Publishing.

Derrida, J. (1981). Implications: Interview with Henri Ronse (pp. 1–14, originally published, 1967). In *Positions* (A. Bass, Trans.). Chicago: University of Chicago Press (original work published 1972).

Derrida, J. (1982). Différance. In *Margins of philosophy* (pp. 1–27). Chicago: University of Chicago Press (original work published 1968)

Ellsworth, E. (1989). Why doesn't this feel empowering? Working through the repressive myths of critical pedagogy. *Harvard Educational Review, 59*, 297–324.

Hall, S. (1992). New ethnicities. In J. Donald & A. Rattansi (Eds.), *Race, culture and difference* (pp. 252–259). Thousand Oaks, CA: Sage.

Hemphill, D. F. (2001). Incorporating postmodernist perspectives into adult education. In V. Sheared & P. A. Sissel (Eds.), *Making space: Merging theory and practice in adult education* (pp. 15–28). Westport, CT: Bergin & Garvey.

Hill, R. J. (2001). Contesting discrimination based on sexual orientation at the ICAE Sixth World Assembly: "Difference" is a Fundamental Human Right, *Convergence, 34*(2–3), 100–116.

Lyotard, J-F. (1984). *The postmodern condition: A report on knowledge* (G. Bennington & B. Massumi, Trans.). Minneapolis, MN: University of Minnesota Press.

Young, I. M. (1990). *Justice and the politics of difference. Princeton*, NJ: Princeton University Press.

Robert J. Hill

Distance Education

In a rapidly changing technological world, distance education has increasingly become a focus of educational design and delivery, providing a dynamic opportunity to reach multiple participants regardless of geographical and time-zone differences. Distance education has the potential of cultivating and advancing individualized and self-directed learning.

Overview

There have been many different forms of distance education over the years, characterized by varying degrees of physical separation between the teacher and learner. These formats have included not only traditional local instruction, but also teaching across different time frames. A myriad of technologies have been used to deliver distance learning, such as Internet and web-based technologies, video conferencing, telephone, email, television, radio, video, audiocassettes, and postal mail (Moore & Kearsley, 1996; Verduin & Clark, 1991). In recent years, the widespread adoption and availability of the Internet in some developed countries has made distance education a major delivery interest and popular option (Cahoon, 1998). Distance education has expanded the opportunity for self-directed learning. However, it does present several issues and challenges of access, equity, and globalization which remain major concerns.

Sorting Out the Confusion: Dimensions of Distance Education

The development of distance education may be categorized across three core dimensions: technology, time, and focus. Improved technology has propelled distance learning developments, providing more readily available and user-friendly technologies over the years. Early examples of widely adopted distance learning initiatives, which are often forgotten today, include postal mail (dating back to the 1840s), radio, television, audiocassettes, and videos. Indeed in many countries some of these methods are still the primary vehicles for distance learning. In the 1960s–1970s the University of Wisconsin's Articulated Instructional Media Project (AIM) and the British Open University were major initiatives and forces in experimenting with nontraditional formats for higher education using multiple technologies and instructional designs including television, telephone, audiocassettes, radio, correspondence, and tutors (Moore & Kearsley, 1996).

Today distance learning is often envisioned as the videoconferencing of the 1980–90s, or the web-based (online) learning which emerged in the 1990s and mainstreamed in the early 2000s. Combining these technologies offers an even more powerful possibility as well; "hybrid" or "blended" formats build on the capabilities of multiple technologies and/or traditional formats (King, 2001; Wallace, 2003). For example, an online class might be combined with face-to-face learning experiences.

Time is another defining dimension of distance education. In some cases students communicate in real-time with the instructor (synchronously). In others, they interact at different times (asynchronously). Videoconferencing tends to be synchronous and has distinct limitations for arranging sessions, such as equipment, scheduling, time-zone differences, technical support, and high cost. In contrast, many of the older technologies and web-based applications are more convenient for learners and teachers alike as they can engage in teaching and learning across 24 hours a day, 7 days a week whenever it fits their schedule. While this flexibility holds great and new benefits for some learners the discipline and responsibility of keeping up with classes and assignments may be difficult obstacles to overcome without the structure of traditional, face-to-face meetings and accountability (Desanctis & Sheppard, 1999; Verduin & Clark, 1991).

This last point leads to the focus of instruction and differentiation of distance education. In other words, is the curriculum designed for independent, self-study or does the learner engage with an instructor and/or classmates? Independently pursued classes can be rich experiences in gaining a knowledge base, technical information, and informal learning; however, when learners engage in dialogue with instructors and other participants the learning can sometimes reach greater depths of reflection, analysis, debate, and application (King, 2001; Palloff & Pratt, 1999; Wallace, 2003). In such discussions, the process of explaining oneself and understanding others holds the potential for more thoroughly understanding one's values, assumptions, and knowledge. Through the assistance of technology and skilled application, distance learning does not have to be an isolated experience, but instead can facilitate dialogue that otherwise might be limited because of many possible constraints.

Altogether these three primary dimensions of distance learning have contributed to the ongoing evolution of design considerations (Berg, 2000; Palloff & Pratt, 2001), and the field has undergone significant changes in delivery formats and expectations. No longer satisfied with independent study as the only possibility, rapid communication, multiple instructional strategies and capabilities, learner collaboration, widely available advanced and more user-friendly technologies have created many possibilities through which distance education design continues to unfold (Berge, 2002; King, 2001; Wallace, 2003).

Major Figures in Recent Development

Major literature in the distance education field has focused on the learning technologies, systems approaches, and community. In 1991 John Verduin and Thomas Clark provided considerable contributions to the field in conceptualizing how it could be framed to include the different developments through the years. Their approach included looking not only at technologies, but also at interaction. Michael Moore and Greg Kearsley (1996) furthered work in this area by articulating a "systems view" of distance learning that examined organizational interactions. Zane Berge (2002) advanced a similar perspective and provides greater delineation among corporate organizational dynamics and issues that need to be addressed in planning and delivery of distance education. In addition, Greg Berg (2000) addressed the interdependence among higher education organizational issues from an administrative decision-making perspective.

For the most part, discussion of learning technologies in distance education has been dominated by how to facilitate teaching and learning. While discussion continues around how best to use the ever-changing technology, the field has also sought to determine how to use it best for instruction. Many articles and books have documented case studies of how their organizations, teachers, and learners used distance education in specific ways and purposes (Berge, 2002; Hopey, 1998).

Throughout the years an emphasis has been placed on the needs of the learner in distance education initiatives. Verduin and Clark (1991) articulated this focus as did Daniel Eastmond (1995). More discussion developed in the late 1990s about the possibilities for online learning to support the development of "communities of learners" beyond the usual boundaries of space and time (Palloff & Pratt, 1999, 2001), and the field actively continues to explore the potential of this area.

Distance Education in Action

Understanding the scope and dynamics of distance education becomes clearer by considering how it has been used in different adult learning contexts. This section briefly examines the practice of distance education in higher education, training, community education, and adult basic education (ABE).

Higher Education

Higher education practitioners find that their adult learners are looking for options to begin, continue, or complete their degree and non-degree studies through distance education. Greater numbers of adults are continuing their higher education studies, in part because modern life demands more time committed to the workplace, more educational credentials, and more knowledge (Berg, 2000). These learners seek ways to fit formal learning into their increasingly complex lives. Today, distance education programs provide more of these opportunities and offer them across disciplines and degrees.

Worldwide, higher education has been utilizing distance education for many years. For example, the United Kingdom's Open University has been prominent in this field for over 40 years spanning satellite-based (alternate site) programs, television, and now online learning. In addition, Australian universities have been leaders in discovering innovative ways to bridge the vast distances that are inherent to their constituency.

The past 10 years have seen widespread and heavily financed commitments to distance learning by universities around the world. While some institutions have become leaders in this arena, others have found the endeavor too costly (Berg, 2000; Carr, 2001). Since 2000, a greater number of corporate-based institutions in the United States gained attention as they moved ahead through technological advances and practical applications in online learning, combined with a more widespread adoption which has resulted in greater visibility in the post-secondary educational market.

Within higher education these dynamics have also included thorny issues such as intellectual property, accreditation, and financial aid. Quite a clash of cultures, expectations, legal rights, and financial compensation has ensued because faculty are accustomed to independent and sole rights to their work, while universities have increasingly addressed distance education curricula as work-for-hire. The issue of accreditation has been challenging, with two major forces at play: (a) traditionally faculty-developed and controlled curricula, and (b) corporate ventures in post-secondary education. The traditional orientation to higher education accreditation has been challenged and developments in this area are ever-evolving. In the past, some nations (like the United States) have had stringent restrictions on the assignment of financial aid to post-secondary distance education study. In 2003, however, there are significant inroads in the United States in loosening these restrictions, and such changes could have a broad impact on enrollment choices and patterns of adult learners (Carnevale, 2003). Corporate training has different dynamics to deal with, but may benefit from examining how these complex issues have been managed through a mixture of personnel, relations, and organizational change.

Training

Within public and private corporations, non-profit agencies, and governmental agencies distance education has many different manifestations. Corporate training has been a significant force in developing and utilizing innovative technologies for teaching and learning (Berge, 2002). Historically having had the greatest resources and highest stakes for training their constituency, corporations have been logical innovators for the field. While video-conferencing and online learning have been widely used in corporate settings for the past 20 years and 10 years respectively, their adoption for adult learning in other contexts has emerged more slowly. Corporate trainers have found the benefits of distance education to include standardizing curricula, reducing travel costs, increasing communication among geographically-dispersed offices, increasing the frequency of training, enhancing workforce knowledge and subject matter expertise, and customizing delivery to meet varying needs. None of these benefits necessarily have come with a small price tag; instead, organizations have invested heavily in not only the technologies, but also in instructional design. With a financial bottom line ultimately driving corporate investments, the emphasis has, at times, seemed to have been more on mass-delivery than individualized instruction. The pressure to meet the training needs of more employees more quickly and with less staff has become a stark reality in today's corporate settings, especially during difficult financial times and global market demands.

Related to these corporate training needs is the proliferation of distance education programs for business degree study. Especially relevant to the time constraints of business executives, these programs offer the possibility and complexities of engaging in study while still on location and managing their organizations full-time (e.g., Desanctis & Sheppard, 1999).

Community Organizations

In comparison, users of distance education in relief organizations and community education projects have had to rely on widely available and inexpensive technologies, such as radio. This limitation poses a great challenge in attempting to develop and deliver instruction that allows timely interaction between teachers and learners, and in many ways these limitations have resulted in communication primarily being the dissemination of information to the public, rather than an interactive instructional process. More recently, worldwide organizations such as UNESCO have developed online resources that are reaching those individuals with Internet access (http://www.unesco.org/education), and as this technology becomes more widely available to more nations, community education programs will be able to build on the experience of corporate training and higher education environments to maximize their use of distance learning in order to reach greater numbers of learners.

ABE–GED–ELL

The adult basic education (ABE) field includes secondary/high-school equivalency study or General Educational Development (GED), English language learning (ELL), and literacy. Throughout history many literacy efforts by non-profit organizations have used distance education technologies to reach the public. For example, religious organizations in particular have used print, radio, and audiocassettes to provide literacy and religious instruction for many years. Additionally, an extensive and successful example of adult education distance learning has been "GED on TV," which began in 1982 through Kentucky Educational Television in the United States and now has online components. More broadly, public television broadcasting emerged in the early 1960s in the United States and, like the British Broadcasting Corporation (BBC), this medium provides a powerful base for formal and informal learning for all ages.

Examining how adults are assisted through such programs provides important groundwork for determining their needs in additional distance learning initiatives.

ABE, GED, ELL, and literacy hold tremendous challenges for distance learning in today's web-based learning formats because they require language and technology literacy. However, ELL has been advancing in this area recently, and a strong force has been, rightly or wrongly, the dominance of English use on the Worldwide Web. This trend has created an even greater need for English language learning, and individuals and programs have been developing how to use the technology itself to meet the need.

Global Differences and Issues

The tendency is to get absorbed with new technological capabilities when considering, planning, and designing distance education; however at least two broader issues are recognized. In a time of tremendous technological advancement the fundamental concern for equity is evident in the issues of access and globalization.

The Digital Divide is a term used to describe the fact that the same racial, socioeconomic, gender, disabilities, and geographical boundaries that control inequitable distribution of other opportunities are evident in disparate technology access (King, 2002). For example, while some prominent countries may seemingly be enjoying widespread adoption and dependence on the Internet, other sectors within those boundaries may not have the necessary skills or access. Additionally, there are still nations today who do not have electrical or transportation infrastructures, sound economic foundations or adequate literacy levels to support the Internet's introduction. While some communities and nations are enveloped in the instant communication and other benefits of this post-information age, with their educational systems building rapidly on its capabilities in other areas, Internet use is an unfamiliar way of life that is, at most, only distantly heard about.

Educators of adults may struggle with these issues within their own organizational and national borders, as learners in different locations and departments may have vastly different technology skill levels and technical capabilities. Not least of these concerns is whether adult learners have access to technology outside of the workplace. Access is the ground-floor concern before distance education can be considered. If access is unattainable or inequitable, organizations and training programs must address these needs prior to being able to deliver distance education initiatives efficiently and effectively. Ignoring these issues would perpetuate unfair delivery systems excluding already underserved individuals and communities.

Globalization issues raise the expansive dimension of economic and cultural variation. In many ways distance technologies bring the distant world within reach. However, at the same time linking the globe means bringing together forces that may have been isolated in the past. Such intersections bear many ramifications for culture, human relations, religion, language, worldviews, politics, and economies (Collis, 1999; Desanctis & Sheppard, 1999). Nations that can participate in this technological environment bring their people and organizations into international relationships and dynamics. In the same way, the educational program that engages in distance education beyond its own organization or usual geographical boundaries may have to cope with these same variables. As the world both contracts and expands with distance technologies, our understanding of adult learners within organizational systems needs to reach new levels.

Future Opportunities

Distance education is not a new phenomenon. However, the increased availability and user-friendliness of technologies that can be used for these purposes has brought it into the experience of more adults than ever before. As a result, adult educators have a tremendous challenge of discerning the training needs of learners and organizations and choosing the best distance education design and delivery options for them (Berg, 2000; Berge, 2002; King, 2002; Lengnick-Hall & Sanders, 1997; Palloff & Pratt, 2001). Rather than technology dictating the choices organizations make in these matters, insight into the history, dimensions, focus, and issues related to distance education enable educators and other decision-makers to further build on their professional insight and expertise.

See also: higher education, literacy, online learning, training.

References and Further Reading

Berg, G. (2000). *Why distance learning?* Westport, CT: Praeger.

Berge, Z. (2002). *Sustaining distance training: Integrating learning technologies into the fabric of the enterprise*. San Francisco: Jossey-Bass.

Cahoon, B. (Ed.). (1998). *Adult learning and the Internet. New Directions for Adult and Continuing Education*, No. 78. San Francisco: Jossey-Bass.

Carnevale, D. (2003). Education Department expands student-aid program for distance education. *The Chronicle of Higher Education* (Dec. 12), *50*(16), A31.

Carr, S. (2001). Is anyone making money in distance education? *The Chronicle of Higher Education* (Feb. 16), *47*(23), A41.

Collis, B. (1999). Designing for differences: Cultural issues in the design of WWW-based course-support sites. *British Journal of Educational Technology*, *30*(3), 201–215.

Desanctis, G., & Sheppard, B. (1999). Bridging distance, time, and culture in executive MBA education. *Journal of Education for Business*, *74*(3), 157–161.

Eastmond, D. (1995). *Alone but together.* Cresskill, NJ: Hampton Press.

Hopey, C. (Ed.). (1998). *Technology, basic skills, and adult education: Info. Series No. 372.* Columbus, OH ERIC Clearinghouse on Adult, Career, and Vocational Education. Retrieved August 20, 2003, from ERIC database (ERIC Document Reproduction Service No. 423420).

King, K. P. (2001). Educators revitalize the classroom "bulletin board:" A case study of the influence of online dialogue on face-to-face classes from an adult learning perspective. *Journal of Research on Computing in Education*, *33*(4), 337–354.

King, K. P. (2002). Testing the waters for distance education in adult education programs. *PAACE Journal of Lifelong Learning*, *11*, 11–24. (Pennsylvania Association for Adult Continuing Education).

Lengnick-Hall, C., & Sanders, M. (1997). Designing effective learning systems for management education. *Academy of Management Journal*, *40*(6), 1,334–1,368.

Moore, M., & Kearsley, G. (1996). *Distance education: A systems view*. Belmont, CA: Wadsworth.

Palloff, R. M., & Pratt, K. (1999). *Building learning communities in cyberspace*. San Francisco: Jossey-Bass.

Palloff, R. M., & Pratt, K. (2001). *Lessons from the cyberspace classroom: The realities of online teaching*. San Francisco: Jossey-Bass.

Verduin, J. R., & Clark, T. A. (1991).

Distance education: The foundations of effective practice. San Francisco: Jossey-Bass.

Wallace, R. M. (2003). Online learning in higher education: A review of research on interactions among teachers and students. *Education, Communication & Information, 3*(2), 241–280.

Kathleen P. King

E

Educational Foundations

There has been no one impetus to the development of North American adult education; it has developed in myriad ways, including through federal initiatives, community-based organized, and local efforts. Yet, one could argue that foundations have played an unprecedented role in defining what adult education is and in funding initiatives that have set the parameters for the field today. The consequences of this role have been both positive and negative. The foundations that have contributed to adult education efforts have often seen it as a way to ameliorate the world's problems. Foundations have led the way in conceptualizing the field of adult education and in pioneering the development of projects for minorities, for under-represented groups, and that have attempted to literally build the field of adult education (Essert, 1960).

Three foundations that have supported adult education directly are the Kellogg Foundation, the Ford Foundation, and the Carnegie Corporation. Each of these three approached adult education in a different fashion and with a different vision. One could argue that each of these visions has pulled the field of adult education in differing ways, resulting in what the sociologist Burton Clark (1968) has called the marginalization of adult education. Central to Clark's view on how adult education has become marginalized, is the idea that adult education has no central, agreed-upon, philosophy and that it is at the whim of economic pressures. While Clark was talking about adult basic education programs in California, his central thesis has pervaded much discussion about adult education in general. For Clark, the principal issue was that adult education's mission seemed to change as funding sources or individual people set divergent goals. In this respect, foundations have certainly been responsible for the ebb and flow of particular ideas related to adult education. Certainly, his view could be expanded to the impact of foundations, in particular, within the field. In this area, adult education professional organizations have either invented themselves (in the case of the Carnegie Corporation) or reinvented themselves. Yet, foundations have helped to lead the way in conceptualizing the field of adult education, have emphasized services to different groups, including minorities, supported community development efforts across the globe, and alternately supported and eschewed literacy programs in North America and around the world. Foundations have also pioneered the development of projects for minorities and under-represented groups, attempting to literally build the field of adult education (Essert, 1960).

Surprisingly, given the vast importance of foundation support to adult education, there has been little research on the central role of foundations in the evolution of the field of adult education, in North America as well as in the development of related phenomena such as community education programs, university programs, and international development efforts. Malcolm Knowles (1977) gives a brief overview of the role of foundations in the development of the field, making clear that foundations have provided what he calls the "risk capital" for ". . . experimentation and new developments, added substantially to its physical plant, greatly expanded its literature, strengthened its leadership, and encouraged it to discover its basis of unity as a discrete dimension of our national educational enterprise" (p. 97).

The Carnegie Corporation

The Carnegie Corporation was the first foundation to see adult education as an entity that could serve as midwife to the birth of a new American society. The Carnegie Corporation was perhaps the most influential in envisioning adult education through financing the founding of the American Association of Adult Education (or A^3E) in 1926. Knowles initially presented this organization as a professional association whose success was short-lived due to the elitist stances it took which excluded vast numbers of adult education providers. In addition to the A^3E, the Carnegie Corporation provided funding for myriad adult education programs covering, among others, African Americans, the Antigonish Movement in Nova Scotia and adult literacy and libraries in various parts of North America. Additionally, the Corporation provided money for the development of the first North American doctoral program in adult education at Teachers College, Columbia University. In particular, a major thrust of funding efforts was to develop community oriented educational efforts that aided the entire community.

The Carnegie concept was that adult education was a unique educational format, lying outside of all traditional educational systems and thus beyond the depredations of the world of public schools. The encouragement of adult education was meant to provide individuals with meaning in their lives, not to help them earn better wages. From the beginning there was some confusion about what the Carnegie Corporation meant to do and whether this goal could be achieved. For example, what we now call adult basic education and English as a second language instruction were initially excluded from the Carnegie definition of adult education. Adult education was seen primarily as a leisure-time activity that would lead to personal growth and development. Lecture series, library programs and individual self-study were all part of the Carnegie mission, yet this mission was never entirely clear. Some saw the creation of the A^3E as a chance to build a professional adult education entity, while those committed to adult education as leisure-time activity eschewed even the possibility of a professional organization for adult educators. Despite this confusion, the Depression and the Second World War demanded a change in emphasis among even the most adamant leisure-time activities. As Morse Cartwright, the Executive Director of the A^3E put it, the national emergency required changes within the organization and the funding of projects. Ultimately this shift led to deep dissatisfaction with Carnegie Corporation adult education projects on the part of the Board of the Carnegie Corporation itself (Stubblefield & Keane, 1994).

The aim was ambitious. In short,

the proponents of adult education meant to develop a system that would go beyond public and higher education, to improve the lot of all people through study, through appreciation of the arts, and for all activities that took individuals beyond the mundane everydayness of their world. In all, the Carnegie Corporation donated $1,596,897 to the A^{3}E between 1926 and 1941. This does not include donations made to arts groups and community groups as well as educational institutions that came under the Carnegie purview.

However, the envisioned world of adult education did not materialize, and instead disparate interests developed that looked to the Carnegie Corporation for funding in a piecemeal, rather than a community development emphasis. Important projects were launched in almost all areas of adult education, including community development in North America and literacy and health education in Africa. Yet the aim of the Carnegie Corporation, which was no less than a re-imagining of American cultural and communal life, was in the end too vast. Its impact was limited and, ironically, it was only in the area of professional leadership development within adult education that the impact was longer lasting (Lagemann, 1989).

The Kellogg Foundation

Although Kellogg involvement in the field has been less studied than that of Carnegie, it may well be that its ultimate impact was greater, at least in the United States. It does not appear to have played a similar role in Canada. The Kellogg Foundation became involved in adult education in 1939 when it expanded its Articles of Association to allow the funding of projects that would promote "the health, education, and welfare of mankind" (cited in Knowles, 1977, p. 95). Until 1945, there was no specific adult education category, but beginning at that point the foundation began to fund specific projects in continuing education. The Kellogg Foundation's vision of continuing education differed substantially from Carnegie's, and there have been three principal eras of Kellogg adult education funding. The first was in the 1950s when the foundation provided the funding for the building of continuing education centers on college campuses; Kellogg Centers for continuing education were built at Michigan State University, the University of Georgia, the University of Chicago, the University of Nebraska, and the University of Oklahoma (Knowles).

In 1976, the Kellogg Foundation provided the funding for the second Wingspread Conference which focused on the future of the adult education field. The result of this conference was a document calling for lifelong learning that would focus on the needs of learners and would perhaps result in a reorganization of the entire field of adult education. Unfortunately this document was never implemented. According to Stubblefield and Keane (1994), the group involved in writing the document became embroiled in association politics and never developed it further.

Finally, in the 1980s and 1990s, the Kellogg Foundation experienced a resurgence of interest in adult education. This interest again focused on colleges and universities, but involved the building of graduate programs in adult education. Programs were funded at Syracuse University and the University of Georgia respectively. Additionally, leadership fellowships were funded in both the 1980s and the 1990s in an effort to help develop cohorts of new adult education professors. Of particular interest was the funding of the Syracuse University History Project, led by Alex Charters, a project which provided the funding for establishment of an archive of adult education history.

Although the Kellogg contribution to adult education remains to be analysed, it is clear that this foundation has funded a diverse array of adult education ventures, many of which have focused on leadership development within the field. Its focus on leadership development in North America and around the world has led to greater cooperation among disparate groups on a worldwide basis. The centers of continuing education were actually part of a worldwide effort that was an extension of the Kellogg vision of community education and community development, a focus which persists until the present-day.

The Ford Foundation

The Ford Foundation's involvement in adult education began in 1951 with the establishing of the Fund for Adult Education (FAE), which was an independent organization formed to encourage activities that focused on "that part of the total educational process which begins when schooling is finished" (cited in Knowles, 1977, p. 96). The Fund for Adult Education provided the funding for a variety of adult education activities which again shaped the contours of adult education in the 1950s and 1960s. The particular aim of the fund was the support of liberal adult education. Grants were made to support educational radio, the development of study materials and programs such as the Great Books Foundation, the Center for the Study of Liberal Education for Adults (CSLEA), and the American Library Association. The Fund was responsible for experiments in discussion-based education as well as research studies connected to adult education. From 1951–61, the Fund provided \$47.4 million dollars to a variety of programs within liberal adult education (Knowles; Stubblefield & Keane, 1994).

In a closely related effort, the Fund financed research on discussion and liberal education, and during the 1950s this was closely allied with anti-communist efforts to promote "free" inquiry and democratic thought. Discussion was seen as a bulwark against totalitarian efforts. While an effort such as this had been discussed in the 1930s, it was not until the 1950s that the funds became available for full-scale dialogue on this issue.

The Fund for Adult Education also brought a liberal education focus to the newly formed Adult Education Association (AEA) of the United States. When the AEA was founded in 1951, it was seen as the answer to the dying A^{3}E, yet, without the support of the Carnegie Corporation there was little financial support available. The FAE provided initial funding for the nascent AEA, yet according to Stubblefield and Keane (1994) this funding eventually split the AEA between different constituents, those allied with liberal education and those most interested in other areas, particularly community development. In essence, the FAE continued the focus of the earlier Carnegie philanthropic efforts, focusing on leisure, intellectual development, and community rather than other more instrumental areas of adult education. Yet, according to Joseph Kett, the FAE experiment was largely a failure. Discussion groups were never fully integrated into the communal life of cities, although the notion of liberal education for adults became incorporated into college programs for adults which grew exponentially at the time that the FAE programs were ebbing (Kett, 1994).

The FAE also provided funding for states to develop state boards of adult education with a state director or superintendent (Edelson, 1991).The antithesis of the earlier Carnegie initiative, this endeavor was to encourage the growth of a state bureaucracy of adult education to match the infrastructure of the pervasive public school boards. Additionally, it was thought that with this seed funding, adult education would receive a greater share of public monies if there were a state organization to receive it. More recently, the Ford Foundation's efforts in adult education have focused almost exclusively on health education, the development of higher education initiatives, and community development efforts in Africa, Asia, and the former Soviet Union. While adult education is not the aim, it is clearly a means towards some of the ends found in current Ford Foundation grants.

Conclusion

North American adult education has a different face than adult education has in other parts of the world. This is in some small part due to the way it has developed, from informal learning opportunities to institutions funded primarily through philanthropic means.

Foundations and various philanthropic efforts provided the seed money for projects that governments (whether state, provincial, local, or federal) could not support. They also sidetracked efforts to move adult education outside of the educational periphery. Each foundation has come to adult education with its own sense of what adult education is and how it fits into a broader educational scheme. Within North America, foundations have supported a vision of adult education that has manifested itself through an emphasis on leisure time and democratic life. Today these ideals are discussed in terms of civil society, whereas in the 1920s it was civic intelligence. The roles of these three foundations (as well as some others) has been to develop and fund innovative programs for educational efforts that individual governments have not been able to support. Along with this aid has gone a particular philanthropic emphasis, whether on leisure pursuits or community development that have had a major impact on the practice and theory of adult education worldwide.This can be seen in the support for non-governmental organizations (NGOs) in other countries.

Thus, the clear message for adult education is that it lies outside of mainstream financial support for education in general. Private foundations have used adult education to ameliorate conditions and develop innovative programs, but for the most part these efforts have not been institutionalized in any meaningful fashion. In fact, one could look at this phenomenon as part of an ever-expanding spiral of adult education. North American foundations have taken adult education as a metaphor; it provides the possibility for redemption. While the positives remain, they can be categorized in terms of program innovation, whilst the negative aspects of this effort lie in the problems encountered when adult education activities must conform to outside prerogatives in order to obtain funding. This is not a simple case of manipulation of a field to achieve an elite agenda, although admittedly parts of this history could be read in this manner. It is more complex than that. In fact, the drama of adult education lies in finding ways to fund innovation while at the same time sustaining it.

See also: higher education, historical inquiry, organizations.

References and Further Reading

Clark, B. R. (1968). *Adult education in transition: A study of institutional insecurity*. Berkeley and Los Angeles: University of California Press.

Edelson, P. (1991). *The Saturation Project – NAPSAE's Silver Bullet for Adult Education*. Paper presented at the Annual Conference of the American Association for Adult and Continuing Education, Montreal, Quebec. Retrieved April 17, 2004 from ERIC database (ERIC Document Reproduction Service No. ED339913).

Essert, P. (1960). Foundations and adult education. In M. S. Knowles (Ed.), *Handbook of adult education in the United States* (pp. 230–237). Washington, DC: Adult Education Association of the USA.

Kett, J. F. (1994). *The pursuit of knowledge under difficulties: From self-improvement to adult education in America, 1750–1990*. Stanford, CA: Stanford University Press.

Knowles, M. S. (1977). *The adult education movement in the United States*. Huntington, NY: Krieger.

Lagemann, E. C. (1989). *The politics of knowledge: The Carnegie Corporation, philanthropy, and public policy*. Middletown, CT: Wesleyan University Press.

Stubblefield, H. W., & Keane, P. (1994) *Adult education in the American experience: From the colonial period to the present*. San Francisco: Jossey-Bass.

Amy Rose

Emancipatory Education

Emancipatory education is a complex term. In general, it refers to the role education plays in helping individuals and social groups to develop new forms of knowledge that will lead to their own greater freedom or "emancipation" in the world. Within the field of adult education, the term was probably made popular by Jack Mezirow (1991) in developing his theory of transformative learning based, in part, on the work of the German critical theorist Jürgen Habermas. Habermas discussed three forms of knowledge: (a) instrumental knowledge which focuses on the nuts and bolts of learning how to do something, such as a technological skill; (b) practical knowledge (often termed communicative) which is related to understanding social norms and human relations; and (c) emancipatory knowledge which is knowledge where learners examine their underlying and often unconscious assumptions about the world, their foundations of knowledge, and their beliefs about themselves and others for the purposes of changing themselves and their worlds. Habermas' concept of emancipatory knowledge is a centerpiece of Mezirow's theory of transformative learning, though Mezirow focused more specifically on the processes by which learners become transformed through emancipatory learning by critically reflecting on assumptions. The unit of analysis in Mezirow's discussion of transformative learning has primarily been *the individual*, and how individuals transform rather than the emancipation of social or cultural groups, which is why many in the field have argued that his theory is not a theory of social emancipation.

While the term emancipatory education was initially made popular in adult education by Mezirow's drawing on Habermas' idea of emancipatory knowledge, more typically in the wider field of education and currently in adult education the term *emancipatory education* is associated with discourses that specifically challenge power relations based on social systems or *structures* of race, gender, class, culture, national origin, religion, sexual orientation, age, or disability in adult and higher education and in popular education. Nearly all of these discussions of emancipatory education are influenced by the work of Brazilian activist and literacy adult educator Paulo Freire (1971), whose focus was on specifically teaching learners to "read the world" and to explicitly challenge power relations based on structural social systems. There are many discourses of emancipatory education with different theoretical influences at their base, and often specific social groups (such as race, gender, and class); however, what all these discourses have in common is their concern for challenging social systems of oppression and privilege based on one or more social structures through inclusive representation in curricula and particular pedagogical strategies. At this juncture, all these discourses have influenced each other; and Black feminist writer bell hooks (1994) refers to the confluence of these various strands of emancipatory education as "radical" or "engaged pedagogy." The major strands of these emancipatory education discourses will be discussed in light of their underlying theoretical frameworks, though the reader needs to bear in mind that there is considerable overlap among these discourses, and should read entries elsewhere in this volume for more specific discussion of these discourses as well as texts that more directly discuss various strands relative to adult education (Dei, Hall, & Rosenberg, 2000; Sheared & Sissel, 2001). Nevertheless, it is helpful in considering any discussion of emancipatory education to bear in mind three questions: (a) *emancipation of whom?*; (b) *for what purposes?*; and (c) *with what strategies?*

Critical Pedagogy

Paulo Freire's (1971) work, which challenged class relations in literacy settings in Brazil, gave rise to the critical pedagogy literature. This literature initially focused on emancipatory education for working-class and poor people (Horton & Freire, 1990), the hope being that through emancipatory educational strategies oppressive class and other relations are challenged to benefit the lives of working-class and poor people or those oppressed based on other structural systems of oppression. In community adult education settings such as the Highlander Center in Tennessee or the Antigonish movement in Canada, the focus has been on using problem-posing educational techniques drawing on learners' life experiences and engaging their passion to build critical thinking skills to analyse political systems and to collectively and communally act on their new understandings to implement changes that challenge oppressive structures. Critical pedagogy has also been discussed and applied in higher education by many authors and scholar activists who teach about social critique and social action (Giroux & McLaren, 1994; Shor, 1996). A strong theoretical base has arisen out of critical pedagogy in higher education, though there has been some critique that it is overly rational and theoretical, offering more in the way of critique than solution (Ellsworth, 1989).

Feminist Pedagogy

Whereas in critical pedagogy the primary unit of analysis has been on social class and on challenging class relations, the primary unit of analysis in feminist pedagogy has been on gender and on challenging gender relations. Feminist educational models initially developed out of two distinct bodies of literature: the literature that focused on women's propensity to connected ways of being and knowing following the work of Belenky, Clinchy, Goldberger, and Tarule (1986), and the critical pedagogy literature with an emphasis on challenging patriarchy and racism, that arose out of women's studies and the writings of thinkers like bell hooks (1994) as well as influences in critical pedagogy. Strategies of feminist pedagogy emphasize the important ways women (and some men) construct knowledge through connection and relationship, and to the role of the affective as well as the rational dimension in learning. Many feminist and womanist writers also discuss the role of gender as it intersects with race, class, culture, national origin and sexual orientation (Hart, 1992; Hayes & Flannery, 2000; hooks; Johnson-Bailey, 2001; Sheared, 1994; Walters & Manicom, 1996). Discussions of feminist pedagogy tend to foreground the five following issues in teaching and learning: (a) the construction of knowledge; (b) voice; (c) authority; (d) how positionality (of both teachers and learners) shapes teaching and learning; and (e) identity as constantly shifting and developing (Maher & Tetreault, 1994; Tisdell, 2000). Educators making use of feminist pedagogy would develop curricula related to these five issues, and emphasize pedagogy and ways of knowing that provide analysis related to these areas in relation to real-life situations as strategies of emancipation for challenging power relations.

Anti-Racist, Cultural, and Culturally Relevant Pedagogies

There is a wide body of literature that deals with challenging systems of oppression based on race, where the primary unit of analysis is race or culture, and the emphasis is education for the emancipation of a particular cultural group. These pedagogies assume that racism exists and is real, and needs to be challenged. Some of these pedagogies are informed by Africentrism (Colin & Guy, 1998) and other race-based social theories, while other scholars emphasize the intersection of race/culture/national origin with language or religion in understanding and challenging systems of oppression for particular cultural groups, such as in the experience of various Latino communities in the USA (Abalos, 1998). Still others (Guy, 1999) discuss teaching for "cultural relevance" where educators challenge themselves and their students to explore their own race or cultural identities (including white identity), as they focus on challenging power relations based on race, color, or culture and at the same time affirming the cultures, identities, and ways of knowing from the specific cultural group that is at the center of analysis. Underpinning all of this literature is the challenging of White privilege and a direct challenge to the implicit assumption that White cultural realities should remain the norm by which all others are judged. In addition, the literature problematizing whiteness in adult and higher education (Manglitz, 2003) is an important part of emancipatory education that specifically challenges White educators to examine their own whiteness as a system of privilege so that they can be allies to people of color in emancipatory educational efforts at social change.

Critical Multicultural, Resistance-Postmodern, and Postcolonial Pedagogies

Closely related to the emancipatory education discourses that focus on race or culture are the critical multicultural education, resistance-postmodern and postcolonial discourses. The term "critical multicultural" here refers specifically to those multicultural education discourses that specifically focus on challenging power relations based on *social structures* of race or culture, gender, class, etc. and on challenging the "isms" that result from those power relations, as in rac*ism* or sex*ism*. *Critical* multiculturalism is distinguished from "multicultural education" approaches that simply focus on individual difference and never deal with directly challenging systemic racism, sexism or heterosexism.

Strongly related to the discourses of critical multiculturalism are the resistance-postmodernist and postcolonial discourses in education in that they focus on how power relations shape our understanding of various aspects of our identity (Sleeter, 1996; Sleeter & McLaren, 1995). The emphasis of postmodernism on deconstructing and understanding how structures of race, gender, class, national origin and sexual orientation, and so on have shaped or constructed our understanding of individual and group-based identities is key to understanding how one can reclaim that identity anew. Unlike ludic versions of postmodernism which simply emphasize deconstruction for its own sake, resistance-postmodernists would see that deconstruction *and reclaiming* of various aspects of one's individual and group-based identities as an important part of challenging power relations (Lather, 1991; Sleeter). The unit of analysis in these resistance-postmodern discourses might be considered *the connections between* social structures and individual identity, and how social structures of race, gender, class, national origin and sexuality inform our identities. Again, some of these resistance-postmodern and postcolonial or global pedagogies may focus more on one social system than another; for example queer pedagogy focus on sexual orientation, and postcolonial and global pedagogies focuses more on national identity in light of globalization and colonization, but neither focus on these to the exclusion of other aspects of identity. The strategies of critical multicultural, resistance-postmodern, and global, and postcolonial approaches to emancipatory education are a confluence of those of critical, feminist, and cultural and anti-racist pedagogies.

Spiritually Grounded Emancipatory Pedagogies

More recently there has been discussion of the role of spirituality in transformative and emancipatory pedagogies in adult and higher education. While many of these discourses focus on the role of spirituality in transformative adult learning, drawing on Mezirow and other transformative learning theories with the individual at the center of analysis (English & Gillen, 2000), others mention the role of spirituality in challenging power relations (O'Sullivan, 1999), whereas others focus specifically on the role of spirituality in learning as it connects directly to challenging power relations based on structural social systems of race, class, gender, culture, religion, sexual orientation, or national origin and working for social justice (Tisdell, 2003). These discourses that focus specifically on the role of spirituality in emancipatory education draw on some discussions of spirituality and/or liberation theology as an underlying force that partially motivated the civil-rights movement in the USA (Cone, 1990), and an underpinning to the work of emancipatory education workers such as Myles Horton, Paulo Freire, and Moses Coady. These discussions make a distinction between spirituality and religion, where spirituality is associated with meaning-making and an internal belief system and experience of the interconnectedness and wholeness of Great Mystery that people call by different names (God, lifeforce, higher power, Great Spirit, Buddha etc.). Religion, on the other hand, is associated with the official belief and creeds of institutionalized religious communities. In any event, those advocating and discussing the importance of spiritually grounded emancipatory pedagogies draw also on a confluence of pedagogical strategies noted in the earlier discussed emancipatory pedagogies. However, rather than necessarily discussing spirituality directly, these writers also call attention to the importance of incorporating forms of knowing through ritual, symbol, art and music that are also cultural, and that sometimes enhance a sense of commitment, community and forms of meaning-making that provide grounding and inspiration and ongoing support to emancipatory work. While some people map the use of such strategies as "spiritual," others do not. The point in these pedagogies is not spirituality itself; rather, the point is to draw on multiple ways of knowing that fuel motivation, inspiration, and a sense of community to continue emancipatory work.

See also: class, critical multiculturalism, critical theory, gender, praxis, race, spirituality.

References and Further Reading

Abalos, D. (1998). *La Communidad Latina in the United States*. Westport, CT: Praeger.

Belenky, M. F., Clinchy, B. M., Goldberger, N. R., & Tarule, J. M., (1986). *Women's ways of knowing, The development of self, voice, and mind*. New York: Basic Books.

Colin, S. A. J., III, & Guy, T. (1998). An Africentric interpretive model of curricular orientations for course development in graduate programs in adult education. *PAACE Journal of Lifelong Learning, 7*, 43–55. (Pennsylvania Association for Adult Continuing Education)

Cone, J. (Ed.). (1990). *A Black theology of liberation*. Maryknoll, NY: Orbis.

Dei, G. J. S., Hall, B. L., & Rosenberg, D. G. (Eds.). (2000). *Indigenous knowledges in global contexts*. Toronto: University of Toronto Press.

Ellsworth, E. (1989). Why doesn't this feel empowering? Working through the repressive myths of critical pedagogy. *Harvard Educational Review, 59*(3), 297–324.

English, L. M., & Gillen, M. A. (Eds.). (2000). *Addressing the spiritual dimensions of adult learning: What educators can do*. New *Directions for Adult and Continuing Education*, No. 85. San Francisco: Jossey-Bass

Freire, P. (1971). *Pedagogy of the oppressed*. (M. Ramos, Trans.) New York: Herder & Herder.

Giroux, H., & McLaren, P. (Eds.). (1994). *Between borders: Pedagogy and the politics of cultural studies*. New York: Routledge.

Guy, T. C. (Ed.).(1999). *Providing culturally relevant adult education: A challenge for the 21st century. New Directions for Adult and Continuing Education*, No. 82. San Francisco: Jossey-Bass.

Hart, M. (1992). *Working and educating for life: Feminist and international perspectives on adult education.* New York: Routledge.

Hayes, E. R., & Flannery, D. D. with Brooks, A. K., Tisdell, E. J., & Hugo, J. M. (2000). *Women as learners: The significance of gender in adult learning.* San Francisco: Jossey-Bass

hooks, b. (1994). *Teaching to transgress.* New York: Routledge.

Horton, M., & Freire, P. (1990). *We make the road by walking: Conversations on education and social change.* Philadelphia: Temple University Press.

Johnson-Bailey, J. (2001). *Sistahs in college: Making a way out of no way.* Malabar, FL: Krieger.

Lather, P. (1991). *Getting smart.* Routledge: New York.

Maher, F., & Tetreault, M. (1994). *The feminist classroom.* New York: Basic Books.

Manglitz, E. (2003). Challenging white privilege in adult education. *Adult Education Quarterly, 53,* 119–135.

Mezirow, J. (1991). *Transformative dimensions of adult learning.* San Francisco: Jossey-Bass.

O'Sullivan, E. (1999). *Transformative learning; Educational vision of the 21st century.* Toronto: University of Toronto Press. London: Zed Books.

Sheared, V. (1994). Giving voice: An inclusive model of instruction – A womanist perspective. In E. R. Hayes & S. A. J., III. Colin (Eds.), *Confronting racism and sexism* (pp. 63–76). *New Directions for Adult and Continuing Education,* No. 61. San Francisco: JosseyBass.

Sheared, V., & Sissel, P. A. (Eds.). (2001). *Making space. Merging theory and practice in adult education.* Westport, CT: Bergin & Garvey.

Shor, I. (1996). *When students have power.* Chicago: University of Chicago Press.

Sleeter, C. (1996). *Multicultural education as social action.* Albany, NY: State University of New York Press.

Sleeter, C., & McLaren, P. (Eds.). (1995). *Multicultural education, critical pedagogy, and the politics of difference.* Albany, NY: State University of New York Press.

Tisdell, E. J. (2000). Feminist pedagogies. In E. R. Hayes & D. D. Flannery with A. K. Brooks, E. J. Tisdell, & J. M. Hugo, *Women as learners: The significance of gender in adult learning* (pp. 155–184). San Francisco: Jossey-Bass.

Tisdell, E. J. (2003). *Exploring spirituality and culture in adult and higher education.* San Francisco: Jossey-Bass.

Walters, S., & Manicom, L. (Eds.). (1996). *Gender in popular education: Methods for empowerment,* London: Zed Books.

Elizabeth J. Tisdell

Embodied Learning

One of the ways in which the hegemony of modern Western culture is expressed is in the privileging of the mind over the body, legitimating rational knowledge and delegitimating knowledge based in the body. The notion of embodied or somatic learning highlights the position of challenges to this norm and argues that the body is a highly significant site and source of knowledge and learning. Embodied learning is a way of recognizing that we *know* with our bodies as well as our minds, to reclaim our wholeness as learners. It also offers powerful ways to expand our effectiveness as adult educators (see also, Clark, 2001).

Western culture has a complex and fundamentally conflicted relationship with the body. The body is normed through social discourses that define the range of acceptability and the criteria for beauty, creating a situation in which the language of desire and indulgence intersects with the language of regulation and control. This conflictual situation makes us uncomfortable with our bodies and gives us further incentive to live in our heads.

This was not the case in earlier centuries. During the Middle Ages in Europe, for example, the process of knowing was much more holistic, more emotional and internal, and people saw themselves as connected to the natural world (Bordo, 1987). Sense-based knowledge was the norm, not rationality. Berman (1989) describes this as a time in which " 'the facts' were first and foremost what happened on a psychic and emotional level" and "the essential truth was an interior one" (p. 111). Knowledge was created with and through the body. This is still the case in our own time in many non-Western cultures. One example is indigenous people, who have "maintained that spirit, mind and body are not separated in experience, that learning is more focused on being than doing, and that experiential knowledge is produced within the collective, not the individual mind" (Fenwick, 2003, p. 129). Collins (1990) likewise argues that the African American way of knowing is embodied within their long history of oppression.

The modern split between mind and body is the legacy of Descartes and the Enlightenment. Rationality is given primacy and a clear distinction is made between the knower and the known. In privileging reason, the body is delegitimated as a mode of knowing. Bordo (1987) points to two dimensions of the Cartesian world view:

> On the one hand, a new model of knowledge is conceived, in which the purity of the intellect is guaranteed through its ability to transcend the body. On the other hand . . . the spiritual and the corporeal are now two distinct substances which share no qualities. (p. 99)

If the body must be transcended in order to construct knowledge, then the body itself becomes suspect as a source of knowing.

The Reemergence of the Body

The body as a source of knowledge is returning and it has taken a number of paths. A major one was the women's movement, since one means by which women have been disempowered and marginalized in Western culture is by associating them with the body. Consciousness-raising groups served as a site of embodied learning as women examined how patriarchy oppressed them through the regulation of their bodies. What had been considered secret and even shameful began to be the object of study and public discourse. This has been developed much more extensively by feminist theorists, who see the body as foundational for women's conceptualization of the self and the construction of knowledge.

There is also the path of our own everyday experience. No-one is a stranger to stress and most of us have had the disconcerting experience, often more than once, of stress manifesting itself in our bodies before our heads fully understand what trouble we're in. Western medicine is increasingly recognizing the mind/body connection in the treatment of disease, and scientists have extensive data on how care of the body (things like proper nutrition, exercise, and sleep) affects brain functioning and thus learning (Weiss, 2001).

The body is also the site of learning what is most true, most authentic, for us as individuals. This is the domain of intuition, of a kind of gut knowing, and it is manifested in decisions big and small. Heshusius and Ballard (1996) offer an unusual and very persuasive example of this. They collected the stories of other scholars who shifted from positivism to interpretivism as their paradigm of research. This, of course, is a very intellectual process, one that involves examining assumptions about reality and the process of knowing, yet they and the other scholars they studied did not come to their new position solely through the application of reason. Instead, each of them began with an inner sense, a gut sense, that they needed to change. "While the dominant assumptions still made sense rationally in terms of how things are done, they no longer made sense somatically and affectively. Something *felt* wrong. Our bodies told us so" (p. 2).

Embodied Learning and Adult Education

The idea of learning being situated in the body is also found in educational theory. The concept of tacit knowing, developed by Polanyi (1969), argues that knowledge actually begins in the body: "Every time we make sense of the world, we rely on our tacit knowledge of impacts made by the world on our body and the complex responses of our body to these impacts. Such is the exceptional position of our body in the universe" (pp. 147–148). In a sense we lead with our body. Kinesthetic knowing is a related though different term, the focus here being on the development of a skill, such as riding a bicycle, that requires more than a cognitive learning process; in a real sense, the body does the learning.

Experiential learning is a broader category within which embodied learning can, to some extent, be situated, but as Fenwick (2003) points out, traditional notions of experiential learning maintain the mind/body split by describing a largely cognitive process – we have an experience, then later we reflect on it – thus locating the learning in the act of reflection and not in the embodied experience. "What becomes emphasized are the supposed conceptual lessons gained from experience, quickly stripped of location and embeddedness in the material and social conditions that produced the knowledge. What is conveniently excised from these lessons is the body" (Fenwick, p. 125). Michelson (1998) argues that the body itself can be the site of the learning. She illustrates this with a story about a woman she calls Mary who is a newly promoted director of a managerial team. At one of her first team meetings, she is angered when one of the senior men rudely dismisses the more junior women on the team, and he then appropriates their ideas himself. She doesn't react to this behavior at the meeting, however, but on her train ride home she consciously reflects on the experience and decides on some strategies to deal with the situation. Michelson argues that Mary's learning happened, not on the train as traditional theorists would claim, but at the meeting: "The understanding that came to Mary on the way home was not a cognitive flash of new learning, but simply the moment in which her mental processes caught up with what her body already knew" (p. 226). Fenwick argues for a reembodied understanding of experiential learning.

The voices for embodied learning in adult education are steadily growing. Two recent examples point to the rich potential of this type of learning for practice. Chapman (2003), working from a Foucaultian analysis of the body, explores how self-writing can be used to expose our own exercise of power over those we teach. And Yorks and Kasl (2002) argue for the practice of whole-person learning, a process that attends more fully to the role of affect. Embodied learning will continue to be an area of rich development in adult education theory and practice.

See also: autobiography, experiential learning, relational learning, writing.

References and Further Reading

Berman, M. (1989). *Coming to our senses: Body and spirit in the hidden history of the West.* New York: Simon & Schuster.

Bordo, S. R. (1987). *The flight to objectivity.* Albany, NY: State University of New York Press.

Chapman, V.-L. (2003). On "knowing one's self": Selfwriting, power and ethical practice: Reflections from an adult educator. *Studies in the Education of Adults, 35*(1), 35–54.

Clark, M. C. (2001). Off the beaten path: Some creative approaches to adult learning. In S. Merriam (Ed.), *The new update on adult learning theory* (pp. 83–91). *New Directions for Adult and Continuing Education,* No. 89. San Francisco: Jossey-Bass.

Collins, P. H. (1990). *Black Feminist thought.* London: Routledge.

Fenwick, T. J. (2003). Reclaiming and re-embodying experiential learning through complexity science. *Studies in the Education of Adults, 35,* 123–141.

Heshusius, L., & Ballard, K. (1996). *From positivism to interpretivism and beyond.* New York: Teachers College Press.

Michelson, E. (1998). Re-membering: The return of the body to experiential learning. *Studies in Continuing Education, 20,* 217–233.

Polanyi, M. (1969). *Knowing and being.* Chicago: University of Chicago Press.

Weiss, R. P. (2001). The mind-body connection in learning. *Training and Development, 55*(9), 60–67.

Yorks, L., & Kasl, E. (2002). Toward a theory and practice for whole-person learning: Reconceptualizing experience and the role of affect. *Adult Education Quarterly, 52*(3), 176–192.

M. Carolyn Clark

English as a Second Language

ESL is an acronym for English as a Second Language, a term referring to the English of those who are acquiring English in a context where it is the dominant language (for example in the United Kingdom, English-speaking Canada, Australia, South Africa and the United States). By contrast, the term EFL (English as a Foreign Language) has traditionally been used to refer to those who are learning English where other languages are dominant (for example, in Europe and Latin America). These terms themselves are contested because of their implicit assumptions, which, some argue, reflect underlying differences in the ways learners are viewed. The terms ESOL (English for Speakers of Other Languages) and EAL (English as an Additional Language) have gained currency recently because, for many learners, English may be a third, fourth or fifth language; these terms are said to reflect the richness and complexity of learners' linguistic competence more adequately than the reductionist binary implicit in "ESL." The term EFL has been challenged on the grounds that there are more similarities than differences in teaching English in various linguistic contexts. Even the notion of a unitary dominant English has been replaced by the concept of Englishes in order to reflect the diversity of English varieties used around the world.

Likewise, terms referring to learners of English reflect ideological differences in how learners are perceived: LEP (Limited English Proficient) is a term commonly used in policy and educational discourses, particularly in the United States, and students have at times been referred to as LEPs, a term which many find offensive because it invokes associations with leprosy, implying illness and outcast status. Because of this deficit connotation, the acronym LEP is increasingly being replaced with ELL – English Language Learner – a more neutral term.

Adult ESL Learners

In many English-dominant countries, ELLs comprise the largest group of learners participating in adult education programming. For example, in the United States in 2000–01, 42% of all participants enrolled in state-administered adult education programs were enrolled in ESL classes (NCLE, 2003, p. 7). This number underestimates the actual number of adult ELLs in that it encompasses only those in ESL classes, not those enrolled in ABE (adult basic education) or ASE (adult secondary education). It is not age that distinguishes this group, but rather immigration status and educational purpose. Adult ESL learners are usually immigrants and refugees who have come to settle in a new country (as opposed to those who come for a limited duration, usually to study, and then return to their homelands). While adult ESL programming may be housed in or administered through tertiary institutions (e.g., community colleges), it usually focuses on English for civic, economic and social rather than academic purposes, although it may lead to English for academic purposes.

Adult ESL learners are a diverse group, coming from a range of backgrounds. They may have been astrophysicists or agricultural workers in their home countries, with advanced degrees or minimal education in their first language. They differ in terms of home languages (including orthographic systems), age, ethnicity, socioeconomic status, family status, immigration experiences, race, literacy proficiencies, immigration status, length of time in the new country, and many other factors. Key pedagogical issues arising from this diversity center around how to teach multilevel classes, whether to teach first-language literacy prior to ESL, when and how to integrate reading and writing with oral language instruction, and what (if any) role the first language should play in ESL classes. ESL literacy has become a field in its own right (Crandall & Peyton, 1993).

The Socio-Economic Context of Adult ESL

Debates over terminology reflect much deeper debates about how adult immigrants and refugees should be taught which, in turn, are rooted in varying conceptions of where learners fit into the socio-economic structures of the receiving countries. Conceptions of what ESL/literacy is intended to accomplish shape pedagogical approaches. The influx of refugees and immigrants to English-dominant countries has historically been closely linked to structural economic needs of those countries. Receiving countries welcome immigration when there is a need for particular kinds of labor; but those policies and laws are often repealed or revised when that need subsides or changes. Thus, in the case of the United States, for example, Chinese immigrants were welcomed in the 1800s to build the railroads and later excluded by law when the railroads were completed. Because manual labor required little use of English, ESL instruction was minimal. Prior to the 1960s, in most English-speaking countries English instruction for adults in non-academic contexts was largely limited to voluntary participation in night-schools taught with traditional grammar-translation methods. The premise of this approach was that language is a neutral skill which can be learned as a formal set of rules (often through memorization and repetition); once people learn the grammar and vocabulary of a language, they will be able to use it in any context.

The field of adult ESL instruction came into its own in the 1960s when large numbers of immigrants and refugees were, on the one hand, pushed from their own countries by war and decolonization, and, on the other, pulled towards the countries of the "center" by the economic needs of the reconfigured global economy. In Britain, for example, "These new immigrants were induced to come here to provide cheap labor that Britain required for the post-war economic building of the countries" (Khanna, Verma, Agnihotri, & Sinha, 1998, p. 9). Likewise, the United States Immigration Act of 1965 established preferences for immigrants to work in occupations with labor shortages – namely, dead-end low-wage unskilled jobs in the industrial and service sectors. Governments of English-speaking countries began mandating participation in English classes as a condition for resettlement subsidies because it was seen as a key to cultural and economic assimilation. Other factors contributing to the post-1960s evolution of the field of adult ESL included: (a) awareness that traditional grammar-focused foreign language instruction was inappropriate for newcomers with little prior education; (b) a general shift away from grammar-translation approaches to more communicative approaches in the field of second-language pedagogy as a whole; and (c) the need to train agrarian workers for new roles in the industrial and service sectors in receiving countries. As the field developed, a key issue differentiating approaches to teaching ESL was how each viewed the social function of ESL: was it to assimilate newcomers into the existing social order, to affirm their cultural strengths and maintain their identities, to assist them in gaining access to powerful discourses, or enable them to challenge and transform oppressive social conditions?

Behavioral and Functional Approaches: English for Assimilation

Among the first departures from grammar-oriented approaches to adult ESL was the functional or competency-based approach. This approach is based on the view that, for immigrants or refugees, the priority is "survival". Thus, where grammar-based approaches value what students *know* about language, this view emphasizes what students can *do* with language. It is concerned with the behaviors and performance demanded in particular domains or roles. The focus might be on life skills like reading want ads, filling out job applications, and preparing for interviews. Proponents of this approach argue that it enables learners to meet the practical demands of work, family and community life, preparing them to "succeed" in the dominant society. The message of this approach is that being able to perform tasks and roles according to socially-defined norms will result in assimilation into the mainstream.

In the early 1980s, functional, survival and competency-based approaches were critiqued on the grounds that they impose cultural values and train immigrants in skills, behaviors, attitudes and values necessary for low-level jobs, socializing them to conform to the demands of the marketplace and to fill dead-end jobs (e.g., Auerbach & Burgess, 1985). The behaviorist orientation, likewise, was seen to preclude dialogue, critical analysis and challenges to the status quo. In the 1980s, a number of alternatives emerged, each claiming to be more learner-centered and empowering than either grammar-translation or functional approaches. However, the means by which each approach proposed fostering these ends differs significantly.

Cognitive Approaches: English for Self-Expression and Meaning-Making

One approach, aligned with the whole language movement in elementary education, emphasizes individual self-expression through reading and writing about lived experience. The focus is on meaningful communication for real, learner-defined purposes. In this approach, reading instruction emphasizes pre-reading, eliciting prior knowledge, and responding to texts in light of personal or cultural experience. Writing is seen as a vehicle for reflection, discovery, and making sense of experience. Common practices in this approach include free writing, using dialogue and learning journals, writing extended narratives, writing poetry and publishing student writing (Peyton & Staton, 1996). Publication of student writing gives writers real audiences and purposes for language use. The message sent in this approach is that learners' lives and voices have value and can become the vehicle for language acquisition as well as self-discovery.

The Social Practices Approach: English for Affirmation

Another perspective coming from the field of literacy studies focuses on *social practices* (rather than functional behaviors or cognitive processes). Literacy ethnographers argue that ways of acquiring and using language/literacy vary from culture to culture, and always depend on context-specific roles and purposes. Advocates of this view propose investigating how people actually use and acquire first and second languages/literacies within specific contexts and communities. Studies of multilingual communities in Canada (Klassen & Burnaby, 1993), South Africa (Prinsloo & Breier, 1996) and the United Kingdom (Martin-Jones & Jones, 2000) document the multiple uses of languages/literacies outside of school contexts. The goal in this view is to build on what people know, and to incorporate their local cultural knowledge and ways of learning into education. Thus, instruction may focus on culture-specific genres, purposes and content as a bridge to new learning. ESL instruction is seen as a vehicle of social and cultural affirmation.

The Genre Approach: English for Access to Powerful Discourses

Another approach argues that both the cognitive and sociocultural approaches to writing instruction, despite claiming to empower learners, assure their continued social/economic exclusion. Advocates of this genre approach argue that because certain literacies yield more power than others, it's not enough for learners to share their stories, find their voices, and celebrate their cultures; they must learn the discourses of power. This approach, popular in England and

Australia, proposes deconstructing powerful genres, analysing them from a linguistic point of view, and reproducing them (Hasan & Williams, 1996). Through overt instruction, students learn to identify specific text types, analyse their structural and linguistic features, and generate their own texts that conform to the conventions of each genre. The message sent by this approach is that mastery of the genres of power will facilitate access to power.

The Critical Approach: English for Community Action and Social Change

A fifth view, which focuses on *social issues and action for change,* posits that it's not enough to celebrate students' voices, affirm their cultures, or teach the language of power: it is crucial to look at the larger institutional and economic forces within which language is acquired. Proponents argue that history shows that factors like gender, ethnicity and race are equally as important as language/literacy proficiency in determining access to power. Inspired by the work of Paulo Freire, problem-posing curricula focus on content drawn from the social context of learners' lives (connecting the word and the world, as Freire would say) and is used in service of action for change (Auerbach, 1992). Caroline Kerfoot (1993), for example, proposed a curriculum development process in which skills for participatory democracy were integrated into ESL instruction in post-apartheid South Africa. The message here is that English classes can become contexts for analysing critical social issues and supporting action to improve conditions in community life. Moreover, the critical approach advocates challenging traditional power relations between students, teachers and program administration through ongoing negotiation and learner participation in curriculum development and decision-making (Campbell & Burnaby, 2001; Wallace, 2001).

New Directions

Regardless of approach, a new direction in ESL instruction is the focus on thematic, content-based learning. Programs and curricula are often structured around themes like family literacy, health, workplace or civic education. How these themes are developed varies ideologically: for example, in workplace programs, functional approaches might focus on skills for following directions, calling in sick, and requesting supplies; cognitive approaches might focus on writing poems or narratives about workplace experiences; social practices approaches might investigate actual literacy practices in a workplace (who does what, with whom, how and why), developing curricula around site-specific practices; genre approaches might deconstruct workplace texts and teach students to analyse them and/or reproduce them; critical approaches might invite students to analyse power dynamics in the workplace and learn the language to take action for improved conditions or asserting rights. In each case, proponents claim that their respective approaches are "learner-centered," but what this means varies: it can mean working on individual goals, promoting self-expression, validating learners' existing practices, or working with communities to change oppressive conditions.

Challenges

Adult ESL educators in English-dominant countries face similar tensions between policy imperatives, research findings and practice: policy-makers are increasingly demanding standardized skills-oriented national curricula designed for workforce preparation in a globalized economy; researchers are focusing on multiple, variable, context-specific language/literacy uses, and practitioners are struggling to maintain professional standards in the face of funding constraints and policy mandates.

See also: attitudes, culturally relevant adult education, literacy, numeracy, race, participation.

References and Further Reading

Auerbach, E. (1992). *Making meaning, making change*. Washington, DC and McHenry, IL: Center for Applied Linguistics and Delta Systems.

Auerbach, E., & Burgess, D. (1985). The hidden curriculum of survival ESL. *TESOL Quarterly*, 19(3), 475–495.

Campbell, P., & Burnaby, B.(Eds.).(2001). *Participatory practices in adult education*. Mahwah, NJ: Lawrence Erlbaum Associates.

Crandall, J. A., & Peyton, J. K. (Eds.). (1993). *Approaches to adult ESL literacy instruction*. Washington, DC & McHenry, IL: Center for Applied Linguistics/Delta.

Hasan, R., & Williams, G. (Eds.). (1996). *Literacy in society*. London, New York: Longman.

Kerfoot, C. (1993). Participatory education in a South African context: Contradictions and challenges. *TESOL Quarterly*, 7(3), 431–447.

Khanna, A. L., Verma, M. K., Agnihotri, R. K., & Sinha, S. K. (1998). *Adult ESOL learners in Britain: A cross-cultural study*. Clevedon, UK: Multilingual Matters.

Klassen, C., & Burnaby, B. (1993). Those who know: Views on literacy among adult immigrants in Canada. *TESOL Quarterly*, 7(3), 377–397.

Martin-Jones, M., & Jones, K. (Eds.). (2000). *Multilingual literacies*. Amsterdam and Philadelphia: John Benjamins.

NCLE (National Center for ESL Literacy Education). (2003). *Adult English language instruction in the 21st Century*. Washington, DC: Center for Applied Linguistics.

Peyton, J., & Staton, J. (1996). *Writing our lives*. Washington, DC and McHenry, IL: Center for Applied Linguistics and Delta Systems.

Prinsloo, M., & Breier, M. (Eds.). (1996). *The social uses of literacy*. Amsterdam and Philadelphia: John Benjamins.

Wallace, C. (2001). Critical literacy in the second language classroom: Power and control. In B. Comber & A. Simpson (Eds.), *Negotiating critical literacies in classrooms* (pp. 209–228). Mahwah, NJ: Lawrence Erlbaum Associates.

Elsa Auerbach

Environmental Adult Education

Environmental adult education makes concrete links between the environment and other social and political dimensions of people's lives. Ecological justice is inextricably linked with social justice concerns such as oppression based on race, gender, sexual orientation, socio-economic class, ethnicity, religion and national origin (Hill, 2003). For example, environmental racism is real, corrosive and pervasive (Tan, 2003). Environmental adult education, or environmental popular education as it is often referred to in Latin America and Asia, emerged as a stream of adult education in 1992 and has grown in both theory and practice worldwide. Although indigenous peoples, women and community educators had been practising forms of environmental adult education for centuries, adult educators have paid little attention to the connections they were making between the natural environment and its resources and human culture, politics, economy, health and social well-being (Clover, 1999).

International Attention to Environmental Adult Education

In 1992 in Rio de Janeiro, the United Nations organized an official global conference on the environment and development which became known as the Earth Summit. In preparation for this event, the International Council for Adult Education (ICAE), an international non-governmental organization, created the Learning for Environmental Action Programme (LEAP) which took the initiative of stimulating a global dialogue on environmental issues and adult learning. This 3-day global forum at the Earth Summit was titled "The International Journey for Environmental Education." Prominent adult educators such as Paulo Freire, Budd Hall and Moema Viezzer were involved. Through workshops, panels, seminars, and the arts, over 300 participants explored the links between global economic dependency on natural resources and increased poverty and inequity, displacement and migration, disease/death and cultural deterioration, social instability and outright war. From their discussions on how to include these issues into their practice, they collectively developed the first Global Treaty on Environmental Education.

From 1992–2000, members of LEAP participated in United Nations conferences and academic fora around the world, developed working papers and booklets, taught courses and facilitated hundreds of local workshops on environmental adult education. As a result of this work, for the first time ever, environmental issues were on the agenda of the Fifth International Conference on Adult Education (CONFINTEA V), a global conference held in Hamburg, Germany in 1997. As further evidence of the international interest in the issue, the ICAE published three special editions (1992, 1995, 2000) of its international journal, *Convergence*, on this theme.

Like adult education, there is no single definition of environmental adult education. However, worldwide there are a collection of commonly shared principles, concepts, frameworks and critical and creative strategies which emerge from and feed into complex historical experiences and contemporary contexts (Clover, 1999). In a poetic essay, Peter Cole (1998, p. 103) asks provocative questions which form the context and rallying point for the critical analysis and socio-ecological learning of environmental adult education. He asks who benefits from oil exploration, commercial enterprise and war. The corrosive impact of the global economy, its insatiable need for natural resources, the destructive methods of extraction, and the inequitable use and ownership of these resources, are often at the root of ill-health, poverty, social unrest, migration, and unemployment. It is argued that "ecological deterioration will soon eclipse ideological conflict as the dominant national security concern throughout the world" (Hill & Clover, 2003, p. 89). African nations are besieged by war and social conflict because of diamonds, and the Middle East has been bombed and invaded because of oil. Fresh water, a key source of life on this planet, is becoming more polluted and scarcer. This latter will result in more inequity and wars in the future (Clarke & Barlow, 2003). Moreover, indigenous peoples and other activists are losing their lives or being forced to flee their homelands because of resources their lands contain (Hill & Clover).

Connections to Gender

The effects of environmental damage are also gendered. Studies show "the relationship between household activities and the environment . . . [and] both urban and rural women make the primary contact with basic resources that provide the basis of family life" (Tabiedi, 2003, p. 75). Therefore, when contemporary neo-liberal development paradigms emphasize wealth-creation through resource depletion and increased pollution rather than human welfare, it is primarily women who are forced to walk further each day to collect fuel and fodder from the receding forests and to spend more time caring for those who become sick from polluted water and air (Strathy & Tabunakawai, 2003). Environmental adult education argues that neither social nor environmental oppressions will be addressed adequately if addressed separately.

Distinct from Environmental Education

While mainstream environmental education focuses on information transmission, environmental adult education, like adult education, works as an engaged and participatory process that begins from a platform of recognizing people(s)' ecological knowledge(s) and bringing these together through dialogue and debate to create new ecological understandings of our world. This ecological epistemological base of women, indigenous peoples, farmers, and fishers comes from daily lived experience and involves a comprehensive understanding of a variety of co-varying environmental features and changes over long periods of time (Clover, 1999). Moreover, while environmental education focuses on individual behavior change, environmental adult education draws attention to the politics of the environment and calls for critical debate and action towards the redemocratization of the political process. Individual behavior change is insufficient as it can easily be undermined by neo-liberal agendas that support wealth-creation and corporate rights over human well-being and collective rights. We can practice the 3Rs (recycle, re-use and reduce), and turn off the tap when we brush our teeth, but the reality is that dramatic and fundamental changes are required in "economic and political structures at national and international levels" (Mikkelson, 1992, p. 72). A primary goal of environmental adult education is to strengthen participatory democracy by helping to develop stronger cross-cultural and intersectoral networks; partnerships amongst educators, environmental and conservation groups, citizen organizations, academics and members of other social movements (Clover).

Learning Strategies and Practices

Environmental adult education also includes respecting and weaving into the learning process spiritualities, ways of knowing and being and cultural practices that are linked to landscape and seascape. The belief that culture and spirit are embedded in the land is often at the root of activities to preserve its value as a source of material existence and spiritual life (Kapoor, 2003). In India the forest is the basis for women's songs of struggle and change. In Newfoundland the culture revolves around a life lived through, in and on the sea (Clover, 2003). In British Columbia, environmental adult educators created a dance that is grounded in the mysteries and ordinariness of the everyday, and the complex symbiotic relationship between humans and place.

Environmental adult education uses a variety of critical and creative practices, strategies and tools in the praxis of learning that encourage critical thinking, debate, celebration and creativity (Clover, Hall, & Follen, 2000). In particular, activities such as mural-making, story-telling, music, dance and theatre are imaginative and aesthetic pathways of socio-ecological learning (Clover, 2000). In Canada and the Philippines, environmental popular theatre was used to "create an entertaining and educational performance about issues of community sustainability that challenged the elite paradigm of sustainable development" (Keough, Carmona, & Grandinetti, 1995, p. 5). Throughout the world, art-based environmental learning is used to bring together unions and environmentalists, filter, organize and give voice to environmental concerns and convert experience into meaning, transforming the contents of consciousness into a collective form that energizes people to act to save our embattled planet (Clover & Markle, 2003).

Drawing from environmental education, environmental adult education places an emphasis on learning through, with, in and about the rest of nature. Grossi (1995) argues that learning in natural settings can help to "recover the positive sides and senses of life, and capture its enthusiasm and pleasure" (p. 40). The rest of nature as a teacher and site of learning can also reveal poignantly the negatives such as poverty, inequality and racism. Learning in and about place creates an eco-epistemological base and a network of meanings, of where and who we are.

Environmental destruction and "deterioration is a cultural issue, a political issue, a feminist issue, an economic issue, a race issue, a workplace/union issue, [and] a global issue" (Clover, 2003, p. 14). Failure to address this was a serious omission in the field of adult education. "Environmental adult education adds another critical lens, an ecological lens, through which we can address environmental problems and give voice to the needs of those who are most affected" (p. 14). It respects and nurtures patterns of knowing and being that are rooted in the spirit and the land, and provides opportunities to critique, reflect and experience from that basis. By connecting social and ecological justice, making stronger links to environmental movements, working at local, national and global levels, and through persistence and imagination, dialogue and debate, creativity and art, environmental adult education attempts to "reassert a vision of the world we want" (p. 14).

See also: gender, problematizing learning, social justice, social movements, social movement learning.

References and Further Reading

Clarke, T., & Barlow, M. (2003). *Blue gold: The battle against corporate theft of the world's water*. Ottawa: Polaris Institute.

Clover, D. E. (1999). *Learning patterns of landscape and life: Towards a theoretical framework of environmental adult education*. Unpublished doctoral thesis. Toronto: OISE/University of Toronto.

Clover, D. E. (2000). Community arts as environmental adult education and activism: A labour and environment case study. *Convergence, 33*(4), 19–30.

Clover, D. E. (Ed.). (2003). *Global perspectives in environmental adult education.* New York: Peter Lang.

Clover, D. E., Hall, B. L., & Follen, S. (2000). *The nature of transformation, environmental adult education.* Toronto: Transformative Learning Centre, OISE/UT and the Learning for Environmental Action Programme.

Clover, D. E., & Markle, G. (2003). Feminist arts practices of popular education: Imagination, counter-narratives and activism on Vancouver Island and Gabriola Island. *New Zealand Journal of Adult Education, 31*(2), 36–52.

Cole, P. (1998). An academic take on "Indigenous traditions and Ecology." *Canadian Journal of Environmental Education, 3,* 100–115.

Grossi, F. V. (1995). Cambios paradigmaticos sociedad ecologica educacion. *Convergence, 28*(4), 31–42.

Hill, R. J. (2003). Environmental justice: Environmental adult education at the confluence of oppressions. In *Environmental adult education, ecological learning: Theory and practice for socioenvironmental change* (pp. 27–38). *New Directions for Adult and Continuing Education Series,* No. 99. San Francisco: Jossey-Bass.

Hill, L. H., & Clover, D. E. (2003). *Environmental adult education, ecological learning: Theory and practice for socioenvironmental change* (pp. 27–38). *New Directions for Adult and Continuing Education,* No. 99. San Francisco: Jossey-Bass.

Kapoor, D. (2003). Indigenous struggles for forests, land and cultural identify in India: Environmental popular education and the democratization of power. In D. E. Clover (Ed.), *Global perspectives in environmental adult education* (pp. 41–58). New York: Peter Lang.

Keough, N., Carmona, E., & Grandinetti, L. (1995). Tales from the Sari-Sari: In search of Bigfoot. *Convergence, 28*(4), 5–11.

Mikkelson, K. (1992). Environmental and adult education – Towards a Danish dimension. *Convergence, 25*(2), 77–74.

Strathy K., & Tabunakawai, K. (2003). Transforming women's lives to "Save the plants that save lives" through environmental adult education. In D. E. Clover (Ed.), *Global perspectives in environmental adult education* (pp. 85–100). New York: Peter Lang.

Tabiedi, S. B. (2003). Women, literacy and environmental adult education in Sudan. In D. E. Clover (Ed.), *Global perspectives in environmental adult education.* (pp. 71–84). New York: Peter Lang.

Tan, S. (2003). Anti-racist environmental education in a trans-global community: Case studies from Toronto. In D. E. Clover (Ed.), *Global perspectives in environmental adult education* (pp. 3–22). New York: Peter Lang.

Darlene E. Clover

Ethics

Ethics is the branch of philosophy – also called moral philosophy – that deals with how we should act in relation to others. Moral philosophy explores the rightness or wrongness, goodness or badness of actions and the beliefs, principles or rules that govern – or should govern – the choices we make.

> As soon as a question is raised about the justifiability of a certain person's or group's moral belief or presupposition, ethical or moral inquiry begins. When people engage in critical inquiry about such matters of disagreement, they *do* ethics or moral philosophy, rather than simply have ethics or morals or a moral philosophy that may or may not be shared with most members of their group . . . (Iannone, 2001, p. 184)

Although distinctions are occasionally made between the two terms, " 'morality' and 'ethics' (and 'moral' and 'ethical') are usually used as synonyms, though 'ethics' is more frequently generally used as the name of the philosophical study of these matters" (Martin, 2002, p. 110). The moral/ethical frameworks that guide our lives have complex origins but some of the more powerful influences include the cultural and religious context of our upbringing, our families, our education and our socialization.

Professional Ethics

If the literature is any indication, adult educators have only recently begun to seriously take up the challenge of identifying and addressing ethical issues of practice. Although there were occasional efforts in the 1960s and 1970s to raise the profile of moral and ethical aspects of the field, it wasn't until the mid-1980s that more sustained and widespread attention became evident. Traditional professions had been concerned with the ethics of practice for decades, so it may be considered odd that adult educators took so long to "awaken" to the moral dimensions of their work. One explanation for this delayed awakening is resistance to "professionalization" of the field, especially the form of professionalization followed by such traditional professions as medicine and law that formalize entry requirements and proscribe behaviors in ways that, some suspect, do more to protect the financial and other interests of the professional than of the less powerful patient/client. To many, adult education is a calling or vocation, not a profession, and is such a diverse and diffuse field that a code of ethics would have to be too broad and general to be of much use to practitioners. Another reason adult educators may be late to consider the ethics of practice is that certain perspectives we bring to our work permit us to avoid ethical issues. Lawson (1979) argued that a "service orientation" and "learner-centered" organizations and teaching techniques permit adult educators to avoid serious engagement with ethical issues by locating the authority for decision-making with learners. This early manifestation of the commodification of knowledge in response to market forces ascendant late in the 20th century puts a great deal of faith in the "market" to regulate behavior and influence what "providers" make available to learners. A third reason is the confusion brought about by postmodernism and the accompanying rejection of metanarratives – like Western, Eurocentric ethical traditions. Several adult educators outside of North America have grappled with what a postmodern ethics might look like (Bagnall, 1995; Jarvis, 1997), but there is no evidence that these ideas have been taken up in any substantial way by others.

During the late 1980s and 1990s, several adult education organizations in the USA developed codes of ethics for their members. Examples include the Academy of Human Resource Development (AHRD), the Association for Continuing Higher Education (ACHE), the Learning Resources Network (LERN) and the Pennsylvania Association for Adult Continuing Education (PAACE). The code developed by AHRD (1999) is readily accessible and is a good example of a carefully prepared document with sufficient scope to cover most of the more obvious ethical issues likely to be encountered in a human resource development context.

There have also been efforts to

develop "universal" codes of ethics that would apply to all adult educators, regardless of context. An abridged version of the most recent attempt (Siegel, 2000) provides a good test of how "universal" such a code can be and whether it is too general to be of much use in guiding decisions about our relationships with learners. Adult educators should:

1. Utilize, to the extent possible, the best available professional knowledge and practices in serving all learners.
2. Respect the ethno-sociocultural heritage, special circumstances, and dignity as human beings of all adult learners.
3. Avoid conflicts of interest, or the appearance of conflicts of interest, in all aspects of their work.
4. Respect, and strive to ensure as appropriate, the need for confidentiality of each learner in interactions between learner and educator.
5. Respect the unique and diverse learning needs of adult learners; respect the need of each learner for honesty, understanding, and fairness; respect the real or perceived disparity in position between educator and learner; and respect the right of learners to participate in any solutions designed to meet their needs.
6. Be cognizant of, remain sensitive to, and communicate the real or perceived negative impact of institutional or organizational policies and procedures on the learners, the institution or organization, and the community as a whole.
7. Present advertising information concerning services and programs that is clear, complete, accurate, and descriptive of the actual services and programs being offered.
8. Present services and programs that are fiscally responsible to all stakeholders, with results based upon objective and honest assessment.
9. Assist in empowering learners to participate actively and effectively to improve the general welfare of their immediate and global communities and to promote the concepts of a just and equitable society.
10. Avoid doing any harm to learners. (pp. 39–64)

A useful test of any ethical framework – whether codified or not – is how consistent it is with several widely-accepted ethical principles that guide many professions including *nonmaleficence* – refraining from harming oneself and others; *beneficence* – bringing about good; *fidelity* – keeping promises; *autonomy* – exercising (and helping others exercise) personal freedom; *veracity* – telling the truth, avoiding deception; and *justice* – distributing benefits and burdens fairly (Purtilo, 1999, pp. 50–59). Some would add *caring* to this set of principles (see Moral Development below).

Codes of ethics are formal expressions of a set of professional values or "oughts" that should guide practice, but these values or oughts can also be developed within a community of practice without producing a formal code. In the best of all worlds following the democratic and participatory traditions of adult education, educators and learners would collaboratively develop such understandings within the context of their teaching–learning relationship.

Some studies have gauged the extent to which practitioners

encounter ethical issues or dilemmas and solicited their views on the desirability of having a code of ethics to guide practice. Gordon and Sork (2001), for example, conducted a survey of Canadian adult educators in British Columbia and compared their responses to an earlier survey of American adult educators in Indiana. They found that practitioners in both countries faced similar ethical issues in such areas as confidentiality, learner–educator relationships, finance, professionalism and competence, conflicts of interest, evaluation of student performance, ownership of instructional materials, intra-organizational concerns, credentials, unsound training design, employment practices, and enrolment and attendance. Fifty-two % of US respondents and 73% of Canadian respondents believed there should be a code of ethics for adult educators, but critics of codes of ethics might well claim that such responses are based on the false hope that a code will provide useful guidance to resolve ethical dilemmas (Cunningham, 1992).

Research Ethics

One important area of concern, especially among university-based adult educators and graduate students, is research ethics. Critics of conventional social science research methods have pointed out the fallacy of the "objective researcher" and castigated researchers for "taking from" but not "giving back" to individuals and groups who agree to participate in studies. In addition, various forms of participatory, action and empowerment research – each of which sets out to change the status quo – raise new and challenging questions about the relationship between the researcher and research participants. Fine, Weis, Weseen, and Wong (2000) offer qualitative researchers a set of ". . . ethical invitations or, put more boldly, ethical injunctions" (p. 125) in the form of 10 reflective questions that capture some of the more vexing problems of method and representation:

1. Have I connected the "voices" and "stories" of individuals back to the set of historic, structural, and economic relations in which they are situated?
2. Have I deployed multiple methods so that very different kinds of analyses can be constructed?
3. Have I described the mundane?
4. Have some informants/constituencies/participants reviewed the material with me and interpreted, dissented, challenged my interpretations? And then how do I report these departures/agreements in perspective?
5. How far do I want to go with respect to theorizing the words of informants?
6. Have I considered how these data could be used for progressive, conservative, repressive social policies?
7. Where have I backed into the passive voice and decoupled my responsibility for my interpretations?
8. Who am I afraid will see these analyses? Who is rendered vulnerable/responsible or exposed by these analyses? Am I willing to show him/her/them the text before publication? If not, why not? Could I publish his/her/their comments as an epilogue? What's the fear?
9. What dreams am I having about the material presented?
10. To what extent has my analysis offered an alternative to the "commonsense" or dominant discourse? What challenges

> might very different audiences pose to the analysis presented? (pp. 126–127)

These questions suggest the ethical complexity of contemporary social science research and the challenges of meeting the informed consent and other requirements of university "ethics boards" whose procedures and forms are sometimes not well-suited to more "activist" undertakings in which participants effectively become co-researchers (van den Hoonaard, 2002).

Technology has also raised novel ethical issues. Researching online learning, for example, wherein there is a complete record of all interactions between instructors and students, raises questions about the definition of informed consent. In more conventional studies, the researcher is observing, interviewing, surveying, and so on, and this "presence" is known to participants. But where is the researcher (or more appropriately, where "isn't" the researcher) in an online course?

Moral Development

A phenomenon of continuing interest to psychologists, philosophers and educators is the process through which people's moral frameworks develop and how these frameworks influence their actions in the world. Arnett (2002) provides an illuminating account of the ethic that guided Paulo Freire's revolutionary literacy work in Brazil linking its development to key features of Freire's biography. Sork (2002) analyses the key influences on the development of "ethical frameworks" that guide the practice of professors of adult education in English-speaking universities in seven countries. Both of these efforts attempt to explain how experiences in the lives of individuals play a role in the formation of a moral point of view and way of reasoning about moral choices.

The early work of Lawrence Kohlberg (1981) on moral development produced what he claimed was a universal "stage theory" wherein the sophistication of a person's moral reasoning could be categorized from Stage 1, where decisions are based on *avoidance of punishment* and *obedience to rules and authority*, to Stage 6, where decisions are based on *universal ethical principles*. Kohlberg's theory was developed from a 20-year longitudinal study of 84 boys. Carol Gilligan (1982) was one of the first to challenge this theory based on the single-gender group Kohlberg studied and the character of the resulting stages which favored justice reasoning over care reasoning. She observed that,

> [a]lthough Kohlberg claims universality for his stage sequence, those groups not included in his original sample rarely reach his higher stages . . . Prominent among those who thus appear to be deficient in moral development when measured by Kohlberg's scale are women, whose judgments seem to exemplify the third stage of his 6-stage sequence. At this stage morality is conceived in interpersonal terms and goodness is equated with helping and pleasing others. (p. 18)

Nel Noddings (1984) followed Gilligan's critique of Kohlberg by proposing an ethic of care that she believed better represented the way women engage with moral issues. For Noddings,

> feminine nonconformity to the Kohlberg model counts against the justification/judgment paradigm and not against women as moral

> thinkers. Women, perhaps the majority of women, prefer to discuss moral problems in terms of concrete situations. They approach moral problems not as intellectual problems to be solved by abstract reasoning but as concrete human problems to be lived and to be solved in living. (p. 96)

Some have accused Gilligan, Noddings and others of overstating the role of gender in moral development. Recent reviews of empirical studies in which gender differences were discussed suggest that the particulars of the situation within which moral decisions are made may play a much more substantial role than gender in explaining differences in outcome (Rooney, 2001).

Concerns have also been raised about the applicability of Kohlberg's theory to other groups not represented in his sample, in particular those from other cultures. Rest, Narvaez, Bebeau, and Thoma (1999) report on several meta-analyses of cross-cultural studies done using Kohlberg's assessment technique. After warning of the problems inherent in translating Kohlberg's methodology and applying it in different cultures, they report a surprising level of support for the universality of at least some of Kohlberg's theory. The most tenuous parts of the theory seem to be the "post-conventional" level of reasoning represented by Stages 5 and 6 and the fact that "justice reasoning" continues to be privileged over "care reasoning" and other forms.

A great deal of empirical and theoretical work has attempted to bring clarity to the process of moral development and how it can be nurtured through education. For adult educators, there remains the thorny question of to what extent an adult's moral development can be influenced by their participation in educational programs. It is a complex and ethically-serious matter to design an educational experience with the intent of bringing about a change in the moral reasoning or behavior of a person. Kohlberg and others believed that the most effective way of promoting such change was through dialogue in a social context. Discussing ethical dilemmas and cases is a well-tested technique for engaging learners in this process.

Rest et al. (1999) present a four-component model that they believe represents the multiple factors that influence moral behavior and these can serve as useful frames for designing programs, although some of the processes lend themselves more to educational intervention that others. "The basic idea behind the four-component model is that various (four) inner psychological processes together give rise to outwardly observable behavior. The four processes, briefly, are . . ."

- Moral *sensitivity* – interpreting the situation, role-taking to experience how various actions would affect the parties concerned, imagining cause–effect chains of events, and being aware that there is a moral problem when it exists.
- Moral *judgment* – judging which action would be most justifiable in a moral sense.
- Moral *motivation* – the degree of commitment to taking the moral course of action, valuing moral values over other values, and taking personal responsibility for moral outcomes.
- Moral *character* – persisting in a moral task, having courage, overcoming fatigue and temptations, and implementing subroutines that serve a moral goal. (p. 101)

This model challenges educators to craft educational experiences that address all four processes while encouraging the social construction of knowledge within a community of adult learners. Such communities, however, are becoming ever-more complex, multicultural and globalized which complicates the educative task enormously.

See also: adult development, philosophy, social justice, vocation.

References and Further Reading

Academy of Human Resource Development (AHRD), Standing Committee on Ethics and Integrity. (1999). *AHRD Standards on Ethics and Integrity* (1st ed.). May, 1999. (http://www.ahrd.org/ahrd/publications/ethics/ethics_standards.PDF)

Arnett, R. C. (2002). Paulo Freire's revolutionary pedagogy: From a story-centered to a narrative-centered communication ethic. In S. L. Bracci & C. G. Christians (Eds.), *Moral engagement in public life: Theorists for contemporary ethics* (pp. 150–170). New York: Peter Lang.

Bagnall, R. G. (1995). *Issues and implications in the epistemology and ethics of adult education events: Selected critiques.* Brisbane, Australia: Centre for Skill Formation Research and Development, Griffith University.

Cunningham, P. M. (1992). Adult education does not need a code of ethics. In M. W. Galbraith & B. R. Sisco (Eds.), *Confronting controversies in challenging times: A call to action* (pp. 107–113). *New Directions for Adult and Continuing Education*, No. 54. San Francisco: Jossey-Bass.

Fine, M., Weis, L., Weseen, S., & Wong, L. (2000). For whom? Qualitative research, representations, and social responsibilities. In N. K. Denzin & Y. S. Lincoln (Eds.), *Handbook of qualitative research* (2nd ed., pp. 107–131). Thousand Oaks, CA: Sage.

Gilligan, C. (1982). *In a different voice: Psychological theory and women's development.* Cambridge, MA: Harvard University Press

Gordon, W., & Sork, T. J. (2001). Ethical issues and codes of ethics: Views of adult education practitioners in Canada and the US. *Adult Education Quarterly, 51*(3), 202–218.

Iannone, A. P. (2001). *Dictionary of world philosophy*. London: Routledge.

Jarvis, P. (1997). *Ethics and education for adults in a late modern society*. Leicester: National Institute for Adult and Continuing Education (England and Wales).

Kohlberg, L. (1981). *E on mode: Volume I.* New York: Harper & Row.

Lawson, K. H. (1979). *Philosophical concepts and values in adult education* (Rev. ed.). Milton Keynes, UK: Open University Press.

Martin, R. M. (2002). *A philosopher's dictionary* (3rd ed.).Peterborough, ON: Broadview Press.

Noddings, N. (1984). *Caring, a feminine approach to ethics and moral education.* Berkeley: University of California Press.

Purtilo, R. (1999). *Ethical dimensions in the health professions* (3rd ed.). Philadelphia, PA: W. B. Saunders.

Rest, J., Narvaez, D., Bebeau, M. J., & Thoma, S. J. (1999). *Postconventional moral thinking: A neo-Kohlbergian approach.* Mahwah, NJ: Lawrence Erlbaum Associates.

Rooney, P. (2001). Gender and moral reasoning revisited: Reengaging feminist psychology. In P. DesAutels & J. Waugh (Eds.), *Feminists doing ethics* (pp. 153–166). Lanham, MD: Rowman & Littlefield.

Siegel, I. S. (2000). Toward developing a universal code of ethics for adult educators. *PAACE Journal of Lifelong Learning, 9*, 39–64. (Pennsylvania Association for Adult Continuing Education.)

Sork, T. J. (2002). Place, time and doing the right thing: The moral geographies of adult education. In J. M. Pettitt (Ed.), *Proceedings of the 43rd Annual Adult Education Research Conference* (pp. 357–361). Raleigh: North Carolina State University.

van den Hoonaard, W. C. (Ed.). (2002). *Walking the tightrope: Ethical issues for qualitative researchers.* Toronto: University of Toronto Press.

Thomas J. Sork

Ethnography

Ethnography is a research methodology for studying the patterns of meaning and behavior that constitute a culture or way of life. It is one of many forms of qualitative research originating in the disciplines of anthropology and sociology. It shares with other forms of qualitative research an interest in understanding the subjective nature of human experience, and the various means by which people make sense out of the world in which they live. Defining features of ethnography are its concern with the cultural context and its emphasis on carrying out research in natural field settings. The common premise is that by entering into close and prolonged interaction with people in their everyday circumstances, ethnographers can better understand the web of implicit beliefs, motivations, and behaviors that constitute the habitual ways of being and doing in that setting. Other terms that are sometimes used synonymously with ethnography include participant observation, naturalistic inquiry, fieldwork, and thick description. In adult education, much of the literature on ethnography comes from allied fields such as educational studies, organizational studies, and cultural studies. Perspectives on ethnography are divided between using ethnography as a data-collection technique, and more critical approaches where ethnography is part of a larger process of ideology critique and activism for social change.

Historical Background

Ethnography is rooted in the discipline of cultural anthropology and developed as an effort of late 19th and early 20th century cultural theorists to discover and understand what the non-Western world was like. As anthropology developed as a form of disciplinary knowledge, ethnography developed alongside it as the investigative branch of the field. To paraphrase Geertz (1973), in anthropology, or anyway social anthropology, ethnography is what the practitioners *do*. One of the earliest examples of ethnographic research and writing is Malinowski's (1922) *Argonauts of the Western Pacific*, which is an account of the cultural norms and practices of the people of the Trobriand Islands, off the coast of Papua New Guinea. Malinowski is also credited with first formulating ethnographic fieldwork into a systematic set of principles and practices (Tedlock, 2000). He articulated the ethnographer's goal as attempting to "grasp the native's point of view" through learning to see, think, and sometimes even act as an insider or native. Other classic ethnographic studies were carried out by such noted pioneers in cultural anthropology as Margaret Mead, Franz Boas, Ruth Benedict, and E.E. Evans-Pritchard. All of these works entailed a prolonged period of immersion in the everyday life of a non-Western, typically remote and so-called primitive, people.

While early anthropologists were carrying out ethnographic studies of foreign and distant cultures, something much like ethnography was also being carried out in the field of sociology as well, typically referred to using the related term of participant observation. Sociologists were conducting extended field research to investigate the everyday beliefs, norms and actions in a number of groups and subgroups closer to home, most notably in the classic studies conducted by Chicago School sociologists such as Everett Hughes, Howard Becker, and William Foote

Whyte. Although anthropologists and sociologists were informed by different theoretical orientations in their study of human group behavior, their fieldwork practices shared a common approach of spending extended periods of time in the daily world of the "other," trying to understand and describe the implicit features of the social environment.

The period from the 1950s until about 1970 has been described by Denzin and Lincoln (2003) as the classic or golden age of qualitative research, where the research and writing practices of ethnography and participant observation flourished in a spirit that evoked very little self-questioning or hard scrutiny. Rosaldo (1993) has described this as the heroic period, where the Lone Ethnographer was in the clear role of the observing authority writing up definitive objective accounts of the lifeways of the subject "other." However, a number of recent developments in critical social thought have increased awareness of the problematic nature of ethnographic fieldwork and representation, assisted by revelations that iconic ethnographic accounts such as those of Malinowski and Mead were riddled with inaccuracy, fabrication and racial prejudice. Clifford and Marcus (1986), among others, assert that ethnographic accounts often reveal more about the culture of the researcher than the researched. A host of other ethical and authorial questions have been raised about power relations in the field, and the socially constructed nature of ethnographic texts (Denzin & Lincoln; Van Maanen, 1988).

Yet, even as ethnography became increasingly subject to debate about its fundamental principles and practices, there has been a widespread expansion of ethnographic research beyond its original disciplinary confines in anthropology and sociology into a number of applied and professional fields, including adult education. This has taken place as part of a broader shift in social science research away from positivistic science towards a more interpretive approach to examining and understanding the social world. The meaning of ethnography remains highly contested and open to several different definitional approaches. It can be defined as: (a) a research process; (b) a way of seeing; (c) a means of social critique; and (d) a representational product or text.

Ethnography: Four Approaches to Definition

Ethnography as a research process

One approach to defining ethnography is to outline the typical procedures and steps involved in conducting ethnographic research. For some, the focus on culture and immersion in the everyday life of a given cultural setting are the hallmarks of the ethnographic research process (Wolcott, 1999). Although a characteristic of all qualitative research methodologies is that the researcher is the research instrument, this is particularly true for ethnography because, when done comprehensively, it involves data acquired through all the senses, where the ambient sights and sounds of a research setting are as important as what research participants have to say. Ethnographic research also entails careful attention to fieldwork relationships and processes, from the initial negotiation of entry into a prospective field site, to identifying key informants, establishing rapport, keeping detailed fieldnotes, and making plans for departure from the field. Ethnographic research is also characterized by its openness to multiple data collection techniques. Merriam and Simpson (1995) identify four procedures for collecting data commonly used in ethnography. These are: participant observation, in-depth interviewing, life history, and document analysis. Extensive research has been carried out in educational and institutional ethnography to examine the cultural norms and practices embedded within schools and workplaces.

Ethnography as a way of seeing

Despite the importance of appropriate field techniques in the ethnographic research process, ethnography is more than a matter of techniques alone. As Geertz (1973) states, "it is not . . . techniques and procedures that define the enterprise. What defines it is the kind of intellectual effort it is: an elaborate venture in, to borrow a notion from Gilbert Ryle, 'thick description.' " (p. 6). For Geertz, it is the interpretation of culture rather than the conduct of fieldwork that makes ethnography distinct. Wolcott (1999) extends this view by stating that ethnography is not primarily a matter of either field technique, length of time in the field, good description, or good rapport with subjects. "The purpose of ethnographic research is to describe and interpret cultural behavior" (p. 43). The essential core of ethnography from this view is the concern for understanding the taken-for-granted beliefs and actions that constitute "commonsense" in a group setting. Although the descriptive tendencies of ethnographic research have been critiqued as being insufficiently theoretical, the perspective of Geertz and others is that ethnographic theorizing is not absent but simply low to the ground, attuned to the particulars of place and circumstance rather than to the abstractions of "grand theory" or broad generalization.

Ethnography as a means of social critique

Another approach to describing ethnography extends beyond field-work and interpretation to address the structures of power and domination embedded within cultural contexts and also within the research process. From this perspective, often referred to as critical ethnography, no research is apolitical, removed from ideology or sociopolitical influence (Carspecken, 1996; Denzin & Lincoln, 2003). The aim of critical ethnography is not simply directed towards the observation and writing of culture, but the disruption of unproblematized hegemonic structures as a first step towards social change. Often in critical ethnography there is an explicit goal of involving participants in the research process to critique and challenge dominant power structures. Feminist ethnography is also situated in the critical tradition, with a particular emphasis on the social construction of gender, highlighting "the knowledge that develops from shifting the ethnographic angle of vision to the everyday lives of women" (Naples, 2003, p. 7). In adult education, critical and feminist approaches to ethnography have been strongly influenced by the Birmingham school of cultural studies, and feminist methodologists Dorothy Smith and Patti Lather.

Ethnography as a representational product or text

Ethnography can also be defined as the written accounts that are produced as an outcome of the research process. From its inception, ethnography has always been a textual enterprise, involving the taking of fieldnotes during the data-collection phase followed by "writing up" the research findings once fieldwork is complete. However, the authorial nature of ethnographic practice raises a number of fundamental questions about whose voice, and whose truths are being told, shaped and validated in the writing process. Atkinson (1990) examines the textual presentation of reality in the construction of ethnographic texts, and Van Maanen (1988) examines the different genres of ethnographic representation from the seemingly objective "realist" tales of the classic period through to more contemporary interpretive and expressive accounts, where the guise of objectivity is surrendered for more reflexive and impressionistic modes of expression. Visual and performance ethnography are now accepted approaches to the interpretation and representation of research findings, along with poetry and fiction. The subjective experience of the researcher is as much a focus of the ethnographic gaze as the experience of research participants, and autoethnography is an increasingly popular form of research into the meaning-making process.

See also: cultural studies, practitioner, research methods.

References and Further Reading

Atkinson, P. (1990). *The ethnographic imagination: Textual constructions of reality*. London: Routledge.

Carspecken, P. (1996). *Critical ethnography in educational research: A theoretical and practical guide*. New York: Routledge.

Clifford, J., & Marcus, G. (1986). *Writing culture: The poetics and politics of ethnography*. Berkeley: University of California Press.

Denzin, N. K., & Lincoln, Y. S. (2003). *The landscape of qualitative research: Theories and issues* (2nd ed.). Thousand Oaks: Sage.

Geertz, C. (1973). *The interpretation of cultures: Selected essays*. New York: Basic Books.

Malinowski, B. (1922). *Argonauts of the Western Pacific*. London: Routledge.

Merriam, S. B., & Simpson, E. L. (1995). A guide to research for educators and teachers of adults (2nd ed.). Malabar, FL: Krieger.

Naples, N. (2003). *Feminism and method: Ethnography, discourse analysis and activist research*. New York: Routledge.

Rosaldo, R. (1993). *Culture and truth: The remaking of social analysis*. Boston: Beacon.

Tedlock, B. (2000). Ethnography and ethnographic representation. In N. Denzin & Y. Lincoln (Eds.), *Handbook of qualitative research* (2nd ed., pp. 455–486). Thousand Oaks, CA: Sage.

Van Maanen, J. (1988). *Tales of the field: On writing ethnography*. Chicago: University of Chicago Press.

Wolcott, H. (1999). *Ethnography: A way of seeing*. Walnut Creek, CA: AltaMira Press.

Jane Dawson

Europe and Adult Education

With the development of the European Union, educational initiatives have been undertaken at both state and European Commission levels. Indeed, Articles 149 and 150 of the original European Treaty specified this – the former being about general education and the latter about vocational education. This article focuses partly upon the European Commission's policy documents that, to some extent, have influenced those of the member states although it could be argued that the reverse is also true. Initially cross-national programs were introduced with many having a school orientation, although adult education was never specifically excluded. From about 1995, however, a wide variety of policy documents about lifelong learning have been introduced, and in addition there have been practical academic initiatives across the Union, with a variety of European-level networks and organizations being formed. Consequently, this entry has three parts: European policy statements, European programs, and trans-national academic organizations and networks.

European Policy Statements

Over the final years of the 20th century there has been a rapid shift in nomenclature: adult education became the education of adults, and then both recurrent and continuing education became the more normal terms – the former contained more radical elements, such as a specified number of years of education post-school as a right, while the latter was much more neutral. Consequently, continuing education gained favor and this term implicitly contained the idea of lifelong education, but, by the mid-1990s, the concept of education was itself falling into disfavor and it was becoming replaced by that of learning. Hence, the idea of lifelong learning emerged recognizing that learning is broader than education and can occur in a wide variety of places, so that terms like learning society, learning organization, learning region, and learning city also appeared (see Jarvis, 2004 for a full discussion of these changes).

It was at about this time that the European Commission adopted a proactive stance on post-school policy on education and training. It could be argued that this was a response to globalization and the emergence of the knowledge economy. Many pan-European initiatives had been started long before this, although it might be argued that these had political aims: the generation of a new united, Europe. A variety of consultation papers were issued and other initiatives taken: for instance, in 1995, the White Paper on *Education and Training* was issued by the Commission, sub-titled *Teaching and Learning: Towards the Learning Society*. (All papers cited here can be obtained from the European Commission and many appear on the Commission's website.) This White Paper notes quite specifically that there are three major changes in European society: the onset of the information society; the development of science and technology; and the internationalization of the economy (p. 5). These implicitly demand the development of a learning society. Each of the three points is dealt with quite fully (pp. 5–10), as well as many other issues, one of main ones being about how people can become employable. The Paper concludes that there are a number of educational principles that have to be considered:

- A broad knowledge base and industrial training are no longer contradictory;
- Bridges need to be built between schooling and industry;
- Equal rights need to be built into education;
- New approaches are needed to teaching. (pp. 22–23)

Thereafter, the White Paper is concerned with how member states of the Union can build a learning society.

That Paper led to a focus on two distinct sets of concerns: lifelong learning, and education and training. A third dimension was also to appear – higher education – in the Bologna Agreement (1999). It may be seen from this that the traditional distinctions between initial, adult and higher education were retained, although it is broadly recognized that learning is a continuous life-span process. The focus of the remainder of this entry will be on lifelong learning, although some reference will be made to education and training.

1996 saw the inauguration of the European Year of Lifelong Learning, which stemmed from another policy source: the Commission's White Paper *Growth, Competitiveness, Employment* (1993). The focus here was on the lifelong aspect of education and vocational training, although four other aspects were mentioned: personal development; integration of people into society; employability; and economic competitiveness. Underlying the Year were the aims of awareness-raising and stimulating a policy debate. The response varied between different member states and their cooperating countries, in which it was recognized that this was a "timely initiative" (*Report from the Commission to the European Parliament, the Council, the Economic and Social Committee and the Committee of the Regions on the Implementation, Results and Overall Assessment of the European Year of Lifelong Learning – 1996*, p. 19).

This was followed by two separate statements: the Cologne Charter, *Aims and Ambitions for Lifelong Learning* (1999), which called on governments of member states to invest in lifelong learning, and the Study Group on Education and Training Report, *Accomplishing Europe Through Education and Training*, recognizing the need to construct European citizenship through education and training, to strengthen European competitiveness, to maintain social cohesion and to recognize the place of education and training in an information society.

Two major reports were soon to follow on lifelong learning: *A Memorandum on Lifelong Learning* (EC 2000; Sec (2000) 1832) and *Making a European Area of Lifelong Learning a Reality* (EC 2001; Com (2001) 678 final). The first suggested that the two main aims of lifelong learning are creating active citizenship and employability. After wide consultation these two aims reverted almost to the same aims as those in *Accomplishing Europe Through Education and Training* (1997), apart from the fact that the fourth one was changed to "developing personal fulfillment." Significantly, as the presidency of the European Union changes every 6 months, it has become a custom that the civil servants responsible for lifelong learning in each country hold a consultation and this is often joined by the European Commission representatives, leaders of relevant non-governmental organizations, and a number of leading academics, so that the policy statements and other initiatives can be discussed. For instance, during the Greek presidency at the start of 2003, the theme was the learning region/city.

It was during Denmark's presidency in 2002 that another major initiative was taken when a joint seminar was organized between these civil servants and those of the Asian countries – the 10 Southeast Asian countries having an economic agreement – on lifelong learning; this was the ASEM conference. The outcome was that cooperation between the two groups should be encouraged, and a final report and three working-party reports were produced and published by the Danish Ministry of Education.

In precisely the same way, policy statements on education and training have emerged including: *The Concrete Future Objectives of Education Systems* (Com (2001) 59 final), *Education and Training in Europe – Diverse Systems, Shared Goals for 2010* (EC 2002), and a call for greater investment in education and training *Investing Efficiently in Education and Training: An Imperative for Europe* (Com (2002) 779 final). In this final document there is a great concern about the enlargement of the European Union in 2004 from 15 to 25 countries, but the major concern was that the "EU suffers from under-investment in human resources" (p. 3) and this included private as well as state funding.

In 2002 there was an EU declaration on vocational education (*the Copenhagen Declaration*) in which the members of the Union (including those about to join) agreed that there should be a stronger European dimension; greater transparency, more information and guidance; transferability in recognition of competencies and recognition of qualifications; and a greater emphasis on quality assurance. This greater cooperation should be achieved by 2010.

An interesting paradox may be seen in nearly all of the documents – while they all recognize the processes of European integration and globalization, they all tend to treat member states as independent sovereign entities, whereas both of these processes are undermining this independence. At the same time, each state does play a major role in developing its own lifelong learning policies, although it may be seen that the consultations that occur between civil servants every 6 months does mean that that there can be a great deal of information exchanged.

Finally, in this section, in 2000 the European Commission also adopted a policy *Towards a European Research Area*, so that there has been funding available for major research and development projects, and these will be discussed in the next section.

European Programs

As is clear from the above, the creation of the European Union has led to a wide variety of policy initiatives, but also a great many cooperative programs. Yet there is recognition that because of national differences, it is impossible to create a single system of lifelong learning. However, it has funded a wide variety of programs, from school-based (under the title of Comenius) to adult, vocational and higher education ones. In addition there has been a great deal of support from the European Social Fund for community education projects and for research.

Adult Education

The Grundtvig Program is designed to support educational providers offering courses that will increase the capacity of adults to play a full and active role in society; improve their employability; and enhance their capacity to access or reenter formal education. This program has four strands to it:

- Grundtvig 1: Cooperative projects in which educational institutions work together, pooling their knowledge and experience, in order to achieve educational outcomes of value to Europe.
- Grundtvig 2: Learning partnerships for small-scale cooperative activities in adult learning.

- Grundtvig 3: Financial support for educational staff working with adults to undertake training activities in a country other than their own.
- Grundtvig 4: Strong networks to operate on a stable basis in either similar themes or joint projects.

Language Programs

The EU has had a policy of encouraging and supporting linguistic diversity across the Union and improving the quality of language teaching throughout individuals' life spans:

- Lingua 1: Aims to raise citizens' awareness of the Union's multilingual wealth and encourage people to learn languages throughout their lifetime, and develop and disseminate innovative techniques and good practices in language teaching. Lingua 1 has three main areas of work:
    - Area 1: raising awareness; motivating individuals towards learning languages; providing information;
    - Area 2: facilitating access; and
    - Area 3: exchanging and disseminating information amongst policy-makers.
- Lingua 2: To ensure that a wide range of language-learning tools are available. Lingua 2 is also concerned with the development of instruments for language teaching and with the assessment of foreign language skills.

Vocational Training

As early as 1975, the EU established the European Centre for the Development of Vocational Training – CEDEFOP (Council Regulation 337/75), a non-profit-making organization independent of the European Commission, but to be of service both to it and the member states. It is now located in Thessalonica, Greece. While CEDEFOP does not run its own programs, it supports the Leonardo da Vinci program for vocational training which began in 1995 and is now in its second phase (2000–06). The program promotes transnational, cooperative projects between various providers of vocational training, and it is regarded as part of the lifelong learning initiative.

Information Technology

Two programs exist in this area: Minerva and Learning. The former has three aims:

- To promote understanding about ICT;
- To ensure pedagogical decisions are fully considered;
- To promote access to methods and educational resources.

The latter is an attempt to stimulate the educational community to introduce innovations into education rapidly.

The European Social Fund

This is of a different nature to the above programs, but it seeks to implement European employment policy into practice. Through it, funding is made available for a wide range of projects to develop people's skills and their potential for work. Like all the other projects, funding is available for partnerships seeking to regenerate people's employment potential.

Apart from all of these programs, there are other initiatives – such as the Tempus program which is a higher education scheme to generate more cooperation in higher education throughout Europe and beyond the boundaries of the EU itself, and the Bologna Agreement in higher education which aims to create a "European higher education area" by 2010. It seeks to simplify the complexity of different European higher education awards, mainly through the European Credit Transfer System (ECTS) which allows for mutual recognition and, therefore, mobility of students and workers throughout Europe. In addition, there are three other projects that deserve mention here:

- The Jean Monnet Project to introduce European integration studies to higher education.
- The College of Europe initiative to provide post-graduate study.
- The European University Institute to undertake research and teaching. This has an EU historical library and offers a number of services Europe-wide.

It is also envisaged that a new program will be introduced supporting European Unions master's courses – to be known as the Erasmus Mundus program. In addition, there are EU official agreements with both the United States and Canada which were established in 1995 in the areas of higher education and vocational training.

Finally, there is a policy to create a research initiative, known as the Framework Program (FP). Framework 5 (FW5) had two parts – one covering research, technological development and demonstration, and the other, Euratom. Funding was available in the first part for quality of life; the information society; sustainable growth and energy, and the environment themes, while other funding was available for the international role of community research, smaller and middle-sized enterprises and improving human research potential. FW6, which is about to be launched, aims to create a Europe of Research.

Trans-National Academic Organizations

A variety of European-wide academic organizations relating to the education of adults have emerged, five of which are mentioned here:

- The European Association for the Education of Adults (EAEA). This is an association of associations and non-governmental organizations concerned with the education of adults, with four major aims:
    - Advocating policy for lifelong learning in Europe.
    - Developing lifelong learning practice through undertaking projects.
    - Providing information and services.
    - Creating international cooperation.

- The European Association for Research on Learning and Instruction (Earli). This is an association in which scholars from around Europe can engage in critical dialogue and share research through conferences and interest groups, and provide a platform for contemporary thought. Amongst its interest groups has been one on the education of adults.
- The European Distance and E-Learning Network (EDEN). This is an association concerned with creating networks for academics and institutions involved in open, distance and e-learning. It holds

an annual conference and has a publication program.

- The European Society for Research on the Education of Adults (ESREA). This is a society that promotes theoretical and empirical research in the education of adults through research networks, conferences and publications.
- The European Universities Continuing Education Network (EUCEN). This is an association of universities concerned with the development of continuing education in Europe. It is an institutional network and holds two conferences per annum.

Finally, there is the European journal *Lifelong Learning in Europe* (LLinE): this is a journal that seeks to span both research and fieldwork projects in Europe. It publishes four editions per annum and is currently sponsored by the Finnish government. In addition, the journal organizes a European conference every year, each of which has been held in Finland.

See also: globalization, lifelong learning, organizations, training.

References and Further Reading

Cooperation on policy issues (n.d). Retrieved on January 12, 2003 from The European Union website: http://europa.eu.int/comm/education/policies/pol/policy_en.html

Jarvis, P. (2004) *Adult education and lifelong learning: Theory and practice* (3rd ed.). London: Routledge.

Peter Jarvis

Evaluation

According to Scriven (2003), evaluation is "the process of determining the merit, worth or significance of things" (p. 15). In adult education the use of the term is complex and confusing. One reason is that evaluation is used to describe different things: the progress and achievement of individual students; the merit, worth and effectiveness of adult education programs; and the validity and significance of any educational experiment, innovation or initiative. Using "evaluation" to make judgements about program quality is widely accepted, although "program review" is also used. For specific aspects of program evaluation, as when judging the quality of teaching, words like "appraisal," "accountability," and "assessment" are used synonymously with "evaluation." Evaluation of programs, experiments and innovations, using formal research processes and professional evaluators, is called "evaluation research." A distinguishing feature of evaluation research is its overriding interest in useful, practical knowledge, enabling action. Perhaps the greatest confusion around "evaluation" concerns evaluation of student learning. Here a number of terms are used interchangeably, including "assessment" (especially in Britain and latterly in the United States), "measurement," "testing," and "grading."

The history of evaluation contributes to its complexity and confusion, and it emerged from at least three different applications. One focused on testing student achievement, initially using constructs from psychology, particularly psychometrics, to accurately measure this. Later, ideas from sociology, including power and social change, entered discussions about evaluating student learning. Another use, dating from the late 1800s in the United States, arose from the requirement to accredit programs and institutions. A third application, dating from the late 1960s, resulted from the increased demand for accountability placed on educational programs by government organizations and other agencies. These demands led to the emergence of evaluation research as a field.

A third reason for the complexity and confusion around evaluation is that, like adult education itself, evaluation is based in different philosophical paradigms. These can be presented as four orientations that resonate with traditions in adult education. One is a positivist, outcome-based orientation that attempts to evaluate the goals and outcomes of programmes and learning using scientific and objective methods. A second is what Scriven (2003) calls a consumer-orientated evaluation process, that evaluates whether program consumers' (learners') needs have been met. A third, postmodern, orientation focuses on uniqueness of context, questioning objectivity, generalizability of data, and places the values and assumptions of the evaluator at the center of the process. Finally, from critical theory there is the view that evaluation must be aimed at the solution of social problems, focusing on identifying and neutralizing the effects of power in evaluation.

It follows that evaluation is not a neutral or absolute process. Embedded within it are philosophies, perspectives and purposes that have cultural, social and political foundations. Consequently the evaluative systems used, the interpretations made, the judgements drawn and the actions taken are influenced by the context. Evaluation in all its guises is political. Its effects may privilege or marginalize certain groups, encourage change, or maintain the status quo.

Evaluation (Assessment) of Student Learning

"Assessment," as a synonym for evaluation of student learning, has growing currency in all parts of the English-speaking world and will be used in this section, which outlines purposes of assessment, frameworks for assessment and issues of defensibility.

One way of thinking about the purposes of assessment in adult education is to think of assessment as summative, formative and diagnostic. Summative assessment usually occurs at the end of a program, aiming to assess the product of learning. Through certification, classification and comparison, decisions and predictions about adults' suitability for employment and potential for future learning are made. Formative assessment usually occurs throughout the learning process, and seeks to guide and correct learning and identify strengths and weaknesses by providing regular and prompt feedback on learner performance. Such assessment may also have the purpose of increasing motivation. Diagnostic assessment identifies both readiness for learning and learning needs. Assessment can also be used to enable learners to gain a critical understanding of the institution they learn in, the industry they work in and the society they live in, with a view to changing the status quo. This requires assessment of higher-order critical thinking and evaluation abilities, and in adult education there are tensions between these purposes. However, it is conceptually difficult to separate them as distinctions between them are blurred. Rarely is an assessment process purely summative, formative or diagnostic. In an age when summative assessment dominates the discourse in many adult education contexts, Crooks (1988) provides a counterpoint:

> Perhaps the most important function of assessment in tertiary teaching is its role in giving students feedback on their progress and achievements; helping them to see their areas of strength and weakness, identifying misconceptions and difficulties they are having, and guiding and encouraging their further development. (p. 8)

Not only do purposes differ, there are different assessment frameworks. While assessment always compares, ways of comparing are often described as fitting within two broad frameworks – norm-referenced assessment, and criterion-referenced assessment (Biggs, 2003). In norm-referenced assessment each learner is compared with others in a particular group. At its simplest, it ranks learners according to their marks, grades or percentages. Sometimes the actual score a learner achieves is adjusted so the group results fit a normal distribution curve, ensuring that a set proportion achieve the top and bottom grades, while most fit around the middle. Criterion-referenced assessment compares an individual's performance with preset standards, stated as learning objectives and defined by performance criteria that clearly describe what a learner has to know or be able to do in order to succeed. All learners can succeed or not, depending on whether they meet the criteria. Two forms of criterion-referenced assessment are identified (Leach, Neutze, & Zepke, 2003): competency-based assessment produces a competent or not-yet-competent result, while achievement-based assessment has arisen out of the criticism that competency-based assessment denies recognition of excellence. To address this, grade-related criteria have been developed.

In addition to purposes and frameworks, assessment raises issues such as defensibility – the ability to withstand the scrutiny of stakeholders. A key consideration here is whether assessment is valid, and validity comes in various forms including content, construct and consequential. Of these, consequential validity seems most pertinent for the adult educator. It is also the most recent and most contested form. It concerns the social context of assessment. To be valid in this way, assessments must reflect learners' social contexts and consider the consequences of their use (Gipps, 1995; Messick, 1993). Consequential validity is contentious as it is open to the charge of relativism, yet it is particularly important in adult education because it recognizes the diversity of adults and their contexts. The acceptance of consequential validity also makes the concept of reliability contentious. Reliability refers to the consistency and reproducibility of assessment results. While it is widely accepted that assessments should be consistent, there may be circumstances in adult education where reliability should not take precedence over consequential validity. Where learning, teaching and assessment center on individual needs rather than set requirements, reliability is not a specific focus.

Assessment practices valued by many adult educators, such as self, peer and group assessments, are particularly in need of defence. Such practices are justified from humanistic and critical orientations but questioned by adherents of outcomes/

summative perspectives. Underpinning this are issues about who should hold power in assessment. Humanists argue that adults, because they are adult, must be involved in assessing their own work, while critical theorists say that adult education must deal with unequal distributions of power in the classroom. Involving learners in assessment is one way of changing balances of power. Opponents observe that such assessment used for summative purposes cannot be objective, reliable or ensure that standards are met. While humanism and critical theory have their own defences, there is also research evidence that supports the validity and reliability of self, peer and group assessment. For example, in a meta-analysis conducted in the late 1980s, Boud and Falchikov (1995), while acknowledging that differences do occur, found considerable similarity in the grading of work between adult learners and their teachers. Also, self, peer, and group assessment are strengthened by a rigorous monitoring regime. Teachers from both inside and outside the institution use random and blind procedures to check grades awarded.

Evaluation of Programs

Program evaluation is not new; people want to know the merit and worth of a program. In the United States the Joint Committee on Standards for Educational Evaluation produced a substantial set of standards for program evaluation (Stufflebeam, 2003), and this section uses and extends ideas from this publication to outline a variety of purposes of program evaluation, describe some conceptual frameworks, and discuss defensibility issues.

Purposes for program evaluation vary, and four primary purposes are outlined. The first, summative in nature, is usually done on behalf of funders, regulators and managers for accountability reasons. Such evaluations may consider the whole future of the program. The second considers to what extent stated program goals have been achieved. Such evaluations also identify the extent to which learners', the public's, industries' and institutional needs have been met. Program improvement is the third purpose of program evaluation, and such evaluations identify program strengths and weaknesses, make judgements about its value and worth, and establish recommendations for change. Finally, program evaluations may initiate social change by examining critically how program objectives facilitate social change.

To achieve these purposes, a number of evaluation frameworks are available (Popham, 1993; Scriven, 2003). Goal-attainment frameworks focus on program objectives, where each is examined rigorously to establish whether it has been achieved. Only when goals are attained is a program deemed successful. In judgement frameworks evaluators have the power to make pronoucements and produce recommendations based on how they interpret the evidence. Decision-facilitation, on the other hand, denies decision-making to the evaluator who conveys information to institutional decision-makers. These frameworks tend to rely on scientific methods and often use quantitative data to make decisions. Within a naturalistic framework, few or no constraints are imposed on the evaluation process. The fewer the preconditions or limitations, the more naturalistic the evaluation. Data are gathered using qualitative methods, and both program participants and outsiders can be involved in this process.

Whatever framework is used, it must be defensible, and if the following five issues are addressed this should be achieved. First, transparency to all stakeholders is essential. Purposes, methods and how the results will be used are clearly stated before the process begins. In high-stakes evaluations, in particular, the possible consequences of a negative evaluation are spelled out. Second, evaluations are useful to stakeholders; they are designed to produce information that leads to actionable decisions. Third, evaluation design is feasible; it takes account of political and practical considerations such as staffing, time, skill levels and resources. The fourth issue concerns the ethics of evaluation, and this takes account of the safety of all stakeholders. Participants have access to information, and are aware of processes that ensure fairness. Finally, evaluation is valid – it evaluates what it claims to evaluate and provides good evidence for recommendations and decisions.

Evaluation Research

Evaluation research is the most recently developed aspect of evaluation, and several of the purposes and defensibility issues outlined are similar to those discussed under evaluation of student learning and programme evaluation.

Like assessment and program evaluation, evaluation research has several purposes. Evaluation for accountability; goal achievement; program improvement; and social change are shared with program evaluation. Additionally, evaluation research can build stakeholder confidence that the evaluation is done professionally by experts using "best-practice" research methods. An overarching purpose is to find evidence that aids decisions leading to action, particularly in relation to cost-effectiveness.

Evaluation research shares with educational research three conceptual frameworks. One is quantitative, where numerical evidence is used to explain and control phenomena and predict consequences. It is based in the natural sciences, sharing with them a desire for objectivity, certainty and generalizability. This approach is often used for accountability evaluations. It suits the purposes of policy-makers and funders because it reduces complex educational interventions to numbers. Critics maintain it ignores important information that cannot be captured as numbers. The second is qualitative, which seeks to understand phenomena using interpretation and illumination. This framework rejects the need for objectivity, seeking instead rich data that enable interpretation of a particular context. It suits evaluation for program improvement and possibly goal attainment. Critics of this framework regret that its findings cannot be generalized and do not offer certainty for action. Defenders welcome its rich and multifaceted data that can lead to well-founded decisions and action. The third framework is critical research. Often described as action research, this goes beyond understanding phenomena, attempting to find ways to change programs and their contexts. Action research is participatory with participants playing a powerful role in the evaluation process. This framework is used to facilitate social change and program improvement. Advocates value the participation and action associated with this framework; critics regret its lack of objectivity and reliability. While these frameworks are separated here, evaluation researchers increasingly use them in combination to achieve research purposes.

Issues that may lead to stakeholder challenges to evaluation research are similar to those noted under program evaluation. Evaluation research must be transparent, useful, feasible, ethical and valid. In addition to these, evaluation researchers need professional credibility, achieved through training and certification.

See also: needs assessment, program planning, research methods.

References and Further Reading

Biggs, J. (2003). *Teaching for quality learning at university* (2nd ed.). Maidenhead: Society for Research into Higher Education and Open University Press.

Boud, D., & Falchikov, N. (1995). What does research tell us about self assessment? In D. Boud (Ed.), *Enhancing learning through self assessment* (pp. 115–166) London: Kogan Page.

Crooks, T. (1988). *Assessing student performance*. Green Guide No. 8, Sydney: Higher Education Research and Development Society of Australasia.

Gipps, C. V. (1995). *Beyond testing: Towards a theory of educational assessment*. London: Falmer.

Leach, L., Neutze, G., & Zepke, N. (2003). Course design and assessment for transformation. In N. Zepke, D. Nuget, & L. Leach (Eds.), *From reflection to transformation* (pp. 155–178). Palmerston North, New Zealand: Dunmore Press.

Messick, S. (1993). Validity. In R.L Linn (Ed.), *Educational measurement* (3rd ed., pp. 13–103). Phoenix: AZ Oryx.

Popham, W. J. (1993). *Educational evaluation* (3rd ed.). Boston: Allyn & Bacon.

Scriven, M. (2003). Evaluation theory and metatheory. In T. Kellaghan, D. L. Stufflebeam & L.A. Wingate (Eds.), *International handbook of educational evaluation* (pp. 15–30). Dordrecht, The Netherlands: Kluwer Academic Publishers.

Stufflebeam, D.L. (2003). Professional standards and principles for evaluations. In T. Kellaghan, D.L. Stufflebeam & L.A. Wingate (Eds.), *International handbook of educational evaluation* (pp. 279–302). Dordrecht, The Netherlands: Kluwer Academic Publishers.

Linda Leach and Nick Zepke

Experiential Learning

Experiential learning is commonly used in two different senses. Firstly, it is used to describe the prior learning that is brought to a new situation arising from the life experiences of the learner. This prior learning then provides the base for any learning that follows. Secondly, but by far the major use of the term, is to refer to learning processes in which the experience of the learner is used as the prime source and stimulus for learning.

Recognizing Prior Learning

Over the past 30 years a movement has been established to recognize the learning that has occurred in nonformal settings to facilitate entry to, or advance standing in, formal educational programs (Chickering, 1986). The term to describe this varies, but it is most frequently known as accreditation of prior experiential learning (APEL), or recognition of prior learning (RPL). Experiential learning is learning that has occurred outside educational settings or as part of nonassessed programs. After reflection and documentation, this experiential learning can be demonstrated to be equivalent to that acquired and assessed as part of an accredited program. Experiential learning in this sense may or may not be used in the programs that follow recognition; it is simply used to access these as an alternative to formally recognized learning outcomes.

As a Philosophy

Experiential learning in its wider usage is both a philosophy and a practice. It is a philosophy in that advocates argue that all learning comes in some sense from experience. That is, learning must take account of the learner and what he or she brings with them from all earlier experience as these not only provide the foundation for dispositions, expectations and motivations, but also establish the base of knowledge and expertise on which new knowledge must build. Thus, learning must necessarily be experience-based. Most representations of this view owe their origins to the work of the early 20th century philosopher, John Dewey (1938).

As a Practice

As a practice, experiential learning is identified with various methods and techniques which include but are not restricted to the following: participatory events, reflective activities, use of feelings, emotions and the whole person, action learning and action-oriented methods, adventure challenges. The common element is that they involve moving away from classroom-based, purely cognitive activities to those which actively utilize experiences (previous or newly provoked), work with them to draw learning from them and locate learning in specific contexts (either authentic or contrived). A common point of reference in much practice is the learning cycle developed by David Kolb from the earlier work of Kurt Lewin (Kolb, 1984), which describes a four-part model focusing on "concrete experience," "reflective observation," "abstract conceptualization" and "active experimentation." Though this has been much discussed and criticized over the years, it is one of the few ideas that is known across the range of practice.

Experiential learning as a practice encompasses a very diverse range of themes and interests. As an illustration of this, at the First International Conference on Experiential Learning (1987) the diversity of the perspectives was such that the editors of the book produced from the conference found it necessary to portray them in terms of four "tribes" of experiential learning (Weil & McGill, 1989). These tribes as located in different "villages" had different cultures and points of reference. The four "villages" are not mutually exclusive, but interact and intersect with each other. Village 1 concerns itself with assessment and accreditation of experiential learning; village 2 sees experiential learning as catalyzing change in education through participative pedagogies; village 3 is concerned with learning from experience as the core of education for consciousnessraising, community action and social change; and village 4 takes as its focus personal growth and development to increase selfawareness and group effectiveness. Each "village" has its own literature and practices, sets of values and terminology for the particular activities used. There is also diversity within each. This diversity between and within practices makes it difficult to characterize experiential learning and ideas associated with it in a simple form.

Fostering Experiential Learning

Given the diversity of practice, it is

not possible to identify a common set of approaches to promoting experiential learning. However, while located in one of the villages identified above, the work of John Heron (1999) provides a conceptual and analytical framework for mapping facilitation practices with applicability across traditions. Also drawing on the different traditions, Boud and Miller (1996), using the term "working with experience," discuss new ways of utilizing the insights of different facilitative practices and argue for a move away from the notion of "facilitator" due to its close association with one tradition, to that of "animator."

Alternative Terms

The field of experiential learning is becoming less distinct and many of the ideas promoted, such as the key role of experience in all learning, have become a part of mainstream educational thinking. Also, much current literature has moved away from the use of "experiential learning" as such to refer to ideas such as "using experience for learning" (Boud, Cohen, & Walker, 1993), "learning from experience" (Miller, 2000) and "learning through experience" (Fenwick, 2003). Usher (1993), however, has distinguished between the terms "learning from experience" and "experiential learning." He argues that learning from experience happens "in everyday contexts as part of day-to-day life, although it is rarely recognized as such." He contrasts this with "experiential learning, on the other hand, that is a key element of a discourse which has this everyday process as its "subject" and which constructs it in a certain way, although it appears to be a term which describes the process" (Usher, p. 169). Usher argues that it is useful to separate the everyday use of experiential learning from the specialized construction in the hands of professional educators.

See also: multiple intelligences, prior learning and assessment recognition, portfolio, reflective learning.

References and Further Reading

Boud, D., Cohen, R., & Walker, D. (Eds.). (1993). *Using experience for learning*. Buckingham, UK: Society for Research into Higher Education and Open University Press.

Boud, D., & Miller, N. (Eds.). (1996). *Working with experience: Animating learning*. London: Routledge.

Chickering, A. W. (1986). *Principles of good practice in assessing experiential learning*. Columbia, MD: Council for Adult and Experiential Learning.

Dewey, J. (1938). *Experience and education*. New York: Collier.

Fenwick, T. J. (2003). *Learning through experience: Troubling orthodoxies and intersecting questions*. Malabar, FL: Krieger.

Heron, J. (1999). *The complete facilitator's handbook*. London: Kogan Page.

Kolb, D. A. (1984). *Experiential learning*. Englewood Cliffs, NJ: Prentice-Hall.

Miller, N. (2000). Learning from experience in adult education. In A. L. Wilson & E. R. Hayes (Eds.). (2000). *Handbook of adult and continuing education* (pp. 71–86). San Francisco: Jossey-Bass.

Usher, R. (1993). Experiential learning or learning from experience: Does it make a difference? In D. Boud, R. Cohen, & D. Walker (Eds.), *Using experience for learning* (pp. 169–180). Buckingham, UK: Society for Reserach into Higher Education and Open University Press.

Weil, S. W., & McGill, I. (Eds.). (1989). *Making sense of experiential learning*. Milton Keynes, UK: Society for Research into Higher Education & Open University Press.

David Boud

Extension

Extension can be best described as a system of non-formal adult education that strives to help people understand the potential merits of scientific information, new technologies, and emergent practices and how the application of this new knowledge can enhance the quality of their lives (Boone, 1989). It strives to do this through a process of technology transfer that induces behavioral changes in its clients. Extension, as a form of adult education dedicated to improving the quality of life of mostly agrarian and rural peoples, is increasingly becoming a contested concept. Its history, firmly rooted in the Renaissance and the Scientific and Industrial Revolutions, has come under intense scrutiny as a result of economic globalization and neo-liberal reform. Both the efficacy and efficiency of traditionally delivered public extension systems has been called into question and as a result we are seeing a variety of different organizations emerging to deliver extension and a variety of different goals for and approaches to extension.

The term extension originated in the second half of the 18th century in England, as Cambridge and Oxford Universities grappled with their role and responsibilities to the increasing populations situated predominately in the industrial, urban areas. The first practical attempt at university extension was in 1867 (Jones & Garforth, 1997), and the term extension education was coined in 1873 by Cambridge University (Blackburn & Flaherty, 1994). While the first endeavors into extension saw lectures delivered on literary and social topics, by the 1890s agricultural topics were being delivered by peripatetic lecturers in rural communities. By the end of the century it had developed into a fully fledged movement.

And while extension has it conceptual origins in the 19th century, practically it has been carried out for hundreds of years. Jones and Garforth (1997) trace the practice of extension back to 1800 BCE Mesopotamia where archeologists unearthed clay tablets with inscribed advice on watering crops and how to eliminate rat populations. They also point to the development of important Latin texts written between the 2nd century BCE to the 4th century CE, whereby practical agricultural information was written down for the expressed purpose of assisting Roman landowners and tenants to improve their estates and revenues. Concurrent developments were also taking place in China during this period as the state became increasingly concerned with assisting landowners and tenants in improving their lands.

Modern extension, however, has its roots in the Renaissance and the beginning of science in the 16th and 17th centuries. As Blackburn and Flaherty (1994) note, there was a desire to use this new knowledge which manifested itself in new movements that attempted to make linkages among science, education and the needs of everyday life. In particular, the roots of European and North American agricultural extension can be traced back to such organizations as the Society of Improvers in the Knowledge of Agriculture founded in Scotland in 1723, the American Philosophical Society founded by Benjamin Franklin in 1744, and the Philadelphia Society for Promoting Agriculture founded in 1785. Of particular note during this period, and one that would reverberate throughout modern agricultural extension in the years to come, was Phillip Emanual von Fellenberg's purchase of the estate known as Wylhof near Bern, Switzerland. He renamed this estate Hofwyl and established one of the first agricultural schools for children which became a model for other schools established before 1850 in Denmark, Germany, France and the United Kingdom. Thus, von Fellenberg influenced the education of a cadre of agriculturalists in Europe (Jones & Garforth, 1997). In addition, he established the first experimental/model farm in Europe at Hofwyl and here he tested and developed husbandry practices and technology. He welcomed visitors to Hofwyl and maintained a voluminous correspondence with these visitors, and as Jones and Garforth note, many of his visitors became active proselytes of his ideas and methods.

Blackburn and Flaherty (1994) report that the first experimental farm in North America was set up by Marc Lescarbot at Port Royal, Nova Scotia. They further argue that within 60 years model farms were becoming popular and the province of Quebec opened Canada's first agricultural school in 1670. By the 1820s itinerant agriculturalists were active in New England and New York, meeting with farmers and offering advice, and by the second half of the 19th century itinerant agriculturalists were being employed throughout North America and Europe.

In the southern hemisphere extension became established in the coastal belts of southern and eastern Australia. By the 1870s and 1880s, and influenced heavily by what was happening in Europe and North America, departments of agriculture had been established with the expressed aim of developing the potential of their territories. Extension work was also established in Japan during this period as a result of modernization policies adopted after the Meiji Restoration in 1868. The Japanese government established two agricultural colleges and state farms where experiments were conducted and new practices and technologies developed. These activities were followed by the development of agricultural societies which were institutionalized through legislation in 1899 and strengthened in 1903, forcing Japanese farmers to belong to local agricultural societies which the government organized into a national network. This led to "forced extension" whereby farmers were compelled to adopt the technical guidance and advice offered by the societies' extension workers.

Extension activities were not confined to temperate countries at this time, and some development took place in tropical countries, particularly those colonized by European countries. As Jones and Garforth (1997) argued, despite the long relationship European countries had with many of these tropical countries, they remained ignorant of many of the tropical agriculture crops. As a result a series of experimental and demonstration botanical gardens were established, the first one in 1821 in Sri Lanka followed by smaller ones in the Caribbean and in some of the Western African territories. One of the more intriguing developments in the African territories was that extension was initiated by missionaries alongside their religious work through the development of church farms (*fermes-chappelles*), first established by the Jesuits in 1895 in the Belgian Congo.

Thus by the beginning of the 20th century, the foundations for the modern extension service had been laid not only in North America and Europe, but around the globe.

Models of the Modern Concept of Extension

As noted, extension as a concept may be described as a system of non-formal education that strives to help people acquire knowledge, and apply that knowledge to meet their needs. Boone (1989) argues that historically there are four models of extension, that are premised on the above description of extension. They are: (a) the typical developing-country extension model; (b) the training and visit system; (c) the farming system research and development model; and (d) the United States cooperative extension system.

Typical Developing Country Extension Model

Historically, these extension systems have been hierarchical, and highly bureaucratic and political. Information flows tend to be from the top of the organization down to the lower levels and are usually firmly entrenched within the Ministry of Agriculture. Furthermore, they tend to exist independent of educational and research institutes, hence technical information and research findings do not circulate within these extension units. In addition, extension staff not only provide education, but their duties include the enforcement of government regulations.

Training and Visit Model (T&V)

This model of extension, developed by Daniel Benor and adopted by the World Bank in the 1970s for developing countries, focuses on small farmers employing traditional methods and low-level technology. Its goal is to help farmers improve production and profits. The role of the village extension agent is to "fill" the knowledge gaps of the farmer. This is accomplished by regular visits to farmers where they teach or illustrate through practice new technologies and methods. There are direct linkages between the extension organization and the village extension agent, who is supported by teams of subject-matter specialists.

Farming Systems Research and Development Model

This approach to extension was premised on the need to understand production within the larger context of the farmer's culture, world view and needs in order to enter into a collaborative relationship with the farmer. The Farming Systems Research and Development Model approaches the farm as a dynamic system that is linked with other systems such as marketing systems, government and educational systems. Its overall aim is to improve production and the quality of farmers' lives. Specifically it (a) targets and researches specific sites; (b) identifies problems and develops research plans; (c) designs and plans on-farm research; (d) carries-out and analyses on-farm research; and (e) disseminates the outcomes of the research (Boone, 1989, p. 4). This approach tends to be multidisciplinary and hence draws on a number of disciplines and/or professions.

United States Cooperative Extension System (USCES)

In the latter half of the 1800s the United States established the land-grant institutions to provide higher education in agriculture. In 1887 experimental stations were established as part of the land-grant institutes, followed in 1914 by the establishment of the Cooperative

Extension Service to provide instruction to farmers and their families in agriculture and home economics. Thus we have an integrated system that links research, education and extension. This model would be difficult to develop in other contexts, according to Boone (1989), because it required a "national commitment to agriculture; political stability that allowed structures and goals to be developed over time, through debate; and bountiful natural resources" (p. 5).

The Decline of Modern Extension

The climate for extension changed drastically starting in the mid-1980s. As Rivera and Zijp (2002) maintain, globalization, new economic systems, trade liberalization, structural adjustment and developments in communication technology forced the reinvention of extension institutions and systems. As they argue, conventional wisdom maintains that current government extension is ineffective and inefficient. Feder, Willett, and Zijp (1999) argue that given the absence of evidence that there is a return on investment in public extension, we need to explore alternative ways of delivering extension services. Given the above, there is an increased emphasis on the contracting of extension (Rivera & Zijp) to either the private sector or third-sector groups such as farmers' organizations. This, however, creates problems for small farmers as they are often in a position where they cannot pay for information from which they might benefit (Kidd, Lamers, Ficarelli, & Hoffmann, 2000). Lightfoot, Alders, and Dolberg (2001) argue that the objective should not be just to save money, but to achieve environmental and socially equitable development. Lightfoot et al. then argue that there is a need for better models of governance at local levels, empowerment of the resource-poor, and stronger democratic institutions, and this means developing capacity within civil society.

Given this backdrop, there are two models of extension that are evolving. The first is predominantly catering to large producers through traditional technology transfer with the difference being that extension services are delivered by private-service providers who are contracted by government to deliver extension, or extension is delivered by private for-profit enterprise (Kidd et al., 2000). The second model is still contracted extension; however, it tends to target small farmers, particularly in developing countries, and focuses on developing capacity within communities through what Lightfoot et al. (2001) describe as the learning approach delivered by third-sector NGOs.

The Learning Approach to Extension

The learning approach to extension is commensurate with the philosophical position of constructionism whereby reality is said to be socially constructed. As Röling and Wagemakers (1998) explain, reality is "created in the discourse of, and negotiations, among people as social actors. Thus the negotiation of social reality becomes the 'objective reality' " (p. 13). They then further argue that this means that the function of extension is to socially reconstruct agrarian reality through the process of communication and information-sharing. It is a form of social learning, a participatory process of social change whereby social transformation is fostered by "critical self-reflection; the development of participatory multi-layer democratic processes; the reflexive capabilities of human individuals and societies; and the capacity for social movements to change political and economic frameworks for the better" (Woodhill & Roling 1998, p. 53).

Lightfoot et al. (2001) maintain that this is a four-phase process. Each phase is characterized by a specific objective from (a) exploring the potential in a learning approach, (b) forming a learning group consisting of various stakeholders, (c) developing local capacity to develop learning tools and processes, and (d) fostering reflection processes, learning indicators and establishing communication networks for peer-to-peer learning. Thus local learners are engaged in a process of knowledge construction within the context of the local environment, and through this process of local knowledge construction they attempt to solve self-identified problems.

See also: community development, historical inquiry, participatory action research, rural learning.

References and Further Reading

Blackburn, D. J., & Flaherty, J. (1994). Historical roots and philosophy of extension. In D. J. Blackburn (Ed.), *Extension handbook: Processes and practices* (pp. 1–10). Toronto: Thompson Educational.

Boone, E. J. (1989). Philosophical foundations of extension. In D. J. Blackburn (Ed.), *Foundations and changing practices in extension* (pp. 1–9). Guelph, ON: University of Guelph.

Feder, G., Willett, A., & Zijp, W. (1999). *Agricultural extension: Generic challenges and some ingredients for solutions*. Policy Research Working Paper no. 2129, The World Bank, Washington, DC.

Jones, G. E., & Garforth, C. (1997). The history, development, and future of agricultural extension. In B.E. Swanson, R.P. Bentz & A.J. Sofranko (Eds.), *Improving agricultural extension: A reference manual* (pp. 3–12). Rome: Food and Agriculture Organization of the United Nations.

Kidd, A. D., Lamers, J. P. A., Ficarelli, P. P., & Hoffmann, V. (2000). Privatising agricultural extension: Caveat emptor. *Journal of Rural Studies*, *16*, 95–102.

Lightfoot, C., Alders, C., & Dolberg, F. (2001). *Linking local learners: Negotiating new development relationships between village, district and nation*. Greve, Denmark: Agroforum.

Rivera, W. M., & Zijp, W. (Eds.). (2002). *Contracting for agricultural extension*. Oxford, UK: CABI Publishing.

Röling, N. G., & Wagemakers, M. A. E. (1998). A new practice: Facilitating sustainable agriculture. In N.G. Röling & M. A. E. Wagemakers (Eds.), *Facilitating sustainable agriculture: Participatory learning and adaptive management in times of environmental uncertainty* (pp. 3–22). Cambridge, UK: Cambridge University Press.

Woodhill, J., & Röling, N. G. (1998). The second wing of the eagle: The human dimension in learning our way to more sustainable futures. In N.G. Röling & M. A. E. Wagemakers (Eds.), *Facilitating sustainable agriculture: Participatory learning and adaptive management in times of environmental uncertain* (pp. 46–72). Cambridge, UK: Cambridge University Press.

Al Lauzon

F

Facilitation

Facilitation describes a range of pedagogical techniques whose shared goal is to guide and assist learning processes, while encouraging high levels of learner ownership and participation. Facilitation places learners at the center of educational activities, values knowledge that learners have acquired through lived experiences, and shifts the focus of processes and activities to the learners themselves. In short, facilitation make learners much more responsible for their learning than more traditional pedagogical approaches.

However, facilitation is not a *laisez-faire* approach to adult education; effective facilitation is active, critical and purposeful (Brookfield, 2000; Brookfield & Preskill, 1999). Facilitation often reflects a constructivist epistemology, and integrates learner subjectivities into the learning process. While facilitation most often uses skills and activities that differ from traditional "banking" approaches to education, the philosophical orientations that inspire this learner-empowered approach are as important as the instructional techniques used. In other words, both "how-to" and "why-to" issues are integral to understanding how effective facilitation happens. Facilitators help make these processes happen, but do not act as gatekeepers or validators of knowledge. Facilitation often involves conceptualizing program objectives and activities in advance, allowing for fluidity during the actual event or program. Conversely, animation (as a particular mode of facilitated learning) seeks to help a group of learners catalyze their objectives as a group, as well as ways to achieve them.

Brookfield (1986) identified six specific principles of effective practice in facilitating learning (pp. 9–11), which are clearly informed by Freire's (e.g., 1983) work:

- Voluntary participation
- Respect for each other's self-worth
- Collaboration
- Praxis
- A spirit of critical reflection
- The nurturing of self-directed empowered adults

These principles are admirable, but does the absence of any one of them make facilitation impossible; can those whose attendance is not initially voluntary become engaged once present? Is facilitation untenable for persons who suffer very low self-esteem, or even self-loathing? Must facilitators gatekeep learner commitments to collaboration, praxis and critical reflection, and exclude those who demonstrate deficits in these areas? And are these principles transferable across cultures, specifically when collectivist notions of identity are valued more highly than individualized ideals like self-direction?

I would argue that these ideals are an excellent rubric by which to query why facilitation in a specific context might not be bringing desired outcomes. But to use these as *a priori* criteria to assess the feasibility of using facilitation as an instructional strategy would render this accessible, adaptable and learner-centered approach inaccessible and inflexible.

A Question of Power

On a continuum created to delineate between instructional approaches, facilitation would lie somewhere between formalist pedagogy and anarchy – but precisely where would be subject to significant debate. Miller, Boud, Brookfield, Brown, Harris, Ireland, Mace, and Tisdell (1997) describe a facilitator as a "supportive person who facilitates learning rather than acting as teacher" (p. 487), reflecting the notion that facilitation is different than being a traditional pedagogue. Brookfield (1986) argues that genuine facilitation "incorporates elements of challenge, confrontation and critical analysis of self and society" (p. vii); but does facilitation always entail the pursuit of changing critical consciousness? Marsick (1991), in describing facilitation as a key component of action learning, argues that facilitation

> ensures that people look at a problem from many perspectives, challenge one another and themselves, ask "stupid" questions, draw contrasts, probe connections, try out new behaviors, see and confront their own dysfunctional behavior, act when they would rather talk, and reflect some more when they are ready to act prematurely to solve a problem that has not been thoroughly considered (p. 44)

Marsick, too, sees criticality as integral to effective facilitation.

Most adult educators espouse a desire to empower and prioritize learner perspectives, but the reality of how this is done is often more challenging. Critical to any differentiation about the role played by instructors (or facilitators or animators) is the question of power in learner–instructor dynamics. Power manifests itself in terms of the dyadic relationship between instructors and individual learners, in the group dynamics of small groups and classrooms, in the institutional conflicts of the activity being facilitated, and often in the learners' and facilitator's real-world lives. Facilitators often espouse a desire to empower learners and place their voice at the center of learning activities. It is often presumed that facilitators find redistributing their power to learners a difficult act; in reality, it is often learners who respond negatively to being asked to take greater responsibility for their (individual and collective) learning: whose job indeed. Similarly, how are issues of power between learners managed? If learners are ostensibly empowered equally, do facilitators bear any responsibility to guard against domineering, offensive or abusive learners? I would argue yes – an integral part of facilitating is accepting an appropriate level of responsibility for group process. Ideally some learners take on this responsibility as necessary, but a good facilitator doesn't avoid tending to these issues. Thus, while adult educators often have specific values or beliefs regarding facilitation, the values and beliefs of learners play a critical role in determining the degree to which such efforts are successful.

But for facilitators, the power issues are often manifest outside learning activities, and involve stakeholders who often don't participate in programs: funders and institutional management, also known as non-participant stakeholders. As Hart (1992) states, "the shaping of communal relations and a corresponding consciousness is as much dependent on institutional support as is the creation of its opposite" (p. 212). In some instances, specific educational endeavors are constrained by content-heavy learning outcomes derived from non-participant stakeholders, making facilitated learning less tenable – and perhaps undesirable. The interests of non-participant stakeholders cannot be disregarded or ignored (Cervero & Wilson, 1994). Constraints in terms of context, funding, and space also inform the extent to which facilitation is tenable as an instructional approach.

A Process Orientation

A good deal of the literature on facilitation focuses on specific techniques for shepherding group activities. These include collaborative learning, consensus-based decision-making, and substantive learner input into program planning. Galbraith (1991) posits that "facilitators and learners constantly re-examine their educational purposes, processes, values, needs and desires in relationship to potential self-growth as well as to the enhancement of society" (p. 1). The process of facilitation, for both facilitator and learner, is iterative rather than static or linear. Facilitating requires accepting the role of change agent rather than disseminator of knowledge. Few in adult education circles would refute the value of inculcating empowered, critical learners; yet often institutional contexts – schools, workplaces, large NGOs – validate more traditional "banking" (Freire, 1983) methods.

See also: needs assessment, practitioner, praxis, program planning, teaching.

References and Further Reading

Brookfield, S. D. (1986). *Understanding and facilitating adult learning: A comprehensive analysis of principles and effective practice*. San Francisco: Jossey-Bass.

Brookfield, S. D. (2000). *The skillful teacher: On technique, trust, and responsiveness in the classroom*. San Francisco: Jossey-Bass.

Brookfield, S. D., & Preskill, S. (1999). *Discussion as a way of teaching: Tools and techniques for democratic classrooms* (1st ed.). San Francisco: Jossey-Bass.

Cervero, R. M., & Wilson, A. L. (1994). *Planning responsibly for adult education: A guide to negotiating power and interests*. San Francisco: Jossey-Bass.

Freire, P. (1983). *Pedagogy of the oppressed* (M. B. Ramos, Trans.). New York: Continuum.

Galbraith, M. W. (1991). *Facilitating adult learning: A transactional process*. Malabar, FL: Krieger.

Hart, M. (1992). *Working and educating for life: Feminist and international perspectives on adult education*. New York: Routledge.

Marsick, V. J. (1991). Action learning and reflection in the workplace. In J. Mezirow (Ed.), *Fostering critical reflection in adulthood: A guide to transformative and emancipatory learning* (pp. 23–46). San Francisco: Jossey-Bass.

Miller, N., & Boud, D. with Brookfield, S. D., Brown, J., Harris, J. B., Ireland, T., Mace, J., & Tisdell, E. J. (1997). From teaching to facilitation to animation: Crossing the boundaries between traditions and perspectives in the promotion of learning from experience. In P. Armstrong, N. Miller, & M. Zukas (Eds.), *Crossing borders, breaking boundaries: Research in the education of adults* (pp. 487–495). Proceedings of the 27th Annual Standing Conference on University Teaching and Research in the Education of Adults (SCUTREA) Conference. London: Centre for Extra-Mural Studies, Birkbeck College, London, UK.

John Egan

Feminism

"Feminism is a movement to end sexism, sexist exploitation, and oppression," writes cultural critic and feminist theorist bell hooks (2000, p. viii). Inherent in this definition, she suggests, is the assumption that all people have been socialized into sexist ideology, and often into particular gender roles and ways of thinking that generally give more institutional, social, and economic power and access to resources to males. Feminism assumes that the problem in the world with regard to gender relations is not men, since feminism is not anti-male. Rather the problem is sexism. Feminism seeks to challenge sexism and sexist ways of thinking that limit both men and women. Everyone has something to gain from the feminist movement, given that its purpose is to create more equitable relations for all people, both women and men.

There are many feminisms, including liberal, radical, psychoanalytic, Marxist, socialist, Black feminist thought, cultural, postmodern, poststructural, postcolonial, global, and third-world feminisms. All focus in some way on working to change the status and opportunities for women worldwide. What they have in common is a recognition of the domination of women through patriarchy, and how to end it. In the following discussion, the range of feminist theories is considered in light of three broad categories of these theoretical frames, with a particular emphasis on what they suggest for adult education (Hayes & Flannery, 2000; Hart, 1992; Miles, 1995, Walters & Manicom, 1996).

Feminist Theories With an Individualistic Focus

Both liberal feminism and psychoanalytic feminism have more of a focus on women as individuals, though liberal feminism does deal with women collectively as a group. Liberal feminism has primarily been concerned with helping women gain access to the institutions and systems of privilege that men have always had access to. Liberal feminism has also been concerned with giving women *as individuals* equal rights and privileges in the current system, especially with regard to education and job opportunities. Rather than provide a systemic critique of the structure of society, liberal feminism focuses more on the rights of women as individuals and on helping women fit in to the current education or employment system. Liberal feminism has its roots in the Enlightenment philosophy of the 19th century. The feminist movement in the 1960s and 1970s, particularly in North America, was fueled by liberal feminism working to give women equal opportunity (Tong, 1998). Many liberal feminists still work for equal education and job opportunities for women, without asking larger systemic questions.

Psychoanalytic feminism, and feminist psychology more generally, also has an individualistic focus but from a psychological perspective. The concern here is more on gender socialization, and on the fact that the system reproduces itself because gender socialization happens through both conscious and unconscious mechanisms. Thus, feminists coming from psychological perspectives focus more on the roots of patriarchy (the domination of women by men) in people's unconscious, arguing that gender relations cannot change unless people deal with the patriarchy in their unconscious. While there is recognition of systemic influences in psychological feminism, the concern is more on change for women at the individual level. From an educational perspective, Belenky, Clinchy, Goldberger, and Tarule's (1986) study, which found that many women emphasized ways of knowing that focused on connection, relationship, and the affective as well as the rational dimension, was conducted largely from a feminist psychological perspective. Their work gave rise to a greater emphasis on ways of teaching and learning that took into account connected forms of knowing for women and men, in both higher and adult education. While educational models based on both liberal and psychological feminisms have contributed greatly to adult education efforts, these feminisms have been critiqued as focusing on the concerns of White middle-class women, because they tend to focus on women as a unitary category, or the generic "woman" who is implicitly White and middle-class.

Structural, Cultural, and Standpoint Feminist Theories

Radical feminism, Marxist feminism, and socialist feminism are structural feminist theories in that they focus on an examination of societal structures and power relations between dominant and oppressed groups that affect women. The concern of radical feminism has been primarily on patriarchy as a form of structural oppression. Unlike liberal feminism, which focuses on equalizing access to rights and privileges for women, radical feminists work to change the system of patriarchy (Tong, 1998). Marxist feminism, on the other hand, argues that there are two primary systems that oppress women: patriarchy and capitalism. According to this frame, one system relies on the other; thus in order to change the oppression of women, one needs to work at changing both capitalism and patriarchy. Socialist feminists would agree that two significant and interrelated systems of oppression to women are both capitalism and patriarchy, but they also discuss the importance of examining other systems of oppression such as racial oppression, and the intersections of gender, race, class, and sexual orientation in women's lives. The units of analysis of these frames are structural as opposed to individual or psychological.

Closely related to structural feminist theories are cultural feminisms, which focus more on challenging power relations, based on race or culture, gender and class, and the lived experience of women, in a particular cultural group. The lived experience of women of that cultural group such as in Black feminist thought (Collins, 1991), or womanism (Sheared, 1994), Latina feminism, Asian/Asian American feminism are at the center of the analysis, rather than in the margins (hooks, 2000). This focus on the dynamics of where women of particular cultural or other groups "stand" in relation to the dominant culture in understanding their lived reality, is why such feminisms are sometimes referred to as *standpoint feminism*. From an educational perspective, strategies of change are incorporated from the critical pedagogy of Paulo Freire and various cultural and feminist pedagogies that incorporate ways of knowing emphasized within the particular cultural community (Maher & Tetreault, 1994).

Poststructural, Postmodern, and Postcolonial Feminist Theories

While poststructuralism, postmodernism, and postcolonialism have considerable differences they have points of connection. These theories draw on structural feminist theories, but the primary differences between structural/cultural and poststructural/modern/colonial feminist theories are twofold. First, the unit of analysis in poststructural/modern/colonial feminist theories is the *connections between* individuals and social structures (of race, gender, class, etc.) rather than the social structure itself. Second, and related, poststructural/modern/colonial feminist theories deal with multiple structures at the same time through the notion of positionality (where one is positioned by virtue of multiple intersecting factors of race, gender, class, culture sexual orientation, age, religion, national origin, dis/ability). There is also a recognition of the shifting nature and understanding of identity in regards to various aspects of one's positionality.

There are many forms of poststructural, postmodern, and postcolonial feminism. Some forms of feminist postmodernism are more influenced by psychoanalysis and deconstruction, whereas poststructural feminism is more influenced by socialist feminism or cultural or standpoint feminisms or other forms of poststructuralism. Postcolonial feminism focuses more on Third World women, and on challenging colonialism. But poststructural/postmodern/postcolonial feminisms attempt to examine the intersections of many forms of oppression and privilege, particularly in regard to how people construct "truth." There is rarely one absolute truth, but each person's "truth" is relative and contextually dependent on these cultural and social factors. From an educational perspective, those who draw on poststructural/modern/colonial feminist theory and pedagogy (Tisdell, 1998) emphasize how positionality (of teachers and learners) shapes teaching and learning in the classroom, and how it affects knowledge production processes in the lives of individuals as well as official knowledge production processes in publication and in curriculum design. There is a rising of consciousness and simultaneous challenge of how structural systems inform thinking, as well as a deconstruction of binary categories such as male/female and affective/rational.

See also: emancipatory education, feminist pedagogy, gender, womanism, women's learning.

References and Further Reading

Belenky, M., Clinchy, B., Goldberger, N., & Tarule, J. (1986). *Women's ways of knowing: The development of self, voice and mind.* New York: Basic Books.

Collins, P. H. (1991). *Black feminist thought.* London: Routledge, Chapman & Hall.

Hart, M (1992). *Working and educating for life: Feminist and international perspectives on adult education.* New York: Routledge.

Hayes, E. R. & Flannery, D. D with Brooks, A. K., Tisdell, E. J., & Hugo, J. M. (2000). *Women as learners: The significance of gender in adult learning.* San Francisco: Jossey-Bass.

hooks, b. (2000). *Feminism is for everybody: Passionate politics.* Cambridge, MA: South End Press.

Maher, F., & Tetreault, M. (1994). *The feminist classroom.* New York: Basic Books.

Miles, A. (1995). *Integrative feminisms: 1960s–1990s.* New York: Routledge

Sheared, V. (1994). Giving voice: An inclusive model of instruction – a womanist perspective. In E. R. Hayes & S. A. J. Colin III (Eds.), *Confronting racism and sexism* (pp. 63–76). San Francisco: Jossey-Bass.

Tisdell, E. J. (1998). Poststructural feminist pedagogies: The possibilities and limitations of a feminist emancipatory adult learning theory and practice. *Adult Education Quarterly*, *48*(3), 139–156.

Tong, R. (1998) *Feminist thought: A more comprehensive introduction*. Boulder, CO: Westview Press.

Walters, S., & Manicom, L. (Eds.). (1996). *Gender in popular education: Methods of empowerment*. London: Zed Books.

Elizabeth J. Tisdell

Feminist Pedagogy

Feminist pedagogy refers broadly to a collection of anti-oppressive theories and educational practices informed by feminist theory, with the goal of empowering women. As Briskin (1994) has argued, feminist pedagogy is a standpoint, rather than a technique. "Feminist pedagogy starts from the acknowledgement of women's oppression and speaks to the gendered character of the classroom, of interactions between students and teachers, of the curriculum itself" (p. 443). Ellsworth (1989, 1992) also speaks about the importance of understanding feminist pedagogy as a relational art that can explore difference and "open up a space where we could construct and support new and provisional social and cultural identities – identities that refused terms and assumptions that come already structured into dominant meanings" (Ellsworth, 1992, p. 9).

Given the dynamic nature of feminist theory and its ongoing critical reflexivity wherein assumptions about women and feminism are continually being debated and augmented with new understandings, defining feminist pedagogy is a dynamic and ongoing project. Indeed, a central aspect of being a feminist educator is the continuous questioning and investigating of one's practice and knowledge. Within this dynamic process of understanding there are several key assumptions that undergird feminist pedagogy. First, education can be both liberating and disempowering; education is not neutral. Much of mainstream learning and teaching is biased towards processes reflecting dominant worldviews which, as a result, contribute to women's (and other non-dominant individuals') disempowerment. Second, the social locations of power relations and the identities and subjectivities of teachers and learners (their gender, race, class, sexuality, culture and language) both within and outside the learning environment matter. The social locations profoundly influence teaching and learning. Third, gender matters; how individuals, societies and cultures interpret the roles and attributes of women and men plays a significant role in learning. Fourth, learners and teachers are not only gendered, but also raced and classed, and their sexualities, dis/abilities, cultures, and languages matter.

Feminist pedagogy shares concerns with critical pedagogy which also regards education as a political, not neutral, process. Critical pedagogy seeks to illuminate how education and learning (teachers as well as learners) are implicated in structures and practices that both reinforce and challenge injustices. Much of the earlier discussions within critical pedagogy focused mainly on issues of class. An example is Paulo Freire's critical approach to literacy which is an example of critical pedagogy in which the curriculum grows from the lived reality of learners and in which the learning process involves learning to read and write, as well as developing critical awareness of the relation between illiteracy and unjust practices in the world. The gender and race-blind elements of critical pedagogy have been challenged by feminists who have called attention to other issues (e.g., sexuality and able-bodiness) that are implicated in inequality. Subsequent critical pedagogy theorizing has begun to address these issues.

Developments in Theorizing Feminist Pedagogy

Feminist pedagogy has grown out of a longstanding feminist concern about women's access to high-quality education. It is important to note when discussing the links between theorizing and social movements, that there was, and is, no single feminist movement. Rather, there exists a diverse set of activities and struggles reflecting the differences that exist within and between women and the different geographic, social, economic, and political contexts in which women live. Centuries ago, the lack of education available for girls and women was a key issue of feminists such as Mary Wollstonecraft. These early contributions, which are still being uncovered, are important aspects of understanding the development of feminist pedagogy.

The 20th century bore witness to a diverse collection of feminist movements which struggled and had some successes, as barriers to education for girls and women (especially middle-class and white) were removed. Feminist movements were important sites of learning from which emerged many aspects of feminist pedagogy. Another important precursor to feminist pedagogy was consciousness raising (CR). In CR groups women came together to share their lived experiences and to engage in critical analysis of how the "personal is political," that is, to understand that their lived experiences of exclusion and oppression were shared by other women. In these groups they also came to understand how their everyday experiences of discrimination were related to systemic sexist practices. Feminist efforts led to legislative and public policy changes in some parts of the world that opened doors to education (mainly for white and middle-class girls and women) that had been previously closed. At the beginning of the 21st century, in North America at least, women make up at least half and sometimes more than half of the post-secondary student population. Studies of participation in adult education activities show that overall women undertake more adult education than men; however, fewer women than men participate in employer-sponsored training. In other parts of the globe, however, doors remain closed. Girls and women continue to face exclusion because of sexist patriarchal practices that are reinforced by capitalist globalization.

As more women gained access, it became apparent that what was happening *inside* educational environments was equally important. The biases of curricula and of teaching and learning practices were studied and questions were raised about curricula that treated the experiences and values of dominant white males as the norm. As attention shifted to what took place *within* the learning environment, particularly women's experiences, feminist pedagogy came into its own. Tisdell (2000) outlines the historical context of feminist pedagogy and the different foci of psychological, structural and post-structural approaches. A psychological orientation emphasizes the development of women's voices and the importance of creating learning supportive contexts that enable women to speak about their experiences and to see themselves as knowers who are capable of producing knowledge. Feminist research in the late 1970s and 1980s fueled this psychological orientation; in particular, *Women's Ways of Knowing* by Belenky, Clinchy, Goldberger and Tarule (1986) examined how "women's self concepts and ways of knowing are intertwined" (p. 3).

Critiques of the psychological orientation pointed to its individualistic orientation and its lack of attention to structural, race and sexuality issues. These critiques reflected the significant contributions made by feminists of color who challenged the assumed homogeneity among women. This work led to deeper appreciation of the differences that exist among women, and in particular to how race, as well as gender, shaped the social relations within and outside classrooms. This discussion became a key focus of feminist pedagogical discussions of the larger extralocal relations of privilege and oppression.

The Difference That Difference Makes

The contributions of feminists of color (e.g., Collins, 1991), indigenous educators (e.g., Graveline, 1994), third-world feminists (e.g., Mohanty, 2003), and queer feminists (e.g., Butler, 1990) have been a key factor in creating deeper understanding of difference and how Eurocentric ways of thinking maintain dominant–subordinate relations, can persist within classrooms, despite "good" intentions. As scholars of color called for feminist pedagogy to focus on race and its intersection with gender and class, in a similar way queer theorists called attention to sexuality, challenging the heterosexual bias of feminist scholarship, including feminist pedagogy. Feminist scholarship generally, and feminist pedagogy specifically, continues to be informed by theorizing and ideas often linked to postmodern and poststructural orientations. This arena of theorizing attempts to address the limitations of earlier efforts that emphasized psychological (based on a sense of a fixed and unified self) and structural factors of teaching and learning.

Poststructural approaches have been concerned with the oppressive outcomes of dichotomous thinking, pointing to how certain categories (male/female, Black/White, rational/emotional, subjective/objective) contribute to injustices, by positioning one side of the pairing as the norm by which the "other" side is judged as inferior or subordinate (Tisdell, 2000). The relationship between structures and individuals, or structure and agency, is another concern of postmodern or poststructural approaches. Using these frameworks, feminist pedagogues invite students to analyse dominant discourses and notions of identity.

Key Themes

Voice and empowerment remain important ideas for feminist pedagogy; a key question is "under what conditions can and do women speak their truths?" Feminist pedagogues are recognizing that given women's differences, different kinds of conditions need to be created. A related issue is that of safety. Earlier discussions within feminist pedagogy emphasized the importance of creating safe learning environments. Again, the recognition of women's differences raises questions about "safe for whom?" The risks of learning are also becoming more recognized. For example, in many literacy or adult basic education contexts, there is growing recognition that many women experience violence in response to their efforts to further their knowledge through education (e.g., Horsman, 1999; Rockhill, 1987; Stalker, 2001). It is also understood that transformative learning involves considerable risk in its challenges to assumptions about identity, privilege and oppression. Women's differences make the issue of "risky learning" or "dangerous knowledge" more complicated. Furthermore, given women's different locations in hierarchies of privilege and oppression, the risks in any given learning situation are often unequally shared, making the job of creating a "safe" learning environment extremely complex and dynamic.

How feminist adult educators interpret silence is another issue being reconsidered. There is growing recognition of the need to explore the multiple meanings of silence; authors note that silence is not inherently oppressive as was suggested in Belenky et al.'s (1986) study. Silence can also be a place of deep learning (when someone is listening and watching carefully) as well as a form of resistance and empowerment (Hayes, 2000; Ropers-Huilman, 1997). Given that successful feminist pedagogy involves creating conditions where oppressive power relations are illuminated and challenged, many students can feel discomfort and can engage in various forms of resistance. Addressing students' resistance to these pedagogical practices is yet another important area of theorizing and strategizing for feminist scholars and adult educators.

Within feminist pedagogy discussions, attention has been drawn to new understandings of social relations (e.g., hooks, 1994), difference, and the fluidity of identity. The social relations between learners and teachers have become another key issue in feminist pedagogy; for hooks, feminist teachers should practice an "engaged pedagogy," in which reciprocity and mutuality are important goals. Another significant development in feminist pedagogy, influenced by postmodern and poststructural orientations, is the challenge to notions of truth and rationality. Honoring the role of emotions in knowledge and learning is only one aspect of feminist pedagogy. Another is challenging narrow conceptions of rationality that regard emotions as problematic and needing to be suppressed in order to remain objective.

The significance of the positionality (race, gender, class, etc.) of the adult educator is being recognized and challenges are being made to discourses that promote the myth that there exists a generic or universal adult educator (Brown, Cervero, & Johnson-Bailey, 2000). Understanding and re-imagining the power and authority of the instructor is also a key element of feminist pedagogy; earlier arguments suggested that feminist teachers should share their power and authority with students or even distance themselves from power and authority. These suggestions have been challenged by postmodern notions that power is not inherently oppressive, that it is something that is exercised. In this view students have power as well as teachers. This orientation also points to the impossibility, in certain institutional contexts, of teachers/educators relinquishing power and authority. The question has shifted to how to use one's authority and power to support students, how to avoid abusing one's power and authority, and how to deal with the problems that occur when instructors abandon their responsibilities.

How students respond to the different social locations of instructors or adult educators also influences teaching and learning processes and outcomes (Duncan & Stasio, 2001). Feminist adult educators of color frequently experience challenges to their credibility and to their power and authority. If they directly take on issues of racism or sexism, studies have shown that students may resist such efforts and see them as an instance of the instructor promoting a personal agenda. Male critical adult educators who are racialized also face challenges to their authority. White, male instructors who bring a critical and feminist approach to their adult education practice face different perceptions of their authority and effectiveness from students, with both male and female students not questioning their approach even when covertly oriented to social justice.

Feminist pedagogy is an approach, a standpoint that must be reflexive and dynamic, reflecting the plurality of learning environments including women's homes and communities, workplaces, cooperatives, literacy classes, and social movements, to name a few. The field and practice of feminist adult education must be understood in a global context. Efforts must be made to disrupt thinking that ignores contexts beyond our own borders. It is important in understanding and practicing feminist pedagogy to avoid producing new orthodoxies in efforts to challenge old ones, to recognize how worldviews are culturally encoded, and to believe that all knowledge is partial.

See also: emancipatory education, feminism, gender, women's learning.

References and Further Reading

Belenky, M. F., Clinchy, B. M., Goldberger, N. R., & Tarule, J. M. (1986). *Women's ways of knowing: The development of self, voice, and mind*. New York: Basic Books.

Briskin, L. (1994). Feminist pedagogy: Teaching and learning liberation. In L. Erwin & D. MacLennan (Eds.), *Sociology of education in Canada: Critical perspectives on theory, research and practice* (pp. 443–470). Toronto: Copp Clark Longman.

Brown, A. H., Cervero, R. M., & Johnson-Bailey, J. (2000). Making the invisible visible: Race, gender and teaching in adult education. *Adult Education Quarterly*, *60*(4), 273–288.

Butler, J. (1990). *Gender trouble: Feminism and the subversion of identity*. New York: Routledge.

Collins, P. H. (1991) *Black feminist thought: Knowledge, consciousness, and the politics of empowerment*. New York: Routledge.

Duncan, K., & Stasio, M. (2001). Surveying feminist pedagogy: A measurement, an evaluation, and an affirmation. *Feminist Teacher*, *13*(3), 225–239.

Ellsworth, E. (1989). Why doesn't this feel empowering? Working through the repressive myths of critical pedagogy. *Harvard Educational Review*, *59*(3), 297–324.

Ellsworth, E. (1992). Teaching to support unassimilated difference. *Radical Teacher*, *42*, 4–9.

Graveline, F. J. (1994) Lived experiences of an aboriginal feminist transforming the curriculum. *Canadian Women's Studies*, *14*(2), 52–55.

Hayes, E. R. (2000). Voice. In E. R. Hayes & D. D. Flannery with A. K. Brooks, E. J. Tisdell, & J. M. Hugo (Eds.), *Women as learners: The significance of gender in adult learning* (pp. 79–109). San Francisco: Jossey-Bass.

hooks, b. (1994). *Teaching to transgress: Education as the practice of freedom*. New York: Routledge.

Horsman, J. (1999). *Too scared to learn: Women, violence, and education*. Toronto: McGilligan.

Mohanty, C. (2003). *Feminism without borders: Decolonizing theory, practicing solidarity*. Durham: Duke University Press.

Rockhill, K. (1987). Literacy as threat/desire: Longing to be SOMEBODY. In J. Gaskell & A. McLaren

(Eds.), *Women and education* (pp. 315–332). Calgary, Alberta: Detselig Enterprises.

Ropers-Huilman, B. (1997). Still waters fun deep: Meanings of silence in feminist classrooms. *Feminist Teacher, 10*(1), 3–7.

Stalker, J. (2001). Misogyny, women and obstacles to tertiary education: A vile situation. *Adult Education Quarterly, 51*(4), 288–305.

Tisdell, E. J. (2000). Feminist pedagogies. In E. R. Hayes & D. D. Flannery with A. K. Brooks, E. J. Tisdell, & J. M. Hugo (Eds.), *Women as learners: The significance of gender in adult learning* (pp. 155–183). San Francisco: Jossey-Bass.

Shauna Butterwick

Folk High Schools

The term folk high school denotes residential schools offering non-formal, often non-vocational, usually full-time and long-term education courses for adults. This Nordic tradition was founded in 1844 by Nikolaj Frederik Severin Grundtvig (1783–1872), a bishop, poet, politician and an eminent personality in Denmark at this time. He was inspired by several visits to English universities where the boarding-school tradition was strong. In several articles in the 1830s Grundtvig proposed the idea of a folk high school in the form of a boarding school in which the authoritarian pedagogy of that time would be replaced by a new way of teaching and learning which relied on "the living word" or oral teaching and communication. Lectures connected with dialogue between student and teacher, and among students themselves, would be an important part of this education. Grundtvig called the folk high school a "school for life" because it had space for singing, music, drama, folk dance, storytelling, and dialogue.

Folk high schools were established some years later in Norway, Finland and Sweden, as well as in a number of European countries, all with different courses and activities. Nordic schools differ, for example, from the German "*Volkshochschulen*" which offer both formal and non-formal adult education in part-time studies. More like the Nordic schools is the German "*Heimvolkshochschule.*" Tanzania uses the term "Folk development college – FDÇ" while countries such as Lithuania and Estonia use the term "folk high school." In the United States, the best-known folk high school is Highlander, which is called a "folk school," although it too is based on the Danish model.

Purpose of the Folk High School

Folk high schools were established in a time when agricultural society was changing into an industrial society, and democracy was beginning to develop. The folk high school was to become very important in the development of a democratic society, as well as in the growth of non-formal, popular and liberal adult education.

For some people in Nordic countries, mainly farmers and the working class, the folk high school was the only way to gain the knowledge needed in everyday life and work. Consequently, folk high schools were called "farmer schools" during the late 19th and early 20th centuries. As more and more folk high schools were established, working-class youth often began their education in them. Folk high schools now offer general civic and political education, as well as vocational education and preparation for higher education studies.

Free and Independent

From the beginning, the folk high schools were free to create their own specializations and curricula in spite of having considerable financial support from the state. The education in these schools is defined as non-formal education because the students do not normally receive a certificate.

The non-formal education at the folk high schools is based on different freedoms (liberties). These include the freedom to choose the specialization of the school; the freedom to choose courses and subjects; the freedom to decide on curricula; the freedom to decide working methods; and the freedom to recruit students and employ teachers.

The Situation in Nordic Countries

In Sweden's 147 folk high schools, about 18,000 students participate in the general courses and 11,000 in special courses, including art, handicraft, media, music, theatre, leadership, international affairs, and creative writing. The general courses are more traditional school-subjects, at different levels and with different aims, which extend from one semester to 1–2 years. All education is free of charge. The folk high school has been assigned a compensatory function as a place for people who have been disfavoured in the traditional school system. This alternative education, based on the needs of the student, is offered by folk high schools and popular education only.

In Denmark the old tradition is still very strong, and today (2005) there are 83 folk high schools in Denmark. At an ideal level, the most important focus in folk high schools is personal development and *"folkeoplysning"* or enlightenment. Some Danish folk high schools are still called "Grundtvig schools," but things are changing. The government wants folk high schools to be part of more traditional adult education, and changes in financial aid from the government have resulted in folk high school closures and a move towards the Swedish model of establishing day schools which give courses in general subjects as a part of formal adult education.

Norway has a long tradition of residential folk high schools which offer courses in both practical and theoretical subjects. The special reform in Norway called *"kompetencereform"* makes it possible for students from folk high schools to receive a special grade which gives them stronger standing when they apply for university.

Finland's folk high schools provide general as well as vocational education, but they also offer courses in ordinary school curricula. Several folk high schools offer special preparatory courses for higher, vocational or professional education in universities.

Folk High Schools in Other Countries

Adult education in the Nordic tradition of folk high schools has inspired countries such as those in the Baltic States – Estonia, Latvia, Lithuania – and also in parts of western Russia. In Lithuania there are three different schools, working within the Swedish tradition but creating courses based on their own needs. Because economic conditions are difficult, these schools have little or no economic support, which means that the courses offered are short, from a few days to 1 or 2 weeks.

Democracy-training, language-training, art and culture are common subjects. In countries of Eastern and

Central Europe, like Poland and Hungary, there is an old tradition of adult education, although this was set aside during the years of dictatorship and stringent governmental control of education. Now they are rebuilding, and the establishment of folk high schools has become important in the development of a new democratic society.

In Germany and in the South European countries, adult education is organized in Adult Education Centres – AECs, which are similar to the folk high school, and to study circles and small groups which meet daily or weekly. Activities are carried on both as vocational training (often for the unemployed) and as personal development, what in Denmark is called "*livsoplysning*" and in Sweden "*folkbildning*" – enlightenment.

Trends and Tendencies

Folk high schools in the Nordic countries have a relatively strong position; they are granted governmental subsidies and they offer education free of charge. In return for these subsidies and in the face of cutbacks, they are sometimes asked to legitimate their existence and their free form. In times of economic crisis their subsidies can be reduced. In Denmark there have been successive adjustments to societal needs which means the folk high schools are asked to take greater responsibility for education of groups such as the unemployed, immigrants and the socially marginalized. This accommodation is considered a deviation from the very free and independent position of the Danish folk high schools. During the last 10 years the number of students has decreased by 25% and about 25 schools have closed, but at same time roughly 10 new schools have opened. It is relatively simple to start new schools in Denmark, if you are willing to follow government regulations for subsidies and student inflow.

A recent competence reform in Norway gives students at folk high schools "competence points," which facilitate their transition to higher education institutions. This order has contributed to an increase in participation in Norwegian folk high schools. Students are required to take part in at least 1 year's education, yet they are free to choose subjects. An important requirement is that the students have to stay at the school during their studies; all Norwegian folk high schools are boarding schools.

See also: popular education, social movements, social movement learning, study circles.

References and Further Reading

Adult Education in Tanzania – Swedish contributions in perspective. Centre for Adult Educators, series no. 10, 1996, University of Linköping.

Andresen, A., & Kvaerndrup, S. (Eds.). (1994). *The Danish folk high school today*. Spausdino: Freka.

Borish, S. M. (1991). *The land of the living. The Danish folk high schools and Denmark's non-violent path to modernization*. Navada City, CA: Blue Dolphin Press.

Folk High Schools in Europe – an important part of free adult education and personal growing. Socrates EU-project FLENOFHS; Reference: 90518-CP-1-2001-1-LT-GRUNDTVIG-G1.

Kulich, J. (2002). *Grundtvig's educational ideas in central and eastern Europe and the Baltic states*. Copenhagen: Forlaget Vartov.

Kuprys, P. (1996). *The Danish folk high school as a democratic personality development phenomenon. A summary of a doctoral dissertation*. Kaunas University of Technology, Lithuania.

Georg Karlsson

G

Gender

Gender is a socially constructed system that uses sex-based categories of male and female to classify, assign, and order society. The study of gender as a political analysis of a system of power is rooted in the 1970s' second-wave feminism. Gendered identities are ascribed by the larger hegemonic society and enforced by society's fundamental unit, the family. Other primary units, such as the church, school, and the workplace also reinforce gendered identities. Set cultural patterns result from these gendered identities and are evident in societal power relations, individual behaviors, conversational exchanges, and in written and spoken language. In some, even many, schools, for example, girls are taught learned helplessness and passivity and boys are taught to believe in their abilities and to practice assertiveness (Sadker & Sadker, 1994). The awareness of how a gender-bound culture shapes educational and learning experiences has a significant influence on how educational researchers approach the study of gender. Overall, the examination of gender in education is focused on how socialization affects females and males in the learning environment. Unlike feminist studies which focus on women, gender studies are distinguished by their concern for how both male and female learning is socially constructed and how males and females relate. It is essential that the adult education field discuss and examine the sociocultural phenomenon of gender and develop an awareness of how gender functions in our society for several reasons: (a) our classrooms are microcosms of the larger society, and gender influences and biases are present in our praxis; (b) one of the expressed missions of the field of adult education is the democratization of the citizenry and gender awareness is essential to achieving this goal; and (c) the majority of adult education practitioners and students are women and the development of gender consciousness and inclusion of gender in the literature and as a research topic is crucial to the development of a healthy and holistic discipline and is respectful of the female students, faculty, and practitioners in the field.

Gender in the Adult Education Literature

Although women make up over half the world's population and over half the learners in higher education and adult education settings, major education and adult education theories were normed on men. The majority of the foundational adult education literature, studies, and theories could be classified as liberal and within the humanistic and behaviorist paradigms. However, during the last decade, a considerable shift has occurred in the field and the literature evidences that critical theory is significantly shaping adult education. According to a review of adult education research studies, the majority of adult education studies do not incorporate gender as a factor in their sample populations (Caffarella & Olson, 1993). Only in the last 30 years has adult education literature and research begun to purposely include women as participants and to consider that women's experiences are qualitatively different than the experiences of men (Hayes & Flannery, 2000). The impetus for the examination and inclusion of women as research participants is the belief that the gendered systems of Western society socialize women and men differently resulting in women and men learning and behaving in dis-similar ways. In accordance, Mary Belenky, Blythe Clinchy, Nancy Goldberger, and Jill Tarule (1986) posited in their groundbreaking text, *Women's Ways of Knowing*, that women and men do not learn in the same way. In the Belenky et al. findings, women were placed on a continuum from silence, to connected knowing, to separate knowing. The majority of the adult education literature that examines gender is produced by feminist scholars, most of whom reject separation or essentialization or women's experience. They have centered the majority of their research on examining the ways that women learn, behave, and or understand information and on the gendered ways that women educators function in the classroom. Primarily, maleness is examined only when contrasted to femaleness. The gendered lives of men are historically represented as generalizable societal experiences. In the hierarchical scheme of patriarchy, the social order of male supremacy and privilege depends on this accepted normalcy to remain invisible and unexamined. Sadker and Sadker (1994) posit that, "Each time a girl opens a book and reads a womanless history, she learns that she is worth less" (p.13). This is a basic and summative analysis of how gender functions in education. Indeed, this premise can be extrapolated to encompass higher and adult education. When literature, theories and studies neglect to address gender they fail at fairness and are intellectually lacking.

Gender is a social construct that affects the distribution of power and privilege in society. An understanding of gender operates in our everyday lives and invariably permeates educational institutions. Therefore, classes, practices, programs, and research reflect what students and teachers have experienced and what they believe about gender. The ways in which adult educators construct practices around gender result in a continuum of privilege and disadvantage.

Major Themes in the Adult Education Gender Literature

Relative to gender, the major themes in the adult education literature are feminist pedagogy, the hidden curriculum, the classroom climate, women's silence, women's voices, and collaborative learning. It is implied in this collective body of literature that women's socialization is manifest in the classroom in a myriad of ways, such as silence and passivity. Furthermore, feminist educational researchers assert that women learn and teach collaboratively and make decisions through consensus. These conclusions regarding women's submissiveness and their proclivity towards consensus-building supports the accepted depiction of women as deferent learners and seemingly reinforces the dominant stereotype that women participate, albeit unknowingly and perhaps unwillingly, in their gender subordination (Hayes & Flannery, 2000).

Feminist pedagogy is defined as a method of teaching and learning that employs a political framework which attends to and/or encourages the following: (a) consciousness-raising; (b) activism; and (c) a caring and safe environment. Implicit in this form of teaching, which is rooted in social justice, is an understanding of the universality of gender oppression. Feminist pedagogy also includes a critique of Western rationality, androcentric theories, structured inequalities, and unequal societal power relations. In addition, the practices that flow from feminist pedagogy center on connected teaching (Belenky et al., 1986), which involves the teacher and students jointly constructing knowledge, engaging in self-reflection, and practicing self-revelation. Feminist pedagogy addresses power issues that are inherent in the classroom and requires academicians to examine their individual practices, curricula, and perspectives relative to issues of gender, race, and class subjugation. Furthermore, feminist pedagogy encourages teaching practices that empower students by asking teachers to develop styles that are non-authoritative and nurturing.

Studies on the circumstances of women in the classroom reveal that adult women students report a "chilly environment" where they are seldom mentored by professors, often interrupted by male students, and frequently treated as less proficient than their male counterparts (Hall & Sandler, 1982). Such conditions occur across the educational landscape and are evident in the formal and informal curriculum (the hidden curriculum). The formal curriculum consists of the intentional components of schooling, such as the program design, textbooks, and structured activities. According to educational theorists, the issues of power are explicitly evident in the ways in which the formal curriculum gives males supremacy and place. When men are the researchers and the study participants, the research findings that are generated represent the male perspective and privilege male experiences. Inevitably this research is extrapolated to women and is represented as the norm. The hidden curriculum, the interpersonal interactions (student/student and professor/student) are directed and shaped by the formal curriculum. Males are privileged in the classroom setting by interpersonal interactions, males are validated by representations in the literature, and males routinely function as the classroom power-brokers. Women are disadvantaged in the classroom in that they are silenced on the psychological and physical level (Gilligan, 1982) and are therefore discouraged from full participation and development.

In the second edition of *Learning in Adulthood*, Sharan Merriam and Rosemary Caffarella (1999) provide a comprehensive overview of the field's research on women learners. They assert that the exciting theories exclude women and caution the field about incorrectly generalizing and applying these theories to women. In addition, Merriam and Caffarella present the research of new voices in the field that offer a woman's perspective in the examination of varied topics, such as feminist pedagogy, spirituality, intuition, non-traditional women in higher education, multicultural education and women in the workplace.

The work of feminist theorists is solidly evident in the research studies being produced by leading adult education researchers in the 1990s. The topic of gender and the perspectives of feminist researchers are emerging foci in the field and are represented at major adult education conferences. For example, at the 2001 Standing Conference on University Teaching and Research in the Education of Adults held in London, there were 10 papers on gender out of 106 conference presentations. At the Adult Education Research Conference in East Lansing, Michigan, there were 9 papers on gender of the 80 presentations. The North American *Handbook of Adult and Continuing Education*'s 42 chapters do not include a single chapter devoted entirely to gender, although the Handbook does include a chapter on race. However, nine of the *Handbook's* chapters do infuse gender as an important component to be considered in the discussion of the primary subject under discussion.

A North American text that focuses solely on gender, *Women as Learners: The Significance of Gender in Adult Learning* by Elisabeth Hayes and Daniele Flannery (2000), offers eight themes as primary to the lives of women learners: identity and self-esteem; voice, connection, transformation, feminist pedagogy, a gendered perspective on practice, and knowledge-creation. This text provides a comprehensive examination of the positionality of women and their gendered place in the educational context as learners and educators. Hayes and Flannery conclude that the field is currently engaged in a dialogue on gender that is long overdue and they challenge the field to assess its perspective on gender in both practice and research. The authors conclude that research on gender runs ahead of the field's practice regarding gender.

Gender Diversity in Adult Education Literature: A North American Text

Research that addresses both gender and race is Vanessa Sheared and Peggy Sissel's (2001) text, *Making Space: Merging Theory and Practice in Adult Education*. To date, this book offers the broadest spectrum of different voices for the field and provides a multicultural inspection of the major areas in adult education.

It is important to note that gender extends beyond the notion that women comprise over half of the world's population. Gender is a social construct with accompanying hierarchical systems that disparately influence the lives of women in all facets of society. The negative influence of gender systems on women is reproduced in adult education learning environments. Adult education can not continue to add gender as an afterthought in research and praxis, but must focus on gender as the field continues to fulfill the mission of democratizing the adult citizenry.

See also: feminism, feminist pedagogy, social constructivism, social justice.

References and Further Reading

Belenky, M. F., Clinchy, B. M., Goldberger, N. R., & Tarule, J. M. (1986). *Women's ways of knowing: The development of self, voice, and mind*. New York: Basic Books.

Caffarella, R. S., & Olson, S. (1993). Psychosocial development of women: A critical review of the literature. *Adult Education Quarterly, 43*(3), 124–151.

Gilligan, C. (1982). *In a different voice: Psychological theory and women's development*. Cambridge, MA: Harvard University Press.

Hall, R., & Sandler, B. (1982). *The classroom climate: A chilly one for women*. Washington, DC: Association of

American Colleges Project on the Status of Women in Education.

Hayes, E. R., & Flannery, D. D., with Brooks, A. K., Tisdell, E. J, & Hugo, J. M. (2000). *Women as learners: The significance of gender in adult learning*. San Francisco: Jossey-Bass.

Merriam, S. B., & Caffarella, R. S. (1999). *Learning in adulthood* (2nd ed.). San Francisco: Jossey-Bass.

Sadker, M., & Sadker, D. (1994). *Failing at fairness: How America's schools cheat girls*. New York: Maxwell McMillan International.

Sheared, V., & Sissel, P. A. (Eds.). (2001). *Making space: Merging theory and practice in adult education*. Westport, CT: Bergin & Garvey.

Juanita Johnson-Bailey

Globalization

Globalization can be broadly defined as a movement of economic integration, of cultural homogenization, and of technological uniformization. This movement has long historical roots, yet, as a large-scale phenomenon, it is basically a product of the past 20 years. Education, in general, and adult education in particular, are part and parcel of this movement, which they have shaped and by which they are both increasingly affected.

What is Globalization?

Depending on how one assesses it, globalization can be seen as having strong historical roots, especially in Western universalistic values (themselves grounded in religion), the technical progress of the Middle Ages, the scientific revolution of the Renaissance, colonialism and Western expansion since the 15th century, as well as the rise of the nation-state, and the Industrial Revolution of the 19th century. All these are indeed significant steps having actively contributed to an ever more widespread and ever-more powerful movement expanding the Western model of civilization to every single corner of this planet.

However, as a more or less coherent yet massive phenomenon, globalization is basically a product of the 1980s, and as such has different strongly intertwined dimensions, not all of which have emerged simultaneously (Falk, 1995, 1999; Held, McGrew, Goldblatt, & Perraton, 1999; Kofman & Youngs, 1996). The main dimensions of globalization are technological (which is potentially universal), financial (resulting from the liberalization of the financial markets during the 1980s), economic (globalization of production and consumption), ecological (increasingly global ecological problems), and cultural (cultural homogenization often along with the local reaction to it).

Indeed, technological developments are inseparable from globalization, as technology is potentially universal. Building on scientific progress, which is essentially universal, technology has quite logically global aspirations. If this is true of technology in general, technological globalization has particularly been boosted by the new information and communication technologies (NICTs), which have emerged since the late 1970s. The NICTs are expanding much more rapidly, as they are less material-based and can be spread through telecommunications networks, satellites, and other wireless devices. It is also these NICTs that significantly accelerated financial and economic globalizations. In short, technology and especially NICTs are global in nature and in turn accelerate globalization.

Financial globalization is the combined result of the NICTs and the liberalization of the financial markets. Indeed, financial deregulation, in particular the abolition of exchange-rate controls, as well as the creation of increasingly global financial markets, have fostered the free flow of capital. Consequently, money is seeking the highest yield no matter where this can be achieved on the planet. Financial globalization, along with emerging stockmarkets, have come to put significant pressures on corporations, pushing them in turn towards globalization. Therefore, and maybe with the exception of the United States, the dynamics of global finance are today beyond national control.

Starting in the 1980s one can observe yet another type of globalization, namely the globalization of ecological problems (Karliner, 1997; Sachs, 1999). Such globalization, which can be seen as a direct consequence of the pursuit of industrial development, takes the form of global ecological problems such as climate change, natural resources depletion, ozone destruction, and many more. Consequently, these global ecological problems call for global solutions, which generally go far beyond the capacities of the nation state.

Economic globalization of both production and consumption is the next step in this process of globalization (Braithwaite & Drahos, 2000; Stiglitz, 2002). Indeed, as a result of technological and financial globalizations, combined with cheap oil – i.e., cheap means of transport – production is delocalizing, while consumption of standardized products is spreading globally (see below). This process is accelerated by all kinds of new managerial methods made possible thanks to the new technologies, especially in the area of logistics, just-in-time management and production, e-business, and the like. Moreover, economic globalization is of course also being boosted thanks to trade liberalization, especially since the end of the Cold War. As a result, nation states are less and less capable of controling industrial production and consumption, and have become more and more subject to global forces governing the movement of goods and services. Furthermore, economic globalization is underpinning the growth of transnational corporations.

It is in this context that one has to mention cultural globalization, which is probably the main force underlying the globalization of consumption. Indeed, technological developments in terms of communications, as well as globalization of transport and tourism, have led to the considerable spread of a "global culture." Such a global culture is generally characterized by the spread of individualism, Western values, and homogenization in general. Yet, simultaneously, cultural globalization is triggering numerous cultural reactions against this very process, leading, among others, to fundamentalism.

Composed of these technological, financial, ecological, economic, and cultural dimensions, the globalization movement of the 1980s can in essence be characterized as a process of commercialization and marketization: through the process of globalization, more or less everything is transformed into potentially commercial products and services (Albrow, 1996; Brand et al., 2000; Fried-man, 2000; Gilpin, 2000; Legrain, 2002). The most lucrative of these products and services will be globalized, while the non- or least-lucrative products and services will be localized (Edwards & Gaventa, 2001).

All societal actors – from individuals to nation states – are in turn forced to redefine themselves in light of this movement, not to mention the fact that globalization gives rise to new global actors, such as for example trans-national corporations (TNCs) and non-governmental organizations (NGOs) (Cable, 1996). Globalization is thus an extremely powerful process, increasingly encompassing all aspects of life. Its pervasiveness has already affected, and will affect even more in the future, the areas of work, leisure, politics and education, to name just a few.

Education and Globalization

The relationship of education to globalization is highly ambiguous (Green, 1997). Indeed, from having been an active contributor to and even a promoter of universalistic values and universally valid (i.e., science-based) knowledge, education has become today, at least to a certain extent, a victim of globalization. At the least, education has to redefine itself in light of the new global era, in part simply because the financial support upon which education still rests is to a large extent being undermined by the very process of globalization (in part via the erosion of the nation state).

To recall, education has been instrumental in promoting universalistic values and "objective" knowledge, which was supposed to be valid regardless of place (and even time). As such, education has made a significant contribution to the spreading of Western civilization, scientific culture, technological progress, and industrial development. While simultaneously having been a positive force, education as a social activity has also actively contributed to the homogenization of the world. This has largely been made possible due to the financial support of the nation state and other state-supported institutions.

Yet, with globalization, education is coming under pressure both in its material and in its philosophical foundations. Indeed, globalization being before all a phenomenon of commercialization, education as a mainly non-lucrative and state-subsidized activity has to give in to financial pressures, i.e., accept downsizing, as well as service and quality reductions in almost every country. Simultaneously, the most lucrative aspects of education – e.g., elite education – are in turn being globalized and thus commercialized. Such commercialization – along with cultural (and increasingly religious) resistance and reactions to globalization – also challenges education on philosophical grounds. Once conceived as a means of secularization, education is today being driven back into the hands of churches, communitarians, and other religious leaders.

Adult Education and Globalization

Adult education is affected by this process of globalization in a quite different way than education in general (Finger & Asún, 2001; Walters, 1997). Having been less tied to the nation state in particular and to the cultural project of Enlightenment in general, adult education seems to be capable of coping with globalization, and actually even taking significant advantage of the process.

On the purely material side, one can observe that adult education as a social practice has never been heavily dependent upon state subsidies, nor has it been instrumentalized by the nation state for its purposes. As a matter of fact, adult education has mainly stayed outside of the state, and as such has its origins in community and social action and development, be it in the labor or the social movements. Since the 1980s, and parallel to growing globalization, adult education has spread into the professional and even executive training arena, by either helping individuals and firms take advantage of commercialization and industrial development, or by supporting individuals in coping with the negative consequences of the same commercial developments. Indeed, a significant portion of adult education has become a repair or support function for the very process of economic and industrial globalization. Adult education, unlike traditional education, has proven to be particularly capable of taking advantage of globalization.

As a result of such "thriving on globalization," adult education practices are increasingly becoming commodified and commercialized. This process is accompanied, not astonishingly, by a loss of adult education's intellectual and theoretical roots, which, to recall, were in essence in social action and social change theory, and also in humanistic psychology and pragmatic philosophy. Adult education practice in the age of globalization increasingly becomes a toolkit for quick fixes by means of tailor-made and individualized short-term, yet lucrative, trainings. Adult education, increasingly, can help repair the shortcomings and even the lacks of initial education, thus taking even further advantage of the negative consequences of globalization on the state, society, and the economy.

But while having been positive for the overall commercial development of adult education, globalization has simultaneously contributed to the erosion of its intellectual and theoretical foundations, its values, and its very identity. Its very success is therefore accompanying its very demise as a field of intellectual thinking. The main challenge for adult education in the age of globalization, therefore, is how to become grounded again in solid intellectual and theoretical roots and values, while simultaneously surviving in a context of growing commercialization, marketization, and commodification. While this is a particularly serious challenge, adult education – given its historical roots and practical experience – nevertheless seems to be much better placed to address it than is traditional education.

See also: civil society, power, theory.

References and Further Reading

Albrow, M. (1996). *The global age*. Stanford: Stanford University Press.

Braithwaite, J., & Drahos, P. (2000). *Global business regulation*. Cambridge, UK: Cambridge University Press.

Brand, U., et al. (2000). *Global governance. Alternative zur neoliberalen Globalisierung*. Münster: Westfählisches Dampfboot.

Cable, V. (1996). *Globalization and global governance: Rules and standards for the world economy*. London: Pinter/Continuum.

Edwards, M., & Gaventa, J. (Eds.). (2001). *Global citizen action*. Boulder: Lynne Rienner.

Falk, R. (1995). *On humane governance: Toward a new global politics*. London: Polity Press.

Falk, R. (1999). *Predatory globalization. A critique*. London: Polity Press.

Finger, M., & Asún, J. (2001). *Adult education at the crossroads, Learning our way out*. London: Zed Books.

Friedman, T. (2000). *The lexus and the olive tree*. New York: Anchor Books.

Gilpin, R. (2000). *The challenge of global capitalism. The world economy in the 21st century*. Princeton, NJ: Princeton University Press.

Green, A. (1997). *Education, globalization and the nation state*. New York: Palgrave Macmillan.

Held, T., McGrew, A., Goldblatt, D., & Perraton, J. (1999). *Global transformations. Politics, economics, and culture.* London: Polity Press.

Karliner, J. (1997). *The corporate planet. Ecology and politics in the age of globalization.* San Francisco: Sierra Club Books.

Kofman, E., & Youngs, G. (Eds.). (1996). *Globalization. Theory and practice.* London: Pinter.

Legrain, P. (2002). *Open world: The truth about globalization.* London: Abacus.

Sachs, W. (1999). *Planet dialectics. Explorations in environment and development.* London: Zed Books.

Stiglitz, J. (2002). *Globalization and its discontents.* London: Allen Lane.

Walters, S. (Ed.).(1997). *Globalization, adult education, and training: Impacts and issues.* London: Zed Books.

Matthias Finger

H

Health Education

Health education is conceptualized as a synthesis of systematic, planned social action and learning experiences designed to empower people by enabling them to exercise control over those factors that influence health and health behavior, as well as the social and environmental conditions that affect their own health status and the health status of others, in order to achieve a state of complete physical, mental and social well-being (Tolsma, 1991). It symbolizes a move away from the narrow reductionist perception of health as simply the absence of infirmity, towards a move at integrating the body, the mind and the socio-environmental conditions as composites of individual and communal health and well-being; and to reflect this in developing and packaging healthcare policies and strategies. Health education epitomizes a new global public health perspective, which is characterized by concern with those physical, psychological, social and environmental factors that enhance or undermine the health status of the individual or the community. It seeks to harness the desirable components of those factors to create and nurture the necessary conditions for developing and sustaining a healthy society. It views the conditions of the surrounding world as central to health. Its goal is encouraging informed personal and communal choices, actions and activities that promote the quality and quantity of life.

Within the field of adult education there has been a reawakening of interest in health education as an important component of adult education, as findings in a recent survey among 52 state directors of adult basic education by the US National Centre for the Study of Adult Learning and Literacy show. They considered health as a content and skill area deserving of relatively high priorities (Garner, 1998). The reasons for this are many. First is the rapidly closing gap between childhood and adulthood with children slipping faster and earlier into adulthood and making choices that affect not only their own health status but also that of the community. Many of them become sexually active and move into parenthood much earlier than in the past. Other reasons include the increasing incidence and emerging pattern of chronic and incurable diseases often caused by unhealthy living; the recognition of the link between parental health choice and the quality of life of their offspring; the rapid growth in the aging population as exemplified by the dramatic increase in the number and proportion of the elderly as a result of increased life expectancy; and the HIV/AIDS pandemic. All these have placed health education at the forefront of adult education because of the recognition that "nothing we can do today to promote and protect health has more to offer than health education" (Tolsma, 1991, p. 27). Thus in the context of adult education, health education seeks to equip adults with the necessary skills, knowledge and attitudes to precipitate positive change in the quality and quantity of their physical, mental, emotional and social lives by inducing desirable health behaviors and health choices; promote responsible choice in child-rearing and child-caring as a factor in promoting optimal health status in the child; and to induce a responsible attitude towards social and environmental issues that affect the health of the individual and that of the community as a strategy for combating the prevailing socio-economic and environmental hazards to health.

Scope and Strategy of Health Education

Health education adopts a multi-sectoral approach in packaging and delivery, involving professionals in the areas of health, education, agriculture, information, industry and so on. Its scope "covers the continuum from disease prevention and promotion of optimal health, detection of illness and treatment, to rehabilitation and long term care" (Glanz, Lewis, & Rimer, 1997, p. 8).

Its activities are not independent and autonomous. They are interactive and interdisciplinary and cover the total scope of the adults' life – mental health, physical fitness, environmental health, sex and reproductive health, nutrition as well as all those factors that promote the general well-being of individuals, prevent the onset of chronic diseases and help the elderly to cope with age-related symptoms to ensure optimal levels of functioning in later years. Health education can be targeted at individuals, organizations or communities and is offered in any conceivable location within the community – hospitals, schools, homes, workplace, religious worship centers, as well as shopping centers and markets. It could also focus on health issues of global concern. A critical issue which has attracted the attention of health educators has been that of HIV/AIDS, the devastating effect of which has seen more than 60 million people affected with the disease and ensured the diversion of resources into HIV/AIDS education. Health education in this area has focused on equipping people with the knowledge to make healthy decisions about their sex lives, familiarizing them with those factors that could expose them to infection, teaching them about their relationship with an infected person, as well as assisting victims to cope, through the development of positive psychological, social and physical attitudes.

The focus of health education is on people and on action, transforming knowledge into practice in the process of engendering attitudinal change in people. The knowledge provided through the education process thus serves as a prerequisite for action. It is characterized by emphasis on information and advice-giving with the aim of educating both the individual and the community. It seeks to strengthen community action by encouraging individuals and communities to work together to improve their health situation.

The traditional process starts with the health educator coming into a community or an organization to interact with its members. The health educator seeks to understand the people – their felt needs, customs and interests; to assess prior knowledge, attitudes and practices and use these as a baseline to develop and implement an education package that addresses the identified health needs of the people.

Language and communication are important components of health education, and the goal of communication in health-education is to facilitate changes in health related practices and consequentially in the health status of the people. Effective communication and language ensures credibility, relevance and clarity of the message in content and context. The language used in health education is usually the language of the target community, and the modes of communication include the mass media (electronic and print) in the form of jingles, press releases, advertisements; visual materials like posters, t-shirts, leaflets; workshops, symposia, seminars, campaigns, rallies; as well as the traditional means of communication – plays, songs, poems and at times the talking drum (within an African context).

A major criticism of the existing traditional strategy is its technist drawback, whereby it really fails to touch the lives of people. It may be prescriptive and alienated from the intended beneficiaries in that it still sees people as clients and consumers in the educational process, is characterized by "advice-giving" (Tones, 1996), and sees the health educator as doing things for the people, not with the people. The contention is that although it seeks to change the level of participation of the people from passive recipients to active participants, it still retains the responsibility for decisions on content and context, as well as on the production of educational materials in the hands of the "experts." Also it often uses predeveloped and prepackaged frameworks and modules that may be incompatible with the socio-economic and cultural realities of the adults within the target community, and that may even sometimes offend their sociocultural sensibility. An instance of this is reflected in a report of the Women's Aid Collective (WACOL, Nigeria, 2003), that lack of progress on and resistance to the provision of safe abortion and post-abortion services in many African countries arise out of the fact that the term "abortion" offends the cultural and religious sensibilities of the people. The move is now towards a rephrasing of the terminology from "abortion" to "procurement of termination of pregnancy," a term found more acceptable to the people. Critics also say that the strategy sometimes uses communication modes that may be inaccessible to the people in the target community (Agha et al., 2003).

Improving Service Delivery in Health Education

In very recent times there has been a move towards improving service delivery in health education within the overall context of adult education. It advocates a move towards a composite human-centered approach to health education, which borrows extensively from the methodology and principles of participatory action research (Horn, 1995; La Machia & Morrish, 1996). It is predicated on the recognition that "the durability of cognitive and behavioral changes is proportional to the degree of active rather than passive participation of the learner" (Green, Kreuter, Deeds, & Partridge, 1980). Participatory action research thus provides a bridge in interdisciplinary communication between participatory action, learning and social change which are at the core of community development theory and practice. The process starts with an equal, collaborative and fully participatory partnership, with the health educator and the people coming together to learn from each other, to jointly identify a health issue in the community, and decide on the appropriate plan, actions and processes to address such issues. The strategy focuses on promoting "real" individual and communal involvement and self-reliance in order to ensure that the change that results from the educational interaction is real, worthwhile and sustainable through integration into practice by the people. Since health education seeks to address the "lived-in" experiences of the adults, the issues that emanate from their daily lives, the participatory action research approach to health education shifts the prerogative for problem identification and management of the change process from the hands of the "experts" to the collective responsibility of the stakeholders and the health educator. The health educator sees the adults as equal partners, not as clients or consumers, in the quest for positive change and works "with them" instead of "for them." Using this strategy they jointly identify health issues that are of importance to the community; locate available resources within the community; plan appropriate responses and interventions; take action and set in motion agreed responses and interventions; articulate how success can be gauged; and disseminate and integrate wider lessons of the educational process (Bernard, 2000). The participatory action research methodology stipulates that the health educator and the adults must jointly develop the educational intervention approach since this will ensure its compatibility with the interests, means and sociocultural sensibilities of the adults within the target community.

Questions abound, however, within a global context on the political and economic practicability of using strictly the participatory action research approach in health education.

See also: culturally relevant adult education, participatory action research.

References and Further Reading

Agha, S., Escudero, G., Keating, J., & Meekers, D. (2003). *Nigeria (Bauchi, Enugu, Oyo). Family planning and reproductive health survey, 2002*. MEASURE Evaluation technical report series, no. 16, USAID & MEASURE Evaluation.

Bernard, M. (2000). *Promoting health in old age, critical issues in self health care*. Buckingham, UK: Open University Press.

Garner, B. (1998). NICSALL's focus on research: Health a relatively high priority. *Focus on Basics*, 2, Issue C.

Glanz, K., Lewis, F. M., & Rimer, B. K. (1997). *Health behaviour and health education – Theory, research and practice*. San Francisco: Jossey-Bass.

Green, L. W., Kreuter, M.W., Deeds, S.G., & Partridge, K.B. (1980). *Health education planning: A diagnostic approach*. Palo Alto, CA: Mayfield.

Horn, M. D. (1995). Linking health and literacy education. Presentation at the American Association of Adult and Continuing Education, Kansas City, MO.

La Machia, J., & Morrish, E. (1996). *Ideas in action: Participatory health and literacy education with adults*. Boston, MA: World Education.

Tolsma, D. D. (1991). Meeting global health challenges. *International Journal of Health Education, 10*(3), 27–29.

Tones, B. K. (1996). The anatomy and ideology of health promotion: Empowerment in context. In A. Scriven & J. Orme (Eds.), *Health promotion: Professional perspectives* (pp. 9–21). London: Palgrave Macmillan.

Women's Aid Collective (WACOL) & School of Public Health of the University of Witwatersrand. (2003). *Report of workshop on advancing abortion advocacy*. Victoria Garden Hotel, Enugu, 24 to 27 October, 2003.

Oluyemisi O. Obilade

Higher Education

The term "higher education," or, alternatively, post-secondary or tertiary education, typically refers to formalized and credentialed learning opportunities offered through institutions such as universities and colleges leading to a degree or diploma. Access is determined by individuals meeting certain standard entry criteria, usually evidence of a required number of high school credits (or its equivalent). For example, in Germany the qualifying entry criterion is the *Abitur* as obtained upon graduation from the *Gymnasium*, and in France it is the *baccalauréat* as obtained upon graduation from the *lycée*.

Many institutions, however, have responded to calls from governments and international agencies highlighting the need to provide greater opportunities for lifelong learning (e.g., World Conference on Higher Education, 1998). Some have begun experimenting with special access routes for mature students and have run such programs for minority groups. Even within mainstream programming, "selectivity" varies considerably from one institution to another in some jurisdictions. The "*Seniorenstudium*" in Germany, where mature learners participate in courses together with students enrolled in degree programs without the former pursuing the degree, is a good example of institutions further broadening their access criteria and placing less emphasis on formal credentialed programs. Institutions of higher education are also major providers of non-formal, non-credit programming in some jurisdictions.

International comparisons reveal both differences and similarities in the *structure* of higher education systems across countries. One focus of these analyses is on the relationships between state regulation of the higher education system (the superstructure) and institutional as well as sub-institutional (department or unit level) governance in an era of declining government funding (Clark, 1983; Reed, Meek, & Jones, 2002). Most federalized countries have decentralized higher education systems from the model of a single system whereby the individual nation state make the most important decisions regarding higher education. Historically-rooted differences exist across countries, most prominently perhaps between countries of an Anglo-Saxon tradition and continental Europe, regarding the degree of state regulation of higher education. More recently, however, researchers have observed an international trend in the direction of a *diminishing role of the state* in the regulation of institutions (based on studies of countries with highly developed economic systems). This phenomenon has been associated with the process of economic globalization and its resultant new demands on education in terms of knowledge and educated labor (e.g., Enders & Fulton, 2002; Amaral, Jones, & Karseth, 2002). As institutions experience declines in government funding, they face growing pressures to demonstrate their legitimacy and purpose. This situation is exacerbated by the fact that higher education is no longer taken for granted as "a public good," but is increasingly evaluated in terms of its effectiveness and efficiency in contributing desired forms of capital in the knowledge-based society. Under such conditions akin to those present in "private industry," individual higher education institutions experience greater autonomy as they are left to compete under market-like conditions on two levels. Firstly, within their own jurisdictions they compete together with other institutions as well as other public sectors for limited private and governmental funding. Secondly, higher education institutions also compete within a common global market for resources, students and graduates (Kivinen, 2002), a process that is set to become even stronger in the years to come as a result of the liberalization of educational markets through the General Agreement on Trade in Services (GATS) (van Vught, van der Wende, & Westerheijden, 2002). Demands for accountability, therefore, are on the rise, as higher education institutions attempt to either preserve a tradition of relatively high autonomy (as is the case, for example, in Canada), or come to terms with the new experience of greater autonomy (as is the case in many European countries). Critical observers of these changes towards a neo liberal agenda with its emphasis on the market, competition, performance accountability and *(new) managerializm,* caution against universities losing sight of their traditional values such as curiosity-driven research, social criticism and the preparation for civic life (Newman, 2000), and warn of the consequences of the academic culture turning into one of *academic capitalism* (Slaughter & Leslie, 1997).

Higher education systems also vary with respect to *diversity* within the system. Though higher education used to be synonymous with university education, many industrialized nations expanded their higher education systems in the 1960s to accommodate the baby boom generation then seeking access to higher education. Next to adding new universities they created alternative institutions (for example polytechnics) whose primary goal was not the advancement but the application of knowledge and direct preparation for specific forms of employment. Most countries, therefore, have higher education systems that are characterized by the simultaneous existence of two or more different types of institutions (sometimes referred to as distinct post-secondary education "sectors"), and it is not uncommon for different "sectors" to operate under the auspices of separate ministries. Higher education systems also vary with respect to transfer arrangements within and across different types of institutions, with some jurisdictions having fluid arrangements and others just beginning to explore such possibilities. Another way of understanding higher education systems is to look at the primary functions of institutions, with some institutions being assigned a key research role and others a stronger teaching role.

Of direct relevance to the rise of a global market for higher education as well as variation in the structure of higher education systems across different countries, is a recent initiative in Europe (the Bologna Declaration), whose major goal is to improve the international competitiveness of European higher education by enhancing its transparency and comparability of degrees (van Vught et al., 2002).

Discussions of the history of higher education often begin uncritically with the founding of the medieval European universities, neglecting higher education's much richer tradition both within as well as outside the Western world (consider, for example, Plato's Academy or Ancient China's Great Academy, the latter informed by Confucian philosophy). Universities, however, are indeed unique institutions in a sense that they have experienced remarkably few changes over the past 1,000 years in their purposes and functions. Though initially primarily teaching institutions preparing students for their role in the clergy, state administration or the professions, by the late 19th and early 20th century universities in many countries experienced the influence of the German (*Humboldtian*) idea of the research university. Within these institutions, the simultaneous advancement and transmission of knowledge, achieved through student involvement in the pursuit of knowledge together with the professor, was considered the fundamental purpose of the academy. Notions of *Lehrfreiheit* (freedom to teach) and *Lernfreiheit* (freedom to learn) became prominent leitmotifs of university education during this era, and ones that the state at the time recognized as essential in supporting the university's economic but also social and cultural role in modern society. The research function of the university experienced a further boom in many industrialized nations in the 1950s after the Soviets launched their first satellite (Sputnik), and advancement in science in particular gained high priority on the agendas of Western governments and, consequently, their universities.

Today, universities, and by extension, the academic work done in those institutions, are typically conceived of in terms of three broad functions: teaching, research and service, whereby the latter refers to service to the institution (as in participation in institutional governance) as well as service to the larger community (as in consultation with industry or through community-based academic programs). Though all three functions are deemed important, research is observed to play a more dominant role particularly, but not exclusively, in institutions which rely heavily on external funding to support their graduate programs and research. More recently, the research imperative has caused some members of the academy to argue that teaching is being undervalued, and has led to calls for a more comprehensive conceptualization of scholarship (Boyer, 1990). As national funding agencies are seen to increasingly exercise power over the daily operations of the university through their allocation of funds on the basis of research productivity rather than excellence in teaching, inquiries into the relationships between research and teaching have developed into a prominent area of research in many countries (Brew, 1999), most significantly in Britain, where the implementation of the Research Assessment Exercise has been vehemently criticized from within the academy (Jenkins, 1995; Lindsay & Rogers, 1998).

Graduate programs in higher education were offered in the United States and Canada as early as the 1950 and 1960s. Europe has a stronger tradition of research centers that are not necessarily attached to teaching programs, though these have become more common. The Centre for Higher Education Policy Studies, CHEPS, at Twente University in The Netherlands, is one of the most significant centers in Europe. Numerous productive centers can be found in North America, among them the Center for the Study of Higher and Postsecondary Education (CSHPE), at the University of Michigan and the Higher Education Research Institute at UCLA. China, too, has a number of excellent centers, the major ones include the Peking University Institute of Higher Education in Beijing, the Research Centre of Higher Education Development, at Xiamen University, in the Fujian Province and the Higher Education

Research Centre at Central China University (Huazhong University) of Science and Technology in Wuhan. The most famous center in Japan is the Research Institute for Higher Education at Hiroshima University. The international Consortium of Higher Education Researchers (CHER) was founded in 1988 and is housed at the University of Kassel, Germany. With about 160 members it is a rather small organization though they represent about 30 countries, approximately a quarter of which are from outside Europe.

Scholarship on higher education has a rather recent history, though the *Journal of Higher Education*, the leading research journal on higher education in North America, has been active for the past 75 years. A large proportion of higher education research, therefore, is conducted not only by centers, but by scholars located in other units within the university and/or those who assume a professional role in the university. This dispersion of scholarship across different departments within the academy gives rise to different subfields of higher education (e.g., teaching and learning in higher education, institutional research and planning, or student affairs), each with its specialized journals. International agencies such as specific subdivisions of UNESCO (e.g., UNESCO-CEPES, the European Centre for Higher Education), OECD, the Council of Europe and the World Bank, also play a significant role in informing and shaping scholarship and policy development on higher education. In the United States, the Carnegie Foundation is a major contributor to research on higher education and an important player within the higher education policy arena.

Higher education scholarship draws on a wide range of primarily social science disciplines including sociology, philosophy, psychology, history and political science and their various subdivisions. Though some higher education research has been primarily descriptive and predictive, higher education phenomena have been analysed from a wide range of epistemological perspectives including, though certainly not limited to, critical, postmodern and poststructuralist theories.

Higher education and adult education are both fields of *practice* and fields of *study*, each with its unique journals, national and international conferences and associations, academic programs, and consequently, its distinct body of scholarship. While a large proportion of higher education scholarship is concerned with very specialized issues unique to the higher education context (e.g., governance and administration; finance; the academic profession; university and industry "partnerships"), there is also considerable convergence between the two fields. Shared interests include participation and access; diversity and inclusion; curricula; teaching and learning; leadership; student change and development; staff development; lifelong learning; university–work links and transitions; and the academic study of adult education itself.

Though conceptualizations vary, higher education is sometimes considered a subset of adult education, and four ways in which higher education can be conceptualized this way are apparent:

- First, institutions of higher learning provide formal education to a student population that is legally defined as "adult." While the adult-status of traditional-aged students has been questioned, there is little doubt that as the student population has been changing with an increasing number of mature and part-time students entering higher education, that higher education institutions are involved in educating adults.

- Second, it is assumed that as adults are involved in higher education programs, they change, develop and learn. Research on the personal, intellectual and moral development of college students is a major area of research in higher education. Problem-based learning, self-directed learning, and cooperative learning in post-secondary education are concepts heavily influenced by adult education scholarship. Educational goals such as citizenship education (e.g., the Carnegie Foundation) and alternative course-delivery approaches such as service learning, experiential education, and community-based education, are influenced by democratic ideals that are in sync with values articulated in the field of adult education. The role of instructional technology in the delivery of programs continues to be extensively researched by scholars from both fields.
- Third, higher education institutions are involved in adult education also in the sense that they offer development opportunities to faculty, academic administrators, and support staff; and such staff development constitute a form of adult education. Particularly with respect to educational (academic) development, a subset of staff development, these programs vary in terms of formality, with Britain, and its national agenda to professionalize teaching, being an example of a country with a very formal and structured program.
- Fourth, universities are those institutions where professional adult educators earn their degrees. Graduate programs offering masters and doctoral degrees in adult education are quite common at universities and some offer bachelor's degrees in adult education.

See also: career education, continuing education, professional education.

References and Further Reading

Amaral, A., Jones, G., & Karseth, B. (2002). Governing higher education: Comparing national perspectives. In A. Amaral, G. Jones, & B. Karseth (Eds.), *Governing higher education: National perspectives on institutional governance* (pp. 279–298). Dordrecht, The Netherlands: Kluwer.

Boyer, E. L. (1990). *Scholarship reconsidered: Priorities of the professoriate* Princeton, NJ: Carnegie Endowment for the Advancement of Teaching.

Brew, A. (1999). Research and teaching: Changing relationships in a changing context. *Studies in Higher Education, 24*(3), 291–300.

Clark, B. (1983). *The higher education system*. Berkeley: University of California Press.

Enders, J., & Fulton, O. (2002). Blurring boundaries and blistering institutions: An introduction. In J. Enders & O. Fulton (Eds.), *Higher education in a globalising world. International trends and mutual observations. A Festschrift in honour of Ulrich Teichler* (pp. 1–17). Dordrecht, The Netherlands: Kluwer.

Jenkins, A. (1995). The research assessment exercise, funding and teaching quality. *Quality Assurance in Education, 3*(2), 4–12.

Kivinen, O. (2002). Higher learning in an age of uncertainty. From postmodern critique to appropriate university practices. In J. Enders & Oliver Fulton

(Eds.), *Higher education in a globalising world. International trends and mutual observations. A Festschrift in honour of Ulrich Teichler* (pp. 191–207). Dordrecht, The Netherlands: Kluwer.

Lindsay, G., & Rogers, T. (1998). Market orientation in the UK higher education sector: The influence of the reform process 1979–1993. *Quality in Higher Education, 4*(2), 159–171.

Newman, F. (2000). Saving higher education's soul. *Change, the Magazine for Higher Education*, September/October, 2–9.

Reed, M., Meek, L., & Jones, G. (2002). Introduction. In A. Amaral, G. Jones, & B. Karseth (Eds.), *Governing higher education: National perspectives on institutional governance* (pp. xv–xxxi). Dordrecht, The Netherlands: Kluwer.

Slaughter, S., & Leslie, L. L. (1997). *Academic capitalism: Politics, policies and the entrepreneurial university*. Baltimore and London: Johns Hopkins University Press.

van Vught, F., van der Wende, M., & Westerhijden, D. (2002). Globalisation or internationalisation: Policy agendas compared. In J. Enders & O. Fulton (Eds.), *Higher education in a globalising world. International trends and mutual observations. A Festschrift in honour of Ulrich Teichler* (pp. 103–121). Dordrecht, The Netherlands: Kluwer.

World Conference on Higher Education (1998). *Higher education in the twenty-first century. Vision and action*. Vol. I, Final Report. Paris: UNESCO Publishing.

Carolin Kreber

Historical Inquiry

Historical inquiry within the ill-defined discipline of adult education has been marginally present since the field emigrated from the worldly trenches to the academy in the mid-1950s. During the heyday (in North America) of professionalization in adult education (from the 1950s to the 1980s), foundational studies, be they philosophy, sociology or history, were hardly in vogue. With a few exceptions (Gordon Selman at the University of British Columbia, J. Roby Kidd at the Ontario Institute for Studies in Education/University of Toronto in the 1960s and 1970s, and Michael Welton at Dalhousie University in the 1980s), historical studies were not perceived as an essential component of the adult educator's professional repertoire. Psychology held promise of providing the discipline with a stable, scientific foundation.

In the 1980s, a new ethos of critique permeated adult education's conference circuits and historical studies gained new importance. Thomas Kelly (1970) and Malcolm Knowles (1977) had written old-fashioned narrative histories of Britain and the United States respectively, largely untouched by the new thinking in the discipline of history. Both writers simply assumed that they could go back into the "past" and discover precursors of present practices. Both thought that the artefacts of the adult education legacy were just there, waiting like seashells to be plucked from the tidal washes.

But the 19th century attempt to establish the historical enterprise on a solid rock of facts collapsed in the late 20th. Linguistically informed historians reexamined conventional ideas about the relationship between language and thought, language and action, and language and history. History was not just about something, it was also written for specific audiences or communities to perform a certain function. All stories were fabrications, invented by the historian to make sense of the facts (themselves representations of never completely uncovered "experience") and propagate particular values in the world. Historians were hybrid artists and scientists (Welton, 2003).

The New Historiography and Adult Education's Problem of the Object

The idea that history – the stories we tell about the past – is not just objective renderings of an unproblematic past, opened the gates for critical scrutiny of old-fashioned narrative writing. Knowles' (1977) history of American adult education history was now perceived to have been written from the vantage point of a self-confident profession of adult education. Knowles showed how the institutional provision of education for adults gradually shed its amateur qualities, becoming more systematic, expert-dominated and technically efficient. For revisionist historians (Rockhill, 1985; Schied, 1991), however, the boundary of the field of adult education had been drawn too narrowly. In the early 20th century, workers' education was an integral part of the larger American adult education enterprise. When adult education found some legitimacy within the academy in the mid-1950s and 1960s, adult educators positioned in the workers' movement and associational lives were nudged out of the field. Adult education was something that professional, university-educated teachers did.

The problem of how to construct the boundary of the study of adult education in the past is not self-evident. One of the discipline's shibboleths – that we can dichotomize the "education of adults" and "adult education" – opens a Pandora's Box of potentially unmanageable problems. This duality uncouples "adult education" (that which is intentionally provided by the professional educator, in identifiable formalized settings) from "adult learning" (learning occurring in a variety of learning sites not conventionally considered as educational).

There are several ways contemporary historians of adult education have grappled with the obvious difficulties of writing learning history (defined, here, as the project of framing historical events and processes in terms of their learning dynamics). First, if one searches for shadowy precedents of the present in the gardens of the past, one will have very little to really think about once one moves beyond Mechanics' Institutes into the early modern, and much earlier periods. If adult education is perceived as "coming of age" in the mid- to-late 20th century, then how and where adults learned in the past fades into irrelevance.

A second way adult education history is rendered manageable is through the arbitrary selecting of a part of adult learning, then letting the part stand for the whole. In the British tradition, the dominant tendency has been to identify adult education history with the history of working-class struggles and initiatives (Simon, 1992). Brian Simon, a leading advocate of this approach, selects "independent education activities" of workers as a historical anchor-point. He then constructs a "line of continuity" from the Corresponding Societies of the 1790s through the heroic days of the Plebs League to the besieged present-day trade union movement. Simon privileges workers' struggles as the motor of social change. The problem, then, with constructing adult education as workers' education is that it also leaves out a large part of empirically ascertainable adult learning.

A third promising route has been to construct adult education history as intellectual history. Harold Stubblefield's *Towards a History of*

Adult Education in America (1988) is exemplary in this regard. Stubblefield's narrative tactic is to identify "formative thinkers" in the early to mid-20th century who shaped their views on the nature of adult education, the social conditions calling for new forms of education, aims to be accomplished, appropriate methods, relation of adult education to society, and what the curriculum should be within an organizing paradigm. This elegant formulation creates several difficulties, however. For one thing, Stubblefield cannot include social movements in his narrative. And we may ask why he has included these particular thinkers. Women and Black thinkers are also excluded from his master narrative. Peter Jarvis's *Twentieth Century Thinkers in Adult Education* (1987) is open to similar questions (Welton, 1991, 1993, 2003).

For Lawrence Cremin (1976), the eminent American educational historian, education is cast as the "deliberate, systematic, and sustained effort to transmit, evoke, or acquire knowledge, skills, values, or sensibilities, as well as any outcomes of that effort" (p. 27). This broad definition allowed him to capture the complex interplay of inter-and-intra-generational transmission. Cremin's definition projects us beyond schools and colleges to the "multiplicity of individuals and institutions that educate" (p. 29). By itself this conceptual move – adding more objects to the field (parents, peers, siblings, libraries, museums, camps, churches, fairs, settlement houses, factories, radio stations, television, newspapers) – is not revolutionary; but Cremin maintains that the educative institutions in any time period form configurations, clusters, or constellations to shape outlook and action.

One cannot search for precursors of what we think adult education is in the present. One must go deeper and ask how adults learned about nature, others and self in ancient tribal societies – before men and women knew that adult education even existed. With this approach (call it learning history), we can, for instance, ask new questions of the historical period of exploration and conquest (the 15th century launches the "age of improvement"). Beginning many thousands of years ago, Amerindian Canadians created an intricate learning system to create and sustain their existence. In the late 15th century, Europeans brought their knowledge maps of the world along with technical skills (navigation, gunpowder, mapmaking, Christianity).

Thus, the encounter between Europe and the Amerindian can be constructed imaginatively as a pedagogical encounter: a confrontation between two developed learning systems (one literate, the other oral). And as we move through time, we can explicate how individuals and groups open up pedagogical space to learn how to make a living, live meaningful lives and find means of self-expression. Once we assume that our troubled, human species is a learning species in its essence, the way is opened for exciting vistas of historical interpretation. In all times and places, human beings must learn to reproduce their existence, live together and with strangers, and bind their worlds into a whole under a sacred canopy. No age or time lived without knowledge of how to order the world.

See also: educational foundations, research methods, social gospel, social movements, women's voluntary organizations.

References and Further Reading

Cremin, L. (1976). *Public education.* New York: Basic Books.

Jarvis, P. (1987). *Twentieth century thinkers in adult education.* London: Croom Helm.

Kelly, T. (1970). *A history of adult education in Great Britain.* Liverpool: Liverpool University Press.

Knowles, M. S. (1977). *A history of the adult education movement in the U.S.* Malabar, FL: Krieger.

Rockhill, K. (1985). Ideological solidification in university adult education: Confrontation over workers' education in the United States. In R. Taylor, K. Rockhill, & R. Fieldhouse, *University adult education in England and the United States* (pp. 175–220). London: Croom Helm.

Schied, F. (1991). Towards reconceptualization of the historical foundations of adult education: The contributions of radical German-Americans to workers' education. Unpublished doctoral dissertation, Northern Illinois University, DeKalb, Illinois.

Simon, B. (Ed.). (1992). *The search for enlightenment: The working class and adult education in the twentieth century.* Leicester: National Institute of Adult Continuing Education.

Stubblefield, H. (1988). *Towards a history of adult education in America: The search for a unifying principle.* London: Croom Helm.

Welton, M. R. (1991). What's new in the history of adult education? *Historical Studies in Education, 3*(2), 285–297.

Welton, M. R. (1993). In search of the object: Historiography and adult education. *Studies in Continuing Education, 15*(2), 133–148.

Welton, M. R. (2003). Decoding Coady: Masters of their own destiny under critical scrutiny. *Studies in Continuing Education, 25*(1), 75–93.

Michael Welton

Human Capital Theory

Human capital theory is invoked to explain wage differentials and to lay the blame for low (or no) wages on the individual, rather than on state policy, supranational fiat or forms of social oppression, such as racism or sexism. Allied with neo-liberal economics, it has become a hegemonic discourse that blames the victim and perpetuates the status quo.

Human capital theory has its origins in the concept of capital itself. Although many, including Karl Marx, have equated capital with money, capital essentially means wealth that creates more wealth. This meaning is reflected in the roots of the word capital, which is connected etymologically to the words "cattle" and "chattel." While capital has enormous potential as a concept for adult education, this potential is squandered in conventional understandings of the term.

The concept of human capital is firmly connected to the field of economics, and generally interpreted from a neo-liberal perspective. Schultz (1981) defines human capital as those abilities and information that have economic value. Pass, Lowes, Davies, and Kronish (1991) add that human capital can be as significant as physical capital in promoting economic growth. This emphasis on economic growth locates human capital within an economic paradigm that ignores planetary limits and recognizes the acquisition of money, not the enhancement of life, as the ultimate guiding value.

This narrowly econometric conception of human capital extends into other forms of capital, such as social capital. While not all understandings of social capital are explicitly linked to neo-liberal economics, Fine (1999) argues that social capital seems to be able to be anything – from public goods and networks to culture; the only proviso is that it should be attached to the economy in a functionally positive way for economic performance, especially growth. Smith, Beaulieu, and Seraphine (1995) highlight the linkage between human capital and social capital when they maintain that "social capital was designed to serve as a conceptual extension of the theory of human capital" (p. 366). And Robert Putnam (1993) also links social capital with human capital, contending that social capital increases the value of human capital.

French sociologist Pierre Bourdieu (1990) broke the econometric conformity concerning understandings of capital with his concept of cultural capital. He used this concept not to reinforce the status quo, but to challenge it by using cultural capital to explain, for example, why upper-class children succeed in school, while lower-class children fail. Cultural capital concerns forms of cultural knowledge, competences or dispositions (Johnson, 1993), but

> cultural competence in all its forms is not constituted as cultural capital until it is inserted into the objective relations set up between the system of economic production and the system producing the producers (which is itself constituted by the relationship between the educational system and the family). (Bourdieu, p. 124)

The concept of cultural capital exposes forms of capital as sources of power, which is unrecognized in human capital theory.

Human Capital Theory

Given the neo-liberal emphasis in concepts of human capital, it is not surprising that human capital theory follows the same narrow, econometric path. Human capital theory rests on the claims that economic performance is linked to education and training, and those investments in human capital are related to earnings. Gary Becker (1993), for example, argues that most investments in human capital raise observed earnings at older ages, because returns are part of earnings then, and lower them at younger ages, because costs are deducted from earnings at that time.

The major problem with human capital theory, according to Johnson (2000), is its assumption that the amount people are paid for their work is based on a rational calculation of their productive worth, with no attention to factors such as race, gender or ethnicity and the vulnerability of such groups to discrimination and exploitation based on prejudice. Other problems include its legitimatization of individualism, its condemnation of people for the defects of the system, its obfuscation of the real conflict of interest between workers and capitalists, and its individualist explanations of economic phenomena (Marshall, 1998). In addition, the ideology of human capital performs a function of reification and legitimization for the new economic order (Bouchard, 1998).

Fine (1999) sees a general, and now uncritical, acceptance of the notion of human capital, which is founded on universalizing the so-called "economic approach" based on utility maximization to all areas of life, including those that are traditionally perceived as lying outside the domain of economics. It is this insidious universalization of neo-liberal economics that makes human capital theory so dangerous to the libratory potential of adult education.

Human Capital Theory and Adult Education

Human capital theory has come to dominate the thinking about education, including adult education, in many societies. Phyllis Cunningham (1996) maintains that human capital formation drives adult education in the United States, turning educators into agents of social control and education into a business. Using Canada as an example of what she refers to as the "factory model of education," she describes how the Saskatchewan Community Colleges have been turned into a corporation with a president who is referred to as a CEO.

While some adult education practitioners have embraced human capital theory, others have rejected it outright. Many practitioners involved in training and preparing adults to compete in the global marketplace follow human capital theory precepts, believing that lack of training alone is the reason people are experiencing employment problems. Critical adult educators disagree with this analysis from a range of perspectives. Transformative feminists have argued that mainstream education is increasingly in the business of human capital formation, with women and other "others" seen mainly as backward elements whose cultures, traditions, knowledge, work and values are ignored (Miles et al., 2000). Schuller and Field (1998) assert that there are a number of serious objections to human capital theory from the perspective of lifelong learning. They point out that treating the consumption of educational materials as leisure spending ignores the evidence of spillover or transfer between one learning domain and another, and is based on a partial picture of economic activity and treats quality-of-life issues as, at best, intangible and, at worst, peripheral. In addition, the more the language of investment dominates, the more it is accepted not only as rational in its own terms but even as the only language, the more difficult it will be for learning activities which cannot show a visible return, and especially a quick return, to justify themselves. Schuller and Field conclude that human capital theory concentrates on individuals, which ignores the wider social context within which much learning takes place, and the relationships – personal and institutional – which actually constitute the vehicles or channels through which learning takes place.

In the realm of training and work, Bouchard (1998) argues that while adult education and training are notions that have been used for proclaiming the intrinsic value of human capital, this contention rests on a series of assumptions that, when viewed in their proper context, are less than convincing. He points out that adult educators are faced with a strange dilemma: after acknowledging the limitations of education and training as cure-all solutions to economic and social inequality, should adult educators abandon their current activities and take on more direct forms of social activism or should they concentrate on providing educational services to those who require them, regardless of the fact that in doing so they may knowingly contribute to the perpetuation of an oppressive cycle? Bouchard concludes that adult educators have three fundamental roles: responsibility to individual learners, to the workplace and to society, with the latter entailing a commitment to certain basic values such as equity, tolerance, cooperation and recognition of the diversity of human experience. He concludes that these roles remind us that adult educators are dynamic actors in the relationship between learners, production organizations and the larger needs of a democratic society.

In terms of policy formation, Joel Spring (1998) argues that education policies based on human capital theory present a number of serious shortcomings. First, they can only address one cause of economic inequality – technological change – while ignoring others such as the weakening of labor unions, the decline of manufacturing jobs, the increase in service jobs and competition from foreign producers and poorly paid immigrants. Second, education policies based on human capital theory imagine humans to be income- and profit-making machines, with human value being defined by an individual's worth in the labor market and the value of education becoming a function of human worth as measured by income. Third, they assume that the global economy is a good thing, and that economic growth and free trade will lead to peace and world prosperity.

Adult education carries the potential of challenge and change: challenge to the lines of power in society and change towards a more equitable world. The kinds of theoretical frameworks that adult educators adopt can help to realize this potential. But Ian Baptiste (2001) contends that human capital theory is so flawed that it is likely to exacerbate rather than alleviate social ills. Baptiste argues that the theory treats humans as lone wolves: radically isolated hedonists, creatures of habit (not intentions) who temper their avarice with economic rationality. In turn, he suggests, education programs that flow from such a theory would be apolitical, adaptive and individualistic. Such programs treat learners as fated beings whose only desires and options are to consume and adapt. Baptiste concludes that human capital theory is socially bankrupt and will never be able to address social inequalities. It is clear that as long as human capital theory remains confined within the parameters of self-maximizing neoliberal market doctrine, the evolving common-wealth that is socially constructed by humans cannot enter into consideration.

See also: class, critical theory, globalization, ideology.

References and Further Reading

Baptiste, I. (2001). Educating lone wolves: Pedagogical implications of human capital theory. *Adult Education Quarterly*, *51*(3), 184–201.

Becker, G. S. (1993). *Human capital: A theoretical and empirical analysis, with special reference to education* (3rd ed.). Chicago: University of Chicago Press.

Bouchard, P. (1998). Training and work: Myths about human capital. In S. M. Scott, B. Spencer, & A. M. Thomas (Eds.), *Learning for life: Canadian readings in adult education* (pp. 128–139). Toronto: Thompson Educational.

Bourdieu, P. (1990). *The logic of practice*. Stanford: Stanford University Press.

Cunningham, P. M. (1996). Race, gender, class, and the practice of adult education in the United States. In P. Wangoola, & F. Youngman (Eds.), *Towards a transformative political economy of adult education: Theoretical and practical* challenges (pp. 139–159). DeKalb, IL: Leadership and Educational Policy Studies (LEPS) Press.

Fine, B. (1999). The developmental state is dead – Long live social capital. *Development and Change*, *30*, 1–19.

Johnson, A.G. (2000). Human capital. *The Blackwell dictionary of sociology: A user's guide to sociological language* (p. 146). Malden, MA: Blackwell.

Johnson, R. (1993). Introduction. In Pierre Bourdieu (Ed.), *The field of cultural production* (pp. 1–25). New York City: Columbia University Press.

Marshall G. (Ed.). (1998). Human capital theory. In *A dictionary of sociology*. Toronto: Oxford University Press. Retrieved May 1, 1997 from Oxford Reference website: http://www.oxfordreference.com

Miles, A., Cunningham, P., Zukas, M., Bhasin, K., Graveline, J., Hart, M., Sheared, V., Thompson J., & Westwood, S. (2000). The politics of transformative feminist adult education: Multi-centred creation of new meanings and new realities. Symposium presented at the 41st Annual Adult Education Research Conference, University of British Columbia, Vancouver.

Pass, S., Lowes, B., Davies L., & Kronish. S. J. (1991). *The HarperCollins dictionary of economics*. New York: HarperCollins.

Putnam, R. D. (1993). The prosperous community: Social capital and public life. *The American Prospect, 13*, 35–42.

Schuller, T. & Field, J. (1998). Social capital, human capital and the learning society. *International Journal of Lifelong Education, 17*(4), 226–235.

Schultz, T. W. (1981). *Investing in people: The economics of population quality*. Los Angeles: University of California Press.

Smith, M., Beaulieu L. J., & Seraphine, A. (1995). Social capital, place of residence and college attendance. *Rural Sociology, 60*(3), 363–380.

Spring, J. (1998). *Education and the rise of the global economy*. Mahwah, NJ: Lawrence Erlbaum Associates.

Jennifer Sumner

Human Resource Development

In 1989, Leonard Nadler and Zeace Nadler defined human resource development (HRD) as "organized learning experiences provided by employers within a specified period of time to bring about the possibility of performance improvement and/or personal growth" (p. 6). At the same time, Patricia McLagan (1989) studied practitioners who explained that the three key roles HRD professionals were working in could be classified as (a) training and development, (b) organization development, and (c) career development. This is an important incident in HRD's history, because it marked the expansion and diversification of HRD roles beyond training.

Wendy Ruona and Richard Swanson (1998) observe that "HRD is viewed by many as a unifying term to overcome a very large conceptual disconnect from the profession's actual practice and its popular title, training" (p. 1). Ruona and Swanson identify key commonalities of HRD definitions as emphasizing development, making multiple interventions to support learning and performance, focusing on the individual, and linking HRD to work.

Richard Swanson and Ed Holton (2001) identify 18 definitions of HRD noting it borrows from several theoretical disciplines including psychology, systems theory, economics, and human performance technology. They emphasize that HRD is a process that relates to individual and organizational learning and performance. They also suggest that the field is establishing itself as a discipline, yet it is questionable whether HRD is best considered as a true discipline or an applied field. There is no uniformity about HRD's aims, goals, or underlying philosophy. Jerry Gilley, Peter Dean and Laura Bierema (2001) suggest that the field is divided and that its practitioners and scholars align themselves with organizational learning, performance, or change. There is also debate over whether HRD should be individually focused (Bierema, 1996), organizationally focused (Swanson & Arnold, 1996), or both (Bierema, 2000).

Names for HRD Practitioners

A practitioner of HRD could have one of many titles such as adult educator, instructional designer, trainer, technical trainer, needs analyst, learning manager, internal consultant, knowledge manager, facilitator, career counselor, manager, coach, organizational and performance consultant, or chief learning officer. Typical HRD functions include: taking a strategic approach to HRD efforts; participating as a key decision-maker; designing organizational infrastructure that supports learning, employees and the organization; attracting, recruiting and retaining a competent, committed workforce; valuing diversity; creating cost-effective policies and practices; and leading organizational change initiatives.

Key People Associated with HRD

Training was practiced even among our most primitive ancestors (Swanson & Holton, 2001), and training in the workplace dates back at least to apprenticeships as well as merchant and craft guilds common during the Middle Ages. Industrialization facilitated the rise of workplace training. Contemporary HRD originates from the Training Within Industry (TWI) Service of the U.S. government from 1940–45, which was an effort to build human resources during wartime, championed by Channing Dooley (Dooley, 1945; Swanson, 2001). The TWI programs gave birth to three contemporary HRD practices: performance-based training, quality improvement, and human relations (Awards Committee, AHRD, 2001). Organization development was created in the 20th century which saw a shift to a human resources perspective (versus capital), the growth of laboratory training, increased use of action research, a recognition of sociotechnical systems and quality of work life, and a new focus on strategic change (Swanson & Holton). Research in the field of HRD is relatively young, establishing a presence in universities only in the late 1900s (Swanson & Holton). Len Nadler is considered to have coined the term "human resource development" in 1969 at George Washington University.

Many people have influenced HRD's emergence, and the Academy of Human Resource Development (AHRD), an international research organization, has inducted the following individuals into its HRD Scholar Hall of Fame: Gary S. Becker (human capital theory), Channing R. Dooley (TWI project), John Clemans Flanagan (critical incident technique), Robert M. Gagne (conditions of learning), Lillian Gilbreth (human aspect of management), Malcolm S. Knowles (adult learning), Kurt Lewin (change theory), Leonard Nadler (foundations of HRD theory), B. F. Skinner (teaching machines), and Donald Super (career development theory). For a full description of these individuals' contributions, see the AHRD website at http://www.ahrd.org/ahrd/ABOUT/awards/h_fame_list.htm.

HRD in Relation to AE

HRD's relationship with adult education could be described as tenuous, but it depends on whom you ask. Some adult educators accuse HRD of allegiance to human capital theory, money and management. Others apply different philosophies to HRD and take a more emancipatory approach to working in organizations. Viewing HRD as management's handmaiden is a narrow view of a field that extends far beyond corporate HR. Today, HRD activities are ongoing in not-for-profit organizations, government, and education.

Some view HRD as a subset of adult education. There have been at least 20 definitions of HRD forwarded and analysed (Weinberger 1998), and most of them are directly related to training and adult education. Others find this subset view too narrow given HRD's heritage and the influence of vocational education, human resource management, and industrial organization

Psychology on the Field

Swanson (Knowles, Holton, & Swanson, 1998) has suggested that the difference between adult education and HRD is locus of control. His proposal is that in adult education, the locus of control resides with the learner, but in HRD it rests with the organization. "Because HRD focuses on performance outcomes, the significance of learning control [by the learner] is viewed as secondary by most professionals in HRD" (p. 124). Adult educators would argue that this dichotomy is too simplistic and narrow given the influence that the social context has on the learning process for adults. Employees make choices such as choosing where to work, what vocation to pursue, and what they learn. In fact, employees are learning all the time, often in spite of management. Workers and their learning are also impacted by positionality: race, gender, class, sexual orientation, religion and many other variables.

HRD: A Name is a Name. The term, human resource development, is distinctly North American, and lacking universal recognition makes forging global understandings of HRD difficult. For this reason and others, there has been argument both for and against changing the name (Ruona, 2002; Walton, 2002). Adult education scholars have criticized the term "human resource" as evoking a dehumanizing, exploitative capitalist view of workers, whilst an HRD professional might argue that the term "resource" recognizes important knowledge and learning people bring to the organization. Russ-Eft (2000) suggests that conflicts emerge when it is debated whether to emphasize *human* development or *resource* development.

Adult Education Critiques of HRD

HRD is often singled out by adult educators as exploiting people based on race, gender, class and other attributes in the name of profit. This simplistic argument and indictment of the HRD field fails to recognize that the power struggles, negotiations and oppression evident in HRD mirror social dynamics present in every social institution. Further, the exploitation critique disregards the tenuous space where HRD professionals reside. HRD practitioners often straddle clashing interests between the employer and employees (or other stakeholders). Finally, the reality that the HRD profession is rather marginalized in the USA is regularly overlooked when leveling criticism about its exploitative nature. Here the majority of practitioners are women and the function often has low organization power.

Another criticism is that human capital theory is the dominant HRD paradigm. Although it has been an influential theoretical lens in HRD, critics tend to focus exclusively on human capital theory, and narrowly conceive HRD to be badly designed and executed training programs intent on maximizing profitability. Alternative frameworks for conceptualizing HRD include systems theory;

field and intervention theory; instructional technology and design; work and design theory; learning organization models; adult education; and critical theory (Watkins, 1991). Watkins concludes that the field needs to take a more systems-oriented approach and draw on multiple theoretical lenses to be effective and future-oriented.

There is a growing recognition of the importance of critically evaluating HRD practice and scholarship (Bierema & Cseh, 2003), yet the field has been relatively uncritical of itself. As the field continues to evolve and expand, there is a need for a more critical HRD that challenges the concept of a performative HRD practice. HRD needs to be more critical and socially conscious and problematize its precepts. The field needs to challenge the commodification of employees, involve multiple stakeholders in HRD activities, contest the nature of power relations, and pursue wide-ranging goals that extend beyond profit. It also needs to create alternative, non-oppressive, holistic models for cultivating development in the work context. Some adult educators reject HRD taking the view that it is exploitative of employees and beholden to management. Yet, HRD could significantly benefit from stronger attention to the issues adult education embraces such as social justice, learner autonomy, and critical thinking. HRD is about *development,* not profit, and HRD professionals need to carefully consider how their work affects human growth, not just the corporate wallet.

See also: action learning, human capital theory, learning organization, organizational learning, training, training organizations, workplace learning.

References and Further Reading

Awards Committee, Academy of Human Resource Development (AHRD). (2001). Induction of Channing R. Dooley into the HRD Scholar Hall of Fame. *Advances in Developing Human Resources, 3*(2), 117–118.

Bierema, L. L. (1996). Development of the individual leads to more productive workplaces. In R. Rowden (Ed.), *Workplace learning: Debating the five critical questions of theory and practice* (pp. 21–28). *New Directions for Adult and Continuing Education,* No. 72. San Francisco: Jossey-Bass.

Bierema, L. L. (2000) Moving beyond performance paradigms in workplace development. In A. Wilson & E. R. Hayes (Eds.), *Handbook of adult and continuing education* (pp. 278–293). San Francisco: Jossey-Bass.

Bierema, L. L., & Cseh, M. (2003). Evaluating HRD research using a feminist research framework. *Human Resource Development Quarterly, 14*(1), 5–26.

Dooley, C. R. (1945). *The training within industry report 1940–1945.* Washington, DC: U.S. War Manpower Commission Bureau of Training. Training Within Industry Service.

Gilley, J. W., Dean, P., & Bierema, L. L. (2001). *Philosophy and practice of organizational learning, performance, and change.* Cambridge, MA: Perseus Publishing.

Knowles, M. S., Holton, E. F., & Swanson, R. A. (1989). *The adult learner: The definitive classic in adult education and human resource development.* Houston, Tx: Gulf.

McLaglan, P. (1989). Models for HRD practice. *Training and Development Journal, 43*(9), 49–59.

Nadler, L., & Nadler, Z. (1989). *Developing human resources: Concepts and a model* (3rd ed.). San Francisco: Jossey-Bass.

Ruona, W. E. A. (2002). What's in a name? Human resource development and its core. In T. M. Egan & S. A. Lynam (Eds.), *Proceedings of the 2002 Academy of Human Resource Development* (pp. 9–16). Honolulu, HI.

Ruona, W. E. A., & Swanson, R. A. (1998).

Foundations of human resource development. In B.R. Stewart & H. C. Hall (Eds.), *Beyond tradition: Preparing HRD educators for tomorrow's workforce* (pp. 1–31). Columbia, MO: University Council for Workforce and Human Resource Education.

Russ-Eft, D. (2000). That old fungible feeling: Defining human resource development. *Advances in Developing Human Resources*, no. 7, 49–53.

Swanson, R. A. (2001). Preface. *Advances in Developing Human Resources, 3*(2), 115.

Swanson, R. A., & Arnold, D. E. (1996). The purpose of human resource development is to improve organizational performance. In R. Rowden (Ed.), *Workplace learning: Debating the five critical questions of theory and practice* (pp. 13–19). *New Directions for Adult and Continuing Education*, No.72. San Francisco: Jossey-Bass.

Swanson, R. A., & Holton, E. F., III. (2001). *Foundations of human resource development*. San Francisco: Berrett-Koehler.

Walton, J. S. (2002). How shall a thing be called? A debate on the efficacy of the term HRD. In T. M Egan & S. A. Lynam (Eds.), *Proceedings of the 2002 Academy of Human Resource Development* (pp. 1–8). Honolulu, HI.

Watkins, K. E. (1991). Many voices: Defining human resource development from different disciplines. *Adult Education Quarterly, 41*(4), 241–255.

Weinberger, L. A. (1998). Commonly held theories of human resource development. *Human Resource Development International, 1*(1), 75–93.

Laura L. Bierema

I

Identity

Identity means sameness and continuity. Adult education has been influential in shaping questions of identity, and identity politics around the world. The question of identity is also forcing discussions of adult learning out of the psychological perspective (most prevalent in North America), and is challenging adult educators to place practice into a social context.

Identity

Stephen Mennell suggests that the term identity can be thought of through a dictum written by Clyde Kluckhohn and Henry Murray, which is that every person is, in certain respects: "like all other[s]" (this shows that human beings share many characteristics with all other members of the species); "like some other[s]" (this draws attention to the characteristics which all human beings share with certain other human beings); "and like no other[s]," which recognizes that there are ways in which every individual human personality is unique (Mennell, 1994, pp. 176–177). The discourse of identity has focused on characteristics that all human beings share in connection with certain other human beings, and the ways in which every individual personality is unique. Identity is thus generally thought of, and discussed in terms of, personal identity, and collective identity.

There are three traditions that are represented in the discourse of identity: essentialism, social constructionism, and deconstructionism. Essentialism holds that identity is given naturally, that an act of individual will produces identity, and that certain transcontextual features produce identity. It follows that the identities of different persons and groups, for all time, in all cases, independent of the economic, sociopolitical context, flow from some natural and fixed features. Social constructionists reject the view that there is an identity that is given naturally, which is an essence endowed by nature. They believe that whatever nature gives is mediated by society, and the mediation gives persons their identities. For deconstructionists, the subject of identity is to be decentered, such that neither nature nor society confers identity; since there is no categorical truth in unmediated nature, neither is there an absolute truth in the mediation of society. (Calhoun, 1994, p. 19).

The strengths and weaknesses of these three traditions problematize attempts to define personal and collective identity, although collective identity is somewhat well described as: "a higher level conscious awareness by members of a group, some degree of reflection and articulation, some positive or negative emotional feelings towards the characteristics (which Nobert Wiley (1994) refers to as "long term abiding qualities, which, despite their importance, may not be part of human nature as such" (p. 130)) which members of a group perceive themselves as sharing and in which they perceive themselves as differing from other groups" (Mennell, 1994, p. 177). The most common forms of identity in the literature are gender, ethnic/racial, national, religious, sexual, generational and worker identities. Concerning personal identity, there are theorists who consider that personal identity exists, or can be, in their conception of the subject in relation to moral accountability. Some attack the individualistic conception of the subject without reference to the social relations that produce it, while others think that personal identity is a fiction. In the discourse of identity, the position that is becoming widespread is that although self-definition and assertion of individuality are essential to empowerment, the self, here, is self in relation, and so the masculinist psychological model of selfhood is rejected. It is therefore thought that it may be worthwhile to avoid a sharp split between personal identity and collective identity.

Also central to the discourse of identity is the fact that individuals inhabit multiple identities. In real life, persons are not just women, or Hispanics or Muslims or aboriginals, gay or poor. There are Ghanain Muslim women, poor African-American men, gay aboriginals and so on. Given that social relations are understood as a complex network of interactions of persons between groups and within groups, it is possible for individuals to take decisions to favor one identity over another, depending on the sociopolitical context in which they find themselves. The discourse of multiplicity of identities addresses the constant pressures that persons are under to favor particular identities – categorical identities. Allied concerns are negotiation/renegotiation and transformation of identities. The thinking is that they are unavoidable, given that persons inhabit multiple identities, given the tenuous nature of most identities, and given the unequal relations of power within groups and between groups, which leads to skewed distribution of rights and resources. When persons are confronted with new experiences, and new realities, they may rethink the principles they hold dear; they may transform their thinking and perhaps turn it into action; they may form new alliances; or they may not take an either–or position. They may look for a third space, where they may at times feel confused, or feel comfortable and thrive, or feel challenged.

Identity Politics

Politics of identity is the struggle over the characteristics attributed socially and institutionally to individuals and groups of individuals. Characteristics, which, when socially and institutionally applied to groups of individuals, define their rights and duties, which then affect the quality of their lives (Wiley, 1994, p. 131). Politics of identity does not take place only between those who claim different identities, it also involves each subject within the group. Whereas subjectivity (the self-conscious perspective of the person or subject), the "I," is supposed to be primary to the person and more immanent, there are too many challenges to the efforts of persons "to attain stable self-recognition or coherent subjectivity" (Calhoun, 1994, p. 20). Critical to the self-conscious perspective of a person is the interrelated problems of self-recognition, and recognition by others. Craig Calhoun makes the point that "it is not just that others fail to see us for who we are sure we really are, or repress us because of who they think we are," we are constantly confronted with discussions of "who it is possible or appropriate or valuable to be" (p. 20). This inevitably affects the way we see ourselves, with the attendant doubts and tensions, and this results in deconstructing certain identities and making strategic claims to others. Identity politics is therefore about seeking recognition, legitimacy, autonomy and power, and it is about resistance. When persons and groups give expression to their belief about who they are sure they are, when they make demands and take actions, they are inviting others to respond. The methods that groups employ in struggles range from: personal interactions to enlightenment campaigns and education programs for group members and others, using different societal institutions and cultural vehicles; to lobbying other groups and state institutions; forming alliances with other oppressed/marginalized or disenchanted groups; to protests, demonstrations and sit-ins; and to violence – verbal violence, terrorist attacks and wars. All the methods reflect different dimensions of power – power within, power with, and power over, that groups use to call attention to their demands and struggles, and influence the outcome of struggles.

The Responses, the Interface, and the Challenges

Adult educators have reported that not everyone admits that race, gender, ethnicity or sexual orientation have any educational relevance, either in terms of the content of education or the instructional techniques used. Some learners get turned off when the issues are raised, preferring a context-free idea of adult learning (Merriam & Caffarella, 1999). There are those who have been involved in identity politics in the past, and/or who are still involved in such struggles, who show intolerance for differences within their groups. Desiree Lewis (2003) points out that the charge of Westernization and cooperation with imperialism is being levied with special virulence against feminists in Africa. This backlash against feminists in Africa is carried on in different learning centers – formal institutions of learning, religious places, and the mass media. In addition, some governments respond to identity politics by appropriating the struggles of groups. For example, in a number of African countries the phenomenon of femocracy (or state feminism) has been reported. Wives of heads of states put themselves forward as the voice of women in their countries and help their husbands to appropriate feminist demands. They organize skills training programs for women, and put together workshops, seminars and conferences to which friends of the government in power are invited.

Multicultural education is another response to identity politics. It is favored because it is thought to have the potential for strengthening relations between different groups of people, given that it is not assimilationist, but it is criticized for glossing over the unequal relations of power between and within groups. For example, the feeling among some non-Western academics is that some academics with some radical persuasion (including feminists) in the Global North, try to mask the unequal relations of power between the two groups by celebrating cultural diversity. There are many non-formal adult education programs that are being supported by philanthropic organizations, religious and intergovernmental organizations all around the world, that are responses to the identity politics of women, environmentalists and first-nation communities. Finally, the responses to some identity politics have been violent, and vehicles of non-formal adult education, which abound in all societies, are turned into vehicles for mobilizing wars, ethnic cleansing and genocide.

Adult education has not always waited to respond to identity politics, and has influenced anti-colonial struggles and the struggles of poor communities. The University of Oxford extra-mural classes introduced to West Africa in 1947 during colonial rule, provided nationalists in Ghana and Nigeria with the knowledge and skills that helped, in part, to forge the sense of national consciousness that was essential to creating independent nations (Benn & Fieldhouse, 1995). Marcie Boucouvalas (1995) has highlighted the role of different agencies of adult education (key personalities, special populations, organized agents and institutional movements), in the development of national consciousness and identity, in the Greek struggle for national independence from Turkey. In Canada, Moses Coady and Jimmy Tompkins, both university teachers, took their skills and resources to the struggling communities of northeastern Nova Scotia.

Identity politics challenges adult educators to take the question of identity seriously and resist the temptation to trivialize it. Identity politics, and the responses to it, have bearing on whether marginalized and discontented persons and groups can attain their full potential, and this has implications for advancing the course of humanity, and world peace. Identity challenges adult educators to imbibe and encourage the dialectical mode of thinking about phenomena, trends and beliefs, in adult learning and in adult education practice. Thus, decisions that adult learners take or are unable to take about participation in adult education programs, for example, are not to be apprehended in antithetical and categorical terms without reference to the internal tensions within individuals about becoming, and without reference to the complexities of the social contexts in which individual learners are positioned, and the relations of power that shape those contexts. Much adult learning is taking place around the world outside formal adult education structures and institutions (that are prevalent in the Global North), that has potential for helping adults to realize themselves. Identity challenges adult educators to explore knowledge systems that differ from the mainstream, to question established definitions and concepts, and to explore and adopt learning styles suited to particular groups (Miles, 1989).

See also: class, feminism, gender, postcolonialism, social constructivism.

References and Further Reading

Benn, R., & Fieldhouse, R. (1995). Adult education and national independence movements in West Africa, 1944–1953. In F. Pöggeler (Ed.), *National identity and adult education – challenge and risk; Vol 25* (pp. 247–259). Frankfurt am Main: Peter Lang.

Boucouvalas, M. (1995). The Greek struggle for independence from Turkish occupation: Contributions of adult education to national identity. In F. Pöggeler (Ed.), *National identity and adult education – challenge and risk; Vol 25* (pp. 219–230). Frankfurt am Main: Peter Lang.

Calhoun, C. (1994). Social theory and the politics of identity. In C. Calhoun

(Ed.), *Social theory and the politics of identity* (pp. 9–36). Oxford: Blackwell.

Lewis, D. (2003). Editorial. *Feminist Africa*. Retrieved June 21, 2002, from Feminist Africa website: http://www.feministafrica.org

Mennell, S. (1994). The formation of we-images: A process theory. In C. Calhoun (Ed.), *Social theory and the politics of identity* (pp. 175–197). Oxford: Blackwell.

Merriam, S. B., & Caffarella, R. S. (1999). *Learning in adulthood: A comprehensive guide* (2nd ed.). San Francisco: Jossey-Bass.

Miles, A. (1989). Women's challenge to adult education, *Canadian Journal for the Study of Adult Education, 3*(1), 1–18.

Wiley, N. (1994). The politics of identity in American history. In C. Calhoun (Ed.), *Social theory and the politics of identity* (pp. 130–149). Oxford: Blackwell.

Olutoyin Mejiuni

Ideology

Ideology is often used now as a simple way of referring to the political viewpoint held by a group, class or even system, for example capitalism, or religion. This simple definition belies the age-old struggle to define the term. *Idéologie* was first used by the French philosopher Destutt de Tracy and his colleagues in the late 1790s to denote their "science of ideas" which, they held, would enable people to understand the bases of common biases and prejudices. But within a few years, the word acquired a more negative meaning when Napoleon Bonaparte dismissed what he called the *idéologues* as impractical visionaries. In the mid-1840s, Karl Marx and Friedrich Engels gave the negative connotation another twist in *The German Ideology*, although the full sense of their uses of the term was not widely appreciated until that work was published in the late 1920s. In brief, they located ideology, as a distortion or misrepresentation of reality, in social contradictions. Thus to them it followed that fundamental social change requires political (revolutionary) action, and not mere critique.

The negative or pejorative notion of ideology is still widely employed. It is often used to refer to any set of illusory beliefs, but more usually beliefs about economic and social relations that can in some way be contrasted with the "real" or "scientific" world. Those holding conservative or even mainstream political views still tend to use it, much like Napoleon, as a way of dismissing oppositional or unfashionable political views and movements. Ideology also may be applied more tightly, mainly from a left perspective, to refer to the fostering, by a specific or dominant class or group, of false or misleading beliefs designed to justify or present as "natural" a particular social order. An example would be politicians' rationalizations for the existence of unemployment and poverty in wealthy, Western countries. This use is sometimes complicated further when the tricky and usually unhelpful notion of "false consciousness" is invoked in order to explain why the poor and disenfranchised opt out of political action.

Since the 1930s, beginning with the work of the sociologist, Karl Mannheim, the negative meaning has coexisted, somewhat awkwardly, with a more neutral sense of ideology that retains the notion of a set of ideas but which tends to discard any sense of illusion or manipulation. Thus ideology can sometimes refer to a set of political ideas (for instance, socialism) or to a way of interpreting the world, or even, when referring to a symbolic or signifying system, as something close to a synonym for a whole way of life or culture. It can also be used in a more active sense to refer to the political philosophy or belief system that motivates a group or class engaged in social action. This use almost always carries quite a strong sense of power, but not necessarily a suggestion of illusion. The term can also be stretched, as Lenin initially did, to refer to not just a social or political movement's underlying philosophy, but also its political project or program. Examples that may contain either a positive or negative connotation would be "socialist" or "neo-liberal" or "feminist" or "ecological" ideology.

From an Adult Education Perspective

These different patterns of use can all be found in the adult education literature. Radicals have long used the term, in a Marxian derived sense, to critique Western liberal capitalist societies in general and, especially, the assumptions that underpin educational practices. More recently, such critique has been extended to neo-liberal or "New Right" philosophies, policies, and practices (Ledwith, 2001). From this perspective, ideology critique, as radical educational practice, can help expose the oppressive dimension of dominant ideas or political cultures. Sheila Rowbotham's (1973) feminist classic, *Hidden from History*, is a good, early example of the ways in which such critique can grow out of and in turn inform radical adult education. Ideology critique gathered momentum throughout the 1970s as the "new sociology of education" spilled into the academic literature. The key work was undoubtedly Jane Thompson's (1980) edited volume, in which authors drew on insights from Paulo Freire and Antonio Gramsci, as well as on more deeply rooted traditions of radical adult education, in order to systematically critique the ways in which current practice in a range of related fields reinforced the ideas and the power of the dominant classes. Of those contributions, none struck more closely at the heart of mainstream adult education than Nell Keddie's (1980) powerful essay, "Adult education: An ideology of individualism." Keddie views ideologies not as "disguised descriptions of the world but rather political bias" (p. 46). Practitioners, she argues, as an interest group located within a particular social structure, are obsessed with an individualistic notion of "needs" that emphasizes adaptation to the existing social order rather than critique and social action.

Within a very short time, several other notions of ideology appeared in the adult education literature. In a response to the Thompson (1980) volume, Kenneth Lawson (1982), a philosopher of adult education, distinguished liberal education, which he claimed was based on rationality and was thus not "ideological," from the politically motivated, ideological perspective offered by the radicals. Peter Jarvis' (1985) valiant attempt to offer a non-ideological sociology of adult education wrestles with these competing uses. Jarvis settles on a simple definition of ideology, the particular viewpoint of a group or class, and he then attempts to match four ideological perspectives (conservative, liberal, reformism, and radical) with three interpretations of the social structure (functionalist, pluralist, and Marxist). But, as the book progresses, he sometimes struggles to keep his own categories stable.

Trends in the social sciences

quickly influence adult education academics. Since the 1980s, the growing influence on the field of European, critical social theory has caused many adult educators to consider in more depth the many subtleties associated with notions of ideology. Stephen Brookfield's (2001) careful, thorough exploration of the place of ideology critique in a critical theory of adult learning is a major contribution. He highlights critical theory's indebtedness to Marx, reflected in its view of ideologies,

> as broadly accepted sets of values, beliefs, myths, explanations, and justifications that appear self-evidently true, empirically accurate, personally relevant, and morally desirable to the majority of the population, but that actually work to maintain an unjust social and political order. (p. 14)

Brookfield also tackles a number of the analytical difficulties with which many academic writers have wrestled in recent years: the implications of Louis Althusser's notions of "dominant" and "dominated" ideologies; the insights offered by Gramsci's notion of "hegemony;" and, briefly, aspects of Michel Foucault's understanding of power.

Foucault eventually concluded that ideology was too limited a concept and that a more encompassing notion of "discourse" offered a better alternative. The extended meaning of that term refers not just to what is said or written with respect to a particular subject, but also to the power relations or implicit rules that govern what can be said, by whom, and with what authority. But while some adult education authors, especially those writing from a left perspective, seem much more comfortable with terms like "hegemony" and "discourse," not all have abandoned ideology. Griff Foley (1999) offers a rich understanding of ideology in which one can find strong echoes of Marx and Engels as well as the influence of Freire and Gramsci. While the role radical education can play in helping to unmask oppressive political cultures is central to Freire's (1981) work, he generally avoids using the term ideology to describe those cultures. But he does use the term in a very positive sense, that of an oppositional ideology, when he refers to Che Guevara's notion of how peasants contribute to a "revolutionary ideology" as a "theory of action" (p. 171). Foley, who discusses both ideology and discourse together, invokes several meanings of ideology. The first is very familiar: the "distorted understanding" of an oppressed group. The second, with which he plays very imaginatively, "refers to the various ways in which social meanings and structures are "produced, challenged, reproduced and transformed in both individual consciousness and social practices and relationships" (p. 14). This active notion of ideology in the context of learning "performs," Foley notes, "both positive and negative functions" (p. 14). Foley accepts the view that discourses play a central role in the production of both dominant and dominated ideologies, but he does not concede to the dominant. Rather, he reaffirms a radical commitment to an emancipatory education that contributes not only to the "unlearning of dominant, oppressive ideologies and discourses," but also to the "learning of insurgent, emancipatory ones . . ." (p. 16).

John Holst (2002) is another contemporary adult education academic who also still advocates studying "the relationship between ideology and politics and the changing nature of the relations of production" (p. 16). In what is proving to be a landmark study, Holst employs a Marxian, substantially Gramscian, perspective to analyse very carefully a wide range of writing on radical adult education and social movements. He identifies a number of authors who affirm the potential of adult education to challenge capitalist ideology; he is especially impressed with Foley's (1999) contribution. While the discussion in Holst refers to hegemony rather than ideology, his observations help bring this discussion to a tidy close. For Holst, one strength of Foley's contribution is his recognition that the social relations within which learning takes place is a "battleground," "is always contested territory and is therefore open, in ever-changing degrees, to the creation of alternative hegemonies" (p. 92). The other strength is Foley's insistence in "bringing us back to political economy as the fundamental analytical tool for understanding this battleground in motion" (p. 92).

While ideology has become unfashionable in much of the social sciences, within adult education the concept is still being developed in a rich and radical way that emphasizes the potential of emancipatory learning.

See also: critical theory, emancipatory adult education, human capital theory, philosophy, theory, social action.

References and Further Reading

Brookfield, S. D. (2001). Repositioning ideology critique in a critical theory of adult learning. *Adult Education Quarterly*, *52*(1), 7–22.

Foley, G. (1999). *Learning in social action*. Leicester: National Institute of Adult Continuing Education.

Freire, P. (1981). *Pedagogy of the oppressed*. (M. B. Ramos, Trans.). New York: Continuum.

Holst, J. D. (2002). *Social movements, civil society, and radical adult education*. Westport: Bergin & Garvey.

Jarvis, P. (1985). The sociology of adult and continuing education. Beckenham, UK: Croom Helm.

Keddie, N. (1980). Adult education: An ideology of individualism. In J. L. Thompson (Ed.), *Adult education for a change* (pp. 45–64). London: Hutchinson.

Lawson, K. H. (1982). *Analysis and ideology: Conceptual essays on the education of adults*. Nottingham: University of Nottingham, Department of Adult Education.

Ledwith, M. (2001). Community work as critical pedagogy: Re-envisioning Freire and Gramsci. *Community Development Journal*, *36*(3), 171–182.

Rowbotham, S. (1973). *Hidden from history*. London: Pluto.

Thompson, J. L. (Ed.). (1980). *Adult education for a change*. London: Hutchinson.

Michael Law

Immigration

Migration is a broad term used to describe the movement of populations from one place to another. Immigration refers to the movement of people from one country to another on a permanent basis. Immigration is an enduring topic of great interest because almost every country is involved in this process as a source, transit or destination country, or all three simultaneously. Adult education plays a prominent role in facilitating immigrants with their settlement and adaptation in a new society.

Immigration as an International Phenomenon

Immigration can be attributed to push and/or pull factors. The former are events or features that drive people away from their home country, such as overpopulation, poverty, natural disasters, war, political and religious persecution, and human-rights abuses. The latter are events or features that attract people to the destination country, including economic opportunities, a higher standard of living, social and political stability, free and accessible social services, a clean environment, and a favorable educational system. While some migrate voluntarily, many are forced to leave their home country. Further, economic globalization and modern communication technology have greatly enhanced the mobility of people across national boundaries. The International Organization for Migration (IOM) (2003) estimates that at the beginning of the 21st century, about 2.9% of the world population, or 170 million people, live outside their countries of birth.

Immigration has always played a central role in the nation-building of receiving countries. For example, in the 19th century massive immigration was used as a strategy to populate and develop Western Canada. Second, immigration has served the economic and demographic interests of the receiving nation. Currently, many advanced nations are facing declining fertility rates, and immigration has been adopted as a strategy to ameliorate aging populations and labor shortages. In addition, immigration has also served as a means of social and ideological control. In deciding who are the most desirable and admissible, the state sets the parameters for the social, cultural and symbolic boundaries of the nation, as manifested in historically racist Canadian and American immigration policies. For example, in 1882 and 1923 respectively, the United States and Canada passed the Chinese Exclusion Act to keep "undesirable" Chinese out. Only since the 1950s have many immigrant-receiving countries shifted immigration criteria from national and racial backgrounds to educational and professional qualifications. Today, developed countries compete for the most talented, skillful and resourceful, but maintain many restrictive strategies to keep out unwanted immigrants and refugee claimants. Such scrutiny and restrictions have increased in the wake of the events of September 11.

Because resources are not equally distributed across the globe, international migration tends to move one way: from less-developed nations to advanced industrial countries. Unfortunately the "brain gain" for many capitalist countries usually means "brain drain" for developing countries. OECD (2004) reports that as of 2001, Australia (23.1%), Canada (18.4%), New Zealand (19.5%), and the United States (11.1%) had the highest foreign-born populations among OECD countries.

The Social Construction of "Immigrant"

At the centre of immigration issues are immigrants themselves. According to Peter Li (2003), the notion of "immigrant" is socially constructed, and he argues that the concept "immigrant" is often associated with people of non-white origin. In the context of Canada, early settlers came mainly from Europe. Only since the "immigrant point system" was introduced in 1967 has Canada attracted an increasing number of immigrants from third-world countries, notably Asia and Africa. Descendents of early European settlers, now long-time Canadians, do not think of themselves as immigrants. As Li puts it, the term "immigrant" becomes a codified word for people of color who come from a different racial and cultural background, who do not speak fluent English, and who work in lower-position jobs. Li maintains that the social construction of immigrant uses skin color as the basis for social marking. Their real and alleged differences (see difference) are claimed to be incompatible with the cultural and social fabric of the "traditional" Canada, and are therefore deemed undesirable. Immigrants are also often blamed for creating urban social problems and racial and cultural tensions in the receiving society. The social construction of the term "immigrant" places uneven expectations on immigrants to conform over time to the norms, values, and traditions of the receiving society.

Challenges for Adult Education

Immigration has posed both challenges and new opportunities for development in adult education. One challenge is related to the cultural and linguistic diversity that immigrant adult learners bring into adult education, and our failure-to-date in integrating this diversity into our system. Two conventional approaches have contributed to this failure: the cultural deficit model and the color-blind approach (Johnson-Bailey & Cervero, 2000; May, 1999). The former views cultural and linguistic differences as deficiencies and as the source of the problem; hence these are subject to assimilation and transformation. The "color-blind" approach assumes universality and sameness among adult learners, normalizes the dominant culture, and discounts the histories, cultures, and life experiences of immigrants; but both approaches work towards the same goal: assimilation. Both may be counterproductive to the goal of building an inclusive model of adult education.

See also: diversity, English as a second language, literacy, social constructivism.

References and Further Reading

International Organization for Migration (IOM) (2003). Facts and figures on international migration. Geneva: IOM.

Johnson-Bailey, J., & Cervero, R. M. (2000). The invisible politics of race in adult education. In A. L. Wilson & E. R. Hayes (Eds.), *Handbook of adult and continuing education* (pp. 147–160). San Francisco: Jossey-Bass.

Li, P. S. (2003). *Destination Canada: Immigration debates and issues*. Don Mills, Ontario: Oxford University Press.

May, S. (1999). Critical multiculturalism and cultural difference: Avoiding essentialism. In S. May (Ed.), *Critical multiculturalism: Rethinking multicultural and antiracist education* (pp. 11–41). London: Falmer.

OECD (2004). *SOPEMI – Trends in international migration: Annual Report 2003 Edition.* Paris: Organization for Economic Co-operation and Development.

Shibao Guo

Indigenous Learning

Indigenous learning refers to learning which occurs with or within indigenous peoples, contexts or worldviews. This learning is a cultural reality, a political contest and an academic discipline. It is affected by Aboriginal worldviews and Western colonial contexts. Multiple and competing narratives of a shared past continue to influence the present struggles to decolonize, and the future visions of what constitutes learning, literacy, empowerment, and activism. Indigenous learning occurred long before colonial powers invaded lands, and continues in spite of and in concert with ongoing assimilationist agendas of educational institutions today. Ancestral teachings, rooted in geographical and spiritual realities, continue to shape and transform lives of indigenous adult educators and learners. Cultural renaissance or the increasing reliance on pedagogies grounded in indigenous worldviews, fuels most exemplary models of indigenous education today. See *Canadian Journal of Native Education* (2002) for a special edition on this theme highlighting Canadian and New Zealand (Maori) programs.

Terminology

Indigenous. To indigenous peoples, naming is a spiritual responsibility that describes and creates realities. Names are given in relation to physical surroundings and personal gifts, and help First Peoples survive and thrive as nations. Naming has become politically contested with people and place-specific colonial terms evolving into common usage, even if derogatory or pejorative. Indigenous peoples resent having to define themselves to outsiders in the languages of intruders. Indigenous peoples can be referred to respectfully by tribal affiliation or by politically preferred terms common to a territory or time frame, like First Nations in Canada, AmerIndian in the United States or Aboriginal in Australia. Indigenous learning, however, can be explored globally by the use of such qualifiers as Aboriginal, Aborigine, Autochthonous, Black, Indian, Métis, Native, minority and multicultural to name a few. These terms may be a construction of the West, but indigenous people are not.

Learning. Adult learning processes, andragogy, are not viewed as distinct from those of children, but rather learning is a lifelong self-directed process of experiencing, processing and reshaping existing knowledge to meet ever-changing demands of environmental contexts. Responsibility for learning comes from within, through acknowledging what medicine or gifts each individual carries, and through building relationships with others, like elders, children, all natural elements, and spirits.

Traditional indigenous learning engages all the senses in the pursuit of knowledge. Dreams, stories, ceremonies, and experiences all present multiple possible lessons. Those seeking knowledge are responsible to consult, use reflective judgment, and undertake innovations or transformations relevant to their current needs, and their abilities to hear, absorb and understand. Traditional indigenous discourse is not appropriately communicated through written methods (Urion,1999).

Western Colonial Contexts

The curriculum and context of indigenous learning has been reshaped through contact with Europeans who have come to spatially, politically, culturally and ideologically dominate our territories. Eurocentric consciousness is a hegemonic way of knowing, seeing, and understanding the world. It is both hidden and expressed, and reinforces past and present superiority of Europeans over all non-Europeans. Used to sustain concrete social, economic and political agendas, Eurocentrism continues to be produced and reproduced in institutions of higher learning.

Colonial education strategies include: dehumanization, forced relocation, re-education, and redefinition through falsification of reality, voice and history. These early educational initiatives fit well within an overall agenda of conquest, conversion, accumulation and control. These tactics were and are supremely profitable for colonizers and their descendants, but impoverishing for indigenous peoples worldwide, who now exist in conditions of imposed internal exile (Geohring, 1993).

Genocidal methods like murder, scalping, disease, destruction of subsistence economies were accompanied by ethnocidal strategies: like persecution and imprisonment of elders, political and spiritual leaders and teachers; destruction, confiscation and museum-izing of ceremonial "artifacts" and teaching tools; enforced residential schooling with regulation of all aspects of life strictly enforced through widespread forms of violence; and widespread apprehension of indigenous children. Indigenous scholars like Dan Paul, Isabelle Knockwood and Ernie Crey have carefully mapped this colonial history in Canada.

Colonial educational history not only contributed to dissolution of indigenous family, clan, and communal learning structures, but its legacy includes far-ranging and intergenerational resistances in higher education contexts today. Built on a shared belief in "indigenous incapacity," the notion that indigenous people are unable to do for themselves, and a religious mission of bringing indigenous peoples "from darkness to light," Western institutions of higher learning continue to reinforce monocultural curricula through: emphasis on replacement of indigenous languages with English; oral tradition with written word; and reinforcement of cognition as separable from affect, spirit and embodiment.

Few curriculum resources exist that are not an appropriation, translation, or distortion of indigenous voices by "experts" in anthropology, history, politics, art, literature and now "native/Indian" and cultural studies. Powerful dominant institutions refuse to publish indigenous work and in some cases reshape indigenous voices through editorial processes to fit "expected" content and conventions. Indigenous peoples are now challenging reification of Euro-expert academic voices through the development of their own publications, like *Gatherings: The En'owkin Journal of First North American People* in Canada. Indigenous artists and visionaries in the *Indigena* collection want educators to read and teach from "first voice" (Graveline, 1998). Others resist the fashion to prescribe that only indigenous people can know and speak about indigenous issues.

Arguments about whose voice is heard in Western educational systems are fueled by culturalism, and in particular scientific culturalism, which is reliance on objectivist scientific research methods to study and describe indigenous cultures. Continued production and reproduction of binary notions of two opposing cultures: indigenous and Western, also contributes to ongoing debates over whether education for indigenous peoples should be indigenous-only, Western-only or a bilingual, bicultural, two-ways, both-ways or integrated approaches, which center around notions of collaboration and partnerships between indigenous peoples and bureaucratic systems. Support amongst indigenous community members and academics for the concept of Western-only education for indigenous students in mainstream schools follows from well-anchored hegemonic beliefs in one right way to educate. Indigenization of social control is a mask of reform, occurring when indigenous peoples are recruited to abandon their identities and their communities, to participate in nation states as citizens without the complications of distinct rights or identity, and to enforce the laws of colonial powers.

Assimilationist Education

Indigenous scholars like Verna Kirkness (1986, 1987) and Marie Battiste (2000) describe how well-meaning efforts to reform education for indigenous learners have resulted in attention being diverted away from issues of colonial relations of power and their consequences, and onto "helping" indigenous peoples transition or succeed, assimilate or be mainstreamed into Western learning environments. Today's ongoing assimilationist education strategies derive theoretical support from literature about indigenous learning styles, motivation and retention and bureaucratic infrastructures such as citizenship-training, vocationalism, literacy programming, competency-based education, standardization of competencies, and nationalization of policies. Liberal curriculum reforms towards more cross-cultural, multicultural, culturally sensitive and inclusive content are frequently additive rather than transformative in their focus. Often historically-frozen romanticized ideals of what indigenous identity "should" be, become measures of both authenticity and levels of deteriorization. Others see links between educational achievement and autonomy, productivity, and dignity, while ignoring restrictive codes that do not allow for development of indigenous knowledges.

For most indigenous peoples, "access" programs are the means by which entry is gained into Western-controlled post-secondary systems. Rapidly increasing birth rates have resulted in a large pool of indigenous youth, and Canadian universities are now actively "courting" students (Bergman, 2002). Ongoing patterns of "official encouragement, institutional discouragement" subject indigenous peoples to marginalization, racialization and tokenization. Indigenous students and scholars are exposed everyday to materials, professors and peers that reinforce hidden and overt messages of inferiority. This "chilly climate" is combined with daily lived experiences of "cultural discontinuity" and lack of culturally appropriate mechanisms to ease transition to university environments.

Indigenous peoples have become notorious for "stepping in and out" of colleges before getting a degree. This pattern has given rise to the National Institute for Native Leadership in Higher Education in Albuquerque, New Mexico and provides incentive for many studies of retention, where indigenous students' success is frequently theorized as "educational resilience", and a positive adaptation in response to adversity. *First Person, First People* (1997) is a collection of indigenous graduates' narratives that documents the perseverance necessary to succeed in the "alien" environment of an Ivy League campus.

Decolonizing Movements

Paulo Freire (1985) names resistance to colonization as universal, as an incredible and dialectical counteraction, a protracted political, cultural, and military struggle. Many indigenous peoples have and are resisting colonization of their lands actively, and are engaged in "primary resistance," taking collective stands against continued military intervention. Indigenous peoples are collectivizing nationally, like "First Nations" – a Canadian nation-wide political movement.

Postcolonial indigenous cultural icons like Russell Means and Leonard Peltier demonstrate how acts of resistance are framed as personal hostility, not as necessary acts of survival. Indigenous peoples worldwide continue to resist assimilatory strategies by: failing to attend schools, which historically led to enforced residential schools; refusing to learn European ways and languages; and using technical abilities of leadership, once learned, to advance decolonizing agendas.

Vine Deloria Jr. (1994), an AmerIndian educator, theorizes and politicizes the safeguarding of spiritual practices by indigenous ancestors: through ignoring – continuing to practice ways when told not to; silence – guarding ancestral secrets; and outward agreement and inner resistance. Introduction of indigenous spiritual practices into Western higher-learning contexts remains highly political and controversial (Graveline 2001, 2002). Other relevant critical multicultural literacies include: globally sharing indigenous resistance strategies and movements; directly challenging slurs and media portrayals; and raising all people's consciousness to recognize and collectivize against structural forces that impact upon indigenous realities.

Many indigenous scholars have entered into a period of "secondary" or "ideological resistance" by taking more time and energy to address indigenous worldviews and less in summarizing and reconfirming the works of the "masters", and making room for non-linear thinking through a holistic worldview emphasizing interaction between the physical, mental, emotional and spiritual. Traditional indigenous pedagogies include the use of story-telling, poetry, metaphor, myth, ceremony, dreams and art; and honoring indigenous elders as "cultural professors" and acknowledging Indigenous contributions to the world, like "native science" (Cajete, 2000), healing medicines and democracy. Indigenous pedagogies broaden an exclusive focus on critique or reason, to bring balance through heightened intuition, creativity and a strengths-oriented perspective. Indigenous research paradigms and methodologies are also being developed and implemented (see *Canadian Journal of Native Education*, 2003).

The Rise of Global Indigenism

Indigenism (Niezen, 2003), the International Movement of Indigenous Peoples, is resulting in widespread development of social, economic, cultural, political, and educational institutions run by and for the benefit of indigenous peoples. Thirty-five tribal colleges, including Red Crow in Canada, belong to the American Indian Higher Education Consortium (AIHEC). The First Nations University of Canada, previously known as Saskatchewan Indian Federated College (SIFC), is the only tribal-controlled university in Canada. At the University of Auckland, New Zealand, the Kaupapa Maori world view, language, culture and politics are revitalized using the principles of Maori scholar Graham Smith. Responding to a dearth of indigenous mentors for graduate students, indigenous scholars like Oscar Kawagly (Alaska), Judy Atkinsen (Australia), Peter Hanohano (Hawaii), and Stan and Peggy Wilson (Canada) are envisioning together an

International Indigenous Graduate Institute.

A central paradox in modernity is the ways that imposed formal education, combined with technology, have shaped and sharpened indigenous peoples' abilities to more effectively collectivize to assert their distinctiveness. Human-rights conventions, multilateral agreements on the environment as well as domestic legislation and policy demonstrate that indigenous peoples' voices must have a place in the development agenda. Only recently have public governments, private-sector and non-governmental organizations begun to realize that traditional knowledge systems and practices that have sustained and nourished cultures for generations have tremendous value for efforts related to sustainable development, medical research, governance and civil society.

Indigenous peoples have consistently demonstrated a willingness to share their knowledge, but often governments, companies and academics have "collaborated" with indigenous groups in ways that have done more harm than good, even if the original intent was legitimate (Battiste & Henderson 2000).

See also: Canada, culturally relevant adult education, New Zealand, post-colonialism, race.

References and Further Reading

Battiste, M. (2000). *Reclaiming indigenous voice and vision*. Vancouver: University of British Columbia Press.

Battiste, M., & Barman, J. (1995). *First Nations education in Canada: The circle unfolds*. Vancouver: University of British Columbia Press.

Battiste, M., & Henderson, J. Y. (2000). *Protecting indigenous knowledge and heritage: A global challenge*. Saskatoon, Saskatchewan: Purich.

Bergman, B. (2002). The chosen peoples: Aboriginal students are now being courted by universities across the county. *Macleans*, January 14, 38–41.

Cajete, G. (2000). *Native science: Natural laws of interdependence*. Santa Fe, NM: Clear Light.

Canadian Journal of Native Education (2002). *Exemplary indigenous education*. Edited by J. Archibald, *26*(1) (special issue).

Canadian Journal of Native Education (2003). *Indigenous research paradigms*. Edited by P. Wilson, *25*(2) (special issue).

Deloria, V., Jr. (1994). *God is red*. Golden, CO: Fulcrum.

First person, first people: Native American college graduates tell their life stories (1997). (A. Garrod & C. Larimore, Eds.). Ithaca, NY: Cornell University.

Freire, P. (1985). *The politics of education: Culture, power, and liberation*. (D. Macedo, Trans.) South Hadley, MA: Bergin & Garvey.

Goehring, B. (1993). *Indigenous peoples of the world*. Saskatoon, Saskatchewan: Purich.

Graveline, F. J. (1998). *Circle works: Transforming Eurocentric consciousness*. Halifax, Nova Scotia: Fernwood.

Graveline, F. J. (2001). Imagine my surprise: Smudge teaches holistic lessons. *Canadian Journal of Native Education*, *25*(6), 6–17.

Graveline, F. J. (2002). Teaching tradition teaches us. *Canadian Journal of Native Education*, *26*(1), 11–29.

Kirkness, V. J. (1986). Native Indian teachers: A key to progress. *Canadian Journal of Native Education*, *13*(1), 47–53.

Kirkness, V. J. (1987). Indian education: Past, present and future. *Professional Journal of NWT Teachers*, *5*(1), 1–14. (Northwest Territories)

McMaster, G., & Martin, L. (Eds.) (1992). *Indigena*.Vancouver: Douglas & McIntyre.

Niezen, R. (2003). *The origins of Indigenism*. Berkeley, CA: University of California Press.

Urion, C. (1999). Changing academic discourse about native education: Using two pairs of eyes. *Canadian Journal of Native Education*,*23*(1), 6–15.

Fyre Jean Graveline

Informal Learning

Informal learning refers generally to the acquisition of new knowledge, understanding, skills or attitudes, which people do on their own and which has not been planned or organized in formal settings such as schools, colleges and universities (see Rothwell & Kazanas, 1990). Informal learning refers to how individuals learn in the workplace and through daily interactions with others. Everyone spends some time pursuing informal activities that permit the acquisition of knowledge. Yet, a universally accepted definition of informal learning continues to challenge specialists in the field and there is an abundance of concepts related to informal learning. Informal learning experts point out that learning activities exist on a continuum and the iceberg of learning is mostly submerged. Between formal and informal learning is non-formal learning, which refers to the semi-structured learning that occurs in workshops, seminars and training events (Coombs, Prosser, & Ahmed, 1973).

Every adult is involved throughout life in activities and experiences that lead to learning. For their survival, humans have always acquired knowledge, skills and attitudes long before the invention of these educational institutions, and they are still doing so. Language, hunting skills, and new songs have been learned and transmitted from generation to generation in informal or intuitive ways such as observation, imitation and teaching by parents and peers. Today, many skills are developed through these informal means, as well as by reading, travelling, and being exposed to mass media. These are important sources for learning what is not taught in formal schools. The work environment, mass media, computers, recreation, household activities, human everyday interactions, and community involvement are situations that trigger such learning. Yet, informal learning does not get the recognition and social value that formal learning receives, as accrediting diplomas.

Formal Learning

Formal learning is the learning that occurs inside the curricula of institutions providing educational activities or programs sanctioned by some kind of formal or official recognition (mostly by a diploma or certification). Objectives, contents, methods of teaching and evaluation, criteria and means, duration and even applications are planned and determined in advance by professionals who choose, impose, apply and supervise these means and processes to be used with students. Teachers make the important decisions and direct tasks to make learning happen, whereas students may have little chance to exercise their own initiative, and must comply by the rules. The control and initiative are mostly in the hands of the institutions. Formal learning is generally age-graded, hierarchically organized, and delivered through a formally constituted system that requires compulsory attendance and provides credentialing programs to certify knowledge or competence (Livingstone, 2004). It is planned and organized in a linear sequential and hierarchical manner starting from basic skills and knowledge to more complex and sophisticated ones. Regularity is a major component of this type of learning. Yet, despite the many controls in these institutions and besides planned formal learning, a great deal of informal, unplanned learning happens, in the schoolyard, for example.

Types of Informal Learning

Self-directed learning is a type of informal learning that has generated intensive research. It is learning in which the learner has initiative and control of the objectives, the means, self-evaluation and the freedom to set the criteria to assess the attainment of satisfactory levels of achievement. Following the works of pioneers like M. Knowles, C. Rogers, and A. Tough, a great deal of theory and research have been devoted to understanding self-directed learning. A large consensus has been reached about the ubiquity and versatility of self-directed learning, but still no satisfactory definition of the concept has been coined. More than 30 different expressions are used indistinctively to refer to this notion, all stressing the dimensions of *self* (self-initiated learning, self-teaching, self-planned learning, etc.), autonomy (autonomous learning, individual learning, autodidactism, etc.), and independence (independent learning, independent study, independent self- education). Learning is also equated with education, instruction, inquiry, study, teaching, mastery, change, and scholarship.

A second type of informal learning is tacit informal learning, which is mostly experiential, unconscious and unplanned learning acquired in everyday life in interactions with others and the environment. It is situationally initiated and can happen anywhere. Socialization or learning of one's language and culture are the best and most widespread aspects of tacit informal learning. Conditions for tacit informal learning can be set by others (parents), or by contingencies of the environment with no prior intent, in what is sometimes called incidental learning (Kerka, 2000; Marsick & Watkins, 1990; Watkins & Marsick, 1992).

A third type is explicit informal learning, which is acquired by the individual's own initiative outside educational programs. The activities that lead to it are self-initiated, deliberate and conscious. For Livingstone (2004), explicit informal learning is distinguished from socialization and tacit informal learning by the fact that the individual consciously chooses or recognizes it as significant learning. The individual seeks the learning and creates the conditions for it by putting himself or herself in situations or with people that make the learning possible. Questioning is the usual vehicle for such explicit informal learning. It can be sustained in the case of an important and extended project, or it can be limited in time and scope. Reading about flower-growing in order to have a nice garden, or asking a mechanic to explain the functioning of our car, why it is broken and how to prevent the break next time, are typical kinds of explicit informal learning.

Yet another type of informal learning, autodidactic learning or self-instruction, refers to learning situations where the learner initiates deliberate learning activities and is responsible for all aspects of the learning process (choosing the subject, fixing the goals, selecting the means and resources, setting the pace, and judging outcomes). Autodidactic learning occurs in the least structured situations with the highest learner autonomy possible. It is learner-initiated and planned. The autodidactic learner is autonomous but not necessarily self-sufficient. He or she may seek experts and resources to help in achieving goals, but planning is quite loose. These situations are the most effective for fulfilling special learning needs when a high degree of autonomy and spontaneity is necessary; formal recognition by accreditation is not necessary (Van Oona, 1992).

Little learning occurs in isolation from the environment, and all types of learning can be hard to distinguish from each other. Yet, informal learning continues, and adult education researchers are still studying it (see also English, 1999).

See also: learning organization, prior learning assessment and recognition, self-directed learning.

References and Further Reading

Coombs, P. H., Prosser, R. C., & Ahmed, M. (1973). *New paths to learning: for rural children and youth.* New York: International Council for Education and Development.

English, L. M. (1999). Learning from changes in religious leadership: A study of informal and incidental learning at the parish level. *International Journal of Lifelong Education, 18*(5), 385–394.

Kerka, S. (2000). Incidental learning. Trends and Issues. Retrieved December 10, 2003, from the ERIC database (ERIC Document Reproduction Service NO. ED446234)http://ericacve.org/docgen.asp? tbl=tia&ID=140

Livingstone, D. W. (2004). Exploring the iceberg of adult learning: Findings of the first Canadian survey of informal learning practices. Retrieved January 1, 2004 from the Ontario Institute for Studies in Education/University of Toronto website: http://tortoise.oise.utoronto.ca/~dlivingstone/icebergs/index.html

Marsick, V. J., & Watkins, K. E. (1990). *Informal and incidental learning in the workplace.* London: Routledge.

Rothwell, W. J., & Kazanas, H. C. (1990). Informal learning in the workplace. *Performance and Instruction, 29*(3), 33–36.

Van Oona, B. (1992). Informal learning on the job. In A. C. Tuijnman & M. Van Der Kamp (Eds.), *Learning across the lifespan: Theories, research, policies* (pp. 125–136). Oxford, UK: Pergamon.

Watkins, K. E., & Marsick, V. J. (1992). Towards a theory of informal and incidental learning in organizations. *International Journal of Lifelong Education, 11*(4), 287–300.

Mohamed Hrimech

International Adult Education

International adult education refers to the efforts of adult educators to work globally in a diversity of contexts in order to educate for liberation, equality and freedom. International adult education shares similarities with comparative adult education and global adult education. In fact adult education has always been an international practice. There are records in the city of Toronto in Canada of a first meeting of the Mechanics' Institute in the mid-19th century. The Mechanics' Institute was created as an English working-men's adult education body in 1815. The Women's Institute, a women's adult education organization in England and in many parts of the Commonwealth, was created in Ontario in the late 19th century. Oscar Olsson, the "father" of the Swedish study-circle movement borrowed many ideas from the late 19th century Chautauqua adult education movement in New York State in the United States. The rise of the modern practice of adult education in Western European countries is linked to the reform movements arising in response to the rapacious nature of early industrial capitalism. The invention of industrial capitalism in Europe began a process of previously unheard of wealth-creation for the small class of owners and investors. And with the creativity, the invention, and the excitement of the mechanical age came an unprecedented call for workers. The rural areas of England and Germany and later elsewhere were depleted with entire villages disappearing into the larger cities. Not only were young men drawn to the factories, but women and even children.

It was not long, however, before those working in the early factories began to call for changes to the smoke and dust-filled workplaces, long hours, and brutal conditions for women and children. Working people and their allies slowly began the collective struggle for shorter working hours, fewer working days, better working conditions and a legal age limit for hiring young people. The systematic study of the lives of working people which are associated with the early work of Marx in Germany and Engels in England supported the aspirations of workers with analytical precision. The rise of organized labor movements as well as the temperance movements was associated with the rise in expectations by women for the vote and by working women and men for the right to learn. The adult education movements of Education Populaire in late 19th century France or the Workers' Education Association of the early 20th century in England and Sweden were more formal responses to social demand for learning by adults, but there were many more local formal and informal ways in which adults began to seek out learning. Ideas, inspiration and practices were shared across borders and languages as a matter of normal practice.

The countries of the majority (often referred to as developing) world have similarly contributed to and benefited from international sharing in the field of adult education. Countries which were part of European empires were influenced by the adult education practices of those empires. The *animation social* of 1960s' Senegal had antecedents in both France and Quebec, whilst the Oxford Extra-Mural Delegacy of England set up university-based adult education centers in most of the British colonial universities. But just as colonial hegemony was being held in place through shared administrative and institutional structures, the newly emerging educated leaders of India, of Africa and elsewhere were sharing dreams of Independence with their counterparts whom they met while studying in the metropolitan countries or locally in evening classes on ideas of democracy. Julius Nyerere, founding president of Tanzania, visited Ruskin College, the workers education college at Oxford in 1964 and used it as a model for Kivukoni College, the political education training center for the Independence movement in his country. The use of non-violence as both a political and an educational tool by Gandhi and his followers in India spread around the world to those who would struggle for freedom everywhere. The cry for widespread accessible education for all became a plank in the pre and post-independence movements of most of the countries of the majority world. Literacy and the right to learn were early rallying cries for adult educators everywhere.

Adult Education in an Age of Globalization

At the global level, the 21st century has similarities with the late 19th-century Europe before the social reforms and legislation. Capital is king; global capital is emperor. The gaps between the rich and the poor at a global level have grown to unprecedented levels. Both high-intensity and low-intensity warfare has spread to many parts of the globe, while entire species of plants and animals are disappearing at an alarming rate. Even when the effects of global industrial life on the biosphere are known, such as the case of global warming, the most powerful corporate interests are able to block large-scale ameliorative measures. Global capitalism renamed as globalization is in its primitive most savage stage. And when global capital is politically aligned as in the United States of America with imperial claims, global capitalism takes on an ugly and violent face (Welton, 2003). The reforming qualities of the early 20th-century labor, health and political reforms have yet to curb the excess of global capital.

Resistance to global capitalism takes many forms; the rise of what some call global civil society (Hall, 2000), the proliferation of global social movements (Edwards & Gaventa, 2001), and the rise of extremist anti-Western organizations (Mojab, 2000). Adult education, like all other forms of human activity, exists as contested terrain at the local, national and international levels. It is a world which is simultaneously, "coming apart and coming together" (Serrano, 1999). Adult education is called upon for many contradictory purposes including: facilitating the global utopia; making the best of the situation; and supporting transformation towards a more humane world (Hall).

Historic International Conferences

The international adult education movement has achieved its highest levels of visibility through a series of international or world conferences. The first such international event took place in Oxford, England in 1929 organized by the now defunct World Association for Adult Education. During the last half of the 20th century and well into the 21st century two organizations have taken the lead in the organizing of these events: UNESCO, the United Nations Educational, Scientific and Cultural Organization made up of the governments of member states, and the ICAE, the International Council for Adult Education. Together they have organized 11 international conferences and world assemblies of adult education. UNESCO international conferences have taken place in 1949 (Elsinsore, Denmark), 1960 (Montreal, Canada), 1972 (Tokyo, Japan), 1985 (Paris), and 1997 (Hamburg). The World Assemblies of Adult Education have taken place in 1976 (Dar es Salaam, Tanzania), 1982 (Marly-le-Roi, France), 1985 (Buenos Aires, Argentina), 1994 (Cairo, Egypt), and 2001 (Ocho Rios, Jamaica). In addition, adult educators have been active in raising the call for adult learning within the many high-level United Nations conferences during the late 20th and early 21st centuries, including the UN Women's Conference (1985, Nairobi, Kenya and 1995, Beijing, China); Environment (1972, Stockholm and 1992 Rio de Janeiro); Social Development (1995, Copenhagen, Denmark); Population (1992, Cairo, Egypt); and Racism and Discrimination (2002, Durban, South Africa).

Adult educators have played a strong role, particularly the women in adult education, both as organizers and as contributors in the various global events associated with the anti-globalization or alternative development movements. These include all of the four World Social Forum events which have taken place in Porto Alegre, Brazil, and one in Mumbai, India in 2004.

International Organizations

The UNESCO Institute for Education (UIE) in Hamburg, Germany is the focal point for United Nations adult education policy developments (www.UNESCO.org/education/uie). The UIE was the organizer of the largest adult education conference in history, the Fifth International Conference on Adult Education which produced the widely quoted Hamburg Declaration (UNESCO, 1997). The UIE publishes the *International Review of Education* and a broad range of studies on adult and lifelong learning. The Organization for Economic Co-operation and Development (OECD), often called the rich-nations club, has taken the lead over the years in research and promulgation of a variety of recurrent and lifelong learning policy studies; it regularly conducts national reviews of adult education policies amongst its members (OECD, 1996). The lead non-governmental organization in the field is the International Council for Adult Education. With member associations in 100 countries and a Secretariat in Montevideo, Uruguay, the ICAE publishes the journal *Convergence*, collaborates with the UIE in the promotion of the exciting and successful United Nations Adult Learning Week activities, and facilitates dialogue and discussion at the international level among civil society and social movement partners (GEO-ICAE, 2003).

The Institute for International Cooperation of the German Adult Education Association, based in Bonn, Germany provides financial support for a wide range of adult education associations in the majority world and in the former Eastern European countries (www.iiz-dvv.de). It publishes the journal *Adult Education and Development*, a twice-yearly journal for adult education in Africa, Asia and Latin America. The *International Journal of Lifelong Education* is a bi-monthly peer-reviewed academic publication which provides an important international forum (www.tandf.co.uk). The Latin American Council for Adult Education (CEAAL), the Asia and South Pacific Bureau for Adult Education (ASPBAE) and the European Adult Education Association (EAA) are active and effective regional bodies. The National Institute of Adult Continuing Education (NIACE) of England and Wales plays a leadership role in support of Adult Literacy Week activities, and publishes the journal *Studies in the Education of Adults*, as well as an extensive list of books.

Trends in International Adult Education

One of the strongest trends is a two-track international policy environment. The wealthy industrialized nations have seen a dramatic growth in the development of wide-ranging and creative policies of lifelong learning (Bélanger & Federighi, 2000), while the poor majority-world countries have seen their aspirations shaped along the lines of the UNESCO and World Bank policies of *Education for All* (Torres, 2003). The EFA policy framework calls for a lowest common denominator approach to universal access for girls and boys at primary education levels and a commitment to basic adult literacy by the year 2015 (UNESCO, 2000).

Another trend is the emergence of new agents of adult learning. Adult education is not limited primarily to organized state-supported formal provision. The business world provides learning opportunities for its employees, which range from direct job-related skills to access to courses for individual creativity and growth (Bélanger & Federighi, 2000, p. 60). The shift from an emphasis on cure to prevention in health has led to a dramatic increase in health-related adult learning and shows signs of increasing further (Bélanger, p. 58). Social movements themselves are increasingly being understood as rich learning environments where new knowledge is created and shared in both formal and informal ways (Hall, Richards, Martin, Paavo, & Philip, 2004).

A final trend is the virtual disappearance of adult education from major international agendas. In spite of the fact that the Hamburg Conference in 1997 had more than 1,600 participants from over 122 countries, adult education has fallen off the agenda of at least two of the most important educational policy statements, the *Education for All Goals* set in Dakar, Senegal in 2000, (UNESCO, 2000) and the *Millennium Development Goals* (MDGs) set forward in the UN *Millennium Declaration.* (United Nations, 2000) There is no *direct* reference to *adult education* in either the *Education for All Goals* or the *MDGs* (Buchert, 2003).

See also: comparative adult education, problematizing learning, social movement learning, social movements .

References and Further Reading

Bélanger, P., & Federighi, P. (2000). *Unlocking people's creative forces: A transnational study of adult learning policies*. Hamburg: UNESCO Institute for Education.

Buchert, L. (2003). Financing adult education: Constraints and opportunities. *Adult Education and Development. 60*, 67–82.

Edwards, M., & Gaventa, J. (Eds.). (2001). *Global citizen action*. Boulder, CO: Lynne Rienner.

GEO-ICAE. (2003). *Education for inclusion throughout life*. Montevideo, Uruguay: International Council for Adult Education.

Hall, B. L. (2000). Global civil society: Theorizing a changing world. *Convergence, 33*(1–2), 33–56.

Hall, B. L., Richards, T., Martin, D., Paavo, A., & Philip S. (2004). The kitchen, the shop floor and the streets: Social movement learning in the 21st century. In D. E. Clover (Ed.), *Proceedings of the Conjoint Conference of the Adult Education Research Conference and the Canadian Association for the Study of Adult Education*, May 27–30 (pp. 541–547). University of Victoria, British Columbia.

Mojab, S. (2000) Adult education in the Middle East: Etatism, patriarchy, and the dynamics of change. *Convergence, 33*(3), 9–24.

OECD. (1996). *Lifelong Learning for All*. Paris: OECD.

Serrano, I. (1999). *Coming apart: Coming together in CIVICUS, Civil society at the millennium*. West Hartford, CN: Kumarian.

Torres, R. M. (2003). Lifelong learning: A new momentum and a new opportunity for adult basic learning and education (ABLE) in the South. *Adult Education and Development*, supplement to no. 60.

United Nations (2000). *Millennium Declaration*. (Declaration of the General Assembly, New York).

UNESCO (1997). *The Hamburg Declaration and the agenda for the future*. Hamburg: Unesco Institute for Education.

UNESCO (2000). *The Dakar Framework for Action: Education for All: Meeting our collective commitments*. Paris: UNESCO.

Welton, M. R. (2003). No escape from the hard things of the world: Learning the lessons of empire. *International Journal of Lifelong Education, 22*(6), 635–651.

Budd L. Hall

Internet Resources

Because of the rapid growth of the Internet, identifying and accessing Internet resources related to adult education and adult learning has become a major challenge. Such resources have proliferated during the past decade and that growth will likely continue. Statistics indicate that the Internet has become a primary method of dissemination for many organizations: between 1998 and 2002, the number of websites grew from 2,636,000 to 8,712,000, a growth of 217%. Public sites with an average size of 441 pages represented 35% of the total sites (O'Neill, Lavoie, & Bennett, 2003). Google, the primary search engine used to search the Internet, indexes 4.3 billion web pages and is searched more than 200 million times daily (Liedke, 2004). Because of the web's loose organization, a number of issues are associated with Internet use as a vehicle for disseminating adult education including locating information and judging its quality. Equitable access to the available resources is also an issue because of lack of technological infrastructure in developing countries.

Categories of Information

Internet resources in adult education and adult learning can be grouped into categories including databases and websites. Several categories exist within websites, including those containing scholarly materials, websites sponsored by adult education-related organizations, and websites with materials that can be used in adult learning. These categories are not mutually exclusive but they serve as a way of organizing what is, on the surface, a rather chaotic library of information.

Databases

Although they predate the Internet by many years, databases are one source of information in adult education available through the Internet, which provide a way of indexing and storing information for easy retrieval. In the United States, they were originally developed in 1890 to store census information using punched cards (National Research Council, 1999). As computer technology advanced during the 20th century, databases became the primary mode of organizing, storing, and retrieving bibliographic information. Some databases, such as ERIC (Educational Resources Information Center), that were developed prior to computerized searching, were initially made available through print indexes. ERIC was also available through online searching using a terminal that did not include a microprocessor (referred to as a "dumb" terminal), and then on CD-ROM. Now, bibliographic databases are routinely made available through the Internet, although access to most is limited to those who are affiliated with a college or university library or a local public library. The ERIC database is the exception since it can be searched directly over the web.

Most databases are also restricted in terms of content because they only include the periodical or journal literature. Again, the ERIC database is an exception because it also includes a large collection of materials such as research reports, conference papers and proceedings, monographs, policy reports, opinion papers, curricular materials, and other publications that might not be readily available. Since its inception in 1966, the ERIC system has included adult education materials, and is widely considered to be one of the most comprehensive sources for adult education. Although ERIC is funded by the United States Department of Education, the adult education collection is international in nature as many English-language materials produced throughout the world have been included in the system. The complete database can be accessed and searched via the Internet at the following URLs (web addresses): http:// www.eduref.org/Eric/ or http:// www.eric.ed.gov/searchdb/index.html. During the past decade, ERIC has moved towards full-text electronic document delivery, but at the present time users must pay a fee for the service. ERIC includes many adult education materials that are available on websites, and which can be retrieved directly from the source using the URL located in the abstract. Currently, the ERIC system is in a transition period with the goal of making more materials available in full text at no charge.

Dissertation Abstracts from UMI (University Microfilms International) is another database that contains information on adult and continuing education. All doctoral dissertations from accredited institutions located in North America plus 200 other institutions are included. Since 1988, Dissertation Abstracts has also included some masters' theses. Because many individuals receiving advanced degrees in adult and continuing education do not produce further published materials on their graduate research, Dissertation Abstracts is an important resource. UMI makes the database available in different versions; the digital version provides a 24-page preview of all entries since 1997; the online version only provides an abstract. The drawback is the limited availability of either version, although by accessing UMI directly at http://www.il.proquest.com/hp/Products/Dissertations.html individuals may search the last 2 years of the digital version. Many institutions, however, have a subscription that allows its students and faculty to search the entire database.

Because adult education draws from a wide variety of disciplines, other online databases may yield relevant information. By becoming familiar with the databases available through either public or institutional libraries, adult educators can learn which are most relevant for their needs.

Websites

The kinds and types of adult education materials available on websites are diverse; the following categories provide an overview with some examples of what can be found.

Scholarly Materials

A number of websites contain scholarly materials, primarily in the form of conference proceedings and reports. In addition to the sites listed below, many professors of adult education maintain personal websites that contain copies of papers and journal articles that they have authored.

- Adult Education Research Conference. http://www.edst.educ.ubc.ca/aerc/ Provides abstracts of papers presented since 1993, and full text of papers presented since 1997. Primarily North American in emphasis.
- Adult Higher Education Alliance Archived Proceedings. http://www.ahea.org/archieved_proceedings.htm The site of this United States organization currently provides full text of proceedings from 1998 through

2001, with plans to make available proceedings since 1984.

- Canadian Association for the Study of Adult Education Conference Proceedings. http://www.oise.utoronto.ca/CASAE/cnfmain/maincnf.html Includes full text of conference proceedings from 1998 onwards.
- National Adult Literacy Database/Full Text Documents. http://www.nald.ca/fulltext/search/ This Canadian site includes full-text reports, directories, articles, and reviews. Many entries are specific to Canada but general subjects also appear.
- National Center for the Study of Adult Learning and Literacy (NCSALL). http://gseweb.harvard.edu/~ncsall/ Results of NCSALL research projects are available in a number of formats on this site including full reports, briefs, and the "Focus on Basics" newsletter. NCSALL is funded by the United States Department of Education.
- New Approaches to Lifelong Learning (NALL). http://www.oise.utoronto.ca/depts/sese/csew/nall/ Housed at the University of Toronto's Ontario Institute for Studies in Education, NALL (funded from 1996 to 2001) was a Canadian National Research Network charged to "study informal learning and its relation to formal and continuing education throughout the life course." Numerous working papers and other documents are available on the site. A successor to NALL, the Work and Lifelong Learning Research Network (WALL) has been funded for 2002 to 2006. WALL can be accessed at http://www1.oise.utoronto.ca/research/wall/
- Standing Conference on University Teaching and Research in the Education of Adults (SCUTREA) Proceedings. http://www.scutrea.ac.uk/links.html The 1997 through 1999 SCUTREA proceedings are available. SCUTREA is a United Kingdom organization.

Adult Education Organizations

Organizations related to adult education host websites that contain a variety of information, and in addition to information related to their activities, many contain full text of publications and links to other resources.

- Adult Learning Australia (ALA). http://www.ala.asn.au/ ALA, the major organization representing adult learning in Australia, contains the full text of a number of research publications and reports as well as general information about the organization. Its links page is divided into several sections, one of which provides links to sites outside of Australia.
- Adult Learning Documentation and Information Network (ALADIN). http://www.unesco.org/education/aladin/ Sponsored by the UNESCO Institute for Education, ALADIN is a worldwide network linking adult education resource centers, libraries, and clearinghouses. Organiza-tions that provide information related to adult learning are listed in its membership directory and the links page points to full-text documents from a host of organizations throughout the world.
- European Society for Research on the Education of Adults (ESREA). http://www.esrea.org ESREA promotes and disseminates research and theory on adult education through research

networks, conferences, and publications.

- Information Network for Adult Education in Southeast Europe. http://www.inebis.com/ This site from the Institute for International Co-operation of the German Adult Education Association provides brief histories and overviews of the state of adult education in Albania, Bosnia/Hertzegovina, Bulgaria, Croatia, Macedonia, Romania, Slovenia, and Yugoslavia.
- International Council for Adult Education (ICAE). http://www.icae.org.uy/ ICAE is an international partnership of adult learners and adult education organizations from throughout the world. A number of documents on lifelong learning and adult education are available in full text through the site.
- National Institute of Adult Continuing Education (NIACE). http://www.niace.org.uk NIACE is the major non-governmental adult learning organization in Great Britain. In addition to information about NIACE activities and publications, the site contains the full text of a number of briefs, many of which present the findings of research studies conducted by NIACE.

Adult Learning Materials/Information

Information available through websites represents a veritable treasure trove of information for use by and with adult learners. By accessing the Internet, adult learners on their own can tap into what has been characterized as "possibly . . . one of the most powerful and important Self-directed learning tools in existence" (Gray, 1999, p. 120). Teachers of adults can also use the Internet as a teaching tool and as a source of learning materials. The sites listed below are representative of the hundreds of thousands of sites that can be accessed for information and materials for adult learning.

- Adult Literacy Core Curriculum. http://www.dfes.gov.uk/curriculum_literacy/ This interactive website is designed to allow teachers to search the literacy curriculum for the United Kingdom, investigate the links for appropriate guidance in Access for All, and then save, store, and/or print appropriate materials for use in learning or lesson plans.
- Adults Learning Mathematics (ALM). http://www.alm-online.org/ ALM is an international research forum that brings together researchers and practitioners in adult mathematics/numeracy teaching and learning to promote the learning of mathematics by adults. Site contains abstracts from conference presentations and full text of newsletters beginning in 1995.
- The Change Agent. http://www.nelrc.org/changeagent/ Subtitled, "Adult Education for Social justice: News, Issues & Ideas," the Change Agent newsletter from the United States provides a resource for teachers and learners that focuses on civic participation and social justice as a part of teaching and learning.
- The Literacy List. http://www.alri.org/literacylist.html/ The Literacy List is a United States-based site that includes a large collection of free adult basic education and English as a second language and English for speakers of other languages websites, listservs, and other Internet resources for adult basic education teachers and learners.

- Making of America (MOA). http://moa.umdl.umich.edu and http://moa.cit.cornell.edu/moa Funded by the Andrew W. Mellon Foundation, MOA uses digital technology to make, preserve, and make available a significant number of primary sources related to the development of the infrastructure of the United States. Those interested in US history can access old letters, diaries, manuscripts and other historically relevant documents that formerly were only available in special library collections.

Related Issues

The use of the Internet as a means of disseminating adult education resources gives rise to several issues. Three that present the greatest challenges or deterrents in making effective use of Internet resources are: locating the information desired, judging the quality of information sources and websites, and access to the Internet.

Searching Skills for Locating Information

"Translating a mental desire for information into an effective" search strategy may be "the greatest challenge of all" (Kline, 2002, p. 252). Whether using an online database or an Internet search engine, individuals looking for information must have some skill in order to locate what they want. Effective searching involves not only knowledge of the particular search tool being used, but also skills in problem-solving, decision-making, and critical thinking (Fitzgerald, Lovin, & Branch, 2003). Research that looked at the attitudes of adult learners towards the Internet found that inadequate knowledge and skills for accessing Internet resources resulted in limited results (Collins & Veal, 2004). Novice searchers, in particular, find searching the Internet to be frustrating, time consuming, and unproductive in terms of finding what they need (Fitzgerald et al.). Searching skills can be improved by spending time learning about the features of Internet search engines and online databases, and through practice. Libraries frequently offer search instruction at no cost.

Judging the Quality of Information

The Internet allows almost instantaneous access to "a wealth of information without the necessity of critique or interaction," but requires skills to "sift through it and use it to produce a creative, balanced, and informed point of view" (Rothenberg, 1999, p. B8). Resources found on the Internet can be evaluated with the same criteria that are used for any other professional resource: author; source or publisher; currency or date; accuracy or quality, including style and tone; objectivity or perspective; and scope are all areas that should be considered in evaluating Internet resources (Tillotson, 2002). Some additional criteria for evaluating websites (based on research on adults' evaluation of websites) include professional design, lack of commercialism, articles that contain references and citations, inclusion of credentials of authors, and contact information for the site host including physical address. (Tillston).

Access

Although access to the Internet has expanded rapidly in industrialized countries, the fact remains that many adult educators and adult learners have either limited access or none at all. "The global potential of information and communication technologies for improving the quality of adult learning continues to be hindered by the lack of requisite infrastructures" (UNESCO Institute for Education, 2003, p. 14). To a large extent, the industrialized countries have succeeded in integrating technology into their adult education systems, whereas developing countries continue to lack policies and resources for doing so (ibid.). Figures on access to and use of the Internet on the Organization for Economic Co-operation and Development's (OECD) website support this statement, for they reveal that Internet access and use is common in the wealthier OECD member nations but drops off in such countries as Turkey and Mexico (http://www.oecd.org/LongAbstract/0,2546,en_2825_495656_2766782_1_1_1_1,00.html). Equitable access to Internet resources across the globe will continue to be an issue for the foreseeable future.

See also: journals.

References and Further Reading

Collins, K. M. T., & Veal, R. E. (2004). Off-campus adult learner's levels of library anxiety as a predictor of attitudes toward the Internet. *Library and Information Science Research, 26*, 5–14.

Fitzgerald, M. A., Lovin, V., & Branch, R. M. (2003). The gateway to educational materials: An evaluation of an online resource for teachers and an exploration of user behavior. *Journal of Technology and Teacher Education, 11*(1), 21–51.

Gray, D. E. (1999). The internet in lifelong learning: Liberation or alienation? *International Journal of Lifelong Education, 18*(2), 119–126.

Kline, V. (2002). Missing links: The quest for better search tools. *Online Information Review, 26*(4), 252–255.

Liedtke, M. (2004, March 23). Microsoft keeps giving ground in battle to set online agenda. *Columbus Dispatch*, p. D1.

National Research Council. (1999). *Funding a revolution: Government support for computing research*. Washington, DC: National Academy Press.

O'Neill, E. T., Lavoie, B. F., & Bennett, R. (2003). Trends in the evolution of the public web. *D-Lib Magazine*, 9(4). Retrieved July 17, 2003 from the Online Computer Library Center website: http:/wcp.oclc.org/

Rothenberg, D. (1999, July 16). Use the web to connect with "ideas in motion." *Chronicle of Higher Education, 45*(45), B8.

Tillotson, J. (2002). Web site evaluation: A survey of undergraduates. *Online Information Review, 26*(6), 392–403.

UNESCO Institute for Education. (2003). *Recommitting to adult education and learning: Synthesis report of the CONFINTEA V midterm review meeting*. September 6–11, 2003. Bangkok, Thailand. Retrieved February 21, 2003 from http://www.unesco.org/education/uie/pdf/recommitting.pdf

Susan Imel

J

Journal Writing

Journals come in many different shapes, sizes, formats and forms, and there are many different purposes for using a journal. Some alternative names for a journal are learning log, diary, notebook, course journal and other more creative terms such as "think place." Portfolio is a word that may sometimes be applicable as well (see below). Journals may be graphic, on audio-tape or video and are now often in electronic form. While for convenience this account will describe written pen-on-paper journals, it is interesting to speculate on how the use of different media can affect the process of writing and the learning that results (Moon, 1999a).

Generally speaking, the features that would distinguish a learning journal from other writing are that it will be written over a period of time, and that it is generally reflective (Moon, 1999a, 2004). A learning journal tends to focus on ongoing issues and there is some intention to learn from either the process or from its results. This suggests that a learning journal is not an events diary or a record or log in the ship-log sense; it also excludes the kinds of portfolio that are simply collections of pieces of work with no reflective commentary.

Learning journals are usually seen as a vehicle for reflection. It seems reasonable to assume that all adults and older children reflect, but some more overtly than others. Some reflect easily and will be familiar with keeping a journal (or diary); some will overtly reflect only when there is an incentive or when guidance or conditions in their environment are conducive. Some will say that they do not reflect at all, and those setting up learning journal activities will need to recognize the difficulties here and take measures to help them. Since it seems likely that reflection is an inherent part of good-quality learning (Moon, 2004), it is not unreasonable to assume that all reflect, but they may find reflective writing unfamiliar.

Although journal writing is becoming more common, there might well be assumptions that the process should primarily be of interest to those working in disciplines that are, in some way, literary. This is not the case. Journal writing can be of use at most stages of education (from 5 or 6 years up), across any discipline (Fulwiler, 1987), and can benefit any situation in which a person is trying to learn something. In higher education, initial work on journals seems to have been done in the context of professional education, but there are examples of journal use in at least 32 disciplines in the literature (Moon, 1999a). Of key importance in the use of journal activities, is the clear and explicit understanding of the purpose for which a journal is being used. Too often, journal activities are set up because they seem a good idea. In a review of more than 100 papers, over 18 purposes for the use of learning journals were found (Moon, 1999a). Most journals will fulfill more than one purpose, and sometimes the purposes set by a tutor are not the same as those that will be perceived by a student. An example of this comes from Salisbury's (1994) research in which the students perceived – rightly or wrongly – that "self-flagellation" was valued by tutors who set their journal work. They purposefully set out to provide plenty of confessional material.

Purposes for Learning Journals

- To record experience and to facilitate learning from experience;
- To support understanding and the representation of understanding;
- To develop critical thinking or a questioning attitude;
- To encourage metacognition (awareness of own learning behavior);
- To increase active involvement in and ownership of learning;
- To increase ability in reflection and thinking and problem-solving;
- To enhance reflective practice or for personal/professional development;
- For therapeutic purposes or as a means of supporting behavior change;
- To enhance creativity and improve self-expression or to give voice;
- To support planning and progress in research or a project.

Journals may be used simply to ensure that learners practice writing, or they can be organized as a collaborative tool so that knowledge about attitudes or processes are shared. Out of the context of formal education, they may be used to accompany "life" projects such as moving house, or aspects of personal development, or projects such as the writing of a book. The work of Field (1951), Rainer (1978) and Progoff (1975) illustrates this.

While there may be different purposes for learning journals and different structures (see below), there are some generalizations that can be made about how we learn from them. Firstly, journal writing encourages reflection, and reflection is associated with good quality learning where the intention of the learner is to develop a personal understanding of the material and to relate it to what is already known. Secondly, we learn because journal writing is a process that accentuates favorable conditions for learning. Learning journals encourage independent learning and because writers "own" the learning, it is likely that it will be more meaningful to them (Moon, 1999b). Writing a journal provides an opportunity to order thoughts and to make sense of situations or of information. Also learning from a journal forces the learner to cope with ideas that are contradictory or not straight-forward; counteracting what can be called "spoon-feeding" in formal education with handouts and lecture notes on the web.

Thirdly, writing in a journal encourages metacognition, which is the understanding of a person about his or her own mental processes. There is evidence to suggest that the learning of those who are more aware of their functioning is generally better. Lastly, the act of writing is associated with learning or the enhancement of learning (Elbow, 1981).

Journals may be structured or unstructured, or may contain both. An unstructured journal consists of free writing. Structure in a journal is a means of focusing either the manner in which a learner works with their journal, or the subject matter itself. A simple form of structure is a request that the learner considers a particular topic – or it may be in the form of a question posed. Sometimes learning journals are structured around the ideas of the Kolb cycle of experiential learning (Kolb, 1984), or the use of imaginary dialogues with people, events, projects and so on. This latter work is derived from Progoff (1975). Moon (1999a) also gives many journal exercises.

Learning journals may require assessment, sometimes because learners would not maintain them unless they were assessed. The design of the assessment procedure should always be rooted in the purpose for which the journal has been set. Within this, it will take into account whether the focus of the learning is on the process of writing a journal (e.g., the development of reflective practice), or on what has been learned as a result of keeping the journal (e.g., learning how to teach). In the latter case any assessment task would suffice – essay, examination and so on. If it is the process of journal writing that is to be assessed, then the task will need to focus more directly on the journal itself; the journal is directly assessed or there is an account written of how the journal demonstrates the process under consideration.

There can be considerable ethical and confidence issues that arise with the use of learning journals in formal educational situations (English & Gillen, 2001). Are they confidential to the learner or are they shown to tutors? If they are shown, what difference does this make to the nature of the writing and reflection? There may also be concerns that material written in journals breaks ethical codes – for example, if it names patients or identifies bad practice in professional situations or breaks confidences. These possibilities need to be taken into account in the design of the journal.

See also: autobiography, ethics, narrative, portfolio, reflective learning, reflective practice, writing.

References and Further Reading

Elbow, P. (1981). *Writing with power: Techniques for mastering the writing process*. New York: Oxford University Press.

English, L. M., & Gillen, M. A. (Eds.). (2001). *Promoting journal writing in adult education. New Directions for Adult and Continuing Education*, No. 90. San Francisco: Jossey-Bass.

Field, J. (1951). *A life of one's own*. Harmonsworth: Penguin.

Fulwiler, T. (1987). *The journal book*. Portsmouth, NH: Heinemann.

Kolb, D. A. (1984). *Experiential learning as the science of learning and development*. Englewood Cliffs, NJ: Prentice Hall.

Moon, J. (1999a). *Learning journals: A handbook for academics, students and professional development*. London: Kogan Page.

Moon, J. (1999b). *Reflection in learning and professional development*. London: Kogan Page.

Moon, J. (2004). *A handbook of reflective and experiential learning*. London: Routledge Falmer.

Progoff, I. (1975). *At a journal workshop*. New York: Dialogue House Library.

Rainer, T. (1978). *The new diary*. Los Angeles: JP Tarcher.

Salisbury, J. (1994). Becoming qualified – an ethnography of a post-experience teacher training course. Unpublished doctoral dissertation. University College of Wales, Cardiff.

Jenny Moon

Journals

Because adult learning takes place in many disciplines and settings, a diverse array of refereed and non-refereed journals publish articles relevant to practice, research, and theory in adult education. Peer-reviewed or refereed journals continue to be privileged as knowledge sources, although their dominance has been challenged in recent years. One factor contributing to the consideration of alternative channels of knowledge production is the rise of electronic journals (e-journals). In 1991, Brockett reported that e-journals were just beginning to appear in adult education, but he foresaw that electronic publishing was likely to have an impact on knowledge dissemination and use in the future. This article reviews some current issues involved in peer review and electronic publishing related to adult education and describes the rich variety of periodicals that publish material useful to adult educators, primarily in English.

Refereed and Non-refereed Journals

In refereed journals, submitted manuscripts are evaluated anonymously by at least two reviewers prior to publication; through an anonymous review process, in which neither the reviewers nor authors know each other's identities (O'Neill & Sachis, 1998). In non-refereed journals, the editor and/or editorial board make publication decisions. In some, such as *New Directions for Adult and Continuing Education*, authors are invited to contribute articles on a theme. Non-refereed journals are important sources of practice descriptions, dialogue, and information about issues in the field (Gadbow, 2002–03). An argument in favor of peer review is that it ensures the quality and integrity of published scholarship (O'Neill & Sachis); reviewers are supposed to have the experience, ability, and reputation that enable them to serve as gatekeepers of quality control (Taylor, Angelique, & Kyle, 2003).

Articles appearing in refereed journals are viewed as significantly more important in tenure and promotion decisions and are considered more credible and prestigious (Crawford 2003; O'Neill & Sachis, 1998). This perspective may vary by discipline; in a survey of Australian scholars (Houghton, Steele, & Henty, 2003), those in science and medical fields had a stronger preference for publishing in peer-reviewed journals and considered the prestige of the publication very important compared to researchers in social sciences, humanities, and the arts. However, concerns have been raised that the gatekeeping function of peer review perpetuates the status quo and limits or bars knowledge from non-traditional sources or scholars (O'Neill & Sachis).

Content analyses of published and rejected articles in adult education journals and analyses of peer-reviewer comments provide some support for this view. Hayes (1992), Hayes and Smith (1994), and Thompson and Schied (1996) found that prior to the 1990s, women's visibility as leaders, and perspectives derived from feminism, were limited in adult education journal articles. Taylor's (2001) analysis of all submissions to *Adult Education Quarterly* from 1989–99 showed that articles by academics, males, and North Americans continued to dominate. Taylor, Beck, and Ainsworth (2001) discovered that, although reviewers of an international adult education journal accepted the validity of qualitative research and were choosing more manuscripts in this area, they appeared to share an implicit set of standards that might indicate a narrow view of what counts as qualitative research. Jacobs (1998) reported the belief of reviewers for *Human Resource Development Quarterly* that qualitative articles do not meet standards of "rigor." Taylor et al. (2003) concluded that authors submitting articles on diversity-focused topics faced an extra, sometimes invisible set of standards and were sometimes subject to reviewers' cultural biases. Thus, although diversity of research perspectives, gender, and knowledge sources is increasing in articles accepted for publication in adult education journals (Taylor), the gatekeeping function of peer review may still be limiting the voices heard in these publications.

Electronic Journals

Electronic journals have been promoted as a way to broaden access to publication channels and widen the narrow gate, as well as drastically reducing the time to publication (Mizzaro, 2003). Yet most e-journals have maintained the format of paper journals (Poliner, 1994) and the small amount of data available indicates that peer review in e-journals is similar to the traditional process (Weller, 2000). In 1991, only 1.1% of 636 e-journals were refereed; in 1997, 11.4% of 9,182 e-journals used the peer review process. The first electronic journal in adult education, *New Horizons in Adult Education*, was established in 1987 as a peer-reviewed journal (Poliner). Some surveys show that publication in e-journals is still less accepted for tenure and promotion (Houghton, Steele, & Henty, 2003; Speier, Palmer, Wren, & Hahn, 1999; Weller 2000); on the other hand, Cronin and Overfelt's (1995) survey concluded that the publication medium may be a non-issue in promotion and tenure decisions.

Through electronic publishing, new modes of knowledge production are emerging that will change research practices and give rise to new information access and dissemination needs (Houghton et al., 2003). There are many uses for the knowledge disseminated in adult education journals, including sharing new information and ideas, fostering professional socialization, promoting critical thinking, and stimulating the development of new knowledge (Brockett, 1991; Gadbow, 2002–03). One measure of the quality of information is its value to audiences, which in adult education includes researchers, practitioners, and students at many levels. For this reason, Brockett calls for a more inclusive view of the knowledge base, citing the value of articles in such publications as the *Journal of Extension* and the *Journal of Continuing Education in Nursing*, the readers of which are largely not in the "mainstream" of adult education. The following list of journals takes a similarly inclusive view of these dissemination channels of adult education knowledge – refereed and non-refereed; electronic and print; mainstream and beyond.

Adult and Continuing Education

- *Adult Education Quarterly* (Sage Publications, http://www.sagepub.com; http://www.coe.uga.edu/aeq/). A quarterly refereed journal committed to advancing the understanding and practice of adult and continuing education.
- *Adult Learning* (American Association for Adult and Continuing Education; http://www.aaace.org). Non-refereed publication with a research-to-practice orientation.
- *Adults Learning* (National Institute of Adult Continuing Education – UK; http://www.niace.org.uk/Publications/Periodicals/Default.htm) Non-refereed publication

that is a forum for debate on all issues affecting adult learning.

- *Australian Journal of Adult Learning* (Adult Learning Australia; http://www.ala.asn.au/pubs/AJAL/ajal.htm). A dual refereed and non-refereed journal publishing articles on the theory, research, and practice of adult and community education with a prime focus on Australia.
- *Canadian Journal for the Study of Adult Education/La Revue Canadienne pour l'étude de l'éducation des Adultes* (Canadian Association for the Study of Adult Education; http://www.oise.utoronto.ca/CASAE/cjsae/cjsaetoc.html). Publishes peer-reviewed reports of research, critical reviews of the literature, and essays on issues in adult and continuing education.
- *Journal of Adult Education* (Mountain Plains Adult Education Association – United States; http://www.mpaea.org/). A refereed journal intended to serve as a voice for the translation of theory into practice.
- *New Directions for Adult and Continuing Education* (Jossey-Bass; http://www.josseybass.com/cda/product/0,,ACE,00.html) A non-refereed sourcebook series that explores issues of common interest to instructors, administrators, counselors, and policy-makers in a broad range of settings.
- *New Horizons in Adult Education* (Nova Southeastern University; http://www.nova.edu/~aed/horizons). The first scholarly refereed electronic journal, it publishes research, thought pieces, book reviews, conceptual analyses, case studies, and invitational columns.
- *New Zealand Journal of Adult Learning* (Massey University). A peer-reviewed forum for debate and analysis of theory, research, and practice related to adults as learners and their contexts, with a focus on New Zealand.
- *PAACE Journal of Lifelong Learning* (Pennsylvania Association for Adult Continuing Education; http://www.paacesite.org). A refereed journal published annually to encourage the improvement of practice in adult, continuing, community, and distance education through the dissemination of theoretical, empirical, historical, philosophical, and practical articles.
- *Perspectives: The New York Journal of Adult Learning* (New York Association of Continuing Community Education and Fordham University; http://www.retc.fordham.edu/perspectives/index.html). A peer-reviewed journal intended to address the areas of adult literacy, adult education, community education, continuing education, workforce training and development, and higher education around the world.

Journals With an International Focus

- *Adult Education and Development* (Institute for International Cooperation of the German Adult Education Association; http://www.iizdvv.de/ englisch/default.htm). A non-refereed journal intended to provide adult educators in Africa, Asia, Latin America, the Pacific, and Central, Southeast and Eastern Europe with a forum for dialogue and professional exchange.
- *Convergence* (National Institute of Adult Continuing Education on behalf of the International Council for Adult Education; http://www.niace.org.uk/Publicat

ions/Periodicals/Default.htm). A worldwide refereed journal of adult education that addresses issues, practices and developments in adult and non-formal education. Articles are in English, French and Spanish.

- *International Journal of Lifelong Education* (Taylor & Francis; http://www.tandf.co.uk/journals/). A peer-reviewed international forum for the debate of the principles and practice of lifelong, continuing, recurrent adult, and initial education and learning.
- *Lifelong Learning in Europe* (KVS Foundation and Finnish Adult Education Research Society; http://www.orivedenopisto.fi/kvs/kansanvalistusseura/lline.htm). Publishes articles in the following categories: research, policy, case studies, projects, information, and book reviews.
- *Studies in the Education of Adults* (National Institute of Adult Continuing Education; http://www.niace.org.uk/Publications/Periodicals/Default.htm). An inter-national refereed academic journal publishing theoretical, empirical, and historical studies from all sectors of post-initial education and training.

Continuing and Higher Education

- *Canadian Journal of University Continuing Education* (Canadian Association for University Continuing Education; http://www.extension.usask.ca/cjuce/cjuce.html). A refereed journal publishing analytical and research papers, reports, reviews, and commentaries of value to professional practice in continuing education, with emphasis on the Canadian context. Articles accepted in either English or French.
- *Continuing Higher Education Review* (Harvard University, on behalf of the University Continuing Education Association). A non-refereed journal on issues of national and international importance in continuing and higher education.
- *International Journal of University Adult Education* (International Congress of University Adult Education; http://www.lib.unb.ca/Texts/JUAE/). A refereed journal publishing articles and research papers related to university adult education.
- *Journal of Adult and Continuing Education* (National Institute of Adult Continuing Education; http://www.niace.org.uk/Publications/Periodicals/Default.htm). A refereed journal publishing theoretical and empirical work in the fields of adult, community, and continuing education.
- *Journal of Continuing Higher Education* (Association for Continuing Higher Education; http://www.acheinc.org/). Refereed journal serving as a forum for the reporting and exchange of information based on research, observations, and experience in continuing higher education.
- *Studies in Continuing Education* (Taylor & Francis; http://www.tandf.co.uk/journals/) Refereed journal concerned with all aspects of continuing, professional, and lifelong learning.

Adult Basic Education and Literacy

- *Adult Basic Education: An Interdisciplinary Journal for Adult Literacy Educators* (Commission on Adult Basic Education; http://www.coabe.org/journal/abe_journal.html). A peer-reviewed journal focused on ABE, ESL, and GED programs and many types of literacy programs.

- *Basic Skills* (Basic Skills Agency-UK; http://www.basic skills.co.uk/). Non-refereed journal intended primarily for anyone teaching basic skills to young people and adults in England and Wales.
- *Exploring Adult Literacy* (Adult Learning Division of the College Reading Association; http://literacy.kent.edu/cra/new.html). A peer-reviewed, interactive electronic journal intended to address the needs of adult literacy practitioners in adult basic education and family and workplace literacy.
- *Focus on Basics* (National Center for the Study of Adult Learning and Literacy; http://ncsall.gse.harvard. edu/fob/). Non-refereed journal dedicated to connecting research with practice in adult learning and literacy.
- *Journal of Adolescent and Adult Literacy* (International Reading Association; http://www.reading.org/publications/jaal/). Peer-reviewed literacy journal focused on the teaching of reading to adolescents and adults.
- *Literacy and Numeracy Studies: An International Journal in the Education and Training of Adults* (Centre for Language and Literacy, University of Technology, Sydney; http://www.education.uts.edu.au/lns/). Peer-reviewed publication focused on the many and complex ways that language, literacy and numeracy are implicated in adult life.
- *RaPAL Bulletin* (Research and Practice in Adult Literacy; http://www.literacy.lancaster.ac.uk/rapal/rapal.htm). Published by a British network of learners, teachers, managers and researchers in adult basic education dedicated to collaborative and reflective research.

English as a Second Language

- *Essential Teacher* (Teachers of English to Speakers of Other Languages, Inc.; http://www.tesol.org/pubs/magz/et.html). Non-refereed journal primarily dedicated to ESL and EFL teaching in pre-K-12, two- and four-year institutions of higher learning, and adult education.
- *ELT Journal* (Oxford University Press; http://www3.oup.co.uk/eltj/). Refereed publication for all those involved in the field of teaching English as a second or foreign language.
- *TESL-EJ* (University of California, Berkeley; http://www-writing.berkeley.edu/TESL-EJ/). E-journal that publishes peer-reviewed articles in English as a second or foreign language research and pedagogy.
- *TESOL Quarterly* (Teachers of English to Speakers of Other Languages, Inc.; http://www.tesol.org/pubs/magz/tq.html) a professional, refereed journal, publishes articles on topics of significance to individuals concerned with the teaching of ESL/EFL and standard English as a second dialect.

Human Resource Development/Training/Organizational Learning

- *Advances in Developing Human Resources* (Sage Publications in association with Academy of Human Resource Development; http://www.sagepub.com). Each issue of this peer-reviewed journal is devoted to a different topic central to the development of human resources.

- *Human Resource Development International* (Taylor & Francis on behalf of the Academy of Human Resource Development and the University Forum for Human Resource Development; http://www.tandf.co.uk/journals/). Peer-reviewed publication that promotes all aspects of practice and research that explore issues of individual, group, and organizational learning and performance.
- *Human Resource Development Quarterly* (Wiley InterScience for the American Society for Training and Development and the Academy of Human Resource Development; http://www3.interscience.wiley.com/cgi-bin/jtoc?ID=74000165). Refereed national forum for interdisciplinary exchange on the subject of HRD.
- *Human Resource Development Review* (Sage Publications in association with Academy of Human Resource Development; http://www.sagepub.com). Publishes non-refereed articles devoted to theory development, foundations of HRD, theory building methods, and integrative reviews of the literature.
- *International Journal of Training and Development* (Blackwell Publishing; http://www.blackwellpublishing.com/journal.asp?ref=1360-3736&site=1). An international, multidisciplinary peer-reviewed forum for the reporting of high-quality research, analysis, and debate for the benefit of the academic, corporate, and public policy communities.
- *Management Learning: The Journal for Managerial and Organizational Learning* (Sage Publications; http://www.sagepub.com). Refereed journal for those concerned with issues of learning, change, and development in organizations.
- *Journal of Workplace Learning* (Emerald; http://www.emeraldinsight.com/jwl.htm). A peer-reviewed journal focused on research into formal, informal, and incidental learning in the workplace for individuals, groups, and teams; work-based learning; and off-the-job learning for the workplace.
- *The Learning Organization* (Emerald; http://www.mcb.co.uk/tlo.htm). Peer-reviewed publication aimed at practitioners, consultants, advisers, researchers, teachers, or students seeking to advance their understanding of what the learning organization is and does.
- *T+D* (American Society for Training and Development; http://www.astd.org/astd/publications/td_magazine). A magazine that covers the art and science of developing people and the systems in which they work to produce results.
- *Training* (VNU Business Publications; http://www. Trainingmag.com/Training/ index.jsp). A professional development magazine for training, human resources, and business management professionals in all industries.

Distance Learning

- *American Journal of Distance Education* (Lawrence Erlbaum Associates; http:// www. erlbaum.com; http:// www. ajde.com). Publishes peer-reviewed articles on the role of print, electronic, telecommunications media and multimedia systems in the field of distance education.

- *Distance Education* (Taylor & Francis on behalf of the Open and Distance Learning Association of Australia; http://www.tandf.co.uk/journals/titles/01587919.asp). A peer-reviewed international journal supporting research and scholarly activities in the broad fields of open, flexible, and distance education and training.
- *International Review of Research in Open and Distance Learning* (Athabasca University; http://www.irrodl.org/) A refereed electronic journal that seeks to advance theory, research, and best practice in distance learning internationally.
- *Journal of Distance Education (*Canadian Association for Distance Education; http://cade.athabascau.ca/). Promotes and encourages Canadian research and scholarly work in distance education through refereed and non-refereed articles in either English or French.
- *Journal of Distance Learning* (Distance and e-Learning Education Association of New Zealand; http://www.deanz. org.nz/journal.htm). Annual refereed journal that includes both theoretical and empirically based research articles and reviews of interest to those involved in distance education and open learning.

Health Sciences/Psychology

- *Ageing International* (Transaction Publishers in cooperation with the International Federation on Ageing; http://www.transactionpub.com/). Non-refereed publication that examines current international aging issues of public concern about aging and older persons.
- *Canadian Journal on Aging* (Canadian Association on Gerontology; http://www.cagacg.ca/english/516_e.htm). A refereed publication that includes articles on aging concerned with biology, educational gerontology, health sciences, psychology, social sciences, and social policy and practice.
- *Education and Ageing* (Triangle Journals; http://www. triangle.co.uk/eda/index.htm). A refereed international journal that publishes scholarly articles addressing the issues of learning in the later years, the teaching of gerontology, and the implications of an aging society.
- *Educational Gerontology* (Taylor & Francis; http://www.tandf. co.uk/journals/). Publishes refereed articles in the fields of gerontology, adult education, and the social and behavioral sciences.
- *International Journal of Aging and Human Development* (Baywood; http://www.baywood.com). Emphasizes the psychological and social studies of aging and older persons and the human side of aging.
- *Journal of Adult Development* (Kluwer in collaboration with the Society for Research in Adult Development; http://www.kluweronline.com/issn/1068 0667/current). A transdisciplinary forum for the publication of peer-reviewed, theoretical and empirical articles on biological, psychological, and/or sociocultural development in young, middle, or late adulthood.
- *Journal of Continuing Education in the Health Professions* (B.C. Decker; http://www.bcdecker.com). Peer-reviewed journal of articles that examine the development, conduct, and evaluation of

continuing education programs in a variety of health professions.

- *Journal of Continuing Education in Nursing* (Slack, Inc.; http://www.slackinc.com/allied/jcen/jcenhome.htm). A bimonthly journal providing peer-reviewed articles on continuing nursing education.

Other Aspects of Adult Learning

- *Action Learning: Research and Practice* (Revans Institute for Action Learning; http://www.tandf.co.uk/journals,). Debuting in 2004, this journal will publish refereed and non-refereed articles designed to advance knowledge and assist the development of practice through the processes of action learning.
- *Action Research International* (Published by the Southern Cross Institute of Action Research and Southern Cross University Press; http://www.scu.edu.au/schools/gcm/ar/ari/arihome.html). A refereed electronic journal of action research that consists of an electronic discussion list to which papers can be submitted for comment and a second list that carries the accepted papers.
- *Action Research* (Sage Publications; http://www.sagepub.co.uk/). An international, interdisciplinary, refereed journal that publishes accounts of action research projects and explorations in the philosophy and methodology of action research.
- *Concept: The Journal of Contemporary Community Education, Practice, Theory* (National Institute of Adult Continuing Education; http://www.niace.org.uk/Publications/Periodicals/Default.htm). A practitioner journal sharing policy and practice in adult learning and contemporary community education.
- *Journal of Access, Policy and Practice* (National Institute of Adult Continuing Education; http://www.niace.org.uk/Publications/Periodicals/Default.htm). Refereed articles that explore educational policy and practice as it affects access to and wider participation in lifelong learning internationally.
- *Journal of Extension* (U.S. Cooperative Extension System; http://www.joe.org). Peer-reviewed e-journal that seeks to expand and update the research and knowledge base for extension professionals and other adult educators to improve their effectiveness.
- *Journal of Transformative Education* (Sage Publications; http://www.sagepub.com). A peer reviewed, scholarly journal focused on advancing the understanding, practice, and experience of transformative education.
- *Reflective Practice* (Carfax/Taylor & Francis; http://www.tandf.co.uk/journals/carfax/14623943.html). A refereed journal publishing papers that explore reflection within and on practice as an individual and collective activity.

See also: Internet resources.

References and Further Reading

Brockett, R. G. (1991). Disseminating and using adult education knowledge. In J. M. Peters & P. Jarvis (Eds.), *Adult education* (pp. 121–144). San Francisco: Jossey-Bass.

Crawford, B. D. (2003). Open-access publishing: Where is the value? *Lancet*, 362(9,395), 1,578–1,580.

Cronin, B., & Overfelt, K. (1995). E-journals and tenure. *Journal of the American Society for Information Science, 46*(9), 700–703.

Gadbow, N. (2002–2003). Adult education journals: Essential tools for professionals. *Perspectives: The New York Journal of Adult Learning, 1*(1), 6–8.

Hayes, E. R. (1992). The impact of feminism on adult education publications: An analysis of British and American journals. *International Journal of Lifelong Education*, 11(2), 125–138.

Hayes, E. R., & Smith, L. (1994). Women in adult education: An analysis of perspectives in major journals. *Adult Education Quarterly, 44*(4), 201–221.

Houghton, J. W. with Steele, C., & Henty, M. (2003). *Changing research practices in the digital information and communication environment*. Canberra, Australia: Australian Department of Education, Science and Training. Retrieved July 26, 2003, from http://www.dest.gov.au/highered/respubs/changing_res_prac/c_res_pract.pdf

Jacobs, R. L. (1998). The role of the "Human Resource Development Quarterly" in shaping the HRD profession: An eight and one-half year perspective. In *Academy of Human Resource Development Conference Proceedings*, edited by R. J. Torraco. Austin, TX: Academy of Human Resource Development. Retrieved February 14, 2004 from ERIC database (ERIC Document Reproduction Service No. ED428251).

Mizzaro, S. (2003). Quality control in scholarly publishing: A new proposal. *Journal of the American Society for Information Science and Technology, 54*(11), 989–1005.

O'Neil, G. P., & Sachis, P. N. (1998). Journal peer review: An endorsement in principle. *Higher Education in Europe, 23*(4), 517–526.

Poliner, E. A. (1994). Development of an operating plan for implementation and evaluation of an adult education network and electronic journal at Nova Southeastern University. Ed. D. Research Project, Nova Southeastern University. Retrieved June 12, 2004 from ERIC database (ERIC Document Reproduction Service No. ED386156).

Speier, C., Palmer, J., Wren, D., & Hahn, S. (1999). Faculty perceptions of electronic journals as scholarly communication: A question of prestige and legitimacy. *Journal of the American Society for Information Science*, 50(6), 537–543.

Taylor, E. W. (2001). *Adult Education Quarterly* from 1989 to 1999: A content analysis of all submissions. *Adult Education Quarterly, 51*(4), 322–340.

Taylor, E. W., Angelique, H., & Kyle, K. (2003). Rising to the occasion: Publishing diversity-focused scholarship in adult education. *International Journal of Lifelong Education, 22*(4), 407–421.

Taylor, E. W., & Beck, J., & Ainsworth, E. (2001). Publishing qualitative adult education research: A peer review perspective. *Studies in the Education of Adults, 33*(2), 163–179.

Thompson, M. M., & Schied, F. M. (1996). Neither polemical nor visionary: Language, professionalization, and the representation of women in the journals of adult education, 1929–1960. *Adult Education Quarterly, 46*(3), 123–141.

Weller, A. C. (2000). Editorial peer review for electronic journals: Current issues and emerging models. *Journal of the American Society for Information Science, 51*(14), 1,328–1,333.

Sandra Kerka

K

Knowledge

The term "knowledge" is a familiar one in adult education in relation to both teaching and research contexts. It is a term, however, that is not easily defined as there are numerous understandings about its nature, its uses, its sources and its relationship with power. These differences have become even more significant in recent times as the word knowledge is increasingly being taken up in non-education contexts and discourses. As a result, epistemological debates, that is, debates about the relationship of knowledge and truth, have increased considerably both in and outside adult education fields. Currently these debates suggest a general shift away from understanding knowledge as absolute and permanent truth to an emphasis on knowledge in relative and context-dependent terms. The debates also reflect an emerging interest in understanding and talking about knowledge in terms of discourse, discursive practices and language (Lee & Poynton, 2000).

Locally Situated Versus Disciplinary Knowledge

The different understandings of knowledge by adult educators reflect the various philosophical, theoretical and political approaches of their work and the fact that practitioners work across various sites and fields of practice. While these variations make it difficult to provide a single characterization of knowledge, in adult education there has been a focus on a strong relationship between knowledge, experience and learning. Within this relationship, individuals' experiences and the site in which learning takes place are considered to produce the most important kind of knowledge – named as experiential or practice-based knowledge (Boud, Cohen, & Walker, 1993) and characterized by its situatedness and the fact that it is relatively unbounded and undisciplined. The focus is on local processes involved in producing knowledge and this draws attention to the relationships between the people involved.

This understanding of knowledge stands in contrast to an understanding of knowledge as foundational or disciplinary (such as science, medicine), which is described as being objective, canonical and hierarchical. The focus is on knowledge as an object, a body, or a thing rather than a process. This kind of knowledge is self-referential and one that can be mastered, transmitted, applied, and built upon.

Practices Around Knowledge

Understanding knowledge either as something that focuses on local and subjective processes or as something that builds on existing bodies of knowledge within a discipline may be rhetorically useful. However, this distinction does not reflect the complexities around knowledge as evident in adult education pedagogical and research practices. An example of this is in the increased use of portfolios and project-based learning in contemporary educational curricula. These practices highlight the movement of people, knowledge and learning across educational and non-educational sites (Boud & Solomon, 2001) and draw attention to an (un)disciplining and (re)institutionalization of knowledge that is being produced. Moreover, the distinction renders invisible other debates about knowledge, in particular in the social sciences, as well as in other science fields. An important example from the scientific world is the work of Kuhn (1970), who questioned the view of science as a cumulative linear construction of knowledge and coined the term paradigm to indicate that understandings of knowledge are not objective or detached but are connected to specific cultures and sets of practices.

Other examples of the changing practices and understandings of knowledge are reflected in the emergence of new areas of study (such as cultural studies) as well as in the naming of knowledge as cross-disciplinary, multidisciplinary, and transdisciplinary. These now-familiar labels recognize a breaking down of boundaries between disciplines, between formal educational knowledge and experience, between the teacher and the learner, and between the researcher and the researched.

Contemporary Influences

These new names for knowledge are signs of a generalized upheaval around knowledge in contemporary society where, in a sense, knowledge is being put to work and questioned in various ways. They draw attention to an understanding of knowledge as fragmented and legitimate in terms of its usefulness rather than its generalizability or scientific rigor (Lyotard, 1984; Usher & Edwards, 1994).

Indeed the current interest in and talk about knowledge in both economic and educational discourses is influencing the practices of adult educators. New terms such as knowledge economy, knowledge management, knowledge worker, knowledge work and knowledge industries have had a number of effects and indicate a legitimatizing of situated knowledge and practices. This is taken up by writers across a number of fields and professional areas, including management writers who link knowledge to changes in the nature of contemporary work; community educators who use this new knowledge discourse to highlight the need to see learning and knowledge as distributed across various settings; and other educators who generate new terms to capture the different emphases and practices in knowledge today (such as working knowledge and new vocationalism in Symes & McIntyre, 2000). The following quote exemplifies a foregrounding of knowledge not as an object but rather as a process: "Knowledge is energy that resides in individuals, groups, practices, technologies, communities, organizations, and nations. We can define knowledge, like physical energy, in terms of the amount of *work* that it can be used to produce" (Gee, Hull, & Lankshear, 1996, pp. 6–7)

This privileging of situated knowledge fits neatly with adult education's interest in contextual and local conditions and practices. It draws attention to and opens up dialogues that question the elitism of objectified traditional knowledge. However, at the same time, knowledge within these discourses has become a commodity to be exchanged, produced, sold and consumed. This commercialization and consumption of knowledge may sit uneasily with some of the radical and political goals of adult education.

Researching Local Knowledge

A concern with the processes of creating new knowledge is a well-known research practice in adult education, exemplified in the practices connected with action research, participatory research, collaborative inquiry and experiential research. While there is variation across and even within each of these, they share a valuing of collaborative processes and the relationships between people including the relationship between the researcher and researched.

More recently, the practices and study of the collaborative process for producing knowledge has been taken up by many other scholars. The work of Gibbons, Limoges, Nowotny, Schwartzman, Scott, and Trow (1994) has proven to be an important text in the discussions that acknowledge and legitimize different ways of producing knowledge. They distinguish between Mode 1 and Mode 2 knowledge, contrasting the attributes of both kinds of knowledge and knowledge production. Mode 1 knowledge, which appears identical with the Newtonian model of scientific methods, is disciplinary, homogeneous, hierarchical in organization and produced in an academically-regulated context. On the other hand, Mode 2 knowledge is transdisciplinary, heterogeneous, heterarchical and carried out in a context of application. Gibbons et al. present Mode 2 as an important and coherent new mode of knowledge production arising out of changing economic and political circumstances and imperatives. Mode 2 is not a replacement for Mode 1, but is "more socially accountable and reflexive. It includes a wider, more temporary and heterogeneous set of practitioners, collaborating on a problem defined in a specific and localised context" (Gibbons et al., p. 3).

While the clear-cut Mode distinctions have been problematized by some writers (Godin, 1998; Edwards, Nicoll, Solomon, & Usher, 2004), the work of Gibbons et al. (1994) usefully draws attention to the different kinds of knowledge-defining and knowledge-producing practices that are currently being discussed. Indeed, these ideas are further legitimized in the work of Stronach and MacLure (1997) who characterize the transformation of academic (non-science) research in terms of three Games. They describe Game 1 as organized within disciplinary boundaries and explicated through traditional academic research methods. This corresponds to Gibbons et al.'s Mode 1. Game 2 represents a transitory stage where academic researchers grapple with satisfying disciplinary demands as well as wider economic (and political) demands. Finally, Game 3 embodies collaborative and commissioned research that disrupts the conventional processes and understandings of research and knowledge (corresponding to Gibbons et al.'s Mode 2). Game 3's kind of knowledge is performative (Lyotard, 1984) and pragmatic, attending to the perceived needs of specific people and/or organizations, and shifting accountability beyond the confines of the academy. The writers suggest that the three Games are operating simultaneously, creating questions about what it is to be a university, as well as ongoing tensions and struggles around academic knowledges and academic identities.

Knowledge and Language

A focus on the situatedness of knowledge production and its concern with the relationships between individuals, institutions and forms of knowledge have been accompanied by what has been named as a linguistic turn in the human sciences. This has seen increasing attention to the significance of language and discourse in the construction of knowledge (Lee & Poynton, 2000). A renewed concern with language and how it is used to produce meanings rather than simply to report on them (du Gay, 1996) suggests a focus on a discursive and textual production of knowledge. A helpful way of understanding *discourse* is that it is a way of talking (or writing) about a topic and a way of producing knowledge about that topic. As du Gay points out, "The term refers both to the production of knowledge through language and representation and the way that knowledge is institutionalized, shaping social practices and setting new practices into play" (p. 43). This kind of talk about knowledge has significant implications for the epistemological debates as it contributes to a disturbance of ideas that propose that reality and knowledge are about single truths.

The questioning about knowledge today reminds adult educators that knowledge, and the accompanying research and pedagogical practices, are neither neutral nor detached from ourselves and the society in which we live. Whether our concern is with knowledge for knowledge's sake or with a hope that knowledge brings progress, it is important that adult educators work with the idea that knowledge "can be a force of good or evil. The point is that knowledge is not innocent; its moral and political implications need to be considered" (Seidman 1994, p. 326).

See also: philosophy, theory.

References and Further Reading

Boud, D., Cohen, R., & Walker, D. (1993). *Using experience for learning.* Buckingham, UK: Society for Research into Higher Education and the Open University Press.

Boud, D., & Solomon, N. (Eds.). (2001). *Work-based learning: A new higher education?* Buckingham: Society for Research into Higher Education and the Open University Press.

du Gay, P. (1996). *Consumption and identity at work*. London: Sage.

Edwards, R., Nicoll, K., Solomon, N., & Usher, R. (2004). *Persuasive Texts*. London: Routledge.

Gee, J. P., Hull, G., & Lankshear, C. (1996). *The new work order: Behind the language of new capitalism*. St. Leonards: Allen & Unwin.

Gibbons, M., Limoges, C., Nowotny, H., Schwartzman, S., Scott, P., & Trow, M. (1994). *The new production of knowledge: The dynamics of science and research in contemporary societies*. London: Sage.

Godin, B. (1998). Writing performative history: The new *New* Atlantis? *Social Studies of Science, 28*(3), 465–483.

Kuhn, T. S. (1970). *The structure of scientific revolutions* (2nd ed.). Chicago: University of Chicago Press.

Lee, A., & Poynton, C. (2000). *Culture & text: Discourse and methodology in social research and cultural studies*. St. Leonards: Allen & Unwin.

Lyotard, F. (1984). *The postmodern condition: A report on knowledge*. Manchester, UK: Manchester University Press.

Seidman, S. (1994). *Contested knowledge: Social theory in the postmodern era*. Oxford: Blackwell.

Stronach, I., & Maclure, M. (1997). *Educational research undone: The postmodern embrace*. Buckingham, UK: Society for Research into Higher Education and the Open University Press.

Symes, C., & McIntyre, J. (Eds.). (2000). *Working knowledge: The new vocationalism and higher education*. Buckingham, UK: Society for Research into Higher Education and the Open University Press.

Usher, R., & Edwards, R. (1994). *Postmodernism and education*. London: Routledge.

Nicky Solomon

L

Labor Education

Labor education refers to education and training offered by labor unions (trade unions) to their full-time officials, working members, and representatives. The extent to which this education is provided directly by unions or by another agency or educational institution for unions varies from country to country and union to union. Labor education attracts more participants than any other form of non-vocational adult education in developed countries, and is one of the most important forms of adult education available to working people. But it is most often under-reported and ignored in discussions about adult learning, labor relations or the role of unions in society.

The term "union education" can be used interchangeably with "labor education" in this entry. (Union education is sometimes reserved for courses run directly by unions as opposed to labor education courses run for unions by other providers – whether or not they are directly sponsored by unions.) An alternative term, "industrial studies", has fallen into disuse. A main purpose of labor education is to prepare and train union lay members to play an active role in the union. Another purpose is to educate activists and members about union policy, about changes in the union environment such as new management techniques, or about changes in labor law. Labor education is also used to develop union consciousness, to build common goals and to share organizing and campaigning experience. Unions often have a small full-time staff and therefore rely on what is essentially voluntary activity of their members to be effective at work and in society; the labor education program is thus a major contributor to building an effective volunteer force.

Most labor union members learn about the union while on the job (what is often referred to as *informal* or *incidental learning*). They probably will learn more and become most active during negotiations, grievances and disputes, but they also learn from union publications and communications, from attending meetings, conferences and conventions, as well as from the union's educational programs. Although labor education caters only to a small number of members in any one year, it is "social," as opposed to personal, education. It is designed to benefit a larger number of members because the course participants are expected to share the learning they have gained with other union members. Labor education has a social purpose – to promote and develop the union presence and purposes so as to advance the union collectively. Labor education can be described as essentially non-vocational, non-formal adult education with its origins rooted in the traditions of workers' education, the seeds of which are more than a century old and predate modern unions.

Unions and Workers' Education

Unions remain the most important and popular form of worker (or working-class) organization in most liberal democracies. Labor unions are regarded as "old" social movements, but as we look back on the past millennium, these unions have to be considered as relatively recent social organizations. If we set aside early forms of workers' associations, "modern" labor or trade unions, with significant membership, probably did not emerge until the 1840s: they are therefore approximately 160 years old. Workers' education in different forms predates modern labor unions, but a substantial offering of "independent working-class education" can only realistically be dated back to the turn of the century (Simon, 1990). Labor education (education with the central purpose of supporting the union organizationally) is no more than 100 years old, and it could probably be argued that the main characteristic of labor or union education – representative training – began no earlier than the 1920s. Labor education draws from earlier forms of workers' education and could simply be treated as part of a continuum rather than a separate entity. Adult education in the West developed from early forms of workers' education such as the Mechanics' Institutes, Workers' Educational Association (WEA), The Plebs League and Labour Colleges, Frontier College and Brookwood Labor College, and even the public provision of "university" education via university extra-mural and extension departments was targeted at the newly enfranchised working classes. For an illustration of these points as they apply to Canada, see Taylor (2001); for the United States see London, Tarr, and Wilson (1990); and for the United Kingdom see Simon.

We should also note that neo-conservative and post-industrial commentators often predict the demise of labor unions but, in fact, unions remain stubbornly present within most liberal democracies. Union membership and union influence may have declined across the spectrum (except in Scandinavia), but it has not vanished. In some cases unions are making a comeback. For example, in Aotearoa, New Zealand a steep decline in the late 1980s and early 1990s, due largely to individualized employment contracts, is being reversed alongside a change in employment law. Organization, representation, negotiation, lobbying, strikes and other forms of union activity still occur worldwide. Labor education also persists and in some ways has been expanded, with, for example, a renewed emphasis on general membership education and on education for union organizing. Labor education has also begun to challenge new management techniques, issues of globalization, and workplace learning (usually interpreted as educating employees to be more valuable human resources). It has responded to calls for international workers" solidarity, to educational challenges posed by widespread computer use and the Internet, and to calls for marrying job preservation to environmental protection. There has also been some rediscovery of the role of traditional workers' education within labor education provision leading to a renewed focus on political economy and social analysis. (International examples of current labor education referred to in this entry can be found in Spencer, 2002.)

Core Labor Education

Most of the labor education courses

provided by unions are *tools* courses (for example, shop-steward training, grievance handling, health and safety representative courses). The next largest category is *issues* courses (for example, sexual harassment, racism, or new human resource management strategies), which often seek to link workplace and societal issues. A third group of courses can be labeled *labor studies*, and they seek to examine the union context (for example, labor history, economics and politics). There is of course overlap between these courses.

Tools courses directly prepare members for active roles in the union, to become representatives of the union, and are targeted at existing or potential union activists. They are provided directly by the unions, by labor federations or by union centrals such as the Canadian Labour Congress (CLC), the United Kingdom Trades Union Congress (TUC) the Swedish Confederation of Trade Unions (LO). Tools courses are also provided for unions by educational institutions (for example by many of the labor studies centers across the United States), collaboratively with the central bodies or individual unions (for example with colleges, universities and the WEA collaborating with the TUC in Britain). They may also be provided by specialized institutions such as the now defunct Australian Trade Union Training Authority (TUTA), or South Africa's Development Institute for the Training, Support and Education of Labour (Ditsela). Many unions layer their courses, with introductory, intermediate and advanced courses and programs.

Some of the introductory tools courses lead on to issue courses (sometimes referred to as "awareness" courses), which are specifically targeted at raising awareness and union action around the issues discussed. In some cases there will not be a strict demarcation between tools and issues courses, nor a requirement to undertake one before the other, but the differentiation between types (and therefore the aims and purposes) of labor education can be useful for analytical purposes.

The union movement also provides more extensive and demanding educational opportunities (labor studies) such as the Harvard Trade Union Program (Bernard, 1991) for lead officials, evening Certificate courses in the United Kingdom and the CLC's 5-week residential Labour College of Canada (LCC). The LCC teaches four courses – labor history, economics, sociology, and politics – at a first-year university level in a 4-week block. Labor law is now taught as a one-week course in the regions.

Although the LCC uses some university educators and takes place in the University of Ottawa, it is a separate entity directly accountable to the CLC. This differs from the Harvard program with its more autonomous structure, from other United States college programs and from the adult residential colleges in the United Kingdom, such as Ruskin and Northern College. These offer year-long programs and are open to union members. Similar labor studies programs can be found in other countries and within some mainstream university offerings (particularly in the United States, Australia, New Zealand and Canada), although these are open to the general public.

Perhaps the most innovative example of a labor studies program offered to union members is the negotiated paid educational leave program developed by the Canadian Autoworkers (CAW) and now also offered by the Canadian Union of Postal Workers. The core offering is four separate but linked one-week units targeted at all members, not just representatives and activists, and funded by an employer levy negotiated at the bargaining table (the unions retain sole control over content).

The intention of the dedicated labor studies courses is to supplement trade union tools and issues courses with a broader educational program, and, in some cases, to provide a research basis for union activity. Some universities are linking directly with unions to offer research collaborations (for example, Leeds in the United Kingdom; Oregon in the United States), or study and research circles (for example, in Sweden). Although unions are usually represented on the "boards of studies" of the university and college offering labor studies programs, they are rarely union-controlled in contrast to the union-run courses. The variations in the nature, structures and delivery of labor education courses are manifold (Spencer, 2002).

The differences between these types of courses are fluid. Some courses will have elements of each type in the one course, for example an introductory course for shop stewards could have a history or political economy component and an issues section. Where unions put their emphasis may vary depending on such factors as the type of union philosophy advocated – business unionism (accommodative/adaptive) versus organizing model (oppositional/militant). The first philosophical approach may result in more emphasis on tools and less on labor studies.

Curriculum and teaching methods for these core labor education courses have been hotly contested over the years, and have been linked in the assertion that labor education should adopt a popular education or Freirian approach. In its extreme form, it was argued that courses would have no specific course content, be experientially based and would respond only to the concerns of course participants attending a particular course, and be led by facilitators rather than teachers. All other educational approaches were dismissed as forms of "banking education." While this debate may have been beneficial in reminding labor educators of the importance of democratic participation in the classroom and in the union and the links between the two, it also distracted attention from issues of course content. The need to address some of the key issues facing union members and discuss information that may be outside of their immediate experience needs a planned course content as well as participatory methods. John McIlroy's chapters in *The Search for Enlightenment* (Simon, 1990) illustrated how the emphasis on participation can mask a retreat into technical training courses denuded of content and represent a move away from the traditions of workers' education committed to establishing an understanding of political economy among labor activists. It is more common now for unions to offer a range of courses with different foci and to incorporate participatory methods and experiential elements as appropriate: some courses are essentially experiential, others are not. Mike Newman (1993) in the *Third Contract* has discussed the question of what adult educational philosophies and teaching methods are appropriate in different kinds of labor education courses and has shown that a range of different educational approaches can be beneficial.

It should also be noted that unions

in different countries do run women-only courses and courses targeted at specific groups of members; for example CAW advertises courses for "workers of color." The intention in these cases is to ensure that those attending are not in a minority and that any issues that are specific to them are not marginalized.

Other Labor Education

While tools, issues and labor studies might describe the majority of labor education.; the definitions do not encompass all labor education offerings. Unions are directly involved in a number of membership education programs, some of them with a basic skills or vocational purpose. In some cases, union-run literacy and second-language courses are tutored by fellow unionists and act as a bridge linking immigrant or illiterate workers to union concerns and publications. Similarly, unions are responsible for a number of worker training programs, which allow the unions to educate workers about union concerns alongside vocational training. In some countries skilled and professional unions have a long history of union-sponsored vocational training and education courses. Unions, including non-craft unions, are becoming much more proactive in responding to company restructuring and deskilling and are arguing for reskilling, skills recognition and skills profiling, as well as challenging employers to live up to their rhetoric of "pay for knowledge."

In some countries unions have developed a comprehensive and integrated education and training program, such as Britain's UNISON Open College, which includes labor education, basic skills, recognition of prior learning and vocational training opportunities for all union members. In Brazil, *Programa Integrar* offers union-sponsored labor education, vocational training and educational opportunities for the unemployed, and is linked to the drive to create worker-owned cooperatives. In other situations, unions are engaging in partnered workplace learning programs, partnered with employers or other agencies (such as NGOs). Unions are also involved in worker health and safety training (this should not be confused with union safety representative tools training); these may be joint management courses, but they often allow unions to argue for a union view (safe workplace) as opposed to a management view (safe worker) of health and safety. In some cases, union-run worker health and safety training has been used as part of union organizing drives.

Nor should we ignore educational provision for full-time officers within our purview of labor education. There has been a growing interest, particularly in Europe, Quebec and Canada generally, in equipping full-time officers with the educational tools needed to conduct union business in a global economy.

Unions have also had some limited involvement in television productions such as "Work Week" or "Working TV" in Canada, or the labor-education programs broadcast in Britain in the late 1960s and early 1970s. Union representatives participate in television and radio programs in an attempt to present union perspectives, influence public opinion and educate their members. Some unions are actively involved in encouraging schools to broaden their curricula to include labor issues by providing packages of materials, and by training and providing speakers for school visits. Nor should we ignore union-sponsored arts and cultural events such as Canada's MayWorks or Manchester, England's labor history museum.

Impact of Labor Education

The extent of labor education varies over time, in some cases just reflecting economic circumstances, in others economic and legal changes. The move to neo-liberal economic policies and globalization of production was accompanied, in many countries, by attacks on the legal rights to paid educational leave for union representatives (particularly in Europe and Australia/New Zealand where these had been most extensive). These educational rights became increasingly narrowly defined as rights to training for industrial relations purposes; they became more limited in the amount of time allowed, and state funding to support this activity was either cut or abolished altogether (for a review of the European experience, see accounts in Bridgford & Stirling, 2000). Yet, studies of effectiveness of labor education show that it continues to be effective.

Over the years a number of studies have been conducted in several countries as to the effectiveness of labor education (for sources and data on Canada see Spencer, 1994, Gereluk, 2001, and for the United Kingdom see Spencer, 1992). In general, studies have found that union members and the unions do benefit from individuals taking union courses; the courses do help members to become more interested in the union; members are able to make better union decisions as a result of attending union courses; and the courses give members the confidence to take on voluntary positions in the union and to challenge arbitrary management decisions. In addition, union education has been found to bolster members' communal, social and political activity. Labor education does support union activism.

See also: class, continuing education, popular education, vocational education.

References and Further Reading

Bernard, E. (1991). Labour programs: A challenging partnership. *Labour/Le Travail, 27*, 199–207.

Bridgford, J., & Stirling, J. (Eds.). (2000). *Trade union education in Europe.* Brussels: European Trade Union College.

Gereluk, W. (2001). *Labour education in Canada today.* Athabasca, Alberta: Athabasca University. Retrieved on September 1, 2001 from http://www.athabascau.ca/wcs/PLAR_Report. pdf

London, S., Tarr, E., & Wilson, J. (Eds.). (1990). *The re-education of the American working class.* New York: Greenwood.

Newman, M. (1993). *The third contract: Theory and practice in trade union training.* Sydney: Stewart Victor Publishing.

Simon, B. (Ed.). (1990). *The search for enlightenment: The working class and adult education in the twentieth century.* London: Lawrence & Wishart.

Spencer, B. (1992). Labour education in the UK and Canada: What do workers do and what should they be offered on union courses? *Canadian and International Education,* 20(2), 55–68.

Spencer, B. (1994). Educating union Canada. *Canadian Journal for the Study of Adult Education, 8*(2), 45–64. Revised version in D. & A. Poonwassie (Eds.), *Fundamentals of adult education* (pp. 214–231). Toronto: Thompson Educational Publishing, 2001.

Spencer, B. (Ed.). (2002). *Unions and learning in a global economy: International and comparative perspectives.* Toronto: Thompson Educational Publishing.

Taylor, J. (2001). *Union learning: Canadian labour education in the twentieth century.* Toronto: Thompson Educational Publishing.

Bruce Spencer

Latin America and Adult Education

Over the past 8 years, the field of adult education in Latin America has been the focus of indepth discussion and activity. With the motivation of the Fifth International Conference on Adult Education (CONFINTEA V) in July 1997, the regional UNESCO office for Latin America and the Caribbean, together with the Latin American Council for Adult Education (CEAAL), designed a process aimed at identifying and assessing national experiences in adult education, carried out by both governments and civil society, in order to develop a regional vision. Thus, in January 1997, the Regional Conference on Adult Education was held in Brasilia, Brazil, with the participation of governments and civil society organizations who jointly drafted an initial regional framework for our participation in CONFINTEA V.

Later, the UNESCO office and CEAAL, together with the Regional Training Center for Latin America (CREFAL) and the National Institute for Adult Education in Mexico (INEA), promoted a process to discuss the *Hamburg Declaration* and action plan at national meetings and three sub-regional gatherings. At these encounters, a key factor to this entire process was guaranteed: the presence and participation of representatives from both governments and civil society.

In November 1998, the countries from the Mercosur sub-region gathered in Montevideo, Uruguay; in January 1999, the Andean countries met in Cochabamba, Bolivia; and in March 1999, the Central American and Caribbean countries met with Mexico to analyse their situation, in Patzcuaro, Mexico. In order to process the collective discussions and reflections generated during these gatherings, a group of seven specialists accompanied this process and held a technical meeting in Santiago, Chile, in August 2000; the results of this process and their contributions generated a book including specific priority themes for Latin America and the Caribbean and a regional framework for action (UNESCO–CEAAL–CREFAL–INEA, 2000).

Subsequently, this process was enriched with national experiences that sought to act upon these regional orientations and more recent contributions have also been made, including a regional report developed by CEAAL for the international meeting to evaluate CONFINTEA V. This international meeting was held in September, 2003, in Bangkok, 6 years after CONFINTEA.

Challenges

The current conditions of inequity and injustice established by the financial and commercial dynamics of globalization have worsened the already perverse effects of the economic and political structures built over time in our region. With the exception of Cuba, deep-rooted social inequalities permeate the rest of the Latin American countries and have been exacerbated by the implementation of neo-liberal economic policies over the past 20 years.

This situation of poverty and social exclusion represents the main challenge for economic and social policies in our countries today. Education cannot develop and thrive independently of this reality. And in the case of adult education, it is clear that educational delay is concentrated within the population characterized by poverty. The 34 million illiterate people and the 110 million people without full primary education are part of the 220 million poor people in our region.

Educational exclusion is another symptom of social and economic exclusion. Thus, the debate on adult education in our countries is necessarily inscribed within the broader debate on how to help activate inclusive social development processes, participation, and empowerment of local organizations through educational action. Any and every educational program that dodges this social and political dimension of its performance will have little impact on the lives of the people it seeks to serve. This certainty situates the debate on adult education within the debate on social policy, the creation of jobs, and the fostering of citizenship in our countries.

If education is a universally recognized human right, then the lack of opportunities and conditions for a person to become educated is a structural violation of this right. Hence, we must emphatically affirm that poverty is currently the broadest and most massive violation of human rights in existence because it impedes full human development for millions of people throughout the world. Consequently, we must affirm that illiteracy and the lack of basic education are also expressions of the violation of people's most elemental human rights. Thus, education as a whole and adult education in particular today are part of the debate about economic, social and cultural rights.

From this perspective, adult education ceased to be a strictly educational issue – although we must undoubtedly continue to strengthen its pedagogical consistency – and has become a key aspect of strategies and policies for economic development, social inclusion, community and political participation, as well as the building of new institutions to guarantee respect for human rights.

The Need to Focus on Adult Education

The term adult education no longer semantically reflects the wealth of practices and fields of action in which we develop our educational practices. Without doubt, in terms of the conceptual debate, the vision that considered adult education to be merely compensatory education oriented to literacy has been surpassed.

At least two situations call for more demanding definitions. The first concerns the fact that in our region, the majority of those matriculated in adult education programs are young people who were unable to continue normal educational cycles. Thus, we have begun to use the term "youth and adult education" (YAE). The second definition has to do with the multiple fields in which youth and adult education are developed, above and beyond the school system. Thus, we have educational processes for capacity-building in local development, the defense and promotion of human rights, the affirmation of indigenous and Afro-Caribbean identities, gender equity, the development of social enterprises, the prevention of HIV/AIDS, the protection of the environment and the democratization of the media, to mention some of the most relevant areas of influence.

If, to this range of practices, we add the concept of basic learning needs, proposed by the Jomtien Conference that situates basic education on the horizon of education for life, together with the concept of lifelong learning, our field of interest is greatly enriched, placing the traditionally entitled adult education in a broader perspective. However, for the purposes of investigation, as well as the design and implementation of effective educational policies, the limits of youth and adult education should be clearly established in order to avoid the risk of becoming all-encompassing, thus diluting its consistency and reducing it to nothing. In this sense, we see the need to broaden our analysis of what we are currently referring to when we say adult education.

The Link with Popular Education

Popular education, systematized as a political and pedagogical proposal by Paulo Freire, has been one of the most original and refreshing contributions that Latin America has made to universal pedagogical thinking. Inspired by Freire (1970), thousands of educational experiences were engendered with youth and adults in every country in our region. Given the political intolerance and closure, together with the execution of dirty wars by military dictatorships throughout almost 2 decades, popular education flourished. It was tied to social movements and popular or grassroots organizations, always in resistance and clear opposition to the governments that were expressions of anti-popular politics.

At present, within the context of still very fragile and restricted democracies, a new relationship between governments and civil society organizations is being built. Also within this context, the link between the contributions of popular education and educational systems and policies – between so-called formal and non-formal education – is being rebuilt. In particular, in the field of youth and adult education, we must build the conditions for civil society engagement and influence upon educational policy and situate the proposals of popular education on the horizon of current debates in order to guarantee quality education for all.

The Agenda in Latin America and the Caribbean

In this process of regional debate, we have identified some priority fields and sectors of the population for the development of educational policies, programs and projects with youth and adults:

1. Our regional perspective situates youth and adult education as a key factor for building citizenship, gender equity, and a culture for the defense and promotion of human rights.
2. This perspective on citizenship should be grounded in the concrete experience of developing and implementing proposals for improving the quality of life in specific locations; in this sense, YAE should help to build capacities for empowerment, in order to influence development policies at the local level.
3. Also, YAE should pay special attention to the development of programs for creating employment and occupational training. Most users of adult education programs are seeking to better their education as a means to obtaining or improving their employment and the quality of their lives.
4. YAE should continue to help overcome illiteracy as one of the basic conditions for indepth lifelong learning.
5. Three sectors of the population are identified as needing special attention and priority: women who tend to hold leadership roles in local processes, youth who

have specific demands regarding employment when they become involved in educational programs, and indigenous peoples who, today in Latin America, are exercising leadership for affirming their cultural identities and demanding justice.

International Dynamics

Undoubtedly, the World Education Forum held in Dakar, Senegal, in April 2000, was an important event for situating the topic of education at the heart of the debate on social development. Of the six commitments established in Dakar, three concern youth and adult education and, together, represent a more comprehensive and demanding vision for guaranteeing education for all boys and girls, women and men. This vision helped to overcome the World Bank's vision during the 1990s that YAE was a non-priority field for investing in child education. Today, this kind of proposal is unsustainable and we recognize a changed vision and interest in thinking of ways to strengthen YAE.

Nonetheless, the risk remains of reducing the package of Dakar commitments to education for boys and girls, along the limited horizon of basic education. The so-called global initiative, led by the World Bank, that seeks to mobilize resources for countries with the greatest financial limitations, places emphasis solely on programs targeting primary education for boys and girls, and thus, in practice, reduces the commitment to other sectors of the population.

In Latin America, we continue to face limitations and a lack of political will on behalf of many governments to commit to promoting new dynamics for YAE. However, new experiences are emerging in which different local governments, committed to social inclusion policies, become associated with civil society experiences and efforts that are contributing to more comprehensive processes in which YAE, both from school environments and systems, as well as within forums for civic participation and organization, is making important contributions to personal development, the exercise of citizenship, and the construction of more equitable relationships.

See also: civil society, popular education, problematizing learning, social policy, South America and adult education, young adult education.

References and Further Reading

Freire, P. (1970). *Pedagogy of the oppressed* (M. B. Ramos, Trans.). New York: Continuum.

UNESCO-CEAAL-CREFAL-INEA. (2000). *La educación de personas jóvenes y adultas en América Latina y el Caribe: Prioridades de acción en el siglo XXI.* Santiago de Chile.

Carlos Zarco Mera

Learning

Learning is a concept that is central to the field of adult education, but most often the term is not defined since it is assumed that its meaning is understood. This is particularly the case when learning is paired with other words, as in "reflexive learning," "situational learning," "workplace learning," "embodied learning," and "accelerated learning." When the term is defined, the definitions are often varied and contested, as they are many.

"Learning defies easy definition

and simple theorizing" (Merriam & Caffarella, 1999, p. 248). For example, the definitions of learning include: both an outcome or a process such as a change in behavior or the potential for change (Hergenhahn & Olson, 1993); the receiving, storing, retrieving and using of knowledge; a process of transforming experience into knowledge, skills, and beliefs (Merriam & Caffarella); a change as a result of imitation and interaction with the environment (Bandura, 1986); and the use of a prior interpretation to make meaning of one's experience in order to guide future action (Mezirow, 2000). The arbitrary application of the term learning poses a challenge for the practitioner and scholar alike when trying to define learning from a particular perspective. To help make sense of this challenge and to find a helpful definition, learning as a construct is analysed from several different perspectives to explain how this field engages with it. This discussion includes four different and overlapping perspectives of learning: theoretical, epistemological, sites of learning, and means of promoting learning.

A Theoretical View

Theory is quite helpful in making sense of the multifaceted nature of learning. It provides an organized set of principles; a framework for research; a model for explaining both simple and complex events; and a mechanism for identifying the underlying dynamics of a learning event. By comparing and critiquing varied theoretical orientations differences emerge, further clarifying the meaning of learning. From a traditional perspective there are three broad, somewhat overlapping, theoretical orientations of learning: behavioristic, cognitive and interactionist (Gredler, 2001). Behaviorism, the most popular and best-known traditional orientation, is based on the following assumptions: learning is an observable external event, rather than internal mental event; it is a response to elements in the environment; and the outcome of learning is seen as a change in behavior (Gredler; Merriam & Caffarella, 1999). Well-known behaviorists are Watson, Tolman, Hull, and Skinner (Driscoll, 1994).

In contrast to behaviorism, a cognitive orientation assumes that the internal mental processes in the human mind are the foremost unit of analysis in understanding learning. A contemporary metaphor for this orientation is a computerized information-processing view of learning where the learning is seen as "information input from the environment, processed and stored in memory, and output in the form of some learning capability" (Driscoll, 1994, p. 68). Contributors to this orientation look at cognition developmentally and culturally (Piaget; Vygotsky), and as metacognitive processes – an awareness of one's own thinking and related cognitive strategies (Flavell; Gardner).

The third traditional theoretical orientation is interactionist, which assumes that the environment, mental processes, and behavior are all involved in learning. Key assumptions about learning from this orientation are best explained in a natural setting, as opposed to a laboratory. Learning involves the observation/modeling of others, a particular environment mediated by internal mental events that influence perception and action; and the outcome of internal symbolic codes that guide future behavior. Contributors include Bandura, Lewin, and Rotter. These traditional theoretical orientations reveal a tension between the meaning of learning as a response to the external environment (behavioral) and learning as an internal experience (cognitive).

As science has advanced, some more contemporary orientations to learning have emerged, including neurophysiological and evolutionary theories of learning. Learning from the neurophysiological orientation is understood in relationship to anatomy, physiology, and the pathology of the brain and its various functions as a physical entity. Learning is seen as physiological change, neuron development and greater activity in various different structures of the brain that previously have been less active (Merriam & Caffarella, 1999; Restak, 1995). Contributors to this orientation include Boucouvalas, Restak, Sylwester, Caine and Caine, and Gardner.

Lastly, the evolutionary orientation, involves understanding the role that evolution plays in conjunction with experience in determining and shaping behavior, such that all organisms, including humans, are predisposed to learn certain things in certain ways. A major assumption of this perspective is that the human mind contains a large number of innate learning mechanisms (Barkow, Cosmides, & Tooby, 1992). These mechanisms evolved over time to solve specific adaptive problems in the ancestral environment. They are triggered by only a narrow range of information, which is transferred through decision rules and manifested in the form of behavior that increased fitness in the past. Contributors to this orientation include Buss, Gazziniga, Pinker, Barkow, Cosmides, and Tooby. The selection of a particular theoretical orientation provides guidance in what questions to ask, where to look for learning (its locus of control), and how it manifests when attempting to make meaning of learning (e.g., behavioral change, internal mental processes, physiological change).

An Epistemological View

A second way to think about learning is through the lens of epistemology, which analyses learning in relationship to the nature of knowledge. The learner is viewed as a knower and learning as a way of knowing. Epistemology means exploring questions such as: What is knowledge? What are legitimate ways of knowing? And, most important to this discussion, is what does it mean to know? How these questions are answered reflect assumptions on how the learner acquires knowledge of and about the world. For example, does the learner acquire knowledge through actual experience or through reason and interpretation? Whereas some learners assert that "knowledge is a matter of internally representing the external world and is primarily acquired through experience . . . others argue that knowledge is a matter of interpretation that learners actively construct by imposing organization on the world about them" (Driscoll, 1994, p. 10). Much of the difference between these two perspectives rests on underlying assumptions held about reality, the nature of truth, and the source of knowledge.

There are several different epistemological perspectives, such as objectivism, pragmatism, and interpretivism. Most significant to the field of adult education is interpretivism, in which reality is seen not as objective and singular, as in the case of objectivism, but instead as constructed, multiple, and holistic. Truth is seen as something that is constructed, contested, and culturally rooted. The primary source of knowledge is reason. From this epistemological perspective the learner does not passively take in and respond to information about the world around him or herself; instead the learner is an active knower and learner, who constructs and makes meaning of information based on a personal interpretation. Conceptions of learning in adult education that are informed by this view of epistemology include: other ways of knowing, situational knowing, relational knowing, and embodied knowing. Similar assumptions are found in adult learning theories, such as transformative learning and constructivism. For example, Mezirow (1996) defines transformative learning "as the process of using prior interpretation to construe a new or revised interpretation of the meaning of one's experience in order to guide future action" (p. 162). Through exploring epistemology and analyzing underlying assumptions about the nature of knowledge and knowing, the contested and varied perspectives of learning are better understood. The selection of a particular theoretical orientation provides guidance in what questions to ask, where to look for learning (its locus of control), and how it manifests, when attempting to make meaning of learning (e.g., behavioral change, internal mental processes, physiological change).

A Situational View

A third way to think about learning is from the perspective of the sites of learning or practice, where learning is being fostered. Examples include rural learning, urban learning, cohort learning, and workplace learning. The fact that learning is being defined from different sites implies that learning is situated and the site plays a unique role in the nature, meaning and/or process of learning. For example, the term cohort learning refers to a shared learning experience that takes place among a supportive peer group over an extended period of time. Learning in this particular context is relational and has been found to be most effective at fostering affective outcomes (e.g., belonging, confidence). Fenwick (2001) identifies several different themes (e.g., situated, cultural, text and discourses) that help explain how learning is conceptualized in the workplace. Since learning is situated, each site of learning has an implicit situated community of practice unique to its particular setting. By participating in a particular community of practice (inclusive of unique tools, activities) learning can be viewed as social as well as " 'tool dependent' because the setting provides the mechanisms (e.g., computers, small groups, paper and pencil) that aid, and more importantly, structure the cognitive process" (Wilson, 1993, p. 73). Wilson notes that it is "the interaction with the setting itself in relation to its social and tool dependent nature that determines the learning" (p. 73).

A third example about the sites of learning emerges in the terms such as formal, nonformal, informal learning, and incidental learning. The meaning of the terms reflects a view of learning emblematic of varying degrees of structure, purposefulness, and self-directedness imposed on or engaged by the learner. Formal learning is usually a highly structured, purposeful, teacher led, classroom-based learning experience, while incidental learning is usually unintentional or unplanned, often not recognized or labeled as learning by learners or others. By exploring the underlying assumptions of the varied site or practice, greater clarity emerges about the meaning of learning.

A Promotional View

A fourth perspective of how learning is engaged in adult education focuses on the various means of promoting learning. These are strategies or approaches to learning, teaching, instructional design, and program development with a goal of fostering learning. Learning from this perspective is seen both as an outcome and as means to an end. Although the meaning of learning itself is often not defined, greater insight into it can be gained by understanding the nature of the approach or strategy and its general intent. Terms that fall within this perspective include reflexive learning, problem-based learning, action learning and accelerated learning. For example, reflexive learning is a metacognitive process, often considered a higher form of learning, where the learner is encouraged to monitor and think about his or her learning as it is happening. Learning is seen as an approach to greater personal understanding, in which the learner is reflecting on the present experience in relationship to prior experiences, replaying events and monitoring feelings associated with the learning experience, and evaluating the experience (Merriam & Caffarella, 1999).

Another example is action learning, a strategy for organizational change which involves learners across sectors of an organization, working in teams, addressing organizational problems by drawing on their varied experiences, and developing solutions (Swanson, York, O'Neil, & Marsick, 1999). A third example is accelerated learning which is an instructional design of educational programs to assist learners to complete courses in a time intensive manner (Wlodkowski & Kasworm, 2003). These examples of learning as an approach or strategy share a common theme that offers insight about the nature of learning in adult education, that of the centrality of experience. Each relies on the importance of prior experience in shaping and making meaning of future actions. It is experience that provides the gist for reflection, for making sense of organizational change, and the cognitive complexity essential for accelerated learning. Through an exploration of varied approaches to learning the different meanings of learning are better understood.

See also: accelerated learning, activity theory/situated cognition, adult learning, cohort learning, embodied learning, informal learning, reflective learning, relational learning, rural learning, urban learning, workplace learning.

References and Further Reading

Bandura, A. (1986). *Social foundations of thought and action: A social cognitive theory*. Englewood Cliffs, NJ: Prentice Hall.

Barkow, J. H., Cosmides, L., & Tooby, J. (1992). *The adapted mind*. New York: Oxford University Press.

Driscoll, M. P. (1994). *Psychology of learning for instruction*. Boston: Allyn & Bacon.

Fenwick, T. J. (2001). Tides of change: New themes and questions in workplace learning. In T. J. Fenwick (Ed.), *Sociocultural perspectives on learning through work* (pp. 3–17). *New Directions for Adult and Continuing Education*, No. 92. San Francisco: Jossey-Bass.

Gredler, M. E. (2001). *Learning and instruction*. Columbus, OH: Merrill Prentice Hall.

Hergenhahn, B. R., & Olson, M. H. (1993).

An introduction to the theories of learning. Englewood Cliffs, NJ: Prentice Hall.

Merriam, S. B., & Caffarella, R. S. (1999). *Learning in adulthood* (2nd ed.). San Francisco: Jossey-Bass.

Mezirow, J. (1996). Contemporary paradigms of learning. *Adult Education Quarterly, 46,* 158–172.

Mezirow, J., & Associates. (2000). *Learning as transformation.* San Francisco: Jossey-Bass.

Restak, R. (1995). *Brainscapes.* New York: Hyperion.

Swanson, R. A., York, L., O'Neil, J., & Marsick, V. (1999). *Action learning: Successful strategies for individual, team, and organizational development.* Baton Rouge, LA: Academy of Human Resource Development.

Wilson, A. L. (1993). The promise of situated cognition. In S. B. Merriam (Ed.), *An update of adult learning theory* (pp. 71–79). *New Directions for Adult and Continuing Education,* No. 57. San Francisco: Jossey-Bass.

Wlodkowski, R. J., & Kasworm, C. (Eds.). (2003). *Accelerated learning for adults: The promise and practice of intensive educational formats. New Directions for Adult and Continuing Education,* No. 97. San Francisco: Jossey-Bass.

Edward W. Taylor

Learning Festival

A learning festival is a collection of mainly public events, organized within territorial boundaries, with the goal of celebrating and promoting lifelong learning. In 2003 there were more than 40 national adult or lifelong learning festivals known to have taken place around the world.

Learning festivals usually aim to support key goals of lifelong learning which are to provide learning opportunities and promote the development of lifelong learners. They are directed at a range of audiences. Firstly, the public in order to give information, guidance and counseling on the range of learning opportunities available and so promote the importance of continuous learning. Secondly, policy-makers in order to advocate for lifelong learning and the resources and institutional support required. Thirdly, current learners in order to celebrate their achievements, provide encouragement, and hear what they think of provision and priorities. Fourthly, educators, trainers, and facilitators, for them to share experiences and new approaches, also build partnerships and cooperation.

The contexts within which the learning festivals take place will determine the underlying rationale, with some having broader political goals while others focus primarily on building learning communities of various kinds.

What Events Make Up a Learning Festival?

Creativity, diversity and novelty have proved to be important features. However, some common activities include workshops and symposia, often drawing in participants from beyond the immediate communities, taster courses, awards to notable achievers, popular lectures, skills demonstrations, cultural events, websites and information phone lines. Popular themes include literacy, civil society and democracy, HIV/AIDS, information, communication technology in general and computers in particular. Another of the features is a conscious attempt to find locations that are not traditionally associated with education but are a part of people's everyday lives. These include pubs and cafes, buses, trams and trains, shopping malls and theatres.

Where do Festivals Take Place?

Of the 40 national learning festivals in 2003, the greatest concentration was in Europe, but there were also several in Africa, as well as some in each of the other continents. The concentration in Europe is perhaps the result of a deliberate focus of the European Union on lifelong learning, with a particular emphasis on the development of democracy and active citizenship. This represents an attempt to integrate marginalized communities as well as to repair, especially in South-eastern Europe, the devastation of widespread war. 2003 saw the first sub-regional festival, based in Macedonia and covering the countries of the former Yugoslavia as well as Albania, Bulgaria and Romania.

Festivals are generally coordinated at a national level with programming and organization taking place locally. At their most developed they can be extensive events, with Germany's festival in 2000 encompassing 2,000 regional festivals, and mobilizing 5,000 providers, and Austria's festival attracting more than 100,000 participants at its peak. They can also be limited, located in one educational institution or province, as with the Learning Cape Festival in South Africa.

What is the History of Learning Festivals?

The current learning festivals movement grew from international literacy events, with the first International Literacy Day taking place in 1967 and the first week taking place in the United States in the late 1980s. The current phase of festivals was launched in the UK in 1992 and has been driven by the National Institute of Adult Continuing Education's (NIACE) Organization for Adult Learning. The development from literacy days to learning festivals was influenced by the new wave of interest in lifelong learning and the promotion of learning societies. Whilst some events are still organized as literacy days or weeks, increasingly they are known as lifelong learning or adult learning festivals. After the World Conference on Adult Education in 1997, UNESCO adopted a resolution in 1999 to officially launch the International Adult Learners Week, embracing International Literacy Day. This development has given added impetus to the growth of learning festivals. The UNESCO Institute for Education (UIE) supports the development of learning festivals, as does the European Union.

How Successful are Learning Festivals?

The impact of learning festivals, especially with their focus on non-formal and informal learning, is hard to measure. Criteria used to assess impact include growth in numbers of events, numbers of participants and geographical spread of festivals, media coverage, effects on policy and organizational development. There are also efforts to assess their impact on the development of learning regions (Walters & Etkind, 2004).

Using these criteria, it is clear that since 1993 there has been consistent growth in terms of the number of countries and the number of locations within countries hosting festivals, plus the number of events within many local festivals. However, there is a smaller counter-tendency, with Germany having abandoned central coordination and Denmark having abandoned its national festival altogether.

Media coverage is both an objective of festivals and a product of them. UNESCO Institute of Education has identified the relationship with the media as key to a festival's success. Approaches to media are diverse, from a literacy storyline in a UK soap opera, to a televised national debate in Slovenia.

Influence on Policy Development

Festivals often aim to enhance the building of partnerships, both amongst education providers and between those providers and government, business and civil society. This directly relates to the perceived need in learning societies for partnership-building as a means of developing "institutional thickness" for intensifying knowledge production and innovation. Learners' forums in the UK have grown to increase the presence and voices of learners in the learning festivals and in society at large. More research is needed into learning festivals and their contributions to the development of lifelong learning and learning societies within different contexts.

See also: civil society, international adult education, learning organization.

References and Further Reading

Bochynek, B. (2002). *The role and impact of adult learners weeks and lifelong learning festivals in Europe, an assessment of European learning festivals as tools for the democratization of lifelong learning.* Hamburg, Germany: UNESCO Institute for Education.

Bochynek, B. (Ed). (2003). *International Adult Learners Week – Six years after CONFINTEA V*. Hamburg, Germany: UNESCO Institute for Education.

Martinez, F., & Weil, M. (Ed.). (2000). *The learning festivals' guide, An internationally-produced communication tool in support of the launch of the International Adult Learners' Week*. Paris: UNESCO.

Slovenian Institute for Adult Education (n.d.). *Widening and strengthening the European dimension of the lifelong learning movement, E-Bulletin.* Retrieved September 17, 2003 from http://www.llw5.org/e-bulletin/

Walters, S., & Etkind, R. (2004). "Developing a learning region: What can learning festivals contribute?" In D. E. Clover (Ed.), Proceedings of the Conjoint Conference of the Canadian Association for the Study of Adult Education and the Adult Education Research Conference (pp. 503–508). University of Victoria, British Columbia, Canada.

Weidemann, D. (2003). *Learning society and knowledge society – conceptualisations in German debates. A Euronet literature review*. Bremen: University of Bremen.

Shirley Walters and Roger Etkind

Learning Organization

The last several decades have seen considerable conceptual speculation about the ability of organizations to learn. In learning organizations, intentional initiatives are undertaken to enhance this ability. This entry defines the learning organization, identifies historical antecedents and common elements, discusses implementation strategies, and highlights critique.

Definitions

Senge (1990) defines the learning organization as one that possesses adaptive capacity and generativity, the ability to create alternative futures. This occurs through the rigorous pursuit of five disciplines: (a) systems thinking, (b) personal mastery, (c) mental models, (d) shared vision, and (e) team learning. Focusing more on the learning of individuals, Pedler, Burgoyne, and Boydell (1991) define the learning organization as "an organization that facilitates the learning of all of its members and continuously transforms itself in order to meet its strategic goals" (p. 1).

Watkins and Marsick (1993) define the learning organization as "one that learns continuously and transforms itself . . . Learning is a continuous, strategically used process – integrated with and running parallel to work" (p. 8). Marsick and Watkins (1999) state that their "model emphasizes three key components: (a) systems-level, continuous learning; (b) that is created in order to create and manage knowledge outcomes; (c) which lead to improvement in the organization's performance, and ultimately its value, as measured through both financial assets and non-financial intellectual capital" (pp. 10–11).

Learning at the Organizational Level

Organizational learning occurs when individuals learn on behalf of the organization and results are embedded in the organization's memory or system. Learning can be tactical (incremental, single-loop) or fundamental (breakthrough, double-loop). Views on how organizations learn vary by discipline. Collective learning is the result of an interactive, interdependent process that involves both tacit social learning and explicit codified knowledge.

Environmental jolts or surprises (such as new regulations, competitors, market changes, technology) trigger organizational learning. Active scanning of the environment, both internal and external, enables the organization to proactively identify needed changes. Culture also serves as a filter to focus the organization's attention. Through their separate functions, key people (separately and collectively) arrive at a strategy for responding to the trigger. The strategy's success, in part, is due to the organization's ability to act cohesively. This requires alignment of vision about what to do, shared meaning about intentions, and the capacity to work together across many different kinds of boundaries. This collaborative capacity leads to collective action. This is a culturally-determined organizational capacity.

Actions have consequences for both individuals and organizations. New learning may be needed to develop new capacity, and knowledge and expertise creation are the net result. What is learned is what the organization retains such as a new capacity, a new understanding of what does not work, or a new procedure or technology.

Some organizations systematically capture and embed new learning in a manner that facilitates widespread dissemination of that learning, both for current and future employees. Our model of the learning organization grew out of this conception of organizational learning. It is built on the idea that change must occur at every level of learning – from individual to group to organizational to environmental – and that these changes must become new practices and routines that enable and support the ability to use learning to improve performance.

Learning at the organizational level is not simply the sum of many people learning. Yet, individuals carry within them a microcosmic portrait of the organization (Argyris & Schön, 1996). Through these portraits, they detect changes in the organization's mental models, shared values, and memory. Individual learning is necessary, but not sufficient, for organizational change. When individuals increase their capacity to learn, they can (collectively) enhance the overall capacity of the organization to learn, as long as the organization is receptive to their efforts and puts in place appropriate mechanisms to enable, support, and reward the use of what is learned. In short, individual learning is related to organizational learning, though not equal to it, and potentially (though not necessarily) interdependent with it. Nevertheless, the essence of the learning organization is the dual focus on individuals and the organization.

What must change for an organization to have learned? Rules, memory, values, the system of relationships or structure, the underlying dynamic or pattern that characterizes the organization can change. Learning organizations embed the capacity to adapt or to respond quickly and in novel ways while working to remove barriers to learning. These organizations increase their capacity to learn by making changes in the four systems that influence learning: strategy, structure, slack, and ideology.

Historical Antecedents and Common Elements

Some critics describe the "learning organization" as a fad. But its core idea is part of a long tradition of different concepts that urge a healthy openness to new information and change. Scholars have described this as open systems (Scott, 2002; Trist & Murray, 1997), adaptive organizations (Haeckel & Slywotsky, 1999), innovative organizations (Pettigrew & Fenton, 2000), and resilient organizations (Wheatley, 2001). A recent focus on knowledge creation (Nonaka & Takeuchi, 1995) and knowledge management examines similar issues from a different perspective. Organizational learning is often described as a process. Knowledge management, which had its roots in information technology management, focuses on the knowledge products that are created, collectively, through learning and shared with others in an organization. Increasingly, knowledge management has moved away from reliance on databases and focused, instead, on social learning.

There will always be tension between forces that support growth and those that close the organization to new information in order to stabilize it and make it more efficient. What remains consistent across conceptualizations for a healthy organization include: (a) openness across boundaries, including an emphasis on environmental scanning, collaboration, and competitor benchmarking; (b) resilience or the adaptability of people and systems to respond to change; (c) knowledge/expertise-creation and sharing; and (d) a culture, systems and structures that capture learning and reward innovation.

Creating the Learning Organization

The most common set of interventions for creating learning organizations is found in handbooks built around Senge's five disciplines (Senge, Roberts, Ross, Smith, & Kleiner, 1994). Most authors, as do we (Marsick & Watkins, 1999; Watkins & Marsick, 1993), eschew "recipes" but rather offer guidelines based on theory and practice because no two organizations are alike. It is not possible to import practices without examining critical success factors. Organizational learning is intricately interwoven with structure, strategy, rewards and culture, so it is best to start with a diagnosis of the organization that will guide choices and identify likely supports and barriers (Watkins & Marsick, 2003). There are many strategies that hold promise for creating a learning organization. Two are highlighted here: action technologies and after-action review. "Action technologies" have roots in action research, founded on Lewin's (1946) belief that people take more effective action by collecting and analysing data together, and using those data to guide and track change. Action research involves iterative cycles of problem formulation, data collection and analysis, intervention, monitoring, assessment and problem reformulation. Some link this data-based decision-making process to democratic participation values and humanitarian goals of social good (Reason & Bradbury, 2001). Variants of action research include action science and action learning.

Action science (Argyris & Schön, 1996) uses a micro-version of action research to analyse the gap between a person's goals (espoused theories) and actual behavior (theories-in-use). Case analysis of what was said versus what was thought or felt but not expressed helps people understand and map causal patterns that interfere with goals. Maps indicate individual learning needs, but they also show how people's behavior is shaped by, and reflects, dysfunctional organizational culture, systems, and practices. Having made dysfunctional patterns explicit, people and organizations can learn new ways to better achieve goals.

Organizational learning is not a quick fix. Interventions typically reveal other systemic problems that must be addressed to reap the benefits of learning. For example, a common learning organization practice is the "after-action review" (AAR), a learning review made popular by the US Army (Sullivan & Harper, 1996). During AARs, key stakeholders talk about whether or not they achieved their goals, what happened, why things happened as they did, and how things can be improved. AARs are only successful if people can talk openly about mistakes without fear of reprisal. Rewards and incentives may need to be introduced to build the AAR habit because people are not used to learning in this way, time is limited, and action is supported more than reflection. Solutions generated by AARs may require change in organization practices. Common learnings in AARs are: that people do not share the same understanding of their goals, they distort facts, and "jump up the ladder of inference" – the "ladder" being a tool introduced by Argyris and Schön (1996) – by making quick judgments and acting on them before they have checked to see if their inference is accurate. AARs are often shared with others in the organization, but experience shows that lessons learned are more valuable for the group generating them. Databases can be built of lessons learned, but they are not often used – a problem in many knowledge management systems that is not unique to AARs.

Critique

A conceptual critique of the learning organization is its lack of a clear, consistent definition. It is differently defined and operationalized within and across disciplines (Dierkes, Berthoin Antal, Child, & Nonaka, 2001), and as a result, research – which is not abundant – is hard to consolidate and compare. Conceptual confusion is not easily dissolved by a review of practice. The same practice implemented in different organizations can have very different outcomes, and one must dig below the labels and look across boundaries over time to track organizational learning. Such studies, however, are seldom undertaken. Moreover, today's global context makes it even more difficult to draw conclusions about effective practices because of cross-cultural and international differences.

Questions are also raised about whose version of the learning organization is being advocated given many different stakeholders. Postmodern scholars feed this critique by unmasking the multiple realities that exist in an organization. Critics frequently note the power imbalances in organizations and ask whether or not the learning organization is simply another tool for managerial domination cast, at times, in benign language but with the age-old purpose of controlling the resources of workers for the benefit of owners. Knowledge is capital in many organizations today; the learning organization urges employees to share that capital even though, by so doing, they may lose control of this resource. The global, decentralized knowledge organization of today thus both requires knowledge sharing and creates additional barriers to sharing, given factors such as international outsourcing and global competition.

See also: action learning, action research, human capital theory, human resource development, organizational learning, training.

References and Further Reading

Argyris, C., & Schön, D. (1996). *Organizational learning II: Theory, method, and practice.* Reading, MA: Addison-Wesley.

Dierkes, M., Berthoin A. A., Child, J., & Nonaka, I. (2001). *Handbook of organizational learning and knowledge.* Oxford: Oxford University Press.

Haeckel, S., & Slywotsky, A. (1999). *Adaptive enterprise: Creating and leading sense-and-respond organizations.* Cambridge, MA: Harvard Business School Press.

Lewin, K. (1946). Action research and minority problems. *Journal of Social Issues, 2*(4), 34–36.

Marsick, V. J., & Watkins, K. E. (1999). *Facilitating learning organizations: Making learning count.* Hampshire, UK: Gower.

Nonaka, I., & Takeuchi, H. (1995). *The knowledge-creating company.* New York: Oxford University Press.

Pedler, M., Burgoyne, J., & Boydell, T. (1991). *The learning company.* London: McGraw-Hill.

Pettigrew, A., & Fenton, E. (2000). *The innovating organization.* Thousand Oaks, CA: Sage.

Reason, P., & Bradbury, H. (2001). *Handbook of action research: Participative inquiry and practice.* Thousand Oaks, CA: Sage.

Scott, R. (2002). *Organizations: Rational, natural, and open systems* (5th ed.). Englewood Cliffs, NJ: Prentice Hall.

Senge, P. M. (1990). *The fifth discipline.* New York: Doubleday Currency.

Senge, P. M., Roberts, C., Ross, R. B., Smith, B. J., & Kleiner, A. (1994). *The fifth discipline fieldbook.* New York: Doubleday Currency.

Sullivan, G. R., & Harper, M. V. (1996). *Hope is not a method.* New York: Broadway Books.

Trist, E. L., & Murray, H. (Eds.). (1997). *The social engagement of social science: A Tavistock anthology: The socio-technical perspective.* Philadelphia, PA: University of Pennsylvania Press.

Watkins, K. E., & Marsick, V. J. (1993). *Sculpting the learning organization.* San Francisco: Jossey-Bass.

Watkins, K. E., & Marsick, V. J. (Eds.). (2003). Making learning count! Diagnosing the learning culture in organizations. *Advances in Developing Human Resources*, 5(2). Thousand Oaks, CA: Sage.

Wheatley, M. (2001). *Leadership and the new science, Discovering order in a chaotic world revised*. San Francisco: Berrett-Koehler.

Victoria J. Marsick and Karen E. Watkins

Learning Region

A learning region is a geographical area, which could be small or big (for example a city, village, or province), which links lifelong learning with economic development to compete globally. It is a response to economic globalization where informal, non-formal and formal learning are recognized as important, for people of all ages, to assist the processes of innovation that can lead to economic distinctiveness. The concept, "learning region," is related to that of the knowledge economy, learning society, and information society.

The European Union has chosen lifelong learning as the overarching concept that, it is hoped, will weld together in one policy, active citizenship and the knowledge economy. Europeans argue that they will not be able to move to a competitive knowledge economy unless there is a sufficient degree of social cohesion in Europe. Lifelong learning therefore needs to assist the processes of social inclusion and to enhance the prospects for innovation. Evidence of this thinking in Europe, Australia, Brazil, India, South Africa or North America has led to numerous towns, cities and regions declaring themselves learning towns, cities or regions. But what they mean by this varies.

Most of the countries developing the concept are high-income countries; however, in middle-income countries like Brazil, India and South Africa, the challenge is to interpret and develop the notion of "learning region" in contexts of widespread poverty and social polarization. Some regions emphasize high-end R&D for economic development, while others argue the importance of social justice and equity as being integral to economic success.

Characteristics of Learning Regions

There are essential characteristics of a learning region. One of these is to have a new understanding of the centrality for economic and social development of all forms of learning – informal, non-formal and formal – for people of all ages and in all sectors and spheres of family, community and work life. A second is to prioritize excellent education and training systems at all levels. A third is to provide frequently updated, easily accessible information and counselling services to enable citizens to maximize their learning opportunities. A fourth is to have world-class systems for collection, analysis, management and dissemination of information in order to monitor progress towards being a learning region. A fifth is the creation of social capital through partnerships and networks.

Human, Social and Cultural Capital

Learning regions emphasize not only human capital, but also cultural and social capital. Traditionally, human resources have been approached from the point of view of reproducing and creating human capital. The model is one of making sure to produce skilled people, as accurately as possible, to fulfill the needs of the economy. This remains a significant exercise, although a difficult one to carry out accurately given variables such as HIV/AIDS, fluctuating financial currencies and migration of people.

Human capital focuses on the individual, while social capital focuses on the collective and social relationships. Cultural capital refers to the credentials and cultural assets embodied in individuals and their families, for example the learning culture in many homes of middle-class people that enhances children's participation in learning. Social capital highlights the networks, norms and trust that are necessary for individuals and institutions to achieve common objectives.

Key words that constantly recur in the literature of social capital are trust, community, partnerships and networks. An example of social systems in which trust resulting from social homogeneity facilitates effective economic transactions, is the savings clubs in poor communities which allow the borrowing of money based on trust.

Social capital is a particularly important concept for the development of the learning region or society as it implies that trusting relationships are good for social cohesion and for economic success. A learning society is dependent on partnerships and collaborations of multiple kinds both for economic development and greater social cohesion.

Partnerships and Networks

The speed of global innovation is intense, and close relationships between different elements in the innovation nexus are required to keep pace. Partnerships and networks are required to make the most of the human capital available and to enable collaboration between those working on similar knowledge areas in different institutions and environments. A constant challenging of traditional knowledge categories to suit rapidly changing social and economic realities is necessary as people are encouraged to move "out of the silos." Expressions of this come in the form of economic clusters or hubs, supported by government, business and higher education, in exploring innovative strategies.

Just as the pace of global innovation is intense, so is that of local need. The same principle of having to make the most of the human capital available, therefore, applies equally to networks around public- sector provision and community development. These networks sometimes grow spontaneously, as meetings of people with similar interests, or simply by accident. However, there is evidence that it is possible to accelerate and focus the processes, for example through incentives or building capacity to enable people to engage across sectors, in partnership development and networking.

Lifelong Learning

Learning societies privilege learning, but often concentrate on formal education and training to the detriment of learning. There is growing recognition that if all learning is represented by an iceberg, then the section above the surface of the water would be sufficient to cover formal learning, but the submerged two-thirds of the structure would be needed to convey the much greater importance of informal learning. This is particularly true in societies where formal schooling levels are low. It is in families, communities, through the media, in books, on the Internet, and at workplaces that informal learning occurs. It is here where children and adults develop a culture of learning or not. Through informal means people learn, for example about informal trading, health, parenting, criminality, budgeting, fixing cars, or civic responsibility. It is in local communities, in townships and villages, on sport fields, religious bodies, or in workplaces that values, skills and cultural practices are often acquired. A learning region therefore needs to be concerned to improve the informal learning cultures.

See also: community education, human capital theory, learning festival, lifelong learning, organizations for adult education, social policy.

References and Further Reading

Coffield, F. (Ed.). (2000a). *Differing visions of a learning society. Research findings Vols. 1 and 2*. Bristol: Policy Press.

Coffield, F. (Ed.). (2000b). *The necessity of informal learning*. Bristol: Policy Press.

Division for Lifelong Learning (2001). *Developing the Learning Cape*. Occasional paper. University of the Western Cape, South Africa.

Keating, J., Badenhorst, A., & Szlachetko, T. (2002). *Victoria as a learning region, background report*, OECD Victoria Learning Cities and Regions Conference. Victoria Department of Education and Training, Australia.

Korsgaard, O., Walters, S., & Andersen, R. (Ed.). (2001). *Learning for democratic citizenship*. Association of World Education and Danish University of Education, Denmark.

Torres, R. M. (2003). Lifelong learning. A new momentum and a new opportunity for adult basic learning and education in the South. In *Adult Education and Development*, supplement to no. 60. Bonn, Institute for International Cooperation of the German Adult Education Association.

Shirley Walters

Learning Styles

Learning styles are preferences for certain conditions or ways of learning, where learning means the development of meanings, values, skills, and strategies. The term learning style is sometimes used interchangeably with cognitive style, but cognitive style (coming from the field of cognitive psychology) usually refers more specifically to the ways that people process information and does not include interpersonal relations, affective preferences, and social conditions. There is no one definition, model, or theory of learning style. It tends to be a practical concept, based on the assessment of individual differences with a view to helping learners and educators understand how best to work together. There are at least 20 commonly used learning-styles inventories in adult education. Interest in learning style was at its height in the 1970s, a time when researchers and theorists were working to understand how individual learner differences interacted with teaching strategies (Cronbach & Snow, 1977). This moved educators away from ability and general intelligence as a way of describing individual differences and provided a value-neutral set of characteristics (no one learning style is better than another). There are at least six approaches to learning style in the adult education literature: (a) experiential, (b) social interaction, (c) personality, (d) multiple intelligences and emotional intelligence, (e) perception, and (f) conditions or needs.

Making Meaning Through Experience

Learners have different styles or preferences when it comes to making meaning out of and learning from their experiences. Within this perspective, Kolb's (1984) work is well-known, and his Learning Style Inventory is one of the most popular approaches to assessing learning style in adult education. Although the Learning Style Inventory has been criticized psychometrically, Kolb conducted considerable research on the learning-cycle model upon which his work is based. He proposes that learners go through four stages: (a) the concrete experience of being involved in a new learning situation, (b) reflective observation of that experience, (c) abstract conceptualization in which concepts and theories are created to explain the observations, and (d) active experimentation in which the theories are used to solve problems and make decisions. Although each individual is seen to go through the entire cycle, learners have preferences for one or more parts of the cycle. The abilities associated with each of these stages combine to form clusters, and learning styles are delineated from these clusters: (a) *convergers* prefer abstract conceptualization and active experimentation which leads them to arrive quickly at specific, concrete solutions, (b) *assimilators* prefer abstract conceptualization and reflective observation which leads them to enjoy the integration of ideas into models and theories, (c) *accommodators* prefer concrete experience and active experimentation meaning that they learn by doing and prefer a trial-and-error approach, and (d) *divergers* prefer concrete experience and reflective observation which leads them to generate ideas, brainstorm, and work well with others but not come quickly to solutions.

Social Interaction

Adults may have preferences for the kind or degree of social interaction they prefer to engage in while learning. This approach may not be as value-neutral as others, especially given the emphasis in adult education on collaboration, discussion, and group learning. Fuhrmann and Jacobs (1980) propose that students may prefer (a) dependence, an expectation that the educator is primarily responsible for learning, (b) collaboration, a preference for shared learning, or (c) independence, an expectation that the learner can set his or her own goals and work toward them. More recently, some authors refer to relational and autonomous learning as two distinct preferences and associate these, at least in part, with gender differences (Hayes, Flannery, & Others, 2000; MacKeracher, 1996)

The Grasha–Riechmann Student Learning Style Scale (Grasha, 1994) is a slightly more complex assessment of social interaction preferences. Six dimensions are addressed: (a) *competitive*, where learners strive to perform better than others, (b) *collaborative*, where students share ideas and talents, (c) *avoidant*, where students express disinterest and prefer not to participate, (d) *participative*, where learners take responsibility and participate when asked to do so, (e) *dependent*, where students learn what is required and look to the educator for guidance, and (f) *independent*, where participants like to think for themselves and work on their own. This system is not value neutral, with the avoidant style being especially negative.

Personality

Models of personality and instruments for the assessment of personality yield a broader picture of the individual than do the models addressing learning style specifically. This approach, especially that derived from Jung's (1921/1971) theory of psychological types, is so commonly used to understand learning style in all facets of adult education that it cannot be ignored here. The Myers–Briggs Type Indicator (Myers, 1985), the Kiersey Temperament Sorter (Kiersey & Bates, 1984), and the PET Type Check (Cranton & Knoop, 1995) are three examples of assessment strategies based on psychological type theory.

Psychological type theory is based on two attitudes towards the world and four functions of living. The introverted attitude focuses on the inner self, and the extraverted attitude focuses on the world outside of the self. When people use the thinking function they make judgments based on logic and analysis; when they use the feeling function, they make judgments based on values. When the sensing function is used, people perceive the world through their five senses, but when the intuitive function is used, individuals rely on hunches, imagination, and possibilities in their perceptions. Depending on which model is followed, these two attitudes and four functions are combined to yield 4, 8 or 16 psychological types. For example, the Myers–Briggs Type Indicator may label a learner as ENTJ (extroverted, intuitive, thinking, and judgmental, with the judgmental categorization meaning that thinking is the most preferred function) or ISFP (introverted, sensing, feeling, and perceptive, with the perceptive function of sensing being dominant) or any one of 16 combinations. The Keirsey Temperament Sorter yields four labels: SP (sensing, perceptive) or the Dionysian Temperament, SJ (sensing, judgmental) or the Epimethean Temperament, NT (intuition, thinking) or the Promethean Temperament, and NF (intuition, feeling) or the Apollonian Temperament. The PET Type Check leads to a profile of preferences with eight possible combinations: extraverted thinking, introverted thinking, extraverted feeling, introverted feeling, extraverted sensing, introverted sensing, extraverted intuition, and introverted intuition.

Learning styles are clearly derived from psychological type preferences. For example, by using extraverted thinking, a person learns through planning, organizing and structuring learning experiences, and by using introverted thinking, a learner is reflective, contemplative, and critical. The feeling function leads to a preference for collaborative and group learning, the sensing function to an interest in learning by doing, and the intuitive function to an inclination for exploratory, unstructured, and imaginative experiences.

Multiple Intelligences and Emotional Intelligence

Although not presented as learning style, Gardner's (1993) notion of multiple intelligence parallels in many ways psychological type theory and clearly contributes to an understanding of learning style. Gardner sees people as having autonomous faculties that can work independently or in concert with each other: (a) musical intelligence, (b) bodily-kinesthetic intelligence, (c) logical-mathematical intelligence, (d) linguistic intelligence, (e) spatial intelligence, (f) interpersonal intelligence, and (g) intrapersonal intelligence. Goleman (1998) focuses on emotional intelligence, which seems to be equivalent to Gardner's conceptualization of interpersonal and intrapersonal intelligence. Emotional intelligence includes knowing and managing one's emotions, motivating oneself, recognizing emotions in others, and handling relationships.

Perception Preferences

When many practitioners think of learning style, they are referring to visual, auditory, and kinesthetic learning preferences. It is standard rhetoric in the how-to guides for adult educators that information should be presented both visually and through auditory channels. Suessmuth (1985) presents a learning style inventory which distinguishes between: (a) language learners who prefer to hear (auditory) or see (visual) language, (b) numerical learners who prefer to hear or see numbers, and (c) auditory-visual-kinesthetic learners who prefer to learn through experiencing and manipulating material.

Conditions or Needs

Yet another approach to learning style takes into account the conditions under which different individuals learn best, and their social and physical needs. Dunn and Dunn's (1977) model contains four categories: (a) environmental conditions such as sound, light, temperature, and design of the learning space, (b) sociological needs including working in groups, in pairs or alone and with or without an instructor presence, (c) physical needs such as time of day, the need for nourishment, and the need for mobility, and (d) emotional conditions such as motivation, persistence, and desire for structure. To some extent, especially with the sociological and emotional needs, this approach overlaps with the social interaction models, but the inclusion of environmental and physical requirements adds a dimension not seen in other learning styles frameworks.

Cultural Issues

Although learning style is presented as value-neutral, the concept of learning style itself is a Euro-American one, and the categorization systems reflect the values of that culture. Anderson (1988) describes the style valued by the male Euro-American culture as independent, analytic, and non-affective. He suggests that Aboriginal, African American, and female Euro-American groups are more field-dependent, relational, holistic, and affective. Bell's (1994) research with African Americans confirms that this group is more likely to demonstrate a holistic and relational style. Swisher's (1991) work with American Indian and Alaskan Native groups also tends to validate Anderson's thinking. Peterson (1997) provides a review of the learning style literature in relation to cultural differences in the area of human resource development; however, it is clear that much work remains to be done in this area. Researchers may need to question the usefulness of conducting cross-cultural comparisons using assessment strategies based on Western conceptualizations of learning style. It is also important to remember that each learning style inventory measures something different and that often there is not a good research base for the reliability and validity claims of existing instruments.

Conceptual, Research, and Practice Issues

There are at least three unresolved issues in the area of learning styles (Merriam & Caffarella, 1999). Conceptually, the definition of learning style is unclear and, with the exception of the work using psychological type, is not derived from a consistent theory (Flannery, 1993).

As a result, whether learning styles change over time with maturity or context, whether they should be consciously developed, or whether they are relatively stable is open to question. From a researcher's perspective, the theoretical foundation of assessment strategies is often not explicit, making it difficult to carry out meaningful investigations. Even whether or not learning style should be studied using quantitative data, as it most often is, is questionable.

Although learning styles are advocated as a means for educators to understand their learners, it is unclear as to whether the educator should adapt to the learning styles of students, construct activities designed to develop non-preferred styles, or simply use a variety of strategies so that some learners can use their preferred style on some occasions.

See also: experiential learning, facilitation, motivation, teaching.

References and Further Reading

Anderson, J. (1988). Cognitive styles and multicultural populations. *Journal of Teacher Education, 39*(1), 2–9.

Bell, Y. R. (1994). A culturally sensitive analysis of Black learning style. *Journal of Black Psychology, 20*(1), 47–61.

Cranton, P., & Knoop, R. (1995). Assessing psychological type: The PET type check. *General, Social, and Genetic Psychological Monographs, 121*(2), 247–274.

Cronbach, L., & Snow, R. (1977). *Aptitudes and instructional methods*. New York: Irvington Publishers.

Dunn, D., & Dunn, K. (1977). How to diagnose learning styles. *Instructor, 87*, 123–144.

Flannery, D. (Ed.). (1993). *Applying cognitive learning theory to adult learning. New Directions for Adult and Continuing Education*, No. 59. San Francisco: Jossey-Bass.

Fuhrmann, B., & Jacobs, R. (1980). *The learning interactions inventory*. Richmond, VA: Ronne Jacobs Associates.

Gardner, H. (1993). *Frames of mind: The theory of multiple intelligences* (10th anniversary edition). New York: Basic Books.

Goleman, D. (1998). *Working with emotional intelligence*. New York: Bantam Books.

Grasha, A. (1994). *Teaching with style: A practical guide to enhancing learning by understanding teaching and learning styles*. Pittsburgh, PA: International Alliance of Teaching Scholars.

Hayes, E. R., Flannery, D. with Brooks, A., Tisdell, E. J. & Hugo, J. M. (2000). *Women as learners: The significance of gender in adult learning*. San Francisco: Jossey-Bass.

Jung, C. (1921/1971). *Psychological types*. Princeton, NJ: Princeton University Press. (originally published in 1921).

Keirsey, D., & Bates, M. (1984). *Please understand me: Character and temperament types*. Delma CA: Prometheus Nemesis Books.

Kolb, D. A. (1984). *Experiential learning*. Englewood Cliffs, NJ: Prentice Hall.

MacKeracher, D. (1996). *Making sense of adult learning*. Toronto: Culture Concepts.

Merriam, S. B., & Caffarella, R. S. (1999). *Learning in adulthood*. San Francisco: Jossey-Bass.

Myers, I. (1985). *Gifts differing* (7th ed.). Palo Alto, CA: Consulting Psychologists Press.

Peterson, L. (1997). International HRD: What we know and don't know. *Human Resource Development Quarterly, 8*(1), 63–79.

Suessmuth, P. (1985). A learning styles inventory. *Training Ideas, 44*, 2–20.

Swisher, K. (1991). American Indian/Alaskan native learning styles: Research and practice. Retrieved April 20, 2004 from ERIC database (ERIC Document Reproduction Service No. ED335175).

Patricia Cranton

Libraries

Libraries or information centers and resource centers, as they are variously known, are often visualized as places with books to read and borrow. While based on experience, this conventional image is also very limiting: libraries perform a more complex function in society by supporting literacy, social action, and lifelong education. Librarians have played a role in the historical development of adult education, and are re-forging this partnership for lifelong learning in the 21st century. While the connections may seem almost intuitive, contemporary literature reveals that little critical attention has been given to this enduring relationship.

Historical Links

Early initiatives in adult education were often intrinsically linked with libraries. During the colonial period in the United States, adult education and libraries were liberal-minded allies in promoting an educated citizenry. The early discussion clubs, such as Benjamin Franklin's Junto, established libraries as part of their programs of self-improvement through education. Later, the Lyceum and Chautauqua movements stimulated interest in the development of public libraries as partners in adult learning. By providing readers' advisory services, librarians assisted individual adults and fostered their varied learning projects. Throughout North America, Britain and Europe, mechanics' and mercantile societies, folk high schools and study clubs also developed specialized library collections to suit the educational interests of their members.

The alliance of libraries with progressive adult education in North America has been somewhat more uneasy. In the early 20th century, Carnegie Foundation support of library and adult education initiatives attempted to reinforce formal linkages between these two emerging professions. Progressive adult educators envisioned a convergence of interests with librarians, but met with reluctance among mainstream librarians to accepting a more socially-engaged role. The entrenchment of liberal ideals for professional library services and a growing emphasis on library "neutrality" constrained the development of the relationship, but did not extinguish it. Both the Highlander Folk School in the United States and the Antigonish Movement in Canada, for example, relied on the active involvement of librarians who saw their work as integral to the social-change stream of adult education.

In the latter half of the 20th century, attempts were made to develop new types of information services that would be more responsive to community learning needs than conventional libraries. Noted adult educator Malcolm Knowles (1976) advocated a new role for the librarian in a learning resource centre, serving as both a vital link to community information resources and as an active agent in structuring learning experiences.

Emergence of Resource Centers

In North America and the United Kingdom, innovative services of this sort were developed on a trial basis in the 1970s. Community resource centers and citizens' advice bureaus supplemented traditional public library services, often taking a more active advocacy role for their patrons.

In countries of the global South, however, some began to question whether the Western library model was fundamentally capable of serving the adult learning and information needs of other regions. The library was seen as an alien institution: a dusty colonial artifact or an insidious tool of imperialism, depending on the perspective and politics of the writer. A profound critique of imposing inappropriate, book-centered models of library service on oral cultures with their own rich heritage of learning was developed.

A wide range of terms is used to describe the services that emerged as alternative centers for information and learning. Among the more common are rural community resource centers, bootstrap libraries, community learning centers, *centres de documentation communautaire*, and community libraries. These centers were often linked with community development, popular education initiatives or social movements, and dismissed the purported neutrality of conventional libraries. In South Africa, for example, resource-centre workers developed a philosophy that encompassed principles of two-way communication, a dialogical process, and recognizing the political dimension of information. Resource centers began to sponsor a variety of learner-centered activities serving to conscientize and empower people in the struggle against apartheid (Karelse, 1991). Similar adult education functions are now common to women's resource centers, environmental resource centers, and a variety of others throughout the world that serve as focal points for learning and activism, and as sites for critically engaged knowledge production and documentation (see Isis, 1997).

Libraries and Adult Learners' Week

As the 20th century ended, a renewed relationship began to develop between adult educators and librarians around the world. Many conventional libraries became more intentional in their support for adult learning activities (see Carr, 1999), viewing themselves not only as venues for learning but as agents in the process. In the United Kingdom, for example, the Library Association's 2001 strategy paper on libraries and lifelong learning committed the association to acting as "champion of the learner" (p. 3) promoting people's entitlement to learning opportunities and access to learning resources.

One aspect of this engagement is the increasing participation of libraries in Adult Learners' Week activities throughout the world (Adams, Krolak, Kupidura, & Pangerc Pahernik, 2002). Libraries from Australia to Botswana, Egypt and Iceland – to name but a few – have chosen to play a significant role in honoring adult learners during this special time. The Learning Cape Festival, a month-long event in South Africa, gives libraries the opportunity to highlight their many adult learning initiatives. In Slovenia, public libraries organize intergenerational activities for Lifelong Learning Week, and offer creative workshops, information access demonstrations, round tables and literary evenings. The often implicit relationship between libraries and adult education is now being formally recognized and celebrated.

Networking of Adult Learning Information Services

Adult education as a discipline has generated its own substantial literature. Despite (or sometimes because of) the pervasive power of information technology, some of this knowledge is marginalized, particularly when it originates outside the presumed centers of power. In 1997 the Fifth World Conference on Adult Education (CONFINTEA V) hosted an historic meeting of adult education documentalists, information specialists and librarians in a workshop that explored networking of adult education information in an international context. Founded on principles of partnership and equity of access, the Adult Learning Documentation and Information Network (ALADIN) now includes approximately 100 information centers worldwide, linking them in their efforts to support and document adult learning. For the UN Literacy Decade, the network has decided to focus on "fostering and supporting grassroots documentation and knowledge production, and will promote the development of dynamic information centers where people can work together for popular action" (Adams et al., 2002, p. 36). In an age of global information exchange, libraries' role in promoting and strengthening adult learning has taken on a new life.

See also: community education, conscientization, learning festivals, social action.

References and Further Reading

Adams, S., Krolak, L., Kupidura, E., & Pangerc Pahernik, Z. (2002). Libraries and resource centers: Celebrating adult learning every week of the year. *Convergence, 35*(2–3), 27–39.

Carr, D. W. (1999). The situation of the adult learner in the library. In P. O. Libutti (Ed.), *Librarians as learners, librarians as teachers: The diffusion of Internet expertise in the academic library* (pp. 18–35). Chicago: American Library Association.

Isis International – Manila (1997). *Living collections*. Manila, Philippines: Isis International.

Karelse, C-M. (1991). The role of resource centres in building a democratic non-racial and united South Africa. *Innovation, 3,* 3–8.

Knowles, M. S. (1976). The future role of libraries in adult education. Paper presented at the Continuing Library Education Network and Exchange Assembly, Chicago, ERIC Document Reproduction Service No. ED118133.

The Library Association (2001). *Libraries and lifelong learning: A strategy 2002–4.* London: The Library Association.

Sue Adams

Life History

Life history is an approach to research that involves the study of the effects of biography and narrative on adults, and has multiple origins and uses. Although researchers have long had an interest in personal writing exposing the dynamics and learnings of adult life, in the last decades the human sciences have extended the applications of life history and developed it as a research methodology. The practice of life history in the field of adult education, however, is more recent. Under the general rubric of the biographical approach, life history has inspired new research on adult learning and development, while biographical narratives have enabled adults in a variety of educational contexts to become aware of how they learn and to make significant changes in their lives.

Brief Historical View

Signs of written life histories existed in Greek as well as Latin culture centuries ago. From Augustine to Rousseau, confessions were a form of writing close to autobiography. However, personal documents and diaries emerged only in the 18th century, giving the writing of autobiography its modern sense. Today, autobiographical narratives have been highly popularized through frequent media presentation.

Life history has a rich philosophical heritage. The work of 19th century philosopher Wilhelm Dilthey is often considered to be the theoretical foundation for the validation of the role of interpretation central to the school of hermeneutics. In the 20th century, the collection and analysis of empirical data constituted the most important aspect of quantitative research, as exemplified in the so-called "hard sciences." Human sciences struggled to ground and validate research that could encompass the complexity of social phenomena. Qualitative and participatory research methodologies emerged in the fields of anthropology and sociology, where Oscar Lewis' book on the Sánchez family (1961) was recognized in anthropology as a classic. Social scientists began to discover the heuristic qualities of the biographical narrative, and it was particularly the influence of the Chicago School of Sociology that encouraged researchers to validate life history as an alternative research approach.

In the field of adult education, life history is used in many countries as an emancipatory methodology sensitizing adult students to the learning resources they need and facilitating self-direction of their own training and development.

Life History in the Field of the Social Sciences

The social and cultural dimensions of immigration have been a major theme in life history studies, and special attention has been given to the historical contexts and cultural roots of refugees and migrants. Thomas and Znaniecke's *The Polish Peasant in Europe and America*, recounting the life histories of immigrants moving from Poland to Chicago, was a pioneering study. Until that time, research had been primarily concerned with the social integration of rural migrant workers in urban areas. At the beginning of the 20th century, however, 30% of Chicago's population were foreign residents, a figure that remains the same in many places in the world today. Issues of intercultural displacement and assimilation became too widespread to be ignored.

In researching the theme of immigration, proponents of qualitative methodology have often favored a variety of versions of the life history approach. Their concern has been to understand complex intercultural differences or violent reactions to uprootedness, for instance, not just through objective observation, description and quantitative analysis, but by giving voice to the immigrants themselves and offering them a protected arena for oral and written narrative as well as social dialogue.

The life history approach has also generated a large body of research focused on the social integration of specific groups or marginal communities. Major examples include: women or gender studies; illiteracy studies; or social-change projects in which role and status are correlated with stages of the life course, such as Erikson's work on adolescence (1982), or Mader's on the aged (1995). Adult development studies have often been based on biographical data or autobiographical narratives. More recently, priority has been given to the analysis of the destructive effects of unemployment and to the impact of a fragmented worklife cycle (Alheit, 1994; Alheit, Bron-Wojciechowska, Brugger, & Dominicé, 1995).

For most authors, life history represents an epistemological choice. The writer attempts to depict what the scholar labels "the lived life." Both writer and researcher seek a comprehensive approach in which the question remains the same: how does one enter a world of different cultural and social references without listening to the individual person in the defined situation or without experiencing the situation oneself?

Life history may be considered today to be both an important tool and a main methodological orientation for social research. Life history researchers speak about a clinical methodology or a methodology leading towards clinical knowledge. Because narratives produced in the life history approach belong to the subjective world of the singular, the question of how many narratives are necessary or how to analyse the narratives has often been debated and remains a key issue. The problems of how to interpret personal narratives and how linguistics could contribute to their analysis are still unresolved.

Educational Practice of Life History

Life history could not have been applied to adult and continuing education without the pioneering work previously accomplished in the social sciences. In France, Bertaux (1981) broke through the confines of empirico-analytical research, as developed in sociology after the Second World War, in order to bring the heritage of life history back to the human sciences. After reading Bertaux's work, Pineau (1983) created a practice of life history which helps participants understand the process of self-education on the basis of how adults tend to construct their lives.

The question of how to identify the learning process of adults (Dominicé, 2000) shares the same theoretical inquiry. In the context of how adults think, how does one relate formal and informal learning? What are the main stages of learning and most important learning events during the course of adult life? What kind of life experiences and meaningful relationships are sources of learning? Pineau and Dominicé, as well as many other colleague-scholars, introduced life history as both a learning and a research tool in the field of adult education.

In the last decade, two international networks have been organized: the International Association of Life History Applied to Adult Education (ASIHVIF) in French-speaking countries, and the European Society for Research in the Education of Adults (ESREA) in Europe.

Educational biography has become a main practice in adult education, based on oral and written narratives shared and discussed in small facilitated groups. This approach has been used in several North American and European universities in the training of trainers, offering an experiential understanding of the ways adults learn. The result of this use of life history is considered basic knowledge for the training of adult educators or instructors.

Life history may also be applied to the guidance of adults entering university programs late in their lives (West, 1996). Writing an autobiography facilitates the reentry to the world of formal learning of adult students questioning their capacity to learn. Already used in lifelong learning programs to validate experiential learning, life history will be increasingly developed in this perspective. And in specific contexts such as library programs, life histories prove valuable as resources for learning by adults of all ages as seen in the Life Stories in Library Programming, a videotape course prepared by Marsha Rossiter and Darlene E. Weingand (1996).

More generally, the practice of life history in adult and continuing education motivates learners to be reflective about how they think and operate. Jack Mezirow & Associates (1990) include educational biography in the panoply of approaches leading to transformative learning. New fields continue to open through life history approaches. Patients of chronic diseases may take better care of themselves by examining how they have always managed their health, and life history work may be helpful in the recall of both painful and joyful events of the past. Life history groups recalling Second World War events have enriched intergenerational dialogue. The life history approach may inspire the recall of a wide variety of significant collective memories of social or political dimensions, and written biographical narratives have been published on such themes.

In the German tradition, biographical narrative is associated with "*Bildung,*" the concept of education and training as life-construction ("*formation*" in French, similar but still slightly different in meaning). Life history is therefore understood within a more global and even spiritual outlook. For some authors, biographical work is considered to be the core of adult education.

In a world perceived as unstable, the main task of adult education becomes the building of a meaningful life course or life history. Such a perspective goes back not just to humanistic psychology as formulated in the 20th century, but to philosophical, social and political roots belonging to the history of mankind. Life history is not just the recounting of a unique personal adventure. The human person constructs the full meaning of life through particular as well as universal social and cultural resources.

See also: autobiography, narrative, older adults' learning, reflective learning, research methods, social constructivism.

References and Further Reading

Alheit, P. (1994). *Taking the knocks: Youth unemployment and biography. A qualitative analysis.* London: Cassel.

Alheit, P., Bron-Wojciechowska, A., Brugger, E., & Dominicé, P. (Eds.). (1995). *The biographical approach in European adult education.* Vienna: Verband Wiener Volksbildung.

Bertaux, D. (Ed.). (1981). *Biography and society.* Beverly Hills: Sage.

Dominicé, P. (2000). *Learning from our lives.* San Francisco: Jossey-Bass.

Erikson, E. H. (1982). *The life cycle completed.* New York: W. W. Norton Co.

Lewis, O. (1961). *The children of Sánchez: Autobiography of a Mexican family.* New York: Random House.

Mader, W. (1995). Thematically guided autobiographical reconstruction. On theory and method of "guided autobiography" in adult education. In P. Alheit, A. Bron-Wojciechowska, E. Brugger, & P. Dominicé (Eds.), *The biographical approach in European adult education* (pp. 244–255). Vienna: Verband Wiener Volksbildung.

Mezirow, J., & Associates (1990). *Fostering critical reflection in adulthood: A guide to transformative and emancipator learning.* San Francisco: Jossey-Bass.

Pineau, G. (1983). *Produire sa vie: Autoformation et autobiographie* (*Creating one's life: Self-development and autobiography*). Montreal, Canada: Editions St. Martin.

Rossiter, M., & Weingand, D. E. (1996). *Life stories in library programming.* Madison: University of Wisconsin.

Thomas, W., & Znaniecke, F. (1974). *The*

Polish peasant in Europe and America: Monograph of an Immigrant group, 2 vols. New York: Octagon (originally published 1918).

West, L. (1996). *Beyond fragments: Adults, motivation and higher education.* London: Taylor & Francis.

Pierre Dominicé

Lifelong Learning

Lifelong learning is a process of learning throughout life. For some, it is considered to be a positive direction taken by governments and individuals since it moves learning from formal institutions to the everyday sphere. The position taken in this entry, however, is that lifelong learning represents an oppressive "regime of truth" (Foucault, 1980), or an attempt to shift responsibility for education from governments to individuals. For some people it is clearly a phenomenon (lifelong learning as a noun); for others it's a process (lifelong learning as a verb). In the UK and other places, adult education now sails under the flag of lifelong learning. But what is lifelong learning? A flag of convenience? Or a template for serious reform?

It is important to distinguish lifelong education from lifelong learning. Lifelong education was a project of UNESCO and activists wanting to strengthen civil society. Lifelong learning, as promoted by the Organization for Economic Co-operation and Development (OECD) (1996) is different. Before jettisoning adult education, there's a need to understand who's doing what to whom under the flag of lifelong learning and how it differs from lifelong education.

Revolting Students

Lifelong education (Faure, 1972) arose from discussions within UNESCO in the 1960s. But it was the French student movements of 1968, the critique of formal education mounted by writers like Ivan Illich, Everett Reimer, Paulo Freire, John Holt, Paul Goodman and others, coupled with the needs of newly independent countries, that led to lifelong education. In *Learning to Be* (Faure, 1972) lifelong education was proposed as a master concept for reform of entire education systems.

A proper application of lifelong education would result in the creation of a learning society where access to and learning in education would be taken-for-granted – an inalienable human right like clean water or a roof over one's head. After 1972, the UNESCO Institute for Education in Hamburg undertook large-scale projects to elaborate what lifelong education meant for teacher training, curriculum reform, evaluation, libraries and other matters (e.g., Cropley, 1977, 1979, 1980).

Lifelong Education in the Learning Society

The learning society can be visualized by drawing a vertical line on a page; at the bottom are the young, and at the top, old people. This is the lifespan aspect of the learning society. Draw a line across the page so it bisects the vertical; this is the horizontal or lifewide aspect of the learning society. On the left non-formal, and on the right formal settings for education. Formal settings are age-graded credential-awarding schools, colleges, universities and similar settings usually under the control of a Ministry of Education. Non-formal are out-of-school educational settings such as community centers, churches, prisons and the workplace.

This mapping yields four equal-sized zones, the two lower zones encompassing education for young people in formal (e.g., school) and non-formal settings (e.g., Boy Scouts, Girl Guides); the two upper zones encompassing education for older people in formal (e.g., universities) and non-formal settings (e.g., community centers or churches). In a learning society there would be a more equal distribution of resources around these four zones. Hence, there would be as much emphasis on the education of old or young people in non-formal as in formal settings. Moreover, a learner would be able to swim back and forth, much like a fish, securing education in a formal setting today, and a non-formal one tomorrow. The emphasis would not be on where a learner gets educated; rather, the focus would be on what is learned. There would also be a more relaxed attitude about prerequisites. Education does not occur in linear ways and learners could secure access to higher levels without always having done (often irrelevant) prerequisites.

Vertical Integration

The vertical dimension refers to the lifespan aspect of the learning society. This is the idea that education should occur throughout life, from cradle to grave. However, there are *psychosocial* and *structural* barriers impeding the ability of people to opt in and out of education throughout their lives. In a vertically integrated system, structural barriers would be removed by passing appropriate legislation such as on paid educational leave. Psychocultural barriers are more formidable. Equal opportunity does not automatically translate into equal learners because audiotapes inside people's heads send negative messages about returning to education as an adult. It is naïve to think facilitating access (as in distance education or distributed learning) will overcome the tendency for formal education to exclude people and reproduce unequal power relations. Access, by itself, is not enough because it fails to overcome adverse psychocultural factors.

Horizontal Integration

Horizontal integration (or interaction) refers to the need to foster education in a plethora of settings. It is intolerable to have a situation where education secured in formal settings results in prestigious credentials, and that gained in non-formal or informal settings attracts few credentials and no status. What is learned is more important than where knowledge is acquired. There should be a more relaxed attitude about the value of what occurs in non-formal and informal settings.

Typically, education in formal settings is paid for by government, well-organized, assigned adequate resources and results in the award of credentials. Education secured in non-formal settings is largely unorganized, struggles with meagre resources and is regarded as outside the mainstream. What Faure (1972) envisaged was not a dismantling of formal settings, rather what was needed (then and now) was a more pluralistic and accessible array of opportunities for education throughout the life-cycle. Integration or interaction is needed.

There are informal, non-formal and formal settings for education. It is confusing to speak of formal or non-formal education because it suggests formality of processes is the issue.

There are many non-formal settings (such as prisons) where the educational processes are as rigid as those found in formal settings such as universities. The intent of this tripartite distinction (formal, non-formal, informal) is to portray learning and education as something that occurs throughout society. But there is no such thing as informal or formal learning.

People learn in informal settings through exposure to media, conversations, casual and incidental encounters in community settings or public awareness campaigns. Although people do learn in informal settings and, in AIDS and other campaigns it is important they do so, this is not education.

Lifelong education requires more than mere tinkering with education systems. What is needed is a complete overhaul of entire educational systems. Hence, as was demonstrated in Tanzania, it is easier to implement in countries where formal education is not well- developed. In developed countries there are entrenched interests (such as schools and universities) unwilling to cooperate with non-formal settings.

Education is a provided service. Lifelong education required someone – often government or other agencies – to develop policy and devote resources to education in a broad array of informal, non-formal and formal settings. Deliberate choices must be made. Lifelong education was a noun – the name of a master concept for educational reform.

Lifelong Learning

Lifelong learning is more of a verb. It denotes a less emancipatory set of relationships than lifelong education. As a discourse, lifelong learning tends to render invisible any obligation on educators to address social conditions. Predatory capitalism is unproblematized. Lifelong learning is nested in an ideology of vocationalism. Learning is for acquiring skills enabling the learner to work harder, faster and smarter and to help their employer compete in the global economy. As discourse, it has spawned allied concepts like the dubious idea that economies and societies are now (but weren't previously) "knowledge-based."

Lifelong learning serves different interests than those envisaged by Faure (1972). It is nested in a notion of the autonomous free-floating individual learner as consumer and mostly abdicates responsibility for the public good. It avoids hard choices by putting learning on the open market. If the learner as consumer does not take advantage of available opportunities it is their own fault. It is easier to blame the victim than overcome structural or psychocultural barriers to learning. Instead, the savvy consumer surfs the Internet to select from a smorgasbord of educational offerings. Learning is an individual activity. Hence, lifelong learning is favored by advocates of an information economy prone to make vast generalizations about technology-mediated forms of learning.

As a regime of truth (Foucault, 1980), lifelong learning is a signifier for adapting to the "needs" of the global economy. It is this that evoked the shift from education to learning. This is a source of concern because "the concept of learning floats free from designated and concrete meanings . . . [and] . . . unless civil societarian adult educators claim 'learning' for themselves, giving it a socially anchored, contextual meaning, the neo-conservatives will run away with it" (Welton, 1997, p. 33).

Misapprehensions

Although the utopian thinking of Faure (1972) still represents an emancipatory template for reform, there is a tendency to dismiss it as "unrealistic." In the meantime, new information technologies have evoked intense competitiveness between educational agencies and the specter of privatized academics and isolated learners tapping keyboards.

By the dawn of the 21st century, neo-liberal notions of lifelong learning had mostly overwhelmed earlier notions of lifelong education. Among many problems associated with this were the following:

- Instead of being a large-scale template for educational reform, lifelong learning was often constructed as a new market for civil society. Hence, there is primary, secondary and civil society – followed by lifelong learning.
- Formal and non-formal settings were still like two parallel railway lines. Both cross the landscape but never touch. Formal settings have little to do with the non-formal. Some people dismiss learning in non-formal and informal settings. It is not "real" education.
- Little is known about high-performing farm-gate learners who, without "benefit" of formal education, learn in non-formal or informal settings and make major achievements (e.g., Peter Jackson, film; Tom Schnackenberg, sailing; Bill Gates, software) (Boshier, 2003).
- Lifelong learning is reduced to an empty slogan or decontextualized set of educational techniques gutted of politicality.
- Lifelong learning is used as a rationale for inflicting (often oppressive and authoritarian) forms of mandatory continuing education on citizens already marginalized and experiencing social difficulties.
- Lifelong learning gets wrongly equated with lifelong schooling.

Promising Developments

As well as misapprehensions there are promising developments. One of these is the notion of learning regions, cities, towns, villages or festivals (Walters & Etkind, 2004), which stems more from a Faure than an OECD ethos. The boisterous and colorful *Pasifika* in Auckland, New Zealand is a good example of a festival that appeals to all ages and collapses boundaries between learning, entertainment and culture.

In a learning city (town or village) there are attempts to foster all forms of learning for citizens old and young in many contexts. The town or city has become a preferred site for learning because of the failure of national plans for educational reform. Learning cities are committed to learning as a core aspect of development. As well as catching dogs and servicing sewers, the city fosters learning. They seek to sustain economic activity by building social capital. By 2005 about 20 communities in Britain had declared themselves as learning cities. In New Zealand, Wanganui and Waitakere went in this direction (Boshier, 2003), and there were similar developments in Australia, Canada, India and Africa. Information technology helps but is not essential. What matters most are local places and spaces. These are both prominent in postmodern reflections on lifelong learning (Edwards, 1997).

A learning city (town or village) is:

> a form of community development in which local people from every community sector act together to enhance the social, economic, cultural and environmental conditions of their community. It is a pragmatic approach that mobilizes the learning resources and expertise of all five community sectors:
>
> - Civic or local government;
> - Economic (private and cooperative enterprise);
> - Public (libraries, recreation commissions, social agencies, arts councils, health bodies, museums, etc.);
> - Education (k[indergarten] to university); and
> - Voluntary/community/individual citizens
>
> The total formal (school, college and university) and nonformal (civic, economic, public and voluntary) learning resources . . . are therefore harnessed . . . according to needs and priorities set by the community . . . local current initiatives are not replaced but rather built upon by the learning community approach. (Faris, 2001, p. 1).

This approach reduces the ambiguities of lifelong education into convivial and, best of all, local operations. It doesn't take citizens long to choose between a knowledge-based society (with its jargon-ridden benchmarks, visions and best practices) or having fun at the local learning festival.

Future in the Past

Apart from developments like learning cities, lifelong learning is mostly infused with false hopes. On the surface, it appears suited to the 21st century, but it is citizens with a broad-based education – and the ability to organize and involve others in respectful, collaborative and convivial ways – that will be best able to function in a global environment.

There is no doubt Faure's vision was derailed (Boshier, 1998). However, although lifelong education is down, it's not out. Faure's architecture for lifelong education is still a worthwhile template for reform. Hence, in a postmodern maneuver, the best hope for the future might reside in the past.

See also: civil society, globalization, learning festival, learning region, organizations for adult education.

References and Further Reading

Boshier, R.W. (1998). The Faure Report: Down but not out. In P. S. Jarvis, J. Holford, & C. Griffin (Eds.), *Lifelong learning in the learning society* (pp. 3–20). London: Kogan Page.

Boshier, R.W. (2003). Heritage learning in the *Back Shed* of the learning city. *New Zealand Journal of Adult Learning, 31*(1), 6–23.

Cropley, A. J. (Ed.). (1977). *Lifelong education: A psychological analysis.* Oxford: Pergamon.

Cropley, A. J. (Ed.). (1979). *Lifelong education: A stock-taking.* Oxford: Pergamon.

Cropley, A. J. (Ed.). (1980). *Towards a system of lifelong education: Some practical considerations.* Oxford: Pergamon.

Edwards, R. (1997). *Changing places? Flexibility, lifelong learning and a learning society.* London: Routledge.

Faris, R. (2001). *Learning communities: Villages, neighbourhoods, towns, cities and regions preparing for a knowledge-based society.* Victoria, BC: Golden Horizon Ventures. Retrieved September 22, 2003 from http://members.shaw.ca/rfaris/docs/LCdigest.pdf

Faure, E. (Chair).(1972). *Learning to be.* Paris: UNESCO.

Foucault, M. (1980). *Truth and power. Power/knowledge: Selected interviews and other writings 1972–1977* (pp. 107–133). Brighton, UK: The Harvester Press.

Organization for Economic Cooperation and Development (OECD). (1996). *Lifelong learning for all.* Paris: OECD.

Walters, S., & Etkind, R. (2004). Developing a learning region: What can learning festivals contribute? In D. E. Clover (Ed.), Proceedings of the Joint International Conference of the Adult Education Research Conference and the Canadian Association for the Study of Adult Education (pp. 503–508). Victoria: University of Victoria, British Columbia.

Welton, M. R. (1997). In defence of civil society: Canadian adult education in neo-conservative times. In S. Walters (Ed.), *Globalization, adult education and training: Impacts and issues* (pp. 27–38). London: Zed Books.

Roger Boshier

Lifespan Development

Development implies growth and progress, not merely change. Lifespan development, then, refers to growth and progress on the full gamut of human dimensions across the lifespan. The study of lifespan development has been concerned with questions such as: What develops? In what sequence? Are there identifiable stages and phases of development? What processes underlie developmental change? What factors enhance or retard development? And to what extent is development socially and culturally determined? An engagement with the literature reveals a range of very different theoretical and empirical approaches to the above questions. Indeed the very notion of development has been challenged (see for example Erica Burman's 1994 work *Deconstructing Developmental Psychology*). Apart from physical development, the human dimensions studied fall into one of two broad categories: cognitive development and self-development (identity).

Cognitive Development

Much of the early work on cognitive and intellectual development focused on child development, either documenting age norms and changes in IQ, or the cognitive capabilities in different ages and stages.

An interest in adult cognitive development did not really occur until the middle of the 20th century. Basically there appear to be three models of cognitive development after maturity. One model, the "stability model," assumes that adult cognition remains essentially stable after maturity; the result of cognitive progress during childhood is the attainment of mature forms of reasoning and thinking which are then applied throughout the adult years. By contrast, the "decrement" model postulates that there is a gradual decrease in the ageing individual's capacity to utilize and organize information, presumably the result of some kind of biological deterioration. Finally, the "decrement with compensation" model accepts the notion of biological deterioration, but also emphasizes the compensatory effects of accumulated experience during adult life (Labouvie-Vief, 1985).

The "decrement" and "decrement plus compensation" models are based on research deriving from a particular tradition in psychology – psychometric theory and methodology – which focuses on testing and measuring intellectual abilities. One of the most influential theories in this tradition is that proposed by Horn and Cattell (1967), in which intellectual ability is separated into two general factors labeled "fluid" and "crystallized" intelligence. Fluid intelligence is measured by tests of complex reasoning, memory and figural relations – tests which are said to be "culture fair" and thereby linked with universal, biological development. Crystallized intelligence is measured by tests of information storage, verbal comprehension and numerical reasoning, those sorts of abilities that are normally associated with experience and acculturation. Horn and Cattell's research reveals that from the teenage years onwards, there is a decrement in fluid intelligence and an increment in crystallized intelligence. The net result is that intellectual functioning remains relatively stable with age, there is simply a shift in the balance between fluid and crystallized intelligence.

In the psychometric tradition, much of the debate about adult intellectual capacity has centered on how to measure and/or interpret the consistent finding that there is a decline with age in performance on "fluid"-type psychometric tests. This was partly a methodological problem and was overcome with the use of studies which control for age, cohort (year of birth), and time-of-measurement effects (the year the tests were administered). In a 21-year study comprising a number of independent cross-sectional studies, Schaie (1983) reported that intelligence does decline with chronological age, but not until relatively later in life. In the Primary Mental Abilities Test, *verbal meaning* increases until age 63, *space* peaks at 46, and *reasoning* only declines after age 60. Moreover, where decline is found, it can normally be reversed through training (Schaie & Willis, 1986). Even though the results of such studies offer a much more optimistic view of adult intellectual capacity, commentators such as Labouvie-Vief (1985) have long argued that we need to reconceptualize what we mean by "intelligence" in its broader sense of "adaptability", and that it is a mistake to think of intelligence along a single quantitative dimension where there is no distinction between how we measure the intelligence, and the adaptability of different age groups.

There have since emerged a number of studies on practical intelligence, and the development of expertise, or even wisdom, as positive aspects of ageing. For example Sternberg et al. (2000) point to the differences between academic and everyday problem solving as a key to understanding adult intelligence.

Self-Development (Identity)

Early theoretical models of the development of identity in adulthood include those of Maslow, Havighurst, Erikson, Levinson, Gould, Loevinger, and Labouvie-Vief. All these approaches attempt to chart the life course in terms of a sequence of phases or stages: periods of stability, equilibrium and balance alternate, in a largely predictable way, with periods of instability and transition. Accepting for the moment that the life course is indeed quite predictable and stable: what is the source of this predictability and stability? Is it the result of a natural psychological unfolding or maturation? Or is it the result of the living out of a set of largely social expectations which vary from one society to another and from one historical period to another? If the latter, to what extent do social and cultural groupings construct and then prescribe the life-course patterns of their members? These are the kinds of questions which were being asked in the mid-1980s within the developmental psychology academy, at the same time that Gilligan (1986) was challenging the gender bias in developmental theories.

Gilligan (1986) put forward a persuasive argument that while the identity of boys is built upon contrast and separateness from their primary caregiver (which in most instances is female), the identity of girls is built on the perception of sameness and attachment to their primary caregiver. Caffarella and Olson (1993), in a review of studies which sought to document the life cycle of women in their own right, confirmed Gilligan's view that women, in contrast to men, place a high value on relationships and interdependence. This research on women's development highlights one of the limitations of the developmental literature: that it does not give sufficient emphasis to the power of social forces in shaping the course of people's lives.

More recently, the work of Gergen (1993), McAdams (1996) and Rose (1996) take up, rather differently, the idea that the self remains situated in history and culture and is continually open to re-inscription and re-formulation. In McAdams' view, identity is self-reflexively authored, made, explored and constructed. An extension of this theme of self as narrative construction is the more postmodern view of selves as residing in narratives which surround and define them, as proposed by Gergen and Rose.

Relevance for Adult and Continuing Education

From a developmental point of view, it is important for adult educators to critically reflect on their practice, one reason being that adult educators are almost always engaged in promoting learning for personal change. Sometimes this is made explicit, for example in programs that aim to improve self-esteem, or self-concept, or that help people discover their authentic selves. Sometimes it is more implicit; for example in programs that address significant social issues such as: gender stereotyping, racial discrimination, migration, domestic violence, environmental concerns, and perhaps health issues; the idea being that individual change is inextricably linked to broader social change. In the workplace, too, most changes imply a reorientation of individuals' values or attitudes or the ways they see themselves; for example, in learning how to implement a new innovation, or a new technology, or a new set of procedures in the workplace, education plays a role in influencing new worker identities.

The conventional view is that adult education cultivates a self that is independent, rational, autonomous, and coherent, but this view of the self has been challenged by theoretical work in developmental psychology. In addition, the problem with such a conventional view is that it is incompatible with inclusive educational practice which needs to take into account a plurality of perspectives and therefore a multiplicity of self-accounts.

See also: adult development, identity, multiple intelligences, older adults' learning, practical intelligence, social constructivism, women's learning, young adult learning.

References and Further Reading

Burman, E. (1994). *Deconstructing developmental psychology*. London: Routledge.

Caffarella, R., & Olson, S. (1993). Psychosocial development of women. *Adult Education Quarterly*, *43*(3), 125–151.

Gergen, K. J. (1993). *Refiguring self and psychology*. Aldershot, Hants: Dartmouth.

Gilligan, C. (1986). *In a different voice*. Cambridge: Harvard University Press.

Horn, J., & Cattell, R. (1967). Age differences in fluid and crystallized intelligence. *Acta Psychologica, 26*, 107–29.

Labouvie-Vief, G. (1985). Intelligence and cognition. In J. E. Birren & K. W. Schaie (Eds.), *Handbook of the psychology of aging* (2nd ed., pp. 500–530). New York: Van Nostrand Reinhold.

McAdams, D. (1996). Personality, modernity, and the storied self: A contemporary framework for studying persons. *Psychological Inquiry, 7*, 295–321.

Rose, N. (1996). *Inventing our selves: Psychology, power and personhood*. Cambridge: Cambridge University Press.

Schaie, K. W. (1983). The Seattle longitudinal study: A 21-year exploration of psychometric intelligence in adulthood. In K. W. Schaie (Ed.), *Longitudinal studies of adult psychological development* (pp. 64–135). New York: Guildford Press.

Schaie, K. W., & Willis, S. (1986). Can adult intellectual decline be reversed? *Developmental Psychology, 22*, 223–232.

Sternberg, R. J., Forsythe, G., Hedlund, J., Horvath, J., Wagner, R., Williams, W., Snook, S., & Grigorenko, E. (2000). *Practical intelligence in everyday life*. Cambridge: Cambridge University Press.

Valsiner, J., & Connolly, K. (Ed.). (2003). *Handbook of developmental psychology*. London: Sage.

Mark Tennant

Literacy

Literacy may be conceptualized as having two dimensions: the ability to perform reading, writing, and numeracy activities – including the ongoing debate on how to measure such skills – and the qualitative dimension of societal judgments on what adults "should," or "need" to know to be considered literate. Few areas of research or practice have engendered more public debate; few have become more contested or politicized in the entire field of adult education. In effect, it has held a mirror to society reflecting its most fundamental knowledge requirements, its loftiest aspirations, and many of its primordial fears for well over 2 centuries.

Looking at the "quantity-side" first, despite its history of campaigns and programs to eradicate illiteracy in nation after nation (Quigley, 1997), no industrialized country achieved full literacy in the 20th century. And, despite assertions such as that of Lê Thánh Khôi (1976) of Vietnam who argues only "revolutionary regimes have . . . been capable of organizing successful mass literacy campaigns" (pp. 125–126), *sustained levels* of high literacy, even sustained high levels of interest in literacy, have been a major challenge around the world. Over the past decade, the 2000 *International Adult Literacy Survey* (IALS) found in "14 out of 20 countries [surveyed], at least 15% of all adults have literacy skills at only the most rudimentary level" (Organization for Economic Co-operation and Development, 2000, p. xiii). Although the IALS studies, too, are contested (e.g., Hamilton, 2001; Sticht, 2001), the 2000 study indicates that the countries with the most adults between 16 and 65 years of age at the lowest level, meaning with more than 15% on the prose tests used, include Australia, Belgium (Flanders), Canada, Chile, Czech Republic, Hungary, Ireland, New Zealand, Poland, Portugal, Slovenia, Switzerland, the United Kingdom, and the United States. Chile indicated that approximately 87% of its adult population is in the two lowest levels, with 51.5% at the lowest; Portugal has approximately 80%, with 49.1% at the lowest level; and Slovenia shows approximately 73%, with

40.9% at the lowest level. By contrast, Sweden, Finland, Norway and The Netherlands, in this order, have the highest levels of adult literacy with each showing less than 15% of the population in level one. The IALS studies have helped put literacy at the forefront of national agendas in these 20 countries and the international Adult Literacy and Lifeskills Survey (ALL) is in process.

If the challenge of the 20th century was to raise the issue of low literacy across nations – including gaining official recognition that some countries have a literacy problem at all – and attempt various approaches to lowering illiteracy, then the challenge of the 21st will be to learn from these disparate national and regional literacy efforts across geographical and institutional borders (e.g., Kozol, 1985; Quigley, 1997). However, the field carries a long and complex social legacy which does not always help in the struggle to lower illiteracy rates, as seen next.

The Evolution of a Social Construct: Literacy History and Hegemony

The ability to read, write and conduct basic numeracy does not necessarily mean one is "literate." As early as 1550, a literate person was thought of as "a liberally educated or learned person" (Little, Fowler, & Coulson, 1970, p. 1,152). Etymologically, the word derives from the Latin term, "*litteratus*," an adjective used in the 8th century to identify adults who had shown themselves "capable of acquiring and sharing written knowledge" (Fischer, 2003, p. 149). However, in this acquiring of basic knowledge, the "accommodation of prevailing values" (Fischer, p. 149) was also required at that time – and still is today. This early requirement was met during the Roman Byzantine Empire by learning to read and write in Latin: "the vehicle of Christendom and all learning" (Fischer, p. 149). Significantly, knowledge of one's own vernacular language was deemed irrelevant and literacy still remains a tenet of the dominant culture today. The term "illiteracy" first appeared in print in 1556 and meant ignorance of letters, or the absence of education. Coming later, by 1648 to be considered "literary," one needed to be considered "liberally educated" (Little et al., p. 1,152). All three constructs derive from the same Latin root; all carry much larger social imperatives than mere skills-acquisition. And it is here – in the debate around "whose imperatives matter most, and as decided by whom, for whom" – that the controversy has raged. If there is a common thread in the evolution of literacy as a construct, it is towards growing recognition of those "being defined" having a role, but the controversy is far from over (Beder, 1991; Sussman, 2003).

Judgments on the "accommodation of prevailing values" have produced centuries of moralizing, politicizing, and rhetoric with little or no interest in the low-literates' actual needs (Quigley, 1997). Rather, low-literate adults have been singled out and stereotyped throughout the history of the Western world as the direct or indirect cause – or, at minimum, as societies' most susceptible recipients – of every conceivable social issue. In the 19th century, every type of sin was laid at the feet of the low-literates; fears ran rampant as illiteracy was seen as arriving with immigrants to North America at the turn of the century (Carlson, 1970); since the Second World War, most of the political rhetoric has been that the economic prospects of Western nations can be turned around if illiterates come to the call of "manpower plans," as invented and reinvented by government after government (Quigley). More concretely, linkages have been made in the popular press and governing policies between illiteracy and social anarchy, communism, Nazism, crime, and, lately, drug abuse and domestic violence (Arnove & Graff, 1987; Quigley). How is it that literacy – the "simple task" of reading, writing, and numeracy – has been so controversial through time? Because, as Levine (1982) put it: "The social and political significance of literacy is very largely derived from its role in creating and reproducing – or failing to reproduce – the social distribution of knowledge" (p. 54). As he concludes: "If this were not so . . . the inability to read would be on a par with tone-deafness, while an ability to write would be as socially inconsequential as a facility for whistling a tune" (pp. 264–265).

Clearly, the history of literacy is not the same as the history of reading, writing and numeracy because literacy carries so many normative values. A few examples are helpful here. While standardized writing and reading systems date to Mesopotamia some 6,000 years ago (Fischer, 2003), the first documented program for the teaching of adults in the English-speaking world was begun by the Bristol Adult School Society in 1812 in Bristol, England. Here, according to Verner (1967) was "undoubtedly the first organization established to promote the education of adults" (p. 71). The Bristol Adult School was begun by an "unlettered" doorkeeper of the local Methodist church, William Smith; and Stephen Prust, a tobacco merchant. They were assisted by Rev. Thomas Martin (Kelly, 1962). Far from merely skills-acquisition, the school's singular purpose was to teach adults to read using the Bible and, thereby: "to moralize and Christianize the minds of men – Instead of idleness, profanities, and vice – They [the Scriptures would] inculcate diligence, sobriety, frugality, piety, and heavenly mindedness" (Verner, p. 18).

The purposes of the first adult schools in North America are also worth noting. The Moonlight Schools of Kentucky, begun in 1911, have been named "the official beginning of literacy education in the United States" (Cook, 1977, p. 13). The superintendent of schools and newspaper editor, Cora Wilson Stewart, is credited with establishing this system where adults were encouraged to come to the local schools if the moon was shining overhead. The evening's literacy lessons would be carried in the next issue of that regional newspaper. A look at the curriculum shows these schools were at least as much about inculcating white, middle-class values as they were about teaching the rudiments of reading and writing (Cook). In Canada, Frontier College, which began in 1899, brought literacy and a civilizing force to the lumber woods and railroad yards (Selman, Cooke, Selman, & Dampier, 1998, p. 186). Through such founding literacy programs, as well as in the massive expansion of citizenship and English-as-a-second-language programs at the turn of the century (Button & Provenzo, 1983), it is clear that the roots of becoming *litteratus* are deeply imbedded in the ever-shifting soil of normative values (Quigley, 2001).

Grabill (2001) observes that "any attempt to understand literate practices without understanding the institutions that make certain practices possible . . . fails to account for how and why literate practices look the way they do" (p. 7). Such growing critiques are indicative of how the literacy literature has become increasingly critical of past assumptions and long-standing hegemonies.

Definitions, Conflicts, and Growing-Pains in Adult Literacy Education

When Canada and the United States began collecting census data, they also began to define and measure literacy. In 1900, 1910, and 1920, the census in the United States defined an illiterate adult in terms of one's ability to read and/or write in one's *native* language (Cook, 1977). By the 1940s these criteria included total years of schooling. Here was the "benchmark approach" to defining and measuring literacy – literacy was a commodity that could be measured, like body weight (Cervero, 1985). In Canada, the first national study on educational and literacy levels (Thomas, 1976) used 1961 and 1971 census data. However, especially since William S. Gray's 1956 UNESCO definition of "functional literacy" (Cervero), a relativist approach has been widely adopted.

Literacy has been envisioned in countless definitions since the 1960s "in terms of adults' ability to function within a social context" (Cervero, 1985, p. 50) and, thus, some qualitative aspects have been added to the quantitative assumptions involved. A transitional example is seen in the US National Literacy Act of 1991: literacy is "an individual's ability to read, write, and speak in English, and compute and solve problems at levels of proficiency necessary to function on the job and in society, *to achieve one's goals, and develop one's knowledge and potential* [italics added]" (Askov, 2001, p. 8). It is only recently that definitions have begun to accept that an adult with low literacy skills might have personal goals or ambitions.

One of the most widely used definitions today comes from the landmark 1993 US *National Adult Literacy Survey* (NALS) (Kirsch, Jungeblut, Jenkins, & Kolstad, 1993), and is seen in the later IALS studies. In the 2000 IALS, literacy is "the ability to understand and employ printed information in daily activities, at home, at work and in the community – to achieve one's goals, and to develop one's knowledge and potential" (IALS, p. x). However, the very attempt to define and, implicitly, "commodify" literacy has been challenged by many (see Hamilton, 2001; Sticht, 2001), including researchers in the New Literacy Studies movement. Lankshear and O'Connor, for instance, have stated that literacy is not a commodity. It is "the practice(s) people engage within routines of daily life" (1999, p. 32).

This slow move to greater respect for adults is paralleled in the evolution of literacy programs. Its salvationist beginnings in the UK and America (Stubblefield & Keane, 1994), its earliest liberatory applications with such as the Gideonites' work with freed slaves following the Civil War (Rachal, 1986; Rose, 1964), and its promise for civic integration, as made by civic institutions such as America's Settlement Houses (Button & Provenzo, 1983), were followed by the first national campaign in North American history: the National Illiteracy Crusade of 1924 under the auspices of the *New York Times*. All of these initiatives saw the illiterate adult as a virtual receptacle for proper values, knowledge, and behaviors.

In Canada, a rather different foundational course ensued with fewer high-profile campaigns, although the purposes were not markedly different. In Canada, education is a provincial/territorial responsibility under the British North America Act of 1867. Early initiatives by organizations such as the YMCA in Upper Canada's Kingston in 1859 (Ross, 1951), the Toronto West End Association of the YMCA (Draper, 1989), and Frontier College, begun in 1899 (Morrison, 1989), are just some of the earliest institutions in the first phase of Canada's literacy education history. Often overlooked, many advances were later made in literacy education by the American and Canadian armed forces during both world wars (Selman, Cooke, Selman, & Dampier, 1998; Stubblefield & Keane, 1994), leading to the major role played since by the GED high-school equivalency tests across North America (Quigley, 1991).

With the space race, growing demands for a better-trained work force, and calls for more national security through the 1950s, literacy education became a continent-wide vehicle for social engineering. In 1962, America passed The Manpower Development and Training Act and Adult Basic Education (ABE) entered the lexicon and the field (Taylor, 1989). The 1964 Economic Opportunity Act provided funding for ABE. Meanwhile, in Canada, the Technical and Vocational Training Assistance Act of 1960 and the Adult Occupational Training Act of 1967 enabled ABE to become part of the fabric of adult literacy education. From the 1960s forward, a plethora of ABE programs have developed across North America, as have a range of community-based literacy programs (Taylor), English as a second language programs (Orem, 1989), and adult secondary programs (Martin & Fisher, 1989).

Today's Ideological Contestation and the Future of Literacy

Half a century of legislation has helped shape literacy both qualitatively and quantitatively, but it has also fueled the historic discourse on "best purposes" for literacy education. Recent debate can be seen as a four-way pull among current ideologies (Belzer & St. Clair, 2003; Quigley, 1997). Many literacy/ABE programs are today funded by governments in order that low-literate adults may acquire the values and knowledge deemed necessary for the workplace. Secondly, some educators, and a few funding agencies, argue that literacy and ABE should provide the essential liberal-progressive knowledge deemed necessary to functioning in today's cultural contexts. Meanwhile, many literacy practitioners argue that literacy should be in the humanist tradition where learners are enabled to build self-esteem and self-reliance. Yet others, often from community-based programs, argue that literacy is a process and perspective that should lead the learner to criticality and action for social and personal liberatory goals (Quigley). However, even in this ideological debate, as Sparks and Peterson (2000) conclude: "Too often missing from the discourse are the voices of those who ultimately determine the outcome of the program – the learners themselves" (p. 274). Here, perhaps, is the greatest challenge for literacy in the 21st century.

See also: class, English as a second language, historical inquiry, human capital theory, lifelong learning, numeracy, religious education, social policy.

References and Further Reading

Arnove, R., & Graff, H. (Eds.). (1987). *National literacy campaigns: Historical and comparative perspectives*. New York: Plenum Press.

Askov, E. N. (2001). What's in a definition? The implications of being defined and strategies for change. *Canadian Journal for the Study of Adult Education, 15*(2), 7–18.

Beder, H. (1991). *Adult literacy education: Issues of policy and practice*. Malabar, FL: Krieger.

Belzer, A., & St. Clair, R. (2003). *Opportunities and limits: An update on adult literacy education*. Columbus, OH: The Ohio State University Center on Education and Training for Employment. Retrieved September 8, 2003 from ERIC database. (ERIC Document Reproduction Service No. ED-99-CO-0013)

Button, H. W., & Provenzo, E. F. (1983). *History of education and culture in America*. Englewood Cliffs, NJ: Prentice Hall.

Carlson, R. (1970). Americanization as an early twentieth century movement. *History of Education Quarterly, 10*, 441–465.

Cervero, R. M. (1985). Is a common definition of adult literacy possible? *Adult Education Quarterly, 36*(1), 50–54.

Cook, W. (1977). *Adult literacy education in the United States*. Newark, DE: International Reading Association.

Draper, J. A. (1989). A historical view of literacy. In M. Taylor & J. Draper (Eds.), *Adult literacy perspectives* (pp. 71–80). Toronto: Culture Concepts.

Fischer, S. (2003). *A history of reading*. London: Reaktion Books.

Grabill, J. (2001). *Community literacy programs and the politics of change*. Albany, NY: State University of New York Press.

Hamilton, M. (2001). Privileged literacies: Policy, institutional process and the life of the IALS. *Language and Education, 14*(2&3), 178–196.

Kelly, T. (1962). *A history of adult education in Great Britain*. Liverpool: Liverpool University Press.

Kirsch, I., Jungeblut, A., Jenkins, L., & Kolstad, A. (1993). *Adult literacy in America: A first look at the results of the National Adult Literacy Survey*. Washington, DC: US Department of Education.

Kozol, J. (1985). *Illiterate America*. New York: Doubleday.

Lankshear, C., & O'Connor, P. (1999). Response to adult literacy: The next generation. *Educational Researcher, 28*(1), 30–36.

Lê Thánh Khôi (1976). Literacy training and revolution: The Vietnamese experience. In L. Bataille (Ed.), *A turning point for literacy* (pp. 125–126). Oxford: Pergamon.

Levine, K. (1982). Functional literacy: False economies and fond illusions. *Harvard Educational Review, 52*, 249–266.

Little, W., Fowler, H., & Coulson, J. (1970). The *shorter Oxford English dictionary*. Oxford: Clarendon Press.

Martin, L., & Fisher, J. (1989). Adult secondary education. In S. B. Merriam & P. M. Cunningham (Eds.), *Handbook of adult and continuing education* (pp. 478–489). San Francisco: Jossey-Bass.

Morrison, J. H. (1989). *Camps & classrooms: A pictorial history of Frontier College*. Toronto: The Frontier College Press.

Orem, R. (1989). English as a second language. In S. B. Merriam & P. M. Cunningham (Eds.), *Handbook of adult and continuing education* (pp. 490–501). San Francisco: Jossey-Bass.

Organization for Economic Co-operation and Development, and Statistics Canada (2000). *Literacy in the information age*. Ottawa: Government of Canada.

Quigley, B. A. (1991). Exception and reward: The history and social policy development of the GED in the US and Canada. *Adult Basic Education, 1*(1), 27–43.

Quigley, B. A. (1997). *Rethinking literacy education*. San Francisco: Jossey-Bass.

Quigley, B. A. (2001). Living in the feudalism of adult basic and literacy education: Can we negotiate a literacy democracy? In C.A. Hansman & P. A. Sissel (Eds.), *Understanding and negotiating the political landscape of adult education* (pp. 55–62). *New Directions for Adult and Continuing Education*, No. 91. San Francisco: Jossey-Bass.

Rachal, J. A. (1986). Freedom's crucible: William T. Richardson and the schooling of the freedmen. *Adult Education Quarterly, 37(1),* 14–22.

Rose, W. (1964). *Rehearsal for Reconstruction*. New York: Bobbs-Merrill.

Ross, M. (1951). *The Y.M.C.A. in Canada.* Toronto: The Ryerson Press.

Selman, G., Cooke, M., Selman, M., Dampier, P. (1998*). The foundations of adult education in Canada (*2nd ed.). Toronto: Thompson Educational.

Sparks, B., & Peterson, E. (2000). Adult basic education and the crisis of accountability. In A. L. Wilson & E. R. Hayes (Eds.), *Handbook of adult and continuing education* (pp. 263–277). San Francisco: Jossey-Bass.

Sticht, T. (2001). The International Adult Literacy Survey: How well does it represent the literacy abilities of adults? *The Canadian Journal for the Study of Adult Education, 15*(2), 19–36.

Stubblefield, H., & Keane, P. (1994*). Adult education in the American experience: From the colonial to the present.* San Francisco: Jossey-Bass.

Sussman, S. (2003). Between a rock and a hard place with literacy rate statistics. *Literacies, 2* (6–8).

Taylor, M. (1989). Adult basic education. In S. B. Merriam & P. M. Cunningham (Eds.), *Handbook of adult and continuing education* (pp. 465–477). San Francisco: Jossey-Bass.

Thomas, A. M. (1976*). Adult basic education and literacy activities in Canada 1975–76*. Toronto: World Literacy of Canada.

Verner, C. (1967). *Poles' history of adult schools*. Washington, DC: Adult Education Association of the USA (original work published 1816).

B. Allan Quigley

M

Marginality

Marginality is social exclusion based on perceived or actual membership in a community or group denigrated, derided or despised. Thus marginality refers to both the individual's experiences on the margins (of community, family, society at-large), as well as the hegemonic forces that often instigate and perpetuate such exclusions (see Egan, 2002). Individuals experience marginalization as members of groups – often where competing and complex notions of identity are at play. In its somewhat benign forms, marginality leads to isolation, limited opportunity and ghettoization; in its extreme, violence and death can occur. Racism or ethnocentrism (particularly towards indigenous peoples), homophobia and hetero-centrism, sexism, ableism, ageism and classism are among the forces behind marginality. Embedded within the notion of marginality is that of identity – particularly when the identity formed is that of an outsider, due to affiliation or membership in a community or constituency outside mainstream society.

The human experience is increasingly pluralized and homogeneity's days are numbered. There are often complex relations of space, place, and affiliation in play when marginality is at issue, particularly as the complexities of identity and affiliation move the human experience farther and farther away from facile, constrictive notions of community. Throughout the world, tensions between various binaries of identity and politic (national versus regional or tribal, monocultural or monoracial, theocratic versus secular, queer versus heterosexist) are giving way to complex, richer, and more nuanced understandings of the human experience. Concomitantly, tensions emerge between those quite invested in specific identities versus those whose lived experiences do not tidily subsume into such categorizations, or who reject such them as too limiting. Regardless, in varied manifestations, often shaped by particular subjectivities around the construction of self, difference occurs, is relevant, and marginality is experienced. How then do adult educators respond to marginality, in learning contexts and larger society?

A Political Question

Marginality is a social injustice; social movements therefore have played a critical role in challenging hegemony and marginality. Arguably giving voice to marginalized learners – in planning, delivery and assessment – is an integral part of bringing marginalized learners out of the margins. Thus the question of one's status as an insider or outsider in a specific context is often of critical importance. As is the question of personal agency: to what extent can individual actors effect change when faced with marginality? How one fights against marginality is often substantively informed by one's socio-political orientation.

According to Jaggar (1983), three

strands of (Western) political thought have contributed both unique analyses of how marginality occurs, and specific ways to eradicate or mitigate its impact. Liberalism, and its obsession with the level playing field, sees marginality as an unfortunate side effect of Western entrepreneurial capitalism. It allows for some adaptation of systems of governance to better balance the scales, but ultimately expects individuals to self-locomote; that is, once a bit of assistance is offered, marginalized folks are expected to pull themselves up by their bootstraps, dust themselves off, and get on with things. Ultimately liberalism embraces the notion of personal agency as problematic and workable – and therefore places great emphasis on individualism and competition.

Marxism sees marginality as integrated – wholly and purposefully – in the capitalist paradigm. So long as capitalism is the system of social and economic order, there will be large numbers of persons on society's margins. Nothing short of revolution will work to make society truly equitable, where individual achievement is harnessed for a more generalized, common good. However this tack does not exactly empower learners (or workers), since personal aspirations and interests are a lower priority. Feminist critiques, while focused on the forces of sexism, have long ago moved beyond the rather narrow realm of second-wave liberal feminism. Issues of power, race, culture and colonialism are more regularly integrated in feminist examinations of marginality: complex analyses which lend themselves to rich and nuanced solutions. Feminism often values material concerns as much as questions of liberty and freedom – are my children well, is our community safe – while integrating the interests of individual women and families. Given feminist scholars' increasing willingness to reflect such complexities in their work, feminist work in this area has made a unique and compelling contribution to adult education literature on marginality. Additionally, so too have postcolonial analyses. Postcolonialism (after colonialism and beyond colonialism) rejects the objectification and dehumanization of those considered incidental to colonial systems. Both the assertion of voice and the pursuit of substantive material change – and the development of cooperative networks of activists and educators that transgress national and international boundaries, often created with colonial (rather than local) interests in mind – have improved the lives of thousands. The de-colonization of marginalized persons has been of particular relevance to indigenous adult educators (see Dei, Hall, & Rosenberg, 2000).

Power Versus Empowerment

Adult educators seeking to redress marginality cannot avoid issues of power (most importantly between themselves and learners) and empowerment. Mechthild Hart (1992) notes that "disrupting and rearranging boundaries means, above all, looking at the experience of those who are usually left out or misrepresented in general analyses" (p. 3). Adult educators working with marginalized learners both endeavor to mitigate such inequities and validate the local as important relevant and good. Therefore the experience of marginality is often not remedied by integration into a larger, more mainstream "whole." Thus adult education which centres on issues of marginality often celebrates diversity and difference, rather than pursues assimilation into the mainstream of society. And how do adult educators respond when their efforts towards conscientization (Freire, 1983; hooks, 1994) of learners are met with resistance? As Jane Thompson (1995) observed "the amelioration and transformation of women's material circumstances requires political consciousness, political resistance and political action. It also requires courage" (p. 133).

For many practitioners, legitimate tensions emerge when the educator's agenda is more liberatory than the learners'. How do we respond when our efforts to inspire and create substantive socio-political change are met with indifference, confusion or hostility? An *a priori* assumption that all learners who might benefit from conscientization will embrace (or acquiesce to) it must be problematized. Some learners seek it, others are amenable to it, but some reject outright the idea that they might not already be empowered citizens. Presuming a shared commitment exists, operational aspects can also be at issue. What sorts of instructional strategies are appropriate? In seeking to give voice to marginal learners, how are tensions between learners and other stakeholders managed? When learners' and others' notions of learning objectives are in conflict, how are such conflicts addressed? Often it is the instigation – or inspiration – of courage that is required of adult educators working with marginalized persons. Quite often fear and resistance are the barriers to shifts in critical consciousness – not unwillingness.

Conclusion

Adult education's espoused commitment to social justice issues is strong, but the particularities of how adult education practice integrates this commitment is less clear – particularly in institutional and hierarchical structures such as the workplace or school. Nevertheless, both our practices and scholarship reflect strong ties to new social movements and ad hoc grassroots activism. Important theoretical work is being done around issues of power, justice and freedom – in contexts around the world – by adult educators. And substantive material, personal, and political change, continues to unfold. Marginality continues to be a negative, corrosive and violent force in the human experience. Adult education often plays a role in mitigating its impact.

See also: conscientization, critical multiculturalism, difference, gender, identity, power, race, social justice.

References and Further Reading

Dei, G. J. S., Hall, B. L., & Rosenberg, D. G. (Eds.). (2000). *Indigenous knowledges in global contexts: Multiple readings of our world.* Toronto: University of Toronto Press.

Egan, J. (2002). Pedagogy of the depressed: Mental health consumers, computers and empowerment. *Convergence, 35*(1), 82–89.

Freire, P. (1983). *Pedagogy of the oppressed* (M. B. Ramos, Trans.). New York: Continuum.

Hart, M. (1992). *Working and educating for life: Feminist and international perspectives on adult education.* New York: Routledge.

hooks, b. (1994). *Teaching to transgress: Education as the practice of freedom.* New York: Routledge.

Jaggar, A. M. (1983). *Feminist politics and human nature.* Totowa, NJ, Sussex: Rowman & Allanheld Harvester Press.

Thompson, J. L. (1995). Feminism and women's education. In M. Mayo & J. L. Thompson (Eds.), *Adult learning critical intelligence and social change* (pp.

124–136). Leicester, UK: National Institute of Adult Continuing Education (NIACE).

John Egan

Meaning-Making

At its simplest, meaning-making refers to a lifelong process of understanding the world and our relationship with it. In adult education, meaning-making is often associated with critical reflection and transformative learning, whereby adults come to understand the psycho-cultural assumptions that affect the way they think and behave (Mezirow, 1981). The concept of meaning-making is fundamental to the hermeneutic approach to research in the social sciences where "access to the facts is provided by the understanding of meaning, not observation" (Habermas, 1971, p. 309).

Predispositions for Meaning-Making by Individuals

Making meaning is about organizing our perceptions of ourselves and the world around us. We engage in the process from the moment we are born, mostly without realizing we are doing so. Early Gestalt psychologists drew attention to the fact that perception is not determined simply by the reception of stimulus patterns in the human eye and brain. Rather, guided by some organizing principle, the brain seems to search actively for the best interpretation of the data available – and that interpretation may be subject to rapid or ongoing change. For example, when looking at patterns of dots equally spaced on a page, most people "organize" them into rows and columns; in a Rorschach inkblot test, people "see" objects rather than randomness; and "Figure–Ground reversing figures," like the famous candlestick or two faces, show how a single pattern of stimulation at the eye can give rise to different interpretations by the same person in successive moments.

In the 1930s, the British psychologist, Sir Frederick Bartlett, suggested that people gradually develop their own mental frameworks, which he called "schemata" (singular: "schema"), to facilitate their organization and interpretation of visual and other sensory experiences. Explaining memory as a creative process of reconstruction drawing on these schemata, Bartlett demonstrated experimentally how readers used schemata to interpret stories from another culture in ways which made sense – meaning – for them, but which often ignored factors that were particularly significant in the "foreign" culture. "Schema theory" remains influential in literacy and literary studies. At one level, it illustrates why proof-reading is important: we often do not notice a repeated word or misspelling because we "see" what previous experience has suggested should be on the page instead of what is actually there. At another, it underpins debates on where the locus of meaning lies in written texts.

Although Lewis Carroll's Humpty Dumpty claimed that words meant whatever he wanted them to, philosophers such as Ludwig Wittgenstein have shown that language is a social construct based on broad agreement about what words mean. However, meaning is itself a problematic term since it can refer to words themselves, as in "verbose" meaning "wordy." Meaning can also refer to the speaker/writer's intention, as in

"What I mean is . . ." Finally, meaning can refer to the value attributed to something, as in "X means a lot to me." Roland Barthes' work has drawn attention to the interrelationships between reader, writer and written text, including the extent to which different styles of writing involve the reader in actively constructing meaning. Writing as a form of professional reflective practice often leads to the discovery of meanings that were not consciously present either in the practice situation or at the start of the writing process.

This is because, in any given moment, there is far more information available to us from our external environment and inner store of memories and associations than we can actively process to discern meaning. The term "mindset" is sometimes used to describe how we "filter" information and therefore make different meanings out of similar situations at different times. Mindsets are like schema but more prone to short-term change. They predispose us to become aware of certain things and ignore others. For example, in an environment full of many other noises a parent will usually hear their own child crying, while a child-free companion remains unaware of it: the parent's mind is "set" to notice such sounds.

Mindsets affect the emotional as well as the physical "reality" that we perceive. Thus, a person suffering from depression may be said to have a "negative mindset," open only to factors that reinforce feelings of low self-esteem regardless of how supportive other people try to be. Mindsets that have become dysfunctional can be changed through educational or therapeutic interventions such as Neuro-Linguistic Programming (NLP).

Educational Implications

Some adult educators regard "coming alongside" other people to help them to understand and articulate their particular forms of intellectual and emotional meaning-making as central to their role. Others criticize this approach as too "psychological," arguing that it focuses on the learner at the expense of subject content, or that it does not pay sufficient attention to the social issues that cause individuals to believe and behave as they do.

Those who adhere to the "psychological approach" often draw heavily on Carl Rogers's work in therapeutic settings. This emphasizes the importance of empathy: the ability to enter temporarily, in a non-judgmental way, into the inner-world of the client to try to sense meanings of which she/he may be barely aware, and to bring these to the surface for discussion. George Kelly's concept of "personal constructs" is also significant. It suggests that we build our inner-worlds by means of dichotomous constructs, such as "hot vs. cold," "happy vs. sad," as a result of past experiences. Even with a "simple" word like "happy," evidence shows that people draw on a wide range of terms to provide its "opposite." Like schemata and mindsets, the constructs we create color our outlook and influence our behavior.

Jack Mezirow (1981) uses the term "meaning perspective" to describe the framework we build out of such constructs and through which we view the world. He speaks of "perspective transformation" as the emancipatory process of becoming critically aware of an existing perspective. This process may involve what Paulo Freire called "problem-posing," making problematic what we take for granted about social roles and expectations and how they should be carried out. Mezirow argues that "Awareness of *why* we attach the meanings we do to reality, especially to our roles and relationships – meanings often misconstrued out of the uncritically assimilated half-truths of conventional wisdom and power relationships assumed as fixed – may be the most distinguishing characteristic of adult learning" (p. 11, original emphasis).

Attempts to understand predispositions to make meaning in certain ways, and their implications for what we know and feel and how we behave, underpin many approaches to professional reflective practice and adult education (see Brookfield, 1995; Hunt, 1998).

Predispositions for Meaning-Making by Groups and Societies

Just as individuals develop meaning perspectives which make them more receptive to some kinds of information than others, so groups and, indeed, whole societies and civilizations, acquire particular ways of thinking about themselves and the nature of "reality." Sometimes known as a "worldview," collective meaning-making of this kind usually changes very slowly and is difficult to challenge. It influences how individuals identify themselves in relation to others who "belong" to different groups, and lies at the root of much intercultural misunderstanding and global conflict.

The way in which much of the Western world currently makes meaning has been shaped for several centuries by the discoveries, developments and methodologies of science and technology. These have reinforced a dualistic worldview based on Newton's vision of a "clockwork universe" which suggests that the physical world is measurable, under the control of humankind, and can best be understood through analysis of its component parts. As Peter Russell (1984) puts it, it also assumes that "I am 'in here,' while the rest of the world is 'out there' . . . All our perceptions and experiences are interpreted on this basis, and we model reality accordingly" (p. 102). It is a very different worldview from the ecclesiastical model which preceded it, in which religious teachings rather than scientific analysis were the primary source of knowledge, and from that held now, for example, by many faith communities and indigenous peoples.

In the early 1960s, Thomas Kuhn (1970) suggested that Western science has itself been shaped by different ways of thinking, which he called "paradigms" (from the Greek *paradeigma,* meaning "pattern"). Significantly, he showed how these change over time, not because of the discovery of any fundamentally new data, but through the interpretation of existing data in a new way. Referring to this process of change as "paradigm shift," he argued that the act of interpreting data differently results in seeing the world differently – literally in a new "World View" (Kuhn, pp. 111–35).

Kuhn's work (1970) has been highly influential, not least in subsequent debates about how understandings in and of science have come to underpin political and social structures. The wider public grasp of recent scientific propositions, such as James Lovelock's *Gaia Hypothesis* and chaos and complexity theories, has led writers like Fritjof Capra (1997) and Henryk Skolimowski (1994) to suggest that we are now on the brink of a new worldview.

This *Gaia*-inspired worldview challenges that of the "clockwork universe" and everything that has followed from it, including the application of mechanistic principles to the natural world and to understandings of the human mind, social behavior and the purpose and processes of education. It envisages the world as an integrated whole rather than a dissociated collection of parts. Referring to it as "deep ecological awareness," Capra argues that such a holistic view, by its very nature, involves "whole-person" understanding and not simply intellectual acknowledgement. It is thus closely linked to ideas in adult education about multiple intelligences and honoring different "ways of knowing." Arguably, these ideas are themselves part of a paradigm shift towards a changed worldview which has profound implications for the future.

Metaphors

It is often possible to identify key metaphors which underpin the ways in which individuals, groups and societies make meaning. Indeed, Gareth Morgan (1997) would argue that all worldviews, theories and perspectives *are* metaphors. Describing metaphor as an "active, constitutive force that leads us to enact the world in a particular manner," he claims that "Metaphor *makes* meaning" (p. 427, original emphasis).

Morgan (1997) provides a useful summary of much of the growing literature on the importance of metaphor (pp. 379–81) and illustrates how using different metaphors to think about organizations leads to very different perspectives on management structures, working practices and work-based personal relationships. He argues that learning to "read" organizations by identifying the metaphors underpinning competing theories and practices facilitates the understanding and articulation of their various strengths and weaknesses and helps in the handling of complex and often-conflicting information. This increases the likelihood of managers being able to create new metaphors and associated actions to suit changing circumstances, rather than being trapped as reactive participants in a preset "text."

Heron (1996) illustrates how metaphors help us to make meaning out of what we sense at a wordless "experiential" level of knowing and enable us to bring it into the shared world of meaning-making that is based on language and "propositional" knowing. Also, he argues that, at the "experiential" level, experience is never *of* something or someone else but always an experience *with* the other. He advocates "co-operative inquiry" as a way of exploring and understanding the human condition by letting go, as far as possible, of preconceived ideas and images and entering fully into "Being" in the moment. In this respect, meaning-making is a spiritual process.

Just as the notion of schemata as "building blocks" of an inner world reflects the imagery of a clockwork universe, so meaning-making as a spiritual process accords with a *Gaian* worldview. It seems impossible to make meaning without a reference point.

See also: multiple intelligences, reflective learning, spirituality, transformative learning.

References and Further Reading

Brookfield, S. D. (1995). *Becoming a critically reflective teacher*. San Francisco: Jossey-Bass.

Capra, F. (1997). *The web of life*. London: Flamingo.

Habermas, J. (1971). *Knowledge and human interests*. Boston: Beacon Press.
Heron, J. (1996). *Co-operative inquiry*. London: Sage.
Hunt, C. (1998). An adventure: From reflective practice to spirituality. *Teaching in Higher Education, 3*(3), 325–337.
Kuhn, T. (1970). *The structure of scientific revolutions* (2nd ed.). Chicago: University of Chicago Press.
Mezirow, J. (1981). A critical theory of adult learning and education. *Adult Education, 32*(1), 3–24.
Morgan, G. (1997). *Images of organization*. London: Sage.
Russell, P. (1984). *The awakening earth*. London: ARK.
Skolimowski, H. (1994). *The participatory mind*. London: Arkana.

Cheryl Hunt

Mediterranean and Adult Education

The Mediterranean is an almost landlocked sea situated between Southern Europe, North Africa and South-west Asia. The area around and also comprising this sea is generally referred to as the Mediterranean Region. The Mediterranean is, in many respects, a *construct*. There are those who define the Mediterranean in a manner that reflects a colonial and Eurocentric conception of the world. Others construct this region differently, attributing to it characteristics of what can be broadly termed the "South" that connotes marginality and has historically been both a partaker of and victim of Western colonization.

There is an emerging visible literature, including literature in English, on education in the various countries of the region. As for adult education, the concentration is, for the most part, on provision in the Southern European and Western-oriented countries, namely Italy, Spain, Portugal (strictly speaking the country does not form part of the Mediterranean since it is on the Atlantic coast but its culture is traditionally regarded as being Southern and Mediterranean), Israel, the countries that previously formed the old Yugoslavia, Greece, Turkey, and to a lesser extent, Cyprus and Malta. There is a paucity of literature in English on adult education in Arab countries.

Adult Education Figures

There are a number of figures, connected with the region, who stand out in the literature on adult education. I would mention Antonio Gramsci (1891–1937), one of the greatest 20th century social and political thinkers/activists, who engaged in adult education and whose concepts influenced the adult education literature, though little attention is devoted to his writings on the Southern question, even though they would seem to be relevant to adult education in the Mediterranean. Ettore Gelpi (1933–2002) is another prominent writer and speaker on adult education who headed UNESCO's Lifelong Education Unit in Paris. Lorenzo Luzuriaga (1889–1959), hailed as the greatest Spanish thinker on adult education, wrote extensively on pedagogy and ways of overcoming illiteracy. We can also mention the Freire-inspired Luiza Cortesao, a contemporary critical educator from Portugal and a symbol of resistance against fascist rule. Martin Buber (1878–1965), a writer, philosopher and organizer of adult education in Palestine, has had (and continues to have) an influence on adult education, especially through his writings on dialogue, notably *I and Thou*. It is not only individuals but also groups and movements that ought to be mentioned with regard to adult education. The *Mediterranean Review (Mediterraneo Un Mare di Donne)*, a bilingual periodical in Italian and English, provides visibility to women's groups and organizations, from the region, that challenge patriarchy at different levels and in different areas. As with most social movements, such organizational work has an adult learning dimension.

Key Projects

Key projects stand out in the international literature on adult education. These include: the Factory Councils in Turin, with their emphasis on industrial democracy; the 150-hours experiment in working-class education in the same country; the concept of the "popular university" which took on various meanings in Italy and Spain, having appeared in the latter country originally as a form of university extension and subsequently as a municipally-funded cultural center (Flecha, 1992); workers' education in the context of self-management in the former Yugoslavia; popular education in Spain and Portugal in the context of the quest for democracy following the fascist period (this also applies to Greek adult education); and the UNESCO-award winning Tehila project in Israel targeting illiteracy especially among women.

Regional Differences

The reference to the old Yugoslavia is particularly significant. The country had a vibrant adult education sector (Soljan, Golubovic, & Krajnc, 1985) with some of its universities, notably those in what are now Serbia and Slovenia, having had strong programs in the field. Scholars such as Dusan Savicevic and Ana Krajnc are well-known in the literature. In Serbia, nowadays, education is equated primarily with schooling. There is a lack of an appropriate organizational structure for adult education; this applies also to many Mediterranean countries. Whereas there existed, in the old Yugoslavia, a network of workers' universities, the emphasis nowadays, in such countries as the former Yugoslav Republic of Macedonia, is on training and retraining. This applies to many countries undergoing the transition from planned to market economies, as with Albania.

In the southern Mediterranean, particularly in Arab states, the emphasis is primarily on literacy with the Arab world estimated to have approximately 70 million illiterates (UNESCO, 2003). Quite prominent are Egyptian efforts in this regard, with numerous projects being developed since the early 1990s (Abel Gawad, 2004). Of special concern is illiteracy among women. The literacy program was stepped up in 2003 following President Mubarak's decree to eliminate illiteracy by 2007 (El-Bakary, 2004). A similar effort is found in Syria with a program covering three stages and targeting, among others, girls and women, especially those living in rural areas and the semi-desert region (Saida, 2004). The Syrian government claims considerable success in reducing illiteracy through this effort, but reports also underscore the problem of literacy retention owing to lack of a literacy-sustaining environment (UNESCO, pp. 32–33). Literacy efforts often involved plans to reach dispersed Bedouin communities through, in the case of Libya, effective use of radio and television (p. 25). Efforts for the spread of literacy are often curtailed in contexts such as Palestine owing to the Israeli occupation that results in curfews, school and road closures and the fear of walking through danger areas (p. 25). It would be interesting to explore the clandestine educational strategies that besieged people often employ in such contexts.

Contextual Issues

Many of the conflicts that characterize this region can have a religious/ethnic basis; this region has given rise to the three great monotheistic religions. Adult Education often has strong links with the various belief systems in the region. For example, excerpts from the Qur'an are used in such literacy programs as the "Read in the name of your God" syllabus in Egypt (Abel Gawad, 2004). In the Ottoman period, mosques and medreses (Muslim theological schools) carried out various adult educational activities in Turkey (Okcabol, 1992, pp. 260–261). In Cyprus, the Christian Orthodox Church has a long tradition of adult education (Symeonides, 1992, p. 210), whereas in Malta and Italy, agencies such as Caritas (also prominent in Egyptian literacy efforts) that form part of the Catholic Church's larger network, are important adult education players.

Significant Issues

One of the key issues confronting adult education in the Mediterranean is that of migration (see also Mayo, 2002). This applies to Arab countries such as Egypt, where English language classes help in the repatriation of Sudanese refugees (El Bakary, 2004), Israel, which since its inception has been a multiethnic state, and Southern European countries which, having previously been net exporters of labor power, have now become net recipients of immigrant labor from the Region's south. With respect to Southern Europe, cultures that have traditionally and problematically been constructed as antagonistic are now expected to coexist in the same geographical space. This can easily create tensions resulting from the fear of *alterity* often resulting from the centuries-old Western demonization and exoticization, based on a sense of "positional superiority," of "the orient." This has implications for efforts in the area of adult education concerning migrants, the challenge being to provide programs that conceive of the immigrant as "subject."

Foreign agencies are playing a key role in adult education in the Mediterranean. Together with support from Arab and Islamic agencies (ALESCO and ISESCO respectively), the Egyptian literacy initiatives, for instance, draw funds from USAID, CIDA and the EU's Social Fund among others. The German Adult Education Association was also instrumental in the funding and organization of the 2002 Cyprus and 2003 Malta conferences on adult education in the Mediterranean, the latter being the second such conference in the country (Wain, 1985). The 2003 Malta conference was concluded with a declaration that, among other things, called for the setting up of a Mediterranean Adult Education Association.

See also: comparative adult education, critical theory, Middle East and adult education.

References and Further Reading

Abel Gawad, O. (2004). Literacy and adult

education in Egypt. In D. Caruana & P. Mayo (Eds.), *Perspectives on lifelong learning in the Mediterranean*. Bonn: International Institute for International Cooperation of the German Adult Education Association (IIZ/DVV).

El Bakary, W. (2004). Adult education in Egypt. Unpublished article, American University in Cairo.

Flecha, R. (1992). Spain. In P. Jarvis (Ed.), *Perspectives on adult education and training in Europe* (pp. 190–203). Leicester: National Institute of Adult Continuing Education (NIACE).

Mayo, P. (2002). General Rapporteur's report. In P. Mayo, K. Symeonides, & M. Samlowski (Eds.), *Perspectives on adult education in the Mediterranean and beyond* (pp. 76–82). Bonn: IIZ-DVV.

Okcabol, R. (1992). Turkey. In P. Jarvis (Ed.), *Perspectives on adult education and training in Europe* (pp. 260–274). Leicester: National Institute of Adult Continuing Education (NIACE).

Saida, M. (2004). Adult education in Syria. D. Caruana & P. Mayo (Eds.), *Perspectives on lifelong learning in the Mediterranean*. Bonn: International Institute for International Cooperation of the German Adult Education Association (IIZ/DVV).

Soljan, N., Golubovic, M., & Krajnc, A. (1985). *Adult education and Yugoslav Society*, Zagreb: Andragoski Centar.

Symeonides, K. (1992). Cyprus. In P. Jarvis (Ed.), *Perspectives on adult education and training in Europe* (pp. 204–218). Leicester: National Institute of Adult Continuing Education (NIACE).

UNESCO (2003). Literacy and adult education in the Arab world. Regional report for CONFINTEA V, Mid-term Review Conference, Bangkok, UNESCO Beirut Regional Office for Education in the Arab States September.

Wain, K. (Ed.). (1985). *Lifelong education and participation. Papers presented at the Conference on Lifelong Education Initiatives in Mediterranean Countries, November 5–7, 1994*. Malta: University of Malta Press.

Peter Mayo

Mentorship

Mentorship is classically understood as a relationship between a more experienced elder and a younger learner in which the mentor provides knowledge, skills, support, challenge, and inspiration. The definition has since been dramatically expanded to include people of all ages as well as peers. This definitional ambiguity has been widely noted. Most definitions, however, include reference to the transfer of knowledge, assistance in career advancement, personal development, and role-modeling.

Mentors have been part of human experience since the emergence of our species, appearing in the role of tribal healer in pre-literate societies and later in the master–apprentice relationship of mediaeval guilds. The archetype of the wise elder echoes through classical and popular literature from Saraswati to Gandalf. The term itself is drawn from Homer's *Odyssey* in which Mentor (an incarnation of Athena) cares for the son of his friend, Odysseus. Mentoring appeared in the mid-1950s in business journals (Grace, personal communication, 2004) but was first brought into popular use by Levinson, Darrow, Klein, Levinson, and McKee (1978) in their study of male psychosocial development.

It is useful to distinguish between *informal* and *formal* approaches to mentoring. Descriptive studies of informal mentoring in the workplace and everyday life are useful for understanding the part mentors play in human development and career advancement, but such studies appear relatively seldom in the adult education literature. Formal programs emphasizing job-training, role-modeling, and career advancement are widespread in the business world, higher and professional education, government, and the non-profit sector. One of the major controversies in such programs concerns the relative effectiveness of assigning mentors to protégés rather than creating contexts in which they may choose one another (Zachary, 2000).

Although the role was pioneered in the 1950s by Goddard College (Vermont), one of the earliest explicit uses of mentors in adult higher education appeared with Empire State College (New York) in 1971. This was a time of dramatic inclusion of older, working "non-traditional" students who demanded more flexible hours, accreditation of experiential learning, and legitimization of new forms of knowing. The traditional "teacher" was no longer adequate for this participatory learning that engaged the whole lives of students. A new role, designated "mentor," took form. Since that time, mentors have proliferated throughout both undergraduate and graduate programs for adult students, often in roles that distinguish them from conventional classroom instructors. While mentors may be faculty members, they frequently hold responsibility for their students' development as well as intellectual learning, necessitating a shift from primary attention to subject matter towards a greater concern for the student's well-being. Where they work with internships or other forms of experiential learning, mentors may assist the student in both articulating and interpreting the meaning of their learning. In some cases, mentors engage their students in discussions of ethics, life choices, and spirituality. This greater emphasis on process over content sharpens their difference from conventional classroom teachers (Daloz, 1999).

Differing Approaches

Approaches to mentoring adult students vary along several dimensions (Galbraith & Cohen, 1995). As faculty advisors, mentors may view their role as anywhere from instrumental to developmental. Some seek to ensure that students make the best course choices for their vocational aspirations or to meet college requirements; others may place greater emphasis on learning experiences that deepen students' self-understanding, critical abilities, or moral and spiritual growth. And some insist that the single most important function of a mentor is to usher learners into critical thought (Parks, 2000).

Another area of variation concerns the degree to which the mentor learns as well as the student (Herman & Mandell, 2004). For some mentors the student's learning is the primary focus of the relationship; for others, the focus lies more with the relationship itself, and the mentor works towards greater mutuality between the two. For still others, the solution lies in new non-hierarchical, networked forms of co-mentoring.

Although recent years have seen welcome attention paid to the effects of gender in mentoring, and although mentoring programs are increasingly strengthening the educational effectiveness of ethnicity and other forms of diversity, critics rightly cite this as an area for further work. As globalization draws us ever closer, cross-race and multicultural mentoring will become both more common and essential (Hansman, 2002).

Research

Efforts to measure the effectiveness of mentoring continue to bear fruit in adult and continuing education. One of the most influential instruments has been Cohen's (1995) "Principles of Adult Mentoring Scale" which yields measures along seven dimensions and is widely used. And while research has tended to focus primarily on mentoring as a one-to-one relationship, there is growing interest in the transformative power of a mentoring culture or community that would include mentors, peers, and institutional context as part of the holding environment (Drago-Severson, 2004).

Not all mentoring serves students well, and an area that remains relatively unexplored concerns the "shadow side" of mentoring. The practical and ethical implications of negative mentor motivation or behavior in adult education call for investigation.

Finally, mentoring is increasingly linked with distance learning programs, particularly the use of such electronic devices as online learning, email, and list servers as well as the use of phone and video. Considerable controversy obtains over the relative effectiveness of these forms of mentoring when compared with the more traditional face-to-face modes. Advocates point to the numerous ways in which richer information can pass between mentor and student more rapidly; critics hold for the centrality of the face-to-face element of mentoring. It seems likely that as we have in the past, we will ultimately co-evolve with our tools and, with Athena's wisdom to guide us, emerge with yet unimagined forms of this nourishing and deeply human relationship.

See also: experiential learning, informal learning, relational learning.

References and Further Reading

Cohen, N. H. (1995). *Mentoring adult learners: A guide for educators and trainers.* Malabar, FL: Krieger.

Daloz, L. (1999). *Mentor: Guiding the journey of adult learners.* San Francisco: Jossey-Bass.

Drago-Severson, E. (2004). *Becoming adult learners: Principles and practices for effective development.* New York: Teachers College Press.

Galbraith, M. W., & Cohen, N. H. (Eds.). (1995). *Mentoring: New strategies and challenges. New Directions for Adult and Continuing Education,* No. 66. San Francisco: Jossey-Bass.

Hansman, C. A. (Ed.).(2002). *Critical perspectives on mentoring: Trends and issues.* Information Series No. 388. ERIC Clearinghouse on Adult, Career, and Vocational Education. Retrieved January 23, 2004 from ERIC database (ERIC Document Reproduction Service No. ED465045).

Herman, L., & Mandell, A. (2004). *From teaching to mentoring: Principle and practice, dialogue and life in adult education.* New York: Routledge Falmer.

Levinson, D. J., with Darrow, C.N., Klein, E.B., Levinson, M. H., & McKee, B. (1978). *The seasons of a man's life.* New York: Knopf.

Parks, S. D. (2000). *Big questions, worthy dreams: Mentoring young adults in their search for meaning, purpose, and faith.* San Francisco: Jossey-Bass.

Zachary, L. (2000). *The mentor's guide: Facilitating effective learning relationships.* San Francisco: Jossey-Bass.

L. A. Parks Daloz

Middle East and Adult Education

The Middle East, extends from Afghanistan and Pakistan in the east to Egypt and Sudan in the west. Although the region is often depicted as the land of oil, sand, Islam and Arabs, it is extremely diverse geographically (mountain ranges, forests, deserts, rivers and lakes), and includes a mosaic of religions (Islam,

Baha'ism, Christianity, Judaism, and many smaller ones), languages (Arabic, Turkish, Persian, Kurdish, Pashtu, and Baluchi), economies (nomadism, agriculture, service sectors, industry), ethnic identities (Arabs, Armenians, Assyrians, Baluches, Kurds and Persians), and political systems (secular republics, theocracies, and monarchies). The region is the birthplace of writing (Iraq), agrarian and urban revolutions, and the first state structures, and it has been the site of the earliest schools and centers of higher learning. Arabic and Persian, the two major classical literary languages, dominated cultural life from India to Morocco.

The Middle East has also been the converging place of African and Euro-Asian cultures, peoples, and civilizations. For instance, the Eastern Mediterranean region became part of the Greek and Roman empires in ancient times, and later Arab-Islamic and Turkic peoples settled throughout the region. In modern times, Western capitalist states scrambled for colonizing the region, and engaged in dismantling the Ottoman Empire, which together with the Persian (Iranian) Empire, dominated the Middle East until 1918.

In spite of its rich natural and human resources, the region suffers from poverty, mass illiteracy, patriarchal violence, dictatorship, neo-colonialism, occupation, war, and genocide. By the late 20th century, it was obvious that the main post-Second World War experiments in nation-building led by nationalists and Islamists had failed to build a prosperous and democratic order. Adult education, thus, is challenged to bridge the gap between a better-educated younger generation and a largely illiterate adult population that demands prosperity, justice, peace, and democracy. However, it is no exaggeration to claim that adult education is one of the least developed areas of education in this region. A huge gap exists between the advances made in adult education research and practice in, for example, Latin America with its unique social-justice orientation, and the rather static status of adult education in the Middle East. Three characteristics distinguish adult education in the Middle East from other regions of the world. First, adult education, like other sectors of education, is planned, financed, and managed by the state. Second, literacy is the dominant feature of adult education. Finally, theoretically, methodologically and pedagogically, adult education research in the Middle East lags behind advances made in the field. In this region, applied and field research are the dominant modes of inquiry, research methods are descriptive, experimental and partly historical, and action research or participatory research are not being commonly used (Abuzeid El-Safi, 1999, p. 63).

Adult Education and Literacy Campaigns

With the rise of anti-colonialist and nationalist movements in the Middle East in the early 20th century, training skilled human resources and building a literate nation became state policy. Both the colonial and postcolonial states exerted a monopoly over formal and non-formal education and planned a massive illiteracy "eradication" campaign, often with symbolic violence against the illiterate population. Poverty, family violence, unequal gender relations, increasing family size, ethnic and religious tensions, were all attributed to illiteracy. State educational planners in the Middle East have continuously failed to develop a vision of a nation based on a regime of citizenry rights and democratic participation. The history of revolutionary and resistance movements in the region (among the most notable ones are movements of women, students, peasants, and workers) and their demands for education rights demonstrate that states, rather than citizens, are the main obstacle to social, economic and political development; the state suppresses social forces in civil society, and seriously constrains the role of education in the process of democratization (Mojab, 2000, pp. 11–14).

It is alarming that while literacy is the dominant trend in adult education in the Middle East, there has been a rise in illiteracy in the last two decades. The Regional Report for the UNESCO CONFINTEA V Mid-term Review Conference (Bangkok, September 2003) states that in Palestine and Iraq, for example,

> due to the deteriorating security situation, drawn-out armed conflicts, economic sanctions, prolonged curfews, the inability of students to reach their schools, the destruction of schools and educational facility and physical degradation of the learning environment . . . there is much concern about the dangers facing education in general and adult education and literacy in those two countries. (p. 9)

The same report concludes:

> If we consider that the Arab region has entered the twenty-first century burdened with over 70 million illiterates over a population of 280 million, and that there are approximately 10 million out-of-school children who will, in no time at all, swell the ranks of the illiterate in the region, then we know we are talking about a catastrophe in the making. (p. 12)

Lebanon is another example of this reversal trend. The report indicates that "[D]uring the 1999–2000 school year, there was a 98.3% enrolment rate in school. However, Ministry of Social Affairs figures indicates that 3.9% of these had dropped out by the end of the school year and did not register for the school year 2000–2001" (p. 10).

A statistical glance at the development of literacy rates in the region shows that in 1990, of the population over 15, 40.7% were illiterate, with the rate for women being more than 51.9%. By the year 2000, still more than 31% of the population over 15 were illiterate, and the rate had reduced to 40.2% among women. The rate of illiteracy is much lower among the age group 15–24. In 1990, more than 22.5% of this group was illiterate; with a rate about 29.9% among women. The illiteracy rate among this population group dropped in 2000 to 15.1%, and for women to 19.4%. Hammoud's (2001) study shows that the illiteracy rate dropped further for the entire region from 48.7% in 1990 to 38.5% in 2000. Further statistical analysis reveals two other educational trends in the region. One is the quantitative expansion of education. The total number of students in the three levels of formal education more than doubled from 23 million in 1975 to 49 million in 1991, and over the same period the average annual rate of growth of first-level school enrolment at 3.8% was higher than the average population growth in the age group 6–11 at 2.8%. Nonetheless, this trend is being endangered by the rising rate of drop-outs. According to a World Bank (1999) report "nearly 5 million children aged 6–10 and another 4 million children aged 11–15 regionwide were out of school in 1995; by 2015, these numbers are expected to grow by over 40 percent, to 7.5 million and 5.6 million respectively" (p. 10; Abuzeid El-Safi 1999, p. 56).

The other trend is the region's public expenditure on education as a percentage of GNP which is among the highest in the world (World Bank, 1999, p. 13; UNESCO 1993, p. 104). However, it is noteworthy that expenditure on education is often overshadowed by military expenditure among most of the regional states. According to the United Nations Development Programme report (1996, pp. 174–5), military expenditures as a percentage of combined health and education expenditures in 1990–91 were as follows: Egypt 52%, Iraq 271%, Iran 38%, Jordan 138%, Kuwait 88%, Oman 293%, Saudi Arabia 151%, Syria 373%, Turkey 87% and Yemen 197%. The percentage for industrial nations overall is 33%, and for the world is 37%.

Gender Parity and Adult Education

Two conflicting forces shape the access and participation of women in education. On the one hand women individually and collectively resist the patriarchal, religious-feudal traditions of their communities and seek education. In many Middle Eastern countries, there is a century-old women's movement which has demanded unrestricted access to education and public life. On the other hand, women face the resistance of patriarchal-religious forces, which deny them many rights including education. Women today count for more than 50% of the illiterate population, with the gender gap more visible in Mauritania (70%), Iraq (77%), Morocco (64%), Egypt (57%), and Sudan (55%) (UNESCO Institute for Statistics, 2002). Patriarchal relations are present in curricula, teaching traditions, educational policies and administration, which together reproduce gender inequality.

Future Research Direction

With the increasing diversification of urban economies, considerable training in information technologies, managerial skills, language proficiencies, customer services, telemarketing, and others is provided by privately owned vocational schools throughout the region. The Regional Report for the CONFINTEA V Midterm Review Conference (2003) also cites examples of best practices of adult literacy in Algeria, Egypt, Lebanon, Morocco, Oman, and Sudan (pp. 15–34), where new programs and curricula have been developed through the cooperation of governmental units, civil society and non-governmental organizations. However, the report identifies a series of internal and external problems which hinder literacy development in the Arab region (p. 13); they include war, militarization, poverty, geopolitics of the region, the role of global powers, digital poverty in the region, a lack of international, national and regional cooperation in education, population growth, and the gender gap. These problems are all interlinked. It is thus difficult to delineate, in the near future, a reversal of the dynamics that reproduce the status quo in a region known as the "cradle of civilization." The region suffers from brain drain, and the Middle East and North Africa ". . . accounts for only about one tenth of 1% of the world's R&D [Research and

Development] spending, less than any other region save sub-Saharan Africa" (World Bank, 1999, p. 7). There is an urgent need to revisit the adult education knowledge-production process in the region. Specifically, there is a need for international and interregional comparative research in adult education; the scope of research needs to be expanded beyond quantitative studies of literacy to incorporate more analysis of adult education and social change, in particular adult education, poverty and democracy. In this new direction, a critical feminist epistemological, theoretical, and methodological framework could be invaluable.

See also: civil society, Europe and adult education, gender, literacy, Mediterranean and adult education, numeracy.

References and Further Reading

Abuzeid El-Safi, H. (Ed.). (1999). Regional study on research trends in adult education in the Arab states. In W. Mauch (Ed.), *World trends in adult education research* (pp. 53–86). Hamburg, Germany: UNESCO Institute for Education.

Hammoud, R. (2001). Non-formal education for girls. UNESCO-Beirut, Regional Office for Education in the Arab States.

Mojab, S. (2000). Adult education in the Middle East: Etatism, patriarchy and civil society. *Convergence, 33*(3), 9–24.

Regional Report for the CONFINTEA V Mid-term Review Conference, Bangkok (2003). Literacy and adult education in the Arab world. UNESCO-Beirut, Regional Office for Education in the Arab States and UNESCO Institute for Education, Hamburg, Germany.

United Nations Development Programme (UNDP), (1996). *Human development report 1996.* New York: Oxford University Press.

UNESCO. (1993). *World education report 1993.* Paris: UNESCO.

UNESCO Institute for Statistics (2002). *Literacy and the non-formal education sector*, July 2002.

World Bank. (1999). *Education in the Middle East and North Africa: A strategy towards learning for development*, April, p. 54ff. World Bank Report Group, Human Development Sector: Middle East and North Africa Region.

Shahrzad Mojab

Military Education

Military education describes instruction for the purposes of intellectual development and the cultivation of wisdom and judgment. It prepares service members to deal with novel situations and is often provided without regard to a student's job assignment in a military unit. A scan of the Internet on 1 January 2004 revealed over 6 million websites worldwide involving the term "military education." This is because confusion in terms abounds and because military education is often, erroneously, thought to include military training. Military training is generally used to identify instruction or study oriented to a particular military job specialty and is designed to develop a technical skill needed by the military. It also includes tactical training of land, sea, and air units. Perhaps the learning process for military personnel can best be understood as a spectrum, with "pure training" (such as a simple exercise in assembling a rifle) at one end, and with "pure education" (involving the highest level of abstraction) on the other (Masland & Radway, 1957, pp. 50–51).

There are two distinct types of military education: professional military education, and voluntary adult and continuing education. Professional military education includes pre-enlistment and pre-induction military preparation activities. It includes professional development for officer and enlisted personnel and civilians who serve as part of the military force structure. Professional military education occurs during various stages in military career development, often in preparation for an individual's advancement. In addition, professional and personal development courses/programs that the military deems essential can loosely be included as professional military education (Anderson, 1989). Professional military education is influenced by each individual country's "sense of national purpose and its acceptance or rejection of militarism" (Harries-Jenkins, 1989, p. 13). Specific educational development of military personnel is related to the wider needs of the parent society. In many countries throughout the world, professional education is associated mostly with career officers within their military force structure. Important journals for professional military education abound; in Canada there is the *Canadian Defense Quarterly*; in the USA there are, among others, *Parameters, US Army War College Quarterly*, and the *Naval Institute Proceedings Magazine*.

Military education should also be understood in the context of adult and continuing education. In the USA, voluntary adult and continuing education in its military is nearly as old as the nation itself. As early as 1778, US military leaders recognized a need for basic academic instruction for its soldiers that went beyond purely military needs. The United States Congress in June 1916 authorized the use of civilian teachers for "instruction of soldiers in addition to Military Training" (Kime, 2003, p. 1). Besides basic and postsecondary education, the law authorized vocational education to include agriculture and the mechanical arts. The rationale for adult, continuing and vocational education for US service personnel was not solely that Military learners would develop personally, enhance their military effectiveness, and facilitate their ability to return to civilian life; there was a perceived requirement to eliminate "idleness" and reduce opportunities for crime and mischief (ibid.).

The transformation from adolescence to adulthood for most enlisted service personnel occurs well outside the confines of a traditional college campus. As opposed to earlier years, many military recruits have a minimum grounding in adult basic education, while living in a global society that maintains a perception that a college degree is important for success. Military organizations in Western Europe, Canada and the United States are able to attract sufficient volunteers to meet their force requirements, in large part by offering increasingly substantial educational opportunities for service members while on active duty. In the USA, service personnel can receive up to 100% tuition assistance to engage in postsecondary education, and in addition they accrue educational benefits that can be accessed after military service as veterans (Kime, 2003).

Warfare and peacetime operations have become increasingly complex. Many military organizations, internationally, have learned that training for specific skills tailored to the military's mission are not sufficient. Even junior personnel are placed in situations that are technically and socially complex; they need critical thinking skills and the broader sociopolitical perspectives of the educated person. Peacekeeping and anti-terror operations require more skills and knowledge than training can provide. The trained automaton who "just follows orders" may not contribute appropriately to mission accomplishment, and may be cause for failure. The military tries to recruit and retain "college-capable" personnel and provide them access to the education needed for a modern military force.

In some countries, including those such as the USA and Canada which have voluntary military service, and Israel which has compulsory service, the military's a large and unique employer, and has been at the leading edge of innovation in adult and continuing education. In the United States the military is a leader in promoting academic recognition of military workplace learning. In fact, the US military is a model for demonstrating that the worker (service member) can be made aware of his or her potential by connecting workplace learning with academic success (Kime & Anderson, 2000).

Leaders in higher education and the United States Department of Defense created Service members Opportunity Colleges (SOC) in 1972 to help bridge the gap between the military and higher education. SOC is a unique civilian–military partnership that involves 15 higher education associations, approximately 1,800 academic institutions, the Office of the Secretary of Defense, and the military services in facilitating service members' access to higher education. This consortium is pledged to assist American service personnel achieve their educational, vocational, and career goals. Its basic principle is that service members should share in postsecondary educational opportunities available to other US citizens. In addition, the US Army, Navy, Marine Corps and Coast Guard have developed and maintain, through Service members Opportunity Colleges, networks of associate and bachelor degree programs to facilitate transfer of credits among member colleges and degree planning for their service personnel (Kime, 2003).

Unlike neighboring countries like Canada, the United States makes a substantial resource commitment to their military and the education of its members. The United States military commits a significant amount to support its Defense Voluntary Education Program; in tuition assistance alone, it spent over $370.8 million in fiscal year 2003 with over 300,000 service personnel participating in postsecondary education (Woods, 2003).

See also: training, vocational education, workplace education.

References and Further Reading

Anderson, C. L. (1989). Educating the United States army. In M.D. Stephens (Ed.), *The educating of armies* (pp. 39–74). London: Palgrave Macmillan.

Harries-Jenkins, G. (1989). The education and training of military elites. In M.D. Stephens (Ed.), *The educating of armies* (pp. 13–38). London: Palgrave Macmillan.

Kime, S. F. (2003). *Servicemembers opportunity colleges 1971–2003*. Washington, DC: Servicemembers Opportunity Colleges.

Kime, S. F., & Anderson, C. L. (2000). Contributions of the military to adult and continuing education. In A. L. Wilson & E. R. Hayes (Eds.), *Handbook of adult and continuing education* (pp. 464–479). San Francisco: Jossey-Bass.

Masland, J. W., & Radway, L. I. (1957). *Soldiers and scholars*. Princeton, NJ: Princeton University Press.

Woods, G. A. (2003). *Military education: A Department of Defense (DoD) update*, Briefing Slides. Washington, DC: Annual NAIMES Meeting, J. W. Marriott Hotel.

Clinton L. Anderson

Motherwork

One of the goals of feminist researchers is to draw attention to the types of work and activities which women engage in that have been traditionally overlooked or devalued within academic discourses. The work of raising children in all cultures is primarily carried out by women. Within adult education, Mechthild Hart (1992, 1995, 1997, 2001) has drawn attention to the significance of *motherwork* in her analysis of how workplace and academic learning have been constructed. Hart's conception of motherwork entails a sophisticated theoretical analysis informed by both feminist and critical thinkers, including Shiva (1989) and Habermas (1987). It is also linked with her practical work in literacy education with poor black mothers (Hart, 1997, 2001).

Hart (1992) argues that subsistence labor, such as motherwork, is continually devalued in academic discourses, noting that this is linked to the glorification of technology and the devaluation of experience-based knowledge. The separation of subsistence and commodity production results in an organization of work and division of labor that marginalizes women's contributions. Women are devalued as workers, whether or not they are mothers, because they are linked with motherhood (Hart, 1995). The privatization of subsistence production is symptomatic in the devaluation of women's labor, and lumping childcare in with other domestic chores is a reflection of the lack of worth assigned to raising children (Hart, 1992, p. 104).

Hart (1992) draws upon Mies to argue that subsistence labor focuses on labor which creates and sustains life. This includes bearing and nursing children, providing shelter, making clothes, preparing food, as well as the psychological and emotional labor of attending to others' well-being. "Subsistence producers are the ones whose labor and production is directly oriented towards life – its creation, sustenance and improvement. They are working with the two most fundamental production forces: land and womb" (Hart, p. 95). Hart challenges cultural critics such as Hannah Arendt who develop a binary between science and nature, whereby science is connected with positive growth while nature and subsistence labor are perceived as detrimental to human evolution.

> Arendt's description of the life processes as threatening, devouring, and as constantly intruding in the human world represents a powerful ideological inversion of the truth, an inversion which for centuries has helped to sanction and to justify precisely the opposite in the name of progress and civilization: the destruction, devouring, and vamporizing of forms of production which are directly oriented towards subsistence, i.e., towards creating, maintaining, and improving life, rather than to the accumulation of capital and the creation of profit. (Hart, p. 115)

Within a masculine framework of values, killing or the destruction of life is symptomatic of power and dominance. Women's capacity for reproduction links them more closely with nature and creates a focus on sustaining life, rather than threatening death. Hart (1992) argues that "the glorification of death is therefore fully linked with the division between masculinity and femininity" (p. 117). In the same way, science and technology afford an opportunity to control and dominate life forces within nature. Patriarchy evolves as "mastery over necessity inevitably seems to translate into mastery over those who take care of the necessities of the life process" (p. 120). Male control over women's labor, and the devaluation of women's engagement in life-sustaining work and production are reflective of a destructive belief system. "Acknowledging that we have bodies and are an integral part of nature would be truly revolutionary" (Hart, 1995, p. 119). To focus on the importance of our connections with the natural world, rather than on how to gain mastery or control over it would lead to a profound shift in values that Hart believes can provide us with an alternative view of living, working, and learning.

With her focus on motherwork, Hart (2001) provides a radical critique of the current focus in education on work for profit and education that is implicitly linked with a capitalist agenda. Hart (1992) argues that "the raising of children, if blessed by social and individual circumstances which acknowledge the importance of nourishing new life, provides numerous parallels for an educational process which is likewise life-oriented" (p. 183). Recognizing the value of subsistence labor, such as the stigmatized motherwork of poor black women, leads to a new form of "literacy" (Hart, 1997). Hart argues that the educational process is woven in relationships between the learner, educator and larger society, influenced by both physical and emotional experience as well as cognitive understanding.

> The epistemology that can be developed out of the experience of mothering is characterized by non-dichotomous relationships between the knower and the object of knowing, between the natural and the social, between critical judgment and empathetic intuition, between reason and emotion, and between the subjective and the objective. (Hart, 1992, p. 190)

Hart's analysis of motherwork raises the importance of examining underlying values that inform educational discourses. It provides a solid theoretical interpretation of critical theory from a feminist perspective, that challenges the way taken-for-granted concepts such as "work" are understood from a masculine perspective (Hart, 1992). In this way, understanding the significance of motherwork becomes a radical way of reconceptualizing educational practices.

See also: critical theory, feminism, gender.

References and Further Reading

Habermas, J. (1987). *The theory of communicative action, Vol. 2.* (T. McCartney, Trans.). Boston, MA: Beacon Press.

Hart, M. (1992). *Working and educating for life: Feminist and international perspectives on adult education.* London: Routledge.

Hart, M. (1995). Motherwork: A radical proposal to rethink work and education. In M. R. Welton (Ed.), *In defense of the lifeworld: Critical perspectives on adult learning* (pp. 99–125). New York: State University of New York Press.

Hart, M. (1997). Life-affirming work, raising children, and education. *Convergence*, 2/3, 128–135.

Hart, M. (2001). *The poverty of life-affirming work: Motherwork, education and social change.* Westport, CN: Greenwood Publishing.

Shiva, V. (1989). *Staying alive women, ecology and development.* London: Zed Books.

Patricia Gouthro

Motivation

In adult education, motivation is a concept widely used to understand and plan for adult learning, instruction, participation, and persistence in training, courses, and programs. Social scientists have created motivation as a hypothetical construct; an invented definition to provide a possible concrete causal explanation of behavior (Baldwin, 1967). Motivation is a referent for the innate human capacity to direct energy in the pursuit of a goal. Psychologists consider intention, attention, concentration, effort, perseverance, and imagination to be motivational processes that provide energy for learning. Engagement in learning, ranging from reflection to skill practice, is the visible outcome of motivation. Although motivation has been studied largely as a psychological concept, as a process it is inseparable from culture (Wlodkowski & Ginsberg, 1995). Understanding an adult's motivation requires a multidisciplinary approach that considers but is not limited to that individual's perspective, ethnicity, family of origin, spiritual beliefs, personal goals, age, economic means, and lifestyle.

Motivation to Learn, and Culture

Since learning is a naturally active and volitional process of constructing meaning from information and experience, motivation contributes the energy and purpose for engaging in learning. Motivational processes such as effort and concentration contribute significantly to learning, particularly for those learning tasks that are challenging. For example, to read a complex article, to write an essay that is substantive and insightful, or to complete a formidable research study requires perseverance and meta-cognitive processes such as reflection and imagination. Motivation not only helps to initiate such activities but mediates them as well. Many social scientists today regard cognitive processes as inherently cultural (Rogoff & Chavajay, 1995).

The language adults use to think and the ways in which adults communicate cannot be separated from cultural practices and cultural context. Motivation is governed to a large extent by emotions. In turn, emotions are socialized through culture. Emotions influence engagement in learning activities such as reading, writing, and solving problems. For example, one person attempting to solve a math problem feels frustrated and stops. Yet another person, with a different set of cultural beliefs, feels frustrated at the task but continues with increased determination. What elicits that frustration or determination may differ across cultures, because cultures differ in their definitions of novelty, failure, opportunity, and gratification and in their definitions of appropriate responses to such experiences and feelings (Kitayama & Marcus, 1994).

An adult's response to a learning activity reflects that adult's culture. In this regard, the internal logic by which an adult understands or does something may not coincide with the instructor's. In this light, religion, myth, ethnicity, and regional and peer group norms have powerful motivational influence. The responses of adults while learning reflect this complexity. There is evidence that instruction that ignores the cultural aspects of learners' behavior and communication provokes their resistance, while instruction that is responsive to cultural perspectives and norms of learners prompts their involvement in learning (Olneck, 1995).

Intrinsic and Extrinsic Motivation

There is continuing debate among psychologists about the merits of using an intrinsic motivation approach to learning versus the merits of using an extrinsic motivation approach to learning. Richard Ryan and Edward Deci (2000) offer a widely accepted definition of intrinsic motivation: "Intrinsic motivation is entailed whenever people behave for the satisfaction inherent in the behavior itself" (p. 16). For example, when people read a book because they find it inherently interesting their motivation is intrinsic; conversely, extrinsic motivation is based on something extrinsic to the activity, often in the form of reward or punishment, for example when people read a book only because the instructor requires it or they believe the activity will gain praise from their instructor their motivation is extrinsic.

The controversy between intrinsic and extrinsic motivation has been explored in numerous studies (Sansone & Harackiewicz, 2000), which illustrate that using extrinsic rewards to motivate someone to do something that the person would have done anyway, undermines subsequent performance quality and motivation for the activity. For example, in experiments where people are paid to solve interesting problems while others solving the same problems are not paid, those who are paid rate the activity as significantly less enjoyable, are less likely to engage in it again, and do not solve the problems as well compared to those people who received no payment for solving the problems. The debate between advocates of intrinsic motivation and advocates of extrinsic motivation remains intense, although progress has been made in the sense that many researchers now perceive a more complex relationship between these two motivational systems and are studying how their effects occur.

At this time, the general principles of the American Psychological Association's Task Force on Psychology in Education (Lambert & McCombs, 1998) support an intrinsic motivation system for learning. The goal of this task force was to determine how psychological knowledge synthesized from research throughout the 20th century could contribute directly to improving learning and designing educational systems. The task force concluded that it is part of human nature to be curious, to be active, to initiate thought and behavior, to make meaning from experience, and to be effective at what people value. These primary sources of motivation reside in all people, across all cultures. In general, when people can see, from their point of view, that what they are learning is important, their motivation emerges. Optimal intrinsic motivation states for learning such as *flow*, where there is intense concentration, loss of self-consciousness, and suspension of anxiety in challenging tasks, have been extensively documented across and within cultures (Csikszentmihalyi & Csikszentmihalyi, 1988).

Motivation Models for Adult Learning

Motivation as a concept is complicated in several respects. It has an array of theories and research that compete and conflict with one another. It also has spawned many principles and variables, that exist apart from any cohesive framework for learning. For example, how does one understand learning using *both* psychoanalytic and operant-conditioning principles or design instruction using both needs and attributions as variables in the lesson plan? In addition, motivation attempts to create an understanding of the behavior of adults whose diversity of perspectives and experiences is vast. Scholars interested in motivation and learning have recognized these complexities and developed models to organize this immense array of content for adult educators. The Motivational Framework for Culturally Responsive Teaching (Wlodkowski, 1999) and the ARCS model (see below) of motivational design (Keller, 1987a, 1987b) are widely used motivation models in adult education.

Raymond Wlodkowski and Margery Ginsburg (1995) created the Motivational Framework for Culturally Responsive Teaching to provide a holistic pedagogy based on intrinsic motivation principles and respect for culturally diverse learners. The framework identifies four motivational conditions that the instructor and learners continuously create or enhance in the learning environment. Instructors act as resources, guides, or partners with adult learners to (a) establish inclusion, (b) develop a positive attitude, (c) enhance meaning, and (d) engender competence. The four conditions work in concert to evoke and sustain intrinsic motivation for learning. Each of these conditions is research-based from applied studies within a number of disciplines (Wlodkowski, 1999).

This model assumes that people, by nature, possess motivation to learn and that learning is multidetermined – resulting from cognition, feelings, and actions that are inseparable from memory, social activity, instructional process, and the ingredients of the setting where the learning takes place (Lave, 1988). Because motivation and learning are seen as interactive and systemic, this model also functions as a means for designing instruction from the beginning to the end of a learning unit. By continually attending to the framework's four conditions the instructor can select strategies from a wide array of theories and literature to enhance motivation in the learning setting (Wlodkowski, 1999). Research indicates this model has applicability in both secondary (French, 2001) and postsecondary settings (Wlodkowski, Mauldin, & Gahn, 2001).

John Keller's ARCS model of motivational design (1987a & 1987b) offers a systematic approach to designing motivational tactics into instruction. Combining an assessment of learner needs and their motivational characteristics with an analysis of instructional objectives and materials, it provides guidance for selecting motivational tactics that are applicable to instructional design (Keller, 1999). Keller's four dimensions of motivation are derived from a synthesis of psychological and educational research; they are attention (A), relevance (R), confidence (C), and satisfaction (S). A number of research studies confirm the applicability of this model (Means, Jonassen, & Dwyer, 1997).

The ARCS model has been used internationally for motivational improvement in computer-based instruction (Keller, 1999). The model recognizes that online programs, after they are packaged, cannot be continuously adjusted for learning, but by implementing a diagnostic approach to instructional design, based on a search for stable motivational elements in the setting, materials, and experience of the learners, it offers a way for distance educators to enhance learning environments even though they cannot control them.

Participation

Participation – what causes adults to undertake learning projects, courses, and programs – enjoys a long history of research in adult education. In most of these studies, motivation is understood as a readiness or desire for learning. There is general agreement among scholars that adult participation in more formal educational settings such as undergraduate degree programs and continuing education courses occurs because of the interaction of individual characteristics such as gender, income, education, and personal needs with social factors such as access to educational and career opportunities, government policies, and social incentives. Some scholars have built generalizable models to test relationships between interacting internal (self) and external (environmental) variables (Boshier & Collins, 1985; Scanlan & Darkenwald, 1984). Although these models have contributed to the evolution of ideas in this area, they have little explanatory value and are not applicable across cultures.

Using telephone interviews and descriptive statistics, Carol Aslanian's research (2001) proposes that adult participation in higher education as well as continuing education is due to a *life transition* that motivates the person to want to learn. The person's actual decision to participate in learning at a particular time is *triggered* by a specific life event. Among seven possible transitions, 85% of the adults in her study named a career transition such as changing or advancing their careers as their reason for wanting to learn. The specific triggers also centered on events in their career lives (71%) such as seeing a job downsized or having to use a computer for the first time. In seeking an education, the adults in her study looked primarily for quality (program, faculty, course, and degree) and convenience (location, schedule, length of time to complete program) as criteria for selecting a college. Since this study was done in the United States, it is likely that, to some extent, life transitions and triggers will vary culturally in other societies.

Persistence

Persistence – what influences adults to continue their involvement in coursework and programs – is a major concern in adult education. Often discussed as *retention* from the perspective of institutions in higher education and government, persistence portrays motivation as willingness and effort to stay or progress in an educational program. In the United States, estimates are that about 60% of adults leave college before graduation. From a government and economic perspective, this attrition is often regarded as a "missed opportunity" that weakens the social resources in a society.

The positive relationship of student academic and social integration to persistence is one of the most widely documented factors in the research literature (New England Adult Research Network, 1999; Tinto, 1998). The more academically and socially involved adult students are, the more they feel connected to other students and faculty, the more likely they are to persist. Since most adults have little extra time to spend in extracurricular activities, collaborative and community learning experiences in the classroom and online offer a pragmatic means to support their inclusion (Wlodkowski, 1999).

Lack of time due to conflict with family and work, and lack of money to finance one's education are well-documented as reasons why adults leave college (Wlodkowski et al., 2001). In this regard, the attraction of convenience as identified by Aslanian (2001) for educational participation probably has persistence effects as well because it reduces stress and cost for adults. Also, pursuit of education may conflict with adult social motivation and responsibilities. Adults may realize they have more satisfaction and fulfillment among their families and in the workplace, than what may be attained within an educational program and its potential rewards.

See also: attitudes, cognition, participation.

References and Further Reading

Aslanian, C. B. (2001). *Adult students today.* New York: The College Board.

Baldwin, A. L. (1967). *Theories of child development.* New York: Wiley.

Boshier, R. W., & Collins, J. B. (1985). The Houle typology after twenty-two years: A large scale empirical test. *Adult Education Quarterly, 35*(3), 113–130.

Csikszentmihalyi, M., & Csikszentmihalyi, I. S. (1988). *Optimal experience: Psychological studies of flow in consciousness.* New York: Cambridge University Press.

French, R. (2001). A tale of four schools. *Journal of Staff Development, 22*(2), 19–23.

Keller, J. M. (1987a). Strategies for stimulating the motivation to learn. *Performance and Instruction, 26*(8), 1–7.

Keller, J. M. (1987b). The systematic process of motivational design. *Performance and Instruction, 26*(9),1–8.

Keller, J. M. (1999). Using the ARCS motivational process in computer-based instruction and distance education. In M. Theall (Ed.), *Motivation from within. Approaches for encouraging faculty and students to excel. New Directions for Teaching and Learning* (pp. 39–47), No. 78. San Francisco: Jossey-Bass.

Kitayama, S., & Markus, H. R. (Eds.).(1994). *Emotion and culture: Empirical studies of mutual influence.* Washington, DC: American Psychological Association.

Lambert, N. M., & McCombs, B. L. (1998). Introduction to learner-centered schools and classrooms as a direction for school reform. In N. M. Lambert & B. L. McCombs (Eds.), *How students learn: Reforming schools through learner-centered education.* (pp. 1–24). Washington, DC: American Psychological Association.

Lave, J. (1988). *Cognition in practice.* Cambridge, UK: Cambridge University Press.

Means, T. B., Jonassen, D. H., & Dwyer, F. M. (1997). Enhancing relevance: Embedded ARCS strategies versus purpose. *Educational Technology Research and Development, 45*(1), 5–18.

New England Adult Research Network (1999). *Factors influencing adult student persistence in undergraduate degree programs.* Amherst, MA: University of Massachusetts.

Olneck, M. R. (1995). Immigrants and education. In J. A. Banks & C. A. M. Banks (Eds.), *Handbook on research in multicultural education* (pp. 310–327). New York: Palgrave Macmillan.

Rogoff, B., & Chavajay, P. (1995). What's become of research on the cultural basis of cognitive development? *American Psychologist, 50*, 859–877.

Ryan, R. M., & Deci, E. L. (2000). When rewards compete with nature: The undermining of intrinsic motivation and self-regulation. In C. Sansone & J. M. Harackiewicz (Eds.), *Intrinsic and extrinsic motivation: The search for optimal motivation and performance* (pp. 13–54). New York: Academic Press.

Sansone, C., & Harackiewicz, J. M. (Eds.). (2000). *Intrinsic and extrinsic motivation: The search for optimal motivation and performance.* New York: Academic Press.

Scanlan, C., & Darkenwald, G. G. (1984). Identifying deterrents to Participation in continuing education. *Adult Education Quarterly, 34*(3), 155–166.

Tinto, V. (1998). Colleges as communities: Taking research on student persistence seriously. *The Review of Higher Education, 21*(2), 167–177.

Wlodkowski, R. J. (1999). *Enhancing adult*

motivation to learn: A comprehensive guide for teaching all adults (Rev. ed.). San Francisco: Jossey-Bass.

Wlodkowski, R. J., & Ginsburg, M. (1995). *Diversity and motivation: Culturally responsive teaching.* San Francisco: Jossey-Bass.

Wlodkowski, R. J., Mauldin, R. J., & Gahn, S. W. (2001). *Learning in the fast lane: Adult learners' persistence and success in accelerated college programs.* Indianapolis, IN: Lumina Foundation for Education.

Raymond J. Wlodkowski

Multiple Intelligences

Multiple intelligences, a theory developed by Howard Gardner (1993), challenges the notion of a fixed "general intelligence" or "IQ," by postulating at least seven types of intelligence. In the late 1970s, when the dominant educational discourses associated with "age and stage" behaviorist and developmental psychology and psychometric testing were beginning to break down, Gardner redefined intelligence as the ability to "solve genuine problems or difficulties" or to "fashion products" valued in at least one cultural setting. He reviewed an extensive literature using several criteria to identify signs of such intelligence, noting that this exercise was "reminiscent more of an artistic judgment than of a scientific assessment" (p. 62), while, as a result, compiling a provisional list of seven different forms of intelligence.

Gardner's Theory of Multiple Intelligences

The first two of Gardner's seven forms of intelligence are what traditional intelligence (IQ) tests have sought to measure. *Linguistic intelligence* involves sensitivity to spoken and written languages, using language to express oneself, remember information and accomplish certain goals, with writers, poets and lawyers among those who draw on this form of intelligence. *Logical-mathematical intelligence* is demonstrated in the analysis of problems through the identification of patterns, deductive reasoning and logical thought; scientists and mathematicians exemplify this type (Smith, 2004).

The next three types of intelligence are often associated with the arts. *Musical intelligence* encompasses appreciation of musical patterns, pitches, tones and rhythms as well as skills in performance and composition. *Bodily-kinesthetic intelligence* uses mental abilities to coordinate bodily movements. *Spatial intelligence* involves the potential to recognize and use patterns.

The final two are "personal intelligences," often particularly valued in education, counseling and organizational leadership and *interpersonal intelligence,* which enables people to work effectively with others by understanding their intentions, motivations and desires. *Intrapersonal intelligence* is about understanding oneself and being able to use this understanding to regulate one's life.

In Gardner's view, although they are distinctive, these seven intelligences rarely operate independently but complement each other as people develop skills and solve problems. There has been much debate about whether there are other forms of intelligence which should be included in (and whether some should be excluded from) Gardner's list. He has since added *naturalist intelligence,* which enables people to recognize, categorize and draw upon features of the environment in problem-solving. Gardner (1999) decided against the inclusion of "spiritual intelligence," largely because of the contested nature of the term "spiritual." However, he acknowledged the importance of people's concerns with "ultimate issues" and considered listing "existential intelligence" as a ninth form. He rejected it, noting: "I find the phenomenon perplexing enough and the distance from the other intelligences vast enough to dictate prudence – at least for now" (p. 66).

Gardner's theory has been criticized because it lacks grounding in empirical research. It has, nevertheless, been embraced by many educators who recognize within it their own professional experiences of working with students' different ways of knowing and learning, and the struggle to accommodate these within curriculum and assessment regimes framed by traditional views of intelligence.

EQ and SQ

Goleman (1996) has built on Gardner's "personal intelligences" to develop the concept of emotional intelligence or emotional quotient (EQ): the ability to understand oneself and others and to deal effectively with emotions and relationships. Goleman points out that, although these socio-emotional aspects of people's lives are generally determinants of happiness and success, they do not feature in traditional views of intelligence/IQ. He argues that EQ underpins the effective use of IQ and should be actively nurtured.

Danah Zohar and Ian Marshall (2000, pp. 3–4) agree, but claim that spiritual intelligence or spirituality quotient (SQ) is what we use to deal with problems of meaning and value: it is therefore "the necessary foundation for the effective functioning of both IQ and EQ. It is our ultimate intelligence" (pp. 3–4). They are somewhat dismissive of Gardner's work, suggesting that his multiple intelligences are merely "variations of the basic IQ, EQ and SQ" (p. 4). Zohar and Marshall contend that the concepts of IQ and EQ fail to take into account the full complexity of human intelligence, including "the vast richness of the human soul and imagination" (p. 5). In their terms, a high IQ affords knowledge of rules and the ability to follow them without making mistakes; a high EQ provides a sense of one's immediate situation and an understanding of how to respond appropriately: both work within the boundaries of a "finite game." SQ enables people to change rules and boundaries and play an "infinite game." It thus has transformative learning potential. It cannot be quantified but it can be engaged with through systematic reflection on life-experiences (pp. 276–81). The process would have been familiar to early pioneers of adult education for whom spirituality, morality and intellectual development were inseparable.

IQ

Aristotle distinguished emotional and moral functions (*orexis*) from the cognitive and intellectual (*dianoia*). Cicero translated the latter term as *intelligentia* (from roots meaning "choose between"). This historical association of intelligence primarily with cognitive processes has shaped the way it has subsequently been understood and investigated.

In 1904, the French psychologist Alfred Binet designed a series of diagnostic tests to measure children's intellectual development, equating this with cognitive, problem-solving abilities. L.M.Terman, at Stanford University, later created the Stanford–Binet Scale to determine mental age. He assumed that the ratio of mental to chronological age would remain constant: multiplied by 100, the ratio represented the child's "intelligence quotient" (IQ).

The development of "intelligence tests" popularized the notion that people have a fixed and measurable "quotient" of intelligence. Sir Cyril Burt claimed that this was largely inherited. Based on studies of identical twins separated at birth and raised apart, his work appeared to reinforce with scientific evidence a common assumption that there is some kind of "natural order" underpinning the inequities of social class and race.

Appointed as the first educational psychologist to the London County Council, Burt created a range of IQ and other educational tests for diagnostic purposes. Such tests were used in Britain for several decades to determine, at the age of 11, what kind of secondary school a child should attend. Only about 20% of each age-cohort passed the so-called "11+" examination, which opened the door to a grammar-school education and the possibility of admission to a university and the professions. IQ test questions were supposedly unbiased. For example, they asked what part was missing from a series of pictures (like a string from a violin or the lines on a tennis court). Until the 1970s, it went largely unremarked that white middle-class children were more likely than those from other cultural and social backgrounds to have had access to the books, information and experiences that would help them to provide the required answers. Evidence that practice in answering test questions improved scores, plus emerging doubts about the basis of Burt's research, eventually contributed to the demise of the 11+, though not of IQ testing.

Shortly after Burt's death in 1971, it was alleged that he might have falsified or misrepresented much of his data, especially that relating to the studies of twins. Controversy has raged about this since, not least because other influential work draws heavily on Burt's ideas, including that of Hans Eysenck and Arthur Jenson, both of whom linked differences in IQ or general intelligence to biological and genetic factors. Stephen Jay Gould (1981), a distinguished biologist, argues that, even before Darwin's theory of evolution, white European men had regarded themselves as the pinnacle of creation. Since then, measurement of various kinds, from cranial size to IQ test scores, has been used to "prove" this assumed superiority and consequent right to educational and other privileges. Gould highlights a range of IQ tests that were manifestly racist in concept: one United States Army test branded black soldiers with an average mental age of 10.

Despite serious concerns about the concept, origins and consequences of IQ tests, they remain in use in a variety of forms. They are sometimes used in medicine to determine possible intellectual impairment following a stroke. A BBC television program called *Test the Nation: The National IQ Test* is extremely popular in the UK. Since the 1940s, Mensa has provided a meeting-place for those who score above 146 on a standard IQ test: approximately 10,000 people in the UK take the supervised entrance test annually, of which about 2,500 gain admission. Membership is approximately two-thirds male and one-third female, which perhaps represents a continued sexist bias in the tests themselves (Thorpe & McKie, 2002).

Application to Adult Education

Interest in intelligence *per se* has waned in adult education. Yet, there is a resurgence of interest in related areas. Work on spirituality of adult education has increased, as has a stress on auto/biography, reflective practice, and inter- and intrapersonal forms of communication. These may be seen as attempts to move beyond the boundaries of cognitive processes and their measurement in order to acknowledge different forms of human knowing and expression.

See also: experiential learning, reflective practice, spirituality, transformative learning.

References and Further Reading

Gardner, H. (1983/1993). *Frames of mind: The theory of multiple intelligences.* New York: Basic Books.

Gardner, H. (1999). *Intelligence reframed: Multiple intelligences for the 21st century.* New York: Basic Books.

Goleman, D. (1996). *Emotional intelligence.* London: Bantam Books.

Gould, S. J. (1981). *The mismeasure of man.* New York: Norton.

Smith, M. K. (2004). Howard Gardner and multiple intelligences. *Encyclopedia of Informal Education.* Retrieved September 1, 2003 from http://www.infed.org/thinkers/gardner.htm

Thorpe, V., & McKie, R. (2002). The rise and fall of IQ, *Observer.* Retrieved September, 23, 2002 from http://observer.guardian.co.uk/focus/story/0,6903,668879,00.html

Zohar, D., & Marshall, I. (2000). *SQ.* London: Bloomsbury.

Cheryl Hunt

N

Narrative

Narrative refers to story, or that which expresses the basic elements of story. In connection with adult education, narrative can be understood as an overarching orientation to knowledge, learning and human development. With roots in multiple disciplines, including literature, theology, and psychology, the narrative orientation is characterized by a focus on story as an organizing structure for human experience and meaning-making. The narrative approach is applied as a way of understanding adult development, as a qualitative research methodology, and as an approach to the facilitation of learning. In all applications, the narrative orientation is defined by its reflection of the temporal, contextual, and interpretive qualities of story (Rossiter, 1999a).

- *Temporality* is an essential element of narrative in that a story, by definition, unfolds over a period of time – it is not one single moment or snapshot of time. We understand the action of a story from the perspective of the present moment, in terms of what has gone before and what we expect might happen next. Because the present moment is ever-changing, narrative meaning is dynamic and fluid rather than static and fixed.
- *Contextuality* is also integral to the narrative orientation at both internal and external levels. In terms of internal narrative coherence, events of a story are understood in relation to each other, that is, in the context of the plot of the story. The events of a story are not simply a listing or chronology, but are connected to one another in a meaningful way. This meaning is defined by the intentionality of the characters and the relative desirability of possible outcomes. At an external level, the narrative orientation is sensitive to the sociocultural milieu within which a story is understood. Indeed, the intelligibility of a story is dependent upon the dominant cultural narratives within which it is told, and upon some level of linguistic and cultural congruence between the story and its audience.
- Stories require *interpretation* because they deal with human intention, as well as action. We make meaning of the story not only on the basis of what we can see, but also in terms of how we understand the intentions of the characters. Our interpretation of the story is some combination of what is told and what we bring to the story.

The narrative orientation has important epistemological implications that distinguish narrative knowing from scientific knowing. As Jerome Bruner (1986) has explained, the narrative and scientific are two fundamentally different ways of making meaning, two approaches to understanding reality. The scientific mode deals with logical argument and deductive reasoning, whereas the narrative mode deals with human intention and action. In the view of narrative scholars such as Donald Polkinghorne (1988, 1996), the scientific mode is appropriate for the physical sciences, which study things outside the realm of human meaning, but it is not necessarily suited to the study of human experience. The natural sciences result in knowledge for the sake of prediction and control, whereas the narrative mode of human science leads to deeper understandings of human experience. Narrative knowing, in contrast to scientific knowing in the positivist tradition, is concerned more with human meaning than with discrete facts, more with coherence than with logic, more with sequences than with categories, and more with understanding than with predictability and control.

Narrative Inquiry

In recent decades adult educators have increasingly explored applications of the narrative orientation to the research endeavor. Broadly speaking, narrative inquiry is a type of qualitative research in which narrative defines both the data and the method of analysis. Narrative data are stories of lived experience told from a first-person point of view. They are most commonly gathered by the researcher as interview transcripts, but are also collected in the form of letters, diaries, or other autobiographical writings. Whatever the form, these accounts function as narrative texts for analysis by the researcher. A distinguishing feature of narrative data is that they are stories that deal with human intention and action *as experienced* by human beings. This reflects the key assumption that subjective experience, instead of being carefully segregated from the research process, is itself a focus of inquiry. A persistent question for narrative researchers has to do with how to interpret narrative data and present findings in a way that remains true to the storyteller's experience. Narrative interpretation involves the confluence of that which is "given" in the story, and that which the listener/reader brings to the story from her or his own experience and knowing. As a result, the product of narrative analysis represents a story that is actually co-constructed by the researcher and the participant.

Narrative analysis is the process of discerning what type of story has been told, and/or the story elements that are expressed in the narrative data. Researchers approach narrative analysis from different theoretical perspectives depending upon their purposes and disciplines such as: psychological, linguistic, and feminist theory. While narrative analysis is growing in popularity, it is *relatively* new as a method of research in education, and as such, is a dynamically evolving approach to inquiry. Ruthellen Josselson (Josselson, Lieblich, & McAdams, 2003) notes that most people who are now doing and teaching narrative analysis have themselves never been taught how to do it. The procedures for narrative analysis are not highly specified and codified but are developing through a wide variety of applications. At a fundamental level, the process involves looking at both what the story is about and what kind of story it is. Lieblich, Tuval-Mashiach, and Zilber (1998) identify four basic approaches to working with narrative data that vary according to whether the focus is on content or form, and according to whether the focus is holistic – looking at the story as a whole – or categorical – focusing on a particular feature, theme or element of the story. Catherine Reissman (1993) describes the process in terms of levels of representation of experience: attending, telling, transcribing, analysing, and reading.

A Narrative Understanding of Human Development

The application of the narrative orientation to an understanding of human development also rests on the premise that narrative is the primary structure through which human beings organize and make meaning of their experience. The basic idea, in connection with development, is that people understand the changes over the course of their own lives narratively, that is, they construct and express meaning in story form. In this orientation, story is the central metaphor for the life course, and development can be understood as a process of constructing and re-constructing the life narrative throughout life (Cohler, 1982). This view differs from the organismic model of development that is generally considered as the framework for stage theories of development, in which the living organism is the underlying metaphor. In stage theory, psychological development is understood in terms of ordered change leading toward a given endpoint – just as the living organism grows physically from birth to maturity in a predictable pattern. In contrast, the narrative perspective does not assume a predictable forward-moving sequence of stages but acknowledges that much change and growth over the life course is not predictable. The narrative approach thus calls into question the endpoints of adult development as identified by stage theory. Narrative psychologists such as Mark Freeman (1991) explain that development is best understood retrospectively, as an ongoing process of reviewing lived experience and interpreting developmental progress in the context of the desired outcomes of individual life narrative. Development is seen as "a never-ending retrospective story of transformation" (Freeman, p. 88).

Because learning is intertwined with developmental change throughout adulthood, the narrative view of development carries important implications for understanding adult learning. Narrative highlights the "inside" perspective on developmental experience as it is lived, rather than the "outside" perspective of the observer (Rossiter, 1999b), and thus it views the adult learner as the expert on her or his own development. For adult educators, this understanding of development suggests the importance of attention to individual learner narratives, rather than focusing on locating the learner within a stage framework. Additionally, narrative identifies the process of "storying" as a means through which learners internalize and make meaning of new ideas and concepts. People explain and cope with change in their lives by creating or revising stories to account for that which is unfamiliar. William Randall (1996) has described "re-storying" the life narrative as the central dynamic of transformative learning. The basic idea is that the telling of and reflection upon life narratives enable learners to locate their experience within larger socio-cultural contexts, and to assess their adequacy. This view of transformative learning is more subjective and interpretive than the perspective transformation as described by Jack Mezirow (1991).

Narrative and Stories in Adult Teaching and Learning

The premise that narrative is integral to human meaning-making points to the centrality and power of narrative-based educational activities. The fundamental assumption of narrative pedagogy is that the most effective way to reach learners with "educational messages" (Hopkins, 1994) is through narrative constructions of meaning, both cultural and individual. The narrative orientation calls for a contextual, interpretive, constructivist approach to teaching and learning. While the ways in which narrative is employed in adult teaching and learning settings are virtually unlimited, they cluster into three areas – narrative interpretation of content, story-telling, and autobiographical activities. First, pedagogical content can be understood as narrative text (Gudmundsdottir, 1995), and learning as the interpretation of that text. The role of the educator is to narrate the content and to bring the learner into an interpretive relationship with it. That is, the educator does not simply tell stories about the subject matter, but actually stories it. In so doing, the narrative educator tries to create an interpretive space in which the learner can interact with the content in much the same way an audience interacts with a movie or novel.

Second, story-telling and the use of stories express the narrative approach to teaching and learning. Case studies, critical incidents, role-playing, and educational drama, are among the story-based learning activities used extensively by adult educators. Throughout history, good teachers have understood that stories are effective as teaching tools. The narrative orientation explains why stories are so powerful. Stories are believable because they deal with human or human-like intention and action, and as such are imbued with the authenticity of human experience. Additionally, stories tend to be rememberable because they are entertaining and because they engage the whole brain – both the left hemisphere associated with logic-based, analytical thought and the right hemisphere, which is associated with visual and symbolic thinking. And, stories are effective as learning activities because they stimulate empathic responses. The detail and particularity of a story, along with the intentionality of the story characters, evokes fuller cognitive and affective engagement by the learner/listener than does a statement of fact, argument, or position statement. Thus stories are a potent supplement to content that is chiefly quantitative or conceptual in nature.

A third area of narrative application in adult education is that of autobiographical learning which, in general terms, has to do with learning from one's own life and is fostered through story-sharing and life-writing. Narrative pedagogy is, above all, grounded in lived experience as situated in the life narratives of the learners. In the view of Irene Karpiak (2000) who works with adult students in higher education, such activity leads to learning and growth as it enables the adult student to bring a sense of order to the life narrative and offers expanded possibilities for self-exploration and meaning-making. Autobiography, as an instructional tool, can facilitate learners' construction and reconstruction of a satisfactory life narrative. Because autobiography involves recounting memories and finding their larger meaning, and to the extent that the activity expands knowledge of self in the world, it is a potent learning dynamic.

See also: autobiography, life history, meaning-making, research methods, writing.

References and Further Reading

Bruner, J. (1986). *Actual minds, possible worlds*. Cambridge, MA: Harvard University Press.

Cohler, B. J. (1982). Personal narrative and the life course. In P.B. Baltes & O.B. Brim Jr. (Eds.), *Life-span development and behavior* (pp. 205–241). New York: Academic Press.

Freeman, M. (1991). Rewriting the self: Development as moral practice. In M. B.Tappan & M. J. Packer (Eds.), *Narrative and storytelling: Implications for understanding moral development* (pp. 83–101). *New Directions for Child Development*, No. 54, San Francisco: Jossey-Bass.

Gudmundsdottir, S. (1995). The narrative nature of pedagogical content knowledge. In H. McEwan & K. Egan (Eds.), *Narrative in teaching, learning, and research* (pp. 24–38). New York: Teachers College Press.

Hopkins, R. L. (1994). *Narrative schooling*. New York: Teachers College Press.

Josselson, R., Lieblilch, A., & McAdams, D. P. (2003). *Up close and personal: The teaching and learning of narrative research*. Washington, DC: American Psychological Association.

Karpiak, I. E. (2000). Writing our life: Adult learning and teaching through autobiography. *Canadian Journal of University Continuing Education, 26*, 31–50.

Lieblich, A., Tuval-Mashiach, R., & Zilber, T. (1998). *Narrative research: Reading, analysis, and interpretation*. Thousand Oaks, CA: Sage.

Mezirow, J. (1991). *Transformative dimensions of adult learning*. San Francisco: Jossey-Bass.

Polkinghorne, D. E. (1988). *Narrative knowing and the human sciences*. Albany, NY: State University of New York Press.

Polkinghorne, D. E. (1996). Narrative knowing and the study of lives. In J.E. Birren, G. M. Kenyon, J-E. Ruth, J. J. F. Schroots & T. Suensson (Eds.), *Aging and biography: Explorations in adult development* (pp. 77–99). New York: Spring Publishing.

Randall, W. L. (1996). Restorying a life: Adult education and transformative learning. In J.E. Birren, G. M. Kenyon, J-E. Ruth, J. J. F. Schroots & T. Suensson (Eds.), *Aging and biography: Explorations in adult development* (pp. 224–247). New York: Spring Publishing.

Riessman, C. K. (1993). *Qualitative research methods: Narrative analysis*, Series 30, Newbury Park, CA: Sage.

Rossiter, M. (1999a). A narrative approach to development: Implications for adult education. *Adult Education Quarterly, 50*, 56–71.

Rossiter, M. (1999b). Understanding adult development as narrative. In M. C. Clark & R. S. Caffarella (Eds.), *An update on adult developmental theory* (pp. 77–85). *New Directions for Adult and Continuing Education*, No. 84. San Francisco: Jossey-Bass.

Marsha Rossiter

Needs Assessment

Needs assessment is the process of identifying gaps or discrepancies between present and more desirable states of affairs, conditions or outcomes. From within the technical-rational tradition of educational planning that has dominated North American adult education for the past 50 years, needs assessment is viewed as an essential task that leads to the development of relevant, responsive and carefully-focused programs for adult learners. From outside that tradition, however, it is an antiquated notion based on misguided assumptions about the origins of "needs" and the romantic belief that conducting a needs assessment democratizes planning and relieves planners from making value judgments. Oddly, needs assessment seems to be a central planning concept only in North America, perhaps because the move to professionalize the field by adopting "scientific" approaches gained a stronger foothold there than in other parts of the world. Needs assessment *can* be a useful concept and powerful planning tool if it is thought about critically and used judiciously.

History and Context

Malcolm Knowles's (1970) influential book *The Modern Practice of Adult Education: Andragogy Versus Pedagogy* referred to assessing needs and interests as a crucially important step in planning. Writers outside of adult education like Roger A. Kaufman (1972) who focused on educational system planning, and Belle Ruth Witkin (1984) who was concerned with planning both educational and social programs, also regarded needs assessment as a central process. Many adult education planning models that followed Knowles', featured needs assessment as an early and necessary step. This was a period in the development of educational theory dominated by the assumptions of technical rationality wherein solutions to most educational and social problems could be found by employing a "scientific" approach that privileged a kind of empirical analysis which avoided, or "controlled for," value judgements and political considerations. Many of these models regarded "needs" as objective conditions that could be identified using empirical tools like questionnaires, tests, interviews, observations, and so on. These models are based on what Sandra Pearce (1998) calls a "functionalist perspective" that "assumes needs can be identified objectively and that they are measurable" (pp. 251–252). This is contrasted with the "empowerment perspective" which is based on a subjectivist world view where social reality is constructed and constantly changing. In many cases, any process that gathered data from learners or others in a position to offer an opinion – about needs, interests, desires, or wants – seemed to be considered a needs assessment even though many of these produced fundamentally different kinds of information for planning purposes. There was a clear preference for involving adult learners in the process, but recognition that this was not always possible. The conventional wisdom in adult education that, whenever possible, learners should be directly involved in planning was complicated by the realization that learners are not always aware of, or able to articulate, what they don't know. From Pearce's empowerment perspective, the point is to involve learners directly in planning so they can take control; without that direct involvement, empowerment is impossible.

As more and more people wrote about needs assessment, a consensus began to emerge that a "need" should be thought of as a gap or discrepancy between a present condition, state of affairs or set of outcomes and a more desirable condition, state of affairs or set of outcomes. This growing consensus brought greater clarity to what a needs assessment might involve empirically and what role value judgments might play, but other concerns emerged that made relying exclusively on the concept of need in planning problematic. One concern was the focus on individual needs to the neglect of community, societal or even global needs. If one only focuses on individual learners in conducting a needs assessment, then how do educational needs affecting a community, society or the planet come to the attention of adult educators? Another concern was the role of value judgments. If part of identifying needs is forming an image of, or making a judgment about, a more desirable state of affairs, then whose views matter? And what happens when there are conflicting or mutually exclusive views about the more desirable state of affairs? Howard Davidson (1995) takes up this issue in his discussion of "needs-making" activities. He rightly points out that needs are often socially constructed to privilege certain domains of life (like the economy) and to provide access of certain learners to educational resources while denying access to others. Adult educators are complicit in this process:

> [W]e cannot dismiss the adult educator as less than a key participant in the emergence and maintenance of needs-making and responding activity. The problem is to analyze how educators perform this work: how they receive claims made by others that a condition be acknowledged as an educational need, how they accumulate resources and employ argot to further these claims and to constitute a response, and how the institutions in which educators work influence the quality of their needs-making and responding activities. (Davidson, 1995, p. 188)

A third concern grows out of a suspicion that conventional need-based approaches to planning further the interests of the already powerful by largely reproducing the status quo. Needs assessment is inherently reactive; it is impossible to identify or "make" needs until there is some discrepancy between a present condition and a desired condition. Needs, therefore, are based on dissatisfaction with the present. Those who control access to resources for planning programs are often in a position to set or imagine the standard to which the present is compared. So it is largely in the hands of those who control these resources to define the desired state of affairs. Two important questions for those doing a needs assessment are, "Whose interests are being served by the way this process is being framed?" and "Whose views matter when determining the desired state of affairs?" It is certainly possible for both learners and educators to articulate a different future that would lead to a more just, peaceful, and sustainable society, but efforts to develop educational programs in support of such goals are subject to complex power dynamics that typically favor the already privileged whose interests may be threatened by fundamental change (Cervero & Wilson, 1996).

One of Many Approaches

Many volumes have been written on different ways of thinking about and conducting a needs assessment. Most of these concentrate on technical aspects including the strengths and weaknesses of various information gathering processes. Witkin and Altschuld (1995), and Altschuld and Witkin (2000), make a distinctive contribution because of the attention they give to the thornier conceptual and methodological issues and the tools they suggest for reducing the reactive character of the process. Examples they provide of methods used by futurists that can be applied to good effect in needs assessment include the Delphi technique, trend analysis, scenario development, cross-impact analysis and future wheels. Each of these is useful for developing a view of the future that is more than the utopian wishes of a select few, or more of the status quo that favors the already privileged. They also offer ways of approaching the priority-setting and resource-allocation process – which they consider part of needs assessment – under the sensible assumption that most needs assessments will uncover more needs than can be addressed with available resources. They do not assume, like many authors, that the resources will somehow appear if a need has been identified.

Those who write for practitioners in human resource development and training tend to situate needs assessment in a strongly technical rational framework. Examples include the planning model of Irwin Goldstein and J. Kevin Ford (2002), and the performance-based approaches of Kavita Gupta (1999) and Allison Rossett (1999) all of which place organizational needs at the centre of the process. In this view, benchmarks or standards for individual performance (desired states of affairs) are linked to the performance of the organization; needs assessments identify performance gaps which may hinder the organization in achieving its mission.

In recent years, writers in adult education have adopted a "softer" approach to the role of needs assessment consistent with a view originally presented in 1972 by Cyril Houle in *The Design of Education* (1972/1996). Houle took the position that there are many different sources of program ideas in adult education. Although he acknowledged that needs assessment *may* be a suitable technique in some situations, he urged educators to decide which approach to use based on the particulars of the context and the nature of the planning task. More recently Pearce (1998), Sork (2001), and Caffarella (2002) proposed a similar position. They point out that needs assessment is *potentially* useful for educational planning, but it is neither the only nor the most appropriate tool for all situations. Rather than assuming that a good planner always conducts a needs assessment, they treat needs assessment as one of several ways of identifying program ideas and determining program substance.

A Framework for Needs Assessment

In the question-based framework to planning he proposes, Sork (2001) urges planners to consider a range of approaches including needs assessment, interest inventory, problem analysis, market testing, trend analysis, and various combinations of these. The decision about which to use should be based on multiple factors including the kind of information needed for decision-making, the time and resources available for planning, and how much is already known about the learners, among others. He defines educational need as "a gap or discrepancy between a present capability (PC) and a desired capability (DC)" (p. 101), and distinguishes, as does Houle (1996), between *felt needs* which are identified or acknowledged by the learners themselves, and *ascribed needs*, which are identified by someone other than the learners. For those who decide that a needs assessment is the preferred approach, he offers a series of questions to guide the process such as: What characteristics of the context and learner community will be especially important to consider as you design the needs assessment and why? Who should be involved in carrying out the needs assessment and what role will they play? Will the assessment identify only felt needs, only ascribed needs or both? What existing information might be useful in the needs assessment and where is it located? Will you use a continuous strategy, a one-time strategy or a combination? How will you determine present and desired capabilities? What process will be used to determine priorities among the needs that you identify and who should be involved? What are the important socio-political and ethical issues you are likely to encounter during the needs assessment and how will you deal with them? (Sork, pp. 105–109)

Regardless of the needs assessment framework adopted, current scholarship in adult education cautions practitioners to be wide awake to the value base of "needs" and the political and ethical implications of whatever process they use to justify and focus their program planning efforts.

See also: facilitation, program planning, teaching.

References and Further Reading

Altschuld, J. W., & Witkin, B. R. (2000). *From needs assessment to action: Transforming needs into solution strategies.* Thousand Oaks, CA: Sage.

Caffarella, R.S. (2002). *Planning programs for adult learners: A practical guide for educators, trainers, and staff developers* (2nd ed.). San Francisco: Jossey-Bass.

Cervero, R. M., & Wilson, A.L. (Eds.). (1996). *What really matters in adult education program planning practice: Lessons in negotiating power and interests. New Directions for Adult and Continuing Education,* No. 69. San Francisco: Jossey-Bass.

Davidson, H. S. (1995). Making needs: Toward a historical sociology of needs in adult and continuing education. *Adult Education Quarterly, 45*(4), 183–196.

Goldstein, I.L., & Ford, J. K. (2002). *Training in organizations: Needs assessment, development and evaluation* (4th ed.). Belmont, CA: Wadsworth/Thomson Learning.

Gupta, K. (1999). *A practical guide to needs assessment.* San Francisco: Jossey-Bass/Pfeiffer.

Houle, C. O. (1996). *The design of education* (2nd ed.). San Francisco: Jossey-Bass.

Kaufman, R. A. (1972). *Educational system planning.* Englewood Cliffs, NJ: Prentice Hall.

Knowles, M. S. (1970). *The modern practice of adult education: Andragogy versus pedagogy.* Chicago: Association Press.

Pearce, S. (1998). Determining program needs. In P. S. Cookson (Ed.), *Program planning for the training and continuing education of adults: North American perspectives* (pp. 249–272). Malabar, FL: Krieger.

Rossett, A. (1999). *First things fast: A handbook for performance analysis.*San Francisco: Jossey-Bass.

Sork, T. J. (2001). Needs assessment. In D. H. Poonwassie & A. Poonwassie (Eds.), *Fundamentals of adult education: Issues and practices for lifelong learning* (pp. 100–115). Toronto: Thompson Educational.

Witkin, B. R. (1984). *Assessing needs in educational and social programs: Using information to make decisions, set priorities, and allocate resources.* San Francisco: Jossey-Bass.

Witkin, B. R., & Altschuld, J. W. (1995). *Planning and conducting needs assessments: A practical guide.* Thousand Oaks, CA: Sage.

Thomas J. Sork

New Zealand and Adult Education

New Zealand is a small democratic country situated in the South Pacific, some 1,200kms from its nearest neighbor, Australia. It has a larger land area than its historical "mother country" Britain, but only one-fifteenth its population. As a country it prides itself on its innovative social developments (the first country to grant women the vote and develop a comprehensive social welfare system) and "farm-gate intellectual innovations" born out of a pioneering attitude and a somewhat skeptical attitude towards formal education (Boshier, 2002).

Pioneering Provision

The indigenous Maori's extensive oral traditions were embedded in an educational system of *whare wananga* (houses of learning), and this attitude to learning transferred readily into engagement with written text and high literacy rates with the arrival of European settlers in the early 1800s. The first European (*pakeha*) adult education institutions were largely transplants from the British adult education tradition – Mechanics' Institutes, literary institutes, athenaeums, mutual improvement societies and the Workers Educational Association (WEA), but soon developed distinctive innovations such as the WEA's "box scheme" of distance provision and traveling libraries (Dakin, 1996). The 1930s economic depression saw extensive cutbacks, but then came a resurgence of interest and enrolment numbers following the Second World War. While some of the initial forms of provision dropped away or disappeared, state-run provision steadily increased in the middle decades of the 20th century, especially with the work of university extension departments at most of the country's seven universities.

The emergence of *lifelong education* under the auspices of UNESCO then ignited a profound new generation of interest in adult education in the 1970s and 1980s (Benseman, 2003b). The Faure Report, *Learning to Be*, was mirrored in a Lifelong Education Committee examining its implications for New Zealand. The education of adults outside formal programs in universities and technical institutes was given unprecedented prominence, leading to milestones such as a senior continuing education appointment in the Department of Education, the revitalization of the National Council of Adult Education as an advocate and professional development agency for the field. In the field existing provision and a series of new innovative developments, such as community colleges (where community education was on an equal footing with vocational education), community learning centers based in schools, a continuing education Unit at Radio New Zealand and Rural Education Activities Programmes (REAP) flourished. Adult education reached new heights of innovative practice, political prominence and practitioner morale during this period, but turbulent times soon dissipated these achievements in the latter part of the 20th century.

The Impact of the New Right

Following a period of budget slashing under the National Government of Robert Muldoon in the early 1980s, the election of a Labor Government in 1985 with a strong commitment to adult education initially led to greater optimism. A subsequent lurch to the political right and strong adherence to New Right policies by successive governments for the next 15 years, however, led adult education to a return to its former marginal status in the New Zealand education system, both in terms of overall policy and funding for provision outside traditional formal institutions (Benseman, 1996).

Current Developments

The election of a centrist Labor

government under Prime Minister Helen Clark in 1999 brought with it more sympathetic ministers (the current Minister of Education is a former REAP adult educator) and policies. Like many other countries, New Zealand has subsequently embraced the concept of lifelong learning that is currently *de rigueur* as the new educational utopia. Alongside a substantial review of all post-school education by the Tertiary Education Advisory Commission (TEAC), have been the first review of adult and community education to be officially accepted by government, and the first ever adult literacy policy (heavily influenced by the country's first national survey as part of the International Adult Literacy Survey). An interesting development to emerge from this flurry of reviews is a new administrative structure, the Tertiary Education Commission (TEC) to administer all post-school provision from non-formal adult education through to universities. While the funding streams are yet to flow significantly higher, adult education has regained recognition within the broader educational sector and there is much debate about the ways and means to achieve the social justice ideals of the *Koia! Koia!* (Ministry of Education, 2001a) adult education report.

Adult Education as a Field

Given its chequered history, it comes as no surprise that adult education as a professional field is still small, underdeveloped, poorly recognized and underfunded – but with a well-developed sense of survival. Career structures for adult educators are patchy and often reliant on short-term, "soft money" and the majority of practitioners and administrators have no formal adult education qualifications. There are a small handful of adult education academics in three of the universities, but a larger number of professional development staff in the polytechnics. Most of the adult education qualifications are taught at the introductory certificate or diploma level, with only a small number of postgraduate degrees.

The small number of adult education academics and postgraduate qualifications is further mirrored in the small amount of research about the field, its practices and issues. A recent review of New Zealand adult literacy research (Benseman, 2003a), for example, identified very few studies of scale or quality. Over the past three decades, the peer-reviewed *New Zealand Journal of Adult Learning* has been the mainstay location of analytical writing, while the national association Adult and Community Education Aotearoa (ACE Aotearoa) has provided ongoing support for practitioners through annual conferences and branch activities.

Participation

Participation rates in New Zealand adult education have been the focus of several national studies, although their scope and accuracy have been inconsistent. In the 1970–1980s there was much public concern about low participation rates (albeit across the post-school spectrum) in comparison to other OECD countries. More recent comparisons have shown, however, national participation rates to be among the highest within the OECD, although the role of the adult education sector within these figures is not differentiated. More importantly, however, some observers (Tobias, 2001) have demonstrated that some underrepresented groups have now achieved rates comparable or even beyond the national norm – Maori participation rates for example have doubled over the past decade.

Tino rangatiratanga – Maori Sovereignty

Probably the most distinctive feature of New Zealand adult education is the role of Maori in terms of policy formation and provision. Fueled by a broader political renaissance in New Zealand society, Maori have increasingly promoted a "by Maori, for Maori" dictum based on their equal political partnership with non-Maori under the founding document of the Treaty of Waitangi signed in 1842. These demands for Maori sovereignty have prompted much debate with the country as a whole and in adult education specifically. Responses have included creating bicultural organizations and structures (such as Literacy Aotearoa, the national adult literacy organization for community-based provision and ACEA) and provision aimed specifically at Maori learners and their needs.

The beginning of the 21st century has signaled a new era of cautious optimism for New Zealand adult education.

See also: higher education, ideology, indigenous learning.

References and Further Reading

Benseman, J. (1996). Thriving and surviving on the fringe: Wither adult and community education in the 1990s? *Access, 15*(2), 1–20.

Benseman, J. (2003a). *Literature review of New Zealand adult literacy research.* Wellington, New Zealand: Ministry of Education.

Benseman, J. (2003b). *New Zealand's journey towards a learning society: Rhetoric and realities of lifelong learning.* Unpublished dissertation. University of Technology Sydney, Australia.

Boshier, R. W. (2002). Farm-gate intellectuals: Intellectuals and the university problem in Aotearoa New Zealand, *Studies in Continuing Education, 24*(1), 5–24.

Dakin, J. (1996). Looking back. In J. Benseman, B. Findsen & M. Scott (Eds.), *The fourth sector: Adult and community education in Aotearoa- New Zealand* (pp. 21–37). Palmerston North, New Zealand: Dunmore Books.

Ministry of Education (2001a). *Koia! Koia! Towards a learning society: The role of adult and community education.* Wellington, New Zealand: Ministry of Education.

Ministry of Education. (2001b). *More than words. The New Zealand adult literacy strategy.* Wellington, New Zealand: Ministry of Education.

Tobias, R. (2001). *Do we have a "great divide" in lifelong learning? Trends in educational participation by adults in Aotearoa-New Zealand, 1977–1996.* Paper presented at the Annual New Zealand Association for Research in Education, Christchurch, New Zealand, December 7–9.

John Benseman

Non-Governmental Organizations

A non-governmental organization (NGO) is an organization created outside the state/government and the market or for-profit organizations. Unlike the education of youth which is predominatly provided for by the state, the education of adults historically owes its presence to sponsorship by independent organizations such as NGOs. They continue to play a key role in adult education, as providers and participants in decision-making processes.

The basis of an NGO is civil society; it is a space between the family and the state (Youngman, 1996), providing a place in which citizens voluntarily form associations and organizations, or organize interest groups to promote collective or community interests (Youngman). In adult education contexts, civil society is an arena for learning and social change; "the site to engage in democratic struggle, social movement and political change" (Murphy, 2001, p. 347). The organizations of civil society include bodies like religious institutions, women's groups, farmers' associations, trade unions, environmental groups, peace groups, community organizations, employers' associations, education and professional bodies. These bodies, popularly called NGOs, are known variously as civil society organizations, private voluntary organizations, community-based organizations, grassroots organizations, professional organizations, and not-for profit organizations.

NGOs vary greatly, and it is difficult to generalize about the sector. However, they can be characterized by one or more of the following: non-profit making, voluntary, service (relief)-oriented or development-oriented; public or private-oriented; a social development nature; independent of external control, democratic, non-sectarian people's organizations; not affiliated to political parties; committed to grassroots issues; and established by and for the community without or with little intervention from the government.

According to Kless (1998), NGOs are a transformative force in promoting more equal, participative and sustainable development in various sectors of social life, including education. Groups such as campaign networks, teacher unions, community associations, research networks, parents' associations, professional bodies, social movements and many others across continents are actively promoting education and development for citizens.

One of the hallmarks of NGOs is voluntarism; NGOs can only invite voluntary involvement in their activities (Edwards & Hulme, 1998). NGOs promote participation and partnership, widening access with communities. They are an essential counterweight to state power in strengthening civil society. NGOs act as a progressive element, empowering citizens to face, resist, and transform unequal developments in their societies (Kless, 1998).

NGOs may be organizations based on community membership or professional membership. Members elect from among themselves office bearers to run their respective organization for a stipulated term of office. Examples of these associations are the American Association for Adult and Continuing Education (AAACE), the Canadian Association for the Study of Adult Education (CASAE), the National Institute of Adult Continuing Education (NIACE), the European Association for the Education of the Adult (EAEA), the Pan-African Association for Literacy and Adult Education (PAALAE), the Asia and South Pacific Bureau of Adult Education (ASPBAE), the Norwegian Association for Adult Education, and so on.

There are also non-membership NGOs, whose governance is through elected boards of trustees, with salaried professionals hired to manage the organizations. Examples include the Bangladesh Rural Advancement Committee (BRAC) and the Academy for Education Development (AED) of the United States. BRAC is a large national NGO with the twin objective of alleviation of poverty and empowering the poor; AED is committed to addressing social issues through education, training, policy analysis, program development and so on.

Functions

Kless (1998) pointed out that the NGO literature provides a variety of distinctions among NGOs and identifies the differences in their functioning: for example, national versus international, Northern versus Southern, community-based, religious-based, or grassroots organizations, and NGOs associated with social movements. Ginsburg (1998) noted the heterogeneity of NGOs with different sectors they serve, their scope and their level of wealth. Although diverse, NGOs fulfill these generic functions: (a) service delivery, for example relief, welfare and basic skills; (b) educational such as basic skills and critical analysis of the social environment; and (c) policy advocacy (Stromquist, 1998).

According to Kabanda (2002), NGOs may function as pressure groups, service deliverers, monitors, innovators, and/or as partners. NGOs may exert pressure from outside 'the tent' in decision-making. They are often seen to represent the disempowered and the marginalized; women, the poor, endangered species, minority groups, and the like. As their champions, NGOs are characterized as opposing the manipulation and distortion imposed by hegemony institutions.

As deliverers, NGOs are responsible for translating policy into program implementation. They are also important players in policy formulation at various levels. For example, on the international scene they played a prominent role in UNESCO's *Jomtien Declaration* (1990) and the Dakar *Framework for Action* (2000). NGOs are leaders and major actors in the provision of non-formal education, particularly that of literacy. They link educational effort with other developmental sectors and programs, for example literacy with poverty alleviation. In their collaborative efforts they build partnerships at different levels and make long-term commitments.

In their capacity as monitors, NGOs assess the allocation and utilization of resources by beneficiaries. They manage their limited funds by observing cost-effectiveness; tracking and accounting for program implementation and outcomes.

NGOs have the advantage of being close to the grassroots, with shorter hierarchical structures, and with less bureaucracy enabling them to be flexible and responsive to local needs. In this way they can be more innovative in their programs and approaches (Kless, 1998). For example, multi-ethnic and religious Malaysian interest in interfaith understanding has increased with recent terrorism issues, and a few NGOs have responded by introducing educational programs on the subject. To remain effective and innovative, NGOs also provide various educational and training programs to supervisors, facilitators and other support staff or volunteers.

NGOs work as partners by collaborating with governments and other players, offering expertise, experience, logistics and other required resources. Meaningful partnership through systematic linkages, collaboration, coordination and dialogue is essential for a program to be accepted by all parties and to maximize the NGOs' limited resources.

Activities

NGOs carry out a broad spectrum of activities (Silliman, 1999). Some are grassroots operations linked to social movements aimed at challenging and transforming unequal social structures (Ginsburg, 1998); others are non-profit businesses run by "professionals" providing work and income opportunities for the disadvantaged in an effort to incorporate them in extant political economic arrangements. Some NGOs are locally-based institutions that operate on limited budgets derived from the resources of those involved, while others are international entities with sizable budgets built from grants and contracts from international organizations (for example development banks, United Nations agencies, and foundations) as well as national governments (foreign as well as domestic to the locale of any particular project being undertaken).

Most NGO activities are related to social and economic services, while others include advocacy and institutional development. Some activities are given greater weight than others, indicating not only the conceptual orientation of NGOs with regard to education, but also showing the fields in which they have a comparative advantage in achieving their goals. Community mobilization, an element in nearly all NGO strategies, is one example. The approach builds on the participation of community members in decisions concerning them, whether in the field of education or development at large. Community involvement is seen as the foundation for ownership of education and development initiatives, and as necessary in democratizing education.

Issues and Challenges

Most countries' education expenditures are low, and a global emphasis on primary education has further marginalized adult education. According to Lovegrove (2003), adult education is "the poor cousin to the poor cousin" (p. 59). NGOs often have limited sources of funding, institutional capacity and expertise. Many organizations see funding of NGOs as a risky option; they are often perceived "as less than professional, less reliable in acquitting funds and often lacking the capacity to handle programs involving large amounts of money" (p. 61). Nonetheless, recently there is an increasing trend among multilateral and bilateral agencies to fund social and economic development. These aid grants help NGOs' work on issues related to their status as a force of social transformation, democratization, legitimacy and accountability (Edwards & Hulme, 1998; Kless, 1998).

Under aid grants, NGOs are likely to shift in status from partners to contractors (Edwards & Hulme, 1998; Kless 1998), and NGO lines of relative autonomy are curtailed as they become bounded by the donors' terms and demands. Projects designed according to donors agenda, imposed from outside and carried out without much consultation with the recipient communities, risk losing the benefits of the traditional partnership approach.

NGOs are often engaged in advocacy to address fundamental inequalities of power and resources, to defend selected groups and to speak out or lobby policy changes. The advocacy role is affected when the NGOs' agenda is no more their own. Wherever there is power, abuse of power prevails, and NGOs are not immune from issues of hegemony and discrimination of the marginal (Hall, 2000). From this perspective, NGOs may function in ways that maintain systemic inequality (Kless, 1998), affecting empowerment, the basic tenet of adult education.

Due to popular support and their self-financing nature, most NGOs have instituted legitimacy and accountability of their own, but such legitimacy and accountability may be affected under aid grants. For example, some Southern NGOs are questioning the right of Northern NGOs to speak for them. The legitimacy of NGOs is based on their core values and volunteerism, but that may change if NGOs become contractors, and beneficiaries become consumers

Although many interventions call for participation by all sectors, some governments have reservations in collaborating with NGOs. This may be partly due to the traditional view that the state knows what is best for the people and how to do it. Some governments are wary of what they perceive to be NGOs' hidden agendas of power and self-interest. Others are outrightly hostile and repressive (Duke, 2003). By depriving an avenue for citizens' voice, such reservations affect the democratic process. On the other hand, although NGOs have espoused ideas about partnership, in reality control over funds and decision-making remains unequal. Cooperation among NGOs themselves also remains a recurring issue.

Through their different roles, NGOs provide an avenue for adult learning. They empower individuals and communities, and assist the state in strengthening civil society. Appropriate strategies enhance their strength and overcome challenges.

See also: civil society, comparative adult education, international adult education, social movement learning.

References and Further Reading

Duke, C. (2003). The year of the sheep – International cooperation for adult education. *Adult Education and Development, 60*, 27–47.

Edwards, M., & Hulme, D. (1998). Too close for comfort? The impact of official aid on nongovernmental organizations. *Current Issues in Comparative Education, 1*(1). Retrieved January 15, 2004 from http://www.tc.columbia. edu/CICE/articles/medh111.htm

Ginsburg, M. (1998). NGOs: What's in an acronym? *Current Issues in Comparative Education, 1*(1). Retrieved February 12, 2004 from http://www.tc.columbia.edu /CICE/ articles/mg111.htm

Hall, B. L. (2000). Global civil society: Theorizing a changing world. *Convergence, 33*(1/2), 10–33.

Kabanda, P. (2002). Role of NGOs in the 3rd world countries. In *Currently Published Articles and Reports from Makerere University*, Kampala, Uganda. Retrieved June 25, 2004 from Electronic Supply of Academic Publications to and From Universities in Developing Regions website: http://bij.hosting. kun.nl/ esap/MAKER/MAKER2/ General/ role-ofngos.php?PHPSESSID=faf8e4a92894928176a8d17670264c6c

Kless, S. J. (1998). NGOs: Progressive force or neo-liberal tool. *Current Issues in Comparative Education, 1*(1). Retrieved June 17, 2001 from http:// www.tc.columbia.edu/CICE/articles/ sjk111. htm

Lovegrove, B. (2003). Dancing with donors: Financing of adult education. *Adult Education and Development, 60*, 59–66.

Murphy, M. (2001). The politics of adult education: State, economy and civil society. *International Journal of Lifelong Education, 20*(5), 345–360.

Silliman, J. (1999). Expanding civil society, shrinking political spaces: The case of women's nongovernmental organization. In J. Silliman & Y. King (Eds.), *Dangerous intersections: Feminist perspectives on populations, environment and development, A project of the committee on women, population and the environment* (pp. 133–162). Cambridge, MA: South End Press.

Stromquist, N. P. (1998). NGOs in a new paradigm of civil society. *Current Issues in Comparative Education, 1*(1).

Retrieved February 17, 2002 from http://www.tc.columbia.edu/CICE/articles/ns111.htm

Youngman, F. (1996). A transformative political economy of adult education: An introduction. In P. Wangoola & F. Youngman (Eds.), *Towards a transformative political economy of adult education* (pp. 3–30). DeKalb, IL: Leadership and Educational Policy Studies (LEPS) Press.

Mazanah Muhamad

Numeracy

Numeracy concerns peoples' mathematical and numerical abilities, knowledge, and beliefs. To be numerate means that one can effectively understand and use a range of mathematical concepts in one's daily life, at home, at work, and in the community. Numeracy is highly valued in industrial societies, commonly recognized as a major determinant for job and career choices, and key to economic productivity and success. Consequently, numeracy is one of the major intended outcomes of schooling, and mathematics occupies a central place in the school curriculum. Despite this, there is a continuing concern that a lack of mathematical ability and awareness prevents many adults from participating as fully in society as they might (Benn, 1997; Steen, 1997).

Public discussion about the mathematical ability of adults is usually couched within the context of debates about adult literacy. Indeed, numeracy and literacy are often linked (as in the notion of "the 3Rs"). Commonly-used standardized literacy tests – such as Comprehensive Adult Student Assessment System (CASAS), Test for Adult Basic Education (TABE) and Adult Basic Learning Examination (ABLE) – and recent literacy surveys – such as International Adult Literacy Survey (IALS) and National Adult Literary Survey (NALS) – all include measures of "quantitative literacy." As a concept, numeracy is often incorporated into a broader concept of literacy; common definitions of literacy usually including some reference to arithmetic skills and abilities. For example, UNESCO defines a literate person as one whose attainments in reading, writing, and arithmetic make it possible for him to use these skills for his own and the community's development. Other definitions describe numeracy in terms of an "at-homeness" with numbers, having an appreciation and understanding of information which is presented in mathematical terms, or possessing the ability to "think mathematically." This latter concept involves the processes of conjecturing, specializing, generalizing, convincing, explaining, and describing, all seen as essential to solving mathematical problems.

There are some noteworthy aspects of these definitions. First, both attitudes, beliefs, knowledge and skills are considered important. Second, the practical application of mathematics is a central criterion; the relevant contexts being provided by the demands and situations of peoples' everyday lives. Third, the appreciation of numerical information is considered as important as technical ability. It is also clear from these definitions that numeracy refers to a much wider range of attributes than simply arithmetic dexterity. It is related to, but not distinct from, language ability. It also implies a certain quality of critical awareness of how mathematics is used in different contexts. To be numerate means not being confused or threatened by numbers and data so that one can critically examine the assumptions that others take for granted, in order to act as informed and productive citizens.

Numeracy and Adult Education

As it is considered such an indispensable attribute for productive citizenship, numeracy should clearly be an important aspect of adult education provision. The prime clientele of Adult Basic Education (ABE) and other adult education programs consist of those who want to improve their previous educational qualifications or who wish to further their education to live constructive and rewarding lives. However, despite the common linkage of numeracy and literacy in popular and policy-oriented discourses, the practice of including numeracy as a central component of literacy programs is far from widespread. Although one might expect numeracy to be considered an integrated component in all North American ABE, General Educational Development (GED) or English-as-a-Second Language (ESL), family literacy and workplace learning programs, it's not. Too few programs focus exclusively on developing adults' numeracy abilities and in those programs that do include numeracy as part of their literacy provision, it tends to be treated as a minor element.

This programmatic dearth is matched by the level of numeracy research. Given how widespread the problem of innumeracy is seen to be, the scarcity of research on adult numeracy or mathematics education for adults is startling. Educators know far too little about how adults do mathematics, how they acquire new mathematical skills, or how they use those skills in their daily lives. There is also very little research on the effectiveness and impact of different approaches to adult numeracy instruction or the development and evaluation of numeracy courses and programs (Gal, 2000). Although extensive research on these topics has been conducted in the corresponding field of adult literacy, few of the approaches, assumptions, topics, or questions that have marked this research, or the insights, applications, or policies that it has generated, have been translated into research on adult numeracy.

What research there is has adopted a predominantly psychological focus. For example, several studies note that low numeracy often correlates with negative emotions about, or attitudes towards, mathematics. Such discussions often centre on the concepts of math anxiety and mathphobia: the need to use mathematics inducing feelings of anxiety, helplessness, fear, guilt, or hostility (Tobias, 1978). In certain cases, people experience a widespread sense of inadequacy or shame if they feel they have not used the proper method, obtained the exact answer, or performed with sufficient speed when solving mathematical problems. Math anxiety and phobia occur at all levels of educational attainment, although they seem to be especially prominent among professionals and those with high academic qualifications who feel that they ought to have a confident understanding of mathematics. Such afflictions also appear to disproportionally affect women and members of ethnic minorities, but this may be due as much to the gendered quality of much mathematics education as it is to any psychological traits (Walkerdine, 1989). Indeed, consideration of the social contexts of numeracy highlights its underlying pattern of inequity: surveys of mathematical abilities among American adults indicate that math performance on tests is often considerably lower among women, working-class, Hispanic, and African American learners.

Why is the preponderance of math anxiety so high and adults' mathematical abilities so low? The widespread and persistent nature of innumeracy suggests that social explanations are more significant than individual causes. It has been suggested that one key contributor is the poor teaching of mathematics in schools. Traditionally, mathematics is taught as an abstract and hierarchical series of objective and decontextualized facts, rules, and answers where knowledge is portrayed as largely separate from learners' thought processes. Predominant teaching methods use largely passive, authoritarian, and individualizing techniques that depend on memorization, rote calculation, and frequent testing which tend to promote competition, individualism and conformity; successful learners are those who best absorb these values. Traditional methods seem to reinforce the notions that mathematics is value-free, devoid of social context, and can be learned by following the textbook and copying what the teacher says. In this way, mathematics education is experienced as a static, rather than dynamic process, and generally tangential to the concerns of daily life.

So what can be done? An alternative approach to numeracy and mathematics education could be based on the different assumption that what is to be learned and how it is learned are both equally important and interrelated. The form of education conveys its aims and purposes as much as does its content. So, if learning mathematics can be changed from the cognitive acquisition of infallible objective knowledge to a more process-oriented inquiry, it can become a catalyst for critical thinking and social empowerment. The importance of using peoples' daily experiences as the context for learning mathematics underlies the recent development of what has been called "critical mathematics" (Frankenstein, 1989). Based on the ideas of Paulo Freire, critical mathematics seeks to empower learners to develop their numeracy skills while also showing how they might be used to challenge hegemonic assumptions about how mathematics, education and society interrelate.

This work forms part of an emerging approach to numeracy that regards mathematics as a personal and social construct rather than a body of objective truth. "Ethnomathematics" draws together mathematics, cultural anthropology, education, history, art, cognitive psychology, and feminist and African studies to explore and describe the mathematics that is created in different cultures and communities. Such an approach encourages learners to reconsider what counts as mathematical knowledge, explore the interactions between culture and mathematics, and uncover the hidden and often distorted histories of mathematical practices and concepts (Powell & Frankenstein, 1997). Adults exposed to these broader mathematical definitions and practices begin to appreciate how "lived" mathematics – that used in people's daily lives – is so much richer than that portrayed in conventional math curricula. By exploring the mathematics of other cultures, they are better able to examine their own and realize that concepts and methods can differ and that they already knew more mathematics than they thought they did, or that standard tests might indicate.

See also: class, literacy, participation, social justice.

References and Further Reading

Benn, R. (1997). *Adults count too: Mathematics for empowerment.* Leicester, UK: National Institute for Adult Continuing Education.

Frankenstein, M. (1989). *Relearning mathematics: A different third R – radical math.* London: Free Association Books.

Gal, I. (Ed.). (2000). *Adult numeracy development: Theory, research, practice.* Cresskill, NJ: Hampton Press.

Powell, A. B., & Frankenstein, M. (Eds.). (1997). *Ethnomathematics: Challenging eurocentrism in mathematics education.* Albany, NY: State University of New York Press.

Steen, L. A. (Ed.).(1997). *Why numbers count.* New York: College Entrance Examination Board.

Tobias, S. (1978). *Overcoming math anxiety.* Boston: Houghton-Mifflin.

Walkerdine, V. (1989). *Counting girls out.* London: Virago Press.

Tom Nesbit

O

Older Adults' Learning

The term older adults' learning describes the vast range of learning activities in which older adults engage in formal, non-formal and informal contexts. Formal contexts are usually highly structured, hierarchical and credentialed, where assessment of learning is graded; non-formal learning consists of structured events in organizations and agencies in which older adults participate but seldom does formal assessment occur; informal learning refers to day-to-day, more incidental learning, in which people are not necessarily cognizant of their learning intentions. While most people attribute "real learning" to formal educational environments, a significant amount of learning occurs for seniors in the non-formal arena such as voluntary organizations, churches, workplaces, and in families (Findsen, 2005).

Terminology Associated With Older Adults' Learning

Older adults do not form a uniform group in society and tend to be more heterogeneous than younger generations. Chronological age in itself is not necessarily the most relevant factor in understanding older adulthood since the aging process is culturally, politically and socially defined. In general, however, the term older adult has more frequently been aligned with people over the age of 55, when most people in Western societies are making decisions about how they will spend their "third age" (Laslett, 1989). The phrase third age has developed considerable international currency to describe that period in an adult's life when the trammels of the second age (full-time work; raising a family) have been left behind. Older people who tend to be in very good health as a cohort, in comparison with prior generations, can extend themselves through education and other pursuits. Unfortunately, the third age, as described by Laslett, is highly romanticized and tends to best apply to the white middle class of the Western world whose economic circumstances are more favorable than the majority of the planet's older citizens. In this humanistic scenario, older adults have seemingly unfettered freedom to extend their minds and enjoy almost full autonomy in what they choose to undertake. This includes their newly-expanded opportunities for continuing education. The reality for many older adults, especially members of the working class and an underclass of disenfranchised minority-group members, is very different. Poverty, discrimination, social welfare dependency and very limited opportunities for education better define their dominant life pattern.

The term older adults' learning (as opposed to older adult education) has been used because it allows for self-directed learning and for learning in non-educational environments. Older adult education refers to the education systems and structures in which older adults tend to be educated by others, usually in educational settings, sometimes for credit. It is a less encompassing concept but nevertheless still widely used.

The phrase "educational gerontology" refers to learning in later years when the focus of learning is on what educators think and do, whereas gerontological education, refers to the practice of "teaching gerontology" (Glendenning, 2000). An example of the former is "instructional gerontology," in which a study can be made of how older people learn, of memory and intelligence, of teaching methods which best suit older adults, and so on. The latter term includes social gerontology wherein a study of stereotypes, popular images of older adults, and the impact of social policy on seniors can be conducted. Blaikie's (1999) excellent treatise, a historical and contemporary analysis of how older people are perceived and treated, *Ageing and popular culture,* is an example of this approach though not directly connected with education itself. A fuller analysis of the differences in the applications of the two terms, educational gerontology and gerontological education, is provided by Glendenning.

Theoretical Positions

Too much discussion of older adults and their learning is couched in deficit terms emphasizing their frailties and dependency. For many writers about seniors and their learning capacities there is a fixation on physiological decline and associated limitations usually linked to implications for practitioners (e.g., Glass, 1996). While there is some truth in the "decline of capacities" story, it tends to cloud the fact that ageing and learning are also socially constructed and that cultural definitions of ageing and older adulthood can play a significant role in promoting and limiting human aspirations and what might be possible. For instance, in the New Zealand context, the norms of older adulthood for urban white middle-class men are vastly different from those of rural Maori (indigenous) women. Hence, the ageing process can be analysed from a wide variety of theoretical perspectives (e.g., Biggs, 1993), and a comprehensive analysis of older adults' learning should include several theoretical positions for a holistic approach.

One theoretical position, conservative in its underlying premises, is functionalism. From this tradition older adults are described with respect to how they fit into the existing social order of which role theory and the disengagement hypothesis are exemplars. In role theory, seniors' social roles are analysed; for example, for gender differences and the impact of changing mores on identity. The disengagement hypothesis promotes the view that older people should segregate or be segregated from the world and its demands for which they are no longer equipped physically or socially. The physical separation of many retirement villages from the hustle and bustle of daily life is an illustration of this thinking. Furthermore, from a functionalist perspective, older adults should render themselves invisible in a youth-oriented society. In effect, this approach argues for a reduction in the scope of older adults' lives and the appropriate form of education for them is that which makes this adjustment palpable.

As is typical of a functionalist paradigm, the political, economic and cultural dynamics of life tend to be missing. As a counter position, writers such as Phillipson (1998) posit that growing old is a social construction and that more account needs to be taken of the political economy of which seniors are a part. Their lives should not be disentangled from the society of which they are still a vital element. From this paradigm, the marginalization of older adults in many societies is acknowledged – they are often financially disadvantaged because of minimal incomes in later life; disenfranchised from decision-making in social policy which affects them; and cut off from educational opportunity by educational providers who render them invisible in their curriculum development. In addition, the state and its apparatus can be a major determinant in what happens to many seniors, often creating "structured dependency."

The term "critical gerontology" has been employed by critical theorists of varying persuasions (such as feminists, neo-Marxists) to capture the importance of the socially-located positioning of older adults with an emphasis on the impact of the state and the economy on their life chances in advanced capitalism. According to Phillipson (2000), at least three elements contribute to the emergence of critical gerontology: the continuance of a political economy perspective; more significant contributions from the humanities; and a growing influence of biographical and narrative approaches.

In the area of critical educational gerontology, the ideas from the critical tradition are employed in analysing educational processes and structures affecting the learning possibilities for older adults. From this approach a range of possible educational studies could emerge: the study of identity reformulation in old age and the repercussions for learning aptitude; the positioning of marginalized older adults in the economy and their levels of educational participation; the changing notions of retirement in society and how these influence older adults' perceptions of what they learn; older adults as volunteers, their training and the impact on what they learn, and so on.

Participation and Providers

Participation of groups of older adults in education follows a familiar pattern in most nations. It is typically rendered as far less than would be expected for their proportions of the population, and it tends to be dominated by those who have already succeeded in the system. In addition, unless the educational activity is more vocationally or technically focused, often there will be more women than men participating. While there are a few exceptions to this trend (such as in the Open University in the UK which has recruited many more older learners proportionately than other tertiary institutions), it is not likely to change unless the ways in which these tertiary providers conduct their activities better matches the realities of older adults' lives (Findsen, 2001). If a wider conception of participation is embraced, then the extent of participation of elders is likely to be much deeper. For instance, there are many institutions that connect closely with seniors' lives (such as war veterans' clubs, sports clubs, cultural centers) where education is a *subsidiary* function. Here older adults engage in activities which are not specifically designed to elicit learning, but which use educational processes to achieve primary objectives. As a consequence, it is likely that participation in education by older adults is largely undocumented and invisible to official bodies.

In terms of effectiveness of learning, arguably the provision of education is best enacted by older adults themselves than by a largely anonymous institution which might guess at their needs and interests. Unsurprisingly, for instance, the University of the Third Age (U3A) has burgeoned since its early beginnings in France and then England. It typifies what is laudable about self-initiated learning by the learners themselves. Essentially, the U3A is a self-help learning agency established to meet the learning aspirations of its older adult membership. Some principles adopted by this educational movement include: the curriculum is usually developed by the learners themselves (that is, they look for teaching expertise from within their own groups); the teacher and the students are virtually interchangeable with minimal differentiation of status; costs are kept to a minimum; administration is virtually non-existent; the pedagogical setting is non-threatening and psychologically supportive (Swindell, 1999). This example of self-determination of older adults for their learning is not restricted to this particular institution though this is an outstanding exemplar. Other excellent examples include Institutes for Learning in Retirement (ILRs) in the United States, and the international movement Elderhostel. More heavily bureaucratized than U3As, the Elderhostel agency encourages older adults to travel and learn, frequently overseas.

A Philosophical Issue

One of the philosophical issues related to older adults' learning is whether older adults should be treated as a separate category of people. Is it more legitimate to speak of "adults" learning rather than "*older*" adults learning? There appears to be no consensus on this issue. If older adults were not specified as a special category of adult deserving of attention then educational provision would likely be even sparser than it is now. Their relative invisibility would be magnified. On the other hand, a world in which older adults need no special attention because resources are fairly distributed would be truly ageless. Discrimination against older adults, in education or in any other social sphere, would be non-existent in such a scenario. Unfortunately, this is still an ideal, not the current reality.

See also: adult development, adult learning, lifespan learning, participation.

References and Further Reading

Biggs, S. (1993). *Understanding ageing: Images, attitudes and professional practice*. Buckingham: Open University Press.

Blaikie, A. (1999). *Ageing and popular culture*. Cambridge UK: Cambridge University Press.

Findsen, B. (2001). Older adults' access to higher education in New Zealand. *Journal of Access and Credit Studies, 3*(2), 118–129.

Findsen, B. (2005). *Learning later*. Malabar, FL: Krieger.

Glass, J. C. (1996). Factors affecting learning in older adults. *Educational Gerontology, 22*, 359–372.

Glendenning, F. (Ed.). (2000). *Teaching and learning in later life: Theoretical implications*. Aldershot: Ashgate Publishing.

Laslett, P. (1989). *A fresh map of life: The emergence of the third age*. London: Weidenfeld & Nicholson.

Phillipson, C. (1998). *Reconstructing old age: New agendas in social theory and practice*. London: Sage.

Phillipson, C. (2000). Critical educational gerontology: Relationships and future developments. In F. Glendenning (Ed.), *Teaching and learning in later life: Theoretical implications* (pp. 25–38). Aldershot: Ashgate.

Swindell, R. (1999). New directions, opportunities and challenges for New Zealand U3As. *New Zealand Journal of Adult Learning, 27*(1), 41–57.

Brian Findsen

Online Learning

Online learning is a broad term used to describe the process of delivering, supporting and assessing teaching and learning through the use of computers and communication networks. Examples of online learning may include the use of any of the following: the World Wide Web (WWW); online resources and materials; electronic libraries; interactive online learning materials; electronic conferencing; synchronous, real time chat or discussions; and group learning activities via email and the Internet. The field of adult education has adopted online learning – the use of these communications technologies, singly or in combination – as a means of providing broader access to learning opportunities for distance learners.

The term online learning is used, at times interchangeably with and at times in place of, many other terms: technology-mediated learning, computer-mediated conferencing, online collaborative learning (OCL), computer-supported collaborative learning (CSCL), telelearning, e-learning, virtual learning, net-based learning, web-based learning. The term online learning is also often used synonymously with terms that have evolved to describe the larger enterprise of distance education, itself a much-discussed term of reference. Distance education, distance learning, open learning, flexible learning, virtual learning, hybrid or blended learning, and distributed learning are all terms that refer to teaching and learning interactions that entail physical separation between learner and instructor.

The term online learning is not used to describe audio-teleconferencing or videoconferencing technologies, although users of both those delivery formats may describe themselves as being "online" when engaged in either of those processes. Similarly, the educational context of online learning that is described here is not considered to apply to commercial enterprises promoting e-training, just-in-time learning, or the development of types of training courses or information technology skills that are available for purchase from Internet-accessible providers. Online learning, in the educational context outlined here, describes distance teaching and learning processes that occur within institutionally-offered courses or programs.

Many traditional educational institutions have incorporated some form of online learning into their program offerings using one, or several, aspects of online technology. A common model might comprise these elements: a web-based course management system (for example WebCT, First Class, or Blackboard); learners at diverse geographical sites; all or some of the course materials mounted on the web; supporting print materials (textbook and/or readings package); various discussion boards for interactive group activity; an instructor/tutor who is responsible for facilitating the course by presenting material, leading discussions, assessing and evaluating learners' performance, and "managing" and motivating learners through content-related discourse and personal interaction (usually by email, often by telephone).

A variation of this model might use the online capability to replace or supplement a group's traditional face-to-face meetings with additional opportunities for interaction and discussion.

Online discussion among learners and instructors may take place asynchronously or synchronously. Asynchronous learning provides learners with more flexibility and control over their learning activities as they can choose when and where – at what time of the day and from what location – to access web-based courses. Synchronous activities that require "real-time" attendance are less favored by, and generally less productive pedagogically for, adult learners.

The Evolution of Online Learning

The evolution of online learning has been paced by developments in technology. Early distance education, print-based and delivered as correspondence courses, is often termed first-generation distance education. As distance technologies have evolved, the labeling of successive generations varies. Currently, although theorists dispute whether online learning falls into third, fourth, or fifth-generation iterations of distance education, it is agreed that learning in this way is characterized by an increased degree of learner control and flexibility, interactive communication and group-oriented processes.

Several factors have contributed to online learning's increased popularity in public and private sectors in recent years. The invention of hypertext and the accessibility of the Internet made appropriate technologies available. Globalization, the internationalization of information, goods and services, integrated new technologies into commercial, economic and political enterprise. In the Western world, the maturation of the baby-boomers defined a comfortable consumer-oriented social class. This combination of forces, while increasing global competition and reducing the apparent impact of geographical distance, has made visible the importance of training, education, and the fluidity of a "wired" information-rich society.

Distance education has long offered ambitious learners opportunities for advancement by removing some of the situational barriers – conditions of time, place, and circumstance – that made accessing educational opportunities difficult. Online learning now makes possible more flexible, often asynchronous learning opportunities that provide both pedagogical and social interaction, that are cost-effective, and that contribute to the development of higher-level thinking and the construction of knowledge. For these reasons, many traditional postsecondary institutions have incorporated some level of online accessibility into their offerings. New private postsecondary institutions also strive to attract learners to virtual programs by offering flexible, online credentialing.

Teaching and Learning Online

Online learning invites educators and program providers to consider new perspectives on teaching and learning since its use of communication technologies provides interactive environments that promote the application of constructivist principles. While recognizing that responsible and thoughtful educators should guard against a "one size fits all" epistemological approach, it is accepted that good online learning is supported by constructivist views of learning that "are focused more on understanding and meaning making than knowledge, knowledge construction rather than instruction, and social interactions rather than behavior" (Jonassen, 2003, p. 6).

Although constructivist principles form the heart of the online teaching and learning dynamic, issues of collaboration and community are also very important. For those who are new to online learning – both teachers and learners – creating or adapting to collaborative, knowledge-building learning communities is challenging, but research studies clearly demonstrate the success of constructivist models of learning.

In the absence of traditional classrooms, where all members of the learning group can physically see each other and relate to each other in accustomed ways, establishing a sense of community – a climate of connectedness, of safety, of trust – is key to successful online learning. Current understandings of online community incorporate notions of learner support that were inherent in earlier models of distance education, along with social-learning theory and community-of-practice theory. In building community, learners find comfort and respite from isolation in their relationships with other learners. At the same time, mature learners assume responsibility for the quality of the knowledge-building that occurs through online dialogue and conversation. With appropriate guidance from mentoring instructors, learners explore the wisdom of their own experiences, relate content to real-world situations, and value the shared experiences of their peers. Ideally, learners' dependence on instructors as sources of information diminishes and the learning environment becomes more collegial, democratic, and interdependent.

The role of the instructor, therefore, following constructivist principles, becomes facilitative rather than didactic. Instructors adapting to teaching online often struggle with notions of control inherent in instructivist models: delivering content and meeting objectives. Online learning more easily supports instructional strategies that encourage learners to think critically and to problem-solve, to accommodate multiple perspectives, and to engage in authentic learning activities that utilize learners' metacognitive skills (Duffy & Jonassen, 1991).

Collins and Berge (1995) indicated four major instructional components of online teaching – pedagogical, social, managerial, and technical. Each of these components assumes a slightly new shape as the online instructional role shifts from that of a "content" expert to that of a "maestro," one who organizes and leads a harmonious group effort.

Pedagogically, instructors are still responsible for the ultimate shape of their course and its assessment, although depending on the level of constructivist activity adopted, learners may assume more control of their learning and of assessment strategies. However, satisfactory delivery of appropriate amounts of content remains a major concern for novice online instructors (Conrad, 2004) who may not recognize, or be unwilling to adapt to, the online learning dynamic that necessitates more instructional attention to managerial, technical, and social roles.

Online learning demands more management because of the separation of learners from each other and from the instructor. Most of this task falls to the instructor, although in some institutions, administrative personnel assist learners in managing the learning process, providing help with registration, orientation, counseling, obtaining materials, and record-keeping. While some level of management has always been a part of teaching and learning, the number of management tasks becomes much more obvious and tangible when learners' questions or transactions are individually directed towards the person with whom they most often interact – the instructor.

Some of the managerial tasks involve or result from the use of the technologies inherent to online learning. Panic-stricken learners, especially those who are new to online learning, often tend to immediately seek help from the instructor. This is problematic as many faculties are not well-versed in technical matters and levels of institutional support vary. Institutions dedicated to distance learning may offer around-the-clock technical assistance to learners, but more traditional, dual-mode institutions often struggle with support services and offer only limited support during daytime hours. Resultant miscommunication or lack of communication in times of technical difficulty creates anxiety for both learners and teachers.

Of the four instructional functions inherent to online teaching and learning, the social function is often the most misunderstood and poorly applied, especially by novice instructors (Conrad, 2004). Instructors, primarily occupied with their pedagogy, are often provided assistance for both managerial and technical tasks, but creating an appropriate social milieu, however, becomes the responsibility of the online group. Learners assume a portion of responsibility for the sense of community that grows within their online group, but also expect some leadership in this area from instructors (Conrad, 2002). Instructor enthusiasm, presence, and promptness all contribute to the growth of a sense of community within the online group. Research repeatedly confirms that learners who learn at a distance are most successful when engaged in learning that offers support, comfort, and the community that comes with a sense of connectedness – to institutions, to other learners, to instructors, and to purpose (Collins & Berge, 1995; Gunawardena, 1995; Richardson & Swan, 2003).

Research in Online Learning

The increased popularity of online learning in recent years is reflected in the literature of distance education (Harasim, Hiltz, Teles, & Turoff, 1996; Pallaf & Pratt, 2001). At the outset of online learning's growth as the predominant distance technology, research understandably focused on the technical aspects that contributed to and enabled the feasibility of its implementation. The efficacy of online learning has now been established and scholarly attention currently addresses a broad range of issues: the pedagogy that underlies this type of learning; program delivery in both private and public sectors; all aspects of the learning transaction, including its very important social dimension and its sub-parts, community and social presence; culture and facilitation styles; and theory-building.

See also: distance education, Internet resources, motivation, participation.

References and Further Reading

Collins, M., & Berge, Z. L. (1995). Introduction to volume two. In Z. L Berge & M. P. Collins (Eds.), *Computer mediated communication and the on-line classroom*, Vol. 2 (pp. 1–10). Cresskill, NJ: Hampton Press.

Conrad, D. (2002). Deep in the hearts of learners: Insights into the nature of online community. *Journal of Distance Education, 17*(1), 1–19.

Conrad, D. (2004). University instructors' reflections on their first online teaching experiences. *Journal of Asynchronous Learning Networks*. Retrieved July 25, 2003 from http:// www.sloan-c.org/publications/jaln/ v8n2/v8n2_conrad.asp

Duffy, T. M., & Jonassen, D. H. (1991). Constructivism: New implications for instructional technology? *Educational Technology, 31*(5), 7–12.

Gunadawardena, L. N. (1995). Social presence theory and implications for interaction and collaborative learning in computer conferences. *International Journal of Educational Telecommunications, 1*(2/3), 147–166.

Harasim, L., Hiltz, S. R., Teles, L., & Turoff, M. (1996). *Learning networks.* Cambridge, MA: Massachusetts Institute of Technology Press.

Jonassen, D. H. (2003). The vain quest for a unified theory of learning. *Educational Technology, 43*(4), 5–8.

Palloff, R. M., & Pratt, K. (2001). *Lessons from the cyberspace classroom: The realities of online teaching.* San Francisco: Jossey-Bass.

Richardson, J. C., & Swan, K. (2003). Examining social presence in online courses in relation to students' perceived learning and satisfaction. *Journal of Asynchronous Learning Networks, 7*(1). Retrieved August 9, 2002 from http://www.aln.org/ publications/jaln/v7n1/v7n1_richardson .asp

Dianne Conrad

Organizational Learning

Organizational learning (OL) is a new field of study and practice straddling business management, education, organizational studies and human resource development. Highly diverse in expression and filled with tensions in perspective, OL is impossible to capture with a single definition. A fundamental tension exists in the OL endeavour to connect *learning*, which increases variety and disorganization, with *organizing*, which attempts to reduce variety. Understandings of OL range widely for two reasons. First, OL literature embraces diverse perspectives ranging from rational-cognitive to cultural, from functional to postmodern. Second, OL literature focuses on different forms and domains of learning in organizations: information processing, product innovation, management of learning, strategic renewal of organizations, politics of knowledge production, and so on. Acquisitional definitions of OL view knowledge as information to be ingested and managed. This rational emphasis on utility and possession leaves aside important questions about learning processes, changing and unpredictable contexts, organizational politics, and the dynamics of knowledge generation in group activities. More recently, these elements are acknowledged as critical in understanding OL. Cultural researchers have influenced the contemporary trend to view OL as located not in individual minds, but in activity. That is, the collective learning process is now frequently referred to as participation in the everyday interactions and practices of particular communities of practice. This shifts the focus of research away from the types of knowledge that are produced in OL and onto the social relationships, identities, meanings, objects, and experiences in an organization. These shape and are shaped by ongoing learning processes.

Historical Development of OL Research

The earliest notions of organizational learning were concerned with organizational continuity, and assumed the essential stability and coherence of the organization. Learning was viewed conservatively as a process to store and retrieve lessons learned on the job, or to improve existing procedures to meet changes in external environments. Early OL research focused on innovation through experimental trial and error, and adaptation. Later approaches viewed organizational learning as a transformative process. Organizational development (OD) has become well-established as a process to help organizations examine and change their own routines and cultural norms. The OD goal was to develop the organization's ability to self-correctively maintain a pattern of homeostasis despite fluctuations in the external environment, through an action science approach. Because the organization was encouraged to incorporate critical thinking into continuous evaluation of its routines and norms – what Chris Argyris called "double-loop learning" – the change process was dynamic and even subversive, although fundamentally conservative. A third group, writing in the 1980s, took a more sophisticated view of learning, clarifying important distinctions between organizational change on the one hand and learning on the other. They described different levels of learning and different learning systems, and acknowledged the complex dynamics of the organization interacting with the various communities and forces comprising its environment. Thus, the concept of learning organization was incubated during growing interest in the nature of collective learning and the notion of an organization as a continuously adaptive and proactive agent.

The second trajectory associated with rising interest in OL was the economic shifts of the 1980s. These shifts had raised considerable alarm: business viewed itself in constant jeopardy in a new competitive climate that moved at fiber-optic speed, embraced global dimensions of cultural and market influences, and communicated through constantly changing technologies. Businesses envisioned themselves caught in a paradigm shift and looked for new organizational structures and leadership approaches. When the link between competitiveness and learning was introduced, OL quickly became the new buzzword.

A third related trajectory was the spread of Total Quality Management (TQM) approaches to organizational development, stressing continuous improvement and knowledge-sharing among teams. Although TQM remained popular, interest in organizational learning had waned by the mid-eighties. Experiential learning processes were not always successful, and overall innovation was found to be unrelated to amount of experimentation.

The Learning Organization

However in 1990, Peter Senge's book *The Fifth Discipline: The Art and Practice of the Learning Organization* inspired unprecedented excitement among managers and organization developers about the concept of a learning organization, "a place where people continually expand their capacity to create the results they truly desire, where new and expansive patterns of thinking are nurtured, where collective aspiration is set free, and where people are continually learning how to act together" (p. 3). The learning organization concept stresses continuous innovation as the key to productivity in an environment of constant change. Senge's book advocated five "disciplines" to cultivate OL: (a) personal mastery among workers, making goals and capacities explicit; (b) a mental model change among workers, instilling critical thinking to help generate innovative solutions; (c) team learning, developing ways to generate and share knowledge effectively in small groups; (d) a shared vision to motivate and unify learning; and (e) systems thinking to help individuals and groups understand their interdependencies and interconnections. Central to these disciplines is the assumption that employees need to engage in critical reflection and open dialogue, exposing their own belief systems and critically challenging others' belief systems, to break free of thinking patterns that perpetuate dysfunction and prevent innovation.

Spurred by the publication of *The Fifth Discipline,* interest in OL suddenly increased. In particular, a new focus was placed on the responsibility of the manager and organizational developer to integrate learning into the organization's activities. OL research expanded to include such diverse perspectives as feminism, activity theory, and organizational symbolism. The first *Handbook of Organizational Learning and Knowledge* (Dierkes, Antal, Child, & Nonaka, 2001) includes a strong representation of European and Japanese perspectives of OL, as well as North American. OL issues for all organizations include generating innovation, integrating new technologies, improving existing processes, predicting and adapting to turbulent conditions, restructuring staff, improving performance, ensuring equitable opportunity, and fostering quality of work.

Theoretical Perspectives of OL

Gherardi and Nicolini (2001) classify contemporary OL literature in five categories corresponding to sociological traditions: conflict, rational-utilitarian, Durkheimian, micro-interactionist, and postmodern theories. First, the conflict tradition examines configurations of power and interests, and their influence on what knowledge is valued in the labor process. Drawing from authors such as Marx and Weber, this perspective highlights the ideologies that circulate in organizations. It also raises issues such as who controls knowledge, the commodification of knowledge, and people's alienation from their own work knowledge.

Second, in the rational-utilitarian tradition, OL is problem-driven, occurring as an organization adapts to its environment. From crises such as a plant explosion to everyday glitches in line operations, this perspective views OL as a rational process dividing the problem into separate parts, and proceeding to find its causes, to close the gap between the actual and the desired performance. These solutions become the learning that is acquired and hopefully integrated into the organization's broader activities. This knowledge must be dispersed, perhaps through information technologies, and managed through policies and legal protection of the organization's "intellectual capital." A branch of strategic OL studies how rational planning processes can increase learning that directly impacts an organization's competitive advantage.

Third is a Durkheimian view of OL as socialization into a specific community in a particular organizational culture. Learning is activated differently by different cultures, whether regulatory, educational, innovative, or interpersonal. Fourth, the micro-interactionist tradition shows how individuals construct as well as become constructed by an organization's activities and norms. The focus is on cultural meanings, values and beliefs and how they come into existence. Analysts like Wenger (1998) have developed this analysis to show OL as a process of individuals' participation in a particular community of practice.

Fifth is an area that Gherardi and Nicolini (2001) call postmodern perspectives. Here, OL is interested in the connection of learning to local and particular contexts. Research explores relationships between power, politics and learning; how knowledge is produced in everyday interactions; how organizational discourses and texts are woven with knowledge; and how changing identities (of individuals, groups, objects, and the whole organization) are created through OL. Knowledge is viewed as circulating continuously, shaped by and shaping people's actions and practices.

Contemporary Issues Within OL

Debates among and even within these views tend to focus on the nature and purposes of organizational learning. The following selected issues appear in contemporary research:

- The first issue is *levels of learning*. Crossan, Lane and White (1999) examine distinctions in process among individual, group, and organizational levels of learning, how these levels are interrelated, and how to enhance learning at these levels. This includes debate about the nature and location of knowledge/learning. Analysts claim that OL has generally moved from a focus on acquiring knowledge to knowledge-as-practice, but questions continue around the combination of cognitive and social processes in OL, and how formal organizational structures influence the location and direction of learning.
- The second issue concerns adaptive–generative and exploration–exploitation aspects. Adaptive learning is accommodating the organization to external changes, while generative learning is creating or refining new processes, skills, products and concepts. Exploration learning is experimenting to produce such innovation. Exploitation learning is the process of integrating the innovation throughout the organization, eventually embedding it within everyday practices and values. Issues for study and debate focus on the processes and mobilizers of these different types of learning, how they are interrelated, and what balance is most desirable among them for different contexts and purposes. Researchers also explore how feedback and feed-forward processes enhance OL, and the extent to which tacit knowledge (skills and knowledge embedded in everyday habits and routines) should be voiced and shared.
- The next issue is *change and learning*. The challenge here is defining the relation between organizational learning, change, performance, and development. Questions continue around the value of distinguishing learning as a concept from organizational change, about the relation between learning and unlearning, about whether OL is more related to performance or to development, and especially about the role of strategic learning or planned change in organizational development.

Power and Politics

Debate has arisen about how power relations construct inequities in access to learning opportunities, who benefits from OL, and what and whose learning is recognized in organizations (and what is suppressed). One position is that OL should create innovations, develop learning capacity and support strategic initiatives to improve performance and increase shareholder value. Others ask, who determines what counts as knowledge and performance, who benefits, and who is excluded? Some argue that the purpose of OL should be transformative and emancipatory for workers aiming to free people from oppression, to take control of their lives. Some have studied how organizational politics shapes the recognition, accreditation, and blockage of new ideas. Others have examined how OL initiatives themselves exacerbate gendered, oppressive and inequitable conditions in organizations.

Knowledge Management (KM) and OL

Debates continue about the boundaries dividing these territories, how the social-cultural aspects of OL might be combined with technical views of KM, and how the more academic, human resource language of OL might be reconciled with the KM language of economics and technicians.

The field of OL directs resources to study and foster continuous learning in the everyday interactions of organizational life, to increase innovation and productivity, and to improve quality of worklife. Major questions continue about how to investigate OL: through micro approaches, or macro positivist studies examining organizational outcomes, or perhaps through case studies using a mix of methods. In adult education, key questions focus on purpose: how educators want to influence OL, and to what end.

See also: action learning, learning organization, training, workplace learning.

References and Further Reading

Crossan, M. M., Lane, H., & White, R. E. (1999). An organizational learning framework: From intuition to institution. *Academy of Management Review, 24*, 522–537.

Dierkes, M., Antal, A. B., Child, J., & Nonaka, I. (Eds.). (2001). *Handbook of organizational learning and knowledge.* Oxford: Oxford University Press.

Gherardi, S., & Nicolini, D. (2001). The sociological foundations of organizational learning. In M. Dierkes, A. B. Antal, J. Child, & I. Nonaka (Eds.), *Handbook of organizational learning and knowledge* (pp. 35–59). Oxford: Oxford University Press.

Senge, P. (1990). *The fifth discipline: The art and practice of the learning organization.* New York: Doubleday.

Wenger, E. (1998). *Communities of practice: Learning, meaning, identity.* Cambridge, UK; New York: Cambridge University Press.

Tara Fenwick

Organizations for Adult Education

There is a degree of ambiguity about this subject because organizations may be seen to be rather tightly bound systems of people working to specific ends, or rather looser networks having similar functions to each other. In addition, the concept of "adult education" is no longer universally employed in the same way that it was some 30 years ago – lifelong learning is gradually supplanting it in many countries of the world. Consequently, the term "adult education organization" is going to be used here to refer to any grouping of people involved in the education of, or in offering learning opportunities for, adults in the broadest possible way. It might be claimed that any wide-ranging discussion on such organizations is an attempt to map the field, but the way in which the term "adult education" itself has changed demonstrates how difficult it is to map a specific field called adult education. This is even clearer in the five-volume work *Adult and Continuing Education* edited by Jarvis (with Griffin) (2003), in which it proved almost impossible to map the field simply. These volumes cover liberal education (2 vols.), vocational education (1 vol.), teaching, learning and research (1 vol.), and adult and continuing education, analysed by other academic disciplines (1 vol.). Each volume has many subsections. This article will, therefore, be divided into two main sections: an historical overview briefly mentioning some of the earlier attempts to cover this subject, and then an examination of other ways of classifying these institutions.

Part 1: Historical Overview

In the past, there have been several attempts to classify adult education organizations and brief reference will be made here to some. In an early edition of the *Handbook of Adult Education* (Knowles, 1960), there was a whole section on "Institutional Programs and Resources" in which 16 chapters deal with different manifestations of adult education, including: associations and councils; business and industry; colleges and universities; governmental agencies; health organizations; independent and residential schools; international organizations; labor organizations, and so on. There is a sense in which Knowles' (1962, revised 1977) celebrated history of the adult education movement in the United States charts the rise of some of these organizations. By this time there were other attempts in the United States to systematize adult education. Schroeder (1970), for instance, suggested four types of agency: those serving the educational needs of adults; those doing the same for young adults; community organizations; and those serving the needs of special groups. By 1989, Apps (in Merriam & Cunningham, 1989) was offering a different approach based on funding which, whilst based on the United States, might have been applicable elsewhere: fully or partially tax-supported agencies; non-profit and self-supporting agencies; for-profit providers; and non-organized learning opportunities. He fully recognized that the boundaries were getting blurred between the different organizations.

Outside of the United States, one of the earliest attempts was Gerver's (in Jarvis, 1992) attempt to classify adult education organizations in Scotland. Around the adult learner, she located the following types: further education colleges; higher education colleges; universities; community education services (which included the traditional adult education organization); libraries and museums; schools; trades unions, voluntary organizations; private training agencies; broadcasting; and private and public sector employees. In addition, she listed the major national organizations involved in the process: national enterprise companies and councils; the national community education council; and the universities council. Significantly, the National Institute of Adult Continuing Education (NIACE, 2003), has published a directory of organizations and resources for adult and continuing education in the United Kingdom – although focusing primarily on England. It has 19 chapters systematizing all the institutions which are affiliated to it in some way or other. These are: government; learning and skills councils; development organizations; local government; learning partnerships; further education; higher education; residential adult education; the voluntary and community sector; adult and community education organizations; workplace-led learning; education regulatedand other organizations; credit awarding bodies; learning guidance providers; the Welsh system; Northern Ireland; Scotland; international institutions; and the media. Since these are only associations affiliated with NIACE, it can now be seen how complex the field is, especially when it can be seen immediately that there are whole areas of society, such as the military, the churches, and so on which are missing from this list of affiliates. It must also be recognized that other countries, such as the United States, would have slightly different classifications, while some societies in less-developed parts of the world might have considerably fewer organizations devoted to adult education.

It is safe, therefore, to conclude that it is impossible to map the field through adult education organizations, and this is becoming an even more problematic exercise as global economies are beginning to dictate much of the provision and policy of lifelong learning. In fact, globalization itself is adding to the complexity of the process. It might be asked whether there are any variables that hold the wide variety of overlapping organizations together that enable them to be called adult education organizations. At the outset of this article it was suggested that, in the broadest sense, organizations that provide education or learning opportunities for adults (itself an undefined term, since it may also include young adults) might be included here.

Part 2: A Classification of Adult Education Organizations

There are at least four major variables may be used to help classify adult education organizations: funding, functions, geographic spread and mode of delivery.

- *Funding*. Here there are two alternative classifications. Firstly, there are non-profit organizations, such as national adult education organizations, and there are *for-profit* organizations such as private residential schools, language schools, and so on. Secondly, the sources of funding might provide a useful criterion, and in this case adult education organizations may be *internationally funded*, such as the European Council projects, the World Bank and UNESCO; *state-funded*, such as national government-funded agencies offering education to adults; *privately funded*, such as a corporate university; or *self-supporting*, such as the churches' educational outreach, or other non-governmental organizations (NGOs).
- *Functions*. Seven different sets of function might be isolated: *academic* (education and training), offering both teaching and

research, as in universities, professional and occupational associations; *advocacy*, where national and professional associations, and NGOs might be included; *consultancy*, organizations that provide professional advice and services in the areas of education and training; *counseling and guidance*, for as learning and educational certificates have become so important in the labor market a variety of organizations have been established to provide guidance and to offer help and support to learners; *policy*, with a variety of organizations advising governments on policy development, including international agencies such as UNESCO, government "think-tanks" and a wide variety of other organizations including networks like the learning-city network; *provision*, – which can be further sub-divided into those organizations that provide educational opportunities for academic credit and those which offer learning opportunities for personal development and interest rather than academic credit; *research and development*, when education and learning needs are researched, or in regional development projects, and so on.

- *Geographic spread*. This category has at least four subdivisions: *international*, such as UNESCO, the OECD (the Organization for Economic Co-operation and Development), the World Bank, or the Commonwealth of Learning; *national*, such as national adult education associations; *regional*, such as the Mid-West Research to Practice Conference on Adult Continuing and Community Education in the United States, and regional development projects throughout the world; or *local*, local government projects and provision, learning towns and learning-city networks, and so on.
- *Mode of delivery*. It was pointed out at the outset that adult education now has to be seen to include both educational organizations and those offering learning opportunities, so that this category can be further subdivided into *teaching organizations* offering face-to-face, distance or mixed-mode delivery, and *learning organizations and networks*, such as the World Wide Web, libraries, museums, and so on. Naturally, some of these, such as museums, offer both teaching and learning opportunities, and others subdivide distance into distance and electronic, such as the European Distance and e-Learning Network (EDEN), which was formerly called the European Distance Education Network.

One final way of classifying adult education organizations within mode of delivery is: *formal*, such as schools and universities; *non-formal*, such as organized systems of mentoring in the workplace and third-age universities; and *informal*, where a wide variety of learning opportunities exist in everyday life.

Conclusion

Naturally, it would have been possible to have discussed each of these categories in much more detail but the complexity is self-evident in the variety of ways in which adult education organizations may be classified. No single approach can cover the whole of this field, which is no longer one separate and distinct field but a wide variety of overlapping areas of education and learning. Indeed, many of the adult education organizations fall into several different categories and sub-categories in the above framework.

See also: community education, higher education, libraries, lifelong learning, non-governmental organizations.

References and Further Reading

Apps, J. W. (1989). Providers of adult and continuing education: A framework. In S. B. Merriam & P. M. Cunningham (Eds.), *Handbook of adult and continuing education* (pp. 275–286). San Francisco: Jossey-Bass.

Gerver, E. (1992). Scotland. In P. Jarvis (Ed.), *Perspectives on education and training in Europe* (pp. 389–404). Leicester: National Institute for Adult Continuing Education.

Jarvis, P. (with Griffin, C.). (Eds.). (2003). *Adult and continuing education: Major themes.* (5 volumes). London: Routledge.

Knowles, M. S. (Ed.). (1960). *Handbook of adult education in the United States.* Washington: Adult Education Association of the United States of America.

Knowles, M. S. (1962/1977). *The adult education movement in the US.* (2nd ed.). Malabar, FL: Krieger.

National Institute of Adult Continuing Education (2003). *Adult learning yearbook 2003* – Leicester: National Institute of Adult Continuing Education.

Schroeder, W. (1970). Adult education defined and described. In R. Smith, G. Aker, & J. Kidd (Eds.), *Handbook of adult education* (pp. 25–43). New York: Macmillan.

Peter Jarvis

P

Participation

Participation refers to formal enrolments in adult education programs (although not necessarily completed), while non-participation refers to non-enrolment. Educational participation is part of the broader concern in civil societies about which citizens take an active part in community life; for example, political scientists study those who participate in voting and protesting, while sociologists are interested in those who participate in volunteer organizations and variations in the use of leisure time. Social theorists such as Putnam (2000) argue that high levels of participation in community life is a significant factor in generating social capital, which is a key factor in forming and maintaining positive living environments and generating economic prosperity.

Participation as an issue has long attracted much debate and research in adult education, where participants are perceived as "volunteers for learning," as opposed to those who are obliged to attend as in compulsory participation in mandatory schooling sectors (Courtney, 1992). Although an ideal of universal educational participation is increasingly implicit in much adult education writing, some writers (such as, most notably, Ohliger, 1974) have challenged the desirability of achieving even medium to high levels of participation among the adult population, especially at the cost of increasing degrees of coercion, that Ohliger argues violates the core ethos of adult education. Ohliger's claim can be seen to have increasing validity in many societies as adults are "sentenced to lifelong learning;" judges, for example, commonly include adult literacy and anger management courses among their sentencing repertoire.

Justifications for Participation

The value of recruiting adults into education is usually taken as an irrefutable self-truth, and interestingly has broad appeal across the political spectrum, albeit for different reasons. McGivney (1990, pp. 32–33) has summarized the range of arguments to justify the extension of participation as lying in four broad areas. The first is equity and social justice; the basic argument is that a system that benefits a small section of the community is morally unjustifiable, and provision should be available to anyone who wants it. Furthermore, many people are not achieving their full potential; education offers a chance to improve lifestyles and life-chances (the "pool of talent" argument). As well, positive action is needed to compensate for previous educational disadvantage, especially schooling, and it is essential to end the "negative intergenerational cycle of disadvantage."

Among the second category of reasons to justify promoting participation are those factors that McGivney (1990) calls pragmatism/expediency. Changing demographics mean that smaller cohorts of young people will be providing for increasing numbers of older people; older people need to remain active in the workforce and maintain a healthy lifestyle to minimize this dependence. This pragmatic category also sees education as a key mechanism to help people adapt to rapidly changing work and lifestyles. A third group of reasons that McGivney provides in support of participation are called national self-interest. Within this worldview, education is a key mechanism to remaining economically competitive internationally against other economies. As well, proponents of this perspective hold that greater participation will lead to increased productivity and material gains. Finally, involvement in education is preferable to paying out welfare benefits.

There have been concerted efforts over recent years to research some of these wider benefits that result from learning throughout the lifespan in areas such as health, mental wellbeing and community life (http://www.learningbenefits. net).

The call to change present patterns of participation has been given added impetus over recent years with the increased prominence of lifelong learning ideals in many countries' educational debates. Central to the concept of lifelong learning and its utopian ideal of a *learning society* is the need not only to increase the numbers of adults participating in education throughout their lifespan, but also to extend the nature of present participation. The latter is about changing patterns from "more of the same" to increase the recruitment of social groups that have been historically underrepresented in programs.

Alongside the development of many new lifelong learning education acts have been some reviews of participation. In Britain for example, one of the key reports prepared as a forerunner to the 1998 *Learning Age* Green Paper (DfEE) was the Kennedy Report, *Learning Works* (1997). Starting with the first chapter entitled "The Case for Widening Participation is Irresistible," the report first outlined the arguments for breaking traditional patterns of participation and then reviewed a range of means for achieving these goals.

As some countries (for example in Scandinavia) are now reaching the position where participants are the majority in their population (albeit usually still a socially select majority), the question arises: what are the upper limits? At what point will a "satisfactory rate of participation" be reached or is universal adult education an increasing possibility? Even the socially selective nature of participation is being fundamentally challenged in some countries. In New Zealand, for example, indigenous Maori have long been underrepresented in post-school education, but over recent years have now attained participation rates above their non-Maori counterparts, due largely to the development of Maori-controlled *whare wananga* (houses of learning), which are committed to provision for Maori in keeping with Maori values and methods.

Overall Patterns of Participation

The research findings on who participates in adult education and who doesn't are remarkably consistent internationally. While there are always variations in different contexts, Johnstone and Rivera's (1965) oft-quoted summary of participants in their American study still holds true in most countries:

> The participant is just as often a woman as a man, is typically under

> 40, has completed high school or better, enjoys an above-average income, works full-time and in a white-collar occupation, is white, Protestant, married and has children, lives in an urbanized area (more likely the suburbs than the city) and is found in all parts of the country, but more frequently on the west coast than would be expected by chance. (p. 8)

Gender participation tends to vary somewhat according to the vocational orientation of the course; in vocationally-oriented courses men tend to dominate, while women dominate in non-vocational courses.

The most striking and ironic feature of this summary statement of participants is the absence of those for whom many adult educators have a commitment – variously called the dispossessed, the forgotten people, the oppressed, but most simply the poor. McGivney (2001, p. 21), for example, provides the following list of social groups who are most underrepresented in adult education: disaffected school leavers and those with poor school experiences; those on low incomes or receiving benefits; those in difficult living circumstances (e.g., homeless); people on the fringes of the labor market; older adults; some groups of ethnic minorities; people with learning difficulties; people with disabilities; and offenders and ex-offenders.

Overall, the single most powerful predictor of participation remains the previous level of education. Those who have already benefited from high levels of schooling and formal tertiary education continue to participate in adult education at rates well above their counterparts who left school early or have not participated in any post-school programs. This pattern both reaffirms adult education's role in maintaining present patterns of social inequality and questions its capacity as an effective means of changing patterns of social inequality.

But despite the best intentions and efforts of many adult educators and their institutions, the above groups remain largely absent among the ranks of learners in adult education programs.

There are two other general points about participation patterns in adult education: firstly, the higher the social status of the course, the greater the degree of social exclusion among its learner population – low status, poorly-funded courses on the margins of adult education are often the most successful in recruiting those traditionally underrepresented. Secondly, even within homogeneous groups of learners (e.g., refugees), participants will tend to be the more advantaged members of that group (e.g., male refugees and those with higher levels of previous education).

Non-Participation

The great majority of participation research has focused on those who participate, rather than those who do not. While this imbalance has probably occurred because of the methodological difficulties in studying non-participants, one resulting difficulty has been that much information about non-participation has been deduced as the inverse of what participants do and believe – for example, because participants may value goal-setting, this does not automatically mean that non-participants do not.

But the few studies of non-participation that have been done have indicated that non-participants are far from a homogeneous group. Indeed, the heterogeneous nature of non-participants provides invaluable insights into how participation can be extended with some of these groups; clearly some non-participants are more easily recruited than others, while others will probably always remain outside the realm of organized provision.

In some adult education areas, there are clear mismatches between the potential pool of learners and those who actually participate. National surveys of adult literacy such as the International Adult Literacy Survey (IALS) have shown the degree of need for these programs, and yet participation data clearly show they cater for only a fraction of those identified in the bottom levels (typically up to 40% of all adults in many countries). For example, Quigley (1997) quotes the United States experience of programs attracting only 8% of those who are eligible.

While many explanations for non-participation have been posited in terms of learner deficiencies (e.g., lack of confidence), others have sought explanations in the selective practices of educational providers (particularly as middle-class-dominated components of status quo class structures). Still others have argued that non-participants actively resist what they see as an extension of the schooling system, which they see as stigmatizing and without merit, and effectively choose alternative subcultures where learning has little to do with formal programs (Quigley, 1997).

Explaining Participation/Non-Participation

Probably the most common explanation posited to explain non-participation has been the concept of *learning barriers* based on the work of Cross (1981). The assumption made here is that participation is hindered by a range of barriers to learning, which can be reduced or eliminated and thereby facilitate the involvement of non-participants. These barriers are usually classified into *situational* barriers relating to a person's particular situation at a given time (e.g., lack of childcare or transport for young parents); *institutional* barriers to do with how providers organize learning opportunities (e.g., timetabling, location of courses); and *dispositional* barriers relating to an individual's attitude to self and learning (e.g., dislike of school, low confidence in learning skills).

These concepts have a certain pragmatic attraction (especially for practitioners) for explaining who enrol in programs and who do not, and provide useful tools for reviewing the effectiveness of learner recruitment. However, there are clear limitations to their ability to explain participation adequately in all cases. For example, one of the most frequent dispositional barriers identified is "lack of time," and many non-participants do have issues around fitting education into their busy daily lives; but often no more than many adult education participants. In other words, learning barriers have a superficial appeal, but do not stand up to rigorous examination. Critics have also criticized this approach for falling too readily into a deficit approach and ignoring the broader social context – individuals' failings are to blame and not the program providers or broader political forces.

From a psychological perspective where the focus is on the individual's motivation to participate, Houle's (1961) study of 22 adults "conspicuously engaged in various forms of continuing learning," (p. 13) spawned many subsequent studies that endeavoured to identify the motivational orientations of learners that lead to their participating in programs. The most extensive development to follow from Houle's seminal study has been Boshier's Educational Participation Scale (Bosher & Collins, 1985), is based originally on a range of between three and seven factors (such as educational preparation, professional advancement, cognitive interest, expectations of others and social stimulation) that have been found to be central to understanding why some participate and others do not.

Sociologists, on the other hand, have studied the social distribution of participation, noting how it matches patterns of inequality found in other sectors of social life such as health and wealth distribution. These social reproduction analyses locate participation in the social context beyond the individual's personal motivation and look to analyses across such factors as ethnicity, gender and social class. In most cases, their conclusions point to adult education's poor performance in countering the inequalities produced by the school system – despite its oft-touted claims to be a mechanism for countering these social inequalities.

None of these approaches has broken the code of participation satisfactorily to date. Hence, many researchers who have grappled with explaining variations in participation have concluded that no one single set of factors or theory will ever fully explain the issue. This conclusion notwithstanding, one of the most useful models to explain participation has been Cross' *Chain of Response* model (Cross, 1981). This model endeavors to include individual motivational factors, the social environment and educational provision in an overview of why some enroll in programs and others don't.

Retention

Allied to the issue of participation is that of retention. In areas such as adult basic education in the United States, withdrawal rates in excess of 50% after 16 weeks are not uncommon (Quigley, 1997, p. 8). Recruiting non-participants counts for little if they subsequently withdraw due to unsatisfactory experiences as learners. In some cases, non-completion may still be judged positively by the learner, but usually it doesn't and simply adds adult education to a long list of educational misadventures in many cases. Successful retention of learners has come under increasing scrutiny in many countries, especially as funding formulae now often include a component for successful completion. One of the most useful analyses on retention has been the work of Tinto (2003), based on force field analysis.

Changing Patterns of Participation

Changing present patterns of participation is neither straightforward or easy, although writers such as McGivney (2001) argue that adult educators already know sufficient to significantly increase the participation of most groups previously underrepresented. The Kennedy Report in Britain argued that market principles (including simply marketing programs better) will not succeed in significant change and that "magic bullets" such as Internet technologies that emerge periodically need to be part of a broader range of strategies. Such strategies need to be proactive in their approach (such as outreach activities), in contrast to institutions' traditional passivity (apart from marketing), and include policy (nationally and institutional) backed by realistic levels of funding. Agencies concerned only with programs for specific target groups (especially where they are run by members of that group) are also more successful than general providers in catering for under-represented groups.

See also: adult learning, attitudes, class, literacy, motivation.

References and Further Reading

Boshier, R. W., & Collins, J. (1985). The Houle Typology after twenty-two years. A large scale empirical test. *Adult Education Quarterly*, *35*(3), 113–130.

Courtney, S. (1992). *Why adults learn: Towards a theory of participation in adult education*. London, New York: Routledge.

Cross, P. (1981). *Adults as learners*. San Francisco: Jossey-Bass.

Department for Education and Employment (DfEE) (1998). *The learning age: A renaissance for a new Britain*. London: British Government.

Houle, C. O. (1961). *The inquiring mind: A study of the adult who continues to learn* (2nd ed.). Madison, WI: University of Wisconsin.

Johnstone, J. & Rivera, R. (1965). *Volunteers for learning: A study of the educational pursuits of American adults*. Chicago, IL: Aldine.

Kennedy, H. (1997). *Learning works – widening participation in further education*. Coventry, UK: Further Education Funding Council.

McGivney, V. K. (1990). *Education's for other people: Access to education for non-participant adults: A research report*. Leicester, UK: National Institute of Adult Continuing Education.

McGivney, V. K. (2001). *Fixing or changing the pattern? Reflections on widening adult participation in learning*. Leicester, UK: National Institute of Adult Continuing Education.

Ohliger, J. (1974). Is lifelong education a guarantee of permanent inadequacy? *Convergence*, *7*(2), 47–58.

Putnam, R. D. (2000). *Bowling alone. The collapse and revival of American community*. New York: Simon & Schuster.

Quigley, B. A. (1997). *Rethinking literacy education: The critical need for practice-based change*. San Francisco: Jossey-Bass.

Tinto, V. (2003). Establishing conditions for student success. In L. Thomas, M. Cooper, & J. Quinn (Eds.), *Improving completion rates among disadvantaged students* (pp. 1–10). Stoke on Trent, UK: Trentham Books.

John Benseman

Participatory Action Research

Participatory action research (PAR) is a composite or a family of research methodologies distinguished and united by shared principles, styles and values, and has evolved in recent times into a major tool for research in adult education. PAR symbolizes and reflects the synthesis of ideas relating to the sociocultural, economic and political rights of people and validates the fundamental human rights of people to contribute to decisions and issues which affect them irrespective of such factors as socio-economic status, gender, class or race. PAR rests on the philosophical distinction between subject and object. The people in PAR research are speaking subjects, not mere inanimate objects or the research tools of the researcher. This philosophical distinction, it is believed, undergirds the legitimacy and credibility of PAR.

PAR emphasizes the creation of positive social change, the extension of knowledge through participatory action and reflection and is the systematic collaborative investigation *in situ* of an issue by the stakeholders (those affected or to be affected by the issue) through a process of planned action, to effect real change and broaden the frontiers of knowledge. It is a bottom-up partnership approach to research and development and rests on the principle that real change (worthwhile, mutually acceptable and sustainable change) occurs only when and if the people concerned are enabled to be inside of the research process. It is a form of action and research about the people, by the people, for the people. It is a horizontal enterprise with the researcher and the stakeholders coming together as partners and co-researchers – planning, taking action, reflecting on and refining plans and strategies together, so that ultimately the people develop an "ownership" feeling for the research outcome (Dick, 2000). PAR has three major components – participation, action, and research with the emphasis in that order. PAR is participatory and is defined by the need for collaborative action geared towards change and the creation of knowledge as a byproduct of the action process.

Within adult education there is an increasing interest in PAR as an effective teaching and research tool, especially within the context of critical pedagogy, which sees the task of adult education as designing programs to promote voluntary participation; respect for self worth; collaborative learning; praxis-activity, reflection and collaborative analysis; a spirit of critical reflection; and the nurturing of empowered, proactive adults (Padamsee, Ewert, & Deshler, 1996). PAR thus provides the conceptual and practical bridge between adult educators and the adult community.

Origin and Evolution: The Ideological and Political Debates

As interest in PAR as a research alternative in adult education keeps growing among scholars and practitioners globally, it becomes worthwhile to examine views on the ideological and political antecedents, how these shape evolving concepts, terminologies and methods, as well as reflect on how these impact the use of PAR methodology in adult education research.

There is some measure of controversy surrounding the origin of PAR. While scholars like Fals-Borda and Rahaman (1991) place the antecedents of PAR firmly within the tradition of liberationist movements and the resultant popular education, peculiar but not exclusive to the developing nations of Latin America, Asia and Africa, and which was popularized on an international scale by Paulo Freire in the 1970s; other scholars like Mebrahtu Kahsay (1996) fault this exclusivity by mainstream development theorists and practitioners. Although they admit the emergence of the current mainstream PAR literature from mostly Latin American revolutionaries, they focus the contributions of many other groups to the evolution of concept and practice of PAR. This group identifies the genesis of the practice of PAR with communist China and cites the writings of Mao Tse-Tung about correct leadership as being from "the masses to the masses" as representing the bottom-up development strategy of PAR. They also emphasize the contributions to the evolution of theory and practice of PAR made by Islamic groups with a social message similar to the Christian liberation theologians of Latin America, as well as the writings and experiences of scholars and practitioners of adult education in Western societies.

The concept of PAR of the radical or revolutionary liberation theologists has as its core value the,

> empowerment [and emancipation] of adults through democratically structured, co-operative study and

> action directed toward achieving more just and peaceful societies within a life sustaining . . . and that the fundamental purpose of education should be social transformation towards full human participation in society through the enlightenment and awakening of the common man. (Hurst, 1995, n. p.)

Adult education in this context becomes a project of resistance, emancipation and empowerment, with PAR as the tool for structural transformation of society and culture thus becoming as much a philosophy of life as a method. The PAR process here requires a revolutionary context; the emphasis is more on the ideological and transformative potentials of PAR.

The liberal PAR scholars, Hall (1984) and Kassam (1982), however, place less emphasis on the political, economic and socio-cultural context. They instead emphasize the role of the researcher and the methods or strategy to be used. This group perceives PAR as a three-pronged activity; ". . . a method of social investigation involving the full participation of the community . . . an educational process, and . . . a means of taking action for development" (Hall, p. 19). Thus one main difference between the two schools is their disposition to the context of the practice of adult education and what to do with that context.

However, despite the variations in theoretical focus and practical commitments brought about by the political and ideological divides among PAR theorists and practitioners, there is a current sign within the PAR community of a move towards a growing convergence of ideas, internationalization and interdisciplinary cooperation and a blurring of barriers. There is recognition of the fact that there are no significant differences between the goals of the two schools for "we are all talking about research that is participatory, and participatory research that unites with action (for transforming reality)" (Fals-Borda, 1991, p. 6). This breaking down of walls has been of immense benefit to research in adult education.

Understanding the Procedure of Participatory Action Research Methodology

The methodology of PAR symbolizes a breakaway from the conventional knowledge production and ownership structure which confers the "experts" an elitism and power over the marginalized and oppressed, perpetuates unequal relations of knowledge and entrenches social and intellectual domination of the ordinary person. It also symbolizes an end to the remoteness of the "space of power" in research and knowledge production by emphasizing the shift of the power base and control of research from the hands of experts to ordinary persons within the community. During the process of research, the researcher becomes both a change agent and a changed agent. PAR has certain characteristics that control the methodology – the research issue must originate within the community, the stakeholders are involved as co-researchers at every stage of the research and are involved in controlling the entire research process; and the goal is effecting social change through structural transformation. This was the case in the Bumpers Cove experience where the adult education model, acting in equal collaborative partnership, was able to use PAR methodology in literacy work to empower the people of the community so as to access and utilize knowledge gained through their personal research efforts to fight a political battle on environmental pollution causing health hazards within their community (Merrifield, 1997). PAR is cyclic and follows a process of dialogue, planning, action, review, critical reflection plus subsequent refining of the earlier cycles to improve the later cycles. Each cycle has four main components; plan – act – observe – reflect – (plan, and so on) (Kemmis & McTaggart, 1988)

The first stage in using the PAR methodology involves researchers coming together at the beginning of a relationship to examine an issue within their environment and identify a research problem. Stage one involves planning, that is negotiating roles and responsibilities as well as agreeing on strategies for actualizing change. The next stage is the action stage when the plan (the change instrument) is activated. This is followed by the observation stage when participants observe the process, impacts and outcomes of the action. The reflection stage is where participants recollect, critique and interpret the research process and outcomes; subsequently using the understanding gained at this stage to challenge and refine the strategy and method of the earlier cycle so as to improve later cycles. The cycles are concentric and dovetail into each other.

Communication is also central to the methodology of PAR and it creatively combines various forms of communication: written, oral and visual, to record and reflect the needs of participants, promote dialogue, encourage action and inform policy (Sohng, 1995). It emphasizes the use of natural languages during the research process, thus enhancing the quality of interaction.

The methodology of PAR offers an immense interest to the field of adult education, and adult education in turn seems to provide an ideal environment for PAR, whether within the context of literacy, work-life, health and environmental education, or community development. It addresses issues emerging from the day-to-day problems of living in the adults' environment and places the opportunity and responsibility to understand issues and consequently activate change in the hands of the adults themselves. When used in adult education research, PAR methodology is particularly suited to the nature of adult learning as it attracts and sustains the interest of adults in the research process through encouraging direct involvement and harnessing their experiences, knowledge and skills in the process of idea generation, planning and implementation, review and interpretation. PAR methodology's emphasis on the use of natural language during the research process aids adults' participation and responsiveness. It makes the whole research process more accessible to the adults' participants and has a carry-over effect in that the adults can develop enough understanding to become more proficient co-researchers in many other situations (Dick, 2000). PAR methodology encourages the adult participant's commitment to research outcomes by involving them as equal partners in the research process and investing them with the responsibility of managing research outcomes, thereby developing a feeling of "ownership" for research outcomes.

Debates on Rigor and Credibility

One criticism of PAR, which borders on credibility and rigour, is that if a research problem derives from the problems faced by adults in a community and these adults are part of the executors of the research, then the credibility of such research methodology and results may be challenged because of its circularity. In other words it could be said that a solution is already reached before the research starts, especially since the research is designed to respond to situations as they occur during the research process. Also there is the problem of objectivity in the PAR mode. The argument here is that research models ought to be objective with respect to researcher, research community and research process and should utilize quantitative data that lands itself to retesting and generalization. In response, other scholars consider these criticisms as bordering on process and not on the substance of PAR, identifying certain components of PAR that ensures credibility and rigour. They posit that participation can generate richer sources of data and allow researchers assumptions to be challenged. They also maintain that the short multiple cycles in the PAR methodology allow for the achievement of rigour as they allow results of earlier cycles to be challenged, tested and refined by later cycles (Dick, 2000).

The PAR approach to research continues to attract the interest of scholars and practitioners in adult education because it demystifies research and transfers control of research from the hands of an "elitist" group of "experts" to the ordinary person within the community, and enhances adults' capacities for mobilization and change through collaborative participation in the research process. Whilst the debate on PAR's credibility and appropriateness as a scientific research method goes on, perhaps a shift in focus from this credibility to improvement of its methodology and application would be more beneficial and immensely enrich the body of adult education research.

See also: action research, international adult education, power, problematizing learning, research methods.

References and Further Reading

Dick, B. (2002). Action research and evaluation on line. Retrieved June 5, 2002 from http://www.scu.edu. au/schools/gcm/ar/areol/areol-intro02.html

Fals-Borda, O., & Rahaman, M. A. (1991). *Action and knowledge: Breaking the monopoly with participatory action research.* New York: Apex Press.

Hall, B. L. (1984). *Participatory research, popular knowledge and power: Two articles by Budd Hall.* Toronto: Participatory Research Group.

Hurst, J. (1995). Popular education. *Educator*, Spring *9*(1). Retrieved April 24, 2001 from http://www-gse. berkeley.edu/Admin/ExtRel/educator/spring95texts/popular.educ.html

Kahsay, M. (1996). PAR and development. NIPARN Discussion Paper No. 1. Nigerian Participatory Action Research Network (NIPARN).

Kassam, Y. (1982). *Participatory research: An emerging alternative methodology in social science research.* New Delhi, India: Society for Participatory Research in Asia.

Kemmis, S., & McTaggart, R. (1988). *The action research planner.* Victoria, Australia: Deaking University.

Merrifield, J. (1997). Knowing, learning, doing: Participatory action research. *Focus on Basics*, vol. 1, issue A.

Padamsee, D. L., Ewert, D. M., & Deshler, J. D. (1996). Participatory Action Research : A strategy for linking rural literacy with community development. *Proceedings of the 1996 World Conference on Literacy*. Philadelphia PA. Available at www.literacyonline.org. products/ ili/pdf/ilprocdp.pdf

Sohng, S. S. L. (1995). Participatory research and community organizing. Working paper presented at The New Social Movement and Community

Organizing Conference, University of Washington, Seattle.
Tse-Tung, M. (1967). Some quotations concerning methods of leadership. *Selected works of Mao Tse-Tung*, Vol. III. Peking: Foreign Language Press.

Oluyemisi O. Obilade

Peace Education

Peace education refers to a system and or process of education that enables participants to empower themselves with knowledge, skills, attitudes, values and beliefs which build cultures of peace, non-violence and sustainability. It enables learners to critically analyse the root causes of violence, wars, conflicts and social injustices, and develop alternatives to violence. Peace education is fundamental to human and earth development. It is quite diverse and dynamic in nature and responds to global development and the knowledge advanced by peace research (Reardon, 1997). Its core principles include a commitment to resolving conflicts non-violently, building cultures of justice, human and earth rights, gender and racial equality and equity, and respect for indigenous peoples' rights.

The contents of peace education are context-specific and depend largely on how peace is defined. Peace is generally defined from two main perspectives – negative peace, which refers to the absence or prevention of war and violent conflicts; and positive peace, which means justice, gender and racial equity and equality, equal distribution of wealth and power within and between families, communities, and states and between the North and South (Turay, 2000). Peace education is interdisciplinary and overlaps with educational initiatives such as education for development, citizenship education, gender training, global education, human-rights education, disarmament education and environmental education (Brock-Utne, 1985; Reardon, 1997). It can take place in formal, non-formal and informal learning situations. Formal peace education is structured and planned, while non-formal peace education is semi-structured and usually takes place in educational institutions. Informal peace education is unstructured and unplanned and generally occurs through the media, social meetings, clubs and associations.

The theory and practices of formal and non-formal peace education have evolved from the work of many prominent philosophers and social theorists. For example, John Comenius, Immanuel Kant, John Dewey, Maria Montessori and Jean-Jacques Rousseau advocated for the principles of peaceful living such as cooperation, tolerance of diversity, reconciliation, non-violence and networking to be integrated into the educational system (Curtis & Boultwood, 1965). In recent times, Johan Galtung has been acknowledged for his immense contribution to theories of structural violence and peace studies. The teachings of Mahatma Gandhi in the 1940s and Martin Luther King Jr. in the 1960s emphasized passive resistance and non-cooperation (Patti & Lantieri, 1999).

Opportunities and Challenges

Adult educators in different global contexts continue to struggle and search for ways of dealing with the social injustices and growing physical and structural violence that continue to erode the social, religious, spiritual, economic, cultural and political fabrics of their societies. Peace education has an important role to play in this search for a more peaceful global community.

In various global contexts, other terms are used instead of peace education. For example, in North America the terms conflict resolution, human-rights education, citizenship education, development education (Reardon, 1997) are also used. In Africa, the term peace education is referred to as inter-religious dialogue, education for democracy, development education and capacity building. Brock-Utne (1985) distinguishes between education for peace and education about peace. She defines education for peace as the teaching and learning of non-violent and peaceful ways of life which begin before birth until death, while education about peace is taught to individuals by an educational institution at some stage in their lives.

Although the content of peace education is debatable, there is a general agreement in the literature with regards its aim. The universal primary purpose of peace education is to transform all forms of violence, including physical, emotional, psychological and structural, and build sustainable cultures of peace at the local and global levels.

Peace education critics argue that the theories and practices of formal peace education have been largely based on Western values (Patti & Lantieri, 1997), which are sometimes insensitive to the cultural and historic contexts of other societies and focus mainly on formal and non-formal aspects. Also, indigenous peoples' peace-building mechanisms are invisible in the mainstream literature. Peace education theoretical frameworks are limited and have a tendency to respond to particular issues and problems instead of being holistic (Reardon, 1997). Brock-Utne (1985) feels peace educators need to deconstruct the warlike nature of men to non-violent men, and recognize that boys and girls are educated differently. Although spirituality is an important element of peace education, the literature is very silent on its role. A critical awareness of the role of spirituality in peace education has the potential of enabling the adult learner and educator to rediscover and value the good in them, other people and their non-human environment (Turay, 2000). Reardon and Brock-Utne both call for more gender-sensitive, inclusive and holistic peace education content and methods.

> Most of the current peace education activities manifest much good will but less theoretical framework and philosophical elaboration concerning the positions, aims, methods, and evaluation of the results and their meanings. (Gur-Ze'ev, 2001, p. 315)

Further research is needed to address these issues.

See also: globalization, international adult education, spirituality.

References and Further Reading

Brock-Utne, B. (1985). *Educating for peace: A feminist perspective*. Willowdale, ON: Pergamon Press.

Curtis, S. J., & Boultwood, M. E. A. (1965). *A short history of educational ideas* (4th ed.). London: University Tutorial Press.

Gur-Ze'ev, I. (2001). Philosophy of peace education in the postmodern era. *Educational Theory, 51*(3), 315–336.

Patti, J., & Lantieri, L. (1999). Peace education: Youth. In L. Kurtz (Ed.), *Encyclopedia of violence, peace, and conflict*. Vol. 2 (pp. 679–689). London: Academic Press.

Reardon, B. A. (1997). Human rights as education for peace education. In G. J. Andreopoulos & R. P. Claude (Eds.), *Human rights education for the twenty-first century* (pp. 21–34). Philadelphia: University of Pennsylvania Press.

Turay, T. M. (2000). Peace research and African development: An indigenous African perspective. In G. J. S. Dei, B. L. Hall, & D. G. Rosenberg (Eds.), *Indigenous knowledges in global contexts: Multiple readings of our world* (pp. 248–264). Toronto: University of Toronto Press.

Thomas Mark Turay

Pedagogic Identity

Pedagogic identity suggests that adult educators see themselves, and are seen, as having some kind of unity which emerges through their long-term participation in practice within pedagogic communities. Both terms, identity and pedagogy, are the subject of debate (see this volume). Here, the use of the term identity suggests that adult educators will draw on a wide, and often contradictory, range of social and discursive pedagogic practices to construct their sense of what it means to be a teacher. This does not imply that teachers have some kind of coherent, unchanging and essential core, or even a name, to attach to this sense of unity between identity and practice. Similarly, the term pedagogy is intended to convey a sense that educational practice is broader than the classroom transaction of teaching: instead it is a situated, multifaceted and complex process, involving multiple relationships with specific and often conflicting purposes, power relations and interests.

Janice Malcolm and Miriam Zukas (2000) first used the notion of pedagogic identity in relation to a range of different versions of the educator that emerged from an analysis of the research literature of adult and higher education. Dan Pratt and his associates (1998) have taken a different approach by elaborating five perspectives on teaching with more of a focus on the individual in relation to teaching, rather than this more social focus. However, there are conceptual overlaps with the five pedagogic identities suggested by Malcolm and Zukas, and these are explored below. The list is by no means comprehensive: for example, educators may privilege disciplinary or vocational identity rather than pedagogic identity; and new identities may also emerge (Chappell, Rhodes, Solomon, Tennant, & Yates, 2003).

Five Pedagogic Identities

The reflective practitioner pedagogic identity derives from the work of Schön (see this volume). The suggestion that practitioners need to improve the quality of their thinking in action through learning by doing and then commenting on their doing underpins many adult education programs. Adult educators are likely to encounter technologies such as the use of reflective journals and coaching in both their own education and in their development of others. Depending on the subject they teach, they may be encouraged or even required to construct themselves as reflective practitioners, modeling reflective practice whilst developing reflective practice in their students.

Those identifying as critical practitioners have borrowed from a range of political traditions to bring a variety of critical, including feminist, social understandings to bear on pedagogy, and to produce various conceptualizations of critical practice. Postmodern and poststructural understandings derive, in part, from these same critical traditions. Critical practitioner identities coalesce around the idea that the content of classroom practice embodies and manifests the power–knowledge relations which exist beyond the classroom (Zukas & Malcolm, 2002a). The purpose or the "why" of adult education, rather than the "what" and the "how," is the dominant concern of critical practitioners.

Lave and Wenger's (1991) conceptualization of learning as participation in communities of practice suggests that adult educators are situated learners in pedagogic communities of practice. Although the terminology is new, the ideas are not: adult educators have emphasized an engagement in legitimate practice for decades. The introduction of performance management tools such as mentoring schemes, appraisals, and continuing professional development requirements emphasize and even demand ongoing learning through practice, thus constructing the educator as lifelong learner. Recently, researchers have been exploring adult educators' situated learning in the pedagogic workplace, with a view to better understanding the relationship between ongoing learning and pedagogic identity (Zukas & Malcolm, 2002b).

A fourth pedagogic identity is based on the idea that some forms of pedagogy can be understood as diagnosis and facilitation. Although the notion of facilitation is familiar, it is contentious to suggest that adult educators might view themselves or be viewed as psycho-diagnosticians. Psycho-metrics and other non-social understandings of the individual deriving from psychology have, until recently, been relatively unpopular in adult education. However, concerns about the measurement and management of learning and learners have resulted in a return to psychological models and understandings, particularly in relation to learning styles and multiple intelligences. Such approaches assume that educators need to diagnose learners' needs, for example by identifying or taking into account learning styles or skills (Zukas & Malcolm, 2002a). Once characteristics and approaches to learning are identified, adult educators facilitate learning by using techniques and tools which meet those needs.

A final version of pedagogic identity has been suggested whereby adult educators become the assurers of organizational quality and efficiency and the deliverers of service to agreed or imposed standards. Monitoring regimes intended to test and maintain the accountability of publicly-funded services are ubiquitous. But the impact of regulation and scrutiny upon adult education pedagogic practices and pedagogic identity is, as yet, under-researched. Nevertheless, in countries where the outcome of inspections, benchmarks and other performance measures determine future funding, adult educators are increasingly encouraged to consider quality and standards first and foremost.

See also: facilitation, higher education, multiple intelligences, teaching.

References and Further Reading

Chappell, C., Rhodes, C., Solomon, N., Tennant, M. C., & Yates, L. (2003). *Reconstructing the lifelong learner: Pedagogy and identity in individual, organisational and social change.* London: Routledge Falmer.

Lave, J., & Wenger, E. (1991). *Situated*

learning: Legitimate peripheral participation. Cambridge, UK: Cambridge University Press.

Malcolm, J., & Zukas, M. (2000). Constructing pedagogic identities: Versions of the educator in adult and higher education. In T. Sork, V.-L. Chapman, R. St-Clair (Eds.), *AERC 2000:* Proceedings of the 41st Adult Education Research Conference (pp. 246–250). Vancouver: University of British Columbia.

Pratt, D.D., & Associates. (1998). *Five perspectives on teaching in adult and higher education.* Malabar, FL: Krieger.

Zukas, M., & Malcolm, J. (2002a). Pedagogies for lifelong learning: Building bridges or building walls? In R. Harrison, F. Reeve, A. Hanson, & J. Clarke (Eds.), *Supporting lifelong learning: Volume 1 – Perspectives on learning.* London: Routledge Falmer.

Zukas, M., & Malcolm, J. (2002b). Playing the game: Regulation, scrutiny and pedagogic identities in post-compulsory education. In J. Seale & D. Roebuck (Eds.), *Envisioning practice – Implementing change: Fifth international conference on post-compulsory education and training, Vol. 3* (pp. 229–236). Brisbane: Australian Academic Press.

Miriam Zukas

Peer Learning

Peer learning is a subset of collaborative learning based on the idea that learning is enriched when it is a synergistic effort among peers. As in collaborative learning, peer learning accentuates the social nature of learning, which involves formal and informal sharing of knowledge, ideas and experience among participants. The emphasis is on the learning process, including the emotional support that learners offer each other, as much as the learning task itself (Boud, Cohen, & Sampson, 2001).

Differences Between Peer Learning and Collaborative Learning

In contrast to collaborative learning, a distinctive feature of peer learning is that it is shared learning among peers. The power dynamics in terms of status is therefore *theoretically* absent in peer learning. Equality is central to Merriam–Webster's (1999) dictionary definition of peer as "one that is of equal standing with another; one belonging to the same societal group especially based on age, grade, or status."

Peer Tutoring

Peer tutoring or peer teaching is one configuration of peer learning. It is the process of interaction in which participants help each other learn through teaching. Peer tutoring is a well-established practice in educational circles whereas peer learning is often perceived as incidental (Boud et al., 2001).

The term "peer tutoring" was coined in the 18th century by Joseph Lancaster and Andrew Bell in the United Kingdom. From its inception, many have considered tutoring programs to be multifaceted experiments in socialization since they engage more people into the process of sharing knowledge. Most peer tutoring is done in pairs although it could also involve work in groups of three or more. The efficacy of peer tutoring rests in the improved performance of the "tutors" as learners. The tutors' learning improves by reviewing, finding meaningful use of the subject-matter, filling in gaps in their own understanding, consolidating learning, and reformulating the information. It also shifts the learning atmosphere away from one of competition towards one of collaboration (Cohen, Kulik, & Kulik, 1982; Goodlad & Hirst, 1989, 1990).

Benefits of Peer Learning

Peer learning has a long tradition in higher education and offers many benefits to participants (Anderson & Boud, 1996). Through peer learning, participants begin to appreciate the content and process dimensions of learning. Radical adult educator Freire (2000) also critiques the separation between content and process and regards a collaborative analysis of individual and collective experience as essential to bringing assumptions into critical consciousness.

Peer learning goes beyond the transfer of knowledge. Learning with others through sharing of ideas and responding to each other sharpens thinking and deepens understanding. Piaget (1950) regards the social relationship of co-operation with others, in the form of discussion, collaboration in work, exchange of ideas and mutual control, to be the basis for the development of logic. He believes that discussion with others gives rise to internalized discussion or deliberation, and reflection. Falchikov (2001) agrees with Piaget and posits that the development of a critical attitude of mind, objectivity and discursive reflection are enhanced through cooperative interaction with peers. The concept of cognitive conflict, which can also occur when students learn on their own and actively engage with the materials by themselves, is more easily stimulated and made more rigorous through interactive engagement with peers.

Critique of Peer Learning

Some of the critiques about peer learning focus on consensus, cognition, as well as role and behavior. Group consensus, according to several writers, is one of the most controversial and misunderstood aspects of peer learning. On the one hand is the fear that consensus generates conformity, stifles individuality, encourages non-controversy, and suppresses creativity and differences. Some critics view consensus synonymously with group-think and peer indoctrination (Trimbur, 1989), whilst others regard groups as an unacceptable form of social control (Mowatt & Siann, 1997). Yet another view is that underlying consensus is a power relationship based on peer pressure that, for example, generates group practices which enable, constrain or suppress the production of knowledge, privilege, and handling of peers.

One of the tenets of peer learning and teaching is that the act of explaining something to someone else requires the one explaining to actively engage in identifying and reorganizing the materials. Cognition is therefore enhanced for the one explaining. De Lisi (2002) cautions, however, that peer learning activities do not guarantee an optimal balanced relationship in the learning of all peers in the group.

Learners with a high need for affiliation are more likely to prefer group learning to individual learning. Conversely, it can also be argued that those who have a low need for affiliation are likely to find learning with others problematic (Goh, 2002). One of the assumptions of peer learning is that all peers are on an equal footing and are free to agree or disagree with each other. However, implementing peer learning may be problematic, as learners bring with them myriad factors such as different personality traits, learning experiences, goal aspirations and motivation, and thus may not always work and learn effectively together. Instead of exercising their right to learn through challenging each other and questioning as equals, peer tutees may resort to adopting the passive behavior of the traditional classroom. Another common problem is role ambiguity, where the peer tutors and tutees are unclear about what they are to do. These problems could, perhaps, be avoided through using reciprocal peer teaching with the tutors and tutees changing roles frequently, as well as providing proper training in peer tutoring.

See also: cohort learning, collaborative learning, higher education, teaching.

References and Further Reading

Anderson, G., & Boud, D. (1996). Extending the role of peer learning in university courses. *Research and Development in Higher Education, 19*, 15–19.

Boud, D., Cohen, R., & Sampson, J. (2001). *Peer learning in higher education: Learning from and with each other*. London: Kogan Page.

Cohen, P. A., Kulik, J. A., & Kulik, C. C. (1982). Educational outcomes of tutoring. *American Educational Research Journal, 19*, 237–248.

De Lisi, P. (2002). From marbles to instant messenger & TM: Implications of Piaget's ideas about peer learning. *Theory into Practice, 41*(1), 5–12.

Falchikov, N. (2001). *Learning together: Peer tutoring in higher education*. London: Routledge Falmer.

Freire, P. (2000). *Pedagogy of the oppressed*. (M. B. Ramos, Trans.) New York: Continuum, 30th anniversary edition.

Goh, H. B. K. (2002). *Exploring the role of peer learning and teaching in supporting learning*. Master of Education thesis. University of Sheffield, UK.

Goodlad, S., & Hirst, H. (1989). *Peer tutoring: A guide to learning by teaching*. London: Kogan Page.

Goodlad, S., & Hirst, H. (1990). *Exploration in peer tutoring*. Cornwall: Blackwell.

Merriam-Webster (1999), *Collegiate dictionary*. (10th ed.). Springfield, MA: Merriam-Webster.

Mowatt, I., & Siann, G. (1997). Learning in small groups. In P.D. Sutherland (Ed.), *Adult learning: A reader* (pp. 94–105). London: Kogan Page.

Piaget, J. (1950). *The psychology of intelligence*. London: Routledge.

Trimbur, J. (1989). Consensus and difference in collaborative learning. *College English, 51*(6), 602–616.

Moira Lee

Phenomenology

Phenomenology as a research method is a qualitative approach whose focus is on meaning; that is, understanding the essence and structures of everyday human experience or "lifeworld." Phenomenological research is a way of deepening our understanding of the phenomena of experience as they present themselves in consciousness. Phenomena are anything that present themselves in consciousness, the basis of all knowledge. This method emphasizes "epoche" and bracketing, that is, the importance of the researcher being aware of the influence of his or her own presuppositions, theories, and opinions about the experience being explored, and limiting their influence to whatever extent possible. The results of phenomenological studies are presented as synthesized textual descriptions of the essence or universal elements (that is, critical aspects of the experience being studied without which it would not be what it is) and structures (that is, relationships among aspects of the essence).

Phenomenological research methods are being increasingly used in adult education settings: adult, teacher and higher education; nursing; psychology; sociology; and business (Bentz & Shapiro, 1998; Denzin

& Lincoln, 1998; Moustakas, 1994). The aims and emerging theories of adult education (for example, understanding meaning-making and knowledge-creation, and transformational learning) and phenomenological research methods share these important perspectives, making this form of inquiry relevant to adult education. For example, adult educators and phenomenological researchers endeavor to enhance the lives of learners, caring for educators and adult education learners (van Manen, 1990).

Roots in Phenomenology as Philosophy

Phenomenological research grew out of phenomenology, a 20th century philosophy, or school of thought, pioneered by the German philosopher Edmund H. Husserl (1859–1938). Husserl (1962) believed that "we can only know what we experience." Phenomenology's aim is to understand the meaning of lived experience, free to whatever extent possible of theories, preconceptions, and prejudgments.

Different schools of phenomenology grew out of Husserl's work, including those led by Heidegger, Scheler, Sartre, Schutz, and Merleau-Ponty. A variety of interpretations is found in Europe – Germany, France, Spain, and England; Australia; and North American movements in Canada and the east and west coasts of the United States (see Embree, 1997).

Phenomenology was criticized as being too mystical, because of its emphasis on the subjective. The main contribution of phenomenology, it has been argued however, is its steadfastness and defense of the role of the subjective view of experience and consciousness as a necessary part of a full understanding of knowledge (Moran, 2000).

Several phenomenological concepts that are directly relevant to research and practice in adult education have been outlined by Michael Collins (1984). For example, critical reflection, observing the mind and its operations, is at the heart of adult education and transformational learning – considered by many to be a central aim of adult education today.

Phenomenology as Research Method

The following describes a transcendental phenomenological research method as found in Clark Moustakas (1994), a contemporary researcher, and applied by the present author (Healy, 2001). This all too brief description entails oversimplifications and generalizations. Phenomenological research is an approach to inquiry, which is to be *lived* rather than steps that one follows. Phenomenological research seeks to understand experience by gaining an understanding of the essence and structures of experience as presented in consciousness. It is designed for exploring little-known phenomena. This approach, based on Husserl's work, returns the focus of study "back to the things themselves."

Essential processes that distinguish a phenomenological analysis include (a) epoche, setting aside prejudgments and assumptions; (b) phenomenological reduction, which includes bracketing – setting aside everything besides the focus of the research, and horizontalization – valuing data such that every statement has equal value; (c) imaginative variation, observing data from varying perspectives; (d) development of individual and composite textual themes; and (e) syntheses of these textual and composite structural descriptions.

Epoche involves developing the researcher's perspective so that he or she will approach the experience with awareness of his or her own preconceptions, frameworks, and expectations and limiting the influence of these preconceptions to whatever extent possible. Epoche is a way of seeing with new eyes, with a beginner's mind. Scholars have mixed opinions about the extent to which this aspect of the process is possible (Pollio, Henley, & Thompson, 1997).

The aim of phenomenological reduction is to describe in textual language the object of examination as well as the experience itself or the internal act of consciousness, focusing on the phenomena with the intention of comprehending its essence. This is done through *bracketing* and *horizontalizing*. Bracketing entails identifying and isolating the phenomena being studied, the most relevant data. The researcher lives with the data, identifies key phrases, interprets the meaning of these phrases, reflects on what these meanings say about the phenomena, and attempts an initial description of the phenomena. Narrowing the researcher's focus still further, through horizontalizing, the researcher views each phenomenon as having equal value. The phenomenon is examined from different angles or vantage points. Irrelevant, overlapping, and repetitive statements are eliminated. These horizons are clustered into themes and organized into textual descriptions.

Imaginative variation moves the data beyond mere description, looking for possible meanings and discovering the structural elements of an experience. The researcher looks creatively at what is known about an experience to identify and describe its essential themes and structures.

Synthesis of meanings and structures involves intuitively bringing together the composite textual and structural descriptions developed through epoche, reduction, and imaginative variation. Structures are the organizing qualities or themes of universal essences. Getting at "the essence of phenomenon from the perspective of those who have experienced it" (Merriam, 2002, p. 93) is an exhaustive and ongoing process but is at the heart of the phenomenological inquiry. Phenomenological research approaches are used to explore a broad range of experiences such as loneliness, nursing, insight meditation as transformational learning, the experience of first time computer users, and so on.

Husserl's work described here is a *transcendental phenomenological method*. Another version of phenomenological research is *heuristic inquiry* (Moustakas, 1990; van Manen, 1990). Heuristic inquiry includes not only the experience being explored, but also an analysis of the researcher's own experience with the phenomena and the text describing the experience. While the emphasis of transcendental phenomenology is description, heuristic inquiry focuses on interpretation. Another type of phenomenological inquiry is *empirical phenomenological psychology*, frequently used for research in psychology (Giorgi, 1985).

Issues/Critiques

Phenomenology as a research method is challenging to understand, perhaps because it is a method that is methodless. That is to say, as an approach to "doing" inquiry, researchers often emphasize how the phenomenological research method must be *lived* and suggest that there are no steps to follow. In spite of this emphasis, processes/steps are provided but with the caution that they cannot be followed in any sequential manner. Disciplined and systematic ways to go about this form of inquiry are provided in great detail.

Misunderstandings arise due to assumptions based on differing epistemology and theoretical perspectives such as using a natural science viewpoint (that values measurement, counting, and is often focused on "why"), when trying to understand the phenomenological viewpoint (valuing the experience, meaning, and focused on "how"). A certain degree of understanding of each other's underlying viewpoints, assumptions, and terminology are necessary to appreciate the value of each other's methodology and methods.

Phenomenological research is criticized for producing texts that are vague and imprecise. However, this criticism goes to the very uniqueness and strength of this form of inquiry that strives to describe experiences in consciousness that are often elusive and subtle. Criteria for precision and exactness in phenomenological texts aim for "fullness and completeness of detail" (van Manen, 1990, p. 17). At times, for example, poetry may be as close as one can come to describing aspects of human experience.

Another critique of phenomenology is that the research is "solipsistic" (Bentz & Shapiro, 1998, p. 102); solipsism being a philosophical school of thought believing that one can only know one's self. Contrary to this critique, however, is the reality that phenomenological research, as does all scholarly work, takes place in a community of fellow scholars. There are many examples of studies carried out by adult educators, sociologists, psychiatrists, and clinical psychologists. Although phenomenological research focuses on personal experience, its goal is to further understanding of the real world.

See also: meaning making, philosophy, research methods.

References and Further Reading

Bentz, V. M., & Sharipo, J. J. (1998). *Mindful inquiry in social research*. Thousand Oaks, CA: Sage.

Collins, M. (1984). Phenomenological perspectives in adult education. In S. B. Merriam (Ed.), *Selected writings on philosophy and adult education* (pp. 179–189). Malabar, FL: Krieger.

Denzin, N. K., & Lincoln, Y. S. (1998). *Strategies of qualitative inquiry*. Thousand Oaks, CA: Sage.

Embree, L. (1997). What is phenomenology? *Center for Advanced Research in Phenomenology*. Retrieved June 11, 2003 from http://www.phenomenologycenter.org/phenom.htm

Giorgi, A. (1985). *Phenomenology and psychological research*. Pittsburg, PA: Duquesne University Press.

Healy, M. (2001). *The insight meditation transformational learning process: A phenomenological study*. Unpublished doctoral dissertation, University of Georgia, Athens, Georgia.

Husserl, E. (1962). *Cartesian meditations: An introduction to phenomenology* (Trans. Dorion Cairns). The Hague: Martinus Nijhoff.

Merriam, S. B. (2002). *Qualitative research in practice*. San Francisco: Jossey-Bass.

Moran, D. (2000). *Introduction to phenomenology*. London: Routledge.

Moustakas, C. (1990). *Heuristic research: Design, methodology, and applications*. Newbury Park, CA: Sage.

Moustakas, C. (1994). *Phenomenological research methods*. Thousand Oaks, CA: Sage.

Pollio, H., Henley, T., & Thompson. C. (1997). *The phenomenology of everyday life*. Cambridge, UK: Cambridge University Press.

van Manen, M. (1990). *Researching lived experience*. London, Ontario, Canada: University of Western Ontario.

Mike Healy

Philosophy

A philosophy is a collection of beliefs, perspectives, explanatory schemas and values that both describes and offers guidelines for the practice of adult education. Philosophizing is something most adult educators do, though they may not call the process by that name. Whenever adult educators ask questions about teaching, learning and educational processes, or about the social, political or spiritual meaning of their work, they are thinking philosophically. Why is this course sequenced this way? Why do we use these admission processes for adult learners? What does it mean for my students to trust me? How could this program be arranged in a more adult way? Although these are all practical questions, they are also philosophical ones in that they ponder why the world is the way it is and how it could be better.

Adult education discourse is often distinguished by a distinction between theory and practice, or philosophy and action. Many in the field who identify themselves as practitioners insist that their focus is on practice, with the implication that philosophizing is the province of an effete elite equipped to breathe the rarified atmosphere of abstract thought. The equipment this elite needs to survive in this stratosphere of conceptual analysis is training in philosophy and logic and an ability to penetrate densely abstract texts far beyond the comprehension of ordinary mortals. Philosophy is thus effectively Balkanized as a marginal activity well outside the "real" world of adult education with its daily concerns of teaching, programming, administration, counseling, and community development.

A more accurate perspective is to see philosophizing as one of the most practical things adult educators do. To adapt Antonio Gramsci's (1971) aphorism that "all men are intellectuals" (p. 9), we can say that all adult educators are philosophers. All adult educators make decisions and come to judgments based on a set of assumptions and understandings. These assumptions and understandings (such as what good adult education looks like, how adult educators should behave and what purposes adult education should serve) comprise a philosophy. Such assumptions and understandings are often implicit but that does not mean they are any the less powerful in shaping action. They are the benchmarks we use to assess whether or not we are doing good work. They are also not developed in isolation. What might appear to be private philosophies of practice are actually connected to, and to some degree shaped by, bodies of philosophical thought in the wider world.

Asking philosophical questions is made easier in an environment where disagreement and speculation are encouraged, or at least not stifled. To quote Magee (1997),

> philosophy begins at the point where dissent starts to be allowed. When people are permitted to criticize the prevailing worldview, and to put forward reasons for their criticisms, and thus inaugurate discussion and debate, the first stirrings of philosophy have occurred. (p. 233)

Conceived of in this way, philosophizing – the asking of critical questions in the company of others – is both a social learning activity and a political process.

One who recognized the political dimension to philosophizing was the critical theorist Herbert Marcuse. In *One Dimensional Man* (1964) Marcuse argued that "critical philosophic thought is necessarily transcendent and abstract" (p. 134). In what he called the administered society, street language – the metaphors, slang and expressions of everyday life – is by definition falsely concrete. It diverts people from considering the possibility of radically different ways of thinking and living. By this logic, philosophical thought is inherently critical, and critical thought is inherently philosophical. Hence, a fundamental task of adult education is to "provide the student with the conceptual instruments for a solid and thorough critique of the material and intellectual culture" (Marcuse, 1969, p. 61). The struggle to think philosophically is always a political struggle to Marcuse, not just a matter of intellectual development. Politics and cognitive movement are partners here in the development of revolutionary consciousness.

Philosophical Schools Framing Adult Education

In a highly influential text first published in 1980, Elias and Merriam (1995) identified six schools of philosophical thought that play an important role in framing adult education practice; behaviorism, liberalism, humanism, progressivism, analytic philosophy and radicalism. Since that time new philosophical movements have emerged that suggest a reformulation of this classification, though Elias and Merriam's categories are still useful. The language of human capital theory, for example, draws strongly on behaviorism, degree-completion programs for adults are grounded in a complex mix of humanism, progressivism and liberalism, whilst many working in adult basic education or community development view themselves as radicals struggling for social change while not being coopted by the system that employs them. But new forms of practice such as online and accelerated learning programs, feminist pedagogy, or racially-based forms of provision, are harder to link directly to any of the six categories outlined above. This entry outlines five philosophical movements that are influential in shaping current practice in the field. Many of these have connections to the categories outlined by Elias and Merriam, though they use different terms to describe their constituent elements. The five are radical humanism, neo-Marxism, Africentrism, postmodernism, and poststructuralism.

Radical humanism is best represented by the work of Paulo Freire, known around the world for his book *Pedagogy of the Oppressed* (1970). Freire is also known in North America for a series of talking books with American adult educators such as Myles Horton and Ira Shor. Radical humanism is grounded in the political analysis of Marxism in that it sees the majority of adults leading lives in which they accept that the world is organized to preserve the interests of a powerful minority. The system is kept intact by different forms of ideological domination. Media, schools, adult education, churches and other institutions of civil society ensure that adults come to see the world as representing some kind of naturally ordained order and as beyond human intervention. Adult education's role is to raise people's consciousness so that they realize their oppression and act to liberate themselves. Radical humanism also draws strongly on the humanistic emphasis on love as a powerful force of change. The oppressors are viewed as deserving of love as much as the oppressed, since the oppressors are themselves caught in a system over which they have no control. An accident of birth might have ensured their membership of the ruling class, but they are seen as being no less alienated and in need of liberation than the oppressed. Freire echoes the critical theorist Erich Fromm's emphasis on *The Art of Loving* (1956) in stressing the need for any revolution to be fuelled by love rather than hate. Although humanist psycho-therapists are not generally cited in Freire's work, their stress on the need to grant every person unconditional positive regard finds a parallel in radical humanism's insistence on the power of love.

Neo-Marxism is firmly grounded in Marxism and the work of subsequent interpreters of Marx such as Gramsci (1971) and Althusser (1971). Neo-Marxism takes Marx's analysis of the contradictions of capitalism, the presence of alienated labor, and the need for class revolution and considers how the conditions of the 20th and 21st centuries alter and refine these analytical categories. Although viewed by some as a discredited doctrine, adult educators in Britain (Allman, 2001) the United States (Holst, 2002) and Africa (Youngman, 2000) have argued forcefully for its continuing relevance. These writers contend that recent developments in practice such as the globalization of adult education and training, the application of human capital theory to models of program development and evaluation, and the increase in corporate-sponsored adult education are well-explained by Marxist theory. Unlike radical humanists, neo-Marxists view organized social movements, and in particular revolutionary political parties, as the engine of change. The role of the individual adult educator is reconfigured as an ally of revolutionary movements. Adult educators work as organic intellectuals, a term coined by Gramsci, to develop critical consciousness among the people in order to combat ruling class hegemony and replace this with proletarian hegemony. In Gramsci's view it is the revolutionary people's party that is the chief site for adult educational work.

The *Africentric paradigm* stands as a counter to the Eurocentric body of work informing radical humanism and neo-Marxism. This position argues for the generation of an alternative discourse – including a discourse of criticality – that is grounded in the traditions and cultures of the African continent. It believes that work drawing on European traditions of thought, however well-intentioned and reframed in terms of African American interests, always neglects the cultural traditions of Africa. Since such traditions are crucial constitutive elements of the identity of African Americans, the Africentric paradigm holds that it is these traditions that should dominate theorizing on behalf of African Americans.

As a philosophical orientation, an Africentric approach to adult education addresses African Americans' striving against racism. To Colin and Guy (1998), the Swahili concept of Nguzo Saba embodies the Africentric paradigm. Its values – *Umoja* (unity), *Kujichagulia* (self-determination), *Ujima* (collective work and responsibility), *Ujamaa* (cooperative economics), *Nia* (purpose), *Kuumba* (creativity) and *Imani* (faith) – stress community, interdependence and collective action. In Colin and Guy's view this differs significantly from traditional Eurocentric perspectives of individualism, competition, and hierarchical forms of authority and decision-making. Africentric values suggest curricular and methodological orientations to adult education that focus on self-ethnic liberation and empowerment. Elaborating a philosophy of self-ethnic reliance, Colin (2002) argues that African American adult education programs must be designed to counteract the sociocultural and the socio-psychological effects of racism. They should be developed by members of the ethnic or racial group that have lived the experience of racism and their curriculum, methods and modes of evaluation must be designed to reflect and affirm the racial identity and traditions of Africans rather than Europeans.

Recent work in Britain (Usher, Bryant, & Johnston, 1997) and Australia (Bagnall, 1999) has explored how the perspective of *postmodernism* challenges many practices uncritically lionized in adult education. Postmodernism is less a philosophy, more an orientation. In fact postmodernism stands against universal modes of abstract philosophizing arguing instead that we should be suspicious of grand narratives such as humanity's universal progress towards increasingly just and humane conditions of life. From a postmodern perspective, attempts to develop a universal theory of adult learning, or to prescribe a universal mode of adult education practice, are naïve. Such theories are described as totalizing and regarded as neglecting to recognize that truth and knowledge are local, partial and subject to continual reinvention. In addition, postmodernists eschew "logocentrism," the idea that at the core of words or symbols are shared, universal meanings that can be understood in the same way by a variety of people. Language is seen as slippery and opaque, with the meanings people take from it held to be beyond the control of the writer or speaker. This contention seriously undercuts the efforts of teachers, materials developers and curriculum designers who work with adults on the assumption that classroom activities or instructional materials will be understood and perceived in roughly the same way by all learners and readers. It also threatens those adult educators who commit themselves to dialogic learning in the belief that mutual, intersubjective understanding is possible between adults who strive to understand each other.

Postmodernism is also skeptical of adult educators' belief that through learning people can come to clearer levels of social and self-awareness. It holds that autobiographical narratives of transformative adult learning are fictional constructions that give our lives the comforting illusion of order, development or progress. The whole concept of the self as a unitary, core identity that can be revealed once the layers of social habit and cultural indoctrination are stripped away is rejected. Identity is seen as infinitely malleable. This perspective raises serious problems for those adult educators who emphasize the importance of self-directed learning as a uniquely adult function. If there is no core self at the center of self-direction, then the idea that self-directed learning projects can be conducted that reflect and affirm one's core inner potential becomes problematic. In its rejection of grand narratives and totalizing theories, postmodernism also emphasizes the situationality and contextuality of adult education practice. Practices of andragogy or conscientization cannot be replicated across diverse contexts. Instead adult educators are enjoined to celebrate the diversity of possible formats and activities suggested by local conditions.

Poststructuralism both builds on, and critiques, the core idea of structuralism that individual actions can be explained by the influence of broader structures (cognitive, linguistic, social, political and economic). Represented by the seminal work of the French theorist Michel Foucault (1980), poststructuralism emphasizes how individuals reproduce themselves as proactive supporters of larger social structures. Foucault argued that the 18th and 19th centuries witnessed the rise of a new form of power – disciplinary power – that was exercised by individuals themselves rather than being enforced from above. Disciplinary power stresses self-surveillance and is seen most explicitly in the functioning of prisons, but its mechanisms are also at play in schools, factories, social service agencies and adult education. Disciplinary power breaks up groups and collectives into separate units – isolated self-directed learners – that can then be inveigled into surveying themselves. Students are separated into individual cubicles and study carrels, or behind individual computer terminals, working on individual, self-directed or self-paced learning projects. Professional examinations are taken, essays written, and adult education graduate theses submitted, as individual acts of intellectual labor. The collective learning represented by graduate students writing a dissertation together as a collaborative project, or adult education professors combining to co-author scholarly articles, is discouraged as a plagiaristic diversion of the intellectually weak. Disciplinary power also breaks down time into separate and adjusted threads by arranging learning in a sequence of discrete stages. Adult training and professional practice are detached from each other, the adult curriculum is divided into elements for which predetermined amounts of time are allocated, and the timetable becomes the pivotal reference point for the organization of adult learners' and adult educators' activities.

Self-surveillance is the most important component of disciplinary power. In a society subject to disciplinary power we discipline ourselves. There is no need for the coercive state apparatus to spend enormous amounts of time and money making sure we behave correctly since we are watching ourselves to make sure we don't step out of line. What makes us watch ourselves so assiduously is not an internal resolve to follow normal ways of thinking and acting, thereby avoiding a fall into disgrace. Instead, we watch ourselves because we sense that our attempt to stay close to the norm is itself being watched by another, all seeing, presence. We carry within us the sense that "out there," in some hidden, undiscoverable location, "they" are constantly observing us. It is hard to deviate from the norm if you feel your thoughts and actions are being recorded (figuratively and sometimes literally) by cameras hidden in every corner of your life. To Foucault it is the fact of being able always to be seen that maintains the disciplined individual in her subjection.

Conclusion

The five broad streams of philosophical thought outlined above have considerable implications for adult education practice. Radical humanism allies the power of love to the political project of democracy. It supports attempts to democratize the classroom, dignifies the knowledge of so-called "ordinary" people, and stresses the need to create practices that help people develop their own responses to their own problems. Neo-Marxism enjoins adult educators to become involved in revolutionary social movements and in revolutionary parties. These movements and parties are the engines of social change and adult educators work within them to help people develop skills and knowledge that can be used for social transformation. Africentrism refocuses adult educators' attention away from European ideas and practices and towards African cultural values. Africentric curricula concentrate on understanding and combating racism and on adult education processes that emphasize collective and communal learning. Post-modernism emphasizes the need for adult educators to avoid standardized models of curriculum and teaching and to develop their own local, situational practices. Post-structuralism cautions us to critically examine the way practices that we judge to be democratic and affirming (such as arranging classroom chairs into a circle) can be experienced by learners as oppressive forms of surveillance. In the coming years we are likely to see other subjugated philosophies such as queer theory, and Latino-critical theory come to play a much greater role in adult education.

See also: Africentrism, feminism, postcolonialism, poststructuralism, postmodernism, practitioner, theory.

References and Further Reading

Allman, P. (2001). *Critical education against global capitalism: Karl Marx and revolutionary critical education.* Westport, CT: Bergin & Garvey.

Althusser, L. (1971). *Lenin and philosophy.* New York: Monthly Review Press.

Bagnall, R. G. (1999). *Discovering radical contingency: Building a postmodern agenda in adult education.* New York: Peter Lang.

Colin, S. A. J., III. (2002). Marcus Garvey: Africentric adult education for self ethnic reliance. In E. A. Peterson (Ed.), *Freedom road: Adult education of African Americans* (pp. 41–65). Malabar, FL: Krieger.

Colin, S. A. J., III, & Guy, T. C. (1998). An Africentric interpretive model of curriculum orientations for course development in graduate programs in adult education. *PAACE Journal of Lifelong Learning* (Pennsylvania Association for Adult Continuing Education), *7*, 43–55.

Elias, J. L., & Merriam, S. B. (1995). *Philosophical foundations of adult education* (2nd ed.). Malabar, FL: Krieger.

Foucault, M. (1980). *Power/knowledge: Selected interviews and other writings, 1972–1977.* New York: Pantheon Books.

Freire, P. (1970). *Pedagogy of the oppressed.* (M. B. Ramos, Trans.) New York: Continuum.

Fromm, E. (1956). *The art of loving: An enquiry into the nature of love.* New York: Harper & Row.

Gramsci, A. (1971). *Selections from the prison notebooks.* In Q. Hoare & G.N. Smith (Eds.). London: Lawrence & Wishart.

Holst, J. D. (2002). *Social movements, civil society, and radical adult education.* Westport, CT: Bergin & Garvey.

Magee, B. (1997). *Confessions of a philosopher: A personal journey through western philosophy from Plato to Popper.* New York: Modern Library.

Marcuse, H. (1964). *One dimensional man.* Boston: Beacon Press.

Marcuse, H. (1969). *An essay on liberation.* Boston: Beacon Press.

Usher, R., Bryant, I., & Johnston, R. (1997). *Adult education and the postmodern challenge: Learning beyond the limits.* New York: Routledge.

Youngman, F. (2000). *The political economy of adult education and development.* New York: Zed Books.

Stephen Brookfield

Popular Education

Popular education refers to a non-formal adult education approach that develops the capacity of learners to critically analyse the root causes of their socioeconomic, political, cultural, spiritual and religious struggles, with the ultimate goal of organizing and taking collective action that will enhance social transformation. The literature describes popular education as an educational philosophy, tool, instrument or approach which creates a learning climate where both the facilitator and adult learner engage in a critically reflective and informed dialogue. Learning cannot be participative and transformative without genuine dialogue (Freire, 1970). An educational process is regarded as popular if it is liberating, accessible, non-elitist, democratic, experiential, participatory, and based on the needs, aspirations and dreams of the disadvantaged people in society. Through this process, the learner develops the ability to perceive and understand his or her reality and how this is linked to mainstream social problems, with the ultimate goal of transforming unjust social conditions (Freire). It is from their concrete location that participants in a popular education process create and interpret their knowledge of the world and work for social change (Freire, 1992).

Historically, popular education theory and practices evolved from different schools of thought. For example, it has been influenced by Marxist theories, particularly with regard to organizing the working class to collectively improve their working conditions by resisting the manipulative and oppressive socio-economic and political systems of the bourgeoisie. In the North American context, popular education in Canada is most clearly seen as having evolved out of the Antigonish Movement in the Atlantic region led by Moses Coady. The Antigonish Movement used popular education techniques to organize fishermen and women to form cooperatives in order to take control of their lives and destinies. Popular education in the United States of America, originated from the human rights and workers' rights movements supported by the Highlander Research and Education Center at Tennessee. This center supported the work of various civil society groups, local community leaders and grassroots organizations committed to the principles and ideals of social justice and good governance. In the Latin American context, popular education became prominent in the 1960s, 1970s and early 1980s as a resistance form of education that helped the working class to tackle the economic exploitation they were faced with (Nadeau, 1996). In the mid-1980s, feminist popular educators emerged and called for the recognition of the role of women, youth, indigenous people and other disadvantaged groups in resisting oppression, violence, exploitation and unjust structures in their societies (Nadeau). They also emphasized that popular education methods should challenge all forms of discrimination related to gender, race, ethnicity, ability, sexual orientation, class and age, and integrate all aspects of human and non-human life, including the spiritual, psychological, emotional and environmental aspects.

The theory of popular education is grounded in Freire's (1970) *Pedagogy of the Oppressed* and begins with indigenous knowledge and experiences, followed by a deeper conscientization process, and finally leads to collective resistance to all forms of oppression and violence. Through popular education, adults develop their capacity to critically analyze their current realities with a commitment to taking collective action that would transform structures that prevent them from realizing the fullness of their human and non-human capacities. Like all forms of formal, informal and non-formal education, popular education is not neutral; rather, it politically collaborates with the poor in their struggle for an active, democratic and informed participation in major-decisions affecting their socioeconomic, political, cultural, spiritual and environmental advancement. This interactive process enables adults to validate their collective knowledge and lived experiences, and strengthens their ability to create new knowledge that would contribute to positive social change. It also enhances people's capacity to question the misuse of power by political leaders and other forces in society. Popular education enables adult learners and their educators to debate and deeply reflect upon contested views and ideas with a view to acknowledging underlying differences and similarities and building common ground for social change.

There are significant variations with regard to how popular education is perceived and practiced around the world. These variations are due to differences in the socio-economic, political, cultural, historical, religious and environmental global contexts. For example, in the 1950s and 1960s popular education methods were used by educators, human rights and political activists to organize the masses to resist military regimes in Brazil, Chile and Mexico. Popular education in these contexts was perceived as resistance education whose main aim was to get rid of the oppressive and brutal military regimes. In the North America context, the term "education for social change" (Arnold, Burke, James, Martin, & Thomas, 1991) is commonly used instead of popular education, although the basic principles of both approaches are the same. The perceptions and practices of popular education in Africa also vary. During the apartheid era in South Africa, terms such as liberating education, emancipatory education and resistance education were used interchangeably with popular education. In West Africa, church-related development practitioners and adult educators have been using the term community development education instead of popular education. This approach to education, also referred to as DELTA (Development Education and Leadership Teams in Action), was developed by Anne Hope and Sally Timmel, authors of *Training for Transformation* (Hope, Timmel, & Hodzi, 1984), primarily from Freire's principles and practices of education. Regardless of what term was used in place of popular education, the main goal was the same – to raise awareness about unjust structures, systems and policies designed to marginalize the masses and mobilize collective action for positive change.

The principles and practices of popular education can be applied and adapted in different adult education contexts. For example, within worker education, the emphasis is on equipping workers with knowledge, skills, attitudes, values and beliefs that promote democratic, accountable, transparent and non-discriminatory organizations. In the promotion of environmental sustainability, popular education enables people to identify and critically analyze the root causes of environmental degradation and strategies for improving such conditions. Popular education can also be used to promote health by helping people to deeply reflect on the root causes of diseases and malnutrition, and find solutions to health problems. In various civil society movements in Africa, popular education is used to strengthen people's capacity to examine the underlying causes of poor governance, corruption, and lack of accountability and transparency, with a view to enabling them to organize themselves and advocate for change. For organizations and/or institutions promoting peace education, participants use popular education techniques to deeply examine and analyze the main causes and effects of violent conflicts both at local and global levels and strategies for building cultures of peace and stability.

The literature reveals that popular education integrates different types of participatory adult learning methods including role-play, games, skits, brainstorming, group discussions and story-telling. From time immemorial, adult educators have also recognized that theatre, especially popular theatre, has played a significant role in the adult education movement and have integrated it in their discourse in order to reach a wider audience, especially the poor. Popular theatre is a participatory, democratic and inclusive popular education technique which uses drama, mimes, folktales, masquerades and puppetry as a means to create awareness among oppressed groups about their struggles, challenging them to mobilize and take action that would improve their lives. In pre-colonial Africa, Asia and South America, indigenous peoples have used this technique as an important non-formal educational tool for the transmission of knowledge, skills, values, attitudes and traditional beliefs from one generation to the other. In postcolonial times, popular theatre has been used in the South as a vehicle for decolonizing the minds of the masses and for facilitating community-based development education. Little wonder it has been generally perceived in the South as a theatre of resistance and social transformation, a theatre for development – as community theatre and people's theatre. Community development practitioners have used this medium to sensitize rural communities about the causes and effects of poor health, poverty, HIV/AIDS, environmental degradation and other related societal problems, and to organize and effect positive change. Augusto Boal, the Brazilian cultural activist and author of *Theatre of the Oppressed*, has been one of the greatest advocates for the integration of popular theatre into popular education theory and practice. His revolutionary cultural teachings greatly contributed to making popular theatre a practical medium for grassroots empowerment and activism (Boal, 1979).

Opportunities and Challenges

There is evidence that popular education has made tremendous contributions to the improvement of the socioeconomic, cultural and political conditions of the masses in Brazil, Chile and Mexico, and popular education activities in these countries continue to grow (La Belle, 1986). In Sub-Saharan Africa, for example, the use of popular theatre through dramas, dances, mimes, story-telling, folktales and communal rituals have helped to educate local rural communities about the root causes and effects of health-related problems, poverty, HIV/AIDS and environmental destruction, and strategies for solving such problems. Unlike many adult education programs which are sometimes designed to maintain the status quo, popular education provides an educational alternative that supports social justice (Burke & Arnold, 1983).

In spite of these successes, popular education has been criticized for several reasons. For example, La Belle (1986) feels that it lacks a strong political base at the grassroots level, and that political, commercial and other interest groups at the local level have not been adequately organized to address the struggles of the poor. The literature on poplar education provides very little of a theoretical and practical framework on how to deal with political and economic influences such as from the major industrialized countries and international organizations such as the World Trade Organization, the World Bank and International Monetary Fund, whose economic policies often do not trickle down to the bulk of the populations they intend to support. In the midst of adversity and opposition from such powerful bodies, popular education seems to lack the theoretical frameworks to guide any structural changes needed (La Belle). There is, therefore, a need for further development of its theory informed by the complexities of globalization and rapidly-growing information technology.

Critics also feel that very little work has been done to critically examine and document the impact of popular education in social transformation both at local and global levels. Although popular education needs to be rooted in local contexts, it has not adequately created global networks that can address the challenges of this dynamic world. Also, "the anti-racist critique of popular education has revealed the limitations of past organizing that not only excluded large groups of marginalized people, but also reinforced racism in its very practice" (Nadeau, 1996, p. 7). Finally, adult educators need to carry out further research on how traditional cultural art forms, especially popular theatre, affect gender, racial and ethnic relations and what should be done to address such issues. Despite these criticisms, popular education remains one of the key critical theories of adult education (Oliver, 2000).

See also: community education, conscientization, international adult education, praxis, social movement learning.

References and Further Reading

Arnold, R., & Burke, B. (1983). *Popular education handbook: An educational experience taken from Central America and adapted to the Canadian context.* Toronto: CUSO and the Ontario Institute for Studies in Education.

Arnold, R., Burke, B., James, C., Martin, D., & Thomas. B. (1991). *Educating for a change*. Toronto: Between the Lines and the Doris Marshall Institute for Education and Action.

Boal, A. (1979). *Theatre of the oppressed.* New York: Urizen Books.

Freire, P. (1970). *Pedagogy of the oppressed* (M. B. Ramos, Trans.). New York: The Seabury Press.

Freire, P. (1992). *Pedagogy of hope: Reliving pedagogy of the oppressed.* (R. R. Barr, Trans.). New York: The Continuum Publishing Company.

Hope, A., Timmel, S., & Hodzi, C. (1984). *Training for transformation: A handbook for community workers.* Gweru, Zimbabwe: Mambo Press.

La Belle, T. J. (1986). *Non-formal education in Latin America and the Caribbean: Stability, reform, or revolution?* New York: Praeger.

Nadeau, D. (1996). *Counting our victories: Popular education and organizing.* New Westminster, British Columbia: Repeal the Deal Productions.

Oliver, B. (2000). Participation in environmental popular education workshops: A case study from Mexico. *Convergence, 33*(4), 44–53.

Thomas Mark Turay

Portfolio

The portfolio in adult higher education is a purposeful compilation of document-supported descriptions of learning outcomes acquired from professional and personal experiences. Portfolios are used in higher education to assess academic progress, act as a career development tool, and encourage reflection. However, credit-bearing portfolios – often referred to as experiential learning portfolios – are most common among adult undergraduates. The portfolio intends to enable adults to gain college credits towards degree completion by reflecting on, analysing, evaluating, communicating, and equating their learning experiences to knowledge gained in traditional classroom settings. Thus, the portfolio serves as a method of prior learning assessment (PLA) designed to help adult students demonstrate college-level learning from real-world settings (Brown, 1999, 2000). It is one of several forms of PLA that also includes standardized tests such as Advanced Placement, CLEP (College Level Examination Program), DANTES (Defense Activity for Non-Traditional Education Support), and university-specific challenge exams.

Portfolios are developed in a variety of media including paper, web-based, and CD ROM or other technological forms. They are utilized in colleges and universities throughout the United States (Flint, 1999), Great Britain, Canada, Australia, Europe and South Africa (Evans, 1999). Outside of the United States, portfolios also serve as a vehicle to satisfy university entry requirements. Regardless of media or location, the use of portfolios as a credit-acquisition strategy has been controversial since its inception over three decades ago in adult non-traditional undergraduate programs. Critics question the variety of processes used by individual institutions to assess and equate experiential learning to academic learning. Proponents argue that experiential learning parallels knowledge gained in the classroom, and the evaluation of learning from experiences is a form of authentic assessment. Supporters also argue that as a teaching strategy for adult learners, portfolio development can produce learning outcomes in and of itself (Brown, 2000; Mandell, 2000).

Background

In the mid-1920s, Lindeman published his groundbreaking book, *The Meaning of Adult Education* (1926/1961), noting the distinctive characteristics of adults as learners. Since then it has become increasingly apparent that adult pedagogy differs from that utilized with children. Younger learners – 5 through 22 years of age – approach the learning environment with fewer life experiences and more teacher-dependency for information than their adult counterparts. Malcolm Knowles, a follower of Lindeman, used the term andragogy in the 1960s as the art of teaching adults (Knowles, 1984). He described several features unique to adult learners that necessitate a different pedagogical approach to instructional program design and teaching. For example, andragogical concepts recognize the breadth and depth of experience brought to the educational environment by adults, the motivation both intrinsic and extrinsic that brings adults to learning venues, the problem-centered orientation to learning by adults, and the adult's readiness to learn combined with self-direction in the knowledge-acquisition process. Knowles' ideas, in addition to influencing the design and execution of adult non-traditional educational programs also support constructivist views on knowledge creation. Thus adult learners are actively engaged in making meaning of their experiences from which learning is derived.

The actual incorporation of portfolios in adult higher education began in the late 1960s and gained greater popularity in the 1970s with an influx of adult learners on college campuses. Today nearly 50% of college students are adults, a number unimagined three decades ago. The motivating factor for the increase of older learners on college campuses focuses primarily on the need for professional credentials for career advancement. Portfolio development was considered a mechanism for demonstrating the how's, what's, and why's of the learning experiences brought to college classrooms by adults.

By the mid-1970s, educators from around the country met at the Educational Testing Service (ETS) site in Princeton, New Jersey to develop guidelines for portfolio prior learning recognition and assessment (Gamson, 1989). Members of the newly organized Cooperative Assessment of Experiential Learning (later to be renamed Council for Adult and Experiential Learning and referred to as CAEL), created standards of good practice in portfolio development and assessment.

These initial efforts were supplemented by the work of David Kolb (1984), who developed a model – that is used extensively in portfolio programs – for explaining how experiences are transformed into learning. It begins with concrete observation of an experience, followed by reflection on the experience, which in turn leads to the formation of abstract conceptualizations, and finally to the application of new concepts to new situations (Baker & Kolb, 1990). In 1989, Urban Whitaker, in conjunction with CAEL, produced the text *Assessing Learning*, which outlines five administrative and five academic standards for portfolio programs used throughout the United States. Currently, CAEL is recognized as the leading professional organization maintaining best practices for portfolio assessment in conjunction with the American Council on Education and other nationally recognized higher education organizations.

International Utilization

Great Britain began portfolio inclusion in higher education in the 1980s (Evans, 1999). Called Accreditation of Prior Experiential Learning, or APEL, England's adoption of prior learning assessment was followed by other countries including Canada, France, Australia, and South Africa. Evans points out that each country that adopted APEL altered it to reflect its own cultural and government systems. For example, when Canada began its own version of APEL – referred to as Prior Learning Assessment and Recognition (PLAR) – in the 1990s, it did so as a collaboration between the Canadian ministries of education and labor. New universities were established that were entirely devoted to adult learners and included prior recognition and assessment of learning as a key component for workforce development. PLAR advocates profess that learning "counts regardless of where it was acquired" (PLAR, 1999). Conferences sponsored by PLAR and the Canadian Board of Labor Force Development tie portfolios to workforce development much as CAEL has done in the last 10 years. More recently, in South Africa, APEL supports access and equity to a workforce that was eliminated from education and economic opportunities under Apartheid (personal communication with Osman, 2003).

Controversy

From its inception, the inclusion of portfolios in adult degree programs has been controversial. The debate in the academy revolves around the assessment of learning experiences and their equation to academic knowledge (CAEL/ACE, 1993; Evans, 1993; Eversoll, 1986; Halpern, 1994). Though most colleges and universities recognize national academic and administrative assessment standards, skepticism remains, especially among faculty who question the correlation of experiential learning outcomes to those gained in college courses (Miller, 1991). This distrust may be due, in part, to the concern that every institution tailors its portfolio program to its particular student body and, in the United States, to various higher education regional accreditation criteria.

Problems arise, both for American and foreign institutions of higher learning, due to the clash of traditional and non-traditional values and objectives of higher education (Bourgeois & Lienard, 1992). Traditionalists find experiential learning, as presented in portfolios, difficult to equate to college-level learning outcomes because of its strong application-over-theory component. Proponents insist that as long as institutions meet standards set forth by regional accreditation agencies and nationally recognized bodies, the assessment process can remain unique to the institution for which it was created. With the debate over assessment taking center-stage, critics have rarely focused on the viability of the portfolio as a teaching strategy potentially producing learning outcomes from the development process (Tucker & Murphy, 1990).

Teaching Strategy

Although portfolio learning outcomes are not measured in a traditional, quantitative manner and present challenges in evaluation, recent studies indicate that portfolio creation goes beyond the identification of prior learning for college credits in that adults often obtain learning outcomes from the development process itself (Brown, 2000, 2002). Jack Mezirow and Associates (1990) defined transformative learning – whether it takes place within professional, personal, or educational settings – as: "the process of learning through critical self-reflection, which results in the reformulation of a meaning perspective to allow a more inclusive, discriminating, and integrative understanding of one's experience. Learning includes acting on these insights" (p. xvi).

Portfolio development can augment critical thinking, reflection and communication competencies among adult learners who often find that the discovery and rediscovery of their abilities produces transformative changes in their perspectives and behavior (Brown, 1999; Charter Oak, 1997; Joerin, 1998).

Research since the time of Knowles on the nature and needs of the adult learner, or andragogy, has influenced the design of college programs that are effective and rewarding for this population (Dick & Robinson, 1992; Hall, 1991). Educators intent on categorizing academic learning in terms of traditional tests and measurements may view portfolio assessment as "too clumsy, subjective ... and time consuming for everyone .... In a world obsessed with searching for a perfect formula for learning and evaluation, the portfolio is just too messy" (Mandell, 2000, pp. 41, 49). Yet, Kolb (1992) reminds us that learning is complex, too complex to fit neatly into quantifiable compartments. Moreover, unlike standardized or multiple choice tests, the portfolio presents a form of authentic assessment (Wiggins, 1998) which connects the learner's performance and learning to the real world, requiring higher learning competencies of critical reflection, analysis, and evaluation while producing a tangible product (Janesick, 2001).

As adult learners continue to enter the academy, non-traditional undergraduate programs with portfolios as a component of degree completion will undoubtedly proliferate. Further research exploring the impact of portfolios on learning and the validity of assessment methods is critically needed in order to evaluate its place in adult higher education.

See also: experiential learning, higher education, informal learning, prior learning and assessment recognition.

References and Further Reading

Baker, R. J., & Kolb, D. A. (1990). *Learning style exercise.* Boston: McBer & Company.

Bourgeois, E., & Lienard, G. (1992). Developing adult education in universities: A political view. *Higher Education Management, 4*(1), 23–30.

Brown, J. O. (1999). *A case study of adults in college who developed an experiential learning portfolio.* Dissertation Abstracts AAG9936897.

Brown, J. O. (2000). The portfolio: A reflective bridge connecting the learner, higher education and the workplace. *Journal of Continuing Higher Education, 49,* 2, 1–13.

Brown, J. O. (2002). Know thyself: The impact of portfolio development on adult learning. *Adult Education Quarterly, 52*(3), 228–245.

Charter Oak State College. (1997). *In-house portfolio survey document.* New Britain, CT: Author.

Council for Adult and Experiential Learning and the American Council on Education (CAEL/ACE) (1993). *Adult degree programs: Quality issues, problem areas, action steps.* Chicago: Council for Adult and Experiential Learning.

Dick, R., & Robinson, B. M. (1992). Assessing self-acquired competency portfolios in speech communication: National and international issues. *ACA Bulletin, 81,* 60–68.

Evans, L. (1993, April). *Development of a student's perceptions instrument to assess contributions of the learning environment to the enhancement of student learning in higher education.* Paper presented at the annual meeting of the American Educational Research Association, Atlanta, GA.

Evans, N. (Ed.) (1999). *Experiential learning around the world.* London: Jessica Kingsley.

Eversoll, D. B. (1986). Institutional planning with successful participants: A "listening ear" for adult baccalaureate degree graduates. *Journal of Continuing Higher Education, 4*(2), 24–26.

Flint, T. (1999). Prior learning assessment: A status report. *Assessment and Accountability Forum, 1*(9), 15–16, 19.

Gamson, Z. M. (1989). *Higher education and the real world: The story of CAEL.* Wolfboro, NH: Longwood Academic.

Hall, J. W. (1991). *Access through innovation: New colleges for new students.* Continuing Higher Education Series. New York: Macmillan. Retrieved November 16, 2003 from ERIC database (ERIC Document Reproduction Service No. ED328178).

Halpern, D. F. (Ed.). (1994). *Changing college classrooms: New teaching and learning strategies for an increasingly complex world.* San Francisco: Jossey-Bass.

Janesick, V. J. (2001). *The assessment debate: A reference handbook.* Santa Barbara, CA: ABC-CLIO Publishers.

Joerin, C. (1998). *Qualitative analysis of the prior learning assessment process at Malaspina University-College.* British Columbia, Canada: Centre for Curriculum, Transfer, and Technology.

Knowles, M. S. (1984). *Andragogy in action.* San Francisco: Jossey-Bass.

Kolb, D. A. (1984). *Experiential learning: Experience as the source of learning and development.* Englewood Cliffs, NJ: Prentice Hall.

Kolb, D. A. (1992). (Keynote address). Paper presented at the annual meeting of the CAEL International Assembly, November 1992, San Diego, CA.

Lindeman, E. C. L. (1961). *The meaning of adult education.* Montreal: Harvest House, originally published in 1926.

Mandell, A. (2000). Saving what is messy: PLA in a world of testing. *Journal of Continuing Higher Education, 47*(1), 49–51.

Mezirow, J., & Associates (1990). *Fostering critical thinking in adulthood: A guide to transformative and emancipatory learning.* San Francisco: Jossey-Bass.

Miller, D. A. (1991). No campus, no problem: Non-traditional degree granting programs. *Adult Learning, 3*(3), 17–19.

PLAR (1999). *Prior Learning and Assessment Recognition Conference Brochure.* Vancouver, BC: PLAR Publisher.

Tucker, R. W., & Murphy, J. D. (1990). *Comprehensive assessment of learning outcomes and processes for working adults.* Paper presented at the meeting of the American Evaluation Association, October 1990, Washington, DC.

Whitaker, U. (1989). *Assessing learning: Standards, principles and procedures.* Philadelphia, PA: Council for Adult and Experiential Learning.

Wiggins, G. (1998). *Educative assessment: Designing assessments to inform and improve student performance.* San Francisco: Jossey-Bass.

Judith O. Brown

Postcolonialism

Postcolonialism can be conceived of as an all-embracing concept accounting for the process of domination that has its basis in European colonization and which incorporates all the different forms taken by colonialism up to the present day (Mayo, Borg, & Dei, 2002). Ashcroft, Griffiths, and Tiffin (1995) use the term "postcolonial" to "represent the continuing process of imperial suppressions and exchanges throughout . . . [a] diverse range of societies, in their institutions and their discursive practices" (p. 3). Studies of this phenomenon are "based in the 'historical fact' of European colonialism, and the diverse effects to which this phenomenon gave rise" (p. 2). The authors stress this point to counter the rather loose use of the term, especially the tendency to use the term with reference to "any kind of marginality" (p. 2).

Effects of Colonialism

Ngugi Wa Thiong'o (1981) argues that colonialism's most important area of domination was "the mental universe of the colonized" (p. 16), and colonial adult education often served this interest. In Malta, to give one example, state-sponsored adult education, which preceded mass public schooling, was encouraged during the British colonial period for the purpose of migration. It included a literacy program that helped the spread of English throughout the country, an important feature of "Anglicization." A smattering of English was provided for those who elected to remain in Malta and those aspiring to emigrate to English-speaking countries. Adult basic education, here, contributed to Anglicization on two fronts. Deference was fostered to the English language both at home and abroad, in the latter case contributing to the consolidation of the dominant White-Anglo culture. Colonial relations between countries are transposed to the country of settlement, with certain cultures being regarded as the norm, because of their relationship to the dominant group, and others being regarded as subaltern. Adult education, especially in the form of English as a second language (ESL) classes for immigrants, is often examined for its role within this process of colonial transposition.

Postcolonialism in Adult Education

Counter-hegemonic approaches to adult education, advocated in the writings of such people as Julius Nyerere, emphasized the validity of subaltern knowledge that had been devalued by colonialists. Others affirm the importance of indigenous forms of knowledge and technologies to rupture the hegemonic presence of Eurocentric thought and values (Dei, Hall, & Rosenberg 2000).

Emphasizing that which is indigenous and popular has been a key feature of the mass adult education programs carried out in post-revolutionary and post-independence contexts. This is often in reaction to the kind of "top to bottom" education provided prior to the change in political climate. Cuba, Tanzania, Nicaragua, Grenada, the Seychelles, Guinea Bissau and Eritrea are among the contexts that feature prominently in the relevant literature. The term "to Grenadize Grenadians," adopted in Grenada by the New Jewel Movement, best captures the spirit characterizing this change in approach, even though, as with most revolutions, there were contradictions (Hickling-Hudson, 1999). The name of Paulo Freire (1983), whose work best exemplifies this spirit is often mentioned with respect to these contexts' literacy campaigns.

Other sources of resistance to various legacies of colonialism and neocolonial encroachment on specific communities include the Movimento dos Trabalhadores Rurais Sem Terra (MST) (Landless Workers Movement) in Brazil; as part of the colonial process, settlers drove people off the land and some of the latter's descendants continue to live in "an impoverished landless limbo" (Young, 2003, p. 45). Popular education, very much inspired by Freire, features prominently in the all-embracing educational work of the MST (Kane, 2001). We can also mention, as another source of resistance to colonialism, the learning through social action of Indian women in the Mira Behn-inspired Chipko movement; they hug trees in defiance of axe-wielding men acting in the interest of foreign capital. The Chipko women resist a process of colonization that renders life unsustainable for the traditional inhabitants (Young, pp. 103–105).

Issues of Identity

Hybridization constitutes an important feature of learning in postcolonial contexts. Aspects of the dominant colonial culture often feature prominently in these forms of popular and anti-colonial education. The classic case is that of appropriating the colonizer's language in adult literacy campaigns, especially when a lingua franca is necessary. The PAIGC's (African Party for the Independence of Guinea Bissau and Cape Verde) use of Portuguese in Guinea Bissau is a case in point. There are instances, as in Tanzania, when

Nordic-European ideas were reinvented to assume, in this case, an African character; the Swedish Folk High Schools influenced the development of communal residential adult education colleges during the Nyerere years. Religious texts, introduced in Latin America as a by-product of European colonization, became instruments for people, in Christian Base Communities, to "read their own world" from their own subaltern standpoint.

Contrapuntal readings, to borrow Edward Said's (1993) favorite adjective from music and literature, allow possibilities for postcolonial takes on texts, especially, in Said's case, literary texts. This seems relevant to adult education given that literature has traditionally featured prominently in liberal adult education programs in certain contexts. The same applies to museums. Edited volumes have focused on their role as sites of adult learning. There is room for adult education initiatives that deconstruct the "orientalist" representations, often found in these museums, to convert these institutions into decolonizing spaces.

See also: English as a second language, identity, philosophy, poststructuralism, postmodernism, practitioner.

References and Further Reading

Ashcroft, B., Griffiths, G., & Tiffin, H. (Eds.). (1995). *The postcolonial studies reader.* London and New York: Routledge.

Dei, G. J. S., Hall, B. L., & Rosenberg, D. G. (2000). *Indigenous knowledges in global contexts. Multiple readings of our world.* Toronto: University of Toronto Press.

Freire, P. (1983). *Pedagogy of the oppressed* (M. B. Ramos, Trans.). New York: Continuum.

Hickling Hudson, A. (1999). Beyond schooling. Adult education in postcolonial societies. In R. F. Arnove & C.A. Torres (Eds.), *Comparative education. The dialectic of the global and the local* (pp. 233–255). Lanham, MD: Rowman & Littlefield.

Kane, L. (2001). *Popular education and social change in Latin America.* London: Latin America Bureau.

Mayo, P., Borg, C & Dei, G. J. S. (2002). Postcolonialism, education and an international forum for debate. *Journal of Postcolonial Education, 1*(1), 3–7.

Ngugi Wa Thiong'o (1981). *Decolonizing the mind. The politics of language in African Literature.* Oxford: James Currey & Heinemann.

Said, E. (1993). *Culture and imperialism.* New York: Knopf.

Young, R.J.C. (2003). *Postcolonialism. A very short introduction.* Oxford: Oxford University Press.

Peter Mayo

Postmodernism

Postmodernism refers to a theoretical perspective on contemporary society that developed during the 1970s and that challenged dominant views about the nature of social progress and development.

The term postmodernism was first applied to the ideas of a group of intellectuals (mainly French) who contested dominant beliefs of modernity. Tracing their intellectual heritage to the late 19th-century philosopher, Friedrich Nietzsche, and drawing their theoretical sustenance from the philosophical tradition called *structuralism*, thinkers like Jacques Lyotard, Michel Foucault, Luce Irigaray, Jacques Derrida, Hélène Cixous, and Jacques Lacan began to question key ideas of the modern world.

By the middle of the 1980s, a loose and varied group of discourses, increasingly identified by the chronically disputed term postmodernism, began to impact the field of adult education. Over the next 15 years, the nature and implications of postmodernism for adult education increasingly became the focus of analysis and debate. Even more impressive than this direct discourse about the term, however, has been the way postmodern sensibilities have infiltrated the fabric of the theories and practices of adult education. For instance, recent feminist, antiracist and queer theory discourses in adult education, which challenge predominant notions about the nature of knowledge and learning, draw extensively on postmodernist modes of critique. Arguably, the full transformative potential of postmodernism is only now being felt in our field.

Postmodernism and its Roots

The term, "postmodernism," was coined to name an architectural movement of the late 1950s. Architecture, at the time, was dominated by a "high-culture" obsession with technological novelty and dismissal of popular and traditional architectural forms. Postmodern architects reasserted the place of more traditional architectural elements, which they recombined into a collage of varied, discontinuous and even contrasting styles.

For the French intellectuals who began using the term more broadly in the 1970s, one of the main targets of their critique was the modern belief that, using reason, human beings could constitute a freer, more sensible and more just world for themselves than what had existed in tradition-bound societies. From the Enlightenment onwards, philosophers posited the human self as unified, rational and autonomous, and the world as objective, knowable and, with the application of the right technology, controllable. With sufficient time and hard-nosed critical/scientific spirit, humans would gradually progress, dispel the prejudices of traditional society, uncover the mysteries of the universe and establish the conditions of truth and justice for all. While Marxists contested the direction that capitalism had taken the dream of the Enlightenment, they did not question its ultimate rational goal.

Postmodern Challenges

By the mid-1980s, under the provocation of the French postmodernists, many of the taken-for-granted certainties of the modern world underwent serious scrutiny. The postmodernists rejected the Enlightenment view of a rational, post-traditional society as simply a "metanarrative" that people refused to see as foundationless. The belief that the world was ultimately knowable and that humans could make systematic progress towards discerning absolute truth was, in the end, indefensible. The world was never simply "objective." Rather, people's view of truth was always conditioned by the historical and power-ridden circumstances of their own cultural conditioning. As beings thoroughly and inescapably locked in a discursive world, humans never possess an unmediated access to truth. Postmodernists likewise challenged the idea that human subjects were autonomous, solitary and rational. Instead of being unified entities, postmodernists held humans to be multiply constituted, fragmented and decentered.

As the 1980s unfolded, postmodernism rapidly attracted adherents, particularly from groups long excluded or marginalized by the grand narratives of modernity. Many feminists, for instance, agreed with postmodernism's criticism of key notions and institutions of patriarchal society. Post-modernism's disparagement of modern reason accorded with many feminists' contentions that patriarchal society depreciated women's ways of knowing. Other critical discourses dealing with issues of race, gender identity, ethnicity, sexual orientation, ability, class and a range of others drew upon and extended the critical insights of postmodernism. They challenged universal claims to truth and celebrated cultural variety and difference.

Critiques of Postmodernism

Detractors have raised concerns about postmodernism on a number of fronts. For instance, early on Jürgen Habermas (1987) raised concerns that postmodernism's attack on Western rationality promoted a relativism that might leave the door open for the development of destructive social and cultural forms (fascism, for instance). Geographer David Harvey (1989) observed that the intellectual sensibilities of postmodernism reflect an underlying transformation in capitalist production from large-scale Fordist industrial processes, to flexible just-in-time computer-mediated post-Fordist production processes. Postmodernism, in this case, is not critical as much as consistent with new forms of social and cultural domination that prevail with globalization. More recently, Margaret Archer (2000) has condemned postmodernism's efforts to "dissolve" the self into "discursive structures" (p. 34), which, she contends, denies humans the capacity for self-conscious agency.

Adult Education and Postmodernism

Perhaps because adult education, itself, was constituted so deeply in service to the aspirations of modernity, debate over the implications of postmodernism for adult education has mostly been amongst a small contingent of specialized theorists of the field (e.g., Bagnall, 1999; Briton, 1996; Plumb, 1995; Usher & Edwards, 1994; Westwood, 1991). Now that the social transformations, which in the early days formed the seedbed of postmodernist discourse, have come to span the globe, mainstream adult education has become more deeply marked by the sensibilities of postmodernism. It may well be that, as adult education adjusts its purpose to fit the aspirations of the new world order, it may become a truly postmodern enterprise.

See also: difference, identity, philosophy, postcolonialism, poststructuralism, theory.

References and Further Reading

Archer, M. S. (2000). *Being human: The problem of agency.* Cambridge, UK; New York: Cambridge University Press.

Bagnall, R. G. (1999). *Discovering radical contingency: Building a postmodern agenda in adult education.* New York: P. Lang.

Briton, D. (1996). *The modern practice of adult education: A postmodern critique.* Albany: State University of New York Press.

Habermas, J. (1987). *The philosophical discourse of modernity: Twelve lectures.* Cambridge, MA: MIT Press.

Harvey, D. (1989). *The condition of postmodernity: An enquiry into the origins of cultural change.* Oxford; New York: Blackwell.

Plumb, D. (1995). Declining opportunities. Adult education, culture, and postmodernity. In M. R. Welton (Ed.),

In defense of the lifeworld: Critical perspectives on adult learning (pp. 157–193). Albany: State University of New York Press.

Usher, R., & Edwards, R. (1994). *Postmodernism and education.* London; New York: Routledge.

Westwood, S. (1991). Constructing the future: A postmodern agenda for adult education. In J. E. Thomas & S. Westwood (Eds.), *Radical agendas?: The politics of adult education* (pp. 54–105). Leicester, UK: National Institute of Adult Continuing Education.

Donovan Plumb

Poststructuralism

Poststructuralism is a body of theory that acts as a resistance to the solidity and surety of the structural movement, or the belief that underneath everything there is a complex and ordered system, not unlike DNA, that controls and directs meaning and operations. Poststructuralism disrupts structuralism's commitment to a world that can be analysed, classified, and mapped. Postructuralism is concerned with the continuous construction of meaning through language and with the constantly fluid, shifting, and political ways in which meaning, identity and power are created (see Dreyfus & Rabinow, 1982).

Postfoundational Approaches

Poststructuralism is one of the many postfoundational theories that gained prominence in the mid to late 20th century. Like other postfoundational approaches such as postcolonialism and postmodernism, the poststructuralist turn interrogates and expresses a disenchantment with the sureties of modernism, universality and a singular truth. In general, the preoccupation with these postfoundational theories reveals a quest for the unknown, a desire to map out the uncharted as opposed to the charted. Although it is not uncommon for researchers to conflate all these postfoundational terms, each is slightly different in its preoccupations and interests: postcolonialism with race, diaspora, and colonization; postmodernism with the metanarrative and the universal truth; and poststructuralism with meaning, discourse, and power. Yet, these descriptors are in themselves problematic since they perpetuate stereotypic readings of each body of thought. Not all poststructuralists, for instance, are concerned with all of power, discourse and meaning.

Poststructuralism exists in many strands and forms, influenced by writers such as Derrida, Lacan, and Foucault. Within adult education, Foucauldian poststructuralism seems to have become the most influential strand (see Brookfield, 2001; Chapman, 2003). Some of the key concepts within this frame are power, discourse, and knowledge (see Foucault, 1988).

Themes in Foucauldian Poststructuralism

Foucauldian poststructuralism challenges any notion of a sovereign, omnipresent power, or an overriding power structure. It offers instead the notion of disciplinary power, which is power embedded in the complex web of relationships and discourses that surround us. This power is exercised in all our interactions with each other. Applied to adult education, this disciplinary power challenges the notion that educators can empower anyone since learners and educators all hold and exercise power in different ways; that is, they use technologies or practices of power such as the learning circle and learning journal to produce effects. This power is capillary, working its way through systems of human interaction and language (Hughes, 2000).

Foucauldian poststructuralism challenges universalisms or regimes of truth, the unwritten laws that govern or operate within adult education. For instance, within women's learning there is a regime of truth that women are relational, empathetic, and caring. Poststructuralism serves as a challenge to these stereotypic and essentialist readings and troubles the notion that women's learning is indeed a unified body of knowledge. Like all knowledge, women's learning is a shifting, multivalent entity. Only some women are heard and some experience is valued, even in the most egalitarian teaching space. Likewise, all knowledge and experience is partial and is ever being produced through discourse.

A key idea in poststructuralism is that there is resistance to the exercises or technologies of power such as facilitation, learning circles and learning journals. We can resist, for instance, reproducing the teacher's knowledge by creating our own. We can resist the adult educationist's use of the teaching circle by being silent. We can resist the reflexive practice of journal writing by challenging it verbally and making visible that it can be problematic and invasive. The resistancies can be written or verbal. Brookfield (2001) points to the circle as a technology of power within adult education, since it produces the effect of self-surveillance or the controlling of speech and action because of fear of who might be watching us. As well, technologies of power such as the encouragement of sharing experience learning, learner reflexivity, and even the seemingly innocuous practice of journal writing come under close scrutiny in poststructuralism because of their confessional nature. They are ways of letting the adult educator know what is in the learners' mind, turning the classroom into a confessional (see Howley & Hartnett, 1992).

Resistance to Poststructuralism

Yet, for all that, poststructuralism, and indeed many postfoundational approaches, are contested, especially by Marxist feminists who see in poststructuralism a challenge to gains made by feminists towards solidarity, truth, and the sovereignty of experience. The uncertainty that marks poststructuralism challenges Marxist notions of the evils of capitalism and the ever present and oppressive power regimes. Poststructuralism makes the identification of the enemy much more difficult and harder to rage against.

Poststructuralism is not a solution; it is a lens that challenges the given, that interrogates assumptions, and that destabilizes what we believe to be true. Its goal is to create a discursive space for knowledge to be produced.

See also: knowledge, philosophy, postcolonialism, postmodernism, power.

References and Further Reading

Brookfield, S. D. (2001). Unmasking power: Foucault and adult learning. *Canadian Journal for the Study of Adult Education, 15*(1), 1–23.

Chapman, V-L. (2003). On "knowing one's self" selfwriting, power, and ethical practice: Reflections from an adult educator. *Studies in the Education of Adults, 35*(1), 35–53.

Dreyfus, H., & Rabinow, P. (1982). *Michel Foucault: Beyond structuralism and hermeneutics. With an afterword by*

Michel Foucault. Chicago: University of Chicago Press.

Foucault, M. (1988). *Politics philosophy culture: Interviews and other writings 1977–1984*. New York: Routledge.

Howley, A., & Hartnett, R. (1992). Pastoral power and the contemporary university: A Foucauldian analysis. *Educational Theory*, *42*(3), 271–283.

Hughes, C. (2000). Resistant adult learners: A contradiction in terms. *Studies in the Education of Adults*, *32*(1), 51–62.

Leona M. English

Power

Definitions of power range from a view of power as brute force, through debates about individual versus structural capacities, to power as a complex social force that exists in, and produces, imbricated networks of shifting and contested relationships. Surprisingly, although adult educators have long recognized power's existence, only recently have they begun to examine how its various manifestations influence their practices. For example, they now explore such questions as: Who benefits from the ways in which adult education is organized? Whose knowledge and ways of knowing are considered legitimate? How does power affect the relationships between educational theories, policies, and practices and the larger society? How is power constituted and how do we think about and change it? (Cervero & Wilson, 2001; Collins, 1991; Forester, 1989).

Power is one of the fundamental realities of human experience, so understanding how it operates is crucial for educational theory and practice. Yet, power and power relationships, although tangibly experienced, are much more difficult to conceptualize and analyse. Indeed, providing one single definition of power without acknowledging the many, and often competing, traditions that have shaped its meaning is next to impossible.

History and Concepts of Power

Historically, the development of the concept of power is marked by several significant shifts. Most early theorists came from a political science orientation, and tended to limit their theories of power to the sphere of politics, disregarding the roles that power can play within the different domains of social life. For example, one of the first aspects of power identified by John Stuart Mill (1859) consisted of two basic inclinations: the desire to exercise power over others, and not to have power exercised over oneself. At this time, a primary goal in political and social theory was to enhance human rights, justice, and democracy. Extending the rights of people was regarded as an enduring principle of human progress and the judicious use of power viewed as the vehicle through which such progress would occur.

With the development of the social sciences in the late 19th century, the overarching concern shifted more to examining the nature of social reality and exploring, understanding, and interpreting how the interplay of various social structures, institutions, practices, and behaviors supports or hinders these fundamental human rights and justice goals. As one contemporary has claimed, "the concept of power plays a fundamental role in describing and evaluating social inequities. Just as the concept of justice plays a significant role in legitimating social institutions, the concept of power plays a fundamental role in their critique" (Wartenberg, 1990, p. 4). By claiming that many of the relationships within society are power relationships, this view acknowledges the existence of hierarchical and typically exploitative relations within society.

The 20th century saw a steady development of the concept of power in social and political theory. Among others, Norbert Elias, Michel Foucault, Anthony Giddens, Henri Lefebvre, Jürgen Habermas, Stephen Lukes, and Raymond Williams have taken some of the early conceptual work of Emile Durkheim, Karl Marx, and Max Weber to further explore the concept of power in society. Others (such as Theodor Adorno, Louis Althusser, Michael Apple, Basil Bernstein, Pierre Bourdieu, Paulo Freire, and Antonio Gramsci) have specifically elaborated theoretical frameworks linking knowledge, power, and education. Of late, other writers (such as Seyla Benhabib, Richard Delgado, Nancy Fraser, David Harvey, Julia Kristeva, Edward Said, and Susan Talburt) have identified how much of the major theorizing on power is gender and racially sanitized and have promoted more divergent and conflicting views.

This rich development reveals four broad interpretive traditions: agentic, structuralist, an integration of agency and structuralism, and a social process tradition. Most discussions of power focus on the relative importance of either human agency or more structural aspects on influencing behavior. In North America, the agentic tradition is by far the most popular because it appeals to everyday and individual "common-sense" experiences of power in social contexts. In this view, power is viewed as the ability of a person or group (an "agent") to make others do whatever the first wants through either the exercise or potential to exercise force. The agentic view is challenged by another, more structural, approach in which power is understood as a supra-individual and irreducible force that better explains and determines behaviors. In this view, power operates unseen and unacknowledged "behind the actor's back" to influence people and their activities. For example, social forces such as class, race, and gender largely determine peoples' actions and thoughts. More recently, efforts have been made to understand power using social constructionist insights that integrate agency and structure and reveal power more as a social process. One prime example is the so-called "three faces of power debate" (Lukes, 1974) which introduces the notion of social construction into the analysis of power. Here, power is described as being both produced and exercised by people in specific social contexts. This view is best represented by the work of Anthony Giddens, whose 1984 structuration theory explains how people, through their participation in social practices, both produce outcomes as well as reproduce their capacities (i.e., power) to act in specific social relations. Finally, power is seen as a productive social process rather than a preexisting agentic or structuralist force, quality, or condition. The chief architect of this approach is Michel Foucault (1980), for whom power as such is neither a "thing" nor a quality, capacity, or possession of particular people. Rather, it only takes shape through the joint agency of all those who participate in a given set of social relations. Foucault's approach challenges the totalizing approaches of other traditions: "it neither falsely subjectivizes power nor falsely elides agency" (Winter, 1996, p. 728). The operation of power is, for Foucault, an all-pervasive process from which no one escapes and in which everyone participates. Thus, because power is constructed in and through social interactions, it is always alterable and vulnerable to disruption. Herein lies the importance of this approach for adult educators: because power can be changed–often by non-violent means–it helps create the possibility of empowerment.

Power in Adult Education

Adult education tends to view itself as an essentially practical endeavor, so it is not surprising its discussions of power concern practical manifestations rather than theoretical statements. Those practical discussions represent three distillate traditions emanating from the broader movements discussed in the previous section: "the political is personal," "the political is practical," and "the political is structural" (Cervero & Wilson, 2001). The first tradition is grounded in humanistic notions about the development of self-actualizing individuals. Here, developmental adult learning – whether andragogical, critical thinking, or transformational – is the chief concern of a dedicated cadre of caring, skilled facilitators. By focusing on the individual adult learner, organizations and society improve because adult educators are helping individual adult learners change. Because of its focus on the individual learner, the political is only personal and not believed to influence educational practice. This view sees adult learning as ideologically neutral in which good intentions go far in making a better world. Because all learning has ideological consequences and because there are no "generic" adult learners, this non-view is non-sustainable in educational theory or practice.

A second tradition (the political as practical), sees power as "the ability to get things done" in an organizational setting. This view understands that power relations influence our practical action but takes those relationships as acceptable in order to concentrate on "satisficing," "making do," and "getting by." Thus, in this view, practitioners are keenly aware of power but focus their attention on the "how to" of getting things done by acting "politically" in organizational contexts rather than asking "what for" questions of what power is, how power works, and for whom. While the view has an understanding of and practical orientation to power, it fails to understand power as characterizing adult education's relationships with, participation in, and reproduction of wider but typically inequitable systems of power (such as those structured by class, race, gender, sexual orientation). Whereas developmental and humanistic adult educators have an interest in adult learners, the practical view lacks any specific social vision of whose interests adult educators should serve other than attention to individual educators' own idiosyncratic interests.

The third tradition (the political as structural), explicitly calls for and works towards a redistribution of power through the practice of adult education. This view recognizes that socially-structured power relations routinely advantage certain social groups while disadvantaging others, and sees as a clear social agenda the redistribution of power, particularly to those who are oppressed by socially-structured economic, gender, racial, and cultural power relations. In this tradition, adult learners have a "face" and adult educators are charged politically and ethically to foster dialogue, democracy, individual and group freedom, and social justice. Whereas this tradition represents a specific politics of adult education with clear social change goals, its understandings of power itself tend to remain traditionalist and inchoate.

Practical and Theoretical Concerns

In general, too many adult educators ignore or downplay issues of power in their own practice. Further, those who do acknowledge its influence still rely upon "folk" theories of power. For example, it is routine to see invocations of "power over" (the force model) counterposed by the allegedly "better," that is, more collaborative model of "power with." Such naïve views are largely unhelpful for understanding or acting in the nuanced social interactions of educational work. Other adult educators are keenly aware of the existence and influence of power in adult education work, yet refrain from or choose not to articulate their theories of power, apparently assuming power is recognizably easy to understand. Recently, however, some analyses of adult learning, adult education history, and adult education program-planning have included or focused on various interpretations of power. Given that the question of power has been pervasive in social theory since the late 19th century, it is some wonder why adult educators continue unable to recognize power as a central dynamic to their work (Wilson & Cervero, 2002).

It is clear that, overall, the discipline has taken little advantage of available theoretical analyses or been reluctant to make much conceptual contribution itself. In our view, without establishing a working analysis of power as a fundamental constituent of adult education practice, that practice will remain impoverished. Despite myriad good intentions, adult educators without explicit analyses of, and responses to, issues of power become unwittingly compliant in the reproduction of dominant and often repressive power regimes.

See also: class, critical theory, gender, knowledge, philosophy.

References and Further Reading

Cervero, R. M., & Wilson, A. L. (Eds.). (2001). *Power in practice.* San Francisco, Jossey-Bass.

Collins, M. (1991). *Adult education as vocation.* London: Routledge.

Forester, J. (1989). *Planning in the face of power.* Berkeley: University of California Press.

Foucault, M. (1980). *Power/knowledge.* New York: Pantheon Books.

Giddens, A. (1984). *The constitution of society: Outline of the theory of structuration.* Berkeley: University of California Press.

Lukes, S. (1974). *Power, a radical view.* New York: Macmillan.

Mill, J. S. (1859). *On liberty.* London: Parker.

Wartenberg, T. E. (1990). The forms of power. Philadelphia, PA: Temple University Press.

Wilson, A. L., & Cervero, R. M. (2002). The question of power in practice (pp. 209–226). In K. Kunzel (Ed.), *International Yearbook of Adult Education,* 30.

Winter, S. L. (1996). The "power" thing. *Virginia Law Review, 82*(5), 721–835.

Tom Nesbit and Arthur L. Wilson

Practical Intelligence

The term practical intelligence has been used to draw attention to the importance of practical thinking – thinking which has a "real-life" end in mind: it seeks to do, to move, to achieve something outside of itself, and works towards that purpose. As Sternberg et al. (2000) explain, "Practical intelligence is what most people call commonsense. It is the ability to adapt, shape, and select everyday environments" (p. xi). The terminology used to describe practical or non-academic intelligence emphasizes practice as opposed to theory, direct usefulness as opposed to intellectual curiosity, procedural usefulness as opposed to abstract knowledge, and commonplace, everyday action or thought which has immediate, visible consequences.

Context

Historically the interest in practical intelligence can be seen as a reaction to the abstract and decontextualized nature of traditional tests of intelligence with their well-documented limitations, including the cultural relativity of IQ items and the poor predictive value of IQ tests for everyday performance. It is closely related to concepts such as tacit knowledge, expertise and wisdom. Tacit knowledge can be seen as an important component of practical intelligence, and practical intelligence can be seen as underpinning the development of expertise and ultimately wisdom. In the development of cognitive psychology there has been growing awareness of the need to take into account the complexities of context in order to understand the functioning of thinking in situ. Thus there has been a general move away from identifying abstract, decontexualized cognitive attributes separated from meaningful action in the world towards a more inclusive understanding of cognition as it operates through engagement in everyday life. It fits well with the everyday observation that there are persons who are not, in conventional terms, academically successful or considered "intelligent," yet are quite capable of operating effectively in the world.

Research

In the literature on practical intelligence and expertise there is a shared presupposition that expertise is built upon the knowledge and skill gained through sustained practice and experience. In all instances there is an interest in documenting the performance capabilities or qualities of the expert or skilled practical thinker. Not surprisingly the most common technique is to contrast the performance of experts with those of novices with a view to developing a model of the nature of expertise and practical intelligence. Studies have sampled a range of professions, trades and skills such as waiting, canoe-building, the magistrates' bench or chess-playing, or particular functions such as decision-making and problem-solving in everyday milieus.

One of the early attempts to systematically study real-life, practical thinking was undertaken by Sylvia Scribner (1986). The Milk Factory studies, so named because they were situated in a large milk product factory in the United States, have generated great interest over the years and in a variety of circles including cognitive psychology, education and adult education.

Scribner's studies resulted in a challenging formulation of thought in context, in which skilled practical thinking is characterized by its flexibility (solving the same problem in different ways yet with each way finely fitted to the particular occasion on hand), fine-tuning to the environment (aspects of the environment, be they people, things or information, are drawn into problem-solving), economy (where least-effort strategies are used), a dependency on setting specific knowledge, and the capacity to formulate problems (rather than solve given problems)

Another early work is that of Ceci and Liker (1986), who in their study of racetrack handicapping found that there was no correlation between successful handicapping (that is, the ability to predict probable favorites) and IQ (Wechsler Adult Intelligence Scale). They make a compelling case for their conclusion that racetrack handicapping is as intellectually demanding as the decision-making apparent among established professions such as science, law and banking. The finding that there was no correlation with this ability and IQ is interpreted as evidence that IQ should not be generalized to non-academic tasks and contexts.

Subsequent work on practical intelligence is well-documented in Sternberg et al.'s (2000) *Practical Intelligence in Everyday Life* that includes studies on the domain-specificity of practical intelligence, tacit knowledge, practical problem-solving, ageing and practical intelligence, and approaches to studying and measuring practical intelligence.

Relevance for Adult and Continuing Education

It is important for adult educators to know as much as possible about the nature and development of expertise, practical thinking and implicit knowledge. In all studies contrasting experts with novices, a consistent funding is that there is a distinct qualitative difference in the ways they function. The implication is that this qualitative shift is an important feature in the acquisition of expertise. Clearly, one cannot be an expert without first being a novice, and as adult educators perhaps we should be as much concerned with teaching people to be novices as we are with teaching people to be experts. Having said this, it is equally important to know the process which makes possible the progression from novice to expert. We can begin to map the way in which experts, as opposed to non-experts, utilize their experiences for learning. In this regard the theoretical and empirical work on situated learning may be useful. As educators, however, we are concerned with how experience is used to become "expert."

See also: cognition, multiple intelligences, practitioner

References and Further Reading

Ceci, S., & Liker, J. (1986). Academic and non-academic intelligence: An experimental separation. In R. J. Sternberg & R. Wagner (Eds.), *Practical intelligence: Nature and origins of competence* (pp. 119–142). Cambridge, UK: Cambridge University Press.

Scribner, S. (1986). Thinking in action: Some characteristics of practical thought. In R. J. Sternberg & R. Wagner (Eds.), *Practical intelligence: Nature and origins of competence* (pp. 13–30). Cambridge, UK: Cambridge University Press.

Sternberg, R., Forsythe, G., Hedlund, J., Horvath, J., Wagner, R., Williams, W., Snook., & Grigorenko, E. (2000). *Practical intelligence in everyday life*. Cambridge, UK: Cambridge University Press.

Tennant, M. C., & Pogson, P. (1995). *Learning and change in the adult years: A developmental perspective.* San Francisco: Jossey-Bass.

Mark Tennant

Practitioner

Practitioner is a term generally used to refer to adult educators in communities of practice as diverse as international adult education, community development, higher education and literacy. The term practitioner is often and erroneously used in contrast to theorist and researcher, both of which are seen to be more intellectually demanding and rigorous pursuits in adult education. However, the implied hierarchy in the terms is increasingly contested (Jarvis, 1999), with attempts being made to find the interconnections between and among them. This is especially true in light of the growing number of practitioners who are using research to inform their practice, especially action research and participatory action research, which are also referred to broadly as practitioner inquiry (Quigley & Kuhne, 1997). Quigley and Kuhne's observation that practitioners do not publish is also changing.

Contemporary Notions of Practice and Practitioner

A considerable group of educators have addressed the relationship of theory and practice by developing models such as that of the intuitive practitioner (Atkinson & Claxton, 2000), the open space practitioner (Owen, 1992), the deliberative practitioner (Forester, 1999), the reflective practitioner (Schön, 1983), and the contemplative practitioner (Miller, 1994). Of these, the most influential is Schön's reflective practitioner, which honors the intuitive, professional know-how that effective professionals evidence in their ability to handle the complex and unpredictable challenges of real-life practice with confidence and skill. According to Schön (1987), professional education programs can be redesigned to foster such capabilities in future professionals. Yet, Schön's focus remains on the how-to of professionalism, and the end result is the creation of yet new dualisms between those who have the ability to use reflection on/in action and those who do not (instrumentalists) (see Ferry & Ross-Gordon, 1998). Furthermore, Schön's focus is on solving crises and problems in the workplace, rather than offering creative alternatives and new epistemologies of practice. Little if any attention is paid to the socio-political context in which the practice takes place.

The Theory–Practice Divide

Jarvis (1999) notes that the typical model of learning theories and then practicing them, is limited. In professional work, the trajectory often begins with the learning of theory, which is then practiced, resulting in the building of new theory. Increasingly, he notes, we need to recognize that practitioners develop their own personal theory or knowledge, and that no matter what they learn in academic settings in professional programs does not become practical knowledge until they implement and test it.

Jarvis (1999) uses the term practitioner-researcher to denote those professionals and practitioners who use research as a way to improve practice. This practitioner-researcher is common in many aspects of adult education, and the implications for teaching and learning are significant. Practitioner-researchers need to engage in continuous learning and those who prepare professionals for this role in their community of practice need to be flexible enough to incorporate methodologies that are more suited for workplaces than academic centers. These methodologies include action research, which Carr and Kemmis (1985) see as a way to improve and understand practices and situations in which people work.

Theoretical Underpinnings and Cautions

Building on the work of Noffke (1995), Jacobson (1998) notes that the construct of practitioner as researcher is simultaneously based on the critical and the constructivist paradigms. Although both paradigms acknowledge the social construction of meaning, the critical in particular draws attention to the power-laden social context in which this practical knowledge is constructed. A critical approach would encourage the recognition and the analysis of power relationships, and the critique of the researchers' role in the research process, as well as the context in which the knowledge is produced.

Usher, Bryant and Johnston (1997) make a related case. They build on the unpublished work of David Kemmis to point to the relationship of theory and practice as being embedded in a social context and process. This social relationship raises the issue of power in practice and points to the complex and complicated ways in which practice is necessarily enacted. Attention to the situatedness of theory and practice moves adult educators away from dualisms and helps situate the discussion in its larger context.

The inherent danger, however, in stressing the value of practice or experience in the practitioner role, is in overvaluing it to the point where theory or theoretical concepts no longer count. Brookfield (1996) points out that experience can teach bigotry and stereotypes, and that theory can help us understand our experiences and name aspects of them. He also notes that theory can help put us in connection with others doing similar work, or expose us to alternative thinking.

An Alternative Practitioner

Third-space practitioners (English, 2004; 2005) serve as a critique to models that are mostly practice-driven and generally silent on the interconnections of theory and practice. The term third space is found in Bhabha's (1994) cultural studies work and is used here to refer to those in-between spaces or marginal places in which there is a fluid movement between the roles of adult educator, researcher, practitioner, or theorist. This third-space practitioner places all these elements into their adult education in a way that incorporates politics, practice, and power, and transcends polarization between theory and practice.

The third-space practitioner is focused on the interconnectedness of ideas but not on consensus. For him or her, contradictions between theory and practice are the new epistemological terrain. Living and practicing in the in-between or hybrid spaces, the practical and the research-oriented, this third-space practitioner refuses to be limited in any way. S/he en/acts hybridity, which is described by Bhabha (1990) as being "precisely about the fact that when a new situation, a new alliance formulates itself, it may demand that you should translate your principles, rethink them, extend them" (p. 216).

See also: action research, identity, postcolonialism, practical intelligence, reflective practice, theory.

References and Further Reading

Atkinson, T., & Claxton, G. (Eds.) (2000). *The intuitive practitioner: On the value of not always knowing what one is doing.* Philadelphia, PA: Open University Press.

Bhabha, H. K. (1990). The third space: Interview with Homi Bhabha. In J. Rutherford (Ed.), *Identity: Community, culture, difference* (pp. 207–221). London: Lawrence & Wishart.

Bhabha, H. K. (1994). *The location of culture.* New York: Routledge.

Brookfield, S. D. (1996). Helping people learn what they do. In D. Boud & N. Miller (Eds.), *Working with experience: Animating learning.* London: Routledge.

Carr, D., & Kemmis, S. (1985). *Becoming critical: Education knowledge and action research.* London: Falmer Press.

English, L. M. (2003). Identity, hybridity, and third space: Complicating the lives of international adult educators. *Convergence, 36*(2), 67–80.

English, L. M. (2004). Third space practice: An alternative practice of adult education. *New Zealand Journal of Adult Learning, 32*(1), 5–17.

English, L. M. (2005). Third-space practitioners: Women educating for justice in the Global South, *Adult Education Quarterly* 55(2), 85–100.

Ferry, N. M., & Ross-Gordon, J. M. (1998). An inquiry into Schön's epistemology of practice: Exploring links between experience and reflective practice. *Adult Education Quarterly, 48*(2), 98–112.

Forester, J. (1999). *The deliberative practitioner: Encouraging participatory planning processes.* Cambridge, MA.: Massachusetts Institute of Technology Press.

Jacobson, W. (1998). Defining the quality of practitioner research. *Adult Education Quarterly, 48*(3), 125–138.

Jarvis, P. (1999). *The practitioner-researcher: Developing theory from practice.* San Francisco: Jossey-Bass.

Miller, J. P. (1994). *The contemplative practitioner.* Westport, CT: Bergin & Garvey.

Noffke, S. (1995). Action research and democratic schooling: Problematics and potentials. In S. Noffke & R. Stevenson (Eds.), *Educational action research: Becoming practically critical* (pp. 1–10). New York: Teachers College Press.

Owen, H. (1992). *Open space technology: A user's guide.* Potomac, MD: Abbott Publishing.

Quigley, B. A., & Kuhne, G. W. (Eds.). (1997). *Creating practical knowledge through action research: Posing problems, solving problems, and improving daily practice* (pp. 3–22). *New Directions for Adult and Continuing Education,* No. 73. San Francisco: Jossey-Bass.

Schön, D. A. (1983). *The reflective practitioner: How professionals think in action.* New York: Basic Books.

Schön, D. A. (1987). *Educating the reflective practitioner: Toward a new design for teaching and learning in the professions.* San Francisco: Jossey-Bass.

Usher, R., Bryant, I., & Johnston, R. (1997). Reconceptualizing theory and practice. In *Adult education and the postmodern challenge* (pp. 122–241). London: Routledge.

Leona M. English

Praxis

Praxis describes the constant interplay of action and reflection, particularly in radically and critically oriented forms of community animation and political activism. Associated with the work of Paulo Freire (1970), praxis informs his much quoted view that action without reflection is mindless activism and reflection without action is verbalism leading only to political quietude. For Freire, praxis is tied to transforming the world. In more scholarly terms praxis is defined as the necessary conjoining of theory and practice, so that theory is seen as both arising within practice while simultaneously informing practice.

Although not explored explicitly by Freire, this exploration of the conjoined theory/practice relationship sometimes exhibits a postmodern tinge in its emphasis on the need for theorizing to be located in specific contexts and locations. In contrast to postmodernism, however, praxis is explicitly transformative and geared to promoting leftist social and political change.

Cooptation of Praxis

There has been something of a coopting of the term within the field of adult education. Just as words such as "empowerment" or "critical" have been torn from the soil of critical theory, so praxis is sometimes a deracinated concept. It is not uncommon to hear praxis spoken of as a methodological orientation involving the integration of reflection and action that can be applied across disciplinary and practice contexts. From this viewpoint praxis is a methodology that can be applied to organizing an executive retreat in which marketing managers are reflecting on the actions they have taken to promote a new clothing line to a particular niche audience. The purpose of such focused reflection is to determine the next steps in the process of keeping production costs down and profit margins as high as possible by selling the maximum number of units. When praxis is conceived of merely as purposeful reflection to improve the effectiveness of action then its origins in revolutionary political movements are erased from the collective professional memory of the field.

Allman (2001) critiques the coopting of praxis and locates it in Marx's theory of consciousness. Allman emphasizes that praxis is a dialectical unity of thought and action rather than a sequence of action, followed by reflection followed by further action, followed by further reflection and so on. She also distinguishes between critical and uncritical praxis. Uncritical praxis is purposeful reflection that leaves dominant capitalist ideology unchallenged. Critical, or revolutionary, praxis questions existing structures and ideology and seeks to transform them through social and political change. In terms of adult educational processes, praxis is seen in the dialectical unity of teaching and learning. Allman and Wallis (1990) argue that a group of adults engaged in praxis are struggling together to change teaching–learning relations in the classroom so that "these two roles, teaching and learning, are held simultaneously by all participants" (p. 23). This requires adult educators to problematize their own practice and not to assume that only they, and not adult learners, clearly perceive the dynamics of oppression.

Engaging With Praxis

Several models for how adult educators might engage in critical praxis are provided by figures in the critical tradition. Foucault (1980) proposes the idea of specific intellectuals who work in specific sites to illuminate the mechanisms and strategies that those in power use to maintain existing systems. One role of intellectuals is to provide instruments of analysis that will help others locate lines of weakness and strength in power configurations. Foucault hoped that intellectuals would produce a topographical and geographical survey of the battlefield comprising power relations. For him any analysis of power that theorists undertake should be understood as an act of solidarity with those who struggle against it, a contribution to a some kind of specific social, cultural or political intervention. So, instead of working on behalf of humanity, the working class, women, the oppressed, non-Whites or any other massive social construct, educators could more fruitfully direct their energies towards specific projects. In Foucault's view educational reforms, teaching practices, housing policies, psychiatric protocols, and prison organization all offered opportunities for intellectuals to intervene in ways that contravened dominant power.

In describing this kind of praxis, Foucault comes close to invoking Gramsci's (1971) notion of organic intellectuals as educators, persuaders and activists working within specific social movements of which they are members. When Gramsci used the word "intellectuals" he was not using it colloquially to refer to a group of sophisticated thinkers intimately familiar with multiple literatures and supposedly operating at a higher theoretical level than the rest of us. For him intellectual work was praxis conducted on behalf of either the oppressor or the oppressed. Intellectuals were organizers, persuaders and opinion leaders who worked either to reproduce dominant ideology or to bring the masses to critical consciousness and organize their political struggle. The dominant group's intellectuals were deputies or subalterns charged with maintaining that group's dominance by working in the institutions of civil society (schools, churches, community associations, and so on) to ensure that the dominant group's conception of the world remained the accepted view of reality. Contrasted to these dominant intellectuals who were primarily concerned with ideological transmission and manipulation was a revolutionary group of intellectuals, organic intellectuals.

Organic intellectuals were elites of a new type who arose directly out of the masses but remained in contact with them. Their praxis focused on formulating and communicating a strategy for political revolution in terms that the working class could understand. The end result of this praxis would be the establishment of a new hegemony reflective of working-class interests. To Gramsci such praxis was especially crucial to the awakening of revolutionary fervor. Organic intellectuals have the responsibility to help people understand the need to contest hegemony. To do this intellectuals need a capacity for empathic identification with how it feels to be oppressed.

In his adumbration of the adult educator as organic intellectual, Gramsci (1971) clearly operated from a very different conception than that of the adult educator as facilitator. To him the job of an organic intellectual was to "organize human masses and create the terrain on which men move, acquire consciousness of their position, struggle etc." (p. 377). There is no pretence at neutrality or objectivity here, no compulsion to see the oppressor's point of view. Praxis entails galvanizing working class opposition with adult education as a site for counter-hegemony in which organic intellectuals can assist the working class in its revolutionary struggle. Gramsci's expression of praxis has been acknowledged as influential by people as different as the Welsh cultural critical Raymond Williams (1977), the African-American philosopher Cornel West (1982) – who views Black pastors and preachers as organic intellectuals – the British Caribbean cultural theorist Stuart Hall (Hall, Gilroy, Grossberg, & McRobbie, 2000), and the aboriginal educator Rick Hesch (1995).

West peppers his works with approving references to Gramsci, describing himself as a Gramscian Marxist and calling Gramsci the most penetrating Marxist theorist of culture in this century. Explaining his affinity to Gramsci, he explains that Gramsci's praxis always places stress on historical specificity, on concrete circumstances and situations. West is drawn to Gramsci's (and later Raymond Williams) idea that hegemony is always contested and open to being undermined by specific actions taken in specific situations. He is drawn also to Gramsci's emphasis on cultural praxis, on using theater, journalism, popular novels (and in contemporary terms films, books, rap music CD's) as vehicles of counter-hegemony (West himself has produced a rap CD). In particular, West refers repeatedly to Gramsci's idea of the organic intellectual as a useful descriptor both for his own work and for the work of critical Black intellectuals in general. In his view Black intellectual praxis is grounded in the concrete experiences and struggles of the African American community while being simultaneously informed by the theoretical wisdom of allies outside that racial group. Such groups include activists of color, feminists, lesbians and gays, Black churches, ecological movements and rank-and-file labor caucuses, and black nationalists. West is clear on the need for critical praxis to be applied to African Americans' philosophizing and organizing and is critical of overly charismatic activists who leave no organizational or community structures in the communities they visit.

An African American Perspective

A specifically African American elaboration of praxis is provided by Angela Davis. Since Davis believes that liberation is not possible without education, it was only natural that she should become a scholar-activist. One of her earliest involvements was in the Liberation School organized by the Los Angeles branch of the Student Non-Violent Coordinating Committee. In her autobiography (Davis, 1974) she describes this as a place where political understanding was forged and sharpened, where consciousness became explicit and was urged in a revolutionary direction. The belief that education is an inherently political praxis has informed all her later work. To her, education as praxis gives people the tools to critique capitalism, penetrate ideology, and help them realize that their individual situations can only be improved if they build alliances across race and gender identities. Transformative education can never be an individual process in Davis' view, and neither can it be successful if it is restricted to a particular group. Over and over again she emphasizes praxis as a collective struggle for social transformation.

At the heart of Davis' praxis is the idea that we "lift as we climb," the motto of the National Association of Colored Women's Clubs (founded in 1896). To "lift as we climb" is to ensure that "we must climb in such a way as to guarantee that all of our sisters, regardless of social class, and indeed all of our brothers, climb with us" (Davis, 1990, p. 5). This effort to build a social movement across lines of race and gender, rather than one based on a single racial or gender identity, is for Davis "the essential dynamic of our quest for power – a principle that must not only determine our struggles as Afro-American women, but also govern all authentic struggles of dispossessed people" (p. 5). One of the most important dimensions of this praxis is the building of a revolutionary, multiracial women's movement that seriously addresses the main issues affecting poor and working-class women. Such a movement would involve Latina, Asian and also White women. Davis clearly sets out her belief that membership of a movement for struggle on behalf of one group is open to people of all groups, not just those immediately affected by an act of dispossession.

Adult educators who use the term praxis to refer to the interplay of action and reflection need to be aware of its origins in Marxism and critical theory and of its call for social and political transformation. From this perspective to be engaged in praxis is to be working to create a qualitatively different form of society, one entailing "the struggle to transform simultaneously not just the socioeconomic and political conditions of our existence but also ourselves" (Allman, 2001, p. 168).

See also: class, conscientization, critical theory, ideology, problematizing learning, social movements.

References and Further Reading

Allman, P. (2001). *Critical education against global capitalism: Karl Marx and revolutionary critical education*. Westport, CT: Bergin & Garvey.

Allman, P., & Wallis, J. (1990). Praxis: Implications for really radical education. *Studies in the Education of Adults*, 22(1), 14–30.

Davis, A. Y. (1974). *Angela Davis: An autobiography*. New York: International Publishers.

Davis, A. Y. (1990). *Women, culture, and politics*. New York: Vintage Books.

Foucault, M. (1980). *Power/knowledge: Selected interviews and other writings, 1972–1977*. New York: Pantheon Books.

Freire, P. (1970). *Pedagogy of the oppressed*. (M. B. Ramos, Trans.). New York: Continuum.

Gramsci, A. (1971). *Selections from the prison notebooks*. (Eds. Q. Hoare & G.N. Smith). London: Lawrence & Wishart.

Hall, S., Gilroy, P., Grossberg, L., & McRobbie, A. (Eds.). (2000). *Without guarantees: Essays in honour of Stuart Hall*. London: Verso.

Hesch, R. (1995). Aboriginal teachers as organic intellectuals. In R. Ng, P. Staton, & J. Scane (Eds.), *Anti-racism, feminism, and critical approaches to education* (pp. 99–128). Westport, CT: Bergin & Garvey.

West, C. (1982). *Prophesy deliverance: An Afro-American revolutionary Christianity*. Philadelphia, PA: The Westminster Press.

Williams, R. (1977). *Marxism and literature*. New York: Oxford University Press.

Stephen Brookfield

Prior Learning Assessment and Recognition

Prior learning assessment and recognition (PLAR) refers to the evaluation and acknowledgment of learning that occurs outside of *formal* credit-awarding training and educational programs. Increasingly, educational and training institutions are utilizing PLAR as a legitimate method of gaining access to, or credit in, formal credential-bearing programs. Students are demanding that learning at work and in society be recognized within the traditional educational institutions when they seek to make the transition to formal higher education or post-secondary training. Educators are increasingly confronted by the question of how to fairly and accurately use PLAR to assess the educational merit of informal learning and non-formal education.

PLAR is the preferred term in Canada; others include prior learning assessment (PLA); accrediting prior learning/assessing prior learning

(APL); accrediting prior experiential learning/assessing prior experiential learning (APEL); and recognition of prior learning (RPL). Although APL is sometimes reserved for transferring previous course learning, and differentiated from APEL, PLAR will be used in this entry to represent all of these terms. PLAR has become a worldwide "movement" encompassing Australia/New Zealand, Southern Africa, Europe and North America with an established International Consortium for Experiential Learning. It attracts those who see PLAR as important for increasing access for previously disadvantaged groups, but also attracts politicians and business leaders, which suggests they may well view PLAR as a mechanism that will help them turn traditional higher education towards meeting the needs, priorities, and interests of the "real" world, as they see it. Adult educators have always valued student experience in the classroom, and while there is broad support for PLAR for adult students there are concerns about processes, the transferability of knowledge, and dilution of the social, emancipatory purposes of education.

There are a number of ways of assessing prior learning; these include challenge exams, portfolio assessment (the most common), and demonstrations of skills and knowledge. Transfer credit is not included here since this essentially refers to the transferring of credit gained from one institution's courses to courses and programs of another. The essence of PLAR is the recognition of non-course learning gained *experientially*, perhaps as a consequence of volunteer or workplace activities or private self-guided study. PLAR can also include recognizing learning in *non-formal* adult courses and ascribing it credit. There are three basic assumptions behind PLAR: significant learning can and does take place outside the classroom; it should be evaluated for credit by educational institutions and by the workplace for hiring and promotion; and education and training practices that force adults to repeat learning are inefficient, costly and unnecessary (HRDC, 1995, p. 1). The process of completing a portfolio is represented as educational in itself, helping students to reflect on experience, gain confidence and redefine goals (European Commission, 2002). Assessing portfolios is, however, problematic and hinges on the students' writing skills and their ability to translate experience into "learning."

The process of PLAR is most often presented as theoretically unproblematic: the vast majority of research focuses on the technical questions of how to measure learning's worth and also how to persuade traditional educational institutions, and "elitist" academics, to accept PLAR credits (European Commission, 2002; Thomas, 1998). The case for PLAR fits best with technical training programs that have identifiable skills and abilities as the course objectives. *Behavioral* learning theories that emphasize *competencies* or *learning outcomes* best fit with this *instrumental* approach to training. Students are encouraged to match their skills to the course outline and outcomes and claim the credits. PLAR can be useful for workers to demonstrate they have knowledge and skills that are needed for promotions or are applied to "laddered" skills-based job categories (for example in Australia). PLAR meets most opposition as a method of gaining credit within academic programs (particularly non-professional or applied); most courses in traditional academic programs are presented as instrumental since the knowledge areas, theories, and learning processes of critical reading and writing they concentrate on are outside of common discourse. Where PLAR is applicable to these programs, it is often easier to grant generic course credits that match up with the broad program goals than to grant specific course credits – similar to French practice (EC, 2002). (Mature student entry to academic programs has been around for some time and is less contested.)

Learning and Knowledge

Adults learn for a whole variety of reasons and in a complex web of settings – the purposes of such learning may be communal or social as much as personal. PLAR raises the question of whether all adult learning should be viewed in terms of what is measurable, exchangeable, and credit-worthy. For example, Briton, Gereluk and Spencer (1998) have argued that the "use value" of certain knowledge is being confused with its "exchange value," what is very useful in one situation may not be "exchangeable" into course credits. It also "undervalues" experiential learning that cannot be transferred. This is not to claim that one kind of knowledge is superior to the other, but different. When an individual decides they need to know more about a certain topic in order to solve a particular problem at work, they are unlikely to be focused on developing critical reading and writing skills. In most cases they are not going to seek out differing perspectives on a problem and then write an assessment of the arguments. Experiential learning can be useful when undertaking course-based learning, but it may be quite legitimate to argue that the prior learning is sufficiently different that it cannot be credited as if the applicant had undertaken the course of study. In these situations *accelerated* courses suited to mature adults may be most useful (many individualized *distance education* programs allow for student self-pacing).

At the core of many PLAR problems is a central contradiction of formal education that is writ even larger when considering experiential learning. The purpose of education is knowledge exploration and creation – the gaining of insights and understandings (in short: learning) – but the outcome and importance of formal education is increasingly seen as the credential. As a result many learners (and educators) substitute the credential for learning as their central objective. For those seeking PLAR, credit recognition can become the only goal. Instead of using PLAR to focus attention on the gaps in skills or knowledge – what is yet to be learned – the emphasis is placed on finding the fastest route to gain a credential.

PLAR emphasizes specific and generic skills as the "outcomes" of learning rather than the gaining of insights and theoretical understandings around a particular area of knowledge. But the transference gained through PLAR into academic (as opposed to applied) credits is mainly based on what knowledge has been gained. Amongst adult education scholars the usual starting point for a discussion about knowledge is Habermas – for example as used by Mezirow in his theory of perspective transformation. Habermas recognizes the importance of beginning with an empirical-analytic framework and of moving beyond that to transforming and liberating the consciousness – hence the importance of critical social sciences (see Spencer, 1998, pp. 62–68 for a discussion and references). Knowledge exploration is also linked to the distinction between critical thinking skills and critical thought (as promoted in critical theory). Critical thought begins by questioning belief systems and by asking who benefits from dominant ideas: its project is educational *and* emancipatory (Burbules & Berk, 1999). It is very difficult to assess these areas of knowledge through PLAR; for example it may be argued (Briton et al., 1998) that this approach to learning will not usually be gained at work, especially given the narrow practices of our modern-day global corporations that demand loyalty and punish criticism (Klein, 2000).

Adult educators have always acknowledged the importance of adult experience in the classroom (Knowles is just one example), but knowledge gained through experience is not unproblematic. For example, Freire's work has been used to justify PLAR, but this reading of Freire ignores his understanding that experience was a starting place, and could be very limiting, leading to a "culture of silence." His argument is for a dialogical and collective education that results in workers "renaming" the world they occupy and eventually organizing to change it. His concern with self-awareness, action and reflection is similar to feminist scholars' approaches to learning that can also be labeled experientially-based, but not experientially limited (Spencer, 1998, pp. 68–70; 90–92).

However, the academy does not have a stranglehold on what counts as knowledge – women's studies, labor studies, indigenous knowledge, cultural studies and the study of adult education all began life outside of the main halls and cloisters of the established universities. And mainstream education today still downplays or ignores the experience of minority groups in society such that their own learning about whom they are and what place they occupy within the dominant culture is undertaken outside the official curriculum (Kelly, 2004). This illustrates that knowledge originating and gained outside of universities is important. Also, working people are capable of breaking through the workplace ideology designed to coopt their compliance and critical experiential learning or non-formal education is relevant to some programs.

Granting Credit

Credit can be granted on a modular or course-by-course basis or as program credits. Building PLAR into programs can have a significant impact resulting in a program tailored to meet mature student needs. However, any claim for extensive transference of experiential learning into higher education credits needs to be critically examined if it is to gain support of academics, as Hanson (1997) has commented, "rigorous though the technical requirements of PLA may be they are of little help without a clear understanding of what they are measuring against and why" (p. 11). Accelerating an adult student to achieve degree completion may result in them missing out on crucial areas of knowledge. On the other hand, adult students do not have to travel the same road to a degree as a high school leaver; for example adult life experiences may legitimately replace elective courses designed to give breadth for younger students, even if it cannot substitute for core courses.

One of the challenges for PLAR advocates and reluctant academics alike is to overcome the "with us or against us" attitude that pervades debate about PLAR and to engage in critical evaluation of the value and applicability of PLAR in particular programs. While PLAR may emphasize access (dramatically illustrated in post-apartheid South Africa but little evidenced in Europe) and has the potential to shake up traditional teaching, the mainstream promotion of PLAR does little to resuscitate the democratic social purposes of adult education: it has the opposite tendency; it emphasizes the argument that learning is essentially about skills and competencies useful for employment. The challenge for progressive educators is to marry the critical experiential learning that working people do engage in to critical theoretical knowledge within the academy: to recognize experiential knowledge when it is appropriate and build on it when needed.

See also: evaluation, experiential learning, higher education, knowledge, portfolio.

References and Further Reading

Briton, D., Gereluk, W., & Spencer, B. (1998). Prior learning assessment and recognition: Issues for adult educators. In M. Taylor (Ed.), *Canadian Association for the Study of Adult Education (CASAE) Conference Proceedings* (pp. 24–28). Ottawa: University of Ottawa.

Burbules, N., & Berk, R. (1999). Critical thinking and critical pedagogy: Relations, differences, and limits. In T. Popkewitz & L. Fendler (Eds.), *Critical theories in education: Changing terrains of knowledge and politics* (pp. 45–65). New York: Routledge.

European Commission (EC). (2002). *Social inclusion through APEL: A learners' perspective. Comparative report.* Glasgow: Glasgow Caledonian University.

Hanson, K. (1997). A university perspective on PLA. *Learning Quarterly, 1*(3), 10–13.

Human Resource Development, Canada (HRDC) (1995). *Prior Learning Assessment Newsletter, 1*(2). Ottawa, Ontario: HRDC.

Kelly, J. (2004). *Borrowed identities.* New York: Peter Lang.

Klein, N. (2000). *No logo: Taking aim at the brand bullies.* Toronto: Random House.

Spencer, B. (1998). *The purposes of adult education: A guide for students.* Toronto: Thompson Educational.

Thomas, A. M. (1998). The tolerable contradictions of prior learning assessment in S. M. Scott, B. Spencer, & A. M. Thomas (Eds.), *Learning for life: Canadian readings in adult education* (pp. 354–364). Toronto: Thompson Educational.

Bruce Spencer

Prison Education

Education programs in prisons are generally expected to form part of a constructive prison regime that may enable prisoners to live a "good and useful life" beyond release. These programs, called prison education in the UK, and in some cases "corrections" education in Canada and the United States, can offer an opportunity for personal development and growth as well as the acquisition of new skills, new knowledge, new ways of thinking and potentially new ways of behaving. For those involved with prison education programs there are therefore particular expectations on the part of prisoner-students, prison service staff and the general public to "deliver" a diversity of outcomes that may range from "correcting" any social and/or deviant problems that an individual prisoner may have, to providing new knowledge and skills in a particular subject area. However, attempts to meet these complex demands meet with varying degrees of success embedded as they are in global cultural networks also characterized by diversity and contradictory ideologies about the role, purpose and function of the prison (Reuss, 1997, 1999, 2000, 2003).

Education programs in prisons can be underpinned by a wide range of issues in terms of what constitutes their aims and objectives. Is their purpose to educate, to inform, to provide opportunities to acquire transferable skills, enhance knowledge and understanding, develop cognitive skills or assist in the process of addressing, challenging and/or changing offending behavior? Arguably, prison education has the potential to deliver all these things and in some correctional institutions it does, but there are many different agendas to satisfy and it is worth remembering that "prisoner" rather than "prison" education (Germanotta in Davidson, 1995, p. 106) is a more accurate term shifting the focus to the experience of imprisonment for the prisoner and not the prison.

Prisoners or Adult Learners?

Prisoner education is about people learning; more importantly it is about an individual learning something as part of a chosen social process that has been embarked upon for a variety of reasons which may have nothing whatsoever to do with "corrections" or anything else that the prison may culturally represent. The vast majority of prisoners in Westernized societies are from lower social classes, 90% have not finished high school or completed any kind of higher education, and visible minorities are over-represented in the population. Latest figures from the UK show that half of all prisoners have the equivalent reading age of an 11-year-old, or are below, whilst two-thirds of the prison population (approximately 75,000 at the time of writing) possess the numeracy skills of an 11-year-old (or below). The same skill levels apply to writing (Prison Reform Trust, 2004). Similarly, when it comes to the issue of possessing qualifications, more than half of male and more than two-thirds of female adult prisoners have no qualifications at all. Attending education in prison may undoubtedly be simply a strategy for survival in an environment characterized in some cases by "psychological violence" (Garland, 1990) or, sadly, even physical violence, but for those who have access to it in the UK (just under a third at any one time), education can have an impact upon tendencies to reoffend – or not – and on reintegration into the community – or not.

However, prisons *are* about punishment. In some societies they are the highest form of sanction used against offenders, excepting the death penalty, so with the ideology of punishment (that at its most basic is embedded in restraint and deprivation of liberty) and ideologies of education (embracing, among other issues, freedom to learn, and status enhancement) standing in direct opposition to each other, it is difficult to assess the effectiveness of any program of education in prisons. Ostensibly the role of the prison is to "control troublesome individuals" in institutions that can inflict, no matter how much people may believe it to be deserved, real hardship, serious deprivation and personal suffering (Garland, 1990). This is no easy task and it makes teaching in prisons within this type of ideological environment difficult too.

The actual practices and delivery of prisoner education vary depending upon the country in question and its educational policies. In the UK, for example, prison teachers are normally employed by colleges of further education which have been contracted to provide educational services to prisons in a specific geographical location. They may be a lower paid tutor employed by government, and some are volunteers. Any higher education (university level) in the UK is delivered by a form of distance learning from what is known as the Open University, although between 1989 and 1998 there was a project in a maximum security prison where prisoners where taught degree-level sociology and social policy (University of Leeds Full Sutton Project). Sadly this closed due to lack of funding. By contrast, in the United States, in the 1990s, prison higher education was a growing field (Williford, 1994).

Prisoner education programs can impact upon students' attitudes, values, thinking and behavior and can also encourage the development of "effective and socially responsible reasoning, problem-solving and decision-making skills" (Duguid, 1986). As adult learners, prisoners on some courses, just like any other students, can and do develop sufficient social and political awareness to the extent that they are perceived as a "threat" once intellectual power shifts in favor of the offender. But does this matter?

Adult prisoners who attend education courses whilst serving their sentences have a personal history and a wide range of existing beliefs, values, knowledge and life experience that they bring to the prison classroom just as any other student. Prisoners are individuals and so have a range of individual educational needs. In this sense it is difficult to agree a specific "profile" relating to the "adult prisoner-student." Is there a profile? In an ideal educationalist's world, any education which is provided for adults is about the promotion of personal growth and self-esteem, but the sociocultural attitudes attached to the labels "prisoner" and "student" are quite diverse, and those prisoners who do attend courses often display a remarkable talent for "switching between different worlds or realities" – the world of prisoner and the world of the student (Reuss, 1997, 1999) – as they deal with the range of interactions they have to face on a daily basis.

Most adult learners, even in a prison setting, are voluntary learners who *choose* to learn and who intend to achieve some kind of goal. However, the typical program today in UK prisons focuses on "basic skills" learning, i.e. numeracy and literacy skills, in an endeavor for the prison to meet prison-service targets. The goal of the prisoner is much more likely to concern the promotion of personal growth, the "full exploitation of the talents of the individual," or it may be about developing a sense of perspective, fostering self-esteem and so on (Rogers, 1986, p. 7). Achieving this goal is difficult since classroom dynamics are complex in a prison context. The dynamics are compounded by issues of rehabilitation, reform, deterrence, and punishment and this can affect any teaching and learning outcomes that characterize any program. There is a sense, though, in which prisoner education is a continuing process that contributes to the learning that never really stops throughout a person's life-course. It is a part of the process of acquiring knowledge across the span of a lifetime (Elias, 1992, p. 47) and is colored by whatever the circumstances are in which one learns, whether as a prisoner or as an adult learner.

Prisoners *as* Adult Learners

The values and practices inherent in adult education underpin prison education practice with the emphasis in this context very often on the so-called disadvantaged adult. In mainstream adult education, the learning outcomes must be valued in a learning context where ". . . real life situations are made by individual personalities, prevailing and changing political, economic, cultural and social conditions" (Elsey, 1986, p. 12). Nowhere is this more apparent than in the prison classroom of adult learners who are perceived as having needs that would undoubtedly correspond with most of the ideas and values about the role and function of adult education, and more besides. In this sense, prisoner education programs may serve the purpose of providing recreation or leisure, providing work training, or even satisfying the criteria of liberal progressive or radical models of education.

Long-term prisoners are generally perceived as having either challenged or deviated from mainstream norms and values to such an extent that any possible transition or integration back into society is going to be problematic. They are often marginalized and excluded beyond the bounds of most people's comprehension. However, many prisoners who choose to study whilst imprisoned do so in the hope that it will facilitate the reintegrative and/or rehabilitative processes they experience as part of prison regimes. Experiences of those regimes, including attending education, however, are a matter for the individual prisoner. For one prisoner, Andrew (personal communication), "being down on education" was a question of "I would like to help black kids in trouble on the streets"; for Trevor (personal communication), education in prison was more a question of "I want to do something just for me."

According to the Prison Reform Trust (2004), in the UK, prison service targets for prisoners who achieved different skills qualifications in 2002–03, were doubled with the British Government's Social Exclusion Unit finding that prisoners who did not have any involvement with education or training being three times more likely to be reconvicted. It was also found that there was a reduction of around 12% in reoffending by those who acquired basic skills learning. Despite this, however, many prisoners feel that education provision for those inside is "second-best," although the efforts and endeavours of educational staff are very much appreciated.

The provision of prison education programs sometimes has to be justified in terms of expenditure for correctional agencies whose primary functions are ideally embedded in security, control and justice. Prisoner education can often be seen as a "luxury" and not a "right" for most prisoners other than those who are young and obliged to complete statutory education. For those with access to courses, prisoner education has a potential to relocate the prisoner within the existing social network. Whilst many prisoners themselves view this as an impossible task, they readily acknowledge that attendance on courses can raise them above their usual social location, which one prisoner, Peter, described as "somewhere below the underclass" (personal communication, 1993).

Adults learning in a prison classroom are involved in a range of classroom dynamics that can potentially provide the basis for all the new opportunities, challenges, ideas and activities that any adult learner will encounter throughout a course (Reuss, 1997). The classroom interaction provides a context in which foundations can be laid for reflexive thinking on a wide variety of subjects – including one's own behavior – and whilst it may be difficult to quantify such processes (Pawson, 2000), it is not impossible. Adult educators in prisons can be seen as "troublesome outsiders" by corrections agencies, but most teachers recognize that adult education in prisons "works" for some people "some of the time."

For the adult learner in prison, to develop existing knowledge, acquire new knowledge, new skills and potentially to acquire new attitudes and opinions is no mean achievement. Education within a prison occurs in a very unique context that is little known and quite often misunderstood and misinterpreted. That context may be an actual physical prison classroom within the prison, complete with other students, that resembles any classroom in any educational setting. However, it probably has alarm bells on the wall (as from my own experiences), uniformed prison staff sitting outside the room, and all the usual prison regime activities taking place in the background. Is it a classroom? One on one? Yet the prison cultural context is as diverse as any other and it is within this context that is acutely divided in terms of power balances (Reuss, 1999) that a great deal of learning takes place. The characteristics of adult learners in prison, their individual differences, and their approaches to learning and teaching, have all to be taken into account in what is a social setting within the prison. This kind of learning can be "inspirational" for some (Rogers, 1986), and most prisoners agree with the view that ". . . prison education can and will change prisoners lives for the better" (Gordon, personal communication, 2000).

See also: class, literacy, motivation, numeracy, participation.

References and Further Reading

Duguid, S. (1986). Selective ethics and integrity: Moral development and prison education. *Journal of Correctional Education, 37*(2), 60–64.

Elias, N. (1992). *Time: An essay.* Oxford: Basil Blackwell.

Elsey, B. (1986). *Social theory perspectives of adult education.* Nottingham, UK: University of Nottingham, Department of Adult Education.

Garland, D. (1990). *Punishment and modern society.* Oxford: Clarendon Press.

Germanotta, D. (1995). Prison education: A contextual analysis. In H. S. Davison (Ed.), *Schooling in a "total institution"* (pp. 103–121). Westport, CN: Bergin & Garvey.

Gordon, R. (2000). One inmate's experience. In D. Wilson & A. Reuss (Eds.), *Prison(er) education* (pp. 158–171). Winchester: Waterside Press.

Pawson, R. (2000). The evaluators tale. In D. Wilson & A. Reuss (Eds.), *Prison(er) education* (pp. 63–83). Winchester: Waterside Press.

Reuss, A. (1997). *Higher education and personal change in prisoners.* Unpublished PhD thesis, University of Leeds.

Reuss, A. (1999). Prison(er) education. *The Howard Journal, 38*(2), 113–127.

Reuss, A. (2000). The researchers' tale. In D. Wilson & A. Reuss (Eds.), *Prison(er) education* (pp. 25–47). Winchester: Waterside Press.

Reuss, A. (2003). Prison education – The potential for change? *The Howard League Magazine, 21*(3), pp. 13ff.

Reuss, A., & Wilson, D. (2000). The way forward. In D. Wilson & A. Reuss (Eds.), *Prison(er) education* (pp. 172–182). Hampshire, UK: Waterside Press.

Rogers, A. (1986). *Teaching adults.* Oxford: Oxford University Press.
Williford, M. (1994). *Higher education in prison: A contradiction in terms?* Phoenix, AZ: Oryx Press.

Anne Reuss

Problematizing Learning

The Brazilian worldwide-known educator Paulo Freire (1972b) placed the educational question of "posing problems" as well as "solving problems" at the centre of the adult learning process. His approach, which may be problematizing learning differs from problem-based learning in that it is deeply rooted in Freire's notion of education for liberation. It is not so much a teaching method as it is a world view of change and freedom. In Freire's liberating education as opposed to banking education, an oppressing social, political, economic and cultural situation faced by educatees in their real life comes to be problematized via an educational strategy – the Freirean dialogue – in order to transform it and liberate people. The ontological principle that sustains such a perspective is that there is a commitment to the creation of a just and democratic world, which implies the recognition and transformation of all forms of oppressive social relations. This commitment is based on a critical assessment of the human condition under capitalism, and also the assessment that human beings have, and often exhibit, the potential to become more fully human. Education is recognized as a fundamental tool for transforming oppressive relations. The epistemological principle here is the adoption of a critical understanding of ideology and commonsense, and a theory of knowledge that allows people to understand reality dialectically. This is based upon criticism of other theories of knowledge and the adoption of the theory of praxis. The pedagogical principles implicit are that (a) the knowable object is the centre of the learning process, and (b) there is a clear intention of questioning the *raison d'être* of the phenomenon under investigation and of seeking or questioning alternatives to transform the relations that determine the phenomenon. As a consequence, it is not the existent knowledge about the object which is the centre of the learning process.

Existent knowledge is used, recreated or negated, as it has to be useful in explaining the historic object under investigation. In critically analysing participants' experience, action already developed and further action needed at local and wider levels should be taken into account. In addition, members' individual needs and skills are considered legitimate but are approached critically. This way to approach knowledge from both experience and extant knowledge leads to the necessity of transforming the traditional roles of and relationship between educator and educatee. They are both seen as subjects of the process of choosing and understanding the knowable object and, consequently, in the process of creating new knowledge and/or a better understanding or criticism of the knowledge already produced. This process must embody the commitment of both educator and educatee to a cooperative process of questioning although they have different roles in relation to the direction of the learning process. Therefore, educators should work *with* students and not *for* them. The educator's commitment to democracy at all levels of his or her duties as well as his or her autonomy to approach any issue critically are crucial principles to guarantee both the educator's radical approach and dialogue. In addition, didactic resources are considered as a means of supporting the transformation of the educator and educatee relationship to knowledge and the power relations involved and not an end in itself.

Dialogue

Dialogue is established as "the seal of the epistemological relationships between subjects in the knowing process" (Freire, 1974, p. 21). The Freirean understanding of dialogue is not the concept of a technique to be applied in order to achieve the participation of those involved in an educational process in discussion. Dialogue is a revolutionary form of communication that enables those involved in the educational process to search for deeper and authentic knowledge. Dialogue expresses the struggle for transformation of the bourgeois patterns of relationship between teacher and learner in relation to knowledge, and in so doing becomes critical praxis. Dialogue is also a form of critical praxis because it represents the struggle to unify, dialectically, reflection and action. Dialogue, therefore is, at the same time, the outcome of transformed relations between teacher and learners and between the two in relation to knowledge, as well as a means of struggle in transforming such relations (Freire, 1972b, 1985).

Problematization

Problematization is an essential process within dialogue. Through dialogue the participants are encouraged to problematize their empirical experience and extant knowledge, then investigate them. The investigation includes discoveries of the historical roots of empirical and produced theoretical knowledge; the relations of the latter to the present context, and the identification of whose social interests are served by the knowledge used in the educational process. The process of investigation also includes people's elaboration of the relevant questions to be addressed for their understanding of reality, and identification of the central problems to be faced within the struggle for social transformation (Freire, 1972b, 1985). Such investigation is a fundamental tool for people to overcome commonsense and, consequently, develop critical praxis. Dialogue, based on this theory of praxis, must start with the actual conceptions of the world which are common to people in order to transform it into a coherent, critical conception of the world. Thus, it is a task for those engaged in dialogue – educator and educatee – to help each other, through problematization, to unveil the ideological forms which are operating in the ways people explain and act upon reality (Freire).

Thus, the dialogical character of education as the practice of freedom does not begin when the teacher-student meets the student-teachers in a pedagogical situation, but rather when the former first asks himself, or herself, what his, or her, dialogue with the latter will be about. And preoccupation with the content of dialogue is really preoccupation with the program content of education (Freire, 1972a, 1972b). Therefore, Freire's understanding of the process of creating and developing educational program content is totally related to his philosophical perspective. That means the process of choosing issues to be studied is understood as a collaborative venture involving the educator and the educatees in their effort to critically understand and change reality.

To help the understanding of the pedagogical process of establishing and developing a program content or a curriculum from such a perspective, a Freirean understanding of the terms "theme" and "generative theme" is crucial (Freire, 1972b). Freire (1985) defines a theme as "a phenomenon that takes place in a concrete reality and that mediates men and women" (p. 112). He also explains that we "need to avoid the Socratic error of regarding the definition of a concept as knowledge of the thing defined" (p. 112). On the contrary, we should assume a committed attitude towards our theme, an attitude of one who does not want to merely describe what goes on as it happens. We want, above all, to transform the real world of our theme so that whatever might be happening now can be changed later (p. 112). The implications of this definition of theme, and our commitment to change or to maintain the phenomenon expressed in a theme, for the curriculum, are: that this has to be a knowing process that is not fragmented, that is able to identify the dialectical contradictions – the opposing themes – and human beings' objectives implicit in the themes (Freire, 1985).

Thus, while we delve into and reveal our understanding of a theme, we also reveal its counterpart, giving us a choice that in turn demands that we commit ourselves to a form of action consonant with the goals implicit in them. The more we get to know the socio-historical reality of the issues in our themes, in their dialectical relation with opposing issues, the more impossible it will be for us to remain neutral (p. 113). Within the same theoretical context, Paula Allman (1989) says, "Nothing could be more antithetical to the principles of dialectic change than the traditional form of curriculum that separates knowledge into distinct disciplines of study" (p. 224). Having said that, it would be worth emphasizing that because most of the radical educational work is developed within given capitalist social relations, even the very thoughts and actions developed from a critical analysis of reality must be analysed critically, as they may become reified knowledge which can lose its critical characteristics. Knowledge becomes reified when the people using it do not check the historical roots that have generated it and its validity in understanding the actual situation. In addition, and as a consequence of that, critical knowledge becomes reified when people lapse into a position wherein they approach knowledge as a thing to be acquired and not to be used.

See also: conscientization, dialogue, praxis, social justice.

References and Further Reading

Allman, P. (1989). *Ideology and the dialectic: Cultural action for socialism.* Nottingham, Unpublished Manuscript.

Freire, P. (1972a). *Cultural action for freedom.* (M. Ramos, Trans.) Harmondsworth: Penguin.

Freire, P. (1972b). *Pedagogy of the oppressed.* Harmondsworth: Penguin.

Freire, P. (1974). Education: Domestication or liberation. In I. Lister (Ed.), *De-schooling: A reader* (pp. 20–21). Cambridge: Cambridge University Press.

Freire, P. (1985). *The politics of education: Culture, power and liberation.* (D. Macedo, Trans.). London: Palgrave Macmillan.

Maria Clara Bueno Fischer

Problem-Based Learning

Problem-based learning (PBL) refers to a method and approach to teaching and curriculum in which learners focus, most often in groups, on a specific problem, identify the issues involved, the resources required to solve it, the learning involved, and then begin the process of solving it. There is no right answer immediately apparent and the learners must muster all resources to find a solution. Problem-*based* learning is distinguished from problem-*centered* teaching strategies and approaches such as project learning, case studies and practice exercises in that it begins with no right answer, the learners are not guided through to the finish, and there is a complex and extended process of discovery and experiential learning involved (Lohman, 2002). The intent of PBL is to foster self-directed inquiry into the world of practice and to better prepare learners for the workplace. Real problems are used to orient learning and to form the nucleus of an extensive educational endeavor to teach professional skills, knowledge, and complex thinking skills. Addressing the problem requires comprehension, application and analysis. Within the PBL framework, the teacher is a facilitator and it is the learners who are in charge of their own learning. The real life problem determines what will be learned and how.

Interest in PBL

Although some educators (Lohman, 2002; Stonyer & Marshall, 2002) have become interested in integrating PBL into workplace education programs, adult educators generally have shown little interest in researching and writing about PBL. By far, the greatest interest in PBL has come from the higher education sector where PBL has formed the basis of a number of curriculum reforms and initiatives in areas such as biology (Harland, 1998) and online comparative education for students in Mexico and Latin America (Valenzuela & Gallardo, 2003). Interest in PBL has grown considerably in professional education programs such as nursing (Murray & Savin-Baden, 2000). One of the more notable practical examples of a PBL curriculum in professional education is at the McMaster Medical School in Ontario, Canada, where all learning is based on practice problems, instead of discrete subject areas. Another example is the curriculum of Renaissance College, an undergraduate liberal arts college in New Brunswick, Canada, which is PBL-based. The subjects and disciplines come into play when they make most sense to do so. The premise is that by collaborating or solving the problem the students will not only learn how to learn, but will also begin the transition to the workplace while still in postsecondary or tertiary education.

Problem-based learning has arisen mainly from a concern that traditional teaching methods have not adequately prepared students for entry into the professions or the workplace. Heightened awareness of the importance of professional know-how and preparing the professionals to be reflective practitioners (Schön, 1987) has increased this concern. Institutions of higher education, in particular, have been viewed as dinosaurs that have reneged on their implicit contract to prepare students for the situations they will encounter in practice. PBL has been proposed as a way to meet this need, given its attention to problems of practice, practitioner know-how, and professional skill.

At the crux of problem-based

learning is the tension between the world of theory and the world of practice, and the attempts of higher education to address the gap by launching PBL initiatives. Should higher education's purpose be to provide skills needed for the workplace today or to prepare learners for both work and lifelong learning? The inevitable tensions between purposes of higher education and the world of work are in question with PBL.

Critiques of PBL

Critics of problem-based learning note that with few exceptions (e.g., Vernon & Blake, 1993) there is little evidence to suggest that PBL is more effective than other approaches to education. Questions remain about whether it increases self-directed learning, whether its graduates are better prepared for the workplace, and whether the considerable investment in PBL is worthwhile. Issues are raised also about the readiness and training of teachers and facilitators to learn to implement the PBL approach (Murray & Savin-Baden, 2000), and especially to assess student learning (see Boud & Feletti, 1997). As well, critics fear that the PBL approach will result in the dissolution of the subject and discipline focus of higher education. Finally, Yoder-Wise (2004) raises the larger question of whether a PBL approach causes learners to focus on problems, to see the world and practice generally as problem-ridden, and to deter attention from the positive. These questions are worth considering.

See also: experiential learning, learning, professional development, transfer of learning, workshops.

References and Further Reading

Boud, D., & Feletti, G. I. (Eds.). (1997). *The challenge of problem-based learning* (2nd ed.). London: Kogan Page.

Harland, T. (1998). Moving towards problem-based learning. *Teaching in Higher Education, 3*(2), 219–230.

Lohman, M. C. (2002). Cultivating problem-solving skills through problems-based approaches to professional development. *Human Resource Development Quarterly, 13*(3), 243–261.

Murray, I., & Savin-Baden, M. (2000). Staff development in problem-based learning. *Teaching in Higher Education, 5*(1), 107–126.

Schön, D. (1987). *Educating the reflective practitioner: Toward a new design for teaching and learning in the professions.* San Francisco: Jossey-Bass.

Stonyer, H., & Marshall, L. (2002). Moving to problem-based learning in the NZ engineering workplace. *Journal of Workplace Learning, 14*(5/6), 190–197.

Valenzuela, J. R., & Gallardo, K. E. (2003). Problem based learning in an online comparative education course. *Canadian and International Education, 32*(1), 77–105.

Vernon, D. T. A., & Blake, R. L. (1993). Does problem-based learning work?: A meta-analysis of evaluation research. *Academic Medicine, 68*, 550–563.

Yoder-Wise, P. S. (2004). The problem with problem-based learning. *Journal of Continuing Education in Nursing, 35*(4), 147.

Leona M. English

Professional Development

Professional development includes not only the initial preparation of educators, but also ongoing learning experiences designed to further their understanding, practice, and growth. The professional development of educators addresses how and what educators learn, and provides opportunities to cultivate and model greater understanding, and personal and professional learning experiences.

Over the centuries, the professional development of educators has taken considerably different forms in different contexts. As a prime example of lifelong learning, professional development includes not only the initial preparation of educators, but also ongoing learning experiences designed to further their understanding, practice, and growth. Educators in this sense come from many settings, including, but not limited to: adult education, training, higher education, and grade schools (K-12). However, what all of these educators have in common is that they actively facilitate teaching and learning processes with other learners. In addition, professional development encompasses many formats including formal workshops and classes, conference participation, certification, continuing education, and academic degree study.

Scope of Professional Development

Professional development of educators has taken several forms based on different contexts. For K-12 educators, professional development has consisted of initial teacher preparation, advanced degree study, and, most frequently, in-service workshops. In workplace and non-education organization settings, trainers gain professional development through workshops, conferences, and a growing number of degree programs in human resource management. In higher education, faculty have traditionally engaged in independent professional development through discipline-specific conferences, and more recently through campus-based faculty development centers which have become more popular. For adult educators working in adult basic education, adult literacy, English language learning, and high school/secondary equivalency programs, professional development has mainly been delivered through workshops, some conferences, and a limited number of degree programs.

As for the "what" or content of professional development, K-12 professional development has focused on pedagogy, child development, specific content areas, and new curricular needs. Within training settings it has centered on industry standards, certifications, management skills, customer service, or other work-determined requirements. Higher education faculty development has again focused on professors' academic disciplines, but has turned increasingly to teaching and learning concerns and techniques. Adult education assistance has often included instructional approaches and requirements, as well as, performance standards mandated by funding agencies. In contrast, academic study in adult education provides a broader foundation in adult learning, adult development, educational philosophy, program planning, research and curricula, to name some major areas.

Impact of Adult Education on Professional Development

Understanding educators of adults as adult learners provides a focus on their prior learning, expectations, contexts, and learners. And, realizing that many educators of adults have limited formal preparation in education underscores the importance of professional development. Teachers of adults may be engaged in working with learners in educational institutions, non-profit organizations, public and private corporations, or other workplace settings. The content areas can span technical knowledge and skills to language learning, management skills, industry standards, legal codes, certification requirements, computer skills, and equipment use, to name a few. The question then becomes, "How do we address this learning in a more holistic manner?"

From an adult education perspective, the key may be recognizing educators as reflective practitioners (Schön, 1983), and finding ways to bring teaching and learning practice into line with expectations and needs. With this perspective, professional development can provide experiences that model and teach how to examine the needs of learners and build learning experiences that dynamically address those needs.

Stephen Brookfield's (1995) work furthered this perspective by casting a vision of educators engaging in personal and professional critical reflection about their assumptions, values, understanding, and work. Focusing on their development as educators and the needs of their learners, he provides personal examples of how to interact with the teaching and learning experience in order to extend expectations and inform practice. Patricia Cranton (1996) provided another dimension to this understanding as she began to talk about how professional development can also be life-changing transformative learning experiences. Kathleen King's (2003) research and model provide specific illustration of how professional development in one content area – learning educational technology – can lead to transformation.

The field also describes how professional development can incorporate adult learning principles (Lawler & King, 2000; Licklider, Schnelker, & Fulton, 1997–98; Smylie, 1995). A specific frame for such professional development is provided through the Adult Learning Model of Faculty Development (Lawler & King), that utilizes an adult learning framework to address the different contexts and needs within higher education faculty development. In further developments, Kathleen King and Patricia Lawler (2003) present how this model can be used and understood among adult educators who work in adult basic education, and higher education, as well as corporate and workplace training.

Challenges and Opportunities

Among the eminent challenges and open questions facing professional development in the years ahead are: How do we emphasize the needs of the educators in a field like adult education, where the learners and focus are already marginalized? Also, how do we raise awareness and build a vision of possibilities of professionalization that the field has been lacking? And, how do we assess the effectiveness and impact of professional development? (King & Lawler, 2003).

Professional development that focuses on the needs of the educators as adult learners integrates their respective contexts and needs. Recognizing the demands of the various organizations and learners within their professional environments, and reaching into new areas, provides a rich basis for creating professional development that will meet their needs in the future.

Additionally, several contextual challenges emerge and need to be addressed in professional development in order to meet the future needs of educators. First, rapidly changing technology means that educators must constantly learn new ways to support and deliver their work. Second, changing economic and global conditions affect educators on at least two levels because of changes in (a) what learners want and need, and (b) what their organizations seek from their employees. Third, educators need to be successful in working with an increasingly diverse group of learners and can benefit from understanding their different contexts, cultures, expectations, and learning styles.

Educators of adults support and lead others in their learning, and herein lies a great opportunity for professional development – its generative power and potential impact. Not only do these professionals benefit from the learning and growth individually, but their experiences may also be multiplied in the lives of the many learners with whom they work. The ways in which we design, pursue, and support their professional development can potentially change the practice of adult learning across a vast array of contexts and people.

In closing, professional development practice needs to be aggressively extended to determine comprehensive, effective approaches to evaluation. Among K-12 educators, this has been a recognized area, but unfortunately not always prominently addressed. For professional development in higher education, the focus has been even less integrated and remains a distinct opportunity for advancement in theory, research, and practice. New directions for opportunity and the impact of teaching and learning can be supported by pursuing research-based evaluation of professional development from a context-sensitive and adult learning perspective.

See also: continuing professional education, higher education, workplace education, workshops.

References and Further Reading

Brookfield, S. D. (1995). *Becoming a critically reflective teacher*. San Francisco: Jossey-Bass.

Cranton, P. (1996). *Professional development as transformative learning*. San Francisco: Jossey-Bass.

King, K. P. (2003). *Keeping pace with technology: Educational technology that transforms. Vol. Two: The challenge and promise for higher education faculty*. Cresskill, NJ: Hampton Press.

King, K. P., & Lawler, P. A. (Eds.). (2003). *New perspectives on designing and implementing professional development for teachers of adults. New Directions in Adult and Continuing Education*, No. 98. San Francisco: Jossey-Bass.

Lawler, P. A., & King, K. P. (2000). *Planning for effective faculty development: Using adult learning strategies*. Malabar, FL: Krieger.

Licklider, B. E., Schnelker, D. L., & Fulton, C. (1997–98). Revisioning faculty development for changing times: The foundation and framework. *Journal of Staff, Program & Organizational Development, 15*(3), 121–133.

Schön, D. A. (1983). *The reflective practitioner: How professionals think in action*. New York: Basic Books.

Smylie, M. A. (1995).Teacher learning in the workplace: Implications for school reform. In T. R. Guskey & M. Huberman (Eds.), *Professional development in education: New paradigms and practices* (pp. 92–113). New York: Teachers College Press.

Kathleen P. King

Program Planning

Program planning has historically been defined as a sequentially and logically ordered set of tasks in which educational planners first assess learning needs, then develop learning objectives from assessed needs, next design learning content and instructional formats to meet the learning objectives, and finally evaluate learning outcomes in terms of whether the objectives were achieved. Within an adult education context often focused on developing programs, analysing planning contexts and administering programs are also typically included tasks. This definition of planning, the conventional view, represents a rational problem-solving process logically linking the technical tasks of assessing needs, developing objectives, designing content, administering programs, and evaluating outcomes. These tasks and their sequential execution (often called "planning steps" and enumerated) thus represent planning principles which prescribe specific procedures planners are supposed to follow when planning educational programs for adults. Planning situations and people vary, however, such that no single set of planning steps or tasks always works in every set of circumstances. Consequently, because planners have to make judgments about which principles and procedures are more likely to produce intended results given the particulars of a planning context, theorists have described planning as a complex decision-making process.

As theorists of planning have focused more on the complex human interactions that planning requires, more critical questions have been raised about how to understand planning contexts and what planners actually do to plan programs. Planning theory has moved from a steady avowal of a linear sequence of idealized planning principles to a more practical understanding of planning work as humans making judgments. Because planning and managing programs is typically considered a major professional focus, adult educators are expected to be knowledgeable about planning theory principles and expert in techniques to implement them. Yet recent research demonstrates that technical competence is insufficient for good planning, for planning also requires political astuteness in negotiating human and organizational relationships as well as ethical sensitivity for recognizing and responding to practical opportunities, challenges, and dilemmas.

History

Most planning theorists tend to discuss planning theory ahistorically. There are, though, different traditions in the history of program planning that can be constructed. One tradition, the conventional history, starts with Ralph Tyler's enormously influential course syllabus from 1949, *Basic Principles of Curriculum and Instruction*, and Malcolm Knowles' 1950 text, *Informal Adult Education* (Sork, 2000; Sork & Caffarella, 1989). Adult educators actually began trying to understand and theorize program planning in American adult education much earlier (Wilson & Cervero, 1997). One of the key principles that help define adult education program planning (as distinguished from K-12 school curriculum planning, from which much adult education program planning derives) appears early in the 20th century as having adult learners self-identify their own learning needs. This characteristically adult dimension to program planning is amply illustrated in Eduard Lindeman's (1926/1961) *The Meaning of Adult Education*, appears often in many other examples in the 1930s and 1940s, and emerges fully articulated in Knowles' 1950 text (Wilson & Cervero). This principle of learner-identified needs, the first "step," has been central to much adult education program planning theory throughout the last century and remains so today. As the conventional history indicates, in the 1950s planning literature began to proliferate. Sork and Buskey's (1986) review of planning literature shows that between 1950 and 1983 nearly 100 publications appeared on program planning in American adult education. The literature has continued apace since the 1980s. Yet amid what many have taken to be a bewildering diversity of planning theories and prescriptions is actually a rather uniform depiction of what has been believed to be the basic principles of program planning. To conduct their review of 93 publications, Sork and Buskey "synthesized" a "generic planning model composed of nine specific steps" (1986, p. 89). Those "nine specific steps," which Sork and Caffarella (1989) subsequently refined as "a six-step basic model" representing "the most common logic found in the literature" (p. 234), directly mirror the sequencing of steps presented as the conventional definition of planning given at the opening of this entry: analysing context, assessing needs, deriving objectives, designing instruction, administering programs, and evaluating outcomes. Wilson and Cervero have demonstrated that this common structure of problem-solving principle and logic has existed in planning theory since the 1920s, and have argued that it promotes a specific professionalization interest of adult educators to use "scientific" problem-solving as a mechanism for controlling what counts as acceptable adult education work.

There are other traditions of planning theory which interweave with and counterpose the conventional history. One, known as the "deliberative" tradition, is only selectively represented in adult education, although its presence has grown (see Caffarella, 2002; Sork, 2000). This is the tradition which represents "practical" theorizing about planning, for practitioners often point out that the rational problem-solving principles upon which conventional planning steps are predicated rarely work in actual planning circumstances. Represented most fully in Cyril Houle's theory of planning in the 1970s, planners are described as analysing their context and then making judgments about what to do to plan programs. The key insight of this tradition is the recognition that while many (but not necessarily all) of the generic planning model steps may be executed in any one planning exercise, they need not be and most likely would not be conducted in the proper order prescribed by conventional planning theory. The notion that planning steps are iterative and that multiple planning tasks can be conducted nearly simultaneously as well as out of order seriously challenges the preferred sequential logic of the conventional view. Whether or not the steps have to be followed sequentially represents the major theoretical debate in the planning literature over the last 50 years (Wilson & Cervero, 1997). The iterative, deliberative view of non-sequential step planning dominates the planning literature today as a way to make conventional theory more practical (see Caffarella, as an example), even as theorists often continue to invoke the sequential logic of the conventional view as the preferred mode.

There is yet another tradition of planning theory, a critical tradition, which emerges most forcefully with Paulo Freire's 1970 *Pedagogy of the Oppressed*. Some have seen implications for planning theory in Freire's *Pedagogy* (Sork, 2000), and others have described it explicitly as a planning model (Boone, Safrit, & Jones, 2002; Wilson & Cervero, 1997). It is indeed both for it contains implicit and specific planning theory and procedures that explicitly derive from Freire's critical questioning of who gets (or does not get) what kinds of education. Freire's program planning shows adult education to be both a political act in challenging repressive power structures and an ethical question of justice for adult educators to ask everyday in their work. I start this history in the "middle" rather than at the "beginning" as I did with the conventional and deliberative histories because Freire's work represents a long historical tradition of planning adult education to redress social and political inequity that continues today (Wilson & Cervero). This history of critical adult education planning has antecedents in 19th and 20th-century adult education in the United Kingdom, Canada, and the United States such as in labor movements, workers education, settlement organizations, churches, civil rights movements, anti-war movements, and other social and political movements that continue in the 21st century wherever people exist in and seek to change repressive social and political regimes. Because adult education always represents a struggle for knowledge and power (Cervero & Wilson, 2001), the various efforts to contest global capitalism such as the World Social Forum, the many contested ends and means for developing a more sustainable world, the efforts to revivify democracy in the West, the education needed to thwart the continuing epidemics of AIDS and other new diseases, all provide fertile ground for understanding and improving the political practice of planning adult education that addresses issues of social justice.

For major reviews of program planning theory for both its historical development as well as selected issues discussed in the next section, readers are urged to consult Boone, Safrit, and Jones (2002); Cervero and Wilson (1994, 2001, in press); Sork (2000); Sork and Caffarella (1989); Sork and Buskey (1986); and Wilson and Cervero (1997).

Issues

Within its several historical traditions, there are any number of key issues which can be examined specifically in the sources just noted. For example, Sork and Buskey (1986) conclude that program planning theory was unsophisticated, that there was little cumulative analysis or integration, that differences among planning theory were more because of contexts than actual differences in planning (hence the "generic model"), and that theory had little to offer in describing what planners do. In developing a "political turn" in theorizing about planning (Sork, 2000), Cervero and Wilson have developed a number of critiques: its inability to develop an account of human action in planning practice in organizational contexts; a comparable problem in its failure to develop a theory of context for practical action; its selective appropriation of scientific ideology to promote professionalization; its continued promotion of a rationalist ideology as the basis for planning action; its continued ideological location as support for the status quo; and a disavowal of its radical social change heritage (Cervero & Wilson, 1994, 2001; in press; Wilson & Cervero, 1997). Likewise, Sork (2000) argues that planning theory has been relatively unaffected by contemporary social theory like feminism, postmodernism, and other forms of critical social theory (with the possible exception of critical theory) and thus tends to serve the status quo because very little planning theory is directed towards social change. It may even be that planning theory is mostly an American phenomenon (witness the discussion here), as other English-speaking countries seem to have a sparser separate discourse on planning theory per se.

Perhaps the most persistent issue is the theory–practice gap. Knowles noted that gap in 1950 when he wrote it was time to get beyond "trial and error" and develop scientific theory about planning education programs for adults. Decades later Sork and Caffarella (1989) argued in the adult education handbook that because the planning literature was largely normative they believed that the "gap that has always existed to some degree between theory and practice has widened" (p. 243) since the previous handbook 10 years prior. They attribute that growing gap to practitioners taking "shortcuts," the influence of context on planning, and/or the increasing irrelevancy of planning theory to planning practice. In his most recent review, Sork (2000) returns to this familiar problem by being "skeptical about the prospects of developing a theory or model" that helps explain what is really going on in planning and helps people be better planners – the classic theory-practice problem (p. 179). So a real problem remains, the split between what theorists prescribe and practitioners do. Experienced practitioners are well-aware of the political, ethical, and technical dilemmas and opportunities that face them daily, while theorists in the main continue to insist on endless iterations of rationalist problem-solving sequences as the only response set to the practical choices educators must routinely make. The practical, empirical, and theoretical question remains: how to integrate the technical, political, and ethical dimensions of planning practice in order to better understand and act in the contexts that planners actually work in (see Caffarella, 2002; Cervero & Wilson, 1994; in press; Sork, 2000, for such integrating efforts).

Relevance

Without well-developed techniques to implement conventional planning principles, the world would have little need of adult educators. Yet conventional theory with its limited focus on principles and procedures only partially helps planners in their actual work. Further, actual planning practice requires more than the deliberative tradition's contribution which illustrates decision-making in planning. In the conventional perspective planners are technically skilled to embody a facilitative role in executing planning steps. In the deliberative tradition, educators are people who make judgments about what to do and how planning is done. Both are unable, however, to provide a working theory of practical action in the lived world of educational planning for adults, for both rely on rational problem-solving as the main foundation for planning work. It is only in the critical tradition that planning theory begins to transcend the rationalist idealism underlying both the conventional and deliberative traditions. It is the critical tradition that understands planners as having to act in real relations of power and interests in which idealized prescriptions for rationality are not reasonable for practice.

Building on Cervero and Wilson (1994), Sork (2000) argues that "being a capable planner involves developing understanding and skills in three closely related domains: the technical, the sociopolitical, and the ethical" (p. 176). In this view, planners have to be more than technically proficient, the major thrust of conventional theory, and more than proficient decision-makers, the major thrust of the deliberative tradition. Although technique and deliberation are important, planners must also be politically aware and ethically responsible. So the same questions face both planning practice and planning theory. In order to plan adult education better, we need to know about not just the technical work, but the political and ethical work as well. For a long time planning theorists have been telling practitioners what they should be doing to plan good education programs for adults, and practitioners have just as earnestly been figuring out their own novel and innovative ways to plan in the technically, politically, and ethically demanding environments in which they work. That we have a great deal of normative but limited discourse about the former and know little about the latter presents a compelling agenda. Adult educators are often more interested in questions about adult learning and teaching, but we also have the responsibility to organize that learning and teaching. So we need to know about how adult educators plan programs because educational planning is what planners have to do if they wish to make a difference in the world.

See also: facilitation, power, practitioner, praxis, theory.

References and Further Reading

Boone, E., Safrit, D., & Jones, J. (2002). *Developing programs in adult education: A conceptual planning model* (2nd ed.). Prospect Heights, IL: Waveland.

Caffarella, R. S. (2002). *Planning programs for adult learners: A practical guide for educators, trainers, and staff developers* (2nd ed.). San Francisco: Jossey-Bass.

Cervero, R. M., & Wilson, A. L. (1994). *Planning responsibly for adult education: A guide to negotiating power and interests*. San Francisco: Jossey-Bass.

Cervero, R. M., & Wilson, A. L. (Eds.). (2001). *Power in practice: Adult education and the struggle for knowledge and power in society*. San Francisco: Jossey-Bass.

Cervero, R. M., & Wilson, A. L. (in press). *Working the planning table: Planning responsibly for adult education* (2nd ed.). San Francisco: Jossey-Bass.

Knowles, M. S. (1950). *Informal adult education: A guide for administrators, leaders, and teachers*. New York: Association Press.

Lindeman, E. C. L. (1961). *The meaning of adult education*. Montreal: Harvest House (first published by New Republic, 1926).

Sork, T. J. (2000). Planning educational programs. In A. L. Wilson & E. R. Hayes (Eds.), *Handbook of adult and continuing education* (pp. 171–190). San Francisco: Jossey-Bass.

Sork, T. J., & Buskey, J. (1986). A descriptive and evaluative analysis of program planning literature, 1950–1983. *Adult Education Quarterly, 36*, 86–96.

Sork, T. J., & Caffarella, R. S. (1989). Planning programs for adults. In S. Merriam & P. Cunningham (Eds.), *Handbook of adult and continuing education* (pp. 233–245). San Francisco: Jossey-Bass.

Tyler, R. W. (1949). *Basic principles of curriculum and instruction*. Chicago: University of Chicago Press.

Wilson, A. L., & Cervero, R. M. (1997). The song remains the same: The selective tradition of technical rationality in adult education program planning theory. *International Journal of Lifelong Education, 16*(2), 84–108.

Arthur L. Wilson

Q

Queer Studies

Since the early 1990s, "queer" has been increasingly used as a descriptor to replace gay and lesbian; indeed it has become an expanded term to include bisexual, intersexual, transgender, and transsexual persons as well as others across the spectrum of sex, sexual, and gender differences. As a historical interpellation, queer has been used to shame the person named or to produce a subject who should be ashamed because they perform and bond outside the parameters of "hegemonic social sanction" or heteronormativity (Butler, 1993, p. 226). In a symbolic act of empowerment, the United States based activist group Queer Nation, founded in 1990, took the term queer back in a transgressive move to revise who queer names and to resignify what it represents (Dilley, 1999; Warner, 1993).

Some queer theorists have also extended the parameters of queer to include foci on outsider differences, like postcolonial nationality, and to interrogate the intersection of queer with other relationships of power like race and ethnicity that rearticulate it (Cohen, 2001; Sedgwick, 1993). Thus queer is emerging as a fluid and expansive term that is dynamic and spacious, resisting prescription and restriction. Queer focuses on positionality, which is the multiple subject's social, political, and cultural locatedness. In terms of advocacy, queer is about strategizing to transgress the limits of heteronormativity (Grace, Hill, Johnson, & Lewis, 2004). It is always open to rearticulation, even when we arbitrarily work with some partial meaning or particular intention of queer to advocate for change in a certain time and space.

The Emergence of Queer Theory and Queer Studies

Queer theory's primary goal is to expose heterosexism and homophobia. It explores how ignorance and fear of queer lead to actual and/or symbolic violence towards queer (or those perceived to be queer) persons. Emerging from ideas found in queer social activism and in multi-perspective theoretical discourses including poststructural feminism and cultural studies, queer theory interrogates systemic and structural relationships shaped by limited understandings of sex, sexuality, and gender (Dilley, 1999; Grace & Hill, 2004; Tierney & Dilley, 1998). It works to dissolve the male/female and homosexual/heterosexual binaries.

Queer studies, as the interpretation and application of queer theory in research and practice, involve confronting the heteronormative culture–language–power nexus, contesting stereotypes and exclusionary history, and learning about queer history and culture as spaces to encounter what queerness (being, believing, desiring, becoming, belonging, and acting queer) might mean. Queer studies are as much about advocacy as they are about theory, research, pedagogy, and practice. They emphasize rearticulation and transgression, and reject alienation and abject compromise. From this perspective, engaging queer is about transforming what Paulo Freire (1998) calls the word and the world, so queer has presence and place.

Eve Kosofsky Sedgwick, Judith Butler, Teresa de Lauretis, Diana Fuss, and Michael Warner are key pioneer theorists in queer theory. Sedgwick's (1990) *Epistemology of the Closet* is usually considered the founding text in queer theory (Gamson, 2000). In this text and in *Tendencies* (1993), Sedgwick engaged queer not only to name and represent a spectrum of sex, sexual, and gender differences, but also to name outsider differences associated with race, ethnicity, and postcolonial nationality. Another text that can vie for the title of founding text is Butler's (1990) *Gender Trouble* in which she viewed gender not as taken-for-granted masculine or feminine essences, but as performative. Butler relates that Queer Nation took up this text while the grassroots activist group Act Up (AIDS Coalition to Unleash Power) employed tactics that resonated with her emerging theory of performativity (Salih & Butler, 2004).

In 1991, de Lauretis edited an issue of *Differences* on queer theory, and Fuss edited *Inside/Out*. These pivotal texts further marked a move away from lesbian and gay studies, which had often been about assimilating or integrating queer persons into heteronormative society, to Queer Studies, which are about transgressing heteronormative space and describing queer on its own terms. Both texts set a clear task for queer theory: to challenge the customary cultural status of heterosexuality as a compulsory identity, practice, and institution that is deemed legitimate and necessary against "the continual predatory encroachments of its contaminated other, homosexuality" (Fuss, 1991, p. 2).

Two other texts central to the emergence of queer theory are Warner's edited collection *Fear of a Queer Planet* and Butler's *Bodies That Matter*, both published in 1993. Warner focused on the question "What do queers want?" (p. vii), and listed these key purposes of queer theory: to show how social structures and ideology influence the sexual order, and how language, themes, and concepts in social theory are generally heteronormalized, thus lacking utility in theorizing queer. In *Bodies That Matter*, Butler encouraged interrogation of queer. Importantly, she questioned what taking queer back means culturally and politically, wondering if the term's repulsive history gets lost in efforts to turn a historical signifier of degradation into a contemporary signifier of a fluid and expanding set of affirmative meanings.

Queer Studies in North American Adult Education

Since the early 1990s there has been a move to make queer history and culture visible in mainstream, critical, and other arenas in North American adult education (Grace, 2001; Grace & Hill, 2004; Hill, 1995, 1996). Historically, the field of study and practice has largely ignored the queer educators, students, and practitioners in its midst. Even critical adult education, which emphasizes the political ideals of modernity – democracy, freedom, and social justice – and ethical practice, has for the most part been complicit in maintaining a heteronormative status quo through its usual omission of queer in its theorizing and practice. In this dim light, Herbert Marcuse's notion of repressive tolerance is actualized across our field of study and practice. While adult educators and learners may believe that sites of learning, research, and practice are open spaces where freedom of speech and expression are pervasive and where the political ideals of modernity are valued, the fact is they are working in a field that keeps a hegemonic status quo through its exclusions, omissions, and enforced silences (Brookfield, 2001). Thus queer and allied adult educators and learners working in queer adult education take considerable risks in the face of colleague and institutional reactions that overtly or subtly dismiss queer work or place sanctions on it (Hill, 2003).

Nevertheless, we persevere and create counterpublic spaces to explore queerness. Of historical importance, one such space was created when Robert J. Hill spearheaded the formation of the Lesbian, Gay, Bisexual, Transgender, Queer & Allies Caucus (LGBTQ & AC) at the 34th Adult Education Research Conference (AERC) held at the Pennsylvania State University, State College in 1993. The Caucus has met every year since and, in 2003, the inaugural LGBTQ & AC Pre-Conference was held at the 44th annual AERC in San Francisco. The Caucus is a site of inclusive education where queer knowledge is built and the resilience of queer and allied adult educators is celebrated.

See also: culturally relevant adult education, cultural studies, critical multiculturalism, difference, identity.

References and Further Reading

Brookfield, S. D. (2001). Traveling from Frankfurt to la la land: Marcuse, repressive tolerance and the practice of learner centred adult education *Proceedings of the 31st Annual Standing Conference on University Teaching and Research in the Education of Adults* (SCUTREA) (pp. 54–57). University of East London, London, UK.

Butler, J. (1990/99). *Gender trouble: Feminism and the subversion of identity*. New York: Routledge.

Butler, J. (1993). *Bodies that matter: On the discursive limits of "sex."* New York: Routledge.

Cohen, C. J. (2001). Punks, bulldaggers, and welfare queens: The radical potential of queer politics? In L. Richardson, V. Taylor, & N. Whittier (Eds.), *Feminist frontiers 5* (pp. 540–556). New York: McGraw-Hill Higher Education.

De Lauretis, T. (Ed.). (1991). Queer theory. *Differences, 3*(2) (special issue).

Dilley, P. (1999). Queer theory: Under construction. *International Journal of Qualitative Studies in Education, 12*(5), 457–472.

Freire, P. (1998). *Teachers as cultural workers: Letters to those who dare teach* (D. Macedo, D. Koike, & A. Oliveira, Trans.). Boulder, CO: Westview Press.

Fuss, D. (1991). Inside/out. In D. Fuss (Ed.), *Inside/out: Lesbian theories, gay theories* (pp. 1–10). New York: Routledge.

Gamson, J. (2000). Sexualities, queer theory, and qualitative research. In N. K. Denzin & Y. S. Lincoln (Eds.), *Handbook of qualitative research* (2nd ed., pp. 347–365). Thousand Oaks, CA: Sage.

Grace, A. P. (2001). Using queer cultural studies to transgress adult educational space. In V. Sheared & P. A. Sissel (Eds.), *Making space: Merging theory and practice in adult education* (pp. 257–270). Westport, CN: Bergin & Garvey.

Grace, A. P, & Hill, R. J. (2004). Positioning Queer in adult education: Intervening in politics and praxis in North America. *Studies in the Education of Adults, 36*(2),

Grace, A. P., Hill, R. J., Johnson, C. W., & Lewis, J. B. (2004). In other words: Queer voices/dissident subjectivities impelling social change. *International Journal of Qualitative Studies in Education, 17*(3), 301–323.

Hill, R. J. (1995). Gay discourse in adult education: A critical review. *Adult Education Quarterly, 45*(3), 142–158.

Hill, R. J. (1996). Learning to transgress: A social-historical conspectus of the

American gay lifeworld as a site of struggle and resistance. *Studies in the Education of Adults, 28*(2), 253–279.

Hill, R. J. (2003). Working memory at AERC: A Queer welcome . . . and a retrospective. *Proceedings of the 1st LGBTQ Pre-Conference at the 44th Annual Adult Education Research Conference (pp. 11–28).* San Francisco: San Francisco State University.

Salih, S., & Butler, J. (2004). *The Judith Butler reader.* Malden, MA: Blackwell.

Sedgwick, E. K. (1990). *Epistemology of the closet.* Berkeley: University of California Press.

Sedgwick, E. K. (1993). *Tendencies.* Durham, NC: Duke University Press.

Tierney, W. G., & Dilley, P. (1998). Constructing knowledge: Educational research and gay and lesbian studies. In W. F. Pinar (Ed.), *Queer theory in education* (pp. 49–71). Mahwah, NJ: Lawrence Erlbaum Associates.

Warner, M. (Ed.). (1993). *Fear of a queer planet: Queer politics and social theory.* Minneapolis, MN: University of Minnesota Press.

André P. Grace

R

Race

The issue of race, what it is and how it makes a difference in adult education, is a complex question which is as relevant in the 21st century as it was in 1903 when W.E. B. DuBois stated that the preeminent problem of the 20th century would be the "color line." The marginalization of African and Latino Americans, Aboriginal Canadians, Aboriginal peoples in Australia, Maori people in New Zealand and Romany people are but a few examples which have a racial root. Early work in eugenics and social Darwinism in the early part of the 1900s attempted to construct race as a physical and biological category. However, we have come to understand race as a social construct which carries with it immense power to shape and define one's world. Race plays a huge role in determining how long a person can expect to live, the quality of that life, the educational possibilities that will or won't open up, and the manner in which that person (by racial affiliation) will be viewed in a given society at a given point in time. Political and historical processes shape race, and, therefore, race is not fixed. Rather, race can be seen as "a critical and defining feature of lived experience that young and old and people of color reflect upon, embody, challenge and negotiate" (Fine, Weis & Powell, 1997, p. 251). There is a perception, based on some physical or cultural characteristic, that a racial group is either superior or inferior. The social construction may be created within the group by the members themselves, but it is frequently the case that those from outside, through the state, create the social construction (Nieto, 1996). Such was the case in Germany where some German Jews, who had long since viewed themselves as fully German, were viewed by the Nazis as Jews.

Race and Ethnicity

Although race and ethnicity are often used interchangeably in the literature there are important differences to consider. Race alone as a construct can blur and smooth over the important differences that exist within one racial group. The construct of Aboriginal Canadian might not allow for the diversity to surface that exists between East Coast Mi'kmaw and Northern Cree. Ethnicity is frequently favored as construct which allows the diversity within a racial group to surface. However, we are cautioned by Anderson (1997) not to lose sight of race since,

> In abandoning the concept of race, there is a serious tendency to abandon discussion of power, domination and group conflict. I cannot help but notice in works on ethnicity how quickly the discussion then turns to matters of culture and identity, and not at all to questions of economic exploitation, political power and powerlessness . . . As such power and domination are central to the study of both race and ethnic relations in the United States. (p. 177)

Finally race cannot be viewed in isolation. It continually interlocks and intersects with other constructs, most notable among them class, gender and ability. Identity is multifaceted and complex, and race represents one important, but not singular, defining feature of that identity.

The question then turns to why the question of race should affect our teaching practice, and it is quite simply answered. "To dismiss a person's race is to misunderstand who that person is in the world as society often mistreats and misunderstands individuals based on racial heritage" (Howard, 2003, p. 175). So, although race is a social construction, it does exist and it has direct impact on the academic achievement of learners. There is robust research worldwide to link the historical and persistent underachievement of certain groups of learners based on their racial affiliation (Banks, 2002; Bear Nicholas, 2001; Binda & Calliou, 2001; Cummins, 2001; Dei, Mazzura, McIsaac, & Zine, 1997; Ladson-Billings, 1994; May, 1999; Tuhiwai Smith, 1999). If we do not acknowledge this reality, then we risk simply reproducing "privilege, dominance and oppression in the guise of neutrality or "color-blindness" (Fine et al., 1997, p. 251).

Having ascertained that race matters in classrooms, we examine the implications of raising the issues of race with adult educators and with learners. What is required of educators is an examination of their own social location and position in relation to the learners they teach. Cummins (2001) suggests that the macro relationships of the larger society (racism) will simply be replicated in the micro relationships of the classroom (racist policies, practices and attitudes) unless the adult educator is acting in a critically reflective manner to "interrupt, disrupt, challenge and unsettle" (Frank, 2001) the hegemonic forces which attempt to shape education. "Educators at all levels need to constantly examine their efforts to determine how their work may actually trivialize race and exacerbate an already dismal situation – they may actually teach racism" (Cross, 2003, p. 209). This requires of the educator a thorough introspection of his/her own identity in relation to the learners s/he is teaching.

Critical teacher reflection is essential to culturally relevant pedagogy because it can ultimately measure a teacher's level of concern and care for their students. A teacher's willingness to ask tough questions about his or her own attitudes toward diverse students can reflect a true commitment toward student's academic success and emotional well-being (Howard, 2003, p. 199).

Confronting Ourselves

While this work needs to be done with all educators, it is perhaps most pressing and difficult for educators who come from the dominant group and who, in many cases, have been socialized not to see themselves as racialized (Calliste, 1999; hooks, 1994; Lee, 1998). In the case of North America, the majority of the teaching force is White and female and these educators are increasingly teaching learners of color (Sleeter, 1995). White educators are challenged to see their "whiteness" as a racial construct and then examine the ways that they can come to recognize, unlearn and diminish their privilege (McIntosh, 1998). When White educators or those of other dominant groups are able to have a "deeper understanding around areas that might otherwise be ignored, misunderstood, misrepresented, misinterpreted or unsettled"

(Howard, 2003, p. 173), they are able to be very effective educators of learners who come from racial groups different than their own (Ladson-Billings, 1994). Milner (2003), Howard (2003), and Cross (2003) suggest various means of critical race reflection, both written and oral, individually and with others, which allow educators to "fight against injustice and racism, barriers that often stifle the growth and learning of students of color" (Milner, p. 176). Such critical awareness allows adult educators, in the spaces they create with learners, to disrupt the "master narrative" that issues of race no longer are of consequence.

Therefore the first step in becoming more culturally responsive to our learners is to come to know our own social construction, examine our own biographies and explore the multifaceted and complex identity that we bring into the classroom setting. The second important step is allowing issues of race (and other interlocking systems of domination such as class and gender) to be welcomed into and become an integral part of the learning experience. Gay (2000) uses the terms "culturally relevant pedagogy" to describe teaching that uses "the cultural knowledge, prior experiences, frames of reference and performance styles of ethnically diverse students to make learning more relevant for them [the learners]. It teaches *to* and *through* strengths of these students. It is culturally validating and affirming" (italics in the original, p. 29). In her work on diversity, Nieto (1996) found that students' high achievement in public school was directly connected to their strong positive sense of cultural integration. Munoz (1997), in her work with young adults, found that the kinds of things that the learners "loved to work on had very much to do with ethnicity, gender, class and sexuality" (p. 172).

Armed with critical reflective awareness as adult educators and a deeper understanding and appreciation of the multifaceted and complex identities of our learners, we are able to make more of a difference in the classrooms in which we teach. We seek to embrace culturally relevant pedagogy whose central premise is "an authentic belief that students from culturally diverse and low-income backgrounds are capable learners" (Ladson-Billings, 1994, p. 197). Geneva Gay (2001) stated that as a learner she became intelligent when she became Black. If we allow our learners to fully bring their whole selves into our classrooms, and if we make space for them to critically reflect on issues of identity and power in their lives, and we explore our own identities as educators alongside of theirs, many of our learners will show up in ways that will surprise us as educators.

See also: Africentrism, class, critical multiculturalism, culturally relevant adult education, difference, gender, womanism.

References and Further Reading

Anderson, M. (1997). Ethnicity and education forum: What difference does difference make? *Harvard Education Review, 67*(3), 169–187.

Banks, J. (2002). *An introduction to multicultural education.* Boston: Allyn & Bacon.

Bear N. A. (2001). Canada's colonial mission: The great white bird. In K.P. Binda & S. Calliou (Eds.), *Aboriginal education in Canada: A study in decolonization* (pp. 9–33). Mississauga, Ontario: Canadian Educators' Press.

Binda, K. P., & Calliou, S. (2001). *Aboriginal education in Canada: A study in decolonization.* Mississauga, Ontario: Canadian Educators' Press.

Calliste, A. (1999). *Anti-racist feminism.* Halifax, NS: Fernwood.

Cross, B. (2003). Learning or unlearning race: Transferring teacher education through curriculum to classroom practices. *Theory Into Practice, 42*(3), 203–209.

Cummins, J. (2001). *Negotiating identities: Education for empowerment in a diverse society.* Ontario, CA: California Association for Bilingual Education.

Dei, G. J. S., Mazzura, J., McIsaac, G., & Zine, J. (1997). *Reconstructing "drop-out." A critical ethnography of the dynamics of black students' disengagement from school.* Toronto: University of Toronto Press.

DuBois, W. E. B. (1903). *The souls of black folks.* New York: Penguin.

Fine, M., Weis, L., & Powell, L. (1997). Communities of difference: A critical look at desegregated spaces created for and by youth. *Harvard Education Review, 67*(3), 247–284.

Frank, B. (2001). *Anti-racist education.* A presentation to the School of Education. St. Francis Xavier University, Antigonish, Nova Scotia, Canada.

Gay, G. (2000). *Culturally responsive teaching.* New York: Teachers College Press.

Gay, G. (2001). *Forum on multicultural education.* Presentation at the American Educational Research Association. Seattle, Washington.

hooks, b. (1994). *Teaching to transgress. Education as the practice of freedom.* New York: Routledge.

Howard, T. (2003). Culturally relevant pedagogy: Ingredients for critical teacher reflection. *Theory Into Practice, 42*(3), 195–202.

Ladson-Billings, G. (1994). *The dreamkeepers: Successful teachers of African American children.* San Francisco: Jossey-Bass.

Lee, E. (1998). Anti-racist education: Pulling together to close the gaps. In E. Lee, D. Menkart, & M. Okazawa-Rey (Eds.), *Beyond heroes and holidays* (pp. 26–34). Washington, DC: Network of Educators on the Americas.

May, S. (1999). *Critical multiculturalism: Rethinking multicultural and antiracist education.* Philadelphia, PA: Falmer.

McIntosh, P. (1998). White privilege: Unpacking the invisible knapsack. In E. Lee, D. Menkart, & M. Okazawa-Rey (Eds.), *Beyond heroes and holidays* (pp. 26–34, 79–82). Washington, DC: Network of Educators on the Americas.

Milner, H. (2003). Teacher reflection and race in cultural contexts: History, meanings and methods in teaching. *Theory Into Practice, 42*(3), 173–179.

Munoz, V. (1997). Ethnicity and education forum: What difference does difference make? *Harvard Education Review: Ethnicity and Education, 67*(3), 169–187.

Nieto, S. (1996). *Affirming diversity. The sociopolitical context of multicultural education.* White Plains, NY: Longman.

Sleeter, C. E. (1995). An analysis of the critiques of multicultural education In J. A. Banks & C. A. Banks (Eds.), *Handbook of research on multicultural education* (pp. 81–94). San Francisco: Jossey-Bass.

Tuhiwai Smith, L. (1999). *Decolonizing methodologies. Research and Indigeneous peoples.* London: Zed Books.

Joanne Tompkins

Reflective Judgment

Reflective judgment describes the process by which adults come to decisions and actions in areas of their lives marked by ambiguity and a lack of dependable protocols. It involves episodes of scanning, gathering and appraisal during which adults learn to recognize the grounds for truth they depend on and the ways in which they come to trust certain knowledge as reliable and valid. Reflective judgment is an important element in models of critical thinking (Brookfield, 1987), practical logic (Sinnott, 1998), critical reflection (Brookfield, 1995), post-formal reasoning (Kincheloe, Steinberg, & Hinchey, 1999) and transformative learning (Mezirow, 1991). It is also often proposed as a distinctively adult mode of cognition. King and Kitchener (1994) define reflective judgment as a developmental progression in the ways people understand the process of knowing and in their ability to respond to ill-structured problems. In adult education, reflective judgment has recently been subsumed in the wider discourse of transformative learning (Mezirow & Associates, 2000) and is seen as part of the process by which adults come to develop meaning schemes and perspectives that are more comprehensive, inclusive and discriminating.

Reflective judgment often begins with an act of apprehension or scanning. Scanning describes the ways we determine the central features of a situation. In scanning we decide what are the situation's boundaries, which patterns of the situation are familiar and grounded in past experience (and which are in new or unusual configurations), and which of the cues that we notice should be attended to. Scanning is the initial sweep or experiential trawl in which we diagnose the big picture. In the gathering phase of reflective judgment we collect the interpretive resources and analytic protocols available to help us understand the situation correctly. These include the general guidelines we have learned as part of our educational preparation or life experience. We remember teachers' instructions regarding what to do in such situations, friends' and colleagues' suggestions we have heard, or practices we have seen. Finally, we call on our own intuition. We attend to the instinctive analyses and responses that immediately suggest themselves as relevant.

In the appraisal phase we sort through the interpretations we have gathered. We decide which seem to fit most closely with the situation we are reviewing and on the basis of these we take action. Reasoning is central to this phase. Scanning and gathering involve looking for patterns and broad similarities between a new situation and previous experiences. But in appraisal we judge the accuracy and validity of the assumptions and interpretations we have gathered. This occurs through a number of interconnected processes – by sifting through past experiences and judging the closeness of their fit to the current situation, by intentionally following prescribed protocols and introducing experimental adaptations of these when they suggest themselves, by consulting peers prior to decisions or in the midst of action, and by attempting to analyse which of our instinctive judgments and readings we should take seriously, and which we should hold in abeyance. As a result of this appraisal we take action regarding those procedures and responses that make the most sense in the current situation.

Appraisal entails a detailed critical review of multiple sources during which we decide to attend to some cues, to discard others, and to reframe those which hold promise but don't entirely explain what we're confronting. In the language of formal research this involves us in determining the accuracy and validity of assumptions and interpretations that we decide are most appropriate to a situation. To King and Kitchener (1994) this is epistemic cognition. In more colloquial terms we try to judge the fit between what we think is happening, the responses that seem to make most sense and the reasons why we trust these responses as accurate guides to action.

One of the most salient features of

reflective judgment is that it is irrevocably context-bound. The same person can be highly open to reexamining one set of practices, but completely closed to critically reappraising another situation or idea. There is also evidence to show that after a breakthrough in reflective judgment people can quite easily revert to an earlier, more naïve, way of thinking and being. So reflective judgment is often best understood, and its development gauged, within a specific context.

Reflective judgment is also an irreducibly social process. It happens best when practitioners enlist the help of others – learners, supervisors, peers and colleagues – to see their ideas and actions in new ways. If reflective judgment is conceived as a social learning process then learners, peers and colleagues become important critical mirrors (Brookfield, 1995). When our peers listen to our stories and then reflect back to us what they see and hear in them, we are often presented with a version of ourselves, and our actions that comes as a surprise. Hearing others' perceptions helps educators gain a clearer perspective on the dimensions to their thoughts and actions that need closer critical scrutiny. It also helps them realize the commonality of their individual experiences as well as the elements of their practice they take for granted. The development and exercise of reflective judgment is likely to remain a central focus of theory building in adult learning as well as an important component of continuing professional education.

See also: cognition, critical thinking, transformative learning.

References and Further Reading

Brookfield, S. D. (1987). *Developing critical thinkers: Challenging adults to explore alternative ways of thinking and acting*. San Francisco: Jossey-Bass.

Brookfield, S. D. (1995). *Becoming a critically reflective teacher*. San Francisco: Jossey-Bass.

Kincheloe, J. L., Steinberg, S., & Hinchey, P. H. (Eds.). (1999). *The post-formal reader: Cognition and education*. New York: Falmer.

King, P. M., & Kitchener, K. S. (1994). *Developing reflective judgment: Understanding and promoting intellectual growth and critical thinking in adolescents and adults*. San Francisco: Jossey-Bass.

Mezirow, J. (1991). *Transformative dimensions of adult learning*. San Francisco: Jossey-Bass.

Mezirow, J., & Associates (2000). *Learning as transformation: Critical perspectives on a theory in progress*. San Francisco: Jossey-Bass.

Sinnott, J. D. (1998). *The development of logic in adulthood: Postformal thought and its applications*. New York: Plenum Press.

Stephen Brookfield

Reflective Learning

Reflective learning seems to lie somewhere around the activities of learning and thinking. It is represented in reflective writing (or drawing or talking or other forms) – but the capacity to write or draw etc. is then also involved. Reflective practice clearly draws on the learner's ability to use reflective learning. In these definitions, we treat the term "reflection" as synonymous with "reflective learning." The reasoning behind the definitions is presented initially in Moon (1999b), and is expanded in Moon (2004).

The following example demonstrates the development of a habit of reflective learning, and some benefits of it in an adult learning situation. A consultant pediatrician was describing his experience of being required to reflect in the context of a brief course. He talked about his initial resistance, how he had seen reflection as "inward-looking and self-destructive indulgence," and how he was afraid that it would "unravel his survival strategies." He went on to talk about how reflection had led him towards a reevaluation of his role and the behaviors traditionally associated with it – of being distant and faintly aggressive. He talked about how those junior to him were now beginning to talk to him and to ask questions, even about other than work matters.

There are three aspects to the definition of reflective learning, all of which need to be taken into account and linked to make full sense of the word and the activity. There is a commonsense use of the word – the "dreaming under the apple tree on a summer day" kind of meaning. There is one which takes into account the implications of using reflective learning in an academic context (an operationalized version), and, furthermore, there are ideas that unify the many uses of "reflective learning" in the very broad literature that relates to it.

The commonsense definition is: Reflection is a form of mental processing – like a form of thinking – that we use to fulfil a purpose or to achieve some anticipated outcome. It is applied to relatively complicated or unstructured ideas for which there is not an obvious solution, and is largely based on the further processing of knowledge and understanding and emotions that we already possess (based on Moon 1999b).

In the formal education situation, we place conditions on the process of reflective learning. We need to recognize these conditions or there is a danger that we make technical an everyday activity. The second definition is in addition to the commonsense definition given above. We add: in the educational context, there is likely to be a conscious and stated purpose for the reflection, with an outcome stated in terms of learning, action or clarification. In this context, it is likely to be preceded by a description of the purpose and/or the subject matter of the reflection. The process and outcome of reflective work is most likely to be written and to be seen by others and both of these factors may influence its nature.

But what of the complex literature that seems to treat reflective learning in many different ways? A general view of the literature suggests that definitions have either accorded with the definitions cited above (e.g., Dewey, 1933) and focus on the process of reflection itself, or they have applied the term and talk about the outcome of the activity instead of the activity of reflective learning itself. An example is Schön (1987), whose focus was professional development.

We pick out particularly significant points in these definitions. Firstly the content of reflection tends to start off with what we know already (Dewey, 1933). It is then a process of reorganizing knowledge and emotional orientations in order to achieve further insights. That we reflect on what we in some way know already tends to contradict the sequence of the well-known model of experiential learning developed by David Kolb (1984). There is also literature that stresses the role of emotion in reflective learning (e.g., Boud, Keogh, & Walker, 1985). An explanation for this may be that while emotion is linked with all learning, in reflective learning, we "allow" it to be expressed (Moon, 2004).

In the last few years, reflective

learning has become a topic of application and interest in professional development, adult and higher education. Increasingly, learners are asked to reflect on their performance, their weaknesses and strengths and future planning. This may be in the context of learning journals (Moon, 1999a), or the development of personal development profiles of some sort. Such developments have not been consistent across the world. Reflection requires independent thought in a learner, and in many countries, instructionism dominates. In some languages there is not a word for "reflection" – which makes it difficult to develop within the educational context.

The increasing requirement for people to engage in reflection has raised issues about the ability of everyone to reflect and the quality of the outcome. These concerns have led to the recognition of the "depth" dimension of reflection. Depth is one pole of a continuum from superficial, descriptive reflection to more profound and broader reflection that takes into account the constructed nature of knowledge and which engages in perspective transformation and other qualities (Hatton & Smith, 1995; Mezirow, 1981, 1991, 1998; Moon, 2004).

See also: critical thinking, experiential learning, journal writing, reflective practice, transformational learning.

References and Further Reading

Boud, D, Keogh, R., & Walker, D. (1985). *Reflection: Turning experience into learning*. London: Kogan Page.

Dewey, J. (1933). *How we think*. Boston, MA: Heath & Co.

Hatton, N., & Smith, D (1995). Reflection in teacher education – towards definition and implementation. *Teaching and Teacher Education, 11*(1), 33–49.

Kolb, D. (1984). *Experiential learning as the science of learning and development*. Englewood Cliffs, NJ: Prentice Hall.

Mezirow, J. (1981). A critical theory of adult learning and education. *Adult Education, 32*(1), 3–24.

Mezirow, J. (1991). *Transformative dimensions of adult learning*. San Francisco: Jossey-Bass.

Mezirow, J. (1998). On critical reflection. *Adult Education Quarterly, 48*(3), 185–199.

Moon, J. (1999a). *Learning journals, a handbook for academics, students and professional development*. London: Kogan Page.

Moon, J. (1999b). *Reflection in learning and professional development*. London: Kogan Page.

Moon, J. (2004). *A handbook of reflective and experiential learning*. London: Routledge Falmer.

Schön, D. A. (1987). *Educating the reflective practitioner*. San Francisco: Jossey-Bass.

Jenny Moon

Reflective Practice

Reflective practice (RP) is an amorphous term which has circulated since the 1980s to describe the many ways that instrumental, critical, poetic, and/or contemplative reflection on the part of professionals and adult educators helps them make meaning and sense out of the tacit knowledge, interactions and experiences of their daily practice with learners and clients; its aim may to be to improve practice, to deepen personal understandings of values and ethics, and to better understand the workings of power in that daily practice. An experienced reflective practitioner purposefully establishes a clearly articulated goal for their RP, makes disciplined use of a personally satisfying method for reflection selected from the many varieties available, regularly assesses what they learn from their reflections, and, above all, makes a commitment to make changes to their practice, personally or professionally, based upon that learning.

Reflective practice is found in as many settings as educators of adults practice, formally, non-formally, and informally. For example, education in reflective practice is offered in pre-service training and continuing education in the fields of education, adult education, the health and social work professions, urban planning, law, and business management. Variants of reflective practice are found in Europe and Latin America, and especially in Britain, Canada, Australia, and the United States. Although corporations and professional organizations tend to be most interested in funding continuing education opportunities that are focused on "updating" the technical knowledge of professionals, adult educators have increasingly voiced great concern for making reflective practice a central component in professional adult education (Cervero, 1998; Frost, 2001; Wilson, 2001).

Introduced by Dewey in the 1930s, the concept of reflective practice was explored by Donald Schön (1983) in the seminal text, *The Reflective Practitioner*. Schön argued that the traditional reliance on scientific knowledge, or technical rationality, as the basis for continuing professional education, was inadequate because it did not address the deeper needs of professionals to more fully understand the "swampy lowlands" of actual practice, where professional judgment requires the practitioner to do more than instrumentally apply a discrete body of technical knowledge to a given problem and arrive at a predictable solution. Schön noted that much more often, professionals are required to engage in "artistry," and that professional judgment, though developed through experience, requires the development of wisdom and ethics. He argued that reflective practice would promote this awareness, and encouraged *reflection-in-action* and *reflection after events*.

Since Schön, adult educators have developed diverse approaches to develop wisdom and artistry and promote change in adult and continuing education through reflective practice, and have encouraged its use (Wilson & Hayes, 2000). A decade ago, Brookfield (1995) complained that the terms reflection and reflective practice were overused, that they had become buzzwords denuded of all real meaning; however, it might be more valuable to assess how much useful scholarship and research in reflective practice has occurred over the last decade, especially in the training of pre-service teachers. Some is proscriptive and instrumentalist in its focus, but newer approaches employing deconstructive and dialogic techniques, promote reflection on the teachers' professional values, practice, improvement and context (Ghaye & Ghaye, 2001), and resonate with adult educators, as do suggestions on how to enhance the "scholarship of teaching" in further and higher education (Palmer, 1998). The interdisciplinary and international journal *Reflective Practice* is devoted exclusively to publishing essays, empirical studies and reviews of reflective practice. Most adult and continuing education journals now carry reports of reflective practice variants, which help differentiate the bewildering array of reflective practice texts, online training courses, conferences, and for-profit seminars offered internationally and across disciplines. Clearly, what reflective practice is not, is cursory reading of course evaluations or client notes, a quick think about it all on the way home and a nice promise to do better next time. Serious and committed reflective practice involves dedication, work and interest. Choosing a focus, a method of reflection and a means of effecting praxis may be a daunting task for adult educators faced with such a plethora of offerings.

Goals for Reflective Practice

The goals of reflective practice fall into several categories. They may include improving practice instrumentally, "just doing it better," by understanding how to apply wisdom, artistry and personal practical knowledge gained through experience, as well as professional, academic knowledge (Frost, 2001; Schön, 1983). Or improving practice through the use of more critical techniques, that is, by better understanding the workings of power and ideology in institutions, practices and structures of work and thus aiming for more equitable and less oppressive conditions (Brookfield, 2000). Or in encouraging transformational learning and perspective shifts (Mezirow, 1998) through reflective techniques. Or, in postmodern and poststructural perspectives, where educators come to understand how the co-construction of subjectivities or categories of identity are intrinsically bound up with how power/knowledge and language/discourse structures operate in relation with others (Chapman, 2003; Usher, Bryant, & Johnston, 1997). Or by enhancing the long-term personal value and holistic appreciation of the professionals' ethical and moral practice (Dawson, 2003). These goals are not mutually exclusive; all may be in play at once – but it is best to select a focus consonant with one's philosophical approach to the practice of adult education in one's professional setting.

For some adult educators, reflective practice requires the practitioner to rigorously examine assumptions regarding practice in a critical, analytic, and rational manner; these theorists distinguish between reflection and critical reflection. Informed by the Frankfurt School of Critical Theory, and defined by Paulo Freire, Myles Horton and Stephen Brookfield, critical pedagogues argue that the purpose of critical reflection is to explore and illuminate power relationships and to uncover hegemonic assumptions within education (Brookfield, 2000). Education is a social activity embedded in a political context, and educators and learners should be about the business of creating a more just and more democratic world. Critical and feminist pedagogues acknowledge the constructed nature of knowledge and the importance of including multiple perspectives and "lenses," but they believe that reflection that does not seek out ideological assumptions, and explore the workings of power in an analytic and rational manner, falls short of its potential for creating change and promoting compassion, inclusion, and justice in adult education. Their commitment is to change and greater democracy, and their underlying belief is in the emancipatory nature of education; they are suspicious of other forms of reflection that promote individualism rather than deepening the awareness of professionals of the political, social, and communal nature of their activities.

Transformational educators do not seek to limit reflection to issues of social justice, power and oppression, though these may well be explored within transformation learning activities, but encourage reflection on psychological, social, logical, ideological or spiritual domains. Transformational educators believe that the primary aim of critically reflective practice should be to emancipate the learner from outmoded, un-useful, and possibly destructive, perspectives and assumptions acquired during childhood in a frequently unjust society, and that transformation has not occurred unless the learner is able to move the transformed perspective into identifiable action. Although critical reflection is usually considered a rational process, recent scholars note that activating events are often provided by exposure to popular media, fiction, poetry, and other artistic expressions, and that learners often desire to express their transformative experience through creative, artistic means (Cranton, 2002).

Poststructural and postmodern scholars encourage personal reflection on the part of the adult educator. They hope the educator will come to awareness that the power operating within relations in their practice is not necessarily negative or oppressive, but that it actually is productive – that is, in power relations, via techniques of practice, and the entwining of language, power/knowledge structures and agreed upon "truths," norms are established that set up expectations for behavior, activity and living. This is a co-construction: learners and educators, clients and professionals, institutions and people, all interact to create the preferred subjectivities or categories of identity in those structures – thus, self awareness can allow the co-creation of more equitable subjectivities, or at the very least, open up the possibility of resistance to prevailing and unfair norms (Chapman, 2003).

Recently, some adult educators have begun to develop holistic approaches to reflective practice that are less proscriptive and less constrained by cognitive, analytic and rational approaches, preferring to illuminate affective and spiritual perspectives towards reflective practice. This is not new. Adult education has always been an applied discipline, drawing from eclectic and often contradictory foundational work in psychology, sociology, humanism, moral education, and organizational theory. Many adult educators reject Cartesian disconnections and dislocations into mind versus body, and are concerned with integrating body, heart and spirit with mind, in the construction/deconstruction of professional and personal practical knowledge, believing that this integration ultimately leads to possibilities for even deeper critical thinking. Although the original goal of Schön's reflective practice was to explore and make explicit the artistry and wisdom of professionals, the models, instruments and language developed for reflective practice are often more closely allied with technical rationality than non-rational human expressions of "art" and "wisdom" and therefore need to be explored using different epistemologies and forms (Winter, Buck, & Sobiechowska, 1999).

Reflective Practice Methods

All reflective practice methods include inquiry, dialogue and intentionality; some are almost exclusively analytic and rational, but other methods now include narrative inquiry, visual, "poetic" or arts-based projects, kinesthetic, and contemplative and meditative techniques which embrace silence.

Many practitioners choose to use writing as a method of reflection, selecting and adapting one of the many genres of narrative inquiry now available to meet their reflective goals (Chapman, 2004). These may include journaling or portfolio production (see Boud, 2001), and useful guidelines exist for making the most of writing about one's practice. In another example, a poststructuralist narrative approach would be based on self-writing, or *askesis*, which Foucault (1997) defines as the discipline and care of the self, with the aim of developing an embodied ethical practice. Rather than trying to move professional knowledge into practice, thereby ignoring the personal, practical wisdom of daily work, the practitioner engaging in askesis, will use two forms of reflective self-writing to surface ethical and philosophical values, and their commitment to change. The first involves the keeping of daily notebooks, and the second, is in correspondence with others about those notes.

Corresponding with others – either face to face, via email, or letters, or even in publications – is a way, Foucault (1997) says, of moving out of self-absorption and narcissism, and into sharing our self with the Other. Reviewing our notebooks nightly, assembling it in a form to communicate to someone else, makes self-writing a social and a critical act. Both kinds of self-writing, will, taken together, reveal an ethic of practice arising from the day-to-day things we actually do, think, read and react to, as opposed to the more traditional method of identifying an ethic to guide our practice, which might not be consonant with our values, assumptions, norms and preferences (Chapman, 2003).

Poetic approaches to reflection, where "poetry" is used in the Artistotlean sense of embracing all the arts, need not require the practitioner be a true poet. Maxine Greene's distinction between art-like and art helps us see that researchers and educators can use art based approaches to produce texts for reflection, and may produce something that is poetry-like, but isn't really poetry. These art-based texts for reflection still hold personal and professional meaning, and opportunities for assessing learning by the artist/teacher/researcher and self-exploring novices. Such poetic approaches may include musical or visual representations, photographs, videos, multi-genre writing and dramatic renderings of events in the professional's practice. Kinesthetic methods of reflection can include, for example, dance, play, Tai-Chi, expressive movement, walking or running; here the practitioner brings the mind-body holistic connection to bear on issues of practice and may then generate poetic or narrative texts for evaluation.

Increasingly, reflective practice is viewed not only as an action, but also as a way of being, an orientation, which must be cultivated (Willis, 1999), and contemplative methods for reflection are emerging. Reflection requires intention, the conscious setting aside of time and space to reflect deeply on one's practice, and includes attention to silence and contemplation, despite the overwhelming busy-ness of professional life (Dawson, 2003), and its proponents emphasize the necessity to engage in substantial, disciplined periods of silence thus producing deep, original and authentic thought. Practices of meditation and contemplation developed over the millennia in spiritual and philosophical traditions around the world allow the practitioner to detach from concerns of the immediate material world and develop an attention to inner authority, or wisdom.

Contemplation can be broadly defined as the disciplined attempt to quiet the mind in order to cultivate concentration, awareness, compassion, connectedness, and inner wisdom. Contemplative practice in professional reflection often results in greater awareness of power relations and critique of dominant cultural patterns, and therefore may also allow for deeply transformative experience, but it is not geared towards such predetermined outcomes. In contemplation, reflective practitioners gain access to knowledge and wisdom from experience, body, intuition, and emotions that is not mitigated by rational, analytic and judgmental modes of thought.

Silence is a complex and elusive concept in Western thought and experience, and it deserves attention (Alerby & Elidottir, 2003). Because contemplation is intentional and purposeful, the practitioner places him-herself into the space of silence, outside of chronological time and beyond temporal experience, and detachment is achieved through prolonged attention to experience of the present moment. The silence of contemplation permits practitioners to know and think beyond the limits of language and rational thought, allowing engagement in multivalent, paradoxical, non-linear, non-hierarchical, and non-rational ways with their world and knowing of the world; practitioners develop the capacity to recognize and respond to inner authority, to find themselves in deep relationship with all of life. This deep sense of connectedness allows them to relinquish quests for isolation, domination, and objectification.

When one develops a contemplative practice of engaging in extended periods of silence, reflection that is neither critical nor instrumental can emerge. Contemplative reflection holds the potential to be more authentic and less geared towards the imperatives and norming powers of the institution. Because the knowledge that comes from contemplative practice is not readily accessible, contemplation needs to be combined with other forms of reflective practice.

Development of contemplation as a basis of reflective practice holds promise for adult education. Scholars in the 1990s were consumed by anxiety over the "crisis of the professions," the loss of professional connection to clients, and the growing attachment to capitalism in the consumerism and commodification of continuing professional education (CPE), and other areas of adult education. Contemplation as the basis of reflective practice, and the understanding of reflective practice as a spiritual exercise, provides a means of rooting adult educators in the pursuit of wisdom, reattaching professionals to clients and educators to learners, resisting credentialism, consumerism and commodification.

Assessing Reflection and Committing to Change

The most important stage of reflective practice is the last: the practitioner must move beyond reflection, and the individualistic and frequently personally satisfying experience of making meaning of their daily work and practice. Reviewing the goals articulated at the beginning of the process, the professional will analyse their reflections – whatever form those take – and make a commitment to change. Questions that might be used in the analysis of the reflection could include: Is it critical, does it reveal power at work? Is it *useful*, does it explain educational phenomena or issue? Is it *valuable*, for practice? Is it *emotive*, and *connective*, will it stimulate resonance and dialogue with peers? Is it *aesthetically pleasing*, will it inspire others in the field? Will it stimulate colleagues or peers or me to praxis, taking action? One may also ask: How can the job be done better? What values need to be questioned? How can the client/learner/professional relationship be deepened? How can I, the professional continue to find value, use and ethical commitment in my daily practice, and sustain my passion and joy in my work? These last questions are best answered in dialogue, in collaboration, and in community with peers, colleagues, mentors, other professionals; learners and clients may also be included in such discussion. Numerous examples abound in the literature (Palmer, 1998), in journals (Daley, 2001), professional organizations and associations of how to set up communities of practice where such dialogue can renew, refresh and reenergize its members.

See also: critical thinking, reflective judgment, reflective learning, practitioner, praxis.

References and Further Reading

Alerby, E., & Elidottir, J. (2003). Sounds of silence: Some remarks on the value of silence in the process of reflection in relation to teaching and learning. *Reflective Practice, 4*(1), 41–51.

Boud, D. (2001). Using journal writing to enhance reflective practice. In L. M. English & M. A. Gillen (Eds.), *Promoting journal writing in adult education* (pp. 9–17). *New Directions for Adult and Continuing Education*, No. 90. San Francisco: Jossey-Bass.

Brookfield, S. D. (1995). *Becoming a critically reflective teacher.* San Francisco: Jossey-Bass.

Brookfield, S. D. (2000). The concept of critically reflective practice. In A. L. Wilson & E. R. Hayes (Eds.), *The handbook of adult and continuing education* (2nd ed.; pp. 33–49). San Francisco: Jossey-Bass.

Cervero, R. M. (1998). Continuing professional education in transition, Symposium on workplace learning and performance in the 21st century. Edmonton, University of Alberta: Institute for Professional Development.

Chapman, V.-L. (2003). On "knowing one's self" selfwriting, power and ethical practice: Reflections from an adult educator. *Studies in the Education of Adults, 35*(1), 35–53.

Chapman, V.-L. (2004). Using critical personal narratives: A poststructural perspective on practice. In R. St. Clair & J. Sandlin (Eds.), *Promoting critical practice in adult education. New Directions in Adult and Continuing Education* No. 102 (pp. 95–103). San Francisco: Jossey-Bass.

Cranton, P. (2002). Teaching for transformation. In J. Ross-Gordon (Ed.), *Contemporary viewpoints on teaching adults effectively* (pp. 63–71). *New Directions for Adult and Continuing Education*, No. 93. San Francisco: Jossey-Bass.

Daley, B. J. (2001). Learning and professional practice: A study of four professions. *Adult Education Quarterly, 52*(1) 39–54.

Dawson, J. (2003). Reflectivity, creativity, and the space for silence. *Reflective Practice, 4*(1), 33–39.

Foucault, M. (1997). Self-writing. In P. Rabinow (Ed.), *Michel Foucault. Ethics, subjectivity and truth. Essential works of Foucault.* New York: The New Press.

Frost, N. (2001). Professionalism, change and politics of lifelong learning, *Studies in Continuing Education, 23*(1) 5–17.

Ghaye, A., & Ghaye, K. (2001). *Teaching and learning through critical reflective practice.* London: David Fulton.

Mezirow, J. (1998). On critical reflection. *Adult Education Quarterly, 48*(3) 185–198.

Palmer, P. (1998). *The courage to teach.* San Francisco: Jossey-Bass.

Schön, D. A. (1983). *The reflective practitioner.* New York: Basic Books.

Usher, R., Bryant, I., & Johnston, R. (1997).

Adult education and the postmodern challenge: Learning beyond the limits. London, New York: Routledge.

Willis, P. (1999). Looking for what it's really like: Phenomenology in reflective practice. *Studies in Continuing Education, 21*(1), 91–101.

Wilson, A. (2001). Professionalization: A politics of identity. In C. A. Hansman & P. A. Sissel (Eds.), *Understanding and negotiating the political landscape of adult education* (pp. 73–83). *New Directions for Adult and Continuing Education,* No. 91. San Francisco: Jossey-Bass.

Wilson, A. L., & Hayes, E. R. (2000). On thought and action in adult and continuing education. In A. L. Wilson & E. R. Hayes (Eds.), *The handbook of adult and continuing education* (pp. 15–32). San Francisco: Jossey-Bass.

Winter, R., Buck, A., & Sobiechowska, P. (1999). *Professional experience and the investigative imagination: The art of reflective writing.* London: Routledge.

Valerie-Lee Chapman and Barbara Shaw Anderson

Relational Learning

Relational learning refers to: (a) learning that occurs within relationships – with one's self, with fellow learners, with teachers and mentors, with the ideas and concepts of the content being studied, and with the larger community and the world; and (b) learning that enables the learner to discern and understand relationships among ideas, concepts and events. While the term "relational learning" itself is not common in the literature of adult education, the tenets of the field reflect a strong emphasis on the relational aspects of adult teaching/learning. Sensitivity to learners' experiences, attention to the mentoring role of learning facilitators, respect for the learning community, and engagement with feminist pedagogies are all areas in which adult education intersects with and expresses relational learning. Four foundational concepts underlie the idea of relational learning: first, humans are by nature relational, social beings; second, knowing itself is relational; third, learners are active participants in the learning process; and fourth, education leads the learner to redefine her or him self in relation to the larger community.

Foundational Concepts

Relational learning begins with the understanding that humans are social beings and that relationship with other human beings is ontologically basic. We construct and develop a sense of self in relationship with people, ideas and transcendent entities. We cannot describe ourselves apart from this network of relationships as they situate and define our lives. We understand our lives, our actions and our knowledge in the context of those social networks, that is, in relation to other human beings. As an activity that involves connection with other human beings and ideas, learning involves a relational dimension.

Second, relational learning is based upon a relational epistemology in which the knower and the known exist in mutual and dynamic relationship. A relational epistemology rejects the objectification and disconnection of knowledge from the knower. Instead it calls for an openness, receptivity and responsiveness to that which is known, not merely mastery of it. The source of knowledge is the impulse towards connection, wholeness and integration. Knowing itself is understood as relational, contextual and dynamic.

The third main idea that underlies relational learning is that learners are active participants in the learning process, not passive receivers of content. Learners engage with content and participate in interactions with other players in the learning experience. In other words, learners are engaged in learning relationships. Learning relationships, like all relationships, entail active participation, maintenance of connection and some level of back-and-forth, give-and-take activity. So relational learning assumes actively engaged learners.

Fourth, relational learning offers a process through which the learner can redefine the self in relation to the community and the world. Learning within relationships with other students, with teachers, and with new ideas develops skill in perspective taking and empathic response. Relational learning emphasizes opportunities for learners to check out emerging perceptions and opinions through feedback from others, and reinforces the recognition that learning does not occur in a vacuum. The process acknowledges the interconnectedness of global issues and fosters the movement to more encompassing and discerning worldview. Students gain insight into themselves and their relationship to the larger community through connection and dialogue with teachers and other learners.

Roots of Relational Learning

The idea of relational learning has emerged from the confluence of several strands of thought in educational philosophy. Perhaps the most foundational is the relational philosophy of Jewish theologian Martin Buber (1970). In Buber's view, humans can enter into two types of relatedness with the world, which he characterizes with two word pairs, I–It and I–You (or, as usually rendered I–Thou). In the I–It mode, one relates partially and conditionally whereas in the I-You relationship one interacts with immediacy and fullness of engagement. The most fundamental way to distinguish these two modes of relating is on the matter of objectification. In the I–It orientation one relates to people, knowledge and the world as object, separate from the self. By contrast, in the I–You mode one moves beyond the subject–object separation into the relationship with a wholeness that does not leave any part of oneself outside the experience to observe and comment on it. The mutuality of the I–You relationship forms the basis of Buber's educational philosophy. Presence and confirmation are two key concepts in Buber's philosophy that relate to relational learning. Presence is the capacity and willingness to present oneself authentically to the other and to be open to receive the authentic presentation of the other in return. Confirmation in the teacher/learner relationship involves not only acceptance of the student as she or he is now at this moment, but a capacity to see and teach to the best self, the potential of the student.

Writer and educational philosopher Nel Noddings (1984) draws from and builds on Buber's description of mutual relationship in the educational experience in her development of a relational pedagogy based on the ethic of care. In her view, the first and primary aim of education is to nurture the ethical ideal – the best self – of the student. Caring is the fundamental relation within which teaching and learning occur. Caring is not regarded as a pedagogical technique but as the fundamental relation upon within which teaching and learning occur. Noddings' view of the educational relationship is grounded in the premise that the student is always more important than the subject. The key components of the educational relationship according to Noddings are modeling, dialogue, practice and confirmation.

Relational Learning in Adult Education

Closely associated with relational learning is writer and teacher-educator Parker Palmer (1983/93) whose well-known book, *To Know as We Are Known,* frames learning in terms of spiritual formation. While prevalent approaches to education historically have been based on individualism and competition, it is the creation of relationship and community that are more truly the role of the education. Palmer notes that among scholars and educators there is a growing recognition that "real learning does not happen until students are brought into relationship with the teacher, with each other, and with the subject" (Palmer, p. xiv). For Palmer, relational learning is supported through educational practices that create community.

Interest in relational education has grown in recent years according to some writers as a result of what Palmer (1993) has termed "the pain of disconnection" in education (p. x). Educators and students alike feel disconnected from one another, from a sense of community in the learning experience, and from the content knowledge.

Aspects of relational learning are implied if not specified in much of the writing about adult teaching and learning. Stephen Brookfield (1991), one of the most highly respected contributors to the literature of the field, has used the terms responsive teaching and grounded teaching to describe relationally oriented approaches. These approaches represent an effort to appreciate the educational encounter from the adult learner's point of view – that is, teaching that is responsive to and grounded in the student's experience of learning. Brookfield's relational approach is sensitive to the emotionality and the fluctuating rhythms of the learning experience.

Relational learning in adult education is frequently associated with feminist theory and women's learning. The themes of self-in-relation, connection, and empowerment that are prevalent in postmodern feminist writing resonate with the foundational concepts of relational learning. The concept of connected knowing from the well-known work *Women's Ways of Knowing* (Belenky, Clinchy, Goldberger, & Tarule, 1986) is essentially and deeply relational in that it refers to knowing that taps the experience and knowledge of others through empathic attunement. The related term connected teaching refers to relational teaching in which the teacher is engaged and implicated as a human being in the educational encounter. The image of teacher as midwife used by these authors suggests an intimate relational connection between teacher and learner in which the learner plays a profoundly active role. The conversation in adult education continues to center around the extent to which connection is reflective of women's learning specifically (Hayes & Flannery, 2000).

Discussions of the mentoring relationship in adult education are another focal point for relational learning in adult education. Laurent Daloz who has worked extensively with adult students returning to higher education articulates a relational view of teaching and learning in his often quoted statement that

"Education is something we neither 'give' nor 'do' to our students. Rather, it is a way we stand in relation to them" (Daloz, 1986, p.xv, underline original). Adult educators see this helping relationship as a means of enabling adult learners to see themselves and life from a different perspective, and to envision an expanded sense of possibility (Daloz; Rossiter, 1999). Norman Cohen (1995) outlines five components of the mentor's role in relationship with adult learners: building a trusting relationship with the learner, gathering accurate information about the learner, facilitating alternative perspectives and options, functioning as a role model, and encouraging learners to envision and develop their full potential (Cohen).

A Model of Relational Learning

Models of relational learning developed as alternative schools for youth offer concise and practice-based principles for relational learning. One such model, RelationaLearning (Otero, 2001) is premised on the conviction that alienation, conflict and a sense of disconnection in modern society results from inadequate relational development. Therefore education should serve as a laboratory for learning within and about relationships. Relational learning in this model helps to recontextualize education by serving as a feedback loop for learners between their knowledge and the world around them. Students gain self-knowledge and understanding through relationships with other learners and with teachers. RelationaLearning helps to recontextualize education by serving as a feedback loop for learners between their knowledge and the world around them. The process involves four levels: recognizing the information, understanding, valuing, and relating. Relational learning is supported by a caring educational environment that uses time, setting and skills to foster relationship building.

What remains unexplored in most discussions of relational learning, however, are the power dynamics and the potential for disharmony. Most writers idealize relational learning and neglect the issues of interpersonal conflict, uneven power relationships, and institutional constraints.

What the literature of adult education does not adequately address are the dynamics of self/other relationship in adult teaching and learning. While adult educators are concerned with relating to learners in an authentic way, some believe that the field does not adequately prepare practitioners to manage the dynamics of those relationships. Specifically, the literature does not sufficiently address the developmental dimension of the adult teacher/learner relationship. Another continuing question about relational learning centers around gender. Some evidence suggests that women are more likely to engage in and prefer connected knowing and relational learning, yet as Flannery points out, there seems to be more difference within than between genders (Hayes & Flannery, 2000).

See also: activity theory, actor-network theory, communities of practice, mentoring, social constructivism, women's learning.

References and Further Reading

Belenky, M. F., Clinchy, B. M., Goldberger, N. R., & Tarule, J. M. (1986). *Women's ways of knowing: The development of self, voice, and mind.* New York: Basic Books.

Brookfield, S. D. (1991). *The skillful teacher.* San Francisco: Jossey-Bass.

Buber, M. (1970). *I and thou* (W. Kaufmann, Trans.), New York: Charles Scribner's Sons.
Cohen, N. H. (1995). *Mentoring adult learners: A guide for educators and trainers.* Malabar, FL: Krieger.
Daloz, L. (1986). *Effective teaching and mentoring.* San Francisco: Jossey-Bass.
Hayes, E. R., & Flannery, D. D., with Brooks, A. K., Tisdell, E. J., & Hugo, J. M. (2000). *Women as learners: The significance of gender in adult learning.* San Francisco: Jossey-Bass.
Noddings, N. (1984). *Caring: A feminine approach to ethics and moral education.* Berkeley: University of California Press.
Otero, G. (2001). *RelationaLearning: Education for mind, body and spirit.* Victoria, Australia: Hawker Brownlow Education.
Palmer, P. J. (1983/93). *To know as we are known: Education as a spiritual journey.* San Francisco: HarperCollins.
Rossiter, M. (1999). Caring and the graduate student: A phenomenological study. *Journal of Adult Development, 5,* 205–216.

Marsha Rossiter

Religious Education

The religious education of adults refers to the teaching and learning that occurs in congregations and other religious institutions within a wide variety of faith traditions such as Judaism, Hinduism, and Christianity. Within Canada, the United States and Australia, the religious educator is referred to variously as catechist, Christian religious educator, Christian educator, and religious instructor. Within these countries, theological education is used as a separate term to describe education that occurs in higher education, especially in schools of theology which typically offer graduate degrees and prepare people for leadership in congregations. In Europe, however, theological education refers to religious education that occurs in congregations, communities of faith, and in schools of theology.

Continued Interest in Religious Education

In the early 20th century, many of the researchers and writers in adult education were concerned with religious education. Britain's Basil Yeaxlee (1925), for instance, worked for the YMCA and wrote about the spiritual values of adult education, which he equated with religious education. This interest has continued, as evidenced by the presence of chapters on religious education in the handbooks of adult education which have been published since 1934. Writers of these chapters have moved from discussions that are mainly descriptive (e.g., Beatty & Hayes, 1989), to ones that are more critical and questioning (English & Gillen, 2000). Acknowledged in all these discussions is the tension of offering education within religious institutions, which are primarily traditional and non-changing.

Trends and Themes

Of late, religious education has received some attention in adult education, especially in the publications of Foltz (1986), Regan (2002), Gillen and Taylor (1995), Jarvis and Walters (1993), Wickett (1991), Schuster (2003), and Elias (1993). In these and other publications, several research interests are discernable. One is an interest in young adult education (see Atkinson, 1995), with its focus on providing meaningful and developmentally appropriate religious education to those in that age group. The other is an interest in educating in congregations and in places of worship (Vogel, 1991). The third interest is in informal religious education (English, 1999). Another trend in North America is lay education, or adult faith and leadership education for those non-ordained members of religious groups. This typically occurs in nonformal seminars and courses, and often in diploma-type programs (see Zeph, 2000), sometimes by church bodies but increasingly in collaboration with universities. The LIMEX (Loyola Institute for Ministry Extension Program) program at Loyola University in New Orleans is a successful example of the latter. Yet the purpose of these lay education programs is contested. The discussion centers, in part, on whether these community-based lay education initiatives are intended to replace traditional higher education and graduate degrees in theology which are the normal route to leadership in religious groups (English, 2002). Issues are raised about the *ad hoc* nature of many of these lay education programs and their providers.

Another discernable trend in adult religious education is in the concern for spirituality, which is a common concern for all religious groups, the general public and many non-religious educators. There is a burgeoning literature on spirituality in adult education, some of which focuses on the spirituality of workplaces (English, Fenwick, & Parsons, 2003).

Journal Publications and Organizations

An English language scholarly publication that focuses specifically on adult religious education is the European publication, *Journal of Adult Theological Education*. In Canada, adult religious education research is published in the Roman Catholic quarterly *Caravan: A Resource for Adult Religious Education* (Canadian Conference of Catholic Bishops: Ottawa); in the United States, the refereed and interfaith journal *Religious Education*, and *Jewish Education*; and in Australia, the ecumenical *Journal of Christian Education*.

On an organizational level in the United States, adult religious education has a significant presence in the interfaith academic organization Association of Professors and Researchers in Religious Education, which meets annually, and includes in its program a task force on adult religious education. In Europe, adult religious education has its own organization, the Ecumenical Association for Adult Education in Europe. Jewish adult educators in North America formed the Alliance for Adult Jewish Learning in the late 1990s, and meet yearly.

See also: continuing education, historical inquiry, meaning making, social gospel, spirituality.

References and Further Reading

Atkinson, H. (Ed.). (1995). *Handbook of young adult religious education*. Birmingham, AB: Religious Education Press.

Beatty, P. T., & Hayes, M. J. (1989). Religious institutions. In S. B. Merriam & P. M. Cunningham (Eds.), *Handbook of adult and continuing education* (pp. 397–409). San Francisco: Jossey-Bass.

Elias, J. L. (1993). *The foundations and practice of adult religious education* (Rev. ed.). Malabar, FL: Krieger.

English, L. M. (1999). Learning from changes in religious leadership: A study of informal and incidental learning at the parish level. *International Journal of Lifelong Education, 18*(5), 385–394.

English, L. M. (2002). Continuing education for lay ministry: Providers, beliefs, issues, and programs. *Canadian Journal of University Continuing Education, 28*(1), 11–30.

English, L. M., Fenwick, T. J., & Parsons, J. (2003). *Spirituality of adult education and training*. Malabar, FL: Krieger.

English, L. M., & Gillen, M. A. (2000). A postmodern approach to adult religious education. In A. L. Wilson & E. R. Hayes (Eds.), *Handbook of adult and continuing education* (pp. 523–538). San Francisco: Jossey-Bass.

Foltz, N. T. (Ed.). (1986). *Handbook of adult religious education*. Birmingham, AL: Religious Education Press.

Gillen, M. A., & Taylor, M. C. (Eds.). (1995). *Adult religious education*. Mahwah, NJ: Paulist.

Jarvis, P., & Walters, N. (Eds.). (1993). *Adult education and theological interpretations*. Malabar, FL: Krieger.

Regan, J. E. (2002). *Toward an adult church: A vision of faith formation*. Chicago: Loyola Press.

Schuster, D. T. (2003). *Jewish lives, Jewish learning: Adult Jewish learning in theory and practice*. New York: Union of American Hebrew Congregations Press.

Vogel, L. J. (1991). *Teaching and learning in communities of faith: Empowering adults through religious education*. San Francisco: Jossey-Bass.

Wickett, R. E. Y. (1991). *Models of adult religious education practice*. Birmingham, AB: Religious Education Press.

Yeaxlee, B. (1925). *Spiritual values in adult education* (2 vols.). London: Oxford University Press.

Zeph, C. (2000). Spiritual dimensions of lay ministry programs. In L. M. English & M. A. Gillen (Eds.), *Addressing the spiritual dimensions of adult learning* (pp. 77–84). *New Directions for Adult and Continuing Education*, No. 85. San Francisco: Jossey-Bass.

Leona M. English

Research Methods

Research methods used in adult education – procedures for gathering data for interpretation, analysis, and knowledge construction – reflect diverse understandings of the nature of the field and the world. "Methods" and "methodology" are sometimes used interchangeably, indicating a lack of agreement about their meanings. As used here, methodology refers to the theoretical and philosophical framework justifying the selection and use of research methods (Clough & Nutbrown, 2002). Research may be defined as a systematic, purposeful, and disciplined process of constructing knowledge (Deshler & Grudens-Schuck, 2000; Merriam & Simpson, 1995). This process takes place within a particular framework or paradigm, the shape of which depends on answers to questions about knowledge and power: Whose knowledge? For whom is it constructed? Who should construct it? How and by whom will it be used? For what purposes? (Deshler & Grudens-Schuck; Merriam & Simpson). Most adult education research is framed by one of three paradigms – positivist, interpretive, and critical, each reflecting a particular stance or worldview – which determines the purpose, design, and methods used and the interpretation of results (Merriam, 1991; Merriam & Simpson).

One way to differentiate among these types of research is to describe the assumptions underlying them (Creswell, 1998), including both philosophical assumptions about the nature of reality and sociological assumptions about the nature of research and the social organization of knowledge (McIntyre, 1993). The vastly simplified discussion that follows is not meant to imply simple dichotomies, but rather continua on which researchers may be located (Onwuegbuzie, 2000).

Ontology

What is the nature of reality? The

positivist research paradigm assumes that there is objective reality subject to natural laws, such as cause and effect, and there are universal truths that can be discovered through inquiry. An interpretivist view is that there are multiple socially constructed realities and inquiry seeks to identify limited patterns that may be culturally specific. A critical paradigm recognizes multiple versions of reality but names and challenges dominant constructions of reality that perpetuate inequality (Cohen, Manion, & Morrison, 2000; Guba & Lincoln, 1994; Merriam & Simpson, 1995).

Epistemology

What is the relationship between the knower and what is known? How do we know what we know? What counts as knowledge? In the positivist paradigm, the object of study is independent of researchers; knowledge is discovered and verified through direct observations or measurements of phenomena; facts are established by taking apart a phenomenon to examine its component parts. An interpretivist view is that knowledge is established through the meanings attached to phenomena studied; researchers interact with the subjects of study to obtain data; inquiry changes both researcher and subject; knowledge is context and time-dependent. From a critical perspective, knowledge is derived from understanding, interrogating, and critiquing actions and interests within the wider context of social structures (Cohen et al., 2000; Guba & Lincoln, 1994; Merriam & Simpson, 1995).

Methodology

How do we find out whatever it is that we believe we know or can come to know? In the positivist paradigm, scientific method is the means of discovering knowledge; theory is used to develop hypotheses, relationships among variables are examined through carefully controlled experimental or quasi-experimental methods, numerical data are analysed, hypotheses are confirmed or disproved through deduction, established facts are used to predict, data represent a specific population and results are generalizable to that population. In interpretivist approaches, the design often evolves during the research; interpretive analysis is applied to narrative data; meanings are sought in specific social/cultural contexts with the possibility of theoretical generalization; and research strategies aim to uncover relations among phenomena, inductively discovering theory out of categories that emerge from research. The critical paradigm, with the goal of transformation and empowerment, is concerned with action informed by reflection. Although defined less by methods than by a critical theoretical perspective, inquiry in this paradigm often includes participatory research, action research, and methods informed by feminism, postmodernism, and poststructuralism (Cohen et al., 2000; Guba & Lincoln, 1994; Merriam & Simpson, 1995; Merriam & Associates, 2002).

Axiology

What is the role of values? In positivism, the research process is considered value-free and methods are structured to reduce error and ensure objectivity and lack of bias. Positivists rarely make their own moral or political stances explicit in reporting research. Interpretivist researchers believe that inquiry is value-bound and research is inevitably value-laden and biased because researchers are influenced by traditions, environments, and personalities. They acknowledge their subjectivities and consider the resulting knowledge valid for a particular time and context rather than for all times and places. A critical researcher undertakes an explicitly ideological approach, critiquing social structures and power relationships and articulating a vision of social justice and equality (Merriam, 1991; Merriam et al., 2002).

Rhetoric

What language and style are used in reporting the research? Reports of positivist-aligned research tend to be written in formal, third-person language that maintains the distance between researcher and phenomenon; data are depicted through tables, graphs, and mathematical models. Qualitative reports in the interpretivist or critical vein use informal, expressive language, metaphor, and narrative; the voices of researchers and participants are evident. Within different paradigms, different persuasive methods are used to convince readers of the trustworthiness of the report (Merriam et al., 2002; Nasser, 2001).

Intent

What is the purpose of knowledge construction? Using Habermas' categories of technical, practical, and emancipatory interests, the positivist researcher has a technical interest in understanding, explaining, predicting, controlling, generalizing and establishing relationships and explaining causes; the interpretivist has a practical interest in understanding phenomena from the participants' perspective for the purpose of application and improvement; the critical researcher's emancipatory interest is in understanding in order to effect empowerment, enhanced self-determination, and social change (Cohen et al., 2000; Quigley, 1997).

Evolution of Adult Education Research Methods

As the field developed over the last 100 years, adult education has manifested diverse forms and functions, a multiplicity of agencies involved in practice, and a varied clientele (Peters & Banks, 1982). Paralleling this diversity of practice are competing perspectives on its purpose – particularly instrumental/technical or social/emancipatory (Grace, 1999; Quigley, 1997), accompanied by differing views of the purpose of research – to improve practice or to extend knowledge. In the 1950s and 1960s, a movement to professionalize and standardize the field emerged; this period saw an increase in graduate programs and a focus on building theory and the knowledge base (Rubenson, 1994). Content analyses of journals and accounts in the periodic handbooks of adult education published in North America show a shift from an early emphasis on project descriptions towards more empirical studies and statistical methods (Deshler & Grudens-Schuck, 2000; Peters & Banks; Rubenson). From the 1950s–1970s, the field's quest for legitimacy as it sought to move from the margins to the mainstream of the educational enterprise led to an emphasis on scientific knowledge-production using methods borrowed from the natural sciences (Grace, 1999). The positivist paradigm predominated because it was seen as a means of producing the knowledge necessary for the field to be classified as a discipline; it may also be due to the emphasis on the individual learner and the psychological orientation of adult education in North America, compared with greater emphasis on social theory in Europe (Merriam, 1991; Rubenson).

However, questions about whether the positivist approaches, used in the natural sciences, were appropriate for the study of social or human issues were raised, particularly among those for whom the social purposes of adult education were paramount (Grace, 1999), and incompatibilities between the positivist paradigm and adult education values were pointed out (Merriam, 1991). The emerging discourses of critical theory, postmodernism, poststructuralism, and feminism began to influence research (Rubenson, 1994). Analyses of research methods used in journal articles and conference papers indicated a shift from the early emphasis on quantitative methodologies to qualitative and combined methodologies (Peters & Banks; Rubenson; Taylor, 2001). The terms "quantitative" and "qualitative" are sometimes used to refer to the positivist and "antipositivist" paradigms themselves, differences between the interpretivist and critical perspectives notwithstanding. On another level the terms refer to the type of research methods used to collect and analyze data and derive generalizations.

Quantitative methods for data gathering include controlled experiments and quasi-experiments (in which the samples occur naturally rather than being artificially manipulated by the researcher), surveys, interviews, and observations. Until the late 1970s, most research in North American adult education used these methods, and they contributed to the knowledge base on participation and adult learning (Merriam, 1991). In contrast, by using qualitative methods "the researcher builds a complex holistic picture, analyzes words, reports detailed views of informants, and conducts the study in a natural setting" (Creswell, 1998, p. 15). Use of these methods, which include biography, phenomenology, ethnography, case study, and narrative inquiry, has steadily grown in adult education in the last three decades (Merriam et al., 2002). Using the methods of critical social science, a group identifies problems or constraints in its social context through dialogue and critique of social conditions, participants undertake a program of education that results in new perspectives on the situation and develop a plan of action to change social conditions (Merriam, 1991). Participatory and action research within a critical framework is only recently emerging in adult education literature, particularly in North America (Little, 1992).

The Paradigm Wars: The Next Wave

The relationship between method and paradigm is not clear-cut, and both qualitative and quantitative techniques are sometimes used regardless of the paradigm framing the study (Cohen et al., 2000). Some methods, for example, historical inquiry or action research, are not as aligned with a particular paradigm as others, such as participatory action research. Selection of research method involves the following factors (Creswell, 1998; Nassar, 2001): the research problem; the training, experience, and psychological attributes of the researcher; the focus of the study; and the needs of the audience. There are many advocates of the use of integrated perspectives and combined methods, taking advantage of the most valuable features of each

(Cohen et al.; Smeyers, 2001). Others make the case for complementarity, suggesting that neither quantitative nor qualitative methods may be sufficient on their own and selection should be based on goodness of fit or appropriateness to the inquiry. Problems and patterns identified by qualitative data can lead to quantitatively defined knowledge construction and vice versa (Deshler & Grudens-Schuck, 2000; McIntyre, 1993).

Although many have called for a truce in the wars over paradigms and methods, recent trends in the United States – including federal legislation that limits research to that which addresses questions using experimental design, randomized field studies, and quantitative rather than qualitative data – suggest that the issue of research methods remains a contested area (Belzer & St. Clair, 2003). One problem with limiting the types and methods of inquiry in adult education is the diversity of contexts, purposes, goals, learners, instructors, and constructions of knowledge, learning, and literacy in the field. A second problem with applying one research approach across every situation lies in the ways practitioners use research, a longstanding concern in adult education. Studies show that "practitioners use research pragmatically in ways that they can apply to their specific needs as practitioners, their working contexts, and the needs of their learners. This use of research does not fit well with the goal of experimental methods that aim to create generalizable findings – practitioners use research in quite the opposite way" (Belzer & St. Clair, p. 11). Practitioners dissatisfied with the usefulness of research findings have taken matters in their own hands by conducting their own inquiries focused on finding answers to practical questions using action research and other methods (Belzer & St. Clair).

At the heart of the disagreements are the questions of what is considered legitimate as knowledge and what constitutes legitimate research. According to Garrison and Shale (1994), the answers to these questions,

> were based on the presumption that truth was to be had only through a particular paradigmatic view of science and research. Although there is now wide recognition of the patently false conclusion that knowledge derived from one source is inherently superior, nonetheless "epistemic privilege" and "methodological imperialism" persist. (p. 23)

Like Garrison and Shale (1994), Quigley (1997) asserts that the debate is over ideology, over differing implicit sociopolitical agendas. In adult education,

> the underlying research issue for the field is not codification of methods. The deeper issue . . . is the conflict among ideological understandings of what the practice of adult education should be for . . . . And, in my view, what types of research and research methods should be acceptable to support the competing purposes of this field constitute the growing academic debate. (Quigley, p. 5)

For Merriam (1991), the issue fades in importance against the larger moral imperative of practice; the struggle is a distraction that leaves pressing practice problems unanswered. That the research question should guide the choice of research methods and techniques is not a new concept. Cohen et al. (2000) cite a 1946 article in which Merton and Kendall suggested that social scientists had already abandoned the "spurious choice" between qualitative and quantitative data (p. 45). Others, however, resist the détente of mixed methods (Lather, 2004). What is the ultimate purpose for research, the reason for seeking knowledge? Gowin (1982) says: "If science is not for the uses of human beings, what justification is there in its pursuit?" (p. 1,415). To which Lather replies: "Science is, like all human endeavor, a cultural practice and the practice of culture" (p. 28).

See also: action research, appreciative inquiry, autobiography, case study, ethnography, life history, narrative, participatory action research, phenomenology.

References and Further Reading

Belzer, A., & St. Clair, R. (2003). *Opportunities and limits: An update on adult literacy education*. Columbus: ERIC Clearinghouse on Adult, Career, and Vocational Education, Ohio State University (ERIC Document Reproduction No. ED482336).

Clough, P., & Nutbrown, C. (2002). *A student's guide to methodology: Justifying enquiry*. London, and Thousand Oaks, CA: Sage.

Cohen, L., Manion, L., & Morrison, K. (2000). *Research methods in education* (5th ed.). London and New York: Routledge Falmer.

Creswell, J. W. (1998). *Qualitative inquiry and research design: Choosing among five traditions*. Thousand Oaks, CA: Sage.

Deshler, D., & Grudens-Schuck, N. (2000). The politics of knowledge construction. In A. L. Wilson & E. R. Hayes (Eds.), *Handbook of adult and continuing education* (pp. 592–611). San Francisco: Jossey-Bass.

Garrison, D. R., & Shale, D. (1994). Methodological issues: Philosophical differences and complementary methodologies. In D. R. Garrison (Ed.), *Research perspectives in adult education*. (pp. 17–37). Malabar, FL: Krieger.

Gowin, D. B. (1982). Philosophy of science in education. In H. E. Mitzel (Ed.), *Encyclopedia of educational research* (5th ed., pp. 1,413–1,416). New York: Free Press.

Grace, A. P. (1999). Building a knowledge base in US academic adult education (1945–70). *Studies in the Education of Adults, 31*(2), 220–236.

Guba, E. G., & Lincoln, Y. S. (1994). Competing paradigms in qualitative research. In N. K. Denzin & Y. S. Lincoln (Eds.), *Handbook of qualitative research* (pp. 105–117). Thousand Oaks, CA: Sage.

Lather, P. (2004). This *IS* your father's paradigm: Government intrusion and the case of qualitative research in education. *Qualitative Inquiry, 10*(1), 15–34.

Little, D. J. (1992). Criteria for assessing critical adult education research. *Adult Education Quarterly, 42*(4), 237–249.

McIntyre, J. (1993). Research paradigms and adult education. *Studies in Continuing Education, 15*(2), 80–97.

Merriam, S. B. (1991). How research produces knowledge. In J. M. Peters, P. Jarvis & Associates (Eds.), *Adult education* (pp. 42–65). San Francisco: Jossey-Bass.

Merriam, S. B., & Associates (2002). *Qualitative research in practice: Examples for discussion and analysis*. San Francisco: Jossey-Bass.

Merriam, S. B., & Simpson, E. L. (1995). *A guide to research for educators and trainers of adults* (2nd ed.). Malabar, FL: Krieger.

Nasser, F. M. (2001). Selecting an appropriate research design. In E. I. Farmer & J. W. Rojewski (Eds.), *Research pathways: Writing professional papers, theses, and dissertations in workforce education* (pp. 91–106). Lanham, MD: University Press of America.

Onwuegbuzie, A. J. (2000). Positivists, post-positivists, poststructuralists, and postmodernists: Why can't we all get along? Towards a framework for unifying research paradigms. Paper presented at the Annual Meeting of the Association for the Advancement of Educational Research, Ponte Vedra, FL. ERIC Document Reproduction Service No. ED 452110.

Peters, J. M., & Banks, B. B. (1982). Adult education. In H. E. Mitzel (Ed.), *Encyclopedia of educational research* (5th ed., pp. 83–87). New York: Free Press.
Quigley, B. A. (1997). The role of research in the practice of adult education. In B. A. Quigley & G. Kuhne (Eds.), *Creating practical knowledge through action research: Posing problems, solving problems, and improving daily practice* (pp. 3–22). *New Directions for Adult and Continuing Education*, No. 73. San Francisco: Jossey-Bass.
Rubenson, K. (1994). Adult education: Disciplinary orientations In T. Husén & T. N. Postlethwaite (Eds.), *International encyclopedia of education* (2nd ed., pp. 120–127). Oxford, UK: Pergamon.
Smeyers, P. (2001). Qualitative versus quantitative research design: A plea for paradigmatic tolerance in educational research. *Journal of Philosophy of Education, 35*(3), 477–495.
Taylor, E. W. (2001). Adult education quarterly from 1989 to 1999: A content analysis of all submissions. *Adult Education Quarterly, 51*(4), 322–340.

Sandra Kerka

Rural Learning

Historically, much of rural learning has been synonymous with extension; however, beginning in the mid-1980s and continuing into the present, rural learning is increasingly becoming synonymous with community capacity-building. Whatever the emphasis, rural learning has always been intimately tied to the history of adult education. For example, Morrison (1999), quoting Alfred Fitzpatrick the founder of the Frontier College in Canada, writes, "The ideal state must educate all the people not a chosen few. Education must be obtainable on the farm, in the bush, on the railway, and in the mines. We must educate the whole family wherever their work is, wherever they earn their living" (p. 7). Clearly Fitzpatrick was arguing that rural and agrarian people could not be forgotten when it came to learning. However, like many concepts in adult education, our understanding of rural learning has varied and changed across time and space as changing social and economic forces gives rise to new understandings and new forms of rural learning.

In order to understand the concept of rural learning we need to understand the concept of rural. First, "rural" is a contested concept with definitions ranging from the spatial definitions of rurality through to postmodernist and poststructuralists who argue that spatial definitions fail to capture the fluidity of rural (Pratt, 1996). It is further argued that rural is best understood as a social and cultural construction that may vary across differing contexts. Others have argued that the nature of rurality is best understood through lay discourse focusing on the experience and beliefs of those people who define themselves as rural (Jones, 1995).

And much like rural, learning too is often a contested concept. Traditionally learning and education were synonymous with an emphasis on the subject–object relationship characterized by pragmatist thought during the 19th and 20th centuries; learning happens as a result of transactions with the world of objects. However, as Woodhill and Röling (1998) maintain, an alternative conceptualization of learning is emerging that emphasizes the relationships among people and what "we experience as 'reality,' and hence knowledge is to a very large extent constructed by social processes" (p. 61). Thus different settings and contexts can give rise to different but equally valid knowledge. Given that the constituent elements of rural learning have varied, our understanding of the compound term rural learning has also varied across time and space as it responds to changing social, economic, cultural and environmental forces.

A Modernist View of Rural Learning

Historically, to understand rural learning is to understand the emergence of the practice of extension, as rural learning, for the most part, has been embedded within systems of non-formal education. And as Nef (1989) points out, to understand extension, and hence understand rural learning, one must recognize the emergence of modern education that was used "to facilitate the movement toward an increasingly secular, industrialized and modern democracy" (p. 39). During the late 19th and 20th centuries there was an infusion of science and technology into education which was directed and guided by an instrumentalist philosophy whereby the focus of learning was on the transfer of "know-how." In this sense there was a separation between knowledge construction, dissemination and application, and thus extension education became the intermediary between those who constructed knowledge and those who applied knowledge. Thus, in North America during the latter part of the 19th century and much of the 20th century, rural learning was equated with extension. From a political perspective it "was an integral part of a successful and unfolding national capitalist project of development under the leadership of the financial and industrial bourgeoisie and played a central role in maintaining the alliance between farmers and industrialists" (Nef, 1989, p. 39).

After the Second World War, extension was seen as a vehicle for national development, reconstruction, and containment, and this was expressed in Europe through the Marshall Plan and the development of the United Nations Food and Agriculture Organization, while in Asia this was expressed through the Colombo Plan (Nef, 1989). Nef goes on to further argue that at this time the promotion of rural learning was a vehicle for preventing political unrest and social revolution.

And while extension and rural learning was playing a part in capitalist North America and Europe, it was also a vehicle for social transformation in the socialist countries by promoting insurgency and consolidating a peasant–worker alliance under the leadership of socialist movements. For example, it was really extension that was at work in Lenin's post-revolutionary modernization of agriculture in an attempt to create a new social order that was based in technology and science. And it was a form of political extension that was at work in Maoist China mobilizing the rural peasant population as a means of radically revamping the socioeconomic structure (Nef, 1989).

Rural learning in the South was also affected by these developments, in particular as large-scale extension systems were developed for the sole purpose to transfer knowledge, tools, skills and values from the "developed" world to the "underdeveloped" world. As Nef (1989) notes, this approach was almost exclusively concerned with the "how-to" without questioning the overall ideological framework or asking the question why. Consequently, rural learning in the South was embedded in hegemonic educational systems that viewed the South as a problem and through the process of "modernization" the developed world could stifle social unrest and at the same time bring the underdeveloped world into the modern era. Thus the educational systems to facilitate rural learning were embedded within an ideological framework whose goal was to further develop the modernist vision, and in particular further the capitalist/ democratic project of the West. Rural learning as fostered by systems of extension was instrumental to this project in the global context.

Structural Changes and Rural Learning

Sumner (2001) has argued that rural communities have experienced significant changes starting in the 1980s and this has continued to the present as a result of economic globalization. First, rural communities in both the North and the South have experienced significant structural changes as a result of economic globalization. After an extensive review of the literature she concludes that rural communities across the globe have been marginalized by unsupportive governments, devastated by international trade agreements, and have been preyed upon by transnational corporations. Hill and Moore (2000) have argued that this places rural communities in a precarious position as they have little influence over the political and economic forces which are shaping their future. They further argue that there is an increasing need for responses at the local and regional level. As Sumner (2003) suggests, rural communities need to learn new ways of engaging the world.

While the modernist vision of rural learning was embedded within non-formal educational systems whose function was to promote the vision and goals of the project of modernity, structural changes have resulted in the articulation of a new paradigm for rural learning known as community capacity-building. In defining this concept, Murray and Dunn (1995) write that capacity-building can be defined "as increasing the ability of people and institutions to do what is required of them. The goal is to secure empowerment of those living in rural areas to better manage their own affairs, thus reducing dependency on state intervention" (p. 91). This approach to rural development and learning, however, is fraught with some difficulties. As Murray and Dunn point out, rural communities have a small population base to draw upon, often lack the specialized knowledge and skills needed within the population base, and are often geographically remote from the necessary intellectual resources that they need to engage in capacity-building. However, limitations aside, community capacity-building is becoming the dominant paradigm for rural learning in both the North and the South (Kaplan, 2000).

Rural Community Capacity-Building

Simpson, Wood, and Daws (2003) argue that rural community capacity-building stresses the importance of "ownership" of development initiatives as a means to sustain rural communities. They further argue that communities must have capacity and these capacities are a sense of efficacy, leadership, norms of trust and reciprocity, social networks, appropriate skills and knowledge, all embedded within a community culture characterized by an openness and a willingness to learn. The underlying argument is that if rural communities are to survive current structural changes, then they must "do so by becoming empowered, by building their existing capacity and by using the skills they have to make their own futures" (Simpson et al., p. 278).

According to Bolger (2000), community capacity-building must operate on the principle that there is broad-based participation in locally driven agendas whereby community action is built on local capacities. However, there is a need for an open culture that promotes ongoing individual and collective learning in order to better adapt the community to ongoing changes. In terms of community capacity development strategies, Bolger argues that there must be a concerted effort on unlearning or eliminating inappropriate capacity, making better use of existing capacity, building and strengthening existing capacity, creating new capacity and all of this must be done in an environment that encourages creativity and innovation. However, the capacity development paradigm recognizes that geographical spaces or government defined spaces/communities do not necessarily define community and hence capacity-building must actively work to develop and enhance social relationships within rural spaces.

Implications for Rural Adult Educators

In the context of the modernist vision, rural learning was viewed as part of a strategy for modernization and was associated with extension education systems. In this context, adult educators were responsible for the dissemination of knowledge and know-how to rural people. Thus the emphasis was on educating rather than learning.

The community capacity paradigm emphasizes not only learning, but knowledge construction. Thus the adult educator is responsible not only for transmitting knowledge to rural people, but is responsible for helping them to facilitate a vision for their community, to help community members identify community assets and to identify additional skills and knowledge needed to realize their vision, and to help communities build and strengthen relationships both within their community and across communities. The rural adult educator is no longer an educator as defined by the transmission of knowledge, but is better understood as the animator of community.

See also: community development, community education, extension, popular education.

References and Further Reading

Bolger, J. (2000). Capacity development. *Occasional Series, 1*(1) (May 2000), Canadian International Development Agency (CIDA) Policy Branch.

Hill, L. H., & Moore, A. B. (2000). Adult education in rural community development. In A.L. Wilson & E.R. Hayes (Eds.), *Handbook of adult and continuing education* (pp. 344–359). San Francisco: Jossey-Bass.

Jones, O. (1995). Lay discourses of the rural: Developments and implications for rural studies. *Journal of Rural Studies, 11*(1), 35–49.

Kaplan, A. (2000). Capacity building: Shifting the paradigms of practice. *Development in Practice, 3, 4* (August), 517–526.

Morrison, J. H. (1999). New introduction: The man, the mission, the book. In A. Fitzpatrick, *The university in overalls: A plea for part-time study* (pp. 7–29). Toronto: Thompson Educational.

Murray, M., & Dunn, L.(1995). Capacity building for rural development in the United States. *Journal of Rural Studies, 11*(1), 89–97.

Nef, J. (1989). Concepts from political science. In D.J. Blackburn (Ed.), *Foundations and changing practices in extension* (pp. 37–46). Media Distribution, University of Guelph, Guelph, Ontario.

Pratt, A. (1996). Discourses of rurality: Loose talk or social struggle? *Journal of Rural Studies, 12*(1), 69–78.

Simpson, L., Wood, L., & Daws, L. (2003). Community capacity building: Starting with people not projects. *Community Development Journal, 38*(4), 277–286.

Sumner, J. (2001). Challenges to sustainability: The impacts of corporate globalization on rural communities. Paper presented at the Canadian Society for Extension, University of Guelph, Ontario.

Sumner, J. (2003). Environmental adult education and community sustainability. In L.H. Hill & D. E. Clover (Eds.), *Environmental adult education: Ecological learning, theory and practice for socioenvironmental change* (pp. 39–45). *New Directions for Adult and Continuing Education*, No. 99. San Francisco: Jossey-Bass.

Woodhill, J., & Röling, N. G. (1998). The second wing of the eagle: The human dimension in learning our way to more sustainable futures. In N. G. Röling & M.A.E. Wagemakers (Eds.), *Facilitating sustainable agriculture: Participatory learning and adaptive management in times of environmental uncertainty* (pp. 46–72). Cambridge, UK: Cambridge University Press.

Al Lauzon

S

Self-Directed Learning

The best-known definition of self-directed learning (SDL) is that of Knowles (1975):

> a process in which individuals take the initiative, with or without the help of others, in diagnosing their learning needs, formulating learning goals, identifying human and material resources for learning, choosing and implementing appropriate learning strategies, and evaluating learning outcomes. (p. 18)

The term self-directed learning seems self-explanatory, yet there is no single, accepted definition. Many terms are used interchangeably, for example: autonomous learning, independent learning, autodidaxy, self-teaching, self-study and self-planned learning, self-regulated learning, learning projects. It is also closely related to andragogy (see Merriam & Caffarella, 1999, for a discussion of both). This creates both confusion and controversy. In spite of this, SDL has been a primary focus of interest in adult education for more than four decades. Central to the debate about definition is whether SDL is learning alone and/or with others and, therefore, whether it can take place in formal contexts or is limited to the non-formal learning that occurs as part of adults' day-to-day living. Discussion has also focused on how learning and teaching in formal contexts can draw on what we know about the SDL adults conduct in their everyday lives. Other discussions highlight issues around goals and processes for SDL; models for SDL; ways to measure readiness for SDL; and critiques of its appropriateness for some people when it is used in formal contexts to foster the development of lifelong, self-directed learners, particularly in an increasingly technological age.

A Brief History

There is a sense in which all learning is self-directed – we learn for ourselves; others cannot learn for us. Arguably, too, adults have always been self-directed learners. It has long been known that adults learn as part of living and self-education has been recognized since the time of the Greeks, preceding formal schooling. The academic field of adult education was established early in the 20th century, but since the 1960s SDL has been a focus of Western adult education. Houle and Tough are usually credited with initiating the study of SDL. Tough's (1971) research built on Houle's work and revealed the extent to which adults take control of the learning projects they conduct outside of formal contexts: 90% engaged in at least one major learning project each year; 80% planned their projects themselves, and only 5% were motivated by formal credit. Building on this work, Knowles developed a set of assumptions and principles for adult learning (andragogy) that centered on SDL: adults had an innate, psychological need to be self-directed, so teaching approaches should allow them to take high levels of control of their whole learning process.

From the early 1980s until 1991, when there were several major publications, research and debate about SDL was a primary focus in adult education. Much of the discussion was published in *Adult Education Quarterly*, and since the 1990s interest in SDL has remained high enough to sustain an annual international symposium on self-directed learning. Indeed, SDL is central to discussions of, for example: adult learning, experiential learning, lifelong learning, popular education, workplace learning, human resource development and methods of teaching in formal contexts. In many countries, both Western and Eastern, government policies are promoting SDL as a way for adults to learn so they can cope with their rapidly changing world and the knowledge society. The assumption that SDL is a desirable goal and process for adults remains firmly embedded in adult education theory and practice.

SDL as Goal and Process

The literature features much discussion of the goals and processes of self-directed learning (Candy, 1991; Merriam & Caffarella, 1999). Separating goal, outcome or product from process or method, Candy identified four distinct phenomena within SDL: two goal-related and two process-related. Personal autonomy (a personal attribute) and self-management (the willingness and ability to manage our own learning) were his goal phenomena; learner control (a mode of organizing instruction in formal settings) and autodidaxy (individual, non-institutional pursuit of learning in natural social settings) were his process phenomena (Candy, p. 23). This allows us to consider SDL in both formal and non-formal contexts. Related to these goals and processes are discussions of the internal and external dimensions of SDL. The external dimension concerns the extent to which adult learners take control of, and responsibility for, their learning processes. The internal dimension focuses on the personal attributes individual adult learners require to be self-directed learners. This internal dimension is also understood as an internal change in consciousness (see Merriam & Caffarella), and as responsibility for constructing meaning (Garrison, 1997). Some SDL models discussed below integrate these two dimensions.

Merriam and Caffarella (1999) identify three goals of SDL: personal growth; transformational learning; and emancipatory learning and social action – and three types of process: linear, interactive and instructional. Tough and Knowles identified a series of stages in SDL, but interactive models deny this linearity and argue that a range of factors impacts on what and how adults learn; for example, learning opportunities adults find in their own environments, the context of their learning, their personality characteristics, and their cognitive suitability for SDL.

Models of SDL

Several different models of SDL are proposed. Tough's (1971) and Knowles' (1975) are the most linear, tracing the steps of the learning process from identifying learning needs to evaluating outcomes. Some models, for example those of both Pratt and Delahaye (Leach, 2000), allow for an individual learner to have different levels of self-direction in different contexts. Later models, for example those of Spear and Mocker, and Brockett and Hiemstra, also take into account factors within the social context (Leach; Merriam & Caffarella, 1999). Spear and Mocker described this as four categories of "organizing circumstances." In their PRO (personal responsibility orientation) model Brockett and Hiemstra (1991) refer to the two dimensions as instructional method (SDL) and personality characteristics (learner self-direction). Integrating the two dimensions results in self-direction *in* learning. Grow (1991) developed a Staged Self-Directed Learning (SSDL) model, that identifies four stages: dependence, interested, involved and self-directed, and proposes matched teaching approaches: authority/ coach, motivator/guide, facilitator and consultant. Garrison (1997) argued for a different view of the internal dimension. He saw it as a meaning construction process and developed a model that incorporated self-management (contextual control), self-monitoring (of cognitive and metacognitive processes) and motivation (both entering and task) as aspects of SDL. The only model that explicitly addresses the emancipatory intention of SDL is that of Hammond and Collins (1991), which incorporates a critical exploration of social, political and environmental contexts and both personal and social learning goals.

Measuring SDL

Instruments to measure SDL have been developed and critiqued (Candy, 1991; Leach, 2000; Merriam & Caffarella, 1999). As early as 1977, Guglielmino's Self-Directed Learning Readiness Scale (SDLRS) triggered a spirited debate. It is a 58-item Likert scale that uses self-reported responses designed to assess the degree to which people perceive themselves as having those skills and attitudes, the personal attributes, usually associated with SDL. While work on the SDLRS has been strongly critiqued as flawed, it remains the best-known. From 1984 a second scale, the Oddi Continuing Learning Inventory (OCLI), attempted to identify personal characteristics that might be associated with SDL (Candy). In 1997 the Self-Directed Learning Perception Scale (SDLPS) was developed by Pilling-Cormick (Leach). It is a 57-item inventory that focuses on environmental characteristics that help or hinder students' ability to be self-directed.

Issues

A number of issues about SDL have been identified. Early debate centered on whether it (and andragogy) applied only to adults. Some argued that children's and adults' learning processes were essentially the same and that self-direction could be found in children. Some also argued that adults' willingness to be self-directed was influenced by a variety of contextual factors and that it varied along a continuum. Closely linked to this debate was another about whether adults were innately self-directed learners. Many adults, particularly when they returned to formal learning, having little domain knowledge, and lacking self-esteem or confidence in their abilities, would become passive and dependent learners, even resisting SDL (Brockett & Hiemstra, 1991; Candy, 1991). There were also differences between what adults would do outside of and within formal institutions (Leach, 2000). Some concluded that self-directed learning was more an ideal than a reality – something to be aimed for rather than assumed; a goal for, rather than a characteristic of, adult learners.

SDL was part of a humanist reaction against the predominant behaviorist views of learning, and this base in humanist psychology has been critiqued for its individualism, its focus on the self, personal choice and freedom. It ignores the complex relationship between the individual and the social; it denies collective action, common interests and human interdependence. It is also argued that SDL does not apply universally to adults. Rather it reflects the context that spawned it – white, middle-class, male, North America. Diversity rather than homogeneity is a feature of adult learners. Culture, gender and class are but three factors of difference, which means that SDL may not apply to those cultures that value the collective over the individual; to women as much as to men; to working class as much as to middle classes. Some research has shown that we are more likely to be self-directed if we are born into cultural groups that value and nurture it (Leach, 2000).

Issues are also raised about whether SDL is emancipatory and/or prescriptive. Knowles' view of SDL has been criticized as prescriptive rather than descriptive (Hartree, 1984), and in danger of requiring learners to conform to existing social and political systems – particularly in human resource development contexts where it can amount to *directed* SDL (see Leach, 2000). On the other hand, writers like Hammond and Collins, Brookfield, and Collins (Merriam & Caffarella, 1999) are committed to emancipatory forms of SDL that result in social action. Related to this is the confusion over whether SDL is understood as learning on your own and/or learning with others (Candy, 1991; Leach; Merriam & Caffarella). Emancipatory forms of SDL require an engagement with others; even in an individualistic approach, we seldom learn entirely on our own.

Finally issues are raised about the "self" in SDL. Usher, Bryant, and Johnston (1997) summarize this as "the government of the self by the self, a freedom from dependence, a situation where one is influenced and controlled only by a source within oneself" (p. 93). This, they argue, requires a self that is individualistic, unitary, rational, pre-given and decontextualized – the monolithic self of Western culture. They criticize this view of SDL, and present a post-modern view of the self as debentured, unable to know itself independently of context and history, a constantly changing self variously represented in different stories rather than a single, "true" self.

Clearly, self-directed learning is contested. There is no agreement in the literature about what it is, to whom it applies or how it might be implemented in practice, particularly in formal education. Rather, we each have to decide how we understand it and how it will play out in our practice.

See also: adult learning, experiential learning, informal learning, motivation, teaching.

References and Further Reading

Brockett, R. G., & Hiemstra, R. (1991). *Self-direction in adult learning: Perspectives on theory, research and practice*. London: Routledge.

Candy, P. C. (1991). *Self-direction for lifelong learning*. San Francisco: Jossey-Bass.

Garrison, D. R. (1997). Self-directed learning: Toward a comprehensive model. *Adult Education Quarterly*, *48*, 18–33.

Grow, G. (1991). Teaching learners to be

self-directed. *Adult Education Quarterly, 41*(3), 125–149.

Hammond, M., & Collins, R. (1991). *Self-directed learning: Critical practice.* London: Nichols/GP Publishing.

Hartree, A. (1984). Malcolm Knowles' theory of andragogy: A critique. *International Journal of Lifelong Education, 3*(3), 203–210.

Knowles, M. S. (1975). *Self-directed learning.* New York: Association Press.

Leach, L. (2000). *Self-directed learning: Theory and practice.* Unpublished doctoral dissertation, University of Technology Sydney, Australia.

Merriam, S. B., & Caffarella, R. S. (1999). *Learning in adulthood: A comprehensive guide* (2nd ed.). San Francisco, Jossey-Bass.

Tough, A. (1971). *The adult's learning projects: A fresh approach to theory and practice in adult learning.* Toronto: Ontario Institute for Studies in Education.

Usher, R., Bryant, I., & Johnston, R. (1997). *Adult education and the postmodern challenge: Learning beyond the limits.* London: Routledge.

Linda Leach

Social Action

Social action occurs when people act collectively to bring about change. In adult education for social action, people consciously engage in teaching and learning in their efforts to bring about change. Learning is used as a tool in the struggle.

Finding a Definition

Social action encompasses the ideas of political action and community action. Political action relates to activities in the arena of ideologies, political parties, and government. Community action is usually associated with an active engagement in local, parochial matters. Social action subsumes both these kinds of action and implies action by people to affect their social, cultural, political and economic worlds. In its turn, adult education for social action subsumes political and community education.

Some forms of adult education are concerned with personal growth or enrichment and, while they may make use of group processes, the focus is on the learner as an individual. This is typically the case of voluntarily attended, non-credit adult education programs. In adult education for social action, while individuals may learn, the concern of the learners and educators is with the learning of the group as a whole.

Some other forms of adult education are concerned with training individuals to perform functions within a system or prevailing set of values, or with achieving the objectives of an organization of which they are members or employees. This is typically the case of workplace and work-based training and human resource development. In contrast, adult education for social action is normally to do with a group of people learning in order to struggle against forces – institutions, political organizations, governments, social mores, ideologies and values – which control, inhibit or constrain them in some way.

And some forms of adult education are to do with responding to disadvantaged members of society and giving them more access to existing social structures. Adult education for social action will have some affinities with education for the disadvantaged, but will be more to do with people learning in order to affect, challenge or change those social structures and so gain more direct control over their own lives.

Adult education for social action is a collective activity. People gather together and cooperate in order to learn. Their motives derive from a common history, a shared oppression, a common membership of an organization, a shared social class, a shared interest or a shared locality, and their aim is not just to learn as a group but to act on their learning as a group. Much adult education for social action, therefore, involves an analysis of existing relations of power. It is concerned with helping learners understand their social, cultural, economic and political context, and is concerned with helping them identify the changes they want and the forces holding them back from making those changes. It is concerned with equipping them with the skills, knowledge, understandings, values and conviction necessary to take action against these forces, and then helping them plan action which will be realistic and effective. We can depict adult education for social action, therefore, as the pitting of various kinds of learning against various forms of social control.

Literature and Histories

There is a literature about adult education for social action to be found under the categories of andragogy, social education, informal education, non-formal education, education for inclusion, radical education, and increasingly under the term popular education. This term has been current for some time in Latin America and Canada, and is now gaining currency in other parts of the world. Paulo Freire (1972, 1994) the Brazilian adult educator, and Myles Horton (1990) the American adult educator, are two key figures whose lives, work, ideas and writings are referred to in discussions of adult education for social action. Both were more concerned with learners who were the victims of injustice, and with the processes of helping them understand and mobilize against that injustice. Others (see for example, Newman, 1999; also Foley, 1999) have written about such learners but have also examined learning for people already motivated to act, such as trade union activists, members of the women's movement, rights activists, environmental activists, and anti-war activists.

Adult education for social action can draw inspiration from a number of different histories in different parts of the world. These include the struggle for an independent working-class education in the first half of the 19th century in England; the use of education in the labor struggles in industrial countries in the latter part of the 19th century and the 20th century; the use of education and learning in liberation struggles against colonial powers in, say, India in the first half of the 19th century, or against the apartheid regime in South Africa in the second half of the 20th century; and the use of popular education in the shanty-towns, villages, churches, workers' groups and BASE communities in Latin America for at least the past 50 years.

Forms

Adult education for social action takes many forms. Working-class activists in England in the 1830s and 1840s made use of the conventional methods of lectures and discussions in halls, Mechanics' Institutes, associations and coffee shops. Some saw a political advantage for their class simply by gaining access to "useful knowledge." Others pursued what was described as "really useful knowledge" in order to understand, for example, why there was continuing poverty in the midst of the extraordinary wealth being accumulated by Britain as it became the leading imperial and industrial power.

In the latter part of the 19th century, folk high schools were established in Denmark and other Scandinavian countries, that made use of reasonably conventional instruction and discussion but were located within rural and often impoverished communities. The programs were non-vocational, and the teaching and learning involved discussion of matters relating to those communities. The folk high school movement was openly concerned with issues of social justice.

Some activists constructed teaching and learning into their activism. In 1930 in India, Gandhi set out on his famous salt march of some 350 kilometers from Sabarmati Ashram to Dandi to illegally harvest a flake of salt, and publicly defy the authority of the British Empire. As part of his act of defiance, each night of the march he would address the ever-increasing crowd of supporters on the values of political freedom.

In Brazil and then in Chile during the 1960s, Freire devised forms of political education making use of themes identified in the discourse of the learners. Educators making use of his ideas re-presented the themes to the learners in images, often in line drawings, and then encouraged an exploratory, creative dialogue. Together the educators and learners defined their lives in terms of problems and challenges instead of givens. Freire described this process as "renaming the world," and talked of shifting his learners from a naïve or fatalistic consciousness to a critical consciousness.

Horton established an adult education center in a farmhouse in the Appalachian mountains in one of the poorest parts of the United States of America in 1931. He invited "natural community leaders" from mining and cotton mill towns to short residential workshops where he encouraged them to share and learn from their experiences of hardship, racism, injustice and struggle, and to take what they had learnt back into their communities.

And in South Africa anti-apartheid activists used covert meetings and classes, poetry and forms of playback theatre in workplaces, and all-night gatherings involving music, dancing and political and educational debate.

Practice and Theory

Adult education for social action continues to be practiced in environmental struggles, anti-war campaigns, literacy programs, campaigns for workers' rights, indigenous people's rights, gay rights, women's rights and refugee rights, and development and community education campaigns across the world. It takes place in workplaces, on housing estates, in small rural communities, on the fringes of big cities, and in websites, chat rooms and activists' lists on the net. Although the terminology used may vary from place to place, adult education for social action is the subject of research and teaching in departments at a number of universities. These include the University of Groningen in the Netherlands, the University of Natal in South Africa, Pennsylvania State University in the United States of America, Chulalongkorn University in Thailand, and the University of Edinburgh in Scotland. And education for social action is discussed at regular conferences, such as those organized by the Popular Education Network in Europe, and a conference of educators and activists held by the Centre for Popular Education every 18 months in Sydney, Australia.

See also: activism, conscientization, folk high schools, popular education, social justice, social movement learning.

References and Further Reading

Foley, G. (1999). *Learning in social action: A contribution to understanding informal learning.* London: Zed Books.

Freire, P. (1972). *Pedagogy of the oppressed.* (M. B. Ramos, Trans.). Harmondsworth: Penguin.

Freire, P. (1994). *Pedagogy of hope: Reliving Pedagogy of the Oppressed.* (R. R. Barr, Trans.) New York: Continuum.

Horton, M. (1990). *The long haul.* New York: Doubleday.

Newman, M. (1999). *Maeler's regard: Images of adult learning.* Sydney: Stewart Victor Publishing.

Michael Newman

Social Constructivism

Although a singular, uniform definition of social constructivism (also labeled social constructionism) is elusive, several characteristics are apparent: (a) suspicion of taken-for-granted/commonsense knowledge; (b) time and location are relevant to meaning-making (historical and cultural specificity and norms condition knowledge); (c) discourse sustains social processes and situates knowledge; and (d) knowledge and social action are linked (i.e., knowledge has material effects on social action). Fundamentally, this analysis is about the social construction of reality. Knowledge is exclusively the result of social processes, especially communication, mediation, and negotiation.

Social constructivism encompasses a variety of expressions, some of which are in conflict. These include postmodernism/poststructuralism, postcolonialism, feminism, and queer theory (Burr, 1995; Lincoln & Guba, 2000). There are strong distinctions between the various schools of social construction. Social constructionist critiques of modernist discourses have generated a number of new social movements, including postmodernism (Seidman, 1993), a collection of disparate notions centered on suspicion of grand narratives about the way the world works. In fact, constructivism makes postmodern analysis possible. The schools of social constructivism are embodied in both modernist (e.g., critical) and postmodernist views.

Constructionists hold the tenet that items have an observer-dependent existence, as opposed to an observer-independent one. As a movement, constructivism "rejects universals and generalizable truths, and focuses instead on the variability of how people interpret their experiences. This strand of thought maintains that events happen to us but that experiences are constructed by us" (Brookfield, 2000a, p. 37). Proponents of constructivism argue that people write their own lives and are authors of their own experiences. Social constructionists contend that "social contexts are so diverse, the possible ways of interpreting experiences will be similarly boundless" (Brookfield, 2000b, p. 53). Perhaps more than a theoretical perspective, social constructivism is an epistemological position – a way that meaning is derived through knowledge and power.

A Reaction to Modernism

Modernism offers the notion that reality exists "out there," external to the observer, and "true" in an absolute sense. With the right tools, methodologies, and means, reality can be discovered, quantified, and ultimately fully understood. Reality is posited as universal rather than particular. This suggests that knowledge itself is fixed, stable, unitary, and can be apprehended – as well as comprehended – in its completeness. The process is not always easy; in fact, this scientific paradigm is based on the belief that nature hoards secrets and, as Francis Bacon offered, must be hounded in her [*sic*] wanderings (Peltonen, 1996). In this paradigm, people come to know only through bold rational pursuit and they are not necessarily responsible for the results of their courageous search. The debate centers around the view that reality, like knowledge itself, is fixed and available to (and for) humans; it is to be discovered and transmitted. A response to this is the opinion that reality, like knowledge, is made by us. Both knowledge and reality are limited, shifting, plural, contingent, fluid, and unstable. Categories such as race, the self, gender, ethnicity, and sexual orientation, are constructed within regimes of power – and not in innocent or naïve ways. Assemblages such as these are constructed classifications.

Social constructivists reject essentialism, the notion that everything has a true essence and that identity can be condensed to an "essential" aspect, constructed in relations to power and knowledge. Essentialism "demands that sources, forms, style, language and symbol all derive from a supposedly homogeneous and unbroken tradition" (Rushdie, 1991, p. 67). Social constructivism is a phenomenon that seeks to subvert the "truths" of modernism.

Discourse Analysis

Social constructivists take up discourse analysis as a tool to interrogate texts and spaces that can be read, or that we occupy – or don't occupy – as a function of our personal positioning on the "uneven and slippery sociohistorical landscape upon which a range of identities are invented, measured and weighed, adopted, negotiated, and contested" (de Castell & Bryson, 1998, p. 97). Discourse constructs social phenomena; it is more than a set of statements, it is composed of the meanings and social relations embedded in those statements. It also includes what remains unsaid in the statements. The purpose of discourse is to produce a specific version of events. It is the "meaningful field that provides the conditions of possibility for experience, thought, and action" (Nash, 2000, p. 274). Scott (1985) suggests that it includes not only specific words and phrases, but a whole set of rules and norms for determining what is true (or not true), what has value (or does not), and what is trivial (or meaningful). For the French philosopher Michel Foucault, discourses construct and make "real" the objects of knowledge they "represent." There is a direct relationship between discourse and power.

Social Constructivism and Adult Education

Consequences of social constructivism for adult education are many. Pratt and Nesbit (2000) situate its impact beginning in the 1980s, offering that it allowed learner's experience to be "the avenue through which teaching gained entry . . . Teaching was about helping people construct better, more complex, differentiated, and integrated cognitive structures" (pp. 120–121). By now the "idea [of social constructivism] is rather commonplace (although not always considered valid) in adult education" (Hayes & Wilson, 2000, p. 671). The work of Stephen Brookfield (2000a, 2000b) reflects the influences of constructivism on criticality. He writes that "this tradition emphasizes the way people learn how to construct, and deconstruct, their own experiences and meanings" (2000a, p. 37).

Adult educators often describe four qualitative research methodologies: positivism, postpositivism, critical theory, and constructivism. In constructivist research, the aim is not so much to discover or uncover what is observed, but rather to create knowledge in an interactive, intra- and inter-personal way. Suspicion of taken-for-granted knowledge and a critique of what constitutes truth and reality position social constructivism as a significant launching site to theorize about learning, learners, education, and identity. It rejects causal models, and discards essentializing practices that imply characteristics are "inherent" within a person.

The influences of social constructivism on recent work in cognition have prompted questions on "the relationship of 'context' and 'learner' as well as between 'learner' and knowledge' and 'knowledge' and 'context' " (Hayes & Wilson, 2000, p. 671). In the *Handbook of Adult and Continuing Education* (Wilson & Hayes, 2000), these authors point out the significant influences of social constructivism in the important work of adult educators. They offer that while the field has undertaken the theoretical work of constructivism, it often misses its application to practice.

In an article on human resource development, Fenwick (2000) points to how experiential learning has been influenced by social constructivist views, for instance in the work of Kolb (1984), Mezirow (1991), Miller and Boud (1996) and Schön (1983). Askov (2000) offers accounts of the impact of social constructivism in adult literacy, including recruitment and retention from a constructivist perspective (see, "Constructivist and social and cultural views of learning," Askov, pp. 255–257). Bounous (1996) shows that in non-formal literacy education, collaborative learning is influenced by the notion that knowledge is socially constructed. The reach of social constructivism has also extended into adult religious education (Goggin, 1995), where a postmodern constructivist theology employs critical reflection, feminism, eco-consciousness, and social justice based on religious believers' cultivation of skepticism and suspicion, uncertainty, fragmentation, notions of life's unruliness, the knowledge that seeing does not always require believing, and an appreciation that individuals live in social disarray.

Social constructivism in a postmodern light offers that learners, and the processes of learning, are always incomplete and constantly shifting. Hemphill (2001) asserts that the "complex cultural and technological changes that are now underway will unavoidably have major effects on how we conceive of knowledge – its construction, conceptualization, storage, transmission, and social function" (p. 27). He warns that "adult education is too important an enterprise to be left to ossify in a decaying [modernist] paradigm" (p. 27). Social constructivists ask that adult educators respect and respond to learners' lives, experiences, beliefs, values and opinions that do not follow normative scripts, and are not simple, linear, predictable, uncomplicated, innocent, ahistorical or asocial. Only then will the field develop schemes of skepticism about regimes of truth that open up new possibilities of being and doing in the world.

See also: feminist pedagogy, knowledge, meaning-making.

References and Further Reading

Askov, E. N. (2000). Adult literacy. In A. L. Wilson & E. R. Hayes (Eds.), *Handbook of adult and continuing education* (pp. 247–262). San Francisco: Jossey-Bass.

Bounous, R. M. (1996). Transforming the teacher–student relationship: Collaborative learning in adult education. In H. Reno & M. Witte (Compilers), Proceedings of the 37th Annual Adult Education Research Conference (pp. 19–24). Tampa, FL: University of South Florida.

Brookfield, S. D. (2000a). The concept of critically reflective practice. In A. L. Wilson & E. R. Hayes (Eds.), *Handbook of adult and continuing education* (pp. 33–49). San Francisco: Jossey-Bass.

Brookfield, S. D. (2000b). Contesting criticality: Epistemological and practical contradictions in critical reflection. In T. J. Sork, V.-L. Chapman, & R. St. Clair (Eds.), Proceedings of the 41st Annual Adult Education Research Conference (pp. 51–55). Vancouver: The University of British Columbia.

Burr, V. (1995). *An introduction to social constructionism*. New York: Routledge.

de Castell, S., & Bryson, M. (1998). Queer ethnography: Identity, authority, narrativity, and a geopolitics of text. In J. L. Ristock & C. G. Taylor (Eds.), *Inside the academy and out: Lesbian/gay/queer studies and social action* (pp. 97–110). Toronto: University of Toronto Press.

Fenwick, T. J. (2000). Putting meaning into workplace learning. In A. L. Wilson & E. R. Hayes (Eds.), *Handbook of adult and continuing education* (pp. 294–311). San Francisco: Jossey-Bass.

Goggin, H. (1995). Process theology and religious education. In R.C. Miller (Ed.), *Theologies of religious education*, (pp. 123–147). Birmingham, AL: Religious Education Press.

Hayes, E. R., & Wilson, A. L. (2000). Reflections on the field. In A. L. Wilson & E. R. Hayes (Eds.), *Handbook of adult and continuing education* (pp. 660–676). San Francisco: Jossey-Bass.

Hemphill, D. F. (2001). Incorporating postmodernist perspectives into adult education. In V. Sheared & P. A. Sissel (Eds.), *Making space: Merging theory and practice in adult education* (pp. 15–28).Westport, CT: Bergin & Garvey.

Kolb, D. A. (1984). *Experiential learning: Experience as the source of learning and development*. Englewood Cliffs, NJ: Prentice Hall.

Lincoln, Y. S., & Guba, E. G. (2000). Paradigmatic controversies, contradictions, and emerging confluences. In N. K. Denzin & Y. S. Lincoln (Eds.), *Handbook of qualitative research* (pp. 163–188). Thousand Oaks, CA: Sage.

Mezirow, J. (1991). *Transformative dimensions of adult learning*. San Francisco: Jossey-Bass.

Miller, N., & Boud, D. (1996). Animating learning from experience. In D. Boud & N. Miller (Eds.), *Working with experience: Animating learning* (pp. 3–24). New York: Routledge.

Nash, K. (2000). *Contemporary political sociology: Globalization, politics, and power*. Malden, MA: Blackwell.

Peltonen, M. (Ed.). (1996). *The Cambridge companion to Bacon*. Cambridge, UK: Cambridge University Press.

Pratt, D. D., & Nesbit, T. (2000). Discourses and cultures of teaching. In A. L. Wilson & E. R. Hayes (Eds.), *Handbook of adult and continuing education* (pp. 117–131). San Francisco: Jossey-Bass.

Rushdie, S. (1991). Commonwealth literature does not exist. In *Imaginary homelands: Essays and criticism 1981–1991*. New York: Grant Books.

Schön, D. A. (1983). *The reflective practitioner: How professionals think in action*. New York: Basic Books.

Scott, J. C. (1985). *Weapons of the weak: Everyday forms of peasant resistance*. New Haven, CT: Yale University Press.

Seidman, S. (1993). Identity and politics in a "postmodern" gay culture: Some historical and conceptual notes. In M. Warner (Ed.), *Fear of a queer planet:*

Queer politics and social theory (pp. 105–142). Minneapolis, MN: University of Minnesota Press.

Wilson, A. L., & Hayes, E. R. (Eds.). (2000). *Handbook of adult and continuing education*. San Francisco: Jossey-Bass.

Robert J. Hill

Social Gospel

The social gospel movement, usually associated within liberal Protestantism during the late 19th and early 20th centuries in North America and Europe, converged with progressive adult education and community leadership as the means for reshaping society into the democratic, Kingdom of God on earth through the development of people (see Fisher, 1997; Kidd, 1975). Adult educators Eduard Lindeman (United States) (1926/1961) and Roby Kidd (Canada) make linkages that tie the social gospel to other social movements of the Progressive era – civil rights for former slaves, women's suffrage, settlement houses, the Chautauqua movement, temperance, and the cooperative movement. Christian socialism was the inspiration for evangelical feminism and for the social gospel in Europe, whereas in academic settings in North America, adult education filtered the social gospel through the lens of theologians such as Washington Gladden, Reinhold Niebuhr and Walter Rauschenbusch (United States), or theologians turned adult educators such as E. A. (Ned) Corbett and Alfred Fitzpatrick (Canada) (Kidd; Lasch, 2001; Walter, 2003). Although the term has fallen into disfavor and disuse in adult education, the influence of the social gospel continues to the present day in non-governmental and voluntary organizations (e.g., YMCA, YWCA, Red Cross, and Women's Institutes) and in harm-reduction programs related to the homeless, child protection, prostitution, substance abuse, safe sex, gambling, and smoking (see Forsythe & Lander, 2003).

Formative Influences

The essentially educational character of Christianity as a social movement and as an ideology predates the social gospel movement; Roslewicz (1999) represents as "popular education" Henry VIII's command to have an English language Bible translation placed in every church in England (p. 42). British historian Richard Johnson (1988) also identifies two strands of adult education rooted in Christianity: the philanthropic educators, for whom religion was a source for "ordering" society and individuals – "God was a kind of policeman in the sky" (p. 5); and, radical educators, for whom Jesus Christ represented a "morality of cooperation among equals . . . turned against inequality and injustice" (p. 5). Reading the Bible and writing from dictation or copies was a central focus of the Quakers' development of the Adult School Movement; the first study of "adult education" in 1816 is attributed to Quaker Thomas Pole (Smith, n.d.). Drawing on Thomas Paine's (1776) influential educational documents of the American Revolution, espousing universal rights and condemning slavery, Law (1996) traces Anglo-American adult education to the "very old English . . . theological precept of equality in the sight of God" (p. 208).

The Progressive era of the 19th century accompanied the shift in adult education to an explicitly social gospel agenda that sought to address the problems of the poor and working classes associated with industrialization and urbanization – and in North America, the influx of immigrants from Europe. Another view was that the social gospel was primarily a religious and intellectual movement. The social gospel influenced the adult education initiative of Frontier College, which Alfred Fitzpatrick, an erstwhile Presbyterian preacher, inaugurated in 1899 to bring literacy and citizenship education to the laboring immigrant men of the remote logging, rail, and mining camps of Canada. A postcolonial perspective on the adult education projects of Anglo-Christianizing, Canadianizing and Americanizing (e.g., literacy, labor, and temperance) reveals a concern for human welfare entangled with a "fear of politically suspect outsiders, and a belief in Anglo-Protestant superiority [that] called for the assimilation of foreigners" (Walter, 2003, p. 56) and indigenous populations.

The Transatlantic forebears of the social gospel movement and institutions of urban immigrant adult education include continental Europe and the United Kingdom. The YMCA and YWCA began in the UK, as did the Workers' Education Association (WEA), whose founders such as Albert Mansbridge and James McTavish were religious activists (Kidd, 1975, p. 237; see also biographies of Basil Yeaxlee and Richard Tawney in Jarvis, 2001). Kidd identifies the Danish folk high school as a major influence, noting that the ideas of its founder, Bishop Grundtvig, were congruent with the social gospel (p. 240). Fisher (1997) indicates that Eduard Lindeman was influenced by Grundtvig. Kidd challenges the exclusively Protestant sources of the social gospel, referencing the social gospel manifestos of the 1920s' Antigonish Movement in passages written by Catholic priests, Jimmy Tompkins and Moses Coady. Social gospel metaphors intertwine with Marxist analysis in the writings of Paulo Freire, in such terms as witness, incarnation, conversion, salvation, faith, hope, trust, love, justice, the Kingdom of God, Jesus Christ, transformation, commitment, humility, sin and reconciliation (Blackwood, 1987, p. 213). "The example of God, who does not violate, dominate, or oppress is the foundational paradigm for Freire" (p. 208). Saint Francis was Dorothy Day's model for the voluntary poverty of lay leaders in the Catholic Worker settlement houses in 1930s' New York. The body of Christ is her preferred metaphor to the social gospel language of Kingdom (Trawick, 2003). Church historians record women's participation in large numbers in religious movements as far back as Christianity, which stands in contrast to their absence in political movements until the 20th century.

Neglected Voices

The social gospel's fall from grace in adult education accompanied charges that as a movement it is fundamentally racist, sexist and clergy-led (Deichmann, Edwards, & De Swarte Gifford, 2003). The dominant sources of the social gospel in adult education, represented by white, Eurocentric, male theological elites, qualify as "authorative knowledge" in Merriam and Simpson's (1995) terms, with the effect that citizens at large take as "truth and reality" what is preached or taught to them through the profession of elites (p. 3). The public speaking and writing voices of evangelical feminism bring some balance to the sexist charge. Social gospelers of the 19th century, such as Frances Willard (United States) and Letitia Youmans (Canada) of the Woman's Christian Temperance Union (WCTU), articulate the "Do Everything" educational practice that spanned not only temperance but everything from women's suffrage and the labor movement, to public water fountains and dress reform. These women were contemporaries of the theologian-adult educators but are seldom named as adult educators or popular educators (see Lander, in press, 2003). Yet their campaigns to have the welfare of women, families, and children addressed by both the church and the state accord with a central task of adult education – that of influencing public policy to effect social and economic justice. Roslewicz (1999) draws attention to the work of Lucretia Coffin Mott, a 19th-century American Quaker minister whose "gospel order" animated her distinctive public speaking and sought to educate adults about abolition of slavery, rights of women, and peaceful ways to address injustice. Social gospel historians represent Jane Addams and her associates in the settlement house movement in the United States as secular reformers because they did not affiliate with religious institutions; yet Jane Addams described her motivation for launching Hull House (between 1889 and 1892) as "a new form of Christianity that was expanding the sacred to include the commonplace" (Sklar, 1999, p. 3).

To illustrate that praxis is at the heart of the social gospel, Lindley (1990) calls attention to the neglected voices of American Christian activists marginalized by race and gender. For example, Nannie Helen Burroughs, a black woman who as corresponding secretary for the Baptist Women's Convention in 1900, raised funds to purchase the site for the National Training School for Women and Girls, which opened in 1909. The so called "School of the 3B's" for bath, Bible and broom, also had the unusual requirement that each student take a course in black history (p. 92).

The Legacy of the Social Gospel

Michael Collins (1991) and Donald Schön (1983) critique technical (instrumental) rationality in adult education, drawing on the ideas of German philosopher Jürgen Habermas, who in turn was inspired by Max Weber, a social gospeler who worked with the Evangelical Social Movement in Europe. The technical-rationality critique in adult education operates as a backlash to the scientific education of the social gospel (see Fisher, 1997).

Social gospel discourses of the 1960s (e.g., scientific temperance instruction) and the social norms marketing discourses of the 21st century have common features (see Forsythe & Lander, 2003) of seeking to effect moral and bodily regulation of young adults by establishing norms of drinking, smoking, and sexual relationships. It is common to cast evangelical youth workers as "indoctrinators" and "brain washers" (Pugh, 1999); however, educators' recognition that both secular and Christian informal education are ideological training towards normative values and ideas of the "good," calls for an emphasis on learning activities that foster democracy and dialogue, a respect for persons, and a commitment to fairness and equality and critical thinking (p. 9).

Recent writings on spirituality in adult education (see English, Fenwick, & Parsons, 2003; Tisdell, 2003) emphasize "public spirituality" or "secular spirituality," echoing

Albert Manbridge's (2001) description of adult education in the 1920s as "la secular gospel" (p. 21). The emphasis on social justice complete with religious metaphors persists, perhaps inevitably, given that the formative years of these North American adult educators were grounded in the Judeo-Christian tradition. Coming from the same tradition, Lander (2003) challenges adult educators to remember our social gospel roots and the unreflective secular use of "crusader" as synonymous with social justice worker, which serves to erase the colonizing, oppressive, and violent effects of the social gospel associated with religious wars or missionary work with indigenous populations and people of color in the Global South.

See also: historical inquiry, folk high schools, non-governmental organizations, popular education, religious education, social justice, social movements, women's voluntary organizations.

References and Further Reading

Blackwood, V. (1987). Historical and theological foundations of Paulo Freire's educational praxis. *Trinity Journal, 8*, 201–232.

Collins, M. (1991). *Adult education as vocation: A critical role for the adult educator.* London: Routledge.

Deichmann, W. J. E., & De Swarte, C. G. (Eds.) (2003). *Gender and the social gospel.* Urbana, IL: University of Illinois Press.

English, L. M., Fenwick, T. J., & Parsons, J. (2003). *Spirituality of adult education and training.* Malabar, FL: Krieger.

Fisher, J. C. (1997). The social gospel: Lindeman's overlooked inspiration? Proceedings of Midwest Research to Practice Conference in Adult, Continuing, and Community Education. Michigan State University, East Lansing, MI. Retrieved November 29, 2003 from http://www.anrecs.msu.edu/research/fisher.htm.

Forsythe, A., & Lander, D. (2003). A reflexive inquiry of two non-smokers: A trans-generational tale of social gospel and social norms marketing. *Reflective Practice, 4*(2), 139–161.

Jarvis, P. (Ed.) (2001). *Twentieth century thinkers in adult and continuing education* (2nd ed.). London: Kogan Page.

Johnson, R. (1988). Really useful knowledge 1790–1850: Memories for education in the 1980s. In T. Lovett (Ed.), *Radical approaches to adult education: A reader* (pp. 3–34). London: Routledge.

Kidd, J. R. (1975). The social gospel and adult education in Canada. In R. Allen (Ed.), *The social gospel in Canada, Papers of the interdisciplinary conference on the social gospel in Canada* (pp. 227–262). Ottawa, ON: National Museums of Canada.

Lander, D. A. (2003). The ribbon workers: (Re)-presenting the colours of the crusades. Proceedings of the 22nd Annual Conference of the Canadian Association for the Study of Adult Education, Charting the Learning Society (Halifax, NS, 2003). Retrieved July 22, 2003 from http://www.oise.utoronto.ca/CASAE/cnf2003/2003_papers/dorothylanderCAS02.pdf

Lander, D. A. (in press). Re-membering mothers as lifelong educators: The art work of the Woman's Christian Temperance Union. *Canadian Journal for the Study of Adult Education.*

Lasch, C. (2001). Religious contributions to social movements: Walter Rauschenbusch, the social gospel and its critics. *Journal of Religious Ethics, 18*(1), 7–25.

Law, M. (1996). Rediscovering hope in a new era: Possibilities for the radical tradition of adult education. In H. Reno & M. Witte (Eds.), Proceedings of the 37th Annual Adult Education Research Conference. Tampa, University of West Florida, ERIC Document Reproduction No. ED 419087.

Lindeman, E. C. L. (1961). *The meaning of adult education.* Montreal: Harvest House, originally published in 1926.

Lindley, S. (1990). Neglected voices and praxis in the social gospel. *Journal of Religious Ethics*, *18*(1), 75–102.

Mansbridge, A. D. (2001). Albert Mansbridge. In P. Jarvis (Ed.), *Twentieth century thinkers in adult and continuing education* (2nd ed., pp. 15–30), London: Kogan.

Merriam, S. B., & Simpson, E. L. (1995). *A guide to research for educators and trainers of adults* (2nd ed.). Malabar, FL: Krieger.

Pugh, C. (1999). *Christian youth work: Evangelism or social action*. London: Informal Education website. Retrieved December 15, 2003 from website: http://www.infed.org/christianeducation/christianyw.htm

Roslewicz, E. A. (1999). *Educating adults through distinctive public speaking: Lucretia Mott, Quaker minister*, Doctoral dissertation. Virginia Polytechnic Institute and State University, Department of Adult Learning and Human Resource Development. Retrieved December 12, 2003 from Digital Library and Archives website: http://scholar.lib.vt. edu/theses/available/etd-042199-022852

Schön, D. A. (1983). *The reflective practitioner: How professionals think in action*. New York: Basic Books.

Sklar, K. K. (1999). Protestant women and social justice activism, 1890–1920. Retrieved December 6, 2003 from Women in Twentieth-Century Protestantism Home Page: http://www.wheaton.edu/isae/Women/sklaressy99.html

Smith, M. K. (n.d.). Quakers and adult schools. Retrieved December 15, 2003 from Informal Education website (n.d.): http://www.infed.org/walking/wa-quak.htm

Tisdell, E. J. (2003). *Exploring spirituality and culture in adult and higher education*. San Francisco: Jossey-Bass.

Trawick, R. (2003). Dorothy Day and the social gospel movement: Different theologies, common concerns. In W. J. Deichmann Edwards & C. DeSwarte Gifford (Eds.), *Gender and the social gospel* (pp. 139–149). Urbana, IL: University of Illinois Press.

Walter, P. (2003). Literacy, imagined nations, and imperialism: Frontier College and the construction of British-Canada, 1899–1933. *Adult Education Quarterly*, *54*(1), 42–58.

Dorothy A. Lander

Social Justice

Social justice involves the assignment of rights and responsibilities within society. How these rights and responsibilities are assigned, and their nature and scope, have long been contested territory. While increasingly invoked in the age of corporate globalization, the meaning of social justice is fluid and often assumed. Over time, it has been associated with a range of complex issues such as human rights, democracy, international trade, sustainable development, health, environment and education.

At the heart of social justice lies the concept of justice itself. This concept has been debated for millennia and forms an important aspect of all religions and philosophies. Christianity, Buddhism and Islam all contain invocations of justice. Ancient Greek philosophers such as Plato and Aristotle discussed justice, as did medieval religious scholars like Thomas Aquinas. In the Anglo-American philosophical tradition, justice is understood in the broadest sense as fairness. Questions of justice, according to philosophers such as David Hume and John Stuart Mill, presuppose conflicts of interest and general principles by which distinctions between competing claims are regulated and justified (Benn, 1967).

Although the concept of justice has a long history of debate, the derivative concept of social justice has a shorter trajectory. According to

Michael Novak (2000), the term social justice was first used in 1840 by a Sicilian priest, Luigi Taparelli d'Azeglio, and was associated with an appeal to the ruling classes to attend to the needs of the new masses of uprooted peasants who had become urban workers. Over the last century and a half, this association with issues of need and fairness has had distinctly political overtones. Historical social forces and dominant ideologies are responsible for shaping certain "truths" relating to the construction of social-justice concerns; that is, the hegemonic constructs of legitimate versus illegitimate issues (Corsianos & Train, 1999).

Understandings of social justice vary widely. For John Rawls (1972), social justice is to be found by self-maximizing contractors behind a "veil of ignorance" (p. 12), choosing principles to bind them fairly in an ordered society of just institutions. Nancy Nagler (2003) sees social justice not only as the underlying principle of many efforts to define and create a civilized society, but also as "a way of doing" involving those affected by policy and those who make policy in partnership to create change. Some understand social justice as including an equitable vision of society, one in which "all members are physically and psychologically safe and secure" (Adams et al., 1997, p. 3). Others consider social justice to be a process of moving towards equality (Smith, 2000) or a shared process of action, commitment and transformation.

Historically, justice has been understood as individual rights and duties in the distribution of social products. Social justice theories, however, are more comprehensive and include the overall order of society's reproduction. *The Charter of the Global Greens* (2001) hints at this wider commitment when it states that the key to social justice is the equitable distribution of social and natural resources, both locally and globally, to meet basic human needs unconditionally, and to ensure that all citizens have full opportunities for personal and social development. John McMurtry (1998) addresses this wider commitment directly when he argues that social justice is a structuring of society to link the realization of human capacities to the fulfillment of vital needs by the evolving institution of the "civil commons" (p. 24), which he defines as any social construct which enables universal access to life goods (the most important of which is society's educational processes).

In addition to a social component, understandings of social justice have evolved to include cultural and relational aspects as well. The connecting of social justice and identity bring to the fore questions concerning our understanding of who we are, the others with whom we identify and those with whom we do not, and how the social groups to which we belong are perceived (Vincent, 2003). Social justice has also stepped outside purely human interests and become linked to environmental issues. For example, the *Charter of the Global Greens* (2001) also declares that "(there is no social justice without environmental justice, and no environmental justice without social justice."

The obverse of social justice is social injustice, understood as "human-spawned, social maladies" (Baptiste, 2000, p. 27). Andre Gunder Frank (2002) probes the question of social injustice, arguing that, at the largest social level, global processes, structures, and institutions seem to generate the greatest injustice. He concludes that there is no end to the issue of social injustice, just as there is no end to the quest and struggle for justice.

Social Justice

In the realm of education, social justice figures prominently in such areas as access, curriculum development, corporate funding, privatization, teaching and learning, and technology. Within these areas, questions of gender, class, race and ethnicity intersect and deepen the complexity of social-justice issues. However, social justice has been an undertheorized concept within education policy: some work simply marginalizes or rejects social-justice concerns, either because of a skeptical postmodernist denial of the tenability and desirability of universalistic principles, or because of an uncritical, problem-solving orientation, or because of a commitment to "value-free" research (Gewirtz, 1998).

The roots of adult education are deeply entwined with the struggle for social justice. From the first Mechanics' Institutes through the outreach of Frontier College to present-day drop-in centers for urban street youth, adult education has stood for and championed some form of social justice. Over the years, adult education has directly addressed such areas of social injustice as unemployment, inequality, racism, homophobia, disability, sweatshops, homelessness, human-rights abuse, sexism, community breakdown, illiteracy, powerlessness, exclusion, and state terrorism. According to Cunningham (1996), the social justice perspective asks adult educators to live by the mission of the field, which is to democratize the citizenry.

In spite of such social commitment on the part of individual adult educators, many forms of adult education decline to engage with social injustice. Michael Newman (1994) contends that a number of fashionable adult education theories are simply too nice, too unfocused, too inward-looking or too mechanistic to define the enemy and address issues of social justice. Taking up Newman's argument, Ian Baptiste (2000) maintains that when perpetrators of violence and injustices fail to readily exhibit self-restraint, when the injuries they inflict are consequential and sustained, adult educators who are serious about redressing social injustices are left with one option: they must try to coercively restrain the perpetrators. By coercive restraint, he means "measured coercion: force appropriate in form and in severity; force that matches the level of conflict" (p. 48). While many adult educators may hesitate to coerce anyone, Baptiste believes that sometimes coercion is our most prudent and ethical response to social injustices, and that these prudent responses can range from mild forms of manipulation, through intimidation, to the use of credible force.

Social-Justice Movements and Adult Education

Although given a name only 150 years ago, the understanding of social justice has been with us for centuries. According to Ted Jackson (1995), the human struggle for social justice, peace, and democracy is timeless and universal, and can be traced far back in history to Lao-Tzu in China, the slave revolts of ancient Rome, and the Levellers in England. In Canada, the 1837 Rebellion in Upper Canada, Riel's Métis rebellion in the West, and the post-Second-World-War social movements led by trade unionists, feminists, environmentalists, peace activists, and anti-racist activists are all part of this tradition.

Adult education has been an integral part of these social-justice movements. Angela Miles (1996) argues that the ideal context for the motivation to learn and for adult education for social change is social movement: "When people are engaged in a collective struggle that they define themselves they also decide what and why they need to learn" (p. 278). In such situations, she maintains, the question for progressive adult educators is how to be relevant to people's desire to learn and how to support their efforts.

Given the documented negative impacts of corporate globalization, the work of social-justice movements becomes crucial to challenging injustices and legitimizing sustainable alternatives to the fatalistic ideology of no alternative. In order to accomplish this work, social-justice movements must also go global and share their learning with other progressive movements. As part of a worldwide expression of globalization from below, these movements can form vital lines of reflexive resistance to the social injustices of globalization from above.

Just as capitalism is becoming universal, so must social justice, without leaving behind considerations of difference and place. "Working out questions of social justice in particular situations might be considered exercises in the contextual thickening of a thin theory with claims to universality" (Smith, 2000, p. 756). Theories of adult education with a political-economy orientation can help to define the enemy and address issues of social justice. Only through critical reengagement with political economy, with our situatedness in relation to capital accumulation, can we hope to reestablish a conception of social justice as something to be fought for as a key value within an ethics of political solidarity built across different places (Harvey, 1996).

See also: activism, philosophy, problematizing learning, social action, social movement learning.

References and Further Reading

Adams, M., Bell, L. A., & Griffin, P. (Eds.). (1997). *Teaching for diversity and social justice: A sourcebook.* New York: Routledge.

Baptiste, I. (2000). Beyond reason and personal integrity: Toward a pedagogy of coercive restraint. *Canadian Journal for the Study of Adult Education, 14*(1), 27–50.

Benn, S. I. (1967). Justice. In P. Edwards (Ed.), *The encyclopedia of philosophy,* Vol. 4. (pp. 298–302). New York: Macmillan & The Free Press.

Charter of the Global Greens, Canberra 2001. Available at: www.europeangreens.org/info/globalgreencharter.html

Corsianos, M., & Train, K. A. (Eds.). (1999). *Interrogating social justice: Politics, culture and identity.* Toronto: Canadian Scholars' Press.

Cunningham, P. M. (1996). Race, gender, class, and the practice of adult education in the United States. In P. Wangoola & F. Youngman (Eds.), *Towards a transformative political economy of adult education: Theoretical and practical challenges* (pp. 139–159). DeKalb, IL: Leadership and Educational Policy Studies (LEPS) Press.

Frank, A. G. (2002). A testimonial contribution to the 25th anniversary issue of *Social Justice. Social Justice, 26*(2), 51–55.

Gewirtz, S. (1998). Conceptualizing social justice in education: Mapping the territory. *Journal of Education Policy, 13*(4), 469–484.

Harvey, D. (1996). *Justice, nature and the geography of difference.* Oxford: Blackwell.

Jackson, T. (1995). Introduction. In D. Smith, *First person plural: A community development approach to social change* (pp. vi–xiv). Montreal: Black Rose Books.

McMurtry, J. (1998). *Unequal freedoms: The global market as an ethical system.* Toronto: Garamond.

Miles, A. (1996). Adult education for global social change: Feminism and women's movement. In P. Wangoola & F. Youngman (Eds.), *Towards a transformative political economy of adult education: Theoretical and practical challenges* (pp. 277–292). DeKalb, IL: Leadership and Educational Policy Studies (LIPS) Press.

Nagler, N. (2003). A framework for social change. *Social justice in Minnesota.* Minneapolis, MN: The Minneapolis Foundation.

Newman, M. (1994). *Defining the enemy: Adult education in social action.* Sydney, Australia: Stewart Victor Publishing.

Novak, M. (2000). Defining social justice. *First Things, 108,* 11–13.

Rawls, J. (1972). *A theory of justice.* Oxford: Clarendon Press.

Smith, D. M. (2000). Social justice. In R.J. Johnston, D. Gregory, G. Pratt, & M. Watts (Eds.), *The dictionary of human geography* (4th ed., pp. 754–758). Malden, MA: Blackwell.

Vincent, C. (2003). Introduction. In C. Vincent (Ed.), *Social justice, education and identity* (pp. 1–13). New York: Routledge Falmer.

Jennifer Sumner

Social Movement Learning

"Social movements are not merely social dramas; they are the social action from where new knowledge including worldviews, ideologies, religions, and scientific theories originate" (Eyerman & Jamison, 1991, p. 14). Social movement learning is both: (a) learning by persons who are part of any social movement; and (b) learning by persons outside of a social movement as a result of actions taken or simply by the existence of social movements. Learning by persons who are part of a social movement may occur in an informal way because of the stimulation and requirements of participation in a movement. Learning by persons who are part of a social movement may also occur as a result of intentional educational activities organized within the movement itself. Learning for those outside a social movement happens both in informal and intentional ways. The study of social movement learning recognizes that whatever else social movements are or do; they are exceedingly rich learning environments. (Clover & Hall, 2000; Finger & Asún, 2001; Foley, 1999; Holford, 1995; & Welton, 1993). Social movements are privileged locations for the creation of new knowledge; they are, as Eyerman and Jamison have said, "epistemic communities" (p. 10).

Learning for persons within a social movement may be informally acquired simply by being surrounded by new understandings of the issues of the movements themselves, such as knowledge of the impact of global warming on the biosphere or the impact of mercury contamination in fish in the case of some environmental movements. It could be the learning about the proliferation of small arms in Africa as members of one or another peace movement organization. It could be about dealing with diverse forms of homophobia or intolerance within the gay and lesbian movements. Informal learning may also take the form of specific organizational skills which are needed to reach social movement goals such as when we take on working with the media, creating websites, raising funds or engaging in public speaking (see Livingstone, 1999). We learn, and we learn at an incredible rate, in both of these cases in action, as a result of the imperatives of social movement activities. For those interested in a fuller discussion of informal learning, the recent work of David Livingstone bears close attention.

Persons within social movements also learn from intentional adult educational efforts to stimulate learning. Trade union movements offer a full range of educational activities for members ranging from ways to interpret the impact of larger political phenomena such as globalization or trade liberalization, to more practical matters such as understanding management, conducting collective bargaining or making grievances (Burke, Geronimo, Martin, Thomas, & Wall, 2002; Martin, 1995; Spencer, 2002; Taylor, 2001).

Perhaps the most significant form of social movement learning is that learning which takes place by persons who are not directly participating as members of a given social movement. For example, many men have learned much about the gendered dimensions of power and perceptions from the women's movement even though they have not been members. Much of what we first learned about the impact of a rapacious and greedy humanity on the rest of nature came from the actions of the environmental movement protesting, for example, the clear cutting of local forests. The tools of social movements, which include poetry, marches, protests, and political theatre are intentionally designed to reach beyond the movements themselves. Such is the power of social movements to reframe the world, that none of us escapes this ongoing democratic flow of energy. To this transformation of vision and imagination we give the name learning.

Vandana Shiva and Mahatma Gandhi of India, Julius Nyerere of Tanzania (Rydstrom, no date), Jimmy Tompkins (Lotz & Welton, 1997) and Moses Coady of Canada (Welton, 2001), Myles Horton and Jane Addams of the United States, Antonio Gramsci of Italy and Paulo Freire of Brazil are but a few of those whose names have been associated with the ideas of social movement learning. Mayo has rendered the most succinct comparative analysis of the work of Gramsci and Freire, who both see the learning process most fully flourishing within social movement contexts. While Gramsci contextualized his work in the notion of a working-class movement of the early 20th century in Italy, Freire's initial work grew out of rural organizing in Northeastern Brazil.

Others whose writing is influenced by social movement learning include: Bélanger and Federighi (2000), Faris (1975), Simon (1992), Smith (1994), and O'Sullivan (1999). The historical roots of adult education in the European tradition have been closely tied to the rise of early social movements such as the labor movements, protection of children's rights, the temperance movement, the struggle for women's rights to vote or the anti-poverty movements. Menconi (2003), Holford (1995), and Welton (1993), have written directly of the linkages between both old and new social movements and adult learning. Welton's (2001) emphasis has been on both older social movements such as the Antigonish Movement and newer movements based on identify and self-expression.

According to Finger and Asún (2001), new social movements such as the environment, are the catalyst for personal transformation and the environment within which transformation occurs. They define the future topics of adult education. Learning, according to Finger and Asún, within these movements has a greater impact than does schooling. Social movement learning theory within the context of endogenous knowledge creation sees learning as a people's tool (political dimension); a democratic right (learning by all) and as learning from the world (epistemological dimension). This is contrasted to exogenous knowledge transmission which sees education as a tool of the system, a package *for* all, and education *about* the world (Finger & Asún).

Welton (1993) argues that new social movements are both personal and collective in form and content. He sees them as "privileged sites" of transformative learning or emancipatory praxis, and asks the question, "What are adults learning?" in new social movements, but does not go much further than outlining some ways of understanding what the new social movements are responding to. He asks one of the key questions which we are trying to answer "Is something of great significance for the field of adult education occurring within these sites"? Menconi (2003) partially responds by writing about learning citizenship within social movements (p. 1)

Eyerman and Jamison (1991) speak of social movements as a location of "cognitive praxis" (p. 10). They suggest that it is "through tensions between different groups and organizations over defining and acting in that conceptual space that the (temporary) identity of a social movement is formed" (p. 22). Through the notion of "cognitive praxis," they emphasize the creative role of consciousness and cognition in all human action, individual and collective. They focus simultaneously on the process of articulating a movement identity (cognitive praxis), on the actors taking part in this process (movement intellectuals), and on the context of articulation (politics, cultures, and institutions). What comes out of social movement action is neither predetermined nor completely self-willed; its meaning is derived from the context in which it is carried out and the understanding that actors bring to it and/or derive from it. *Learning in Social Action* by the Australian Griff Foley (1999) offers a wide-reaching exploration of informal learning within the context of a variety of social movement settings such as an environmental campaign, a Brazilian women's organization and an African liberation struggle. He notes that informal learning occurs in social action. Particpants learn: alternative organizational forms; the links between spiritual and political action; the power of a small group of committed people; that expertise can be acquired from outside; that social action as a part of local struggles is stressful and creates a need for mutual support; and that learning deepens in the context of the community action itself (pp. 40–45).

Clover, Follen, and Hall (2000) in their study, *The Nature of Transformation*, have looked at a wide range of lessons about learning that have been gleaned from and contributed back into the environmental movement. Their principles include: passionate reconnection with the rest of nature through all our senses; critical examination of unjust power relations behind contemporary social and environmental trends; learning from where we are; taking responsibility for personal and collective action in our communities; transcending the limits of top-down educational models and learning through the creativity of music, poetry, story-telling and more (p. 23).

There are rich sources of documentation related to learning within specific social movements. Roy (2004) of Trent University writes on the learning of Canada's "Raging Grannies." The Raging Grannies are older women who turn the stereotypes of old age upside down as they sing satirical and well-researched songs of political protest on the steps of the legislature while dressed in old fashioned bonnets and dresses. Dekeyser (2000) of the Katholieke Universitet in Belgium has looked at 10 years of learning in social movements in the Netherlands and Belgium. Schugurensky (2003) writes of the learning of citizens within the special participatory democracy experiences in Porto Alegre, Brazil. Barndt (1990) documents the social movement learning of Nicaragua during the Sandínista years. Parajuli (1999) writes of ecological ethnicities in Asia from a social movement learning framework. Cunningham and Curry (1997) write of the urban African American movements. Butterwick (1998) and Clover (2002) write of women's creative learning. Hill (1996) articulates social movement learning issues as a member of both the environmental and gay-lesbian movements. At the global level, today's social movements are not phenomena taking place in isolation or narrowly limited to a single issue or actor; they seem to be cognizant of a variety of overlapping issues (Edwards & Gaventa, 2001; Hall, 2000). Hence today's movements are radical, complex, visionary, and inclusive of different identities more than any existing social movement theories have been able to capture (Hunter, 1993; Melucci, 1989).

There is much to be learned from the local and global movements for those with an interest in adult education. From the perspective of social movements, the study of social movement learning can help answer the question of how best to use scarce resources for movement purposes. Reflection on the tacit skills being learned by social movement activists is of critical use for strengthening and extending the power and reach of social movements today.

See also: activism, environmental adult education, popular education, problematizing learning, Queer studies, social movements.

References and Further Reading

Barndt, D. (1990). *To change this house: Popular education under the Sandinistas*. Toronto. Between the Lines.

Bélanger, P., & Federighi, P. (2000). *Unlocking people's creative forces: A transnational study of adult learning policies*. Hamburg: UNESCO Institute for Education.

Burke, B., with Geronimo, J., Martin, D., Thomas, B., & Wall, C. (2002). *Education for changing unions*. Toronto: Between the Lines.

Butterwick, S. (1998). Lest we forget: Uncovering women's leadership in adult education. In G. Selman, M. Cooke, M. Selman, & P. Dampier, *The foundations of adult education in Canada* (2nd ed., pp. 103–116). Toronto: Thompson Educational.

Clover, D. (2002). Women, community arts and popular education. Paper prepared for the Popular Education Network Conference, Barcelona, September.

Clover, D. E., with Follen, S., & Hall, B. L. (2000). *The nature of transformation: Environmental adult education* (2nd ed.). Toronto: Department of Adult Education, Community Development and Counseling Psychology.

Clover, D. E., & Hall, B. L (2000). In search of social movement learning: The growing jobs for living project, *New Approaches to Adult Learning*. Retrieved September 29, 2003 from Ontario Institute for Studies in Education/ University of Toronto website: http://www.oise.utoronto.ca/depts/sese/csew/nall/res/18insearchof.htm

Cunningham, P. M., & Curry, R. (1997). Learning within a social movement:

The Chicago African-American experience. Proceedings of the Adult Education Research Conference (AERC). Retrieved May 21, 2003 from University of British Columbia Department of Education website: http://www.edst.educ.ubc.ca/aerc/1997/97cunningham.htm

Dekeyser, L. (2000). Lessons about adult learning to be drawn from different types of social movements. Paper prepared for the International Conference About Education and Social Action Sydney, Australia December 2000.

Edwards, M., & Gaventa, J. (2001). *Global citizen action*. Boulder, CO: Lynne Rienner.

Eyerman, R., & Jamison, A. (1991). *Social movements: A cognitive approach*. University Park, PA: Pennsylvania State University Press.

Faris, R. (1975). *The passionate educators*. Toronto: Peter Martin Associates.

Finger, M., & Asún, J. M. (2001). *Adult education at the crossroads: Learning our way out*. London: Zed Books.

Foley, G. (1999). *Learning in social action: A contribution to understanding informal education*. London: Zed Books.

Hall, B. L. (2000). Global civil society: Theorizing a changing world. *Convergence, 33*(1–2), 10–32.

Hill, R. J. (1996). Learning to transgress: A sociohistorical conspectus of the American gay life world as a site of struggle and resistance. *Studies in the Education of Adults, 28*(2), 253– 279.

Holford, J. (1995). Why social movements matter: Adult education theory, cognitive praxis and the creation of knowledge. *Adult Education Quarterly, 45*(2), 95–111.

Hunter, A. (1993). Rethinking revolution in light of the new social movements. In M. Darnovsky, B. Epstein, & R. Flacks (Eds.), *Cultural politics and social movements* (pp. 320–346). Philadelphia, PA: Temple University Press.

Livingstone, D. W. (1999). Exploring the icebergs of adult learning: Findings of the first Canadian survey of informal learning practices. *Canadian Journal for the Study of Adult Education, 13*(2), 49–72.

Lotz, J., & Welton M. R. (1997). *Father Jimmy: Life and times of Jimmy Tompkins*. Wreck Cove, Cape Breton Inland, NS: Breton Books.

Martin, D. (1995). *Thinking union: Activism and education in Canada's labour movement*. Toronto: Between the Lines.

Melucci, A. (1989). *Nomads of the present: Social movements and individual needs in contemporary society*. Philadelphia, PA: Temple University Press.

Menconi, M. (2003). *Beyond bowling alone: Learning democracy in social movements and in deliberative democracy*. Paper presented at the Transformative Learning Centre Conference, October 2003. Teachers College, Columbia University, New York.

O'Sullivan, E. (1999). *Transformative learning: Educational vision for the 21st century*. London: Zed Books.

Parajuli, P. (1999). *Tortured bodies and altered earth: Ecological ethnicities in the regime of globalization*. Lanham, MD: Rowman & Littlefield.

Roy, C. (2004). *The Raging Grannies: Wild hats, cheeky songs and witty action for a better world*. Montreal: Black Rose Books.

Rydstrom, G. (Ed.). *Adult education in Tanzania: Swedish contributions*. Linköpings University, Sweden: Vuxenutbildarcentrum.

Schugurensky, D. (2003). Learning societies and the question of democracy: Pedagogy of engagement. In P. Cranton (Ed.), Canadian Association for the Study of Adult Education (CASAE-ACEEA) Annual Conference Proceedings (pp. 180–186). Retrieved January 27, 2003 from http://www.oise.utoronto.ca/CASAE/cnf2003/2003_papers/danielschugurenskyCAS03.pdf

Simon, B. (Ed.). (1992). *The search for enlightenment: The working class and adult education in the twentieth century*. Leicester, UK: National Institute of Adult Continuing Education

Smith, D. (1994). *First person plural*. Ottawa: Mapleview Press.

Spencer, B. (Ed.). (2002). *Unions and learning in a global economy: International and comparative perspectives*. Toronto: Thompson Educational.

Taylor, J. (2001). *Union learning: Canadian labour education in the twentieth century*. Toronto: Thompson Educational.

Welton, M. R. (1993). Social revolutionary learning: The new social movements as learning sites. *Adult Education Quarterly*, *43*(3), 152–164.

Welton, M. R. (2001). *Little Mosie from the Margaree: A biography of Moses Michael Coady*. Toronto: Thompson Educational.

Budd L. Hall and Darlene E. Clover

Social Movements

The term social movement is used to describe a wide variety of collective attempts to bring about a change in social institutions or to create a new social order. In the 19th and early 20th centuries, "social movement" was applied almost solely to the movements of the emerging industrial working class, for example the emerging trade union and other broader political movements, aimed at achieving a new social order that would abolish the social exclusion and economic exploitation of working people.

Later, the term came to be used to describe the full range of organized collective activities, such as the peace, environmental, women and civil-rights movements, all of which were designed to effect fundamental societal change. Also, it came to be recognized that not all social movements were necessarily progressive in nature. Such anti-progressive social movements include the anti-immigrant movements of the 19th century, fascism, white supremacist movements, fundamentalist religious movements, and the racist/ethno-nationalist movements of 1990s. Social movements are now seen as a specific kind of concerted action group. They are not as organized as formally constituted organizations. However, a social movement may be made up of a series of formally constituted associations or groups. For instance the broad labor movement is made up of a number of formal established trade unions, various affiliated bodies, and political groupings. A much more significant defining factor, than the degree of formality, is the development of a sense of group consciousness, a feeling of belonging and solidarity among the members of the movement. This is an essential characteristic of the ideal type movement, though in real movements such a sense occurs to varying degrees.

Adult education and its relationship with social movements may be thought of at three levels of generality; though, of course, there is a great deal of overlap and some controversy as to where best to place particular examples in terms of these levels. Firstly, all social movements, to some extent, have an adult educational dimension. Secondly, some adult education initiatives were or are social movements. Thirdly, to some activists, all of adult education, as they define it, is a social movement. In this entry the major emphasis is on the second level of generality: adult education initiatives that are themselves social movements.

The Adult Educational Dimension of all Social Movements

Many of the great changes in the social order that have occurred during the past 200 plus years are largely (either directly or indirectly) the results of the efforts of social movements. Even if a movement did not achieve all of its goals, and very few movements actually do, parts of its program will have become incorporated into the ever-changing social order. While the achievement of its stated goals must be seen as its primary function, a social movement also has very significant secondary functions. Two of these are predominantly adult educational in nature: the movement provides educational activities for its members and the general public in regard to the issues involved, and it provides training for the leaders within the movement.

There are countless examples of innovative and effective adult education and learning that grew out of these social movements. The Socialist Sunday schools of the early labor movement provided much really useful education and produced a whole generation of labor leaders. The Nazi movement raised public informational education (or more correctly mis-education) to new levels of effectiveness using all the then available media of mass communication. The women's movement of the late 19th/early 20th centuries produced many educational innovations both in terms of content and process for both men and women and across many fields of endeavor. The teach-ins of the student movement, the consciousness-raising sessions of the feminist and the gay-rights movement, the intensive workshops of the environmental movement, and the confrontist training techniques of the civil rights and the anti-war movements, all provided adult education and learning experiences of the highest quality.

Social Movements for Adult Education

The 19th and early 20th centuries were an important formative period in the development of adult education. The period was characterized by a high level of innovation, the creation of many new institutional forms, the refinement of significant educational practices, and the extension of participation in organized adult learning to new social groups. These developments are often referred to as adult education movements (Hake, 2000).

At the beginnings of the 19th century, various adult education projects were established by members of the "well-meaning" British middle classes to extend the benefits of reading and writing and a sound knowledge of the Bible to the industrial working class. These initiatives, generally described as the adult school movement, are usually seen as being the first formal provision of modern adult education. They were largely intended as a means of domesticating this new class, which stood threateningly outside both the traditional patterns of authority and deference and the more rational patterns of the emerging modern nation state. It was thought advisable, by their betters, that such workers should: learn habits of sobriety, industry and thrift; acquire basic vocational skills; and develop a greater sense of commitment and loyalty to the emerging capitalist state and its institutions (Kelly, 1970).

While the remote origins of that social movement known as the Mechanics' Institute movement may never be untangled, and that the movement's final emergence was the result of the convergence of a great many factors, George Birkbeck is generally acknowledged as its founder. In 1800, as Professor of Natural Philosophy at the Anderson Institute in Glasgow, he began a special course of lectures "solely for persons engaged in the practical exercise of the mechanical arts." The Mechanics' Institute was an idea whose time had come, and soon purpose-built schools/institutes were spreading across the English-speaking world (Inkster, 1985, pp. 3–19). While, again like the adult schools movement, the Institute's movement was largely an initiative of the progressive middle class, there were genuine working-class advocates of such adult education. They were from within the longstanding but largely inchoate tradition of independent working-class education. Radicals like Thomas Hodgkins battled, largely unsuccessfully, the middle-class domination of the institute's movement, writing in 1825 that "men had better be without education than be educated by their rulers . . .". Though generally condemned for this and a range of other reasons as a "glorious failure," the Mechanics' Institute movement should be regarded as a modest success (see Collins, 1992, pp. 324–325). The Institutes emphasized the importance of design in vocational education, popularized the idea of science and progress, promoted the concept of individual responsibility in learning, and provided basic infrastructure for the later development of formal technical education and local public libraries.

The first Danish folk high schools were founded in 1844. The key figure in their founding was N.F.S. Grundtvig, who planned a network of self-governing residential adult education institutions which would create a new type of community consciousness among the Danish people (Borish, 1991). He saw the folk high school as a place where adults could learn basic subject matter, but more importantly as places where they could come together to discuss their concerns and learn to participate as democratic citizens. It is strongly believed that it was this view of the cooperative community as nurtured in the folk high school movement that laid the foundations for the Danish welfare state and Denmark's well-known global perspective of world community.

In the 19th century, there emerged a widespread self-improvement movement. Local reading, study and discussion groups were founded, often in conjunction with a nonconformist protestant church, having largely developed out of those churches' longstanding regular Bible study classes. A variant of this idea was the Chautauqua Movement, which grew out of the Sunday school summer institutes held by the Methodist Church in upstate New York. In 1873, it was proposed that general, as well as religious, education, be provided at these institutes (Knowles, 1962). Soon thousands were attending 8-week summer sessions to hear lectures, to attend classes, to discuss issues, to listen to orchestras, bands and glee clubs and to see plays. In 1878, the movement initiated home reading and discussion groups as part of the Chautauqua idea. Soon, there were 10, 000 reading circles in towns all across the United States. In the early 1900s, "traveling Chautauquas" were organized with tent shows moving from town to town during the summer offering education and entertainment.

The local reading and discussion group idea reached a high level of development in the Swedish study circle (Oliver, 1987), which is usually defined as a group of friends or associates assembled for the common planned study of a predetermined subject or problem area. Oscar Olsson established the first such circle in 1902. He was inspired by a visit to the United States and his experience of the Chautauqua Movement. The study circle movement soon became the principal vehicle for adult education in Sweden and was adopted by the government as the principal means of providing public education on a range of emerging social issues. Sweden has been described as a "study circle democracy."

The WEA (Workers' Educational Association) was founded in 1903. The WEA believed that a network of local adult education classes organized by the association but taught by university staff would permit able working-class persons to breach the barriers of social stratification. Its founder, Albert Mansbridge, was a son of the working class who had been strongly influenced by the cooperatives movement, university extension, and the teachings of his church. The association grew rapidly. Local branches were largely autonomous, and members decided democratically what it was they wished to study. The only commitment expected of members was to the ideals of the WEA, that is a commitment to objectivity in study. The non-party-political and unsectarian nature of the association was stressed at every opportunity. Without such a stance, it was argued, the WEA could not appeal to workers of all persuasions, secure the goodwill of all the major political parties, and a share of public education funding. However, the WEA did demand radical educational reform. So the WEA's official ideology was a strong, even strident, demand for educational reform coupled with rigid neutrality, as an organization, on more general political issues. Right from the beginnings there were difficulties with this approach. Internally, many activists believed that the Association needed to adopt a more pro-worker stance. Externally, many left-wing critics regarded the WEA as merely a tool of the ruling classes, accepting public funding and acting in collusion with the universities (Fieldhouse, 1989)

As the WEA movement spread, so did the more radical alternative to its moderate stance, the labor workers' college movement. This movement was much more rooted within the working class and presented a much more class-conscious and militant view of workers' education (Millar, 1980). In Britain, the National Council of Labour Colleges (NCLC) was a revolutionary educational movement with a rigid Marxist approach as opposed to the WEA's more traditional liberal approach. The NCLC declined as the leadership of the unions became more right-wing and withdrew their financial support. But, to some extent, they had also lost the support of their potential students to the WEA, which was seen as less dogmatic, and more democratic and flexible. In the United States a number of workers' colleges were founded, largely by immigrant groups, during the latter part of the 19th century (Schied, 1993). While the workers' college movement flourished until well into the 1920s, providing general education within the Marxist tradition and sound training in more practical skills required by labor activists, they, too, were opposed by the more conservative union officials and they had largely faded from the scene by the 1930s.

From within this same tradition, there emerged, in the early 1930s, the Highlander Folk School in Tennessee, which was established by Myles Horton. Later, it was to be renamed the Highlander Research and Education Centre (Horton, 1990). Over the years since, Highlander has trained generations of community, civil rights and trade union activists. Believing that educators should learn from the people and start the educational process where the learners were,

Highlander was less rigid, less interested in intellectual purity and more flexible, more interested in finding practical collective solutions to real community problems than the more ideologically driven workers' colleges.

Another North American adult education movement of the 1930s, directed at the poor and downtrodden, but from within a completely different tradition, was the Antigonish Movement of Nova Scotia, Canada. It advocated a program of adult education, self-help and cooperative development to assist the miners, fishermen, and farmers of this impoverished province. Its leading figures were two Roman Catholic priests, Father Moses Coady and Father Jimmy Tompkins (Welton, 2001). For the Antigonish Movement, adult education was an aggressive agent of change, a means of reform, and the peaceful path to social change. The movement was populist and strongly anti communist but had a firm vision of a new, better society. The movement, through a wide range of educational activities including mass meetings, study clubs, radio discussion groups, kitchen meetings, formal courses, conferences and leadership institutes, created a range of alternative institutions of a cooperative nature to empower impoverished communities.

Today, many of the goals of these adult education movements have been achieved. Indeed, to some extent at least, aspects of their work have been incorporated into the normal functioning of their societies. They may have, to varying degrees, become institutionalized. Their time may have passed, their prime goals may have changed dramatically, but their achievements are impressive.

Adult Education as a Social Movement

For some adult educators (Newman, 1994), all of adult education is, itself, a broad social movement. To these adult educators the fundamental purpose of adult education is to reach those adults who have been ruthlessly sifted out by the formal education system and excluded from full participation in society. These adult educators believe that knowledge is power and that it is social knowledge that will free people from oppression and exploitation. Adult education is not only about extending opportunities, it is about making learning part of the process of social change itself. What is needed is an understanding of social forces, a participation in the struggle for social improvement and a recognition that the fulfillment of personal desires depends upon the reformation of society. It is the achievement of this state of mind on the part of the learner – not academic pleasure, not vocational competence, not personal social advancement, not romantic escapism – that is the true purpose of adult education.

See also: folk high schools, social movement learning, study circles

References and Further Reading

Borish, S. M. (1991). *The land of the living*. Nevada City, NV: Blue Dolphin.

Collins, M. (1992). Thomas Hodgskin and the Mechanics' Institutes. Proceedings of the Thirty-Third Annual Adult Education Research Conference. Saskatoon, Saskatchewan, Canada, May 15–17, ERIC Document Reproduction Service No. ED368856.

Fieldhouse, R. (1989). Great Britain: The workers' education association. In A. N. Charters & R. J. Hilton (Eds.), *Landmarks in international adult education: A comparative analysis*. London: Routledge.

Hake, B. J. (2000). Social movements and adult education in a cross cultural perspective. In A. Cooke & A. MacSween (Eds.), *The rise and the fall of adult education institutions and social movements* (pp. 17–32). Frankfurt am Main: Peter Lang.

Horton, M. (with J. & H. Kohl) (1990). *The long haul*. New York: Doubleday.

Inkster, I. (Ed.). (1985). *The steam intellect societies: Essays on culture, education and industry*. Nottingham, UK: Department of Adult Education, University of Nottingham.

Kelly, T. (1970). A *history of adult education in Great Britain*. Liverpool, UK: Liverpool University Press.

Knowles, M. S. (1962). *The adult education movement in the United States*. New York: Holt, Rinehart & Winston.

Millar, J. P. M. (1980). *The labour college movement*. London: National Council of Labour Colleges (N.C.L.C.) Publishing Society.

Newman, M. (1994). *Defining the enemy*. Sydney: Stewart Victor Publishing.

Oliver, L. P. (1987). *Study circles*. Washington, DC: Seven Locks Press.

Schied, F. M. (1993). *Learning in social context: Workers and adult education in nineteenth century Chicago*. DeKalb, IL: Leadership and Educational Policy Studies (LEPS) Press, Northern Illinois University.

Welton, M. R. (2001). *Little Mosie from the Margaree: A biography of Moses Michael Coady*. Toronto: Thompson Educational.

Roger K. Morris

Social Policy

Social policy is the instrument of the state's involvement in people's lives through education, health, and social services. Such involvement has sometimes led to disasters for nations or for groups of citizens; the "major disasters of mankind . . . produced by the narrowness of men with good methodology," as Alfred North Whitehead (cited in Grattan, 1955) once described it. Social policy refers to the formal (legislated) and informal (common practices) policies that are operative in areas such as health, education and literacy, that directly affect the quality of life of citizens. However, some of the lasting changes that have truly lifted and benefited humankind throughout history have arisen from vision and the application of *good methodology*. Whether the results have led to democratic societies, to disaster or to social benefit, in democratic nations most of these methodologies will have involved governmental policies. And, if those same policies focused on the redistribution or creation of resources in the three areas of education, health, and social services, they typically were social policies.

Throughout our history as a field of research and practice, the critical question has been the extent to which we should play a part in social policy formation and implementation. Indeed, some in adult education believe, or assume, we should have no direct role. For instance, many oriented to the behaviorist and humanist schools of adult education philosophy (Merriam & Brockett, 1997) will agree that the sharing and creation of knowledge, and effectively responding to learner needs, are the overarching purposes of this field. In such a "learners-first" view, if governmental or institutional polices are somehow ultimately affected by a more enlightened, "self-actualized," learner population, then so much the better. However, in this view, government and policy formation is typically deemed to be foreign territory.

On the other hand, for many who see the mission of adult education from a liberal or libratory viewpoint (Quigley, 1997) – or what Beder

(1989) calls the position of "countercritique" (p. 45) – involvement in matters of democracy and the common good should be, and has been, our founding purpose. From this perspective, it is fallacious to think otherwise. Carlos Torres (1990), for instance, has argued that it is "the state that defines adult education and is the principal beneficiary of its effective implementation" (p. x). Nor can we be immune from its effects. The impact of social policy on us, our field, and our learners is pervasive even if it goes unnoticed. For those in the countercritique, we are, instead, too often the unwitting accomplices of its implementation (Quigley, 1989, 2000). As Britain's Colin Griffin (1987) noted, we are today seeing social policy agendas being "set *for* rather than *by* adult education" (p. 32).

Adult Educators' Direct and Indirect Declining Influence

Scholars such as Thomas (1987) have argued that our direct involvement in social policy has declined through past decades. Fewer and fewer adult educators were being involved in the design and passage of landmark social policy legislation through the 1970s and 1980s, he says. Selman, Cooke, Selman, and Dampier (1998) have recently looked back on the last century and reached the conclusion that: "at one time [adult education] had its own vision of the kind of society it was helping to define and to bring about" but it is "increasingly losing its philosophical roots" (p. 9). Herein lies the unresolved, but central, question facing this field as we enter a new millennium. What role, if any, will we play in the social policy of societies into the future?

If we consider that people such as the 19th century British economist and industrialist, Sir Josiah Stamp, claimed the role of adult education was to assist adults "to earn a living, to live a life and to *mould a world*" (as cited in Selman, 1995; italics added), it would seem we have drifted far from our collective purpose. We have not fulfilled the promise of this field and never will (Quigley, 1989). However, it is also important to say that many in adult education found that the last two decades of the 20th century served as harsh reminders of not just what we have done, but what we have failed to do. If we are to play a significant role in creating and sustaining a more responsive democracy, a more equitable economy, a more just society, and a perfect world, we cannot continue as we have been.

Many adult education scholars (e.g., Collins, 1991; Welton, 1995) have argued that the recent erosion of a focus on systemic, economic, and sociocultural issues within our field is enfeebling us and reducing this field into reductionist professional technicism and an insipid ideology of individualism. Derek Briton (1996), for example, argues that "Adult education is a cultural practice with moral and political consequences that reach far beyond the walls of the classroom" (p. 33). And, within our classroom walls, Merriam (1991) has argued that "programs of graduate study should present research as a value-laden, moral activity" (pp. 60–61). Cervero and Wilson (1994) have introduced terms such as "responsible planning," "ethical decision-making," and "morals" into the program-planning vocabulary. There is also a rising new literature on adult education and spirituality (e.g., English & Gillen, 2000), and Stephen Brookfield (1998) has written on topics such as moral learning. Clearly, in theory, research and practice, the field is being exhorted to return to its moral, ethical center and become more directly involved in seeking a more just society.

It can only be hoped that the sum of these disparate parts will add up to and mean a greater focus on what governments do through policies, why they choose to do it, and how they go about it. It can only be hoped that, as Colin Griffin put it in 1987: "By adopting a social policy perspective . . . adult education theory and discourse may regain a degree of intellectual coherence, and adult education provision a better defence" (p. 253).

Public Policy and Social Policy

These arguments are not arguments for an enhanced focus on *public policy* – a term often confused with social policy and one widely used in the Untied States where public policy often subsumes social policy. Public policy has traditionally held a far wider public mandate than social policy. Public policy extends from highways to the legal system to a nation's currency rates. It is typically far less concerned with the redistribution of valued resources, or "life chances," as Griffin calls them. While there is more than one social policy model (e.g., Marshall, 1965), social policy typically involves the ways and means that the state can improve societies through the creation and redistribution of valued scarce resources through education, health, and social services. Titmuss (1974) has broadened this understanding to all redistributive means by which societies and their governments "can redistribute command over material and non-material resources from the poor to the rich; from one ethnic group to another ethnic group; from working life to old age, within income groups and social classes" (p. 26), but social policy is the mainstay of governments in their ability or inability – their willingness or unwillingness – to enhance life chances throughout societies.

In discussing social policy, it is important to be reminded that adult education has a long, proud, history of helping to "mould a world," as Stamp put it. For instance, following the First World War, the famous 1919 Report of the British Ministry for Reconstruction presented lifelong learning as essential to the policies that would rebuild war-torn Britain (Adult Education Committee, 1919). Through the 1950s, 1960s and into the 1970s, Canada's and Britain's respective fields of adult education were involved in multiple consultations, conferences, white paper discussions, and adult programs for the common good through social policies (Selman et al., 1998). Scandinavian countries have long employed "good methodologies" such as study circles and the folk school model to inform social policy. The list of examples arising from Britain's welfare state period are many (Jarvis, 1985). With the exception of the United States, every industrialized nation has developed a national healthcare plan, and adult education has supported the training and the policies that made this possible (Selman et al., 1998). Adult literacy education social policies in every industrial nation have risen and fallen with governments, and may be said to play a far larger role in literacy education than literacy educators play in their own literacy policies, but they play a role nevertheless (i.e., Benseman, Findsen, & Scott, 1996; Crowther, Hamilton, & Tett, 2001; Tennant, 1991; Quigley, 1997).

Two Emerging Patterns in Adult Education Discourse

In the midst of the often contradictory discourse, if there are two emerging patterns, it seems that one is that there is agreement that the role adult education must play into the future – to the extent it chooses to have one at all – must, by current necessity, be based more on levels of direct pressure and confrontation, less on the collaborative and educational approaches of the last century. At the risk of oversimplification, it seems that the literature around this trend is falling into three categories. Budd Hall (2001) and others in international advocacy movements are perhaps the most optimistic in the quest for a collaborative although critical move towards social change. For instance, Hall has written about the Fifth International Conference on Adult Education held in Hamburg in 1997 as "the most remarkable meeting in the history of the adult education movement" (p. 116), and he points to hopeful examples where, he believes, environmental adult educators, indigenous adult educators, and citizen's movements are working effectively to change multinational agreements and ill-conceived social, public and international policies. Less sanguine, Michael Welton (1997) and others forcefully argue that far more adult educators must become directly involved in the current rise of civil society and work for systemic and attitudinal change on a wide scale. Movements are not enough. As Welton sees it, nothing less than "the transformative potential of late modern societies hinges on the rediscovered and reinvigorated concept of civil society" (p. 68). Meanwhile, Ian Baptiste (2000) has gone the furthest on the spectrum of confrontational positionality as he argues against the liberal and humanist hegemony that has virtually held our field "hostage." He argues adult education should "seek out our enemies and try to coercively restrain them" (p. 34). Baptiste argues against liberal and humanist "romanticism," and would undoubtedly agree that "some of the major disasters of mankind have been produced by the narrowness of men with good methodology," but would surely add that these methodologies include andragogy, self-directed learning, transformative learning, and the field's willingness to assist in the "pernicious acts" (p. 40) of corporations. For Baptiste, adult education must practice much more of what it preaches, including fighting power with any and all power this field can muster.

In each of these three emerging sub-categories of positionality, we see a gathering sense that social policies will not, of themselves, somehow simply arise out of political or corporate "largesse" to serve everyone's best interests. It is clear from these authors that believing education will mean enlightenment at the policy level is naïve.

The second emerging trend can be seen in the powerful European analysis which has gained adherents at an international level. Jansen and Van Der Veen (1997) have argued that Western societies are now being subjected to a shift into individualism, which means that as people become less and less connected, less unified in communities and collectivism: "The processes of individualization will drive society and individuals apart" (p. 267). The fear is that, despite the calls for advocacy as mentioned: "individuals will drift apart from each other and the civil society and citizenship, solidarity, and shared values and norms will become utterly meaningless as a result (Jansen & Van Der Veen, p. 267). In this analysis, adult education is clearly playing the enabler for the slide to separateness when we champion individualism in our textbooks, our graduate programs, and our vision of purpose. Welton (1995) strongly agrees with this analysis. He has argued against what he calls the "andragogical consensus" (p. 128) that he sees in adult education. He says adult education's vocational and humanist infatuation with andragogy is indicative of a misguided focus on individuals: not on the affects of state and corporate power; not on inequities in cultural colonization and racism, not on gender discrimination, and not on the oppressive impact that socioeconomic policies and hegemonies can have on these same learners.

In both of these trends, the indirect shift is back to concern for the social policies that affect us all. Little did postmodernist Jean-François Lyotard realize when, in 1984, he claimed the 20th century has given us as "much terror as we can take" (pp. 81–82). With the September 11, 2001 terrorist attacks on the United States World Trade Center and the resultant wars on terrorism and Muslim nations, we see rising public fear, division of public opinion, and cynicism growing towards governments and their policies; including governmental neglect of education, health and social services. Is a focus on social policy the way forward for those of us in this field? I believe it is. Finch (1984) tells us that social policy is "action designed by government to engineer social change; a mechanism for identifying human needs and devising the means to meet them; a mechanism for solving social problems; [and a means for] redistributive justice" (p. 4). If we are to believe in democracy, we need actively to participate in it. I believe there has never been a point in our history when adult education's early mission has been more needed, or a time when adult education has had a clearer responsibility to become involved in the social policies that can create life chances. Whether by critiquing and participating in social policy; challenging social policies through civil society activism; or, by subscribing to Baptiste's (2000) argument for coercive restraint, to think we can ignore the very policies that define us and our field is a fallacy. The choice is ours.

See also: activism, civil society, pedagogic identity, social justice, social movement learning.

References and Further Reading

Adult Education Committee, British Ministry of Reconstruction. (1919). *The 1919 Report: The final and interim reports of the Ministry of Reconstruction*. London: Her Majesty's Stationery Office.

Baptiste, I. (2000). Beyond reason and personal integrity: Towards a pedagogy of coercive restraint. *Canadian Journal for the Study of Adult Education, 14*(1), 27–50.

Beder, H. (1989). Purposes and philosophies of adult education. In S. Merriam & P. Cunningham (Eds.), *Handbook of adult and continuing education* (pp. 37–50). San Francisco: Jossey-Bass.

Benseman, J., Findsen, B., & Scott, M. (1996). *The fourth sector: Adult and community education in Aotearoa/New Zealand*. Palmerston North, NZ: Dunmore Press.

Briton, D. (1996). *The modern practice of adult education: A post-modern critique*. Albany: State University of New York Press.

Brookfield, S. D. (1998). Understanding and facilitating moral learning in adults. *Journal of Moral Education, 7*(3), 283–296.

Cervero, R. M., & Wilson, A. L. (1994).

Planning responsibly for adult education. San Francisco: Jossey-Bass.

Collins, M. (1991). *Adult education as vocation*. New York: Routledge.

Crowther, J., Hamilton, M., & Tett, L. (2001). *Powerful literacies*. Leicester, UK: National Institute of Adult Continuing Education.

English, L. M., & Gillen, M. A. (Eds.). (2000). *Addressing the spiritual dimensions of adult learning. New Directions for Adult and Continuing Education*, No. 85. San Francisco: Jossey-Bass.

Finch, J. (1984). *Education as social policy*. London: Longman.

Grattan, H. (1955). *In quest of knowledge: A historical perspective on adult education*. New York: Association Press.

Griffin, C. (1987). *Adult education as social policy*. New York: Croom Helm.

Hall, B. L. (2001). The politics of globalization: Transformative practice in adult education graduate programs In R. M. Cervero, A. L. Wilson & Associates (Eds.), *Power in practice* (pp. 107–125). San Francisco: Jossey-Bass.

Jansen, T., & Van Der Veen, R. (1997). Individualization, the new political spectrum and the functions of adult education. *International Journal of Lifelong Education, 16*(4), 264–276.

Jarvis, P. (1985). *The sociology of adult and continuing education*. London: Croom Helm.

Lyotard, J-F. (1984). *The postmodern condition*. Minneapolis, MN: University of Minnesota Press.

Marshall, T. (1965). *Social policy in the twentieth century*. London: Hutchinson.

Merriam, S. B. (1991). How research produces knowledge. In J. Peters & P. Jarvis (Eds.), *Adult education: Evolution and achievements in a developing field of study* (pp. 42–65). San Francisco: Jossey-Bass.

Merriam, S. B., & Brockett, R. G. (1997). *The profession and practice of adult education*. San Francisco: Jossey-Bass.

Quigley, B. A. (Ed.). (1989). *Fulfilling the promise of adult and continuing education. New Directions for Adult and Continuing Education*, No. 44. San Francisco: Jossey-Bass.

Quigley, B. A. (1997). *Rethinking literacy: The critical need for practice-based change*. San Francisco: Jossey-Bass.

Quigley, B. A. (2000). Adult education and democracy: Reclaiming our voice through social policy. In A. L. Wilson & E. R. Hayes (Eds.), *Handbook of adult and continuing education* (pp. 208–223). San Francisco: Jossey-Bass.

Selman, G. (1995). *Adult education in Canada: Historical essays*. Toronto: Thompson Educational.

Selman, G., Cooke, M., Selman, M., & Dampier, P. (1998). *The foundations of adult education in Canada* (2nd ed.). Toronto: Thompson Educational.

Tennant, M. C. (1991). *Adult and continuing education in Australia: Issues and practices*. New York: Routledge.

Thomas, A. M. (1987). Policy development for adult education: The law In W. Rivera (Ed.), *Planning adult learning: Issues, practices and directions* (pp. 57–64). New York: Croom Helm.

Titmuss, R. M. (1974). *Social policy: An introduction* (B. Abel-Smith & K. Titmuss, Eds.). London: Allen and Unwin.

Torres, C. (1990). *The politics of nonformal education in Latin America*. New York: Praeger.

Welton, M. R. (1995). *In defense of the lifeworld: Critical perspectives on adult learning*. Albany, NY: State University of New York Press.

Welton, M. R. (1997). Globalization, internationalization, regionalization: A challenge for adult education. In O. Korsgaard (Ed.), *Adult learning and the challenges of the 21st century* (pp. 67–75). Odense, DK: Odense University Press.

B. Allan Quigley

South America and Adult Education

In line with international conceptions, adult educators and researchers in South America, and Latin America as a whole, see adult education as including formal, non-formal and informal educational processes and programs undertaken with adults (according to the understanding of adulthood adopted by each country). This broad concept is not necessarily assumed in the official adult and youth education public/state policies and legislation. More recently, as a result of a phenomenon called *"juvenização"* adult education (and practice) has been widened to include the youth population, and is now labelled *adult and youth education.*

Given the well-known levels of economic, social and cultural inequalities in South America and other continent-specific historical characteristics (the popular education movement, for instance), adult and youth education is an educational practice oriented to the working class and the poor. In formal education, activities are delivered to offer a second chance for people who have dropped out from the regular educational system, to achieve higher levels of schooling, and are delivered by state agencies. With respect to non-formal education, educational programs are delivered by different organisations – NGOs, social movements, universities, and firms – to respond to various demands and aims according to the agency and the audience involved. In addition, policy-makers, educators and other people involved in the area of adult and youth education have increasingly assumed that informal education is a fundamental educational process.

As in other parts of the world, non-formal and informal learning, which are not subject to the rules of schooling, have been included under the label of continuing education. The main forms that adult and youth education take are literacy and post-literacy programs – primary and secondary school special courses – vocational education and popular-education-oriented programs. The methodologies used to work with adults vary, ranging from adult education activities based on the pedagogical principles of teaching children, to Freire's literacy methods, to traditional training programs developed by firms or vocational schools. State and civil society providers of education for adult and youth education have developed an ongoing networking process. Some of the networks are: CEAAL, the Mercosur regional network, and the Andes network, both of which are regional UNESCO organisations.

Some current challenges can be pointed out: (a) the need for more conceptual precision in the field of adult and youth education; (b) the demand for formal education to break its isolation from other modalities of adult education; (c) the need for a critical analysis of the limits and possibilities of popular education and its relation to adult and youth education; (d) the requirement of developing a pedagogy more appropriate to the audience, which implies educating the educators; (e) the urgent need for professionalization of adult educators (working conditions, proper training programs); (f) the demand for improving research in the field; (g) the need to tackle specific contemporary themes (for instance, peace, gender, ecology, culture); (h) the demand for analysis and the development of new paradigms with which to understand the relationship between the state and civil society and (i) the necessity of developing more permanent state/public policies in addition to temporary governmental policies.

Agency and Adult and Youth Education in the Region

These general characteristics of adult education in South America are rooted in the history of the region. There has been a historical tension between the state and civil society in the process of conceiving policies and practices of adult and youth education. Behind the scenes are the questions: education for whom? For what? In other words, what is the purpose of this modality of education? South America, for a long period, was inhabited by indigenous people with unique cultures and forms of education. One should consider, for example, the ancient Inca civilization in Peru. South America was invaded and colonized mainly by Portugal and Spain in the 16th century, so that today Spanish is the main language spoken in the vast majority of the countries; the exception being Brazil, where the official language is Portuguese. Such rich culture has been recovered in some current adult education social movements proposals and official curricula. Political independence was achieved, in the majority of the countries, at the beginning of the 19th century. One shouldn't forget, though, the significant cultural, economical and political influence of the United States of America on South America in the last century. The peripheral geopolitical condition in relation to the central capitalist countries, as a result of its history, has been maintained and even improved in new forms, such as: the recent implementation of neoliberal reforms in the continent. As part of this broad scenario and as a result of the class struggle within each country, South America's countries have been: submitted to military dictatorships; experimented with national development projects, and with popular and socialist revolutionary movements; and have developed a creative and intense social movement, for example, the *campesinos'* struggle for land reform. These elements have had a direct relationship to what has been proposed, conceptualized and practiced regarding the education of youth and adults in South America. A particularly interesting area has been the relationship between popular education and adult education in the continent.

There has been a strong influence of the popular education tradition in the field of adult and youth education. Some important principles of popular education, as it has been understood from the 1960s, have been transferred in one way or another into the field: (a) the ontological assumption of the incomplete nature of the human being; (b) the assumption of the political nature of education, and the firm belief that there is a mutual relationship among the vocational, political and ideological educational dimensions; (c) the assumption of the Freirean perspective of *dialogue*, and, therefore *problematization*, and, consequently, a redefinition of educator and educatee roles to become educatee-educator and educator-educatee; and (d) the recognition of the value and the limits of popular knowledge as well as of extant knowledge, which means recognising and dealing with the concept of ideology.

Education is considered as a tool to help people to become conscious historical subjects. The influence of these ideas on the field led Paulo Freire in 1985 to affirm that adult education in its formal modality would be better understood, and would have a wider perspective, if it was considered as part of popular education (*Movimento de Educação de Jovens e Adultos* – MOVA). Of course, not everybody who works in formal, non-formal and informal education with adults agrees with Freire's ideas. The field of adult education embodies a permanent tension between cooptation and autonomy in relation to the status quo: the state and ruling classes. What is clear is that there are a number of popular education providers (NGOs or social movements, for instance) whose initiatives, labelled by them as adult education, involve schooling processes – even with certification – and, at the same time, the political and pedagogical perspective of popular education. But these social actors are still active in developing popular education networks such as CEAAL – the Latin America and Caribbean Adult Education Council – that is the main non-governmental forum committed to the idea of political education. Established in 1982, it is associated with the International Council of Adult Education – ICAE. Its main aims are to discuss, systematize and develop policies, theories and methodologies for emancipation of the poor. Therefore, the right of adults and young adults to be formally educated and, at the same time, to develop a critical reading of the world is part, at least since the 1960s, of the struggle of educators and educatees to develop this field locally and at the international level. Educational programs and policies for adults, developed by state or civil society organizations have, to a great extent, been characterized by this intertwined struggle for the individual and collective right of human beings to affirm their humanity. Therefore vocational, formal education and political education *with* (and not *for*) adults and young adults are a means for a broader strategic collective liberating perspective that demands collective and individual *subjects*. If, 30 years ago the focus was helping adults living in the countryside critically to understand the world and organize themselves, nowadays poor and working-class adults living in urban areas, with their plural and interrelated identities involving gender, race and class, are also target groups for popular adult education. If, some years ago, revolution was the horizon, perhaps nowadays peace, non-violence, ecology, and sustainability are the dreams that may connect formal educational programs with those who are more popular education-oriented.

See also: civil society, international adult education, Latin America and adult education, popular education, problematizing learning.

References and Further Reading

Freire, P. (1985). *The politics of education: Culture, power and liberation*. (D. Macedo, Trans.). New York: Bergin & Garvey.

Kane, L. (2001). *Popular education and social change in Latin America*. London: Latin America Bureau.

Rivero, J. (1997). Educação de Jovens e Adultos no Contexto das Reformas Educativas Contemporâneas". In Seminário internacional educação de Jovens e Adultos/Instituto Brasileiro de Estudos e Apoio Comunitário (1996: São Paulo). Trabalhos apresentados no Seminário Internacional Educação de Jovens e Adultos/Instituto Brasileiro de Estudos e Apoio Comunitário Brasília: MEC, pp. 19–69.

UNESCO/CEAAL/CREFAL/INEA (2000). Prioridades de acción en el siglo XXI: la educación de personas jóvenes y adultas en América Latina y el Caribe. Santiago de Chile: Oficina Regional de Educación de la UNESCO para América Latina y el Caribe UNESCO-Santiago.

Maria Clara Bueno Fischer

Spirituality

Spirituality refers to an awareness of something greater than ourselves, a sense that we are connected to all human beings and to all of creation. Historically, spirituality has been in the domain of religious groups, which were charged with meeting the spiritual needs of humans through ritual, sacred writings and traditions. Postmodern scholars such as Kristeva and Spretnak point to the need to break down these historical barriers between religious and secular, and religious and spiritual. Whereas spirituality was seen as the giver of meaning, and religion as the giver of rules (Ó Murchú, 1998), the postmodern trend in spirituality is to move away from these divisions and to embrace intersections.

Increasingly, adults have come to seek spiritual guidance and growth and have either adapted practices from existing religions or created their own. Critics fear that much of this spiritual searching, or search for meaning, is being met by a wide range of spiritual expressions ranging from an amorphous, unreflected new-age teaching, to cooptation of things spiritual by human resource development to fundamentalism (English & Gillen, 2000).

Within adult education, interest in spirituality was traditionally relegated to the study and practice of religious education. That has changed as mainline adult educators have become interested in holistic and experiential education, meaning-making, and the implications of acknowledging the spiritual as well as the aesthetic, social, emotional, physical, intellectual, and other dimensions of the learner. There is a growing awareness that to omit the spiritual dimension is to ignore the importance of a holistic approach to adult learning, in addition to the complexity of the adult learner.

Interest in the spirituality of adult education is apparent in the growing body of field research on the spirituality of adult education or learning (see English, 2003). Tisdell's (2003) work on culture and spirituality is a prime example of qualitative work in this area. Meanwhile, other adult educators have been researching related themes such as values in adulthood, effective teaching and mentoring, meaning-making, transformative learning, and autobiography, as well as ethical decision-making and responsible action. All seem to be concerned about the integrity of adult educators' lives, the search to find meaning, and the need to address the personal/spiritual dimensions of practice, as well as how to integrate this with a concern for the common good.

Within workplace education, there is an increasing emphasis on the notion of spirituality, and an emphasis on corporate retreats, ethics-based decision-making and worker reflection. Critics suggest the need for a guard against this movement because of the potential to encroach on the lifeworld of the participants, invade the personal space of the individual, and manipulate spirituality so that it can increase the bottom line by manipulating the worker (English, Fenwick, & Parsons, 2003).

For some, the renewed interest in spirituality represents a return to adult education's roots in community action (Coady, 1939), social development (Lindeman, 1926/1961), and religion-based initiatives (Yeaxlee, 1925). Moses Coady and Jimmy Tompkins, leaders in the Antigonish Movement, fostered the goals of spiritual development. In *Masters of Their Own Destiny*, Moses Coady gave expression to his dream that people lead lives that are "good and beautiful, be it economic, political, social, cultural, or spiritual" (Coady, p. 163). Coady and Tompkins drew on thousands of years of spiritual thought in formulating their operational principles and sets of assumptions. Spirituality was significant also to the lives of Freire and Horton, and was the driving force behind adult education institutions such as Chautauqua, Mondragon, and Highlander (English, in press). Current research in the field tries to recover the early concerns of education for the common good and to investigate the motivation and support for practice – this research signals a way to move the field from a technical-rational orientation to a more ethical vision.

While history serves as a source of insight on spirituality for some, others look to Native education and social movements. Orr (2000) examines spiritual practices drawn from Native ways of knowing, recognizing that the art of communion with the earth, which is so basic to Native ways of knowing, is also basic to all spiritual development. Yet others note that the spiritual ideals of justice, service, caring, cooperation, and the dignity of the human person are the bedrock on which international and community development are built.

Practical Dimensions

Practitioners are continuously searching for ways to incorporate a spiritual dimension into their work. Jane Vella (2000) suggests that educators look to a "spirited epistemology," or a practice of teaching that focuses on adult learners as subjects or decision-makers of their own learning. Others insist that a spiritual approach that honors the experience of each person and leaves room for mystery can lead to transformative teaching/learning that engages the transcendent in ways that grow out of different faith traditions. From this perspective, the educators' task is to encourage the exploration of our inner lives for insights that inform our questions and our answers; tapping our spiritual lives in ways that are life-giving, open to difference, and accepting of other; and recognizing that our spiritual lives are nurtured through story, tradition, ritual, hope, creativity, and imagination.

Whether the debates about the place of spirituality in workplace education, community development, or training are resolved, the quest for ultimate significance and meaning still stirs the interest of adult educators. Questions remain about the authentic intersection of spiritually and adult education research and practice and given the influence of spirituality in adult education, further exploration about this issue is essential.

See also: meaning making, peace education, reflective learning, religious education, transformative learning.

References and Further Reading

Coady, M. (1939). *Masters of their own destiny*. New York: Continuum.

English, L. M. (2002). Learning how they learn: International adult educators in the global sphere. *Journal of Studies in International Education, 6*, 230–248.

English, L. M. (Ed.). (2003). Contestations, Invitations, and Explorations: Spirituality in Adult Learning. *Adult Learning, 12*(3), special issue.

English, L. M. (in press). Historical and contemporary explorations of the social change and spiritual directions of adult education. *Teachers College Record*.

English, L. M., Fenwick, T. J., & Parsons, J. (2003). *Spirituality of adult education and training*. Malabar, FL: Krieger.

English, L. M., & Gillen, M. A. (Eds.). (2000). *Addressing the spiritual dimensions of adult learning: New Directions for Adult and Continuing Education*, No. 85. San Francisco: Jossey-Bass.

Lindeman, E. C. L. (1926). *The meaning of adult education*. New York: Continuum.

Ó Murchú, D. (1998). *Reclaiming spirituality*. New York: Crossroad.

Orr, J. (2000). First Nations education. In L. M. English & M. A. Gillen (Eds.), *Addressing the spiritual dimensions of adult learning* (pp. 59–66). *New Directions for Adult and Continuing Education*, No. 85. San Francisco: Jossey-Bass.

Tisdell, E. J. (2003). *Exploring spirituality and culture in adult and higher education*. San Francisco: Jossey-Bass.

Vella, J. (2000). Spirited epistemology. In L. M. English & M. A. Gillen (Eds.), *Addressing the spiritual dimensions of adult learning* (pp. 7–16). *New Directions for Adult and Continuing Education*, No. 85. San Francisco: Jossey-Bass.

Yeaxlee, B. (1925). *Spiritual values in adult education*, 2 vols. London: Oxford University Press.

Leona M. English

Study Circles

Study circles emanated in the context of popular movements in early 20th century Scandinavia. In the beginning, the study circle was understood as an activity in which a group of people came together and decided to study a topic. Around 10 persons typically gathered, either at a popular movement centre or some participant's home, often to have conversations around texts. Therefore, access to a library, which covered a broad range of subjects including fiction, was linked to the study circle process. These movement-based libraries became an effective link between literature and the workers, farmers and those who would not normally have any contact with books other than religious texts. The conversations focused on the personal appropriation of the message in the texts. Equality between participants was emphasized instead of the notion of a teacher as leader who organized the dialogue and whose suitability was not necessarily based on having more knowledge than other participants. There were no examinations or tests, and no points to be gained from participating. The general attitude was open, and study circles varied in order to meet the needs of movements with members who had a thirst for all kinds of knowledge.

The study circle has changed a great deal from the middle of the 20th century. The link to a library disappeared and movement-based libraries were actually closed. The popular movements as bases from which to recruit study circle participants have also become less pronounced. Instead, the study associations, which were started as special branches within different popular movements, eventually began to recruit participants outside of the movements. This openness to new members probably helped them from being negatively affected by the crisis of popular movements, which has been discussed since the 1950s. Rather, a growth in participation in the circles has made them into a mass-phenomenon; their activities have also been institutionalized, with an elaborate administration and paid staff to lead the study circles.

Historical Background

The study circle can best be understood as a tradition whose identity varies. It was developed as a part of the early 20th-century popular movements, which at first were in conflict with the dominant culture and power structures. The Swedish educationist, politician and leader in the temperance movement, Oscar Olsson, is considered to have contributed most to the establishment of the idea of the study circle. As a key person in the temperance movement, Olsson proposed in 1902 that study circles should be used in the Order of Good Templars. He was inspired by the North American Chautauqua educational movement as well as by practical experiments within the temperance movement. Olsson's proposal ignited other movements that shared not only the same needs, but also the same conditions such as lack of money. Study circles soon became a popular way to organize study activities in popular movements in other Scandinavian countries. The labor movement was quick to adopt the idea. Later other movements started study circles within their own organizations. Also, universities eventually developed structures for organizing study circles for the general public, which have remained relatively marginal in Sweden, although they have become more important in Norway. Study circles eventually emerged as a well-known activity in all Scandinavian countries. The idea also spread to other countries, but did not attain such a strong position elsewhere.

Contemporary Characteristics

One can depict the ideal study circle as having the following characteristics:

(a) There are no examinations and normally no merits to be gained. This can be viewed as a key to understanding the experiences that participants have; participants do not participate out of an instrumental interest in gaining rewards, but rather because of a personal interest in the topic. This also positively affects the power relation between participants and leaders.

(b) Participation is voluntary. The effect is a personal commitment to the study activity. Some study circles are organized by the participants, who choose the topic, leader, and the location, but most are organized by study associations or popular movements' organizations. The variation in background and knowledge among participants can be considerable.

(c) Circles operate with the expectation of a limited number of persons in the group, normally somewhere between 5–10 persons. This size allows space for a higher level of active participation than in ordinary classes. It is also the basis for commonly expressed social qualities, such as a feeling of togetherness. Study circles can also function as important social arenas where these are otherwise scarce, as in the countryside.

(d) Study circles will often meet for 10–15 weeks for 3 hours once a week with a break in the middle. They are often an evening activity, which makes it possible to participate after work.

(e) A circle will have a leader, who does not have to be an expert – in fact the leader may be one of the participants. On the other hand there are often experts acting as leaders.

(f) Communication within the study circle should be shared equally with a focus on the topic; yet the ideal is difficult to achieve, especially when the leader is an expert. An informal atmosphere is the norm, however.

(g) There are very broad parameters for what can be the content of studies, and the lack of restriction on what counts as content has meant that study circles have been very responsive towards participants' varying needs. In this respect the study circle tradition is very different from formal education, which is generally very restricted regarding what counts as content.

(h) Study circles can be linked to various political, religious, and social interests and perspectives, making them arenas for cultural diversity.

(i) Persons of different ages often mix in the circles, and statistics from Sweden show relatively even rates of participation in different age groups. For the older half (50+) of the adult population, study circles are almost the only available alternative, since other forms of adult education focus on younger adults.

Knowledge Interests

Study circles were originally part and parcel of the democratically ruled popular movements, which gave them a unique quality. They promoted self-education, that is, education was in the hands of the collective that constituted the movement. Oscar Olsson described the study circle as providing an education "for and through the people." During the first part of the 20th century this "movement culture" or life-form was very strong. To be part of, for instance, the workers' movement often meant some kind of involvement in a conglomerate of organizations and their activities; for example, political participation, union activities, study circles, youth clubs, consumers' cooperatives, as well as entertainment such as theatre and ballroom dancing. In this context, democracy was something very explicit.

The disintegration of this popular movement culture during the mid-20th century was paralleled by study-circle participation becoming more and more autonomous from participation in movements. Participation increased; study circles became open to everyone, and were often publicized widely. No longer did participants pay as much attention to the social movement that was organizing the study circle. The original mission to change society has also been overshadowed by other motives for participation. Although, study circles are still used by old and new social movements as instruments to develop useful knowledge for activists, such use is very small. Another change has been that content from the cultural sector has come to dominate, such as handicrafts, music and art, a change which has also challenged the definition of a study circle in that many are not following the ideal type.

A third change is a strong quantitative expansion during the second half of the 20th century, though it is difficult to quantify the exact amount of expansion. The organizations in charge of study circles operate with a very generous definition, which results in an over-estimation of the actual number of study circles. On the other hand, there are a lot of study circle activities that are self-organized. Official statistics from Sweden give an estimate of more than 300,000 study circles, with around 2.6 million participants for the year 2002. Since the same person can participate in several circles, it is estimated that between 1.5–2 million of a population of just 9 million participated in one or several study circles in 2002; 75% of the adult population had participated at least once. Norway, with a population of 5 million, reported more than 0.6 million participants for the year 2000. More women than men participate in both countries. Denmark and Finland have lower rates of participation. One reason for the high levels of participation in the Scandinavian countries is financial support from the state for the study associations. A second reason is probably the long tradition, which has established study circles as a mass phenomenon, a pedagogy that is well-known and accepted as part of everyday community life. However, study circles do exist in other countries: a well-documented example is in Slovenia. Study circles are organized in many other countries, including the United States. Dialogic literary circles in Spain also seem to have traits in common with study circles.

Study Circles and Civil Society

Study circles are often discussed as a form of democratic education and at least two aspects can be discerned here. First, the study-circle tradition is in principle linked to civil society; it emanated within the context of popular movements and the content is normally not subservient to the market, state or local government. In this way, study circles are in principle a platform for cultivating opinions independent of the state and the corporate market interest. They are also an arena for people to learn more about things they care about, without any consideration of their usefulness to the state, or as a provider to the market sector, or as a reward in a meritocratic society. They can therefore in principle contribute to strengthening civil society and contribute to democracy. Some have noticed the similarities between the processes in a study circle and those supposed to happen in a deliberative democracy. Habermas' description of the conditions and ideals of communicative action also seem to look like the ideal of a study circle. From the perspective of these theories of democracy, the conditions and inner life of study circles become relevant. The lack of an instrumental rationality linked to examinations as well as the personal interest in the topic creates the conditions for studies related to the life-world of the participants rather than the needs of the economic and administrative system. However, if the deliberations should lead to political and social action, study circles seldom result in efforts to take action. Most study circles in the Nordic countries are related to individual interests, and the relation to collective action outside the study circle context remains unclear. In other countries, e.g., the United States, study circles are portrayed as related to political activism. In Slovenia it is well-documented that study circles result in action, but often action that is related to community development. Another angle is the space study circles provide for diversity and pluralism, which is often argued to be the contemporary challenge for democratic thinking. Diverse interests and identities, creating a fabric of collectives that individuals are involved in, can strengthen their positions through study circles. In that case study circles will promote democracy by making society more pluralistic through supporting diversity.

See also: civil society, community education, popular education, social movement learning.

References and Further Reading

Arvidsson, L. (1989). Popular education and educational ideology. In S.J. Ball & S.Larsson (Eds.), *The struggle for democratic education. Equality and participation in Sweden* (pp. 149–168). Basingstoke, UK: Falmer.

Byström, J. (1988). *The study circle. A brief introduction*. Stockholm: Brevskolan.

Klemencic, S. (1998). Evaluation research of study-circles as agents for the development of local communities in Slovenia. In G. Bisovsky, E. Bourgois, M. Bron, G. Chivers, & S. Larsson (Eds.), *Adult learning and social participation* (pp. 153–183). Wien: Verband Wiener Volksbildung.

Larsson, S. (1998). Defining the study circle tradition. In A. Bron, J. Field, & E. Kurantowicz (Eds.), *Adult education and democratic citizenship II* (pp. 50–70). Krakow: Impuls Publishers.

Larsson, S. (2001). Seven aspects of democracy as related to study circles. *International Journal of Lifelong Education, 20*(3), 199–217.

Oliver, L. P. (1987). *To understand is to act: Study circles. Coming together for personal growth and social change*. Washington, DC: Seven Locks Press.

Sundgren, G. (1999). Identity and civic virtues – as a result of study circle participation. In C. A. Säfström (Ed.), *Identity* (pp. 117–134). Lund: Studentlitteratur.

Staffan Larsson

T

Teaching

Teaching refers to the intentional facilitation of someone's learning. Teaching adults can be an exhilarating, frustrating and dizzying ride; it is common for adult educators to feel both unbounded excitement and serious doubt about their teaching, all within the span of one course. Spirits and confidence rise when things go well; but euphoria can easily switch to doubt when things don't go well. To make matters worse, and against all logic, a string of positive experiences in teaching can be negated by just one knotty teaching episode. And yet, we all know that potholes are to be expected along the bumpy road to becoming a teacher of adults. The "power of one" depends on its valence! Why do teachers experience such doubt and uncertainty in their teaching? Why is the reflective gaze of teachers so easily confused when turned upon one's self? Why do adult educators succumb to such negative interpretations of their own teaching? What is it that teachers are reflecting upon when they draw mixed judgments of their teaching? And how might we approach the puzzle of understanding the teaching of adults in the 21st century?

Part of the answer to the puzzle resides in the nature of teaching itself. Although the concept of teaching is relatively unproblematic, the term "teaching" is not. Different regions of the world use different terms to refer to the concept of teaching (Kember, 1997; Pratt, Kelly, & Wong, 1999). Anyone who has worked in different countries, especially those that cross linguistic and cultural boundaries of significance, knows the problems that can easily arise from using the wrong word to refer to "teaching." As a result, there is a rather wide "cultural geography" of related terms, all of which refer to teaching, including: andragogy, facilitation, instruction, pedagogy, and training. Indoctrination is sometimes included in such a list, but is excluded here.

Moving from andragogy towards training there is a falling off of the centrality of a philosophy of teaching that is based upon learners' prior experience, their immediate needs and the assumption of an egalitarian relationship between teacher and learner. Yet, within every term, from andragogy to training, teaching is assumed to be more than just a technical matter. Teaching requires knowledge of learners, content, curriculum, pedagogy (or andragogy), society and a special form of content knowledge that distinguishes between subject matter experts and teachers of that subject, called "pedagogical content knowledge" (Shulman, 1987). However, it also requires knowledge of self and of the moral aspects of teaching, as will be shown.

There is too little room here to review all the forms of knowledge that are related to effective teaching. Instead, this entry will describe three aspects of teaching that characterize much of the work in adult education today. One of these aspects is well-known; the other two are comparatively new, but increasingly recognized as central to responsible teaching. The three aspects of teaching are: technical tools; personal styles; and philosophical belief.

Each aspect is important and has its role within the craft of teaching. Until recently, adult education has been most vocal on the technical aspects and comparatively silent on the other two. Even today, much of the literature is silent on the interactive effects and artful balance of all three aspects of teaching. Yet, it is in the interaction of these three aspects that we find a place from which to better understand paths to effectively reflect on teaching. It is also here, in the interactions of all three aspects, that we are more likely to gain insight into the often erratic and emotionally charged experience of teaching.

Technical Tools: The Technical Aspect of Teaching

Every profession, every craft, has its tools. Whether one is a plumber, surgeon, musician, gardener, lawyer, engineer, nurse or teacher, there are tools that one must learn to use with proficiency. Tools such as a hammer, cello, knife, computer, scissors, or a series of questions used by a teacher, mediate between the worker and the work to be done. It is only through the skillful use of such tools that the work can be done.

Teachers first learn how to use tools by watching others. As students, they served a long and varied apprenticeship in teaching, watching a veritable parade of teachers pass before them. Each time they watched, they learned how tools were employed, which tools worked and whether the same tool worked differently for different teachers. From this apprenticeship or mentoring, they formed impressions and drew conclusions about the tools that might be useful to them long before they knew that they, too, would be teachers.

The tools of teaching include a wide range of instructional techniques, questions, methodological arrangements and devices. Tools are the means by which teachers engage learners in the content or with each other in pursuit of some learning goals. Many authors on teaching adults focus on the tools of teaching, and three in particular offer excellent guidelines on how to use specific instructional tools: Jerry Apps (1991), Peter Renner (2004), and Richard Tiberius (1990). These authors also acknowledge the larger picture of teaching, for example, that teaching techniques are not recipes to be followed precisely as described. Tools are simply the means to particular educational ends; they are "what teachers use until the real teacher arrives" (Palmer, 1998 p. 5). The next section is about finding that "real teacher."

Personal Styles: The Personal Aspect of Teaching

In shifting our gaze from the technical to the personal, we move from that which is most generalizable (technical) to that which is most individualistic (style). The personal aspect of teaching addresses fundamental questions such as: "Who is the self that teaches?" and "What does it mean to be authentic as a teacher?" "What is the nature of "self" to which one must be true if one is to be authentic as a teacher?" Exploring authenticity and the self-as-teacher is an important part of the journey towards understanding what Parker Palmer (1998) means when he says, "We teach who we are" (p. 4).

Several adult educators have written convincingly about the self as teacher. Patricia Cranton (2001) writes of authenticity in teaching as the expression of the genuine self in relation to a specific community. She suggests that teachers get to know themselves as teachers by coming to know their own preferences within the social context of their work. She sees teaching, in this sense, as "authentic" when those involved are speaking genuinely and honestly rather than with intent to manipulate or deceive. Stephen Brookfield (1990) suggests that authenticity in teaching means, among other things, owning up to the fact that we do not have all the answers and that we can and will make mistakes. Peter Jarvis (1992) suggests that authenticity in teaching arises out of a genuine intention to foster dialogue and mutual learning between teachers and learners. And Dirkx and Gilley (2004) write more broadly of the inner work of adult educators, in classrooms and in the workplace, as they struggle to develop congruence between their work and their authentic self. The common theme among these authors is that authenticity in teaching can only arise out of an understanding of how we wish to be in relation with others.

How, then, does the search for personal style and authenticity relate to the doubt and uncertainty that teachers experience, described at the outset of this chapter? Teachers often look back upon a teaching episode reviewing the events and in the process constructing a narrative of what happened, why they think that happened, and what they will do about it (reflection on action, Schön, 1983). They may or may not tell anyone else their narrative, but it forms the basis for further exploration of their self-as-teacher. And because the subject of this narrative is their emerging self-as-teacher, much of their reflection is indirectly, if not directly, focused on their identity as teacher rather than on technique. Indeed, this is why a single negative episode can be so troubling; the object of reflection is the self, not the technique.

Teachers work in contexts populated with classroom discursive practices that may do battle with their narratives and emerging sense of self (Pratt & Nesbit, 2000). Novices are particularly vulnerable because the three aspects of teaching are only partially formed or not yet in harmony with each other. As well, the borders between borrowing and constructing a personal teaching style are blurred. Teaching styles witnessed in earlier years remain as vague mythical models and borrowed personal scripts that don't always fit the emerging self that is trying to stand on its own and proclaim "This is MY teaching style." That declaration needs yet another aspect of firm footing before its claim can be made with commitment and confidence. It is to that aspect we turn next.

Philosophical Beliefs: The Philosophical Aspect

Teaching is more than an intellectual act; it is also a moral and philosophical undertaking (Fenstermacher, 1990). It is moral because it is guided by a sense of what is right, good, or just. It is philosophical because it requires a critical examination of the underlying beliefs and values that guide teaching towards particular purposes; asking why those ends are justified and by what means they might be reasonably and appropriately accomplished.

Beliefs about the means and the ends of education represent a commitment to underlying values. As such, they are held with varying degrees of clarity, confidence, and centrality. Some are vague and implicit; others are clear and readily explained. Some are held tentatively; others are considered incontestable. Some are marginal to the way a person thinks; others are central and even dominant. When they are central or dominant they represent the core of one's philosophical aspect of teaching.

Teaching involves not just intellectual purposes, but social purposes and responsibilities that are morally and intellectually grounded. It is not possible to talk about teaching without, at least implicitly, adopting some view of knowledge and learning in relation to those intellectual and moral purposes. What is meant by "knowledge" and "learning" is usually taken for granted. It is either assumed that educators are "in agreement" on what they mean, or that these concepts are not particularly relevant to the question of how to teach.

Beliefs regarding knowledge and learning are some of the most central beliefs related to teaching. Beliefs about knowledge determine what will be taught, how it will be rendered, and what will be accepted as evidence people have learned. Beliefs about learning shape not only the teacher's selection and adaptation of tools, they also shape the way in which one's professional knowledge and identity will be called forth and used during moments of teaching.

Several educators have addressed this aspect of teaching, and the best-known is Paulo Freire (1998). However, three other, lesser-known works are worth mentioning: Arnold, Burke, James, Martin, and Thomas (1991), Glazer (1999), and Nesbit (1998). The book by Arnold et al. is unusual for its ability to join technique with philosophy; its collection of ideas and tools is grounded in a strong commitment to social justice. Steven Glazer's book (1994) includes chapters by Huston Smith, Rachel Naomi Remen, Parker Palmer, the Dalai Lama, bell hooks, Rabbi Zalman Schactger-Shalomi, and other well-known activists. With a chorus of inspiration, these authors show how learning and teaching can (and must) have regard for the moral, as well as the intellectual character of teaching and of the self as teacher. Tom Nesbit's chapter (1998) is singled out because it does something that few books or chapters do: it reveals the moral workings of teaching in a most unlikely arena – the teaching of math. As one of five perspectives on teaching in a book by Pratt and Associates (1998), Nesbit provides an exceptional example of how one can seek social change through teaching math. Each of these works discusses a philosophical aspect of teaching – sometimes without saying so – and explains the essential role of beliefs in responsible teaching.

Seeking Harmony

Moving from competence to conscience in teaching, much of the literature on teaching adults addresses one and sometimes two of the aspects so far discussed. Rarely does it address all three. As a result, exchange of knowledge about teaching can be problematic. Emphasizing the technical aspect of teaching, for example, can be problematic for several reasons: First, it separates the tools from the person using them, animating the tools and thus suggesting the tools have the power to facilitate learning. Second, the same tool can be used by different teachers or at different times with markedly different results. A teaching tool is like a musical instrument awaiting the musical score and magical hands of the teacher to bring it to life. Third, without a genuine connection to the self and the moral and philosophical aspect of teaching, it can be difficult to justify one's approach to teaching.

Excessive emphasis on the self can become narcissistic, where everything reflected upon turns inward and becomes a question about "me." Most sessions are neither as good nor as bad as teachers think they were; they are somewhere in-between. But when teachers dwell on the last session too much, either on how wonderful or how dreadful it was, they tend to exaggerate or distort both the evidence that might suggest such effects and the importance of it in the larger scheme of things. In all instances, teaching is about the self, but always about the self in relation to a body of knowledge, a set of learners, and particular moral and intellectual ends that are justified.

Excessive emphasis on philosophical aspects can become an exercise in eloquence, devoid of practical application. Rather, the power and purpose of understanding the philosophical aspect of teaching lies not in the eloquence of its statement or in its fit with some current discourse of teaching, but in its ability to reveal what is hidden, yet essential, to understanding someone's teaching. At its best, the philosophical aspect can be a map to the deeper structures of a teacher's values, revealing both origins and destinations of their teaching.

To approach teaching without considering the relationship between the philosophical, personal and technical aspects of teaching is to be forever at the mercy of the dizzying ride of teaching. In the beginning, tools are very important because they help structure the work of teaching amidst complexity and uncertainty. However, at this stage the tools are the master and the self is the servant. As teachers mature, the relationship shifts and tools become servant and the self becomes master. Then, as the self finds root in commitment, it moves towards even greater authenticity and harmony with a greater understanding of the values and beliefs that form an underlying philosophy of teaching.

The goal is to develop harmony between the three aspects of teaching. Harmony means that each aspect is defined in relation to the other two, and the collective is greater than the sum of its parts. When teachers become truly effective, they have found a comfortable blend of competence and conscience, and they have moved from technical knowledge to craft knowledge in how they use their self in concert with the tools of teaching. Craft knowledge means the tools are no longer separate from the actor; they have been adapted, not adopted, and become integrated with the self in the role of teacher, and in service of the beliefs that guide teaching.

See also: andragogy, authenticity, facilitation, motivation, pedagogic identity, program planning.

References and Further Reading

Apps, J. W. (1991). *Mastering the teaching of adults*. Malabar, FL: Krieger.

Arnold, R., Burke, B., James, C., Martin, D., & Thomas, B. (1991). *Educating for a change*. Toronto: Doris Marshall Institute for Education and Action.

Brookfield, S. D. (1990). *The skillful teacher*. San Francisco: Jossey-Bass.

Cranton, P. (2001). *Becoming an authentic teacher in higher education*. Malabar, FL: Krieger.

Dirkx, J. M., & Gilley, J. (2004). Change theory: Toward a holistic view of learning and change in work. *Advances in Human Resource Development*, *6*(1), 34–51. Sage Publications.

Fenstermacher, G. D. (1990). Some moral considerations on teaching as a profession. In J. Goodlad, R. Soder, & K. Sirotnik (Eds.), *The moral dimensions of teaching* (pp. 130–151). San Francisco: Jossey-Bass.

Freire, P. (1998). *Pedagogy of freedom: Ethics, democracy, and civic courage.* (P. Clarke, Trans.) Lanham, MD: Rowman & Littlefield.

Glazer, S. (Ed.). (1999). *The heart of learning: Spirituality in education.* New York: Jeremy Tarcher.

Jarvis, P. (1992). *Paradoxes of learning: On becoming an individual in society.* San Francisco: Jossey-Bass.

Kember, D. (1997). A reconceptualization of the research into university academics' conceptions of teaching. *Learning and Instruction, 7*(3), 255–275.

Nesbit, T. (1998). The social reform perspective: Seeking a better society. In D.D. Pratt & Associates, *Five perspectives on teaching in adult and higher education* (pp. 173–199). Malabar, FL: Krieger.

Palmer, P. (1998). *The courage to teach: Exploring the inner landscape of a teacher's life.* San Francisco: Jossey-Bass.

Pratt, D. D., & Associates (1998). *Five perspectives on teaching in adult and higher education.* Malabar, FL: Krieger.

Pratt, D. D., Kelly, M., & Wong, W. S. S. (1999). Chinese conceptions of "effective teaching" in Hong Kong: Towards culturally sensitive evaluation of teaching. *International Journal of Lifelong Education, 18*(4), 241–25.

Pratt, D. D., & Nesbit, T. (2000). Discourses and cultures of teaching. In E. Hayes & A. Wilson (Eds.), *Handbook of adult and continuing education* (pp. 117–131). San Francisco: Jossey-Bass.

Renner, P. (2004). *The art of teaching adults: How to become an exceptional instructor and facilitator.* Vancouver: Training Associates.

Schön, D. A. (1983). *The reflective practitioner: How professionals think in action.* New York: Basic Books.

Shulman, L. S. (1987). Knowledge and teaching: Foundations of the new reform. *Harvard Educational Review, 57*(1), 1–22.

Tiberius, R. G. (1990). *Small group teaching: A trouble-shooting guide.* Monograph Series 22. Toronto: OISE Press, The Ontario Institute for Studies in Education.

Daniel D. Pratt

Theory

To engage in some form of systematic reflection on an issue is to engage with theory as a resource and with theorizing as a practice. In theorizing we are trying to understand and explain phenomena, which takes us beyond the immediate and day-to-day. This involves abstraction, contemplation, critical engagement and imagination. Thus, although sometimes dismissed as irrelevant or involving unnecessary jargon in areas of practice, such as adult education, theory cannot be avoided. To address an issue of practice, such as how best to provide opportunities for adults with literacy challenges, requires some form of systematic and critical reflection on the lessons to be learned from existing literature on the subject of literacy and the practical experience of teaching such adults. This is what Donald Schön (1983) refers to as reflection-on-action. Not to theorize is to engage in practice as some sort of unthinking activity, which is undesirable in adult education.

However, it is often understandable why theory is not engaged with systematically and this is because there is not one single theory, but many theories, each of which is an arena for debate in its own right. In adult education, practices are informed by theories of humanistic, cognitive and sociocultural psychology, Marxism, feminism, poststructuralism, postcolonialism, postmodernism and many others. Some of these theories will be more influential in some geographical and work locations than others. For instance, labor educators in the OECD countries might draw upon Marxism, while feminist adult educators in less developed countries might well draw upon postcolonial and feminist thinking. For workplace trainers, theories of human resource development and their psychological underpinnings might be brought to the fore.

Within and between each of these theories, there is much debate, as they point towards different adult education practices and ways of explaining them and assessing their significance and consequences. Adult educators influenced by feminism will look at the implications of practices for gender. Environmental practitioners will look at the consequences of practice for the environment. This tends to produce further debate, which moves us closer to questions of epistemology and ontology, in other words, the philosophy of education. While philosophical issues tend to be irresolvable in any complete sense, theorizing helps us to question our own belief systems and assumptions and provides alternative ways for understanding our practices.

The Emergence of Theory

Modern conceptions of theory started to emerge in the Western Enlightenment of the 17th and 18th century. With the waning of the religious orders in Europe and the growth of secularism, there was the need to try to understand the world in ways that did not rely on religion and appeals to a higher order. The growth of theory itself contributed to that challenge to religion and, over time, became institutionalized in the disciplines of the social sciences in the universities. During the 19th century, positivism was a predominate theory in many places, the view that through a scientific approach social life could be improved. In general, two sorts of theory emerged: ones that worked to improve the status quo, such as positivism and functionalism, and those which sought to challenge the status quo, such as Marxism and radical feminism.

Theory can take many forms, and Edwards (n.d.) identifies five different understandings of theory:

- theory as explanation;
- theory as testable;
- theory as abstraction;
- theory in relation to the real world; and
- theorizing as a human activity.

For many adult educators, it is the relationship between theory and practice that is important; in particular the often perceived gap between the two. However, this is to already invoke a particular form of theorizing, which suggest the existence of two separate realms – theory and practice – and a relationship between them. An alternative formulation suggests that adult education practitioners are already involved in a form of *informal* theorizing in practice that acts as a starting point for more systematic theorizing, once subject to critical evaluation (Usher, 1989). In discussing theory in different ways therefore we are already involved in theorizing. Thus, the French sociologist Pierre Bourdieu refers to theory as the reflexive exploration of the unthought categories of thought.

Theory is not cumulative. Insofar as theorizing is an attempt to provide a more systematic understanding of the world and what goes on in it, changes in the world are also to be found in theory. Thus, for instance, the changing relations and roles of women in OECD countries in the 19th century witnessed also an upsurge of feminist theory. As Anthony Giddens, the British sociologist, suggests then, theory is not insulated from its subject matter; it changes and mutates and takes many forms. It is also in particularly unsettled times that theory comes to greater prominence, as taken-for-granted assumptions come up for question. This state of upheaval in the contemporary period has gone so far that those associated with a postmodern perspective suggest that theory itself can no longer help us to establish what is true or how to improve practice, but can only point to the provisionality and instability of understanding. For many adult educators with strong value systems committed to improving the lot of the people with whom they work, this is not a very comfortable form of theorizing.

Theories pose questions to commonsense or taken for granted assumptions about the world. For instance, why do many adult educators work with groups of students in circles rather than use other approaches? Why is experience given such prominence in the teaching of adults? Why do some prefer to talk of facilitation rather than teaching? However, not all theories or theorists reflexively engage with their own taken-for-granted assumptions.

The Clash of Theories

In adult education, like education more generally, much theory is drawn from the wider social sciences rather than generated from within. This has both benefits and drawbacks. It both results in dynamic possibilities for engagement upon the nature, purpose and practices of adult education, but also results in a theoretical eclecticism within the field. Thus, for instance, the ways in which post-structuralism have developed in America and Europe are very different, so even within theories there can be many interpretations depending on the situation and location of the person theorizing. In the American critical pedagogy of Henry Giroux, postmodernism, poststructuralism, and critical theory have been melded together into a single theory, whereas in Europe, poststructuralism and critical theory are positioned as distinctive theories. Similarly, in recent decades, there has been much debate about the increased significance of communication – e.g., the media, the Internet, in social life. This is reflected in an increased significance in the UK and Australia being given to questions of language in theory and what has become known as the linguistic turn in the social sciences (MacLure, 2003). This is less the case in much of North American adult education. The resulting theoretical eclecticism has implications for adult education practice and research, which are themselves not always brought to the fore.

Many theoretical debates are not "simply" theory, but reflect significant issues about continuity and change in social and historical practices, including those in adult education. One fundamental question that occurs in a lot of adult education literature is the extent to which different practices contribute to or challenge inequalities. For instance, does community outreach work merely keep people literally and metaphorically in their place? There being no settled position on the theory through which to examine these issues, the question of inequality and how best to address or challenge it remains continually open to question.

Theorizing, Theorists and Theory

As with theories of knowledge and learning more generally, the notion of theory can appear to be a universal and decontextualized body of understanding. Thus, for instance, feminism and postcolonialism might be read as a complete body of knowledge upon which to draw. This is the discourse of "-isms" "-ists" and "-ologies" in adult education discourse, but what this often does is to set up broad categories as the basis for making comparisons of changing circumstances and practices. Thus, for instance, people write of the premodern, modern and postmodern in order to identify broad differences associated with each. Within this approach to theory the specific arguments of specific actors/writers/speakers tend to get lost and complex arguments are reduced to slogans (Edwards & Usher, 2001). This is not very helpful for adult educators. More helpful is an engagement with specific actors, whether those engaged in more speculative work or those reflecting systematically on practice. However, this involves more engagement with theorists and theories than would be the case at present in much adult education practice.

It also points to theorizing as a situated practice. Depending on the practices in which we engage and our locations, the theoretical and materials resources available to us differ. To theorize is to interpret, to make a sense of practices. Others may make a different sense of the same practices; we may come to view things differently ourselves. Widening participation to educational opportunities may appear to be an unconditional good, but this depends upon the opportunities accessed and the outcomes for students. Adult education remains a powerful set of practices that reproduce inequalities more than they are challenged. Such issues cannot be challenged in theories alone, but without theorizing, they will not be challenged at all.

See also: pedagogic identity, philosophy, practitioner, praxis.

References and Further Reading

Edwards, C. (n.d.). Educational theory is troublesome stuff. Retrieved November 25, 2003 from http://s13a.math.aca.mmu.ac.uk/ Chreods/Issue_9/Cherry/Cherry.html

Edwards, R., & Usher, R. (2001). Lifelong learning: A postmodern condition of knowledge. *Adult Education Quarterly*, *51*(4), 273–87.

MacLure, M. (2003). *Discourse in educational and social research*. London: Sage.

Ritzer, G., & Smart, B. (Eds.). (2001). *Handbook of social theory*. London: Sage.

Schön, D. A. (1983). *The reflective practitioner: How professionals think in action*. London: Temple Smith.

Usher, R. (1989). Locating adult education in the practical. In B. Bright (Ed.), *Theory and practice in the study of adult education: The epistemological debate* (pp. 65–93). London: Routledge.

Richard Edwards

Training

Training is the procedure whereby knowledge is transmitted with an instrumental and operational vision of the learning process and of its expected results. Training is usually related to achieving precise objectives: applied to animals, it is meant to make them obey; in sports, it is meant to help athletes win; in the army, it is meant to make soldiers physically tough and morally compliant. In formal education, training refers to professional and vocational activities carried out both in technical schools and in adult education institutions. In all these situations, the purpose is to develop in trainees an enhanced standard of behavior and efficiency. This explains why training has been mostly related to the world of work; as a way of accomplishing economic objectives. In this globalization society, the concept is closely linked with skills and expected performance that individuals have to maximize in the labor market and in the workplace. The planning and the organization of training activities follow general rules and require that providers and trainers have expertise in the field of knowledge they transmit.

From an epistemological point of view, the behaviorist framework offers a clear understanding of training. Descartes' identification of voluntary and involuntary behavior in the 17th century was followed by Pavlov's famous experiments with conditioned reflexes. Skinner's (1968) concept of reinforcement has been a mainstay of the educational system and has opened the doors both to principles of behavioral objectives, like skills, and to principles underlying instruction rules, from the specification of goals to the evaluation of results. The existing forms of training programs, in the main, incorporate these basic principles.

Another way to understand the idea of training is to compare it to other concepts, as Nadler (1979) has done. In the business and industry contexts, he distinguishes training that is preparing workers for specific current jobs; education that is preparing workers for future jobs; and development that is encouraging workers to explore non-job-related activities. These distinctions are conceptually consistent with the behaviorist understanding of training. Within the global economy landscape, the use of the word training has changed in recent decades to embrace all the teaching activities related to work, even if it is still associated with practical performance expectations. The concept of education has also evolved to be used mostly in connection with the process of learning and rarely with direct work contingencies. Many adult educators see training as the opposite of education, with the former being seen as too behaviorist and the latter as emancipatory. Consequently, many adult educators in North America, for instance, avoid using the word training. In Europe, at the present time, the word training is usually added to the expression "vocational education" and gives rise to a new independent concept, Vocational Education and Training or VET. VET is "the process [used] to acquire knowledge and skills with outcomes, attitudes and behavior patterns which have a practical bearing on potential or actual roles in the economic and social division of labor" (Cedefop, 2000, p. 66). This new concept combining two notions is integrated in the European Union's new vision of lifelong learning.

Training Practices: Historical Overview

Throughout the ages, aspiring young artists and craftspeople learned by watching experienced masters and by practicing under their watchful instruction, with the aim of producing a beautiful object that they could be proud of. We can call this the beginning of on-the-job training practices. On a more organized level, from the 17th century onwards there was the rise of the famous organizations of journeymen in Europe, who specialized in various crafts. A very high level of competence was required to satisfy the criteria for completion of training and a high degree of discipline to achieve it. This type of teaching approach became generalized and institutionalized in the 19th century: "technical experts" were trained through apprenticeships dispensed by technical schools, whereby the main part of the teaching program was given in the workplace rather than in the classroom. These training practices spread like wildfire during the process of industrialization. In industry, training was and is still focused on the performance of specific technical jobs and it offers learners a level of vocational proficiency. At the present time, apprenticeship practices, which are widely used in Germany and Switzerland, are attracting great interest from other countries where the educational system is still primarily based on the principle of general studies.

The period of industrialization was also the period of work rationalization. Taylorism, advocating as little training as possible for the workers, set the rules for a reductionist idea of training: first, designers determine what is required, then, they develop a single, simple procedure for the workers to learn in order to obtain the result. Training was therefore conceived as the adaptation of workers to a defined task in terms of spatial and temporal criteria, and was part of a global strategy to match the economic life with standards. During the 20th century, with its two world wars, work became a central value in life. After the First World War, training programs were set up in Europe as short-term and temporary measures for women, young people and veterans, all of them perceived as having a handicap and difficulty in entering or reentering the labor market. These training programs concentrated mostly on preparing people for unskilled jobs or for sectors needing a labor force. Following the economic crash, work camps were established mainly in English-speaking countries, as described by Field (1992). First set up in Britain, then in Canada, the United States, in Australia and New Zealand, these camps had a program of training and work, mostly with a view to rehabilitation following a period of unemployment or readaptation related to immigration.

Nowadays, training is still viewed as an adaptation process but the ultimate purposes are different. In technology, economy and the social arena, training is viewed as the road to survival. Rapid advances in information and communication technologies and the whole field of electronics, oblige not only designers and manufacturers but also customers to learn how to deal with these technologies. The wide range of available computer training corroborates this need. The present economic philosophy, still based on human capital theories, sees training as an effective tool and an answer to world competition and quality requirements. Thus, it is with the clear objective of obtaining maximum efficiency and competitiveness that training programs are offered, ranging from managerial training in the business sector to security and safety programs in industry. In the private sphere, training is of importance to individuals as well as to the community because of the role that training can play in increasing employment opportunities or developing autonomous career plans for a flexible job market. In the most general sense, undergoing training can be perceived as an act of looking to the future and not just as an act of remedying a situation or adapting to change.

Close Links to Work

Training has always been connected with a task to be performed. In the educational system, training gives learners the possibility to touch, to do, and to become familiar with something they did not know before. In continuing education, the purpose of training for learners facing an unfamiliar task is the same; but in addition, it is also intended to help them adapt to new circumstances in their environment, for instance to new technologies. Training can also be an organizational strategy in a number of cases: as a remedy, when workers are unable to undertake new responsibilities due to their lack of skills; as part of organizational planning, training may be required in connection with changes in the organization or methods of work, such as the introduction of team-work, quality groups, critical event analysis or task analysis. In cases such as these, where the learning objectives are work-based, training takes place in the company and is called in-house learning, or workplace learning, and is intimately related to the work situation.

Training can also take other forms. In most occupational fields, the initial training and training as part of continuing education enables learners to become proficient in the tasks they are expected to perform, whatever the complexity of the task or the social status of the particular occupation. In the health professions, this applies to doctors, nurses, and also nurses' aides. Part of the training is dispensed in the classroom (off the job), the rest takes place in the healthcare institutions (on-the-job training). This implies that graduate educational institutions such as vocational and technical schools, as well as universities, have a responsibility to offer training programs which fit workplace expectations and requirements. In the universities, this comes under the heading "working knowledge" (Symes & McIntyre, 2002).

The general framework of dual training ("*formation en alternance*" in French) is increasingly considered to be of great value as it gives trainees the opportunity to move back and forth between theory and practice. In a sense, this educational policy is a modern form of the apprenticeship model, even though it is no longer limited to trades, but now also applies to the more highly qualified, and to the technical professions as well as to other work sectors.

Training Procedure and Trainers

Researchers and teachers see training as an opportunity for learners to experience a learning process. Training also involves a procedure which training designers must follow in order for it to fulfil its operational objectives. In Europe, it is generally called "training engineering," or training architecture in America. The procedure involves several stages, or steps, which have universal validity. The first step is the determination of the training needs, based on the identification of problem issues related to the organization, to the work situation, and/or to the individuals involved, with a view to finding appropriate solutions through the training program. While training-needs analysis was formerly focused mainly on persons in a stable economic context, today it is centered primarily on performance requirements from an organizational point of view. The second step is the identification of short-term and long-term goals. This step is necessary in order to design the training program – its scope, the time frame, and the contents – in accordance with the ultimate goal of the project. The third step is drawing up the instruction process: choosing the form training will take, whether in-company training or school courses, or workshops. The fourth step, relating to the training course itself, involves the choice of methods and pedagogical strategies to be implemented by the trainers. The fifth and last step is evaluation, to assess the results of the training. Evaluation measures factors ranging from indicators of satisfaction to attested observable behavioral results. Human resources and training managers sometimes like to use sophisticated evaluation tools in order to gather evidence of the worth and usefulness of training, without recognizing that training is only one among many factors that generate behavioral changes.

These steps or stages are a regular part of the curriculum in the training courses for trainers in Western countries. The presentation may differ to some extent, but the classification always covers the pre-training preparatory stage, the training stage itself, and the post-training steps. The subject is even specially covered in the training manuals prepared for distribution and sale by major training organizations, as, for instance, the recent TCA, "Training Competency Architecture," distributed by the Canadian Society for Training and Development (CSTD, 2002). In connection with trainers' competencies, this handbook lists five headings: analysing performance and training needs, designing the training procedure, facilitating/instructing, evaluating the results, and coaching the application of training. These principles of training–engineering can produce high-quality results; however, enterprises must be aware of the advantages of training and must be willing to offer it as an investment, rather than considering it simply as an expenditure on their budget.

See also: continuing professional education, human capital theory, human resource development, training organizations, work-based learning, workplace learning.

References and Further Reading

Canadian Society for Training and Development (CSTD) (2002). *TCA: Training Competency Architecture Toolkit*. Toronto: Canadian Society for Training and Development.

Cedefop (2000). *Comparative vocational education and training research in Europe: Balance and perspectives*. Frankfurt am Main/Thessaloniki: Cedefop.

Field, J. (1992). *Learning through labor: Training, education and the state 1890–1939*. Leeds, UK: Leeds Studies in Continuing Education, University of Leeds.

Nadler, L. (1979). *Developing human resources*. Austin, TX: Learning Concepts Ltd.

Skinner, B. F. (1968). *The technology of teaching*. New York: Appleton Century Crofts.

Symes, C., & McIntyre, J. (2002). *Working knowledge: The new vocationalism and higher education*. Buckingham: Society for Research into Higher Education (SRHE) & Open University Press.

Edmée Ollagnier

Training Organizations

Training organizations are bodies whose primary objective is to give training prominence, and to highlight its social and economic value. We can distinguish among them international and governmental organizations, which concentrate on elaborating training policies; organizations which offer training, training providers; and professional organizations of trainers. It is the latter which play a key role in many Western countries in determining the quality of training offered and the competence of trainers.

Training Policies Through Public Organizations

At the international level, the IBE

(International Bureau of Education) and ILO (International Labor Organization) deal with global training issues. The IBE focuses most of its activity on primary and secondary schools, and professional schools; while the ILO seeks to promote training as a key factor to enhance employability and the development of skills through a department which collects quantified data, analyses the situation in various countries in light of priority issues, and finances missions to poor countries. In Europe, the European Union's Training Foundation, based in Italy, offers a venue to political decision-makers, researchers in adult education, as well as training organizations and individuals engaged in training to meet and elaborate their ideas on training. For this European foundation and the ILO, the principal objective is to promote and give prominence to training as an asset that countries can take advantage of, for social and economic development.

At the national level, some countries have specialized entities dealing exclusively with training issues; these, known as "national training organizations," are in some cases part of the Ministry of Labor. Their mission is to formulate, to develop and to implement national training policies in accordance with the respective government's socioeconomic priorities. Often, these entities are also the repositories of information, not only on the legislation and the structures of the country in question, but also on the training products that are available. While they are mostly governmental structures, they are supported in their activities by partnerships with employers' organizations, labor unions, and other training organizations. Being entrusted with the implementation of training policies on the national level, they have authority to make decisions which have repercussions for their partners: for example, for employers on whom an obligation is placed to pay for training, or for training-provider organizations who have to observe the quality requirements that have been defined.

Organizations Providing Training

Depending on the contents and objectives of the specific training, providers belong to different sectors of activity; broadly speaking in the three categories listed in the European Union's databases (Masson, 2000). The first category includes commercial training providers for whom training is a product for sale: in the main, they produce training products in specialized fields, ranging from literacy programs to advanced technologies. The second category includes all the education institutions, public or private, that have been granted government recognition as training institutions and authorized to issue diplomas to trainees either in basic or in continuing education, or both. The third category relates to the manufacturers of equipment who organize training sessions to accompany the sale of products requiring technical instruction for use. In each of these situations, the person in charge of instruction is a trainer. Trainers are usually professionals in a specialized field of knowledge or occupation, who become trainers not on the basis of any specific instructional training, but because of their expertise in a field or of their gifts for interpersonal relations.

Training, like other marketable services, is now part of the economic scene and is subject to competition, and struggles over territory and dominance. In this respect, the manufacturers of equipment may be left out, as their training is an integral part of their customer service. But those in the first category, who offer training as saleable merchandise, are, without a doubt, the most exposed to the pressures of competition. Their number is difficult to estimate due to the lack of statistical data. The legal registration status of these organizations varies widely: there are associations, foundations, private companies, incorporated companies, and others. The clientele to whom they sell their services (their training) is equally varied: small and medium-sized enterprises at home and abroad, governments, community groups or labor organizations. They earn their reputation on the basis of the quality of their services, and usually remain specialized in a particular area. As regards the educational institutions in the second category, the universities in particular, enterprises and governments place great expectations on their training activities (Walshok, 1995, p. 41). Being in a position to make demands, they want these educational institutions to prepare people for employment who are not only well-trained, but also able to satisfy work-performance expectations. This raises questions: should universities, by virtue of their continuing education department and other faculty departments be considered training organizations? Do they want that? Or will it lead them into competition with private training organizations, which are usually governed by considerations other than education and knowledge?

Professional Training Organizations

Trainers and training-providers join local or national associations in order to share information and exchange views on their practices and experience. These associations, being representative of the profession, have considerable weight in the partnership with public authorities, and play an important role in establishing training practices and standards. These associations or professional groups are led mainly by training managers and have connections both to training and to human resource development. This is the case with the large North American societies: the ASTD (American Society for Training and Development), which has just formed an alliance with the OSTD (Ontario Society for Training and Development), and the CSTD (Canadian Society for Training and Development). The ASTD "is the world's leading association of workplace learning and performance professionals, forming a world-class community of practice" (ASTD, 2003). It has 70,000 members from 15,000 organizations: multinational corporations, medium- and small-sized businesses, government, the academic world, consulting firms and product and service suppliers. These societies organize conferences, publish periodicals, and list job openings in training and human development. They operate separately from the American Association for Adult and Continuing Education (AAACE), which is composed mostly of researchers and academics, who focus on adult learning and the training of adult educators.

In Europe, the organizations of training professionals are much more modest both in terms of their membership and in terms of their activities. Nevertheless they play a similar role at local or national levels. The essential difference is that American organizations are explicitly oriented towards training as a tool to achieve financial results, while European structures have a two-fold outlook: they address all the issues connected with workplace training, as in America, and in addition they view training as a right to pursue continuous learning throughout the lifetime, whatever the subject's cultural, financial, or educational background. An example is the FSEA, the "Fédération Suisse d'Education des Adultes" in Switzerland, whose members are training professionals, and which publishes a periodical in addition to organizing meetings and lectures on pertinent topics. But all these structures in the Western world have in common two poles of interest and practice: the certification of trainers, and the certification of training organizations. Yet, in Europe research societies like ESREA (European Society for Research on the Education of Adults) are distinguished from practitioners' associations.

Training Quality

Nobody in the 1970s, neither the public authorities nor the training professionals, had given any thought to setting the guiding principles and operational rules for training. At the present time, however, like all other products and services competing for a market, training has to adhere to standards of quality. The professional training organizations in some countries have elaborated reference criteria for the certification of quality, which, though specific to the profession, are based on the same principles as the ISO (International Organization for Standardization) quality standards. These organizations are usually authorized to become certifying organizations, a task they perform in addition to their ordinary activities.

In Canada, the CSTD offers a certification program that sets the standards of practice for the training profession. In Switzerland, the FSEA (Fédération Suisse d'Education des Adultes) made its "Eduqua" certification program public in 2000. Without this certification, Swiss training bodies cannot obtain public subsidies for their courses, even though these may be recognized as being of public utility. The conditions for certification include criteria relating to needs analysis and evaluation procedures, as well as to the qualification of trainers. In England, a certification body, the IRCA (International Register for the Certification of Auditors), recently created a certification procedure for training organizations with two additional protocols: an approval as a certified training organization, and a certification of certified training courses. These innovations prove that training is looked upon as a commercial product on a par with others, with the same obligation to adhere to standardized, and sometimes rigid, rules in order to be of service not only to commercial enterprises but also to public authorities in their planning of training projects and budgets.

The Training of Trainers

In some European countries, like Switzerland, training quality standards are going to include the qualification of trainers (Ollagnier, 2003). Consequently, the professionalization of trainers is gaining greater importance than ever before: trainers will not only have to be good professionals in their fields, but will also need to learn the basic principles of adult education. This is an encouraging development, but considering the growing importance attached to professional training organizations and their influence on the market, one may wonder what principles the trainers of tomorrow are going to follow and what kind of trainers' practices society will encourage. Their organizations push trainers to ever greater economic efficiency in the face of the demands of the market. For instance, the last ASTD Congress held at San Diego in 2003 offered workshops with such topics as: "Careers: Guiding Yourself, Guiding Others;" "E-learning;" "Leadership and Management Development;" "Performance Consulting;" and "Personal and Professional Effectiveness." The publications of the ASTD cover similar ground: "Leadership Training," "Coaching Training," "Customer Service Training," and "Technology for Trainers." Thus, these organizations provide trainers with tools and techniques, and also offer them the certification for this type of professional learning.

Aside from those described above, programs for the training of trainers are also offered in universities, but from a different learning perspective. University courses typically involve, first, a discussion of the basic principles of adult education and a critical review of training practices (Brookfield, 1988), and only later the discussion of performance goals in training. These universities are fully authorized to offer professionals sound training and background knowledge that will be useful to them in the practice of their trade, as envisaged by the AAACE. But how can trainers find their bearings amidst these complementary, but often also contradictory, currents of thought and educational practices?

The development of new training functions and of the competencies of trainers related thereto, as well as the higher requirements set for qualification and certification for professional recognition, allow us to predict that training organizations are going to continue their growth in many countries. Nonetheless, it is to be hoped that trainers will, despite the power and influence of professional training structures, continue to obtain training instruction in universities so as to acquire as full an understanding as possible of what the trainer's work involves. In light of the above, training could progress and turn into a practice in which the trainer becomes an educator, while the learner is at least equal in importance to the expected economic results.

See also: competency-based education, human resource development, professional development, training, vocational education.

References and Further Reading

ASTD (2003). *News release.* Alexandria, VA: ASTD Media.

Brookfield, S. D. (Ed.). (1988). *Training educators of adults.* London, New York: Routledge.

Masson, J. R. (Ed.). (2000). *Involvement in the EU lifelong learning policy: Achievements, gaps and challenges.* Torino: European Training Foundation Report.

Ollagnier, E. (2003). *Higher education or vocational training system for trainer's APEL: The debate in Switzerland.* Glasgow, Scotland: Centre for Research in Lifelong Learning. Conference Proceedings, Glasgow.

Walshok, M. L. (1995). *Knowledge without boundaries: What America's research universities can do for the economy, the workplace and the community.* San-Francisco: Jossey-Bass.

Websites:

AAACE (American Association for Adult and Continuing Education): www.aaace.org

ASTD (American Society for Training and Development): www.astd.org

CSTD (Canadian Society for Training and Development): www.cstd.ca

ESREA (European Society for Research on the Education of Adults): www.esrea.org

European Training Foundation: http://europa.eu.int/agencies/etf/index_en.htm

FSEA (Fédération Suisse d'Education des Adultes): www.alice.ch

Edmée Ollagnier

Transfer of Learning

Transfer of learning is a term used to describe the process by which learners apply, in settings outside of an adult educational setting, the skills and knowledge they have learned within that setting. Cantor (1992) distinguishes between positive and negative transfer, with positive transfer occurring when learners apply the skills they have been taught. Negative transfer, according to Cantor, occurs when learners do not apply what has been taught, but desired outcomes occur anyway. To Cantor, key factors in positive transfer are the ability of adult educators to help learners link new information to information they already know, and the ability of educators to demonstrate to learners the relevance for them of the skills and knowledge being taught. Demonstrating the successful transfer of learning becomes a particular necessity for program survival when budgets are being pruned and provision being cut back. As calls for accountability grow louder within the field, the pressures on program planners and teachers to show the utility and applicability of learning in the "real world" become irresistible. Vella, Berardinelli, and Burrow (1998) see transfer of learning as one of the three dimensions of accountability, the others being changes in learners' knowledge, skill or attitudes that result from a program, and changes in the learner's organization that result from new learning. However, transfer of learning is not a simple process of replication across contexts. As Caffarella (1994) points out, critics who complain that adult educational programs cannot show a clear and direct transfer of learning sometimes fail to recognize the existence of institutional, political and community factors that prevent this from happening.

Critiquing the Discourse

One of the critiques of the discourse of transfer of learning is that such a discourse commodifies the complex process of learning. Commodification is an idea often associated with Marx (1961) and has been highly influential within critical theory, describing the process by which a human quality or relationship becomes regarded as a product, good or commodity to be bought and sold on the open market. The concept of the transfer of learning is one that supports the notion of commodification. Thinking of learning as something that can be transferred means thinking of it as an object that exists apart from us. Learning thus becomes conceptualized as a package of decontextualized skills and knowledge that is transferred from one context (the adult educational setting) to another (the workplace, community, family and so on) with the implication that it has some existence that can be measured and recognized outside of the teachers' and learners' own identities. In the commodity-exchange economy, the dynamic of exchange – I give you this, you give me that in return – determines all human relationships and how people think of their labor (including their intellectual labor of learning). The exchange value of a thing (what it's worth in monetary terms) overshadows its use value (its value assessed by how it helps satisfy a human need or desire). For example, the exchange value of learning to read in adulthood (how such learning will help the adult become more successful in the job market) overshadows its use value (how it helps the adult develop self-confidence, draw new meanings from life, and be opened to new perspectives on the world). Although the use value of learning is important to adult learners and adult educators, it is primarily the exchange value that policy-makers and purse-holders consult when determining whether or not programs should be funded and how they should be evaluated. In the exchange economy the ability of adult educators to demonstrate the successful transfer and use value of learning becomes imperative for program survival. Not surprisingly, then, the transfer of learning is a process that is often commodified, with the learning to be transferred viewed as if it existed as an object in a world located outside our emotions or positionality.

One of the most articulate commentators on commodification is the Frankfurt School theorist Erich Fromm (1976). Fromm argued that the education system tries to train people to *have* knowledge as a possession, by and large commensurate with the amount of property or social prestige they are likely to have in later life. Educational institutions give each student a certain amount of cultural property, what Fromm called a "luxury-knowledge package" (p. 49), with the size of each package being in accord with the person's probable social prestige. This luxury-knowledge package becomes, in effect, the learning that is transferred to contexts outside the institution. In this analysis of transfer of learning, knowledge becomes equated with content, with "fixed clusters of thought, or whole theories" (Fromm, p. 37) that students store, and teachers are reduced to bureaucratic dispensers of knowledge to be transferred. This commodified content, transferred bureaucratically, is alienated from learners' lives and experiences. In Fromm's view, "students and the content of the lectures remain strangers to each other, except that each student has become the owner of a collection of statements made by somebody else" (p. 37). In determining what learning is to be transferred, little attention is paid to subjugated knowledge; that is, knowledge not deemed legitimate or scientific enough to be part of the "official" curriculum.

A second critique of the concept of transfer of learning focuses on how it ignores the ways in which the learner's own positionality (her class, gender, race, ideology), habitual modes of cognitive processing, emotional rhythms and subjective experience frame how learning is understood and applied. Studies of situated cognition, dialectical thinking, reflective judgment, embedded logic, everyday cognition, post-formal thinking and practical reasoning (Sinnott, 1998) emphasize that modes of thought and analysis learned in formal education are reframed and skewed by learners to fit the contexts through which they move. Studies of the workings of practical logic explore how mothers and children solve problems together, how sports fans understand the nuances of cricket or baseball games, and how punters make decisions in betting shops on which horses to back. These studies show how skills and models of decision-making, problem-solving and logical analysis learned in formal educational institutions are changed, some would say distorted, to fit the specific contexts and imperatives of adult life. Adults are acting logically but not based on the straight transfer of forms of logical reasoning learned in school and college. The logic they apply is a form of practical logic that springs from a deep understanding of the context of the situation (whether this be placing a bet or deciding whether to alter a patient's medication). It is a logic that does not follow formal rules of deductive reasoning, but that is experiential and inferential. It involves being aware of, and attending seriously to, very subtle cues whose importance only becomes apparent to those who have the benefit of a lengthy and mindful immersion in experience.

A third critique of the discourse surrounding the transfer of learning stresses the role played by oppressive social and political structures in preventing the transfer of knowledge and skills outside the classroom. This is particularly relevant in explorations of the transfer of critical thinking skills. One may learn to recognize and question familiar assumptions in the relatively supportive environment of the classroom, only to find that the exercise of these skills is actively discouraged or punished outside. In families, communities and workplaces, the adult who starts to question accepted values and practices can easily commit cultural suicide without being aware that this is happening (Brookfield, 1995). As with any transfer of learning, a key component of success in this regard is preparing the learner, as much as possible, to survive the barriers and animosities that exercising new learning often entails. Questioning racism, sexism and homophobia in class, or learning to recognize one's own collusion in hegemony, is something that can be done without incurring great penalty in a classroom where the teacher is supportive of those learning processes. Doing the same things outside the classroom with one's own family, friends and colleagues, or with those who hold positional power over you, is a very different matter. Such new behaviors learned in class can cause divorces, get you fired (or passed over for promotion), ensure you lose friends, split your family or subject you to physical and mental violence. Adult educators who see their classrooms as temporary zones of liberation, in which students learn to recognize hegemony, challenge ideology and practice democracy, frequently warn of the dangers accompanying the transfer of this learning to sites in the outside world (Shor & Freire, 1987). At the Highlander Folk School the use of extensive role-plays and simulations was stressed by Myles Horton as an important means by which activists could prepare themselves to face the animosity and hostility they would encounter in applying skills learned at Highlander in their activist work (Jacobs, 2003).

Finally, postmodern perspectives challenge the epistemology undergirding the concept of transfer of learning. This epistemology holds that a single fixed standardized meaning exists that is embedded in an act of learning occurring in a classroom and that this single fixed meaning can be applied or replicated in other contexts (Bagnall, 1999). Such an epistemology is undeniably modernist. Modernism holds that if we spend enough time paying careful attention to how we speak and what we say or write, we can cut down the ambiguities in human communication and come to clear meanings and understandings that can be shared with others. By implication, modernism holds that a set of skills or knowledge learned in the adult education classroom can, if such learning is facilitated in an unambiguous, transparent manner, allow such learning to be transferred to other contexts carrying the same meaning ascribed to it by learners in the classroom. Postmodernism rejects this view, which it regards as grounded in the Anglo Saxon tradition of transparency whereby clarity of speech and writing is valued above all. It eschews logocentrism – the idea that at the core of words is a shared, universal meaning. Language, meaning, and consequently transfer of learning, is seen as slippery and opaque. Even the very words and symbols that we use to communicate new learning to students are compromised, from a postmodern perspective. Adult educators can strive to invest the words they speak or write with certain meanings, but they can never find exactly the right words to express what they feel and think. Then, the words they use as teachers are interpreted in multifarious ways by those who hear and read them as learners. The speakers/writers/educators have absolutely no control over the meanings adult learners take from their words, no matter how much effort they make to be as unambiguous and transparent as possible. Similarly, from a postmodern perspective, adult educators have virtually no control over the ways skills, knowledge, insights and meanings learned in the classroom are understood and applied – that is to say, transferred – in the world outside. To judge the success of programs by the transfer of learning they enable is, from this perspective, based on a false understanding of the nature of communication.

See also: continuing professional education, critical theory, human capital theory, training.

References and Further Reading

Bagnall, R. G. (1999). *Discovering radical contingency: Building a postmodern agenda in adult education*. New York: Peter Lang.

Brookfield, S. D. (1995). *Becoming a critically reflective teacher*. San Francisco: Jossey-Bass.

Caffarella, R. S. (1994). *Planning programs for adult learners: A practical guide for educators, trainers and staff developers*. San Francisco: Jossey-Bass.

Cantor, J. A. (1992). *Delivering instruction to adult learners*. Middletown, OH: Wall & Emerson.

Fromm, E. (1976). *To have or to be*. London: Sphere Books.

Jacobs, D. (2003). *The Myles Horton reader: Education for social change*. Knoxville, TN: University of Tennessee Press.

Marx, K. (1961). *Economic and philosophical manuscripts* (T.B. Bottomore, Trans.). In E. Fromm (Ed.), *Marx's concept of man*. New York: Frederick Ungar.

Shor, I., & Freire, P. (1987). *A pedagogy for liberation: Dialogues on transforming education*. Westport, CT: Bergin & Garvey.

Sinnott, J. D. (1998). *The development of logic in adulthood: Postformal thought and its applications*. New York: Plenum.

Vella, J., Berardinelli, P., & Burrow, J. (1998). *How do they know? Evaluating adult learning*. San Francisco: Jossey-Bass.

Stephen Brookfield

Transformative Learning

Transformative learning is a process by which previously uncritically assimilated assumptions, beliefs, values, and perspectives are questioned and thereby become more open, permeable, and better validated (Cranton, 2000; Mezirow, 2000).

Mezirow's (1978) original presentation of perspective transformation was based on a study of the experiences of women returning to college, where they found many of their assumptions, about their roles, challenged. The theory has since been extended to define transformation in more complex ways, but in 1978 perspective transformation referred to a structural reorganization of the way a person looks at himself or herself. At its core, the idea of transformative learning is elegant in its simplicity. People make meaning out of the world through experiences. What happens once, they expect to happen again. Through this process, they develop habits of mind or a frame of reference for understanding the world, much of which is uncritically assimilated. Individuals absorb, in the process of daily living, values, assumptions, and beliefs about how things are. When a person encounters something unexpected, he or she either rejects the new information or begins to question the previously held assumptions. This has the potential to be transformative.

Critical Self-Reflection

The centrality of critical reflection to transformative learning theory is due in part to the theory and research being based almost exclusively in the North American culture, where rationality is strongly valued. The primary texts on transformative learning and the *Journal of Transformative Education* are published in North America, and the International Conference on Transformative Learning is held in North America. Although the key role of critical reflection in transformation has been debated, it remains at the core of Mezirow's conceptualization. People transform frames of reference through critical reflection on their own and others' assumptions and beliefs. Although reflection need not lead to transformation, when it does the frame of reference becomes more open and better justified. The process is not about changing one's mind from one thing to another, or adopting the "right" point of view, but rather about becoming more open.

When something different happens, people can be led to question their way of seeing the world by asking, "What happened here?" (content reflection), "How did I come to think this way?" (process reflection), and, "Why is this important?" (premise reflection). It is premise reflection that is most likely to lead to transformed habits of mind; here, we question the very validity of the assumptions underlying how we see the world. Critical self-reflection may not be linear or sequential, but it is essentially a rational process of seeing that previously-held views no longer fit – they are too narrow, too limiting.

Merriam (2003) points out that a certain level of cognitive development is necessary before individuals can engage in critical reflection. She also reminds us that transformative learning is, in itself, developmental; critical self-reflection leads to developmental outcomes. Mezirow (2000) distinguishes between transformative learning that occurs through objective and subjective reframing. When critical reflection occurs on the assumptions of others (questioning things heard in the media, for example), it can lead to objective reframing, and when critical self-reflection occurs on one's own assumptions (questioning one's behavior in interpersonal relationships, for example), it can lead to subjective reframing. He also distinguishes between epochal (sudden and dramatic) transformation and incremental (gradual, over time) transformation. It is not clear how the nature of critical reflection varies between these two kinds of transformation.

Discourse

Ideas and evidence from others help us to consider our own views in a new light. Discourse is a specialized use of dialogue that has as its goal reaching a common understanding and justification of an interpretation or belief. People present reasons for their beliefs, weigh the evidence given in others' arguments, and consider alternative perspectives. Together, people come to a tentative best judgment. Mezirow (2000) points out that effective participation in discourse requires emotional maturity and clear thinking. He says that in order for learners to freely and fully engage in discourse, they should ideally: (a) have accurate and complete information, (b) be free from coercion and distorting self-deception, (c) be open to alternative points of view and have empathy and concern about how others think and feel, (d) have the ability to weigh evidence and assess arguments, (e) be aware of the context of ideas and be able to reflect on assumptions (f) have an equal opportunity to participate in the various roles of discourse, and (g) be willing to seek understanding and agreement and accept a resulting best judgment as a test of validity. Again, Merriam (2003) reminds us that such a sophisticated level of discourse mandates a certain level of cognitive development on the part of the learner.

Frame of Reference

A frame of reference is a meaning perspective, the web of assumptions and expectations through which we filter the way we see the world (Mezirow, 2000). A frame of reference has two dimensions – a habit of mind and the resulting points of view. Habits of mind are the broad predispositions we use to interpret experience. Mezirow lists six kinds of habits of mind, each overlapping and influencing the other. Epistemic habits of mind relate to the way we come to know things and the way we use that knowledge. Sociolinguistic perspectives are the way we view social norms, culture, and how we use language. Psychological perspectives include our self-concept, personality, emotional responses, and our personal images and dreams. Moral-ethical habits of mind incorporate our conscience and morality. Philosophical habits of mind are based on religious doctrine or world view. Aesthetic habits of mind include our tastes and standards about beauty.

A habit of mind is expressed as a point of view. A point of view is a cluster of meaning schemes, and meaning schemes are habitual, implicit rules for interpreting experiences.

Domains of Learning

Becoming critically reflective of assumptions occurs in both instrumental and communicative learning. Mezirow draws on Habermas's (1971) work on kinds of knowledge to form a foundation for transformative learning theory. *Instrumental knowledge* is that which allows us to manipulate and control the environment, predict observable physical and social events, and take appropriate actions. Empirical or natural scientific methodologies produce technically useful knowledge, the knowledge necessary for industry and production in modern society. In this paradigm, knowledge is established by reference to external reality. There is an objective world made up of observable phenomena. Physical and social systems are seen to operate independently of human perceptions. Habermas criticizes instrumental rationality when it becomes such a pervasive ideology that we believe all knowledge is instrumental. In the Age of Enlightenment, the application of reason was seen as the way to solve the world's problems. As a result, empirical scientific methods were viewed as superior to subjective, qualitative, or spiritual ways of knowing. Only recently has modernism (the reign of logic) been criticized in the social sciences and education as not allowing a deeper, more open understanding of human interactions.

The second kind of knowledge is based on our need to understand each other through language. Habermas (1971) calls this *practical or communicative knowledge*. Human beings have always been social creatures, instinctively forming groups, tribes, communities, cultures, and nations in order to satisfy their mutual needs. In order for people to survive together in groups and societies, they must communicate with and understand each other. There are no scientific laws governing these communications – when we communicate with others, we interpret what they say in our own way. This does not mean that communicative knowledge is entirely individual. All societies share and transmit social knowledge, that is, a code of commonly accepted beliefs and behavior, including standards and values, moral and political issues, educational and social systems, and government actions. Habermas argues that people may misinterpret the world around them based on distorted assumptions about themselves or society. We want social knowledge to be objective and concrete and therefore stop questioning the systems around us.

The third kind of knowledge, which derives from a questioning of instrumental and communicative knowledge, Habermas calls *emancipatory*. By nature, people are interested in self-knowledge, growth, development, and freedom. Gaining emancipatory knowledge is dependent on our abilities to be self-determining and self-reflective. Self-determination can be described as the capacity to both be aware and critical of ourselves and of our social and cultural context. Self-reflection involves being aware and critical of our subjective perceptions of knowledge and of the constraints of social knowledge. Emancipatory knowledge is gained through a process of critically questioning ourselves and the social systems within which we live. The philosophical foundation of emancipatory knowledge lies in critical theory. In this paradigm, instrumental and communicative knowledge are not rejected but are seen as limiting. If we do not question current scientific and social theories and accepted truths, we may never realize how we are constrained by their inevitable distortions and errors (the world is flat, the Aryan race is superior). Without the possibility of critical questioning of ourselves and our beliefs, such constraining knowledge can be accepted by entire cultures.

Phases of Transformation

Transformative learning follows some variation of 10 phases (Mezirow, 2000). Not all researchers find evidence of all phases and some researchers have proposed additional phases, but there appear to be somewhat consistent patterns. Some unexpected event or disorienting dilemma begins the learning experience. This can be as simple as hearing or reading about a point of view that is different from one's own, or as traumatic as serious illness or the death of a spouse. Self-examination follows, sometimes with feelings of fear, anger, or guilt, depending on the context. This examination may lead to a critical assessment of assumptions. In dialogue with others, learners share their experience and gather different ideas and interpretations. This makes the exploration of options for new roles, relationships, and actions possible. If transformative learning occurs, and a person revises his or her assumptions, a new course of action may be chosen. In this process, it is sometimes necessary to acquire new knowledge and skills and to experiment with new roles and relationships. Finally, the new perspective is integrated into a person's life.

The nature of these phases implies a sequential process, something that is questioned by those theorists who see transformation as involving intuition, imagination, and insight more so than rationality.

Individual Differences

Psychological predispositions form one kind of habit of mind, and there are two dimensions to this that are relevant to transformative learning theory. First, as Dirkx (2000) and others argue, as people develop, they individuate: they separate themselves from the collective of humanity. This process is transformative; it is a reconstruction of the frame of reference related to the self. Second, psychological predispositions influence the way learners experience transformation. When people question a frame of reference, they do so using their psychological traits. Cranton (2000) uses Jung's ([1921] 1971) theory of psychological types to propose that individuals differ in the ways in which they engage in transformative learning.

Jung describes two attitudes or ways of relating to the world. Introversion is a preference for the self or the inner world, and extraversion is a preference for the world external to the self. The introverted attitude leads to the personalization or subjectification of experiences, which would be similar to Mezirow's subjective reframing in transformative learning. The extraverted attitude is demonstrated by an objective reaction to experiences, which is parallel to objective reframing.

Jung delineates four functions of living, two of which are judgmental and two of which are perceptive. In order to make judgments, a person may use the thinking function, which is logical and analytical, or the feeling function, which relies on value-based reactions of acceptance or rejection in which logic plays no part. When perceiving things, a person may use the sensing function, which perceives through the five senses or the intuitive function, which follows hunches, images, and possibilities.

Mezirow's (2000) understanding of transformative learning calls primarily on the use of the thinking function, either introverted or extraverted. Critical reflection and critical self-reflection, as described in the traditional theory, is logical and analytical. Arguments are weighed, evidence is assessed, and judgments are made. Intuition may play a secondary role in exploring options and envisioning alternative points of view, but the thinking function operates at the core of the process. Cranton (2000) suggests that people who have psychological type preferences other than thinking may experience tranformative learning in different ways. Other learning styles, models or other approaches to understanding differences among people could also be used to explore alternative transformative processes, but this has not been addressed in this way very often in the literature. Belenky and Stanton (2000), for example, distinguish between separate knowing (following a line of reasoning and looking for flaws in logic) and connected knowing (working to understand and empathize with another person's view) and conclude that transformative learning as described by Mezirow relies on separate knowing. They suggest that it is "clear that there are other processes that are equally vital but less well described in this body of work" (p. 91). Separate knowing parallels the use of the thinking function, and connected knowing parallels the use of the feeling function in Jung's theory of psychological types.

Extrarational Approaches

Several alternatives to the cognitive, rational approach have been proposed. Boyd (1991), for example, suggests that transformation is an inner journey of individuation, the process of learning through reflection on the psychic structures (anima, animus, ego, shadow, collective unconscious, and so forth) that make up one's uniqueness. In working to understand the role of imagination in transformative learning, Dirkx (2000) relies on the process of individuation as well. He argues that transformation is the stuff of ordinary, everyday occurrences much more than it is a "burning bush" phenomenon in which we use reason to "wrest knowledge from the throes of ignorance"(p. 247). Individuation, Dirkx suggests, is an ongoing psychic process that occurs in everyone whether we are conscious of it or not. When we participate in it consciously and imaginatively, we develop a deepened sense of self, an expansion of consciousness, and an engendering of soul.

Transformation is the Emergence of the Self

Taylor (1998) suggests it is not critical reflection that is at the center of transformative learning, but discernment – a holistic orientation including receptivity, recognition, and grieving. Grieving, an emotional facet of transformation, is stressed in Scott's (1997) work. Daloz (1999) explores the notion of transformation as being a response to some change in our world which "suddenly forces us to relate to it in a sharply different way" (p. 135). That is, we have an experiential facet to the process – transformative learning is a response to an experience.

Social Change

Another facet of transformative learning is highlighted in the debate between those scholars who view social action as central to transformative learning (for example, Cunningham, 1992; Newman, 1994) and those who see the individual's development as the primary focus. Mezirow (1991) sees the educator's role as being one of helping the individual become aware of, question, and work to change oppressive social norms. He distinguishes this from larger scale political, social, and economic transformation. The tasks of education are different than the tasks of political mobilization (Brookfield, 2000). Others hold that critical reflection without social action is meaningless.

Daloz (2000) represents this view well when he explores the nature of transformative learning that occurs as a person develops a sense of social responsibility. He sees transformative learning as a deep shift in that person's frame of reference. Our social context plays an extremely important role in defining who we are. Daloz says that emancipatory learning is "not about escape from but rather about a deeper immersion into the rough-and-tumble of human relationship" (p. 120). Our responsibility as adult educators is to work to bring about transformation at both the individual and the social level. We need to pay attention to transformative learning for the common good, and not place our own welfare ahead of that of the larger community. Similarly, O'Sullivan (2003) stresses that transformative learning cannot be concerned only with the individual. We are responsible for the future of the planet, he says, and all educational ventures must be judged within this.

See also: adult development, critical thinking, dialogue, emancipatory education, knowledge, reflective learning.

References and Further Reading

Belenky, M. F., & Stanton, A. (2000). Inequality, development, and connected knowing. In J. Mezirow & Associates (Eds.), *Learning as transformation: Critical perspectives on a theory in progress* (pp. 71–102). San Francisco: Jossey-Bass.

Boyd, R. (1991). *Personal transformation in small groups*. London: Routledge.

Brookfield, S. D. (2000). Transformative learning as ideology critique. In J. Mezirow & Associates (Eds.), *Learning as transformation: Critical perspectives on a theory in progress* (pp. 125–148). San Francisco: Jossey-Bass.

Cranton, P. (2000). Individual differences and transformative learning. In J. Mezirow & Associates (Eds.), *Learning as transformation: Critical perspectives on a theory in progress* (pp. 181–204). San Francisco: Jossey-Bass.

Cunningham, P. M. (1992). From Freire to feminism: The North American experience with critical pedagogy. *Adult Education Quarterly*, *42*(3), 180–191.

Daloz, L. (1999). *Mentor: Guiding the journey of adult learners* (2nd ed.). San Francisco: Jossey-Bass.

Daloz, L. (2000). Transformative learning for the common good. In J. Mezirow & Associates (Eds.), *Learning as transformation: Critical perspectives on a theory in progress* (pp. 103–123). San Francisco: Jossey-Bass.

Dirkx, J. (2000). After the burning bush: Transformative learning as imaginative engagement with everyday experience. In C. Wiessner, S. Meyer, & D. Fuller (Eds.), *Challenges of practice: Transformative learning in action*. Proceedings of the Third International Conference on Transformative Learning. New York: Teachers College, Columbia University.

Habermas, J. (1971). *Knowledge and human interests*. (Trans. J. J. Shapiro). Boston: Beacon Press.

Jung, C. (1971). *Psychological types*. Princeton, NJ: Princeton University Press, originally published in 1921.

Merriam, S. B. (2003). Cognitive development and transformational learning: A research agenda. In C. Wiessner, S. Meyer, N. Pfhal, & P. Neaman (Eds.), *Transformative learning in action: Building bridges across contexts and disciplines*. Proceedings of the Fifth International Conference on Transformative Learning. New York: Teachers College, Columbia University.

Mezirow, J. (1978). Perspective transformation. *Adult Education, 28*, 100–110.

Mezirow, J. (1991). *Transformative dimensions of adult learning*. San Francisco: Jossey-Bass.

Mezirow, J. (2000). Learning to think like an adult: Core concepts of transformation theory. In J. Mezirow & Associates (Eds.), *Learning as transformation:*

Critical perspectives on a theory in progress (pp. 3–33). San Francisco: Jossey-Bass.

Newman, M. (1994). *Defining the enemy: Adult education in social action*. Sydney, Australia: Stewart Victor Publishing.

O'Sullivan, E. (2003). The ecological terrain of transformative learning: A vision statement. In C. Wiessner, S. Meyer, N. Pfhal, & P. Neaman (Eds.), *Transformative learning in action: Building bridges across contexts and disciplines*. Proceedings of the Fifth International Conference on Transformative Learning. New York: Teachers College, Columbia University.

Scott, S. M. (1997). The grieving soul in the transformation process. In P. Cranton (Ed.), *Transformative learning in action* (pp. 41–50). *New Directions for Adult and Continuing Education*, No. 74. San Francisco: Jossey-Bass.

Taylor, E. W. (1998). *The theory and practice of transformative learning: A critical review*. Information Series No. 374. ERIC Clearinghouse on Adult, Career and Vocational Education, Ohio State University. Retrieved February 20, 2004, from ERIC database (ERIC Document Reproduction Service No. ED423422).

Patricia Cranton

U

The United States and Adult Education

Adult education in the United States comprises a complicated mosaic of unevenly shaped and haphazardly arranged pieces. Programmatically and conceptually it is a contested field. Programmatically, adult education activities are claimed by their proponents to be located in an incredible array of settings. Chief amongst these are community colleges, high schools, corporations, the military, community action groups, churches, the health system, political campaigns and proprietary online universities. The contents of the decennial handbooks of adult education (published by the American Association of Adult and Continuing Education and summarized in its millennial edition) provide a vivid illustration of the field's diversity (Wilson & Hayes, 2000). Conceptually, a major schism exists between those who define adult education as the provision of organized education and training opportunities for adults wherever this occurs, and those who claim that for an activity to be an example of adult education it must exhibit certain intrinsic features. Members of this latter group often claim that adult education is defined by a certain methodological stance such as andragogy, democratic process, self-direction, conscientization or collaborative learning; that adult education must be geared towards certain predefined objectives such as transformative learning, critical reflection or democratic social change; or that adult education should be conducted with a certain moral or political tone (that usually stresses respect for learners' personhood and experiences as well as viewing the teacher as a co-learner and co-creator of knowledge).

For the first half of the 20th century, American adult education's traditional identity was as part of a movement to create and sustain *The Democratic Way of Life* (Lindeman & Smith, 1951). In the 21st century this identity has splintered. For many who see themselves as adult educators the chief concern of the field is to introduce adult educational principles and practices in the capitalist workplace. Terms such as workplace learning or organizational learning are viewed by many as synonymous with adult learning, whilst the argument is often advanced that supporting adult education will assist in the regeneration of ailing companies and in America's attempt to compete in the global marketplace. The prevalence of training activities within corporations and government agencies, and the explosion of online learning programs, promoted by proprietary schools explicitly devoted to selling services within a competitive marketplace, might seem to suggest that the field has become essentially the engine of capitalist development. Yet, even as capitalist discourses (with learners as customers or consumers) dominate some sectors of the field, other voices critical of this cooptation have emerged (Sheared & Sissel, 2001). Much attention has been given to the role of adult education in oppositional social and political movements and revolutionary organizations. Pre-conferences at the annual Adult Education Research Conference have explored how the Africentric paradigm can reframe adult educational practices, on the still meaningful connections between adult education and the labor movement, and on the existence of gay, lesbian and transgendered learners, practitioners and discourses in the field. Postmodern, queer, feminist and Africentric discourses have de-centered the field's implicit assumption that a unitary theory of adult learning and a unitary methodology of adult education can be discovered or advanced. Recently a concern has emerged to explore the spiritual dimensions to adult learning and education.

In the 20th century, adult education scholars spent considerably energy striving to establish a theory of adult learning which they could claim represented their own empirical territory. The *raison d'être* of this effort was to assert that adulthood as a time of life brings with it a way of learning (and a corresponding set of practices for facilitating this learning) that is not paralleled at earlier stages of the lifespan. Adult learning has been claimed to be a separate, distinct and discrete phenomenon, something that stands alone as the clear object of theory development. For many in the field, establishing the distinctive nature of adult learning has had important professional ramifications. If they could establish irrefutable proof that adults learned in a way that differed in kind from the learning undertaken by children and adolescents, then at a stroke they could lay claim to an area of research (adult learning) and a set of practices (adult education) that were undeniably their own. They could hold conferences, establish journals, write books, create departments and award degrees – in short create a whole professional career structure – based on their familiarity with the conceptual and empirical territory claimed as unique to the field. The emerging discourse of lifelong learning undercuts the separateness previously claimed for adult learning. In this discourse learning is conceived as a lifelong process with important connections established between schooling, higher education, and universities of the "third age." The position that has ensured adult educators' professional credibility in the past – the position that adult learning is a discrete and separate domain – is now challenged.

A dominant discourse that many in American adult education believe holds the most promise for developing a distinctive, unitary theory within the field is that of transformative learning. Researchers in transformative learning have built on the groundbreaking work of Mezirow (1991) to produce numerous replication studies, critiques and conceptual extensions of his ideas. In line with the splintering of the field's identity, however, different strands within this discourse have emerged. Some locate transformative learning primarily within developmental psychology, some focus on transformation's connections to the soul, some see transformation as the answer to corporate malaise, and still others view it as a form of ideology critique. As the millennium unfolds it is likely that adult education's unpredictable and constantly changing mosaic will continue to assume new and unpredictable patterns.

See also: andragogy, lifelong learning, transformative learning.

References and Further Reading

Lindeman, E.C.L., & Smith, T.V. (1951). *The democratic way of life*. New York: New American Library.

Mezirow, J. (1991). *Transformative dimensions of adult learning*. San Francisco: Jossey-Bass.

Sheared, V., & Sissel, P. A. (Eds.). (2001). *Making space: Merging theory and practice in adult education*. Westport, CT: Bergin & Garvey.

Wilson, A.L., & Hayes, E. R. (Eds.). (2000). *Handbook of adult and continuing education*. San Francisco: Jossey-Bass.

Stephen Brookfield

Urban Adult Education

Urban adult education, sometimes used interchangeably with the term inner-city education, concerns the problems, practices, and adult education programming for urban communities. Beyond its geographic designation, the concept of "urban" entails the demographic variables of density of population, low socioeconomic status, and ethnic or racial minority groups (Martin, 2004). Thus, other terms used in reference to urban suggest ethnic or racial community and social and economic segregation (e.g., the terms "ghetto" and "barrio"). Furthermore, the concept of urban signals social issues such as comparatively high levels of crime, drug dependency, unemployment, poverty, school dropout, and low literacy rates.

Urbanization has occurred at different times and for different reasons in various parts of the world. Historically, the largest cities in the United Kingdom and Europe have been transformed by waves of immigrants from former colonial nations in Asia, Latin America, the Caribbean, and Africa. In North America, European immigration to the United States and Canada as well as the northern migration of millions of African Americans have transformed cities into diverse and highly stratified communities often segregated along racial and ethnic lines. More recently, migration due to economic and political dislocation has further diversified American and European cities. In Africa, large urban areas have developed largely as a result of colonization that has transformed traditional African societies to highly urbanized and industrialized areas.

As centers of economic, ethnic, racial, cultural and linguistic diversity, Negre and Bernet (1993) have conceptualized the city as an agent of education. They argue that the city is a source of learning and socialization for its residents. Dense urban populations foster communicative opportunities and the possibility for the combination of cultural elements in new an unforeseen ways. Informal learning associated with intercultural exchanges at public venues such as stadiums, cinemas, malls, parks, and music auditoriums create crossroads where the city dwellers occupied different spaces can interact and cross borders. As a complex network of human relations the city has an educative and socializing effect on its residents.

However, densely populated urban areas create living conditions that undermine formal educative efforts and are thus associated with low levels of formal educational attainment, illiteracy, unemployment, crime and violence. Some lines of research in urban adult education have focused on sociological and demographic factors that affect urban communities (Guy, 2004; Martin, 2004). Urban violence, owing to gang affiliation, deculturation, and differences in generational perspectives on life chances and economic opportunities, has led to increasing levels of urban violence. Adult education strategies have therefore turned to addressing the underlying social issues through peace education initiatives as, for example, in Colombia (Mina, 2002) and Nigeria (Apanpa, 2004). Other program initiatives have focused on women's issues and the socioeconomic status of women in urban areas. Often women are left in family situations where they are responsible as heads of households, living in poverty, and having little opportunity open to them for educational or economic advancement.

Other lines of research have focused on programming, especially in adult basic education and literacy, and the relative lack of sufficient resources to support adult education programs in urban communities (Peterson, 1999; Sheared, 1994). Related to this line of research is the focus on the inadequacy of educational policy, as well as related policies that impact upon education such as welfare reform, to produce the kinds of improvements in social conditions and educational services and educational outcomes necessary to make a significant improvements in the lives of urban adults. Rogers and Hansman (2004) identify five issues that negatively influence adult education policy in urban communities: (a) inadequate, unclear, and uncoordinated policy; (b) poor understanding of urban low-income adults by policy-makers; (c) little emphasis on combining and continuing supportive education with work; (d) no recognition of the marginalization of urban adult education programs and providers; and (e) multiple sources of, and tension in, accountability for practitioners in urban programs.

Urban adult education is further understood as juxtaposing the poor and the rich. Martin (2004) distinguishes between adult education programs that target resource-rich and resource-poor urban communities. Resource-rich communities have a whole range of programming options available to them offered by a range of providers, formal, informal, and nonformal. Resource-poor communities have few options available to them through formal institutional offerings, and are frequently either economically unable to access them or are unwilling to participate in due to their failure to meet the needs of the urban poor (Sparks, 1994).

See also: class, culturally relevant adult education, literacy.

References and Further Reading

Apanpa, O. (2004). *Towards conflict resolution in the Niger-Delta region Nigeria: Proposal for a peace education curriculum at the primary school level.* Paper delivered at the One People, Multiple Dreams of a Different World International Conference at the Source of the Nile, Jinja, Uganda, June 9, 2004.

Guy, T. C. (2004). Gangsta rap and adult education. In L. Martin & E. Rogers (Eds.), *Adult education in an urban context: problems, practices, and programming for inner-city communities* (pp. 43–57). *New Directions for Adult and Continuing Education*, No. 101. San Francisco: Jossey-Bass.

Martin, L. (2004). Adult education in the urban context. In L. Martin & E. Rogers (Eds.), *Adult education in an urban context: Problems, practices, and programming for inner-city communities* (pp. 3–16). *New Directions for Adult and Continuing Education*, No. 101. San Francisco: Jossey-Bass.

Mina, J. G. (2002). Simulation-games as educational strategy for social harmony. Athens, GA: The University of Georgia Department of Adult Education and the Cyril O. Houle Scholars Program.

Negre, J. S., & Bernet, J. T. (1993). *L'education en milieu urban: La ville educatrice.* Paris: UNESCO.

Peterson, E. (1999). Creating a culturally relevant dialogue for African American adult educators. In T. C. Guy (Ed.), *Providing culturally relevant adult education: A challenge for the twenty first century* (pp. 79–92). *New Directions for Adult and Continuing Education,* No. 82. San Francisco: Jossey-Bass.

Rogers, E., & Hansman, C. A. (2004). Social and cultural issues in urban communities. In L. Martin & E. Rogers (Eds.), *Adult education in an urban context: Problems, practices, and programming for inner-city communities* (pp. 17–27). *New Directions for Adult and Continuing Education,* No. 101. San Francisco: Jossey-Bass.

Sheared, V. (1994). Giving voice: An inclusive model of instruction – a womanist perspective. In E. R. Hayes & S. A. J. Colin, III (Eds.), *Confronting racism and sexism in adult and continuing education* (pp. 27–37). San Francisco: Jossey-Bass.

Sparks, B. (1994). *Structural-cultural factors of nonparticipation in adult basic education by Chicano/adults in urban communities in Colorado.* Final Section 353 Project Report (CE 70673). Denver: Colorado Statement Department of Education. Washington DC: US Department of Education, Office of Vocational and Adult Education.

Talmadge C. Guy

V

Vocation

The term vocation is derived from the Latin word *vocare*, which means to invite, welcome, or call by name. In current usage it has several meanings, depending on the context, all pertaining in different ways to the special characteristics of a particular person or distinct course of action. It is often used synonymously with the word "calling" to refer to a sense of mission or purpose. Within religious, predominantly Christian, traditions it is often tied to a sense of spiritual prompting and the relationship between a person and God. In the context of religious discourse it often takes the form of a specific calling to ordination as a priest or profession as a member of a religious order. However, the term is also used frequently in a more secular context to refer to specific jobs or professions, with a particular association with technical occupations and the skilled trades. Beyond the confines of these distinct religious and occupational discourses, the word vocation is also often used to designate either the unique practices and virtues of a given area of work or thought (Gerth & Mills, 1946; Gumport, 1990; Stehlik, 2003), or as a personal sense of talent and suitability for a chosen livelihood (Fox, 1995). All of these meanings are present in adult education, with the result that it can sometimes be used to connote radically different and sometimes opposing sensibilities.

The Religious Context

In the context of adult religious education the term vocation retains much of its original meaning as a call to ministry or monastic life. "In the medieval church the usage of the word prevailed that those called were persons chosen for the life of clerics or religious" (Elias, 2003, p. 298), and this usage is little changed in the Catholic tradition to the present day. Although other meanings of vocation in Catholic life (such as a vocation to married life, a chosen career path, or the process of spiritual growth in general) have become more prevalent, according to Elias, "praying for vocations still means praying for more priests, sisters or brothers" (p. 299). In Christian discourse, adult education pertaining to the matter of vocation typically suggests a process of discernment regarding either a specific career in priestly or consecrated life, or more broadly the way that one might feel called to live and be in the world most fully.

The Secular Context

With the growth of secular society, the religious meaning of vocation has become separated from other usages of the term as it has been lifted out of the religious context and expanded to include all walks of life and all manner of work and worldly occupations. Historically, this is associated with the advent of the Protestant reformation, a central feature of which was Martin Luther's criticism of the monastic vocation on the grounds that holiness was accessible to everyone and in every form of work, not just to those who had taken holy orders. This view was amplified in the work of John Calvin and Thomas Carlyle, who came to invest work with the same spiritual overtones that had once been the exclusive preserve of priests and monastics. According to the early sociologist Max Weber (1930), it was this development that led to the advent of the Protestant work ethic as the spiritual ally of capitalist economics. This is also the historical underpinning of current understandings of vocation that pertain to the world of work and occupations.

The Academic/Vocational Divide

In adult education, vocational education and training refer exclusively to the preparation of people for participation in the workforce. In particular, the meaning of vocation in this context has a strong association with the realm of technical occupations and the skilled trades, with a clear distinction made between academic education in the sciences and liberal arts, and vocational education for the workplace. The academic/vocational divide has been a longstanding topic of much discussion and debate in adult education and educational studies more broadly (Kincheloe, 1999). According to many education critics, this two-track system is a reflection of deep-seated class differences in capitalist society, where academic study holds a privileged position and vocational study is equated with lower educational attainment and the working class. Changes in the contemporary workplace with the advent of globalization and new technologies have led many educators to call for changes in vocational education away from the narrow job skills orientation of the past towards a more integrated curriculum combining academic and vocational areas of skills and knowledge. However, as Kincheloe contends, any changes in educational provision must still take into account the persistent influence of race, class and gender inequalities in the workplace and, in the United States in particular, stark disparities in income between executive and worker pay. Vocational education is still a term that is heavily freighted with class bias and the negative connotations of second-class training for working-class jobs.

Adult Education and the Issue of "Vocation"

In addition to the specific meanings of vocation in the context of religious life and occupational training, there are a number of other ways in which the term is used in adult education discourse. In some cases, it refers to the formation and character of the field itself, in other cases to the contribution of the teaching profession to the social good, and in other cases to the nature of the learning process.

In the first instance, Selman, Cooke, Selman, and Dampier (1998) describe the history of the field of adult education in Canada as developing a sense of vocation as it becomes more professionalized. The authors state that although the activities that have come to be defined as adult education or the teaching of adults have gone on for centuries, the development of the field as a distinct area of theory and practice is a relatively recent phenomenon. In the North American context, "it is generally agreed that a sense of vocation in the field of adult education, at least one which spanned many of the settings in which adult education functioned, emerged in the inter-war period, and most strongly in the United States" (Selman et al., 1998, p. 296). The authors associate the growing sense of vocation in the field with the advent of professional training, specifically in the form of academic departments of adult education, and the establishments of professional organizations, publications and conferences focused on adult education as a coherent and self-conscious enterprise. Notably, they cite the American educator Webster Cotton's observation that it is when adult education becomes "essentially an *educational* enterprise concerned with the life of the mind, with ideas and the use of intelligence" rather than an instrument of social change (Cotton, as cited in Selman et al., p. 297, italics in the original) that it begins to attain its distinct status as a vocation.

This view of adult education's distinct vocation stands in marked contrast with the sense of vocation articulated by Michael Collins (1990) and Ian Martin (2001). Both authors claim that it is precisely the trend towards professionalization that has contributed to the loss of vocation in the field. Collins equates the idea of retrieving a sense of vocation with retrieving a sense of mission and passionate devotion to education for social justice in a spirit of critical, self-reflective practice. The route towards professionalization has led to undue emphasis on technique and careerism at the expense of an ongoing commitment to "the ethical notion of adult education as "friends educating each other . . . in a dialectical process where the teacher is also a learner and the learner, in learning, teaches the teacher" (p. 48). Martin similarly identifies the vocation of adult education with the social-purpose tradition, committed to "the interests of social and political change: change towards more justice, equality and democracy" (p. 15), rather than the narrower interests of professionalization, individualistic pedagogy, and normative economic policy. The notion of vocation in this usage is what Martin styles as a dissenting vocation, with a goal of fostering critical dialogue, and challenging the dominant interests of the status quo.

The Role of the Educator

In addition to these contrasting perspectives about vocation pertaining to the adult education field as a whole, there is also a body of literature where the term vocation refers more specifically to the role of the educator and the moral dimensions of teaching practice (Elias, 2003; Estola, Erkkila, & Syrjala, 2003; Hansen, 1994; hooks, 2003; Palmer, 2000). This is part of a wider body of scholarship on vocation which explores questions of career choice and commitment in a number of social contexts, with an emphasis on the relationship of the self and work for the common good (Fox, 1995; Kovan & Dirkx, 2003). The term is frequently used to refer to the quest for meaningfulness in life and work. Vocation represents "an active stance towards the meaning of our lives and our outer work, a form of ongoing learning and inner work" (Kovan & Dirkx, p. 101).

In this larger sense of the quest for meaningful and engaged existence, some usages of vocation encompass both the teacher and learner alike. This finds expression in the philosophical writings of such luminaries as John Dewey and Paulo Freire. For Dewey (1959), each individual has many vocations in his or her relationships with family, work, and community. Ultimately, each person has a vocation to be the best they can be, and through this contribute to the overall well-being of society. Similarly, Freire (1970) speaks of each person having an inherent "vocation of becoming more fully human" (p. 28). Although Dewey and Freire take different approaches to the pedagogical processes involved in helping people to fulfill their vocation, their views contain a shared sense of hopefulness about the potential of human kind. Indeed, despite the range of meanings of vocation inside and outside the literature of adult education, the common idea underpinning all of them is the concern for meaningfulness of action as the hallmark of purposeful individual and social existence.

See also: meaning-making, religious education, spirituality, teaching.

References and Further Reading

Collins, M. (1990). *Adult education as vocation: A critical role for the adult educator*. London: Routledge.

Dewey, J. (1959). *Dewey on education*. (M. Dworkin, Ed.). New York: Teachers College Press.

Elias, J. L. (2003). Reflections on the vocation of a religious educator. *Religious Education, 98*(3), 297–310.

Estola, E., Erkilla, R., & Syrjala, L. (2003). A moral voice of *vocation* in teachers' narratives. *Teachers and Teaching, 9*(3), 239–257.

Fox, M. (1995). *The reinvention of work: A new vision of livelihood for our time*. New York: HarperCollins.

Freire, P. (1970). *Pedagogy of the oppressed* (Trans. M. B. Ramos). New York: Continuum.

Gerth, H. H., & Mills, C. W. (Eds.). (1946). *From Max Weber: Essays in sociology*. New York: Oxford University Press.

Gumport, P. (1990). Feminist scholarship as a vocation. *International Journal of Higher Education and Educational Planning, 20*(3), 231–243.

Hansen, D. (1994). Teaching and the sense of vocation. *Educational Theory, 44*(3), 259–276.

hooks, b. (2003). *Teaching community: A pedagogy of hope*. New York: Holt.

Kincheloe, J. L. (1999). *How do we tell the workers? The socioeconomic foundations of work and vocational education*. Boulder, CO: Westview Press.

Kovan, J. T., & Dirkx, J. M. (2003). Being called awake: The role of transformative learning in the lives of environmental activists. *Adult Education Quarterly, 53*(2), 99–118.

Martin, I. (2001). Lifelong learning: For earning, yawning or earning. *Adults Learning, 13*(2), 14–18.

Palmer, P. (2000). *Let your life speak: Listening for the voice of vocation*. San Francisco: Jossey-Bass.

Selman, G., Cooke, M., Selman, M., & Dampier, P (1998). *The foundations of adult education in Canada* (2nd ed.). Toronto: Thompson Educational.

Stehlik, T. (2003). Parenting as a *vocation*: Lifelong learning can begin in the home. *International Journal of Lifelong Education, 22*(4), 367–380.

Weber, M. (1930). *The Protestant ethic and the spirit of capitalism* (Trans. T. Parsons). London: Allen & Unwin.

Jane Dawson

Vocational Education

Vocational education is essentially education to prepare individuals for a vocation, specialist occupation or work. Because it involves education of people for work, vocational education is closely linked to effective production and the international competitiveness of nations. There has been increasing recognition by government policy-makers, since the early 1990s when human capital theory became fashionable, that skills are the only sustainable source of advantage in international competitiveness, and hence most countries have sought to gain a competitive edge by realigning education and labor-market policies. Internationally there have been changed expectations for vocational education programs with governments attempting to raise skill standards and accountability.

Social Class and Vocational Education

All specialist occupational areas have evolved specific learning programs to develop essential skills and knowledge that characterize successful practice in that area. Many of these areas are not generally categorized as vocational education, although this is their intended purpose. University specializations such as medicine, law, engineering, veterinary science, teaching and dentistry are definitely vocational, but in common usage the term vocational education is often restricted to non-university education or training.

Income and social status are closely linked to occupational choice, hence issues of status and social class underlie vocational education practices and policy issues. There has long been a tendency in human society to avoid hard or dirty physical labor because the former in particular destroys the body (Ainley, 1993). Furthermore, manual labor is a discriminating factor in the categorization of occupations (and ascription of social status), for example in the *Canadian Classification and Dictionary of Occupations* (CCDO) and the *American Dictionary of Occupational Titles* (DOT).

Historically, the responsibility of educating managerial classes has fallen to universities, while vocational education offered in other institutes has educated the working classes to varying degrees of skillfulness. Currently in the UK post-compulsory vocational education is referred to as Further Education, whereas university education is distinguished as higher education. In the United States the term "vocational education" carried such social stigma, with those undertaking vocational education generally considered as lacking any academic ability, that vocational education has been renamed "technical and career education" (e.g., Castellano, Stringfield, & Stone, 2003). By contrast, German society recognizes the importance of skilled practitioners, and assigns considerable status to vocational education. The term "master craftsman" is still used to distinguish more highly skilled individuals and in France and Germany denotes officially recognized status. In short, there are widely differing cultural and class values concerning the worth and status of vocational education in a society.

Challenges Created by Recent Changes in Technology and the Nature of Work

Major changes to the nature of work and knowledge have created new challenges in policy-making and educational thinking concerning vocational education. Superior forms of mechanization have removed much of the dirty and dangerous work of even 50 years ago in many developed countries, as in the mining industry, where comparatively fewer people now tend to be employed in that industry but with higher levels of skilling evident. The application of computer technology to many skill areas, such as automobiles and other forms of transport, has transformed skill and knowledge requirements in more cognitively demanding ways involving more abstract reasoning and problem-solving (Zuboff, 1988). Further, post-Fordist management theory has highlighted the fact that effective business expansion and creative production of goods and services require the cooperation of individuals of diverse specializations with sound knowledge of theory and real-world practice. Increased performance and learning demands are leading to greater recognition in industrially advanced countries that vocational education should no longer be seen as the dumping ground for those who cannot succeed in academically challenging areas.

Sites and Forms of Vocational Education

Since vocational education encompasses all forms of education other than academic, it occurs in many different forms in many different sites. Sites for the teaching of vocational education extend from schools to various colleges, universities, and workplaces in business and industry with on- and off-the-job learning and involving private and public providers.

Historically, apprenticeships have been the most important avenue for learning substantial vocational skills in trade and crafts areas, with the period of training extending over several years. Older forms of apprenticeship involved indentured training with an employer and usually some off-site formal training in a college. These traditional forms of apprenticeship in English-speaking countries like Australia and the UK have experienced a decline in numbers (Wolf, 2002). Governments have supplemented traditional apprenticeship numbers with traineeships of short duration called new apprenticeships, with these generally involving considerable on-site workplace training. These new apprenticeships also encompass areas such as retail not previously covered by traditional apprenticeships. Traditionally apprenticeships involved younger teenage, early school-leavers, but increasingly adults are to be found taking up apprenticeships. Other changes, as in Germany with a strong commitment to vocational education, involve employers offering the opportunity for more advanced general education as part of apprenticeships in order to attract more desirable employees (see Wolf).

Schools are seen again as important sites for vocational preparation of teenagers/young adults for adult life in many Anglo countries, although this has not always or consistently been the case and contrasts markedly with many European countries where the theory–practice and academic–vocational divides are not a cultural issue. Research generally points to greater motivation, understanding and continued education as adults, along with enhanced employment opportunities, for those experiencing effective vocational education in schools.

Adult community colleges under various names in different countries, often operating in the evening, provide a mixture of both vocational learning and academic learning along with personal development through hobby/interest courses. Workers' Education Associations (WEA) and Mechanics' Institutes, although historically oriented more towards general education and personal development, also provide a range of subjects and courses with more or less vocational relevance depending upon individual subjects. In post-industrial societies, hobbies and specialist interests often form the basis for employment and hence have come to overlap into the vocational.

Currently there is much interest in workplace learning in many countries, since the workplace is the most likely context in which learning will result from the application of new technology and organizational practices. Consequently there are many very different learning sites all influenced by the culture of the organization or business and the occupational specialization. In Anglo countries with traditions of Mechanics' Institutes, there has long been a separation of opportunities for learning from the workplace. This stance is based upon the realistic understanding that pressures for economy and efficiency in business are not necessarily conducive to effective, meaningful learning. Current research is often supportive of this position (see Castellano et al., 2003) with future research into human resource development in business in Holland indicating that this situation is unlikely to change (Streumer, Van Der Klink, & Van Der Brink, 1999).

In Germany, strong cultural traditions and careful regulation result in significant and generally successful workplace learning through apprenticeship and more general education via their Dual System (Wolf, 2002). However, in Australia there is evidence that, even with legal protection of apprentices supposedly to ensure effective learning, there has been a lack of willingness to enforce legal requirements with consequent ineffective learning often resulting within large industries like hospitalities/commercial cookery (Cornford & Gunn, 1998). Deep-seated traditions in some countries and industries ensure the dominance of employer interests over student learning needs.

General Education Versus Vocational Education Challenges

The educational policy challenges to achieve relevance and quality of education in the 21st century apply very specifically to vocational education. Ongoing technological changes have created problems for the nature of initial education programs and maintenance of skill currency. Consistent challenges in Anglo countries remain: the selection of the most valuable content for programs, and the interrelationship of theory and practice to produce meaningful learning with the deep understanding and the problem-solving skills characteristic of truly skilled, professional performance. Genuinely liberal vocational education programs need to cover the areas of personal development, the teaching of specific work skills and the process of socialization for effective work performance. In the United States this often translates as focus upon education through work, education about work and education for work (Castellano et al., 2003). The appropriate balance of these elements remains unresolved, as do the best combinations of approaches to achieve the most effective, longer-term learning.

Changed patterns of education in most Anglo countries over the last decade of the 20th century show higher university enrolments at the expense of vocational education courses as students opt for education of greater status, while also benefiting from a more general education that allows them to keep career options open in an era of considerable occupational change (e.g., see Wolf, 2002). Government attempts to sell the value of university education have succeeded, however there is good reason to believe that many going directly from school to university are not suited to this form of higher education and could benefit from better career counseling. Ironically, Australian research has indicated that, for every individual who moves from Technical and Further Education colleges to university level, there are somewhere between five to eight who move from university to the more practical, specifically applied, vocational programs. With credible projections of multiple career changes for individuals in the 21st century, the challenges for policy-makers and educational administrators are how to combine more general academic and vocational education, and to keep pathways open for when individuals change career paths and move between different types of educational institutions.

Adaptive career changes seem to be facilitated through good general education. It is thus not surprising that generic skills have been focused upon by policy-makers in the UK, Australia and many other countries, with such skills seen as a means of ensuring continuing relevance of initial training through personal adaptation. Unfortunately, policy-makers as yet do not appear cognizant of the problems of transfer of learning that are inherent in any generic approach.

Generally there is increased recognition by policy-makers of the need for lifelong learning. In Europe, in particular, lifelong learning issues are deeply permeating many aspects of educational policy in significant ways. However, effective lifelong learning is dependent upon effective learning-to-learn skills. These skills are of particular relevance for vocational education students who are subjected most to technological and workplace change, hence need to keep learning to maintain employability. A practical solution would appear to reside in the explicit teaching in school and post-compulsory education of learning-to-learn strategies to vocational education students, who are frequently attracted to vocational education on account of their lack of success with academic subjects, as well as to other, more academically oriented students (Cornford, 2002). Nonetheless, cautions about the role of vocational education in lifelong learning and adult education remain. Finger and Asún (2001) typify those who critique vocational education as part of the instrumentalization of learning. They see this as part of the "race to the bottom" (p. 110) for adult education in that it has become part of instrumentalization and commodification of the learner and quality of life.

See also: human capital theory, training, transfer of learning, vocation, work-based learning.

References and Further Reading

Ainley, P. (1993). *Class and skill*. London: Cassell.

Castellano, M., Stringfield, S., & Stone, J. R., III (2003). Secondary career and technical education and comprehensive school reform: Implications for research and practice. *Review of Educational Research, 73*, 231–272.

Cornford, I. R. (2002) Learning-to-learn strategies as a basis for effective lifelong learning. *International Journal of Lifelong Education, 21*, 357–368.

Cornford, I. R., & Gunn, D. (1998). Work-based learning of commercial cookery apprentices in the New South Wales hospitalities industry. *Journal of Vocational Education and Training, 50*, 549–568.

Finger, M., & Asún, J. (2001). *Adult education at the crossroads: Learning our way out*. New York, London: Zed Books.

Streumer, J. N., Van Der Klink, M. R., & Van Der Brink, K. (1999). The future of

HRD. *International Journal of Lifelong Education, 18*, 259–274.
Wolf, A. (2002). *Does education matter? Myths about education and economic growth*. London: Penguin.
Zuboff, N. (1988). *In the age of the smart machine: The future of work and power*. New York: Basic Books.

Ian R. Cornford

Voluntary Organization

Lord Beveridge's report, *Voluntary Action*, defined a voluntary organization as an organization which, whether its workers are paid or unpaid, is initiated and governed by its own members without external control (1948, pp. 8–10). This definition is as helpful today as then.

Voluntary organization is notoriously difficult to define, yet is a fundamental aspect of adult education and lifelong learning. According to the landmark 1919 *Report on Adult Education*, a voluntary organization counteracts "the sterilizing effects inherent in organized education;" "safeguards the freedom of both students and teachers;" and is "vital to the continuance and progressive development of adult education" (Adult Education Committee, 1919, p. 113). But what is it, and how does it make such a contribution?

To begin it is worth distinguishing between voluntary organizations as: individual activity; a feature of group life; and as an institutional form. As an individual activity voluntary organization shares much with notions such as self-direction. It involves people in freely-chosen planned activity. This may be directed towards self-advancement and improvement, perhaps in the form of autodidaxy; or concerned with service to others and social improvement. Examples of the latter include John Pounds (1766–1839) who pioneered, without establishing an organization, what became known in Britain as "ragged schooling;" and the individual acts of service to neighbours that Friedrich Engels described as "working class philanthropy".

Voluntary organization can also be approached as a component of certain forms of group life. Groups generally involve people joining together in companionship or undertaking some task, which necessarily requires some attention given to making the group satisfying for its members and to the achievement of the task. Often groups are established by others and require people to participate in some way. Obvious examples here include work teams and book clubs. However, participation in many groups is freely chosen. These groups may not have a separate institutional existence – neighbours with a regular "badminton night," the quiz team, friends going out clubbing on a Friday night – but they all involve some organization. Joining them involves the often implicit, but sometimes explicit, assumption that members will take a hand in making arrangements.

Perhaps the most obvious use of the term "voluntary organization" is to delineate a particular type of institution that is neither a direct part of the state nor a profit-taking business. While there have been various definitional debates as to what might constitute a voluntary organization in this context, it is possible to map out the ground. Here it is still worth returning to Lord Beveridge's (1948) report, *Voluntary Action*, where he employed a definition of a voluntary organization as an organization which, whether its workers are paid or unpaid, is initiated and governed by its own members without external control (pp. 8–10). This required a set of rules, a membership involving some formal act of joining, and a declared purpose. It also entailed an associational structure with officers, committees and elections of some sort. The two main motives identified for action here were mutual aid and philanthropy. To these, Beveridge added personal thrift (saving to have money at one's own command, saving for personal independence). This motive, when combined with mutual aid, allowed for the development of institutions such as friendly societies.

Beveridge (1948) also discussed a fourth motive, "the pursuit of a livelihood or of gain for oneself in meeting the needs of one's fellow citizens" ("the business motive"). When linked to mutual aid, he argued, it had led to the establishment of some organizations of "portentous scale" (p. 10). However, in his view voluntary organizations are essentially not-for-profit. This flowed from a belief in the paramouncy of mutual aid and philanthropy as motives for action in his (and subsequent) conceptions of voluntary organization.

Being uninhibited by the profit motive, voluntary organizations are potentially "free to concentrate their energies" (Prochaska, 1988, p. 6). However, the way in which business thinking and managerialism permeated many larger voluntary organizations such as the YM/YWCA in the last quarter of the 19th century has altered their character and many have come to represent business organizations in all but overt profit-taking. In North America, for example, it can be argued that "professionally managed advocacy groups and institutions" have come to the fore, "while representatively governed, nation-spanning voluntary membership federations . . . have lost clout in national public affairs and faded from the everyday life of most Americans" (Skocpol, 2003, p. 4).

Just as voluntary organization is essentially not-for-profit, so it has to be distanced from the state to fall within common definitions. Indeed, this is reflected in the nomenclature used for voluntary organizations by the United Nations and in many Southern countries – non-governmental organizations (NGOs). Their associational nature and relative separation from the state provide a "democratic safeguard" that rescues citizens "from the state's standardizing process" (Prochaska, 1988, pp. 5–6). However, while being detached in organizational terms from the state; many voluntary organizations such as women's resource centers have become increasingly dependent upon government funding. As a result they have frequently lost a significant degree of discretion in their activities. This has been exacerbated by the turn to a contract culture, and a rise in state direction, intervention and monitoring in social policy within many countries. Subjected to inappropriate degrees of external control, and increasingly managerial in their orientation and functioning, they have become organizations that Beveridge would have had difficulty recognizing as "voluntary."

Given the above analysis it would be easy to be pessimistic about the future of voluntary organization, and researchers such as Robert Putnam (1999) have identified a significant decline in people's involvement in voluntary organization and local social networks. However, a large number of individuals and groups remain active in them. For example, Elsdon, Reynolds, and Stewart (1995) have estimated that around 12 million women and men were involved in running 1.3 million bodies in Britain. Participation in such bodies, and the social capital generated as a result, brings considerable benefit to both the individuals involved and to local communities. To appreciate the significance for adult education and lifelong learning in this respect it is helpful to examine the learning and benefits involved in simple participation in the life of voluntary organizations (*la vie associative*); the extent to which voluntary organizations have been a vehicle for mutual improvement and organizing around enthusiasms; and the educative possibilities of philanthropy.

La Vie Associative

It has been argued, at least since the inception of Mechanics' Institutes, that associations, whether they be enthusiast groups, tenants' organizations or community associations, have what might be called an "educative tendency" (Hole 1860). Elsdon et al. (1995), for example, have commented on "the great range of learning, change and satisfaction over and above those which are deliberate, inherent in the organization's objectives, and expected by their members" (p. 47). In their research, the benefit given almost universal priority, and seen as being of greater importance than the "content objective of the organization," was growth in confidence, and

> its ramifications and secondary effects of self-discovery, freedom in forging relationships and undertaking tasks, belief in oneself and in one's potential as a human being and an agent, and ability to learn and change both in the context of the organization's objectives *and* in others. (Elsdon, p. 47)

This finding is mirrored by Putnam's (1999) extensive collation of research concerning the membership of groups within the United States. As well as enhancing confidence, group membership brought considerable health benefits and a substantial growth in personal happiness. Regular club attendance, volunteering, entertaining, or church attendance, he assessed as the "happiness equivalent" of getting a college degree or more than doubling someone's income (p. 333).

In addition to having an impact on individuals, associational life can have considerable educative power with regard to communal affairs. Such groups can become, in Malcolm Knowles' (1950) words, "laboratories of democracy" – places where people have the experience of learning to live cooperatively. "Attitudes and opinions," he wrote, "are formed primarily in the study groups, work groups and play groups with which adults affiliate voluntarily." He continued, "These groups are the foundation stones of our democracy" (Knowles, p. 9). As well as being places where people experience cooperative activity, voluntary organizations are also the means by which many, probably most, engage with the traditional political arena. They are a direct vehicle for engagement with local issues, and into wider political debates through affiliation to regional and national bodies.

Mutual Aid, Mutual Improvement and Organizing Around Enthusiasms

One key expression of voluntary organization within British adult education can be found in the growth of mutual improvement societies during the 19th century. Fundamentally, a "venture in cooperative education," a mutual improvement society typically consisted of between 6 and 100 men from both the working and lower-middle classes "who met periodically, sometimes in their own homes but commonly under the auspices of a chapel or church" (Rose, 2001, p. 58). The basic form comprised a paper or lecture on some subject (the range was immense) followed by an open discussion. These groups put the standard teacher-student hierarchy on one side, and provided an opportunity for a large number of men to develop their interests and ability to explore and make arguments. Other examples of mutual improvement activity, often linked to chapels and churches and involving women as well as men, included the establishment of reading circles, dramatic societies, art groups, and adult schools. This explosion of club, friendly society and voluntary endeavor in the central half of the 19th century touched the vast majority of working-class families.

The mutual improvement tradition continues in various forms including book groups, study circles and in the pursuit of various cultural and leisure activities. Some of these groups are formed with a clear improving and educational purpose. They may even be part of large national movements such as is the case with Women's Institutes. (The first UK Institute was formed in 1915, the 5,000th in 1933. Today there are approximately 7,500 Institutes with around 220,000 members in England and Wales). Other groups may be organized around enthusiasms. Obvious examples focus on sports, hobbies, and arts and crafts. Such groupings of enthusiasts provide opportunities for creating "collective rather than individual products," for example in drama productions, and the chance for people to meet together and make friends (Bishop & Hoggett, 1986, p. 33). Crucially, they make possible and encourage the exchange of information, and facilitate informal guidance and training. They also provide a setting for more formal learning opportunities through short courses, talks and events.

Running alongside the development of mutual improvement societies in the 19th century was a massive growth in more general mutual aid activity. Friendly societies, where people (largely men) could club together to save and to establish funds to cover, for example, basic health benefits, unemployment support, and burial costs became a familiar part of working-class life. Indeed, by 1880 somewhere between 75 and 80% of all male workers belonged to one (Rose, 2001, p. 58). The expansion of voluntary collectivism in the workplace in the form of trade unionism, and in the marketplace through consumer cooperation, also demanded associational activity and brought with it both informal and formal educational elements. Friendly societies, trade unions and cooperative societies established programs both to train officers and to inform members about issues and questions related to their interests.

Philanthropy

Philanthropy can be defined as "love of one's fellow man, an action or inclination which promotes the well-being of others" (Prochaska, 1988, p. 7). Much philanthropy is unseen. It is local and spontaneous and takes the shape of caring for a sick relative, helping a neighbor to fill in a form, taking someone to hospital and so on. Classically it has been disproportionately undertaken by women.

Where philanthropy takes a more organizational and associational form it has frequently entered the field of education in an innovatory and far-reaching way. In the 19th century it was voluntary organization in the form of ragged schools and Sunday schools, Mechanics' Institutes, youth's institutes, social settlements and adult schools (to name but a few institutions) that defined, promoted and almost totally provided post-school educational opportunities for the working classes. Later, dedicated voluntary organizations such as the Workers' Educational Association and the Women's Institutes were large-scale providers of learning opportunities. Today voluntary organizations still provide a significant environment for the formal cultivation of lifelong learning – but these do not often take the form of courses and are frequently not directed at accreditation. Here it is worth highlighting four arenas of activity:

- The first is non-vocational education. Many voluntary organizations continue to offer non-vocational courses and schemes of various kinds to the general public. These include programs of liberal education: for example around Black history, environmental issues and classical studies; religious education including the study of sacred texts; and basic and literacy education.
- Another is vocational and professional training. Voluntary organizations such as settlements and community centers frequently offer opportunities to develop general work skills, for example, around it. However, many voluntary agencies are linked into programs of training and education that are linked to their particular specialties. They may provide courses and events for volunteer workers, and host placements and parts of professional training programs in areas such as social work, community and youth work, and social care.
- A third is social pedagogy. Significant elements of the work within some of the larger units such as settlements and those linked into national organizations such as The Children's Society are similar to what may be described in Germany as social pedagogy. This includes a wide range of educative practice within settings such as youth projects, crèches and nurseries, daycare centers, work with offenders and some areas of church work. These are not usually course-based and will often take the form of activities and discussion groups. Examples of work include health promotion, social skills training, and developmental opportunities for those with disabilities and learning difficulties.
- A fourth is animation. Animation, particular in countries like Italy and France, is usually linked to the activities of community workers and arts workers. It can include, for example, using theatre and play as a means of self-expression and learning with community groups, children and people with special learning needs (sometimes called creative-expressive animation); working with people and groups so that they participate in and manage the communities in which they live (sometimes called sociocultural animation); and developing learning opportunities for preschool and schoolchildren such as adventure playgrounds, toy

libraries, outdoor activity centers, and organized sports activities (sometimes called leisure-time animation) (see Lorenz, 1994).

See also: civil society, community education, labor education, nongovernmental organizations, study circles, women's voluntary organizations.

References and Further Reading

Adult Education Committee, British Ministry of Reconstruction (1919). *Final Report.* Chaired by Arthur L. Smith and commonly known as "The 1919 Report." Cmnd 321 (1919), London: His Majesty's Stationary Office.

Beveridge, L. (1948). *Voluntary action: A report on methods of social advance.* London: George Allen & Unwin.

Bishop, J., & Hoggett, P. (1986). *Organizing around enthusiasms. Mutual aid in leisure.* London: Comedia.

Elsdon, K. T., with Reynolds, J., & Stewart, S. (1995). *Voluntary organizations. Citizenship, learning and change.* Leicester: National Institute of Adult Continuing Education.

Hole, J. (1860). *Light, more light on the present state of education amongst the working classes of Leeds.* London: Longman, Green, Longman & Roberts.

Knowles, M. S. (1950). *Informal adult education.* New York: Association Press.

Lorenz, W. (1994). *Social work in a changing Europe.* London: Routledge.

Prochaska, F. (1988). *The voluntary impulse. Philanthropy in modern Britain.* London: Faber & Faber.

Putnam, R. D. (1999). *Bowling alone. The collapse and revival of American community.* New York: Simon & Schuster.

Rose, J. (2001). *The intellectual life of the British working classes.* New Haven, CT: Yale University Press.

Skocpol, T. (2003). *Diminished democracy. From membership to management in American civic life.* Norman: University of Oklahoma Press.

Mark K. Smith

W

Womanism

Womanism represents a global ideology and philosophy that addresses the reality and consciousness of the African woman, celebrates African essence and womanhood, and concerns itself with all those structures that subjugate and oppress Africans and people of African descent. Womanism is a "coming to voice" of the African woman (whether in the African continent or the diaspora), an attempt to use her voice to properly name herself and her movement; to exercise her right and obligation to give nomenclature to a philosophical ideology that adequately addresses those factors that are central to her survival and the survival of her community. It encapsulates the totality of African womanhood, its feminine self-expression, self-retrieval and self-assertion anchored and expressed in positive cultural ways that are compatible with the reality of her experiences and existence (Amdahl, 1997; Kolawole, 1997).

Womanism represents a reaction of women of African descent not only to the perceived exclusivity of Western mainstream feminism, but also its non-sensitivity to African values and ideals. Womanists allege that mainstream feminism failed to address the root cause of the diverse, simultaneous and embracing oppressions plaguing women of African descent. This arises through its unwillingness to incorporate racism, class, colonialism, postcolonialism, patriarchy and African traditions into the feminist agenda, preferring instead to focus on a gender-based analysis alone.

Womanism also resists certain components of Western mainstream feminism that are considered antagonistic to an African worldview; a worldview shared and sustained by Africans and people of African descent, that is predominantly family-oriented, that recognizes the centrality of the family, that cherishes the family, the children and the home as the stable pivot upon which the society is anchored. In essence, womanists insist on an inclusive agenda that focuses on and is committed to the survival and wholeness of entire people, whether male or female, and the community in which they live. The womanist sees her womanhood as having its roots deep inside the family, and her allegiance is firmly tied to those cultural components that sustain her life and her community. In this regard, womanism exhibits a shared vision with adult education which focuses on enhancing the quality of life of all members of the community by harnessing and utilizing all physical, material and social capital existing within the community. Thus womanism did not emerge as a result of a lack of commitment to woman's inequality, but to the African woman's vision of the interconnectedness of her life as a woman of African descent and her perception that mainstream feminism has been ". . . too narrow to encompass it" (Walker, 1983, pp. 135–136).

Womanism thus represents a conscious and determined refusal of African women and women of African descent to operate a foreign agenda within the framework of Western mainstream feminism. The womanist's operational ideological principle could be compared to the Senegalese concept of "*sani-baat*," an exercise in throwing her voice; a refusal to allow her voice to be submerged by existing feminist discourses, to sing other people's songs, dance other people's dances or speak to other people's agendas; a refusal to engage in the ventriloquism of parroting or rote imitation of other people's voices (Kolawole, 1997). It epitomizes a determination to set an inclusive feminist agenda and feminist theory that reflects and is relevant to her needs, the needs of her community, the realities of her existence and the inherent hope for the survival of her community and her race. Womanism, within the precinct of adult education theory and practice, would seem to represent a move away from approaching women's issues solely from a gender-based discourse to one that recognizes and addresses the multidimensional realities of African women/women of African descent's oppression.

Womanism, Black Feminism, Woman of Color Feminism: Contestations, Divergences and Convergences

There are convergences and divergences of opinion regarding the interchangeability of the terms Womanism, Black feminism and Woman of Color feminism. The proponents of convergences (Omolade, 1994; Walker, 1983) believe that womanists are Black feminists and subsequently defined a womanist as a Black (African) feminist or feminist of color (Walker). These people observe no difference between the terminologies since they all speak to a common agenda of Black women's self-definition and self-determination; are concerned with struggles against sexism and racism by Black women who are themselves part of the Black community's efforts to achieve equity and liberty (Omolade); redefine and name African ideologies, experiences and worldview within a raced political context rooted positively in culture and enunciating the consciousness of women of African descent; and recognize the inseparability of the individual and communal experience and to ultimate survival. The quibbling on nomenclature is thus seen as divide-and-rule philosophy, an attempt to weaken the whole by emphasizing the differences.

On the other side of the debate are scholars who position womanism as being distinct from Black feminism. They believe that deeply rooted cultural characteristics within the African/African American communities, and shared with African/Black nationalism, set womanism apart from Black feminism and underlies the difference. This they submit makes womanism a more acceptable means by which women of African descent can express their interest in woman-oriented ideology (Amdahl, 1997)

In the middle of the debate are those scholars who see the divergences and arguments as arising from the emergence of long-standing differences among Black (African) women structured along axes of sexuality, social class, nationality, religion and region (Collins, 1996). They advocate the need to accommodate diversity among women of African descent, chart a mid-point by reconciling the pressures for diversity and differences with those for integration and community (Tong, 1989). They believe, like Kolawole (1997), that the African worldview permits many roads to the same goal.

Whichever way the debates are resolved, the implications of the ideology for adult education theory, policies and practice remain of utmost significance.

See also: Africa, feminism, women's learning.

References and Further Reading

Amdahl, J. (1997). My voice, my choice: Identity issues in Black feminist/womanist discourse. Retrieved March 20, 2003 from http://www.ksu.edu/english/janette/ geffb/GEFFB

Collins, P. H. (1996). What's in a name? Womanism, Black feminism and beyond. *The Black Scholar*, 26(1), 9–18.

Kolawole, M. E. M. (1997). *Womanism and African consciousness*. Trenton, NJ: Africa World Press.

Omolade, B. (1994). *The rising song of African American women*. New York: Routledge.

Tong, R. (1989). *Feminist thought*. San Francisco: Westwood.

Walker, A. (1983). *In search of our mother's gardens*. New York: Harcourt, Brace, Jovanovich.

Oluyemisi O. Obilade

Women's Learning

Women's learning can be broadly defined as the understandings, knowledge, and skills acquired by those who have attained the gender of "woman." In the Western world, until well into the 19th century, many women did not have access to formal credentialed settings in which learning opportunities occurred. However, this did not mean that we did not learn. For centuries, and much like the women of today, we learned within communities of women, in the home and through our religious and voluntary involvements. We learned about motherhood, menstruation, menopause, craftwork and how to be effective keepers of our cultures and our homes. Today, these areas of learning have shifted only slightly and indeed have been enlarged to include responsibilities to learn within the paid workplace and formal credentialed settings.

Within the Field of Adult Education Literature

Despite the far-reaching extent of women's learning, it is only more recently that the concept has gained prominence in the field of adult education. It replaces discussions of adult learning in which all adults were presumed to learn in the same ways, and women as a distinct group of learners were ignored. The research of Gilligan (1982), and Belenky, Clinchy, Goldberger, and Tarule (1986) significantly shifted this thinking. Based in psychological and socio-psychological analyses, they fundamentally argued that women can be differentiated from men in the ways in which they absorb, process, and act upon information, knowledge, attitudes, and skills. They identified women's preferences for connected, relational and collaborative knowing and meaning-creation. Although their studies were critiqued later for their White, middle-class approaches, they made important contributions to guiding the study of adult learning into issues of gender. Since then, the study of women's learning has developed, although many might argue too slowly and with too many remaining gaps in the literature. The purpose of this contribution is to identify the six key themes which exist in the study of women's learning.

Approaches to the Concept

There are three key approaches or ideological positions to the concept of women's learning. First, is the notion that women learners should be treated as a homogenous group who consistently share a particular approach to learning. This is often complemented by the supposition that women's learning is inherently different from men's learning. This dichotomous positioning of women's learning in relation to men's learning is associated with the idea that learning is a biological or psychological event. This view suggests that men and women acquire cognitive abilities, such as verbal, spatial, mathematical and general knowledge and skills, more or less successfully according to their sex. Authors writing with this approach support the assumptions which flow from this position, such as "women naturally prefer collaborative approaches."

The second key approach to the concept of women's learning revolves around a critique of the approach above. Certainly in its early days, the concept was hailed, in part, because it valued women and at least inserted female perspectives into adult learning theories. More recently, however, as researchers, practitioners and theoreticians engage with postmodern ideas, they are critiquing it for its oversimplification of a complex activity. They reject the notion of homogenous women and homogenous learning, and instead attempt to value the implications for women's learning of our diverse class, color, ethnicity, sexual orientation, and ability. Authors writing with this approach reject as overly-crude, the notion's assumption that women's learning is inherently different from men's learning. Many scholars are wary of this dichotomous positioning and argue that it usually results in women being judged as "less than" relative to the "norm" defined by men. They critique this view of learning as being one-dimensional and suggest instead that learning differences are socially constructed as a result of gendered differences. They seek political, economic, social and cultural explanations rather than psychological and biological explanations to women's "natural" learning styles, preferences and so on.

Today, a third approach is evolving. It is located at the intersection of the approaches above. Researchers are attempting to recognize and value the uniqueness of women's learning without tying it into rigid models. They are trying to recognize the distinctiveness and exceptionality of women's learning in the global context of women's collective experiences of inequality. They are striving to keep women learners' struggle for equality paramount, yet acknowledge the complexity of intervening variables (Hayes & Colin III, 1994; Hayes & Flannery, 2002; Luttrell, 1989; Tisdell, 1993). It is not an easy task.

Limitations on Our Understandings of Women's Learning

Many of the historical, embedded, understandings we have about women's learning are limited by two factors. The first factor concerns the frequent location of "female" as a tidy demographic variable within large quantitative studies on motivation to learn, obstacles to learning and so on. This has meant that women were treated homogenously and in opposition to men. Simultaneously, the research focus, design, methodology, and analysis could not accommodate differences between the contexts within which men and women responded to the research. Over time, research that focused exclusively on women evolved from these studies, but frequently the research process duplicated the original approaches with all their inherent difficulties of dichotomous positioning.

Second, as hinted at in the opening statements, our understandings have been shaped by researchers' preoccupation with institutionalized learning. Responses from women learners readily accessible through universities, evening classes and programs, and more lately paid workplaces, have formed the basis of much of our data. Although studies into learning in "garage" and "kitchen table" contexts have increased, the emphasis remains on women in institutionalized settings or those attempting to enter them. Furthermore, studies are frequently specific to a particular kind of setting. This means that there is limited holistic knowledge about women learners.

Obstacles That Prevent Women's Learning

Adult educators' understanding about the obstacles or barriers which prevent women from learning has been shaped by our preoccupation with institutionalized learning. Thus, responses from readily accessible learners form the basis of our data. Parallel studies which are more women-specific evolved from these wider studies, but tend to deal with mature students/paid workers and "their" problems as they enter institutions.

Many researchers continue to stress obstacles to learning such as lack of self-esteem, awareness, confidence, and childcare/home responsibilities. This "blame the victim" approach has been challenged. Theoretical and empirical research shifts the focus away from the individual to broader contextual obstacles such as misogyny and patriarchy (Stalker, 2001), and to the impact of trauma and violence on women's learning (Horsman, 2000). This tendency to examine obstacles in terms of the grim realities of many women's lives has been broadened to include wars, political conflicts and the resultant rapes and abuses of women as obstacles to our learning.

Strategies to Enhance Women's Learning

The proliferation of literature in the area of obstacles, leads naturally to literature which proposes to overcome those obstacles and to enhance women's learning. Many of the studies parallel the literature on obstacles, which focuses on the individual. They thus present strategies to "fix" women learners, that is, how to improve their self-esteem, assertion, study skills, confidence and so on. This individualistic, deficit approach to women learners is not the sole approach, fortunately. At the organizational level, the emphasis is on improving the andragogy and curricula to better accommodate women learners. A fundamental strategy is to establish a learning environment free of threat which suits the unique nature of women learners. However, this treatment of women learners as homogeneous is challenged by those who advocate diverse strategies appropriate for diverse kinds of women. Finally, a few authors present more macro-level strategies to address the political, economic, social and cultural milieus within which women learn.

Outcomes

Much of what we know about the outcomes of women's learning has been gleaned indirectly from literature with a slightly different orientation. For example, a considerable amount of literature approaches women's learning through the study of our socialization into our roles, responsibilities and positions within society. It is fundamentally literature about identity-formation and learning gender. Much of this literature is imbued with a tone that suggests that these learnings are both negative and inevitable. Jane Thompson's (1983) classic contribution to the discourse gives a different interpretation of women's learning. She re-focuses on women learning liberation and deals with women learners as more active agents with the ability to resist and (re)define our lives. She discusses how we can learn our way out of oppressive male lifeworlds constructed primarily by patriarchs who hold power unapologetically. Thompson introduces into a predominantly psychological schema, broader political, economic, social and cultural perspectives.

Majority ("developing") and minority ("developed") countries extend the concept of outcomes even further. Increasingly, they link women's learning with the achievement of outcomes which benefit the nation. The World Bank, for example, implements strategies in which women's learning is an essential part of their funded projects for "engendered" national strength, stability, (re)construction, and development.

Ways Forward

There is consensus among many adult educators that the literature on women's learning is underdeveloped. At women's international conferences there are two discussions about women's learning which are gaining prominence. First is the need to explore women's learning in a way which is specific to the day-to-day lived experiences of women; this is the study of women's rights. These include experiences which are different from men in the areas of unequal pay, domestic violence, legislated restrictions, overwork in the paid and unpaid workplaces, to name a few. Women's learning is linked inextricably to these sites of learning and its study in relation to those issues is seen to be essential.

The second discussion area concerns the need for the study of women's learning to extend beyond the individual, beyond the organization, beyond immediate political, economic, social and cultural milieus. Increasingly, this encompasses the study of women learning their identities and responsibilities as a cross-boundary activity. It is cross-boundary in both the literal and intellectual senses. It also addresses women's learning in the global context of fundamentalism, conflict, reproduction technologies, and trade zones. It also includes women's learning in relation to international trafficking and the global assemblyline (Heng, 1997). It crosses intellectual areas of study research to extend and widen our study of women learners of differing class, color, ethnicity and ability, to accept women learners who are transsexual, homosexual and transgendered. It includes the overlap between women and men's learning as they seek to learn a way forward as allies. Finally, it embraces the notion of women unlearning optimistic views that the struggle for equality has been successful and re-learning that patriarchy, oppression, and abuse still exist despite generations of effort to the contrary.

See also: cultural learning, feminism, gender, learning, social constructionism.

References and Further Reading

Belenky, M. F., Clinchy, B. M., Goldberger, N. R., & Tarule, J. M. (1986). *Women's ways of knowing: The development of self, voice, and mind.* New York: Basic Books.

Gilligan, C. (1982). *In a different voice: Psychological theory and women's development.* Cambridge, MA: Harvard University Press.

Hayes, E. R., & Colin, S. A. J. III (Eds.). (1994). *Confronting racism and sexism. New Directions for Adult and Continuing Education.* No. 61. San Francisco: Jossey-Bass.

Hayes, E. R., & Flannery, D. D., with Brooks, A. K., Tisdell, E. J., & Hugo, J. M. (2002). *Women as learners: The significance of gender in adult learning.* San Francisco: Jossey-Bass.

Heng , L., & Chan, L. (1997). Women on the global assembly line. In S. Walters (Ed.), *Globalization, adult education and training. Impacts and issues* (pp. 79–88). London: Zed Books.

Horsman, J. (2000). *Too scared to learn: Women, violence, and education.* Mahwah, NJ: Lawrence Erlbaum Associates.

Luttrell, W. (1989). Working-class women's ways of knowing: Effects of gender, race, and class. *Sociology of Education, 62*, 33–46.

Stalker, J. (2001). Misogyny, women and obstacles to tertiary education: A vile situation. *Adult Education Quarterly, 51*(4), 288–305.

Thompson, J. L. (1983). *Learning liberation: Women's response to men's education.* London: Croom Helm.

Tisdell, E. J. (1993). Feminism and adult learning: Power, pedagogy and praxis. In S. B. Merriam (Ed.), *An update on adult learning theory* (pp. 91–103). *New Directions for Adult and Continuing Education*, No. 57. San Francisco: Jossey-Bass.

Walters, S., & Manicom, L. (Eds.). (1996). *Gender in popular education: Methods for empowerment.* London: Zed Books.

Joyce Stalker

Women's Voluntary Organizations

Women's voluntary organizations – feminist and non-feminist, historical and contemporary, rural and urban – are of interest to adult education, as sites of both women's individual learning, and educational leadership. They contribute to, or challenge, a democratic model of societal change. Common principles of voluntary organizations in the UK (Elsdon, Reynolds, & Stewart, 1995) and Canada (Meinhard & Foster, 2003) are personal membership, self-governance, non-profit-making and internally evolved objectives. Women participate in these variously named organizations (e.g., civil society organizations, NGOs) as leaders and facilitators of lifelong learning from birth to death and are inclined to focus on learning for life rather than "learning for earning" (Cunningham, 1992).

Women's History of Organizing

By the end of the 19th century, a vast number of women's clubs and associations emerged in Britain and Ireland, many around leisure needs and welfare, sometimes in combination (Smith, 2001). The rise of evangelism or "Bible Christianity" from the late 18th century on, with its focus on the family, social piety and moral fervour, created the climate for women's charitable organizations. Jane Addams (1850–1935) and Ida B.

Wells (1862–1931) were involved in the Chicago Woman's Club movement and settlement house movements. Munro (1999) describes how these educator-activists broadened the definitions of progressive education by providing "sites in which people of various classes, races, and ethnicities could come together to learn from each other" (p. 43). The pioneer women's clubs in the 1930s Middle West America are credited with giving rise to many of the first extension divisions in state universities (Ely & Chappell, 1938). In the late 1970s, the Women's Education Centre in Southampton (UK) grew from the university's adult education department's community education program and provided educational opportunities based upon such principles as: women-only classes; teaching-learning experiences that disrupt hierarchies of "experts" and "others"; the validation of personal experience; good childcare; flexible timing; minimal fees; and, freedom from male interference (Mayo, 1997, p. 142).

Many of Butterwick's (1998) exemplars of women's leadership in Canadian adult education exist alongside, or in an ancillary role, with male-led voluntary organizations or social movements often led by a visionary male leader (e.g., the Antigonish Movement, Frontier College, and the Canadian Association for Adult Education). In 1983, the Black Women's Coalition of Atlanta sought to recover and interpret women's activism in the civil rights movement (Nasstrom, 1999, p. 115); for untold numbers of Americans, Dr. Martin Luther King, Jr., *was* the civil rights movement. This coalition of activists focuses on the ongoing meaning of the movement, whereby "disseminators of information themselves become historical actors who intervene between the past and present, continually reframing the movement" (p. 134).

Likewise Stromquist (2000) agrees with Touraine's observation that women's coalition-building in developing countries, although establishing the strong link between private life and social action, remains on the periphery of organized political forces. She notes that women's organizing strategies of small workshops, public demonstrations, participation in global conferences, and elaboration of governmental agreements and action plans rely on distant others for implementation (p. 423). With reference to DAWN (Development Alternatives for Women with a New Era), a feminist network focused on the daily experiences of poor women living in the economic South, Antrobus (2002) describes the major challenge that women continue to face in gaining space for their specific concerns at the global level and within mainstream, male-led networks. Conversely, the International Women's Media Founda-tion (IWMF) established in 1990 in Washington, D.C., to strengthen the role of women in the news media around the world, used appreciative inquiry to evaluate its 3-year-old program at the African Women's Media Center (AWMC), headquartered in Senegal, West Africa. They were surprised to learn how much the center had achieved in terms of the unique and important role for African women journalists, and their sustainability – AWMC's membership has grown to 648 individuals since its launch in 1997 (Catsambas & Webb, 2003).

Troubling Taxonomies of Organizing Women

In the Canadian context, Butterwick's (1998) chronological taxonomy distinguishes between first-wave 19th-century women's organizations (e.g., YWCA, Women's Institutes, WCTU, the Women's International League for Peace and Freedom, and the Elizabeth Fry Society) and second-wave organizations (e.g., the Canadian Congress for Learning Opportunities for Women; Association for Community Based Education for Women; and Women in Trades networks) that began in the 1960s and 1970s. Meinhard and Foster's (2003) study of executive directors of 351 women's organizations and 294 "other" (gender-neutral) organizations to gauge their responses to changing public policy in Canada, grouped Canadian women's organizations into three categories – social services (e.g., Elizabeth Fry Society), health services (e.g., Women's Health Clinic), and a cluster labelled education/advocacy/lobbying (e.g., National Anti-Poverty Association) (p. 376). Auretto (2001) classifies social change organizations into four categories depending on their orientation towards the dominant society: reformative organizations, like the National Organization of Women (NOW); separatist or alternative groups, like the home schooling movement; redemptive groups, like charismatic Christians; and transformative organizations dedicated to the structural transformation of society (p. 42).

Other taxonomies provide qualitative criteria. For example, Elsdon et al.'s (1995) UK study distinguishes among the dynamic organization (observably learning and developing), the static (not undergoing any changes), and the divergent (manifesting some kind of disadvantageous position in relation to their declared objectives) (p. 97). The National Women's Register (NWR) and the Women's Institutes exemplified the dynamic, the National Association of Widows exemplified the static, and no women's organization registers as divergent according to their taxonomy. Giraldo's (2002) qualitative study of formal and informal social and cultural learning for political action focused on two women's organizations in Colombia – the Association of Daycare Mothers and the Community Mothers – and interpreted results according to: ethic of care; ethic of justice; the political (system of values and representations that exercise power); participation in public arena and private arena; and women's social organization.

Leist's (1998) research into how women experience membership in branches of the American Association of University Women identifies four stages of increasing social activism and responsiveness to the national agenda of equity, lifelong education, and positive societal change. In the first stage, *Participating*, members attended meetings and took part in activities. During the second stage, *Supporting*, members promoted education opportunities by setting up study groups. During the third stage, *Facilitating*, members disseminated information in the community regarding the association's issues. This leads to the fourth stage, *Advocating*, in which members worked in the community to effect changes consistent with the issues identified nationally. Riger (1994) also provides a stage model of feminist organizations: the *creation stage* marked by effort and excitement of the founders; the *collectivity stage* marked by the "family" feeling of high group morale; the *formalization stage* that presses towards institutionalization of the organization's policies and procedures and a hierarchy of authority; and, *elaboration of structure* characterized by expansion, delegation, and coordination as well as a need to decentralize.

The 19th-century doctrine of "separate spheres" endures as a gender ideology (and taxonomy) of contemporary women's organizations. Reminiscent of the so-called maternal feminism of women's organizations that emerged in the 19th century (e.g., Women's Institutes, Woman's Christian Temperance Union), Gouthro's (2000) current research develops the explicit link between the homeplace and women's educative activities in civil society. Gouthro and Hernández (1997) critique the separate spheres doctrine that pervades Habermasian writings on civil society. "The system/lifeworld faithfully mirrors the public/private divide. . . . [I]t tends to diminish women's labor and societal contributions" (Gouthro, p. 64). *Las Madres*, the Argentinian mothers of the "disappeared" children that had been murdered by the despotic government and the army, provide Gouthro with an exemplar of "homeplaces" and "motherwork," and Hernández with an exemplar of the "feminist public counter-sphere." Both highlight the active learning that is part of the traditional division between the public and private (p. 43).

Mary Belenky traveled to the homeplaces to interview leaders and members of grassroots organizations, including Mothers' Centers in New York and Germany, the National Congress of Neighborhood Women (NCNW), an anti-racist community action group in Brooklyn, and the Center for Cultural and Community Development (CCCD), which grew out of the work of southern African American women (Belenky, Bond, & Weinstock, 1991). Antrobus (2002) also oversteps the public/private divide to categorize the essentially embodied and spatial nature of women's organizing. She identifies four spaces for linking local work to advocacy at the global level: consciousness-raising groups or women's circles; caucuses; coalitions; and campaigns. Antrobus credits the women's circle with the "speak bitterness" campaigns of China after 1948, protesting the practices of foot-binding and concubinage. Contemporary adult education research on motherwork and public homeplaces parallels Tamboukou's (2003) research on 19th-century women teachers in the UK, which effectively destabilizes the coherence of oppositional and separate spheres.

Lander (2002) notes four overlapping conceptual frames of women's protest. *Civil society* is exemplified by *Les Madres* of Argentina, which grew to a collective force of "politicized motherhood" standing for human rights for all children. Paradoxically, *feminist popular education*, which builds on the experiential knowledge of learners themselves (Walters & Manicom, 1996), is exemplified by "Women Against Pit Closures" (Elliott, 2000), a non-institutionalized and non-feminist example of women's protest against the 1984 UK miners' strike. Unlike the women's movement of the 1970s, this women's organization was supportive of family, rooted in the working class, and "heterosexualized" (p. 10). Mary Leigh's activism in the British suffragette movement, specifically the Women's Social and Political Union (WSPU), in which women's bodies make a powerful display of dissent, exemplifies *performativity*; words and symbolic acts have effects, and in this case they perform citizenship (Parkins, 2000). *Carnival* or the suspension of official rules is the strategy of the Women's Institute (WI) in Yorkshire, which produced a calendar in which the women were pictured stark naked doing traditional WI things such as jam-making (see Michelson, 1999). Similarly, the Raging Grannies, a Canadian institution of antinuclear protest, acts as a " 'laughing chorus' in opposition to official dogma" (Heikinen, 1998, p. 2; see Roy, 2000).

Naming the Educator

In the context of women's organizations, the learning *from* direct action (see Lander, 2003) seems to get more attention than the equally important educative actions *of* women. Martin (2000) critiques the emphasis on the non-directive "facilitation" of individual and individualized learning insofar as it renders invisible the purposeful educational interventions of women's leadership in civil society organizations. Puigvert (2001) decries the ignored social justice contributions of women's organizations, including those led by non-academic women. The Research Network, born in 1999 and composed of academic women, seeks to radicalize democracy internationally through the extension of lifelong education and training for women with low academic levels (p. 45). Members of the Research Network include: the Women's Group FACEPA, a federation of adult education associations in Catalonia that manage their own projects; Drom Kotar Mestipen (Women's Gypsy Association) working for equality and against the discrimination of the Roma women; Mothers of the Plaza de Mayo (Argentina); and Insha Allah, an association of Muslim women from different countries with diverse academic levels.

Non-directive facilitation is an implicit value embedded in Foley's (1999) case studies of social movements. He laments that the largely informal and often incidental *learning* in social movements is ignored. This learning is "tacit, embedded in action . . . is often not recognized as learning" (p. 3), nor as education, adds Lander (2003). The *learning* of the founders and educators is also the emphasis in Welton's (1991) study of Canadian women's organizations (e.g., Women's Institutes, Home and School Associations, Imperial Order Daughters of the Empire). However, Ross-Gordon and Dowling's (1995) research into contemporary African-American women's voluntary organizations records instances of how members *both* educated others *and* learned through their experiences.

See also: civil society, motherwork, non-governmental organizations, social action, voluntary organizations, women's learning.

References and Further Reading

Antrobus, P. (2002). Building global networks: Women-led alternatives. In O. Gladkikh (Ed.), *Coady International Institute Learning and Innovations Institute on Democracy and Active Citizen Engagement: Best practices in advocacy and networking* (pp. 105–113). Antigonish, NS: St. Francis Xavier University.

Auretto, V. (2001). Social change movements and transformative learning. *PAACE Journal of Lifelong Learning, 10,* 41–53. (Pennsylvania Association of Adult Continuing Education).

Belenky, M. F., Bond, L. A., & Weinstock, J. A. (1991). *A tradition that has no name: Nurturing the development of people, families, and communities*. New York: Basic Books.

Butterwick, S. (1998). Lest we forget: Uncovering women's leadership in adult education. In G. Selman, M. Cooke, M. Selman, & P. Dampier (Eds.), *The foundations of adult education in Canada* (2nd ed., pp. 103–116). Toronto: Thompson Educational.

Catsambas, T. T., & Webb, L. D. (2003). Using appreciative inquiry to guide an evaluation of the international women's media foundation Africa program. In H. Preskill & A. T. Coghlan (Eds.), *Using appreciative inquiry in evaluation* (pp. 41–51). *New Directions for Evaluation*, No. 100. San Francisco: Jossey-Bass.

Cunningham, P. M. (1992). From Freire to feminism: The North American experience with critical pedagogy. *Adult Education Quarterly, 42*(3), 180–191.

Elliott, J. (2000). The challenge of lifelong learning as a means of extending citizenship for women, *Studies in the Education of Adults, 32*(1). Retrieved December 10, 2003 from ProQuest database.

Elsdon, K. T., with Reynolds, J., & Stewart, S. (1995). *Voluntary organizations: Citizenship, learning and change.* Leicester, UK: National Institute for Adult Continuing Education.

Ely, M. L., & Chappell, E. (1938). *Women in two worlds.* New York: American Association for Adult Education.

Ferree, M., & Martin, P. (Eds.). (1995). *Feminist organizations: Harvest of the new women's movement.* Philadelphia, PA: Temple University Press.

Finger, M. (1995). Adult education and society today. *International Journal of Lifelong Education, 14*(2), 110–119.

Foley, G. (1999). *Learning in social action: A contribution to understanding informal education.* London: Zed Books.

Giraldo, M. A. (2002). Contributions for strengthening and promoting processes of social organizations into organizations with political processes. In R. M. Cervero, B. C. Courtenay, & C. H. Monaghan (Eds.), *The Cyril O. Houle Scholars in Adult and Continuing Education Program: Global Research Perspectives, Volume 2.* Retrieved January 10, 2004 from http://www.coe.uga.edu/hsp/monographs2/giraldo.pdf (ERIC Document Reproduction Service No. ED470936).

Gittell, M., Ortega-Bustamante, I., & Steffy, T. (2000). Social capital and social change: women's social activism. *Urban Affairs Review, 36*(2), 123–147.

Gouthro, P. A. (2000). Globalization, civil society and the homeplace. *Convergence, 33(1/2)*, 57–77.

Heikinen, T. (1998). From Freire to Bakhtin: The role of carnival in the composition classroom. *Journal of Critical Pedagogy, 1*(2). Retrieved March 21, 2002 from http://www.coedu.usf/chandler/ Critical Pedagogy/critical_pedagogy. html

Hernández, A. (1997). *Pedagogy, democracy and feminism: Rethinking the public sphere.* Albany: State University of New York Press.

Lander, D. A. (2002). Women's ways of protesting: Activism, feminism, or witnessing across separate spheres. In S. Mojab & W. McQueen (Eds.), *Proceedings of the 21st Annual Conference of the Canadian Association for the Study of Adult Education, Adult Education and the Contested Terrain of Public Policy* (pp. 159–164). Retrieved August 31, 2003 from the Ontario Institute for Studies in Education /University of Toronto website: http://www.oise.utoronto. ca/CASAE/cnf2002/2002_Papers/lander2002w.pdf

Lander, D. A. (2003). Activist women as action learners: A visual genealogy of community organizing for lifelong learning (pp. 246–253). *Proceedings of International Conference on Researching Learning Outside the Academy.* Glasgow: Centre for Research in Lifelong Learning.

Lander, D. A. (in press). Re-membering mothers as lifelong educators: The art work of the Woman's Christian Temperance Union. *Canadian Journal for the Study of Adult Education.*

Leist, M. T. (1998). *Increasing stages of social activism and responsiveness to the national agenda: How women experience membership in branches of the American Association of University Women.* Doctoral dissertation, Department of Adult Education, Virginia Polytechnic Institute and State University, Blacksburg, VA. Retrieved December 14, 2003 from http://www.scholar.lib.vt.edu/theses/available/etd-31398-153455/unrestricted/etd.pdf

Martin, I. (2000). Reconstituting the agora: Towards an alternative politics of lifelong learning. *Concept, 2*(1), 4–8.

Mayo, M. (1997). *Imagining tomorrow: Adult education for transformation.* Leicester, UK: National Institute of Adult Continuing Education.

Meinhard, A. G., & Foster, M. K. (2003). Differences in the responses of women's voluntary organizations to shifts in Canadian public policy. *Nonprofit and Voluntary Sector Quarterly, 32*(3), 366–396.

Michelson, E. (1999). Carnival, paranoia and experiential learning. *Studies in the Education of Adults, 31*(2), 140–154.

Munro, P. (1999). Political activism as teaching: Jane Addams and Ida B. Wells. In M. S. Crocco, P. Munro, & K. Weiler (Eds.), *Pedagogies of resistance: Women educator activists, 1880–1960* (pp. 19–45). New York: Teachers College Press.

Nasstrom, K. L. (1999). Down to now: Memory, narrative, and women's leadership in the civil rights movement in Atlanta, Georgia. *Gender and History, 11*(1), 113–144.

Parkins, W. (2000). Protesting like a girl: Embodiment, dissent and feminist agency. *Feminist Theory, 1*, 59–78.

Puigvert, L. (2001). Dialogic feminism: Other women's. Contributions to the social transformation of gender relations (pp. 29–60). In E. Beck-Gernsheim, J. Butler, & L. Puigvert (Eds.), *Women and social transformation* (J. Vaida, Trans.). New York: Peter Lang.

Riger, S. (1994). Challenges of success: Stages of growth in feminist organizations. *Feminist Studies, 20*(2), 275–300.

Ross-Gordon, J. M., & Dowling, W. D. (1995). Adult learning in the context of African-American women's voluntary organizations. *International Journal of Lifelong Education, 14*(4), 306–319.

Roy, C. (2000). Raging Grannies and environmental issues: Humour and creativity in educative protests. *Convergence, 32*(4), 6–17.

Smith, M. K. (2001). Club work. In *The Encyclopedia of Informal Education*, The Informal Education website. Retrieved December 15, 2003 from http://www.infed.org/association/club-work.htm.

Stromquist, N. (2000). Voice, harmony, and fugue in global feminism. *Gender and Education, 12*(4), 419–433.

Tamboukou, M. (2003). *Women, education and the self: A Foucauldian perspective.* New York: Palgrave Macmillan.

Walters, S., & Manicom, L. (Eds.). (1996). *Gender in popular education: Methods for empowerment.* London: Zed Books.

Welton, M. R. (Ed.). (1991). *Education for a brighter day: Women's organizations as learning sites.* Halifax, NS: Dalhousie University.

Dorothy A. Lander

Work-Based Learning

Work-based learning refers to learning that is undertaken at work or directly for purposes of work. Such learning is also typically utilized as part of some educational qualification or credit towards a qualification. The term workplace learning is more commonly used when there is no connection with an academic or vocational award and learning is solely for the purposes of work (Billett, 2001). Work, as used here, is not necessarily paid or full-time, but includes any activity that is productive or involves a service to others.

While there are many variations of the exact terms used, and there is no universal consistency of use, work-based learning commonly encompasses two categories of activity.

These categories are identified with regard to whether the learner starts from the position of being a student who then engages in work-related learning, or from the position of a worker who engages in work-related study. In the first, the learner has the prime identity of student, in the second case the learner has the prime identity as worker, though in both cases mixtures of working and studying are involved.

The first category of work-based learning (labeled here as work-based learning for students) involves students who are enrolled in an educational program undertaking part of that program in a workplace. This may be termed a work placement, work experience, internship or practicum. When it is a major part of a degree program it is sometimes called cooperative education (as distinct from cooperative learning) or a sandwich course: work experience is sandwiched between periods of formal study in an educational institution. In this first category of use, work-based learning is one element of a wider program which includes substantial formal study as part of the total curriculum. The experience of work is part of preparation for future employment by those who identify mainly as "student." Identity as "employee" or "volunteer" is an additional identity taken on temporarily during the period of placement.

The second category of use (labeled here as work-based learning for workers) occurs when those in work undertake a program of study in which they use the learning opportunities of their own work, or work within their own organization, as part of a program of study. This may be undertaken in order to extend their learning within their existing role, or, more frequently, to equip themselves to taken on new responsibilities within their organization. In this case, work defines what is studied and learning outcomes are judged in terms of organizational relevance. Until the last decade such types of learning were confined within the realm of organizations. However, there has been a new involvement of educational institutions in this form of work-based learning in recent times with the rise of work-based learning partnerships (Boud & Solomon, 2001). These partnerships are formal arrangements between an organization and an educational institution, often a university, in which learning arising from work is supported by both the work organization and the educational institution. This learning is then accredited as a formal course. The identity of those who undertake work-based learning in the second sense is that "workers" (employees, practitioners, staff, volunteers) who take on an additional identity as "learners" without foregoing their ongoing identity as workers.

Reading of literature on work-based learning is complicated by the fact that most practitioners of one of the categories of use seem unaware of its use by the other community of practice. Not only do proponents of one position take their own use of the term to be definitive, but they often ignore the very existence of the other position.

Work-Based Learning for Students

Programs using work placements are of very long standing and many different traditions have been established depending on the profession or occupation into which students are being introduced. Terminology varies greatly as almost every group has their own language for this practice. For example, "clinical placements" are commonly used in the health sciences and teaching practice or the "practicum" in teacher education. The various elements of these practices are also characterized in various ways. In addition to the practices within specific professions, there is also a generic practice of cooperative education that is often used when there is not a mandated requirement for professional practice as an intrinsic component of gaining qualified status (as is the case in teaching and the health professions).

Cooperative education has become the accepted term in many countries for the practice of students spending a complete semester or year in a working environment as part of their course. The *Journal of Cooperative Education* is the well-established journal in this area. Such placements were designed to provide students who had little experience of work life with an authentic taste of working in an area in some way connected with the focus of their main study. Traditionally, there have been only loose linkages between the part of the program undertaken in the educational institution and that undertaken in the workplace. In many cases, the work component was not seen officially as part of the course and did not gain full credit as there were no requirements for students to undertake assessed work during their placement. This has changed considerably in recent years.

Work experience was often unsystematic, unregulated and not organized in ways that ensured any particular learning outcome. Students experienced whatever was to be had in the environment in which they were placed, which led to wide variations in types of experience and what was learned. In an attempt to provide a minimum quality of outcome for such placements, more systematic approaches have been created. This has typically involved the specification of desired learning outcomes, the development of learning plans involving three-way agreements between student, workplace supervisor and educational advisor, and the formal assessment of what has been learned. Learning contracts (Anderson, Boud, & Sampson, 1996; Knowles, 1975) are commonly used to provide a framework for learning and to increase students' sense of agency when confronted with often complex and demanding situations. Also, briefing and debriefing activities before and after placement and greater acknowledgement of work experience in other parts of the curriculum are now found.

In recent years attempts have been made to conceptualize student work experience – an undertheorized and under-researched area – in terms of contemporary learning theory (Guile & Griffiths, 2001) and pedagogy (Tynjälä, Välimaa, & Sarja 2003).

Work-Based Learning for Workers

Programs for employees are widespread, particularly at management level, and the term work-based learning has become attached to some of these. In many ways these involve a rebadging and systemization of familiar activities within organizations. These include the use of action learning sets, mentorships, coaching and various reflection practices. However, the labeling of this group of practices as work-based learning does enable these practices to be identified collectively as an important element of learning at work (Raelin, 2002).

In contrast to this new grouping of work-based learning activities, and work-based learning for students, credentialed work-based learning as part of formal educational qualifications for those already in work is a relatively recent phenomenon. Opportunities for workers to take courses for credit either in-house or in an educational institution are widespread, but this is not what is being referred to when the term work-based learning is used. Work-based learning in the second use of the term involves the enrolment of those already working for a particular organization in an educational program that takes work itself as the curriculum. That is, the workplace is used not as a site for developing an understanding of already codified disciplinary or professional knowledge, but as a site of understanding new forms of transdisciplinary knowledge which are not part of existing educational programs. Work-based learning involves an epistemological shift from engaging with what Gibbons et al. (1994) term Mode 1 knowledge production (problems set and solved in context governed by interests of a specific academic community), to Mode 2 knowledge production (knowledge understood in a context of application). This is a radical shift of position that challenges many of the taken-for-granted assumptions of educational institutions. Education is required to respond to the knowledge demands of actual work rather than frame knowledge for use in work.

In this case, work defines what is studied and learning outcomes are judged against both the learning demands of work and a generic framework of levels and standards according to the kind of qualification sought. Work-based activities may constitute the entire program of study. However, in practice, work-based learning may involve a combination of elements drawn from the existing program of offerings of an educational institution and substantial work-located learning projects which are of benefit to the individual and the organization in which they operate.

In work-based learning programs of this kind, the starting point and educational level of the program is established after learners have engaged in a process of recognition of current competencies and identification of the learning they wish to engage in. This is in contrast to conventional practice in which the level of the program is predetermined and students may gain recognition of prior learning through the accreditation of their prior experiential learning against an existing course specification.

See also: cooperative learning; prior learning assessment and recognition, training, workplace learning.

References and Further Reading

Anderson, G., Boud, D., & Sampson, J. (1996). *Learning contracts: A practical guide*. London: Kogan Page.

Bailey, T. R., Hughes, K. L., & Moore, D. T. (2004). *Working knowledge: Work-based learning and education reform*. London: Routledge Falmer.

Billett, S. (2001). *Learning in the workplace: Strategies for effective practice*. Sydney: Allen & Unwin.

Boud, D., & Solomon, N. (Eds.) (2001). *Work-based learning: A new higher education?* Buckingham: Society for Research into Higher Education Education (SRHE) and Open University Press.

Gibbons, M., Limoges, C., Nowotny, H., Schwartzman, S., Scott, P., & Trow, M. (1994). *The new production of knowledge: The dynamics of science and research in contemporary societies*. London: Sage.

Guile, D., & Griffiths, T. (2001). Learning through work experience. *Journal of Education and Work, 14*(1), 113–131.

Knowles, M. S. (1975). *Self-directed learning: A guide for learners and teachers*. New York: Associated Press.

Raelin, J. A. (2002). *Work-based learning: The new frontier of management development*. Englewood Cliffs, NJ: Prentice Hall.

Tynjälä, P., Välimaa, J. & Sarja, A. (2003). Pedagogical perspectives on the relationships between higher education and working life. *Higher Education, 46*, 147–166.

David Boud

Workplace Learning

Workplace learning signifies human change in consciousness or behavior occurring primarily in activities and contexts of work, however defined and located. The assumption is that learning and knowledge associated with work are embedded in material and social activity, highly contextual, fluid, and not necessarily connected with educational initiatives.

Work – paid and unpaid, organizational or independent – is well-recognized as a significant developmental site for adult learning, change, and resistance. This is perhaps the main reason why workplace learning deserves recognition by adult educators as a distinct field of research, theory and practice. But are learning processes in work so different from learning in community, classroom, or everyday life that they deserve distinction? Beckett and Hager (2002) assert that: unlike instructional contexts, workplace learning occurs in "hot action," when decisions are taken on the run, relying on know-how and practical judgments, with the nagging doubt that action might be superficial, hasty or inappropriate. But furthermore, the study of learning/education in and through work has the potential to open alternate approaches to understanding experiential learning processes and their links to social relations, identity, and language. Workplace learning also poses a significant challenge to the academy's authority over the legitimation of knowledge, and to the largely rational discourses of critical thinking and constructivist meaning-making that tend to characterize understandings of adult learning derived from classroom settings. Thus, sociologists, organization theorists, economists and cultural researchers have joined educators in a rising interdisciplinary tide of research being swept along by massive changes in the nature of work and its meaning for 21st-century workers. Most are committed to informing policies and practices that enable more life-giving, democratic, and productive workplace education.

Issues of Language and Definition

Definition is difficult. In discussing cognition and changes experienced by human beings through work, should we examine the phenomenon more culturally as one of social "knowledge production," or more psychologically as one of individual "learning"? The notions of "useful knowledge" and "effective learning practice" fluctuate according to the position, power and purpose of individual perspectives, whether worker, manager, owner, educator, unionist, or some combination. The terms "work" and "workplace" are also problematic, for their conventional usage tends to ignore important spheres of unpaid work in homes and communities, and to assume that work is based in unitary, identifiable, geographically-organized places.

Changing Contexts of Work

Influences on workplace learning begin with globalization, which has accelerated competition among corporations. As they jostle for position to meet changing consumer tastes, pressure increases for innovation to produce endless variation in customized goods and services. At the same time, international standards have helped homogenize and instrumentalize "method," and contributed to an obsession with accountability in work. As well as the information technology revolution has transformed modes of doing business, the nature of services and products, the meaning of time in work, and the processes of learning. Flexibility is endemic in job structures, skill demands, pay, and learning. Workers are expected to accept constant change as a given, to forego expectation of stable employment and organizational loyalty, and to assume personal responsibility for adapting to organizations' changing needs for skills and labor.

At the organizational level, increasing examples of post-Fordist workplaces are appearing, where people work in self-directed teams rather than command-and-control hierarchies, and where meaning, mission and values are emphasized to create communities of learning. But workplaces are still driven by hierarchical power structures and divisions of labor. Thus the workplace is highly political, where flexibility, specialization, new technologies, globalization, emphasis on innovation and knowledge management, and particular cultural norms affect both work demands and learning processes.

Contemporary Workplace Learning Research

Perspectives in workplace learning research are wide-ranging, from neo-Marxist to utilitarian, and from technical to poststructural. Leaving aside an explanation of these theoretical standpoints, the following discussion presents prominent topics grouped into five strands. The first three are outlined very briefly. The last two are described in more detail, as they have attracted a significant body of research.

Understanding the relation of learning to changing forms of work

As the continuous changes in work have led to a focus on workers' skill upgrading, researchers have become interested in both the types of skills produced by these efforts, and workers' responses to skill training and assessment. Some researchers focus on ways to recognize and assess skills that workers have developed on the job. Others have highlighted the phenomenon of under-employment due to undervaluing of workers' knowledge. Still others examine forms of individual learning occurring in diverse forms and activities of work – contingent and self-employed work, technology in work, labor struggles, and the learning embedded in new textual practices required in workplaces such as self-directed teams. A related area examines how learning is shaped by particular written texts in a workplace, such as documents, policies, forms for record-keeping, reports, and so on. Such discourse analysis reveals how texts have the power to standardize what counts as knowledge, thus controlling the work practices and working relations of people.

Understanding people's life histories in work

Researchers have used life history methods to understand connections among individuals' learning at work and their overall career development, identity and social relations. Some focus on professionals' learning and others on working-class identities and knowledge. Questions are raised about both limitations and possibilities afforded to human identity by particular workplace conditions, activities and relationships. What identity categories are considered "normal" and "deviant" or "other than normal" in a workplace? How do people "learn" coherent identities amidst the fragmentation, anxiety and constant change of their work conditions?

Educational initiatives in work

Workplace initiatives to promote learning include mentorship, team structures, guided learning opportunities, job-redesign or rotation to increase exposure to new projects, and paid educational leave. A popular approach is action learning, an on-the-job problem-solving process whereby workers identify an issue together, experiment with solutions in practice, then critically reflect on the consequences. Labor educators have also studied popular education and emancipatory learning opportunities in work to determine methods that best foster people's development of a critical consciousness. Others have examined ways of fostering a people-centered workplace and quality of worklife through educational initiatives focused on increasing gender equity, combating racism, and helping people recognize and value their own working knowledge.

Understanding processes of practice-based (informal) learning

Some researchers have argued that workplace learning develops through reflection in the "swamp" of uncertain, contradictory dilemmas of everyday work. Reflection during and after the "doing" transforms experience into knowledge, which can then be represented and generalized to new contexts. Critics say that this emphasis on reflection is simplistic and reductionist. It overemphasizes rational thought and understates the messiness of everyday practice. Practice-based perspectives of workplace learning believe that learning is rooted in the particular *activity, situation* and *community* in which people participate, and not merely in people's heads. Building on the participative metaphor, different models of workplace learning have been proposed. Beckett and Hager (2002) focus on developing know-how in the workplace, particularly through making practical judgments. Valuable working knowledge is "anticipative action" in particular situations, a back-and-forth dynamic between means and ends as a worker makes judgments in the "hot action" of work situations. Billett (2001) advocates a model of guidance (direct, indirect, and environmental) that moves workers towards fuller participation in workplace activity, and therefore to more comprehensive and critical knowledge as actors in their community of practice.

Complexity theory is also gaining acceptance as a useful conceptualization of the activity and knowledge that emerge together as part of the process of workplace learning. Individual interactions and meanings form part of the workplace context itself: they are interconnected systems nested within the larger systems in which they act. As workers are influenced by symbols and actions in which they participate, they adapt and learn. As they do so, their behaviors and thus their effects upon the systems change. The focus is not on the components of experience (which other perspectives might describe in fragmented terms: person, experience, tools, and activity), but on the *relationships* binding them together. Workplace learning is thus cast as continuous invention and exploration in complex systems.

Equity and ethics in workplace learning

Concern for workers' well-being is driving much inquiry into workplace learning, although there is considerable debate about how to facilitate this in equitable, non-exploitive terms. The notion of worker "empowerment," once associated with transforming workplaces into democratic learning communities, has become a target of considerable criticism. Many wonder just how democratic an organization can pretend to be when it views workers as resources valued only for what they add to the organization's productivity. Critical case studies demonstrate that learning organization initiatives are sometimes wielded for worker subjugation and control.

Analysts have also shown how current organizing of work and workplace education cultivates inequality by widening the chasm between workers and management. Studies demonstrate how class- and colorblindness in workplace learning has marginalized large groups of workers (Kincheloe, 1999). This form of inequity has narrowed our understandings of what it means to be skilled, what is useful knowledge, what is success, and what identities are recognized and rewarded in the workplace. Women continue to confront gendered work knowledges and structures as they negotiate workplace cultures of male-oriented values, communication patterns and work styles (Probert, 1999). There is also some evidence of gendered distribution of learning opportunities and control of learning purposes in the workplace.

These writers have focused attention on access to learning opportunities in work. They show forms of exclusion that circulate in the knowledge and language of a workplace community of practice. They ask, What learning experiences, and whose, are most valued? How do existing policies about work and learning reinforce social and economic inequities? Through what processes can people critically interrogate exclusive organizational practices, and agitate for more inclusive policies and practices?

Directions for Future Exploration

Recent research in workplace learning blends theoretical perspectives in the sociology and political economy of work, cultural analyses of workplace practice, human narratives, and psychology of learning and reflection. Research also is underway to generate more multifaceted methods for observing and analysing people's learning in practice-based work activity. Symes and McIntyre (2000) suggest that the following questions are guiding new scholarship in workplace learning:

- What is the nature of working knowledge, and how does workplace learning challenge our existing theories of knowledge?
- How is knowledge formed and learned at work?
- How is working identity configured in the learning process?
- What are the conditions bringing about workplace learning?
- How adequate are our explanations of "new modes" of contemporary work knowledge production, such as knowledge situated in communities of practice?
- What should be the role and practice of educators in light of these understandings of working knowledge and workplace learning?

Clearly, workplace learning embraces a wide range of engagements: both intentional and unintentional learning resulting from coping with routine and nonroutine problems and practices. Learning can produce desirable and undesirable outcomes, and can be experienced at personal, group, or organizational levels. Learning is ongoing but it can be reactive or proactive, producing knowledge about how to act, who to be, what to believe, and where to position oneself. As skill demands continue shifting, knowledge-production expanding, and the link between learning and work success growing tighter, the question of the role and practice of educators becomes particularly critical.

See also: action learning, activity theory, complexity theory, knowledge, learning organization, organizational learning, training, work-based learning.

References and Further Reading

Beckett, D., & Hager, P. (2002). *Life, work and learning: Practice in postmodernity*. London: Routledge.

Billett, S. (2001). *Learning in the workplace: Strategies for effective practice*. Sydney: Allen & Unwin.

Kincheloe, J. L. (1999). *How do we tell the workers? The socioeconomic foundations of work and vocational education*. Boulder, CO: Westview.

Probert, B. (1999). Gendered workers and gendered work: Implications for learning. In D. Boud & J. Garrick (Eds.), *Understanding learning in work* (pp. 98–116). New York and London: Routledge.

Symes, C., & McIntyre, J. (Eds.). (2000). *Working knowledge: Higher education and the new vocationalism*. Buckingham, UK: Society for Research into Higher Education and Open University Press.

Tara Fenwick

Workplace Literacy

Workplace literacy generally refers to the skills needed by employees at work; these typically include reading, writing and oral communication skills. The term "workplace basic skills" is also frequently used to describe the above skills, as well as numeracy or basic mathematics. Further, skills such as teamwork, leadership, problem-solving and ICT skills are also sometimes included in the definition of workplace basic skills. In what follows, the more generic term "workplace basic skills" will be used, as much of the work that has been carried out in this area is relevant to a broader range of workplace basic skills, rather than just literacy. It is, however, important to stress that there is considerable debate about the terminology and that a host of terms with similar meanings can be found in the literature, for example, "essential skills," "key skills" or "workplace education." The latter, in particular, is often preferred by educators as it is considered to be free of the more negative overtones of the terms literacy or basic skills.

Workplace Basic Skills Training Programs

The motivation behind the development of workplace basic skills programs in the late 1980s and 1990s has been the assumed link between basic skills and productivity. Specifically, it is argued that increased levels of literacy, language and numeracy can, among other things, reduce the number of errors at work, improve communication between colleagues, supervisors and managers and increase customer satisfaction. Further, it has also been argued that the move towards a knowledge-based economy has led to a demand for higher levels of basic skills in a large number of occupations (see for example Hull & Grubb, 1999). In addition, workplace basic skills programs are thought to be potentially more motivating and effective in improving skill levels compared to more conventional provision, for example in further education or community colleges. Such arguments led to the development of major, government-funded workplace basic skills programs, such as the National Workplace Literacy Program started in 1988 in the United States, and the Basic Skills at Work Programme in 1991 in the UK (ALBSU, 1993). More recent initiatives in the UK include: Skills for Life, the national adult literacy and numeracy strategy, and the Employer Training Pilots, a pilot scheme operating in 12 areas in England offering incentives to employers (such as compensation for releasing staff) for providing basic skills and low-level vocational training to their employees (HM Treasury, 2002).

Specific training programs or courses can either be tailored to particular job or sector requirements (job-specific) or be more generic and broader in scope. There is, however, little information on the exact number, nature and scope of basic skills programs offered at the workplace in any country or region.

There is some evidence that in England sizeable numbers of employers are making some provision for their workers to improve their basic skills where necessary. The *Learning and Training at Work 2002* survey (Spilsbury, 2003) asked a sample of over 3,000 employers in England which learning opportunities they offered to employees at the location. Among all workplaces with five or more employees the survey found that basic numeracy was offered by 14% of employers and basic literacy by 13%. Further, the likelihood that each type of learning opportunity, including literacy and numeracy, would be available increased with the size of the workplace. Among establishments with 100 to 199 employees, 26% offered basic literacy and 25% offered basic numeracy. The proportions rose to 33% for both numeracy and literacy for workplaces of between 200 and 499 employees, while in workplaces with 500 or more employees 49% offered basic numeracy and 50% basic literacy. Looking at the same data by industry sector of the employer, the survey found that employers in the "transport, public administration and other services" sector were more likely to offer basic numeracy and literacy training (15% and 16% respectively), while those in the "agriculture, mining, utilities and construction" sectors were the least likely (9% and 10% respectively for numeracy and literacy). There are no further details in the *Learning and Training at Work* survey about how basic skills courses were delivered, how they were funded, whether they were general or job-specific in scope, or what number or type of employees attended them. With regards to the latter point, there is some preliminary evidence from the first year evaluation report of the Employer Training Pilots (ETPs) (Hillage & Mitchell, 2003) that basic skills learners are more likely to be from an ethnic minority, be younger than the average worker, have a disability, and be a member of a trade union. This information is based on a total of 1357 basic skills learners participating in the basic skills part of the ETP scheme.

Economic Impact of Workplace Basic Skills Programs

The major possible benefits of basic skills training from the point of view of the employers are (higher) productivity, (lower) turnover and (greater) safety. However, despite the sizeable number of workplace training schemes now available, there is very little evidence on how basic skills training influences any of these outcomes.

One well-structured quantitative study of the impact of such training was conducted by Krueger and Rouse (1998). They compared outcomes such as earnings, staff turnover and absenteeism levels between two groups of employees in two mid-sized United States companies: one group had received a 16-month basic skills course, the other had not. The authors found small effects of the program on all outcomes investigated. For example, there was some evidence that participants in one company were 7% more likely to apply for and gain internal promotion, and that those in the other company were more frequently nominated for or won a performance award, compared to non-participants. Workers who had participated in the program also had slightly lower absenteeism rates during the weeks in which they had classes and for 2 months after the end of the course. Finally, there was no evidence that participation in training made workers either more or less likely to leave the company after training. Krueger and Rouse further investigated a number of "subjective" variables by asking employees a series of questions on their attitudes towards their jobs, their desire to take additional classes, and their self-perceived productivity. In one of the two companies, self-perceived productivity was greater among trainees, but for almost all the other variables measured differences between course participants and non-participants did not reach conventional significance levels.

Pearson (1996) reports the results of a survey of 30 different Australian workplaces representing 13 industries across five states. The study found that language and literacy training was considered to have had a positive effect on five aspects of the workplace: direct cost savings; access to and acceptability of further training; participation in teams and meetings; promotion and job flexibility; and the value of training (which included issues such as worker morale, confidence to communicate). When respondents were asked to provide a quantitative estimate of savings, 70% of them identified that their organization had made perceptible cost savings as a result of the language and literacy training. Typically, these were related to time-saving when carrying out a literacy or language work task and to more accurate and fuller completion of workplace documentation.

Bloom et al. (1997) report the qualitative feedback of 21 Canadian companies on the benefits of literacy training to their organization. The employers indicated which benefits they had observed in their employees as a result of literacy training. The most frequently cited benefits were: increased ability to handle training on the job; better team performance; improved labor-management relations; and increased quality of work.

New Literacy Studies

Another strand of research in the area of workplace literacy is "New Literacy Studies" (NLS) (see for example, Barton, 1994). Research within this framework approaches literacy as a social practice rather than as a series of technical skills to be learned in a formal education context and emphasizes the social relations and institutions within which literacy is embedded. Different literacies are associated with different domains of life and the workplace is one such domain where literacy practices take place. Barton and Hamilton (2000) use the example of cooks, whose literacy practices, they argue, may be quite different at home and at the workplace (that is, in institutional kitchens), as the latter will involve a different division of labor, scale of operations, health and safety precautions, and so on. Jackson (2000) describes the work in this framework as bringing attention to the complexity of the work situation and of moving the emphasis away from the individual skilled worker.

Researchers in NLS generally draw on ethnographic research traditions in terms of methodology. One detailed case study of a workplace literacy program using such a methodology is reported by Gowen (1992), who studied a 9-month long workplace literacy program offered to front-line hospital workers in the southern United States. The data she collected as part of her research included interviews with employees receiving the program, notes on staff meetings and class sessions, and her own written observations of the general hosptial culture. The research themes she investigated included: defining literacy behaviors, worker/employer relations, interpreting resistance and making and displaying knowledge. Gowen's overarching research question was how beliefs about language, learning and work are shaped by the variety of interests in the program. She describes the political forces that influence the design and success of the program and which determine how much employees can improve their prospects after attending a literacy course. Gowen recommends a more participatory model of workplace education that involves all stakeholders, including the employees themselves.

More recently, Searle (2001) reports a case study of an Australian construction company implementing the nationally endorsed training package for the civil construction sector, which includes literacy and numeracy competencies. Through a series of semi-structured interviews with personnel from the Training Depart-ment, Searle investigated the way literacy and numeracy were understood within the training and assessment programs of the company. She concludes that literacy and numeracy skills are essential at today's workplaces, where employees increasingly need to become multiskilled, keep up-to-date with new technology, and assume managerial responsibilities.

See also: literacy, numeracy, training, workplace learning.

References and Further Reading

ALBSU (1993). *The cost to industry basic skills and the workforce.* London: Adult Literacy and Basic Skills Unit (ALBSU).

Barton, D. (1994). *Literacy: An introduction to the ecology of written language.* Oxford: Blackwell.

Barton, D., & Hamilton, M. (2000). Literacy practices. In D. Barton, M. Hamilton & R. Ivanic (Eds.), *Situated literacies: Reading and writing in contex* (pp. 7–15). London: Routledge.

Bloom, B.M., Burrows, M., Lafleur, B., & Squires, R. (1997). *The economic benefits of improving literacy skills in the workplace.* Ottawa: Conference Board of Canada. Retrieved January 10, 2004, from ERIC database (ERIC Document Reproduction Service No. ED412340).

Gowen, S. G. (1992). *The politics of work-*

place literacy: A case study. New York: Teachers College Press.

Hillage, J., & Mitchell, H. (2003). *Employer training pilots. First year evaluation report.* London: Department for Education and Skills (DfES).

HM Treasury (2002). *Developing workforce skills: Piloting a new approach*. London: HM Treasury.

Hull, G., & Grubb, N. (1999). Literacy, skills and work. In D. Wagner, R. Venezky & B. Street (Eds.), *Literacy: An international handbook* (pp. 311–317). Boulder, CO: Westview Press.

Jackson, N. (2000). Writing-up people at work: Investigations of workplace literacy. *Literacy and Numeracy Studies, 10*(1), 5–22.

Krueger, A., & Rouse, C. (1998). The effect of workplace education on earnings, turnover, and job performance. *Journal of Labor Economics, 16*(1), 61–94.

Pearson, G.(1996). *More than money can say: The impact of ESL and literacy training in the Australian workplace*. Canberra: Department of Employment, Education, Training and Youth Affairs.

Searle, J. (2001). Constructing literacies in the new work order. *Literacy and Numeracy Studies, 11*(1), 21–40.

Spilsbury, D. (2003). *Learning and training at work 2002*. Research Report No 399. London: Department for Education and Skills (DfES).

Katerina Ananiadou

Workshops

Workshops are formally arranged educational situations that usually have some general characteristics in common, though there can be broad variations (Moon, 2001). They tend to be of short duration (e.g., from a few hours to a day or two), and there tends to be a practical orientation. They are usually more than a straightforward presentation by one person, and participants tend to be involved in greater mental or physical activity than simple accumulation of information. An "active" element is usually present and they are facilitated rather than "taught." This implies that there is greater account taken of the existing and developing knowledge of the participants than in many other teaching situations (see the framework below). In addition, the subject matter of a workshop is concentrated (Parlett & King, 1971) – participants do not study a variety of subject matter, but focus on one topic. There might be a series of workshops on specified aspects of a particular topic, and there are some activities that typically distinguish workshops from formal teaching situations in institutions (e.g., warm-up sessions; brainstorming work). However they are run, the effectiveness or impact of workshops is an issue.

Much of the literature on workshops emanates from the training and development field and workshops often become the main means of delivery of continuing professional education programs. The Kolb cycle of experiential learning (Kolb, 1984) has been strongly influential in that field and tends to be used as the theoretical underpinning to the learning processes. The cycle suggests that reflection, in effect, turns an experience into learning (Boud, Keogh, & Walker, 1985), and effective learning is ensured by a further stage of "active experimentation." There are good reasons why the Kolb cycle leads to effective learning that are not related directly to the cycle as such (Moon, 2004).

Impact

An alternative to the Kolb (1984) cycle as an underpinning to successful workshops is the concept of impact – the idea that a workshop is only effective if participants can demonstrate knowledge of something, or can do something differently as a result of attendance at the workshop (Moon, 2001; Willis, 1993). If there is no impact, then the workshop was not effective and not worth attending. This maxim should apply equally to workshops run in the context of adult education or workplace training and education. There are some general principles related to the concept of impact, the most important of which is that workshops are short and time is at a premium. To have impact, there should be clarity, precision and awareness of the topic, the learners and the purpose (or anticipated impact). A second principle, that will be evident below, is that there should be a clear understanding of the difference between the activities of instruction (under which heading is also included teaching, facilitation, direction, tuition, etc.) and the process of learning. Learning is what the learner does and is of central importance to the process of a workshop. Learning is guided and facilitated by instruction – but these are separate activities, engaged in by different people involved in a workshop. The focus should be on whatever helps the learner to learn in accordance with the purpose of the workshop.

The Effectiveness of Learning in a Workshop

The effectiveness of learning in workshops is influenced by a number of factors in their planning and execution. The first of these is the manner in which aims and anticipated outcomes (or objectives) are expressed and used to guide the progress of a workshop. It is important to have a general aim, which can be expressed as a general intention of instruction or what the workshop is to cover (i.e., the subject matter). Learning outcomes are the expression of what it is hoped that the learners will learn as a result of the workshop, and their expression may be influenced by designated standards such as the level structure of formal education (Moon, 2001).

The learning outcome might be introduced by the following: "at the end of the workshop, it is anticipated that the learners will be able to . . .," with the following words clearly and precisely describing what learning it is anticipated will have occurred. If there is any assessment of the learning that results from the workshop, the assessment criteria should relate directly to the learning outcome statements. The method used to assess the learning will be chosen for the manner in which it tests the assessment criteria, as well as feasibility and convenience. It is also important to recognize that an assessment process can be a source of learning in itself (Angelo & Cross, 1990).

A second factor in the promotion of an effective workshop is the facilitator's understanding of the process of learning that s/he is hoping will occur in the participants. A common view of learning is that we progressively accumulate knowledge, replacing erroneous or old knowledge with new knowledge as one might replace a brick in a wall. A more common view of knowledge to underpin workshop practice is the constructivist view which considers learning as a process of continuous modification of previous knowledge (i.e., of changing conceptions) (Marton, Hounsell, & Entwistle, 1997). Constructivists usually recognize that while learning is ultimately an individual process, there is a strong social element because concepts are socially generated and agreed in social groups and mediated by the commonality of language. Workshops may particularly engage the social aspects of learning by supporting discussion and sharing of conceptions of the subject matter.

Another aspect of learning relevant to the impact of a workshop is the quality of the learning. Most workshop leaders want learners to move beyond a superficial approach to the subject matter and to retain the new concepts and skills that they have been taught in the workshop. The construct of deep and surface approaches to learning is well-researched in higher education literature and can support effective learning and facilitation practices (Martin & Booth, 1997).

The third factor in the promotion of an effective workshop follows from the second and relates to the process of facilitation (instruction/teaching/direction, etc.). In one sense good facilitation is what encourages and supports good quality learning, and is based on an explicit or intuitive understanding of what learners need. However, there are some further features that are particularly relevant in short and purposeful workshops and these concern the management of the workshop process. There needs to be a holistic view of the whole workshop and its learning outcomes – how it all fits together. Because a workshop is short, it is also important to get the balances right in terms of time and workload, recognizing the needs of learners and the limitations of time. The facilitator needs to manage the emotional climate of the workshop (Moon, 2004) as well as monitor the quality and progress of the learning. Beyond the skills of facilitation of learning, and the management of the workshop, there are some "technical skills" required of the facilitator, including the good use of voice, building credibility with the learners, explaining and presenting clearly, being organized, and conveying enthusiasm for the subject matter (Heron, 1996).

A fourth factor for effective workshops is to ensure that the overall design of the workshop is geared towards having an impact on the participants so that they know or are able to do something differently as a result of their learning. This is a matter of taking account of the state of knowledge/skills of participants at the beginning of the workshop and the hoped-for state at the end. Moon offers a design framework that was suggested by the observation of nurses going to health-education workshops, and returning to their workplace with new knowledge but little incentive or opportunity to put the new ideas into practice. The framework supports a workshop by posing questions that need to be taken into account in its design, which consists of four phases. In the first phase there is development of awareness of the nature of current practice/knowledge/understanding (p/k/u). The question is: what is the current p/k/u with reference to the subject matter of the workshop? In the second phase, there is clarification of the new learning and how it relates to current p/k/u. The question then is: what is the anticipated learning on the workshop and how does it improve the current practice/knowledge/understanding? In the third phase there is integration of the new learning and current p/k/u and the question is: how does the new learning relate to the current p/k/u? How does it modify or extend it? In the fourth phase there is anticipation or the imagining of the nature of the improved p/k/u. The question is: how will participants act differently as a result of the learning from the workshop? (Framework based on Moon, 1999, 2001).

The main features of this framework is that it takes good account of current practice, requires that the workshop attend to the integration of this practice with the new learning, and requires that attention be paid to the context of the new practice, not just leaving it to chance.

The fifth factor that can contribute to the impact of a workshop is ensuring that, in the short time space of a workshop, each component of a workshop contributes to the achievement of the purposes of the workshop. This thinking arose from the observation of workshop activities that were conducted for reasons of habit, rather than because they significantly contributed to learning (Moon, 2001). An example is "warm-up" activities conducted because "they are expected." Some components of a workshop – that must contribute to the outcomes – are: (a) workshop planning and administration (e.g., considerations of the location, timing, etc.); (b) activities that involve actual instruction or the delivery of information (e.g., presentations, mini lectures); (c) activities that facilitate group functioning to improve the learning of the participants (e.g., introductory activities, ensuring sociable tea breaks, etc.); (d) activities that support the learning of participants and enable them to change their knowledge/practice/understanding (e.g., paying attention to the framework above); (e) provision of overviews of the workshop content (e.g., introductory or summary activities at appropriate points in the proceedings); and (f) activities to enable or to deepen integration of learning. A significant aspect of this would be the inclusion of opportunity for reflective activities of a group and/or individual nature; activities to support individual learning or coping behaviors (e.g., providing an opportunity to deal with the difficulties of individuals); and assessment activities to evaluate the achievement of learning outcomes of the workshop. These may be conducted formally or informally. Lastly, there are likely to be workshop evaluation activities.

See also: evaluation, experiential learning, facilitation, prior learning assessment and recognition, program planning, training.

References and Further Reading

Angelo, T., & Cross, K. (1990). *Classroom assessment techniques*. San Francisco: Jossey-Bass.

Boud, D., Keogh, R., & Walker, D. (1985). *Reflection: turning experience into learning*. London: Kogan Page.

Heron, J. (1996). Helping whole people learn. In D. Boud & N. Miller (Eds.), *Working with experience: Animating learning* (pp. 75–91). London: Routledge.

Kolb, D. A. (1984). *Experiential learning as the science of learning and development*. Englewood Cliffs, NJ: Prentice Hall.

Martin, F., & Booth, S. (1997). *Learning and awareness*. Mahwah, NJ: Lawence Erlbaum.

Martin, F. & Hounsell, D., & Entwistle, N. (1997). *The experience of learning*. Edinburgh, Scotland: Scottish Academic Press.

Moon, J. (1999). *Reflection in learning and professional development*. London: Kogan Page.

Moon, J. (2001). *Short courses and workshops: Improving the impact of learning in training and professional development*. London: Kogan Page.

Moon, J. (2004). *A handbook of reflective and experiential learning*. London: Routledge Falmer.

Parlett, M., & King, J. (1971). *Concentrated study*. London: Society for Research into Higher Education (SRHE).

Willis, M. (1993). *Managing the training process*. Maidenhead, UK: McGraw-Hill.

Jenny Moon

Writing

The practice of writing is a thread that runs through adult education in a range of applications including from adult basic education and literacy (Hull, 1997; Mace, 1996), professional writing (Hiemstra & Brier, 1994; Rankin, 2001), and popular education (Von Kotze, 1996) to educational research (Usher, Bryant, & Johnston, 1997). References to writing in early studies of adult education typically equate writing and reading at a "functional" level with literacy and its opposite, illiteracy. Recent adult literacy research highlights the complexity of writing and offers a nuanced class analysis – by defining literacies in the plural as a social practice (Hull, 1997; Mace) that exists at the nexus of power and knowledge in any learning setting. Usher (1993) acknowledges that the academic text is the dominant form of writing in adult education, and challenges the field to recognize the capacity of writing for questioning and subverting its own social practices and discourses that effect power-knowledge formations (p. 113). Creative writing workshops with factory workers in South Africa take up this challenge, adapting popular education to feminist pedagogy: women learners take control of their "weaving of words" and "interrogate, destabilize and disorganize dominant strategies of power . . . through the act of writing" (Von Kotze, p. 166).

"Writing as a social practice" signals that it is socially constructed and deeply embedded in "organized beliefs about how reading and writing might be, or should be, used to serve particular social and personal purposes and ends" (Hull, 1997, p. 19). Moreover, moments of illiteracy are a common experience, as is the experience of turning to others to act as our writers or scribes (Mace, 2002, p. xii). Different kinds of status are associated with the role of the scribe in different societies and can range from the professional status of scribes outside the post offices in North Sudan – who charge different prices for a request for *Zakat* (alms) from the destitute and applications to the judiciary – to the family responsibility of accurately copying a phone message, to the researcher's task of producing a distilled version of the many voices in a group inquiry (p. xii).

Writing as Learning

In the context of formal education, a writing task in a public adult-learning setting can intimidate learners (Mace, 1996, p. 180), and is symptomatic of the "imposter syndrome" (Brookfield, 1990) in which adult learners feel that they are returning to an educational setting under false pretenses and fear that their true (and inadequate) identities will be found out. Remarkably consistent across cultural contexts, the imposter syndrome manifests as "resistance to learning, [which] may occur because of a feeling that it is occurring in an overly public forum rather than their dislike for the focus of the learning itself" (p. 153).

Elbow (1997) makes the distinction between high-stakes writing and low-stakes writing, which is determined by how much a piece of writing *matters* or *counts* (p. 5), and is often linked to its public versus private purposes. Journal writing constitutes low-stakes writing because it is often informal and private. Although excerpts may be shared with co-learners and teachers – in the case of dialogue journals – journal writing is not intended for the public domain, and is not judged for grammar, spelling, syntax, or adherence to a style manual. Related to the "imposter syndrome" (Brookfield, 1990) and learners' fears that their true (and inadequate) identities will be found out, are the ethical issues of who will judge and respond to the learners' journal writing, a concern that adult educators Leona English (2001) and Tara Fenwick (2001) discuss. Writing online in distance education programs confuses give-and-take scribing (Mace, 2002): notions of the safe and democratic classroom where every voice can be heard in e-mail messages and chat rooms coexist with issues of isolation and motivation that are frequent in (dis)embodied and (dis)located learning (see English & Lander, 2000; Lander & English, 2000). Teachers/advisors and learners tease out each other's metaphors in the back-and-forth responses to written work, such as writing a qualitative thesis in adult education (Lander, 2000a); as co-inquirers, they push their "mixed metaphors" to their limits – and identify when they fall apart (Neilsen, 2001).

Writing as Research

Writing as the essence of research (e.g., Lander, 2002; Usher et al., 1997) calls the adult educator-researcher-writer to engage as a reflective practitioner and attend to the reflexivity of the researcher so that "writing the self and the world . . . encourage[s] the production of a text which is alien neither to author nor audience" (Usher et al., p. 213). In a self-study research project, Forsythe and Lander (2003) adapted Brookfield's (1995) critical-incident questionnaire and engaged reflexively with their teenage autobiographies around smoking – in the 1990s and 1960s respectively – to compose their third-person "collective theorizing" on the situated learning and communities of practice that influence teen smoking. Increasingly, self-writing and autobiography are favored by women adult educators as embodied ethical practices for representing their research. These forms of writing serve to highlight the contradictory discourses and transitional spaces in which women not only resist and negotiate power relations, but also compromise, in order to shape their lives and ways of being in the world as learners, teachers, managers, and researchers (Chapman, 2003; Lander, 2000b; Tamboukou, 2003).

Writing as research is high-stakes writing. In Lander's (2002) appreciative inquiry approach to adult education, practitioners write as part of their orientation to research-based graduate studies. Adult learners are encouraged to judge for themselves their "quality moments" of writing in practice. To demonstrate "research literacies" (Neilsen, 1998), adult learners and teachers together tell stories about writing, which serves to sensitize researchers to the consequences of writing: "To the potential consequences of all of our writing by bringing home . . . the ethics of representation" (Richardson, 2001, p. 932), which implies "writing as witness" (Lander, 2001). Neilsen (2001) challenges the high-stakes writing assignments of the academy and calls for artful writing of qualitative research, which refuses exclusionary practices, and does not need a vocabulary test: "we simply write what we see (and hear and touch and smell and sense) . . . creating from our many emerging and imagining selves lines to connect beyond" (p. 267). Writing thus becomes a holistic learning practice that does not divide mind, body, and spirit (see Michelson, 1998) and which focuses on what we know.

See also: appreciative inquiry, ethics, journal writing, literacy, practitioner, reflective learning.

References and Further Reading

Brookfield, S. D. (1990). *The skillful teacher.* San Francisco: Jossey-Bass.

Brookfield, S. D. (1995). *Becoming a critically reflective teacher.* San Francisco: Jossey-Bass.

Chapman, V.-L. (2003). On knowing ones' self, self-righting, power and ethical practice: Reflections from an adult educator. *Studies in the Education of Adults, 35*(11), 35–54.

Elbow, P. (1997). High stakes and low stakes in assigning and responding to writing. In M. D. Sorcinelli & P. Elbow (Eds.), *Writing to learn: Strategies for assigning and responding to writing across the disciplines* (pp. 5–130). *New Directions for Teaching and Learning*, No. 69. San Francisco: Jossey-Bass.

English, L. M. (2001). Ethical concerns related to journal writing. In L. M. English & M. A. Gillen (Eds.), *Promoting journal writing in adult education* (pp. 27–36). San Francisco: Jossey-Bass.

English, L. M., & Lander, D. A. (2000). Increasing reflection and dialogue in distance learning. *Journal of the Art of Teaching, 7*(1), 85–96.

Fenwick, T. J. (2001). Responding to journals in a learning process. In L. M. English & M. A. Gillen (Eds.), *Promoting journal writing in adult education* (pp. 37–48). *New Directions for Adult and Continuing Education*. No. 90. San Francisco: Jossey-Bass.

Forsythe, A., & Lander, D. A. (2003). A reflexive inquiry of two non-smokers: A trans-generational tale of social gospel and social norms marketing. *Reflective Practice, 4*(2), 139–161.

Hiemstra, R, & Brier, E. M. (1994). *Professional writing: Processes, strategies, and tips for publishing in educational journals.* Malabar, FL: Krieger.

Hull, G. (Ed.). (1997). *Changing work, changing workers: Critical perspectives on language, literacy and skills.* Albany: State University of New York Press.

Karpiak, I. E. (2000). Writing our life: Adult learning and teaching through autobiography. *Canadian Journal of University Continuing Education, 26*(1), 31–50.

Lander, D. A. (2000a). Mixed metaphors for reading and writing the qualitative thesis in adult education. *Studies in the Education of Adults, 32*(2), 148–165.

Lander, D. A. (2000b). Re-pairing knowledge worker and service worker: A critical autobiography of stepping into the shoes of my other. In C. Prichard, R. Hull, M. Chumer, & H. Willmott (Eds.), *Managing knowledge: Critical investigations of work and learning* (pp. 141–157). London: Palgrave Macmillan.

Lander, D. A. (2001). Writing as witness: Doing justice to participants' testimony. *Adult Learning, 12*(3), 17–19 (special issue on spirituality).

Lander, D. A. (2002). Teaching and learning research literacies in graduate adult education: Appreciative inquiry into practitioners ways of writing. *Canadian Journal of University Continuing Education, 28*(1), 31–55.

Lander, D. A., & English, L. M. (2000). Doing research "with": Reading and writing our difference. *Reflective Practice, 1*(3), 343–358.

Mace, J. (1996). Writing and power: Influence and engagement in adult literacies. In D. Boud & N. Miller (Eds.), *Working with experience: Animating learning* (pp. 171–183). London: Routledge.

Mace, J. (2002). *The give and take of writing: Scribes, literacy and everyday life.* Leicester, UK: National Institute of Adult Continuing Education.

Michelson, E. (1998). Re-membering: The return of the body to experiential learning. *Studies in Continuing Education, 20* (2), 217–234.

Neilsen, L. (1998). *Knowing her place: Research literacies and feminist occasions.* Great Tancook Island, NS: Backalong Books.

Neilsen, L. (2001). Scribbler: Notes on writing and learning inquiry. In L. Neilsen, A. L. Cole, & J. G. Knowles (Eds.), *The art of writing inquiry* (pp. 253–272). Halifax, NS: Backalong Books.

Rankin, E. (2001). *The work of writing.* San Francisco: Jossey-Bass.

Richardson, L. (2001). Getting personal: Writing-stories. *Qualitative Studies in Education, 14*(1), 33–38.

Tamboukou, M. (2003). *Women, education and the self: A Foucauldian perspective.* New York: Palgrave Macmillan.

Usher, R. (1993). From process to practice: Research, reflexivity and writing in adult education. *Studies in Continuing Education, 15*(2), 98–116.

Usher, R., Bryant, I., & Johnston, R. (1997). Writing and learning about research. In *Adult education and the post-modern challenge: Learning beyond the limits* (pp. 212–232). London: Routledge.

Von Kotze, A. (1996). The creaking of the word: A feminist model? In S. Walters & L. Manicom (Eds.), *Gender in popular education: Methods for empowerment* (pp. 149–168). London: Zed Books.

Dorothy A. Lander

Y

Young Adult Education

Youth lasts from puberty until the preconditions for a more or less stable adulthood are established, typically through relatively permanent relationships with partners and work, or through a consciousness of not wanting to enter into such relationships. It is a characteristic of present-day society that the period of youth is longer than it has ever been, and has a very fluid transition to adulthood; it is quite within the bounds of normality for youth to finish anywhere between the ages of 20 and 35. The end of it will often be incomplete, with a degree of connection to the youth phase being carried over into adulthood.

Although youth has not always been perceived as existing as a life stage in its own right, as long as it has existed it has been linked with a particular need for socially-necessary learning and personal development. With Erik Erikson's (1968) *Identity, Youth and Crises*, the conception of youth came to be that youth is primarily a period of more or less crisis-determined development of personal identity or self comprehension. However, recent decades have seen a further expansion of the youth period, and in addition, youth has become very much idealized – and commercialized – as the age of freedom, no responsibilities and happiness, while at the same time, the personal and societal problems linked with youth seem to be steadily increasing. The frame of reference and the empirical studies behind this entry are the behavior of young people in Western societies and in Western economies.

Understanding and Relating to Youth

Young people of today behave differently from the way in which those who are a little older did, and often completely differently from the way in which the latter expect and are immediately prepared to accept. For this reason, conflict can occur when the generations meet, especially within the educational system and in the workplace. Adults – teachers, supervisors, planners, employers, managers, trained workers etc. – are sometimes confronted with behavior on the part of young people which they have difficulty in regarding as other than spoiled and demanding. At the same time, adults simply have to relate to the new ways of being young (Simonsen, 2000).

Empirical Work on Youth

According to empirical studies carried out by Birgitte Simonsen and Noemi Katznelson (Katznelson et al., 2000), young people behave differently on two levels: in general with respect to their attitude to education and future jobs, and also in everyday life concerning school work, places of work and social behavior. According to these studies, some adults see the frequent youth mobility between jobs and schooling as an expression of young people's lack of interest in education and work, but this is often an inaccurate perception. Young people are extremely interested in their choice of education and training and in their future work. They prioritize education very highly and have great expectations with respect to their working life. What is lacking is thus not the motivation to get an education or a good job, but rather a strong need to have an exciting, challenging and interesting job. The small number of young people who want quite ordinary manual jobs also state as their motivation that they find it interesting and would like to do it. The reasons they express for working tend to go in the direction of work as personal development, as opposed to work as necessary for survival. Practically all of them want to work, and have expectations with respect to work, basically that it should be fun and interesting. But the labor market cannot always meet these expectations and young people have a difficult time accepting this. This will have consequences for the education system, which is only now starting to adapt itself to this situation.

Theoretical Perspectives

Widely accepted theoretical sources such as Erikson (1968), Ziehe (Ziehe & Stubenrauch, 1982), and Giddens (1990, 1991) suggest that young adulthood centres on the development of a personal identity – although some postmodernists claim that this is not possible (Gergen, 1991; Shotter 1993; Usher, 2000). Anyway, the demands on the formation of identity have undergone an explosive growth in line with late-modernity – it is definitely not by chance that in Danish we often talk of "identity work," which young people have to do, as well as getting through their education, forming relationships with a partner, and finding their place in society.

Previously there was family affiliation, a gender role, class attachment, and often an attachment to a particular profession, as well as a mass of given values and norms that the young person was expected to take on, perhaps through a somewhat rebellious process; now this structure is disintegrating or becoming redundant, and young people must find their own way. Not only must they decide about education, careers, partners and homes; but also about lifestyles and personal identities. Development in these areas has been overwhelming, and young people and society have to struggle with new, untried processes, the conditions of which change from day to day – new educational opportunities, new consumer opportunities, new communication systems and new lifestyle choices make themselves felt in an almost chaotic confusion. Everything seems possible, and yet young people perceive countless limitations, for many opportunities are completely inaccessible for the vast majority – only very few can become actors or sports heroes, even though many secretly wish for it and do what they can in the hope of achieving it.

Learning in Youth

According to Piaget (Illeris, 2002), human beings are cognitively fully developed from puberty, i.e., we have reached the formal operational stage and are equipped to think logically and deductively. In terms of learning, the first part of the youth period is still subject to compulsory education, later it is virtually a requirement to go through some youth education, and, as a rule, also some further education of a more vocational nature. Although this would appear to be education with a specific subject content, all learning in the youth period from the age of about 12 or 13 onwards is very much oriented towards the formation of identity and can only be understood in this light.

This contradictory relationship leads to a number of problems, because the school and education system are developed primarily to deal with subject learning, while matters of identity in its broadest sense are what young people are concerned about. Therefore, young people often react more or less reluctantly to the academic subject requirements, which they feel are forced upon them and which they find outdated, while the representatives of the system attempt to concentrate on the academic work, which they themselves are trained in, committed to, and under an obligation to uphold.

Adult Education Perspective

The education of young adults is seen to present particular issues. One of the most striking effects of these factors is the dramatic drop in applications to technical and scientific courses, degrees, and programs. Even though these courses bring employment opportunities with high status in society and good salaries, many young people tend to go in other directions, typically towards humanistic, social, pedagogical and societal subjects, for these provide far better opportunities for establishing an interaction between the academic content and the formation of identity (Katznelson et al., 2000; Ulriksen, 2001).

The identity process for most young people today is far more important and far more urgent than career orientation, and in one way it is also a precondition for the choice of career. So, from the perspective of young people, there is good reason for the many searching activities, shifts, and years out, that the system views as expensive delays in the education process.

The most important things for young people to learn today are: to be able to orient themselves, to be able to make choices that can be answered for, not to waste their lives on the wrong thing, and to be able to make good decisions. Society and employers also demand maturity, independence, responsibility, and academic qualifications. Yet no-one can predict which academic qualifications will be relevant in 5 or 10 years' time, so youth must be prepared to continue their learning throughout most of life. The best security for the future is to be ready to change and take hold of what is relevant in many different situations. Uncertainty cannot be countered by stability, but only by being open, flexible and constantly oriented to learning (Simonsen, 2000).

How Youth Learn

As to the question whether young adults learn differently than middle-aged adults and older adults the following general answers can be given: for more traditional kinds of learning theory dealing with internal mental learning processes, the answer is no, the learning processes are in principle the same. This is because these theories are based on the assumption that learning occurs by means of certain innate mental mechanisms that have been generated throughout the history of our species' struggle for survival. In general, these mechanisms are at the disposal of any normal human being, although the ability to fully practise them only gradually ripens during the years of childhood. But in recent decades, some learning theories have included social aspects in a new way and, most radically in social constructivism, such processes as learning are primarily or exclusively regarded as social processes (e.g., Gergen 1991). In this case, age certainly influences the learning processes, as the ways in which the individual is involved in social processes are strongly influenced by age.

To sum up the differences in life age and learning: children want to capture their world; the fundamental characteristics of childhood learning are that it is uncensored and confident, the child aims at learning what there is to learn and has to rely on the support of adults. Late-modern society has, indeed, led to growing complexity and even confusion, but still the open and confident approach must be recognized as the starting point.

Young people want to construct their own identity, which is different from that of adults. In terms of learning, the main orientation in adulthood is broadly towards the management of the life course and its challenges, typically centering on family and work, and more broadly on interests, lifestyle and attitudes.

The beginning of the adult period may typically be marked by external events such as starting a family or finishing education. There are no decisively new cognitive opportunities; what happens in terms of learning and consciousness is that the person takes on the management of, and responsibility for, his or her own life, with this normally occurring gradually as a long process throughout the years of youth and into adulthood.

See also: adult development, identity, lifespan learning, social constructivism.

References and Further Reading

Erikson, E. H. (1968). *Identity, youth and crises*. New York: Norton.

Gergen, K. J. (1991). *The saturated self: Dilemmas of identity in contemporary life*. New York: Basic Books.

Giddens, A. (1990). *The consequences of modernity*. Stanford, CA: Stanford University Press.

Giddens, A. (1991). *Modernity and self-identity*. Cambridge: Polity Press.

Illeris, K. (2002). *The three dimensions of learning*. Copenhagen: Roskilde University Press.

Katznelson, N., Illeris, K., & Simonsen, B. (2000). Working identities and inner logics in motion. In European Commission, Targetes Socio-Economic Research: *Balancing Competencies: Enhancing the participation of young adult in economic and social processes* (pp. 63–86). Brussels: European Commission.

Shotter, J. (1993). *Cultural politics of everyday life*. Buckingham, UK: Open University Press.

Simonsen, B. (2000). New young people, new forms of consciousness, new educational methods. In K. Illeris (Ed.), *Adult education in the perspective of the learners* (pp. 137–156). Copenhagen: Roskilde University Press.

Ulriksen, L. (2001). *Expectations of university studies. Students, teachers and institution*. Paper presented at the Annual Meeting of the Society for Research into Higher Education. Cambridge, UK.

Usher, R. (2000). Impossible identities, unstable boundaries: Managing experience differently. In K. Illeris (Ed.), *Adult education in the perspective of the learners* (pp. 178–198). Copenhagen: Roskilde University Press.

Ziehe, T., & Stubenrauch, H. (1982). *Plädoyer für ungewöhnliches Lernen*. [*Plea for unusual learning*]. Reinbek: Rowohlt.

Birgitte Simonsen

Term Index

Name Index

Notes: **bold** = either an article by the writer or an extended discussion of their work

Subject Index

Notes: **bold** = extended discussion (or a heading or a word emphasized in the main text)